Lecture Notes in Computer Science 8205

Commenced Publication in 1973
Founding and Former Series Editors:
Gerhard Goos, Juris Hartmanis, and Jan van Leeuwen

Advanced Research in Computing and Software Science

Subline of Lectures Notes in Computer Science

Yehuda Afek (Ed.)

Distributed Computing

27th International Symposium, DISC 2013
Jerusalem, Israel, October 14-18, 2013
Proceedings

 Springer

Volume Editor

Yehuda Afek
Tel-Aviv University
Blavatnik School of Computer Sciences
Ramat Aviv, Tel-Aviv, Israel
E-mail: afek@cs.tau.ac.il

ISSN 0302-9743   e-ISSN 1611-3349
ISBN 978-3-642-41526-5   e-ISBN 978-3-642-41527-2
DOI 10.1007/978-3-642-41527-2
Springer Heidelberg New York Dordrecht London

Library of Congress Control Number: 2013950637

CR Subject Classification (1998): F.2, C.2, E.1, E.2, G.2, D.2

LNCS Sublibrary: SL 1 – Theoretical Computer Science and General Issues

Typesetting: Camera-ready by author, data conversion by Scientific Publishing Services, Chennai, India

Printed on acid-free paper

Springer is part of Springer Science+Business Media (www.springer.com)

Preface

DISC, the International Symposium on DIStributed Computing, is an international forum on the theory, design, analysis, implementation, and application of distributed systems and networks. DISC is organized in cooperation with the European Association for Theoretical Computer Science (EATCS).

This volume contains the papers presented at DISC 2013, the 27th International Symposium on Distributed Computing, held during October 15–17, 2013, in Jerusalem, Israel. The volume also includes the citation for the 2013 Edsger W. Dijkstra Prize in Distributed Computing, and the 2013 Principles of Distributed Computing Doctoral Dissertation Award, both jointly sponsored by the EATCS Symposium on Distributed Computing (DISC) and the ACM Symposium on Principles of Distributed Computing (PODC), and were presented at DISC 2013 in Jerusalem. The Dijkstra Prize was given to Nati Linial, for his work on locality in distributed graph algorithms, and the Doctoral Dissertation Award was given jointly to Shiri Chechik and Danupon Nanongkai for their respective dissertations.

There were 142 regular papers submitted to the symposium (in addition to a large number of abstract-only submissions). The Program Committee selected 37 contributions out of the 142 full-paper submissions for regular presentations at the symposium. Each presentation was accompanied by a paper of up to 15 pages in this volume (with one exception of two papers whose presentation was merged into one presentation). Every submitted paper was read and evaluated by at least three members of the Program Committee. The committee was assisted by about 180 external reviewers. The Program Committee made its final decisions in discussions carried out mostly over the Web, using EasyChair, from June 25 to July 12, 2013. Revised and expanded versions of several selected papers will be considered for publication in a special issue of the journal *Distributed Computing*.

The Best Paper Award of DISC 2013 was presented to Mohsen Ghaffari and Fabian Kuhn for their paper "Distributed Minimum Cut Approximation."

Although the best paper awardee is also a student paper (Mohsen Ghaffari is a full time student) the Program Committee selected an additional paper as the Best Student Paper of DISC 2013 and that award was given to Shahar Timnat for the paper "Lock-Free Data Structure Iterators," co-authored with Erez Petrank.

The Program Committee also considered about 44 papers for brief announcements, among the papers that were submitted as brief announcements, as well as the regular submissions that generated substantial interest from the members of the committee, but could not be accepted for regular presentations. This volume contains 16 brief announcements. Each two-page announcement presents ongoing work or recent results, and it is expected that these results will appear as full papers in later conferences or journals.

The program also featured two invited lectures, presented by Ravi Rajwar from Intel and Nati Linial from the Hebrew University, the Dijkstra awardee. Abstracts of these invited lectures are included in these proceedings.

In addition, the program included a tutorial given by Teemu Koponen from VMware discussing "The Evolution of SDN and How Your Network Is Changing".

Five workshops were co-located with the DISC symposium this year: the First Workshop on Biological Distributed Algorithms (BDA), organized by Ziv Bar-Joseph, Yuval Emek, and Amos Korman, on October 14; the Second Workshop on Advances on Distributed Graph Algorithms (ADGA) chaired by Jukka Suomela, on October 14; the 5th Workshop on the Theory of Transactional Memory (WTTM 2013) organized by Alessia Milani, Panagiota Fatourou, Paolo Romano, and Maria Couceiro, on October 14; the 9th Workshop on Foundations of Mobile Computing (FOMC), organized by Keren Censor-Hillel and Valerie King, during October 17–18; and the 5th Workshop on Theoretical Aspects of Dynamic Distributed Systems (TADDS), organized by Lélia Blin and Yann Busnel, on October 18.

August 2013   Yehuda Afek

Organization

DISC, the International Symposium on Distributed Computing, is an annual forum for presentation of research on all aspects of distributed computing. It is organized in cooperation with the European Association for Theoretical Computer Science (EATCS). The symposium was established in 1985 as a biannual International Workshop on Distributed Algorithms on Graphs (WDAG). The scope was soon extended to cover all aspects of distributed algorithms and WDAG came to stand for International Workshop on Distributed AlGorithms, becoming an annual symposium in 1989. To reflect the expansion of its area of interest, the name was changed to DISC (International Symposium on DIStributed Computing) in 1998, opening the symposium to all aspects of distributed computing. The aim of DISC is to reflect the exciting and rapid developments in this field.

Program Committee Chair

Yehuda Afek   Tel-Aviv University, Israel

Program Committee

Ittai Abraham	Microsoft Research, USA
Dan Alistarh	MIT, USA
Chen Avin	Ben-Gurion University, Israel
Anat Bremler-Barr	IDC, Herzelia, Israel
Xavier Defago	JAIST, Ishikawa, Japan
Michael Elkin	Ben-Gurion University, Israel
Yuval Emek	ETH Zurich, Switzerland
Pascal Felber	Université de Neuchâtel, Switzerland
Pierre Fraigniaud	CNRS and University of Paris Diderot, France
Juan Garay	AT&T Labs - Research, USA
Shafi Goldwasser	MIT, USA
Maurice Herlihy	Brown University, USA
Adrian Kosowski	Inria, University of Bordeaux, France
Victor Luchangco	Oracle Labs, USA
Dahlia Malkhi	Microsoft Research, USA
Rotem Oshman	University of Toronto, Canada
Dmitri Perelman	Facebook, USA
Yvonne Anne Pignolet	ABB Corp. Research, Switzerland
Michel Raynal	IUF and IRISA (University of Rennes), France
Andrea Richa	Arizona State University, USA
Alexander A. Shvartsman	University of Connecticut, USA
Michael Spear	Lehigh University, USA

Jukka Suomela   University of Helsinki, Finland
Corentin Travers   LaBRI, France
Jennifer Welch   Texas A&M University, USA
Masafumi Yamashita   Kyushu University, Japan

Steering Committee

Marcos K. Aguilear   Microsoft Research, USA
Shlomi Dolev   Ben-Gurion University, Israel
Antonio Fernandez Anta   Institute IMDEA Networks, Spain
Achour Mostefaoui   University of Rennes, France
Nancy Lynch   MIT, USA
David Peleg   Weizmann Institute, Israel
Sergio Rajsbaum (Chair)   UNAM, Mexico

Organization

Chen Avin (Publicity chair)   Ben-Gurion University, Israel
Danny Dolev (Co-chair)   Hebrew University Israel
Suzie Eid (Administrative support)   Technion, Israel
Seth Gilbert (Tutorials and Workshops
   chair)   NUS, Singapore
Idit Keidar (Co-chair)   Technion, Israel

External Reviewers

Sergio Arevalo   Eli Brosh
James Aspnes   Venkat Chakaravarthy
Hagit Attiya   Jeremie Chalopin
David A. Bader   Nishanth Chandran
Mahesh Balakrishnan   Ioannis Chatzigiannakis
Roberto Baldoni   Eden Chlamtac
Oana Balmau   Hyun Chul Chung
Carlos Baquero   Colin Cooper
Leonid Barenboim   Alejandro Cornejo
Dmitry Basin   Eliyahu Dain
Udi Ben-Porat   Ajoy Datta
Annette Bieniusa   Seda Davtyan
Marcin Bienkowski   Yuval Degani
François Bonnet   Dariusz Dereniowski
Michael Borokhovich   David Dice
Anastasia Braginsky   Stephan Diestelhorst
Philipp Brandes   Alex Dimakis
Joshua Brody   Michael Dinitz

Nicolas Nicolaou

Fukuhito Ooshita

Merav Parter

Omry Pazi

Fernando Pedone

Daniel Peek

David Peleg

Franck Petit

Erez Petrank

Tal Rabin

Rajmohan Rajaraman

Nimrod Rappoport

Dror Rawitz

Etienne Riviere

Luis Rodrigues

Adi Rosen

Guy Rothblum

Matthieu Roy

Joel Rybicki

Yogish Sabharwal

Thomas Sauerwald

Gabriel Scalosub

Michael Schapira

Christian Scheideler

Stefan Schmid

Johannes Schneider

Michael Scott

Jochen Seidel

Alexander Shraer

Anita Sobe

Moshe Sulamy

Pierre Sutra

Edward Talmage

Tami Tamir

Stefano Tessaro

Gilles Tredan

John Tristan

Shimrit Tzur-David

Jara Uitto

Yogev Vaknin

Vincent Villain

Wojciech Wawrzyniak

Yaron Welner

Donglin Xia

Yukiko Yamauchi

Neal Young

Métivier Yves

Igor Zablotchi

Marek Zawirski

Akka Zemmari

Jin Zhang

Vassilis Zikas

Ofri Ziv

Sponsoring Organizations

European
Association for
Theoretical
Computer Science

Google Inc.

vmware

Facebook

i-core

Microsoft Research

Oracle

Cisco

 Technion

 The Hebrew University

 Ben-Gurion University

 Tel-Aviv University

 Weizmann Institute of Science

 Technion Computer Engineering

DISC 2013 acknowledges the use of the EasyChair system for handling submissions, managing the review process, and compiling these proceedings.

The 2013 Edsger W. Dijkstra Prize in Distributed Computing

The Dijkstra Prize Committee has selected **Nati Linial** as the recipient of this year's Edsger W. Dijkstra Prize in Distributed Computing. The prize is given to him for his outstanding paper "Locality in distributed graph algorithms", published in SIAM Journal on Computing, 21 (1992) 193-201.

The Edsger W. Dijkstra Prize in Distributed Computing is awarded for an outstanding paper on the principles of distributed computing, whose significance and impact on the theory and/or practice of distributed computing has been evident for at least a decade.

This paper has had a major impact on distributed message-passing algorithms. It explored the notion of *locality* in distributed computation and raised interesting questions concerning the locality level in various problems, in terms of their time complexity in different classes of networks. Linial developed a clean model for studying locality that ignores message sizes, asynchrony and failures. The model allowed researchers to isolate the effects of locality and study the roles of distances and neighborhoods, as graph theoretic notions, and their interrelations with algorithmic and complexity-theoretic problems.

Linial's paper also presents an $O(\Delta^2)$-coloring algorithm for graphs with degree at most Δ that runs in $O(\log^* n)$ time. It is based on a new connection between extremal set theory and distributed computing. This result serves as a cornerstone for other coloring algorithms, including the current best algorithm. Whether one can get an $O(\Delta^{2-\epsilon})$-coloring within the same time bound remains a major open problem.

His paper also proves that, for any function f, any $f(\Delta)$-coloring algorithm requires $\Omega(\log^* n)$ time. Moreover, the same bound is shown for 3-coloring an oriented path or cycle. To obtain these lower bounds, Linial introduced the concept of the *neighborhood graph* of a distributed network and analyzed it. An enhanced form of his technique was recently used for establishing the best known lower bounds for Maximal Independent Set and Maximal Matching.

In summary, Linial's paper opened new approaches to distributed symmetry breaking and remains one of the most important papers in this area.

The Prize is sponsored jointly by the ACM Symposium on Principles of Distributed Computing (PODC) and the EATCS Symposium on Distributed Computing (DISC). This prize is presented annually, with the presentation taking place alternately at PODC and DISC. This year it was presented at DISC.

Dijkstra Prize Committee 2013

Yehuda Afek,	Tel-Aviv Univ.
Faith Ellen,	Univ. of Toronto
Boaz Patt-Shamir,	Tel-Aviv Univ.
Sergio Rajsbaum,	UNAM
Alexander Shvartsman,	Univ. of Connecticut
Gadi Taubenfeld,	IDC, Chair

The 2013 Principles of Distributed Computing Doctoral Dissertation Award

The abundance of excellent candidates made the choice very difficult. Even after narrowing the list down, the committee still decided to split the award between two winners, listed next alphabetically by last name. Dr. Shiri Chechik completed her thesis "Fault-tolerant structures in graphs" in 2012 under the supervision of Prof. David Peleg at the Weizmann Institute of Science. Dr. Danupon Nanongkai completed his thesis "Graphs and geometric algorithms on distributed networks and databases" in 2011 under the supervision of Prof. Richard J. Lipton at the Georgia Institute of Technology.

The thesis of Dr. Chechik includes a comprehensive and deep body of work on fault-tolerant graph spanners and related structures. It contains many strong results, one of which received a best student paper award, and one solved a long-standing open problems. In one of these results, Dr. Chechik shows that it is possible to compute, ahead of time, a compact routing table that provides good routes even if several edges fail. The thesis targets an area of research that has been well studied, but Dr. Chechik's contributions advances the area significantly and promises to have a deep and long-lasting impact.

The thesis of Dr. Nanongkai shows a useful approach to make communication complexity a powerful tool for establishing lower bounds bounds for distributed computing. It also contains several sophisticated almost matching upper bounds. The thesis shows that this tool is applicable in diverse contexts, such as random walks, graph problems, and more.

Besides being technically deep, the thesis combines distributed computing, communication complexity, and theory of random walks, in natural and novel ways. These results suggest and open the path for much exciting follow-up work on distributed communication complexity and distributed random walks.

The award is sponsored jointly by the ACM Symposium on Principles of Distributed Computing (PODC) and the EATCS Symposium on Distributed Computing (DISC). This award is presented annually, with the presentation taking place alternately at PODC and DISC. This year it was presented at DISC.

Principles of Distributed Computing Doctoral
Dissertation Award Committee, 2013

Marcos K. Aguilera,	Microsoft Research
Rachid Guerraoui,	EPFL
Shay Kutten (Chair),	Technion
Michael Mitzenmacher,	Harvard
Alessandro Panconesi.	Sapienza

DISC 2013 Tutorial: The Evolution of SDN and How Your Network Is Changing

Teemu Koponen

VMware

Network data planes have greatly evolved since the invention of Ethernet: the port densities, forwarding latencies and capacities of modern switches are all at levels no one would have predicted. Yet at the same time, the principles of network control planes have remained unchanged; control planes have largely been a story of distributed algorithms and manual configuration of individual network elements.

As seen in the trade press and networking conference proceedings, Software Defined Networks (SDN) is quickly changing this, and in networking, the past few years have been all about the evolution of the control plane, almost to the point that it's difficult to tell what SDN is!

In this tutorial, I'll cover the evolution of the SDN: its beginning, current state, and where it might be heading next. Using the industry use cases as examples I'll discuss the management challenges SDN is solving today, as well as how the implementation of SDN control planes has evolved and most importantly how SDN has opened new avenues for control plane design. While SDN revolves around the idea of replacing distributed route computation with logical centralization, the practical requirements for scalability and availability do necessitate distribution of functionality. To this end, networking community might be more interested in distributed algorithms than ever before – however, this time they are not for route computation.

DISC 2013 Invited Lecture:
Adventures in Parallel Dimensions

Ravi Rajwar

Intel Corporation

Historically, transparent hardware improvements meant software just ran faster. However, the slowing growth in single-thread performance has meant an increasingly parallel future – involving parallelism across data, threads, cores, and nodes.

In this talk, I'll explore some of the dimensions of parallelism and their growing interplay with software, discuss the resulting system challenges, and share some experiences.

DISC 2013 Invited Lecture: Simplicial Complexes - Much more than a Trick for Concurrent Computation Lower Bounds

Nati Linial

The Hebrew University

As (hopefully) everyone in this audience knows simplicial complexes are very useful in distributed computing. It is not hard to understand the reason for this success. Graphs are the perfect tool in the modeling of systems that are driven by pairwise interactions. In contrast, distributed systems are all about multiway interactions involving many processors at once. This suggests the search for the high-dimensional counterparts of many basic concepts and ideas from graph theory. What plays the role of trees? What is the analog of graph connectivity? Of expansion? Is there a good theory that resembles the theory of random graphs? In this lecture I will describe work done in recent years to address these questions.

I have many excellent partners and collaborators in this research effort: Lior Aronshtam, Tomasz Luczak, Roy Meshulam, Ilan Newman, Tahl Nowik, Yuval Peled, Yuri Rabinovich and Mishael Rosenthal

Table of Contents

Crypto, Trust, and Influence

Networking

Brief Announcements

Distributed Minimum Cut Approximation

Mohsen Ghaffari[1] and Fabian Kuhn[2]

[1] Computer Science and Artificial Intelligence Lab, MIT, USA
ghaffari@mit.edu
[2] Department of Computer Science, University of Freiburg, Germany
kuhn@cs.uni-freiburg.de

Abstract. We study the problem of computing approximate minimum edge cuts by distributed algorithms. We use a standard synchronous message passing model where in each round, $O(\log n)$ bits can be transmitted over each edge (a.k.a. the CONGEST model). The first algorithm is based on a simple and new approach for analyzing random edge sampling, which we call the *random layering technique*. For any weighted graph and any $\epsilon \in (0, 1)$, the algorithm with high probability finds a cut of size at most $O(\epsilon^{-1}\lambda)$ in $O(D) + \tilde{O}(n^{1/2+\epsilon})$ rounds, where λ is the size of the minimum cut and the $\tilde{O}$-notation hides poly-logarithmic factors in n. In addition, based on a centralized algorithm due to Matula [SODA '93], we present a randomized distributed algorithm that with high probability computes a cut of size at most $(2 + \epsilon)\lambda$ in $\tilde{O}((D + \sqrt{n})/\epsilon^5)$ rounds for any $\epsilon > 0$.

The time complexities of our algorithms almost match the $\tilde{\Omega}(D + \sqrt{n})$ lower bound of Das Sarma et al. [STOC '11], thus leading to an answer to an open question raised by Elkin [SIGACT-News '04] and Das Sarma et al. [STOC '11].

To complement our upper bound results, we also strengthen the $\tilde{\Omega}(D + \sqrt{n})$ lower bound of Das Sarma et al. by extending it to unweighted graphs. We show that the same lower bound also holds for unweighted multigraphs (or equivalently for weighted graphs in which $O(w \log n)$ bits can be transmitted in each round over an edge of weight w). For unweighted simple graphs, we show that computing an α-approximate minimum cut requires time at least $\tilde{\Omega}(D + \sqrt{n}/\alpha^{1/4})$.

1 Introduction

Finding minimum cuts or approximately minimum cuts are classical and fundamental algorithmic graph problems with many important applications. In particular, minimum edge cuts and their size (i.e., the edge connectivity) are relevant in the context of networks, where edge weights might represent link capacities and therefore edge connectivity can be interpreted as the throughput capacity of the network. Decomposing a network using small cuts helps designing efficient communication strategies and finding communication bottlenecks (see, e.g., [20,27]). Both the exact and approximate variants of the minimum cut problem have received extensive attention in the domain of centralized algorithms (cf. Section 1.1 for a brief review of the results in the centralized setting). This line of research has led to (almost) optimal centralized algorithms with running times $\tilde{O}(m+n)$ [19] for the exact version and $O(m+n)$ [24] for constant-factor approximations, where n and m are the numbers of nodes and edges, respectively.

As indicated by Elkin [6] and Das Sarma et al. [4], the problem has remained essentially open in the distributed setting. In the LOCAL model [26] where in each round, a

Y. Afek (Ed.): DISC 2013, LNCS 8205, pp. 1–15, 2013.
© Springer-Verlag Berlin Heidelberg 2013

message of unbounded size can be sent over each edge, the problem has a trivial time complexity of $\Theta(D)$ rounds, where D is the (unweighted) diameter of the network. The problem is therefore more interesting and also practically more relevant in models where messages are of some bounded size B. The standard model incorporating this restriction is the CONGEST model [26], a synchronous message passing model where in each time unit, B bits can be sent over every link (in each direction). It is often assumed that $B = \Theta(\log n)$. The only known non-trivial result is an elegant lower bound by Das Sarma et al. [4] showing that any α-approximation of the minimum cut in weighted graphs requires at least $\Omega(D + \sqrt{n/(B \log n)})$ rounds.

Our Contribution: We present two distributed minimum-cut approximation algorithms for undirected weighted graphs, with complexities almost matching the lower bound of [4]. We also extend the lower bound of [4] to unweighted graphs and multigraphs.

Our first algorithm, presented in Section 4, with high probability[1] finds a cut of size at most $O(\varepsilon^{-1}\lambda)$, for any $\epsilon \in (0,1)$ and where λ is the edge connectivity, i.e., the size of the minimum cut in the network. The time complexity of this algorithm is $O(D) + O(n^{1/2+\epsilon} \log^3 n \log \log n \log^* n)$. The algorithm is based on a simple and novel approach for analyzing random edge sampling, a tool that has proven extremely successful also for studying the minimum cut problem in the centralized setting (see, e.g., [20]). Our analysis is based on *random layering*, and we believe that the approach might also be useful for studying other connectivity-related questions. Assume that each edge $e \in E$ of an unweighted multigraph $G = (V, E)$ is independently sampled and added to a subset $E' \subset E$ with probability p. For $p \leq \frac{1}{\lambda}$, the graph $G' = (V, E')$ induced by the sampled edges is disconnected with at least a constant probability (just consider one min-cut). In Section 3, we use random layering to show that if $p = \Omega(\frac{\log n}{\lambda})$, the sampled graph G' is connected w.h.p. This bound is optimal and was known previously, with two elegant proofs: [23] and [15]. Our proof is simple and self-contained and it serves as a basis for our algorithm in Section 4.

The second algorithm, presented in Section 5, finds a cut with size at most $(2 + \varepsilon)\lambda$, for any constant $\varepsilon > 0$, in time $O((D + \sqrt{n} \log^* n) \log^2 n \log \log n \cdot \frac{1}{\varepsilon^5})$. This algorithm combines the general approach of Matula's centralized $(2+\varepsilon)$-approximation algorithm [24] with Thurimella's algorithm for sparse edge-connectivity certificates [29] and with the famous random edge sparsification technique of Karger (see e.g., [16]).

To complement our upper bounds, we also extend the lower bound of Das Sarma et al. [4] to unweighted graphs and multigraphs. When the minimum cut problem (or more generally problems related to small edge cuts and edge connectivity) are in a distributed context, often the weights of the edges correspond to their capacities. It therefore seems reasonable to assume that over a link of twice the capacity, we can also transmit twice the amount of data in a single time unit. Consequently, it makes sense to assume that over an edge of weight (or capacity) $w \geq 1$, $O(w \log n)$ bits can be transmitted per round (or equivalently that such a link corresponds to w parallel links of unit capacity). The lower bound of [4] critically depends on having links with (very) large weight over which in each round only $O(\log n)$ bits can be transmitted. We generalize the approach of [4] and obtain the same lower bound result as in [4] for the weaker setting where edge weights correspond to edge capacities (i.e., the setting that can be modeled using

---

[1] We use the phrase *with high probability* (w.h.p.) to indicate probability greater than $1 - \frac{1}{n}$.

unweighted multigraphs). Formally, we show that if Bw bits can be transmitted over every edge of weight $w \geq 1$, for every $\lambda \geq 1$ and every $\alpha \geq 1$, there are λ-edge-connected networks with diameter $O(\log n)$ on which computing an α-approximate minimum cut requires time at least $\Omega\left(\sqrt{n/(B \log n)}\right)$. Further, for unweighted simple graphs, we show that computing an α-approximate minimum cut in λ-edge-connected networks of diameter $O(\log n)$ requires at least time $\Omega\left(\frac{\sqrt{n/(B \log n)}}{(\alpha\lambda)^{1/4}}\right)$.

In addition, our technique yields a structural result about λ-edge-connected graphs with small diameter. We show that for every $\lambda > 1$, there are λ-edge-connected graphs G with diameter $O(\log n)$ such that for any partition of the edges of G into spanning subgraphs, all but $O(\log n)$ of the spanning subgraphs have diameter $\Omega(n)$ (in the case of unweighted multigraphs) or $\Omega(n/\lambda)$ (in the case of unweighted simple graphs). As a corollary, we also get that when sampling each edge of such a graph with probability $p \leq \gamma/\log n$ for a sufficiently small constant $\gamma > 0$, with at least a positive constant probability, the subgraph induced by the sampled edges has diameter $\Omega(n)$ (in the case of unweighted multigraphs) and $\Omega(n/\lambda)$ (in the case of unweighted simple graphs). For lack of space, the details about these results are deferred to the full version [10].

1.1 Related Work in the Centralized Setting

Starting in the 1950s [5, 8], the traditional approach to the minimum cut problem was to use max-flow algorithms (cf. [7] and [20, Section 1.3]). In the 1990s, three new approaches were introduced which go away from the flow-based method and provide faster algorithms: The first method, presented by Gabow [9], is based on a matroid characterization of the min-cut and it finds a min-cut in $O(m + \lambda^2 n \log \frac{n}{m})$ steps, for any unweighted (but possibly directed) graph with edge connectivity λ. The second approach applies to (possibly) weighted but undirected graphs and is based on repeatedly identifying and contracting edges outside a min-cut until a min-cut becomes apparent (e.g., [14, 20, 25]). The beautiful *random contraction algorithm* (RCA) of Karger [14] falls into this category. In the basic version of RCA, the following procedure is repeated $O(n^2 \log n)$ times: contract uniform random edges one by one until only two nodes remain. The edges between these two nodes correspond to a cut in the original graph, which is a min-cut with probability at least $1/O(n^2)$. Karger and Stein [20] also present a more efficient implementation of the same basic idea, leading to total running time of $O(n^2 \log^3 n)$. The third method, which again applies to (possibly) weighted but undirected graphs, is due to Karger [18] and is based on a "semiduality" between minimum cuts and maximum spanning tree packings. This third method leads to the best known centralized minimum-cut algorithm [19] with running time $O(m \log^3 n)$.

For the approximation version of the problem (in undirected graphs), the main known results are as follows. Matula [24] presents an algorithm that finds a $(2 + \varepsilon)$-minimum cut for any constant $\varepsilon > 0$ in time $O((m + n)/\varepsilon)$. This algorithm is based on a graph search procedure called *maximum adjacency search*. Based on a modified version of the random contraction algorithm, Karger [17] presents an algorithm that finds a $(1 + \varepsilon)$-minimum cut in time $O(m + n \log^3 n/\varepsilon^4)$.

2 Preliminaries

Notations and Definitions: We usually work with an undirected weighted graph $G = (V, E, w)$, where V is a set of n vertices, E is a set of (undirected) edges $e = \{v, u\}$ for $u, v \in V$, and $w : E \to \mathbb{R}^+$ is a mapping from edges E to positive real numbers. For each edge $e \in E$, $w(e)$ denotes the weight of edge e. In the special case of unweighted graphs, we simply assume $w(e) = 1$ for each edge $e \in E$.

For a given non-empty proper subset $C \subset V$, we define the cut $(C, V \setminus C)$ as the set of edges in E with exactly one endpoint in set C. The size of this cut, denoted by $w(C)$ is the sum of the weights of the edges in set $(C, V \setminus C)$. The edge-connectivity $\lambda(G)$ of the graph is defined as the minimum size of $w(C)$ as C ranges over all nonempty proper subsets of V. A cut $(C, V \setminus C)$ is called α-*minimum*, for an $\alpha \geq 1$, if $w(C) \leq \alpha\lambda(G)$. When clear from the context, we sometimes use λ to refer to $\lambda(G)$.

Communicaton Model and Problem Statements: We use a standard *message passing model* (a.k.a. the CONGEST model [26]), where the execution proceeds in synchronous rounds and in each round, each node can send a message of size B bits to each of its neighbors. A typically standard case is $B = \Theta(\log n)$.

For upper bounds, for simplicity we assume that $B = \Theta(\log n)^2$. For upper bounds, we further assume that B is large enough so that a constant number of node identifiers and edge weights can be packed into a single message. For $B = \Theta(\log n)$, this implies that each edge weight $w(e)$ is at most (and at least) polynomial in n. W.l.o.g., we further assume that edge weights are normalized and each edge weight is an integer in range $\{1, \ldots, n^{\Theta(1)}\}$. Thus, we can also view a weighted graph as a multi-graph in which all edges have unit weight and multiplicity at most $n^{\Theta(1)}$ (but still only $O(\log n)$ bits can be transmitted over all these parallel edges together).

For lower bounds, we assume a weaker model where $B \cdot w(e)$ bits can be sent in each round over each edge e. To ensure that at least B bits can be transmitted over each edge, we assume that the weights are scaled such that $w(e) \geq 1$ for all edges. For integer weights, this is equivalent to assuming that the network graph is an unweighted multigraph where each edge e corresponds to $w(e)$ parallel unit-weight edges.

In the problem of computing an α-*approximation of the minimum cut*, the goal is to find a cut $(C^*, V \setminus C^*)$ that is α-minimum. To indicate this cut in the distributed setting, each node v should know whether $v \in C^*$. In the problem of α-*approximation of the edge-connectivity*, all nodes must output an estimate $\tilde{\lambda}$ of λ such that $\tilde{\lambda} \in [\lambda, \lambda\alpha]$. In randomized algorithms for these problems, time complexities are fixed deterministically and the correctness guarantees are required to hold with high probability.

2.1 Black-Box Algorithms

In this paper, we make frequent use of a *connected component identification* algorithm due to Thurimella [29], which itself builds on the minimum spanning tree algorithm of Kutten and Peleg [22]. Given a graph $G(V, E)$ and a subgraph $H = (V, E')$ such that

---

[2] Note that by choosing $B = b \log n$ for some $b \geq 1$, in all our upper bounds, the term that does not depend on D could be improved by a factor $\sqrt{b}$.

$E' \subseteq E$, Thurimella's algorithm identifies the connected components of H by assigning a label $\ell(v)$ to each node $v \in V$ such that two nodes get the same label iff they are in the same connected component of H. The time complexity of the algorithm is $O(D + \sqrt{n} \log^* n)$ rounds, where D is the (unweighted) diameter of G. Moreover, it is easy to see that the algorithm can be made to produce labels $\ell(v)$ such that $\ell(v)$ is equal to the smallest (or the largest) id in the connected component of H that contains v. Furthermore, the connected component identification algorithm can also be used to test whether the graph H is connected (assuming that G is connected). H is not connected if and only if there is an edge $\{u, v\} \in E$ such that $\ell(u) \neq \ell(v)$. If some node u detects that for some neighbor v (in G), $\ell(u) \neq \ell(v)$, u broadcasts *not connected*. Connectivity of H can therefore be tested in D additional rounds. We refer to this as Thurimella's *connectivity-tester* algorithm. Finally, we remark that the same algorithms can also be used to solve k independent instances of the connected component identification problem or k independent instances of the connectivity-testing problem in $O(D + k\sqrt{n} \log^* n)$ rounds. This is achieved by pipelining the messages of the broadcast parts of different instances.

3   Edge Sampling and the Random Layering Technique

Here, we study the process of random edge-sampling and present a simple technique, which we call *random layering*, for analyzing the connectivity of the graph obtained through sampling. This technique also forms the basis of our min-cut approximation algorithm presented in the next section.

Edge Sampling: Consider an arbitrary unweighted multigraph $G = (V, E)$. Given a probability $p \in [0, 1]$, we define an *edge sampling experiment* as follows: choose subset $S \subseteq E$ by including each edge $e \in E$ in set S independently with probability p. We call the graph $G' = (V, S)$ *the sampled subgraph*.

We use the *random layering technique* to answer the following *network reliability* question: "How large should p be, as a function of minimum-cut size λ, so that the sampled graph is connected w.h.p.?"[3] Considering just one cut of size λ we see that if $p \leq \frac{1}{\lambda}$, then the probability that the sampled subgraph is connected is at most $\frac{1}{e}$. We show that $p \geq \frac{20 \log n}{\lambda}$ suffices so that the sampled subgraph is connected w.h.p. Note that this is non-trivial as a graph has exponential many cuts. It is easy to see that this bound is asymptotically optimal [23].

Theorem 1. *Consider an arbitrary unweighted multigraph $G = (V, E)$ with edge connectivity λ and choose subset $S \subseteq E$ by including each edge $e \in E$ in set S independently with probability p. If $p \geq \frac{20 \log n}{\lambda}$, then the sampled subgraph $G' = (V, S)$ is connected with probability at least $1 - \frac{1}{n}$.*

We remark that this result was known prior to this paper, via two different proofs by Lomonosov and Polesskii [23] and Karger [15]. The Lomonosov-Polesskii proof [23] uses an interesting coupling argument and shows that among the graphs of a given

---

[3] A rephrased version is, how large should the edge-connectivity λ of a network be such that it remains connected w.h.p. if each edge fails with probability $1 - p$.

edge-connectivity λ, a cycle of length n with edges of multiplicity $\lambda/2$ has the smallest probability of remaining connected under random sampling. Karger's proof [15] uses the powerful fact that the number of α-minimum cuts is at most $O(n^{2\alpha})$ and then uses basic probability concentration arguments (Chernoff and union bounds) to show that, w.h.p., each cut has at least one sampled edge. There are many known proofs for the $O(n^{2\alpha})$ upper bound on the number of α-minimum cuts (see [19]); an elegant argument follows from Karger's *random contraction algorithm* [14].

Our proof of Theorem 1 is simple and self-contained, and it is the only one of the three approaches that extends to the case of random vertex failures[4] [2, Theorem 1.5].

Proof (Proof of Theorem 1). Let $L = 20 \log n$. For each edge $e \in E$, we independently choose a uniform random *layer number* from the set $\{1, 2, \ldots, L\}$. Intuitively, we add the sampled edges layer by layer and show that with the addition of the sampled edges of each layer, the number of connected components goes down by at least a constant factor, with at least a constant probability, and independently of the previous layers. After $L = \Theta(\log n)$ layers, connectivity is achieved w.h.p.

We start by presenting some notations. For each $i \in \{1, \ldots, L\}$, let S_i be the set of sampled edges with layer number i and let $S_{i-} = \bigcup_{j=1}^{i} S_j$, i.e., the set of all sampled edges in layers $\{1, \ldots, i\}$. Let $G_i = (V, S_{i-})$ and let M_i be the number of connected components of graph G_i. We show that $M_L = 1$, w.h.p.

For any $i \in [1, L-1]$, since $S_{i-} \subseteq S_{(i+1)-}$, we have $M_{i+1} \leq M_i$. Consider the indicator variable X_i such that $X_i = 1$ iff $M_{i+1} \leq 0.87 M_i$ or $M_i = 1$. We show the following claim, after which, applying a Chernoff bound completes the proof.

Claim. For all $i \in [1, L-1]$ and $T \subseteq E$, we have $\Pr[X_i = 1 | S_{i-} = T] \geq 1/2$.

To prove this claim, we use *the principle of deferred decisions* [21] to view the two random processes of sampling edges and layering them. More specifically, we consider the following process: first, each edge is sampled and given layer number 1 with probability p/L. Then, each remaining edge is sampled and given layer number 2 with probability $\frac{p/L}{1-p/L} \geq p/L$. Similarly, after determining the sampled edges of layers 1 to i, each remaining edge is sampled and given layer number $i + 1$ with probability $\frac{p/L}{1-(i\,p)/L} \geq p/L$. After doing this for L layers, any remaining edge is considered not sampled and it receives a random layer number from $\{1, 2, \ldots, L\}$. It is easy to see that in this process, each edge is independently sampled with probability exactly p and each edge e gets a uniform random layer number from $\{1, 2, \ldots, L\}$, chosen independently of the other edges and also independently of whether e is sampled or not.

Fix a layer $i \in [1, \ldots, L-1]$ and a subset $T \subseteq E$. Let $S_{i-} = T$ and consider graph $G_i = (V, S_{i-})$. Figure 1 presents an example graph G_i and its connected components. If $M_i = 1$ meaning that G_i is connected, then $X_i = 1$. Otherwise, suppose that $M_i \geq 2$. For each component $\mathcal{C}$ of G_i, call the component *bad* if $(\mathcal{C}, V \setminus \mathcal{C}) \cap S_{i+1} = \emptyset$. That is, $\mathcal{C}$ is bad if after adding the sampled edges of layer $i + 1$, $\mathcal{C}$ does not get connected to any other component. We show that $\Pr[\mathcal{C} \text{ is bad}] \leq \frac{1}{e}$.

---

[4] There, the question is, how large the vertex sampling probability p has to be chosen, as a function of vertex connectivity k, so that the vertex-sampled graph is connected, w.h.p. The extension to the vertex version requires important modifications and leads to $p = \Omega(\frac{\log n}{\sqrt{k}})$ being a sufficient condition. Refer to [2, Section 3] for details.

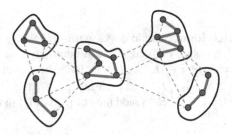

Fig. 1. Graph G_i and its connected components. The green solid links represent edges in S_{i-} and the blue dashed links represent $E \setminus S_{i-}$.

Since G is λ-edge connected, we have $w(C) \geq \lambda$. Moreover, none of the edges in $(C, V \setminus C)$ is in S_{i-}. Thus, using the principle of deferred decisions as described, each of the edges of the cut $(C, V \setminus C)$ has probability $\frac{p/L}{1-(ip)/L} \geq p/L$ to be sampled and given layer number $i+1$, i.e., to be in S_{i+1}. Since $p \geq \frac{20 \log n}{\lambda}$, the probability that none of the edges $(C, V \setminus C)$ is in set S_{i+1} is at most $(1 - p/L)^{\lambda} \leq 1/e$. Thus, $\Pr[C \text{ is bad}] \leq 1/e$. Having this, since each component that is not bad gets connected to at least one other component (when we look at graph G_{i+1}), a simple application of Markov's inequality proves the claim, and after that, a Chernoff bound completes the proof. See [10] for details.   □

Theorem 1 provides a very simple approach for finding an $O(\log n)$-approximation of the edge connectivity of a network graph G in $O(D + \sqrt{n} \log^2 n \log^* n)$ rounds, simply by trying exponentially growing sampling probabilities and checking the connectivity. The proof appears the full version [10]. We note that a similar basic approach has been used to approximate *the size* of min-cut in the streaming model [1].

Corollary 1. *There exists a distributed algorithm that for any unweighted multi-graph* $G = (V, E)$, *in* $O(D + \sqrt{n} \log^2 n \log^* n)$ *rounds, finds an approximation* $\tilde{\lambda}$ *of the edge connectivity such that* $\tilde{\lambda} \in [\lambda, \lambda \cdot \Theta(\log n)]$ *with high probability.*

4   Min-Cut Approximation by Random Layering

Now we use random layering to design a min-cut approximation algorithm. We present the outline of the algorithm and its major ideas but defer putting the pieces together to the proof of Theorem 2 in the full version [10].

Theorem 2. *There is a distributed algorithm that, for any* $\epsilon \in (0, 1)$, *finds an* $O(\epsilon^{-1})$-*minimum cut in* $O(D) + O(n^{0.5+\epsilon} \log^3 n \log \log n \log^* n)$ *rounds, w.h.p.*

4.1   Algorithm Outline

The algorithm is based on closely studying the sampled graph when the edge-sampling probability is between the two extremes of $\frac{1}{\lambda}$ and $\frac{\Theta(\log n)}{\lambda}$. Throughout this process, we identify a set $\mathcal{F}$ of $O(n \log n)$ cuts such that, with at least a 'reasonably large probability', $\mathcal{F}$ contains at least one 'small' cut.

The Crux of the Algorithm: Sample edges with probability $p = \frac{\epsilon \log n}{2\lambda}$ for a small $\epsilon \in (0,1)$. Also, assign each edge to a random layer in $[1, \ldots, L]$, where $L = 20 \log n$. For each layer $i \in [1, \ldots, L-1]$, let S_i be the set of sampled edges of layer i and let $S_{i-} = \bigcup_{j=1}^{i} S_j$. For each layer $i \in [1, \ldots, L-1]$, for each component $\mathcal{C}$ of graph $G_i = (V, S_{i-})$, add the cut $(\mathcal{C}, V \setminus \mathcal{C})$ to the collection $\mathcal{F}$.

We show that with probability at least $n^{-\epsilon}/2$, at least one of the cuts in $\mathcal{F}$ is an $O(\epsilon^{-1})$-minimum cut. Note that thus repeating the experiment for $\Theta(n^{\epsilon} \log n)$ times is enough to get that an $O(\epsilon^{-1})$-minimum cut is found w.h.p.

Theorem 3. *Consider performing the above sampling and layering experiment with edge sampling probability $p = \frac{\epsilon \log n}{2\lambda}$ for $\epsilon \in (0,1)$ and $L = 20 \log n$ layers. Then, $\Pr[\mathcal{F}$ contains an $O(\epsilon^{-1})$-minimum cut$] \geq n^{-\epsilon}/2$.*

Proof. Fix an edge sampling probability $p = \frac{\epsilon \log n}{2\lambda}$ for an $\epsilon \in (0,1)$ and let $\alpha = 40\epsilon^{-1}$. We say that a sampling and layering experiment is *successful* if $\mathcal{F}$ contains an α-minimum cut or if the sampled graph $G_L = (V, S_{L-})$ is connected. We first show that each experiment is *successful* with probability at least $1 - \frac{1}{n}$. The proof of this part is very similar to that of Theorem 1.

For an arbitrary layer number $1 \leq i \leq L-1$, consider graph $G_i = (V, S_{i-})$. If $M_i = 1$ meaning that G_i is connected, then G_L is also connected. Thus, in that case, the experiment is successful and we are done. In the more interesting case, suppose $M_i \geq 2$. For each component $\mathcal{C}$ of G_i, consider the cut $(\mathcal{C}, V \setminus \mathcal{C})$. If any of these cuts is α-minimum, then the experiment is successful as then, set $\mathcal{F}$ contains an α-minimum cut. On the other hand, suppose that for each component $\mathcal{C}$ of G_i, we have $w(\mathcal{C}) \geq \alpha\lambda$. Then, for each such component $\mathcal{C}$, each of the edges of cut $(\mathcal{C}, V \setminus \mathcal{C})$ has probability $\frac{p/L}{1-(ip)/L} \geq p/L$ to be in set S_{i+1} and since $w(\mathcal{C}) \geq \alpha\lambda$, where $\alpha = 20\epsilon^{-1}$, the probability that none of the edges of this cut in set S_{i+1} is at most $(1 - p/L)^{\alpha\lambda} \leq e^{\frac{p}{L}\cdot\alpha\lambda} = e^{-\frac{\epsilon \log n}{2\lambda}\cdot\frac{1}{L}\cdot\frac{40}{\epsilon}\cdot\lambda} = 1/e$. Hence, the probability that component $\mathcal{C}$ is *bad* as defined in the proof of Theorem 1 (i.e., in graph G_{i+1}, it does not get connected to any other component) is at most $1/e$. The rest of the proof can be completed exactly as the last paragraph of of the proof of Theorem 1, to show that

$$\Pr[\textit{successful experiment}] \geq 1 - 1/n.$$

Using a union bound, we know that

$$\Pr[\textit{successful experiment}] \leq \Pr[\mathcal{F} \text{ contains an } \alpha\text{-min cut}] + \Pr[G_L \text{ is connected}].$$

On the other hand,

$$\Pr[G_L \text{ is connected}] \leq 1 - n^{-\epsilon}.$$

This is because, considering a single mininmum cut of size λ, the probability that none of the edges of this cut are sampled, in which case the sampled subgraph is disconnected, is $(1 - \frac{\epsilon \log n}{2\lambda})^{\lambda} \geq n^{-\epsilon}$. Hence, we can conclude that

$$\Pr[\mathcal{F} \text{ contains an } \alpha\text{-min cut}] \geq (1-1/n) - (1-n^{-\epsilon}) = n^{-\epsilon} - 1/n \geq n^{-\epsilon}/2. \qquad \square$$

Remark: It was brought to our attention that the approach of Theorem 3 bears some cosmetic resemblance to the technique of Goel, Kapralov and Khanna [11]. As noted by Kapralov [13], the approaches are fundamentally different; the only similarity is having $O(\log n)$ repetitions of sampling. In [11], the objective is to estimate the *strong-connectivity* of edges via a streaming algorithm. See [11] for related definitions and note also that strong-connectivity is (significantly) different from (standard) connectivity. In a nutshell, [11] uses $O(\log n)$ iterations of sub-sampling, each time further sparsifying the graph until at the end, all edges with strong-connectivity less than a threshold are removed (and identified) while edges with strong connectivity that is a $\Theta(\log n)$ factor larger than the threshold are preserved (proven via Benczur-Karger's sparsification).

4.2 Testing Cuts

So far we know that $\mathcal{F}$ contains an α-minimum cut with a reasonable probability. We now need to devise a distributed algorithm to read or test the sizes of the cuts in $\mathcal{F}$ and find that α-minimum cut, in $O(D) + \tilde{O}(\sqrt{n})$ rounds.

Consider a layer i and the graph $G_i = (V, S_{i-})$. Notice that we do not need to read the exact size of the cut $(\mathcal{C}, V \setminus \mathcal{C})$. Instead, it is enough to devise a *test* that *passes* w.h.p. if $w(C) \leq \alpha\lambda$, and *does not pass* w.h.p. if $w(C) \geq (1 + \delta)\alpha\lambda$, for a small constant $\delta \in (0, 1/4)$. In the distributed realization of such a test, it would be enough if all the nodes in $\mathcal{C}$ consistently know whether the test passed or not. Next, we explain a simple algorithm for such a test. This test itself uses random edge sampling. Given such a test, in each layer $i \in [1, \ldots, L - 1]$, we can test all the cuts and if any cut passes the test, meaning that, w.h.p., it is a $((1 + \delta)\alpha)$-minimum cut, then we can pick such a cut.[5]

Lemma 1. *Given a subgraph $G' = (V, E')$ of the network graph $G = (V, E)$, a threshold κ and $\delta \in (0, 1/4)$, there exists a randomized distributed cut-tester algorithm with round complexity $\Theta\left(D + \frac{1}{\delta^2}\sqrt{n}\log n \log^* n\right)$ such that, w.h.p., for each node $v \in V$, we have: Let C be the connected component of G' that contains v. If $w(C) \leq \kappa/(1+\delta)$, the test passes at v, whereas if $w(C) \geq \kappa(1 + \delta)$, the test does not pass at v.*

For pseudo-code, we refer to the full version [10]. We first run Thurimella's connected component identification algorithm (refer to Section 2.1) on graph G for subgraph G', so that each node $v \in V$ knows the smallest id in its connected component of graph G'. Then, each node v adopts this label *componentID* as its own id (temporarily). Thus, nodes of each connected component of G' will have the same id. Now, the test runs in $\Theta(\log^2 n/\delta^2)$ *experiments*, each as follows: in the jth experiment, for each edge $e \in E \setminus E'$, put edge e in set E_j with probability $p' = 1 - 2^{-\frac{1}{\kappa}}$. Then, run Thurimella's algorithm on graph G with subgraph $H_j = (V, E' \cup E_j)$ and with the new ids twice, such that at the end, each node v knows the smallest and the largest id in its connected component of H_j. Call these new labels $\ell_j^{min}(v)$ and $\ell_j^{max}(v)$, respectively. For a node v of a component C of G_i, we have that $\ell_j^{min}(v) \neq v.id$ or $\ell_j^{max}(v) \neq v.id$ iff at least one of the edges of cut $(\mathcal{C}, V \setminus \mathcal{C})$ is sampled in E_j, i.e., $(\mathcal{C}, V \setminus \mathcal{C}) \cap E_j \neq \emptyset$. Thus, each node v of each component $\mathcal{C}$ knows whether $(\mathcal{C}, V \setminus \mathcal{C}) \cap E_j \neq \emptyset$ or not.

---

[5] This can be done for example by picking the cut which passed the test and for which the related component has the smallest id among all the cuts that passed the test.

Moreover, this knowledge is consistent between all the nodes of component $\mathcal{C}$. After $\Theta(\log n/\delta^2)$ experiments, each node v of component $\mathcal{C}$ considers the test *passed* iff v noticed $(\mathcal{C}, V \setminus \mathcal{C}) \cap E_j \neq \emptyset$ in at most half of the experiments. We defer the calculations of the proof of Lemma 1 to of the full version [10].

5   Min-Cut Approximation via Matula's Approach

In [24], Matula presents an elegant centralized algorithm that for any constant $\varepsilon > 0$, finds a $(2 + \varepsilon)$-min-cut in $O(|V| + |E|)$ steps. Here, we explain how with the help of a few additional elements, this general approach can be used in the distributed setting, to find a $(2 + \varepsilon)$-minimum cut in $O((D + \sqrt{n}\log^* n)\log^2 n \log\log n \cdot \frac{1}{\varepsilon^5})$ rounds. We first recap the concept of *sparse certificates for edge connectivity*.

Definition 1. *For a given unweighted multi-graph $H = (V_H, E_H)$ and a value $k > 0$, a set $E^* \subseteq E_H$ of edges is a* sparse certificate *for k-edge-connectivity of H if (1) $|E^*| \leq k|V_H|$, and (2) for each edge $e \in E_H$, if there exists a cut $(\mathcal{C}, V \setminus \mathcal{C})$ of H such that $|(\mathcal{C})| \leq k$ and $e \in (\mathcal{C}, V \setminus \mathcal{C})$, then we have $e \in E^*$.*

Thurimella [29] presents a simple distributed algorithm that finds a sparse certificate for k-edge-connectivity of a network graph G in $O(k(D + \sqrt{n}\log^* n))$ rounds. With simple modifications, we get a generalized version, presented in Lemma 2. Details of these modification appear in the full version of this paper [10].

Lemma 2. *Let E_c be a subset of the edges of the network graph G and define the virtual graph $G' = (V', E')$ as the multi-graph that is obtained by contracting all the edges of G that are in E_c. Using the modified version of Thurimella's certificate algorithm, we can find a set $E^* \subseteq E \setminus E_c$ that is a sparse certificate for k-edge-connectivity of G', in $O(k(D + \sqrt{n}\log^* n))$ rounds.*

Following the approach of Matula's centralized algorithm[6] [24], and with the help of the sparse certificate algorithm of Lemma 2 and the random sparsification technique of Karger [15], we get the following result.

Theorem 4. *There is a distributed algorithm that, for any constant $\varepsilon > 0$, finds a $(2 + \varepsilon)$-minimum cut in $O((D + \sqrt{n}\log^* n)\log^2 n \log\log n \cdot \frac{1}{\varepsilon^5})$ rounds.*

Proof (Proof Sketch). We assume that nodes know a $(1 + \varepsilon/10)$-factor approximation $\tilde{\lambda}$ of the edge connectivity λ, and explain a distributed algorithm with round complexity $O((D + \sqrt{n}\log^* n)\log^2 n \cdot \frac{1}{\varepsilon^4})$. Note that this assumption can be removed at the cost of a $\Theta(\frac{\log\log n}{\log(1+\varepsilon/10)}) = \Theta(\log\log n \cdot \frac{1}{\varepsilon})$ factor increase in round complexity by trying $\Theta(\frac{\log\log n}{\varepsilon})$ exponential guesses $\tilde{\lambda}(1 + \varepsilon/10)^i$ for $i \in [0, \Theta(\frac{\log\log n}{\varepsilon})]$ where $\tilde{\lambda}$ is an $O(\log n)$-approximation of the edge-connectivity, which can be found by Corollary 1.

For simplicity, we first explain an algorithm that finds a $(2 + \varepsilon)$-minimum cut in $O(\lambda(D + \sqrt{n}\log^* n)\log n \cdot \frac{1}{\varepsilon^2})$ rounds. Then, we explain how to reduce the round complexity to $O((D + \sqrt{n}\log^* n)\log^2 n \cdot \frac{1}{\varepsilon^4})$.

---

[6] We remark that Matula [24] never uses the name *sparse certificate* but he performs *maximum adjacency search* which indeed generates a sparse certificate.

Pseudo-code is given in the full version [10]. First, we compute a sparse certificate E^* for $\tilde{\lambda}(1+\varepsilon/5)$-edge-connectivity of G, using Thurimella's algorithm. Now consider the graph $H = (V, E \setminus E^*)$. We have two cases: either (a) H has at most $|V|(1-\varepsilon/10)$ connected components, or (b) there is a connected component $\mathcal{C}$ of H such that $w(\mathcal{C}) \le \frac{2\lambda(1+\varepsilon/10)(1+\varepsilon/5)}{1-\varepsilon/10} \le (2+\varepsilon)\lambda$. Note that if (a) does not hold, case (b) follows because H has at most $(1+\varepsilon/5)\tilde{\lambda}|V|$ edges.

In Case (b), we can find a $(2+\varepsilon)$-minimum cut by testing the connected components of H versus threshold $\kappa = \tilde{\lambda}(2+\varepsilon/3)$, using the Cut-Tester algorithm presented in Lemma 1. In Case (a), we solve the problem recursively on the virtual graph $G' = (V', E')$ that is obtained by contracting all the edges of G that are in $E_c = E \setminus E^*$. Note that this contraction preserves all the cuts of size at most $\tilde{\lambda}(1+\varepsilon/5) \ge \lambda$ but reduces the number of nodes (in the virtual graph) at least by a $(1-\varepsilon/10)$-factor. Consequently, $O(\log(n)/\varepsilon)$ recursions reduce the number of components to at most 2 while preserving the min-cut.

The dependence on λ can be removed by considering the graph $G_S = (V, E_S)$, where E_S independently contains every edge of G with probability $\Theta\left(\frac{\log n}{\varepsilon^2\lambda}\right)$. It can be shown that the edge connectivity of G_S is $\Theta(\log(n)/\varepsilon^2)$ and a min-cut of G_S gives a $(1+O(\varepsilon))$-min-cut of G. The details appear in the full version [10].   □

6   Lower Bounds

In this section, we describe a lower bound that allows to strengthen and generalize some of the lower bounds of Das Sarma et al. from [4]. Our lower bound uses the same basic approach as the lower bounds in [4]. The lower bounds of [4] are based on an n-node graph G with diameter $O(\log n)$ and two distinct nodes s and r. The proof deals with distributed protocols where node s gets a b-bit input x, node r gets a b-bit input y, and apart from x and y, the initial states of all nodes are globally known. Slightly simplified, the main technical result of [4] (Simulation Theorem 3.1) states that if there is a randomized distributed protocol that correctly computes the value $f(x, y)$ of a binary function $f : \{0, 1\}^b \times \{0, 1\}^b \to \{0, 1\}$ with probability at least $1 - \varepsilon$ in time T (for sufficiently small T), then there is also a randomized ε-error two-party protocol for computing $f(x, y)$ with communication complexity $O(TB \log n)$. For our lower bounds, we need to extend the simulation theorem of [4] to a larger family of networks and to a slightly larger class of problems.

6.1   Generalized Simulation Theorem

Distributed Protocols: Given a weighted network graph $G = (V, E, w)$ ($\forall e \in E : w(e) \ge 1$), we consider distributed tasks for which each node $v \in V$ gets some private input $x(v)$ and every node $v \in V$ has to compute an output $y(v)$ such that the collection of inputs and outputs satisfies some given specification. To solve a given distributed task, the nodes of G apply a distributed protocol. We assume that initially, each node $v \in V$ knows its private input $x(v)$, as well as the set of neighbors in G. Time is divided into synchronous rounds and in each round, every node can send at most $B \cdot w(e)$ bits over each of its incident edges e. We say that a given (randomized) distributed protocol solves a given distributed task with error probability ε if the computed outputs satisfy the specification of the task with probability at least $1 - \varepsilon$.

Graph Family $\mathcal{G}(n, k, c)$: For parameters n, k, and c, we define the *family of graphs* $\mathcal{G}(n, k, c)$ as follows. A weighted graph $G = (V, E, w)$ is in the family $\mathcal{G}(n, k, c)$ iff $V = \{1, \ldots, n\}$ and for all $h \in \{1, \ldots, n\}$, the total weight of edges between nodes in $\{1, \ldots, h\}$ and nodes in $\{h + k + 1, \ldots, n\}$ is at most c. We consider distributed protocols on graphs $G \in \mathcal{G}(n, k, c)$ for given n, k, and c. For an integer $\eta \geq 1$, we define $L_\eta := \{1, \ldots, \eta\}$ and $R_\eta := \{n - \eta + 1, \ldots, n\}$. Given a parameter $\eta \geq 1$ and a network $G \in \mathcal{G}(n, k, c)$, we say that a two-party protocol between Alice and Bob η-solves a given distributed task for G with error probability ε if a) initially Alice knows all inputs and all initial states of nodes in $V \setminus R_\eta$ and Bob knows all inputs and all initial states of nodes in $V \setminus L_\eta$, and b) in the end, Alice outputs $y(v)$ for all $v \in L_{n/2}$ and Bob outputs $y(v)$ for all $v \in R_{n/2}$ such that with probability at least $1 - \varepsilon$, all these $y(v)$ are consistent with the specification of the given distributed task. A two-party protocol is said to be *public coin* if Alice and Bob have access to a common random string. The proof of the following theorem appears in the full version [10].

Theorem 5 (Generalized Simulation Theorem). *Assume we are given positive integers n, k, and η, a parameter $c \geq 1$, as well as a subfamily $\tilde{\mathcal{G}} \subseteq \mathcal{G}(n, k, c)$. Further assume that for a given distributed task and graphs $G \in \tilde{\mathcal{G}}$, there is a randomized protocol with error probability ε that runs in $T \leq (n - 2\eta)/(2k)$ rounds. Then, there exists a public-coin two-party protocol that η-solves the given distributed task on graphs $G \in \tilde{\mathcal{G}}$ with error probability ε and communication complexity at most $2BcT$.*

We now describe a generic construction to obtain graphs of the family $\mathcal{G}(n, k, c)$. Given some integer $n > 0$, we define $T_n = (V, E_T)$ to be a fixed unweighted binary tree on the nodes $V = \{1, \ldots, n\}$ with depth $\lceil \log_2 n \rceil$ where an *in-order DFS traversal* of T_n (starting at the root) reproduces the natural order $1, 2, \ldots, n$. The tree T_n can thus be seen as a binary search tree: Given any node i, for all nodes j of the left subtree of i, it holds that $j < i$ and for all nodes j of the right subtree of i, it holds that $j > i$.

Lemma 3. *Given an integer $p \in \{1, \ldots, n - 1\}$, consider the cut $(S_p, V \setminus S_p)$, where $S_p = \{1, \ldots, p\}$. For every $p \in \{1, \ldots, n - 1\}$, the number of edges between over the cut $(S_p, V \setminus T_p)$ is at most $\lceil \log_2 n \rceil$.*

Using the tree T_n, we can construct graphs from the family $\mathcal{G}(n, k, c)$ for $c = \lceil \log_2 n \rceil$. Let $\mathcal{H}(n, k)$ be the family of weighted graphs $H = (V, E_H, w_H)$ with node set $V = \{1, \ldots, n\}$ such that for all edges $\{i, j\} \in E_H$, $|j - i| \leq k$. Given a graph $H \in \mathcal{H}(n, k)$, we define a graph $G(H) = (V, E, w)$ with node set $V = \{1, \ldots, n\}$ as follows: (a) The edge set E of $G(H)$ is $E := E_H \cup E_T$. (b) The weight $w(e)$ of an edge $e \in E$ is given as $w(e) := \max\{1, w_H(e)\}$.

Lemma 4. *Given a graph $H \in \mathcal{H}(n, k)$, graph $G(\tilde{H}) \in \mathcal{G}(n, k, c)$ for $c = \lceil \log_2 n \rceil$. Further, the diameter of $G(H)$ is $O(\log n)$.*

6.2 Lower Bound for Approximating Minimum Cut

We start by proving a lower bound on approximating min-cut in weighted graphs (or equivalently in unweighted multigraphs).

Theorem 6. *In weighted graphs, for any $\alpha \geq 1$ and any $\lambda \geq 1$, computing an α-approximate minimum cut requires at least $\Omega\big(D + \sqrt{n/(B \log n)}\big)$ rounds.*

Proof. We prove the theorem by reducing from the two-party set disjointness problem [3,12,28]. Assume that as input, Alice gets a set X and Bob get a set Y such that both X and Y are of size p and the elements of X and Y are from a universe of size $O(p)$. It is known that for Alice and Bob need to exchange at least $\Omega(p)$ bits to determine whether X and Y are disjoint [12,28]. This lower bound holds even for public coin randomized protocols with constant error probability and it also holds if Alice and Bob are given the promise that if X and Y intersect, they intersect in exactly one element [28]. As a consequence, if Alice and Bob receive sets X and Y of size p as inputs such that $|X \cap Y| = 1$, finding $X \cap Y$ also requires Alice and Bob to exchange $\Omega(p)$ bits.

Assume that there is a protocol to find an α-minimum cut or to α-approximate the size of a minimum cut in time T with a constant error probability ε. In both cases, we show that Alice and Bob can use this protocol to efficiently solve set disjointness by simulating the distributed protocol on a special network.

We now describe the construction of this network. Let a and b be two positive integer parameters. We construct a graph $G \in \mathcal{G}(n, \lambda, O(\log n))$ as follows: First, we construct a weighted graph $H = (V_H, E_H, w_H) \in \mathcal{H}(a, 1)$ where the node set of H is $V_H = \{1, \ldots, a\}$ and there is an edge e of weight $w_H(e) = \alpha\lambda + 1$ between nodes i and j if and only if $|i-j| = 1$. By Lemma 4, we can then get a graph $G(H) \in \mathcal{G}(a, 1, O(\log n))$. To get a graph G, we add b additional copies of graph H. Call node i in the original copy $(i, 0)$ and node i in the jth additional copy node (i, j). In each copy $j \geq 1$, we connect node $(1, j)$ with node $(1, 0)$ by an edge of weight λ. By renaming node (i, j) to $\kappa(i, j) := j + (i-1)(b+1)$, we can see that graph G is in $\mathcal{G}(a(b+1), b+1, O(\log n))$. In the following, let $n = a(b+1)$ be the number of nodes of G. The first $b+1$ nodes of G are nodes $(1, j)$ for $0 \leq j \leq b$, the last $b+1$ nodes of G are nodes (a, j) for $0 \leq j \leq b$. Note that graph G is exactly λ-edge connected as any of the edges $\{(1, j), (1, 0)\}$ defines a cut of size λ. Note also that every cut which divides one of the copies of H into two or more parts has size at least $\alpha\lambda + 1$.

Assume that Alice and Bob need to solve a set disjointness instance where $X \subset \{1, \ldots, b\}$, $Y \subset \{1, \ldots, b\}$, $|X \cap Y| \leq 1$, and $|X|, |Y| = \Omega(b)$. The graph G is extended such that the minimum cut problem in G represents the given set cover instance. For each $x \notin X$, the weight of the edge $\{(1, x), (1, 0)\}$ is increased to $\alpha\lambda + 1$. Further, for every $y \notin Y$, we add an edge $\{(a, y), (a, 0)\}$ of weight $\alpha\lambda + 1$. Now, if and only if $X \cap Y = \emptyset$, every copy of H is connected to the first copy by a link of weight $\alpha\lambda + 1$. Therefore, if X and Y are disjoint, the size of a minimum cut is at least $\alpha\lambda + 1$ and if X and Y intersect, there is a cut of size λ.

Alice knows the initial states of nodes (i, j) for all $i < a$ and thus for the nodes (i, j) with $1 \leq \kappa(i, j) < n - b$ (i.e., all except the last $b + 1$ nodes) and Bob knows the initual states of nodes (i, j) for all $i > 1$ and thus for the nodes (i, j) with $b + 1 < \kappa(i, j) \leq n$ (i.e., all except the first $b + 1$ nodes). If we have $T < (n - 2)/(2(b+1)) =$

$O(n/b) = O(a)$ for the time complexity T of the distributed minimum cut approximation protocol, Theorem 5 implies that Alice and Bob can $(b + 1)$-solve the distributed task of α-approximating the minimum cut with total communication complexity at most $O(TB \log n)$. As a consequence, Alice and Bob can also solve the given set disjointness instance using the same protocol and from the known set disjointness communication complexity lower bound, we therefore get $TB \log n = \Omega(b)$. Choosing $a = \Theta(\sqrt{n/(B \log n)})$ and $b = \Theta(\sqrt{nB \log n})$ this implies the claimed lower bound for approximating the size of the minimum cut. Assuming that Alice and Bob already know that $|X \cap Y| = 1$, the communication complexity lower bound on finding $X \cap Y$ also implies the same lower bound for finding an α-minimum cut, even if the size λ of the minimum cut is known. □

We now present our lower bound about min-cut approximation in unweighted simple graphs.

Theorem 7. *In unweighted simple graphs, for any $\alpha \geq 1$ and $\lambda \geq 1$, computing an α-approximate minimum cut requires at least $\Omega\left(D + \sqrt{\frac{n}{B\sqrt{\alpha\lambda}\log n}}\right)$ rounds.*

Proof (Proof Sketch). The proof is essentially done in the same way as the proof of Theorem 6. We therefore only describe the differences between the proofs. Because in a simple unweighted graph, we cannot add edges with different weights and we cannot add multiple edges, we have to construct the graph differently. Let us first describe the simple, unweighted graph H' corresponding to H in the construction of Theorem 7. Instead of a being path of length a with edges of weight $\alpha\lambda + 1$, H' is a sequence of a cliques of size $\lceil\sqrt{\alpha\lambda + 1}\rceil$. Adjacent cliques are connected by complete bipartite graphs (with at least $\alpha\lambda + 1$ edges). We again have $b + 1$ copies of H', where copy 0 is augmented with a complete binary tree by using Lemma 4. Each edge $\{(1,0),(1,j)\}$ of weight λ is replaced by λ edges between clique $(1,0)$ and clique $(1,j)$. Edges of weight $\alpha\lambda + 1$ between nodes $(1,0)$ and $(1,j)$ and between nodes $(a,0)$ and (a,j) are replaced by complete bipartite graphs between the respective cliques. Again, by simulating a minimum cut approximation algorithm on the constructed graph, Alice and Bob can solve a given set disjointness instance for a universe of size b. However, the number of nodes of the network in this case is $\Theta(ab\sqrt{\alpha\lambda})$ leading to the lower bound claimed by the theorem. □

Acknowledgment. We thank David Karger for helpful discussions in the early stages of this work and thank Michael Kapralov for discussing cosmetic similarities with [11].

References

1. Ahn, K.J., Guha, S., McGregor, A.: Graph sketches: sparsification, spanners, and subgraphs. In: Proc. of the 31st Symp. on Princ. of Database Sys., PODS 2012, pp. 5–14 (2012)
2. Censor-Hillel, K., Ghaffari, M., Kuhn, F.: A new perspective on vertex connectivity. arXiv (2013), http://arxiv.org/abs/1304.4553
3. Chattapodhyay, A., Pitassi, T.: The story of set disjointness. SIGACT News Complexity Theory Column 67 (2011)

4. Das Sarma, A., Holzer, S., Kor, L., Korman, A., Nanongkai, D., Pandurangan, G., Peleg, D., Wattenhofer, R.: Distributed verification and hardness of distributed approximation. SIAM J. on Comp. 41(5), 1235–1265 (2012)
5. Elias, P., Feinstein, A., Shannon, C.E.: Note on maximum flow through a network. IRE Transactions on Information Theory IT-2, 117–199 (1956)
6. Elkin, M.: Distributed approximation: a survey. SIGACT News 35(4), 40–57 (2004)
7. Ford, L.R., Fulkerson, D.R.: Flows in Networks. Princeton Univ. Press (2010)
8. Ford, L.R., Fulkersonn, D.R.: Maximal flow through a network. Canad. J. Math. 8, 399–404 (1956)
9. Gabow, H.N.: A matroid approach to finding edge connectivity and packing arborescences. In: Proc. 23rd ACM Symposium on Theory of Computing (STOC), pp. 112–122 (1991)
10. Ghaffari, M., Kuhn, F.: Distributed minimum cut approximation. arXiv (2013), http://arxiv.org/abs/1305.5520
11. Goel, A., Kapralov, M., Khanna, S.: Graph sparsification via refinement sampling. arXiv (2010), http://arxiv.org/abs/1004.4915
12. Kalyanasundaram, B., Schnitger, G.: The probabilistic communication complexity of set intersection. SIAM J. Discrete Math. 5(4), 545–557 (1992)
13. Kapralov, M.: Personal communication (August 2013)
14. Karger, D.R.: Global min-cuts in $\mathcal{RNC}$, and other ramifications of a simple min-out algorithm. In: Prc. 4th ACM-SIAM Symp. on Disc. Alg. (SODA), pp. 21–30 (1993)
15. Karger, D.R.: Random sampling in cut, flow, and network design problems. In: Proc. 26th ACM Symposium on Theory of Computing (STOC), STOC 1994, pp. 648–657 (1994)
16. Karger, D.R.: Random sampling in cut, flow, and network design problems. In: Proc. 26th ACM Symposium on Theory of Computing (STOC), pp. 648–657 (1994)
17. Karger, D.R.: Using randomized sparsification to approximate minimum cuts. In: Proc. 5th ACM-SIAM Symposium on Discrete Algorithms (SODA), pp. 424–432 (1994)
18. Karger, D.R.: Minimum cuts in near-linear time. In: Proc. 28th ACM Symp. on Theory of Computing (STOC), pp. 56–63 (1996)
19. Karger, D.R.: Minimum cuts in near-linear time. J. ACM 47(1), 46–76 (2000)
20. Karger, D.R., Stein, C.: An $\tilde{O}(n^2)$ algorithm for minimum cuts. In: Proc. 25th ACM Symposium on Theory of Computing (STOC), pp. 757–765 (1993)
21. Knuth, D.E.: Stable Marriage and Its Relation to Other Combinatorial Problems: An Introduction to the Mathematical Analysis of Algorithms. AMS (1996)
22. Kutten, S., Peleg, D.: Fast distributed construction of k-dominating sets and applications. In: Proc. of the 14th Annual ACM Symp. on Principles of Dist. Comp., PODC 1995, pp. 238–251 (1995)
23. Lomonosov, M.V., Polesskii, V.P.: Lower bound of network reliability. Problems of Information Transmission 7, 118–123 (1971)
24. Matula, D.W.: A linear time $2 + \varepsilon$ approximation algorithm for edge connectivity. In: Proc. of the 4th Annual ACM-SIAM Symposium on Disc. Alg., SODA 1993, pp. 500–504 (1993)
25. Nagamochi, H., Ibaraki, T.: Computing edge-connectivity in multigraphs and capacitated graphs. SIAM J. Discret. Math. 5(1), 54–66 (1992)
26. Peleg, D.: Distributed Computing: A Locality-Sensitive Approach. SIAM (2000)
27. Picard, J.C., Queyranne, M.: Selected applications of minimum cuts in networks. Infor. 20, 19–39 (1982)
28. Razborov, A.A.: On the distributional complexity of disjointness. Theor. Comp. Sci. 106, 385–390 (1992)
29. Thurimella, R.: Sub-linear distributed algorithms for sparse certificates and biconnected components. Journal of Algorithms 23(1), 160–179 (1997)

When Distributed Computation
Is Communication Expensive*

David P. Woodruff[1] and Qin Zhang[2]

[1] IBM Research Almaden
dpwoodru@us.ibm.com
[2] Indiana University Bloomington
qinzhang@cse.ust.hk

Abstract. We consider a number of fundamental statistical and graph problems in the message-passing model, where we have k machines (sites), each holding a piece of data, and the machines want to jointly solve a problem defined on the union of the k data sets. The communication is point-to-point, and the goal is to minimize the total communication among the k machines. This model captures all point-to-point distributed computational models with respect to minimizing communication costs. Our analysis shows that exact computation of many statistical and graph problems in this distributed setting requires a prohibitively large amount of communication, and often one cannot improve upon the communication of the simple protocol in which all machines send their data to a centralized server. Thus, in order to obtain protocols that are communication-efficient, one has to allow approximation, or investigate the distribution or layout of the data sets.

1 Introduction

Recent years have witnessed a spectacular increase in the amount of data being collected and processed in various applications. In many of these applications, data is often distributed across a group of machines, referred to as *sites* in this paper, which are connected by a communication network. These sites jointly compute a function defined on the union of the data sets by exchanging messages with each other. For example, consider the following scenarios.

1. We have a set of network routers, each observing a portion of the network, and periodically they want to compute some functions defined on the global network which can be used to determine the overall condition/health of the network. Concrete functions include the number of distinct source IP addresses, the set of most frequent destination IP addresses, etc.
2. The massive social network graphs are usually stored in many sites, and those graphs are keeping changing. To answer queries such as whether the whole graph is connected, or whether the graph exhibit a particular property (e.g., bipartiteness, cycle-freeness), we have to synthesize data from all the sites.

---

* Most of this work was done when the author was at IBM Research Almaden.

Y. Afek (Ed.): DISC 2013, LNCS 8205, pp. 16–30, 2013.
© Springer-Verlag Berlin Heidelberg 2013

In distributed computational models for big data, besides traditional measurement like local CPU processing time and the number of disk accesses, we are also interested in minimizing two other objectives, namely, the *communication cost* and the *round complexity*. The communication cost, which we shall also refer to as the communication complexity, denotes the total number of bits exchanged in all messages across the sites during a computation. The round complexity refers to the number of communication rounds needed for the computation, given various constraints on what messages can be sent by each site in each round.

The communication cost is a fundamental measure since communication is often the bottleneck of applications (e.g., applications mentioned above), and so it directly relates to energy consumption, network bandwidth usage, and overall running time. The round complexity is critical when the computation is partitioned into rounds and the initialization of each round requires a large overhead. In this paper we will focus on the communication complexity, and analyze problems in an abstract model called the message-passing model (see the definition in Section 1.1) that captures all models for point-to-point distributed computation in terms of their communication costs. In particular, our lower bound results hold even if the communication protocol sends only a single bit in each message, and each site has an unbounded amount of local memory and computational power. Note that this means our lower bounds are as strong as possible, not requiring any assumptions on the local computational power of the machines. We also present several upper bounds, all of which are also locally computationally efficient, meaning the protocols we present do not need extra memory beyond what is required to accommodate the input. We will briefly discuss the issue of round-efficiency in Section 7.

Common sources of massive data include numerical data, e.g., IP streams and logs of queries to a search engine, as well as graph data, e.g., web graphs, social networks, and citation graphs. In this paper we investigate the communication costs for solving several basic statistical and graph problems in the message-passing model. Solving these problems is a minimal requirement of protocols seeking to solve more complicated functions on distributed data.

We show that if we want to solve many of these problems exactly, then there are no better solutions than the almost trivial ones, which are usually quite communication-inefficient. The motivation of this work is thus to deliver the following message to people working on designing protocols for solving problems on distributed systems: for many statistical and graph problems in the distributed setting, if we want efficient communication protocols, then we need to consider the following relaxations to the original problem:

1. Allow for returning an approximate solution. Here, approximation can be defined as follows: for a problem whose output is a single numerical value x, allowing an approximation means that the protocol is allowed to return any value $\tilde{x}$ for which $\tilde{x} \in [(1 - \varepsilon)x, (1 + \varepsilon)x]$, for some small user-specified parameter $\varepsilon > 0$. For a problem whose output is YES or NO, e.g., a problem deciding if a certain property of the input exists or not, we could instead allow the protocol to return YES if the input is close to having the property (under some problem-specific notion of closeness) and NO if the input is far from having that property. For example, in the

graph connectivity problem, we return YES if the graph can be made connected by adding a small number of edges, while we return NO if the graph requires adding a large number of edges to be made connected. This latter notion of approximation coincides with the *property testing* paradigm [12] in the computer science literature. By allowing certain approximations we can sometimes drastically reduce the communication costs. Concrete examples and case studies will be given in Section 2 and Section 6.

2. Use well-designed input layouts. Here are two examples: (1) All edges from the same node are stored in the same site or on only a few sites. In our lower bounds the edges adjacent to a node are typically stored across many different sites. (2) Each edge is stored on a unique (or a small number) of different sites. Our results in Table 1 show that whether or not the input graph has edges that occur on multiple sites can make a huge difference in the communication costs.

3. Explore prior distributional properties of the input dataset, e.g., if the dataset is skewed, or the underlying graph is sparse or follows a power-law distribution. Instead of developing algorithms targeting the worst-case distributions, as those used in our lower bounds, if one is fortunate enough to have a reasonable model of the underlying distribution of inputs, this can considerably reduce communication costs. An extreme example is that of a graph on n vertices - if the graph is completely random, meaning, each possible edge appears independently with probability p, then the k sites can simply compute the total number of edges m to decide whether or not the input graph is connected with high probability. Indeed, by results in random graph theory, if $m \geq 0.51n \log n$ then the graph is connected with very high probability, while if $m \leq 0.49n \log n$ then the graph is disconnected with very high probability [8]. Of course, completely random graphs are unlikely to appear in practice, though other distributional assumptions may also result in more tractable problems.

1.1 The Message-Passing Model

In this paper we consider the message-passing model, studied, for example, in [23,26]. In this model we have k sites, e.g., machines, sensors, database servers, etc., which we denote as $P_1, \ldots, P_k$. Each site has some portion of the overall data set, and the sites would like to compute a function defined on the union of the k data sets by exchanging messages. There is a two-way communication channel between all pairs of players P_i and P_j. Then, since we will prove lower bounds, our lower bounds also hold for topologies in which each player can only talk to a subset of other players. The communication is point-to-point, that is, if P_i talks to P_j, then the other $k - 2$ sites do not see the messages exchanged between P_i and P_j. At the end of the computation, at least one of the sites should report the correct answer. The goal is to minimize the total number of bits and messages exchanged among the k sites. For the purposes of proving impossibility results, i.e., lower bounds, we can allow each site to have an infinite local memory and infinite computational power; note that such an assumption will only make our lower bounds stronger. Further, we do not place any constraints on the format of messages or any ordering requirement on the communication, as long as it is point-to-point.

The message-passing model captures all point-to-point distributed communication models in terms of the communication cost, including the BSP model by Valiant [25], the $\mathcal{MRC}$ MapReduce framework proposed by Karloff et al. [19], the generic MapReduce model by Goodrich et al. [13], and the Massively Parallel model by Koutris and Suciu [20].

Remark 1. We comment that in some settings, where the primary goal is to parallelize a single computation on a big dataset, communication may not be the only bottleneck; CPU time and disk accesses are also important. However, in this paper we are mainly interested in the following setting: The data has already been distributed to the sites, and perhaps keeps changing. The goal is to periodically compute some function that is defined on the dataset (e.g., queries). In this setting, communication is usually the most expensive operation, since it directly connects to network bandwidth usage and energy consumption.

1.2 Our Results

We investigate lower bounds (impossibility results) and upper bounds (protocols) of the exact computation of the following basic statistical and graph problems in the message-passing model.

1. Statistical problems: computing the number of distinct elements, known as F_0 in the database literature; and finding the element with the maximum frequency, known as the ℓ_∞ or iceberg query problem. We note that the lower bound for ℓ_∞ also applies to the heavy-hitter problem of finding all elements whose frequencies exceed a certain threshold, as well as many other statistical problems for which we have to compute the elements with the maximum frequency exactly.
2. Graph problems: computing the degree of a vertex; testing cycle-freeness; testing connectivity; computing the number of connected components (#CC); testing bipartiteness; and testing triangles-freeness.

For each graph problem, we study its lower bound and upper bound in two cases: with edge duplication among the different sites and without edge duplication. Our results are summarized in Table 1. Note that all lower bounds are matched by upper bounds up to some logarithmic factors. For convenience, we use $\tilde{\Omega}(f)$ and $\tilde{O}(f)$ to denote functions of forms $f/\log^{O(1)}(f)$ and $f \cdot \log^{O(1)}(f)$, respectively. That is, we hide logarithmic factors.

We prove most of our lower bound results via reductions from a meta-problem that we call THRESH_θ^r. Its definition is given in Section 4.

In Section 6 we make a conjecture on the lower bound for the diameter problem, i.e., the problem of computing the distance of the farthest pair of vertices in a graph. This problem is one of the few problems that we cannot completely characterize by the technique proposed in this paper. We further show that by allowing an error as small as an additive-2, we can reduce the communication cost of computing the diameter by roughly a $\sqrt{n}$ factor, compared with the naive algorithm for exact computation. This further supports our claim that even a very slight approximation can result in a dramatic savings in communication.

Table 1. All results are in terms of number of bits of communication. Our lower bounds hold for randomized protocols which succeed with at least a constant probability of $2/3$, while all of our upper bounds are deterministic protocols (which always succeed). k refers to the number of sites, with a typical value ranging from 100 to 10000 in practice. For F_0 and ℓ_∞, n denotes the size of the element universe. For graph problems, n denotes the number of vertices and m denotes the number of edges. d_v is the degree of the queried vertex v. We make the mild assumption that $\Omega(\log n) \le k \le \min\{n, m\}$. Let $r = \min\{n, m/k\}$. Except for the upper bound for cycle-freeness in the "without duplication" case, for which $m \ge n$ implies that a cycle necessarily exists (and therefore makes the problem statement vacuous), we assume that $m \ge n$ in order to avoid a messy and uninteresting case-by-case analysis.

Problem	With duplication		Without duplication	
	LB	UB	LB	UB
F_0	$\tilde{\Omega}(kF_0)$	$\tilde{O}(k(F_0 + \log n))$	–	–
ℓ_∞	$\tilde{\Omega}(\min\{k, \ell_\infty\}n)$	$\tilde{O}(\min\{k, \ell_\infty\}n)$	–	–
degree	$\tilde{\Omega}(kd_v)$	$O(kd_v \log n)$	$\tilde{\Omega}(k)$	$O(k \log n)$
cycle-freeness	$\tilde{\Omega}(kn)$	$\tilde{O}(kn)$	$\Omega(\min\{n, m\})$	$\tilde{O}(\min\{n, m\})$
connectivity	$\tilde{\Omega}(kn)$	$\tilde{O}(kn)$	$\tilde{\Omega}(kr)$	$\tilde{O}(kr)$
#CC	$\tilde{\Omega}(kn)$	$\tilde{O}(kn)$	$\tilde{\Omega}(kr)$	$\tilde{O}(kr)$
bipartiteness	$\tilde{\Omega}(kn)$	$\tilde{O}(kn)$	$\tilde{\Omega}(kr)$	$\tilde{O}(kr)$
triangle-freeness	$\tilde{\Omega}(km)$	$\tilde{O}(km)$	$\Omega(m)$	$\tilde{O}(m)$

1.3   Related Work

For statistical problems, a number of approximation algorithms have been proposed recently in the *distributed streaming* model, which can be thought of as a dynamic version of the one-shot distributed computation model considered in this paper: the k local inputs arrive in the streaming fashion and one of the sites has to continuously monitor a function defined on the union of the k local inputs. All protocols in the distributed streaming model are also valid protocols in our one-shot computational model, while our impossibility results in our one-shot computational model also apply to all protocols in the distributed streaming model. Example functions studied in the distributed streaming model include F_0 [7], F_2 (size of self join) [7,26], quantile and heavy-hitters [15], and the empirical entropy [3]. All of these problems have much lower communication cost if one allows an approximation of the output number x in a range $[(1 - \varepsilon)x, (1 + \varepsilon)x]$, as mentioned above (the definition as to what ε is for the various problems differs). These works show that if an approximation is allowed, then all these problems can be solved using only $\tilde{O}(k/\varepsilon^{O(1)})$ bits of communication. A suite of (almost) matching lower bounds for approximate computations was developed in [26]. For exact F_0 computation, the best previous communication cost lower bound was $\Omega(F_0 + k)$ bits. In this paper we improve the communication cost lower bound to $\tilde{\Omega}(kF_0)$, which is optimal up to a small logarithmic factor.

For graph problems, Ahn, Guha and McGregor [1,2] developed an elegant technique for *sketching* graphs, and showed its applicability to many graph problems including connectivity, bipartiteness, and minimum spanning tree. Each sketching step in these algorithms can be implemented in the message-passing model as follows: each site computes a sketch of its local graph and sends its sketch to P_1. The site P_1 then combines these k sketches into a sketch of the global graph. The final answer can be obtained based on the global sketch that P_1 computes. Most sketches in [1,2] are of size $\tilde{O}(n^{1+\gamma})$ bits (for a small constant $\gamma \geq 0$), and the number of sketching steps varies from 1 to a constant. Thus direct implementations of these algorithms in the message-passing model have communication $\tilde{O}(k \cdot n^{1+\gamma})$ bits. On the lower bound side, it seems not much is known. Phillips et al. [23] proved an $\Omega(kn/\log^2 k)$ bits lower bound for connectivity. Their lower bound proof relies on a well-crafted graph distribution. In this paper we improve their lower bound by a factor of $\log k$. Another difference is that their proof requires the input to have edge duplications, while our lower bound holds even if there are no edge duplications, showing that the problem is hard even if each edge occurs on a single site. Very recently in an unpublished manuscript, Huang et. al. [14] showed that $\Omega(kn)$ bits of communication is necessary in order to even compute a constant factor approximation to the size of the maximum matching of a graph. Their result, however, requires that the entire matching has to be reported, and it is unknown if a similar lower bound applies if one is only interested in estimating the matching size.

Besides statistical and graph problems, Koutris and Suciu [20] studied evaluating conjunctive queries in their massively parallel model. Their lower bounds are restricted to one round of communication, and the message format has to be tuple-based, etc. Some of these assumptions are removed in a recent work by Beame et al. [5]. We stress that in our message-passing model there is no such restriction on the number of rounds and the message format; our lower bounds apply to *arbitrary* communication protocols. Recently, Daumé III et al. [16,17] and Balcan et al. [4] studied several problems in the setting of distributed learning, in the message-passing model.

1.4   Conventions

Let $[n] = \{1, \ldots, n\}$. All logarithms are base-2. All communication complexities are in terms of bits. We typically use capital letters $X, Y, \ldots$ for sets or random variables, and lower case letters $x, y, \ldots$ for specific values of the random variables $X, Y, \ldots$. We write $X \sim \mu$ to denote a random variable chosen from distribution μ. For convenience we often identify a set $X \subseteq [n]$ with its characteristic vector when there is no confusion, i.e., the bit vector which is 1 in the i-th bit if and only if element i occurs in the set X.

All our upper bound protocols are either deterministic or only using private randomness. We make a mild assumption that $\Omega(\log n) \leq k \leq \min\{n, m\}$, where for F_0 and ℓ_∞, n denotes the size of the element universe; and for graph problems, n denotes the number of vertices and m denotes the number of edges.

1.5   Roadmap

In Section 2, we give a case study on the number of distinct elements (F_0) problem. In Section 3, we include background on communication complexity which is needed for understanding the rest of the paper. In Section 4, we introduce the meta-problem THRESH_θ^r and study its communication complexity. In Section 5 and Section 6, we show how to prove lower bounds for a set of statistical and graph problems by performing reductions from THRESH_θ^r. We conclude the paper in Section 7.

2   The Number of Distinct Elements: A Case Study

In this section we give a brief case study on the number of distinct elements (F_0) problem, with the purpose of justifying the statement that approximation is often needed in order to obtain communication-efficient protocols in the distributed setting.

The F_0 problem requires computing the number of distinct elements of a data set. It has numerous applications in network traffic monitoring [9], data mining in graph databases [22], data integration [6], etc., and has been extensively studied in the last three decades, mainly in the data stream model. It began with the work of Flajolet and Martin [11] and culminated in an optimal algorithm by Kane et al. [18]. In the streaming setting, we see a stream of elements coming one at a time and the goal is to compute the number of distinct elements in the stream using as little memory as possible. In [10], Flajolet et al. reported that their HyperLogLog algorithm can estimate cardinalities beyond 10^9 using a memory of only 1.5KB, and achieve a relative accuracy of 2%, compared with the 10^9 bytes of memory required if we want to compute F_0 exactly.

Similar situations happen in the distributed communication setting, where we have k sites, each holding a set of elements from the universe $[n]$, and the sites want to compute the number of distinct elements of the union of their k data sets. In [7], a $(1 + \varepsilon)$-approximation algorithm (protocol) with $O(k(\log n + 1/\varepsilon^2 \log 1/\varepsilon))$ bits of communication was given in the distributed streaming model, which is also a protocol in the message-passing model. In a typical setting, we could have $\varepsilon = 0.01$, $n = 10^9$ and $k = 1000$, in which case the communication cost is about 6.6×10^7 bits [1]. On the other hand, our result shows that if exact computation is required, then the communication cost among the k sites needs to be at least be $\Omega(kF_0/\log k)$ (See Corollary 1), which is already 10^9 bits even when $F_0 = n/100$.

3   Preliminaries

In this section we introduce some background on communication complexity. We refer the reader to the book by Kushilevitz and Nisan [21] for a more complete treatment.

In the basic two-party communication complexity model, we have two parties (also called sites or players), which we denote by Alice and Bob. Alice has an input x and Bob has an input y, and they want to jointly compute a function $f(x, y)$ by communicating with each other according to a protocol Π. Let $\Pi(x, y)$ be the transcript of the protocol, that is, the concatenation of the sequence of messages exchanged by Alice and Bob, given the inputs x and y. In this paper when there is no confusion, we abuse notation by using Π for both a protocol and its transcript, and we further abbreviate the transcript $\Pi(x, y)$ by Π.

The *deterministic communication complexity* of a deterministic protocol is defined to be $\max\{|\Pi(x, y)| \mid$ all possible inputs $(x, y)\}$, where $|\Pi(x, y)|$ is the number of bits in the transcript of the protocol Π on inputs x and y. The *randomized communication complexity* of a randomized protocol Π is the maximum number of bits in the transcript of the protocol over all possible inputs x, y, together with all possible random tapes of

---

[1] In the comparison we neglect the constants hidden in the big-O and big-Ω notation which should be small.

the players. We say a randomized protocol Π computes a function f correctly with error probability δ if for all input pairs (x, y), it holds that $\Pr[\Pi(x, y) \neq f(x, y)] \leq \delta$, where the probability is taken only over the random tapes of the players. The randomized δ-*error communication complexity* of a function f, denoted by $R^{\delta}(f)$, is the minimum communication complexity of a protocol that computes f with error probability δ.

Let μ be a distribution over the input domain, and let $(X, Y) \sim \mu$. For a deterministic protocol Π, we say that Π computes f with error probability δ on μ if $\Pr[\Pi(X, Y) \neq f(X, Y)] \leq \delta$, where the probability is over the choices of $(X, Y) \sim \mu$. The δ-*error* μ-*distributional communication complexity* of f, denoted by $D_{\mu}^{\delta}(f)$, is the minimum worst-case communication complexity of a deterministic protocol that gives the correct answer for f on at least $(1-\delta)$ fraction of all inputs (weighted by μ). We denote $ED_{\mu}^{\delta}(f)$ to be the δ-*error* μ-*distributional expected communication complexity*, which is define to be the minimum expected cost (rather than the worst-case cost) of a deterministic protocol that gives the correct answer for f on at least $(1 - \delta)$ fraction of all inputs (weighted by μ), where the expectation is taken over distribution μ.

We can generalize the two-party communication complexity to the multi-party setting, which is the message-passing model considered in this paper. Here we have k players (also called sites) $P_1, \ldots, P_k$ with P_j having the input x_j, and the players want to compute a function $f(x_1, \ldots, x_k)$ of their joint inputs by exchanging messages with each other. The transcript of a protocol always specifies which player speaks next. In this paper the communication is point-to-point, that is, if P_i talks to P_j, the other players do not see the messages sent from P_i to P_j. At the end of the communication, only one player needs to output the answer.

The following lemma shows that randomized communication complexity is lower bounded by distributional communication complexity under any distribution μ. We include a proof in Appendix A, since the original proof is for the two-party communication setting.

Lemma 1 (Yao's Lemma [28]). *For any function f, any $\delta > 0$, $R^{\delta}(f) \geq \max_{\mu} D_{\mu}^{\delta}(f)$.*

Therefore, one way to prove a lower bound on the randomized communication complexity of f is to first pick a (hard) input distribution μ for f, and then study its distributional communication complexity under μ.

Note that given a $1/3$-error randomized protocol for a problem f whose output is 0 or 1, we can always run the protocol $C \log(1/\delta)$ times using independent randomness each time, and then output the majority of the outcomes. By a standard Chernoff bound (see below), the output will be correct with error probability at most $e^{-\kappa C \log(1/\delta)}$ for an absolute constant κ, which is at most δ if we choose C to be a sufficiently large constant. Therefore $R^{1/3}(f) = \Omega(R^{\delta}(f)/\log(1/\delta)) = \Omega(\max_{\mu} D_{\mu}^{\delta}(f)/\log(1/\delta))$ for any $\delta \in (0, 1/3]$. Consequently, to prove a lower bound on $R^{1/3}(f)$ we only need to prove a lower bound on the distributional communication complexity of f with an error probability $\delta \leq 1/3$.

Chernoff Bound. Let $X_1, \ldots, X_n$ be independent Bernoulli random variables such that $\Pr[X_i = 1] = p_i$. Let $X = \sum_{i \in [n]} X_i$. Let $\mu = \mathsf{E}[X]$. It holds that $\Pr[X \geq (1+\delta)\mu] \leq e^{-\delta^2 \mu/3}$ and $\Pr[X \leq (1 - \delta)\mu] \leq e^{-\delta^2 \mu/2}$ for any $\delta \in (0, 1)$.

4 A Meta-problem

In this section we discuss a meta-problem THRESH_θ^r and we derive a communication lower bound for it. This meta-problem will be used to derive lower bounds for statistical and graph problems in our applications.

In THRESH_θ^r, site P_i $(i \in [k])$ holds an r-bit vector $x_i = \{x_{i,1}, \ldots, x_{i,r}\}$, and the k sites want to compute

$$\text{THRESH}_\theta^r(x_1, \ldots, x_k) = \begin{cases} 0, & \text{if } \sum_{j \in [r]} (\vee_{i \in [k]} x_{i,j}) \leq \theta, \\ 1, & \text{if } \sum_{j \in [r]} (\vee_{i \in [k]} x_{i,j}) \geq \theta + 1. \end{cases}$$

That is, if we think of the input as a $k \times r$ matrix with $x_1, \ldots, x_k$ as the rows, then in the THRESH_θ^r problem we want to find out whether the number of columns that contain a 1 is more than θ for a threshold parameter θ.

We will show a lower bound for THRESH_θ^r using the symmetrization technique introduced in [23]. First, it will be convenient for us to study the problem in the *coordinator* model.

The Coordinator Model. In this model we have an additional site called the coordinator [2], which has no input (formally, his input is the empty set). We require that the k sites can only talk to the coordinator. The message-passing model can be simulated by the coordinator model since every time a site P_i wants to talk to P_j, it can first send the message to the coordinator, and then the coordinator can forward the message to P_j. Such a re-routing only increases the communication complexity by a factor of 2 and thus will not affect the asymptotic communication complexity.

Let $f : \mathcal{X} \times \mathcal{Y} \to \{0, 1\}$ be an arbitrary function. Let μ be a probability distribution over $\mathcal{X} \times \mathcal{Y}$. Let $f_{\text{OR}}^k : \mathcal{X}^k \times \mathcal{Y} \to \{0, 1\}$ be the problem of computing $f(x_1, y) \vee f(x_2, y) \vee \ldots \vee f(x_k, y)$ in the coordinator model, where P_i has input $x_i \in \mathcal{X}$ for each $i \in [k]$, and the coordinator has $y \in \mathcal{Y}$. Given the distribution μ on $\mathcal{X} \times \mathcal{Y}$, we construct a corresponding distribution ν on $\mathcal{X}^k \times \mathcal{Y}$: We first pick $(X_1, Y) \sim \mu$, and then pick $X_2, \ldots, X_k$ from the conditional distribution $\mu \mid Y$.

The following theorem was originally proposed in [23]. Here we improve it by a $\log k$ factor by a slightly modified analysis, which we include here for completeness.

Theorem 1. *For any function $f : \mathcal{X} \times \mathcal{Y} \to \{0, 1\}$ and any distribution μ on $\mathcal{X} \times \mathcal{Y}$ for which $\mu(f^{-1}(1)) \leq 1/k^2$, we have $D_\nu^{1/k^3}(f_{\text{OR}}^k) = \Omega(k \cdot \text{ED}_\mu^{1/(100k^2)}(f))$.*

Proof. Suppose Alice has X and Bob has Y with $(X, Y) \sim \mu$, and they want to compute $f(X, Y)$. They can use a protocol $\mathcal{P}$ for f_{OR}^k to compute $f(X, Y)$ as follows. The first step is an input reduction. Alice and Bob first pick a random $I \in [k]$ using shared randomness, which will later be fixed by the protocol to make it deterministic. Alice simulates P_I by assigning it an input $X_I = X$. Bob simulates the coordinator and the remaining $k - 1$ players. He first assigns Y to the coordinator, and then samples $X_1, \ldots, X_{I-1}, X_{I+1}, \ldots, X_k$ independently according to the conditional distribution $\mu \mid Y$, and assigns X_i to P_i for each $i \in [k] \setminus I$. Now $\{X_1, \ldots, X_k, Y\} \sim \nu$. Since

---

[2] We can also choose, for example, P_1 to be the coordinator and avoid the need for an additional site, though having an additional site makes the notation cleaner.

$\mu(f^{-1}(1)) \leq 1/k^2$, with probability $(1 - 1/k^2)^{k-1} \geq 1 - 1/k$, we have $f(X_i, Y) = 0$ for all $i \in [k] \setminus I$. Consequently,

$$f_{\text{OR}}^k(X_1, \ldots, X_k, Y) = f(X, Y). \tag{1}$$

We say such an input reduction is *good*.

Alice and Bob construct a protocol $\mathcal{P}'$ for f by independently repeating the input reduction three times, and running $\mathcal{P}$ on each input reduction. The probability that at least one of the three input reductions is good is at least $1 - 1/k^3$, and Bob can learn which reduction is good without any communication. This is because in the simulation he locally generates all X_i ($i \in [k] \setminus I$) together with Y. On the other hand, by a union bound, the probability that $\mathcal{P}$ is correct for all three input reductions is at least $1 - 3/k^3$. Note that if we can compute $f_{\text{OR}}^k(X_1, \ldots, X_k, Y)$ correctly for a good input reduction, then by (1), $\mathcal{P}$ can also be used to correctly compute $f(X, Y)$. Therefore $\mathcal{P}$ can be used to compute $f(X, Y)$ with probability at least $1 - 3/k^3 - 1/k^3 \geq 1 - 1/(100k^2)$.

Since in each input reduction, $X_1, \ldots, X_k$ are independent and identically distributed, and since $I \in [k]$ is chosen randomly in the two input reductions, we have that in expectation over the choice of I, the communication between P_I and the coordinator is at most a $2/k$ fraction of the expected total communication of $\mathcal{P}$ given inputs drawn from ν. By linearity of expectation, if the expected communication cost of $\mathcal{P}$ for solving f_{OR}^k under input distribution ν with error probability at most $1/k^3$ is C, then the expected communication cost of $\mathcal{P}'$ for solving f under input distribution μ with error probability at most $1/(100k^2)$ is $O(C/k)$. Finally, by averaging there exists a fixed choice of $I \in [k]$, so that $\mathcal{P}'$ is deterministic and for which the expected communication cost of $\mathcal{P}'$ for solving f under input distribution μ with error probability at most $1/(100k^2)$ is $O(C/k)$. Therefore we have $D_\nu^{1/k^3}(f_{\text{OR}}^k) = \Omega(k \cdot \text{ED}_\mu^{1/(100k^2)}(f))$.

4.1 The 2-DISJ^r Problem

Now we choose a concrete function f to be the set-disjointness problem. In this problem we have two parties: Alice has $x \subseteq [r]$ while Bob has $y \subseteq [r]$, and the parties want to compute 2-DISJ$^r(x, y) = 1$ if $x \cap y \neq \emptyset$ and 0 otherwise. Set-disjointness is a classical problem used in proving communication lower bounds. We define an input distribution τ_β for 2-DISJ^r as follows. Let $\ell = (r + 1)/4$. With probability β, x and y are random subsets of $[r]$ such that $|x| = |y| = \ell$ and $|x \cap y| = 1$, while with probability $1 - \beta$, x and y are random subsets of $[r]$ such that $|x| = |y| = \ell$ and $x \cap y = \emptyset$. Razborov [24] proved that for $\beta = 1/4$, $D_{\tau_{1/4}}^{(1/4)/100}(2\text{-DISJ}^r) = \Omega(r)$, and one can extend his arguments to any $\beta \in (0, 1/4]$, and to the expected distributional communication complexity where the expectation is take over the input distribution.

Theorem 2 ([23], Lemma 2.2). *For any $\beta \in (0, 1/4]$, it holds that* $\text{ED}_{\tau_\beta}^{\beta/100}(2\text{-DISJ}^r)$ $= \Omega(r)$, *where the expectation is taken over the input distribution.*

4.2 The OR-DISJ^r Problem

If we choose f to be 2-DISJ^r and let $\mu = \tau_\beta$ with $\beta = 1/k^2$, then we call f_{OR}^k in the coordinator model the OR-DISJ^r Problem. By Theorem 1 and Theorem 2. We have

Theorem 3. $D_\nu^{1/k^3}(OR\text{-}DISJ^r) = \Omega(kr)$.

The Complexity of THRESH$_\theta^r$. We prove our lower bound for the setting of the parameter $\theta = (3r-1)/4$. We define the following input distribution ζ for THRESH$_{(3r-1)/4}^r$: We choose $\{X_1, \ldots, X_k, Y\} \sim \nu$ where ν is the input distribution for OR-DISJ^r, and then simply use $\{X_1, \ldots, X_k\}$ as the input for THRESH$_\theta^r$.

Lemma 2. *Under the distribution ζ, assuming $k \geq c_k \log r$ for a large enough constant c_k, we have that $\bigvee_{i \in [k]} X_{i,j} = 1$ for all $j \in [r] \backslash Y$ with probability $1 - 1/k^{10}$.*

Proof. For each $j \in [r] \backslash Y$, we have $\bigvee_{i \in [k]} X_{i,j} = 1$ with probability at least $1 - (1 - 1/4)^k$. This is because $\Pr[X_{i,j} = 1] \geq 1/4$ for each $j \in [r] \backslash Y$, by our choices of X_i. By a union bound, with probability $1 - (3/4)^k \cdot |[r] \backslash Y| = 1 - (3/4)^k \cdot (3r-1)/4 \geq 1 - 1/k^{10}$. (by our assumption $c_k \log r \leq k \leq r$ for a large enough constant c_k), we have $\bigvee_{i \in [k]} X_{i,j} = 1$ for all $j \in [r] \backslash Y$.

Theorem 4. $D_\zeta^{1/k^4}(THRESH_{(3r-1)/4}^r) = \Omega(kr)$, *assuming $c_k \log r \leq k \leq r$ for a large enough constant c_k.*

Proof. By Lemma 2, it is easy to see that any protocol $\mathcal{P}$ that computes THRESH$_{(3r-1)/4}^r$ on input distribution ζ correctly with error probability $1/k^4$ can be used to compute OR-DISJ^r on distribution ν correctly with error probability $1/k^4 + 1/k^{10} < 1/k^3$, since if $(X_1, \ldots, X_k, Y) \sim \nu$, then with probability $1 - 1/k^{10}$, we have

$$OR\text{-}DISJ^r(X_1, \ldots, X_k, Y) = THRESH_{(3r-1)/4}^r(X_1, \ldots, X_k).$$

The theorem follows from Theorem 3.

5   Statistical Problems

For technical convenience, we make the mild assumption that $c_k \log n \leq k \leq n$ where c_k is some large enough constant. For convenience, we will repeatedly ignore an additive $O(1/k^{10})$ error probability introduced in the reductions, since these will not affect the correctness of the reductions, and can be added to the overall error probability by a union bound.

5.1 F_0 (#Distinct-Elements)

Recall that in the F_0 problem, each site P_i has a set $S_i \subseteq [n]$, and the k sites want to compute the number of distinct elements in $\bigcup_{i \in [k]} S_i$.

For the lower bound, we reduce from THRESH$_{(3n-1)/4}^n$. Given $\{X_1, \ldots, X_k\} \sim \zeta$ for THRESH$_{(3n-1)/4}^n$, each site sets $S_i = X_i$. Let σ_F be the input distribution of F_0 after this reduction.

By Lemma 2 we know that under distribution ζ, with probability $1 - 1/k^{10}$, for all $j \in [n] \backslash Y$ (recall that Y is the random subset of $[n]$ of size $(n+1)/4$ we used to construct $X_1, \ldots, X_k$ in distribution ζ), $\bigvee_{i \in [k]} X_{i,j} = 1$. Conditioned on this event, we have $\text{THRESH}_{(3n-1)/4}^n(X_1, \ldots, X_k) = 1 \iff F_0(\cup_{i \in [k]} S_i) > (3n-1)/4$. Therefore, by Theorem 4 we have that $D_{\sigma_F}^{1/k^4}(F_0) = \Omega(kn)$. Note that in this reduction, we have to choose $n = \Theta(F_0)$. Therefore, it makes more sense to write the lower bound as $D_{\sigma_F}^{1/k^4}(F_0) = \Omega(kF_0)$. The following corollary follows from Yao's Lemma and the discussion following it.

Corollary 1. $R^{1/3}(F_0) = \Omega(kF_0/\log k)$.

An almost matching upper bound of $O(k(F_0 \log F_0 + \log n))$ can be obtained as follows: the k sites first compute a 2-approximation F_0' to F_0 using the protocol in [7] (see Section 2), which costs $O(k \log n)$ bits. Next, they hash every element to a universe of size $(F_0')^3$, so that there are no collisions among hashed elements with probability at least $1 - 1/F_0$, by a union bound. Finally, all sites send their distinct elements (after hashing) to P_1 and then P_1 computes the number of distinct elements over the union of the k sets locally. This step costs $O(kF_0 \log F_0)$ bits of communication.

5.2 ℓ_∞ (MAX)

In the ℓ_∞ problem, each site P_i has a set $S_i \subseteq [n]$, and the k sites want to find an element in $\bigcup_{i \in [k]} S_i$ with the maximum frequency.

For the lower bound, we again reduce from $\text{THRESH}_{(3n-1)/4}^n$. Recall that in our hard input distribution for $\text{THRESH}_{(3n-1)/4}^n$, there is one special column that contains zero or a single 1. The high level idea is that we try to make this column to have the maximum number of 1's if originally it contains a single 1, by flipping bits over a random set of rows. Concretely, given an input $\{X_1, \ldots, X_k\} \sim \zeta$ for $\text{THRESH}_{(3n-1)/4}^n$, the k sites create an input $\{S_1, \ldots, S_k\}$ as follows: first, P_1 chooses a set $R \subseteq [k]$ by independently including each $i \in [k]$ with probability $7/8$, and informs all sites P_i ($i \in R$) by sending each of them a bit. This step costs $O(k)$ bits of communication. Next, for each $i \in R$, P_i flips $X_{i,j}$ for each $j \in [n]$. Finally, each P_i includes $j \in S_i$ if $X_{i,j} = 1$ after the flip and $j \notin S_i$ if $X_{i,j} = 0$. Let σ_L be the input distribution of ℓ_∞ after this reduction.

They repeat this input reduction independently T times where $T = c_T \log k$ for a large constant c_T, and at each time they run $\ell_\infty(\cup_{i \in [k]} S_i)$. Let $R_1, \ldots, R_T$ be the random set R sampled by P_1 in the T runs, and let $O_1, \ldots, O_T$ be the outputs of the T runs. They return $\text{THRESH}_{(3n-1)/4}^n(X_1, \ldots, X_k) = 1$ if there exists a $t \in [T]$ such that $O_t \geq |R_t| + 1$ and 0 otherwise.

We focus on a particular input reduction. We view an input for $\text{THRESH}_{(3n-1)/4}^n$ as a $k \times n$ matrix. The i-th row of the matrix is X_i. After the bit-flip operations, for each column $j \in [n] \backslash Y$, we have for each $i \in [k]$ that $\Pr[X_{i,j} = 1] \leq 7/8 \cdot \left(1 - \frac{(n+1)/4 - 1}{(3n-1)/4}\right) + 1/8 \cdot \frac{(n+1)/4}{(3n-1)/4} < 3/4$. By a Chernoff bound, for each $j \in [n] \backslash Y$, $\sum_{i \in [k]} X_{i,j} < 13k/16$ with probability $1 - e^{-\Omega(k)}$. Therefore with probability at least $(1 - e^{-\Omega(k)} \cdot n) \geq (1 - 1/k^{10})$ (assuming that $c_k \log n \leq k \leq n$ for a large enough constant c_k), $\sum_{i \in [k]} X_{i,j} < 13k/16$ holds for all $j \in [n] \backslash Y$.

Now we consider columns in Y. We can show again by Chernoff bound that $|R| > 13k/16$ with probability $(1 - 1/k^{10})$ for all columns in Y, since each $i \in [k]$ is included into R with probability $7/8$, and before the flips, the probability that $X_{i,j} = 1$ for an i when $j \in Y$ is negligible. Therefore with probability $(1 - 1/k^{10})$, the column with the maximum number of 1s is in the set Y, which we condition on in the rest of the analysis.

In the case when $\text{THRESH}^n_{(3n-1)/4}(X_1, \ldots, X_k) = 1$, then with probability at least $1/8$, there exists a column $j \in Y$ and a row $i \in [k] \backslash R$ for which $X_{i,j} = 1$. If this happens, then for this j we have $\sum_{i \in [k]} X_{i,j} \geq |R| + 1$, or equivalently, $\ell_\infty (\cup_{i \in [k]} S_i) \geq |R| + 1$. Otherwise, if $\text{THRESH}^n_{(3n-1)/4}(X_1, \ldots, X_k) = 0$, then $\sum_{i \in [k]} X_{i,j} = |R|$ for all $j \in Y$. Therefore, if $\text{THRESH}^n_{(3n-1)/4}(X_1, \ldots, X_k) = 1$, then the probability that there exists a $t \in [T]$ such that $O_t \geq |R_t| + 1$ is at least $1 - (1 - 1/8)^T > 1 - 1/k^{10}$ (by choosing c_T large enough). Otherwise, if $\text{THRESH}^n_{(3n-1)/4}(X_1, \ldots, X_k) = 0$, then $O_t = |R_t|$ for all $t \in [T]$.

Since our reduction only uses $T \cdot O(k) = O(k \log k)$ extra bits of communication and introduces an extra error of $O(1/k^{10})$, which will not affect the correctness of the reduction. By Theorem 4, we have that $D^{1/k^4}_{\sigma_L}(\ell_\infty) = \Omega(kn)$. Note that in the reduction, we have to assume that $\Theta(\ell_\infty) = \Theta(k)$. In other words, if $\ell_\infty \ll k$ then we have to choose $k' = \Theta(\ell_\infty)$ sites out of the k sites to perform the reduction. Therefore it makes sense to write the lower bound as $D^{1/k^4}_{\sigma_L}(\ell_\infty) = \Omega(\min\{\ell_\infty, k\}n)$. The following corollary follows from Yao's Lemma and the discussion following it.

Corollary 2. $R^{1/3}(\ell_\infty) = \Omega(\min\{\ell_\infty, k\}n/\log k)$.

A simple protocol that all sites send their elements-counts to the first site solves ℓ_∞ with $O(\min\{k, \ell_\infty\}n \log n)$ bits of communication, which is almost optimal in light of our lower bound above.

6 Graph Problems

Due to the space constraints, we defer this section to the full version of this paper [27]. We refer readers to Table 1 for all the results.

7 Concluding Remarks

In this paper we show that exact computation of many basic statistical and graph problems in the message-passing model are necessarily communication-inefficient. An important message we want to deliver through these negative results, which is also the main motivation of this paper, is that a relaxation of the problem, such as an approximation, is necessary in the distributed setting if we want communication-efficient protocols. Besides approximation, the layout and the distribution of the input are also important factors for reducing communication.

An interesting future direction is to further investigate efficient communication protocols for approximately computing statistical and graph problems in the message-passing model, and to explore realistic distributions and layouts of the inputs.

One question which we have not discussed in this paper but is important for practice, is whether we can obtain round-efficient protocols that (almost) match the lower bounds which hold even for round-inefficient protocols? Most simple protocols presented in this paper only need a constant number of rounds, except the ones for bipartiteness and (approximate) diameter, where we need to grow BFS trees which are inherently sequential (require $\Omega(\Delta)$ rounds where Δ is the diameter of the graph). Using the sketching algorithm in [1], we can obtain a 1-round protocol for bipartiteness that uses $\tilde{O}(kn)$ bits of communication. We do not know whether a round-efficient protocol exists for the additive-2 approximate diameter problem that could (almost) match the $\tilde{O}(kn^{3/2})$ bits upper bound obtained by the round-inefficient protocol in Section 6.

References

1. Ahn, K.J., Guha, S., McGregor, A.: Analyzing graph structure via linear measurements. In: Proceedings of the Twenty-Third Annual ACM-SIAM Symposium on Discrete Algorithms, pp. 459–467. SIAM (2012)
2. Ahn, K.J., Guha, S., McGregor, A.: Graph sketches: sparsification, spanners, and subgraphs. In: Proc. ACM Symposium on Principles of Database Systems, pp. 5–14 (2012)
3. Arackaparambil, C., Brody, J., Chakrabarti, A.: Functional monitoring without monotonicity. In: Albers, S., Marchetti-Spaccamela, A., Matias, Y., Nikoletseas, S., Thomas, W. (eds.) ICALP 2009, Part I. LNCS, vol. 5555, pp. 95–106. Springer, Heidelberg (2009)
4. Balcan, M.-F., Blum, A., Fine, S., Mansour, Y.: Distributed learning, communication complexity and privacy. Journal of Machine Learning Research - Proceedings Track 23, 26.1–26.22 (2012)
5. Beame, P., Koutris, P., Suciu, D.: Communication steps for parallel query processing. In: PODS, pp. 273–284 (2013)
6. Brown, P., Haas, P.J., Myllymaki, J., Pirahesh, H., Reinwald, B., Sismanis, Y.: Toward automated large-scale information integration and discovery. In: Härder, T., Lehner, W. (eds.) Data Management (Wedekind Festschrift). LNCS, vol. 3551, pp. 161–180. Springer, Heidelberg (2005)
7. Cormode, G., Muthukrishnan, S., Yi, K.: Algorithms for distributed functional monitoring. ACM Transactions on Algorithms 7(2), 21 (2011)
8. Erdos, P., Renyi, A.: On the evolution of random graphs, pp. 17–61. Publication of the Mathematical Institute of the Hungarian Academy of Sciences (1960)
9. Estan, C., Varghese, G., Fisk, M.: Bitmap algorithms for counting active flows on high-speed links. IEEE/ACM Trans. Netw. 14(5), 925–937 (2006)
10. Flajolet, P., Fusy, É., Gandouet, O., Meunier, F.: Hyperloglog: the analysis of a near-optimal cardinality estimation algorithm. DMTCS Proceedings (1) (2008)
11. Flajolet, P., Martin, G.N.: Probabilistic counting algorithms for data base applications. Journal of Computer and System Sciences 31(2), 182–209 (1985)
12. Goldreich, O., Goldwasser, S., Ron, D.: Property testing and its connection to learning and approximation. Journal of the ACM 45(4), 653–750 (1998)
13. Goodrich, M.T., Sitchinava, N., Zhang, Q.: Sorting, searching, and simulation in the mapReduce framework. In: Asano, T., Nakano, S.-i., Okamoto, Y., Watanabe, O. (eds.) ISAAC 2011. LNCS, vol. 7074, pp. 374–383. Springer, Heidelberg (2011)
14. Huang, Z., Radunović, B., Vojnović, M., Zhang, Q.: The communication complexity of approximate maximum matching in distributed data (manuscript 2013), http://research.microsoft.com/apps/pubs/default.aspx?id=188946

15. Huang, Z., Yi, K., Zhang, Q.: Randomized algorithms for tracking distributed count, frequencies, and ranks. In: Proc. ACM Symposium on Principles of Database Systems, pp. 295–306 (2012)
16. Daumé III, H., Phillips, J.M., Saha, A., Venkatasubramanian, S.: Efficient protocols for distributed classification and optimization. In: Bshouty, N.H., Stoltz, G., Vayatis, N., Zeugmann, T. (eds.) ALT 2012. LNCS, vol. 7568, pp. 154–168. Springer, Heidelberg (2012)
17. Daumé III, H., Phillips, J.M., Saha, A., Venkatasubramanian, S.: Protocols for learning classifiers on distributed data. Journal of Machine Learning Research - Proceedings Track 22, 282–290 (2012)
18. Kane, D.M., Nelson, J., Woodruff, D.P.: An optimal algorithm for the distinct elements problem. In: Proc. ACM Symposium on Principles of Database Systems, pp. 41–52 (2010)
19. Karloff, H.J., Suri, S., Vassilvitskii, S.: A model of computation for mapreduce. In: Proc. ACM-SIAM Symposium on Discrete Algorithms, pp. 938–948 (2010)
20. Koutris, P., Suciu, D.: Parallel evaluation of conjunctive queries. In: Proc. ACM Symposium on Principles of Database Systems, pp. 223–234 (2011)
21. Kushilevitz, E., Nisan, N.: Communication Complexity. Cambridge University Press (1997)
22. Palmer, C.R., Gibbons, P.B., Faloutsos, C.: Anf: a fast and scalable tool for data mining in massive graphs. In: Proc. ACM SIGKDD International Conference on Knowledge Discovery and Data Mining, pp. 81–90 (2002)
23. Phillips, J.M., Verbin, E., Zhang, Q.: Lower bounds for number-in-hand multiparty communication complexity, made easy. In: Proc. ACM-SIAM Symposium on Discrete Algorithms (2012)
24. Razborov, A.A.: On the distributional complexity of disjointness. In: Paterson, M.S. (ed.) Proc. International Colloquium on Automata, Languages, and Programming. LNCS, vol. 443, pp. 249–253. Springer, Heidelberg (1990)
25. Valiant, L.G.: A bridging model for parallel computation. Communications of the ACM 33(8), 103–111 (1990)
26. Woodruff, D.P., Zhang, Q.: Tight bounds for distributed functional monitoring. In: Proc. ACM Symposium on Theory of Computing (2012)
27. Woodruff, D.P., Zhang, Q.: When distributed computation is communication expensive. CoRR, abs/1304.4636 (2013)
28. Yao, A.C.: Probabilistic computations: Towards a unified measure of complexity. In: Proc. IEEE Symposium on Foundations of Computer Science (1977)

A   Proof for Lemma 1

Proof. The original proof is for two players, though this also holds for $k > 2$ players since for any distribution μ, if Π is a δ-error protocol then for all possible inputs $x^1, \ldots, x^k$ to the k players,

$$\Pr\nolimits_{\text{random tapes of the players}}[\Pi(x^1, \ldots, x^k) = f(x^1, \ldots, x^k)] \geq 1 - \delta,$$

which implies for any distribution μ on $(x^1, \ldots, x^k)$ that

$$\Pr\nolimits_{\text{random tapes of the players}, (x^1, \ldots, x^k) \sim \mu}[\Pi(x^1, \ldots, x^k) = f(x^1, \ldots, x^k)] \geq 1 - \delta,$$

which implies there is a fixing of the random tapes of the players so that

$$\Pr\nolimits_{(x^1, \ldots, x^k) \sim \mu}[\Pi(x^1, \ldots, x^k) = f(x^1, \ldots, x^k)] \geq 1 - \delta,$$

which implies $D_\mu^\delta(f)$ is at most $R^\delta(f)$.

Use Knowledge to Learn Faster:
Topology Recognition with Advice*

Emanuele Guido Fusco[1], Andrzej Pelc[2,**], and Rossella Petreschi[1]

[1] Computer Science Department, Sapienza, University of Rome, 00198 Rome, Italy
{fusco,petreschi}@di.uniroma1.it
[2] Département d'informatique, Université du Québec en Outaouais,
Gatineau, Québec J8X 3X7, Canada
pelc@uqo.ca

Abstract. Topology recognition is one of the fundamental distributed tasks in networks. Each node of an anonymous network has to deterministically produce an isomorphic copy of the underlying graph, with all ports correctly marked. This task is usually unfeasible without any a priori information. Such information can be provided to nodes as *advice*. An oracle knowing the network can give a (possibly different) string of bits to each node, and all nodes must reconstruct the network using this advice, after a given number of rounds of communication. During each round each node can exchange arbitrary messages with all its neighbors and perform arbitrary local computations. The time of completing topology recognition is the number of rounds it takes, and the size of advice is the maximum length of a string given to nodes.

We investigate tradeoffs between the time in which topology recognition is accomplished and the minimum size of advice that has to be given to nodes. We provide upper and lower bounds on the minimum size of advice that is sufficient to perform topology recognition in a given time, in the class of all graphs of size n and diameter $D \leq \alpha n$, for any constant $\alpha < 1$. In most cases, our bounds are asymptotically tight. More precisely, if the allotted time is $D - k$, where $0 < k \leq D$, then the optimal size of advice is $\Theta((n^2 \log n)/(D-k+1))$. If the allotted time is D, then this optimal size is $\Theta(n \log n)$. If the allotted time is $D+k$, where $0 < k \leq D/2$, then the optimal size of advice is $\Theta(1 + (\log n)/k)$. The only remaining gap between our bounds is for time $D + k$, where $D/2 < k \leq D$. In this time interval our upper bound remains $O(1 + (\log n)/k)$, while the lower bound (that holds for any time) is 1. This leaves a gap if $D \in o(\log n)$. Finally, we show that for time $2D+1$, one bit of advice is both necessary and sufficient.

Our results show how sensitive is the minimum size of advice to the time allowed for topology recognition: allowing just one round more, from D to $D + 1$, decreases exponentially the advice needed to accomplish this task.

Keywords: topology recognition, network, advice, time, tradeoff.

* This research was done during the visit of Andrzej Pelc at Sapienza, University of Rome, partially supported by a visiting fellowship from this university.
** Partially supported by NSERC discovery grant and by the Research Chair in Distributed Computing at the Université du Québec en Outaouais.

Y. Afek (Ed.): DISC 2013, LNCS 8205, pp. 31–45, 2013.
© Springer-Verlag Berlin Heidelberg 2013

1   Introduction

The Model and the Problem. Learning an unknown network by its nodes is one of the fundamental distributed tasks in networks. Once nodes acquire a faithful labeled map of the network, any other distributed task, such as leader election [19, 26], minimum weight spanning tree construction [5], renaming [4], etc. can be performed by nodes using only local computations. Thus constructing a labeled map converts all distributed problems to centralized ones, in the sense that nodes can solve them simulating a central monitor.

If nodes are a priori equipped with unique identifiers, they can deterministically construct a labeled map of the network, by exchanging messages, without any additional information about the network. However, even if nodes have unique identities, relying on them for the task of learning the network is not always possible. Indeed, nodes may be reluctant to reveal their identities for security or privacy reasons. Hence it is important to design algorithms reconstructing the topology of the network without assuming any node labels, i.e., for anonymous networks. In this paper we are interested in deterministic solutions.

Ports at each node of degree d are arbitrarily numbered $0, \ldots, d - 1$, and there is no assumed coherence between port numbers at different nodes. A node is aware of its degree, and it knows on which port it sends or receives a message. The goal is, for each node, to get an isomorphic copy of the graph underlying the network, with all port numbers correctly marked. There are two variants of this task: a weaker version, that we call *anonymous topology recognition*, in which the nodes of the reconstructed map are unlabeled, and a stronger version, that we call *labeled topology recognition*, in which all nodes construct a map of the network assigning distinct labels to all nodes in the same way, and know their position in this map. Even anonymous topology recognition is not always feasible without any a priori information given to nodes, as witnessed, e.g., by the class of oriented rings in which ports at each node are numbered 0,1 in clockwise order. No amount of information exchange can help nodes to recognize the size of the oriented ring and hence to reconstruct correctly its topology. Thus, in order to accomplish (even anonymous) topology recognition for arbitrary networks, some information must be provided to nodes. This can be done in the form of *advice*. An oracle knowing the network gives a (possibly different) string of bits to each node. Then nodes execute a deterministic distributed algorithm that does not assume knowledge of the network, but uses message exchange and the advice provided by the oracle to nodes, in order to reconstruct the topology of the network by each of its nodes.

In this paper we study tradeoffs between the *size of advice* provided to nodes and the *time* of topology recognition. The size of advice is defined as the length of the longest string of bits given by the oracle to nodes. For communication, we use the extensively studied $\mathcal{LOCAL}$ model [25]. In this model, communication proceeds in synchronous rounds and all nodes start simultaneously. In each round each node can exchange arbitrary messages with all its neighbors and perform arbitrary local computations. The time of completing a task is the number of rounds it takes. The central question of the paper is: *what is the minimum size of*

advice that enables (anonymous or labeled) topology recognition in a given time
T, in the class of n-node networks of diameter D?

Our Results. We provide upper and lower bounds on the minimum size of
advice sufficient to perform topology recognition in a given time, in the class
$\mathcal{C}(n, D)$ of all graphs of size n and diameter $D \leq \alpha n$, for any constant $\alpha < 1$.
All our upper bounds are valid even for the harder task of labeled topology
recognition, while our lower bounds also apply to the easier task of anonymous
topology recognition. Hence we will only use the term *topology recognition* for all
our results. We prove upper bounds $f(n, D, T)$ on the minimum size of advice
sufficient to perform topology recognition in a given time T, for the class $\mathcal{C}(n, D)$,
by providing an assignment of advice of size $f(n, D, T)$ and an algorithm, using this advice, that accomplishes this task, within time T, for any network in
$\mathcal{C}(n, D)$. We prove lower bounds on the minimum size of advice, sufficient for a
given time T, by constructing graphs in $\mathcal{C}(n, D)$ for which topology recognition
within this time is impossible with advice of a smaller size.

The meaningful span of possible times for topology recognition is between 0
and $2D + 1$. Indeed, while advice of size $O(n^2 \log n)$ permits topology recognition
in time 0 (i.e., without communication), we show that topology recognition in
time $2D + 1$ can be done with advice of size 1, which is optimal.

For most values of the allotted time, our bounds are asymptotically tight. This
should be compared to many results from the literature on the advice paradigm
(see, e.g., [9,12,13,15,24]), which often either consider the size of advice needed
for feasibility of a given task, or only give isolated points in the curve of tradeoffs
between resources (such as time) and the size of advice.

We show that, if the allotted time is $D - k$, where $0 < k \leq D$, then the optimal
size of advice is $\Theta((n^2 \log n)/(D - k + 1))$. If the allotted time is D, then this
optimal size is $\Theta(n \log n)$. If the allotted time is $D + k$, where $0 < k \leq D/2$, then
the optimal size of advice is $\Theta(1 + (\log n)/k)$. The only remaining gap between
our bounds is for time $D + k$, where $D/2 < k \leq D$. In this time interval our
upper bound remains $O(1 + (\log n)/k)$, while the lower bound (that holds for
any time) is 1. This leaves a gap if $D \in o(\log n)$.

Our results show how sensitive is the minimum size of advice to the time
allowed for topology recognition: allowing just one round more, from D to $D + 1$,
decreases exponentially the advice needed to accomplish this task. Our tight
bounds on the minimum size of advice also show a somewhat surprising fact
that the amount of information that nodes need to reconstruct a labeled map
of the network, in a given time, and that needed to reconstruct an anonymous
map of the network in this time, are asymptotically the same in most cases.

Due to the lack of space, most proofs are omitted.

Related Work. Providing nodes with information of arbitrary type that can be
used to perform network tasks more efficiently has been proposed in [1,7,9–16,
18,20–22,24,27]. This approach was referred to as algorithms using *informative
labeling schemes*, or equivalently, algorithms with *advice*. Advice is given either to
nodes of the network or to mobile agents performing some network task. Several

authors studied the minimum size of advice required to solve the respective network problem in an efficient way. Thus the framework of advice permits to quantify the amount of information needed for an efficient solution of a given network problem, regardless of the type of information that is provided.

In [9] the authors investigated the minimum size of advice that has to be given to nodes to permit graph exploration by a robot. In [22], given a distributed representation of a solution for a problem, the authors investigated the number of bits of communication needed to verify the legality of the represented solution. In [13] the authors compared the minimum size of advice required to solve two information dissemination problems using a linear number of messages. In [14] the authors established the size of advice needed to break competitive ratio 2 of an exploration algorithm in trees. In [15] it was shown that advice of constant size permits to carry on the distributed construction of a minimum spanning tree in logarithmic time. In [11] the advice paradigm was used for online problems. In [12] the authors established lower bounds on the size of advice needed to beat time $\Theta(\log^* n)$ for 3-coloring of a cycle and to achieve time $\Theta(\log^* n)$ for 3-coloring of unoriented trees. In the case of [24] the issue was not efficiency but feasibility: it was shown that $\Theta(n \log n)$ is the minimum size of advice required to perform monotone connected graph clearing.

Distributed computation on anonymous networks has been investigated by many authors, e.g., [2, 3, 6, 17, 23, 25, 28] for problems ranging from leader election to computing boolean functions and communication in wireless networks. Feasibility of topology recognition for anonymous graphs with adversarial port labelings was studied in [28]. The problem of efficiency of map construction by a mobile agent, equipped with a token, exploring an anonymous graph has been studied in [8]. In [10] the authors investigated the minimum size of advice that has to be given to a mobile agent, in order to enable it to reconstruct the topology of an anonymous network or to construct its spanning tree. Notice that the mobile agent scenario makes the problem of map construction much different from our setting. Since all the advice is given to a single agent, it is impossible to break symmetry. Hence reconstructing a labeled map in an anonymous network is usually impossible, and even anonymous map construction often requires to provide a large amount of information to the agent, regardless of the exploration time. To the best of our knowledge, tradeoffs between time and the size of advice for topology recognition have never been studied before.

2   Preliminaries

Unless otherwise stated, we use the word *graph* to mean a simple undirected connected graph without node labels, and with ports at each node of degree d labeled $\{0, \ldots, d-1\}$. Two graphs $G = (V, E)$ and $G' = (V', E')$ are *isomorphic*, if and only if, there exists a bijection $f : V \longrightarrow V'$ such that the edge $\{u, v\}$, with port numbers p at u and q at v is in E, if and only if, the edge $\{f(u), f(v)\}$ with port numbers p at $f(u)$ and q at $f(v)$ is in E'.

The size of a graph is the number of its nodes. Throughout the paper we consider a fixed positive constant $\alpha < 1$ and the class of graphs of size n and diameter $D \leq \alpha n$. We use log to denote the logarithm to the base 2. For a graph G, a node u in G, and any integer t, we denote by $N_t(u)$ the set of nodes in G at distance at most t from u.

We will use the following notion from [28]. The *view* from node u in graph G is the infinite tree $\mathcal{V}(u)$ rooted at u with unlabeled nodes and labeled ports, whose branches are infinite sequences of port numbers coding all infinite paths in the graph, starting from node u. The *truncated view* $\mathcal{V}^l(u)$ is the truncation of this tree to depth $l \geq 0$.

Given a graph $G = (V, E)$, a function $f : V \longrightarrow \{0, 1\}^*$ is called a *decoration* of G. Notice that an assignment of advice to nodes of G is a decoration of G. For a given decoration f of a graph G we define the *decorated graph* G_f as follows. Nodes of G_f are ordered pairs $(v, f(v))$, for all nodes v in V. G_f has an edge $\{(u, f(u)), (v, f(v))\}$ with port numbers p at $(u, f(u))$ and q at $(v, f(v))$, if and only if, E contains the edge $\{u, v\}$, with port numbers p at u and q at v.

We define the *decorated view* at depth l of node v in G, according to f, as the truncated view at depth l of node $(v, f(v))$ in the decorated graph G_f.

The following two lemmas will be used in the proofs of our upper bounds.

Lemma 1. *Let G be a graph and let r be a positive integer. There exists a set X of nodes in G satisfying the following conditions.*

- *For any node w of G there is a node $u \in X$ such that the distance between w and u is at most r.*
- *For each pair $\{u, v\}$ of distinct nodes in X, the distance between u and v is larger than r.*

Lemma 2. *Let G be a graph of diameter D and let A be an injective decoration of G. Then each node u in G can accomplish topology recognition using its view, decorated according to A, at depth $D + 1$, even without knowing D a priori.*

The following proposition can be easily proved by induction on the round number. Intuitively it says that, if two nodes executing the same algorithm have the same decorated views at depth t, then they behave identically for at least t rounds.

Proposition 1. *Let G and G' be two graphs, let u be a node of G and let u' be a node of G'. Let A be a decoration of G and let A' be a decoration of G'. Let $\mathcal{A}$ be any topology recognition algorithm. Let σ_t be the set of triples $\langle p, r, m \rangle$, where m is the message received by node u in round $r \leq t$ through port p when executing algorithm $\mathcal{A}$ on the graph G, decorated according to A. Let σ'_t be defined as σ_t, but for u', G', and A' instead of u, G, and A. If the view of u at depth t, decorated according to A is the same as the view of u' at depth t, decorated according to A', then $\sigma_t = \sigma'_t$.*

We will use the above proposition to prove our lower bounds as follows. If the size of advice is too small, then there are two non-isomorphic graphs G and G' resulting, for some node u in G and some node u' in G', in the same decorated view at the depth equal to the time available to perform topology recognition. Hence either u or u' must incorrectly reconstruct the topology (even anonymous) of G or G'.

3   Time $2D + 1$

We start our analysis by constructing a topology recognition algorithm that works in time $2D + 1$ and uses advice of size 1. Since we will show that, for arbitrary $D \geq 3$, there are networks in which topology recognition without advice is impossible in any time, this shows that the meaningful time-span to consider for topology recognition is between 0 and $2D + 1$.

Algorithm TR-1
Advice: The oracle assigns bit 1 to one node (call it v), and bit 0 to all others. Let A be this assignment of advice.
Node protocol: In round i, each node u sends its view at depth $i-1$, decorated according to A, to all its neighbors; it receives such views from all its neighbors and constructs its view at depth i, decorated according to A. This task continues until termination of the algorithm.

Let t be the smallest round number at which node u sees a node with advice 1 in its view decorated according to A (at depth t). Node u assigns to itself a label in round t as follows. The label $\ell(u)$ is the lexicographically smallest shortest path, defined as a sequence of consecutive port numbers (each traversed edge corresponds to a pair of port numbers), from u to any node with advice 1, in its decorated view at depth t. (Notice that since there can be many shortest paths between u and v, this node can appear many times in the decorated view at depth t of u.) Let A^* be the decoration corresponding to the labeling obtained as above. (We will show that labels in A^* are unique.)

After round t, node u starts constructing its decorated view, according to decoration A^*. In any round $t' > t$, node u sends both its view, decorated according to A, at depth t', and its view, decorated according to A^*, at the largest possible depth. Messages required to perform this task are piggybacked to those used for constructing views, decorated according to A, at increasing depths. In each round t', node u checks for newly discovered values of A^*. As soon as there are no new values, node u reconstructs the labeled map and outputs it. Then node u computes the diameter D of the resulting graph and continues to send its views, decorated according to A and according to A^*, at increasing depths, until round $2D + 1$. After round $2D + 1$ node u terminates.   ◇

Proposition 2. *Algorithm TR-1 completes topology recognition for all graphs of size n and diameter D in time $2D + 1$, using advice of size 1.*

The following proposition shows that advice of size 1, as used by Algorithm TR-1, is necessary, regardless of the allotted time. As opposed to the n-node rings mentioned in the introduction as graphs that require at least one bit of advice, but whose diameter is $\lfloor n/2 \rfloor$, the class of graphs we will use to prove the proposition allows greater flexibility of the diameter.

Proposition 3. *Let $D \geq 3$ and let $n \geq D + 6$ be an even integer. The size of advice needed to perform topology recognition for the class of all graphs of size n and diameter D is at least 1.*

4   Time above D

In this section we study the size of advice sufficient to perform topology recognition in arbitrary time larger than D, i.e., large enough for allowing each node to see all nodes and edges of the graph. We first give an algorithm using advice of size $O(1 + \log(n)/k)$ that performs topology recognition in time $D + k$.

Algorithm TR-2
Advice: Let G be a graph of size n and diameter D. Let $t = \lceil k/4 \rceil - 1$. If $t = 0$ then the oracle gives a unique label of size $\lceil \log n \rceil$ as advice to each node. Suppose that $t \geq 1$. The oracle picks a set of nodes X satisfying Lemma 1, for $r = 2t$. Then it chooses a unique label $\ell(v)$ from the set $\{0, \ldots, n-1\}$ for each node v in X. For any node $u \in N_{t-1}(v)$ let $\pi_v(u)$ be the lexicographically smallest shortest path (coded as a sequence of consecutive port numbers) from u to v. Sort the nodes u in $N_{t-1}(v)$ in the increasing lexicographic order of $\pi_v(u)$. The binary representation of $\ell(v)$ is partitioned into $|N_{t-1}(v)|$ consecutive segments, each of length at most $\lceil (\log n)/|N_{t-1}(v)| \rceil$. The oracle assigns the first segment, with a trailing bit 1, as advice to node v. For $1 < i \leq |N_{t-1}(v)|$, the i-th segment, with a trailing bit 0, is assigned as advice to the i-th node of $N_{t-1}(v)$. (Notice that some nodes in $N_{t-1}(v)$ could receive only the trailing bit 0 as advice.) All other nodes get the empty string as advice. Let A_1 be the above assignment of advice.
Node protocol: We first describe the protocol when $t \geq 1$. In round i, each node u sends its view at depth $i - 1$, decorated according to A_1, to all its neighbors; it receives such views from all its neighbors and constructs its view at depth i, decorated according to A_1. This task continues until termination of the algorithm.

Each node u whose advice has a trailing bit 0 assigns to itself a temporary label $\ell'(u)$ as follows. Let s be the smallest round number at which node u sees a node with advice with a trailing bit 1 in its view decorated according to A_1 (at depth s). The label $\ell'(u)$ is the lexicographically smallest shortest path, defined as a sequence of consecutive port numbers, from u to any node with advice with a trailing bit 1 in its view, decorated according to A_1, at depth s.

Let u be a node whose advice has a trailing bit 0. After reconstructing its label $\ell'(u)$, node u sends $(\ell'(u), A_1(u))$ to the node $v \in X$ closest to it, along the lexicographically smallest shortest path that determined label $\ell'(u)$. Nodes along this path relay these messages piggybacking them to any message that they should send in a given round.

Each node $v \in X$ (having a trailing bit 1 in its advice) computes t as the first depth in which its view, decorated according to A_1 contains nodes without any advice. In round $2t$ each such node reconstructs its label $\ell(v)$ from messages $(\ell'(u), A_1(u))$ it received (which it sorts in the increasing lexicographic order of $\ell'(u)$), and from $A_1(v)$.

Let A_2 be the decoration of G where each node v in the set X is mapped to the binary representation of its unique label $\ell(v)$, and each node outside of X is mapped to the empty string.

Nodes outside of X start constructing their decorated view, according to A_2. This construction is put on hold by a node v in X until the time when it reconstructs its unique label $\ell(v)$. Upon reconstructing its label $\ell(v)$, each node $v \in X$ starts constructing its view decorated according to A_2, hence allowing its neighbors to construct their view, decorated according to A_2, at depth 1. This process continues for $2t$ steps, during which nodes construct and send their views at increasing depth, decorated according to A_2.

Each node u assigns a label $\ell''(u)$ to itself as follows. Let s' be the smallest depth at which the view of u, decorated according to A_2, contains a node v with label $\ell(v)$ and let $\lambda(u, v)$ be the lexicographically smallest path connecting u to such a node v (coded as a sequence of consecutive port numbers). Node u sets $\ell''(u) = (\lambda(u, v), \ell(v))$.

Let A_3 be the decoration of G where each node u is mapped to $\ell''(u)$. (We will prove that A_3 is an injective function.) Upon computing its value in A_3 each node starts constructing its decorated view, according to A_3. In each round t', node u checks for newly discovered values of A_3. As soon as there are no new values, node u reconstructs the labeled map and outputs it. Then node u computes the diameter D of the resulting graph and continues to send its views, decorated according to A_1, according to A_2, and according to A_3, at increasing depths, until round $D + 4t + 1$. After round $D + 4t + 1$ node u terminates.

If $t = 0$, the protocol consists only of the last step described above, with decoration A_3 replaced by the assignment of advice given to nodes by the oracle.   ◇

Theorem 1. *Let $0 < k \leq D$. Algorithm* TR-2 *completes topology recognition for all graphs of size n and diameter D within time $D + k$, using advice of size $O(1 + (\log n)/k)$.*

We now provide a lower bound on the minimum size of advice sufficient to perform topology recognition. This bound matches the upper bound given by Algorithm TR-2 in the time-interval $[D + 1, \ldots, 3\lfloor D/2 \rfloor]$.

Theorem 2. *Let $2 \leq D \leq \alpha n$ and $0 < k \leq D/2$. The size of advice needed to perform topology recognition in time $D + k$ in the class of graphs of size n and diameter D is in $\Omega((\log n)/k)$.*

Proof. Our lower bound will be proved using the following classes $\mathcal{B}(n, D, k)$ of graphs of size n and diameter D, called *brooms*. We define these classes for n sufficiently large and for $k < \log n$. Nodes in a broom $B \in \mathcal{B}(n, D, k)$ are partitioned into three sets, called the *bristles*, the *stick*, and the *handle*. Let m be the largest even integer such that $km + D - k < n$.

The set bristles consists of km nodes, partitioned into m pairwise disjoint sets $B_1, \ldots, B_m$, each of size k. The stick consists of $D - k$ nodes, and the remaining $n - (km + D - k)$ nodes are in the handle. Hence the bristles, the stick, and the handle are non-empty sets. We now describe the set of edges in each part.

Edges of the bristles are partitioned into two sets, E_1 and E_2. Edges in E_1 connect nodes of each set B_i into a path with port numbers 0 and 1 at each edge. We call *head* of each set B_i the endpoint of the path to which port number

1 has been assigned, and *tail* the other endpoint (to which port number 0 has been assigned). Notice that sets B_i can be of size 1, in which case heads coincide with tails. Edges in E_2 form a perfect matching M among tails of the bristles. These edges have port number 1 at both endpoints.

Edges of the stick form a path of length $D - k - 1$ with port numbers 0 and 1 at each edge. (Notice that this path is of length 0, i.e., the stick consists of a single node, when $D = 2$.) The handle has no edges.

The bristles, the stick, and the handle are connected as follows. Let u be the endpoint of the stick to which port number 1 has been assigned, and let v be the other endpoint of the stick (to which port number 0 has been assigned). Nodes v and u coincide when $D = 2$. Node v is connected to the head of each set B_i by an edge with port numbers i at v and 0 at each head. Node u is connected to each node in the handle. Port numbers at u corresponding to these connecting edges are numbered $\{0, 2, \ldots, n - (km + D - k)\}$, if $u \neq v$, and $\{0, m + 1, \ldots, n - (k - 1)m - 2\}$, if $u = v$. Nodes in the handle are of degree 1, so they have a unique port with number 0. See Figure 1 for an example of a broom in $\mathcal{B}(23, 6, 3)$. Notice that all brooms in $\mathcal{B}(n, D, k)$ are defined over the same set of nodes and share the same edges, apart from those in sets forming perfect matchings among tails of the bristles. Moreover notice that growing the length of the bristles above $\lfloor D/2 \rfloor$ would result in a graph of diameter larger than D, which explains the assumption $k \leq D/2$.

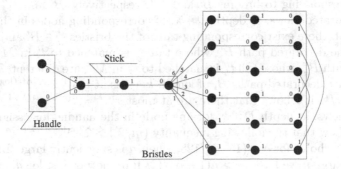

Fig. 1. A broom in $\mathcal{B}(23, 6, 3)$

For two brooms B' and B'' in $\mathcal{B}(n, D, k)$ we define *corresponding* nodes as follows. Let h' and h'' in B' and B'', respectively, be the nodes in the handles whose only incident edge has port number 0 at both endpoints. Node $u' \in T'$ corresponds to node $u'' \in T''$, if and only if, the (unique) shortest path (defined as the sequence of port numbers on consecutive edges) from h' to u' is the same as the shortest path from h'' to u''.

The idea of the proof is to show that if the size of advice is smaller than $c(\log n)/k$, for a sufficiently small constant $0 < c < 1$, then there exist two brooms in $\mathcal{B}(n, D, k)$, whose corresponding nodes receive the same advice, for which the decorated view at depth $D + k$ of each node in the handle remains the same in both brooms. Since different brooms are non-isomorphic, this will imply the theorem, in view of Proposition 1.

Observe that for $k \in \Omega(\log n)$, we have that $c(\log n)/k$ is constant, and $\Omega(1)$ is a lower bound on the size of advice for topology recognition, regardless of the allowed time. Hence we do not need to define brooms when $k \geq \log n$ to prove the theorem.

We now provide a lower bound on the size of the class $\mathcal{B}(n, D, k)$. This size depends on the number m of tails of the bristles among which perfect matchings M can be defined. For given n and k, the size of the class $\mathcal{B}(n, D, k)$ cannot increase when D grows. Hence the class is smallest for the largest considered value of D, i.e., $D = \lfloor \alpha n \rfloor$. We do the estimation for this value of D.

The number of perfect matchings among tails is at least $(m - 1) \cdot (m - 3) \cdot (m - 5) \cdot \ldots \cdot 3 \cdot 1 > (m/2)!$.

Suppose, from now on, that the size of advice is bounded by $c(\log n)/k$, for some constant $0 < c < 1$. Then there are at most $2^{(c(\log n)/k+1)n}$ ways of assigning advice to nodes of a broom in $\mathcal{B}(n, D, k)$. Hence there are at least $(m/2)!/2^{(c(\log n)/k+1)n}$ brooms in $\mathcal{B}(n, D, k)$ for which corresponding nodes get the same advice. Fix one such assignment A of advice.

We now provide an upper bound on the number of distinct decorated views, at depth $D + k$, of any node in the handle, when advice is assigned to nodes according to A. Consider two brooms B' and B'' in $\mathcal{B}(n, D, k)$, decorated according to assignment A. Let M' and M'' be the perfect matchings among tails of the bristles corresponding to brooms B' and B'', respectively. B' and B'' result in distinct decorated views, at depth $D + k$, of corresponding nodes in the handle, if and only if, there exist corresponding tails of the bristles $t'_i \in B'$ and $t''_i \in B''$, such that the decorated path B'_j, whose tail t'_j is matched to t'_i in M' and the decorated path B''_h, whose tail t''_h is matched to t''_i in M'', are different. The number of distinct decorated paths B_i of length $k - 1$ is at most $x = 2^{(c(\log n)/k+1)k}$. Since $m \leq n/k$, it follows that there are at most $x^{n/k} = 2^{(c(\log n)/k+1)n}$ distinct decorated views, at depth $D + k$, for any node in the handle, for assignment A.

We will show that the following inequality $(m/2)! > 2^{2(c(\log n)/k+1)n}$ which we denote by $(*)$, holds for $c < (1 - \alpha)/128$, when n is sufficiently large. Indeed, for sufficiently large n we have $m > n(1 - \alpha)/(2k)$; in view of $k < \log n$, taking the logarithms of both sides we have

$$\log \left(\frac{m}{2}! \right) > \frac{m}{4} \log \frac{m}{4} > \frac{n(1 - \alpha)}{8k} \log \frac{n(1 - \alpha)}{8k} \geq 2 \left(\frac{c \log n}{k} + 1 \right) n.$$

Inequality $(*)$ implies that $(m/2)!/2^{(c(\log n)/k+1)n} > 2^{(c(\log n)/k+1)n}$. Hence the number of brooms from $\mathcal{B}(n, D, k)$, decorated according to assignment A, exceeds the number of distinct decorated views, at depth $D + k$, of any node in the handle, for these brooms. It follows that some decorated view corresponds to different brooms from $\mathcal{B}(n, D, k)$. In view of Proposition 1, this proves that (even anonymous) topology recognition in time $D + k$, for the class of graphs of diameter D and size n, requires advice of size at least $(1 - \alpha)(\log n)/(128k) \in \Omega(\log n/k)$. □

Since the lower bound $\Omega(1)$ on the size of advice holds regardless of time, theorems 1 and 2 imply the following corollary.

Corollary 1. *Let $D \leq \alpha n$ and $0 < k \leq D/2$. The minimum size of advice sufficient to perform topology recognition in time $D + k$ in the class of graphs of size n and diameter D is in $\Theta(1 + (\log n/k))$.*

5 Time D

In this section we provide asymptotically tight upper and lower bounds on the minimum size of advice sufficient to perform topology recognition in time equal to the diameter D of the network. Together with the upper bound proved in Theorem 1, applied to time $D + 1$, these bounds show an exponential gap in the minimum size of advice due to time difference of only one round.

Algorithm TR-3

Advice: The oracle assigns a unique label $\ell(u)$ from the set $\{0, \ldots, n-1\}$ to each node u. The advice given to each node u consists of the diameter D, the label $\ell(u)$, and the collection of all edges incident to u, coded as quadruples $\langle \ell(u), p, q, \ell(v) \rangle$, where p is the port number at node u corresponding to edge $\{u, v\}$, and q is the port number at node v corresponding to this edge.

Node protocol: In round i, each node sends to all its neighbors the collection of edges learned in all previous rounds. After D rounds each node reconstructs the topology and stops. $\diamond$

Proposition 4. *Algorithm TR-3 completes topology recognition for all graphs of size n and diameter D in time D, using advice of size $O(n \log n)$.*

The following lemma will be used for our lower bound.

Lemma 3. *There are at least $(\prod_{i=1}^{n-1} i! i^i)/n!$ non-isomorphic cliques of size n.*

We define the following classes $\mathcal{L}(n, D)$ of graphs of size n and diameter $D \leq \alpha n$, called *lollipops*. These graphs will be used to prove our lower bounds for time D and below. Nodes in a lollipop $L \in \mathcal{L}(n, D)$ are partitioned into two sets, called the *candy* and the *stick*. The candy consists of $n - D$ nodes; for the purpose of describing our construction we will call these nodes $w_1, \ldots, w_{n-D}$. The stick consists of the remaining D nodes.

Nodes in the candy are connected to form a clique; port numbers for these edges are assigned arbitrarily from the set $\{0, \ldots, n - D - 2\}$. Edges of the stick form a path of length $D - 1$ with port numbers 0 and 1 at each edge. The stick and the candy are connected as follows. Let v be the endpoint of the stick to which port number 1 has been assigned and let u be the other endpoint of the stick (to which port number 0 has been assigned). Notice that u and v coincide, when $D = 1$. Node v is connected to all nodes in the candy. The port number, at node v, corresponding to edge $\{v, w_i\}$ is 0, if $i = 1$. For $i > 1$ this port number is i, when $u \neq v$ and $i - 1$, when $u = v$. The port number, at all nodes w_i, corresponding to edge $\{v, w_i\}$ is $n - D - 1$.

Since, for $D \leq \alpha n$, the size of the candy of a lollipop in $\mathcal{L}(n, D)$ is at least $\lceil n(1 - \alpha) \rceil$, Lemma 3 implies the following corollary:

Corollary 2. *The size of the class* $\mathcal{L}(n, D)$, *for* $D \leq \alpha n$ *is at least*
$(\prod_{i=1}^{\lceil n(1-\alpha)\rceil-1} i!i^i)/\lceil n(1-\alpha)\rceil!$.

Theorem 3. *Let* $D \leq \alpha n$. *The size of advice needed to perform topology recognition in time* D *in the class of graphs of size* n *and diameter* D *is in* $\Omega(n \log n)$.

Proof. If we consider a lollipop of diameter $D \leq \alpha n$, then there are $\Omega(n^2)$ edges of the candy that are outside of the view at depth D of the endpoint u of the stick. The idea of the proof is based on the fact that information about these edges has to be assigned to nodes of the graph as advice that will become available to u within time D.

First observe that the view at depth D of the endpoint u of the stick is the same for all lollipops in $\mathcal{L}(n, D)$. Hence, if the size of advice is at most $cn \log n$, then the number of distinct decorated views of node u is at most $2^{cn^2 \log n + n} < 2^{cn^2(\log n + 1)}$. We will show that, if $c < (1 - \alpha)^2/7$, then, for sufficiently large n, the number of lollipops in $\mathcal{L}(n, D)$ exceeds this bound. Indeed, by Corollary 2, the size of the class $\mathcal{L}(n, D)$ is at least $\frac{\prod_{i=1}^{\lceil n(1-\alpha)\rceil-1} i!i^i}{\lceil n(1-\alpha)\rceil!}$. For sufficiently large n we have

$$\frac{\prod_{i=1}^{\lceil n(1-\alpha)\rceil-1} i!i^i}{\lceil n(1-\alpha)\rceil!} > \prod_{i=1}^{\lceil n(1-\alpha)\rceil-2} i!i^i > \left(\left(\frac{n(1-\alpha)}{2}\right)! \left(\frac{n(1-\alpha)}{2}\right)^{n(1-\alpha)/2}\right)^{n(1-\alpha)/3}.$$

It is enough to show that $\left(\frac{n(1-\alpha)}{2}\right)^{n^2(1-\alpha)^2/6} > 2^{n^2(\log n + 1)(1-\alpha)^2/7}$, which is immediate to verify by taking the logarithm of both sides.

It follows that the same decorated view at depth D of node u corresponds to different lollipops from $\mathcal{L}(n, D)$. In view of Proposition 1, this proves that (even anonymous) topology recognition in time D, for the class of graphs of size n and diameter $D \leq \alpha n$, requires advice of size at least $(n \log n)(1-\alpha)^2/7 \in \Omega(n \log n)$.
□

Proposition 4 and Theorem 3 imply the following corollary.
Corollary 3. *Let* $D \leq \alpha n$. *The minimum size of advice sufficient to perform topology recognition in time* D *in the class of graphs of size* n *and diameter* D *is in* $\Theta(n \log n)$.

6   Time below D

In this section we study the minimum size of advice sufficient to perform topology recognition when the time allotted for this task is too short, for some node, to communicate with all other nodes in the network.

Algorithm TR-4
Advice: Let G be a graph of size n and diameter D. The oracle assigns a unique label $\ell(v)$ from $\{0, \ldots, n-1\}$ to each node v in the graph G. It codes all edges of the graph as quadruples $\langle \ell(u), p, q, \ell(v) \rangle$, where $\ell(u)$ and $\ell(v)$ are the labels of two adjacent nodes u and v, p is the port number at node u corresponding to

edge $\{u, v\}$, and q is the port number at node v corresponding to this edge. Let E be the set of all these codes.

Let $t = \lfloor (D - k)/3 \rfloor$. If $t = 0$, then the advice provided by the oracle to each node u is: $\ell(u)$, the collection E of all edges, and the integer 0.

If $t \geq 1$, then the oracle picks a set X of nodes in G satisfying Lemma 1, for $r = 2t$. Let $z(x) = |N_t(x)|$. Moreover, let $E_1, \ldots, E_{z(x)}$ be a partition of the edges in E into $z(x)$ pairwise disjoint sets of sizes differing by at most 1. Let $v_1, \ldots, v_{z(x)}$ be an enumeration of nodes in $N_t(x)$. The advice given by the oracle to node $v_i \in N_t(x)$ consists of the label $\ell(v_i)$, of the set E_i, and of the integer t. Every other node u only gets $\ell(u)$ and t as advice. Let A be the resulting assignment of advice.

Node protocol: Let t be the integer received by all nodes as part of their advice. In round i, with $1 \leq i \leq 3t$, each node sends to all its neighbors the collection of edges learned in all previous rounds. (In particular, if $t = 0$, then there is no communication.) After $3t$ rounds of communication each node reconstructs the topology and stops.   ◇

Theorem 4. *Let $0 < k \leq D$. Algorithm TR-4 completes topology recognition for all graphs of size n and diameter D within time $D - k$, using advice of size $O((n^2 \log n)/(D - k + 1))$.*

The following lower bound shows that the size of advice used by Algorithm TR-4 is asymptotically optimal.

Theorem 5. *Let $D \leq \alpha n$ and $0 < k \leq D$. The size of advice needed to perform topology recognition in time $D - k$ in the class of graphs of size n and diameter D is in $\Omega((n^2 \log n)/(D - k + 1))$.*

Theorems 4 and 5 imply the following corollary.

Corollary 4. *Let $D \leq \alpha n$ and $0 < k \leq D$. The minimum size of advice sufficient to perform topology recognition in time $D - k$ in the class of graphs of size n and diameter D is in $\Theta((n^2 \log n)/(D - k + 1))$.*

7   Conclusion and Open Problems

We presented upper and lower bounds on the minimum size of advice sufficient to perform topology recognition, in a given time T, in n-node networks of diameter D. Our bounds are asymptotically tight for time $T = 2D + 1$ and, if $D \leq \alpha n$ for some constant $\alpha < 1$, in the time interval $[0, \ldots, 3D/2]$. Moreover, in the remaining time interval $(3D/2, \ldots, 2D]$ our bounds are still asymptotically tight if $D \in \Omega(\log n)$. Closing the remaining gap between the lower bound 1 and the upper bound $O(1 + (\log n)/k)$ in this remaining time interval, for graphs of very small diameter $D \in o(\log n)$, is a natural open problem. In particular, it would be interesting to find the minimum time in which topology recognition can be accomplished using advice of constant size, or even of size exactly 1.

Other open problems remain in the case of networks with very large diameter, those which do not satisfy the assumption $D \leq \alpha n$ for some constant $\alpha < 1$, or equivalently those for which $n - D \in o(n)$. Our upper bounds do not change in this case (we did not use the assumption $D \leq \alpha n$ in their analysis), while our lower bounds change as follows, using the same constructions. The lower bound for time above D, i.e., when $T = D + k$, where $0 < k \leq D$, becomes $\Omega((\log(n - D))/k)$; our lower bound for time D becomes $\Omega(((n - D)^2 \log(n - D))/n)$; the lower bound for time below D, i.e., when $T = D - k$, where $0 < k \leq D$, becomes $\Omega(((n - D)^2 \log(n - D))/(D - k + 1))$. It remains to close the gaps between these lower bounds and the upper bounds that we gave for each allotted time.

Finally, let us address the issue of node identities vs. advice given to nodes. We did our study for unlabeled networks, arguing that nodes may be reluctant to disclose their identities for security or privacy reasons. As we have seen, however, for anonymous networks some advice has to be given to nodes, regardless of the allotted time. Does the oracle have to provide new distinct labels to nodes? Our results show that for time above D this is not the case, as the minimum size of advice enabling topology recognition in this time is too small for assigning a unique identifier to each node. Hence, in spite of not having been given, a priori, unique identifiers, nodes can perform labeled topology recognition in this time span. On the other hand for time at most D, the minimum size of advice is sufficiently large to provide distinct identifiers to nodes, and indeed our oracles inserted unique identifiers as part of advice. However, this should not raise concerns about security or privacy, as these identifiers may be arbitrary and hence should be considered as "nicknames" temporarily assigned to nodes.

References

1. Abiteboul, S., Kaplan, H., Milo, T.: Compact labeling schemes for ancestor queries. In: Proc. 12th Annual ACM-SIAM Symposium on Discrete Algorithms (SODA 2001), pp. 547–556 (2001)
2. Angluin, D.: Local and global properties in networks of processors. In: Proc. 12th Annual ACM Symposium on Theory of Computing (STOC 1980), pp. 82–93 (1980)
3. Attiya, H., Snir, M., Warmuth, M.: Computing on an anonymous ring. Journal of the ACM 35, 845–875 (1988)
4. Attiya, H., Bar-Noy, A., Dolev, D., Koller, D., Peleg, D., Reischuk, R.: Renaming in an asynchronous environment. Journal of the ACM 37, 524–548 (1990)
5. Awerbuch, B.: Optimal distributed algorithms for minimum weight spanning tree, counting, leader election and related problems. In: Proc. 19th Annual ACM Symposium on Theory of Computing (STOC 1987), pp. 230–240 (1987)
6. Boldi, P., Vigna, S.: Computing anonymously with arbitrary knowledge. In: Proc. 18th ACM Symposium on Principles of Distributed Computing (PODC 1999), pp. 181–188 (1999)
7. Caminiti, S., Finocchi, I., Petreschi, R.: Engineering tree labeling schemes: a case study on least common ancestor. In: Halperin, D., Mehlhorn, K. (eds.) ESA 2008. LNCS, vol. 5193, pp. 234–245. Springer, Heidelberg (2008)
8. Chalopin, J., Das, S., Kosowski, A.: Constructing a map of an anonymous graph: Applications of universal sequences. In: Lu, C., Masuzawa, T., Mosbah, M. (eds.) OPODIS 2010. LNCS, vol. 6490, pp. 119–134. Springer, Heidelberg (2010)
9. Cohen, R., Fraigniaud, P., Ilcinkas, D., Korman, A., Peleg, D.: Label-guided graph exploration by a finite automaton. ACM Transactions on Algorithms 4 (2008)

10. Dereniowski, D., Pelc, A.: Drawing maps with advice. Journal of Parallel and Distributed Computing 72, 132–143 (2012)
11. Emek, Y., Fraigniaud, P., Korman, A., Rosen, A.: Online computation with advice. Theoretical Computer Science 412, 2642–2656 (2011)
12. Fraigniaud, P., Gavoille, C., Ilcinkas, D., Pelc, A.: Distributed computing with advice: Information sensitivity of graph coloring. Distributed Computing 21, 395–403 (2009)
13. Fraigniaud, P., Ilcinkas, D., Pelc, A.: Communication algorithms with advice. Journal of Computer and System Sciences 76, 222–232 (2010)
14. Fraigniaud, P., Ilcinkas, D., Pelc, A.: Tree exploration with advice. Information and Computation 206, 1276–1287 (2008)
15. Fraigniaud, P., Korman, A., Lebhar, E.: Local MST computation with short advice. Theory of Computing Systems 47, 920–933 (2010)
16. Fusco, E., Pelc, A.: Trade-offs between the size of advice and broadcasting time in trees. Algorithmica 60, 719–734 (2011)
17. Fusco, E., Pelc, A.: How much memory is needed for leader election. Distributed Computing 24, 65–78 (2011)
18. Gavoille, C., Peleg, D., Pérennes, S., Raz, R.: Distance labeling in graphs. Journal of Algorithms 53, 85–112 (2004)
19. Hirschberg, D.S., Sinclair, J.B.: Decentralized extrema-finding in circular configurations of processes. Communications of the ACM 23, 627–628 (1980)
20. Ilcinkas, D., Kowalski, D., Pelc, A.: Fast radio broadcasting with advice. Theoretical Computer Science 411, 1544–1557 (2012)
21. Katz, M., Katz, N., Korman, A., Peleg, D.: Labeling schemes for flow and connectivity. SIAM Journal of Computing 34, 23–40 (2004)
22. Korman, A., Kutten, S., Peleg, D.: Proof labeling schemes. Distributed Computing 22, 215–233 (2010)
23. Kranakis, E., Krizanc, D., van der Berg, J.: Computing Boolean functions on anonymous networks. Information and Computation 114, 214–236 (1994)
24. Nisse, N., Soguet, D.: Graph searching with advice. Theoretical Computer Science 410, 1307–1318 (2009)
25. Peleg, D.: Distributed computing, a locality-sensitive approach. SIAM Monographs on Discrete Mathematics and Applications, Philadelphia (2000)
26. Peterson, G.L.: An $O(n \log n)$ unidirectional distributed algorithm for the circular extrema problem. ACM Transactions on Programming Languages and Systems 4, 758–762 (1982)
27. Thorup, M., Zwick, U.: Approximate distance oracles. Journal of the ACM 52, 1–24 (2005)
28. Yamashita, M., Kameda, T.: Computing on anonymous networks: Part I - characterizing the solvable cases. IEEE Transactions on Parallel and Distributed Systems 7, 69–89 (1996)

An $O(\sqrt{n})$ Space Bound
for Obstruction-Free Leader Election

George Giakkoupis[1,*], Maryam Helmi[2], Lisa Higham[2], and Philipp Woelfel[2,**]

[1] INRIA Rennes – Bretagne Atlantic, France
george.giakkoupis@inria.fr
[2] Department of Computer Science, University of Calgary, Canada
{mhelmikh,higham,woelfel}@ucalgary.ca

Abstract. We present a deterministic obstruction-free implementation of leader election from $O(\sqrt{n})$ atomic $O(\log n)$-bit registers in the standard asynchronous shared memory system with n processes. We provide also a technique to transform any deterministic obstruction-free algorithm, in which any process can finish if it runs for b steps without interference, into a randomized wait-free algorithm for the oblivious adversary, in which the expected step complexity is polynomial in n and b. This transformation allows us to combine our obstruction-free algorithm with the leader election algorithm by Giakkoupis and Woelfel [21], to obtain a fast randomized leader election (and thus test-and-set) implementation from $O(\sqrt{n})$ $O(\log n)$-bit registers, that has expected step complexity $O(\log^* n)$ against the oblivious adversary.

Our algorithm provides the first sub-linear space upper bound for obstruction-free leader election. A lower bound of $\Omega(\log n)$ has been known since 1989 [29]. Our research is also motivated by the long-standing open problem whether there is an obstruction-free consensus algorithm which uses fewer than n registers.

Keywords: leader election, test-and-set, shared memory model, randomized algorithms, obstruction-free algorithms.

1   Introduction

One of the fundamental theoretical questions in shared memory research is whether certain standard primitives can be simulated from other ones (given certain progress conditions), and if yes, how much resources (usually time and space) are necessary for such simulations. Perhaps the best studied problem in this context is that of *consensus*, where each process receives an input and processes have to agree on one of their inputs. Consensus cannot be solved deterministically with wait-free progress in shared memory systems that provide

* This work was funded in part by INRIA Associate Team RADCON and ERC Starting Grant GOSSPLE 204742.
** This research was undertaken, in part, thanks to funding from the Canada Research Chairs program and the HP Labs Innovation Research Program.

Y. Afek (Ed.): DISC 2013, LNCS 8205, pp. 46–60, 2013.
© Springer-Verlag Berlin Heidelberg 2013

only shared atomic registers [20]. The study of which primitives can be used to solve consensus deterministically in systems with a certain number of processes has led to Herlihy's famous wait-free hierarchy [24]. Randomized algorithms can solve consensus and guarantee randomized wait-freedom even if only registers are available. The randomized step complexity of the consensus problem has been studied thoroughly and is well understood for most of the common adversary models [8–13].

On the other hand, it is still open how many registers are needed in a system with n processes to have a randomized wait-free implementation of consensus, or even an obstruction-free one. Fich, Herlihy and Shavit [18] showed that at least $\Omega(\sqrt{n})$ registers are necessary, but no obstruction-free algorithm that uses fewer than n registers is known. (The lower bound holds in fact even for the weaker progress condition of nondeterministic solo termination, and for implementations from any historyless base objects.) The space complexity of other fundamental primitives has also been investigated, e.g., the implementation of timestamp objects from registers and historyless objects [17, 23], or that of a wide class of strong primitives called perturbable objects such as counters, fetch-and-add and compare-and-swap from historyless objects [25].

In this paper we consider *leader election*, another fundamental and well-studied problem, which is related to consensus but is seemingly much simpler. In a leader election protocol for n processes, each process has to decide on one value, win or lose, such that exactly one process (the leader) wins. The problem is related to *name consensus*, where processes have to agree on the ID of a leader—whereas in leader election each process only has to decide whether it is the leader or not. Leader election is also closely related to, and in most models equally powerful as, the *test-and-set (TAS)* synchronization primitive. TAS is perhaps the simplest standard shared memory primitive that has no wait-free deterministic implementation from registers. A TAS object stores one bit, which is initially 0, and supports a TAS() operation which sets the bit's value to 1 and returns its previous value. It has consensus number two, so it can be used together with registers to solve deterministic wait-free consensus only in systems with two processes. TAS objects have been used to solve many classical problems such as mutual exclusion and renaming [4–6, 14, 15, 26, 28]. Processes can solve leader election using one TAS object by simply calling TAS() once, and returning win if the TAS() call returned 0, or lose otherwise. On the other hand a very simple algorithm using a leader election protocol and one additional binary register can be used to implement a linearizable TAS object, where for a TAS() operation each process needs to execute only a constant number of operations in addition to the leader election protocol [22].

Significant progress has been made in understanding the step complexity of randomized leader election [2, 3, 6, 21, 30]. In particular, in the oblivious adversary model (where the order in which processes take steps is independent of random decisions made by processes), the most efficient algorithm guarantees that the expected step complexity (i.e., the expected maximum number of steps executed by any process) is $O(\log^* k)$, where k is the contention [21].

Little is known, however, about the space complexity of randomized wait-free or obstruction-free leader election. For the much weaker progress condition of deadlock freedom, it is known that the space complexity of leader election is $\Theta(\log n)$ [29]. Clearly, this implies also a space lower bound of $\Omega(\log n)$ for randomized wait-free and obstruction-free leader election. Still, prior to our work presented here, no obstruction-free (or even nondeterministic solo terminating) algorithm was known for solving leader election with fewer than n registers.

We devise the first deterministic obstruction-free algorithm for leader election (and thus for TAS) which uses only $O(\sqrt{n})$ registers. The algorithm is simple but elegant.

Theorem 1. *There is an obstruction-free implementation of a leader election object for n processes from $\sqrt{2n} + o(\sqrt{n})$ atomic $O(\log n)$-bit registers.*

This result raises the question whether it is also possible to obtain a fast randomized wait-free algorithm for leader election. The relation between wait-freedom and obstruction-freedom has been investigated before: Fich, Luchangco, Moir, and Shavit [19] showed that obstruction-free algorithms can be transformed to wait-free ones in the unknown-bound semi-synchronous model.

In this paper we follow a different approach, as we use randomization, but stay in the fully asynchronous model. It is easy to see that any deterministic obstruction-free algorithm can be transformed into an algorithm which is randomized wait-free against the oblivious adversary: Whenever a process is about to perform a shared memory step in the algorithm, it can flip a coin, and with probability $1/2$ it performs the step of the algorithm (called "actual" step), while with the remaining probability it executes a "dummy" step, e.g., reads an arbitrary registers. Suppose a process is guaranteed to finish the obstruction-free algorithm if it performs b unobstructed steps. Any execution of length bn (i.e., where exactly bn shared memory steps are performed) must contain a process that executes at least b steps, and with probability at least $1/2^{bn}$ that process executes b actual steps while all other processes execute just dummy steps. Then during an execution of length $bn \cdot 2^{bn} \cdot (\log n + c)$ some process runs unobstructed for at least b actual steps with probability $1 - O(1/2^c)$. Hence, the algorithm is randomized wait-free.

This naive transformation yields exponential expected step complexity. We provide a slightly different but also simple transformation (which requires a more sophisticated analysis) to show the following result.

Theorem 2. *Suppose there is a deterministic obstruction-free algorithm which guarantees that any process finishes after it has executed at most b steps without interference from other processes. Then the algorithm can be transformed into a randomized one that has the same space complexity, and for any fixed schedule (determined by an oblivious adversary) each process returns after at most $O(b(n+b)\log(n/\delta))$ of its own steps with probability at least $1-\delta$, for any $\delta > 0$ that can be a function of n.*

As mentioned above, Giakkoupis and Woelfel [21] have recently presented a randomized leader election algorithm which has $O(\log^* k)$ expected step complexity against the oblivious adversary, where k is the contention. The algorithm requires $\Theta(n)$ registers, but with high probability (*w.h.p.*) processes access only the first poly-logarithmic number of them. The idea is now to reduce the space requirements of this algorithm by removing the registers which are not needed in most executions, and then in the unlikely event that processes run out of registers, they switch to the algorithm obtained by applying the transformation of Theorem 2 to the algorithm from Theorem 1.

Theorem 3. *There is a randomized implementation of leader election from $\sqrt{2n} + o(\sqrt{n})$ atomic $O(\log n)$-bit registers which guarantees that for any fixed schedule (determined by an oblivious adversary), the maximum number of steps executed by any process is $O(\log^* k)$ in expectation and $O(\log n)$ w.h.p., where k is the contention.*

Model and Preliminaries

We consider the standard asynchronous shared memory model where up to n processes communicate by reading and writing to shared atomic multi-reader multi-writer $O(\log n)$-bit registers. Processes may fail by crashing at any time.

An algorithm may be deterministic or randomized. If it is randomized, then processes can use local coin-flips to make random decisions. For randomized algorithms, the scheduling and process crashes are controlled by an adversary, which at any point of an execution decides which process will take the next step. In this paper we only deal with the *oblivious adversary*, which determines the entire (infinite) schedule ahead of time, i.e., before the first process takes a step.

A deterministic algorithm is *wait-free* if every process finishes in a finite number of its own steps. It is *obstruction-free*, if it guarantees that any process will finish if it performs enough steps alone (i.e, without interference from other processes). If the algorithm is randomized, and every process finishes in an *expected* finite number of steps, then the algorithm is *randomized wait-free* [24].

Our algorithms use an obstruction-free and linearizable scan() operation, which returns a view of an M-element array R (a view is the vector of all array entry values). Implementations of M-component *snapshot* objects which provide M-element arrays supporting linearizable scan() operations are well-known [1, 7, 16]. But in order to achieve our space upper bounds we need a snapshot implementation that uses only $O(M)$ bounded registers. The wait-free implementation by Fich, Fatourou, and Ruppert [16] has space-complexity $O(M)$ but uses unbounded registers. In Appendix A we present a linearizable obstruction-free implementation of a linearizable snapshot object from $M + 1$ $O(\log n)$-bit registers, where each scan() operation finishes after $O(M)$ unobstructed steps.

2   Obstruction-Free Leader Election

We present an obstruction-free implementation of leader election from $O(\sqrt{n})$ registers. The algorithm proceeds in phases, during which processes have access

---

Algorithm 1. Pseudocode for process p.

```
/* Let m = √2n + c⁴√n, where c > 0 is a suitable constant        */
```

```
shared: array R[0...m] of pairs (process_ID, phase_number) initialized to (0,0)
```

1 $\phi \leftarrow 1$ /* p's current phase number */
2 **while** $\phi \leq m$ **do**
3 | $r[0 \ldots m] \leftarrow R.\text{scan}()$
4 | **if** $\exists i, p', \phi' > \phi : r[i] = (p', \phi')$
5 | **or** $\big(|\{j : r[j] = (p, \phi)\}| \leq 1$ **and** $\exists q \, |\{j : r[j] = (q, \phi)\}| \geq 2\big)$ **then**
6 | | **return lose**
7 | **else if** $r[0 \ldots \phi] = [(p, \phi) \ldots (p, \phi)]$ **then**
8 | | $\phi \leftarrow \phi + 1$ /* proceed to the next phase */
9 | **else**
10 | | Let i be the smallest index such that $r[i] \neq (p, \phi)$.   /* $i \leq \phi$ */
11 | | $R[i] \leftarrow (p, \phi)$
12 | **end**
13 **end**
14 **return win**

---

to a shared array $R[0 \ldots m]$ of registers, where $m = \sqrt{2n} + o(\sqrt{n})$. Each register of R stores a pair (process ID, phase number). In phase $1 \leq \phi \leq m$, process p tries to write value (p, ϕ) on all registers $R[0 \ldots \phi]$. After each write, p obtains a view r of array R using a $\text{scan}()$.

Process p loses if one of the two happens: (i) some entry of view r contains a phase number larger than p's phase ϕ; or (ii) two (or more) entries of r have the same value (q, ϕ) for some $q \neq p$, while at most one entry has value (p, ϕ). If neither (i) nor (ii) happens, then p picks the smallest i such that $i \leq \phi$ for which $r[i] \neq (p, \phi)$ and writes (p, ϕ) to $R[i]$. If no such i exists, i.e., all entries of $r[0 \ldots \phi]$ are equal to (p, ϕ), then p enters the next phase, $\phi + 1$. A process wins when it reaches phase $m + 1$. Pseudocode is given in Algorithm 1.

The above algorithm is not wait-free: First of all, our $\text{scan}()$ operation is only obstruction-free. But even if we used wait-free snapshot objects, no process may finish the algorithm for certain schedules. E.g., suppose two processes alternate in executing the while-loop of Algorithm 1 (and each of them executes the entire loop without obstruction). Then whenever one of them scans R in line 3, $R[0]$ does not contain that process' ID, so the process remains in phase 1 and writes to $R[0]$ in line 11. We show below that our algorithm is obstruction-free.

The proof of Theorem 1 unfolds in a series of lemmas. First we show that not all processes lose; thus at least one process wins or does not finish. Then we argue that a process finishes if it runs without interruption for long enough. Last, we show that no two processes win.

To distinguish between the local variables of different processes, we may explicitly state the process as a subscript, e.g., ϕ_p.

Lemma 1. *There is no execution in which all participating processes lose.*

Proof. Suppose, towards a contradiction, that there is some non-empty execution in which all participating processes lose. Let $\phi_{\max}$ be the largest phase in which any process participates in this execution. Clearly $\phi_{\max} \leq m$, because if for some process p we have $\phi_p = m + 1$ then ϕ_p must have increased from m to $m + 1$ in line 8, and after that p cannot lose as it does not do another iteration of the while-loop. Among all processes participating in phase $\phi_{\max}$, consider the last process p that executes a `scan()` in line 3, i.e., the linearization point of the `scan()` by p is after the corresponding linearization points of the `scan()` operations by any other process participating in phase $\phi_{\max}$. After p has executed line 3 for the last time, r_p must satisfy the condition of the if-statement in the next line (otherwise p does not lose), i.e., either (i) $\exists i, p', \phi' > \phi_{\max} \colon r[i] = (p', \phi')$, or (ii) we have

$$|\{j \colon r_p[j] = (p, \phi_{\max})\}| \leq 1 \ \wedge \ \exists q \ |\{j \colon r_p[j] = (q, \phi_{\max})\}| \geq 2. \tag{1}$$

By $\phi_{\max}$'s definition, condition (i) does not hold; hence, condition (ii) holds. Consider now a process q that realizes this condition, and consider the last `scan()` by that process. Then by the same argument as for p, after this `scan()` we have that r_q satisfies

$$|\{j \colon r_q[j] = (q, \phi_{\max})\}| \leq 1 \ \wedge \ \exists w \ |\{j \colon r_q[j] = (w, \phi_{\max})\}| \geq 2. \tag{2}$$

Since q does not execute any write to R after its `scan()`, and since we have assumed that the last `scan()` by p linearizes after the `scan()` by q, it follows that $\{j \colon r_p[j] = (q, \phi_{\max})\} \subseteq \{j \colon r_q[j] = (q, \phi_{\max})\}$. However, the cardinality of the set to the left is at least 2 by (1), and the cardinality of the set to the right is at most 1 by (2). We have thus reached the desired contradiction. □

Lemma 2. *For any reachable configuration C, an execution started at C in which just a single process p takes steps finishes after at most $O(n^{3/2})$ steps.*

Proof. The step complexity of the execution is dominated by the step complexity of the `scan()` operations by p, in line 3. Each of these operations is completed in $O(m)$ steps, as p runs solo. Further, for each phase ϕ in which p participates it performs (at most) $\phi + 1$ iterations of the while-loop, until it overwrites all entries of $R[0 \ldots \phi]$ by (p, ϕ), in line 11. It follows that p finishes after a number of steps bounded by $O\left(\sum_{1 \leq \phi \leq m} \phi m\right) = O(m^3) = O(n^{3/2})$. □

Lemma 3. *There is a constant $c > 0$ such that if $m \geq \sqrt{2n} + c\sqrt[4]{n}$, then in any execution at most one process wins.*

Proof. For each $1 \leq \phi \leq m + 1$, let N_ϕ be the set of processes that participate in phase ϕ and let $n_\phi = |N_\phi|$. To simplify notation, we assume that there is also phase 0, in which all n processes participate by default, and phases $\phi > m + 1$ in which no process participates; we extend the definitions of N_ϕ and n_ϕ to those dummy phases as well. Clearly, the sequence of n_ϕ, $\phi \geq 0$, is non-increasing. Below we analyze how fast this sequence decreases.

We show that the number k of phases after phase ϕ, until at most k processes are left is bounded by $\sqrt{2n_\phi} + O\left(\sqrt[4]{n_\phi}\right)$, and at most $n_\phi + 1$ phases are needed after ϕ to be left with a single process. Formally, for any $0 \leq \phi \leq m$ we show

(a) $\min\{k \colon n_{\phi+k} \le k\} \le \sqrt{2n_\phi} + O\left(\sqrt[4]{n_\phi}\right)$; and

(b) $\min\{k \colon n_{\phi+k} \le 1\} \le n_\phi + 1$.

From this claim, Lemma 3 follows easily: For $\phi = 0$ it follows from (a) that $n_{k_1} \le k_1$ for some $k_1 \le \sqrt{2n_0} + O(\sqrt[4]{n_0}) = \sqrt{2n} + O(\sqrt[4]{n})$. Applying (a) again, for $\phi = k_1$, yields $n_{k_1+k_2} \le k_2$ for some $k_2 \le \sqrt{2n_{k_1}} + O(\sqrt[4]{n_{k_1}}) \le \sqrt{2k_1} + O(\sqrt[4]{k_1}) = O(\sqrt[4]{n})$. Finally, for $\phi = k_1 + k_2$, we obtain from (b) that $n_{k_1+k_2+k_3} \le 1$ for some $k_3 \le k_2 + 1$. Therefore, $n_\phi \le 1$ for $\phi = k_1 + k_2 + k_3 \le \sqrt{2n} + O(\sqrt[4]{n})$.

It remains to prove (a) and (b). We start with the proof of (b), which is more basic. Suppose that $n_\phi = \ell > 1$. We must show that $n_{\phi+\ell+1} \le 1$. Assume, for the sake of contradiction, that $n_{\phi+\ell+1} \ge 2$, and let p be the first process to enter phase $\phi + \ell + 1$, i.e., p's last `scan()` operation in phase $\phi + \ell$ precedes the corresponding operations of other processes from $N_{\phi+\ell+1}$. This `scan()` returns a view r of R in which all entries of $r[0 \ldots \phi+\ell]$ have value $(p, \phi+\ell)$. We claim that after this happens no other process can enter phase $\phi + \ell + 1$, thus contradicting the assumption that $n_{\phi+\ell+1} \ge 2$. Observe that each process writes to R at most once before it executes a `scan()` on R. Further at most $n_\phi - 1 = \ell - 1$ processes $q \ne p$ can write to $R[\phi \ldots \phi+\ell]$. Thus, if any such process q executes a `scan()` on R, it will find at least two entries with values (p, k), for $k \ge \phi + \ell$, and at most one entry $(q, \phi + \ell)$, and thus q will lose.

Next we prove (a). We proceed as follows. For a phase $i = \phi + k$, if $n_i - n_{i+1} < k$ (i.e., fewer than k of the processes participating in phase i fail to enter the next phase, $i + 1$), we argue that during the time interval in which the last $d_i = k - (n_i - n_{i+1})$ processes enter phase $i + 1$, at least some minimum number of processes from N_ϕ perform their "final" write operation to R. We show that this minimum number of processes is at least $d_i(d_i - 1)/2$ if $n_i \ge k$, and observe that the total number of such processes for all $i \ge \phi$ is bounded by n_ϕ. Further, we have that the sum of the differences $k - d_i$ is also bounded by n_ϕ. Combining these two inequalities yields the claim.

We give now the detailed proof. Consider a phase $i \ge \phi$, let $k = i - \phi$, and suppose that $n_i \ge k$. Let $d_i = \max\{0, k - (n_i - n_{i+1})\}$. Suppose that $d_i \ge 2$, and consider the last d_i processes from N_i to enter phase $i + 1$. Let t_i be the time when the first of these d_i processes enters phase $i + 1$, and t_i' be the time when the last one does. We argue now that at least $\sum_{1 \le j < d_i} j = d_i(d_i - 1)/2$ processes from N_ϕ perform their last write operation between times t_i and t_i'. First note that no process enters a phase other than $i+1$ between times t_i and t_i'. Suppose now that the j-th of the d_i processes has just entered phase $i + 1$, where $1 \le j < d_i$, and let p be that process. Then, right after p's `scan()` we have that all entries in $R[0 \ldots i]$ are equal to (p, i). Unless all but at most one of the entries $R[\phi \ldots i]$ are subsequently overwritten by processes in phase i or smaller, no other process can enter phase $i + 1$. Since p is not the last process to enter phase $i+1$, and the number of processes left in phase i is $(d_i - j) + (n_i - n_{i+1}) = k - j$, it follows that to overwrite $i - \phi = k$ of the $k + 1$ entries of $R[\phi \ldots i]$ at least $k - (k - j) = j$ of them must be overwritten by processes that are in phases smaller than i; this will be the final write for those processes. It follows that at least $\sum_{1 \le j < d_i} j = d_i(d_i - 1)/2$ processes from N_ϕ perform their last write operation between t_i and t'_i, as desired. Note that this result holds also when $d_i < 2$, as in this case the above sum is 0. Observe now that for two distinct i with $d_i \geq 2$ the intervals $[t_i, t'_i]$ do not overlap, and thus the sets of processes that do their final write to each of these intervals are distinct. It follows that the total number of processes from N_ϕ that do a final write in the execution is at least $\sum_{\phi \leq i < \kappa} d_i(d_i - 1)/2$, where $\kappa = \min\{k : n_{\phi+k} \leq k\}$. Since this number cannot exceed the size of N_ϕ, we have

$$n_\phi \geq \sum_{\phi \leq i < \phi+\kappa} d_i(d_i - 1)/2. \tag{3}$$

In addition to the above inequality, we have that

$$n_\phi = \sum_{\phi \leq i < \phi+\kappa} (n_i - n_{i+1}) + n_{\phi+\kappa} \geq \sum_{\phi \leq i < \phi+\kappa} (n_i - n_{i+1})$$

$$\geq \sum_{\phi \leq i < \phi+\kappa} (i - \phi - d_i) = \kappa(\kappa - 1)/2 - \sum_{\phi \leq i < \phi+\kappa} d_i. \tag{4}$$

(The second inequality follows from the definition of d_i.)

We now combine the two inequalities above to bound κ. Let $\lambda = \sum_{\phi \leq i < \phi+\kappa} d_i$. Then (3) gives

$$n_\phi \geq \sum_{\phi \leq i < \phi+\kappa} d_i^2/2 - \lambda/2 \geq \lambda^2/(2\kappa) - \lambda/2 \quad \text{(by Cauchy-Schwarz Inequality)}.$$

Solving for λ gives $\lambda \leq (\kappa + \sqrt{\kappa^2 + 8\kappa n_\phi})/2$. Applying this bound of $\lambda = \sum_{\phi \leq i < \phi+\kappa} d_i$ to (4) and rearranging gives $\kappa^2 \leq 2n_\phi + 2\kappa + \sqrt{\kappa^2 + 8\kappa n_\phi}$. Solving for κ yields $\kappa \leq \sqrt{2n_\phi} + O(\sqrt[4]{n_\phi})$. This completes the proof of (a) and the proof of Lemma 3. □

Lemmas 1-3 imply that Algorithm 1 is a correct obstruction-free leader election algorithm using $2\sqrt{n} + o(\sqrt{n})$ registers, proving Theorem 1.

Remark 1. We can use an early termination criterion, in which p exits the while-loop (and wins) if the condition of line 7 is satisfied and, in addition, p has seen no process other than itself during phases ϕ and $\phi - 1$: Since p does not see another process during phase $\phi - 1$, it follows that no process finishes phase $\phi - 1$ before p. And since p does not see any process during phase ϕ either, it follows that no process finishes phase $\phi - 1$ before p finishes phase ϕ. Thus, no process other than p ever completes phase ϕ. The detailed argument is straightforward and is omitted due to space constraints. Applying this early termination criterion achieves that each process p finishes after $O(n)$ instead of $O(n^{3/2})$ solo steps.

3   Obstruction Freedom vs. Randomized Wait Freedom

We present now a simple technique that transforms any deterministic obstruction-free algorithm into a randomized one that has the same space complexity and is randomized wait-free against the oblivious adversary. In particular, if the deterministic implementation guarantees that any process finishes after executing at most b steps without interference, then the randomized implementation guarantees that any process finishes w.h.p. after a number of steps that is bounded by a polynomial function of n and b, namely, $O(b(n + b) \log n)$.

We apply the above transformation to Algorithm 1 presented in Section 2, to obtained a randomized implementation for leader election that has the same $O(\sqrt{n})$ space complexity, and polynomial step complexity against the adaptive adversary. Then we explain how this randomized implementation can be combined with known faster randomized leader election implementation to achieve simultaneously both space- and time-efficiency.

Next we describe the simple transformation technique. Suppose we are given a deterministic obstruction-free algorithm which guarantees that any participating processes p finishes its execution after it takes a sequence of at most b steps during which no other process takes steps. (E.g., from Lemma 2, we have that $b = O(n^{3/2})$ for Algorithm 1.) The randomized implementation we propose is as follows. Every process p flips a biased coin before its first step, and also again every b steps. Each coin flip returns heads with probability $1/n$ and tails with probability $1 - 1/n$, independently of other coin flips. If the outcome of a coin flip by p is heads, then in the next b steps following the coin flip, p executes the next b steps of the given deterministic algorithm; if the outcome is tails then the next b steps of p are *dummy* steps, e.g., p repeatedly reads some shared register.

Analysis. We show that the requirements of Theorem 2 are met by the randomized implementation described above, i.e., a process flips a coin every b steps and with probability $1/n$ it executes the next b steps of the deterministic algorithm, while with probability $1 - 1/n$ it takes b dummy steps instead.

Let $\sigma = (\pi_1, \pi_2, \dots)$ be an arbitrary schedule determining an order in which processes take steps. We assume that σ is fixed before the execution of the algorithm, and in particular before processes flip their coins. For technical reasons we assume that after a process finishes it does not stop, but it takes *no-op* steps whenever it is its turn to take a step according to σ. Also the process continues to flip a coin every b steps; the outcome of this coin flip has no effect on the execution, but is used for the analysis.

We start with a rough sketch of the proof. We sort processes participating in schedule σ in increasing order in which they are scheduled to take their (λb)-th step, where $\lambda = \Theta\big((n + b) \log(n/\delta)\big)$. Let p_i denote the i-th process in this order. We will argue about p_1 first. We define λ disjoint *blocks* of σ, where the ℓ-th block starts with the first step of p_1 after its ℓ-th coin flip, and finishes after the last step of p_1 before its $(\ell + 1)$-th coin flip. Let m_ℓ denote the number of steps contained in block ℓ; then $\sum_\ell m_\ell \leq n\lambda b$ by p_1's definition. Further, the number of coin flips that occur in block ℓ is at most $O(m_\ell/b + n)$. These coin flips, plus at most n additional coin flips preceding the block (one by each process), determine which of the steps in the block are actual steps and which ones are dummy. If all these coin flips by processes other than p_1 return tails, we say that the block is *unobstructed*. Such a block does not contain any actual steps by processes other than p_1. It follows that the probability of block ℓ to be unobstructed is at least $(1 - 1/n)^{O(m_\ell/b + n)}$. The expected number of unobstructed blocks is then

$\sum_\ell (1 - 1/n)^{O(m_\ell/b+n)}$, and we show that this is $\Omega(\lambda)$ using that $\sum_\ell m_\ell \le n\lambda b$. We then show that this $\Omega(\lambda)$ bound on the number of unobstructed blocks holds also w.h.p. This would follow easily if for different blocks the events that the blocks are unobstructed were independent; but they are not, as they may depend on the outcome of the same coin flip. Nevertheless we observe that the dependence is limited, as each coin flip affects steps in at most b different blocks and each block is affected by at most $O(n)$ coin flips on average. To obtain the desired bound we use a concentration inequality from [27], which is a refinement of the standard method of bounded differences. Once we have established that $\Omega(\lambda)$ blocks are unobstructed, it follows that the probability that process p_1 flips heads at the beginning of some unobstructed block is $1 - (1 - 1/n)^{\Omega(\lambda)} = 1 - e^{-\Omega(\lambda/n)} \ge 1 - \delta/n$ for the right choice of constants. Hence with at least this probability, p_1 finishes after at most λb steps.

Similar bounds are obtained also for the remaining processes: We use the same approach as above for each p_i, except that in place of σ we use the schedule σ_i obtained from σ by removing all instances of p_j except for the first λb ones, for all $1 \le j < i$. We conclude that with probability $1 - \delta/n$, p_i finishes after taking at most λb steps, assuming that each of $p_1, \ldots, p_{i-1}$ also finishes after at most λb steps. The theorem then follows by combining the results for all processes.

We give now the detailed proof. Let $\lambda = \beta(n+b)\ln(n/\delta)$, for a constant $\beta > 0$ to be quantified later. Let $p_1, \ldots, p_k$ be the processes participating in schedule σ, listed in the order in which they are scheduled to take their (λb)-th step; processes that take fewer steps than λb are not listed. Let σ_i, for $1 \le i \le k$, be the schedule obtained from σ after removing all instances of p_j except for the first λb ones, for all $1 \le j < i$. For each $1 \le i \le k$, we identify λ disjoint blocks of σ_i, where the ℓ-th block, denoted $\sigma_{i,\ell}$, starts with p_i's step following its ℓ-th coin flip, and finishes after the last step of p_i before its $(\ell + 1)$-th coin flip. By $|\sigma_{i,\ell}|$ we denote the number of steps contained in $\sigma_{i,\ell}$. We have $\sum_\ell |\sigma_{i,\ell}| \le n\lambda b$, i.e., blocks $\sigma_{i,1}, \ldots, \sigma_{i,\lambda}$ contain at most $n\lambda b$ steps in total, namely, λb steps by each of processes $p_1, \ldots, p_i$, and fewer than λb steps by each of the remaining processes.

Observe that if p_i has not finished before block $\sigma_{i,\ell}$ begins, and if p_i's coin flip before block $\sigma_{i,\ell}$ returns heads, then p_i is guaranteed to finish during $\sigma_{i,\ell}$ if all other steps by non-finished processes during $\sigma_{i,\ell}$ are dummy steps.

We say that a coin flip *potentially obstructs* $\sigma_{i,\ell}$ if it is performed by a process $p \ne p_i$, and at least one of the b steps by p following that coin flip takes place during $\sigma_{i,\ell}$. This step will be an actual step only if the coin flip is heads (this is not 'if and only if' because p may have finished, in which case it does a no-op). We say that block $\sigma_{i,\ell}$ is *unobstructed* if all coin flips that potentially obstruct this block are tails. The number of coin flips that potentially obstruct $\sigma_{i,\ell}$ is bounded by $|\sigma_{i,\ell}|/b + 2n$, because if process $p \ne p_i$ takes $s > 0$ steps in $\sigma_{i,\ell}$, then the coin-flips by p that potentially obstruct $\sigma_{i,\ell}$ are the at most $\lceil s/b \rceil$ ones during $\sigma_{i,\ell}$, plus at most one before $\sigma_{i,\ell}$.

From the above, the probability that $\sigma_{i,\ell}$ is unobstructed is at least $(1 - 1/n)^{|\sigma_{i,\ell}|/b+2n}$. Thus the expected number of unobstructed blocks among

$\sigma_{i,1}, \ldots, \sigma_{i,\lambda}$ is at least $\sum_\ell (1 - 1/n)^{|\sigma_{i,\ell}|/b+2n}$. Using now that $\sum_\ell |\sigma_{i,\ell}| \leq n\lambda b$, and that $(1 - 1/n)^{x+2n}$ is a convex function of x, we obtain that the above sum is minimized when all λ blocks have the same size, equal to nb. Thus, the expected number of unobstructed blocks is at least

$$\sum_\ell (1 - 1/n)^{|\sigma_{i,\ell}|/b+2n} \geq \lambda(1 - 1/n)^{(nb)/b+2n} \geq \lambda(1 - 1/n)^{3n} > \lambda/4^3 = \lambda/64.$$

Next we use Theorem 4, from Appendix B, to lower bound the number of unobstructed blocks w.h.p. Let the binary random variables $X_1, X_2, \ldots$ denote the outcome of the coin flips that potentially obstruct at least one block $\sigma_{i,1}, \ldots, \sigma_{i,\lambda}$ ($X_j = 1$ if and only if the j-th of those coin flips is heads). Then, $\Pr[X_j = 1] = 1/n$. Let $f(X_1, X_2, \ldots)$ denote the number of unobstructed blocks. We showed above that $\mathbf{E}[f(X_1, X_2, \ldots)] \geq \lambda/64$. Further, we observe that changing the value of X_j can change the value of f by at most the number of blocks that X_j potentially obstructs; let c_j denote that number. Then, $\max_j c_j \leq b$. Finally, since each block $m_{i,\ell}$ is potentially obstructed by at most $|\sigma_{i,\ell}|/b + 2n$ coin flips, $\sum_j c_j \leq \sum_\ell (|\sigma_{i,\ell}|/b + 2n) \leq 3n\lambda$, as $\sum_\ell |\sigma_{i,\ell}| \leq n\lambda b$, and thus $\sum_j c_j^2 \leq (3n\lambda/b) \cdot b^2 = 3nb\lambda$. Applying now Theorem 4 for $t = \lambda/128 \leq \mathbf{E}[f(X_1, X_2, \ldots)]/2$ gives $\Pr\left(f(X_1, \ldots, X_n) \leq t\right) \leq 2\exp\left(-\frac{t^2}{6b\lambda+2tb/3}\right)$. Substituting $t = \lambda/128 = (\beta/128)(n+b)\ln(n/\delta)$ and letting $\beta = 2(6 \cdot 128^2 + 2 \cdot 128/3)$ yields $\Pr\left(f(X_1, \ldots, X_n) \leq \lambda/128\right) \leq 2e^{-2\ln(n/\delta)} < \delta/(2n)$. Thus, with probability at least $1 - \delta/(2n)$ at least $\lambda/128$ of the blocks $\sigma_{i,1}, \ldots, \sigma_{i,\lambda}$ are unobstructed. The probability that process p_i flips heads in at least one unobstructed block is then at least $\left(1 - \delta/(2n)\right) \cdot \left(1 - (1 - 1/n)^{\lambda/128}\right)$. Since $1 - (1 - 1/n)^{\lambda/128} \geq 1 - e^{\lambda/(128n)} > 1 - \delta/(2n)$, the above probability is at least $\left(1 - \delta/(2n)\right)^2 \geq 1 - \delta/n$.

We have just shown that for any $1 \leq i \leq k$, with probability at least $1 - \delta/n$ process p_i finishes after at most λb steps *assuming schedule σ_i*. However, schedules σ and σ_i yield identical executions if processes $p_1, \ldots, p_{i-1}$ all finish after executing at most λb steps (the executions are identical assuming that the same coin flips are used in both). Then, by the union bound, the probability that *all* processes p_i finish after executing no more than λb steps each is at least $1 - n \cdot \delta/n = 1 - \delta$. This concludes the proof of Theorem 2.

Randomized Leader Election. From Theorem 2 and Lemma 2 it follows that Algorithm 1 can be transformed into a randomized leader election implementation with step complexity $O(n^3 \log n)$.

Corollary 1. *There is a randomized variant of Algorithm 1 that has the same space complexity, and for any fixed schedule (determined by an oblivious adversary), w.h.p. every process finishes after at most $O(n^3 \log n)$ steps.*

If we use a variant of Algorithm 1 which employs the early termination criterion described in Remark 1 on page 53, then $b = O(n)$ and thus the step complexity of the randomized algorithm obtained is $O(n^2 \log n)$ w.h.p.

Giakkoupis and Woelfel [21] proposed a randomized implementation for leader election from $\Omega(n)$ registers with expected step complexity $O(\log^* n)$ against the oblivious adversary. Next we give an overview of this algorithm, and explain how to combine it with the randomized variant of Algorithm 1 to reduce space complexity to $O(\sqrt{n})$, without increasing the asymptotic step complexity.

The algorithm in [21] uses a chain of n group-election objects $G_1, \ldots, G_n$ alternating with n deterministic splitters $S_1, \ldots, S_n$, and a chain of n 2-process leader election objects $L_1, \ldots, L_n$. Each group-election object G_i guarantees that at least one of the processes accessing G_i gets elected, and if k processes access G_i then $O(\log k)$ get elected in expectation. Each splitter S_i returns one of the three outcomes: win, lose, or cont (for continue). It guarantees that if k processes access it, then at most one wins, at most $k-1$ lose, at most $k-1$ continue; thus, if only one process accesses the splitter, that process wins.

A process p proceeds by accesses the group-election objects in increasing index order. If p accesses G_i and fails to get elected, it loses immediately; if it does get elected, it then tries to win splitter S_i. If it loses S_i, it loses also the implemented leader election; if it returns cont it continues to the next group-election object, G_{i+1}; and if it wins S_i, it switches to the chain of 2-process leader election objects. In the last case it subsequently tries to win $L_i, L_{i-1}, \ldots, L_1$ (in this order). If it succeeds, it wins the implemented leader election, else it loses.

The analysis of the above algorithm given in [21] shows that in expectation only the first $O(\log^* n)$ group-election objects are used. Further, for any $i = \omega(\log^* n)$, the probability that S_i is used is bounded by $2^{-\Omega(i)}$.

We propose the following simple modification to this algorithm: For an index $K = \Theta(\log^2 n)$, we replace group-election object G_K with the randomized variant of Algorithm 1, and then remove all objects G_i, S_i, and L_i, for $i > K$. Clearly, the first modification does not affect the correctness of the algorithm, since any leader election algorithm is also a group-election algorithm. This modification guarantees that at most one process will ever access S_K. It follows that objects G_i, S_i, and L_i for $i > K$ will never be used, and thus are no longer needed. Hence, the space complexity of the new implementation is equal to that of Algorithm 1 plus $O(\log^3 n)$ registers, as each group-election object can be implemented from $O(\log n)$ registers. Further, the step complexity of the algorithm is the same as that of the original algorithm from [21], because a process reaches G_K with probability at most $2^{-\Omega(\log^2 n)} = n^{-\Omega(\log n)}$, and when this happens at most $O(n^3 \log n)$ additional steps are needed w.h.p., by Corollary 1. Thus, we have proved Theorem 3.

4   Conclusion

We provided a randomized wait-free algorithm for leader election (and thus test-and-set) from $O(\sqrt{n})$ registers and with $O(\log^* n)$ expected step complexity against the oblivious adversary. To obtain our result we first developed an obstruction-free algorithm with $O(\sqrt{n})$ space complexity. Then we devised and applied a general construction that shows how any deterministic obstruction-free algorithm can be transformed to a randomized wait-free one, such that the expected step complexity is polynomial in n and in the maximum number of unobstructed steps a process needs to finish the obstruction-free algorithm.

We are not aware of any other obstruction-free implementation of an object with consensus number two or higher from $o(n)$ registers. Perhaps the most interesting open questions remains to be whether there is a consensus algorithm that needs only sub-linear many registers. While it is not clear whether our techniques can help developing such an algorithm, we believe that it yields interesting insights. Finding an $o(n)$-space algorithm for consensus would seem hopeless if it weren't even possible for the seemingly simpler problem of leader election.

References

1. Afek, Y., Attiya, H., Dolev, D., Gafni, E., Merritt, M., Shavit, N.: Atomic snapshots of shared memory. J. of the ACM 40(4), 873–890 (1993)
2. Afek, Y., Gafni, E., Tromp, J., Vitányi, P.: Wait-free test-and-set. In: Segall, A., Zaks, S. (eds.) WDAG 1992. LNCS, vol. 647, pp. 85–94. Springer, Heidelberg (1992)
3. Alistarh, D., Aspnes, J.: Sub-logarithmic test-and-set against a weak adversary. In: Peleg, D. (ed.) DISC. LNCS, vol. 6950, pp. 97–109. Springer, Heidelberg (2011)
4. Alistarh, D., Aspnes, J., Censor-Hillel, K., Gilbert, S., Zadimoghaddam, M.: Optimal-time adaptive strong renaming, with applications to counting. In: Proc. of 30th PODC, pp. 239–248 (2011)
5. Alistarh, D., Aspnes, J., Gilbert, S., Guerraoui, R.: The complexity of renaming. In: Proc. of 52nd FOCS, pp. 718–727 (2011)
6. Alistarh, D., Attiya, H., Gilbert, S., Giurgiu, A., Guerraoui, R.: Fast randomized test-and-set and renaming. In: Lynch, N.A., Shvartsman, A.A. (eds.) DISC 2010. LNCS, vol. 6343, pp. 94–108. Springer, Heidelberg (2010)
7. Anderson, J.H.: Composite registers. Dist. Comp. 6(3), 141–154 (1993)
8. Aspnes, J.: Randomized consensus in expected $o(n^2)$ total work using single-writer registers. In: Peleg, D. (ed.) DISC. LNCS, vol. 6950, pp. 363–373. Springer, Heidelberg (2011)
9. Aspnes, J.: Faster randomized consensus with an oblivious adversary. In: Proc. of 31st PODC, pp. 1–8 (2012)
10. Aspnes, J.: A modular approach to shared-memory consensus, with applications to the probabilistic-write model. Dist. Comp. 25(2), 179–188 (2012)
11. Attiya, H., Censor, K.: Tight bounds for asynchronous randomized consensus. J. of the ACM 55(5) (2008)
12. Attiya, H., Censor-Hillel, K.: Lower bounds for randomized consensus under a weak adversary. SIAM J. on Comp. 39(8), 3885–3904 (2010)
13. Aumann, Y.: Efficient asynchronous consensus with the weak adversary scheduler. In: Proc. of 16th PODC, pp. 209–218 (1997)
14. Buhrman, H., Panconesi, A., Silvestri, R., Vitányi, P.: On the importance of having an identity or, is consensus really universal? Dist. Comp. 18(3), 167–176 (2006)
15. Eberly, W., Higham, L., Warpechowska-Gruca, J.: Long-lived, fast, waitfree renaming with optimal name space and high throughput. In: Kutten, S. (ed.) DISC 1998. LNCS, vol. 1499, pp. 149–160. Springer, Heidelberg (1998)
16. Ellen, F., Fatourou, P., Ruppert, E.: Time lower bounds for implementations of multi-writer snapshots. J. of the ACM 54(6) (2007)
17. Ellen, F., Fatourou, P., Ruppert, E.: The space complexity of unbounded timestamps. Dist. Comp. 21(2), 103–115 (2008)

18. Fich, F., Herlihy, M., Shavit, N.: On the space complexity of randomized synchronization. J. of the ACM 45(5), 843–862 (1998)
19. Fich, F.E., Luchangco, V., Moir, M., Shavit, N.N.: Obstruction-free algorithms can be practically wait-free. In: Fraigniaud, P. (ed.) DISC 2005. LNCS, vol. 3724, pp. 78–92. Springer, Heidelberg (2005)
20. Fischer, M., Lynch, N., Paterson, M.: Impossibility of distributed consensus with one faulty process. J. of the ACM 32(2), 374–382 (1985)
21. Giakkoupis, G., Woelfel, P.: On the time and space complexity of randomized test-and-set. In: Proc. of 31st PODC, pp. 19–28 (2012)
22. Golab, W., Hendler, D., Woelfel, P.: An $O(1)$ RMRs leader election algorithm. SIAM J. on Comp. 39, 2726–2760 (2010)
23. Helmi, M., Higham, L., Pacheco, E., Woelfel, P.: The space complexity of long-lived and one-shot timestamp implementations. In: Proc. of 30th PODC, pp. 139–148 (2011)
24. Herlihy, M.: Wait-free synchronization. ACM Trans. Program. Lang. Syst. 13(1), 124–149 (1991)
25. Jayanti, P., Tan, K., Toueg, S.: Time and space lower bounds for nonblocking implementations. SIAM J. on Comp. 30(2), 438–456 (2000)
26. Kruskal, C., Rudolph, L., Snir, M.: Efficient synchronization on multiprocessors with shared memory. ACM Trans. Program. Lang. Syst. 10(4), 579–601 (1988)
27. McDiarmid, C.: Concentration. In: Habib, M., McDiarmid, C., Ramirez-Alfonsin, J., Reed, B. (eds.) Probabilistic Methods for Algorithmic Discrete Mathematics, pp. 195–248. Springer (1998)
28. Panconesi, A., Papatriantafilou, M., Tsigas, P., Vitányi, P.: Randomized naming using wait-free shared variables. Dist. Comp. 11(3), 113–124 (1998)
29. Styer, E., Peterson, G.: Tight bounds for shared memory symmetric mutual exclusion problems. In: Proc. of 8th PODC, pp. 177–191 (1989)
30. Tromp, J., Vitányi, P.: Randomized two-process wait-free test-and-set. Dist. Comp. 15(3), 127–135 (2002)

Appendix A: Obstruction-Free M-Component Snapshots

We present an obstruction-free implementation of an M-component snapshot object from $M+1$ bounded registers. Formally, an M-component snapshot stores a vector $V = (V_1, \ldots, V_M)$ of M values from some domain D. It supports two operations; scan() takes no parameter and returns the value of V, and update(i,x), $i \in \{1, \ldots, M\}$, $x \in D$, writes x to the i-th component of V and returns nothing.

Our implementation uses an array $A[1 \ldots M]$ of shared registers and a register S. Each array entry $A[i]$ stores a triple (w_i, p_i, b_i), where $w_i \in D$ represents the i-th entry in the vector V of the snapshot object, p_i is a process ID or $\perp$ which identifies the last process that wrote to $A[i]$, and $b_i \in \{0,1\}$ is a bounded (modulo 2) sequence number. Initially, $S = \perp$ and each array entry $A[i]$ has the value $(w_i, \perp, 0)$ for some fixed $w_i \in D$.

Now suppose process p calls update(i, x), and this is p's j-th update of the i-th component of V. To perform the update, p first writes its ID to S and then it writes the triple $(x, p, j \bmod 2)$ to $A[i]$.

To execute a scan(), process p first writes its ID to S. Then it performs a collect (i.e., it reads all entries of A) to obtain a *view* $a[1 \ldots M]$, and another collect to obtain a second view $a'[1 \ldots M]$. Finally, the process reads S. If S does not contain p's ID or if the views a and a' obtained in the two collects differ, then p starts its scan() over; otherwise it returns view a.

Obviously scan() is obstruction-free, and update() is even wait-free. Note also that a process which runs without obstruction can finish each operation in $O(M)$ steps.

To prove linearizability, we use the following linearization points: Each update(i, x) operation linearizes at the point when the calling process writes to $A[i]$, and each scan() operation that terminates linearizes at the point just before the calling process performs its last collect during its scan(). (We don't linearize pending scan() operations.)

Consider a scan() operation by process p which returns the view $a = a[1 \ldots M]$. Let t be the point when that scan() linearizes, i.e., just before p starts its last collect. To prove linearizability it suffices to show that $A = a$ at point t.

For the purpose of a contradiction assume that this is not the case, i.e., there is an index $i \in \{1, \ldots, M\}$ such that at time t the triple stored in $A[i]$ is not equal to $a[i]$. Let t_1 and t_2 be the points in time when p reads the value $(w, q, b) = a[i]$ from $A[i]$ during its penultimate and ultimate collect, respectively. Then $t_1 < t < t_2$. Since $A[i] \neq (w, q, b)$ at time t but $A[i] = (w, q, b)$ at times t_1 and t_2, process q writes (w, q, b) to $A[i]$ at some point in the interval $(t, t_2) \subseteq (t_1, t_2)$. Since p does not write to A during its scan(), this implies $q \neq p$.

First suppose q writes to $A[i]$ at least twice during (t_1, t_2). Each such write must happen during an update() operation by q. Since each update() operation starts with a write to S, q writes its ID to S at least once in (t_1, t_2). But since the penultimate collect of p's scan() starts before t_1 and the ultimate collect finishes after t_2, S cannot change in the interval (t_1, t_2), which is a contradiction.

Hence, suppose q writes to $A[i]$ exactly once in (t_1, t_2); in particular it writes the triple (w, q, b) to $A[i]$ at some point $t^* \in (t_1, t_2)$. Recall that each time q writes to $A[i]$ it alternates the bit it writes to the third component. Hence, at no point in $[t_1, t^*]$ the second and third component of $A[i]$ can have value q and b. In particular, $A[i] \neq (w, q, b)$ at point t_1, which is a contradiction.

Appendix B: A Concentration Inequality

The next result follows from [27, Theorem 3.9], which is an extension to the standard method of bounded differences.

Theorem 4. *Let* $X_1, \ldots, X_n$ *be independent 0/1 random variables with* $\Pr(X_i = 1) = p$. *Let* f *be a bounded real-valued function defined on* $\{0, 1\}^n$, *such that* $|f(x) - f(x')| \leq c_i$, *whenever vectors* $x, x' \in \{0, 1\}^n$ *differ only in the* i-*the coordinate. Then for any* $t > 0$,

$$\Pr\left(|f(X_1, \ldots, X_n) - \mathbf{E}[f(X_1, \ldots, X_n)]| \geq t\right) \leq 2 \exp\left(-\frac{t^2}{2p \sum_i c_i^2 + 2t \max_i\{c_i\}/3}\right).$$

Distributed Protocols for Leader Election:
A Game-Theoretic Perspective

Ittai Abraham[1], Danny Dolev[2,*], and Joseph Y. Halpern[3,**]

[1] Microsoft Research, Silicon Valley
ittaia@microsoft.com
[2] The Hebrew University of Jerusalem, Jerusalem, Israel
dolev@cs.huji.ac.il
[3] Computer Science Department, Cornell University, Ithaca, NY 14853, USA
halpern@cs.cornell.edu

Abstract. We do a game-theoretic analysis of leader election, under the assumption that each agent prefers to have some leader than to have no leader at all. We show that it is possible to obtain a *fair* Nash equilibrium, where each agent has an equal probability of being elected leader, in a completely connected network, in a bidirectional ring, and a unidirectional ring, in the synchronous setting. In the asynchronous setting, Nash equilibrium is not quite the right solution concept. Rather, we must consider *ex post* Nash equilibrium; this means that we have a Nash equilibrium no matter what a scheduling adversary does. We show that ex post Nash equilibrium is attainable in the asynchronous setting in all the networks we consider, using a protocol with bounded running time. However, in the asynchronous setting, we require that $n > 2$. We can get a fair ϵ-*Nash* equilibrium if $n = 2$ in the asynchronous setting, under some cryptographic assumptions (specifically, the existence of a pseudo-random number generator and polynomially-bounded agents), using ideas from bit-commitment protocols. We then generalize these results to a setting where we can have deviations by a coalition of size k. In this case, we can get what we call a fair k-resilient equilibrium if $n > 2k$; under the same cryptographic assumptions, we can a get a k-resilient equilibrium if $n = 2k$. Finally, we show that, under minimal assumptions, not only do our protocols give a Nash equilibrium, they also give a *sequential* equilibrium [23], so players even play optimally off the equilibrium path.

1 Introduction

As has been often observed, although distributed computing and game theory are interested in much the same problems—dealing with systems where there are many agents, facing uncertainty, and having possibly different goals—in practice, there has been a

* Incumbent of the Berthold Badler Chair in Computer Science. Part of the work was done Supported in part by The Israeli Centers of Research Excellence (I-CORE) program, (Center No. 4/11), by NSF, AFOSR grant FA9550-09-1-0266, and by the Google Inter-University Center for Electronic Markets and Auctions.
** Supported in part by NSF grants IIS-0534064, IIS-0812045, and IIS-0911036, IIS-0911036, and CCF-1214844, AFOSR grants FA9550-08-1-0438, FA9550-09-1-0266, and FA9550-12-1-0040, and ARO grant W911NF-09-1-0281.

Y. Afek (Ed.): DISC 2013, LNCS 8205, pp. 61–75, 2013.

significant difference in the models used in the two areas. In game theory, the focus has been on rational agents: each agent is assumed to have a utility on outcomes, and be acting so as to maximize expected utility. In distributed computing, the focus has been on the "good guys/bad guys" model. The implicit assumption here is that there is a system designer who writes code for all the processes in the system, but some of the processes may get taken over by an adversary, or some computers may fail. The processes that have not been corrupted (either by the adversary or because of a faulty computer) follow the designer's protocol. The goal has typically been to prove that the system designer's goals are achieved, no matter what the corrupted processes do.

More recently, there has been an interest in examining standard distributed computed problems under the assumption that the agents are *rational*, and will deviate from the designer's protocol if it is in their best interest to do so. Halpern and Teague [19] were perhaps the first to do this; they showed (among other things) that secret sharing and multiparty communication could not be accomplished by protocols with bounded running time, if agents were using the solution concept of iterated admissibility (i.e., iterated deletion of weakly dominated strategies). Since then, there has been a wide variety of work done at the border of distributed computing and game theory. For one thing, work has continued on secret sharing and multiparty computation, taking faulty and rational behavior into account (e.g., [1,10,17,18,28]). There has also been work on when and whether a problem that can be solved with a trusted third party can be converted to one that can be solved using *cheap talk*, without a third party, a problem that has also attracted the attention of game theorists (e.g., [1,2,4,6,11,16,20,21,25,29,34,35,36]). This is relevant because there are a number of well-known distributed computing problems that can be solved easily by means of a "trusted" mediator. For example, if fewer than half the agents are corrupted, then we can easily do Byzantine agreement with a mediator: all the agents simply tell the mediator their preference, and the mediator chooses the majority. Another line of research was initiated by work on the *BAR* model [3]; see, for example, [30,37]. Like the work in [1,2], the BAR model allows Byzantine (or faulty) players and rational players; in addition, it allows for *acquiescent* players, who follow the recommended protocols.[1] Traditional game theory can be viewed as allowing only rational players, while traditional distribution computing considers only acquiescent and Byzantine players.

In this paper, we try to further understand the impact of game-theoretic thinking on standard problems in distributed computing. We consider the classic distributed computing problem of electing a leader in an anonymous network (a network where, initially, each process knows its own name, but does not know the name of any other process). Leader election is a fundamental problem in distributed computing. Not surprisingly, there are numerous protocols for this problem (see, e.g., [9,14,24,27,32]) if we assume that no agents have been corrupted; there have also been extensions that deal with corrupted agents [15,22]. Much of this work focuses on leader election in a ring (e.g., [9,14,24,27,32]).

In this paper we study what happens if we assume that agents are rational. It is easy to show that if all agents (a) prefer to have a leader to not having a leader and

---

[1] Originally, the "A" in "BAR" stood for *altruistic*, but it was changed to stand for "acquiescent" [37].

(b) are indifferent as to who is the leader, then all the standard distributed computing protocols work without change. This can be viewed as formalizing the intuition that in the standard setting in distributed computing, we are implicitly assuming that all the agents share the system designer's preferences. But what happens if the agents have different preferences regarding who becomes the leader? For example, an agent may prefer that he himself becomes the leader, since this may make the cost of routing to other agents smaller. In this case, the standard protocols (which typically assume that each agent has a distinct id, and end up electing the agent with the lowest id, or the agent with the highest id, as the leader) do not work; agents have an incentive to lie about their id. Nevertheless, there is always a trivial Nash equilibrium for leader election: no one does anything. Clearly no agent has any incentive to do anything if no one else does. We are thus interested in obtaining a *fair* Nash equilibrium, one in which each agent has an equal probability of being elected leader. Moreover, we want the probability that someone will be elected to be 1.[2] In the language of the BAR model, we allow acquiescent and rational players, but not Byzantine players.

It is easy to solve leader election with a mediator: the agents simply send the mediator their ids, and the mediator picks an id at random as the leader and announces it to the group. We cannot immediately apply the ideas in the work on solving the problem with a mediator and then replacing the mediator with cheap talk to this problem because all these results assume (a) that agents have commonly-known names, (b) that the network is completely connected, and (c) the network is synchronous. Nevertheless, we show that thinking in terms of mediators can be helpful in deriving a simple protocol in the case of a completely connected network that is a fair Nash equilibrium in which a leader is elected with probability 1. We can then modify the protocol so that it works when the network is a ring. We also show that our protocol is actually *k-resilient* [1,2]: it tolerates coalitions of size k, as long as $n > k$. This forms an interesting contrast to work on Byzantine agreement, where it is known that the network must be $2k + 1$ connected to tolerate k Byzantine failures [12]. But we can tolerate coalitions of k rational players even in a unidirectional ring.

These protocols work if the network is synchronous. What happens in an asynchronous setting? Before answering this question, we need to deal with a subtlety: what exactly a Nash equilibrium is in an asynchronous setting? To make sense of Nash equilibrium, we have to talk about an agent's best response. An action for an agent i is a best response if it maximizes i's expected utility, given the other agents' strategies. But to compute expected utility, we need a probability on outcomes. In general, in an asynchronous setting, the outcome may depend on the order that agents are scheduled and on message-delivery times. But we do not have a probability on these. We deal with these

---

[2] Without the last requirement, the existence of a fair Nash equilibrium follows from well-known results, at least in the case of a completely connected network. We can model our story as a symmetric game, one where all agents have the same choice of actions, and an agent's payoff depends only on what actions are performed by others, not who performs them. In addition to showing that every game has a Nash equilibrium, Nash also showed that a symmetric game has a symmetric Nash equilibrium, and a symmetric equilibrium is clearly fair. However, in a symmetric equilibrium, it may well be the case that there is no leader chosen. For example, a trivial symmetric equilibrium for our game is one where everyone chooses a candidate leader at random. However, in most cases, agents choose different candidates, so there is no leader.

problems in this setting by using the standard approach in distributed computing. We assume that an adversary chooses the scheduling and chooses message-delivery times, and try to obtain a strategy that is a Nash equilibrium no matter what the adversary does. This intuition gives rise to what has been called in the literature an *ex post Nash equilibrium*. We provide a simple protocol that gives a fair ex post Nash equilibrium provided that $n > 2$. More generally, we provide a fair ex post k-resilient equilibrium as long as $n > 2k$. We then show that these results are optimal: there is no fair k-resilient ex post Nash equilibrium if $n \leq 2k$.

The lower bounds assume that agents are not computationally bounded. If we assume that agents are polynomially-bounded (and make a standard assumption from the cryptography literature, namely, that a pseudorandom number generator exists), then we can show, using ideas of Naor [31], that there is a fair ex post ϵ-*Nash* equilibrium in this case (one where agents can gain at most ϵ by deviating) for an arbitrarily small ϵ; indeed, we can show that there is a fair ex post ϵ–k-resilient equilibrium as long as $n > k$.

Finally, we show that, under minimal assumptions, not only do our protocols give a Nash equilibrium, they also give a *sequential* equilibrium [23], so players even play optimally off the equilibrium path.

2   The Model

We model a network as a directed, simple (so that there is at most one edge between each pair of nodes), strongly connected, and finite graph. The nodes represent agents, and the edges represent communication links. We assume that the topology of the network is common knowledge, so that if we consider a completely connected network, all agents know that the network is completely connected, and know that they know, and so on; this is similarly the case when we consider unidirectional or bidirectional rings. Deviating agents can communicate only using the network topology; there is no "out of band" communication. We assume that, with each agent, there is associated a unique id, taken from some commonly-known name space, which we can take to be a set of natural numbers. Initially agents know their ids, but may not know the id of any other agent. For convenience, if there are n agents, we name them $1, \ldots, n$. These are names used for our convenience when discussing protocols (so that we can talk about agent i); these names are not known by the agents. Message delivery is handled by the channel (and is not under the control of the agents). Agents can identify on which of their incoming links a message comes in, and can distinguish outgoing links.

When we consider synchronous systems, we assume that agents proceed in lockstep. In round m, (if $m > 0$) after all messages sent in round $m - 1$ are received by all agents, agents do whatever internal computation they need to do (including setting the values of variables); then messages are sent (which will be received at the beginning of round $m + 1$). [3] In the asynchronous setting, agents are scheduled to move at arbitrary times by a (possibly adversarial) scheduler. When they are scheduled, they perform the same kinds of actions as in the synchronous case: receive some messages that were sent to them earlier and not yet received, do some computation, and send some messages. For ease of exposition, we assume that the message space is finite. While we assume that

---

[3] Thus, the synchronous model assumes no "rushing".

all messages sent are eventually received (uncorrupted), there is no bound on message delivery time. Nor do we make any assumption on the number of times one agent can be scheduled relative to another, although we do assume that agents are scheduled infinitely often (so that, for all agents i and times t, there will be a time after t when i is scheduled).

For leader election, we assume that each agent i has a variable $leader_i$ which can be set to some agent's id. If, at the end of the protocol, there is an id v such that $leader_i = v$ for all agents i, then we say that the agent with id v has been elected leader. Otherwise, we say that there is no leader. (Note that we are implicitly requiring that, when there is a leader, all the players know who that leader is.) We assume that each agent i has a utility on outcomes of protocols. For the purposes of this paper, we assume that agents prefer having a leader to not having one, in the weak sense that each agent i never assigns a higher utility to an outcome where there is no leader than to one in which there is a leader (although we allow the agent to be indifferent between an outcome where there is no leader and an outcome where there is a leader). We make no further assumptions on the utility function. It could well be that i prefers that he himself is the leader rather than anyone else; i could in addition prefer a protocol where he sends fewer messages, or does less computation, to one where he sends more messages or does more computation. Nevertheless, our eassumptions require that player i never prefers an outcome where there is no leader to one where there is, even if the latter outcome involves sending many messages and a great deal of computation (although in fact our protocols are quite message-efficient and do not require much computation). Note that our assumptions imply that agent i can "punish" other agents by simply setting $leader_i$ to $\perp$; this ensures that there will be no leader. In the language of [6], this means that each agent has a *punishment strategy*.

A strategy profile (i.e., a strategy or protocol for each agent) is a *Nash equilibrium* if no agent can unilaterally increase his expected utility by switching to a different protocol (assuming that all the other agents continue to use their protocols). It is easy to see that if all the agents are indifferent regarding who is the leader (i.e., if, for each agent i, i's utility of the outcome where j is the leader is the same for all j, including $j = i$), then any protocol that solves leader election is a Nash equilibrium. Note that it is possible that one Nash equilibrium *Pareto dominates* another: all agents are better off in the first equilibrium. For example, if agents are indifferent about who the leader is, so that any protocol that solves leader election is a Nash equilibrium, all agents might prefer an equilibrium where fewer messages are sent; nevertheless, a protocol for leader election where all agents send many messages could still be a Nash equilibrium.

For the remainder of this paper, we assume that each agent has a *preference for leadership*: agent i's utility function is such that i does not give higher utility to an outcome where there is no leader than to one where there is a leader. (Agent i may also prefer to be the leader himself, or have preferences about which agent j is the leader if he is not the leader; these preferences do not play a role in this paper.)

3   The Protocols

We consider protocols in three settings: a completely connected network, a unidirectional ring, and a bidirectional ring. We also consider both the synchronous case and the asynchronous case.

3.1   Completely Connected Network, Synchronous Case

Consider leader election in a completely connected network. First suppose that we have a mediator, that is, a trusted third party. Then there seems to be a naive protocol that can be used: each agent tells the mediator his id, then the mediator picks the highest id, and announces it to all the agents. The agent with this id is the leader. This naive protocol has two obvious problems. First, since we assume that the name space is commonly known, and all agents prefer to be the leader, agents will be tempted to lie about their ids, and to claim that the highest id is their id. Second, even if all agents agree that an agent with a particular id v is the leader, they don't know which agent has that id.

We solve the first problem by having the mediator choose an id at random; we solve the second problem by having agents share their ids. In more detail, we assume that in round 1, agents tell each other their ids. In round 2, each agent tells the mediator all the set of ids he has heard about (including his own). In round 3, the mediator compares all the sets of ids. If they are all the same, the mediator chooses an id v at random from the set; otherwise, the mediator announces "no leader". If the mediator announces that v is the leader, each agent i sets $leader_i = v$ (and marks the incoming link on which the id v was originally received); otherwise, $leader_i$ is undefined (and there is no leader).

It is easy to see that everyone using this protocol gives a Nash equilibrium. If some agent does not send everyone the same id, then the mediator will get different lists from different agents, and there will be no leader. And since a leader is chosen at random, no one has any incentive not to give his actual id. Note that this protocol is, in the language of [1,2], k-resilient for all $k < n$, where n is the number of agents. That is, not only is it the case that no single agent has any incentive to deviate, neither does any coalition of size k. Moreover, the resulting Nash equilibrium is *fair*: each agent is equally likely to be the chosen leader.

Now we want to implement this protocol using cheap talk. Again, this is straightforward. At round 1, each agent i sends everyone his id; at round 2, i sends each other agent j the set of ids that he (i) has received (including his own). If the sets received by agent i are not all identical or if i does not receive an id from some agent, then i sets $leader_i$ to $\perp$, and leader election fails. Otherwise, let n be the cardinality of the set of ids. Agent i chooses a random number N_i in $\{0, \ldots, n - 1\}$ and sends it to all the other agents. Each agent i then computes $N = \sum_{i=1}^{n} N_i \pmod{n}$, and then takes the agent with the Nth highest id in the set to be the leader. (If some agent j does not send i a random number, then i sets $leader_i = \perp$.) Call this protocol for agent i $LEAD_i^{cc}$. The formal pseudocode of the protocol appears in the full paper, available at http://www.cs.cornell.edu/home/halpern/papers/leader.pdf. Let $\mathbf{LEAD}^{cc}$ denote the profile $(LEAD_1^{cc}, \ldots, LEAD_1^{cc})$ (we use boldface for profiles throughout the paper). Clearly, with the profile $\mathbf{LEAD}^{cc}$, all the agents will choose the same leader. It is also easy to see that no agent (and, indeed, no group of size $k < n$) has any incentive to deviate from this strategy profile.

Theorem 1. $\mathbf{LEAD}^{cc}$ *is a fair, k-resilient equilibrium in a completely connected network of n agents, for all $k < n$.* [4]

---

[4] All proofs can be found in the full paper.

Up to now we have implicitly assumed that each agent somehow gets a signal regarding when to start the protocol. This assumption is unnecessary. Even if only some agents want to start the protocol, they send a special round 0 message to everyone asking them to start a leader election protocol. The protocol then proceeds as above.

3.2   Unidirectional Ring, Synchronous Case

We give a Nash equilibrium for leader election in a unidirectional ring, under the assumption that the ring size n is common knowledge. This assumption is necessary, for otherwise an agent can create k sybils, for an arbitrary k, and pretend that the sybils are his neighbors. That is, i can run the protocol as if the ring size is $n + k$ rather than n, simulating what each of his sybils would do. No other agent can distinguish the situation where there are n agents and one agent has created k sybils from a situation where there are actually $n + k$ agents. Of course, if any of i's sybils are elected, then it is as if i is elected. Thus, creating sybils can greatly increase i's chances of being elected leader, giving i an incentive to deviate. (However, the overhead of doing may be sufficient to deter an agent from doing so. See the discussion in Section 4.) Note that in the case of a completely connected network, given that the topology is common knowledge, the number of agents is automatically common knowledge (since each agent can tell how many agents he is connected to).

The protocol is based on the same ideas as in the completely connected case. It is easy to ensure that there is agreement among the agents on what the set of agents is; implementing a random selection is a little harder. We assume that the signal to start leader election may come to one or more agents. Each of these agents then sends a "signed" message (i.e., a message with his id) to his neighbor. Messages are then passed around the ring, with each agent, appending his id before passing it on. If an agent receives a second message that originated with a different agent, the message is ignored if the originating agent has a lower id; otherwise it is passed on. Eventually the originator of the message with the highest id gets back the message. At this point, he knows the ids of all the agents. The message is then sent around the ring a second time. Note that when an agent gets a message for the second time, he will know when the message should make it back to the originator (since the system is synchronous and he knows the size of the ring).

At the round when the originator gets back the message for the second time, each agent i chooses a random number $N_i < n$ and sends it around the ring. After n rounds, all agents will know all the numbers $N_1, \ldots, N_n$, if each agent indeed sent a message. They can then compute $N = \sum_{i=1}^{n} N_i \pmod{n}$, and take the agent with the Nth highest id in the set to be the leader. If agent i does not receive a message when he expects to, then he aborts, and no leader is elected. For example, if an agent who originated a message does not get his message back n rounds and $2n$ rounds after he sent it, or gets a message from an originator with a lower id, then he aborts. Similarly, if an agent who forwarded an originator's message does not get another message from that originator n rounds later or get a message from another originator with a lower id, then he aborts. Finally, for each of the n rounds after the originator with the highest id gets back his message for the second time, each agent i should get a random number from the appropriate agent (i.e., k rounds after the originator with the highest id gets back his message for the second time, agent i should get agent j's random number, j is k steps before i on the ring). If any of these checks is not passed, then i aborts, and no leader is chosen. Call this protocol for agent i $LEAD_i^{uni}$. The formal pseudocode of this and all other protocols mentioned in this paper appear int the full paper.

We would now like to show that $\mathbf{LEAD}^{uni}$ gives a k-resilient fair Nash equilibrium. But there is a subtlety, which we already hinted at in the introduction. In a Nash equilibrium, we want to claim that what an agent does is a best response to what the other agents are doing. But this implicitly assumes that the outcome depends only on the strategies chosen by the agents. But in this case, the outcome may in principle also depend on the (nondeterministic) choices made by nature regarding which agents get an initial signal. Thus, we are interested in what has been called an *ex post* Nash equilibrium. We must show that, no matter which agents get an initial signal, no agent has any incentive to deviate (even if the deviating agent knows which agents get the initial signal, and knows the remaining agents are playing their part of the Nash equilibrium). In fact, we show that no coalition of $k < n$ agents has any incentive to deviate, independent of nature's choices.

Theorem 2. $\mathbf{LEAD}^{uni}$ *is a fair, k-resilient (ex post) equilibrium in a unidirectional ring with n agents, for all $k < n$.*

3.3   Bidirectional Ring, Synchronous Case

It is easy to see that the same protocol will work for the case of the bidirectional ring. More precisely, if there is agreement on the ring orientation, each agent implements the protocol above by just sending left, ignoring the fact that he can send right. If there is no agreement on orientation, then each originating agent can just arbitrarily choose a direction to send; each agent will then continue forwarding in the same direction (by forwarding the message with his id appended to the neighbor from which he did not receive the message). The originator with the highest id will still be the only one to receive his original message back. At that point the protocol continues with round 2 of the protocol for the unidirectional case, and all further messages will be sent in the direction of the original message of the originator with the highest id. Since it is only in the second round that agents append their random numbers to messages, what happened in the first round has no effect on the correctness of the algorithm; we still get a Nash equilibrium as before.

3.4   Asynchronous Ring

We now consider an asynchronous setting. It turns out to be convenient to start with a unidirectional ring, then apply the ideas to a bidirectional ring. For the unidirectional ring, we can find a protocol that gives an ex post Nash equilibrium provided that there are at least 3 agents in the ring.

Consider the following protocol. It starts just as the protocol for the unidirectional case in the synchronous setting. Again, we assume that the signal to start a leader election may come to one or more agents. Each of these agents then sends a message with his id to his neighbor. Messages are then passed around the ring, with each agent appending his id before passing it on. If an agent receives a second message that originated with a different agent, the message is ignored if the originating agent has a lower id; otherwise it is passed on. Eventually the originator of the message with the highest id gets back the message. The originator checks to make sure that the message has n (different) ids, to ensure that no "bogus" ids were added. The message is then sent around the ring a second time. When an agent i gets the message the second time, he chooses a random number N_i mod n and sends it to his neighbor (as well as passing on the list of names). Agent i's neighbor does not pass on N_i; he just keeps it. Roughly speaking, by sending N_i to his neighbor, agent i is committing to the choice. Crucially, this commitment must be made before i knows any of the random choices other than that of the agent j of whom i is the neighbor (if i is not the originator). When the originator gets the message list for the second time (which means that it has gone around the ring twice), he sends it around the ring the third time. This time each agent i adds his random choice N_i to the list; agent i's neighbor j checks that the random number that i adds to the list is the same as the number that i sent j the previous time. When the originator gets back the list for the third time, it now includes each agent i's random number. The originator then sends the list around the ring for a fourth time. After the fourth time around the ring, all agents know all the random choices. Each agent then computes $N = \sum_{i=1}^{n} N_i \pmod{n}$, and then takes the agent with the Nth highest id in the set to be the leader. Each time an agent i gets a message, he checks that it is compatible with earlier messages that he has seen; that is, the second time he gets the message, all the ids between the originator and his id must be the same; the third time he gets the message, all the ids on the list must be the same as they were the second time he saw the message; and the fourth time he gets the message, not only must the list of ids be the same, but all the random choices that he has seen before can not have been changed. If the message does not pass all the checks, then agent i sets $leader_i$ to $\perp$.

Clearly this approach will not work with two agents: The originator's neighbor will get the originator's random choice before sending his own, and can then choose his number so as to ensure that he becomes leader. (We discuss how this problem can be dealt with in Section 3.7.) As we now show, this approach gives a fair ex post Nash equilibrium provided that there are at least three agents. In an asynchronous setting, nature has much more freedom than in the synchronous setting. Now the outcome may depend not only on which agents get an initial signal, but also on the order in which agents are scheduled and on message delivery times. Ex post equilibrium implicitly views all these choices as being under the control of the adversary; our protocol has the property that, if all agents follow it, the distribution of outcomes is independent of the adversary's choices. However, for the particular protocol we have given, it is easy to see that, no matter what choices are made by the adversary, we have a Nash equilibrium. While considering ex post Nash equilibrium seems like a reasonable thing to do in asynchronous systems (or, more generally, in settings where we can view an adversary as making choices, in addition to the agents making choices), it is certainly not the only solution concept that can be considered. (See Section 4.)

What about coalitions? Observe that, for the protocol we have given, a coalition of size two does have an incentive to deviate. Suppose that i_1 is the originator of the message, and i_1 is i_2's neighbor (so that i_2 will be the last agent on the list originated by i_1). If i_1 and i_2 form a coalition, then i_2 does not have to bother sending i_1 a random choice on the second time around the ring. After receiving everyone's random choices, i_2 can choose N_{i_2} so that he (or i_1) becomes the leader. This may be better for both i_1 and i_2 than having a random choice of leader.

We can get a protocol that gives a k-resilient (ex post) Nash equilibrium if $n > 2k$. We modify the protocol above by having each agent i send his random choice k steps around the ring, rather than just one step (i.e., to his neighbor). This means that i is committing N_i to k other agents. In more detail, we start just as with the protocol presented earlier. Each agent who gets a signal to start the protocol sends a message with his id to his neighbor. The messages are then passed around the ring, with each agent appending his id. If an agent receives a second message that originated with a different agent, the message is ignored if the originating agent has a lower id; otherwise it is passed on. Eventually the originator of the message with the highest id gets back the message. The originator checks to make sure that the message has n ids, to ensure that no "bogus" ids were added. The message is then sent around the ring a second time; along with the message, each agent i (including the sender) sends a random number N_i. Agent i's neighbor does not pass on N_i; he just keeps it, while forwarding the list of ids. When the originator gets the message the third time, he forwards to his neighbor the random number he received in the previous round (which is the random number generated by his predecessor on the ring). Again, his neighbor does not forward the message; instead he sends to his successor the random number he received (from the originator) on the previous round. At the end of this phase, each agent knows his random id and that of his predecessor. We continue this process for k phases altogether. That is, to when the originator gets a message for the third time, he sends this message (which is the random number chosen by his predecessor's predecessor) to his successor. Whenever an agent gets a message, he forwards the message he received in the previous phases. At the end of the jth phase for $j \leq k$, each agent knows the random numbers of his j closest predecessors. After these k phases complete, the sender sends his random number to his neighbor; each agent then appends his id to the list, and it goes around the ring twice. Each agent checks that the random numbers of his k predecessors agree with what they earlier told him. At the end of this process, each agent knows all the random numbers. As usual, each agent then computes $N = \sum_{i=1}^{n} N_i \pmod{n}$ and chooses as leader the agent with the Nth highest id.

Each time an agent i gets a message, he checks that that it is compatible with earlier messages that he has seen; that is, the second time he gets the message, all the ids between the originator and his id must be the same; the third time he gets the message, all the ids on the list must be the same as they were the second time he saw the message; and the fourth time he gets the message, not only must the list of ids be the same, but all the random choices that he has seen before can not have been changed. He also checks that he has gotten the random choices of his k predecessors on the ring. If the message does not pass all the checks, then agent i sets $leader_i$ to $\perp$. Call this protocol for agent i A-$LEAD_i^{uni}$.

Theorem 3. *If $n > 2k$, then* **A-LEAD**^{uni} *is a fair, k-resilient ex post equilibrium in an asynchronous unidirectional ring.*

We can also use this approach to get a fair Nash equilibrium in a bidirectional network. If agents know the network orientation, they send all their messages in only one direction, implementing the protocol in the unidirectional case. If they do not know the orientation, they first proceed as in the synchronous, exchanging ids to determine who has the highest id. That agent then chooses a direction for further messages, and again they can proceed as in the unidirectional case.

3.5 Asynchronous Completely Connected Network

We can use the ideas above to get a protocol for a completely connected network, embedding a unidirectional ring into the network, but now the added connectivity hurts us, rather than helping. When we embed a ring into the network, each coalition member may be able to find out about up to k other random choices. Since now coalition members can talk to each other no matter where they are on the ring, we must have $n > k(k + 1)$ to ensure that a coalition does not learn all the random choices before the last member announces his random choice. We can do better by using ideas from secure multi-party computation and secret sharing [5].

To do secret sharing, we must work in a finite field; so, for ease of exposition, assume that n is a power of a prime. As in the synchronous case, agents start by sending their ids to all other agents, and then exchanging the set of ids received, so that they all agree on the set of ids in the system. (Of course, if an agent i does not get the same set of ids from all agents, then i sets $leader_i = \perp$.) We denote by agent i the agent with the ith largest id. Each agent i chooses a random value $N_i \in \{0, \ldots, n - 1\}$ and a random degree-$(k + 1)$ polynomial f_i over the field $F_n = \{0, \ldots, n - 1\}$ such that $f_i(0) = N_i$. Then i sends each agent j the message $f_i(j)$. Once i receives $f_j(i)$ from all agents j, then i sends $DONE$ to all agents. Once i receives $DONE$ messages from all agents, i sends $s_i = \sum_{j=1}^n f_j(i)$ to all agents. After receiving these messages, i will have n points on the degree-$(k + 1)$ polynomial $\sum_{j=1}^n f_j$ (if no agents have lied about their values). After i has received the messages s_j for all agents j, i checks if there is a unique polynomial f of degree $k + 1$ such that $f(j) = s_j$ for $j = 1, \ldots, n$. If such a polynomial f exists, and $f(0) = N$, then i takes the agent with the Nth highest id as leader; otherwise, i sets $leader_i$ to $\perp$. Call this protocol $A\text{-}LEAD_i^{cc}$.

Theorem 4. *If $n > 2k$ then* **A-LEAD**^{cc} *is a fair, ex post k-resilient equilibrium in an asynchronous completely connected network.*

3.6 A Matching Lower Bound

We now show that Theorems 3 and 4 are the best we can hope for; we cannot find a fair ex post k-resilient strategy if $n \leq 2k$.

Theorem 5. *If $n \leq 2k$, then there is no fair, ex post k-resilient equilibrium for an asynchronous unidirectional ring (resp., bidirectional ring, completely connected network).*

Observe that all the protocols above are *bounded*; although they involve randomization, there are only boundedly many rounds of communication. This is also the case for the protocol presented in the next section. If we restrict to bounded protocols, using ideas of [8,33], we can get a stronger result: we cannot even achieve an ϵ-k-resilient equilibrium (where agents do not deviate if they can get within ϵ of the utility they can get by deviating) for sufficiently small ϵ.

Theorem 6. *If $n \leq 2k$, then there exists an $\epsilon > 0$ such that for all ϵ' with $0 < \epsilon' < \epsilon$, there is no fair, ex post $\epsilon'-k$ resilient equilibrium for an asynchronous unidirectional ring (resp., bidirectional ring, completely connected network).*

3.7 Doing Better with Cryptography

In the impossibility result of Section 3.6, we implicitly assumed that the agents were computationally unbounded. For example, even though our proof shows that, in the 2-agent case, one agent can always do better by deviating, it may be difficult for that agent to recognize when it has a history where it could do better by deviating. As we now show, if agents are polynomially-bounded and we make an assumption that is standard in cryptography, then we can get a fair $\epsilon-k$-resilient equilibrium in all these topologies, even in the asynchronous settings, as long as $n > k$. Our solution is based on the bit-commitment protocol of Naor [31]. Bit commitment ideas can be traced back to the coin-flipping protocol of Blum [7].

The key idea of the earlier protocol is that i essentially commits N_i to his neighbor, so that he cannot later change it once he discovers the other agents' random choices. We can achieve essentially the same effect by using ideas from *commitment* protocols [31]. In a commitment protocol, an agent Alice commits to a number m in such a way that another agent Bob has no idea what m is. Then at a later stage, Alice can reveal m to Bob. Metaphorically, when Alice commits to m, she is putting it in a tamper-proof envelope; when she reveals it, she unseals the envelope.

It should be clear how commitment can solve the problem above. Each agent i commits to a random number N_i. After every agent has received every other agents' commitment, they all reveal the random numbers to each other. This approach will basically work in our setting, but there are a few subtleties. Naor's commitment protocol requires agents to have access to a *pseudorandom* number generator, and to be polynomially bounded. We can get an $\epsilon-k$-resilient protocol for ϵ as small as we like (provided that Bob is polynomially bounded) by choosing a sufficiently large security parameter for the pseudorandom number generator, but we cannot make it 0. Thus, we actually do not get a fair ex post Nash equilibrium, but a fair ex post ϵ-*Nash* equilibrium.

In the full paper, we show how the protocol in the synchronous setting for the unidirectional ring can be modified by using Naor's commitment scheme to get a protocol $A\text{-}LEAD_i^{ps,uni}$ that works in the asynchronous setting. There is another subtlety here. It is not enough for the commitment scheme to be secure; it must also be *non-malleable* [13]. Intuitively, this means that each choice made by each agent j must be independent of the choices made by all other agents. To understand the issue, suppose that the agent i just before the originator on the ring knows every other agent j's random choice N_j before committing to his own random choice; metaphorically, i has an envelope containing N_j for each agent $j \neq i$. (This is actually the case in our protocol.) Even if i cannot compute N_j, if he could choose N_i in such a way that $\sum_{i=1}^{n} N_i \pmod{n}$ is 3, he could then choose his id to be 3. If the scheme were malleable, it would be possible for j's choice to depend on the other agents' choices even if j did not know the other agents' choices. Indeed, we want not just non-malleability, but *concurrent* non-malleability. In the protocol, agents engage in a number of concurrent commitment protocols; we do not want information from one commitment protocol to be used in another one. We assume for ease of exposition that Naor's scheme is *concurrently pseudo-non-malleable*;

not only can no agent guess other agents' bit with probability significantly greater than $1/2$, they also cannot make a choice dependent on other agents' choices with probability significantly greater than $1/2$, even running many instances of the protocol concurrently. (Note that concurrent non-malleable commitment schemes are known; see [26] for the current state of the art.)

Theorem 7. *For all ϵ, if agents are polynomially bounded and pseudorandom number generators exists, then $A\text{-}LEAD^{ps,uni}$ (with appropriately chosen security parameters) is a fair, ϵ–k-resilient ex post equilibrium in an asynchronous unidirectional ring, for all $k < n$.*

The same result holds in the case of a bidirectional ring and completely connected network; we can simply embed a unidirectional ring into the network, and run $A\text{-}LEAD^{ps,uni}$.

4   Discussion and Open Questions

The paper illustrates some issues that might arise when trying to apply game-theoretic approaches to distributed computing problems. Perhaps what comes out most clearly in the case study is the role of *ex post* Nash equilibrium, both in the upper bounds and lower bounds. To us, the most important question is to consider, when applying game-theoretic ideas to distributed computing, whether this is the most appropriate solution concept. While it is the one perhaps closest to standard assumptions made in the distributed computing literature, it is a very strong requirement, since it essentially means that players have no incentive to deviate even if they know nature's protocol. Are there reasonable distributions we can place on adversary strategies? Do we have to consider them all?

Besides this more conceptual question, there are a number of interesting technical open problems that remain. We list a few here:

- We have focused on the case that agents are rational. In [1,2], we also considered agents who were faulty. Our protocols break down in the presence of even one faulty agent. It is well known that Byzantine agreement is not achievable in a graph of connectivity $\leq 2f$, where f is the number of failures. This suggests that we will not be able to deal with one faulty agent in a ring. But it may be possible to handle some faulty agents in a completely connected network.
- We have focused on leader election. It would be interesting to consider a game-theoretic version of other canonical distributed computing problems. We believe that the techniques that we have developed here should apply broadly, since many problems can be reduced to leader election.
- In [2], it is shown that, in general, if we can attain an equilibrium with a mediator, then we can attain the same equilibrium using cheap talk only if $n > 3k$. Here we can use cheap talk to do leader election in the completely connected asynchronous case (which is implicitly what was assumed in [2]) as long as $n > k$. Thus, we beat the lower bound of [2]. There is no contradiction here. The lower bound of [2] shows only that there exists a game for which there is an equilibrium with a mediator that cannot be implemented using cheap talk if $n \leq 3k$. It would be

interesting to understand what it is about leader election that makes it easier to implement. More generally, can we refine the results of [1,2] to get tighter bounds on different classes of problems?

- We have focused on "one-shot" leader election here. If we consider a situation where leader election is done repeatedly, an agent may be willing to disrupt an election repeatedly until he becomes leader. It would be of interest to consider appropriate protocols in a repeated setting.
- We made one important technical assumption to get these results in rings: we assumed that the ring size is known. As we argued earlier, this assumption is critical, since otherwise an agent can create sybils and increase his chances of becoming leader. However, this deviation comes at a cost. The agent must keep simulating the sybils for all future interactions. This may not be worth it. Moreover, ids must also be created for these sybils. If the name space is not large, there may be an id clash with the id of some other agent in the ring. This will cause problems in the protocols, so if the probability of a name clash is sufficiently high, then sybils will not be created. It would be interesting to do a more formal game-theoretic analysis of the role of sybils.

References

1. Abraham, I., Dolev, D., Gonen, R., Halpern, J.Y.: Distributed computing meets game theory: robust mechanisms for rational secret sharing and multiparty computation. In: Proc. 25th ACM Symp. Principles of Distributed Computing, pp. 53–62 (2006)
2. Abraham, I., Dolev, D., Halpern, J.Y.: Lower bounds on implementing robust and resilient mediators. In: Canetti, R. (ed.) TCC 2008. LNCS, vol. 4948, pp. 302–319. Springer, Heidelberg (2008)
3. Aiyer, A.S., Alvisi, L., Clement, A., Dahlin, M., Martin, J.P., Porth, C.: BAR fault tolerance for cooperative services. In: Proc. 20th ACM Symp. Operating Systems Principles (SOSP 2005), pp. 45–58 (2005)
4. Barany, I.: Fair distribution protocols or how the players replace fortune. Mathematics of Operations Research 17, 327–340 (1992)
5. Ben-Or, M., Goldwasser, S., Wigderson, A.: Completeness theorems for non-cryptographic fault-tolerant distributed computation. In: Proc. 20th ACM Symp. Theory of Computing, pp. 1–10 (1988)
6. Ben-Porath, E.: Cheap talk in games with incomplete information. Journal of Economic Theory 108(1), 45–71 (2003)
7. Blum, M.: Coin flipping by telephone a protocol for solving impossible problems. SIGACT News 15, 23–27 (1983)
8. Boppana, R.B., Narayanan, B.O.: Perfect-information leader election with optimal resilience. SIAM Journal on Computing, 1304–1320 (2000)
9. Chang, E., Roberts, R.: An improved algorithm for decentralized extrema-finding in circular configurations of processes. Communications of the ACM 22(5), 281–283 (1979)
10. Dani, V., Movahedi, M., Rodriguez, Y., Saia, J.: Scalable rational secret sharing. In: Proc. 30th ACM Symp. Principles of Distributed Computing, pp. 187–196 (2011)
11. Dodis, Y., Halevi, S., Rabin, T.: A cryptographic solution to a game theoretic problem. In: Bellare, M. (ed.) CRYPTO 2000. LNCS, vol. 1880, pp. 112–130. Springer, Heidelberg (2000)
12. Dolev, D.: The Byzantine generals strike again. Journal of Algorithms 3(1), 14–30 (1982)
13. Dolev, D., Dwork, C., Naor, M.: Non-malleable cryptography. SIAM Journal on Computing 30(2), 391–437 (2000)

14. Dolev, D., Klawe, M., Rodeh, M.: An $o(n \log n)$ unidirectional distributed algorithm for extrema finding in a circle. Journal of Algorithms 3(3), 245–260 (1982)
15. Feldman, P., Micali, S.: An optimal probabilistic protocol for synchronous Byzantine agreement. SIAM Journal on Computing 26, 873–933 (1997)
16. Forges, F.: Universal mechanisms. Econometrica 58(6), 1341–1364 (1990)
17. Fuchsbauer, G., Katz, J., Naccache, D.: Efficient rational secret sharing in standard communication networks. In: Micciancio, D. (ed.) TCC 2010. LNCS, vol. 5978, pp. 419–436. Springer, Heidelberg (2010)
18. Gordon, D., Katz, J.: Rational secret sharing, revisited. In: SCN (Security in Communication Networks) 2006, pp. 229–241 (2006)
19. Halpern, J.Y., Teague, V.: Rational secret sharing and multiparty computation: extended abstract. In: Proc. 36th ACM Symp. Theory of Computing, pp. 623–632 (2004)
20. Heller, Y.: A minority-proof cheap-talk protocol (2005) (unpublished manuscript)
21. Izmalkov, S., Lepinski, M., Micali, S.: Perfect implementation. Games and Economic Behavior 71, 121–140 (2011)
22. Katz, J., Koo, C.-Y.: On Expected Constant-Round Protocols for Byzantine Agreement. In: Dwork, C. (ed.) CRYPTO 2006. LNCS, vol. 4117, pp. 445–462. Springer, Heidelberg (2006)
23. Kreps, D.M., Wilson, R.B.: Sequential equilibria. Econometrica 50, 863–894 (1982)
24. Le Lann, G.: Distributed systems—towards a formal approach. In: IFIP Congress, vol. 7, pp. 155–160 (1977)
25. Lepinski, M., Micali, S., Peikert, C., Shelat, A.: Completely fair SFE and coalition-safe cheap talk. In: Proc. 23rd ACM Symp. on Principles of Distributed Computing, pp. 1–10 (2004)
26. Lin, H., Pass, R.: Constant-round non-malleable commitments from any one-way function. In: Proc. 21st International Joint Conf. on Artificial Intelligence (IJCAI 2009), pp. 153–158 (2009)
27. Lynch, N.A.: Distributed Algorithms. Morgan Kaufmann, San Francisco (1997)
28. Lysyanskaya, A., Triandopoulos, N.: Rationality and adversarial behavior in multi-party computation. In: Dwork, C. (ed.) CRYPTO 2006. LNCS, vol. 4117, pp. 180–197. Springer, Heidelberg (2006)
29. McGrew, R., Porter, R., Shoham, Y.: Towards a general theory of non-cooperative computing. In: Theoretical Aspects of Rationality and Knowledge: Proc. Ninth Conf. (TARK 2003), pp. 59–51 (2003)
30. Moscibroda, T., Schmid, S., Wattenhofer, R.: When selfish meets evil: Byzantine players in a virus inoculation game. In: Proc. 25th ACM Symp. Principles of Distributed Computing, pp. 35–44 (2006)
31. Naor, M.: Bit commitment using pseudorandomness. Journal of Cryptology 4, 151–158 (1991)
32. Peterson, G.L.: An $O(n \log n)$ unidirectional distributed algorithm for the circular extrema problem. ACM Trans. Progr. Lang. Syst. 4(4), 758–762 (1982)
33. Saks, M.E.: A robust noncryptographic protocol for collective coin flipping. SIAM Journal on Discrete Mathemantics, 240–244 (1989)
34. Shoham, Y., Tennenholtz, M.: Non-cooperative computing: Boolean functions with correctness and exclusivity. Theoretical Computer Science 343(1-2), 97–113 (2005)
35. Urbano, A., Vila, J.E.: Computational complexity and communication: coordination in two-player games. Econometrica 70(5), 1893–1927 (2002)
36. Urbano, A., Vila, J.E.: Computationally restricted unmediated talk under incomplete information. Economic Theory 23(2), 283–320 (2004)
37. Wong, E.L., Levy, I., Alvisi, L., Clement, A., Dahlin, M.: Regret freedom isn't free. In: Fernàndez Anta, A., Lipari, G., Roy, M. (eds.) OPODIS 2011. LNCS, vol. 7109, pp. 80–95. Springer, Heidelberg (2011)

Compact Deterministic Self-stabilizing Leader Election
The Exponential Advantage of Being Talkative

Lélia Blin[1,3] and Sébastien Tixeuil[2,3]

[1] Université d'Evry Val d'Essonne, France
[2] UPMC Sorbonne Universités, France, Institut Universitaire de France
[3] LIP6-CNRS UMR 7606
{lelia.blin,sebastien.tixeuil}@lip6.fr

Abstract. This paper focuses on *compact* deterministic self-stabilizing solutions for the leader election problem. When the protocol is required to be *silent* (i.e., when communication content remains fixed from some point in time during any execution), there exists a lower bound of $\Omega(\log n)$ bits of memory per node participating to the leader election (where n denotes the number of nodes in the system). This lower bound holds even in rings. We present a new deterministic (non-silent) self-stabilizing protocol for n-node rings that uses only $O(\log \log n)$ memory bits per node, and stabilizes in $O(n \log^2 n)$ time. Our protocol has several attractive features that make it suitable for practical purposes. First, the communication model matches the one that is expected by existing compilers for real networks. Second, the size of the ring (or any upper bound for this size) needs not to be known by any node. Third, the node identifiers can be of various sizes. Finally, no synchrony assumption besides a weak fair scheduler is assumed. Therefore, our result shows that, perhaps surprisingly, trading silence for exponential improvement in term of memory space does not come at a high cost regarding stabilization time, neither it does regarding minimal assumptions about the framework for our algorithm.

1 Introduction

This paper is targeting the issue of designing efficient self-stabilization algorithm for the leader election problem. *Self-stabilization* [13,14,29] is a general paradigm to provide forward recovery capabilities to distributed systems and networks. Intuitively, a protocol is self-stabilizing if it is able to recover from any transient failure, without external intervention. *Leader election* is one of the fundamental building blocks of distributed computing, as it permits to distinguish a single node in the system, and thus to perform specific actions using that node. Leader election is especially important in the context of self-stabilization as many protocols for various problems assume that a single leader exists in the system, even when faults occur. Hence, a self-stabilizing leader election mechanism permits to run such protocols in networks where no leader is a priori given, by using simple composition techniques [14].

Y. Afek (Ed.): DISC 2013, LNCS 8205, pp. 76–90, 2013.
© Springer-Verlag Berlin Heidelberg 2013

Most of the literature in self-stabilization is dedicated to improving efficiency after failures occur, including minimizing the stabilization time, i.e., the maximum amount of time one has to wait before recovering from a failure. While stabilization time is meaningful to evaluate the efficiency of an algorithm in the presence of failures, it does not necessarily capture the overhead of self-stabilization when there are no faults [1], or after stabilization. Another important criterium to evaluate this overhead is the *memory space* used by each node. This criterium is motivated by two practical reasons. First, self-stabilizing protocols require that *some* communications carry on forever (in order to be able to detect distributed inconsistencies due to transient failures [7,12]). So, minimizing the memory space used by each node enable to minimize the amount of information that is exchanged between nodes. Indeed, protocols are typically written in the state model, where the state of each node is available for reading to every neighbor, and all existing stabilization-preserving compilers [28,10,4,9] expect this communication model. Second, minimizing memory space enables to significantly reduce the cost of redundancy when mixing self-stabilization and replication, in order to increase the probability of masking or containing transient faults [21,20]. For instance, duplicating every bit three times at each node permits to withstand one randomly flipped bit. More generally, decreasing the memory space allows the designer to duplicate this memory many times, in order to tolerate many random bit-flips.

A foundational result regarding memory space in the context of self-stabilization is due to Dolev*et al.* [15]. It states that, n-node networks, $\Omega(\log n)$ bits of memory are required for solving global tasks such as leader election. Importantly, this bound holds even for the ring. A key component of this lower bound is that it holds only whenever the protocol is assumed to be *silent*. (Recall that a protocol is silent if each of its executions reaches a point in time beyond which the registers containing the information available at each node do *not* change). The lower bound can be extended to *non-silent* protocols, but only for specific cases. For instance, it holds in anonymous (uniform) unidirectional rings of prime size [19,8]. As a matter of fact, most deterministic self-stabilizing leader election protocols [3,16,2,5,11] use at least $\Omega(\log n)$ bits of memory per node. Indeed, either these protocols directly compare node identifiers (and thus communicate node identifiers to neighbors), or they compute some variant of a hop-count distance to the elected node (and this distance can be as large as $\Omega(n)$ to be accurate).

A few previous work [27,24,6,25] managed to break the $\Omega(\log n)$ bits lower bound for the memory space of self-stabilizing leader election algorithms. Nevertheless, the corresponding algorithms exhibit shortcomings that hinder their relevance to practical applications. For instance, the algorithm by Mayer *et al.* [27], by Itkis and Levin [24], and by Awerbuch and Ostrovstky [6] use a constant number of bits per node only. However, these algorithms guarantee *probabilistic* self-stabilization only (in the Las Vegas sense). In particular, the stabilization time is only *expected* to be polynomial in the size of the network, and all three algorithms make use of a source of random bits at each node. Moreover, these algorithms are designed for a communication model that is more powerful than the classical state model used in this paper. (The state model is the model used in most available compilers for actual networks [28,10,4,9]). More specifically, Mayer *et al.* [27] use the message passing model, and Awerbuch and Ostrovsky [6] use the link-register model, where communications between neighboring nodes are carried out through dedicated registers. Finally, Itkis and Levin [24] use the state model augmented with reciprocal pointer to neighbors. In this model, not only a node u is able to distinguish a particular neighbor v (which can be done using local labeling), but also this distinguished neighbor v is aware that it has been selected by u. Implementing this mutual interaction between neighbors typically requires distance-two coloring, link coloring, or two-hops communication. All these techniques are impacting the memory space requirement significantly [26]. It is also important to note that, the communication models in [6,24,27] allow nodes to send different information to different neighbors, while this capability is beyond the power of the classical state model. The ability to send different messages to different neighbors is a strong assumption in the context of self-stabilization. It allows to construct a "path of information" that is consistent between nodes. This path is typically used to distribute the storage of information along a path, in order to reduce the information stored at each node. However, this assumption prevents the user from taking advantage of the existing compilers. So implementing the protocols in [6,24,27] to actual networks requires to rewrite all the codes from scratch.

To our knowledge, the only *deterministic* self-stabilizing leader election protocol using sub-logarithmic memory space in the classical model is due to Itkis *et al.* [25]. Their elegant algorithm uses only a constant number of bits per node, and stabilizes in $O(n^2)$ time in n-node rings. However, the algorithm relies on several restricting assumptions. First, the algorithm works properly only if the size of the ring is *prime*. Second, it assumes that, at any time, a *single* node is scheduled for execution, that is, it assumes a *central* scheduler [18]. Such a scheduler is far less practical than the classical *distributed* scheduler, which allows any set of processes to be scheduled concurrently for execution. Third, the algorithm in [25] assumes that the ring is *oriented*. That is, every node is supposed to possess a consistent notion of left and right. This orientation permits to mimic the behavior of reciprocal pointer to neighbors mentioned above. Extending the algorithm by Itkis *et al.* [25] to more practical settings, i.e., to non-oriented rings of arbitrary size, to the use of a distributed scheduler, etc, is not trivial if one wants to preserve a sub-logarithmic memory space at each node. For example, the existing transformers enabling to enhance protocols designed for the central scheduler in order to operate under the distributed scheduler require $\Theta(\log n)$ memory at each node [18]. Similarly, self-stabilizing ring-orientation protocols exist, but those which preserve sub-logarithmic memory space either works only in rings of odd size for deterministic guarantees [22], or just provide probabilistic guarantees [23]. Moreover, in both cases, the stabilization time is $O(n^2)$, which is pretty big.

To summarize, all existing self-stabilizing leader election algorithm designed in a practical communication model, and for rings of arbitrary size, without a priori orientation, use $\Omega(\log n)$ bits of memory per node. Breaking this bound, without introducing any kind of restriction on the settings, requires, beside being non-silent, a completely new approach.

Our results. In this paper, we present a deterministic (non-silent) self-stabilizing leader election algorithm that operates under the distributed scheduler in non-anonymous undirected rings of arbitrary size. Our algorithm is non-silent to circumvent the lower bound $\Omega(\log n)$ bits of memory per node in [15]. It uses only $O(\log \log n)$ bits of memory per node, and stabilizes in $O(n \log^2 n)$ time.

Unlike the algorithms in [27,24,6], our algorithm is deterministic, and designed to run under the classical state-sharing communication model, which allows it to be implemented by using actual compilers [28,10,4,9]. Unlike [25], the size of the ring is arbitrary, the ring is not assumed to be oriented, and the scheduler is distributed. Moreover the stabilization time of our algorithm is smaller than the one in [25]. Similarly to [27,24,6], our algorithm uses a technique to distribute the information among nearby nodes along a sub-path of the ring. However, our algorithm does not rely on powerful communication models such as the ones used in [27,24,6]. Those powerful communication models make easy the construction and management of such sub-paths. The use of the classical state-sharing model makes the construction and management of the sub-paths much more difficult. It is achieved by the use of novel information distribution and gathering techniques.

Besides the use of a sub-logarithmic memory space, and beside a quasi-linear stabilization time, our algorithm possesses several attractive features. First, the size (or any value upper bound for this size) need not to be known to any node. Second, the node identifiers (or identities) can be of various sizes (to model, e.g., Internet networks running different versions of IP). Third, no synchrony assumption besides weak fairness is assumed (a node that is continuously enabled for execution is eventually scheduled for execution).

At a high level, our algorithm is essentially based on two techniques. One consists in electing the leader by comparing the identities of the nodes, bitwise, which requires special care, especially when the node identities can be of various sizes. The second technique consists in maintaining and merging trees based on a parenthood relation, and verifying the absence of cycles in the 1-factor induced by this parenthood relation. This verification is performed using small memory space by grouping the nodes in hyper-nodes of appropriate size. Each hyper-node handles an integer encoding a distance to a root. The bits of this distance are distributed among the nodes of the hyper-nodes to preserve a small memory per node. Difficulties arise when one needs to perform arithmetic operations on these distributed bits, especially in the context in which nodes are unaware of the size of the ring. The precise design of our algorithm requires overcoming many other difficulties due to the need of maintaining correct information in an environment subject to arbitrary faults.

To sum up, our result shows that, perhaps surprisingly, trading silence for exponential improvement in term of memory space does not come at a high cost regarding stabilization time, neither it does regarding minimal assumptions about the communication framework.

2   Model and Definitions

Program syntax and semantics. A distributed system consists of n processors that form a communication graph. The processors are represented by the nodes of this graph, and the edges represent pairs of processors that can communicate directly with each other. Such processors are said to be *neighbors*. This classical model is called *state-sharing communication model*. The *distance* between two processors is the length (i.e., number of edges) of the shortest path between them in the communication graph. Each processor contains variables, and rules. A variable ranges over a fixed domain of values. A rule is of the form

$$\langle label \rangle : \langle guard \rangle \longrightarrow \langle command \rangle.$$

A *guard* is a boolean predicate over processor variables. A *command* is a sequence of assignment statements. A command of processor p can only update its own variables. On the other hand, p can read the variables of its neighbors. An assignment of values to all variables in the system is called a *configuration*. A rule whose guard is **true** in some system configuration is said to be *enabled* in this configuration. The rule is *disabled* otherwise. An atomic execution of a subset of enabled rules results in a transition of the system from one configuration to another. This transition is called a *step*. A *run* of a distributed system is a sequence of transitions.

Schedulers. A *scheduler*, also called *daemon*, is a restriction on the runs to be considered. The schedulers differ among them by different execution semantics, and by different fairness in the activation of the processors [18]. With respect to execution semantics, we consider the least restrictive scheduler, called the *distributed scheduler*. In the run of a distributed scheduler, a step can contain the execution of an arbitrary subset of enabled rules of correct processors. With respect to fairness, we use the least restrictive scheduler, called *weakly fair scheduler*. In every run of the weakly fair scheduler, a rule of a correct processor is executed infinitely often if it is enabled in all but finitely many configurations of the run. That is, the rule has to be executed only if it is continuously enabled. A *round* is the smallest portion of an execution where every process has the opportunity to execute at least one action.

Predicates and specifications. A predicate is a boolean function over network configurations. A configuration *conforms* to some predicate R, if R evaluates to **true** in this configuration. The configuration *violates* the predicate otherwise. Predicate R is *closed* in a certain protocol P, if every configuration of a run of P conforms to R, provided that the protocol starts from a configuration conforming to R. Note that if a protocol configuration conforms to R, and the configuration resulting from the execution of any step of P also conforms to R, then R is closed in P.

A *specification* for a processor p defines a set of configuration sequences. These sequences are formed by variables of some subset of processors in the system. This subset always includes p itself. A *problem specification*, or *problem* for short, defines specifications for each processor of the system. A problem specification in the presence of faults defines specifications for correct processors only. Program P *solves* problem S under a certain scheduler if every run of P satisfies the specifications defined by S. A closed predicate I is an *invariant* of program P with respect to problem S if every run of P that starts in a state conforming to I satisfies S. Given two predicates l_1 and l_2 for program P with respect to problem S, l_2 is an *attractor* for l_1 if every run that starts from a configuration that conforms to l_1 contains a configuration that conforms to l_2. Such a relationship is denoted by $l_1 \triangleright l_2$. A program P is *self-stabilizing* [13] to specification S if every run of P that starts in an arbitrary configuration contains a configuration conforming to an invariant of P with respect to problem S. That is, this invariant is an attractor of predicate *true*.

Leader election specification. Consider a system of processors where each processor has a boolean variable leader. We use the classical definition of *leader election*, which specifies that, in every protocol run, there is a suffix where a single processor p has $\text{leader}_p = true$, and every other processor $q \neq p$ satisfies $\text{leader}_q = false$.

3 A Compact Leader-Election Protocol for Rings

In this section, we describe our self-stabilizing algorithm for leader election in arbitrary n-node rings. The algorithm will be later proved to use $O(\log \log n)$ bits of memory per node, and to stabilize in quasi-linear time, whenever the identities of the nodes are between 1 and n^c, for some $c \geq 1$. For the sake of simplicity, we will assume that the identifiers are in $[1, n]$. Nevertheless, the algorithm works without assuming any particular range for the identifiers. We first provide a general overview of the algorithm, followed by a more detailed description in Section 3.2.

3.1 Overview of the Algorithm

As many existing deterministic self-stabilizing leader election algorithms, our algorithm aims at electing the node with maximum identity among all nodes, and, simultaneously, at constructing a spanning tree rooted at the elected node. The main constraint imposed by our wish to use sub-logarithmic memory is that we cannot exchange or even locally use complete identifiers, as their size $\Omega(\log n)$ bits does not fit in a sub-logarithmic size memory. As a matter of fact, we assume that individual bits of its identifier can be accessed by every node, but only a constant number of them can be simultaneously stored and/or communicated to neighbors at a given time. Our algorithm will make sure that every node stores the current position of a particular bit of the identifier, referred to as a *bit-position* in the sequel.

Selection of the leader. Our algorithm operates in phases. At each phase, each node that is a candidate leader v reveals some bit-position, different from the ones at the previous phases, to its neighbors. More precisely, let Id_v be the identity of node v, and assume that $\mathsf{Id}_v = \sum_{i=0}^{k} b_i 2^i$. Let $I = \{i \in \{0, ..., k\}, b_i \neq 0\}$ be the set of all non-zero bit-positions in the binary representation of Id_v. Let us rewrite $I = \{p_1, ..., p_j\}$ with $0 \leq p_1 < p_2 < ... < p_j \leq k$. Then, during Phase i, $i = 1, ..., j$, node v reveals p_{j-i+1} to its neighbors, which potentially propagate it to their neighbors, and possibly to the whole network in subsequent phases. During Phase i, for $j + 1 \leq i \leq \lfloor \log n \rfloor + 1$, node v either becomes passive (that is, stops acting as a candidate leader) or remains a candidate leader. If, at the beginning of the execution of the algorithm, all nodes are *candidate* leaders, then during each phase, some candidate leaders are eliminated, until exactly one candidate leader remains, which becomes the actual leader. More precisely, let $p_{max}(i)$ be the most significant bit-position revealed at Phase i among all nodes. Then, among all candidate leaders still competing for becoming leader, only those whose bit-position revealed at Phase i is equal to $p_{max}(i)$ carry on the electing process. The other ones become passive.

If all identities are in $[1, n]$, then the communicated bit-positions are less than $\lceil \log n \rceil$, and thus can be represented with $O(\log \log n)$ bits. The difficulty is to implement this simple "compact" leader election mechanism in a self-stabilizing manner. In particular, the nodes may not have same number of bits encoding their identifiers, the ring may not start from a configuration in which every node is a candidate leader, and the distributed scheduler may lead nodes to operate at various paces.

An additional problem in self-stabilizing leader election is the potential presence of *impostor* leaders. If one can store the identity of the leader at each node, then detecting an impostor is easy. Under our memory constraints, nodes cannot store the identity of the leader, nor read entirely their own identifier. So, detecting impostor leaders becomes non trivial, notably when an impostor has an identity whose most significant bit is equal to the most significant bit of the leader. To overcome this problem, the selection of the leader must run perpetually, leading our algorithm to be non-silent.

Spanning tree construction. Our approach to make the above scheme self-stabilizing is to merge the leader election process with a tree construction process. Every candidate leader is the root of a tree. Whenever a candidate leader becomes passive, its tree is merged to another tree, until there remains only one tree. The main obstacle in self-stabilizing tree-construction is to handle an arbitrary initial configuration. This is particularly difficult if the initial configuration yields a cycle rather than a spanning forest. In this case, when the leader election subroutine and the tree construction subroutine are conjointly used, the presence of the cycle implies that, while every node is expecting to point to a neighbor leading to a leader, there are no leaders in the network. Such a configuration is called *fake* leader. In order to break cycles that can be present in the initial configuration, we use an improved variant of the classical distance calculation [17]. In the classical approach, every node u maintains an integer variable d_u that stores the distance from u to the root of its tree. If v denotes the parent of u, then typically $d_v = d_u - 1$, and if $d_v \geq d_u$, then u deletes its pointer to v. If the topology of the network is a ring, then detecting the presence of an initial spanning cycle, instead of a spanning forest, may involve distance variables as large as n, inducing $\Omega(\log n)$ bits of memory.

In order to use exponentially less memory, our algorithm uses the distance technique but modulo $\log n$. More specifically, each node v maintains three variables. The first variable is an integer denoted by $d_v \in \{0, ..., \lfloor \log n \rfloor\}$, called the "distance" of node v. Only candidate leaders v can have $d_v = 0$. Each node v maintains $d_v = 1 + (\min\{d_u, d_{u'}\} \bmod \lfloor \log n \rfloor)$ where u and u' are the neighbors of v in the ring. Note that nodes are not aware of n. Thus they do not actually use the value $\lfloor \log n \rfloor$ as above, but a potentially erroneous estimation of it.

The second variable is p_v, denoting the parent of node v. This parent is its neighbor w such that $d_v = 1 + (d_w \bmod \lfloor \log n \rfloor)$. By itself, this technique is not sufficient to detect the presence of a cycle. Therefore, we also introduce the notion of *hyper-node*, defined as follows:

Definition 1. *A hyper-node X is a set $\{x_1, x_2, \cdots, x_{\lfloor \log n \rfloor}\}$ of consecutive nodes in the ring, such that $d_{x_1} = 1$, $d_{x_2} = 2$,..., $d_{x_{\lfloor \log n \rfloor}} = \lfloor \log n \rfloor$, $p_{x_2} = x_1$, $p_{x_3} = x_2$, ..., $p_{x_{\lfloor \log n \rfloor}} = x_{\lfloor \log n \rfloor - 1}$ and $p_{x_1} \neq x_2$.*

The parent of a hyper-node $X = \{x_1, x_2, \cdots, x_{\lfloor \log n \rfloor}\}$ is a hyper-node $Y = \{y_1, y_2, \cdots, y_{\lfloor \log n \rfloor}\}$ such that $p_{x_1} = y_{\lfloor \log n \rfloor}$. By definition, there are at most $\lceil n/\lfloor \log n \rfloor \rceil$ hyper-nodes. If n is not divisible by $\lfloor \log n \rfloor$, then some nodes can be elements of an incomplete hyper-node. There can be several incomplete hyper-nodes, but if the parent of a (complete) hyper-node is an incomplete hyper-node, then an error is detected. Incomplete hyper-nodes must be leaves: there cannot be incomplete hyper-nodes in a cycle.

The key to our protocol is that hyper-nodes can maintain larger distance information than simple nodes, by distributing the information among the nodes of an hyper-node. More precisely, we assume that each node v maintains a bit of information, stored in variable dB_v. Let $X = \{x_1, x_2, \cdots, x_{\lfloor \log n \rfloor}\}$ be an hyper-node, the set $\mathbb{B}_X = \{dB_{x_1}, dB_{x_2}, ..., dB_{x_{\lfloor \log n \rfloor}}\}$ can be considered as the binary representation of an integer on $\lfloor \log n \rfloor$ bits, i.e., between 0 and $2^{\lfloor \log n \rfloor} - 1$. Now, it is possible to use the same distance approach as usual, but at the hyper-node level. Part of our protocol consists in comparing, for two hyper-nodes X and Y, the distance $\mathbb{B}_X$ and the distance $\mathbb{B}_Y$. If Y is the parent of X, then the difference between $\mathbb{B}_X$ and $\mathbb{B}_Y$ must be one. Otherwise an inconsistency is detected regarding the current spanning forest. The fact that hyper-nodes include $\lfloor \log n \rfloor$ nodes implies that dealing with distances between hyper-nodes is sufficient to detect the presence of a cycle spanning the n-node ring.

This is because $2^{\lfloor \log n \rfloor} \geq n/\log n$. (Note that hyper-nodes with k nodes such that $2^k \geq n/k$ would do the same).

In essence, the part of our algorithm dedicated to checking the absence of a spanning cycle generated by the parenthood relation boils down to comparing distances between hyper-nodes. Note that comparing distances between hyper-node involves communication at distance $\Omega(\log n)$. This is another reason why our algorithm is non-silent.

3.2 Detailed Description

Notations and Preliminaries. Let $C_n = (V, E)$ be the n-node ring, where V is the set of nodes, and E the set of edges. A node v has access to an unique identifier, but can only access to this identifier one bit at a time, using the $\mathrm{Bit}(x, v)$ function, that returns the position of the xth most significant bit equal to 1 in Id_v. This position can be encoded with $O(\log \log n)$ bits when identifiers are encoded using $O(\log n)$ bits, as we assume they are. A node v has access to local port number associated to its adjacent edges. The variable parent of node v, denoted by p_v, is actually the port number of the edge connecting v to its parent. In case of n-node rings, $\mathsf{p}_v \in \{0, 1\}$ for every v. (We do not assume any consistency between the port numbers). In a correct configuration, the structure induced by the parenthood relation must be a tree. The presence of more than one tree, or of a cycle, correspond to illegal configurations. We denote by N_v the set of the neighbors of v in C_n, for any node $v \in V$.

The variable distance, denoted by d_v at node v, takes values in $\{-1, 0, 1, ..., \lfloor \log n \rfloor\}$. We have $\mathsf{d}_v = -1$ if all the variables of v are reset. We have $\mathsf{d}_v = 0$ if the node v is a root of some tree induced by the parenthood relation. Such a root is also called candidate leader. Finally, $\mathsf{d}_v \in \{1, ..., \lfloor \log n \rfloor\}$ if v is a node of some tree induced by the parenthood relation, different from the root. Such a node is also called passive. Note that we only assume that variable d can hold *at least* (and not *exactly*) $\lfloor \log n \rfloor + 1$ different values, since nodes are not aware of how many they are in the ring, and just use an estimation of n. The children of a node v are returned by the macro $\mathrm{Ch}(v)$, which returns the port number(s) of the edges leading to the child(ren) of v.

To detect cycles, we use four variables. First, each node maintains the variable dB introduced in the previous section, for constructing a distributed integer stored on an hyper-node. The second variable, $\mathsf{Add}_v \in \{+, \mathrm{ok}, \emptyset\}$, is used for performing additions involving values stored distributively on hyper-nodes. The third variable, MC_v, is used to send the result of an addition to the hyper-node children of the hyper-node containing v. Finally, the fourth variable, MV_v, is dedicated to checking the hyper-node bits. Variables MC_v and MV_v are either empty, or each composed of a pair of variables $(x, y) \in \{1, ..., \lfloor \log n \rfloor\} \times \{0, 1\}$.

For constructing the tree rooted at the node with highest identity, we use three additional variables. After convergence, we expect the leader to be the unique node with distance zero, and to be the root of an inward directed spanning tree of the ring, where the arc of the tree is defined by the parenthood relation.

$$
\begin{array}{lll}
\mathbb{R}_{\text{Error}} & : \ \mathbb{T}\text{Er}(v) & \rightarrow \text{Reset}(v); \\
\mathbb{R}_{\text{Start}} & : \neg\mathbb{T}\text{Er}(v) \wedge (d_v = \text{-}1) \wedge \neg\mathbb{T}\text{Reset}(v) \wedge \mathbb{T}\text{Start}(v) & \rightarrow \text{Start}(v); \\
\mathbb{R}_{\text{Passive}} & : \neg\mathbb{T}\text{Er}(v) \wedge (d_v > \text{-}1) \wedge \neg\mathbb{T}\text{Reset}(v) \wedge \mathbb{T}\text{Pass}(v) & \rightarrow \text{Passive}(v); \\
\mathbb{R}_{\text{Root}} & : \neg\mathbb{T}\text{Er}(v) \wedge (d_v = 0) \wedge \neg\mathbb{T}\text{Pass}(v) \wedge \mathbb{T}\text{StartdB}(v) & \rightarrow \text{StartdB}(v); \\
 & \ \ \neg\mathbb{T}\text{Er}(v) \wedge (d_v = 0) \wedge \neg\mathbb{T}\text{Pass}(v) \wedge \mathbb{T}\text{Inc}(v) & \rightarrow \text{Inc}(v); \\
\mathbb{R}_{\text{Update}} & : \neg\mathbb{T}\text{Er}(v) \wedge (d_v > 0) \wedge \neg\mathbb{T}\text{Pass}(v) \wedge (\text{ME}_v \neq \text{ME}_{p(v)}) \wedge \mathbb{T}\text{Update}(v) & \rightarrow \text{Update}(v); \\
\mathbb{R}_{\text{HyperNd}} & : \neg\mathbb{T}\text{Er}(v) \wedge (d_v > 0) \wedge \neg\mathbb{T}\text{Pass}(v) \wedge (\text{ME}_v = \text{ME}_{p(v)}) \wedge & \\
 & \ \ (\text{Add}_v = \emptyset) \wedge \mathbb{T}\text{Add}(v) & \rightarrow \text{BinAdd}(v); \\
 & \ \ (\text{Add}_v \neq \emptyset) \wedge \mathbb{T}\text{Broad}(v) & \rightarrow \text{Broad}(v); \\
 & \ \ \mathbb{T}\text{Verif}(v) & \rightarrow \text{Verif}(v); \\
 & \ \ \mathbb{T}\text{CleanM}(v) & \rightarrow \text{CleanM}(v);
\end{array}
$$

Fig. 1. *Formal description of algorithm* **CLE**

To satisfy the leader election specifications, we introduce the variable $\text{leader}_v \in \{0, 1\}$ whose value is 1 if v is the leader and 0 otherwise. Since we do not assume that the identifiers of every node are encoded on the same number of bits, simply comparing the i-th most significant bit of two nodes is irrelevant. So, we use variable $\overline{B}$, which represents the most significant bit-position of all the identities present in the ring. This variable will also be locally used at each node v as an estimate of $\lfloor \log n \rfloor$. Only the nodes v whose variable $\overline{B}_v$ is equal to the most significant bit of the Id_v carry on participating to the election. Finally, variable ME is the core of the election process. Let r be the root of the tree including node v. Then, the variable ME_v is a 4-tuple which stores the position of the most significant bit of Id_r, the current phase number i, the bit-position of Id_r at phase i, and one additional bit dedicated to the control of the updating of the variable (we call "bit-control" this latter variable).

The Compact Leader Election Algorithm CLE. Algorithm **CLE** is presented in Figure 1. In this figure, a rule of the form

$$label : guard_0 \wedge (guard_1 \vee guard_2) \longrightarrow (command_1; command_2)$$

where $command_i$ is performed when $guard_0 \wedge guard_i$ is true, is presented in several lines, one for the common guard, and one for each alternative guards, with their respective command. Figure 1 describes the rules of the algorithm. **CLE** is composed of six rules:

- The rule $\mathbb{R}_{\text{Error}}$, detects at node v the presence of inconsistencies between the content of its variables and the content of its neighboring variables. If v has not reset its variables, or has not restarted, the command $\text{Reset}(v)$ is activated, i.e all the content of all the variables at node v are reset, and the variable d_v is set to -1.
- The rule $\mathbb{R}_{\text{Start}}$, makes sure that, if an inconsistency is detected at some node, then all the nodes of the network reset their variables, and restart. Before restarting, every node v waits until all its neighbors are reset or have restarted. A node v that restarts sets $d_v = 0$, and its election variables ME_v appropriately, with current phase 1.

- The rule $\mathbb{R}_{\text{Passive}}$, is dedicated to the election process. A node v uses command $\text{Passive}(v)$ when one of its neighbors has a bit-position larger than the bit-position of v, at the same phase.
- The rule $\mathbb{R}_{\text{Root}}$, concerns the candidate leaders, i.e., every node v with $d_v = 0$. Such a node can only execute the rule $\mathbb{R}_{\text{Root}}$, resulting in that node performing one of the following two commands. Command $\text{StartdB}(v)$ results in v distributing the bit dB to its neighboring hyper-nodes. Command $\text{Inc}(v)$ results in node v increasing its phase by 1. This happens when all the nodes between v and others candidate leaders in the current tree are in the same phase, with the same election value ME_v.
- The rule $\mathbb{R}_{\text{Update}}$, is dedicated to updating the election variables.
- The rule $\mathbb{R}_{\text{HyperNd}}$, is dedicated to the hyper-nodes distance verification.

Hyper-nodes Distance Verification. Let us consider two hyper-nodes X and Y with X the parent of Y. Our technique for verifying the distance between the two hyper-nodes X and Y, is the following (see an example on Figure 2). X initiates the verification. For this purpose, X dedicates two local variables at each of its nodes: Add (to perform the addition) and MC (to broadcast the result of this addition inside X). Similarly, Y uses the variable MV for receiving the result of the addition.

The binary addition starts at the node holding the last bit of X, that is node x_k with $k = \overline{B}_v$. Node x_k sets $\text{Add}_{x_k} := +$. Then, every node in X, but x_k, proceeds as follows. For $k' < k$, if the child $x_{k''}$ of $x_{k'}$ has $\text{Add}_{x_{k''}} = +$ and $\text{dB}_{x_{k''}} = 1$, then x'_k assigns $+$ to $\text{Add}_{x_{k''}}$. Otherwise, if $\text{Add}_{x_{k''}} = +$ and $\text{dB}_{x_{k''}} = 0$, the binary addition at this point does not generate a carry, and thus $x_{k'}$ assigns "ok" to $\text{Add}_{x_{k'}}$. Since $\text{Add}_{x_{k'}} = ok$, the binary addition is considered finished, and $x_{k'}$'s ancestors (parent, grand-parent, etc.) in the hyper-node assign "ok" to their variable Add. However, if the first bit of X (that is, dB_{x_1}) is equal to one, then the algorithm detects an error because the addition would yield to an overflow. The result of the hyper-node binary addition is the following: if a node x_k has $\text{Add}_{x_k} = ok$, then it means that node y_k holds the appropriate bit corresponding to the correct result of the addition if and only if $\text{dB}_{y_k} = \text{dB}_{x_k}$. Otherwise, if $\text{Add}_{x_k} = +$, then the bit at y_k is correct if and only if $\text{dB}_{y_k} = \overline{\text{dB}}_{x_k}$[1].

The binary addition in X is completed when node x_1 satisfies $\text{Add}_{x_1} = +$ or $\text{Add}_{x_1} = ok$. In that case, x_1 starts broadcasting the result of the addition. For this purpose, it sets $\text{MC}_{x_1} = (1, \text{dB}_{y_1})$ where dB_{y_1} is obtained from Add_{x_1} and dB_{x_1}. Each node x_i in X, $i > 1$, then successively perform the same operation as x_1. While doing so, node x_i deletes Add_{x_i}, in order to enable the next verification. When the child of a node x_i publishes $(d_{x_i}, \text{dB}_{x_i})$, node x_i deletes MC_{x_i}, in order to, again, enable the next verification. From $i = 1, \ldots, k$, all variables MC_{x_i} in X are deleted. When y_i sets $\text{MV}_{y_i}[0] = dy_i$, node y_i can check whether the bit in $\text{MV}_{y_i}[1]$ corresponds to dB_{y_i}. If yes, then the verification carries on. Otherwise y_i detects a fault.

---

[1] If $\text{dB}_x = 0$ then $\overline{\text{dB}}_x = 1$, and if $\text{dB}_x = 1$ then $\overline{\text{dB}}_x = 0$.

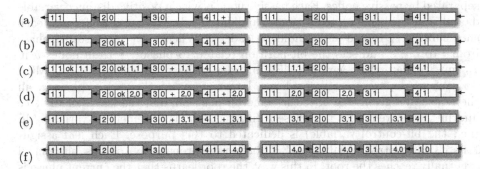

Fig. 2. An example of distance verification between the hyper-node X and its child Y. Hyper-nodes are here composed of four nodes. The memory of each node is represented by four boxes storing, respectively, the distance of the node, the bit distance of the hyper-node, the binary addition information, and the information for the bit verification. (a) The last node of X starts the addition. (b) The addition in X is completed. (c) The first node of X starts the verification. (d) The second node v of Y checks dB_v. (e) The third node v of Y checks dB_v. (f) The last node of Y detects an error.

Leader Election and Tree Construction. As previously mentioned, our leader election protocol simultaneously performs, together with the election of a leader, the construction a tree rooted at the leader. The leader should be the node whose identifier is maximal among all nodes in the ring. Our assumptions regarding identifiers are very weak. In particular, identifiers may be of various sizes, and the total number n of different identifiers is not known to the nodes. In our algorithm, we use the variable $\overline{B}$ to estimate (to some extent) the network size, and the variable $\mathsf{ME}[0]$ to propagate this estimation in the ring. More precisely, $\overline{B}$ represents the most significant bit-position among all identities present in the ring, and we consider that all variables ME that do not carry the right value of $\overline{B}$ are not valid. During the execution of the algorithm, only nodes whose identifiers match the most significant bit-position remain candidate leaders. Moreover, only candidate leaders broadcast bit-position during subsequent phases.

Let us detail now the usage of the variable ME_v. Again, this variable is essentially meant to represent the current bit-position of the candidate leaders. The first element of ME_v represents the most significant bit-position among all identifiers, which must be in agreement with variable $\overline{B}_v$ to assess the validity of ME_v. The second and third elements of ME_v are the current phase i, and the corresponding bit-position revealed by a candidate leader during phase i, respectively. The comparison of bits-positions is relevant only if these bits-positions are revealed at the same phase. Hence, we force the system to proceed in phases.

If, at phase i, the bit-position ρ_v of node v is smaller than the bit-position ρ_u of a neighboring node u, then node v becomes passive, and v takes u as parent. It is simple to compare two candidate leaders when these candidate leaders are neighbors. Yet, along with the execution of the algorithm, some nodes become passive, and therefore the remaining candidate leaders can be far away, separated by passive nodes. Each passive node is with a positive distance variable d, and is in a subtree rooted at some candidate leader. Let us consider now each such subtree T_v rooted at a candidate leader v. Whenever v increases its phase from i to $i + 1$, and sets the bit-position related to phase $i + 1$, all nodes u in T_v must update their variable ME_u in order to have the same value as ME_v. At each phase, trees are merged into larger trees. At the end of phase i, all the nodes in a given tree have the same bit-position, and the leaves of the tree inform their parent that the phase is finished. The last element of variable ME (i.e., the bit-control variable) is dedicated to this purpose. Each leaf assigns 1 to its bit-control variable, and a bottom-up propagation of this bit-control eventually reaches the root. In this way, the root learns that the current phase is finished. If the largest identifiers are encoded using $\log n$ bits, each phase results in halving the number of trees, and therefore of candidate leaders. So within at most $\log n$ phases, a single leader remains. To avoid electing an impostor leader, the (unique) leader restarts the election at the first phase. This is repeated forever. If an arbitrary initial configuration induces an impostor leader l, either l has not the most significant bit-position in its identifier or this impostor leader has its most significant bit-position equal to the most significant bit-position of the (real) leader. In the former case, the error is detected by a node with the most significant bit-position. In the latter case, then error is detected by at least one node (the true leader), because there exists at least one phase i where the bit-position of the leader is superior to the bit-position of the impostor.

The process of leader election and spanning tree construction is slowed down by the hyper-node construction and management. When a node v changes its parents, it also changes its variable dB_v, in order not to do impact the current construction of the tree. The point is that variable dB_v should be handled with extra care to remain coherent with the tree resulting from merging different trees. To handle this, every candidate leader assigns bits for its children into its variable MC. More precisely, if a root v has not children, then v publishes the bit for its future children with variable distance equal to one. If root v has children with distance variable equal to one, then v publishes the bit for the children u with $\mathsf{d}_u = 2$, and so on, until the distance variable of v becomes $\overline{\mathsf{B}}_v$. On the other hand, a node cannot change its parent if its future new parent does not publish the bit corresponding to its future distance variable. When the hyper-node adjacent to the root is constructed, the hyper-node verification process takes care of the assignment of the bits to the node inside the hyper-node.

4   Correctness

In this section, we briefly sketch the proof of correctness of our Algorithm.

Theorem 1. *Algorithm* **CLE** *solves the leader election problem in a self-stabilizing manner for the n-node ring, in the state-sharing model, with a distributed weakly-fair scheduler. Moreover, if the n node identities are in the range $[1, n^c]$ for some $c \geq 1$, then Algorithm* **CLE** *uses $O(\log \log n)$ bits of memory per node, and stabilizes in $O(n \log^2 n)$ rounds.*

The main difficulty for proving this theorem is to prove detection and complete removing of a possibly initial cycle generated by the parenthood relation. Let Γ be the set of all possible configurations of the ring, under the set of variables described before in the paper. First, we prove that Algorithm **CLE** detects the presence of "level-one" errors, that is, inconsistencies between neighbors. Second, we prove that, after removing all these level-one errors (possibly using a reset), the system converges and maintains configurations without level-one errors. The set of such configurations is denoted by Γ_{TEF} where TEF stands for "Trivial Error Free". From now on, we assume only configurations from Γ_{TEF}.

The core of the proof regarding correct cycle detection is based on proving the correctness of the hyper-node distance verification process. This verification process is the most technical part of the algorithm, and proving its correctness is actually the main challenge in the way of establishing Theorem 1. This is achieved by using proofs based on invariance arguments.

Once the correctness of the hyper-node distance verification process has been proved, we establish the convergence of Algorithm **CLE** from an arbitrary configuration in Γ_{TEF} to a configuration where there exist no spanning cycles, and all hyper-node distances are correct. Configurations with no spanning cycles form the set Γ_{CF} (where CF stands for "Cycle Free"), and configurations in which all hyper-node distances are correct form the set Γ_{HVEF} (where HVEF stands for "Hyper-node Verification Error Free"). Whenever we restrict ourselves to configuration in Γ_{HVEF}, we prove the correctness of our mechanisms to detect and remove impostor leaders. We denote by Γ_{IEF} (where IEF stands for "Impostor leader Error Free") the set of configurations with no impostors. Finally, assuming a configuration in Γ_{IEF}, we prove that the system reaches and maintains a configuration with exactly one leader, which is in addition the node with maximum identifier. Moreover, we prove that the structure induced by parenthood relation is a tree rooted at the leader, and spanning all nodes. We denote by Γ_L the set of configurations where the unique leader is the node with maximum identity. In other words, we prove that **CLE** is self-stabilizing for Γ_L.

References

1. Adamek, J., Nesterenko, M., Tixeuil, S.: Evaluating practical tolerance properties of stabilizing programs through simulation: The case of propagation of information with feedback. In: Richa, A.W., Scheideler, C. (eds.) SSS 2012. LNCS, vol. 7596, pp. 126–132. Springer, Heidelberg (2012)
2. Afek, Y., Bremler-Barr, A.: Self-stabilizing unidirectional network algorithms by power supply. Chicago J. Theor. Comput. Sci. (1998)
3. Arora, A., Gouda, M.G.: Distributed reset. IEEE Trans. Computers 43(9), 1026–1038 (1994)
4. Arumugam, M., Kulkarni, S.S.: Prose: A programming tool for rapid prototyping of sensor networks. In: S-CUBE, pp. 158–173 (2009)
5. Awerbuch, B., Kutten, S., Mansour, Y., Patt-Shamir, B., Varghese, G.: A time-optimal self-stabilizing synchronizer using a phase clock. IEEE Trans. Dependable Sec. Comput. 4(3), 180–190 (2007)
6. Awerbuch, B., Ostrovsky, R.: Memory-efficient and self-stabilizing network reset. In: PODC, pp. 254–263. ACM (1994)

7. Beauquier, J., Delaët, S., Dolev, S., Tixeuil, S.: Transient fault detectors. Distributed Computing 20(1), 39–51 (2007)
8. Beauquier, J., Gradinariu, M., Johnen, C.: Randomized self-stabilizing and space optimal leader election under arbitrary scheduler on rings. Distributed Computing 20(1), 75–93 (2007)
9. Choi, Y., Gouda, M.G.: A state-based model of sensor protocols. Theor. Comput. Sci. 458, 61–75 (2012)
10. Dalton, A.R., McCartney, W.P., Ghosh Dastidar, K., Hallstrom, J.O., Sridhar, N., Herman, T., Leal, W., Arora, A., Gouda, M.G.: Desal alpha: An implementation of the dynamic embedded sensor-actuator language. In: ICCCN, pp. 541–547. IEEE (2008)
11. Kumar Datta, A., Larmore, L.L., Vemula, P.: Self-stabilizing leader election in optimal space under an arbitrary scheduler. TCS 412(40), 5541–5561 (2011)
12. Devismes, S., Masuzawa, T., Tixeuil, S.: Communication efficiency in self-stabilizing silent protocols. In: ICDCS 2009, pp. 474–481. IEEE Press (2009)
13. Dijkstra, E.W.: Self-stabilizing systems in spite of distributed control. Commun. ACM 17(11), 643–644 (1974)
14. Dolev, S.: Self-stabilization. MIT Press (March 2000)
15. Dolev, S., Gouda, M.G., Schneider, M.: Memory requirements for silent stabilization. Acta Inf. 36(6), 447–462 (1999)
16. Dolev, S., Herman, T.: Superstabilizing protocols for dynamic distributed systems. Chicago J. Theor. Comput. Sci. (1997)
17. Dolev, S., Israeli, A., Moran, S.: Resource bounds for self-stabilizing message-driven protocols. SIAM J. Comput. 26(1), 273–290 (1997)
18. Dubois, S., Tixeuil, S.: A taxonomy of daemons in self-stabilization. Technical Report 1110.0334, ArXiv eprint (October 2011)
19. Fich, F.E., Johnen, C.: A space optimal, deterministic, self-stabilizing, leader election algorithm for unidirectional rings. In: Welch, J.L. (ed.) DISC 2001. LNCS, vol. 2180, pp. 224–239. Springer, Heidelberg (2001)
20. Gouda, M.G., Cobb, J.A., Huang, C.-T.: Fault masking in tri-redundant systems. In: Datta, A.K., Gradinariu, M. (eds.) SSS 2006. LNCS, vol. 4280, pp. 304–313. Springer, Heidelberg (2006)
21. Herman, T., Pemmaraju, S.V.: Error-detecting codes and fault-containing self-stabilization. Inf. Process. Lett. 73(1-2), 41–46 (2000)
22. Hoepman, J.: Self-stabilizing ring-orientation using constant space. Inf. Comput. 144(1), 18–39 (1998)
23. Israeli, A., Jalfon, M.: Uniform self-stabilizing ring orientation. Inf. Comput. 104(2), 175–196 (1993)
24. Itkis, G., Levin, L.A.: Fast and lean self-stabilizing asynchronous protocols. In: FOCS, pp. 226–239. IEEE Computer Society (1994)
25. Itkis, G., Lin, C., Simon, J.: Deterministic, constant space, self-stabilizing leader election on uniform rings. In: Helary, J.-M., Raynal, M. (eds.) WDAG 1995. LNCS, vol. 972, pp. 288–302. Springer, Heidelberg (1995)
26. Masuzawa, T., Tixeuil, S.: On bootstrapping topology knowledge in anonymous networks. ACM Transactions on Adaptive and Autonomous Systems 4(1) (2009)
27. Mayer, A.J., Ofek, Y., Ostrovsky, R.l., Yung, M.: Self-stabilizing symmetry breaking in constant-space (extended abstract). In: STOC, pp. 667–678 (1992)
28. McGuire, T.M., Gouda, M.G.: The Austin Protocol Compiler. Advances in Information Security, vol. 13. Springer (2005)
29. Tixeuil, S.: Algorithms and Theory of Computation Handbook, pp. 26.1–26.45. CRC Press, Taylor & Francis Group (2009)

Time Optimal Synchronous Self Stabilizing Spanning Tree

Alex Kravchik and Shay Kutten*

Technion, Information Systems Engineering, IE, Haifa, Israel
alex.kravchik@gmail.com
kutten@ie.technion.ac.il

Abstract. In this research, we present the first time-optimal self stabilizing algorithm for synchronous distributed spanning tree construction, assuming the standard shared registers size ($O(\log n)$ bits, where n stands for the number of processes in the system), or, similarly, standard message size. Previous algorithms with $O(diameter)$ stabilization time complexity assumed that a larger message can be sent through each link in one time unit. Hence, when assuming the standard message size, the time complexity of previous algorithms was not $O(diameter)$. The current algorithm stabilizes in $O(diameter)$ time without having previous knowledge of the network size or diameter. The only assumption we make is that we have some polynomial (possibly very large) given upper bound on the network size. However, the time complexity of the algorithm does not depend on that upper bound. Using our results, most known distributed global tasks, such as distributed reset, can be performed in a relatively easy way and in optimal time. As a building block, we present a new self stabilizing silent phase clock algorithm for synchronous networks (based on a known non-silent algorithm). It is optimal in time too. We believe it may be an interesting contribution by itself.

1 Introduction

The construction of a spanning tree is a basic task in communication networks. In this task, it is required to mark at each node, one edge as the route to the *parent* node. The marked edges must form a spanning tree - a tree composed of all the nodes and some (or perhaps all) of the edges, when every vertex lies in the tree. Most known distributed global tasks, such as reset, leader election, broadcast, etc. become much easier using a spanning tree. This makes spanning tree construction an important task.

A strong property one would like a distributed spanning tree algorithm to possess is self-stabilization. First introduced by Dijkstra in [18], this property implies the ability of a system to stabilize from any initial state. It is desirable that such an algorithm will be efficient in terms of time - meaning, able to stabilize in a short time after the occurrence of failures or topological changes in the system.

---

* Supported in part by the Israel Science Foundation and the Technion TASP fund.

Y. Afek (Ed.): DISC 2013, LNCS 8205, pp. 91–105, 2013.

There has been a considerable amount of research in the area of self stabilizing spanning trees. In [2, 3], the authors present two self stabilizing spanning tree protocols for asynchronous systems. The protocol of [3] is randomized. Their protocols have $O(n^2)$ time complexity and $O(\log n)$ space complexity, where n is the size of the network. In [31], a randomized spanning tree protocol for anonymous systems is given. Its expected time complexity is $O(\text{diameter} \times \log n)$. In [5], the authors present a self stabilizing spanning tree algorithm for ID-based network. The time complexity in [5] is $O(N^2)$, where N is a known upper bound on the size of the network. In [10], a self stabilizing spanning protocol and a reset protocol (which utilizes the spanning tree) are presented. The time complexity of the spanning tree protocol is $O(n)$, the space complexity is $O(\log n)$ A fault containing self stabilizing spanning tree algorithm was presented in [23]. Its time complexity is affected by the number and type of faults. In [1], the algorithm uses verification messages ("power supply") from the root for the purpose of the algorithm stabilization. In [16], a self stabilizing leader election algorithm that constructs a spanning tree is presented. Using unbounded space, it stabilizes in $O(\text{diameter})$ time units.

Several papers deal with the semi-uniform model, meaning there is a distinguished root. In [20], an algorithm that uses fine-grained atomic operations is proposed. In [14], a time optimal algorithm in a semi-uniform model is presented. This algorithm also requires the knowledge of the network size n for constructing BFS spanning tree.

Some algorithms require previous knowledge of an upper bound on the network diameter - D. For example, in [9, 12], the authors present self stabilizing algorithms with $O(\text{diameter})$ time complexity, but the messages of those protocols are $O(\log n \log D)$ bits long. In the current study, we assume the most common assumption that sending a message of $O(\log n)$ bits takes 1 unit of time (using the *Congest* model as defined in [29]). Hence, sending an $O(\log n \log D)$ bits message takes $\log D$ time, and $O(\text{diameter})$ time in the model of [9, 12] translates into $O(\text{diameter} \times \log D)$ time. If D is very large (much larger than the diameter), the time complexity of the algorithm grows significantly.

In [4], the authors present an algorithm which does not require any information about the network topology and stabilizes in $O(\text{diameter})$ rounds. However, the message size in this protocol is strongly influenced by the faults and is not bounded, so the messages can grow unbounded above the traditional $O(\log n)$ size. If we assume that sending a message of $O(\log n)$ bits takes 1 unit of time, the time complexity of [4] is not bounded. The algorithm of [4] uses an approach that is different than the one used for the other distributed spanning tree algorithms. Instead of "dismantling" existing trees that contain fake roots, it tries to preserve them, as will be explained later. This approach is referred as "path preservation". We use the same approach in our algorithm.

In [15], the author present a new stabilizing solution for the construction of an arbitrary spanning tree. This algorithm runs in $\Theta(n)$ rounds and $\Theta(n^2)$ steps.

Distributed spanning tree algorithms are important even without self stabilization. In the seminal paper of [22], the authors present a spanning tree algorithm for a static case. Their algorithm constructs a minimum spanning tree in a network with unique weighted edges. In [28], the authors present a time optimal spanning tree algorithm for anonymous networks. In [7], there is a spanning tree algorithm for a dynamic case, which is optimal in terms of the amortized message complexity. In [27], the presented protocol iteratively rebuilds a spanning tree of a maximal connected component, when an edge fails. The time complexity of that protocol is $O(d^*)$, when d^* stands for the diameter of the maximal connected component, adding an extra poly-logarithmic term.

In the independent research of [21], the authors present a speculative global mutual exclusion algorithm. It is optimal in time (though under different assumptions) in a synchronous system. We mention this work since the task of global mutual exclusion is related to the leader election task, and hence, to the distributed spanning tree construction task. In addition, the algorithm of [21] is based on the synchronizer algorithm of [13]. We also use the results of that research.

Another leader election algorithm is presented in [17].

We present a time-optimal self stabilizing spanning tree algorithm, which requires no prior knowledge about the system's topology, except for the not necessarily tight upper bound on the network size; this upper bound does not affect the time complexity of the algorithm. The algorithm uses shared registers of size $O(\log n)$ bits.

Paper Organization. In Section 2, we formalize the model and present some notations. In Section 3, we present a new self-stabilizing synchronous phase clock algorithm, later used in the spanning tree algorithm. In Section 4, we describe the spanning tree algorithm informally, outlining the ideas adopted from [4] and presenting the new ones. In Section 5, we formalize the algorithm. In Section 6, we present the proof of correctness and performance analysis. In Section 7, we conclude and present some questions and ideas for future research.

2   Model and Notations

The system topology is represented by an undirected graph $G = (V, E)$, where nodes represent the system's processes and edges represent communication links between them. We denote the number of nodes by $n = |V|$. The actual diameter of the network is denoted by d. Both n and d are unknown to the processes. We assume that each node $v \in V$ has a unique identity value, denoted by UID, which cannot be corrupted by the adversary. For each $v \in V$, every node u such that $(v, u) \in E$ is called a *neighbor of v*. The collection of v's neighbors is denoted by $\mathcal{N}(v) = \{u : (v, u) \in E\}$, $\overline{\mathcal{N}}(v) = \mathcal{N}(v) \bigcup \{v\}$. We denote the distance in hops (the number of edges on the shortest path) between two nodes u, v as $d(u, v)$.

Each node has a constant set of registers and constants, each of size $O(\log n)$ bits. Each register or constant x of node v is denoted by x_v. We shall omit the subscript when the subject node's identity is clear from the context.

We do make the rather common assumption that we have some given upper bound on n, denoted by N. Without this knowledge, it is impossible to use bounded registers, since every chosen register size x will become insufficient for representing a node's ID, if the number of nodes grows larger than 2^x. It is enough that this upper bound is polynomial in n, so the size of the registers is $O(\log n)$ bits. It is important to notice that the time complexity of the current algorithm does not depend on that upper bound on n.

We assume that there might be faults during the execution. We abstract those faults as a result of an *adversary* action. The adversary might change the values of registers and destroy edges or nodes (causing topology changes).

We use the *shared registers* model. For each $v \in V$, its registers are visible to every $u \in \mathcal{N}(v)$. All registers are of $O(\log n)$ size. Note that in terms of message passing (not used here), their values can be sent over an edge in one time unit. In synchronous systems, when assuming that a communication line can contain one message at a time, the message passing model is equivalent to the shared registers model.

The system is a synchronous network. All the processes perform their actions synchronously in grained periods of time called *rounds*. Every process receives a "pulse" which marks the beginning of a new round of execution. All the pulses in the system are generated simultaneously. We denote the round $k = 0$ as the first round of execution after the adversary actions. At every round k, each process v can read the values of all v's neighbors registers, perform computations, and update its own registers. The results of those updates are visible to all v's neighbors at round $k+1$.

Each protocol is presented as an infinite loop, performed repeatedly by all the processes. It is infinite, since the protocols are supposed to overcome new failures and maintain the system in a legal global state forever. At each round, the loop is performed exactly once. The number of rounds that is required for the system to reach the desired state marks the time complexity of the algorithm.

The *local state* of node v consists of the values of all v's registers. A *Global state* γ_t is the set of all local states at round t of the execution. We denote the local state of a node v at global state γ as $\gamma.v$, and the value of any register x of a node v at global state γ as $\gamma.x_v$.

We use the notation $x[y]$ for "x modulo y".

3   Self-Stabilizing Silent Synchronizer - SS-Sync

A *synchronous algorithm* is an algorithm that is designed to work correctly in a synchronous system. When executed in an asynchronous system, its result is unpredicted. A *synchronizer* is originally defined in [6] as a distributed algorithm that enables synchronous algorithms to be executed correctly in an asynchronous system, simulating the "pulse" property. Pulse $i + 1$ ($i \geq 0$) is generated on process p after all neighbors executed all actions at pulse i. We say that the synchronizer maintains a *strict pulse counter*, if each pulse has its own unique index. However, a synchronizer may not maintain a strict pulse counter. For example, [6] uses a pulse number modulo 3.

In a broader sense, a synchronizer is a distributed algorithm which synchronizes the execution of some action on different processes. In this sense, synchronizer may be useful even in synchronous systems [13].

A *phase clock* in a distributed system is an algorithm that maintains synchronized clock (or pulse) counters on each process. Those clocks are said to move in *unison* ([24]), and the task of maintaining phase clocks is also called *unison task*. There are two possible *unison* definitions. The clocks are said to be in *strong unison*, if all the clocks in the system are supposed to have strictly the same value. This can be only achieved in a synchronous system. The clocks are said to be in *weak unison*, if the clock value of neighboring processes are allowed to differ one from another by at most ±1.

The task of maintaining phase clocks was shown to be non trivial even in synchronous systems ([25]).

In [8], the authors present a time optimal self stabilizing synchronizer for asynchronous model, that also supplies a phase clock. However, that algorithm uses unbounded registers. A related example of maintaining distributed clocks using bounded registers is [19]. In [11] and [13], the authors present a group of synchronous and asynchronous synchronizers with phase clocks, which use bounded registers. In addition, the authors present a detailed study of optimality in terms of space for any algorithm that uses bounded registers for the unison task, and provide space-optimal algorithms for various topologies and models.

We propose a new self stabilizing synchronization and unison algorithm for synchronous systems - *SS-Sync*. It is based on the algorithms of [11] and [13]. It stabilizes in $O(d)$ rounds, and provides both a synchronization mechanism and a phase clock. The clocks in the system are maintained in weak unison.

This is the first unison algorithm that both stabilizes in O(diameter) time and is *silent*. A silent unison algorithm [11] that does not receive any outside input stabilizes such that (1) the phase clocks in all the processes contain the same number x for some x and (2) the value of the phase clocks never changes after the stabilization. Of course, the value may change because of faults. However, a silent unison algorithm may receive as an input requests from some other algorithm (at one or more processes). If a request is made, the value grows by one (eventually, at all the processes).

A silent unison algorithm in general, and SS-Sync in particular can be used as a tool for some upper layer algorithm. Intuitively, the upper layer algorithm may use SS-Sync in order to synchronize some action among different processes. The semantics is given more formally below. Again, intuitively, if no synchronized action is issued, then the silent unison algorithm assigns some value to the phase clocks at all the processes, and stops. It increases this value only if a request for a synchronized action is issued. In such a case, the phase clocks are advanced, and then the silent algorithm stops again (and the phase clocks cease advancing until yet another synchronized action is issued).

Somewhat more formally, SS-Sync provides the following interface to the upper layer algorithm:

1. An externally visible *clock* read-only register, which indicates the current phase clock value.
2. A writeable pointer to a procedure *SynchronizedAction* - the action which execution is synchronized by SS-Sync.
3. Boolean writeable flag *act*. When the upper layer assigns $act \leftarrow true$, SS-Sync is committed to advance the clock and to execute SynchronizedAction.
4. Boolean function *IsSynchronized*, indicating whether clock is in weak unison with all neighbor's clocks.

Every process u advances its clock, if the following conditions hold:

1. The advancing of the clock does not break the weak unison with u's neighbors.
2. There exists $v \in \mathcal{N}(u)$ with a higher clock value, or $act_u = true$.

As mention above for silent algorithms, if there is no process where the upper layer algorithm asks for SynchronizedAction execution (by setting $act = true$), then all the clocks in the system gradually (in $O(d)$ rounds) synchronize with the maximum one and stop advancing. Hence, the algorithm is *silent*.

In order to implement the clock with bounded registers, SS-Sync uses a construct called *Finite Incrementing System* [11]. FIS allows the maintaining of a self stabilizing and infinitely advancing phase clock, using bounded registers. FIS is detailed below.

Finite Incremented System - FIS. Let K be a strictly positive integer, $K \geq 3$. Two integers a and b are said to be *congruent modulo K*, denoted by $a \equiv b[K]$ if and only if $\exists \lambda \in \mathbb{N}, b = (a + \lambda)K$. The distance $d_K(a, b) = \min(x \geq 0, (a - b) \equiv x[K] \vee (b - a) \equiv x[K])$. Two integers a and b are said to be *locally comparable*, denoted as $a \backsim b$, if and only if $d_K(a, b) \leq 1$. The *local order relation* for locally comparable integers, denoted by $\leq_l$, is defined as follows: $a \leq_l b \iff 0 \leq (b - a)[K] \leq 1$.

A *Finite Incrementing System* is defined by the pair (χ, φ). The set χ is the range of all possible register values, defined as follows: $\chi = \{-\alpha, ..., 0, ..., K-1\}$, where α is some positive integer, defined later. The function φ is an **incrementing** function, defined as follows:

$$\varphi(x) = \begin{cases} x + 1, \text{if } x < 0 \\ (x + 1)[K], \text{if } x \geq 0 \end{cases}$$

We define $tail = \{-\alpha, ..., 0\}$, $tail^- = \{-\alpha, ..., -1\}$ and $ring = \{0, ..., K - 1\}$. A *reset* on a node's clock consists of enforcing any value of χ to $-\alpha$.

In [11], the authors prove that a self stabilizing FIS implementation on network G is only possible if $K \geq C_G$, when C_G is the size of the longest cycle in the graph, and $\alpha \geq T_G$, when T_G is the size of the longest chordless cycle (hole) in the graph. Since T_G and C_G are unknown, but we do have an upper bound on the size of the network (N), we define $K = \alpha = N + 1$.

The main procedure of SS-Sync for process i is presented in figure 1. Register *clock* is defined within the range of χ. Lines 2-9 are executed if $\forall v \in$

$\overline{N}(i), clock_v \backsimeq clock_i$, so the system appears to be stabilized for node i. This code section is called *NormalAction*. If $\exists v \in \mathcal{N}(i) : clock_v \not\backsimeq clock_i$ (so the system is not stabilized), either *ResetAction* (lines 12-14) or *StabilizationAction* (lines 16-20) is executed. Boolean function *IsStabilized* on node v returns *true* iff $\forall u \in \mathcal{N}(v), clock_u \backsimeq clock_v$.

SS-Sync is self-stabilizing, hence, after $O(d)$ rounds, all neighbouring processes' *clock* values are locally comparable. Moreover, after SS-Sync stabilizes, every process is guaranteed to be able to execute the SynchronizedAction in $O(d)$ round after it was asked to do so by the upper layer algorithm.

SS-Sync Formal Description. Each process i carries a constant *UID*, unique in the system. Each process i maintains the following registers:

- *clock* - The value of the clock at process i.
- *act* - A boolean flag, accessible (writeable) by external (upper·layer) protocols at i, which uses SS-Sync.
- *SynchronizedAction* - A pointer to an external procedure, executed by SS-Sync during NormalAction, if $act_i = true$. This register is assigned by an external (upper layer) protocols, which uses SS-Sync.

```
 1: if ∀v ∈ N̄(i), clock_v ≃ clock_i then
 2:     if (∃v ∈ N(i) | clock_v = φ(clock_i) or act = true) and ¬∃u ∈ N(i) | clock_i =
        φ(clock_u) then
 3:         /* NormalAction */
 4:         clock_i ← φ(clock_i);
 5:         if act = true then
 6:             SynchronizedAction;
 7:         end if
 8:         act ← false;
 9:     end if
10: else
11:     if ∀v ∈ N̄(i), clock_v ∈ ring then
12:         /* ResetAction */
13:         clock_i ← −α;
14:         act ← false;
15:     else
16:         /* StabilizationAction */
17:         /* there must be a neighbor with clock in tail */
18:         let m = MIN(clock_v : v ∈ N̄(i));
19:         clock_i ← φ(m);
20:         act ← false;
21:     end if
22: end if
```

Fig 1. SS-Sync procedure - executed in every round for node i

SS-Sync correctness and complexity analysis is very similar to those of the algorithms of [11] and [13]. The detailed analysis is deferred to the full paper.

4 The Main Ideas behind the Spanning Tree Construction Algorithm

Like most distributed spanning tree algorithms, our algorithm relies on the paradigm of *ID adoption* from the distributed Bellman-Ford algorithm [1, 10, 31]. Let us first describe the main ideas behind the Bellman-Ford approach: each tree gets an ID which is the UID of the tree root. Such an adopted identity is called *TID*. A process v that detects a neighbour u who belongs to a tree T with a higher TID than its own, joins that tree as a leaf by adopting the TID of T and adopting u as a parent. There might be more than one process with equal TID and distance from root; in this case, assuming a process's edges are numbered, the neighbor with the maximum edge connecting to it is chosen. Ideally (without state faults), the system will eventually reach the state where the process with the maximum ID is the root of the tree that spans the entire network. Every process maintains, in addition to the *TID* register, also two other registers: a pointer to the parent in the spanning tree (*parent*), and the estimated distance to the root in hops (*distance*). The value of the *parent* registers of the roots is *null*. In a legal state, the graph induced by the *parent* pointers of all the system processes is supposed to form a spanning tree.

However, it is well known [30], that by itself, this "pure" approach of the basic Distributed Bellman Ford is not self-stabilizing, unless some additional measures are taken. Due to faults, the *TID* registers of some processes might contain faulty data, saying that those processes belong to a tree with some high TID α. Since TID is the UID of the root, this implies that those processes belong to a tree rooted at a process whose UID is α. However, such a process may not exist. We term α a *fake root*. This could cause the *count to infinity* problem ([26, p.315]).

There are several approaches for solving the problem of fake roots. For example, in [5, 20] a known upper bound on the tree's height is assumed, which is based on the assumed upper bound on the diameter of the network. The use of this approach in previous works caused the time complexity of the algorithm to depend on that bound. Since the tightness of that bound can't be assured, time complexity of the algorithms could grow very large. Another approach, utilized in [1–3], is to send verifications from the root to it's children.

In [4], a different approach is presented. The TID of the tree doesn't have to be equal to the tree root UID. When a process detects that it belongs to a tree whose root might be missing, it declares itself the root, adopting the existing TID. This way, there is no need to "dismantle" a tree that may already have been built, just because root's ID is a fake root. This was shown in [4] to save time.

This approach raised another problem: since the TID may be different from the UID of the root, there may be multiple trees with an equal TID - *ID collision*. Had no additional action been taken in such a situation in [4], no tree would have overrun the other, and the algorithm would have failed to achieve the goal of constructing a spanning tree.

To overcome this, [4] proposes the *DETECT-OTHER-TREES* mechanism, so that every root finds whether there is another tree with the same TID. If such a tree exists, both roots perform an *Extend-ID* operation. During the *Extend-ID* operation in the anonymous model, a random value is concatenated to the TID of the root, and in the deterministic version, the UID of the root itself is concatenated to the TID. This way, the algorithm breaks the symmetry and, eventually, one of the trees will overrun all other trees and will become the spanning tree.

We use an approach inspired by [4] rather than by the others due to its time efficiency. The other approaches first dismantle the "fake" trees (those that contain fake roots), before building the new one. The dismantling may take more time than the diameter, because these fake trees may be deeper than the diameter (since the adversary composed those trees). In the current study, a new tree can be constructed while overcoming the old trees, instead of waiting for their dismantling.

A disadvantage of the algorithm described in [4] lies in the mechanism of *Extend-ID*. Since this action concatenates a value to the TID each time there is an ID Collision, the TID of such a tree becomes a sequence of values of an unbounded length. In other words, the adversary might initialize the TID of one of the trees to be very long, much longer than $O(\log n)$. In this case, the actual time complexity of the algorithm won't be $O(d)$, since the messages won't be of $O(\log n)$ bits length. Just bounding the length of TID would not solve the problem. Had we just bounded it, the adversary might have initialized multiple roots to have the maximum ID, causing an ID collision, and the size bounding would make it impossible to overcome such a collision.

To overcome this problem, we propose a different approach for solving the ID Collision in the deterministic model. The *TID* is a fixed size register. In addition, we use the SS-Sync mechanism for synchronizing and stabilizing the algorithm. We use the *clock* value of SS-Sync as an indicator of priority over neighbors when constructing the spanning tree.

Unlike the algorithm in [4], there is no mechanism for ID collision detection. Every root v with $TID_v \neq UID_v$ performs an *Increment-ID* operation by initiating a synchronized action of SS-Sync (that is, v sets $act_v \leftarrow true$). During the execution of *SynchronizedAction* of *SS-Sync*, $clock_v$ is advanced and $TID_v \leftarrow UID_v$. This way, v increases its priority (detailed later) and makes the tree TID unique, since the UID of v is unique.

Priority Relation. Let u and v be two processes in the system. A mutual neighbour w prefers to join as a child of the process with the higher priority, defined as follows. When we compare two processes' priority, we use the $\prec$ notation. The meaning of $v \prec u$ is:

$$clock_v <_l clock_u$$
$$\text{or}$$
$$clock_v = clock_u \text{ and } TID_v < TID_u$$
$$\text{or}$$
$$clock_v = clock_u \text{ and } TID_v = TID_u \text{ and } distance_v > distance_u$$

Since *clock* implements a Finite Incrementing System, priority relation on *clock* values $<_l$ is defined for locally comparable values only. If there are more than one neighboring processes with equal priority, then, assuming a process's edges are numbered, the neighbor with the maximum edge connecting to it is chosen.

5 The Algorithm Formal Description

Each process i carries a constant *UID*, unique in the system. Each process i maintains the following variables:

- *TID* - The TID of the tree.
- *parent* - A pointer to the process which is supposed to be the parent of i in the tree.
- *distance* - This is supposed to represent the distance over the tree to the root r. It is measured by the number of hops between i and r.

Each process i maintains SS-Sync mechanism. SS-Sync main procedure is executed explicitly by the spanning tree algorithm main procedure. Each process i executes the procedure *Main* (figure 2) on each round of execution. The procedure *Main* calls the procedure *Maximize-Priority* (figure 3) and the SS-Sync main procedure (figure 1). In figure 4, the *SynchronizedAction* of SS-Sync is presented.

```
 1: /* Read all neighbors' variables */
 2: LOOK − AT − NEIGHBORS;
 3: if SS − Sync.IsStabilized then
 4:    /* The code of Maximize − Priority appears in figure 3 */
 5:    Maximize − Priority;
 6:    SS − Sync.act_i ← false;
 7:    /*If p is root and has to increment its TID */
 8:    if distance_i ≐ 0 and TID_i ≠ UID_i then
 9:       /* Increment − ID */
10:       SS − Sync.act_i ← true;
11:    end if
12: end if
13: SS − Sync Main Procedure;
```

Fig. 2. Main - Executed in every round for process i

```
1: /* Join the tree with highest TID and address the fake roots problem */
2: /* l - pointer to the neighbor with maximum priority */
3: let l ← MAX(u ∈ N̄(i));
4:
5: /* If there is a neighbor with higher priority than i, join it as a child. Otherwise
   become root */
6: if i ≺ l then
7:    TID_i ← TID_l;
8:    distance_i ← distance_l + 1;
9:    parent_i ← l;
10: else
11:    distance_i ← 0;
12:    parent_i ← null;
13: end if
```

Fig. 3. Maximize-Priority for process i

```
1: TID_i ← UID_i;
```

Fig. 4. SynchronizedAction - executed by SS-Sync during NormalAction if $act_i = true$

6   Correctness and Complexity Proofs

We prove that after $O(d)$ rounds, the graph induced by the *parent* pointers forms a spanning forest. Then we prove that from this state on, the number of roots can only reduce, and that no new roots appear. We prove that eventually, after $O(d)$ rounds there remains only one root and that the graph induced by the *parent* pointers forms a shortest path spanning tree. Moreover, from this round on that graph will not change.

By the properties of SS-Sync, there exists a round $t \geq 0$, where all processes' *clock* values are locally comparable, and remain locally comparable from this round on as long as no new failures occur. We analyse the behavior of spanning tree algorithm starting from $t_1 \equiv t + 1$.

Lemma 1. *After round t_1, for any process v, v's priority at any round t cannot decrease with the respect to v's priority at round $t - 1$.*

Proof. During Maximize-Priority, a process can became a child of a higher priority process (causing increase of priority), or a root (also causing increase of priority). During SS-Sync action (following Maximize-Priority), the only enabled action is NormalAction, increasing priority also. Note, that by the definition of the $<_l$ operator, this holds also if *clock* value overlaps.   □

Lemma 2. *After round t_1, for any processes v, u:*
   $parent(u) = v \Rightarrow u \prec v$

Proof. After executing Maximize-Priority, every process becomes a child of a higher priority process, or becomes a root. Hence, if at round t, a process p becomes a child of q, then $\gamma_t.p \prec \gamma_{t-1}.q$. By lemma 1, $\gamma_{t-1}.q \prec \gamma_t.q$. Hence, $\gamma_t.p \prec \gamma_t.q$. □

Theorem 3. *After round t_1, the graph induced by the parent pointers forms a spanning forest.*

Proof. Let us assume there is a cycle $p_1, p_2, ..., p_n$ in the graph induced by the parent pointers. In this case, by transitivity of priority relation and lemma 1 there must be two processs p_k, p_{k+1}, where $p_{k+1} \prec p_k$. This contradicts lemma 2. □

Lemma 4. *After round t_1, a non-root process cannot become a root.*

Proof. After t_1, every non-root v has a parent u with higher priority by lemma 2. Let us assume by contradiction that v becomes a root at round $t > t_1$. The only way for v to become a root is to become the highest priority process among $\overline{\mathcal{N}}(v)$. Since no neighbor of v decrease its priority (by lemma 1), v had to increase its priority. The only way for a non-root to increase priority is by executing NormalAction of SS-Sync. Let us assume that at round $t - 1$, the process v executed NormalAction, which caused v to become a root at round t. Thus, at round $t - 1$, v has at least one neighbor u, such that $clock_u = \varphi(clock_v)$ (see line 3 in figure 1). Let us assume that u has the maximal priority among such neighbors. Thus, at round $t-1$, v had to become u's child (see lines 3-6 in figure 3). After executing *NormalAction*, $v \prec u$ (since $distance_v = distance_u + 1$), hence v can't become a root at round t. □

Lemma 5. *After round t_1, a root r performs Increment-ID at most once.*

Proof. After performing *Increment-ID*, $TID_r \equiv UID_r$. Hence, another *Increment-ID* will not be executed (see line 8 in figure 2). The value of TID_r might change after performing *Increment-ID* only if r joins a higher priority tree as a child. In this case, *Increment-ID* will not be performed either, since only roots can perform it. □

Lemma 6. *If at round t_1 there is a root r, such that $TID_r \neq UID_r$, then in at most $O(d)$ rounds, TID_r becomes equal to UID_r (unless r becomes a non-root).*

Proof. In this case, r performs $act_r \leftarrow true$, asking *SS-Sync* to execute the synchronized action. By the properties of SS-Sync, it will be executed in at most $O(d)$ rounds, performing $TID_r \leftarrow UID_r$. □

Lemma 7. *Let t_2 be the round when all roots executed their Increment-ID action. Then, after t_2, in at most $O(d)$ rounds, all clock values in the system become equal. Moreover, from this round on, clock values are not changed any more.*

Proof. Since no root needs to perform an additional Increment-ID action (by lemmas 5 and 6), and there are no new roots by lemma 4, no process performs

$act \leftarrow true$. Hence, by the properties of SS-Sync, in $O(d)$ rounds all the clocks in the system become equal. After this, no action of SS-Sync is enabled on any process. Hence, the *clock* values don't change any more.   □

Let t_3 be the round when all the clocks in the system become equal, as described in lemma 7.

Theorem 8. *In $O(d)$ rounds after t_3, only one root remains, and the graph induced by parent pointers forms a spanning tree.*

Proof. After round t_3, the graph induced by *parent* pointers is a spanning forest (by theorem 3), and every root (and tree) has a unique TID (by lemma 6). From this point on, the algorithm acts similar to the basic Distributed Bellman-Ford algorithm, and the graph induced by parent pointers forms a spanning tree in $O(d)$ rounds.   □

7   Conclusion and Future Research

In this research, we propose the first time-optimal spanning tree algorithm for synchronous systems in the common model with a standard register size (or, similarly, message size) of $O(\log n)$ bits. It is efficient in terms of time, stabilizing in $O(d)$ rounds.

In addition, we present a self stabilizing time optimal silent synchronous synchronizer with a phase clock - SS-Sync, and show an application of a synchronizer with a phase clock for spanning tree construction. SS-Sync is a multi-purpose tool, which can be used for a variety of tasks, like mutual exclusion and synchronization.

It may seem that SS-Sync implements a self-stabilizing *reset* algorithm. Unfortunately, this is not the case, since the the ResetAction of SS-Sync may not affect all the processes in the system (since it affects only those processes whose *clock* values are in *stab*).

However, using the spanning tree, the task of *distributed reset* becomes quite easy, as shown in [10]. The reset operation can be controlled by the root, making it time optimal.

Note, that the spanning tree algorithm itself can be executed successfully in an asynchronous system, given a silent asynchronous self stabilizing phase clock algorithm replacing SS-Sync. For example, replacing SS-Sync with the silent algorithm of [11], would give us an asynchronous self-stabilizing spanning tree algorithm with standard message size, which stabilizes in $O(d + \alpha)$ time units, where α stands for the upper bound on the size of the largest hole in the system. Hence, finding a time-optimal silent asynchronous self stabilizing phase clock algorithm may be the main point of interest in the future work.

Another interesting task might be adjusting the current algorithm for *anonymous* systems, where the nodes do not possess unique IDs. Since [4] deals with such systems, this goal seems to be achievable using the same method suggested there.

References

1. Afek, Y., Bremler-Barr, A.: Self-stabilizing unidirectional network algorithms by power supply. Chicago J. Theor. Comput. Sci. (1998)
2. Afek, Y., Kutten, S., Yung, M.: Memory-efficient self stabilizing protocols for general networks. In: van Leeuwen, J., Santoro, N. (eds.) WDAG 1990. LNCS, vol. 486, pp. 15–28. Springer, Heidelberg (1991)
3. Afek, Y., Kutten, S., Yung, M.: The local detection paradigm and its application to self-stabilization. Theor. Comput. Sci., 199–229 (1997)
4. Aggarwal, S., Kutten, S.: Time optimal self-stabilizing spanning tree algorithms. In: Shyamasundar, R.K. (ed.) FSTTCS 1993. LNCS, vol. 761, pp. 400–410. Springer, Heidelberg (1993)
5. Arora, A., Gouda, M.G.: Distributed reset. In: Veni Madhavan, C.E., Nori, K.V. (eds.) FSTTCS 1990. LNCS, vol. 472, pp. 316–331. Springer, Heidelberg (1990)
6. Awerbuch, B.: Complexity of network synchronization. J. ACM 32(4), 804–823 (1985)
7. Awerbuch, B., Cidon, I., Kutten, S.: Optimal maintenance of a spanning tree. J. ACM 55(4) (2008)
8. Awerbuch, B., Kutten, S., Mansour, Y., Patt-Shamir, B., Varghese, G.: A time-optimal self-stabilizing synchronizer using a phase clock. IEEE Trans. Dependable Sec. Comput. 4(3), 180–190 (2007)
9. Awerbuch, B., Mansour, Y., Kutten, S., Patt-Shamir, B., Varghese, G.: Time optimal self-stabilizing synchronization. In: STOC, pp. 652–661 (1993)
10. Awerbuch, B., Patt-Shamir, B., Varghese, G.: Self-stabilization by local checking and correction. In: FOCS, pp. 268–277 (1991)
11. Boulinier, C., Petit, F., Villain, V.: When graph theory helps self-stabilization. In: PODC, pp. 150–159 (2004)
12. Burman, J., Kutten, S.: Time optimal asynchronous self-stabilizing spanning tree. In: Pelc, A. (ed.) DISC 2007. LNCS, vol. 4731, pp. 92–107. Springer, Heidelberg (2007)
13. Petit, F., Boulinier, C., Villain, V.: Synchronous vs. asynchronous unison. Algoritmica 51(1), 61–80 (2008)
14. Chen, N.-S., Yu, H.-P., Huang, S.-T.: A self-stabilizing algorithm for constructing spanning trees. Inf. Process. Lett., 147–151 (1991)
15. Cournier, A.: A new polynomial silent stabilizing spanning-tree construction algorithm, 141–153 (2009)
16. Datta, A.K., Larmore, L.L., Piniganti, H.: Self-stabilizing leader election in dynamic networks. In: Dolev, S., Cobb, J., Fischer, M., Yung, M. (eds.) SSS 2010. LNCS, vol. 6366, pp. 35–49. Springer, Heidelberg (2010)
17. Datta, A.K., Larmore, L.L., Vemula, P.: An o(n)-time self-stabilizing leader election algorithm. J. Parallel Distrib. Comput. 71(11), 1532–1544 (2011)
18. Dijkstra, E.W.: Self stabilization in spite of distributed control. Comm. ACM 17, 167–180 (1974)
19. Dolev, D., Shavit, N.: Bounded concurrent time-stamping. SIAM J. Comput., 418–455 (1997)
20. Dolev, S., Israeli, A., Moran, S.: Self-stabilization of dynamic systems assuming only read/write atomicity. In: PODC, pp. 103–117 (1990)
21. Dubois, S., Guerraoui, R.: Introducing speculation in self-stabilization: an application to mutual exclusion. In: PODC, pp. 290–298 (2013)

22. Gallager, R.G., Humblet, P.A., Spira, P.M.: A distributed algorithm for minimum-weight spanning trees. ACM Trans. Program. Lang. Syst. 5(1), 66–77 (1983)
23. Gosh, S., Gupta, A., Pemmaraju, S.V.: A fault containing self stabilizing algorithm for spanning trees. Journal of Computing and Information 2, 322–338 (1996)
24. Gouda, M.G., Herman, T.: Stabilizing unison. Inf. Process. Lett. 35(4), 171–175 (1990)
25. Herman, T., Ghosh, S.: Stabilizing phase-clocks. Inf. Process. Lett. 54(5), 259–265 (1995)
26. Kurose, J.F., Ross, K.W.: Computer Networking: A Top-Down Approach, 2nd edn. Addison Wesley (2003)
27. Kutten, S., Porat, A.: Maintenance of a spanning tree in dynamic networks. In: Jayanti, P. (ed.) DISC 1999. LNCS, vol. 1693, pp. 342–355. Springer, Heidelberg (1999)
28. Matias, Y., Afek, Y.: Simple and efficient election algorithms for anonymous networks. In: Bermond, J.-C., Raynal, M. (eds.) WDAG 1989. LNCS, vol. 392, pp. 183–194. Springer, Heidelberg (1989)
29. Peleg, D.: Distributed computing: a locality-sensitive approach. Society for Industrial and Applied Mathematics (2000)
30. Perlman, R.J.: Fault-tolerant broadcast of routing information. Computer Networks 7, 395–405 (1983)
31. Dolev, S., Israeli, A., Moran, S.: Uniform dynamic self-stabilizing leader election. In: Toueg, S., Kirousis, L.M., Spirakis, P.G. (eds.) WDAG 1991. LNCS, vol. 579, pp. 167–180. Springer, Heidelberg (1992)

Proving Non-opacity

Mohsen Lesani and Jens Palsberg

UCLA, University of California, Los Angeles
{lesani,palsberg}@ucla.edu

Abstract. Guerraoui and Kapalka defined opacity as a safety criterion for transactional memory algorithms in 2008. Researchers have shown how to prove opacity, while little is known about pitfalls that can lead to non-opacity. In this paper, we identify two problems that lead to non-opacity, we present automatic tool support for finding such problems, and we prove an impossibility result. We first show that the well-known TM algorithms DSTM and McRT don't satisfy opacity. DSTM suffers from a write-skew anomaly, while McRT suffers from a write-exposure anomaly. We then prove that for direct-update TM algorithms, opacity is incompatible with a liveness criterion called local progress, even for fault-free systems. Our result implies that if TM algorithm designers want both opacity and local progress, they should avoid direct-update algorithms.

1 Introduction

Transactional Memory. Atomic statements can simplify concurrent programming that involves shared memory. Transactional memory (TM) [24, 35] interleaves the bodies of atomic statements as much as possible, while guaranteeing noninterleaving semantics. Thus, the noninterleaving in the semantics can coexist with a high degree of parallelism in the implementation. TM aborts an operation that cannot complete without violating the semantics. The use of TM provides atomicity, deadlock freedom, and composability [21], and increases programmer productivity compared to use of locks [30,32]. Researchers have developed formal semantics [1, 26, 29] and a wide variety of implementations of the TM interface in both software [9, 10, 22, 23, 33] and hardware [2, 18]. IBM supports TM in its Blue Gene/Q processor [19], and Intel supports transactional synchronization primitives in its new processor microarchitecture Haswell [7].

Safety. A TM interface consists of the operations `read`, `write`, and `commit`. The task of a TM algorithm is to implement those three operations. What is a correct TM algorithm? The traditional safety criterion for database transactions is strict serializability [31]. For TM algorithms, strict serializability [34] requires that committed transactions together have an equivalent sequential execution, that is, an execution that could also happen if the transactions execute noninterleaved. However, to ensure semantic correctness, active and aborted transactions should execute correctly too. This observation has led researchers to define the stronger safety criteria opacity [13], VWC [25], and TMS1 [11]. We will focus on opacity,

Y. Afek (Ed.): DISC 2013, LNCS 8205, pp. 106–120, 2013.

which is the strongest safety criterion and requires that *all* transactions together have an equivalent sequential execution.

Verification. Researchers have shown how to verify the safety of TM algorithms. In pioneering work, Tasiran [36] proved serializability for a class of TM algorithms. Cohen et al. [5,6] were the first to use a model checker to verify strict serializability of TM algorithms for a bounded number of threads and memory locations. Later, Guerraoui and Kapalka [17] proved opacity of two-phase locking with a graph-based approach that is related to an earlier approach to serializability. Guerraoui et al. [14–16] used a model checker to verify opacity of TM algorithms that use an unbounded number of threads and memory locations. Their approach relies on four assumptions about TM algorithms. In follow-up work, Emmi et al. [12] used a theorem prover to generate invariants that are sufficient to prove strict serializability. Their proofs work for TM algorithms that use an unbounded number of threads and memory locations. Later, Lesani et al. [27] presented a TM verification framework based on IO automata and simulation. We identify specific pitfalls that lead to non-opacity and show how a tool can automatically find such pitfalls.

The Problem: Which pitfalls lead to non-opacity?

Our Results: We identify two problems that lead to non-opacity, we present a tool that automatically finds such problems, we find problems with DSTM and McRT, and we prove an impossibility result.

We show that the well-known TM algorithms DSTM and McRT don't satisfy opacity. These results may be surprising because previous work has proved that DSTM and McRT satisfy opacity [15,16]. However, there is no conflict and no mystery: the previous work focused on abstractions of DSTM and McRT, while we work with specifications that are much closer to original formulations of DSTM and McRT. Thus, we experience a common phenomenon: once we refine a specification, we may lose some properties.

Let us recall common terminology. A TM algorithm is a *deferred-update* algorithm if every transaction that writes a value must commit before other transactions can read that value. All other TM algorithms are *direct-update* algorithms. DSTM is a deferred-update algorithm while McRT is a direct-update algorithm.

DSTM suffers from a write-skew anomaly, while McRT suffers from a write-exposure anomaly. The write-skew anomaly is an incorrectness pattern that is known in the setting of databases [3]. The write-exposure anomaly happens when a direct-update TM algorithm exposes written values to other transactions before the transaction commits.

We present fixes to both DSTM and McRT that we conjecture make the fixed algorithms satisfy opacity. Interestingly, we note that writers can limit the progress of readers in the fixed McRT algorithm. This is an instance of a general pattern: we prove that for direct-update TM algorithms, opacity is incompatible with a liveness criterion called local progress [4], even for fault-free systems.

Our result implies that if TM algorithm designers want both opacity and local progress, they should avoid direct-update algorithms.

We hope that our observations and tool can help TM algorithm designers to avoid the write-skew and write-exposure pitfalls, and to be aware that if local progress is a goal, then deferred-update algorithms may be the only option.

The Rest of the Paper. In Section 2 we recall the definition of transaction histories, and in Section 3 we introduce bug patterns that violate opacity. In Section 4, we introduce our tool and in Section 5, we show how our tool automatically finds that DSTM and McRT don't satisfy opacity. In Section 6, we prove that for direct-update TM algorithms, opacity and local progress are incompatible. The full version of the paper has appendices in which we give a formal definition of opacity, prove our theorems, and give details of DSTM, McRT, base objects, and our tool.

2   Histories

Guerraoui and Kapalka [13] defined opacity in terms of *transaction histories*. A transaction history is a record of what happened at the interface of a TM. For example, $H_{WS}, H_{WE}, H_{WE2}, H_1, H_2$ are all transaction histories:

$$H_{WS} = Init \cdot read_{T_1}(1){:}v_0 \cdot read_{T_2}(1){:}v_0 \cdot read_{T_1}(2){:}v_0 \cdot read_{T_2}(2){:}v_0 \cdot$$
$$write_{T_1}(1, -v_0) \cdot write_{T_2}(2, -v_0) \cdot$$
$$inv_{T_1}(commit_{T_1}) \cdot inv_{T_2}(commit_{T_2}) \cdot ret_{T_1}(\mathbb{C}) \cdot ret_{T_2}(\mathbb{C})$$
$$H_{WE} = Init \cdot inv_{T_1}(read_{T_1}(2)) \cdot write_{T_2}(2, v_1) \cdot ret_{T_1}(v_1) \cdot$$
$$inv_{T_2}(read_{T_2}(1)) \cdot write_{T_1}(1, v_1) \cdot ret_{T_2}(v_1) \cdot$$
$$inv_{T_1}(commit_{T_1}) \cdot inv_{T_2}(commit_{T_2}) \cdot ret_{T_1}(\mathbb{A}) \cdot ret_{T_2}(\mathbb{A})$$
$$H_{WE2} = Init \cdot inv_{T_1}((write_{T_1}(1, v_1)) \cdot read_{T_2}(1){:}v_1 \cdot ret_{T_1}(ok) \cdot$$
$$write_{T_1}(1, v_2) \cdot commit_{T_1}(){:}\mathbb{C} \cdot commit_{T_2}(){:}\mathbb{A}$$
$$H_1 = Init \cdot H_0 \cdot write_{T_2}(2, j) \cdot read_{T_1}(2){:}j \cdot write_{T_1}(1, j) \cdot read_{T_2}(1){:}\mathbb{A}$$
$$H_2 = Init \cdot H_0 \cdot write_{T_2}(2, j) \cdot read_{T_1}(2){:}j \cdot write_{T_1}(1, j) \cdot read_{T_2}(1){:}j$$

where $Init$ is described below and H_0 is a transaction history that does not contain a write operation that writes value j.

The invocation event $inv_T(o.n_T(v))$ denotes the invocation of method n on object o in thread T with the argument v. The response event $ret_T(v)$ denotes a response that returns v in the thread T. We will use the term completed method call to denote a sequence of an invocation event followed by the matching response event (with the same thread identifier). We use $o.n_T(v){:}v'$ to denote the completed method call $inv_T(o.n_T(v)) \cdot ret_T(v')$. We use $o.write_T(i, v)$ as an abbreviation for $o.write_T(i, v){:}ok$. Let i range over the set of memory locations, v range over the set of values, and t range over the set of transactions. The interface of a transactional memory object has three methods $read_t(i)$, $write_t(i, v)$ and $commit_t$ and we write calls to those methods without a receiver object. The current object *this* is the implicit receiver of these calls and thus they are called *this* method calls. The method call $read_t(i)$ returns the value of location i or $\mathbb{A}$ (if the transaction is aborted). The method $write_t(i, v)$ writes v to location i and returns *ok* or returns $\mathbb{A}$. The method $commit_t$ tries to commit transaction t and returns $\mathbb{C}$ (if the transaction is successfully committed) or returns $\mathbb{A}$ (if it is aborted). In general, a transaction history H is of the form $Init \cdot H'$, where $Init$ is the transaction $write_{T_0}(1, v_0), \ldots, write_{T_0}(m, v_0), commit_{T_0}{:}\mathbb{C}$ that initializes every location to v_0, and for all $T \in H'$: $H'|T$ is a prefix of $O.F$ where O is a sequence of reads $read_T(i){:}v$ and writes $write_T(i, v)$ (for some T, i, and v) and F is one of the following sequences: (1) $inv_T(read_T(i))$, $ret_T(\mathbb{A})$ (for some T and i), (2) $inv_T(write_T(i, v))$, $ret_T(\mathbb{A})$ (for some T i, and v), (3) $inv_T(commit_T)$, $ret_T(\mathbb{C})$, or (4) $inv_T(commit_T)$, $ret_T(\mathbb{A})$ (for some T). For a history H, we use $H|T$ to denote the subsequence of all events of T in H. Note that H' is an interleaving of the invocation and response events of different transactions.

3   Opacity and Bug Patterns

Guerraoui and Kapalka [17] defined *final-state opaque* transaction histories. In their earlier, seminal paper on opacity [13], they used the shorter term *opaque* for such histories; we will use opaque and final-state opaque interchangeably. In Appendix A, we formalize opacity as a set of histories called *FinalStateOpaque* and we prove that none of the transaction histories $H_{WS}, H_{WE}, H_{WE2}, H_1, H_2$ are opaque.

Theorem 1. $\{H_{WS}, H_{WE}, H_{WE2}, H_1, H_2\} \cap FinalStateOpaque = \emptyset$.

We say that H_{WS}, H_{WE}, H_1, H_2 are *bug patterns*, because if a TM can produce any of them, then the TM violates opacity. Let us now focus on H_{WS}, H_{WE} and later turn to H_{WE2}, H_1, H_2.

Write-skew Anomaly. The transaction history H_{WS} is evidence of the write-skew anomaly. Let us illustrate the write-skew anomaly with the following narrative.

Assume that a person has two bank accounts that are stored at locations i_1 and i_2 and that have the initial balances v_0 and v_0, where $v_0 > 0$. Assume also that the regulations of the bank require the *sum* of a person's accounts to be positive or zero. Thus, the bank will authorize a transaction that updates the value of one of the accounts with the previous value of the account minus the sum of the two accounts because the transaction makes the sum of the two accounts zero.

Now we interpret the narrative in the context of H_{WS}, which is a record of the execution of two "bank-authorized" transactions. In H_{WS} the transaction T_1 reads the values of both accounts and updates i_1 with $v_0 - (v_0 + v_0) = -v_0$. Similarly, the transaction T_2 reads the values of both accounts and updates i_2 with $-v_0$. But in H_{WS} both transactions commit, which results in a state that violates the regulations of the bank: $-v_0$ is the balance of both accounts.

The problem with H_{WS} stems from that the TM that produced H_{WS} doesn't guarantee noninterleaving semantics of the transactions. In a noninterleaving semantics, either T_1 executes before T_2, or T_2 executes before T_1. However, if we order T_1 before T_2, then the values read by T_2 violate correctness; and if we order T_2 before T_1, then the values read by T_1 violate correctness.

Experts may notice that since H_{WS} is not opaque and all the transactions in H_{WS} are committed, H_{WS} is not even serializable. However, H_{WS} does satisfy *snapshot isolation*, which is a necessary, though not a sufficient, condition for serializability. A history satisfies snapshot isolation if its reads observe a consistent snapshot. Snapshot isolation prevents observing some of the updates of a committing transaction before the commit and some of the rest of the updates after the commit. Algorithms that support only snapshot isolation but not serializability are known to be prone to the write-skew anomaly, as shown by Berenson et al. [3]. Note that H_{WS} satisfies snapshot isolation but suffers from the write-skew anomaly. A TM algorithm that satisfies serializability (and opacity) must both provide snapshot isolation and prevent the write-skew anomaly.

Write-Exposure Anomaly. The transaction history H_{WE} is evidence of the write-exposure anomaly. The two locations i_1 and i_2 each has initial value v_0 and no *committed* transaction writes a different value to them, and yet the two read operations return the value v_1. Write-exposure happens when a transaction that eventually fails to commit *writes* to a location i and *exposes* the written value to other transactions that read from i. Thus, active or aborting transactions can read inconsistent values. This violates opacity even if these transactions are eventually prevented from committing.

4   Automatic Bug Finding

We present a language called Samand in which a program consists of a TM algorithm, a user program, and an assertion. A Samand program is *correct* if every execution of the user program satisfies the assertion. Our tool solves constraints to decide whether a Samand program is correct. Our approach is reminiscent of bounded model checking: we use concurrency constraints instead of Boolean constraints, and we use an SMT solver instead of a SAT solver.

Our Language. We present Samand via two examples. We will use a sugared notation, for simplicity, while in an appendix of the full paper, we list the actual Samand code for both examples. The first example is

$$(\text{Core DSTM}, P_{WS}, \neg WS)$$

where Core DSTM (see Figure 1) is a core version of the TM algorithm DSTM, and the user program and assertion are:

$$P_{WS} = \{read_{T_1}(1){:}r_{11} \ read_{T_1}(2){:}r_{12} \ write_{T_1}(0, v_1) \ commit_{T_1}(){:}c_1\} \ ||$$
$$\{read_{T_2}(1){:}r_{21} \ read_{T_2}(2){:}r_{22} \ write_{T_2}(1, v_1) \ commit_{T_2}(){:}c_2\}$$
$$WS = (r_{11} = v_0 \ \wedge \ r_{12} = v_0 \ \wedge \ r_{21} = v_0 \ \wedge \ r_{22} = v_0 \ \wedge \ c_1 = \mathbb{C} \ \wedge \ c_2 = \mathbb{C})$$

Note that the assertion WS specifies a *set* of buggy histories of the user program; the history H_{WS} is a member of that set. The second example is

$$(\text{Core McRT}, P_{WE}, \neg WE)$$

where Core McRT (see Figure 2) is a core version of the TM algorithm McRT, and the user program and assertion are:

$$P_{WE} = \{read_{T_1}(2):r_1 \;\; write_{T_1}(1, v_1) \;\; commit_{T_1}():c_1\} \;\|$$
$$\{write_{T_2}(2, v_1) \;\; read_{T_2}(1):r_2 \;\; commit_{T_2}():c_2\}$$
$$WE = (r_1 = v_1 \wedge r_2 = v_1 \wedge c_1 = \mathbb{A} \wedge c_2 = \mathbb{A})$$

Like above, the assertion WE specifies a *set* of buggy histories of the user program; the history H_{WE} is a member of that set.

Samand enables specification of loop-free user programs. Every user program has a finite number of possible executions and those executions all terminate.

Each of Core DSTM and Core McRT has three parts: declarations, method definitions, and a program order. Let us take a closer look at these algorithms.

Core DSTM has two shared objects *state* and *start*, and one thread-local object *rset*. Samand supports five types of objects namely `AtomicRegister`, `AtomicCASRegister`, `Lock`, `TryLock`, and `BasicRegister`, as well as arrays and records of such objects. Atomic registers, atomic compare-and-swap (cas) registers, locks, and try-locks are linearizable objects, while basic registers behave as registers only if they are not accessed concurrently. Core DSTM declares one record type *Loc* that has three fields.

Core DSTM has five methods *read*, *write*, *commit*, *stableValue*, and *validate*. Among those, a user program can call the first three, while the *read* method calls the last two, and the *commit* method calls *validate*. Each method is a list of labeled statements that can be method calls on objects, simple arithmetic statements, dynamic memory allocation statements, and if and return statements. The **new** operator dynamically allocates an instance of a record type and returns a reference to it.

Core McRT has three shared objects, two thread-local objects, four methods, and a specification of the program order.

Core McRT specifies the program order $R03 \prec_p R04$, $C03 \prec_p C04$. The idea is to enable out-of-order execution yet maintain fine-grained control of the execution. The execution of the algorithm in a Samand program can be any out-of-order execution that respects the following: the program control dependencies, data dependencies, lock happens-before orders, the declared program orders, that each linearizable object satisfies the linearizability conditions, and that each basic register behaves as a register if it is not accessed concurrently. A method call m_1 is data-dependent on a method call m_2 if an argument of m_1 is the return variable of m_2. If a method call m_2 is data-dependent on a method call m_1 then m_1 must precede m_2 in any execution. For example, in Core McRT, the statement $R03$ must precede $R04$ in any execution. Each statement of the if and else blocks of an if statement is control-dependent on the if statement.

Intuitively, a program execution must respect both the wishes of the programmer and the guarantees of the objects. We can use fences to implement the declared orders.

Constraints. Our tool uses the following notion of constraints to decide whether a Samand program is correct. Let l, x, v range over finite sets of labels, variables, and values, respectively. Let the *execution condition* of a statement be the conjunction of all enclosing if (or else) conditions. A constraint is an assertion about transaction histories and is generated by the following grammar:

$$
\begin{aligned}
a ::= &\ obj(l) = o \mid name(l) = n \mid thread(l) = T \mid && \text{Assertion} \\
&\ arg1(l) = u \mid arg2(l) = u \mid retv(l) = x \mid \\
&\ cond(l) = c \mid exec(l) \mid l \prec l \mid \neg a \mid a \wedge a \\
u ::= &\ v \mid x && \text{Variable or Value} \\
c ::= &\ u = u \mid u < u \mid \neg c \mid c \wedge c && \text{Condition}
\end{aligned}
$$

The assertions $obj(l) = o$, $name(l) = n$, $thread(l) = T$, $arg1(l) = u$, $arg2(l) = u$, $retv(l) = x$ and $cond(l) = c$ respectively assert that the receiver object of l is o, the method name of l is n, the calling thread of l is T, the first argument of l is u, the second argument of l is u, the return value of l is x, and the execution condition of l is c. The assertion $exec(l)$ asserts that l is executed. The assertion $l \prec l'$ asserts that l is executed before l'.

The satisfiability problem is to decide, for a given constraint, whether there exists a transaction history that satisfies the constraint. One can show easily that the satisfiability problem is NP-complete.

From Programs to Constraints. We map a Samand program to a set of constraints such that the Samand program is correct if and only if the constraints are unsatisfiable.

Let us first define the run-time labels for a program. A run-time label denotes a run-time program point and is either a program label (if the program point is at the top level) or a concatenation of two program labels (if the program point is in a procedure). In the latter case, the additional label is the program label of the caller.

Let us now define the labels and variables that we use in the constraints for a Samand program. For each call we define two labels: the run-time label of the call concatenated with Inv and with Ret, respectively. For other statements we have a single label, namely the run-time label. For each local variable, we define a family of constraint variables, namely one for each caller: each constraint variable is the concatenation of the program label of the caller and the name of the local variable.

Next, we define two auxiliary concepts that are helpful during constraint generation. The *program order* is a total order on program labels. We define the program order to be the transitive closure of the following orders: the control and data dependencies, the declared program order, the orders imposed by locks, that each invocation event is before its matching response event and that each method call inside a *this* method call is before the invocation and after the response event of the *this* method call. The *execution order* is the ordering of labels in a particular history.

We have five sources of constraints: the method calls, the execution conditions, the program order, the base objects, and the assertion.

First, for each run-time label of a method call, we generate constraints that assert the receiver object, the method name, the calling thread, the arguments, the return variable, and the execution condition. For each *this* method call, we generate constraints that assert that the actual parameters and the formal parameters are equal, that the response event of the *this* method call is executed if and only if one (and only one) of its return statements are executed, and that if a return statement is executed, the argument of the return statement is equal to the returned variable of the *this* method call.

Second, we generate constraints that assert that a statement is executed if and only if its execution condition is valid and no prior return statement is executed.

Third, we generate constraints that assert that if l_1 is before l_2 in the program order and the statements with labels l_1, l_2 are both executed, then l_1 is before l_2 in the execution order.

Fourth, we generate constraints that assert the safety properties of the base objects. For each linearizable object, there should be a linearization order of the executed method calls on the object. For example, consider an atomic register. The *write* method call that is linearized last in the set of *write* method calls that are linearized before a *read* method call R is called the *writer* method call for R. The return value of each *read* method call is equal to the argument of its writer method call. For a second example, consider an atomic cas register. A *successful write* is either a *write* method call or a successful *cas* method call. The *written value* of a successful write is its first argument, if it is a *write* method call or is its second argument, if it is a *cas* method call. For a method call m, the successful write method call that is linearized last in the set of successful write method calls that are linearized before m is called the *writer* method call for m. The return value of each *read* method call is equal to the written value of its writer method call. A *cas* method succeeds if and only if its first argument is equal to the written value of its writer method call. For a third example, consider a lock object. The last method call linearized before a *lock* method call is an *unlock* method call. Similarly, the last method call linearized before an *unlock* method call is a lock method call. For a fourth example, consider a try-lock object. We call a *lock* method call or successful *tryLock* method call, a *successful lock* method call. We call a *lock* method call, successful *tryLock* method call or *unlock* method call, a *mutating* method call. The last *mutating* method call linearized before a successful *lock* method call is an *unlock* method call. Similarly, the last *mutating* method call linearized before an *unlock* method call is a *successful lock* method all. A *tryLock* succeeds if the last *mutating* method before it in the linearization order is an *unlock*. It fails otherwise (if the last *mutating* method before it in the linearization order is a *successful lock*). The rules for the return value of *read* method calls are similar to the rule for *tryLock* method calls.

Fifth, we map the assertion in the Samand program to the *negation* of that assertion. As a result, we can use a constraint solver to search for a transaction history that violates the assertion in the Samand program.

Our Tool. Our tool maps a Samand program to constraints in SMT2 format and then uses the Z3 SMT solver [8] to solve the constraints. If the constraints are unsatisfiable, then the Samand program is correct. If the constraints are satisfiable, then the Samand program is incorrect and the constraint solver will find a transaction history that violates the assertion in the Samand program. Our tool proceeds to display that transaction history as a program trace in a graphical user interface. Our tool and some examples are available at [28].

5   Experiments

We will now report on running our tool on the two example Samand programs. Our first example concerns Core DSTM.

The Context. We believe that Core DSTM matches the *paper* on DSTM [23]. While we prove that Core DSTM doesn't satisfy opacity, we have learned from personal communication with Victor Luchangco, one of the DSTM authors, that the *implementation* of DSTM implements more than what was said in the paper and most likely satisfies opacity.

The Bug. DSTM provides snapshot isolation by validating the read set (at $R10$) before the read method returns but fails to prevent write skew anomaly. When we run our tool on $(CoreDSTM, P_{WS}, \neg WS)$, we get an execution trace that matches H_{WS}. Figure 3(a) presents an illustration of the set of DSTM executions that exhibit the bug. Note that this set is a subset of the set of executions that the bug pattern describes. In Figure 3(a), each transaction executes from top to bottom and the horizontal lines denote "barriers", that is, the operations above the line are finished before the operations below the line are started and otherwise the operations may arbitrarily interleave. For example, $read_{T_1}(2){:}v_0$ should finish execution before $write_{T_2}(2, -v_0)$ but $read_{T_1}(1){:}v_0$ and $read_{T_2}(1){:}v_0$ can arbitrarily interleave. In Figure 3(a), T_1 writes to location 1 after T_2 reads from it so T_2 does not abort T_1. T_1 invokes commit and finishes the validation phase ($C01 - C04$) before T_2 effectively commits (executes the *cas* method call at $C05$). The situation is symmetric for transaction T_2. During the validation, the two transactions still see v_0 as the stable value of the two locations; thus, both of them can pass the validation phase. Finally, both of them succeed at *cas*. Note that the counterexample happens when the two commit method calls interleave between $C04$ and $C05$.

The Fix. We learned from Victor Luchangco that the *implementation* of DSTM aborts the *writer* transactions of the locations in the read set $rset_T$ during validation of the commit method call. We model this fix by adding the following lines between $C01$ and $C02$ in Core DSTM:

foreach $(i \in dom(rset_t))$ {
    $st := start[i].read();\ t' := st.writer.read();$ **if** $(t \neq t')\ state[t'].cas(\mathbb{R}, \mathbb{A})$ }

$state : AtomicCASRegister[LocCount]$ init $\mathbb{R}$	
$start : AtomicCASRegister[TransCount]$ init $new\ Loc(T_0, 0, 0)$	
$rset : ThreadLocal\ Set$ init $\emptyset$	
$Loc\ \{writer, oldVal, newVal : BasicRegister\}$	

$R01:$ **def** $read_t(i)$	$W01:$ **def** $write_T(i, v)$
$R02:$ $s := state[t].read()$	$W02:$ $s := state[t].read()$
$R03:$ **if** $(s = \mathbb{A})$	$W03:$ **if** $(s = \mathbb{A})$
$R04:$ **return** $\mathbb{A}$	$W04:$ **return** $\mathbb{A}$
$R05:$ $st := start[i].read()$	$W05:$ $st := start[i].read()$
$R06:$ $v := stableValue_t(st)$	$W06:$ $wr := st.writer.read()$
$R07:$ $wr := st.writer.read()$	$W07:$ **if** $(wr = t)$
$R08:$ **if** $(wr \neq t)$	$W08:$ $st.newVal.write(v)$
$R09:$ $rset_t.add((i, v))$	$W09:$ **return** ok
$R10:$ $valid := validate_t()$	$W10:$ $v' := stableValue_t(st)$
$R11:$ **if** $(\neg valid)$	$W12:$ $st' := new\ Loc(T, v', v)$
$R12:$ **return** $\mathbb{A}$	$W13:$ $b := start[i].cas(st, st')$
$R13:$ **return** v	$W14:$ **if** (b)
$C01:$ **def** $commit_t$	$W15:$ **return** ok
$C02:$ $valid := validate_t()$	$W16:$ **else**
$C03:$ **if** $(\neg valid)$	$W17:$ **return** $\mathbb{A}$
$C04:$ **return** $\mathbb{A}$	$V01:$ **def** $validate_t()$
$C05:$ $b := state_t.cas(\mathbb{R}, \mathbb{C})$	$V02:$ **foreach** $((i, v) \in rset_t)$
$C06:$ **if** (b)	$V03:$ $st := start[i].read()$
$C07:$ **return** $\mathbb{C}$	$V04:$ $t' := st.writer.read()$
$C08:$ **else**	$V05:$ $s' := state[t'].read()$
$C09:$ **return** $\mathbb{A}$	$V06:$ **if** $(s' = \mathbb{C})$
$CV01:$ **def** $stableValue_t(st)$	$V07:$ $v' := loc.newVal.read()$
$CV02:$ $t' := st.writer.read()$	$V08:$ **else**
$CV03:$ $s' := state[t'].read()$	$V09:$ $v' := loc.oldVal.read()$
$CV04:$ **if** $(t' \neq t \wedge s' = \mathbb{R})$	$V10:$ **if** $(v \neq v')$
$CV05:$ $state[t'].cas(\mathbb{R}, \mathbb{A})$	$V11:$ **return** $false$
$CV06:$ $s'' := state[t'].read()$	$V12:$ $s := state[t].read()$
$CV07:$ **if** $(s'' = \mathbb{A})$	$V13:$ **return** $(s = \mathbb{R})$
$CV08:$ $v := loc.oldVal.read()$	
$CV09:$ **else**	
$CV10:$ $v := loc.newVal.read()$	
$CV11:$ **return** v	
$R05 \prec_p R10, C02 \prec_p C05$	

Fig. 1. Core DSTM

Those lines prevent H_{WS} because each transaction will abort the other transaction and thus both of them abort.

Our second example concerns Core McRT.

The Context. McRT [33] predates the definition of opacity [13] and wasn't intended to satisfy such a property, as far as we know. Rather, McRT is serializable by design. Still, we prove that Core McRT doesn't satisfy opacity.

$r : BasicRegister[LocCount]$	
$ver : AtomicRegister[LocCount]$ init 0	
$l : TryLock[LocCount]$ init $\mathbb{R}$	
$rset : ThreadLocal\ Map$ init $\emptyset$	
$uset : ThreadLocal\ Map$ init $\emptyset$	

$R01 :$ **def** $read_t(i)$	$C01 :$ **def** $commit_t()$
$R02 :$ **if** $(i \notin dom(uset_t))$	$C02 :$ **foreach** $((i \mapsto rver) \in rset_t)$
$R03 :$ $rver := ver[i].read()$	$C03 :$ $locked := l[i].read()$
$R04 :$ $locked := l[i].read()$	$C04 :$ $cver := ver[i].read()$
$R05 :$ **if** $(locked)$	$C05 :$ **if** $(locked \lor rver \neq cver)$
$R06 :$ **return** $abort_t()$	$C06 :$ **return** $abort_t()$
$R07 :$ **if** $(i \notin dom(rset_t))$	$C07 :$ **foreach** $(i \in dom(uset_t))$
$R08 :$ $rset_t.put(i, rver)$	$C08 :$ $cver := ver[i].read()$
$R09 :$ $v := r[i].read()$	$C09 :$ $ver[i].write(cver + 1)$
$R10 :$ **return** v	$C10 :$ $l[i].unlock()$
$W01 :$ **def** $write_t(i, v)$	$C11 :$ **return** $\mathbb{C}$
$W02 :$ **if** $(i \notin dom(uset_t))$	$A01 :$ **def** $abort_t()$
$W03 :$ $locked := l[i].tryLock()$	$A02 :$ **foreach** $((i \mapsto v) \in uset_t)$
$W04 :$ **if** $(\neg locked)$	$A03 :$ $r[i].write(v)$
$W05 :$ **return** $abort_t()$	$A04 :$ $l[i].unlock()$
$W06 :$ $v' := r[i].read()$	$A05 :$ **return** $\mathbb{A}$
$W07 :$ $uset_t.put(i, v')$	
$W08 :$ $r[i].write(v)$	
$W09 :$ **return** ok	
$R03 \prec_p R04,\ C03 \prec_p C04$	

Fig. 2. Core McRT

The Bug. When we run our tool on $(CoreMcRT, P_{WE}, \neg WE)$, we get an execution trace that matches H_{WE} in about 20 minutes. Figure 3(b) presents an illustration of the set of executions that exhibit the bug. Like above, this set is a subset of the set of executions that the bug pattern describes. Figure 3(b) uses the same conventions as Figure 3(a). The execution interleaves $write_{T_2}(2, v_1)$ between statements $read_{T_1}(2).R01 - R04$ and $read_{T_1}(2).R05 - R10$ such that the old value of $l[2]$ (unlocked) and the new value of $r[2]$ (the value v_1) are read. Also, $commit_{T_2}.C01 - C04$ are executed before $commit_{T_1}.C05 - C06$ such that T_2 finds $l[1]$ locked and aborts. The situation is symmetric for transaction T_1.

The Fix. The validation in the commit method ensures that only transactions that have read consistent values can commit; this is the key to why Core McRT is serializable. Our fix to Core McRT is to let the read method do validation, that is, to insert a copy of lines $C03 - C06$ between line $R09$ and line $R10$ in Core McRT.

Let us use Fixed Core MrRT to denote Core McRT with the above fix. When we run our tool on $(FixedCoreMcRT, P_{WE}, \neg WE)$, our tool determines that the algorithm satisfies the assertion, that is, Fixed Core McRT doesn't have the write-exposure anomaly. The run takes about 10 minutes.

T_1	T_2
$read_{T_1}(1){:}v_0$	$read_{T_2}(1){:}v_0$
$read_{T_1}(2){:}v_0$	$read_{T_2}(2){:}v_0$
$write_{T_1}(1,-v_0)$	$write_{T_2}(2,-v_0)$
$commit_{T_1}.C01{-}C04$	$commit_{T_2}.C01{-}C04$
$commit_{T_1}.C05{-}C09$	$commit_{T_2}.C05{-}C09$

(a) DSTM counterexamples

T_1	T_2
$read_{T_1}(2).R01{-}R04$	
	$write_{T_2}(2,v_1)$
$read_{T_1}(2).R05{-}R10$	
	$read_{T_2}(1).R01{-}R04$
$write_{T_1}(1,v_1)$	
	$read_{T_2}(1).R05{-}R10$
$commit_{T_1}.C01{-}C04$	$commit_{T_2}.C01{-}C04$
$commit_{T_1}.C05{-}C06$	$commit_{T_2}.C05{-}C06$

(b) McRT counterexamples

Fig. 3. Counterexamples

Note though that in the fixed algorithm, a sequence of writer transactions can make a reader transaction abort an arbitrary number of times. This observation motivated the next section's study of progress for direct-update TM algorithms such as McRT.

6   Local Progress and Opacity

We will prove that for direct-update TM algorithms, opacity and local progress are incompatible, even for fault-free systems.

Local Progress. We first recall the notion of local progress [4]. Intuitively, a TM algorithm ensures local progress if every transaction that repeatedly tries to commit eventually commits successfully. A *process* is a sequential thread that executes transactions with the same identifier. A process T is *crashing* in an infinite history H if $H|T$ is a finite sequence of operations (not ending in an abort $ret_T(\mathbb{A})$ or commit $ret_T(\mathbb{C})$ response event). A crashing process may acquire a resource and never relinquish it. A process T is *pending* in infinite history H if H has only a finite number of commit response $ret_T(\mathbb{C})$ events. A process *makes progress* in an infinite history, if it is not pending in it. A process T is *parasitic* in the infinite history H if $H|T$ is infinite and in history $H|T$, there are only a finite number of commit invocation $inv_T(commit_T())$ or abort response $ret_T(\mathbb{A})$ events. In other words, a parasitic process is a process that from some point in time keeps executing operations without being aborted and without attempting to commit. A process is *correct* in an infinite history if it is not parasitic and not crashing in the history. A process that is not correct is *faulty*. An infinite history satisfies *local progress*, if every infinite correct process in it makes progress. A TM algorithm ensures *local progress*, if every infinite history of it satisfies local progress and every finite history of it can be extended to an infinite history of it that satisfies local progress. A system is *fault-prone* if at least one process can be crashing or parasitic.

The Seminal Result. Theorem 2 is the seminal result on the incompatibility of opacity and local progress.

Theorem 2. (Bushkov, Guerraoui, and Kapalka [4]) *For a fault-prone system, no TM algorithm ensures both opacity and local progress.*

Considering a fault-prone system, the proof uses strategies that result in either a crashing or parasitic process.

Fault-Prone Versus Fault-Free. The large class of fault-prone systems presents a formidable challenge for designers of TM algorithms who want some form of progress. A crashing or parasitic process may never relinquish the ownership of a resource that another process must acquire before it can make progress. Bushkov, Guerraoui, and Kapalka [4] consider a liveness property called *solo progress* that guarantees that a process that eventually runs alone will make progress. They conjecture that obstruction-free TM algorithms (as defined in [23]) ensure solo progress in parasitic-free systems, and that lock-based TM algorithms ensure solo progress in systems that are both parasitic-free and crash-free. Those conjectures embody the following idea and practical advice.

> **Bushkov, Guerraoui, and Kapalka's advice [4, paraphrased]:**
> If designers of TM algorithms want opacity and progress, they must consider either weaker progress properties or fault-free systems.

TM algorithms for fault-free systems can rely on that no processes are crashing or parasitic.

Local Progress for Fault-Free Systems. Following the advice embodied in the paper by Bushkov, Guerraoui, and Kapalka [4], we study liveness in the setting of fault-free systems. Our main result is that an entire class of TM algorithms cannot ensure both opacity and local progress for fault-free systems.

We need two definitions before we can state our result formally. A TM algorithm is a *deferred-update* algorithm if every transaction that writes a value must commit before other transactions can read that value. All other TM algorithms are *direct-update* algorithms. For example, DSTM is a deferred-update algorithm while McRT is a direct-update algorithm.

Our main result is Theorem 3 which says that direct-update TM algorithms cannot ensure both opacity and local progress for fault-free systems.

Theorem 3. *For a fault-free system, no direct-update TM algorithm ensures both opacity and local progress.*

The proof of Theorem 3 is different from the proof of Theorem 2 because the proof of Theorem 3 cannot use crashing or parasitic processes. The proof of Theorem 3 considers a arbitrary direct-update TM algorithm for a fault-free system and exhibits a particular program that uses the TM. The program leads to transaction histories that are either H_1, H_2, or easily seen to violate local progress. In Theorem 1 we showed that H_1 and H_2 violate opacity.

We can now refine Bushkov, Guerraoui, and Kapalka's advice.

> **Our advice:** If designers of TM algorithms want opacity and *local progress*, they might have success with *deferred-update* TM algorithms that work for fault-free systems.

7   Conclusion

We have identified two problems that lead to non-opacity and we have proved an impossibility result. Our proofs of non-opacity for Core DSTM and Core McRT show that even if an algorithm satisfies opacity at a high level of abstraction, it may fail to satisfy opacity at a lower level of abstraction. Our impossibility result implies that if local progress is a goal, then deferred-update algorithms may be the only option.

Our tool is flexible and can accommodate a variety bug patterns such as H_{WE2} that was suggested by a DISC reviewer (thank you!). Our tool outputs an execution trace of Core McRT that matches H_{WE2} in about 7 minutes. Our tool handles small bug patterns efficiently; scalability is left for future work.

We hope that our observations and tool can help TM algorithm designers to avoid the write-skew, write-exposure, and other pitfalls. We envision a methodology in which TM algorithm designers first use our tool to avoid pitfalls and then use a proof framework such as the one by Lesani et al. [27] to prove correctness. Our tool can be used also during maintenance of TM algorithms. For example, a set of bug patterns can serve as a regression test suite. Additionally, our tool can be used to avoid pitfalls in other synchronization algorithms.

References

1. Abadi, M., Birrell, A., Harris, T., Isard, M.: Semantics of transactional memory and automatic mutual exclusion. In: POPL, pp. 63–74 (2008)
2. Scott Ananian, C., Asanovic, K., Kuszmaul, B.C., Leiserson, C.E., Lie, S.: Unbounded transactional memory. In: HPCA (2005)
3. Berenson, H., Bernstein, P., Gray, J., Melton, J., O'Neil, E., O'Neil, P.: A critique of ANSI SQL isolation levels. SIGMOD Rec. 24(2), 1–10 (1995)
4. Bushkov, V., Guerraoui, R., Kapalka, M.: On the liveness of transactional memory. In: PODC, pp. 9–18 (2012)
5. Cohen, A., O'Leary, J.W., Pnueli, A., Tuttle, M.R., Zuck, L.D.: Verifying correctness of transactional memories. In: FMCAD (2007)
6. Cohen, A., Pnueli, A., Zuck, L.D.: Mechanical verification of transactional memories with non-transactional memory accesses. In: Gupta, A., Malik, S. (eds.) CAV 2008. LNCS, vol. 5123, pp. 121–134. Springer, Heidelberg (2008)
7. Intel Corporation. Intel architecture instruction set extensions programming reference. 319433-012 (2012)
8. de Moura, L., Bjørner, N.S.: Z3: An efficient SMT solver. In: Ramakrishnan, C.R., Rehof, J. (eds.) TACAS 2008. LNCS, vol. 4963, pp. 337–340. Springer, Heidelberg (2008)
9. Dice, D., Shalev, O., Shavit, N.N.: Transactional locking II. In: Dolev, S. (ed.) DISC 2006. LNCS, vol. 4167, pp. 194–208. Springer, Heidelberg (2006)
10. Dice, D., Shavit, N.: TLRW: Return of the read-write lock. In: SPAA (2010)
11. Doherty, S., Groves, L., Luchangco, V., Moir, M.: Towards formally specifying and verifying transactional memory. In: Formal Aspects of Computing (2012)
12. Emmi, M., Majumdar, R., Manevich, R.: Parameterized verification of transactional memories. In: PLDI, pp. 134–145 (2010)
13. Guerraoui, R., Kapalka, M.: On the correctness of transactional memory. In: PPOPP, pp. 175–184 (2008)

14. Guerraoui, R., Henzinger, T.A., Jobstmann, B., Singh, V.: Model checking transactional memories. In: PLDI, pp. 372–382 (2008)
15. Guerraoui, R., Henzinger, T.A., Singh, V.: Software transactional memory on relaxed memory models. In: Bouajjani, A., Maler, O. (eds.) CAV 2009. LNCS, vol. 5643, pp. 321–336. Springer, Heidelberg (2009)
16. Guerraoui, R., Henzinger, T.A., Singh, V.: Model checking transactional memories. Distributed Computing (2010)
17. Guerraoui, R., Kapalka, M.: Principles of Transactional Memory. Morgan and Claypool Publishers (2010)
18. Hammond, L., Wong, V., Chen, M., Carlstrom, B.D., Davis, J.D., Hertzberg, B., Prabhu, M.K., Wijaya, H., Kozyrakis, C., Olukotun, K.: Transactional memory coherence and consistency. In: ISCA (2004)
19. Haring, R., Ohnmacht, M., Fox, T., Gschwind, M., Sattereld, D., Sugavanam, K., Coteus, P., Heidelberger, P., Blumrich, M., Wisniewski, R., Gara, A., Chiu, G.-T., Boyle, P., Chist, N., Kim, C.: The IBM Blue Gene/Q compute chip (2012)
20. Harris, T., Larus, J., Rajwar, R.: Transactional Memory, 2nd edn. Morgan and Claypool Publishers (2010)
21. Harris, T., Marlow, S., Jones, S.P., Herlihy, M.: Composable memory transactions. In: PPOPP, pp. 48–60. ACM Press (2005)
22. Herlihy, M., Luchangco, V., Moir, M.: A flexible framework for implementing software transactional memory. In: OOPSLA, pp. 253–262 (2006)
23. Herlihy, M., Luchangco, V., Moir, M., Scherer III, W.N.: Software transactional memory for dynamic-sized data structures. In: PODC (2003)
24. Herlihy, M., Moss, J.E.B.: Transactional memory: Architectural support for lock-free data structures. In: ISCA, pp. 289–300 (1993)
25. Imbs, D., de Mendivil, J.R., Raynal, M.: Brief announcement: virtual world consistency: a new condition for STM systems. In: PODC, pp. 280–281 (2009)
26. Koskinen, E., Parkinson, M., Herlihy, M.: Coarse-grained transactions. In: POPL, pp. 19–30 (2010)
27. Lesani, M., Luchangco, V., Moir, M.: A framework for formally verifying software transactional memory algorithms. In: Koutny, M., Ulidowski, I. (eds.) CONCUR 2012. LNCS, vol. 7454, pp. 516–530. Springer, Heidelberg (2012)
28. Lesani, M., Palsberg, J.: Proving non-opacity,
    http://www.cs.ucla.edu/~lesani/companion/disc13
29. Moore, K.F., Grossman, D.: High-level small-step operational semantics for transactions. In: POPL, pp. 51–62 (2008)
30. Pankratius, V., Adl-Tabatabai, A.-R., Otto, F.: Does transactional memory keep its promises? results from an empirical study. Technical Report 2009–12, Institute for Program Structures and Data Organization (IPD), University of Karlsruhe (September 2009)
31. Papadimitriou, C.H.: The serializability of concurrent database updates. Journal of the ACM 26(4), 631–653 (1979)
32. Rossbach, C.J., Hofmann, O.S., Witchel, E.: Is transactional programming actually easier? SIGPLAN Notices 45(5) (January 2010)
33. Saha, B., Adl-Tabatabai, A.-R., Hudson, R.L., Minh, C.C., Hertzberg, B.: McRT-STM: a high performance software transactional memory system for a multi-core runtime. In: PPoPP (2006)
34. Scott, M.L.: Sequential specification of transactional memory semantics. In: TRANSACT (2006)
35. Shavit, N., Touitou, D.: Software transactional memory. In: PODC (1995)
36. Tasiran, S.: A compositional method for verifying software transactional memory implementations. Technical Report MSR-TR-2008-56, Microsoft Research (2008)

Exploiting Locality in Lease-Based Replicated Transactional Memory via Task Migration

Danny Hendler[1], Alex Naiman[1], Sebastiano Peluso[2], Francesco Quaglia[2],
Paolo Romano[3], and Adi Suissa[1]

[1] Ben-Gurion University of the Negev, Israel*
[2] Sapienza University of Rome, Italy
[3] Instituto Superior Técnico, Universidade de Lisboa/INESC-ID, Portugal

Abstract. We present LILAC-TM, the first locality-aware Distributed Software Transactional Memory (DSTM) implementation. LILAC-TM is a fully decentralized lease-based replicated DSTM. It employs a novel self-optimizing lease circulation scheme based on the idea of dynamically determining whether to migrate transactions to the nodes that own the leases required for their validation, or to demand the acquisition of these leases by the node that originated the transaction. Our experimental evaluation establishes that LILAC-TM provides significant performance gains for distributed workloads exhibiting data locality, while typically incurring little or no overhead for non-data local workloads.

1 Introduction

Transactional Memory (TM) has emerged as a promising programming paradigm for concurrent applications, which provides a programmer-friendly alternative to traditional lock-based synchronization. Intense research work on both software and hardware TM approaches [16,22], and the inclusion of TM support in world-leading multiprocessor hardware and open source compilers [17,21] extended the traction it had gained in the research community to the mainstream software industry.

Distributed Software TM (DSTM) systems extend the reach of the TM model to distributed applications. An important lesson learnt by the deployment of the first enterprise-class TM-based applications [6,19] is that, in order to permit scalability and meet the reliability requirements of real-world applications, DSTMs must support data replication. As a result, several replication techniques for distributed TM have been proposed, deployed over a set of shared-nothing multi-core systems [1,2,11,20], as typical of cloud computing environments.

A key challenge faced by replicated DSTMs, when compared with more conventional transactional systems (such as relational databases), is the large increase of the communication-to-computation ratio [19]: unlike classical DBMSs, DSTMs avoid disk-based logging and rely on in-memory data replication to

---

* Partially supported by the Israel Science Foundation (grant number 1227/10) and by the Lynne and William Frankel Center for Computing Science at Ben-Gurion University.

Y. Afek (Ed.): DISC 2013, LNCS 8205, pp. 121–133, 2013.

achieve durability and fault-tolerance; further, the nature of the programming interfaces exposed by DSTMs drastically reduces the latencies of accessing data, significantly reducing the duration of typical TM transactions, when compared to typical on-line transaction processing (OLTP). Overall, the reduction of the transaction processing time results in the growth of the relative cost of the distributed (consensus-based [14]) coordination activities required by conventional replication protocols, and in a corresponding increase of their relative overhead.

Model and Background: We consider a classical asynchronous distributed system model [14] consisting of a set of processes $\Pi = \{p_1, \ldots, p_n\}$ that communicate via message passing and can fail according to the fail-stop (crash) model. We assume that a majority of processes is correct and that the system ensures sufficient synchrony for implementing a *View Synchronous Group Communication Service* (GCS) [10].

GCS provides two complementary services: group membership and multicast communication. Informally, the role of the *group membership service* is to provide each participant in a distributed computation with information about which process is active (or reachable) and which is failed (or unreachable). Such information is called a *view* of the group of participants. We assume that the GCS provides a *view-synchronous primary-component group membership service* [5], which maintains a single agreed view of the group at any given time and provides processes with information on whether they belong to the primary component.

We assume that the *multicast communication* layer offers two communication services, which disseminate messages with different reliability and ordering properties: *Optimistic Atomic Broadcast* (OAB) [12] and *Uniform Reliable Broadcast* (URB) [14]. URB is defined by the primitives *UR-broadcast(m)* and *UR-deliver(m)*, and guarantees causal order and uniform message delivery. Three primitives define OAB: *OA-broadcast(m)*, which is used to broadcast message m; *Opt-deliver(m)*, which delivers message m with no ordering or reliability guarantees; *TO-deliver(m)*, which delivers message m ensuring uniform and total order guarantees.

The ALC (Asynchronous Lease Certification) protocol [8] is based on the *lease* concept. A *lease* is an ownership token that grants a node temporary privileges on the management of a subset of the replicated data-set. ALC associates leases with data items indirectly through *conflict classes*, each of which may represent a set of data items. This allows flexible control of the granularity of the leases abstraction, trading off accuracy (i.e., avoidance of aliasing problems) for efficiency (amount of information exchanged among nodes and maintained in-memory) [3].

With ALC, a transaction is executed based on local data, avoiding any inter-replica synchronization until it enters its commit phase. At this stage, ALC acquires a lease for the transaction's accessed data items, before proceeding to validate the transaction. In case a transaction T is found to have accessed stale data, T is re-executed without releasing the acquired leases. This ensures that, during T's re-execution, no other replica can update any of the data items accessed during T's first execution, which guarantees the absence of remote conflicts on the subsequent re-execution of T, provided that the same set of conflict classes accessed during T's first execution is accessed again.

To establish lease ownership, ALC employs the OAB communication service. Disseminating data items of committed transactions and lease-release messages is done using the URB service. The ownership of a lease ensures that no other replica will be allowed to successfully validate any conflicting transaction, making it unnecessary to enforce distributed agreement on the global serialization order of transactions. ALC takes advantage of this by limiting the use of atomic broadcast exclusively for establishing the lease ownership. Subsequently, as long as the lease is owned by the replica, transactions can be locally validated and their updates can be disseminated using URB, which can be implemented in a much more efficient manner than OAB.

Our Contributions: In this paper, we present an innovative, fully decentralized, LocalIty-aware LeAse-based repliCated TM (LILAC-TM). LILAC-TM aims to maximize system throughput via a distributed self-optimizing lease circulation scheme based on the idea of dynamically determining whether to migrate transactions to the nodes that own the leases required for their validation, or to demand the acquisition of these leases by the transaction's originating node.

LILAC-TM's flexibility in deciding whether to migrate data or transactions allows it not only to take advantage of the data locality present in many application workloads, but also to further enhance it by turning a node N that frequently accesses a set of data items D into an attractor for transactions that access subsets of D (and that could be committed by N avoiding any lease circulation). This allows LILAC-TM to provide two key benefits: (1) limiting the frequency of lease circulation, and (2) enhancing contention management efficiency. In fact, with LILAC-TM, conflicting concurrent transactions have a significantly higher probability of being executed on the same node, which prevents them from incurring the high costs of distributed conflicts.

We conducted a comprehensive comparative performance analysis, establishing that LILAC-TM outperforms ALC by a wide margin on workloads possessing data locality, while incurring little or no overhead for non-data local workloads.

2   LILAC-TM

Figure 1 provides an overview of the software architecture of each replica of LILAC-TM, highlighting in gray the modules that were either re-designed or that were not originally present in ALC.

The top layer is a wrapper that intercepts application level calls for transaction demarcation without interfering with application accesses (read/write) to the transactional data items, which are managed directly by the underlying local STM layer. This approach allows transparent extension of the classic STM programming model to a distributed setting.

The prototype of LILAC-TM has been built by extending the ALC implementation shipped in the GenRSTM framework [7]. GenRSTM has been designed to support, in a modular fashion, a range of heterogeneous algorithms across the various layers of the software stack of a replicated STM platform. LILAC-TM inherits this flexibility from GenRSTM. In this work, we use TL2 [13] as the local STM layer.

The Replication Manager (RM) is the component in charge of interfacing the local STM layer with its replicas deployed on other system nodes. The RM is responsible of coordinating the commit phase of both remote and local transactions by: (i) intercepting commit-request events generated by local transactions and triggering a distributed coordination phase aimed at determining transactions' global serialization order and detecting the presence of conflicts with concurrently executing remote transactions; and (ii) validating remote transactions and, upon successful validation, committing them by atomically applying their write-sets in the local STM.

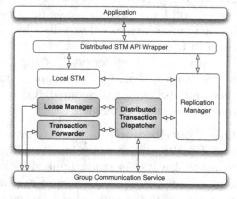

Fig. 1. Middleware architecture of a LILAC-TM replica

At the bottom layer we find a GCS (Appia [18] in our prototype), which, as mentioned in Section 1, provides the view synchronous membership, OAB and URB services.

The role of the Lease Manager (LM) is to ensure that no two replicas simultaneously disseminate updates for conflicting transactions. To this end, the LM exposes an interface consisting of two methods, GETLEASE() and FINISHEDX-ACT(), which are used by the RM to acquire/release leases on a set of data items. This component was originally introduced in ALC and has been re-designed in this work to support *fine-grained leases*. As we explain in more detail in Section 2.1, fine-grained leases facilitate the exploitation of locality and consequently reduce lease circulation.

The Transaction Forwarder (TF) is responsible for managing the forwarding of a transaction to a different node in the system. The transaction forwarding mechanism represents an alternative mechanism to the lease-based certification scheme introduced in ALC. Essentially, both transaction forwarding and lease-based replication strive to achieve the same goal: minimizing the execution rate of expensive Atomic Broadcast-based consensus protocols to determine the outcome of commit requests. ALC's lease mechanism pursues this objective by allowing a node that owns sufficient leases to validate transactions and disseminate their writesets without executing consensus protocols. Still, acquiring a lease remains an expensive operation, as it requires the execution of a consensus protocol.

The transaction forwarding scheme introduced in this work aims at reducing the frequency of lease requests triggered in the system, by migrating the execution of transactions to remote nodes that may process them more efficiently.

This is the case, for instance, if some node n owns the set of leases required to certify and commit a transaction T originated on some remote node n'. In this scenario, in fact, n could validate T locally, and simply disseminate its writeset in case of success. Transaction migration may be beneficial also in subtler scenarios in which, even though no node already owns the leases required to certify a transaction T, if T's originating node were to issue a lease request for T, it would revoke leases that are being utilized with high frequency by some other node, say n''. In this case, it is preferable to forward the transaction to n'' and have n'' acquire the lease on behalf of T, as this would reduce the frequency of lease circulation and increase throughput in the long term.

The decision whether to migrate a transaction's execution to another node or to issue a lease request and process it locally is far from being a trivial one. The transaction scheduling policy should take load balancing considerations into account and ensure that the transaction migration logic avoids excessively overloading any subset of nodes in the system. In LILAC-TM, the logic for determining how to manage the commit phase of transactions is encapsulated by the Distributed Transaction Dispatching (DTD) module. In this paper, we propose two decision policies based on an efficiently solvable formulation in terms of an Integer Linear Programming optimization problem.

In the following we describe the key contributions of this paper, i.e. the fine-grained lease management scheme, the TF and the DTD.

2.1 Fine-Grained Leases

In ALC, a transaction requires a *single lease object*, associated with its data set in its entirety. A transaction T, attempting to commit on a node, may reuse a lease owned by the node only if T's data set is a subset of the lease's items set. Thus, each transaction is tightly coupled with a single lease ownership record. This approach has two disadvantages: i) upon the delivery of a lease request by a remote node that requires even a single data item from a lease owned by the local node, the lease must be released, causing subsequent transactions accessing other items in that lease to issue new lease requests; ii) if a transaction's data set is a subset of a union of leases owned by the local replica but is not a subset of any of them, a new lease request must be issued. This forces the creation of new lease requests, causing extensive use of *OA-broadcast* and *TO-deliver*.

To exploit data-locality, we introduce a new lease manager module that decouples lease requests from the requesting transaction's data set. Rather than having a transaction acquire a single lease encompassing its entire data set, each transaction acquires a set of fine-grained *Lease Ownership Records* (LORs), one per accessed conflict class.

Implementation Details: ALC's *Replication Manager* (RM) was not changed. It interfaces with the LM via the GETLEASE() and FINISHEDXACT() methods for acquiring and releasing leases, respectively. As in ALC, LILAC-TM maintains the indirection level between leases and data items through conflict classes. This allows flexible control of the leases abstraction granularity. We ab-

---

Algorithm 1. Lease Manager at process p_i

```
 1  FIFOQueue<LOR> CQ[NumOfCCs]={⊥,...,⊥}      19  upon Opt-deliver([LeaseRequest, req])
 2  Set<LOR> GetLease(Set DataSet)                    from p_k do
 3  │ ConflictClass[] CC = getCCs(DataSet)       20  │ freeLocalLeases(req.cc)
 4  │ if (∃(Set<LOR>)S⊆CQ s.t. ∀cc∈CC(∃lor∈S :   21  upon TO-deliver([LeaseRequest, req])
    │ (lor.cc=cc ∧ lor.proc=p_i ∧ ¬lor.blocked)))      from p_k do
    │ then                                        22  │ Set<LOR> S = createLorsForCCs(req.cc)
 5  │ │ foreach lor∈S do                          23  │ foreach lor∈S do CQ[lor.cc].enqueue(lor)
 6  │ │ │ lor.activeXacts++                       24  upon UR-deliver([LeaseFreed, Set<LOR>
 7  │ else                                            S]) from p_k do
 8  │ │ Set<LOR> S = createLorsForCCs(CC)         25  │ foreach lor∈S do CQ[lor.cc].dequeue(lor)
 9  │ │ LeaseRequest req = new LeaseRequest(p_i,S) 26  void freeLocalLeases(ConflictClass[]
10  │ │ OA-broadcast([LeaseRequest,req])              CC)
11  │ wait until isEnabled(S)                     27  │ Set<LOR> lorsToFree
12  │ return S                                    28  │ foreach cc ∈ CC do
                                                  29  │ │ if ∃lor in CQ[cc] s.t. lor.proc=p_i then
13  void FinishedXact(Set<LOR> S)                 30  │ │ │ lor.blocked=true
14  │ Set<LOR> lorsToFree                         31  │ │ │ if (CQ[lor.cc].isFirst(lor) ∧
15  │ foreach lor∈S do                                │ │ │ lor.activeXacts=0) then
16  │ │ lor.activeXacts--                         32  │ │ │ │ lorsToFree=lorsToFree ∪ lor
17  │ │ if (lor.blocked ∧ lor.activeXacts=0) then 33  │ if (lorsToFree ≠ ∅) then
    │ │ lorsToFree=lorsToFree ∪ lor                   │ UR-broadcast([LeaseFreed,lorsToFree])
18  │ if (lorsToFree ≠ ∅) then                    34  boolean isEnabled(Set<LOR> S)
    │ UR-broadcast([LeaseFreed,lorsToFree])       35  │ return ∀lor∈S : CQ[lor.cc].isFirst(lor)
                                                  36
```

---

stract away the mapping between a data item and a conflict class through the `getConflictClasses()` primitive, taking a set of data items as input parameter and returning a set of conflict classes.

As in ALC, each replica maintains one main data structure for managing the establishment/release of leases: CQ (Conflict-Queues), an array of FIFO queues, one per conflict class. The CQ keeps track of conflict relations among lease requests of different replicas. Each queue contains LORs, each storing the following data: (i) **proc**: the address of the requesting replica; (ii) **cc**: the conflict class this LOR is associated with; (iii) **activeXacts**: a counter keeping track of the number of active local transactions associated with this LOR, initialized to 1 when the LOR is created; and (iv) **blocked**: a flag indicating whether new local transactions can be associated with this LOR - this flag is initialized to false when the LOR is created (in the `createLorsForConflictClasses` primitive), and set to true as soon as a remote lease request is received.

Algorithm 1 presents the pseudo-code of LILAC-TM's LM. The method GETLEASE() is invoked by the RM once a transaction reaches its commit phase. The LM then attempts to acquire leases for all items in the committing transaction's data set. It first determines, using the `getCCs()` method, the set CC of conflict classes associated with the transaction's data set (line 3). It then checks (in line 4) whether CQ contains a set S of LORs, associated with all the conflict classes in CC, such that i) the LORs were issued by p_i, and ii) additional transactions of p_i may still be associated with these LORs (this is the case if none of

these LORs is blocked). If the conditions of line 4 are satisfied, the current transaction can be associated with all LORs in S (lines 5–6). Otherwise, a new lease
request, containing the set of LORs, is created and is disseminated using OAB
(lines 7–10). In either case, p_i waits in line 11 until S is enabled, that is, until
all the LORs in S reach the front of their corresponding FIFO queues (see the
ISENABLED() method). Finally, the method returns S and the RM may proceed
validating the transaction.

When a transaction terminates, the RM invokes the FINISHEDXACT() method.
This method receives a set of LORs and decrements the number of active transactions within each record (line 16). All blocked LORs that are not used by local
transactions are then released by sending a single message via the UR-$broadcast$
primitive (lines 17–18).

Upon an Opt-$deliver$ event of a remote lease request req, p_i invokes the FREE-
LOCALLEASES() method, which blocks all LORs owned by p_i that are part of req
by setting their $blocked$ field (line 30). Then, all LORs that are blocked and are no
longer in use by local transactions are released by sending a single UR-$broadcast$
message (lines 31–33). Other LORs required by req that have local transactions
associated with them (if any) will be freed when the local transactions terminate.
Blocking LORs is required to ensure the fairness of the lease circulation scheme.
In order to prevent a remote process p_j from waiting indefinitely for process
p_i to relinquish a lease, p_i is prevented from associating new transactions with
existing LORs as soon as a conflicting lease request from p_j is Opt-$delivered$ at
p_i.

Upon a TO-$deliver$ of a lease request req (line 21), p_i creates the corresponding
set of LORs, and enqueues these records in their conflict class queues. The logic
associated with a UR-$deliver$ event (line 24) removes each LOR specified in the
message from its conflict class queue.

2.2 Transaction Forwarder

The TF is the module in charge of managing the process of migrating transactions between nodes. If at commit time the set S of conflict classes accessed by
a transaction T is not already owned by its origin node, say n, the DTD may
decide to avoid requesting leases for T, and forward its execution to a different
node n'. In this case node n' becomes responsible for finalizing the commit phase
of the transaction. This includes establishing leases on S on behalf of transaction T, which can be achieved avoiding any distributed coordination, in case n'
already owns all the leases required by T'. Else, if some of the leases requested
by T' are not owned by n', n' has to issue a lease request on behalf of T via the
OAB service.

Next we can use a remote validation optimization and let n' perform T's final
validation upon arrival (without re-executing T) in order to detect whether T
has conflicts with concurrently committed transactions.[1] In case of successful

---

[1] In order to use this remote validation optimization, the TF module must be augmented with a TM-specific validation procedure and append the appropriate meta-

validation, T can be simply committed, as in ALC, by disseminating a Commit message via the *UR-Broadcast*. Additionally, in LILAC-TM, this has the effect of unblocking the thread that requested the commit of T on node n. On the other hand, if T fails its final validation, it is re-executed on node n' until it can be successfully committed, or until it fails for a pre-determined number of attempts. In this latter case, the origin node is notified of the abort of T, and the user application is notified via an explicit exception type. Note that, in order to commit the transaction associated with the re-execution of T, which we denote as T', n' must own the set of conflict classes accessed by T'. This may not be necessarily true, as T' and T may access different sets of conflict classes. In this case, LILAC-TM prevents a transaction from being forwarded an arbitrary number of times, by forcing n' to issue a lease request and acquire ownership of the leases requested by T'.

It must be noted that, in order to support the transaction forwarding process, the programming model exposed by LILAC-TM has to undergo some minor adaptations compared, e.g., with the one typically provided by non-replicated TM systems. Specifically, LILAC-TM requires that the transactional code is replicated and encapsulated by an interface that allows to seamlessly re-execute transactions originating at different nodes.

2.3   Distributed Transaction Dispatching

The DTD module allows encapsulating arbitrary policies to determine whether to process the commit of a transaction locally, by issuing lease requests if required, or to migrate its execution to a remote node. In the following we refer to this problem as the *transaction migration problem*. This problem can be formulated as an Integer Linear Programming (ILP) problem as follows:

(1) $\min \sum_{i \in \Pi} N_i \cdot C(i, S)$
subject to: (2) $\sum_{i \in \Pi} N_i = 1$, (3) $CPU_i \cdot N_i < maxCPU$

The above problem formulation aims at determining an assignment of the binary vector N (whose entries are all equal to 0 except for one, whose index specifies the selected node) minimizing a generic cost function $C(i, S)$ that expresses the cost for node i to be selected for managing the commit phase of a transaction accessing the conflict classes in the set S. The optimization problem specifies two constraints. Constraint (2) expresses the requirement that a transaction can be certified by exactly a single node in Π. Constraint (3) is used to avoid load imbalance between nodes. It states that a node i should be considered eligible for re-scheduling only if its CPU utilization (CPU_i) is below a maximum threshold ($maxCPU$).

We now derive two different policies for instantiating the above ILP formulation, which are designed to minimize the long-term and the short-term impact of the decision on how to handle a transaction. We start by defining the cost

---

data to forwarding messages. TM-specific adaptation and overhead can be avoided by simply always re-executing the forwarded transaction once it is migrated to n'.

function $LC(i, S)$, which models the *long-term cost* of selecting node i as the node that will execute the transaction as the sum of the frequency of accesses to the conflict classes in S by every other node $j \neq i \in \Pi$:

$$LC(i, S) = \sum_{x \in S} \sum_{j \in \Pi \vee j \neq i} \mathcal{F}(j, x)$$

where $\mathcal{F}(j, x)$ is defined as the per time-unit number of transactions originated on node j that have object x in their dataset.

In order to derive the *short-term policy*, we first define the function $SC(i, S)$, which expresses the immediate costs induced at the GCS level by different choices of where to execute a transaction:

$$SC(i, S) = \begin{cases} c_{URB} & \text{if } i = O \wedge \forall x \in S : \mathcal{L}(i, x) = 1 \\ c_{AB} + 2c_{URB} & \text{if } i = O \wedge \exists x \in S : \mathcal{L}(i, x) = 0 \\ c_{p2p} + c_{AB} + 2c_{URB} & \text{if } i \neq O \wedge \exists x \in S : \mathcal{L}(i, x) = 0 \\ c_{p2p} + c_{URB} & \text{if } i \neq O \wedge \forall x \in S : \mathcal{L}(i, x) = 1 \end{cases}$$

where we denote by O the node that originated the transaction, and by c_{URB}, c_{AB} and c_{p2p} the costs of performing a URB, an AB, and a point-to-point communication, respectively. The above equations express the cost of the following scenarios (from top to bottom): i) the originating node already owns all the leases required by it; ii) the originating node does not own all the necessary leases and issues a lease request; iii) the originating node forwards the transaction to a node that does not own all the necessary leases; iv) the transaction is forwarded to a node that owns the leases for all required conflict classes. The DTD can be configured to use the long-term or the short-term policy simply by setting the generic cost function $C(i, S)$ in (1) to, respectively, $LC(i, S)$ or $SC(i, S)$.

It is easily seen that the ILP of Equation 1 can be solved in $O(|\Pi|)$ time regardless of whether the long-term or the short-term policy is used. The statistics required for the computation of the long-term policy are computed by gathering the access frequencies of nodes to conflict classes. This information is piggybacked on the messages exchanged to commit transactions/request leases. A similar mechanism is used for exchanging information on the CPU utilization of each node. For the short-term policy, we quantify the cost of the P2P, URB and OAB protocols in terms of their communication-steps latencies (which equal 1, 2, and 3, resp.).

3   Experimental Evaluation

In this section, we compare the performance of LILAC-TM with that of the baseline ALC protocol. Performance is evaluated using two benchmarks: a variant of the *Bank* benchmark [15] and the *TPC-C* benchmark [23]. We compare the following algorithms: ALC (using the implementation evaluated in [7]), FGL (ALC using the fine-grained leases mechanism), MG-ALC (ALC extended with the transaction migration mechanism), and two variants of LILAC-TM (transaction migration on top of ALC using fine-grained leases), using the short-term (LILAC-TM-ST) and the long-term (LILAC-TM-LT) policies, respectively. The source code of ALC, LILAC-TM and the benchmarks used in this study is publicly available [4].

All benchmarks were executed running 2 threads per node, and using a cluster of 4 replicas, each comprising an Intel Xeon E5506 CPU at 2.13 GHz and 32 GB of RAM, running Linux and interconnected via a private Gigabit Ethernet.[2]

Bank. The *Bank* benchmark [9,15] is a well-known transactional benchmark that emulates a bank system comprising a number of accounts.

We extended this benchmark with various types of read-write and read-only transactions, for generating more realistic transactional workloads. A *read-write transaction* performs transfers between randomly selected pairs of accounts. A *read-only transaction* reads the balance of a set of randomly-selected client accounts. Workloads consist of 50% read-write transactions and 50% read-only transactions of varying lengths.

We introduce data locality in the benchmark as follows. Accounts are split into *partitions* such that each partition is logically associated with a distinct replica and partitions are evenly distributed between replicas. A transaction originated on replica r accesses accounts of a single (randomly selected) partition associated with r with probability P, and accounts from another (randomly selected) remote (associated with another replica) partition with probability $1-P$. Larger values of P generate workloads characterized by higher data-locality and smaller inter-replica contention. Hence, the optimal migration policy is to forward a transaction T to the replica with which the partition accessed by T is associated. We therefore implement and evaluate a third variant of LILAC-TM (called LILAC-TM-OPT) using this optimal policy.[3]

Figure 2(a) shows the throughput (committed transactions per second) of the algorithms we evaluate on workloads generated by the Bank application with P varying between 0% and 100%.

Comparing ALC and FGL, Figure 2(a) shows that, while ALC's throughput remains almost constant for all locality levels, FGL's performance dramatically increases when locality rises above 80%. This is explained by Figure 2(b), that shows the *Lease Reuse Rate*, defined as the ratio between the number of read-write transactions which are piggy-backed on existing leases and the total number of read-write transactions.[4] A higher lease reuse rate results in fewer lease requests, which reduces in turn the communication overhead and the latency caused by waiting for leases. FGL's lease reuse rate approaches 1 for high locality levels, which enables FGL and FGL-based migration policies to achieve up to 3.2 times higher throughput as compared with ALC and MG-ALC.

When locality is lower than 80%, the FGL approach yields throughput that is comparable to ALC. Under highly-contended low-locality workloads, FGL's throughput is even approximately 10%-20% lower than that of ALC. This is because these workloads produce a growing demand for leases from all nodes. FGL releases the leases in fine-grained chunks, which results in a higher load on URB-communication as compared with ALC.

---

[2] Evaluation using 4 threads per node shows similar trends. For lack of space, we report on this evaluation in our technical report: http://arxiv.org/abs/1308.2147.

[3] Our MG-ALC implementation also uses this optimal migration policy.

[4] Read-only transactions never request leases.

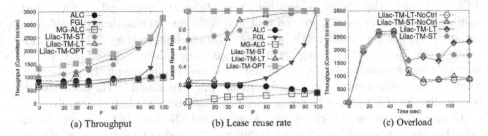

(a) Throughput   (b) Lease reuse rate   (c) Overload

Fig. 2. Bank Benchmark

The adverse impact of low-locality workloads on transaction migration policies, however, is much lower. Migrating transactions to replicas where leases might already be present (or will benefit from acquiring it), increases the lease reuse rate, which increases throughput in turn. Indeed, as shown by Figure 2(a), LILAC-TM achieves speed-up of 40%-100% even for low-locality workloads (0%-60%) in comparison with ALC. For high-locality workloads, both FGL and LILAC-TM converge to similar performance, outperforming ALC by a factor of 3.2.

Comparing the performance of ALC and MG-ALC shows that using transaction migration on top of ALC does not improve the lease reuse rate as compared with ALC. This is because migration only helps when used on top of the fine-grained leases mechanism. The slightly lower throughput of MG-ALC vs. ALC is due to the overhead of the TF mechanism.

Next, we evaluate the ability of LILAC-TM to cope with load imbalance. To this end, we set the benchmark to access with 20% probability a single partition, p, from all the nodes, except for the single node, say n, associated with p, which accesses only p. In these settings, with all the considered policies, n tends to attract all the transactions that access p. At second 40 of the test, we overload node n by injecting external, CPU-intensive jobs. The plots in Fig. 2(c) compare the throughput achieved by LILAC-TM with and without the mechanism for overload control (implementing Inequality (3)), and with both the long-term and the short-term policies. The data highlights the effectiveness of the proposed overload control mechanism, which significantly increases system throughput. In fact, the schemes that exploit statistics on CPU utilization (LILAC-TM-ST and LILAC-TM-LT) react in a timely manner to the overload of n by avoiding further migrating their transactions towards it, and consequently achieve a throughput that is about twice that of uninformed policies (LILAC-TM-ST-NoCtrl and LILAC-TM-LT-NoCtrl).

TPC-C. We also ported the TPC-C benchmark and evaluated LILAC-TM using it. The TPC-C benchmark is representative of OLTP workloads and is useful to assess the benefits of our proposal even in the context of complex workloads that simulate real world applications. It includes a wider variety of transactions that simulate a whole-sale supplying *items* from a set of *warehouses* to *customers* within sales *districts*. We ported two of the five transactional profiles offered by

TPC-C, namely the *Payment* and the *New Order* transactional profiles, that exhibit high conflict rate scenarios and long running transactional workloads, respectively. For this benchmark, we inject transactions to the system by emulating a load balancer operating according to a geographically-based policy that forwards requests on the basis of the requests' geographic origin. In particular, requests sent from a certain geographic region are dispatched to the node that is responsible for the warehouses associated with the users of that region. To generate more realistic scenarios we also assume that the load balancer can make mistakes by imposing that with probability 0.2 a request sent from a certain region is issued by users associated with warehouses that do not belong to that region.

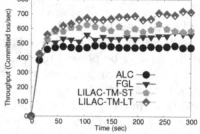

In Figure 3, we present the throughput obtained by running a workload with 95% Payment transactions and 5% New Order transactions. We show the throughput varying over time in order to better assess the convergence of the reschedule policies. We first notice that even in this complex scenario FGL performs better than ALC due to better exploitation of the application, and a

Fig. 3. TPC-C

higher leases reuse rate. In addition, using the migration mechanism, driven by either the short-term (ST) or the long-term (LT) policy, over FGL, achieves speedups of between 1.2 and 1.5 when compared to ALC. However, unlike the Bank Benchmark, in this case the ST policy achieves only minor gains compared to the LT policy, due to TPC-C's transactional profiles that generate more complex access patterns. In fact, even when the data set is partitioned by identifying each partition as a *warehouse* and all the objects associated with that *warehouse*, TPC-C's transactions may access more than one partition. This reduces the probability that the ST policy can actually trigger a reschedule for a transaction on a node that already owns all the leases necessary to validate/commit that transaction. On the other hand, the LT policy can exploit application locality thus noticeably reducing lease requests circulation, i.e. the number of lease requests issued per second.

4   Conclusions

In this paper we introduced LILAC-TM, a fully decentralized, LocalIty-aware LeAse-based repliCated TM. LILAC-TM exploits a novel, self-optimizing lease circulation scheme that provides two key benefits: (1) limiting the frequency of lease circulation, and (2) enhancing the contention management efficiency, by increasing the probability that conflicting transactions are executed on the same node.

By means of an experimental evaluation based on both synthetic and realistic benchmarks we have shown that LILAC-TM can yield significant speed-ups, reaching peak gains of up to 3.2 times with respect to the previous state of the art lease-based replication protocol.

References

1. Aguilera, M.K., Merchant, A., Shah, M., Veitch, A., Karamanolis, C.: Sinfonia: a new paradigm for building scalable distributed systems. In: SOSP 2007, pp. 159–174 (2007)
2. Allen, E., Chase, D., Hallett, J., Luchangco, V., Maessen, J.-W., Ryu, S., Steele, G.L., Tobin-Hochstadt, S.: The Fortress Language Specification. Technical report, Sun Microsystems, Inc., Version 1.0. (March 2008)
3. Amza, C., Cox, A., Rajamani, K., Zwaenepoel, W.: Tradeoffs between false sharing and aggregation in software distributed shared memory. In: PPoPP 1997 (1997)
4. Aristos Project (2013), http://aristos.gsd.inesc-id.pt
5. Bartoli, A., Babaoglu, O.: Selecting a "primary partition" in partitionable asynchronous distributed systems. In: SRDS 1997, pp. 138–145 (1997)
6. Cachopo, J.: Development of Rich Domain Models with Atomic Actions. PhD thesis, Technical University of Lisbon (2007)
7. Carvalho, N., Romano, P., Rodrigues, L.: A generic framework for replicated software transactional memories. In: NCA 2011, pp. 271–274 (2011)
8. Carvalho, N., Romano, P., Rodrigues, L.: Asynchronous lease-based replication of software transactional memory. In: Gupta, I., Mascolo, C. (eds.) Middleware 2010. LNCS, vol. 6452, pp. 376–396. Springer, Heidelberg (2010)
9. Carvalho, N., Romano, P., Rodrigues, L.: Scert: Speculative certification in replicated software transactional memories. In: SYSTOR, p. 10 (2011)
10. Chockler, G.V., Keidar, I., Vitenberg, R.: Group communication specifications: a comprehensive study. ACM Comput. Surv. 33(4), 427–469 (2001)
11. Couceiro, M., Romano, P., Carvalho, N., Rodrigues, L.: D^2STM: Dependable Distributed Software Transactional Memory. In: PRDC 2009, pp. 307–313 (2009)
12. Defago, X., Schiper, A., Urban, P.: Total order broadcast and multicast algorithms: Taxonomy and survey. ACM Computing Surveys 36(4), 372–421 (2004)
13. Dice, D., Shalev, O., Shavit, N.N.: Transactional locking II. In: Dolev, S. (ed.) DISC 2006. LNCS, vol. 4167, pp. 194–208. Springer, Heidelberg (2006)
14. Guerraoui, R., Rodrigues, L.: Introduction to Reliable Distributed Programming. Springer (2006)
15. Herlihy, M., Luchangco, V., Moir, M.: A flexible framework for implementing software transactional memory. In: OOPSLA 2006, pp. 253–262 (2006)
16. Herlihy, M., Moss, J.E.B.: Transactional memory: architectural support for lock-free data structures. In: ISCA 1993, pp. 289–300 (1993)
17. Intel Corporation. Intel® 64 and IA-32 Architectures Optimization Reference Manual. Number 248966-018 (March 2009)
18. Miranda, H., Pinto, A., Rodrigues, L.: Appia, a flexible protocol kernel supporting multiple coordinated channels. In: ICDCS 2001, pp. 707–710 (2001)
19. Romano, P., Carvalho, N., Rodrigues, L.: Towards distributed software transactional memory systems. In: LADIS 2008 (2008)
20. Saad, M.M., Ravindran, B.: Transactional forwarding: Supporting highly-concurrent stm in asynchronous distributed systems. In: SBAC-PAD, pp. 219–226. IEEE (2012)
21. Schindewolf, M., Cohen, A., Karl, W., Marongiu, A., Benini, L.: Towards transactional memory support for GCC. In: GROW 2009 (2009)
22. Shavit, N., Touitou, D.: Software transactional memory. Distributed Computing 10(2), 99–116 (1997)
23. TPC Council. TPC-C Benchmark, Revision 5.11 (February 2010)

Generic Multiversion STM*

Li Lu and Michael L. Scott

Computer Science Department, University of Rochester
Rochester, NY 14627-0226 USA
{llu,scott}@cs.rochester.edu

Abstract. Multiversion software transactional memory (STM) allows a transaction to read old values of a recently updated object, after which the transaction may serialize *before* transactions that committed earlier in physical time. This ability to "commit in the past" is particularly appealing for long-running read-only transactions, which may otherwise starve in many STM systems, because short-running peers modify data out from under them before they have a chance to finish.

Most previous approaches to multiversioning have been designed as an integral part of some larger STM system, and have assumed an object-oriented, garbage-collected language. We describe, instead, how multiversioning may be implemented on top of an almost arbitrary "word-based" STM system. To the best of our knowledge, ours is the first work (for any kind of STM) to combine bounded space consumption with guaranteed wait freedom for read-only transactions (in the form presented here, it may require writers to be blocking). We make no assumptions about data or metadata layout, though we do require that the base system provide a hash function with certain ordering properties. We neither require nor interfere with automatic garbage collection. Privatization safety can be ensured—without compromising wait freedom for readers—either by forcing privatizing writers to wait for all extant readers or by requiring that programmers explicitly identify the data being privatized.

1 Introduction

Transactional memory (TM) raises the level of abstraction for synchronization, allowing programmers to specify what should be made atomic without specifying *how* it should be made atomic. The underlying system then attempts to execute nonconflicting transactions in parallel, typically by means of speculation. Hardware support for TM has begun to reach the market, but software implementations (STM) can be expected to remain important for many years.

In both hardware and software TM, strategies for detecting and recovering from conflicts differ greatly from one implementation to another. Most systems, however,

---

* This work was supported in part by the National Science Foundation under grants CCR-0963759, CCF-1116055, and CNS-1116109.

Y. Afek (Ed.): DISC 2013, LNCS 8205, pp. 134–148, 2013.
© Springer-Verlag Berlin Heidelberg 2013

have particular trouble accommodating long-running transactions. When *writer* transactions (those that update shared data) conflict with one another (or appear to conflict due to limitations in the detection mechanism) users will presumably not be surprised by a lack of concurrency: in the general case, conflicting updates must execute one at a time. When writers conflict with *readers*, however (i.e., with transactions that make no changes to shared data), one might in principle hope to do better, since there is a moment in time (the point at which it starts) when a reader could execute to completion without interfering with the writer(s).

The problem, of course, is that changes made by writers after a reader has already started may prevent the reader from completing. Specifically, if transaction R reads location x early in its execution, it will typically be able to commit only if no other thread commits a change to x while R is still active. Since readers are "invisible" in most STM systems (they refrain from modifying metadata, to avoid exclusive-mode cache misses), writers cannot defer to them, and a long-running reader may starve. To avoid this problem, most systems arrange for a long-running reader to give up after a certain number of retries and re-run under the protection of a global lock, excluding all other transactions and making the reader's completion inevitable.

A potentially attractive alternative, explored by several groups, is to keep old versions of objects, and allow long-running readers to "commit in the past." Suppose transaction R reads x, transaction W subsequently commits changes to x and y, and then R attempts to read y. Because the current value of y was never valid at the same time as R's previously read value of x, R cannot proceed, nor can it switch to the newer value of x, since it may have performed arbitrary computations with the old value. If, however, the older version of y is still available, R can safely use that instead. Assuming that the STM system is otherwise correct, R's behavior will be the same as it would have been if it completed all its work before transaction W, and then took a long time to return.

Multiversioning is commonplace in database systems. In the STM context, it was pioneered by Riegel et al. in their SI-STM [21] and LSA [20] systems, and, concurrently, by Cachopo et al. in their JVSTM [3, 4]. SI-STM and LSA maintain a fixed number of old versions of any given object. JVSTM, by contrast, maintains all old versions that might potentially be needed by some still-running transaction. Specifically, if the oldest-running transaction began at time t, JVSTM will keep the newest version that is older than t, plus all versions newer than that.

In all three systems, the runtime deletes no-longer-wanted versions explicitly, by breaking the last pointer to them, after which the standard garbage collector will eventually reclaim them. More recently, Perelman et al. demonstrated, in their SMV system [17], how to eliminate explicit deletion: they distinguish between *hard* and *weak* references to an object version v, and arrange for the last hard reference to become unreachable once no running transaction has a start time earlier than that of the transaction that overwrote v.

Several additional systems [1, 2, 11, 16, 18] allow not only readers but also writers to commit in the past. Unfortunately, because such systems require visible readers and complex dependence tracking, they can be expected to have significantly higher constant overheads. We do not consider them further here.

SI-STM, LSA, JVSTM, and SMV were all implemented in Java. While only SMV really leverages automatic garbage collection, all four are "object-based": their meta-data, including lists of old versions, are kept in object headers. One might naturally wonder whether this organization is a coincidence or a necessity: can we create an efficient, multiversion STM system suitable for unmanaged languages like C and C++, in which data need not be organized as objects, and in which unwanted data must always be explicitly reclaimed?

Our GMV (Generic MultiVersioning) system answers this question in the affirmative. It is designed to interoperate with any existing "word-based" (i.e., hash-table–based) STM system that provides certain basic functionality. It is also, to the best of our knowledge, the first mechanism to simultaneously (a) guarantee wait-free progress for all read-only transactions, and (b) bound total space consumption—specifically, to $O(nm)$, where n is the number of threads and m is the space consumed by an equivalent nontransactional, global-lock-based program (this assumes reasonable space consumption in the underlying STM system). Finally, GMV can preserve both privatization safety (for writers) and wait freedom for readers if we are willing either to force privatizing writers to wait for extant readers, or to require programmers to explicitly label the data being privatized.

As a proof of concept, we have implemented GMV on top of the TL2-like [6] "LLT" back end of the RSTM suite [19]. Experiments with microbenchmarks confirm that GMV eliminates starvation for long-running readers, yielding dramatically higher throughput than single-version systems for workloads that depend on such transactions.

We focus in this paper on the formal properties of GMV. We describe the algorithm, including its interface to the underlying STM system and its impact on privatization, in Section 2. In Section 3 we outline proofs of strict serializability, bounded space consumption, and wait-free readers. We also consider the impact of GMV on the liveness of writers. Section 4 summarizes the performance of our prototype implementation. We conclude in Section 5.

2   GMV Design

We refer to a transaction as a "reader" if it is known in advance to perform no updates to shared locations. Otherwise it is a "writer." On behalf of readers, and with limited cooperation from writers, GMV maintains four key data structures: a global timestamp variable, gt, that tracks the serialization order of writer transactions; an array ts of local timestamps, indexed by thread id; a history_table that holds values that have been overwritten by writers but may still be needed by active readers; and an array, hp, of "helping structures," also indexed by thread id. Variable gt can be shared with the underlying STM system (the *host*), if that system is timestamp-based. The history table, likewise, can be merged with the table of ownership records (Orecs) in the host, if it has such a table. Array hp is used to let the garbage collection process (invoked by writer threads) cooperate with reader transactions. Each reader records its history table inquiries in hp. If a writer needs to perform a potentially conflicting collection on a history list, it first completes the reader's request and stores the result in hp. GMV uses a type-preserving memory allocator for history nodes; this convention, together with the monotonicity of timestamps, allows a reader to notice if its search has conflicted with a writer, and to retrieve the answer it was looking for from the helping array.

We characterize both GMV and the host as linearizable concurrent objects. The host provides methods for use by writers; GMV is oblivious to these. The host must also provide two methods to be called by GMV. GMV, for its part, exports four methods: two to be called by readers, the other two by the host. Readers make no direct calls to the host

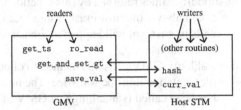

Fig. 1. GMV interface routines

(Fig. 1). Our pseudocode assumes that memory is sequentially consistent, but it can easily be adapted to more relaxed machines.

GMV tracks overwritten values at word granularity, in a hash table keyed by memory address. Each bucket of the hash table is a dummy head node for a list of *history nodes* whose locations share a hash value. Each (real) node n in turn has three fields: a location loc, an old_value formerly contained in loc, and the global time (gt value) overwrite_time when this value was overwritten. A special-purpose, built-in garbage collector reclaims nodes that are no longer needed.

2.1 GMV–Host Interface

GMV provides two methods to be called by the host STM:

get_and_set_gt(): This method atomically increments gt and returns the new value. The host must guarantee that the serialization order of writers is consistent with the values returned. These values provide a well-defined meaning for "writer W serializes at time t," and "value v was written to location l at time t." Note that spurious calls to get_and_set_gt() are harmless: every committed writer must obtain a unique timestamp, but not every timestamp must correspond to a unique committed writer.

save_val(loc, old_value, overwrite_time): After calling get_and_set_gt(), and before allowing its thread to proceed with post-transaction execution, a writer must call this method for every location it has modified, passing the value returned by get_and_set_gt() as its overwrite_time. A call with a given location must not be made until all calls with a smaller overwrite_time and a location with the same hash value have already returned.

Code for these routines is trivial: get_and_set_gt performs a fetch_and_increment on gt and returns the result plus one; save_val writes its arguments into a newly allocated history node, which it then pushes, in the manner of a Treiber stack [24], onto the beginning of history list hash(l). We assume that the memory allocator employed by save_val tracks the total number of extant history nodes. Each writer checks this number at commit time. If it exceeds some predetermined threshold (we used $100K$ in our experiments), the writer invokes a garbage collection algorithm, described in Section 2.3.

GMV in turn requires two methods from the host:

hash(loc): Values returned by this function are used as indices into the history table. As noted above, the host must ensure that if two locations have the same hash value, calls to save_val will happen in timestamp order, even if they are made by different transactions.

curr_val(loc): GMV calls this method to obtain values not found in a history list. Its implementation must be wait-free. The host must guarantee that (1) if save_val(l, v, t) has been called (something that GMV of course can see), then the value v' returned by a subsequent call to curr_val(l) must have been written at some time $t' \geq t$, and (2) if curr_val(l) has returned v' and save_val(l, v'', t'') is subsequently called, then v' must have been written at some time $t' < t''$.

The implementation of curr_val depends on the nature of the host STM, but will often be straightforward. In a redo-log based STM, curr_val(l) can simply return the value at location l in main memory. In an undo-log based STM, it may need to access the log of some active writer W: it cannot require the reader to abort, nor can it wait for W to complete. It may also need to access the log of an active writer in a nonblocking STM [9, 12], where locations may be "stolen" without every having been written back to main memory. (The ordering requirements on calls to save_val are a bigger concern than save_val in nonblocking systems; we return to this subject in Section 3.3.)

2.2   Read-only Transactions

Aside from calls to curr_val, GMV handles reader transactions. At the beginning of reader R, executed by thread i, GMV stores the current global timestamp gt into local timestamp ts$[i]$. To read location l, R then calls ro_read(l) (Algorithm 1). When R commits, ts$[i]$ is set to infinity.

At line 2 of ro_read, reader_history_list_search(h, l, i) looks for the last (oldest) node in history list h whose location field is l and whose overwrite time is greater (newer) than ts$[i]$. It returns $\perp$ if such a node does not exist. Code for this helper method appears in Algorithm 2. (The similar code in Algorithm 3 will be needed in Algorithm 4.) To enable helping by a garbage-collecting writer, ro_read maintains its current request—the location and time it's looking for—in hp$[i]$. During list traversal, if the reader sees a node with a larger than expected timestamp, it knows that a writer has interfered with its search, and that the answer it is looking for can be found in hp$[i]$.

Algorithm 1. ro_read

Require: location l, thread id i
1: $h :=$ history_table$[$hash$(l)]$
2: $v :=$ reader_history_list_search(h, l, i)
3: **if** $v \neq \perp$ **then**
4:      **return** v
5: $c :=$ curr_val(l)
6: **if** $h =$ history_table$[$hash$(l)]$ **then**
7:      **return** c
8: $v :=$ reader_history_list_search(h, l, i)
9: **if** $v \neq \perp$ **then**
10:     **return** v
11: **else**
12:     **return** c

Like other multiversion STM systems, GMV avoids reader transaction aborts by allowing them to "commit in the past." Where a writer transaction obtains its serialization time by calling get_and_set_gt when it is ready to commit, a reader obtains its serialization time by reading gt when it first begins execution. If reader R is long-running, it may

Algorithm 2. reader_history_list_search

Require: history list h, location l, thread id i

```
1:  v := ⊥;  n := h.next
2:  hp[i] := ⟨l, ts[i]⟩
3:  pt := ∞ {previous node timestamp}
4:  while n ≠ null do
5:      if n→overwrite_time > pt then
6:          {GC has interfered}
7:          v := hp[i]
8:          break
9:      if n→overwrite_time ≤ ts[i] then
10:         {no further nodes will be useful}
11:         break
12:     if n→loc = l then
13:         v := n→old_value
14:     pt := n→overwrite_time
15:     n := n→next
16: hp[i] := ⊥
17: return v
```

Algorithm 3. GC_history_list_search

Require: hash value k, location l, time t

```
1:  while true do
2:      v := ⊥;  n := history_table[k].next
3:      pt := ∞ {previous node timestamp}
4:      while n ≠ null do
5:          nl := n→loc;  nv := n→old_value
6:          nn := n→next
7:          nt := n→overwrite_time
8:              {read overwrite_time last}
9:          if nt > pt then
10:             {another GC thread has interfered}
11:             continue while loop at line 1
12:         if nt ≤ t then
13:             {no further nodes will be useful}
14:             break
15:         if nl = l then
16:             v := nv
17:         pt := nt;  n := nn
18: return v
```

serialize before a host of writer transactions whose implementations commit before it does. This "early serialization" resembles that of mainstream systems like TL2 [6], but multiversioning avoids the need to abort and restart read-only transactions that attempt to read a location that has changed since the transaction's start time. Early serialization stands in contrast to systems like RingSTM [23] and NOrec [5], which serialize readers at commit time, and to systems like TinySTM [22] and SwissTM [7], which dynamically update their "start time" in response to commits in other transactions, and may therefore serialize at some internal transactional read.

2.3 Garbage Collection

To avoid unbounded memory growth, history lists must periodically be pruned. If readers are never to abort, this pruning must identify and reclaim only those list nodes that will never again be needed. In GMV, a node may still be needed by reader i if it is the earliest node for its location that is later than $ts[i]$. Nodes that do not satisfy this property for some thread i are reclaimed by the GC.

The core of the garbage collection algorithm appears in Algorithm 5. It is invoked from save_val, and can be executed concurrently by multiple writers. It has been designed to be lock free, and to preserve the wait freedom of readers. Writers synchronize with each other using a simplified version of the Harris [10] and Michael [14] lock-free list algorithm (simplified in the sense that insertions occur only at the head of the list). To support this algorithm, next pointers in history lists contain both a *count* and a *mark*.

The count, which is incremented whenever the pointer is modified, avoids the ABA problem. The mark indicates that a node is garbage and can be unlinked from the list; when set, it inhibits updating the pointer to link out the successor node.

As noted in Section 2.2, thread i begins a reader transaction by copying the global timestamp gt into ts$[i]$. It ends by resetting ts$[i]$ to infinity (maxint). To identify garbage nodes (Algorithm 6), we collect the entries in ts, sort them into descending order (with an end-of-list sentinel value), and then compare them to the timestamps of nodes in each history list via simultaneous traversal. The collect need not be atomic: nodes that transitioned from useful to garbage after the beginning of the scan may not necessarily be reclaimed, but the monotonicity of timestamps implies that anything that was garbage at the beginning of the scan is guaranteed to be recognized as such. If another writer finds that memory is getting low, it will call GC, discover nodes that can be freed, and keep the space bound by freeing them.

To delete node n from a history list (having already read its predecessor's next pointer), we first mark n's next pointer. We then update the predecessor's next pointer to link n out of the list. We add n to a thread-local set of to-be-reclaimed nodes. Traversing the history list from head to tail, we effectively convert it to a tree. Any reader that is actively perusing the list will continue to see all useful successor nodes beyond ("above") it in the tree.

Algorithm 4. help_readers
Require: hash value k
1: **for** each thread id i **do**
2: $\quad x := \mathsf{hp}[i]$
3: $\quad$ **if** $x \neq \bot$ **then**
4: $\quad\quad \langle l, t \rangle := x$
5: $\quad\quad$ **if** hash$(l) = k$ **then**
6: $\quad\quad\quad$ (void) CAS(&hp$[i]$, x,
7: $\quad\quad\quad\quad$ GC_history_list_search(k, l, t))

Before we can actually reclaim the garbage nodes, however, we must ensure, via help_readers and GC_history_list_search (Algorithms 4 and 3) that no reader is still using them. We peruse the global helping array, hp. If we discover that reader R is searching for location l, and l hashes to the current history list, we complete R's search on its behalf, and attempt to CAS the result back into the helping array (in our pseudocode, this changes the type of hp$[i]$, which is effectively a union). If the CAS fails, then either R has moved on or some other writer has already helped it. We can then safely reclaim our to-be-deleted nodes (moving them to a lock-free global free list), provided that we first update the timestamp in each so that a reader will recognize (line 5 of Algorithm 2) that it no longer belongs in the previous list.

2.4 Privatization Safety

It is generally recognized that any STM system for an unmanaged language must be *privatization safe* [13]. That is, if a transaction renders datum x accessible only to thread T, the STM system must ensure that (1) subsequent nontransactional writes of x by T cannot compromise the integrity of "doomed" transactions that may access x before aborting, and (2) delayed cleanup in logically committed transactions cannot compromise the integrity of nontransactional post-privatization reads of x by T.

We may safely assume that problem (2) is addressed by the host STM; the addition of GMV introduces no new complexity. Problem (1), however, is a challenge: if a privatizer writes to formerly shared data, and doesn't update the history table, an active

Algorithm 5. Garbage collection	**Algorithm 6.** find_garbage_nodes
1: array st := sort(ts $\cup \{-1\}$), descending)	**Require:** hash val k, sorted time array st
2: **for** k in hash range **do**	1: $start\_time$:= gt {global timestamp}
3: node set G := find_garbage_nodes(k, st)	2: **while true do**
4: node set U := $\varnothing$ {unlinked nodes}	3: node set G := $\varnothing$ {garbage nodes}
5: **while true do**	4: mapping[location$\Rightarrow$node] M := $\varnothing$
6: p := &history_table[k]	5: i := 0; n := history_table[k]
7: n := $p \rightarrow$next	6: pt := ∞ {prev. node timestamp}
8: pt := ∞ {previous node timestamp}	7: **while** $n \neq$ null and
9: **while** $n \neq$ null **do**	$n \rightarrow$overwrite_time > $start\_time$ **do**
10: nn := $n \rightarrow$next	8: {never reclaim nodes newer than
11: nt := $n \rightarrow$overwrite_time	$start\_time$}
12: **if** $nt > pt$ **then**	9: n := $n \rightarrow$next
13: {another GC thread has interfered}	10: **while** $st[i] \neq -1$ and $n \neq$ null **do**
14: **continue while** loop at line 5	11: nl := $n \rightarrow$loc; nn := $n \rightarrow$next
15: **if** $n \in G$ and $\neg$is_marked(nn) **then**	
16: **if** $\neg$CAS(&$n \rightarrow$next, nn, mark(nn))	12: nt := $n \rightarrow$overwrite_time
then	13: {read overwrite_time last}
17: {another GC has interfered}	14: **if** $nt > pt$ **then**
18: **continue while** loop at line 5	15: {another GC has interfered}
19: $flag$:= $false$	16: **continue while** loop at line 2
20: **if** is_marked(nn) **then**	17: **if** $nt > st[i]$ **then**
21: **if** CAS(&$p \rightarrow$next, n, nn) **then**	18: m := $M[nl]$
22: U += n	19: **if** $m \neq$ null **then**
23: $flag$:= **true**	20: G += m
24: **if** $|U| \geq U_{MAX}$ **then**	21: $M[nl]$:= n; n := nn
25: help_readers(k)	22: pt := nt
26: **for** n in U **do**	23: **else**
27: $n \rightarrow$overwrite_time := ∞	24: i++; M := $\varnothing$
28: reclaim all nodes in U	25: **while** $n \neq$ null **do**
29: U := $\varnothing$	26: nn := $n \rightarrow$next
30: **else**	27: nt := $n \rightarrow$overwrite_time
31: {another GC has interfered}	28: {read overwrite_time last}
32: **continue while** loop at line 5	29: **if** $nt > pt$ **then**
33: **if** not $flag$ **then**	30: {another GC has interfered}
34: p := n; pt := nt	31: **continue while** loop at line 2
35: n := nn	32: G += n; n := nn
36: **break**	33: **break**
37: help_readers(k)	34: **return** G
38: **for** n in U **do**	
39: $n \rightarrow$overwrite_time := ∞	
40: reclaim all nodes in U	

reader that needs to commit at some past time t may see the wrong value if calls curr_val. One possible solution is to require a privatizing writer to wait for all active readers to commit before it continues execution. This, of course, sacrifices nonblocking progress for writers (a subject to which we will return in Section 3.3). Even in a blocking system, it may induce an uncomfortably long wait. Alternatively, if the source program explicitly identifies the data being privatized, GMV could push the current values into the history table, where they would be seen by active readers. This option sacrifices the transparency of privatization. In a similar vein, if the compiler can identify data that *might* be sharable, it can instrument nontransactional writes to update the history list. This option compromises the performance benefit of privatization.

3   GMV Properties

In this section we sketch proofs of our claims of GMV safety, bounded space, and wait-free progress for read-only transactions ("readers"). We also consider the impact of GMV on the liveness of writers.

3.1   Safety

Theorem 1. *When GMV is correctly integrated into a strictly serializable host STM, the resulting STM remains strictly serializable.*

Proof. As described in Section 2.1, GMV requires the host STM, H, to ensure that (1) the serialization order of writer transactions is consistent with the values returned by get_and_set_gt, (2) a writer calls save_val(l, v, t) for every location it modifies, and (3) the calls for all locations with the same hash value occur in timestamp order. These rules ensure that history list nodes are ordered by timestamp, and that if $n_2 = \langle l, v_2, t_2 \rangle$ and $n_1 = \langle l, v_1, t_1 \rangle$ are consecutive nodes for location l $(t_2 > t_1)$, then a reader transaction that sees v_2 at location l can correctly serialize at any time t such that $t_2 > t \geq t_1$.

Since nodes are removed from history lists only when there is no longer any reader transaction that can use them, the only remaining concern is for readers that call curr_val. In this case, as again described in Section 2.1, GMV requires H to ensure that any call to curr_val linearizes within H (1) after any method of H that calls save_val for the same location and a same or earlier timestamp, and (2) before any method of H that calls save_val for the same location and a later timestamp. These rules ensure that curr_val is called only when there is no appropriate history node, and that any writer that would cause curr_val to return a "too new" value calls save_val to create an appropriate history node first.

Taken together, the requirements on H ensure that a GMV reader sees exactly the same values it would have seen if executed as a writer in timestamp order within H. This in turn implies that the combined system remains strictly serializable.   □

3.2   Space Consumption

Lemma 1. *In the wake of a call to Algorithm 5, started at time t, the total space consumed in history lists by nodes with timestamp less than t (denoted TS_t) is in $O(nm)$,* *where n is the total number of threads in the system, and m is the space consumed by a nontransactional, global lock-based program.*

Proof. Algorithm 5 retains nodes that may be used by a concurrent reader. Therefore, for each location l, the GC retains a constant number of history list nodes for each currently active reader. We assume that the size of history_table (and hence of the extra head nodes) is bounded by $O(m)$. Since the total number of distinct locations is also in $O(m)$, and the total number of active readers is in $O(n)$, the total space for all nodes on all lists is clearly in $O(nm)$.   □

Lemma 2. *Algorithm 5 is lock free*

Proof. We assume that the routines to allocate and reclaim list nodes are lock free. Given that history lists are noncircular, the traversal loops at Algorithm 3 line 4, Algorithm 5 line 9, and Algorithm 6 lines 7, 10, and 25 must all complete within a bounded number of steps. The remaining potential loops are the various **continue** statements: Algorithm 3 line 11; Algorithm 5 lines 14, 18, and 32; and Algorithm 6 lines 16 and 31. In most of these cases, execution of the **while true** loop continues when a GC thread encounters a node that has been reclaimed by some other thread (one whose timestamp appears larger than that of its predecessor); in these cases the system as a whole has made forward progress, and lock freedom is not endangered. The only tricky cases occur at Algorithm 5 lines 18 and 32, in the wake of a failed CAS. Here again the system as a whole has made progress: failure to mark or unlink a node indicates that some other thread has done so, and a marked node can be unlinked by any GC writer.   □

Theorem 2. *The total space TS consumed by history lists is in $O(nm)$.*

Proof. Garbage collection will be started by any writer that discovers, at commit time, that the number of extant history nodes exceeds some predetermined threshold. Progress of the collection cannot be delayed or otherwise compromised by readers. Moreover any writer that attempts to commit before a GC pass has updated its statistics will also execute GC. By Lemma 2, so long as some thread continues to execute, some GC thread will make progress. By Lemma 1, a GC pass that starts at time t guarantees that TS_t is bounded by $O(nm)$. The only remaining question is then: what is the maximum value of $TS - TS_t$, the space that may be consumed, at the end of the GC pass, by history nodes that are unlinked but not reclaimed, or that have timestamp $\geq t$? This value is clearly the number of history nodes that may be generated by writers that are already in their commit protocol when the GC pass begins (TS_{added}), plus the number of nodes held by non-progressing GC threads (TS_{hold}, privatized at Algorithm 5 line 22). Since the number of writers is in $O(n)$, and the number of history nodes generated by any given writer is in $O(m)$, we know that TS_{added} is in $O(nm)$. For TS_{hold}, since each blocked GC may hold at most U_{MAX} nodes at a time (Algorithm 5 line 24), the total number of nodes held by non-progressing GC threads is in $O(n)$. It follows that $TS - TS_t$ is in $O(nm)$, and therefore so is TS.   □

3.3 Liveness

Theorem 3. *GMV readers are wait free.*

Proof. Straightforward: by Theorem 2, the number of history nodes is bounded, and therefore so is the time spent traversing any given list in ro_read. We also require curr_val to be wait free. There are no other waits, loops, or aborts in the reader code. So all readers in GMV are wait free.   □

By way of comparison, both SI-STM [21] and LSA [20] require readers to abort if the historical version they need has been reclaimed, so readers may in principle starve. JVSTM [3, 4] and SMV [17] never reclaim versions that may still be needed, but an active writer may create an unbounded number of history nodes for a reader to traverse. Systems that revert to inevitability for long-running readers are of course fundamentally blocking: a reader cannot start until active writers get out of the way.

Nonblocking writers. Ideally, we should like to be able to guarantee that if GMV were added to a lock-free (or obstruction-free) STM system, writers in the combined system would remain lock free (obstruction free). The GMV API functions are all lock free, which is certainly a good start: get_and_set_gt() is trivially lock free: its internal fetch_and_increment fails only if some other caller's succeeds. In a similar vein, calls to save_val() loop only when the Treiber-stack push fails because another thread's push succeeded. By Lemma 2, the garbage collection process called by save_val() is also lock free. Therefore save_val() is lock free.

Unfortunately, we must also consider the constraints we have placed on calls to these API functions. In particular, we have insisted that if $t_1 < t_2$ and $\mathsf{hash}(l_1) = \mathsf{hash}(l_2)$, then any call of the form $\mathsf{save\_val}(l_1, v_1, t_1)$ must occur before any call of the form $\mathsf{save\_val}(l_2, v_2, t_2)$. This requirement is similar to asking transactions that modify locations with the same hash value to write their updates back to main memory in serialization order. It is not at all clear how a nonblocking system might do so. In particular, WSTM [8, 9] and MM-STM [12] (to our knowledge the only extant nonblocking word-based systems) both allow a transaction to "steal" an ownership record (Orec); values of locations that hash to that Orec may then be written back to memory out of order, up until the next time that the Orec is quiescent (if it ever is).

We believe we could obtain a (nonblocking) multiversion variant of WSTM or MM-STM by requiring the thread that steals an Orec to maintain the prefix of the history list corresponding to that Orec's locations. Method ro_read would begin by consulting the Orec: if quiescent, it would consult the usual history list; otherwise, it would first consult the stealer's list prefix. This solution would require that GMV be integrated into the underlying system in a way that no longer merits the term "generic." We leave the details to future work.

4   Performance of a Proof-of-Concept Implementation

We implemented a proof of concept system, GMV+, for GMV. This implementation is based on the LLT back end, a TL2 [6]-like STM, in the RSTM suite [19].

GMV+ differs from GMV only in the addition of a "fast path" for garbage collection. This path reclaims only the tails of history lists, in a region known to be ignored by all still-running readers, thereby eliminating the need for helping. If memory consumption is still beyond the preset threshold after execution of the fast path, GMV+ returns to execute the normal "slow path" GC algorithm, with helping. In our experiments, the slow path was very rarely needed.

We tested GMV+ on a two-processor Intel Xeon E5649 machine. Each processor has 6 cores running at 2.53 GHz, and 2 hardware threads per core. Each core has 32 KB of L1 D-cache and 256 KB of L2 cache; the cores of a given processor share 12 MB of on-chip L3 cache. Microbenchmark results indicate that the maintenance of history lists increases the overhead of writers by approximately 50%. In return, multiversioning reaps significant benefits when the workload has long-running readers. We modified a hash table microbenchmark that performs lookup, insert, and remove operations, to also include long-running "sum" operations, which traverse the entire table and add up all its elements. Unlike lookup operations, which are small and fast, sum operations take long enough that they almost always conflict with concurrent writers, and will starve unless something special is done.

Figure 2 (top) present results for a read-heavy test with sum, lookup, and update (insert and delete) operations in a ratio of 1:79:20. We compare the throughput (transactions/second) of LLT, GMV+, and two variants of the simpler NOrec algorithm [5]. Because NOrec serializes transaction write-back using a global lock, it supports a trivial implementation of inevitability (irrevocability). In the "NOrec inevitable" experiments we use inevitable mode to run the sum transactions. We also test a (non-general) extension of LLT (labeled "LLT inevitable") in which the checker thread acquires a global lock. Other threads read this lock; if it is held they abort, and wait to retry.

When running our microbenchmark, GMV+ outperforms the other tested algorithms, with speedup out to the full count of hardware threads. While inevitability avoids starvation of readers, it also limits scalability: neither algorithm with inevitability speeds up with additional threads.

We also evaluate GMV+'s performance on a modified version of the "Vacation" benchmark from the STAMP suite [15]. Vacation simulates a concurrent travel inquiry / reservation system. Most threads, as in the original version, repeatedly perform read / write / update operations on price tables (for cars, flights and rooms), and read / write operations on the reservation table. At the same time, we add a dedicated "checker" thread that periodically runs a transaction to checksum the reservation table. Note that in contrast to the hash table microbenchmark, here long-running read-only transactions are confined to a single thread. Overall system throughput is displayed in the bottom half of Figure 2.

We run this benchmark with 4 queries per normal transaction and 65536 initial relations in each price table. 98% of normal transactions are for reservations; the other 2% update price tables. The benchmark's "query range" parameter is set to 60% for normal transactions, which the application's authors consider "high contention." We run the checker every 100 ms in this test. Without inevitability, checker transactions routinely starve in both LLT and NOrec. We omitted results for these configurations in the figure. With inevitability, the checker can almost always complete within 100 ms. It usually completes within this interval for GMV+ as well, at least at low thread counts.

Overall transaction throughput for GMV+ is roughly 20% higher than for LLT with inevitability, presumably because the checker thread, when running, does not exclude concurrent writers. Throughput peaks at 12 threads (the number of cores) on the

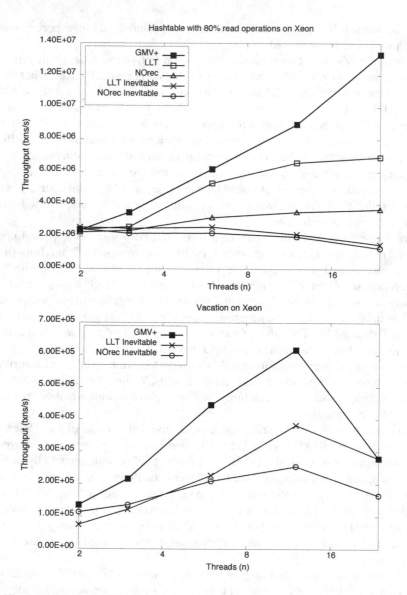

Fig. 2. Throughput of GMV+ for hash table (top) and augmented Vacation (bottom)

testing machine. The default scheduling discipline places successive threads on alternating processors, so inter-chip communication is occurring even at low thread counts. In this situation NOrec's scalability is limited by contention on the lock that serializes writer commits.

Performance results for GMV+ confirm that multiversioning is an attractive alternative to inevitability for applications with long-running read-only transactions. Multiversioning allows long-running readers to complete without aborting, and to co-exist with short transactions that continue to scale to the limits otherwise imposed by the STM runtime and hardware coherence fabric.

5 Conclusions

We have proposed a generic multiversion STM system, GMV. Unlike previous integrated systems, it can be layered on top of most existing word-based STM. To the best of our knowledge, GMV is the first STM system to combine bounded space consumption with guaranteed wait freedom for read-only transactions. It neither requires nor interferes with automatic garbage collection. Privatization can be ensured—without compromising wait freedom for readers—either by blocking writers or by requiring that programmers explicitly identify the data being privatized.

We also described a proof-of-concept implementation of GMV. With roughly 50% overhead to maintain history lists, our implementation eliminates reader starvation, and generates up to $2\times$ speedup on workloads with long-running readers. With further implementation effort, the instrumentation overhead could probably be reduced, but for small transactions it will always be higher than the baseline. Topics for future work include (1) integration with nonblocking word-based STM; (2) automatic mechanisms to choose when a read-only transaction should use the history lists (as opposed to acting as a writer); and (3) a mechanism to choose (on a global basis), when writers should maintain the history lists.

Acknowledgment. We are grateful to the anonymous referees for identifying several bugs in the pseudocode, and for prodding us to clarify our thinking on the issue of nonblocking writers.

References

1. Aydonat, U., Abdelrahman, T.: Serializability of Transactions in Software Transactional Memory. In: 3rd ACM SIGPLAN Wkshp. on Transactional Computing, Salt Lake City, UT (February 2008)
2. Bieniusa, A., Fuhrmann, T.: Consistency in Hindsight: A Fully Decentralized STM Algorithm. In: Proc. of the 24th Intl. Parallel and Distributed Processing Symp., Atlanta, GA (April 2010)
3. Cachopo, J., Rito-Silva, A.: Versioned Boxes as the Basis for Memory Transactions. Science of Computer Programming 63(2), 172–185 (2006)
4. Cachopo, J., Rito-Silva, A.: Versioned Boxes as the Basis for Memory Transactions. In: Proc., Wkshp. on Synchronization and Concurrency in Object-Oriented Languages, in conjunction with OOPSLA 2005, San Diego, CA (October 2005)
5. Dalessandro, L., Spear, M.F., Scott, M.L.: NOrec: Streamlining STM by Abolishing Ownership Records. In: Proc. of the 15th ACM Symp. on Principles and Practice of Parallel Programming, Bangalore, India (January 2010)
6. Dice, D., Shalev, O., Shavit, N.: Transactional Locking II. In: Proc. of the 20th Intl. Symp. on Distributed Computing, Stockholm, Sweden (September 2006)
7. Dragojević, A., Guerraoui, R., Kapałka, M.: Stretching Transactional Memory. In: Proc. of the SIGPLAN 2009 Conf. on Programming Language Design and Implementation, Dublin, Ireland (June 2009)

8. Fraser, K., Harris, T.: Concurrent Programming Without Locks. ACM Trans. on Computer Systems 25(2), article 5 (May 2007)
9. Harris, T., Fraser, K.: Language Support for Lightweight Transactions. In: OOPSLA 2003 Conf. Proc., Anaheim, CA (October 2003)
10. Harris, T.L.: A Pragmatic Implementation of Non-Blocking Linked-Lists. In: Welch, J.L. (ed.) DISC 2001. LNCS, vol. 2180, pp. 300–314. Springer, Heidelberg (2001)
11. Keidar, I., Perelman, D.: On Avoiding Spare Aborts in Transactional Memory. In: Proc. of the 21st ACM Symp. on Parallelism in Algorithms and Architectures, Calgary, AB, Canada (August 2009)
12. Marathe, V.J., Moir, M.: Toward High Performance Nonblocking Software Transactional Memory. In: Proc. of the 13th ACM Symp. on Principles and Practice of Parallel Programming, Salt Lake City, UT (February 2008) Expanded version available as TR 932 Dept. of Computer Science, Univ. of Rochester (March 2008)
13. Marathe, V.J., Spear, M.F., Scott, M.L.: Scalable Techniques for Transparent Privatization in Software Transactional Memory. In: Proc. of the 2008 Intl. Conf. on Parallel Processing, Portland, OR (September 2008)
14. Michael, M.M.: High Performance Dynamic Lock-Free Hash Tables and List-Based Sets. In: Proc. of the 14th ACM Symp. on Parallel Algorithms and Architectures, Winnipeg, MB, Canada (August 2002)
15. Minh, C.C., Chung, J., Kozyrakis, C., Olukotun, K.: STAMP: Stanford Transactional Applications for Multi-Processing. In: Proc. of the 2008 IEEE Intl. Symp. on Workload Characterization, Seattle, WA (September 2008)
16. Napper, J., Alvisi, L.: Lock-Free Serializable Transactions. Technical report TR-05-04, Dept. of Computer Sciences, Univ. of Texas at Austin (February 2005)
17. Perelman, D., Byshevsky, A., Litmanovich, O., Keidar, I.: SMV: Selective Multi-Versioning STM. In: Proc. of the 25th Intl. Symp. on Distributed Computing, Rome, Italy (September 2011)
18. Perelman, D., Fan, R., Keidar, I.: On Maintaining Multiple Versions in STM. In: Proc. of the 29th ACM Symp. on Principles of Distributed Computing, Zurich, Switzerland (July 2010)
19. Reconfigurable Software Transactional Memory Runtime. Project web site, `code.google.com/p/rstm/`
20. Riegel, T., Felber, P., Fetzer, C.: A lazy snapshot algorithm with eager validation. In: Dolev, S. (ed.) DISC 2006. LNCS, vol. 4167, pp. 284–298. Springer, Heidelberg (2006)
21. Riegel, T., Fetzer, C., Felber, P.: Snapshot Isolation for Software Transactional Memory. In: 1st ACM SIGPLAN Wkshp. on Transactional Computing, Ottawa, ON, Canada (June 2006)
22. Riegel, T., Fetzer, C., Felber, P.: Time-based Transactional Memory with Scalable Time Bases. In: Proc. of the 19th ACM Symp. on Parallelism in Algorithms and Architectures, San Diego, CA (June 2007)
23. Spear, M.F., Michael, M.M., von Praun, C.: RingSTM: Scalable Transactions with a Single Atomic Instruction. In: Proc. of the 20th ACM Symp. on Parallelism in Algorithms and Architectures, Munich, Germany (June 2008)
24. Treiber, R.K.: Systems Programming: Coping with Parallelism. RJ 5118, IBM Almaden Research Center (April 1986)

Practical Parallel Nesting
for Software Transactional Memory

Nuno Diegues and João Cachopo

INESC-ID Lisboa / Instituto Superior Técnico
Universidade de Lisboa, Portugal
ndiegues@gsd.inesc-id.pt, joao.cachopo@ist.utl.pt

Abstract. Transactional Memory (TM) provides a strong abstraction to tackle the challenge of synchronizing concurrent tasks that access shared state. Yet, most TMs do not allow a single transaction to contain parallel code. We propose an efficient parallel nesting algorithm to explore existing latent parallelism within a transaction. If this intra-transaction parallelism has reduced conflict probability (compared to the inter-transaction parallelism), then it may be worthy to execute less transactions at a given time, but have each one parallelized and using several available cores.

We provide practical support for parallel nesting in the first lock-free parallel nesting algorithm with support for multi-versions. Our prototype builds over an available multi-version TM, which we outperform on standard benchmarks by up to 2.8×. We show improvements over parallel nesting alternatives of up to 3.6×.

Keywords: Transactional memory, Parallel Nesting, Abort reduction, Lock-freedom.

1 Introduction

Transactional Memory (TM), originally proposed in hardware [12], promises to tackle a major challenge in the development of concurrent programs: How to synchronize concurrent tasks accessing shared mutable state. Years of research led the microprocessor industry to adopt Hardware Transactional Memory (HTM) [5,20], bringing TM to the forefront of concurrent programming due to its accessibility in commodity processors.

But TM only solves part of the challenges, namely, that of synchronizing concurrent accesses. Identifying concurrent tasks and boundaries of transactions is still left to the programmer. Devising applications in a way that allows small, uncontended, and correct transactions, can be a challenging task rivalling that of using fine-grained locks. It is thus tempting for programmers to use long transactions bundling many actions.

The problem is that this predictable usage of TM is directly in contradiction with the reality of HTMs available in the market. Hardware vendors have opted for a paradigm of best-effort semantics, in which no guarantee is given that a transaction will ever make progress. One of the main reasons for such weak semantics is the difficulty in dealing with arbitrarily large transactions, while preserving a simple hardware design [14]. The adopted alternative is to use software fallback paths, namely to a Software Transactional Memory (STM) implementation.

Y. Afek (Ed.): DISC 2013, LNCS 8205, pp. 149–163, 2013.

Therefore, it is crucial to ensure that large, possibly contending transactions can be dealt with efficiently in STMs. The extent to which this challenge can be overcome is highly dependent on the given workload and concurrency patterns. There is a limit to which a TM can avoid spurious aborts and remain correct. It is in this context that we propose a radically different approach: To diminish abort rates by reducing the inter-transaction parallelism (i.e., executing fewer transactions at a time), and instead explore additional levels of intra-transaction parallelism (by parallelizing each transaction). Clearly, this can be beneficial under two assumptions: (1) there is a level of intra-transaction parallelism that has reduced conflict probability; and (2) it must be possible to exploit such arbitrary levels of parallelism without inducing excessive overheads in the concurrency control mechanism. In this paper we show that parallel nesting can be used effectively to tackle these problems.

Example. To illustrate the problem, consider a graph of transactional objects as represented in Fig. 1b: There are root objects that provide access to one or more other objects, such that an object accessible from a root may also be accessible from another root. This arbitrary structure is representative of the state of transactional programs.

In Listing 1a, we show a simple transactional program manipulating that state. The method updateGraph traverses all the objects in the graph and updates some of them, whereas the method changeStatus traverses only a few objects and modifies at most one of them. Both methods should execute atomically. This means that updateGraph is very likely to cause a conflict with any other transaction manipulating the graph (such as changeStatus). In some sense, this kind of workload challenges the optimistic concurrency model used by most TMs: As updateGraph calls continuously conflict and restart, they will accumulate and get delayed; any attempt to enforce their successful execution will hinder concurrency and the throughput of the application.

But this is no longer true if we reduce the top-level parallelism and simultaneously parallelize each of the fewer transactions with the model of parallel nesting. This is done in this example by parallelizing the transaction in updateGraph (shown in Listing 1c), namely by traversing the graph in parallel. Note that there is no guarantee of conflict-freedom, as we may find conflicts even in intra-transaction parallelism. For this reason, the parallel nesting model fits perfectly given its focus on concurrency control even within each single transaction. As a result of this technique, we are able to exploit to the same extent the underlying available hardware parallelism, albeit with much more efficiency in terms of reducing transactional aborts.

Contributions. In this paper, we explore this novel approach for long, conflict-prone transactions. Very few TMs support parallel nesting and, as we shall see, they cannot be used efficiently to solve this problem: A key requirement for profitable parallel nesting is that its overhead does not cancel out the gains of finer-grained parallelism.

The main contribution of this paper is a practical parallel nesting algorithm that integrates with a full-fledged STM [9]. It exploits common cases and fast paths to be efficient, and is the first proposal with support for multi-versions. In addition, it also preserves the lock-freedom progress guarantee of the underlying STM.

Our implementation of parallel nesting allows us to get significant performance gains in a variety of highly-conflicting workloads, and it achieves that by adding low

```
@Atomic void updateGraph() {
  for (Root r: getRoots())
    updateIfNeeded(r);
}

void updateIfNeeded(Node source) {
  if (source.needsUpdate())
    source.update();

  for (Node n : source.children())
    updateIfNeeded(n);
}

@Atomic void changeStatus(int id) {
  for (Root r : getClosestRoots(id)) {
    Node n = r.find(id);
    if (n != null)
      return n.changeStatus();
  }
}
```

(a) Program that manipulates the graph represented in Fig. 1b and that is synchronized with TM

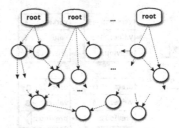

(b) Graph of transactional objects in an application

```
@Atomic void updateGraph() {
  @Parallel
  for (Root r: getRoots())
    updateIfNeeded(r);
}
```

(c) Parallelizing the transaction in updateGraph method

Fig. 1. Example of transactional application where both inter- and intra-transaction parallelism is explored

overhead when exploring intra-transaction parallelism and no overhead when only inter-transaction parallelism is explored.

In the following section, we overview our solution and its strengths. In Section 3, we formalize the properties of our proposal. In Section 4, we present an experimental evaluation of an implementation of our proposal. Then, we discuss the related work and conclude with some remarks in Sections 5 and 6, respectively.

2   A New Design for Parallel Nesting

We consider a lazy write-back STM underlying our algorithm. In particular, we used the Java Versioned STM (JVSTM) [9], a multi-version STM. JVSTM uses Versioned Boxes (VBox) to represent transactional locations. Each VBox holds a history of values corresponding to some of its past versions. Fig. 2 shows this scheme (for now, only the permanent versions). Its garbage collection algorithm guarantees that a version is preserved as long as an active transaction may require it. The access to VBoxes is always mediated by transactions, which record the accesses in their local read- and write-sets. If the read-set is still valid at commit time, the tentative writes logged in the write-set are written back, producing a new version for each of the boxes written and publicizing the new values in a lock-free manner [9].

The original design of the JVSTM follows a linear nesting model, in which a thread that is executing a transaction may start, execute, and commit a nested transaction (which itself may do the same), effectively forming a nesting tree with only one active branch at a time. The leaf of that active branch represents an active nested transaction

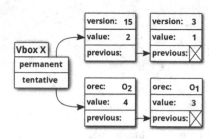

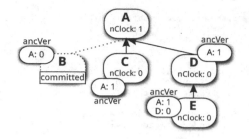

Fig. 2. A transactional location in the JVSTM

Fig. 3. Part of the state maintained in a nesting tree. C and D were spawned concurrently by A after the commit of B.

that is guaranteed to be the only one accessing and modifying the read- and write-sets of that nesting tree. Yet, this simple model does not allow the decomposition of long transactions into concurrent parts.

In our proposal, we build on the model of closed nesting as described by Moss [16], in which two nested transactions are said to be siblings if they have the same parent. Thus, in parallel nesting, we allow siblings to run concurrently. We consider that each top-level transaction may unfold a nesting tree in which a transaction performs transactional accesses only when all its children are no longer active.[1] Conceptually, in this model, a nested transaction maintains its own read- and write-sets, much in the same way of a top-level transaction. Yet, given the compositional nature of transactions, the read of a transactional location within a nested transaction T must obtain the value most recently written to that location in the sequence of operations performed by T and by all of its ancestors (but not by any of its siblings). This means that a read operation may encounter a globally uncommitted value that resulted from the commit of a sibling (or the execution of its ancestors). Therefore siblings must synchronize and validate their commits to respect the correctness criterion (herein assumed to be opacity [10]).

The parallel nesting algorithm that we propose in this paper extends VBoxes so that transactions may now write directly to the VBoxes rather than having to maintain a private write-set mapping each location written to its new value. But we need to distinguish between globally committed values and the tentative values of ongoing transactions. Thus, a VBox now contains both *permanent* and *tentative* versions, as shown in Fig. 2: A permanent value has been consolidated via a commit of some top-level transaction, whereas a tentative value belongs to an active top-level transaction (or any of its children nested transactions) and is thus part of its write-set.

Additionally, each tentative write points to an ownership record (**orec**) that encapsulates the **owner** (a transaction), the version of the write (referred to as **nestedVer**), and the **status** of the owner. Each writing transaction creates one such *orec* and propagates it to the transaction's parent when it commits. Fig. 3 also shows two other important metadata kept in each transaction T: The **nClock** (incremented by the commit of each

---

[1] This restriction simplifies the model and does not impose any significant limitation to its expressive power, because a transaction that needs to execute concurrently with its children may spawn a nested transaction to execute its own code.

direct nested child of T) and the **ancVer** (a map computed when T starts, by adding its parent's current *nClock* to the parent's *ancVer*). Using the example of Fig. 3, this means that transaction E can read tentative writes owned by A with *nestedVer* up to (and including) 1, but not writes owned by C. This is dictated by the **ancVer** map computed at each nested transaction T, which defines the versions of the ancestors of T that are available for it to read safely.

The algorithm that we propose in this work[2] has three major features that make it efficient: (1) a fast path in the read operation that is performed in constant time (independently of the nesting depth); (2) a fast mode for writing, backed up by a slow mode for fallbacks; and (3) a commit operation that is independent of the write-set size. The next subsections address each of the previous points, but, for space constraints, we omit some of the details of our solution, which can be found in an extended version of this paper serving as a companion technical report [6].

2.1 Reading a VBox

When reading a VBox, we have to take into account a possible read-after-write. For this reason, the pseudo-code presented in Algorithm 1 either returns a tentative value written by some transaction in this nesting tree, or a global value, represented by a consolidated version in a VBox.

Lines 5-8 correspond to the fast path that we have mentioned: When the last tentative write was made by a transaction that finished before this one started, then we can be sure that this is not a read-after-write. In that case, a permanent value is returned (committed by a top-level transaction), in a lightweight operation with constant time. Note that this is the typical case, in which we manage to bypass the costly check of writes from ancestors. If this fast path is not used, then the algorithm iterates over the tentative writes of the VBox until one of the following conditions is verified:

1. The owner of the tentative write is the transaction attempting the read (T), in which case no further checks are needed to read that entry (lines 12-14).
2. The owner of the tentative write is an ancestor of T. When this happens, T may read that entry only if the entry was made visible by its owner before T started (lines 16-20). This is enforced by looking up in the *ancVer* of T what is the maximum version readable from that ancestor. If the write has a more recent version than T can read, T causes a chain abort up to that ancestor such that those nested transactions restart with the most recent versions on their *ancVer* map.

The algorithm presented here stops iterating when a nested transaction finds a tentative write that it may read, returning that value. This is correct because our algorithms were designed to ensure the following invariant: Given a read operation of a VBox, as soon as the nested transaction reaches a tentative write that it may read, then it is guaranteed that no other write further down the list has to be read instead of that one to maintain correctness. Because of this invariant, we are able to shorten traversals as most transactions will read only the first tentative write.

---

[2] The source code for the integration with the full-fledged JVSTM is publicly available at: https://github.com/inesc-id-esw/JVSTM

Algorithm 1. Read procedure in a parallel nested transaction.

1: GETBOXVALUE(T, vbox):
2:   wInplace ← vbox.tentative
3:   status ← wInplace.orec.status
4:   ▷ *fast path if this cannot be a read-after-write; positive status means the owner is* COMMIT
5:   **if** status > 0 ∧ status ≤ T.startVersion **then**
6:     T.globalReads.add(vbox)
7:     **return** *readFromPermanent*(vbox)   ▷ *fast path confirmed that is not a read-after-write*
8:   **end if**
9:   ▷ *it is possible to be a read-after-write*
10:   **while** wInplace ≠ null **do**
11:     owner ← wInplace.orec.owner
12:     **if** owner = T **then**
13:       **return** wInplace.value   ▷ T *is the owner, confirms a read-after-write*
14:     **end if**
15:     **if** T.ancVer.contains(owner) **then**
16:       **if** wInplace.orec.nestedVer > T.ancVer.get(owner) **then**
17:         abortUpTo(T, owner)   ▷ *confirms a read-after-write: vbox is owned by ancestor*
                                        of T but is not visible to the snapshot of T
18:       **end if**
19:       T.nestedReadSet.put(vbox, wInplace)
20:       **return** wInplace.value   ▷ *read-after-write, visible with safety to the snapshot of T*
21:     **end if**
22:     wInplace ← wInplace.previous   ▷ *try an older version, as this is owned by a different*
                                          branch of the nesting tree (not an ancestor of T)
23:   **end while**
24:   value ← rootWriteSet.get(vbox)   ▷ *no in-place write to be read, check fallback set*
25:   **if** value ≠ NONE **then**
26:     **return** value   ▷ *do not need to register the read in this case*
27:   **end if**
28:   T.globalReads.add(vbox)
29:   **return** *readFromPermanent*(vbox)   ▷ *not a read-after-write, but had to go through the*
                                              slow path to confirm it

2.2   Writing to a VBox

Algorithm 2 presents the pseudocode of the write operation of a parallel nested transaction. When writing to a VBox, it fetches the tentative write at the head and reads its *orec* (lines 2-3) to tell whether that VBox is currently owned by the transaction. In that case it simply overwrites the previous write. Otherwise, after line 7, the algorithm running for a transaction T follows one of these cases:

− The VBox owner finished before transaction T started, in which case T attempts to acquire ownership of the tentative write at the head of the list of that VBox (lines 9-14). To do so, T attempts a compare-and-swap (CAS) to change the ownership of the first tentative write. If the CAS fails, the algorithm proceeds to the fallback in line 21 (because some other transaction acquired the ownership of the box). If, on the other hand, the previous owner finished after T started, then no transaction in this nesting tree (and particularly T) will ever be able to write to that VBox in-place. In that case the algorithm also proceeds to the fallback mechanism. This is what allows us to maintain the fast path in the read operation.

- The VBox is owned by an ancestor of T (line 15). In this case, T attempts to enqueue a new in-place tentative write by performing a CAS on the head of the tentative list of that VBox. If this CAS fails, then some other transaction in this nesting tree succeeded, in which case the algorithm proceeds to the fallback.
- We are left with the fallback (line 21). If we get to this case, there must exist a concurrent transaction owning the VBox, and, therefore, this transaction must write in an alternative way, which we describe at the end of this section.

Much of the complexity of this operation arises from the fact that we are maintaining multi-versions in the nesting tree. But this is required due to partial aborts (as we explain in our technical report [6]), in which a parallel nested transaction aborts due to concurrency internal to the nesting tree. Therefore, this choice is largely independent of the fact that the baseline TM algorithm uses multi-versions.

Note that the algorithm that we provide detects write-write conflicts. To better understand this design choice, consider an example where transactions B and C are concurrent siblings that write to x. Assume that B writes first, but then C commits before B into their parent (A). At this point in such execution, the first tentative write of VBox x would be the one written by C, because C performed the most recent write. Yet,

---

Algorithm 2. Write procedure in a parallel nested transaction.

```
 1: SETBOXVALUE(T, vbox, value):
 2:   wInplace ← vbox.tentative
 3:   orec ← wInplace.orec
 4:   if orec.owner = T then
 5:     wInplace.value ← value   ▷ write-after-write by T, no synchronization needed
 6:     return
 7:   end if
 8:   if orec.status ≠ ALIVE then
 9:     ▷ attempt to acquire ownership of the tentative slot
10:     if orec.status ≤ T.startVersion ∧ wInplace.CASorec(orec, T.orec) then
11:       wInplace.value ← value   ▷ T was successful, so it may write in the tentative slot
12:       T.boxesWritten.add(vbox)
13:       return
14:     end if
15:   else if T.ancVer.contains(orec.owner) then
16:     ▷ belongs to an ancestor of T, so the tentative slot is owned by this nesting tree
17:     if vbox.CAStentative(wInplace, new Tentative(value, T.orec, wInplace)) then
18:       return   ▷ successfully enqueued a new tentative write in the slot owned by this tree
19:     end if
20:   end if
21:   executeAsTopLevel(T)   ▷ cannot write in-place, fallback mechanism
```

the most recent commit was B's, which consequently should make its writes the most recently publicized to the parent A.

Therefore, the underlying problem is one of lag between the write-time and the commit-time. To maintain the invariant mentioned in Section 2.1 for faster reads, the solution is to perform work proportional to the size of the write-set at commit-time [8]. We avoid such expensive strategy by precluding nested write-write concurrency. This is a beneficial trade-off because, as we show in our companion report, this design decision does not hinder concurrency in real workloads [6]. The main reason is that transactions typically write a datum after reading it. Therefore, if concurrent transactions B and C both write to x, then they must have both read it (non-serializably), for which reason pure write-write concurrency is rare.

The fallback path (line 21) takes care of the case in which there is write-write contention. Due to space constraints we refer to our technical report [6] for details. Briefly, it aborts the nested transaction up to the root ancestor. Then it re-executes the affected nested transactions (in the chain) in the context of the root top-level transaction (after all its other children are finished). That re-execution flattens those transactions such that the code re-executed is encapsulated in the top-level transaction of the nesting tree. The key difference is that top-level transactions maintain a traditional write-set, which we call *rootWriteSet*, to use when the in-place slots are controlled by another nesting tree. Therefore, the write that triggered the fallback, if repeated, will be performed by the top-level transaction in that fallback write-set. This explains why the read operation checks the *rootWriteSet* in lines 24-27 of Algorithm 1.

2.3   Commit of a Parallel Nested Transaction

At commit-time we are left with two tasks: To ensure that all the reads are still up-to-date, and to make the read-set and the write-set of the transaction visible to its parent. The key idea is that a parallel nested transaction propagates to its parent only the *orecs* that it owns. This means that, after validating its read-set (and its children's), it changes the ownership of each *orec* it controls. This also entails updating the *nestedVer* of those *orecs* to the version acquired from the *nClock* of the parent during that commit. As a result, the commit procedure performs independently of the write-set size and is very lightweight in practice.

Space prevents us from delving into details, but in [6] we present a lock-free design that implements the idea above. Briefly, the idea is to use a lock-free queue where transactions obtain the commit order. We use such a queue for each nesting tree, conceptually associated with the root top-level transaction. As a result, a nested transaction attempting to commit either succeeds, or helps one of its siblings that managed to win the race to the queue.

3   Formal Guarantees

We now address the consequences of supporting parallel nesting in a TM. Namely, we look into which correctness and progress guarantees of TMs our parallel nesting algorithm allows.

Theorem 1. *The proposed parallel nesting algorithm ensures opacity [10].*

Proof. Our parallel nesting algorithm performs concurrency control using a known strategy, present in JVSTM: A write transaction commits successfully if the versions read have not been overwritten by the time it (atomically) commits. Moreover, any transaction always reads the most recent version available in a stable prefix of versions (called a snapshot), which is determined by using the global clock available at the start of the transaction. This value defines the versions that belong to the snapshot, as it is also the value used to version new data items. We can see this strategy in our algorithm: There is a clock in each transaction (**nClock**) to regulate the commits of its direct children; each transaction maintains a multi-dimensional snapshot, one per level of nesting, by using the map **ancVer** (to always read consistently); and nested transactions fail validation if they read a data item that has been overwritten within the nesting tree (to always commit consistently). □

Theorem 2. *The proposed parallel nesting algorithm ensures lock-freedom.*

We omit this proof due to space constraints (it is available in [6], where we describe the commit procedure in more detail). This property is of practical relevance, given that STMs are likely to remain as the fallback of best-effort HTMs.

Theorem 3. *The proposed parallel nesting algorithm ensures mv-permissiveness [17].*

Proof. Considering an mv-permissive TM, as our underlying JVSTM, a read-only transaction T must always commit. Suppose that T uses parallel nesting to speed its execution, and that T_c is one of its children. Alg. 1 only aborts a nested transaction T_c in the read operation if some VBox is owned by some ancestor T'. But we said that T is read-only, so no children T' of T will ever own a VBox. Thus, read-only transactions never abort, even if parallelized. Moreover, a write transaction T may only abort if faced with a conflict. A nested transaction T_c, child of T, aborts only when it attempts to read or write a VBox concurrently written by another transaction. Together, these two facts show that we preserve mv-permissiveness. □

We designed the support for parallel nesting with specific care to preserve the strong properties of JVSTM, namely opacity for safety, lock-freedom for progress and mv-permissiveness. As we can see from the previous analysis, our support for parallel nesting does not preclude any such property. An important consequence is that we can adapt this algorithm in TMs with weaker properties without suffering performance penalties.

4   Experimental Evaluation

The results presented in this section were obtained on a machine with four AMD Opteron 6168 processors (48 cores total) with 128GB of RAM and Oracle's JVM 1.6.0_24. Every experiment reports the average of five runs of each benchmark.

Our evaluation is split in two parts. First, in Section 4.1, we present results for several benchmarks that we modified to parallelize their transactions and, therefore, explore finer-grained parallelism through parallel nesting; the goal is to show that we may get performance gains when using parallel nesting, thereby validating that our algorithm is practical. Then, in Section 4.2, we compare our implementation with the implementation of two other state-of-the-art STMs that support parallel nesting.

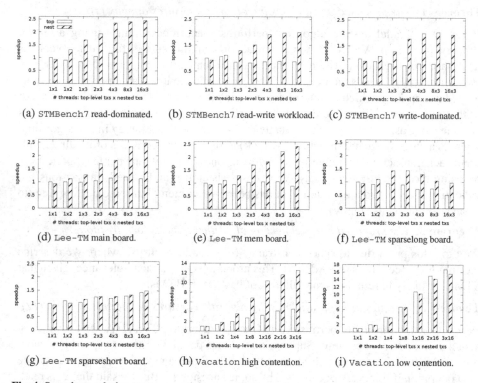

Fig. 4. Speedups relative to a sequential transaction. nest uses $t \times n$ as the configuration: t top-level transactions with each one parallelized into n children. top uses the product of t and n as top-level transactions.

4.1 Parallel Nesting versus Top-Level Only

To understand how effective our parallel nesting algorithm is, we compare the performance obtained with JVSTM when using only top-level transactions against fewer top-level transactions, with each one using parallel nesting. Fig. 4 shows the speedup of both approaches relatively to a sequential transaction in three standard benchmarks.

STMBench7 [11]: In Figs. 4a, 4b, and 4c, we show the results for the three existing workloads with long traversals enabled. The long traversals access most of the object graph of the benchmark, both with read and write accesses. This precludes much of the possible concurrency, as TMs have to detect conflicts in most concurrent accesses with these traversals. For this reason, we can see that adding more top-level transactions scales very poorly. We exploited the inner parallelism in each of those traversals (identified in the benchmark as $T2a, T2b, T2c, T3a, T3b, T3c, T5$). For this, we identified the parts of those traversals to be ran in parallel, similarly to the example provided in the beginning of this paper. At 48 threads, this yielded an increase of 102% in the read-dominated workload; 129% in the read-write workload; and 131% in the write-dominated workload.

Lee-TM [2]: In Figs. 4d, 4e, 4f, and 4g, we perform the same experiment as above, using different boards available in Lee-TM. We used parallel nesting by parallelizing the expansion phase in the boards, and this approach also yielded improvements, namely 119% and 170% for `mainboard` and `memboard`, respectively. In the case of the `sparseshort` board, the transactions are very small, which makes the time spent managing nested transactions an overhead that supplants the gains obtained from less conflicts. Therefore, parallel nesting only obtained 4% improvement in that board. This example stresses the requirement of efficiently supporting parallel nesting, which we achieved in our algorithm.

Vacation [15]: In this benchmark we explored the parallelism in the transactions by parallelizing the cycle that repeats the operations for (potentially) different objects in the vacation manager. Fig. 4h uses the high contention workload where it becomes increasingly hard to obtain improvements in terms of performance by adding more threads (and correspondingly top-level transactions). Therefore, parallel nesting yielded 173% increase in performance. With a low contention workload, shown in Fig. 4i, the top-level transactions scale properly as the thread count increases. Thus, applying the parallel nested transactions does not yield any extra performance. In this case we measured a slight overhead from executing the transactions with some nesting: The overhead ranges from 3% to 8% and is on average 5%. This also strengthens our claim that this algorithm adds very little overhead when no additional parallelism is being explored.

Across these experiments we can see that added benefit is obtained by exploiting both the inter- and the intra-parallelism of transactions. This supports the idea of using TM at both levels of parallelism to ease the synchronization effort.

4.2 Comparison with Other Parallel Nesting Algorithms

We compare our algorithm with both NesTM [3] and PNSTM [4], which represent different design spaces in the state of the art. NesTM is not opaque, but our benchmarks have invariant checks to ensure correct executions (aborting a transaction if inconsistent reads are observed). Other existing proposals are either theoretical [1,13] or captured by the designs of these two [19,18]. Fig. 5a presents the throughput of each STM in a scenario with high-contention in `Vacation`. Looking at the dashed lines we may see that the JVSTM is considerably faster than the alternatives when using only top-level transactions. In particular, it obtains 1.58 speedup over NesTM and 5.41 speedup over PNSTM with a single top-level transaction. Note that our JVSTM already has support for parallel nesting, albeit it does not introduce any noticeable overhead for top-level transactions. Given that the baseline JVSTM is already faster than NesTM and PNSTM, it is expected that using parallel nesting is also faster in JVSTM. We can see that in the full lines. Still, the actual improvement (for 48 threads) is greater for JVSTM (2.8×) than for NesTM (2.2×) and PNSTM (no improvements).

We also show a comparison between the three STMs in a write-dominated workload of the `STMBench7` benchmark, with long-traversals enabled. The results are shown in Fig. 5b, where we may see that JVSTM is again faster already with only one thread: It obtains a speedup of 3.6 and 4.4 over NesTM and PNSTM, respectively, when using only top-level transactions. Moreover, even though we do not show them, the results are very similar across the other workloads of the `STMBench7`. Yet, unlike the results

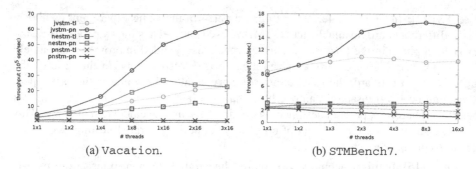

(a) Vacation.   (b) STMBench7.

Fig. 5. Comparison between three STMs, both using only top-level transactions (*tl*) or exploiting intra-transaction parallelism (*pn*) in a high contention workload in Vacation and in the write-dominated workload of the STMBench7 benchmark with long-traversals enabled

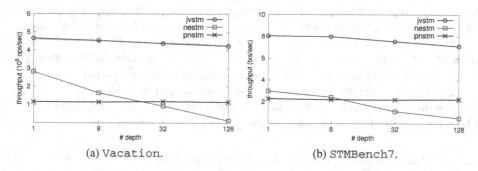

(a) Vacation.   (b) STMBench7.

Fig. 6. Throughput obtained with a single nested transaction at an increasing depth

obtained in Vacation, in this case the parallel nesting algorithm of NesTM is unable (together with PNSTM) to obtain improvements over top-level transactions alone, whereas our solution more than doubles its throughput when using parallel nesting.

Finally, we modified both benchmarks so that they execute all of their transactions entirely within a single nested transaction at a certain depth. This yields a nesting tree with a single branch that is increasingly deeper. We present this experiment for STMBench7 and Vacation in Fig. 6, where we may see how each STM performs when the nesting depth increases. We also obtained similar results in this experience when using 16 threads.

These results are consistent with the theoretical complexity bounds of each STM [7]. Namely, PNSTM performs independently of the nesting depth, whereas the others degrade their performance. However, JVSTM not only performs significantly better, but it also degrades at a much slower rate than NesTM. So, just as PNSTM gets better results than NesTM for a sufficiently high depth, we expect the same to happen also, at some depth, with regard to JVSTM. Yet, given the slow decay of the JVSTM, it requires a much higher nesting depth (note the horizontal axis growing exponentially). In fact, we argue that such depth would seldom, if at all, exist in real applications.

5   Related Work

Some TM implementations provide support for linear nesting, which limits a transaction to have only one nested transaction active at a given time. In this case, nested transactions are used only for their compositional properties, as transactions cannot parallelize their contents by running concurrent children. Thus, in the following, we consider only TMs with support for parallel nesting.

The CWSTM [1], which builds on the Cilk language, introduced the combination of the parallel and spawn constructs to create new threads with assigned nested transactions. It was the first work to show a depth-independent nesting algorithm, but did not provide any implementation or evaluation. In a different setting, the Sibling STM [18] considered that sibling nested transactions may have relationships and be dependent among each other under the notion of coordinated sibling transactions. Yet, they do not provide the underlying algorithm, which prevents more detailed comparisons.

Another approach is NePalTM [19], which was built on top of OpenMP and Intel's STM to integrate parallel and atomic blocks. The authors propose to have direct children of top root atomic blocks (shallow nested transactions) proceeding optimistically (using transactions) while deep nested parallel transactions run sequentially in mutual exclusion. As a result, its model is not too powerful, but still allows unveiling some concurrency in transactions as long as they only compose within one level of depth.

Conversely, in the Nested STM [3] the authors extended their earlier work to allow parallel nested transactions. Yet, their algorithm synchronizes commits with mutual exclusion on the parent, which may cause performance penalties when many transactions attempt to commit and the owner of the lock is delayed. The authors also identified that it is possible for their nested transactions to livelock, which they attempt to solve with heuristics. Moreover, their property of invisible reads incurs in an effort that is proportional to the depth of the nesting tree because they need to revalidate the read-set for each access. HParSTM [13] allows a parent to execute concurrently with its nested transactions, but failed to present any evaluation. Finally, PNSTM [4] was based on the ideas that CWSTM pioneered. It provided an efficient depth-independent algorithm, but all accesses are assumed to be writes, which precludes read-only concurrency.

A common trait of all this previous work is that it uses single-version, whereas the implementation that we describe in this paper has support for multi-versions. Moreover, our solution also yields better results than the state-of-the-art alternatives with support for parallel nesting while providing a stronger progress guarantee (lock-freedom). This is a key factor to make parallel nesting useful.

6   Conclusions

In this paper we proposed a novel algorithm for parallel nesting. This algorithm is lock-free and was designed to add minimal overhead to the underlying STM. This was accomplished by designing the operations of parallel nested transactions with fast paths that correspond to the common cases of a transactional application using parallel nesting. Moreover, these operations do not affect the operations for top-level transactions.

Our experiments with various benchmarks show that, on one hand, we can get significant performance gains with parallel nesting, and, on the other hand, parallel nesting does not add significant overhead into an application that does not benefit from it. A key observation of our evaluation is that the best results are attained when two conditions are met: (1) top-level transactions fail to deliver significant improvements with the increase of parallel threads, because of contention among the transactions that inhibits the optimistic concurrency severely; and (2) top-level transactions contain substantial computation that is efficiently parallelizable.

Finally, we showed that our algorithm yields considerable improvements over alternative TMs with support for parallel nesting while providing a stronger progress guarantee. As a result, this parallel nesting algorithm can be used effectively to improve the performance of applications with long transactions. This approach answers the main concern of the lack of progress guarantees given by HTMs available in the market. In the near future, we look forward to integrate these techniques in the software fallback path of the HTMs soon to be available.

Acknowledgements. This work was supported by national funds through Fundação para a Ciência e Tecnologia under project PEst-OE/EEI/LA0021/2013, by RuLAM project (PTDC/EIA-EIA/108240/2008), and by Cloud-TM project (co-financed by the European Commission through the contract no. 257784).

References

1. Agrawal, K., Fineman, J.T., Sukha, J.: Nested parallelism in transactional memory. In: Proceedings of the 13th ACM SIGPLAN Symposium on Principles and Practice of Parallel Programming, PPoPP 2008, pp. 163–174. ACM (2008)
2. Ansari, M., Kotselidis, C., Watson, I., Kirkham, C., Luján, M., Jarvis, K.: Lee-TM: A nontrivial benchmark suite for transactional memory. In: Bourgeois, A.G., Zheng, S.Q. (eds.) ICA3PP 2008. LNCS, vol. 5022, pp. 196–207. Springer, Heidelberg (2008)
3. Baek, W., Bronson, N., Kozyrakis, C., Olukotun, K.: Implementing and evaluating nested parallel transactions in software transactional memory. In: Proceedings of the 22nd ACM Symposium on Parallelism in Algorithms and Architectures, SPAA 2010, pp. 253–262. ACM (2010)
4. Barreto, J., Dragojević, A., Ferreira, P., Guerraoui, R., Kapalka, M.: Leveraging parallel nesting in transactional memory. In: Proceedings of the 15th ACM SIGPLAN Symposium on Principles and Practice of Parallel Programming, PPoPP 2010, pp. 91–100. ACM (2010)
5. Intel Corporation. Intel Architecture Instruction Set Extensions Programming Reference. 319433-012 edn. (February 2012)
6. Diegues, N., Cachopo, J.: Practical Parallel Nesting for Software Transactional Memory. Technical Report RT/22/2013, INESC-ID Lisboa (July 2013)
7. Diegues, N., Cachopo, J.: On the design space of Parallel Nesting. In: The 4th Workshop on the Theory of Transactional Memory, WTTM 2012 (2012)
8. Diegues, N., Fernandes, S., Cachopo, J.: Parallel Nesting in a lock-free multi-version Software Transactional Memory. In: The 7th ACM SIGPLAN Workshop on Transactional Computing, TRANSACT 2012 (2012)
9. Fernandes, S., Cachopo, J.: Lock-free and scalable multi-version software transactional memory. In: Proceedings of the 16th ACM symposium on Principles and Practice of Parallel Programming, PPoPP 2011, pp. 179–188. ACM (2011)

10. Guerraoui, R., Kapalka, M.: On the correctness of transactional memory. In: Proceedings of the 13th ACM SIGPLAN Symposium on Principles and Practice of Parallel Programming, PPoPP 2008, pp. 175–184. ACM (2008)
11. Guerraoui, R., Kapalka, M., Vitek, J.: STMBench7: a benchmark for software transactional memory. In: Proceedings of the 2nd ACM EuroSys European Conference on Computer Systems 2007, EuroSys 2007, pp. 315–324. ACM (2007)
12. Herlihy, M., Moss, J.E.B.: Transactional memory: architectural support for lock-free data structures. In: Proceedings of the 20th Annual International Symposium on Computer Architecture, ISCA 1993, pp. 289–300. ACM (1993)
13. Kumar, R., Vidyasankar, K.: HParSTM: A hierarchy-based STM protocol for supporting nested parallelism. In: The 6th ACM SIGPLAN Workshop on Transactional Computing, TRANSACT 2011 (2011)
14. Liu, Y., Diestelhorst, S., Spear, M.F.: Delegation and nesting in best-effort hardware transactional memory. In: Proceedings of the 24th Annual Symposium on Parallelism in Algorithms and Architectures, SPAA 2012, pp. 38–47 (2012)
15. Minh, C.C., Chung, J., Kozyrakis, C., Olukotun, K.: STAMP: Stanford transactional applications for multi-processing. In: IEEE International Symposium on Workload Characterization, IISWC 2008, pp. 35–46 (2008)
16. Moss, J.E.B., Hosking, A.L.: Nested transactional memory: model and architecture sketches. Science of Computer Programming 63(2), 186–201 (2006)
17. Perelman, D., Fan, R., Keidar, I.: On maintaining multiple versions in stm. In: Proceedings of the 29th ACM SIGACT-SIGOPS Symposium on Principles of Distributed Computing, PODC 2010, pp. 16–25. ACM (2010)
18. Ramadan, H., Witchel, E.: The Xfork in the road to coordinated sibling transactions. In: The 4th ACM SIGPLAN Workshop on Transactional Computing, TRANSACT 2009 (2009)
19. Volos, H., Welc, A., Adl-Tabatabai, A.-R., Shpeisman, T., Tian, X., Narayanaswamy, R.: NePaLTM: design and implementation of nested parallelism for transactional memory systems. In: Proceedings of the 14th ACM SIGPLAN Symposium on Principles and Practice of Parallel Programming, PPoPP 2009, pp. 291–292. ACM (2009)
20. Wang, A., Gaudet, M., Wu, P., Amaral, J.N., Ohmacht, M., Barton, C., Silvera, R., Michael, M.: Evaluation of blue Gene/Q hardware support for transactional memories. In: Proceedings of the 21st International Conference on Parallel Architectures and Compilation Techniques, PACT 2012, pp. 127–136. ACM (2012)

Asynchronous Resilient Linearizability

Sagar Chordia[1], Sriram Rajamani[2], Kaushik Rajan[2],
Ganesan Ramalingam[2], and Kapil Vaswani[2]

[1] IIT Bombay
[2] Microsoft Research India
chordiasagar14@gmail.com
{sriram,krajan,grama,kapilv}@microsoft.com

Abstract. We address the problem of implementing a distributed data-structure
that can tolerate process crash failures in an asynchronous message passing system, while guaranteeing correctness (linearizability with respect to a given sequential specification) and resiliency (the operations are guaranteed to terminate,
as long as a majority of the processes do not fail). We consider a class of data-
structures whose operations can be classified into two kinds: *update* operations
that can modify the data-structure but do not return a value and *read* operations
that return a value, but do not modify the data-structure. We show that if every
pair of update operations commute or nullify each other, then resilient linearizable
replication is possible. We propose an algorithm for this class of data-structures
with a message complexity of two message round trips for read operations and
$O(n)$ round trips for update operations. We also show that if there exists some
reachable state where a pair of idempotent update operations neither commute
nor nullify each other, resilient linearizable replication is not possible.

1 Introduction

In this paper, we focus on a standard asynchronous message-passing distributed computing setting with n processes, in the presence of non-byzantine (stopping) process
failures. The standard correctness criterion in this setting is linearizability [8] with respect to a sequential specification. A desirable progress guarantee in this setting is *t-
resiliency*, which guarantees that all operations terminate as long as no more than t
processes fail. We consider the case where t is $\lceil n/2 \rceil - 1$: i.e., a majority of the n processes do not fail. We address the question of when (i.e., for which data-structures or
sequential specifications) a resilient linearizable algorithm is possible in this setting.

We consider a class of data-structures whose operations can be classified into two
kinds: *update* operations that may modify the data-structure but do not return a value
and *read* operations that return a value, but do not modify the data-structure. We show
that if every pair of update operations commute or nullify each other, then resilient linearizable replication is possible. We propose a algorithm for this class of data-structures
with a message complexity of two message round trips for read operations and $O(n)$
round trips for update operations. The algorithm is based on the insight that if all operations commute, the order in which operations are applied is irrelevant for the final
state produced by a given set of update operations. This reduces the problem to that of

Y. Afek (Ed.): DISC 2013, LNCS 8205, pp. 164–178, 2013.

ensuring that reads observe monotonically increasing sets of operations and respecting the real time ordering between non-concurrent operations. The extension for nullifying operations is more complex, but is based on the intuition that when an earlier operation is nullified by a later operation, the execution of the earlier operation is optional.

We also show that if there exists some reachable state where a pair of idempotent update operations neither commute nor nullify each other, resilient linearizable replication is not possible. This result is based on a reduction from consensus to resilient linearizable state machine replication.

These results show that resilient linearizability is possible for some interesting data-structures. We also show how these results help design certain data-structure specifications so that a resilient linearizable implementation is possible, by addressing the design of a simple graph data-structure. We present two closely related graph specifications, where resilient linearizability is possible for one specification but not the other.

2   The Problem

We assume a standard asynchronous computation setting with non-byzantine (stopping) process failures. We have n processes that communicate via messages. All messages are assumed to be eventually delivered, but no bound is assumed on the time taken for a message to be delivered and no assumptions are made about the order in which messages are delivered. We are interested in $(\lceil n/2 \rceil - 1)$-resilient algorithms: algorithms that guarantee progress as long as a majority of the n processes do not fail. In the sequel, we will use the term resilient as short-hand for $(\lceil n/2 \rceil - 1)$-resilient.

State machine replication is a general approach for implementing data-structures that tolerate process failures by replicating state across multiple processes. The key challenge in state machine replication is to execute data-structure operations on all replicas such that linearizability is guaranteed.

A state machine models a system that implements an interface consisting of a set of procedures. Every procedure has a set of parameters and we assume that the parameters are of primitive type. In the sequel, we will use the term *operation* to refer to a tuple of the form $(p, a_1, \cdots, a_n)$ consisting of the name p of the procedure invoked as well as the actual values $a_1, \cdots, a_n$ of the parameters. A state machine m consists of a set of states Σ_{m}. The semantics of an operation is given by a function that maps an input state to an output state as well as a return value.

UQ State Machines. In this paper, we consider a special class of state machines we refer to as *Update-Query* (UQ) state machines. We assume that operations of the state machine can be classified into two kinds: *updates* (operations that modify the state) and *queries* (also called *reads*) (operations that do not modify the state, but return a value). Furthermore, the operations on the data-structure are assumed to be deterministic. The semantics of an update operation op is given by a function $[\![op]\!] : \Sigma_{\mathrm{m}} \to \Sigma_{\mathrm{m}}$.

Note that a UQ state machine does not allow for any operation that modifies the state and returns a value. While this is a convenient simplification, it does not restrict expressiveness, as long as we are able to associate every update operation invocation with an unique identifier. We can then use a separate query operation, with the unique identifier as a parameter, to obtain the return-value associated with the corresponding update operation.

NC State Machines. We say that two update operations op_1 and op_2 *commute* iff $op_1(op_2(\sigma)) = op_2(op_1(\sigma))$ for every state σ. We say that an operation op_1 *nullifies* an operation op_2 iff $op_1(op_2(\sigma)) = op_1(\sigma)$ for every state σ: in other words, op_1 nullifies op_2 iff $op_1 \circ op_2 = op_1$. We write $op_1 > op_2$ to denote that op_1 nullifies op_2. We say that two operations op_1 and op_2 *nullify* if $op_1 > op_2$ or $op_2 > op_1$.

A UQ state machine is said to be a *NC state machine* if for any pair of operations f and g, f and g commute or f nullifies g or g nullifies f.

Lemma 1. $>$ *is a transitive relation: if $f > g$ and $g > h$, then $f > h$.*

Proof. We omit proofs due to space constraints. Please refer to [5] for all proofs.

We say that a partial-ordering $\leq_s$ on a set of update operations (of the given state machine) is an NC-ordering if it satisfies the following conditions, where we write $x <_s y$ as shorthand for $x \leq_s y$ and $x \neq y$:

1. if $op_1 <_s op_2$, then op_2 nullifies op_1.
2. if $op_1 \not<_s op_2$ and $op_2 \not<_s op_1$, then op_1 and op_2 commute.

Lemma 2. *Every NC State Machine has a NC-ordering on the set of all its update operations.*

Many well known data-structures like read-write registers, read-write memory, counters, maps, sets are NC state machines. Details of these and other such data-structures can be found in [5].

3 Replication for NC State Machines

We now describe our replication algorithm for an NC state machine. Assume that we have n replicas (processes). External clients may submit operations (either updates or reads) to any replica. Note that the same operation (e.g., an increment operation on a counter) may be invoked multiple times in an execution. We refer to each distinct invocation of an update operation as a *command*.

Our algorithm makes use of a resilient linearizable add-only set that provides an operation $add(v)$ to add an element v to the set and an operation $read()$ that returns the current value of the set. We describe an implementation of this data-type in Section 4.

The basic idea behind our algorithm, presented in Algorithm 1, is as follows. We utilize the add-only set to maintain the set of all commands executed so far, referred to as *cset* below. Executing an update operation involves adding an element, representing this operation invocation, to *cset*. Read operations are realized by getting the current value S of *cset*, and then materializing the state σ_S corresponding to this set S of commands.

The key challenge is in defining σ_S so that the desired consistency criterion (linearizability) is satisfied.

Algorithm 1. NC State Machine Replication Algorithm (Process k)

DistributedSet cset = {}

procedure ExecuteUpdate(op)
    let ts = get-time-stamp() **in**
    cset.add ((ts,op))

procedure State LinearizableRead()
    let S = cset.read() **in**
    return Apply(S)

procedure int get-time-stamp()
    let S = cset.read() **in**
    return (S, k) // k is this process' id

procedure State Apply(S)
    let $cmd_1, \cdots , cmd_k$
        = topological-sort($S, \prec_{tn}$) **in**
    let $(ts_i, op_i) = cmd_i$ **in**
    let s_0 = initial-state **in**
    let $s_i = op_i(s_{i-1})$ **in**
    return s_k

Capturing Ordering Constraints between Non-overlapping Operations

Linearizability requires that any execution π of a set of commands be equivalent to some sequential execution π_s of the same set of commands. Furthermore, this sequential execution π_s must preserve the order of non-overlapping commands in π.

We associate a *timestamp* with each command. This timestamp serves two purposes. First, it lets us conservatively identify non-overlapping commands, as explained soon. Second, it ensures that different invocations of the same operation are represented by different command instances. This is important since *cset* is a set and not a multi-set.

Specifically, a replica k that receives an update operation o augments it with a timestamp t and represents the command as a pair (t, o). The *timestamp* is a pair consisting of the current value of *cset*, obtained by replica k via a read operation, paired with the unique-id k of the replica. The replica-id distinguishes between different concurrent invocations of the same operation at different replicas. (Each replica processes its requests sequentially.) We refer to the ordered pair (t, o) as an *update command*. Given any update command $c = (t, o)$, we define $op(c)$ to be o. The set *cset* is used to track the set of all executed update commands.

We define a relation $\prec_t$ on commands, as follows: $c_1 = ((cset_1, id_1), o_1) \prec_t c_2 = ((cset_2, id_2), o_2)$ iff $cset_1 \in cset_2$. We say that $c_1 \parallel c_2$ iff $(c_2 \not\prec_t c_1) \wedge (c_1 \not\prec_t c_2)$. These relations help determine whether two update commands are concurrent and the ordering relation between non-concurrent update commands, as follows. Thus, the representation lets us determine the order in which non-overlapping operations must be executed.

Lemma 3. *For any two commands c_1 and c_2 in an execution, if c_1 completes before c_2 starts, then $c_1 \prec_t c_2$. Hence, if $c_1 \parallel c_2$, then the execution of c_1 and c_2 overlap.*

Lemma 4. *Let X denote the value of* cset *at some point during an execution and let Y denote the value of* cset *at a later point in the same execution. Then, (a) $X \subseteq Y$, and (b) there exists no $x \in X, y \in (Y \setminus X)$ such that $y \prec_t x$.*

Consistently Ordering Concurrent Operations

Linearizability permits concurrent operations to be executed in any order. The challenge, however, lies in ensuring that all replicas execute these operations in the same order. In other words, we need a scheme for ordering operations which satisfies the following constraints. Let $Y_1 \subseteq Y_2 \cdots Y_k$ denote some sequence of values of $cset$ during an execution. Then the ordering scheme must ensure that (a) different processes that evaluate the same set Y_i produce the same state, and (b) states obtained by evaluating each of the sets $Y_1, \cdots Y_k$ must correspond to states produced by the execution of increasing prefixes of a single sequential execution of the update commands in Y_k. We now describe a way to order concurrent operations in a $cset$ that satisfies the above requirements.

Concurrent Commuting Operations. It is not necessary to determine the order in which two commuting update operations in a $cset$ must be executed, as the resulting state is independent of the order in which commuting updates are applied.

Concurrent Non-Commuting Operations. However, we must determine a unique ordering among non-commuting concurrent update operations so that we have a well-defined notion of the state σ_S corresponding to a set S of commands (i.e., to ensure requirement (a) above). We utilize the NC-ordering relation on the update operations for this purpose. Let $\prec_s$ be a NC partial-order on the set of all update operations.

Given a $cset$ value Y, we define the relation $\prec_n^Y$ on elements of Y recursively as follows:

$$c_1 \prec_n^Y c_2 \text{ iff } c_1 \parallel c_2 \wedge (op(c_1) \prec_s op(c_2)) \wedge (\nexists c_3. c_2 \prec_n^Y c_3 \prec_t^* c_1).$$

More precisely, we define the relation $\prec_n^Y$ inductively, by considering pairs of elements (c_1, c_2) in topological sort order, with respect to $\prec_t$, so as to satisfy the above constraint. Intuitively, we consider any pair of commands c_1 and c_2 that are concurrent (i.e., $c_1 \parallel c_2$). If these commands do not commute, then we utilize the static nullification ordering relation between the operations of c_1 and c_2 to determine the $\prec_n^Y$ ordering between them. However, we do not add this extra ordering constraint if we have already established an ordering constraint $c_2 \prec_n^Y c_3$ that transitively (in combination with $\prec_t$) establishes an ordering between c_1 and c_2.

We further define a "combined" ordering relation $\prec_{tn}^Y$ to be the union of $\prec_t$ and $\prec_n^Y$:

$$c_1 \prec_{tn}^Y c_2 \text{ iff } c_1 \prec_t c_2 \vee c_1 \prec_n^Y c_2.$$

If no confusion is likely, we will abbreviate $\prec_n^Y$ to $\prec_n$ and $\prec_{tn}^Y$ to $\prec_{tn}$.

The following example illustrates the use of this recursive constraint, which is meant to ensure that the combined relation $\prec_{tn}$ does not have cycles. Consider an execution history consisting of three commands c_1, c_2, and c_3 such that $c_1 \parallel c_2$, $c_2 \parallel c_3$, while $c_1 \prec_t c_3$. Further assume that $op(c_3) \prec_s op(c_2) \prec_s op(c_1)$. In this case, we add the constraint $c_2 \prec_n c_1$, since c_2 and c_1 are concurrent and c_2 is nullified by c_1. However, we do not add the constraint $c_3 \prec_n c_2$ even though c_3 and c_2 are concurrent and c_3 is nullified by c_2 because we already have: $c_2 \prec_n c_1 \prec_t c_3$.

Lemma 5. *If $a \prec_n^Y b \prec_n^Y c$, then we must have $a \prec_{tn}^Y c$.*

Lemma 6. *$\prec_{tn}^Y$ is an acyclic relation (i.e., the transitive closure of $\prec_{tn}^Y$ is irreflexive.)*

Let $\prec_{tn}^*$ denote the transitive closure of $\prec_{tn}$. We will write $a \parallel_{tn} b$ to denote that $(a \nprec_{tn}^* b) \wedge (b \nprec_{tn}^* a)$.

Lemma 7. *If* $a \parallel_{tn} b$, *then* $op(a)$ *and* $op(b)$ *commute.*

Given a sequence π of update commands, let state$[\pi]$ denote the state produced by the execution of the updates in π in order.

Lemma 8. *Let S denote the value of cset at some point in an execution. Let π_1 and π_2 denote any two topological sort ordering of S with respect to the acyclic relation $\prec_{tn}$. Then,* state$[\pi_1]$ = state$[\pi_2]$.

Given a set of update commands S, let $\overrightarrow{S}$ denote any sequence obtained by topologically sorting S with respect to the partial ordering $\prec_{tn}$. We define the state σ_S to be the state state$[\overrightarrow{S}]$ obtained by executing the update commands in $\overrightarrow{S}$ in order. It follows from the previous lemma that σ_S is well-defined.

Consistency Across Csets. We now have a precise definition of the state σ_S produced by a set of commands S. This ensures that different replicas will produce the same state for the same set of commands. However, this is not sufficient for correctness. We need to establish that this way of constructing the state of a *cset* also ensures that the values produced by different sets of commands are consistent with each other. Note that as the *cset* is linearizable if two reads return different *csets* then one must necessarily be a subset of the other and all commands in the smaller *cset* will necessarily be $\prec_t$ or $\parallel$ with respect to commands in the larger *cset*.

Lemma 9. *Let $X \subseteq Y$ be two values of cset in an execution. Then,* $\prec_{tn}^{X} = \prec_{tn}^{Y} \cap (X \times X)$. *(Thus, the ordering between elements of X does not change over time.)*

Let $A \subset B$ denote two different values of *cset*. We need to show that the values σ_A and σ_B are consistent with each other: i.e., that σ_A and σ_B are states produced by executing some sequential executions π_A and π_B, respectively, where π_A is a prefix of π_B. We now show how we can construct these witness sequences π_A and π_B.

The simple case is when there is no pair of operations $op_1 \in A$ and $op_2 \in (B \setminus A)$ such that $op_2 \prec_s op_1$. In this case, we can let π_A be $\overrightarrow{A}$ (a topological-sort ordering of A) and π_B be a topological-sort ordering of B that is also consistent with π_A.

The case where $op_2 \prec_s op_1$ for some $op_1 \in A$ and $op_2 \in (B \setminus A)$ requires more careful consideration. Note that the value σ_A is produced by executing op_1 but not op_2. However, our scheme above requires executing op_2 before op_1 when computing σ_B. We exploit the *nullification* property to deal with this issue. Note that the definition of a NC-ordering requires that op_1 nullify op_2 if $op_2 \prec_s op_1$. Hence, even though σ_A was computed without executing op_2, the nullification property guarantees that $\sigma_A = \sigma_{A'}$ where $A' = A \cup \{op_2\}$. Hence, we simply let π_B be $\overrightarrow{B}$ and we let π_A be the smallest prefix of π_B that includes all elements of A. We can show that the state produced by executing π_A is the same as the state σ_A produced by executing $\overrightarrow{A}$. Hence σ_A and σ_B are still consistent with each other. Based on the above discussion the following lemma can be proved.

Lemma 10. *Let $X \subseteq Y$ be two values of cset in an execution. Then,* state$[\overrightarrow{Y} \downarrow X]$ = state$[\overrightarrow{X}]$, *where $\overrightarrow{Y} \downarrow X$ is the smallest prefix of $\overrightarrow{Y}$ that includes all elements of X.*

Theorem 1. *The NC state machine replication algorithm (Algorithm 1) is both linearizable and resilient.*

4 A Resilient Linearizable Add-Only Set

Our algorithm in Section 3 makes use of a resilient linearizable add-only set. Such a set can be realized as sketched in Faleiro *et al.* [6], which presents a resilient algorithm for solving the generalized lattice agreement problem and shows how that can be used to implement a UQ state machine in which all update operations commute. The Faleiro *et al.* algorithm has a complexity of $O(n)$ message delays for both reads and updates. We now present a modified algorithm (Figure 1) that realizes reads with four message delays (two round trips) while retaining the $O(n)$ complexity for updates.

4.1 Notation

We use the following language constructs to keep the algorithm description simple and readable. We introduce a Majority Vote construct "QVote $[f]$ g" where f is a "remote delegate", denoting code to be executed at other processes and g is a "callback" that represents the code to be executed locally to process the return values of f. On invocation of the QVote construct at process P a message containing sufficient information to execute the remote delegate is broadcast to all other processes. Every process that receives this message executes the delegate and sends back the result of evaluating this delegate to p. Process p evaluates every received value x by applying the function g to x. The execution of the QVote construct terminates when a majority (at least $\lceil n + 1 \rceil / 2$) of the responses from other processes have been received and processed by p. Finally, every execution of f and g executes atomically.

The remote delegate may access/modify the state variables of the remote process where it is executed. The references to the variables of the remote process are denoted "r!var". The remote-delegate may also contain read-only references to the variables of the local process (the process executing the QVote construct), which are denoted "l!var". The values of these local variables are evaluated when the QVote construct starts executing. The callback is only allowed read the return value of f and read/modify local state. As for the other code, any code that needs to execute atomically is explicitly wrapped in an "atomic" construct.

The construct asyncmap f executes the remote-delegate f in every process. It is asynchronous: the construct completes execution once it sends the necessary messages and does not wait for the completion of the remote delegate execution. The construct when cond stmt is a conditional atomic statement that executes when cond is true. It is equivalent to atomic { if (cond) then stmt else retry } .

4.2 The Algorithm

Read. The local variable current of every process represents the latest value of the set that it is aware of. A process p processes a request for the current value of the set as follows (as shown in procedure read). It sends a request to every (other) process to get their own copy of current. It computes the union of the values returned by a majority of the processes. Once the responses of a majority of the processes have been received and processed, p has a correct (linearizable) value to be returned. However, before returning this value, it broadcasts this value to all other processes. Every recipient updates its own value of current (to be the union of its current value and the new value) and sends an ack back. Once p receives an ack back from a majority of the processes, it can complete the read operation.

Add. Every process tracks elements to be added to the set using a variable buffer. A process p processes a request to add an element e to the set by first adding it to its own buffer and broadcasting a request to all other processes to add e to their own buffers. Elements to be added to the set are processed in batches by each process sequentially. If p is in the middle of processing the previous batch of elements (as indicated by the status variable passive being false), it then waits until the previous batch is processed.

Every process uses a local variable proposed to store its proposed (i.e., candidate) next value for the set and a local variable accepted that represents the join of all the proposed values it has seen so far. Process p begins by adding all elements in its buffer to the proposed new value. It then sends the proposed value to all other processes. Every recipient compares the proposed value with its accepted value. If the proposed value is a superset of its accepted value, it sends back an ACK. Otherwise, it sends back a NACK. In either case, it updates its accepted value to include the newly proposed value.

If process p gets back responses from a majority of the processes, and these are all ACKs, then p has succeeded. It updates its current value to be the last value it proposed. If p receives any NACKs, then it updates its proposed value to include the accepted value indicated by the NACK.

Process p exits the loop when the element e to be added is contained in its current value. Then, p broadcasts its current value and waits until a majority of the processes update their own current value appropriately. Then, the add operation is complete.

4.3 Correctness and Complexity

Consider any history (i.e., execution) of the algorithm. The following terminology is relative to a given history. We refer to the execution of the QVote in line [18] as a *proposal round* and the value of 1!proposed as the *proposed* value of the round. We say that the proposal round is *successful* if it terminates without receiving any NACK and we say that the proposal round *failed* otherwise. We identify any successful proposal round by a pair (P, Q), where P is the proposed value and Q is the set of processes that accepted the proposal with an ACK. Note that Q constitutes a quorum: i.e., it consists of a majority of the processes. We say that a set value P has been *chosen* if it is the proposed value of a successful proposal.

The following key property of the algorithm is the basis for correctness. If (P_1, Q_1) and (P_2, Q_2) are two successful proposals in a single execution, then P_1 and P_2 must be comparable: that is, either $P_1 \subseteq P_2$ or $P_2 \subseteq P_1$. (This follows since $Q_1 \cap Q_2$ must be non-empty, as both Q_1 and Q_2 consist of a majority of the processes. Since every process ensures that the values it ACKs form an increasing chain, the result follows.) It follows that all chosen values form a chain in the powerset lattice.

We say that a set value P has been *learnt* iff P is a chosen value and the value of current $\supseteq P$ for a majority of the processes. It follows that the set of all learnt values also form a chain. The *maximal learnt value*, at any point in time, represents the latest learnt value: it represents the current state/value of the distributed set.

```
1   Set current = {}, proposed = {}, accepted = {};
2   boolean passive = true;
3
4   Set read() {
5      Set result = {};
6      QVote [r!current] (λx. result := result ∪ x);
7      QVote [r!current := r!current ∪ l!result](λack. ())
8      return result;
9   }
10
11  void add(e) {
12     atomic {buffer := buffer ∪ {e}};
13     asyncmap [r!buffer := r!buffer ∪ {l!e}];
14     when (passive} { passive := false; }
15     atomic {proposed := proposed ∪ buffer};
16     while (e ∉ current) {
17        NACKrecvd = false;
18           QVote [let x = r!accepted ⊆ l!proposed in
19                 r!accepted := r!accepted ∪ l!proposed;
20              if (x) then (ACK, r!accepted) else (NACK, r!accepted)]
21           (λ(x,s). if (x = NACK) then NACKrecvd := true;
22                 proposed := proposed ∪ s);
23        if (!NACKrecvd) then current = current ∪ proposed;
24     }
25     QVote [r!current := r!current ∪ l!current](λack. ())
26     passive := true;
27  }
```

Fig. 1. The Add-Only Set

It can be shown that the following properties hold:

1. Any chosen value consists only of elements e for which an add operation has been invoked.
2. The value of the variable current, of any process, is always a chosen value.
3. When an invocation of add(e) completes, e belongs to the maximal learnt value (as ensured by line [24]).
4. The value R returned by a read operation is a learnt value.
5. The value R returned by an invocation of read contains the maximal learnt value at the point of the invocation of the read operation.
6. The value R returned by an invocation of read is contained in the maximal learnt value at the point of completion of the read operation. (as ensured by line [7]).

Linearizability We can show that the given history is linearizable by constructing an equivalent sequential history as follows.

1. For any two operations add(x) and add(y), we order add(x) before add(y) if there exists a chosen value that contains x but not y.

2. For any two read operations op_1 and op_2, we order op_1 before op_2 if the value returned by op_1 is properly contained in the value returned by op_2.
3. For any two operations add(x) and read(), we order the add operation before the read operation iff the read operation returns a value containing x and the add operation was initiated before the read operation completed.

Resiliency and Complexity Every invocation of QVote is guaranteed to terminate as long as a majority of the processes are correct and all messages between correct processes are eventually delivered (and every correct process eventually processes all received messages). It follows that every read operation requires four message delays (two round-trips). The proof of termination of the while loop in the add operation is more involved.

A proposal round in this loop may fail if multiple incomparable values are being concurrently proposed (by different processes). In the worst case, all of these concurrent proposals may fail. However, whenever a proposal by a process fails, a strictly greater value will be proposed by the same process in the next proposal round. As a result, it can be shown that we can have at most n successive proposal rounds before at least one of the processes succeeds in its proposal. Since every add operation begins by broadcasting the value to be added to all other processes, and any process that successfully completes a proposal round is guaranteed to include all values it has received in its next proposal, every add operation is guaranteed to terminate. A careful analysis shows that the complexity of the add operation is $O(n)$ message delays.

5 Impossibility Results

Suppose we have a state machine with two operations op_1 and op_2 such that they do not commute with each other and neither operation nullifies the other operation. Our algorithm from Section 3 does not apply in this case. We now show that if we make somewhat stronger assumptions about op_1 and op_2 no resilient linearizable algorithm is possible for such a state machine.

Consider a state machine with an initial state σ_0. Let op_1 and op_2 be two operations on the state machine. Let σ_i denote the state $op_i(\sigma_0)$ and let $\sigma_{i,j}$ denote the state $op_j(op_i(\sigma_0))$. We say that op_1 and op_2 are *2-distinguishable* in state σ_0 iff $\{\sigma_1, \sigma_{1,1}, \sigma_{1,2}\} \cap \{\sigma_2, \sigma_{2,1}, \sigma_{2,2}\} = \phi$. This essentially means that the state produced by execution of op_1, optionally followed by the operation op_1 or op_2, is distinguishable from the state produced by the execution of op_2, optionally followed by the operation op_1 or op_2.

Theorem 2. *A state machine with 2-distinguishable operations op_1 and op_2 in its initial state can be used to solve consensus for 2 processes. Thus, it has a consensus number of at least 2.*

Proof. Assume that we have a resilient linearizable implementation of the given state machine. Reduction 1 shows how we can solve binary consensus for two processes using the state machine implementation. Consider the execution of Reduction 1 by two

Reduction 1. 2-distinguishable opera-tions	**Reduction 2.** k-distinguishable opera-tions

procedure Consensus (Boolean b)
   if (b) **then** $op_1()$ **else** $op_2()$ **endif**
   s = read()
   return($s \in \{\sigma_1, \sigma_{1,1}, \sigma_{1,2}\}$)
	procedure Consensus (Boolean b)
	   if (b) **then** $op_1()$ **else** $op_2()$ **endif**
	   s = read()
	   return($s \in \Sigma_1$)

processes p and q. Since the state machine implementation is resilient, the above algorithm will clearly terminate (unless the executing process fails).

We first show that when neither process fails, both processes will decide on the same value (*agreement*) and that this value must be one of the proposed values (*validity*). Let s_x denote the value read by process x (in line [3]). To establish agreement, we must show that $s_p \in \{\sigma_1, \sigma_{1,1}, \sigma_{1,2}\}$ iff $s_q \in \{\sigma_1, \sigma_{1,1}, \sigma_{1,2}\}$.

Let f_x denote the update operation performed by process $x \in \{p, q\}$ (in line [2]). Without loss of generality assume that the update operation f_p executes before f_q (in the linearization order). If f_q executes before the read operation by p, then both processes will read the same value and agreement follows.

Thus, the only non-trivial case (for agreement) is the one where p executes its read operation before q executes its update operation (f_q). Thus, $s_p = f_p(\sigma_0)$ while $s_q = f_q(f_p(\sigma_0))$. Without loss of generality, we can assume that the operation f_p is op_1 (since the other case is symmetric). Operation f_q can, however, be either op_1 or op_2. Thus, $s_p = \sigma_1$, while s_q is either $\sigma_{1,1}$ or $\sigma_{1,2}$. Hence, agreement holds even in this case.

Validity follows since the algorithm *decides* on the value proposed by the process that first executes its update operation. Specifically: the value read by either process will belong to $\{\sigma_1, \sigma_{1,1}, \sigma_{1,2}\}$ iff the first update executed is op_1.

Hence, both validity and agreement holds when both processes are correct. If either process fails, then agreement is trivially satisfied. Validity holds as explained above.

We can extend the above result to n processes as follows. Let $\gamma = [e_1, \cdots, e_k]$ be a sequence where each element e_i is either op_1 or op_2. Define $\gamma(\sigma)$ to be $e_k(\cdots (e_1(\sigma)) \cdots)$. Define $first(\gamma)$ to be e_1. Let Γ_k denote the set of all non-empty sequences, of length at most k, where each element is either op_1 or op_2.

We say that op_1 and op_2 are k-distinguishable in state σ_0 if for all $\gamma_1, \gamma_2 \in \Gamma_k$, $\gamma_1(\sigma_0) = \gamma_2(\sigma_0)$ implies $first(\gamma_1) = first(\gamma_2)$. In other words, if γ_1 and γ_2 are two sequences in Γ_k such that $first(\gamma_1) \neq first(\gamma_2)$, then the final states produced by executing γ_1 and γ_2 should be different. Loosely speaking, the first operation executed has a "memory effect" that lasts for at least $k - 1$ more operations.

Define Σ_i to be $\{\gamma(\sigma_0) \mid \gamma \in \Gamma_k, first(\gamma) = op_i\}$, where $i \in \{1, 2\}$. Note that op_1 and op_2 are k-distinguishable in state σ_0 iff Σ_1 and Σ_2 are disjoint.

Theorem 3. *A state machine with k-distinguishable operations op_1 and op_2 in its initial state can be used to solve consensus for k processes. Thus, it has a consensus number of at least k.*

Proof. We use Reduction 2 a generalization of our previous reduction scheme. The proof follows as before.

We now show that the k-distinguishability condition reduces to a simpler non-commutativity property for *idempotent* operations. We say that an operation *op* is *idempotent* if repeated executions of the operation *op* have no further effect. We formalize this property as follows. Let γ be a sequence of operations. Define $\gamma!op$ to be the sequence obtained from γ by omitting all occurrences of *op* except the first one. We say that *op* is idempotent if: for all sequences γ, $\gamma(\sigma_0) = (\gamma!op)(\sigma_0)$.

Let op_1 and op_2 be two idempotent operations. Then, for any $k \geq 2$, op_1 and op_2 are k-distinguishable in σ_0 iff op_1 and op_2 are 2-distinguishable in σ_0. This condition can be further simplified to: $\{\sigma_1, \sigma_{1,2}\} \cap \{\sigma_2, \sigma_{2,1}\} = \phi$.

Note that the above condition can be equivalently viewed as follows:

1. op_1 and op_2 behave differently in σ_0: $op_1(\sigma_0) \neq op_2(\sigma_0)$.
2. op_1 and op_2 do not commute in σ_0: $op_1(op_2(\sigma_0)) \neq op_1(op_2(\sigma_0))$.
3. op_1 does not nullify op_2 in σ_0: $op_1(op_2(\sigma_0)) \neq op_1(\sigma_0)$.
4. op_2 does not nullify op_1 in σ_0: $op_2(op_1(\sigma_0)) \neq op_2(\sigma_0)$.

Note that the notions of commutativity and nullification used above are with respect to a single initial state.

State machines in a distributed setting are often designed to be *idempotent* (i.e., all its operations are designed to be idempotent) since a client may issue the same operation multiple times in the presence of message failures. This may simply require clients to associate a unique identifier to each request they make so that the system can easily identify duplicates of the same request. (Recall that an operation, as defined earlier, includes all the parameters passed to a procedure.)

Theorem 4. *A state machine with 2-distinguishable idempotent operations op_1 and op_2 in its initial state can be used to solve consensus for any number of processes. Thus, it has a consensus number of ∞.*

Extension. The above theorems immediately tell us that resilient linearizable implementations of certain data-structures or state-machines are not possible in an asynchronous model of computation (in the presence of process failures). The above theorem requires 2-distinguishable idempotent operations in the initial state. We can generalize this to state-machines where such operations exist in states other than the initial states.

We say that a state σ is a *reachable* state iff there exists a sequence of operations γ such that $\sigma = \gamma(\sigma_0)$. We say that a state σ is an *idempotently reachable* state iff there exists a sequence of idempotent operations γ such that $\sigma = \gamma(\sigma_0)$.

Theorem 5. *Consider a state machine that has an idempotently reachable state σ and two idempotent operations op_1 and op_2 such that op_1 and op_2 are 2-distinguishable in σ. Then, the given state machine can be used to solve consensus for any number of processes. Thus, it has a consensus number of ∞.*

Proof. Since state σ is reachable, there exists a sequence γ_0 of idempotent operations $[f_1, \cdots, f_m]$ such that $[f_1, \cdots, f_m](\sigma_0) = \sigma$. We use the following reduction: The proof follows as before. Let γ_1 denote the sequence of update operations γ_0 followed by op_1. Let γ_2 denote the sequence of update operations γ_0 followed by op_2. Note that

---

Reduction 3. 2-distinguishable operations in idempotently reachable state

1:    **procedure** Consensus (Boolean b)
2:        $f_1(); \cdots ; f_m();$
3:        **if** (b) **then** $op_1()$ **else** $op_2()$ **endif**
4:        s = read()
5:        **return**$(s \in \{op_1(\sigma), op_2(op_1(\sigma))\})$

---

every process executes either the sequence γ_1 or γ_2 followed by a read. The idempotence property lets us ignore repeated execution of the same operation. Consider the first process p that executes statement 3. We can show that at this point, the state must be σ (the state produced by the sequence γ_0). Execution of statement 3 by p will produce either state $op_1(\sigma)$ or $op_2(\sigma)$. Suppose p executes op_1 producing state $op_1(\sigma)$. The only subsequent operation that can change the state is op_2, which will produce the state $op_2(op_1(\sigma))$. Thus, the state read in line 4 by any process will belong to the set $\{op_1(\sigma), op_2(op_1(\sigma))\}$. Dually, if p executes op_2, then the state read in line 4 by any process will belong to the set $\{op_2(\sigma), op_1(op_2(\sigma))\}$. It follows that all processes will decide on the same value, depending on the operation p executes.

Idempotent stacks, certain forms of multi-writer registers and many other examples are impossible to realize in a linearizable and resilient manner. Please refer to the technical report [5] for details.

Generalization. Our preceding results assume that the state machine includes a read operation that returns the entire state. It is possible to generalize the definitions and proofs to deal with state machines that provide restricted read operations. In particular, the notion of 2-distinguishability requires that resulting states must be distinguishable by some read operation.

6 Applications

Both our positive result (Theorem 1) and negative result (Theorem 5) may help in crafting data-structure APIs so as to enable a resilient linearizable implementation. We illustrate this by considering the design of a graph data-structure API.

Graph-1. Let U denote any countable set of vertex identifiers (such as the natural numbers or integers). The *graph* data-structure provides the following update operations:

$$U = \{\, \text{removeVertex}(u) \mid u \in U \,\} \cup$$
$$\{\, \text{addEdge}(u, v), \text{removeEdge}(u, v) \mid u, v \in U \,\}$$

The state consists of only a set of edges. The formal specification of the operations is shown in Specification 1. Most of the graph operations commute with each other. The only non-commuting operations are discussed below. Operations addEdge(u, v) and removeEdge(u, v) nullify each other. Operation removeVertex(u) nullifies the operations addEdge(u, x) and addEdge(x, u) (for any x).

Specification 1. Graph-1	**Specification 2.** Graph-2

Set $\langle U \times U \rangle$ E;
addEdge(u, v) { $E = E \cup \{(u, v)\}$ }
removeEdge(u, v) { $E = E \setminus \{(u, v)\}$ }
removeVertex(u)
  { $E = \{(x, y) \in E \mid x \neq u, y \neq u\}$ }
	Set $\langle U \rangle$ V; Set $\langle U \times U \rangle$ E;
	addEdge(u, v) { $V = V \cup \{u, v\}$;
	  $E = E \cup \{(u, v)\}$ }
	removeEdge(u, v) { $E = E \setminus \{(u, v)\}$ }
	removeVertex(u) { $V = V \setminus \{u\}$;
	  $E = \{(x, y) \in E \mid x \neq u, y \neq u\}$ }

It follows that Graph-1 is a NC state machine and that a resilient linearizable implementation of Graph-1 is possible. However, we now present a very similar specification for a Graph for which no resilient linearizable algorithm is possible.

Graph-2. This specification provides the same set of operations as Graph-1. However, the semantics of the operations are slightly different. The state in this case consists of both a set of vertices V and a set of edges E. The operations maintain the invariant that for any edge $(u, v) \in E$, the vertices u and v are in V (a sort of *referential integrity* constraint). The formal specification is shown in Specification 2. It turns out that Graph-2 is not a NC state machine. The operations $op_1 = $ addEdge(u, v) and $op_2 = $ removeVertex(u) neither commute nor nullify in state $G = (\{u, w\}, \{(u, w)\})$ consisting of two vertices u and w and the edge (u, w). It can be verified that the operations op_1 and op_2 are 2-distinguishable in state G. It follows from Theorem 5 that a idempotent version of Graph-2 cannot be realized resiliently.

Discussion. At first glance, it might appear that the key difference between Graph-1 and Graph-2 is that Graph-2 maintains a set of vertices in addition to a set of edges. Even though Graph-1 does not provide for an explicit representation of the vertex set, the edge set implicitly encodes a vertex set as well (namely the endpoints of the edges in the edge-set). Graph-1 even permits encoding of graphs with isolated vertices (as a self-loop of the form (u, u)). Thus, Graph-1 is, in some sense, as expressive as Graph-2. The key difference between Graph-1 and Graph-2 that leads to the possibility/impossibility distinction above is the subtle change in the semantics of the operations.

7   Related Work

State machine replication is a general approach for implementing data-structures that can tolerate process failures. One common way to implement state machine replication is by using consensus to order all commands If the state machine is deterministic, each correct process is guaranteed to generate the same responses and reach the same state. As consensus is impossible in the presence of process failures [7] this approach does not guarantee progress.

Shapiro *et al.* [10] exploit properties of data structures like commutativity to build efficient replicated data structures. However, they do not seek to achieve linearizability. Many of the implementations they propose are not linearizable.

Faleiro *et al.* [6] show that a weaker form of agreement namely lattice agreement and a generalized version of it (GLA) can be solved in asynchronous message passing systems. They also show that GLA can be used to implement linearizable and resilient UQ state machines as long as all updates commute. This paper shows that even data structures in which not all updates commute can be implemented in a linearizable and resilient manner. In addition we show that certain UQ state machines are impossible to implement in a linearizable and resilient manner.

Wait free implementations of other specific data structures like atomic snapshot objects have been studied in literature [4,9]. Attiya *et al.* [2] show how a wait free linearizable atomic register for a shared memory system can be emulated in a message passing system so long as only a minority of processes fail.

Our feasibility result is closely related to the result of [1] that wait-free linearizable algorithms are possible in a shared-memory setting for a similar class of problems. The key differences are that we address the problem in a message-passing model. Our approach distinguishes updates from reads, unlike [1]. This also allows us to achieve a more efficient algorithm for read-operations. We also present impossibility results, which are new. In the context of shared memory systems, Vechev et al [3] show that it is impossible to build a linearizable implementation of an object with a non-commutative method without using strong synchronization (barrier, fence or locks).

References

1. Aspnes, J., Herlihy, M.: Wait-free data structures in the asynchronous pram model. In: Proceedings of the Second Annual ACM Symposium on Parallel Algorithms and Architectures, SPAA 1990, pp. 340–349. ACM, New York (1990)
2. Attiya, H., Bar-Noy, A., Dolev, D.: Sharing memory robustly in message-passing systems. J. ACM 42 (1995)
3. Attiya, H., Guerraoui, R., Hendler, D., Kuznetsov, P., Michael, M.M., Vechev, M.T.: Laws of order: expensive synchronization in concurrent algorithms cannot be eliminated. In: POPL, pp. 487–498 (2011)
4. Attiya, H., Herlihy, M., Rachman, O.: Atomic snapshots using lattice agreement. Distrib. Comput. 8 (March 1995)
5. Chordia, S., Rajamani, S., Rajan, K., Ramalingam, G., Vaswani, K.: Asynchronous resilient linearizability. Technical Report MSR-TR-2013-71, Microsoft Research
6. Faleiro, J.M., Rajamani, S., Rajan, K., Ramalingam, G., Vaswani, K.: Generalized lattice agreement. In: Proceedings of the 2012 ACM Symposium on Principles of Distributed Computing, PODC 2012, pp. 125–134. ACM, New York (2012)
7. Fischer, M.J., Lynch, N., Paterson, M.S.: Impossibility of distributed consensus with one faulty process. Journal of the ACM 2(32), 374–382 (1985)
8. Herlihy, M.P., Wing, J.M.: Linearizability: a correctness condition for concurrent objects. ACM Transactions on Programming Languages and Systems 12, 463–492 (1990)
9. Jayanti, P.: An optimal multi-writer snapshot algorithm. In: Proceedings of the Thirty-Seventh Annual ACM Symposium on Theory of Computing, STOC 2005, pp. 723–732. ACM, New York (2005)
10. Shapiro, M., Preguiça, N., Baquero, C., Zawirski, M.: Convergent and commutative replicated data types. Bulletin of the European Association for Theoretical Computer Science (EATCS) (104), 67–88 (2011)

Fair Synchronization

Gadi Taubenfeld

The Interdisciplinary Center, P.O. Box 167, Herzliya 46150, Israel
tgadi@idc.ac.il

Abstract. Most published concurrent data structures which avoid locking do not
provide any fairness guarantees. That is, they allow processes to access a data
structure and complete their operations arbitrarily many times before some other
trying process can complete a single operation. Such a behavior can be prevented
by enforcing fairness. However, fairness requires waiting or helping. Helping
techniques are often complex and memory consuming. Does it mean that for enforcing fairness it is best to use locks? The answer is negative. We show that it
is possible to automatically transfer any non-blocking or wait-free data structure
into a similar data structure which satisfies a strong fairness requirement, without
using locks and with limited waiting. The fairness we require is that no beginning process can complete two operations on a given resource while some other
process is kept waiting on the same resource. Our approach allows as many processes as possible to access a shared resource at the same time as long as fairness
is preserved. To achieve this goal, we introduce and solve a *new* synchronization
problem, called *fair synchronization*. Solving the new problem enables us to add
fairness to existing implementations of concurrent data structures, and to transform any solution to the mutual exclusion problem into a fair solution.

Keywords: Synchronization, fairness, concurrent data structures, non-blocking,
wait-freedom, locks, mutual exclusion.

1 Introduction

Motivation

Concurrent access to a data structure shared among several processes must be synchronized in order to avoid interference between conflicting operations. Mutual exclusion
locks are the de facto mechanism for concurrency control on concurrent data structures:
a process accesses the data structure only inside a critical section code, within which
the process is guaranteed exclusive access. However, using locks may degrade the performance of synchronized concurrent applications, as it enforces processes to wait for
a lock to be released.

A promising approach is the design of data structures which avoid locking. Several progress conditions have been proposed for such data structures. Two of the most
extensively studied conditions, in order of decreasing strength, are wait-freedom [17]
and non-blocking [19]. Wait-freedom guarantees that every process will always be able
to complete its pending operations in a finite number of its own steps. Non-blocking
(which is sometimes also called lock-freedom) guarantees that some process will always be able to complete its pending operations in a finite number of its own steps.

Y. Afek (Ed.): DISC 2013, LNCS 8205, pp. 179–193, 2013.

Wait-free and non-blocking data structures are not required to provide fairness guarantees. That is, such data structures may allow processes to complete their operations arbitrarily many times before some other trying process can complete a single operation. Such a behavior may be prevented when fairness is required. However, fairness requires waiting or helping. Using helping techniques (without waiting) may impose too much overhead upon the implementation, and are often complex and memory consuming. Does it mean that for enforcing fairness it is best to use locks? The answer is negative. We show how any wait-free and any non-blocking implementation can be automatically transformed into an implementation which satisfies a very strong fairness requirement without using locks and with limited waiting.

We require that no beginning process can complete two operations on a given resource while some other process is kept waiting on the same resource. Our approach, allows as many processes as possible to access a shared resource at the same time as long as fairness is preserved. To achieve this goal, we introduce and solve a new synchronization problem, called *fair synchronization*. Solving the fair synchronization problem enables us to add fairness to existing implementations of concurrent data structures, and to transform any solution to the mutual exclusion problem into a fair solution.

Fair Synchronization

The fair synchronization problem is to design an algorithm that guarantees fair access to a shared resource among a number of participating processes. Fair access means that no process can access a resource twice while some other process is kept waiting. There is no limit on the number of processes that can access a resource simultaneously. In fact, a desired property is that as many processes as possible will be able to access a resource at the same time as long as fairness is preserved.

It is assumed that each process is executing a sequence of instructions in an infinite loop. The instructions are divided into four continuous sections: the remainder, entry, critical and exit. Furthermore, it is assumed that the entry section consists of two parts. The first part, which is called the *doorway*, is *fast wait-free*: its execution requires only a (very small) *constant* number of steps and hence always terminates; the second part is a *waiting* statement: a loop that includes one or more statements. Like in the case of the doorway, the exit section is also required to be fast wait-free. A *waiting* process is a process that has finished its doorway code and reached the waiting part of its entry section. A *beginning* process is a process that is about to start executing its entry section.

A process is *enabled* to enter its critical section at some point in time, if sufficiently many steps of that process will carry it into the critical section, independently of the actions of the other processes. That is, an enabled process does not need to wait for an action by any other process in order to complete its entry section and to enter its critical section, nor can an action by any other process prevent it from doing so.

The **fair synchronization problem** is to write the code for the entry and the exit sections in such a way that the following three basic requirements are satisfied.

- **Progress:** *In the absence of process failures and assuming that a process always leaves its critical section, if a process is trying to enter its critical section, then some process, not necessarily the same one, eventually enters its critical section.*

The terms deadlock-freedom and livelock-freedom are used in the literature for the above progress condition, in the context of the mutual exclusion problem.

- **Fairness:** *A beginning process cannot execute its critical section twice before a waiting process completes executing its critical and exit sections once. Furthermore, no beginning process can become enabled before an already waiting process becomes enabled.*

It is possible that a beginning process and a waiting process will become enabled at the same time. However, no beginning process can execute its critical section twice while some other process is kept waiting. The second part of the fairness requirement is called *first-in-first-enabled*. The term *first-in-first-out* (FIFO) fairness is used in the literature for a slightly stronger condition which guarantees that: no beginning process can pass an already waiting process. That is, no beginning process can enter its critical section before an already waiting process does so.

- **Concurrency:** *All the waiting processes which are not enabled become enabled at the same time.*

It follows from the *progress* and *fairness* requirements that *all* the waiting processes which are not enabled will eventually become enabled. The concurrency requirement guarantees that becoming enabled happens simultaneously, for all the waiting processes, and thus it guarantees that many processes will be able to access their critical sections at the same time as long as fairness is preserved. We notice that no lock implementation may satisfy the concurrency requirement.

The processes that have already passed through their doorway can be divided into two groups. The enabled processes and those that are not enabled. It is not possible to always have all the processes enabled due to the fairness requirement. All the enabled processes can immediately proceed to execute their critical sections. The waiting processes which are not enabled will eventually simultaneously become enabled, before or once the currently enabled processes exit their critical and exit sections. We observe that the stronger FIFO fairness requirement, the progress requirement and concurrency requirement cannot be mutually satisfied (see [36] for a proof).

Fair Synchronization is a deceptive problem, and at first glance it seems very simple to solve. The only way to understand its tricky nature is by trying to solve it. We suggest the readers to to try themselves to solve the problem, assuming that there are only three processes which communicate by reading and writing shared registers.

Contributions

Our model of computation consists of an asynchronous collection of n processes that (in most cases) communicate by reading and writing atomic registers. In few cases, we will also define and consider stronger synchronization primitives. With an atomic register, it is assumed that operations on the register occur in some definite order. That is, reading or writing an atomic register is an indivisible action. Our contributions are:

Fair synchronization. We define a new synchronization problem – called fair synchronization – for concurrent programming, show how it can be solved and demonstrate its importance. The problem is to design a highly concurrent algorithm that guarantees that no beginning process can access a resource twice while some other process is kept waiting on the same resource.

Algorithms. We present the first fair synchronization algorithm for n processes. The algorithm uses $n + 1$ atomic registers: n 4-valued atomic registers plus one atomic bit. We also explained how to construct a fast and adaptive versions of the algorithm.

Fair data structures. We define the notion of a fair data structure and prove that by composing a fair synchronization algorithm and a non-blocking or a wait-free data structure, it is possible to construct the corresponding fair data structure.

Fair mutual exclusion algorithms. A fair mutual algorithm, in addition to satisfying the mutual exclusion and deadlock freedom requirements (Section 4), guarantees that no beginning process can access its critical section twice while some other process is kept waiting. We prove that by composing a fair synchronization algorithm and a deadlock-free mutual exclusion algorithm, it is possible to construct a fair mutual algorithm.

A space lower bound. We show that $n - 1$ registers and conditional objects are necessary for solving the fair synchronization problem for n processes. Compare-and-swap and test-and-set are examples of conditional objects.

Related Work

Mutual exclusion locks were first introduced by Edsger W. Dijkstra in [8]. Since than, numerous implementations of locks have been proposed [30,32]. Various other types of locks, like ℓ-exclusion locks [13,12] and read/write locks [7], were considered in the literature. For each type of a lock it is *a priori* defined how many processes and/or which processes (i.e., a reader process or a writer process) cannot be in their critical sections at the same time. In the case of the fair synchronization problem no such a priori requirement exists. The fair synchronization algorithm, presented in Section 2, uses some ideas from the mutual exclusion algorithm presented in [33].

Implementations of data structures which avoid locking have appeared in many papers, a few examples are [9,14,15,27,31,37]. Several progress conditions have been proposed for data structures which avoid locking. The most extensively studied conditions are wait-freedom [17] and non-blocking [19]. Strategies that avoid locks are called lockless [16] or lock-free [26]. (In some papers, lock-free means non-blocking.) Consistency conditions for concurrent objects are linearizability [19] and sequential consistency [22]. A tutorial on memory consistency models can be found in [1].

In order to improve wait-free object implementations, in [3,4], it is suggested to first protect a shared object by an ℓ-exclusion lock; processes that passed the ℓ-exclusion lock, rename themselves before accessing the object. This enables the usage of an object that was designed only for up to ℓ processes, rather than a less efficient object designed for n processes. The implementation uses strong synchronization primitives.

An algorithm is *obstruction-free* if it guarantees that a process will be able to complete its pending operations in a finite number of its own steps, if all the other processes hold still long enough (that is, in the absence of interference from other processes) [18]. Transformations that automatically convert any obstruction-free algorithm into a non-blocking or a wait-free algorithm are presented in [10,34], for a model where it is assumed that there is a (possibly unknown) upper bound on memory access time.

Contention-sensitive data structures in which the overhead introduced by locking is eliminated in the common cases, when there is no contention, or when processes with non-interfering operations access it concurrently, are introduced in [35]. Hybrid implementations of concurrent objects in which lock-based code and lock-free code are merged in the same implementation of a concurrent object, are discussed in [29].

2   The Fair Synchronization Algorithm

We use one (multi-writer multi-reader) atomic bit, called *queue*. The first thing that process i does in its entry section is to read the value of the *queue* bit, and to determine to which of the two queues (0 or 1) it should belong. This is done by setting i's single-writer register $state_i$ to the value read.

Once i chooses a queue, it waits until its queue has priority over the other queue and then it enters its critical section. The order in which processes can enter their critical sections is defined as follows: If two processes belong to different queues, the process whose queue, as recorded in its *state* register, is *different* from the value of the bit *queue* is enabled and can enter its critical section, and the other process has to wait. If all the active processes belong to the same queue then they can all enter their critical sections.

Next, we explain when the shared *queue* bit is updated. The first thing that process i does when it leaves its critical section (i.e., its first step in its exit section) is to set the *queue* bit to a value which is *different* from the value of its $state_i$ register. This way, i gives priority to waiting processes with belong to the same queue that it belongs to.

Until the value of the *queue* bit is first changed, all the active processes belong to the same queue, say queue 0. The first process to finish its critical section flips the value of the *queue* bit and sets it to 1. Thereafter, the value read by all the new beginning processes is 1, until the queue bit is modified again. Next, *all* the processes which belong to queue 0 enter and then exit their critical sections possibly at the same time until there are no active processes which belong to queue 0. Then all the processes from queue 1 become enabled and are allowed to enter their critical sections, and when each one of them exits it sets to 0 the value of the *queue* bit, which gives priority to the processes in queue 1, and so on.

The following registers are used: (1) a single multi-writer atomic bit named *queue*, (2) an array of single-writer atomic registers $state[1..n]$ which range over $\{0, 1, 2, 3\}$. To improve readability, we use below subscripts to index entries in an array. At any given time, process i can be in one of four possible states, as recorded in it single-writer register $state_i$. When $state_i = 3$, process i is not active, that is, it is in its remainder section. When $state_i = 2$, process i is active and (by reading *queue*) tries to decide to which of the two queues, 0 or 1, it should belong. When $state_i = 1$, process i is active and belongs to queue 1. When $state_i = 0$, process i is active and belongs to queue 0.

The statement **await** *condition* is used as an abbreviation for **while** $\neg condition$ **do** *skip*. The *break* statement, like in C, breaks out of the smallest enclosing *for* or *while* loop. Finally, whenever two atomic registers appear in the same statement, two separate steps are required to execute this statement. The algorithm is given below.[1]

Algorithm 1. A FAIR SYNCHRONIZATION ALGORITHM: process i's code $(1 \leq i \leq n)$

Shared variables:
　　$queue$: atomic bit; the initial value of the queue bit is immaterial.
　　$state[1..n]$: array of atomic registers, which range over $\{0, 1, 2, 3\}$
　　Initially $\forall i : 1 \leq i \leq n : state_i = 3$　　/* processes are inactive */

```
1    state_i := 2                                    /* begin doorway */
2    state_i := queue             /* choose queue and end doorway */
3    for j = 1 to n do                             /* begin waiting */
4        if (state_i ≠ queue) then break fi      /* process is enabled */
5        await state_j ≠ 2
6        if state_j = 1 − state_i                 /* different queues */
7        then await   (state_j ≠ 1 − state_i) ∨ (state_i ≠ queue) fi
8    od                                              /* end waiting */
9    critical section
10   queue := 1 − state_i                           /* begin exit */
11   state_i := 3                                     /* end exit */
```

In line 1, process i indicates that it has started executing its doorway code. Then, in *two* atomic steps, it reads the value of $queue$ and assigns the value read to $state_i$ (line 2).

After passing its doorway, process i waits in the *for loop* (lines 3–8), until all the processes in the queue to which it belongs are simultaneously enabled and then it enters its critical section. This happens when either, $(state_i \neq queue)$, i.e. the value the $queue$ bit points to the queue which i does *not* belong to (line 4), or when all the waiting processes (including i) belong to the same queue (line 7). Each one of the terms of the await statement (line 7) is evaluated separately. In case processes i and j belong to different queues (line 6), i waits until either (1) j is not competing any more or j has reentered its entry section, or (2) i has priority over j because $state_i$ is *different* than the value of the $queue$ bit.

In the exit code, i sets the $queue$ bit to a value which is different than the queue to which it belongs (line 10), and changes its state to not active (line 11). We notice that the algorithm is also correct when we replace the order of lines 9 and 10, allowing process i to write the queue bit immediately before it enters its critical section. The order of lines 10 and 11 is crucial for correctness.

We observe that a *non* beginning process, say p, may enter its critical section ahead of another waiting process, say q, twice: the first time if p is enabled on the other queue, and the second time if p just happened to pass q which is waiting on the same queue and enters its critical section first. We point out that omitting lines 1 and 5 will result

---

[1] To simplify the presentation, when the code for a fair synchronization algorithm is presented, only the entry and exit codes are described, and the remainder code and the infinite loop within which these codes reside are omitted.

an incorrect solution. It is possible to replace each one of the 4-valued single-writer atomic registers, by three *separate* atomic bits. In the full version [36], we present this variant of the algorithm which uses $3n + 1$ separate bits. Below we discuss two other interesting variants of Algorithm 1.

A Fast Fair Synchronization Algorithm. A fast algorithm is an algorithm which its time complexity, in the absence of contention, is a constant [24]. Thus, a fair synchronization algorithm is fast if, in the absence of contention, the maximum number of times (i.e., steps) a process may need to access the shared memory in its entry and exit codes. It is not difficult to make the fair synchronization algorithm (Algorithm 1) fast, using an additional atomic counter. The value of the counter is initially 0. The first step of a process is to atomically increment the counter by 1. After the process finishes executing its doorway (i.e., lines 1 and 2), it reads its value. If the returned value is 1, the processes can safely enter its critical section, otherwise, the process continues to the waiting code (line 3). In the last step of its exit code the process decrements the counter by 1.

An Adaptive Fair Synchronization Algorithm. An adaptive algorithm is an algorithm which its time complexity is a function of the actual number of participating processes rather than a function of the total number of processes. In [2], a new object, called an *active set* was introduced, together with an implementation which is wait-free, adaptive and uses only atomic registers. The authors have shown how to transform the Bakery algorithm [21] into its corresponding adaptive version using the active set object. In [33], it was shown how to transform the Black White Bakery algorithm into its corresponding adaptive version using the same technique. It is rather simple to use the same transformation to make also the fair synchronization algorithm (Algorithm 1) adaptive.

Correctness Proof

We prove below the correctness of the fair synchronization algorithm.

Theorem 1. *The fair synchronization algorithm for n processes (Algorithm 1) satisfies the progress, fairness and concurrency requirements, and uses $n + 1$ atomic registers: n 4-valued single-writer atomic registers plus one multi-writer atomic bit. The total number of bits used is $2n + 1$.*

The following lemma captures the effect of the queue a process belongs to, on the order in which processes enter their critical sections.

Lemma 1. *For any two waiting processes i and j, if $state_i \neq queue$ and $state_j = queue$, then i must enter its critical section and complete its exit section before j can enter its critical section.*

Proof. A waiting process, say i, is *enabled* to enter its critical section only when one of the following two condition holds: (1) the value of $state_i \neq queue$. In such a case, i will break out of the for loop after executing line 4; or (2) for all processes $j \neq i$, $state_j \neq 1 - state_i$. That is, no process belongs to a different queue than the queue i belongs to. In such a case, i will execute the loop n times and will exit. If non of these two conditions holds, i will eventually have to wait in line 7, until either the value of the queue bit changes of the processes which belong to the other queue change the values of their state registers.

Until the value of the *queue* bit is first changed, all the active processes belong to the same queue $v \in \{0, 1\}$. Hence, as explained above, they are all enabled. The first process to finish its critical section flips the value of the *queue* bit and sets it $1 - v$. Thereafter, the value of the queue bit read by all the new beginning processes is $1-v$. As explained in the previous paragraph, non of these new beginning processes can become enabled until either, the value of the queue bit changes again, or all the processes which belong to the queue v complete their exit sections. Since all the processes which belong to the queue v set the queue bit to $1 - v$ on their exit, the disabled processes will have to wait until all the enabled processes with state registers equal v exit.

Only then all the active processes belong to the same queue $1 - v$, and hence will all become enabled. When they exit they change back to v the value of the *queue* bit, and so on. As we can see in the above explanation, for any two waiting processes i and j, if $state_i \neq queue$ and $state_j = queue$, then i is enabled and j is disabled, and i and all the processes which belong to the same queue as i will enter their critical sections and complete their critical and exit sections before j can enter its critical section.   □

Proof of Theorem 1. The correctness of the claims about the number and size of the registers are obvious. Assume a beginning process i overtakes a waiting process j in entering its critical section. It follows from Lemma 1, that this can happen only if both i and j belong to the same queue (i.e., $state_i = state_j$) at the time when i has completed executing line 2. On exit i (and possibly other processes) will set the value of the *queue* bit to $1 - state_i$. Thereafter, by Lemma 1, the value of the queue bit will not change (at least) until j completes its exit section. If i will try to enter its critical section again while j has not completed its exit section yet, then after passing through its doorway i will belong to a different queue than j (i.e., $state_i \neq state_j$) and the value of the *queue* bit will be the same as the value of $state_i$. Thus, by Lemma 1, i will not again become enabled until j - the process it has overtaken - completes its exit section and changes the value of its $state_j$ register. Thus, the algorithm satisfies *fairness*.

Next we assume to the contrary that the algorithm does not satisfy progress and show how this assumption leads to a contradiction. Assuming that the algorithm does not satisfy progress means that all the active processes are forced to remain in their entry sections forever. There are two possible cases: (1) the values of the state registers of all the active processes are the same, and (2) it is not the case that the values of the state registers of all the active processes are the same. In the first case, all the active processes are enabled and they all can proceed to their critical sections. In the later case, all the processes which their state register is different from the value of the queue bit can proceed to their critical sections. In either case, some process can proceed. A contradiction. Thus, the algorithm satisfies *progress*.

We prove that the algorithm satisfies the concurrency requirement. As we have already explained in the proof of Lemma 1, a waiting process, say i, is *enabled* to enter its critical section only when one of the following two condition holds: (1) the value of $state_i \neq queue$; in such a case, i will break out of the for loop after executing line

4; or (2) for all processes $j \neq i$, $state_j \neq 1 - state_i$. That is, no process belongs to a different queue than the queue i belongs to. In such a case, i will execute the loop n times and will exit. Thus, it follows that if two waiting processes, say i and j, are disabled then it must be the case that $state_i = state_j$. Lets assume that i becomes enabled. If i becomes enabled because the value of the queue bit has changed then also j must become enabled for that reason. If i becomes enabled because no process belongs to a different queue than the queue i belongs to, then also j must become enabled for that reason. Thus, the algorithm satisfies *concurrency*.   □

3   Fair Data Structures

In order to impose fairness on a concurrent date structure, concurrent accesses to a data structure can be synchronized using a fair synchronization algorithm: a process accesses the data structure only inside a critical section code. Any data structure can be easily made fair using such an approach, without using locks and with limited waiting.

We name a solution to the fair synchronization problem a (finger) *ring*.[2] Using a single *ring* to enforce fairness on a concurrent data structure, is an example of coarse-grained *fair* synchronization. In contrast, fine-grained *fair* synchronization enables to protect "small pieces" of a data structure, allowing several processes with *different* operations to access it completely independently. For example, in the case of adding fairness to an existing wait-free queue, it makes sense to use two rings: one for the enqueue operations and the other for the dequeue operations.

Coarse-grained fair synchronization is easier to program but might be less efficient compared to fine-grained fair synchronization. When using coarse-grained fair synchronization, operations that do not conflict may have to wait one for another, precluding disjoint-access parallelism. This can be resolved when using fine-grained fair synchronization.

3.1   Definitions

An implementation of each operation of a concurrent data structure is divided into two continuous sections of code: the doorway code and the body code. When a process invokes an operation it first executes the doorway code and then executes the body code. The *doorway* is *fast wait-free*: its execution requires executing only a *constant* number of instructions and hence always terminates.

A *beginning* process is a process that is about to start executing the doorway code of some operation. A process has *passed* its doorway, if it has finished the doorway code and reached the body code. A process is *enabled* while executing an operation on a given data structure, if by executing sufficiently many steps it will be able to complete its operation, independently of the actions of the other processes. That is, an enabled process does not need to wait for an action by any other process in order to complete its operation, nor can an action by any other process prevent it from doing so.

---

[2] Many processes can simultaneously pass through the ring's hole, but the size of the ring may limit their number.

The problem of implementing a **fair data structure** is to write the doorway code and the body code in such a way that the following four requirements are satisfied,

- **Starvation-freedom (progress):** *In the absence of process failures, if a process is executing the doorway code or the body code, then this process, must eventually complete its operation.*

- **Fairness:** *No beginning process can complete an operation twice while some other process which has already passed the doorway has not completed its operation yet. Furthermore, no beginning process can become enabled before a process that has already passed its doorway becomes enabled.*

- **Concurrency:** *All the processes that have passed their doorway and are not enabled, become enabled at the same time.*

To keep things simple, we have not separated between the different types of operations a data structure may support. It is possible to refine the definition and, for example, require fairness only among operations of the same type.

3.2 A Composition Theorem

By composing a fair synchronization algorithm and a non-blocking or a wait-free linearizable data structure, it is possible to construct a *fair* linearizable data structure. Linearizability is a consistency condition which means that although operations of concurrent processes may overlap, each operation should appear to take effect instantaneously, and operations that do not overlap should take effect in their "real-time" order [19]. The doorway code of the composed fair data structure is the doorway of the fair synchronization algorithm. The body is the waiting code of the fair synchronization algorithm followed by the code of the data structure, followed by the exit section.

Theorem 2. *Let A be a fair synchronization algorithm and let B be a non-blocking or a wait-free data structure. Assume that the registers of A are different from the registers of B. Let C be a data structure obtained by replacing the critical section of A with the data structure B. Then, C is a fair data structure. Furthermore, if B is linearizable, then also C is linearizable.*

The correctness proof appears in [36]. Using Theorem 2, it is now possible to construct new fair data structures from existing non-blocking or wait-free data structures.

4   Fair Mutual Exclusion

The mutual exclusion problem is to design an algorithm that guarantees mutually exclusive access to a critical section among a number of competing processes [Dij65]. As before, it is assumed that each process is executing a sequence of instructions in an infinite loop. The instructions are divided into four continuous sections: the remainder, entry, critical and exit. The entry section consists of two parts: the *doorway* which is *wait-free*, and the waiting part which includes one or more loops. Recall that a *waiting* process is a process that has finished its doorway code and reached the waiting part, and a *beginning* process is a process that is about to start executing its entry section. Like in the case of the doorway, the exit section is also required to be wait-free. It is assumed that processes do not fail, and that a process always leaves its critical section.

4.1 Definitions

The *mutual exclusion problem* is to write the code for the entry and the exit sections in such a way that the following *two* basic requirements are satisfied.

Deadlock-freedom: *If a process is trying to enter its critical section, then some process, not necessarily the same one, eventually enters its critical section.*

Mutual exclusion: *No two processes are in their critical sections at the same time.*

Satisfaction of the above two properties is the minimum required for a mutual exclusion algorithm. For an algorithm to be fair, satisfaction of an additional condition is required.

k-**fairness:** *A beginning process cannot execute its critical section $k + 1$ times before a waiting process completes executing its critical and exit sections once.*

We notice that 1-fairness implies that no beginning process can execute its critical section twice while some other process is kept waiting. The terms first-in-first-out (FIFO) is used for 0-bounded-waiting: no beginning process can pass an already waiting process. The term *linear-waiting* is used in the literature for the requirement that no (beginning or not) process can execute its critical section twice while some other process is kept waiting.

The **fair mutual exclusion problem** is to write the code for the entry and exit sections in such a way that the deadlock-freedom, mutual exclusion and 1-fairness requirements are satisfied. Solving the fair synchronization problem enables to transform *any* solution for the mutual exclusion problem into a fair solution.

4.2 A Composition Theorem

By composing a fair synchronization algorithm (FS) and a deadlock-free mutual exclusion algorithm (ME), it is possible to construct a *fair* mutual exclusion algorithm (FME). The entry section of the composed FME algorithm consists of the entry section of the FS algorithm followed by the entry section of the ME algorithm. The exit section of the FME algorithm consists of the exit section of the ME algorithm followed by the exit section of the FS algorithm. The doorway of the FME algorithm is the doorway of the FS algorithm.

Theorem 3. *Let A be a fair synchronization algorithm and let B be a deadlock-free mutual exclusion algorithm. Assume that the registers of A are different from the registers of B. Let C be the algorithm obtained by replacing the critical section of A with the algorithm B. That is, the code of C is:* **loop forever** *remainder code (of C);* entry *code of A;* entry *code of B;* critical section; *exit code of B;* exit code of A **end loop.** *Then, C is a fair mutual exclusion algorithm.*

The correctness proof appears in [36]. Using Theorem 3, it is now possible to construct new interesting fair mutual exclusion algorithms. For example, the One-bit algorithm that was devised independently in [5,6] and [23], is a deadlock-free mutual exclusion algorithm for n processes which uses n shared bits. By Theorem 3, using the fair synchronization algorithm from Section 2 which uses $2n + 1$ bits together with the One-bit algorithm which uses n bits, we can construct an elegant and simple fair mutual exclusion algorithm which uses a $3n + 1$ bits.

Several techniques for designing FIFO mutual exclusion algorithms have been used in [20,23,25]. It is interesting to note that while the doorway of the above new fair mutual exclusion algorithm includes only three steps (accessing $state_i$ twice and $queue$ once), the doorway of the various FIFO mutual exclusion algorithms [20,23,25] is not fast wait-free as it takes at least n steps, where n is the number of processes. Next we use Theorem 3 for proving a space lower bound for the fair synchronization problem.

5   A Space Lower Bound for Fair Synchronization

In Section 2, we have shown that $n + 1$ atomic registers are sufficient for solving the fair synchronization problem for n processes. In this section we show that $n - 1$ registers and conditional objects are necessary for solving the fair synchronization problem for n processes. A conditional operation is an operation that changes the value of an object only if the object has a particular value. A *conditional object* is an object that supports only conditional operations. Compare-and-swap and test-and-set are examples of conditional objects.

A compare-and-swap operation takes a register r, and two values: *new* and *old*. If the current value of the register r is equal to *old*, then the value of r is set to *new* and the value *true* is returned; otherwise r is left unchanged and the value *false* is returned. A compare-and-swap object is a register that supports a compare-and-swap operation. A test-and-set operation takes a registers r and a value *val*. The value *val* is assigned to r, and the old value of r is returned. A test-and-set bit is an object that supports a reset operation (i.e., write 0) and a restricted test-and-set operation where the value of *val* can only be 1.

Theorem 4. *Any fair synchronization algorithm for n processes using only atomic registers and conditional objects must use at least $n - 1$ atomic registers and conditional objects.*

Proof. A deadlock-free mutual exclusion algorithm using a single test-and-set bit is defined as follows. It uses a test-and-set bit called x. In its entry section, a process keeps on accessing x until, in one atomic step, it succeeds to change x from 0 to 1. Then, the process can safely enter its critical section. The exit section is simply to reset x to 0. By Theorem 3, it is possible to construct a fair mutual exclusion algorithm (FMX) by composing any fair synchronization algorithm and the above deadlock-free mutual exclusion algorithm.

A starvation-free mutual exclusion is an algorithm that satisfy the mutual exclusion requirement and guarantees that, in the absence of process failures, any process that tries to enter its critical section eventually enters its critical section. Clearly, any FMX algorithm is also a starvation-free mutual exclusion algorithm.

In [28], it is proven that any starvation-free mutual exclusion algorithm for n processes using only atomic registers and test-and-set bits must use at least n atomic registers and test-and-set bits. In [11] it is proven that any starvation-free mutual exclusion algorithm for n processes using only atomic registers and conditional objects must use at least n atomic registers and conditional objects. Since, a FMX algorithm is also a starvation-free mutual exclusion algorithm, the above lower bound holds also for FMX algorithms.

It follows from the two facts that (1) we can construct a FMX algorithm using any fair synchronization algorithm plus a single test-and-set bit, and that (2) any FMX algorithm for n processes using only atomic registers and conditional objects must use at least n atomic registers and conditional objects, that any *fair synchronization* algorithm for n processes using only atomic registers and conditional objects must use at least $n - 1$ atomic registers and conditional objects.   □

6   Discussion

We have considered the problem of enforcing fairness in a shared-memory algorithm, by preventing a process from accessing a shared resource twice while another process is waiting to get the resource. We have proposed to enforce fairness as a wrapper around any concurrent algorithm, and studied the consequences. We have formalized the fair synchronization problem, presented a solution, and then showed that existing concurrent data structures and mutual exclusion algorithms can be encapsulated into a fair synchronization construct to yield algorithms that are inherently fair. A linear space lower bound has been obtained for the problem.

Wait-free algorithms are frequently criticized for sacrificing performance compared to non-blocking algorithms. When enforce fairness as a wrapper around a concurrent algorithm, it is better that the concurrent algorithm be an efficient non-blocking algorithms rather than a wait-free algorithm. Since many processes may enter their critical sections simultaneously, it is expected that using fair synchronization algorithms will not degrade the performance of concurrent applications as much as locks. However, as in the case of using locks, slow or stopped processes may prevent other processes from ever accessing their critical sections.

There are several interesting variants of the fair synchronization problem which can be defined by strengthening or weakening the various requirements. For example, it is possible to require that a solution be able to withstand the slow-down or even the crash (fail by stopping) of up to $\ell - 1$ of processes. In that variant, the (stronger) progress condition is: If strictly fewer than ℓ processes fail (are delayed forever) then if a process is trying to enter its critical section, then some process, not necessarily the same one, eventually enters its critical section. Solving the problem with such a strong progress requirement, should be possible only by weakening the fairness requirement.

According to our definition of fairness, there is no overtaking. It seems that allowing limited amounts of overtaking (e.g., a process accessing a shared resource for a constant number of times while another is spinning on it) would not be detrimental. Some version of the two composition theorems would still hold for such weaker versions, and this might be closer to what happens in real life. Put another way, it is possible to replace the fairness requirement by k-fairness (as defined in Section 4) for some $k > 1$.

Like in the case of mutual exclusion, it would be interesting to solve the fair synchronization problem using synchronization primitives other than atomic registers, prove time complexity bounds, and find local spinning, symmetric, self stabilizing and fault-tolerant solutions.

References

1. Adve, S.V., Gharachorloo, K.: Shared memory consistency models: A tutorial. IEEE Computer 29(12), 66–76 (1996)
2. Afek, Y., Stupp, G., Touitou, D.: Long-lived adaptive collect with applications. In: Proc. 40th IEEE Symp. on Foundations of Computer Science, pp. 262–272 (October 1999)
3. Anderson, J.H., Moir, M.: Using k-exclusion to implement resilient, scalable shared objects. In: Proc. 14th ACM Symp. on Principles of Distributed Computing, pp. 141–150 (August 1994)
4. Anderson, J.H., Moir, M.: Using local-spin k-exclusion algorithms to improve wait-free object implementations. Distributed Computing 11 (1997)
5. Burns, J.E., Lynch, A.N.: Mutual exclusion using indivisible reads and writes. In: 18th Annual Allerton Conference on Communication, Control and Computing, pp. 833–842 (October 1980)
6. Burns, J.N., Lynch, N.A.: Bounds on shared-memory for mutual exclusion. Information and Computation 107(2), 171–184 (1993)
7. Courtois, P.L., Heyman, F., Parnas, D.L.: Concurrent control with Readers and Writers. Communications of the ACM 14(10), 667–668 (1971)
8. Dijkstra, E.W.: Solution of a problem in concurrent programming control. Communications of the ACM 8(9), 569 (1965)
9. Easton, W.B.: Process synchronization without long-term interlock. In: Proc. of the 3rd ACM Symp. on Operating Systems Principles, pp. 95–100 (1971)
10. Fich, F.E., Luchangco, V., Moir, M., Shavit, N.N.: Obstruction-free algorithms can be practically wait-free. In: Fraigniaud, P. (ed.) DISC 2005. LNCS, vol. 3724, pp. 78–92. Springer, Heidelberg (2005)
11. Fich, F.E., Hendler, D., Shavit, N.: On the inherent weakness of conditional synchronization primitives. In: Proc. 23rd ACM Symp. on Principles of Distributed Computing, pp. 80–87 (2004)
12. Fischer, M.J., Lynch, N.A., Burns, J.E., Borodin, A.: Distributed FIFO allocation of identical resources using small shared space. ACM Trans. on Programming Languages and Systems 11(1), 90–114 (1989)
13. Fischer, M.J., Lynch, N.A., Burns, J.E., Borodin, A.: Resource allocation with immunity to limited process failure. In: Proc. 20th IEEE Symp. on Foundations of Computer Science, pp. 234–254 (October 1979)
14. Fomitchev, M., Ruppert, E.: Lock-free linked lists and skip lists. In: Proc. 23rd ACM Symp. on Principles of Distributed Computing, pp. 50–59 (2004)
15. Harris, T.L.: A pragmatic implementation of non-blocking linked-lists. In: Welch, J.L. (ed.) DISC 2001. LNCS, vol. 2180, pp. 300–314. Springer, Heidelberg (2001)
16. Hart, T.E., McKenney, P.E., Brown, A.D.: Making lockless synchronization fast: Performance implications of memory reclamation. In: Proc. of the 20th International Parallel and Distributed Processing Symp. (2006)

17. Herlihy, M.P.: Wait-free synchronization. ACM Trans. on Programming Languages and Systems 13(1), 124–149 (1991)
18. Herlihy, M.P., Luchangco, V., Moir, M.: Obstruction-free synchronization: Double-ended queues as an example. In: Proc. of the 23rd International Conference on Distributed Computing Systems, p. 522 (2003)
19. Herlihy, M.P., Wing, J.M.: Linearizability: a correctness condition for concurrent objects. Toplas 12(3), 463–492 (1990)
20. Katseff, H.P.: A new solution to the critical section problem. In: Proc. 10th ACM Symp. on Theory of Computing, pp. 86–88 (May 1978)
21. Lamport, L.: A new solution of Dijkstra's concurrent programming problem. Communications of the ACM 17(8), 453–455 (1974)
22. Lamport, L.: How to make a multiprocessor computer that correctly executes multiprocess programs. IEEE Trans. on Computers 28(9), 690–691 (1979)
23. Lamport, L.: The mutual exclusion problem: Part II – statement and solutions. Journal of the ACM 33, 327–348 (1986)
24. Lamport, L.: A fast mutual exclusion algorithm. ACM Trans. on Computer Systems 5(1), 1–11 (1987)
25. Lycklama, E.A., Hadzilacos, V.: A first-come-first-served mutual exclusion algorithm with small communication variables. ACM Trans. on Programming Languages and Systems 13(4), 558–576 (1991)
26. Massalin, H., Pu, C.: A lock-free multiprocessor OS kernel. Technical Report CUCS-005-91, Columbia University (1991)
27. Michael, M.M., Scott, M.L.: Simple, fast, and practical non-blocking and blocking concurrent queue algorithms. In: Proc. 15th ACM Symp. on Principles of Distributed Computing, pp. 267–275 (1996)
28. Peterson, G.L.: New bounds on mutual exclusion problems. Technical Report TR68, University of Rochester (February 1980) (Corrected, November 1994)
29. Raynal, M.: Concurrent Programming: Algorithms, Principles, and Foundations, 515 pages. Springer (2013) ISBN 978-3-642-32027-9
30. Raynal, M.: Algorithms for mutual exclusion. The MIT Press (1986); Translation of: Algorithmique du parallélisme (1984)
31. Sundell, H., Tsigas, P.: Lock-free and practical doubly linked list-based deques using single-word compare-and-swap. In: Higashino, T. (ed.) OPODIS 2004. LNCS, vol. 3544, pp. 240–255. Springer, Heidelberg (2005)
32. Taubenfeld, G.: Synchronization Algorithms and Concurrent Programming, 423 pages. Pearson/Prentice-Hall (2006) ISBN 0-131-97259-6
33. Taubenfeld, G.: The black-white bakery algorithm and related bounded-space, adaptive, local-spinning and FIFO algorithms. In: Guerraoui, R. (ed.) DISC 2004. LNCS, vol. 3274, pp. 56–70. Springer, Heidelberg (2004)
34. Taubenfeld, G.: Efficient transformations of obstruction-free algorithms into non-blocking algorithms. In: Pelc, A. (ed.) DISC 2007. LNCS, vol. 4731, pp. 450–464. Springer, Heidelberg (2007)
35. Taubenfeld, G.: Contention-sensitive data structures and algorithms. In: Keidar, I. (ed.) DISC 2009. LNCS, vol. 5805, pp. 157–171. Springer, Heidelberg (2009)
36. Taubenfeld, G.: Fair Synchronization, 2013. The full version is http://www.faculty.idc.ac.il/gadi/Publications.htm
37. Valois, J.D.: Implementing lock-free queues. In: Proc. of the 7th International Conference on Parallel and Distributed Computing Systems, pp. 212–222 (1994)

Gossip Protocols for Renaming and Sorting

George Giakkoupis[1,*], Anne-Marie Kermarrec[1], and Philipp Woelfel[2,**]

[1] INRIA Rennes – Bretagne Atlantic, France
{george.giakkoupis,anne-marie.kermarrec}@inria.fr
[2] Department of Computer Science, University of Calgary, Canada
woelfel@ucalgary.ca

Abstract. We devise efficient gossip-based protocols for some fundamental distributed tasks. The protocols assume an n-node network supporting point-to-point communication, and in every round, each node exchanges information of size $O(\log n)$ bits with (at most) one other node.

We first consider the *renaming* problem, that is, to assign distinct IDs from a small ID space to all nodes of the network. We propose a renaming protocol that divides the ID space among nodes using a natural push or pull approach, achieving logarithmic round complexity with ID space $\{1, \ldots, (1 + \epsilon)n\}$, for any fixed $\epsilon > 0$. A variant of this protocol solves the *tight* renaming problem, where each node obtains a unique ID in $\{1, \ldots, n\}$, in $O(\log^2 n)$ rounds.

Next we study the following *sorting* problem. Nodes have consecutive IDs 1 up to n, and they receive numerical values as inputs. They then have to exchange those inputs so that in the end the input of rank k is located at the node with ID k. Jelasity and Kermarrec [20] suggested a simple and natural protocol, where nodes exchange values with peers chosen uniformly at random, but it is not hard to see that this protocol requires $\Omega(n)$ rounds. We prove that the same protocol works in $O(\log^2 n)$ rounds if peers are chosen according to a non-uniform power law distribution.

Keywords: renaming, sorting, gossip protocols, epidemic protocols, distributed algorithms, randomized algorithms, network algorithms.

1 Introduction

Today's highly distributed systems are based on networks of massive scale. Such networks often suffer from link and node failures, and from limited computational capabilities of their nodes. For example, peer-to-peer and mobile ad-hoc networks are inherently highly dynamic, with nodes joining and leaving the system frequently; or sensor networks are often used in harsh environments leading to communication disruptions, and their nodes have little computational power.

* This work was funded in part by INRIA Associate Team RADCON and ERC Starting Grant GOSSPLE 204742.
** This research was supported in part by a Discovery Grant and the Canada Research Chair Program of the Natural Sciences and Engineering Research Council of Canada (NSERC), and in part by the HP Innovation Research Program.

Y. Afek (Ed.): DISC 2013, LNCS 8205, pp. 194–208, 2013.

Gossip (or *epidemic*) protocols have emerged as an important communication paradigm for these networks. In gossip protocols nodes repeatedly contact random neighbors and exchange small amounts of information in order to distribute and gather information. Such protocols are usually simple, scalable, and fault-tolerant. They generally offer small communication overhead and modest demands on the nodes' storage space and computational power. Even though they only provide probabilistic guarantees, the probability of failure typically converges quickly to 0 with the time the protocol is run.

The classical problem solved with gossip protocols is *rumor spreading* [10] in the random phone-call model [22]. In this model, nodes exchange information in synchronous parallel communication rounds, using either push, pull, or push-pull communication with peers chosen uniformly at random among all nodes (or just among the node's neighbors, if the network topology is not a complete graph). Such rumor spreading protocols have been shown to be very efficient, requiring only a logarithmic number of rounds for the complete graph and various other topologies [22,19,14,18,7,12,13].

Later, gossip protocols have been used to solve node aggregation problems [6,23,28,8]. Here, the goal is to compute the value $f(x_1, \ldots, x_n)$ of some aggregation function f (e.g., sum, average, or extrema), where x_i is an input to the i-th node. Most gossip protocols for aggregation need only poly-logarithmic many rounds in the complete graph before nodes know the value of the aggregation function (with sufficient accuracy) with high probability. In the design of gossip protocols it is often assumed that any given node can in each round exchange information with a peer selected uniformly at random from all nodes, independently of the network topology. In practice [17], this is usually realized by a peer-sampling service [21], which can be singled out from the application.

In the present paper, we study practical and fundamental problems that cannot be expressed by aggregation functions. First, we study the problem of *renaming*. Here, every node must obtain a unique ID from an *ID space* $\{1, \ldots, m\}$ of size $m \geq n$. The renaming problem has been studied extensively in the distributed computing literature, especially in the areas of shared memory and message passing (see, e.g., [2] and references therein). Many distributed tasks can only be solved if the participants have unique IDs, and often the complexity of algorithms depends on the size of the domain from which those IDs are chosen. For example, an algorithm to construct overlay networks in peer-to-peer networks proposed by Angluin et al. [3] has expected round complexity $O(W \log n)$, where W is the bit-length of node IDs. Another application is the unique assignment of a small number of resources (e.g., servers or printers) to processors (nodes). Nodes can also use their IDs as "tags" to mark their presence in some data structure (e.g., a priority queue), so that a node can distinguish whether itself or some other node has placed the tag [4]. We solve both, the *loose renaming* problem, where $m = (1 + \epsilon)n$ for some constant $\epsilon > 0$, and the *tight renaming* problem, where $m = n$, with simple protocols that have respectively $O(\log n)$ and $O(\log^2 n)$ round complexity with high probability, and logarithmic message-size complexity. Both protocols assume that each node can contact a uniform random node in a round. The tight renaming protocol assumes further that a node can contact an arbitrary node directly, if it knows its network address (see Section 1.1). Note that non-gossip based algorithms, e.g., algorithms based on leader election protocols, can be used to solve tight renaming in $O(\log n)$ time. But contrary to our gossip based solution, such algorithms require "exact" communication, and tolerate no or almost no transmission faults.

Then we consider the problem of *sorting* n input values $x_1, \ldots, x_n$, each one given to a distinct node. Here we assume that the n nodes have consecutive IDs in $\{1, \ldots, n\}$. Nodes must exchange their input values in multiple communication rounds, such that in the end the value of rank k is located at the node with ID k. Jelasity and Kermarrec [20] proposed the following simple gossip protocol for this problem: In each round, a node contacts a peer chosen uniformly at random, and both nodes exchange their values, if they are out of order with respect to their IDs. However, this protocol may need in expectation $\Omega(n)$ rounds until all input values are sorted. For example, suppose node 1 holds value 2 and node 2 holds value 1, and each node $i \geq 3$ holds value i. Then it takes $\Omega(n)$ rounds in expectation before nodes 1 and 2 contact each other and resolve their inversion. (There are other input instances for which it takes up to $\Omega(n \log n)$ rounds with high probability before all input values are sorted.) We show that the round complexity drops to $O(\log^2 n)$, if peers are not chosen *uniformly* at random, but rather from a power law distribution: A node with ID x chooses a peer with ID y with a probability inversely proportional to $|x - y|$. (A similar distribution for sampling peers is used in Kleinberg's small-world graph routing scheme [26,25], and also in the spatial gossip algorithms proposed by Kempe et al. [24].)

Our protocols for renaming and sorting are very simple and natural, however, their analysis is non-trivial and is based on potential function arguments. Further, the protocols can tolerate random transmission faults, similar to the standard rumor spreading protocols [15]. I.e., if communication channels fail to be established between parties independently with a probability of q, then the round complexity increases only by a factor of at most $1/(1 - q)$, which is the expected number of trials before a connection is established.

1.1   Model and Practical Considerations

We assume that the network supports the abstraction of point-to-point communication. That is, each node has a unique network *address* from some arbitrary domain, and node u can contact any other node v, if u knows v's address. Nodes do not know the addresses of other nodes in advance, but they can find out during the course of the protocol. When two nodes have established a communication channel, both can reliably exchange information for one round.

We assume further that the abstraction of a *random peer-sampling service* is supported. Each time this service is invoked it returns a node chosen independently and uniformly at random among all nodes. In a large-scale dynamic system it is unrealistic that nodes maintain complete tables of network addresses of peers, from which they can sample at random. To overcome this obstacle, various distributed designs of peer-sampling services have been proposed and studied experimentally by the systems community (see, e.g., [21]). The use of such services has become a standard practice in the implementation of gossip-based systems [17]. This service is often implemented by building and maintaining a random overlay network, that changes over time by having nodes exchange random fractions of their list of neighbors with other (randomly selected) neighbors. For related theoretical results on this problem see, e.g., [16,9].

Our loose renaming algorithm relies only on the assumption that in each round a node can contact some uniformly random node. The tight renaming algorithm has the additional requirement that a node can contact a node by its address. Initially, nodes do not know the address of any other node, but a node can add its own address to a message (or the address of another node it knows of), thus allowing the recipients of that message to contact the node directly in future rounds. We stress that addresses may come from an arbitrary large space that may be much larger than n, thus they cannot be used themselves as IDs.

For the sorting algorithm we assume that nodes already have IDs 1 up to n. Similar to the loose renaming algorithm, the sorting algorithm does not use network addresses directly. However, it requires a non-uniform peer-sampling service, which allows each node with ID i to choose a random node with ID j according to a probability distribution that depends on $|i - j|$. Precisely, the probability of choosing j needs to be inversely proportional to $|i-j|$. A DHT-like overlay network can be used to provide this service: By overlaying the network with a Chord topology [29], peer-sampling with the required power-law distribution can be achieved in such a way that it does not increase the overall asymptotic round complexity of our sorting protocol.[1] If the non-uniform peer-sampling abstraction is provided by other means, then no overlay network is required for the sorting protocol.

In order to solve the sorting problem, one could also follow a different approach that is not gossip-based: One can construct a (perfect) Chord overlay on top of the network, and then implement a sorting network, where each comparator is replaced with a link between two peers in the network. If one uses a Bitonic sorter [5], the comparators correspond to Chord links, and thus no lookups in Chord are necessary. This would yield a sorting algorithm with the same round complexity as ours. (One could even use an AKS [1] sorting network to obtain, with some additional tricks, a round complexity of $O(\log n)$, but AKS networks are considered impractical due to the extremely large constant factors [27].[2]) Most sorting networks, however, provide no inherent fault-tolerance (with the exception of the AKS sorting network). Our gossip-based algorithm is naturally fault-tolerant in the sense that it still works without an increase in the asymptotic round complexity, if any two peers fail to establish a communication

---

[1] This requires nodes to sample multiple peers at the beginning of the protocol and leads to a poly-logarithmic increase in the message size complexity.

[2] In our analysis of the sorting algorithm we have not tried to optimize the constant multiplicative factor in front of $\log^2 n$. This analysis gives an upper bound of roughly 100 on this constant, and a more careful analysis yields a bound of roughly 25. We believe, however, that the actual value is much smaller.

with constant probability. By repeating comparators (cf. [30]) one can also make sorting networks fault-tolerant, but the repetition of comparators increases the depth of the sorting network (and thus the round complexity in our application) by a factor of $\Omega(\log n)$ in order to allow for a constant failure probability for each communication/comparator. Note also that we only need to use an overlay network to provide the non-uniform peer sampling service, while such an overlay seems inherent for a sorting network based approach.

To bound the message-size complexity of our protocols, we assume that each network address is a W-bit string, where $W = O(\log n)$. If W is super-logarithmic, then the complexity increases by an additive term of $O(W)$.

We present our protocols in terms of synchronous rounds. The synchrony assumption is not really necessary for the definition of the protocols. Instead, nodes may simply follow their own clocks in deciding when to initiate connections. We expect that the running time of our protocols should not be affected, as long as (most) nodes take steps at roughly the same rate, e.g., in the standard asynchronous model where each node takes steps at times determined by a poisson process with a fixed rate for all nodes.

2   Renaming Protocols

2.1   Loose Renaming

We present an algorithm that assigns IDs to n nodes from the integer interval $[1..(1 + \epsilon)n]$, for some $\epsilon > 0$; ϵ can be a function of n, but the running time increases linearly with $1/\epsilon$. At any time, each node stores zero or more IDs, and each ID is stored at exactly one node. If node u has one or more IDs at a given time, then one of them is permanently stored by u, and is the ID assigned to u by the algorithm, while the remaining IDs, if any, are u's *free IDs*. The free IDs of a node are *consecutive*, and thus they can be stored using at most $2 \log n$ bits. We present two versions on the algorithm: a *pull* algorithm, and a *push* algorithm.

In round 0, a *starting* node sends the ID interval $[1..(1+\epsilon)n]$ to itself.[3] If node u receives interval $[a..b]$ in round $t \geq 0$, and it has not received any IDs prior to that, then ID a is assigned to u. Further, if $a \neq b$ then the interval $[a + 1..b]$ of remaining IDs will be the free IDs of u for the next round.

In the *pull* version of the algorithm, in every round $t \geq 1$, each node u that has no free IDs (u may or may not have been assigned an ID yet) sends a request to a random node v. If v has an interval $[a..b]$ of free IDs, then it chooses an arbitrary node u' among the nodes from which it received requests in round t, and sends to u' half of $[a..b]$, precisely, the interval $[\lceil (a + b)/2 \rceil..b]$. If $a \neq b$ then v is left with the interval $[a..\lceil (a + b)/2 \rceil - 1]$ of free IDs, while if $a = b$ (i.e., u had only one free ID) then v has no free IDs in the next round.

---

[3] The starting node can be chosen randomly via a gossip-based sampling procedure and the network size n can also be estimated via gossip (see, e.g., [23]).

The *push* algorithm is symmetric: In round $t \geq 1$, each node u that has at least one free ID sends half of its interval $[a..b]$ of free IDs, i.e., $[\lceil (a+b)/2 \rceil..b]$, to a randomly chosen node v. If v has no free IDs at the time, then it accepts (an arbitrary) one of the ID intervals it receives in round t, and rejects the remaining ones; if v already has some free IDs then it rejects any ID intervals it receives. If the interval that u sent is rejected, then u keeps the whole interval $[a..b]$ of free IDs, thus no IDs are 'lost'.

From the analysis of the pull protocol presented below, it follows that a node which has been assigned an ID but has no free IDs may as well stop sending requests after the first t_1 rounds, for some $t_1 = \Theta(\log n)$, without affecting the performance guarantees of the protocol. Then, only nodes with no assigned IDs continue to send requests. This offers a natural stopping condition for the protocol. The push algorithm, on the other hand, does not have a natural way to determine when nodes that have free IDs should stop trying to push those IDs. A drawback of pull is that nodes must be notified when the protocol starts so that they can begin to send pull request.

Theorem 1. *The loose renaming protocol described above for distributing a set of $(1+\epsilon)n$ IDs to n nodes guarantees that all nodes acquire IDs after at most $O\left(\frac{(1+\epsilon)n}{\epsilon n+1} \cdot \log n\right)$ rounds with probability $1 - n^{-\beta}$ for any $\epsilon \geq 0$ and any fixed $\beta > 0$.*

Proof. We prove the theorem for the pull algorithm. The proof for push is almost the same and is omitted. We start with an overview of the proof. We define a potential function Φ_t, which measures the unbalance in the distribution of free IDs among nodes, and we show that Φ_t drops by a constant factor per round on average, as long as most nodes have 0 or 1 IDs. On the other hand, when most nodes have 2 or more IDs, we observe that the number of nodes with 0 IDs decreases by a constant factor on average per round. We combine these two results to show that w.h.p. in $O(\log n)$ rounds either all nodes have acquired IDs or the free IDs are fairly balanced among nodes. In the latter case we bound the additional number of steps until all nodes obtain IDs, by looking at a single node and bounding the steps until it contacts some node that has free IDs.

Next we give the detailed proof. Let $X_{u,t}$ denote the number of IDs that node u has after round t (including its assigned ID). Let $X_t = \{X_{u,t}\}_u$ be the vector of all $X_{u,t}$ for a given round t. Let $N_t^k = |\{u: X_{u,t} = k\}|$ be the number of nodes that have exactly k IDs after round t, and let $N_t^{\geq k} = |\{u: X_{u,t} \geq k\}|$ and $N_t^{\leq k} = |\{u: X_{u,t} \leq k\}|$.

We define the potential $\Phi_{u,t}$ of node u after round t, as $\Phi_{u,t} = (X_{u,t} - 2)^2$ if $X_{u,t} \geq 3$, and $\Phi_{u,t} = 0$ if $X_{u,t} \leq 2$. The (total) potential after round t is then

$$\Phi_t = \sum_u \Phi_{u,t} = \sum_{u: X_{u,t} \geq 3} (X_{u,t} - 2)^2.$$

The next lemma bounds the expected potential difference in a single round.

Lemma 1. $\mathbf{E}[\Phi_{t+1} \mid X_t] \leq \Phi_t \left(1 - \frac{N_t^{\leq 1}}{4n}\right).$

Proof. Fix X_t, and let u be a node with $X_{u,t} \geq 3$. Suppose that u receives a request in round $t+1$ to share its $X_{u,t}-1$ free IDs, and thus sends $\lceil (X_{u,t}-1)/2 \rceil$ of them to some node v with $X_{v,t} \in \{0,1\}$. We show that

$$\Phi_{u,t+1} + \Phi_{v,t+1} \leq \Phi_{u,t}/2. \tag{1}$$

We have

$$X_{u,t+1} = X_{u,t} - \lceil (X_{u,t}-1)/2 \rceil = \begin{cases} X_{u,t}/2 + 1/2, & \text{if } X_{u,t} \text{ is odd;} \\ X_{u,t}/2, & \text{if } X_{u,t} \text{ is even; and} \end{cases}$$

$$X_{v,t+1} = X_{v,t} + \lceil (X_{u,t}-1)/2 \rceil \leq 1 + \lceil (X_{u,t}-1)/2 \rceil = \begin{cases} X_{u,t}/2 + 1/2, & \text{if } X_{u,t} \text{ odd;} \\ X_{u,t}/2 + 1, & \text{if } X_{u,t} \text{ even.} \end{cases}$$

It follows that if $X_{u,t}$ is odd (recall also that $X_{u,t} \geq 3$), then

$$\Phi_{u,t+1} + \Phi_{v,t+1} \leq (X_{u,t}/2 + 1/2 - 2)^2 + (X_{u,t}/2 + 1/2 - 2)^2$$
$$= (X_{u,t} - 3)^2/2 \leq (X_{u,t} - 2)^2/2 = \Phi_{u,t}/2;$$

and, similarly, if $X_{u,t}$ is even (and thus $X_{u,t} \geq 4$) then

$$\Phi_{u,t+1} + \Phi_{v,t+1} \leq (X_{u,t}/2 - 2)^2 + (X_{u,t}/2 + 1 - 2)^2$$
$$= (X_{u,t} - 4)^2/4 + (X_{u,t} - 2)^2/4 \leq (X_{u,t} - 2)^2/2 = \Phi_{u,t}/2.$$

Thus, in both cases, Eq. (1) holds. We can now bound the total potential, Φ_{t+1}. From (1), if a node u with $X_{u,t} \geq 3$ shares its free IDs with some node v then $\Phi_{u,t+1} + \Phi_{v,t+1} \leq \Phi_{u,t}/2$, while if u does not share its free IDs then $\Phi_{u,t+1} = \Phi_{u,t}$. Further, all other nodes have zero potential. Therefore, if Y_u is a 0/1 random variable with $Y_u = 1$ iff u shares its free IDs in round $t+1$, we have

$$\Phi_{t+1} \leq \sum_{u:\, X_{u,t} \geq 3} \left(Y_u \Phi_{u,t}/2 + (1 - Y_u)\Phi_{u,t} \right) = \sum_{u:\, X_{u,t} \geq 3} (1 - Y_u/2)\Phi_{u,t}.$$

Taking the expectation (recall that we have fixed X_t), yields

$$\mathbf{E}[\Phi_{t+1}] \leq \sum_{u:\, X_{u,t} \geq 3} (1 - \mathbf{E}[Y_u]/2)\Phi_{u,t}. \tag{2}$$

Since $\mathbf{E}[Y_u]$ is the probability that u receives a request in round $t+1$ from at least one of the $N_t^{\leq 1}$ nodes v with $X_{v,t} \leq 1$, we have

$$1 - \mathbf{E}[Y_u] = (1 - 1/n)^{N_t^{\leq 1}} \leq e^{-N_t^{\leq 1}/n} \leq 1 - N_t^{\leq 1}/n + (N_t^{\leq 1}/n)^2/2 \leq 1 - N_t^{\leq 1}/(2n).$$

Thus, $\mathbf{E}[Y_u] \geq N_t^{\leq 1}/(2n)$. Applying this to (2) completes the proof of Lemma 1. $\qquad \square$

Next we bound the expected drop in a round of the number N_t^0 of nodes that have no IDs.

Lemma 2. $\mathbf{E}[N_{t+1}^0 \mid X_t] \leq N_t^0 \left(1 - \frac{N_t^{\geq 2}}{en}\right)$.

Proof. Fix X_t, and suppose that $X_{v,t} = 0$ for some node v. In order to have $X_{v,t+1} > 0$ it suffices that v sends its request in round $t + 1$ to some node u with $X_{u,t+1} \geq 2$, and u does not receive a request from any other node. The probability that v sends its request to some u with $X_{u,t+1} \geq 2$ is $N_t^{\geq 2}/n$; and the probability that no node sends a request to the same node as v is

$$(1 - 1/n)^{N_t^{\leq 1}-1} \geq (1 - 1/n)^{n-1} \geq 1/e.$$

Thus, the probability of $X_{v,t+1} > 0$ is at least $N_t^{\geq 2}/(en)$. From the linearity of expectation then we get $\mathbf{E}[N_t^0 - N_{t+1}^0] \geq N_t^0 N_t^{\geq 2}/(en)$, which proves Lemma 2. ☐

Consider now the product $Z_t := \Phi_t N_t^0$. From Lemma 1 and the fact that $N_{t+1}^0 \leq N_t^0$, it follows

$$\mathbf{E}[Z_{t+1} \mid X_t] \leq N_t^0 \cdot \mathbf{E}[\Phi_{t+1} \mid X_t] \leq N_t^0 \Phi_t \left(1 - \frac{N_t^{\leq 1}}{4n}\right),$$

and similarly, from Lemma 2 and the fact that $\Phi_{t+1} \leq \Phi_t$,

$$\mathbf{E}[Z_{t+1} \mid X_t] \leq \Phi_t \cdot \mathbf{E}[N_{t+1}^0 \mid X_t] \leq \Phi_t N_t^0 \left(1 - \frac{N_t^{\geq 2}}{en}\right).$$

Thus,

$$\mathbf{E}[Z_{t+1} \mid X_t] \leq Z_t \left(1 - \max\left\{\frac{N_t^{\leq 1}}{4n}, \frac{N_t^{\geq 2}}{en}\right\}\right),$$

and since $N_t^{\leq 1} + N_t^{\geq 2} = n$, we can easily compute that $\max\left\{\frac{N_t^{\leq 1}}{4n}, \frac{N_t^{\geq 2}}{en}\right\} \geq \frac{1}{e+4} \geq \frac{1}{7}$. Therefore, we have that $\mathbf{E}[Z_{t+1} \mid X_t] \leq (6/7)Z_t$. It follows $\mathbf{E}[Z_t] \leq (6/7)^t Z_0 \leq (6/7)^t n^3$. For

$$t_1 = (\beta + 3)\log_{7/6} n + \log_{7/6} 2 = O(\log n), \tag{3}$$

we obtain then that $\mathbf{E}[Z_{t_1}] \leq n^{-\beta}/2$. And by Markov's Inequality, $\Pr(Z_{t_1} > 0) = \Pr(Z_{t_1} \geq 1) \leq n^{-\beta}/2$. Thus, we have that $N_{t_1}^0 = 0$ or $\Phi_{t_1} = 0$, with probability at least $1 - n^{-\beta}/2$.

Suppose first that $\epsilon > 1$. Then $\Phi_{t_1} > 0$, for otherwise, no node has more than two IDs after round t_1, which is not possible as there are $(1 + \epsilon)n > 2n$ IDs in total. It follows that $N_{t_1}^0 = 0$ with probability $1 - n^{-\beta}/2$, and thus all nodes obtain IDs in $t_1 = O(\log n) = O\left(\frac{(1+\epsilon)n}{\epsilon n+1} \cdot \log n\right)$ rounds; this proves the theorem.

For the remainder of the proof we assume that $\epsilon \leq 1$. Suppose that $\Phi_{t_1} = 0$. We will compute a t_2 such that $N_{t_1+t_2}^0 = 0$ with probability $1 - n^{-\beta}/2$. Since $\Phi_{t_1} = 0$, no node has more that 2 IDs after round t_1. It follows that $N_t^2 = \epsilon n + N_t^0$, for all $t \geq t_1$. If $X_{v,t} = 0$ for some node v and round $t \geq t_1$, then the probability of $X_{v,t+1} > 0$ is bounded from below by the probability of the event that in round $t + 1$, v sends a request to one of the $N_t^2 \geq \epsilon n + 1$ nodes with free IDs, and this node does not receive any other request. This probability is at least

$$\frac{\epsilon n + 1}{n} \cdot \left(1 - \frac{1}{n}\right)^{N_t^{\leq 1} - 1} \geq \frac{\epsilon n + 1}{n} \cdot \left(1 - \frac{1}{n}\right)^{n-1} \geq \frac{\epsilon n + 1}{en}.$$

It follows that for any node v, the probability of $X_{v,t_1+k} = 0$ is at most $\left(1 - \frac{\epsilon n + 1}{en}\right)^k \leq e^{-k(\epsilon n + 1)/(en)}$. For

$$t_2 = ((\beta + 1) \ln n + 1) en/(\epsilon n + 1) = O(n \log n / (\epsilon n + 1)),$$

we obtain then that $X_{v,t_1+t_2} = 0$ with probability at most $n^{-\beta}/(2n)$. Hence, by the union bound, we have that $X_{v,t_1+t_2} \neq 0$ for *some* v (i.e., $N_{t_1+t_2}^0 \neq 0$) with probability at most $n^{-\beta}/2$. This probability is conditional on $\Phi_{t_1} = 0$, i.e., formally, $\Pr(N_{v,t_1+t_2}^0 \neq 0 \mid \Phi_{t_1} = 0) \leq n^{-\beta}/2$. It follows

$$\Pr(N_{v,t_1+t_2}^0 \neq 0 \wedge \Phi_{t_1} = 0) = \Pr(N_{v,t_1+t_2}^0 \neq 0 \mid \Phi_{t_1} = 0) \cdot \Pr(\Phi_{t_1} = 0) \leq n^{-\beta}/2.$$

And since we showed earlier that $\Pr(\Phi_{t_1} N_{t_1}^0 \neq 0) \leq n^{-\beta}/2$, we get

$$\Pr(N_{v,t_1+t_2}^0 \neq 0) = \Pr(N_{v,t_1+t_2}^0 \neq 0 \wedge \Phi_{t_1} = 0) + \Pr(N_{v,t_1+t_2}^0 \Phi_{t_1} \neq 0) \leq n^{-\beta}. \quad (4)$$

Finally, observing that $t_1 + t_2 = O\left(\log n + \frac{n \log n}{\epsilon n + 1}\right) = O\left(\frac{(1+\epsilon)n}{\epsilon n + 1} \cdot \log n\right)$, completes the proof of Theorem 1. □

2.2   Tight Renaming

The previous protocol cannot be used to solve efficiently tight renaming, in which the size of the ID space is exactly n: If there are just n IDs, then once there are only few nodes left that have not received an ID, there are also only few nodes that still have a non-empty interval of free IDs. Then it takes a long time, until a node that needs an ID contacts one with a free ID. We solve the tight renaming problem by adding a second phase to the loose renaming algorithm. In this phase, any node that has not been assigned an ID yet, periodically broadcasts (via rumor spreading) "requests" for an ID to the network; the requests contain the network address of the node. When requests of different nodes "meet" at some node, only one of them (the most recent one) survives. Thus, not all requests reach all nodes, but each node receives at least some requests. This approach ensures that message sizes and the information that each node stores is just $O(\log n)$ bits. Nodes that receive requests in this second phase and have free IDs respond by sending to the requesting node some of their free IDs. (They can do so, as the request message contains the address of the requesting node.)

More precisely, in the first phase, nodes run the algorithm described in the previous section for $t_1 = \Theta(\log n)$ rounds.[4] In the second phase, a node u that has not acquired an ID yet, generates a request every $O(\log n)$ rounds and sends this

---

[4] This is the same t_1 as that defined in Eq. (3).

request to itself. The request contains u's network address and an age counter (which increases in each round). Each node keeps only the most recently generated request it has received, choosing arbitrarily among requests with the same age. In every round, each node holding a request sends a copy of it to a randomly chosen node. When a node v that has free IDs receives a request generated by node u, it responds by sending to u directly half of its interval of free IDs (similar to the loose renaming algorithm). Node u accepts the interval if it has not already acquired an ID from some other node that also responded to its requests, or rejects the offer otherwise.

We stress that is not required for different nodes to generate their requests in the same round, or with the same frequency. The only requirement is that each node generates a new request every $O(\log n)$ rounds for as long as it has no IDs.

Theorem 2. *The tight renaming protocol described above for distributing IDs to n nodes guarantees that all nodes acquire IDs after at most $O(\log^2 n)$ rounds with probability $1 - n^{-\beta}$ for any fixed $\beta > 0$.*

Proof. We will use the same notation as in the proof of Theorem 1, namely, $X_{u,t}$, X_t, N_t^k, and Φ_t. Recall that for tight renaming the ID space has size exactly n.

We have shown in the proof of Theorem 1 that with probability at least $1 - n^{-\beta}/2$, we have $N_{t_1}^0 = 0$ or $\Phi_{t_1} = 0$.

Suppose that $\Phi_{t_1} = 0$, and thus no node has more than 2 IDs after round t_1. We will lift this assumption only at the end of the proof. Suppose that node u has no ID yet after round $t \geq t_1$, and it sends a request in round $t + 1$. We show that with some constant probability, either u acquires an ID by round $t + \log n$, or the number of nodes with no IDs drops by a constant factor by that time.

Lemma 3. *Let $t \geq t_1$. If a node u with $X_{u,t} = 0$ sends a request in round $t+1$, then with some probability $p = \Omega(1)$ we have $X_{u,t'} \neq 0$ or $N_{t'}^0 \leq N_t^0/2$, for $t' = t + \log(n/N_t^0) + 1$.*

Proof. Fix X_t. Let A_i, for $i \geq 0$, denote the set of nodes that have received u's request and still have it at the end of round $t + i$. Recall that nodes keep only the most recently generated request they have received. Let B_i be the set of nodes which, at the end of round $t + i$, have a request generated after round t by a node other than u. Further, let $a_i = |A_i|$ and $b_i = |B_i|$. Then,

$$a_i \leq 2^{i-1} \quad \text{and} \quad b_i \leq (N_t^0 - 1)2^{i-1}.$$

Next we show for $i = \log(n/N_t^0)$ that $a_i = \Omega(2^i) = \Omega(n/N_t^0)$ with constant probability. Further, we show that if $a_i = \Omega(n/N_t^0)$ and $N_{t+i}^0 \geq N_t^0/2$ and also u has still no ID after round $t + i$, then in the next round u acquires an ID with probability $\Omega(1)$. The claim then follows.

To show the lower bound on a_i, we first bound $\mathbf{E}[a_i]$. Given a_i and b_i, we bound the conditional expectation of a_{i+1} as follows: The expected number of nodes $v \notin A_i \cup B_i$ that receive u's request (and possibly other requests) in round $t + i + 1$ is at least $a_i(n - 2a_i - b_i)/n$ (we subtract $2a_i$ instead of a_i to account for collisions). The probability that a given one of these node does not receive a request pushed by a node in B_i in this round is $(1 - 1/n)^{b_i} \geq (1 - b_i/n)$. Combining these yields

$$
\begin{aligned}
\mathbf{E}[a_{i+1} \mid a_i, b_i] &\geq (a_i + a_i(n - 2a_i - b_i)/n) \cdot (1 - b_i/n) \\
&= 2a_i(1 - a_i/n - b_i/2n) \cdot (1 - b_i/n) \\
&\geq 2a_i(1 - a_i/n - 3b_i/2n) \\
&\geq 2a_i(1 - 3N_t^0 2^{i-2}/n),
\end{aligned}
$$

where for the last relation we used the upper bounds for a_i and b_i we mentioned earlier. Applying the above inequality repeatedly and using that $a_1 = 1$ gives

$$
\mathbf{E}[a_i] \geq 2^{i-1} \left(1 - 3N_t^0 \sum_{j=1}^{i-1} 2^{j-2}/n \right) \geq 2^{i-1} \left(1 - 3N_t^0 2^{i-2}/n \right).
$$

For $i^* = \log(n/N_t^0)$ we get $\mathbf{E}[a_{i^*}] \geq 2^{i^*-1}(1 - 3/4) = 2^{i^*-3}$, and by Markov's Inequality,

$$
\Pr(a_{i^*} \leq 2^{i^*-4}) = \Pr(2^{i^*-1} - a_{i^*} \geq 2^{i^*-1} - 2^{i^*-4}) \leq \frac{2^{i^*-1} - 2^{i^*-3}}{2^{i^*-1} - 2^{i^*-4}} = 6/7.
$$

Next suppose that $a_{i^*} \geq 2^{i^*-4} = n/(2^4 N_t^0)$ and $N_{t+i^*}^0 \geq N_t^0/2$. The conditional probability of $X_{t+i^*+1} \neq 0$ is lower-bounded by the probability that some node from A_{i^*} chooses some node v with free IDs (there are $N_{t+i^*}^2 = N_{t+i^*}^0 \geq N_t^0/2$ such nodes) and at the same time no other node chooses v. Thus, this probability is at least

$$
\left(1 - \left(1 - (N_t^0/2)/n \right)^{n/(2^4 N_t^0)} \right) (1 - 1/n)^{n-1} \geq \left(1 - e^{1/2^5} \right)(1/e) \geq (1/2^6)(1/e).
$$

We can now use the above bounds to prove the lemma. Define the events: $\mathcal{X} = (X_{u,t'} \neq 0)$, $\mathcal{N} = (N_{t+i^*}^0 < N_t^0/2)$, and $\mathcal{A} = (a_{i^*} \geq 2^{i^*-4})$. We have shown that $\Pr(\mathcal{A}) \geq 1 - 6/7$, and $\Pr(\mathcal{X} \mid \neg\mathcal{N} \wedge \mathcal{A}) \geq (1/2^6)(1/e)$. The probability we want to lower-bound is

$$
\begin{aligned}
\Pr(\mathcal{X} \vee \mathcal{N}) &= \Pr(\mathcal{N}) + \Pr(\mathcal{X} \wedge \neg\mathcal{N}) \\
&\geq \Pr(\mathcal{N} \wedge \mathcal{A}) + \Pr(\mathcal{X} \wedge \neg\mathcal{N} \wedge \mathcal{A}) \\
&= 1 \cdot \Pr(\mathcal{N} \wedge \mathcal{A}) + \Pr(\mathcal{X} \mid \neg\mathcal{N} \wedge \mathcal{A}) \cdot \Pr(\neg\mathcal{N} \wedge \mathcal{A}) \\
&\geq \Pr(\mathcal{X} \mid \neg\mathcal{N} \wedge \mathcal{A}) \cdot \left(\Pr(\mathcal{N} \wedge \mathcal{A}) + \Pr(\neg\mathcal{N} \wedge \mathcal{A}) \right) \\
&= \Pr(\mathcal{X} \mid \neg\mathcal{N} \wedge \mathcal{A}) \cdot \Pr(\mathcal{A}) \\
&\geq (1/2^6)(1/e)(1 - 6/7).
\end{aligned}
$$

This completes the proof of Lemma 3.   □

We can now finish the proof of the theorem as follows. Assume that $X_{u,t_1} = 0$, and let $r_0 < r_1 < \ldots$ be the rounds after which u is supposed to send requests (if it has not yet an ID by that round, i.e., $X_{u,r_i} = 0$). W.l.o.g. we assume

$r_{i+1} - r_i \geq \log n$, otherwise we can achieve that by omitting some of these times. Further, from the algorithm we have $r_{i+1} - r_i = O(\log n)$.

Define the random variables Y_i, $i \geq 0$, such that $Y_i = N_{r_i}^0$ if $X_{u,r_i} = 0$, and $Y_i = 0$ if $X_{u,r_i} \neq 0$. Note that $Y_i \neq 0$ iff $X_{u,r_i} = 0$. From Lemma 3 it follows

$$\mathbf{E}[Y_{i+1} \mid Y_i] \leq pY_i/2 + (1-p)Y_i = (1-p/2)Y_i;$$

and thus $\mathbf{E}[Y_i] \leq (1-p/2)^i N_{r_0}^0$. Choosing $i^* = (2/p)((\beta+1)\ln n + 1)$ gives $\mathbf{E}[Y_{i^*}] \leq n^{-\beta-1}/2$, and from Markov's Inequality, $\Pr(Y_{i^*} \neq 0) = \Pr(Y_{i^*} \geq 1) \leq n^{-\beta-1}/2$. It follows that for

$$t^* = r_{i^*} = t_1 + O(i^* \log n) = t_1 + O(\log^2 n) = O(\log^2 n)$$

we have $\Pr(X_{u,t^*} = 0) \leq n^{-\beta-1}/2$, as we observed earlier that $Y_i \neq 0$ iff $X_{u,r_i} = 0$. From this and the union bound over all u, it follows that $\Pr(N_{t^*}^0 \neq 0) \leq n^{-\beta}/2$. Recall that we have assumed $\Phi_{t_1} = 0$. But since $\Pr(\Phi_{t_1} N_{t_1}^0 \neq 0) \leq n^{-\beta}/2$ as we saw at the beginning, we can obtain similar to Eq. (4) that the unconditional probability that $N_{t^*}^0 \neq 0$ is bounded by $n^{-\beta}$. This completes the proof of Theorem 2.   □

3   Sorting Protocol

For the sorting problem we assume that nodes have consecutive IDs, $1, \ldots, n$, and each node has an input value from some totally ordered domain. W.l.o.g. we assume that the input values are numbers, and nodes have distinct inputs. We will say 'node i' to refer to the node with ID i. The goal is to redistribute the values to nodes (one value per node) so that for each i, node i stores the value of rank i, that is, the i-th smallest one among the input values.

In every round of the protocol, each node chooses to be *active* independently with probability $1/2$. Each active node i picks a node at random, choosing node j with probability proportional to $1/|i-j|$. If a non-active node j is contacted by one or more active nodes, then it chooses one of them, say node i, and the two nodes compare their values. Let X_i and X_j be the values of i and j respectively, at the time. If $(i-j)(X_i - X_j) < 0$ then the two nodes swap their values; otherwise, the do nothing. If an active node is contacted by another active node, it does not respond to it.

Theorem 3. *The sorting protocol described above sorts the inputs of all n nodes in $O(\log^2 n)$ rounds with probability $1 - n^{-\beta}$ for any fixed $\beta > 0$.*

Proof. The proof uses a potential function argument. For each node i, we consider the distance between i and the node that should have the value stored by node i. We claim that the sum of the squares of these distances drops by a factor of $1 - \Omega(1/\log n)$ in expectation in each round; and thus it becomes zero after $O(\log^2 n)$ rounds.

For each node i, let $X_{i,t}$ be the value that node i has after round t, and let $R_{i,t} = \text{rank}(X_{i,t})$ be the rank of that value. Hence, $R_{i,t}$ is equal to the ID of the node at which value $X_{i,t}$ should be stored eventually. Further, let $d_{i,t} = |R_{i,t} - i|$ be the distance between nodes $R_{i,t}$ and i. We define the potential $\Psi_{i,t}$ of node i after round t to be $\Psi_{i,t} = d_{i,t}^2$. The (total) potential after round t is then

$$\Psi_t = \sum_i \Psi_{i,t} = \sum_i d_{i,t}^2.$$

Lemma 4. $\mathbf{E}[\Psi_{t+1} \mid \Psi_t] \leq (1 - c/\ln n)\,\Psi_t$, *for some constant* $c > 0$

Proof. The drop in the potential when two nodes i and j swap their values in round $t + 1$ is

$$\Psi_{i,t} + \Psi_{j,t} - \Psi_{i,t+1} - \Psi_{j,t+1} = (R_{i,t} - i)^2 + (R_{j,t} - j)^2 - (R_{i,t} - j)^2 - (R_{j,t} - i)^2$$
$$= 2(i - j)(R_{j,t} - R_{i,t})$$
$$= 2|i - j| \cdot |R_{j,t} - R_{i,t}|,$$

where the last equality holds because $2(i - j)(R_{j,t} - R_{i,t}) > 0$, as nodes i and j swap values only if $(i - j)(X_{i,t} - X_{j,t}) < 0$, and the differences $R_{j,t} - R_{i,t}$ and $X_{j,t} - X_{i,t}$ have the same sign.

Below we assume w.l.o.g. that $i \leq R_{i,t}$. Consider the two sets of nodes $U = [(i + d_{i,t}/3)..n]$ and $W = [1..(R_{i,t} - d_{i,t}/3)]$. The intersection of the two sets has size $|U \cap W| = d_{i,t}/3$. It follows that there are at least $d_{i,t}/3$ nodes $j \in U$ for which $R_{j,t} \in W$. Fix one of these nodes j. If node i is active in round $t + 1$, which happens with probability $1/2$, then the probability that i chooses j is $1/(|i - j| \cdot \nu_i)$, where ν_i is the normalizing factor $\sum_{1 \leq k \leq n,\, k \neq i}(1/|i - k|)$, which is in the range $\ln n < \nu_i < 2\ln n$. Thus, i chooses j with probability $1/(|i - j| \cdot 2\nu_i) \geq 1/(|i - j| \cdot 4\ln n)$. Further, the probability that node j is not active and not chosen by any other node $k \neq i$ in the round is

$$\frac{1}{2} \prod_{1 \leq k \leq n,\, k \neq i,j} \left(1 - 1/(|i - k| \cdot 2\nu_j)\right) \geq \frac{1}{2}\left(1 - \sum_{1 \leq k \leq n,\, k \neq i,j} 1/(|i - k| \cdot 2\nu_j)\right) \geq 1/4.$$

From all the above it follows that the expected drop in the potential as a result of the likelihood of i choosing j and swapping values with it is at least

$$2|i - j| \cdot |R_{j,t} - R_{i,t}| \cdot \left(1/(|i - j| \cdot 4\ln n)\right)(1/4) = |R_{j,t} - R_{i,t}|/(8\ln n).$$

We saw earlier that there are at least $|U \cap W| = d_{i,t}/3$ such nodes j, and for each we have $R_{i,t} - R_{j,t} \geq d_{i,t}/3$ since $R_{j,t} \in W$. It follows that the expected decrease in the potential as a result of i choosing and swapping values with *some* inactive node in round $t + 1$ it at least $(d_{i,t}/3)(d_{i,t}/3)/(8\ln n) = \Psi_{i,t}/(72\ln n)$. Therefore, the total expected potential difference is $\mathbf{E}[\Psi_t - \Psi_{t+1} \mid \Psi_t] \geq \sum_i \Psi_{i,t}/(72\ln n) = \Psi_t/(72\ln n)$. This completes the proof of Lemma 4. $\qquad\square$

Applying Lemma 4 repeatedly and using that $\Psi_0 < n^3$, we obtain for $t^* = (\beta + 3)(\ln n)^2/c$,

$$\mathbf{E}[\Psi_{t^*}] \leq (1 - c/\ln n)^{t^*}\Psi_0 \leq e^{-ct^*/\ln n}\Psi_0 \leq e^{-(\beta+3)\ln n}n^3 = n^{-\beta}.$$

Markov's Inequality then yields $\Pr(\Psi_{t^*} > 0) = \Pr(\Psi_{t^*} \geq 1) \leq n^{-\beta}/1$, and thus $\Pr(\Psi_{t^*} = 0) \geq 1 - n^{-\beta}$. Since $\Psi_{t^*} = 0$ implies that sorting is completed in at most t^* rounds, Theorem 3 follows. □

4 Conclusion

We presented and analyzed gossip-based protocols for two fundamental tasks, renaming and sorting. The protocols are simple and natural, and they are fault-tolerant in the sense that they still succeed even if a (random) constant fraction of the communication channels fail to get established. For our sorting protocol it is necessary to use *non-uniform* peer-sampling in order to achieve polylogarithmic round complexity. A DHT-like overlay network can be used to implement this service, but we suggest that further research on non-uniform peer-sampling should be pursued.

The probability distribution that we chose for the peer-sampling in our sorting algorithm is the same power law distribution as the one used in Kleinberg's small world graph model [26,25]. There, the distribution determines additional edges (long range contacts) to augment the ring network, in order to achieve decentralized greedy routing in $O(\log^2 n)$ expected time. It is known that no other distance-based probability distribution for those augmentations can achieve faster greedy routing time [11]. Since sorting is intuitively harder than routing, it seems unlikely that a faster sorting algorithm can be obtained by a change in the probability distribution of the peer-sampling mechanism.

References

1. Ajtai, M., Komlós, J., Szemerédi, E.: An $O(n \log n)$ sorting network. In: Proc. 15th STOC, pp. 1–9 (1983)
2. Alistarh, D., Aspnes, J., Gilbert, S., Guerraoui, R.: The complexity of renaming. In: Proc. 52nd FOCS, pp. 718–727 (2011)
3. Angluin, D., Aspnes, J., Chen, J., Wu, Y., Yin, Y.: Fast construction of overlay networks. In: Proc. 17th SPAA, pp. 145–154 (2005)
4. Attiya, H., Bar-Noy, A., Dolev, D., Peleg, D., Reischuk, R.: Renaming in an asynchronous environment. J. ACM 37(3), 524–548 (1990)
5. Batcher, K.E.: Sorting networks and their applications. In: AFIPS Spring Joint Computing Conference, pp. 307–314 (1968)
6. Bawa, M., Garcia-Molina, H., Gionis, A., Motwani, R.: Estimating Aggregates on a Peer-to-Peer Network. Technical report, Stanford University (2003)
7. Berenbrink, P., Elsässer, R., Friedetzky, T.: Efficient randomized broadcasting in random regular networks with applications in peer-to-peer systems. In: Proc. 27th PODC, pp. 155–164 (2008)
8. Boyd, S.P., Ghosh, A., Prabhakar, B., Shah, D.: Randomized gossip algorithms. IEEE Trans. Inf. Theory, 52(6), 2508–2530 (2006)
9. Cooper, C., Dyer, M.E., Handley, A.J.: The flip markov chain and a randomising P2P protocol. In: Proc. 28th PODC, pp. 141–150 (2009)

10. Demers, A.J., Greene, D.H., Hauser, C., Irish, W., Larson, J., Shenker, S., Sturgis, H.E., Swinehart, D.C., Terry, D.B.: Epidemic algorithms for replicated database maintenance. In: Proc. 6th PODC, pp. 1–12 (1987)
11. Dietzfelbinger, M., Woelfel, P.: Tight lower bounds for greedy routing in uniform small world rings. In: Proc. 41st STOC, pp. 591–600 (2009)
12. Doerr, B., Fouz, M.: Asymptotically optimal randomized rumor spreading. In: Aceto, L., Henzinger, M., Sgall, J. (eds.) ICALP 2011, Part II. LNCS, vol. 6756, pp. 502–513. Springer, Heidelberg (2011)
13. Doerr, B., Fouz, M., Friedrich, T.: Social networks spread rumors in sublogarithmic time. In: Proc. 43rd STOC, pp. 21–30 (2011)
14. Doerr, B., Friedrich, T., Sauerwald, T.: Quasirandom rumor spreading: Expanders, push vs. Pull, and robustness. In: Albers, S., Marchetti-Spaccamela, A., Matias, Y., Nikoletseas, S., Thomas, W. (eds.) ICALP 2009, Part I. LNCS, vol. 5555, pp. 366–377. Springer, Heidelberg (2009)
15. Elsässer, R., Sauerwald, T.: On the runtime and robustness of randomized broadcasting. Theor. Comput. Sci. 410(36), 3414–3427 (2009)
16. Feder, T., Guetz, A., Mihail, M., Saberi, A.: A local switch Markov chain on given degree graphs with application in connectivity of peer-to-peer networks. In: Proc. 47th FOCS, pp. 69–76 (2006)
17. Felber, P.: Epidemic algorithms: A "systems" perspective. Talk at the Dagstuhl Seminar 13042, Epidemic Algorithms and Processes: From Theory to Practice (February 2013), Slides available online at http://www.dagstuhl.de/mat/Files/13/13042/13042.FelberPascal.Slides.pdf
18. Fountoulakis, N., Huber, A., Panagiotou, K.: Reliable broadcasting in random networks and the effect of density. In: Proc. 29th INFOCOM, pp. 2552–2560 (2010)
19. Giakkoupis, G.: Tight bounds for rumor spreading in graphs of a given conductance. In: Proc. 28th STACS, pp. 57–68 (2011)
20. Jelasity, M., Kermarrec, A.-M.: Ordered slicing of very large-scale overlay networks. In: Peer-to-Peer Computing, pp. 117–124 (2006)
21. Jelasity, M., Voulgaris, S., Guerraoui, R., Kermarrec, A.-M., van Steen, M.: Gossip-based peer sampling. ACM Trans. Comput. Syst. 25(3), 8 (2007)
22. Karp, R.M., Schindelhauer, C., Shenker, S., Vöcking, B.: Randomized rumor spreading. In: Proc. 41st FOCS, pp. 565–574 (2000)
23. Kempe, D., Dobra, A., Gehrke, J.: Gossip-based computation of aggregate information. In: Proc. 44th FOCS, pp. 482–491 (2003)
24. Kempe, D., Kleinberg, J.M., Demers, A.J.: Spatial gossip and resource location protocols. J. ACM 51(6), 943–967 (2004)
25. Kleinberg, J.M.: Navigation in a small-world. Nature, 845 (2000)
26. Kleinberg, J.M.: The small-world phenomenon: An algorithm perspective. In: Proc. 32nd STOC, pp. 163–170 (2000)
27. Knuth, D.E.: The Art of Computer Programming, 2nd edn. Sorting and Searching, vol. 3. Addison-Wesley, Reading (1998)
28. Mosk-Aoyama, D., Shah, D.: Fast distributed algorithms for computing separable functions. IEEE Trans. Inf. Theory 54(7), 2997–3007 (2008)
29. Stoica, I., Morris, R., Liben-Nowell, D., Karger, D.R., Kaashoek, M.F., Dabek, F., Balakrishnan, H.: Chord: a scalable peer-to-peer lookup protocol for internet applications. IEEE/ACM Trans. Netw. 11(1), 17–32 (2003)
30. Yao, A.C.-C., Yao, F.F.: On fault-tolerant networks for sorting. SIAM J. Comput. 14(1), 120–128 (1985)

Faster Rumor Spreading:
Breaking the log n Barrier[*,**]

Chen Avin[1] and Robert Elsässer[2]

[1] Communication Systems Engineering, Ben Gurion University of the Negev, Israel
avin@cse.bgu.ac.il
[2] Department of Computer Sciences, University of Salzburg, Austria
elsa@cosy.sbg.ac.at

Abstract. $O(\log n)$ rounds has been a well known upper bound for rumor spreading using push&pull in the *random phone call* model (i.e., uniform gossip in the complete graph). A matching lower bound of $\Omega(\log n)$ is also known for this special case. Under the assumptions of this model and with a natural addition that nodes can call a partner once they learn its address (e.g., its IP address) we present a new distributed, address-oblivious and robust algorithm that uses push&pull with pointer jumping to spread a rumor to all nodes in only $O(\sqrt{\log n})$ rounds, w.h.p. This algorithm can also cope with $F = o(n/2^{\sqrt{\log n}})$ node failures, in which case all but $O(F)$ nodes become informed within $O(\sqrt{\log n})$ rounds, w.h.p.

1 Introduction

Gossiping, or rumor-spreading, is a simple stochastic process for dissemination of information across a network. In a *round* of gossip, *each* node chooses a single, usually random, neighbor as its *communication partner* according to a *gossip algorithm* (e.g., selecting a random neighbor). Once a partner is chosen the node *calls* its partner and a limited amount of data is transferred between the partners, as defined by the gossip *protocol*. Three basic actions are considered in the literature: either the caller pushes information to its partner (push), pulls information from the partner (pull), or does both (push&pull). In the most basic information dissemination task, a token or a rumor in placed arbitrary in the network and we are interested in the number of rounds and message transmissions until all nodes in the networks receive the rumor. The selection of the protocol can lead to significant differences in the performance. Take for example the star graph, let nodes call a neighbor selected uniformly at random and assume the rumor is placed at one of the leafs. It is easy to see that both push and pull will require $\omega(n)$ rounds to complete the spreading of a single rumor while push&pull will take only two rounds.

---

[*] This work was partially supported by the Austrian Science Fund (FWF) under contract P25214-N23 *"Analysis of Epidemic Processes and Algorithms in Large Networks"*.

[**] The main result of this paper emerged from an open problem presented at Dagstuhl Seminar 13042 *"Epidemic Algorithms and Processes: From Theory to Applications"*.

Y. Afek (Ed.): DISC 2013, LNCS 8205, pp. 209–223, 2013.
© Springer-Verlag Berlin Heidelberg 2013

Somewhat surpassingly, but by now well understood, randomized rumor-spreading turned out to be very efficient in terms of time and message complexity while keeping robustness to failures. In addition, this type of algorithms are very simple and distributed in nature so it is clear why gossip protocols have gained popularity in recent years and have found many applications both in communication networks and social networks. To name a few examples: updating a database replicated at many sites [6,16], resource discovery [15], computation of aggregate information [17], multicast via network coding [5], membership services [13], or the spread of influence and gossip in social networks [18,3].

In this paper we consider the most basic scenario, the *random phone call model* [16], where the underlying network is the complete graph and nodes can call a random neighbor according to some given distribution. In addition, the model requires the algorithm to be *distributed* and *address-oblivious*: it cannot use the address of the current communication partners to determine its state (for an exact definition see Section 2). For example this setting fits well to applications which require communication over the internet such as peer-to-peer protocols and database synchronization. A node can pick and call any (random or given) neighbor via its IP address, but it is desired to keep the algorithm address-oblivious otherwise it may have critical points of failure. For example agreeing before hand on a leader to contact (by its IP address) is *not* an address-oblivious algorithm. Furthermore, such a protocol is also highly fragile, although it leads to efficient information spreading (as pointed out in the star graph example above).

The random phone call model was thoroughly studied in the literature starting with the work of Frieze and Gimmet [11] and following by Pittel [22] who proved an upper bound of $O(\log n)$ rounds for push in the complete graph. Demers et al. [6] considered both push and pull as a simple and decentralized way to disseminate information in a network and studied their rate of progress. Finally, Karp et al. [16] gave a detailed analysis for this model. They used push&pull to optimize the message complexity and showed the robustness of the scheme. They proved that while using only push the communication overhead is $\Omega(n \log n)$, their algorithm only requires $O(n \log \log n)$ message transmissions by having a running time of $O(\log n)$, even under arbitrary oblivious failures. Moreover they proved that any address-oblivious algorithm (that selects neighbors uniformly at random) will require $\Omega(n \log \log n)$ message transmissions.

1.1   Our Contribution

We consider the same assumptions as in the random phone call model: the algorithm needs to be distributed, address-oblivious and it can select neighbors at random. In addition we use the fact that given an address of a node (e.g., its IP address) the caller can call directly on that address. This slight addition leads to a significant improvement in the number of rounds from $O(\log n)$ to $O(\sqrt{\log n})$, but still keeps the algorithm robust. The main result of the paper is the following theorem:

Theorem 1. *At the end of the algorithm Jumping-Push-Pull (JPP), all but $O(F)$ nodes are informed w.h.p.[1], where F is the number of failed nodes (as described in the text). The algorithm has running time $O(\sqrt{\log n})$ and produces a* **bit** *communication complexity of $O(n(\log^{3/2} n + b \cdot \log\log n))$, w.h.p., where b is the bit length of the message.*

Clearly, if there are no failures (i.e., $F = 0$), then all nodes become informed in the number of rounds given in Theorem 1. As mentioned, we inform all nodes in $O(\sqrt{\log n})$ rounds vs. $O(\log n)$ rounds achieved by the algorithm of Karp et al. Our message complexity is $O(n\sqrt{\log n})$ compared to $O(n \log\log n)$ and if the rumor is of bit length $b = \Omega(\frac{\log^{3/2} n}{\log\log n})$ both of the algorithms bit complexity is $\Omega(b \cdot n \log\log n)$. Moreover, if there are $\Omega(n)$ messages to be distributed in the network, then the first term in the expression describing the bit communication complexity is amortized over the total number of message transmissions (cf. [16]), and we obtain the same communication overhead as in [16].

Few words on the basic idea of the algorithm are in place. In a nutshell our approach has two phases: first we try to build an infrastructure, a virtual topology, that is efficient for **push&pull**. Second, we perform a simple **push&pull** on the virtual topology. The running time is the combination of both these tasks. For example, constructing a random star would be preferable since the second phase will then take only a constant number of rounds, but as it turns out the cost of the first phase, in this case, is too high. Interestingly, our algorithm results in balancing these two phases where each task requires $O(\sqrt{\log n})$ rounds. Instead of a star with a single leader, our algorithm builds a virtual topology with about random $n/2^{\sqrt{\log n}}$ leaders and each leader is connected to about $2^{\sqrt{\log n}}$ nodes we call *connectors* (a node is either a leader or a connector). Each connector is then linked to two leaders after a process of pointer jumping [19]. This simple 2-level hierarchy results in a very efficient information spreading. Leaders are a source of fast **pull** mechanism and connectors are essential for fast spreading among leaders using **push**. Our approach was motivated from similar phenomena in social networks [10,1] (see the related work section for a more detailed description of these results).

2 Model and Preliminaries - Rumor Spreading

Let $G(V, E)$ be an undirected graph, with V the set of nodes and E the set of edges. Let $n = |V|$ and $m = |E|$. For $v \in V$, let $N(v) = \{u \in V \mid (vu) \in E\}$ the set of neighbors of v and $d(v) = |N(v)|$ the degree of v. Initially a single arbitrary node holds a rumor (i.e., a token) of size b bits; then the process of rumor-spreading (or gossiping) progresses in synchronous *rounds*. At each round, each node v selects a single *communication partner*, $u \in N(v)$ from its neighbors and v calls u. The method by which v choses u is called the *goosip algorithm*. The algorithm is called *address-oblivious* if v's state in round t does not depend on the

---

[1] In this paper with high probably or w.h.p. is with probability at least $1 - n^{-1-\Omega(1)}$.

addresses of its communication partners at time t. Meaning, any decision about if, how and what to send in the current round is made before the current round. Nevertheless, v's state can still depend on the addresses of its communication partners from previous rounds [16].

Randomized gossip is maybe the most basic address-oblivious algorithm, in particular, when the communication partners are selected uniformly at random the process is known as *uniform gossip*. A well studied such case is the *random phone call model* [16] where G is the complete graph and u is selected u.a.r from $V \setminus v$. Upon selecting a communication partner the *gossip protocol* defines the way and which information is transferred between v and u. Three basic options are considered to deliver information between communication partners: push, pull and push&pull. In push the calling node, v, sends a message to the called node u, in pull a message is only transferred the other way (if the called node, u, has what to send) and in push&pull each of the communication partners sends a message to the node at the other end of the edge. The content of the messages is defined by the protocol and can contain only the rumor (in the simplest case) or additional information like counters or state information (e.g., like in [16]).

After selecting the graph (or graph model), the gossip algorithm and protocol, the main metrics of interest are the dissemination time and the message complexity. Namely how many rounds and messages are needed until all vertices are informed[2] (on average or with high probability), even under node failures. The *bit complexity* is also a metric of interest and counts the *total* number of bits sent during the dissemination time. This quantity is a bit more involved since it depends also on b (the size of the rumor) and messages at different phases of the algorithms may have different sizes.

A *pointer jumping* is a classical operation from parallel algorithm design [19] where the destination of your next round pointer is the pointer at which your current pointer points to. Our algorithm uses pointer jumping by sending the addresses (i.e., pointers) of previous communication partners to current partners (see Section 4 for a detailed description).

3   Related Work

Beside the basic random phone call model, gossip algorithms and rumor spreading were generalized in several different ways. The basic extension was to study *uniform gossip* (i.e., the called partner is selected uniformly at random from the neighbors lists) on graphs other than the clique. Feige et. al. [9] studied randomized broadcast in networks and extended the result of $O(\log n)$ rounds for push to different types of graphs like hypercubes and random graphs models. Following the work of Karp et al. [16], and in particular in recent years the push&pull protocol was studied intensively, both to give tight bounds for general graphs and to understand its performance advantages on specific families of graphs. A lower bound of $\Omega(\log n)$ for uniform gossip on the clique can be conclude from

---

[2] A call, in which no data is sent (e.g., the rumor, or a pointer), is not considered as a message.

[24] that studies the sequential case. We are not aware of a lower bound for general, address-oblivious push&pull.

Recently Giakkoupis [12] proved an upper bound for general graphs as a function of the *conductance*, ϕ, of the graph, which is $O(\phi^{-1} \log n)$ rounds. Since the conductance is at most a constant this bound cannot lead to a value of $o(\log n)$, but is tight for many graphs. Doerr et al. [7] studied information spreading on a known model of social networks and showed for the first time an upper bound which is $o(\log n)$ for a large family of natural graphs. They proved that while uniform gossip with push&pull results in $O(\log n)$ rounds in these social networks, a slightly improved version where nodes are not allowed to repeat their last call results in a spreading time of $O(\frac{\log n}{\log \log n})$. Following this, Fountoulakis et al. [10], considered a spreading to all but a small ϵ-fraction of the population. For random power law graphs [4] they proved that push&pull informs all but an ϵ-fraction of the nodes in $O(\log \log n)$ rounds. Their proof relies on the existence of many *connectors* (i.e., nodes with low degree connected to high degree nodes) which amplify the spread of the rumor between high degree nodes, and this influenced our approach; in some sense our algorithm tries to imitate the structure of the social network they studied.

Another line of research was to study push&pull (as well as push and pull separately) but not under the uniform gossip model. Censor-Hillel et al. [2], gave an algorithm for all-to-all dissemination in arbitrary graphs which eliminates the dependency on the conductance. For unlimited message sizes (essentially you can send everything you know), their randomized algorithm informs all nodes in $O(D + \text{polylog}(n))$ rounds where D is the graph diameter; clearly this is tight for many graphs. Quasi-random rumor spreading was first offered by Doerr et al. in [8] and showed to outperform the randomize algorithms in some cases. Most recently Haeupler [14] proposed a completely deterministic algorithm that spread a rumor with $2(D + \log n) \log n$ rounds (but also requires unlimited message size).

In a somewhat different model (but similar to ours), where nodes can contact any address as soon as they learn about it, Harchol-Balter et. al. [15] considered the problem of resource discovery (i.e., learning about all nodes in the graph) starting from an arbitrary graph. They used a form of one hop pointer jumping with push&pull and gave an upper bound of $O(\log^2 n)$ rounds for their algorithm. It will be interesting to extend our result to this case (starting from an arbitrary graph and not the complete graph).

Another source of influence to our work was the work on pointer jumping with push&pull in the context of efficient construction of peer-to-peer networks [20].

4   Jumping-Push-Pull in $O(\sqrt{\log n})$-time

First, we present the algorithm, which disseminates a rumor by push&pull in $O(\sqrt{\log n})$ time, w.h.p. Then, we analyze our algorithm, show its corectness, and prove the runtime bound.

4.1   Algorithm - Rumor Spreading with Pointer Jumping

First, we provide a high-level overview of our algorithm. At the beginning, a message resides on one of the nodes, and the goal is to distribute this message (or rumor) to every node in the network. We assume that each node has a unique address (which can be for example its IP-address), and every node can select a vertex uniformly at random from the set of all nodes (i.e., like in the random phone call model). Additionally, a node can store a constant number of addresses, out of which it can call one of them in a future round. However, a node must decide in each round whether it chooses an address uniformly at random or from the pool of the addresses stored before the current round.

In our analysis, we assume for simplicity that every node knows n exactly. However, a slightly modified version of our algorithm also works if the nodes have an estimate of $\log n$, which is correct up to some constant factor. We discuss this case in Section 5.

The algorithm consists of five main *phases* and these phases may contain several *rounds* of communication. Basically there are two type of nodes in the algorithm, which we call *leaders* and *connectors*, and the algorithm is:

Phase 0 - each informed node performs push in every step of this phase. The phase consists of $c \log \log n$ steps, where c is some suitable constant. According to e.g. [16], the message is contained in $\log^2 n$ many nodes at the end of this phase.

Phase 1 - each node flips a coin to decide whether it will be a leader, with probability $1/2^{\sqrt{\log n}}$, or a connector, with probability $1 - 1/2^{\sqrt{\log n}}$.

Phase 2 - each connector chooses leaders by preforming five pointer jumping sub-phases, each for $c\sqrt{\log n}$ rounds. At the end, all but $o(n)$ connectors will have at least 2 leader addresses stored with high probability. Every such connector keeps exactly 2 leader addresses (chosen uniformly at random) and forgets all the others. A detailed description of this phase is given below.

Phase 3 - each connector opens in each round of this phase a communication channel to a randomly chosen node from the list of leaders received in the previous phase. However, once a connector receives the message, it only transmits once in the next round using push communication to its other leader. The leaders send the message in each round over all incoming channels during the whole phase (i.e., the leaders send the message by pull). The length of this phase is $c\sqrt{\log n}$ rounds.

Phase 4 - every node performs the usual push&pull (median counter algorithm according to [16]) for $c\sqrt{\log n}$ rounds. All informed nodes are considered to be in state B_1 at the beginning of this phase (cf. [16]).

The second phase needs some clarification: it consists of 5 sub-phases in which connectors chose leaders. In each sub-phase, every connector performs so called pointer-jumping [19] for $c\sqrt{\log n}$ rounds, where c is some large constant. The leaders do not participate in pointer jumping, and when contacted by a connector, they let it know that it has reached a leader. The pointer jumping sub-phase works as follow: in the first round every connector chooses a node uniformly at random, and opens a communication channel to it. Then, each (connector or leader) node, which has incoming communication channels, sends its address by **pull** to the nodes at the other end of these channels. In each round $i > 1$ of this sub-phase, every connector calls on the address obtained in step $i - 1$, and opens a channel to it. Every node, which is incident to an incoming channel, transmits the address obtained in step $i - 1$. Clearly, at some time t each node stores only the address received in the previous step $t - 1$ of the current sub-phase, and the addresses stored at the end of the previous sub-phases. If in some sub-phase a connector v does not receive a leader address at all, then it forgets the address stored in the last step of this sub-phase. In this case we say that v is "black" in this sub-phase. The idea of using connectors to amplify the information propagation in graphs has already been used in e.g. [10].

From the description of the algorithm it follows that its running time is $O(\sqrt{\log n})$. In the next section we show that every node becomes informed with probability $1 - n^{-1 - \Omega(1)}$.

4.2   Analysis of the Algorithm

For our analysis we assume the following failure model. Each node may fail (before or during the execution of the algorithm) with some probability $o(1/(2^{\sqrt{\log n}} \cdot \log n))$. This implies that e.g. $n^{1-\epsilon}$ nodes may fail in total, where $\epsilon > 0$ can be any small constant. If a node fails, then it does not participate in any pointer- or message-forwarding process. Moreover, we assume that the other nodes do not realize that a node has failed, even if they contact him directly. That is, all nodes which contact (directly or by pointer-jumping) a failed node in some sub-phase are also considered to be failed.

First, we give a high-level overview of our proofs. Basically, we do not consider phases 0 and 1 in the analysis; the resulting properties on the set of informed nodes are straight-forward, and have already been discussed in e.g. [16]. Thus, we know that at the end of phase 0, the rumor is contained in at least $\log^2 n$ nodes, and at the end of phase 1 there are $n/2^{\sqrt{\log n}} \cdot (1 \pm o(1))$ leaders, w.h.p. Lemma 1 analyzes phase 2. We show that most of the connectors will point to a leader after a sub-phase, w.h.p. To show this, we bound the probability that for a node v, the choices of the nodes in the first step of this sub-phase lead to a cycle of connectors, such that after performing pointer jumping for $c\sqrt{\log n}$ steps, v will point to a node in this cycle. Since we have in total 5 sub-phases, which are run independetly, we conclude that each connector will point to a leader, after at least 2 sub-phases. At this point we do not consider node failures.

In Lemma 2, we basically bound the number of nodes pointing to the same leader. For this, we consider the layers of nodes, which are at distance 1, 2, etc... from an arbitrary but fixed leader u after the first step of a sub-phase. Since we know how many layers we have in total, and bound the growth of a layer i compared to the previous layer $i - 1$ by standard balls into bins techniques, we obtain an upper bound, which is polynomial in $2^{\sqrt{\log n}}$.

In Lemma 3 we show that most of the connectors share a leader address at the end of a sub-phase with $\Omega(2^{\sqrt{\log n}} / \log n)$ many connectors, w.h.p. Here, we start to consider node failures too. To show this, we compute the expected length of the path from a connector to a leader after the first step of a sub-phase. However, since these distances are not independent, we apply Martingale techniques to show that for most nodes these distances occur with high probability.

Lemma 4 analyzes then the growth in the number of informed nodes within two steps of phase 3. What we basically show is that after any two steps, the number of informed nodes is increased by a factor of $2^{\sqrt{\log n}/2}$, w.h.p., and most of the newly informed nodes are connected to a (second) leader, which is not informed yet. Thus, most connectors which point to these leaders are also not informed. These will become informed two steps later.

The main theorem then uses the fact that at the end of phase 3 a $2^{7\sqrt{\log n}}$ fraction of the nodes is informed, w.h.p. Then, we can apply the algorithm of [16] to inform all nodes within additional $O(\sqrt{\log n})$ steps, w.h.p.

Now we start with the details. In the first lemma we do not consider node failures. For this case, we show that, w.h.p., there is no connector which is "black" in more than two sub-phases of the second phase. Let $r(v)$ be the choice of an arbitrary but fixed connector node v in the first round of a sub-phase. Furthermore, let $R(v)$ be the set of nodes which can be reached by node v using (directed) edges of the form $(u, r(u))$ only. That is, a node u is in $R(v)$ iff there exist some nodes $u_1, \ldots, u_k$ such that $u_1 = r(v)$, $u_{i+1} = r(u_i)$ for any $i \in \{1, \ldots, k-1\}$, and $u = r(u_k)$.

Clearly, if there are no node failures, then only one of the following cases may occur: either a leader u exists with $u \in R(v)$, or $R(v)$ has a cycle. We prove the following lemma.

Lemma 1. *For an arbitrary but fixed connector v, the set $R(v)$ has a cycle with probability $O\left(\frac{2^{2\sqrt{\log n}} \log^2 n}{n}\right)$. Furthermore, the size of $R(v)$ is $|R(v)| = O(2^{\sqrt{\log n}} \log n)$, w.h.p.*

Proof. Let $P(v)$ be a directed path $(v, u_1, \ldots, u_k)$, where $u_1 = r(v)$, $u_{i+1} = r(u_i)$ for any $i \in \{1, \ldots, k-1\}$, and $u_i \neq u_j, v$ for any $i, j \in \{1, \ldots, k\}$, $i \neq j$. Then, $r(u_k) \in \{v, u_1, \ldots, u_{k-1}\}$ with probability $k/(n-1)$. Let this event be denoted by A_k. Furthermore, let B_k be the event that $r(u_k)$ is not a leader (B_1 is the event that neither $r(v)$ nor $r(u_1)$ is a leader). If L is the set of leaders, then since communication partners are selected independently we have

$$Pr[\overline{A_k} \wedge B_k \mid \overline{A_1} \wedge B_1 \wedge \cdots \wedge \overline{A_{k-1}} \wedge B_{k-1}] = \frac{n - |L| - k}{n-1} \text{ and}$$

$$Pr[\overline{A_1} \wedge B_1] = \frac{n - |L|}{n-1} \cdot \frac{n - |L| - 1}{n-1}.$$

Simple application of Chernoff bounds imply that $|L| = n(1 \pm o(1))/2^{\sqrt{\log n}}$, w.h.p. We condition on the event that this bound holds on $|L|$, and obtain for some $k > c \cdot 2^{\sqrt{\log n}} \log n$ that

$$Pr[\overline{A_1} \wedge B_1] \cdot Pr[\overline{A_2} \wedge B_2 \mid \overline{A_1} \wedge B_1] \cdots \cdots$$
$$\cdot Pr[\overline{A_k} \wedge B_k \mid \overline{A_1} \wedge B_1 \wedge \cdots \wedge \overline{A_{k-1}} \wedge B_{k-1}]$$
$$\leq \left(1 - \frac{1}{2^{\sqrt{\log n}}} \right)^{c \cdot 2^{\sqrt{\log n}} \log n} \leq n^{-3 - \Omega(1)},$$

whenever c is large enough. The first inequality follows from $|L| = \omega(k)$. This implies that the size of $R(v)$ is at most $c \cdot 2^{\sqrt{\log n}} \log n$, w.h.p.

Now we prove that

$$Pr[R(v) \text{ contains a cycle}] = O \left(\frac{2^{2\sqrt{\log n}} \log^2 n}{n} \right).$$

We know that

$$Pr[A_i \mid \overline{A_0} \wedge B_0 \wedge \cdots \wedge \overline{A_{i-1}} \wedge B_{i-1}] = \frac{i}{n-1},$$

where B_0 is the event that $r(v) \notin L$ and $A_0 = \emptyset$. Then, $|R(v)|$ has a cycle, with probability less than

$$\sum_{i=1}^{n-|L|-1} Pr[A_i \mid \overline{A_0} \wedge B_0 \wedge \cdots \wedge \overline{A_{i-1}} \wedge B_{i-1}] \cdot Pr[\overline{A_0} \wedge B_0 \wedge \cdots \wedge \overline{A_{i-1}} \wedge B_{i-1}]$$
$$\leq \frac{(c2^{\sqrt{\log n}} \log n)^2}{n} + O(n^{-2-\Omega(1)}).$$

$\square$

From the previous lemma we obtain the following corollary.

Corollary 1. *Assume there are no node failures. After phase 2, every connector stores the address of at least 2 leaders, with probability at least $1 - n^{-2}$.*

We can also show the following upper bound on the number of connectors sharing the same leader address. This bound also holds in the case of node failures, since failed nodes can only decrease the number of connectors sharing the same leader address.

Lemma 2. *Each connector shares the same leader address with $O(2^{3\sqrt{\log n}})$ other connectors, w.h.p.*

Proof. Let S be a set of nodes, and let $r(S) = \{v \in V \mid r(v) \in S\}$. We model the parallel process of choosing nodes in the first round of a fixed sub-phase by the following sequential process (that is, the first round of the sub-phase is modeled by the whole sequence of steps of the sequential process). In the first step of the sequential process, all connectors choose a random node. We keep all edges between $(u, r(u))$ with $r(u) \in L$, and release all other edges. Let L_1 denote the set of nodes u with $r(u) \in L$. In the ith step, we let each node of $V \setminus \cup_{j=0}^{i-1} L_j$

choose a node from the set $V \setminus \cup_{j=0}^{i-2} L_j$ uniformly at random, where $L_0 = L$. Clearly, the nodes are not allowed to choose themselves. Then, L_i is the set of nodes u with $r(u) \in L_{i-1}$, and all edges $(u, r(u))$ (generated in this step) with $r(u) \notin L_{i-1}$ are released.

Obviously, the sequential process produces the same edge distribution on the nodes of the graph as the parallel process. If now $S \subset L_{i-1}$, then the probability for a node $v \in V \setminus \cup_{j=0}^{i-1} L_j$ to choose a node in S is $|S|/|V \setminus \cup_{j=0}^{i-2} L_j|$. Then, according to [23] the number of nodes v with $r(v) \in S$ is at most $|S| + O(\log n + \sqrt{|S| \log n})$, w.h.p.

Similar to the definition of L_i, for a leader u the nodes v with $r(v) = u$ are in set $L_1(u)$, the nodes v with $r(r(v)) = u$ are in set $L_2(u)$, and generally, the nodes v with $r(v) \in L_{i-1}(u)$ define the set $L_i(u)$. Then, according to the arguments above $|L_{i+1}(u)| = |L_i(u)| + O(\log n + \sqrt{|L_i(u)| \log n})$, w.h.p. We assume now that $|L_1(u)| = \Theta(\log n)$ (from [23] we may conclude that $|L_1(u)| = O(\log n)$, w.h.p.). Then, for any $i \leq c \cdot 2^{\sqrt{\log n}} \log n$, we assume the highest growth for $|L_{i+1}(u)|$, i.e., $|L_{i+1}(u)| = |L_i(u)| + O(\sqrt{|L_i(u)| \log n})$, where c is some constant. This leads to $|L_{c \cdot 2^{\sqrt{\log n}} \log n}(u)| < 2^{2\sqrt{\log n}}/\log n$. Since $|R(v)| = O(2^{\sqrt{\log n}} \log n)$ for any v (cf. Lemma 1), we obtain the claim.   □

Let us fix a sub-phase. We allow now node failures (i.e., each node may fail with some probability $o(1/(2^{\sqrt{\log n}} \log n)))$, and prove the following lemma.

Lemma 3. *There are $n(1 - o(1))$ connectors, which store the address of at least two leaders, and each of these leader addresses is shared by at least $\Omega\left(\frac{2^{\sqrt{\log n}}}{\log n}\right)$ connectors, w.h.p.*

Proof. First, we consider the case in which no node failures are allowed. Then, we extend the proof. Now let us assume that no failures occur. We have shown in Lemma 1 that the length of a path $(v, u_1, \ldots, u_k, u)$ from a node v to a leader u is $O(2^{\sqrt{\log n}} \log n)$, w.h.p., where $u_1 = r(v)$, $u_i = r(u_{i-1})$ for any $i \in \{2, \ldots, k\}$, and $u = r(u_k)$. Let u be a leader, and let $L_i(u)$ be the set of connectors which have distance i from u after a certain (arbitrary but fixed) sub-phase of the second phase. Furthermore, let $L_i(L) = \cup_{u \in L} L_i(u)$. For our analysis, we model the process of choosing nodes in the first step of this sub-phase by a sequential process (similar to the proof of the previous lemma), in which first v chooses a node, then $r(v)$ chooses a node, then $r(r(v))$ chooses a node, etc... In step i of this sequential process the i node u_{i-1} on the path $P(v)$ chooses a node. For some $i = O(2^{\sqrt{\log n}}/\log n)$ we have

$$Pr[v \notin \cup_{j=1}^{i} L_j(L) \mid \overline{A_1} \wedge \cdots \wedge \overline{A_{i-1}}] \geq \left(1 - \frac{|L|}{n - i - 1}\right)^i,$$

Since $Pr[v \in \cup_{j=1}^{n-1} L_j(L)] = 1 - O(2^{2\sqrt{\log n}} \log^2 n/n)$ (cf. Lemma 1), we obtain that, given $R(v) \cap L \neq \emptyset$, a node has a path of length $\Omega(2^{\sqrt{\log n}}/\log n)$ to a leader with probability $1 - o(1)$, and thus the expected number of such nodes is $n(1-o(1))$.

Now we consider node failures. A node v is considered failed, if it fails as described at the beginning with probability $o(1/(2^{\sqrt{\log n}} \log n))$, or there is a node in $R(v)$, which fails with this probability. Since $|R(v)| = O(2^{\sqrt{\log n}} \log n)$, a node of $R(v)$ fails with probability $o(1)$. However, these probabilities are not independent. Nevertheless, the expected number of nodes, which will not be considered failed **and** have a path of length $\Omega(2^{\sqrt{\log n}}/\log n)$ to a leader, is $n(1 - o(1))$.

Now, consider the following Martingale sequence. Let $v_1, \ldots, v_{n-|L|}$ denote the connectors. In step j, we reveal the directed edges and nodes from node v_j to all nodes in all $R(v_j)$ obtained from the different sub-phases. Given that $|R(v_j)| = O(2^{\sqrt{\log n}} \log n)$, we apply the Azuma-Hoeffding inequality [21], and obtain that a $1 - o(1)$ fraction of the nodes is connected to a leader by a path of length $\Omega(2^{\sqrt{\log n}}/\log n)$ and will not be considered failed, w.h.p.

Summarizing, a $1 - o(1)$ fraction of the nodes store at the end of the first phase the address of at least two leaders, and such a connector shares each of these addresses with $\Omega(2^{\sqrt{\log n}}/\log n)$ other connectors, w.h.p.   □

Applying pointer jumping on all connectors as described in the algorithm, we obtain the following result.

Observation 1. *If in an arbitrary but fixed sub-phase of the second phase $R(v) \cap L \neq \emptyset$ for some connector v, then v stores the address of a leader u at the end of this phase, w.h.p.*

This observation is a simple application of the pointer jumping algorithm [19] on a directed path of length $|R(v)|$. According to Lemma 1, $|R(v)| = O(2^{\sqrt{\log n}} \log n)$, w.h.p.

Now we concentrate on the third phase. We condition on the event that each connector has stored at least two and at most 5 different leader addresses. Furthermore, an address stored by a connector is shared with at least $\Omega(2^{\sqrt{\log n}}/\log n)$ other connectors, with probability $1 - o(1)$. Out of these connectors, let C be the set of nodes v with the following property. The first time a leader of v receives the message, v will contact this leader in the next step, pulls the message, and in the next step it will push the message to the other leader. Clearly, for a node v this event occurs with constant probability, independently of the other nodes. Therefore, the total number of nodes in C with at least two different leader addresses, where each of these addresses is shared by at least $\Omega(2^{\sqrt{\log n}}/\log n)$ other connectors, is $\Theta(n)$, w.h.p. We call the set of these nodes $\tilde{C}$. Now we have the following observation.

Observation 2. *Let C_i be the set of nodes which store the same (arbitrary but fixed) leader address after a certain subsphase, and assume that $|C_i| = \Omega(2^{\sqrt{\log n}}/\log n)$. Then, $|C_i \cap \tilde{C}| = \Theta(|C_i|)$, w.h.p.*

The proof of this observation follows from the fact that if two nodes share the same address after a certain subphase, then each of these nodes will share with probability $1 - o(1)$ a leader address obtained in some other subphase with at least $\Omega(2^{\sqrt{\log n}}/\log n)$ other connectors. However, these events are not independent.

Let now C_j be some other set, which contains a node $v \in C_i$. Since $|C_i|, |C_j| = O(2^{3\sqrt{\log n}})$ (see Lemma 2), there will be with probability at least $1 - n^{-2}$ at most 4 nodes in $C_i \cap C_j$. Conditioning on this, we apply for the nodes of $C_i \cap C$ the same Martingale sequence as in the proof of Lemma 3. By taking into account that in this case the Martingale sequence satisfies the 4-Lipschitz condition (the nodes of C_i are part of the Martingale only), we obtain the statement of the observation.

Now we are ready to show the following lemma.

Lemma 4. *After the third phase the number of informed nodes is at least $\frac{n}{2^{7\sqrt{\log n}}}$, w.h.p.*

Proof. For a node $v \in \tilde{C}$, let $C_v^{(1)}$ and $C_v^{(2)}$ represent two sets of nodes, which store the same leader address as v (obtained in the same sub-phases of the second phase), and for which we have $|C_v^{(1)}|, |C_v^{(2)}| = \Omega(2^{\sqrt{\log n}}/\log n)$. We know that each node has exactly 2 leader addresses. Since after phase 0 at least $\log^2 n$ nodes are informed, we may assume that at the beginning of this phase a node $w \in \tilde{C}$ is informed, and w pushes the message exactly once. That is, after two steps all nodes of $C_w^j \cap \tilde{C}$ are informed, where j is either 1 or 2 (we may assume w.l.o.g. that $j = 1$). Furthermore, we assume that these are the only nodes which are informed after the second step.

Now, we show by induction that the following holds. After $2i$ steps, the number of informed nodes $I(i)$ in $\tilde{C}$ is at least $\min\{2^{\sqrt{\log n} \cdot i/2}, n/2^{7\sqrt{\log n}}\}$, w.h.p. Furthermore, there is a partition of the set $\{C_v^{(j)} \cap \tilde{C} \mid v \in I(i), j \in \{1,2\}\}$, into the sets $E^{(j)}(i)$ and $F^{(j)}(i)$, where $E^{(j)}(i)$ are the sets $C_v^{(j)} \cap \tilde{C}$ with $|C_v^{(j)} \cap \tilde{C} \cap I(i)| = O(\log n)$, and $F^{(j)}(i)$ are the sets $C_v^{(j)} \cap \tilde{C}$ with $C_v^{(j)} \cap \tilde{C} \cap I(i) = C_v^{(j)} \cap \tilde{C}$. Roughly speaking, the sets belonging to $E^{(j)}(i)$ contain some nodes, which have just been informed in the last time step, and most of the nodes from these sets are still uninformed. If now these nodes perform push, and in the next step the nodes of the sets in $E^{(j)}(i)$ a pull, then these nodes become informed as well. Our assumption is that the number of sets $E_v^{(j)}(i)$ is $\Omega(|I(i)|/\log n)$, w.h.p. This obviously holds before the first or after the second step.

Assume that the induction hypothesis holds after step $2i$ and we are going to show that it also holds after step $2(i+1)$. Clearly, if U is some set of nodes which have the same leader address after an arbitrary but fixed subphase of the second phase, where $|U| = \Omega(2^{\sqrt{\log n}}/\log n)$, then we have $|U \cap \tilde{C}| = \Theta(|U|)$, w.h.p. (see Observation 2). On the other hand, there are at least $\Omega(n/2^{3\sqrt{\log n}})$ such sets U with $U \notin \cup_{j=1,2} F^{(j)}(i)$, w.h.p., since the largest set we can obtain has size $O(2^{3\sqrt{\log n}})$, w.h.p. (cf. Lemma 2). According to our induction hypothesis, at least $\Omega(|I(i)|/\log n)$ and at most $O(|I(i)|)$ of these sets are elements of $E^{(j)}(i)$, where $v \in I(i)$.

Clearly, a node $v \in \tilde{C} \setminus I(i)$ will be in at most one of these sets, w.h.p. Since any of these sets accomodates at least $\Theta(2^{\sqrt{\log n}}/\log n)$ nodes from $\tilde{C}$, w.h.p., the number of informed nodes increases within two steps by at least a factor of $\Theta(2^{\sqrt{\log n}}/\log^2 n) \gg 2^{\sqrt{\log n}/2}$, which leads to $|I(i+1)| \geq 2^{\sqrt{\log n} \cdot (i+1)/2}$, w.h.p.

The induction step can be performed as long as $|I(i)| \leq n/2^{7\sqrt{\log n}}$. Now we concentrate on the distribution of these nodes among the sets $U \notin \{E_v^{(j)}(i) \mid v \in I(i), j \in \{1,2\}\}$. Note that each such node belongs to two sets; one of these sets is an element of $E_v^{(j)}(i)$ for some $v \in I(i)$, while the other one is not. Since the total number of nodes in some set of $E(j)(i)$ is $O(2^{3\sqrt{\log n}})$, w.h.p., we have $|I(i+1)| = O(2^{3\sqrt{\log n}} \cdot |I(i)|) = O(n/2^{4\sqrt{\log n}})$. As argued above, there are at least $\Omega(n/2^{3\sqrt{\log n}})$ sets U with $U \notin \{F_v^{(j)}(i+1) \mid v \in I(i+1), j \in \{1,2\}\}$, w.h.p., where U is some set of nodes which have the same leader address after an arbitrary but fixed subphase of the second phase, and $|U| = \Omega(2^{\sqrt{\log n}}/\log n)$. Thus, a node $v \in (I(i+1) \setminus I(i)) \cap \tilde{C}$ is assigned to a fixed such U with probability $O(1/|I(i+1)|)$. Therefore, none of the sets $E_v^{(j)}(i+1)$ will accomodate more than $O(\log n)$ nodes from $(I(i+1) \setminus I(i)) \cap \tilde{C}$, w.h.p. [23], and the claim follows. $\square$

Now we are ready to prove our main theorem, which also compares the communication overhead of the usual push&pull algorithm of [16] to our algorithm. Note that the **bit** communication complexity of [16] w.r.t. one rumor is $O(nb \cdot \log \log n)$, w.h.p., where b is the bit length of that rumor. We should also mention here that in [16] the authors assumed that messages (so called updates in replicated databases) are frequently generated, and thus the cost of opening communication channels amortizes over the cost of sending messages through these channels. If in our scenario messages are frequently generated, then we may also assume that the cost of the pointer jumping phase is negligable compared to the cost of sending messages, and thus the communication overhead in our case would also be $O(nb \log \log n)$. In our theorem, however, we assume that one message has to be distributed, and sending the IP-address of a node through a communication channel is $O(\log n)$. Also, opening a channel without sending messages generates an $O(\log n)$ communication cost.

Theorem 1. *At the end of the JPP algorithm, all but $O(F)$ nodes are informed w.h.p., where F is the number of failed nodes as described above. The algorithm has running time $O(\sqrt{\log n})$ and produces a **bit** communication complexity of $O(n(\log^{3/2} n + b \cdot \log \log n))$, w.h.p., where b is the bit length of the message.*

Proof. At the end of the third phase, there are at least $n/2^{7\sqrt{\log n}}$ informed nodes, w.h.p. (cf. Lemma 4). Clearly, the communication overhead w.r.t. the rumor is $O(n \cdot b)$ in the third phase. Then, the median counter algorithm informs all nodes within $O(\sqrt{\log n})$ steps, w.h.p., and the number of message transmissions is $O(n \log \log n)$ [16], leading to a bit complexity of $O(nb \cdot \log \log n)$ in the fourth phase. The communication overhead w.r.t. the addresses sent by the nodes in the pointer jumping phase is upper bounded by $O(n\sqrt{\log n} \cdot \log n)$, where $\sqrt{\log n}$ stands for the number of steps in the second phase, while the $\log n$ term describes the bit size of a message (an address is some polynomial in n). $\square$

5   Discussion - Non-exact Case

As mentioned in Section 4.1, a modified version of our algorithm also works if the nodes only have an estimate of $\log n$, which is accurate up to some constant factor. In this case, we introduce some dummy sub-phases between any two phases and any sub-phases of phase 2. Now, for a node v the length of sub-phase i of phase 2 will be $\rho^{2i}c\sqrt{\log n_v}$, and between sub-phase i and $i+1$, there will be a dummy sub-phase of length $\rho^{2i+1}c\sqrt{\log n_v}$. Here n_v is the estimate of n at node v. Accordingly, the dummy sub-phase between phase 1 and 2 will have length $\rho c\sqrt{\log n_v}$, between phases 2 and 3 length $\rho^{11}c\sqrt{\log n_v}$, and between 3 and 4 length $\rho^{13}c\sqrt{\log n_v}$. The length of phase 3 will be $\rho^{12}c\sqrt{\log n_v}$, and that of phase 4 will be $\rho^{14}c\sqrt{\log n_v}$. Here ρ will be a large constant, such that $\rho^i \gg \sum_{j=0}^{i-1}\rho^j$ for any $i < 15$. Furthermore,

$$\sum_{j=0}^{i}\rho^j c\min_{v\in V}\sqrt{\log n_v} \gg \sum_{j=0}^{i-1}\rho^j c\max_{v\in V}\sqrt{\log n_v} + c\max_{v\in V}\sqrt{\log n_v},$$

where $i \in \{1,\ldots,15\}$.

The role of the dummy sub-phases is to synchronize the actions of the nodes. That is, no node will enter a phase or sub-phase before the last node leaves the previous phase or sub-phase. Accordingly, no node will leave a phase or a sub-phase, before the last node enters this phase or sub-phase. Moreover, the whole set of nodes will be together for at least $c\sqrt{\log n}$ steps in every phase or sub-phase. This ensures that all the phases and sub-phases of the algorithm will work correctly, and lead to the results we have derived in the previous section. Note that, however, the communication overhead might increase to some value $O(n(\log^{3/2} n + b\sqrt{n}))$.

References

1. Avin, C., Lotker, Z., Pignolet, Y.-A., Turkel, I.: From caesar to twitter: Structural properties of elites and rich-clubs. CoRR abs/1111.3374 (2012)
2. Censor-Hillel, K., Haeupler, B., Kelner, J., Maymounkov, P.: Global computation in a poorly connected world: Fast rumor spreading with no dependence on conductance. In: Proc. 44th ACM Symposium on Theory of Computing, pp. 961–970 (2012)
3. Chaintreau, A., Fraigniaud, P., Lebhar, E.: Opportunistic spatial gossip over mobile social networks. In: Proc. 1st Workshop on Online Social Networks, pp. 73–78 (2008)
4. Chung, F., Lu, L.: Connected components in random graphs with a given degree expected sequence. Annals of Combinatorics 6, 125–145 (2002)
5. Deb, S., Médard, M., Choute, C.: Algebraic gossip: a network coding approach to optimal multiple rumor mongering. IEEE Transactions on Information Theory 52(6), 2486–2507 (2006)
6. Demers, A., Greene, D., Hauser, C., Irish, W., Larson, J., Shenker, S., Sturgis, H., Swinehart, D., Terry, D.: Epidemic algorithms for replicated database maintenance. In: Proc. 6th Annual ACM Symposium on Principles of Distributed Computing, pp. 1–12 (1987)
7. Doerr, B., Fouz, M., Friedrich, T.: Social networks spread rumors in sublogarithmic time. In: Proc. 43rd Annual ACM Symposium on Theory of Computing, pp. 21–30 (2011)

8. Doerr, B., Friedrich, T., Sauerwald, T.: Quasirandom rumor spreading. In: Proc. 19th Annual ACM-SIAM Symposium on Discrete Algorithms, pp. 773–781 (2008)
9. Feige, U., Peleg, D., Raghavan, P., Upfal, E.: Randomized broadcast in networks. Random Struct. Algorithms 1(4), 447–460 (1990)
10. Fountoulakis, N., Panagiotou, K., Sauerwald, T.: Ultra-fast rumor spreading in social networks. In: Proc. 23rd Annual ACM-SIAM Symposium on Discrete Algorithms, pp. 1642–1660 (2012)
11. Frieze, A.M., Grimmett, G.R.: The shortest-path problem for graphs with random arc-lengths. Discrete Applied Mathematics 10(1), 57–77 (1985)
12. Giakkoupis, G.: Tight bounds for rumor spreading in graphs of a given conductance. In: 28th International Symposium on Theoretical Aspects of Computer Science, pp. 57–68 (2011)
13. Gurevich, M., Keidar, I.: Correctness of gossip-based membership under message loss. SIAM Journal on Computing 39(8), 3830–3859 (2010)
14. Haeupler, B.: Simple, fast and deterministic gossip and rumor spreading. In: Proc. 24th Annual ACM-SIAM Symposium on Discrete Algorithms, pp. 705–716 (2013)
15. Harchol-Balter, M., Leighton, T., Lewin, D.: Resource discovery in distributed networks. In: Proc. 18th Annual ACM symposium on Principles of Distributed Computing, pp. 229–237 (1999)
16. Karp, R., Schindelhauer, C., Shenker, S., Vöcking, B.: Randomized rumor spreading. In: Proc. 41st Annual Symposium on Foundations of Computer Science, pp. 565–574 (2000)
17. Kempe, D., Dobra, A., Gehrke, J.: Gossip-based computation of aggregate information. In: Proc. of the 44th Annual IEEE Symposium on Foundations of Computer Science, pp. 482–491 (2003)
18. Kempe, D., Kleinberg, J., Tardos, É.: Maximizing the spread of influence through a social network. In: Proc. 9th ACM SIGKDD International Conference on Knowledge Discovery and Data Mining, pp. 137–146 (2003)
19. Leighton, F.T.: Introduction to parallel algorithms and architectures. Morgan Kaufmann, San Francisco (1992)
20. Mahlmann, P., Schindelhauer, C.: Distributed random digraph transformations for peer-to-peer networks. In: Proc. 18th Annual ACM Symposium on Parallelism in Algorithms and Architectures, pp. 308–317 (2006)
21. Mitzenmacher, M., Upfal, E.: Probability and Computing: Randomized Algorithms and Probabilistic Analysis. Cambridge University Press, New York (2005)
22. Pittel, B.: On spreading a rumor. SIAM Journal on Applied Mathematics 47(1), 213–223 (1987)
23. Raab, M., Steger, A.: "Balls into bins" - A simple and tight analysis. In: Rolim, J.D.P., Serna, M., Luby, M. (eds.) RANDOM 1998. LNCS, vol. 1518, pp. 159–170. Springer, Heidelberg (1998)
24. Sauerwald, T.: On mixing and edge expansion properties in randomized broadcasting. Algorithmica 56(1), 51–88 (2010)

Lock-Free Data-Structure Iterators*

Erez Petrank and Shahar Timnat

Dept. of Computer Science, Technion - Israel Institute of Technology, Haifa, Israel
{erez,stimnat}@cs.technion.ac.il

Abstract. Concurrent data structures are often used with large concurrent software. An *iterator* that traverses the data structure items is a highly desirable interface that often exists for sequential data structures but is missing from (almost all) concurrent data-structure implementations. In this paper we introduce a technique for adding a linearizable wait-free iterator to a wait-free or a lock-free data structure that implements a set. We use this technique to implement an iterator for the wait-free and lock-free linked-lists and for the lock-free skip-list.

Keywords: concurrent data structures, lock-freedom, wait-freedom, linked-list, skiplist, iterator, snapshot.

1 Introduction

The rapid deployment of highly parallel machines resulted in the design and implementation of a variety of lock-free and wait-free linearizable data structures in the last fifteen years. However, almost none of these designs support operations that require global information on the data structure, such as counting the number of elements in the structure or iterating over its nodes. In general, operations such as these will be trivially enabled if snapshot operations are supported because snapshot operations enable a thread to obtain an atomic view of the structure. But creating a "consistent" or linearizable snapshot without blocking simultaneous updates to the data structure is a difficult task. The main focus of this study is to obtain such a view in a wait-free manner.

A common interface in many lock-free and wait-free data structures consists of the INSERT, DELETE and CONTAINS operations. An INSERT operation inserts an integer key (possibly associated with a value) into the data structure, if it is not already present (otherwise it just returns false). A DELETE operation removes a key from the structure, or fails (returning false) if there is no such key, and a CONTAINS operation returns true (and possibly a value associated with this key) if the key is in the list, and false otherwise. Examples of data structures implementing this interface are the lock-free linked-lists [9,8], the wait-free linked-lists [15], the lock-free skiplist [10], and search trees [6,4]. None of these structures implements an iterator.

In this work we present a design which allows the construction of wait-free, highly efficient iterators for concurrent data structures that implement sets. We use this design to implement iterators for the linked-list and skiplist. The iterator is implemented by first obtaining a consistent *snapshot* of the data structure, i.e., an atomic view of all the

---

* This work was supported by the Israeli Science Foundation grant No. 283/10.

Y. Afek (Ed.): DISC 2013, LNCS 8205, pp. 224–238, 2013.

nodes currently in it. Given this snapshot, it is easy to provide an iterator, or to count the number of nodes in the structure.

A well-known related problem is the simpler *atomic snapshot object* of shared memory [1], which has been extensively studied in the literature. An atomic snapshot object supports only two types of operations: UPDATE and SCAN. An UPDATE writes a new value to a register in the shared memory, and a SCAN returns an atomic view of all the registers.

Unfortunately, existing snapshot algorithms cannot support a (practical) data structure iterator. Three problems hinder such use. First, atomic snapshot objects are designed for pre-allocated and well-defined memory registers. Therefore, they are not applicable to concurrent data structures that tend to grow and shrink when nodes are added or removed. Second, the UPDATE operation in the classic snapshot object algorithms [1,3] requires O(n) steps (n is the number of threads), which is too high an overhead to impose on all operations that modify the data structure. Finally, many atomic snapshot objects do not support an efficient READ operation of the shared memory. This lack of support allows linearization arguments that would fail in the presence of a read. But it is hard to imagine a practical data structure that does not employ a read operation, and instead relies on obtaining a full snapshot just to read a single field in the structure.

The first problem is the least bothersome, because one could imagine borrowing ideas from snapshot objects, generalizing them, and building a snapshot algorithm for a memory space that grows and shrinks. But the other two problems are harder to eliminate. The classic algorithms for an atomic snapshot can be easily extended to support a READ operation, but they require O(n) steps for each UPDATE operation, which is too high. Later snapshot algorithms support UPDATE in O(1) steps. Examples are the coordinated collect algorithm of Riany et al. [14], later improved to the interrupting snapshots algorithm [2], and the time optimal snapshot algorithms of Fatourou and Kallimanis [7]. However, these algorithms do not support a READ operation. This lack of support seems inherent as the algorithms employ unusual linearization properties, which sometimes allow the linearization point of an UPDATE to occur before the new value has actually been written to *any* register in the memory. Thus, it is not clear how to add a READ operation that does not require a substantial overhead.

Another wait-free algorithm that supports UPDATE operations in O(1) is the algorithm of Jayanti [11]. Jayanti's algorithm does not support a read operation, and it is not trivial to add an efficient read to it, but our work builds on ideas from this algorithm. An UPDATE operation of Jayanti's algorithm first updates the memory as usual, and then checks whether a SCAN is currently being taken. If so, the update operation registers the update in a designated memory register. In this work we extend this basic idea to provide a snapshot that supports an efficient read as well as the INSERT, DELETE, and CONTAINS operations, which are more complex than the simple UPDATE operation. This facilitates the desirable iterator operation for the data structure. The simplest algorithm of Jayanti, from which we start, is described in Section 2.

Although most lock-free data structures do not provide iterators, one notable exception is the recent CTrie of Prokopec et al. [13]. This lock-free CTrie efficiently implements the creation of a snapshot, but the performance of updates deteriorates when concurrent snapshots are being taken, because each updated node must be copied, together with the path from the root to it. Another recent work presenting a concurrent data structure supporting snapshot operations is the practical concurrent binary search tree of Bronson et al. [5]. But their work uses locks, and does not provide a progress guarantee.

In this paper, we present a wait-free snapshot mechanism that implements an $O(1)$ update and read operations. We have implemented a linked-list and skiplist that employ the snapshot and iterator and measured the performance overheads. In our implementation we made an effort to make updates as fast as possible, even if iterations take a bit more time. The rational for this design is that iterations are a lot less frequent than updates in typical data structures use. It turns out that the iterator imposes an overhead of roughly 15% on the INSERT, DELETE, and CONTAINS operations when iterators are active concurrently, and roughly 5% otherwise. When compared to the ad-hoc CTrie iterator of [13], our (general) iterator demonstrates lower overhead on modifications and read operations, whereas the iteration of the data structure is faster with the ad-hoc CTrie iterator.

2   Jayanti's Single Scanner Snapshot

Let us now review Jayanti's snapshot algorithm [11] whose basic idea serves the (more complicated) construction in this paper. This basic algorithm is limited in the sense that each thread has an atomic read/write register associated with it (this variant is sometimes referred to as a single-writer snapshot, in contrast to a snapshot object that allows any thread to write to any of the shared registers). Also, it is a single scanner algorithm, meaning that it assumes only one single scanner acting at any point in time, possibly in parallel to many updaters. In [11], Jayanti extends this basic algorithm into more evolved versions of snapshot objects that support multiple writers and scanners. But it does not deal with the issue of a READ operation, which imposes the greatest difficulty for us. In this section we review the basic algorithm, and later present a snapshot algorithm that implements a read operation (as well as eliminating the single-writer and single-scanner limitations), and combines it with the INSERT, DELETE, and CONTAINS operations.

Jayanti's snapshot object supports two operations: UPDATE and SCAN. An UPDATE operation modifies the value of the specific register associated with the updater, and a SCAN operation returns an atomic view (snapshot) of all the registers. Jayanti uses two arrays of read/write registers, A[n], B[n], initialized to null, and an additional read/write binary field, which we denote *ongoingScan*. This field is initialized to false. The first array may be intuitively considered the main array with all the registers. The second array is used by threads that write during a scan to report the new values they wrote. A third array of n registers, C[n], is never read in the algorithm; it is used to store the snapshot the scanner collects. The algorithm is depicted in figure 1. When thread number k executes an UPDATE, it acts as follows. First, it writes the new value to A[k]. Second, it reads the ongoingScan boolean. If it is set to false, then the thread simply exits. If it is set to true, then the threads *reports* the new value by also writing it to B[k], and then it exits.

When the scanner wants to collect a snapshot, it first sets the ongoingScan binary field to true. Then, in the second step, it sets the value of each register in the array B to

```
A[n], B[n], C[n]: arrays of read/write          Scan()
registers initiated to Null                      1.  ongoingScan = 1
ongoingScan: a binary read/write register        2.  For i in 1..n
initiated to 0.                                   3.      B[i] = NULL
                                                  4.  For i in 1..n
                                                  5.      C[i] = A[i]
Update(tid, newValue)                             6.  ongoingScan = 0
     1.  A[tid] = newValue                        7.  For i in 1..n
     2.  If (ongoingScan==1)                       8.      If (B[i] != NULL)
     3.      B[tid]=newValue                        9.         C[i] = B[i]
                                                 10.  Array C now holds the Snapshot
```

Fig. 1. Jayanti's single scanner snapshot algorithm

null (in order to avoid leftovers from previous snapshots). Third, it reads the A registers one by one and copies them into the C array. Fourth, it sets the ongoingScan to false. This (fourth) step is the linearization point for the SCAN. At this point array C might not hold a proper snapshot yet, since the scanner might have missed some updates that happened concurrently with the reading of the A registers. To rectify this, the scanner uses the reports in array B; thus in the final step, it reads the B registers one by one, and copies any non-null value into C. After that, C holds a proper snapshot.

The linearizability correctness argument is relatively simple [11]. The main point is that any UPDATE which completes before the linearization point of the SCAN (line 6) is reflected in the snapshot (either it was read in lines 4-5 or will be read in lines 7-9), while any UPDATE that begins after the linearization point of the SCAN is not reflected in the snapshot. The remaining updates are concurrent with each other and with the scan since they were all active during the linearization point of the SCAN (line 6). This gives full flexibility to reorder them to comply with the semantics of the snapshot object ADT.

3   From Single Scanner Snapshot to Multiple Iterators

Our goal is to add an iterator to existing lock-free or wait-free data structures. We are interested in data structures that support three standard operations: INSERT, DELETE, and CONTAINS. Similarly to the scanner object, threads executing the INSERT, the DELETE, or the CONTAINS operations cooperate with a potential scanner in the following way.

– Execute the operation as usual.
– Check whether there exists a parallel ongoing scan that has not yet been linearized.
– If the check is answered positively, report the operation.

Two major complications that do not arise with a single scanner snapshot algorithm arise here: the need to report operations of other threads, and the need to support multiple concurrent iterators.

3.1   Reporting the Operations of Other Threads

The first problem stems from dependency of operations. Suppose, for example, that two INSERT operations of the same value (not currently exist in the data structure) are executed concurrently. One of these operations should succeed and the other should fail. This creates an implicit order between the two INSERTS. The successful INSERT must be linearized before the unsuccessful INSERT. In particular, we cannot let the second operation return before the linearization of the snapshot and still allow the first operation not to be visible in the snapshot. Therefore, we do not have the complete flexibility of linearizing operations according to the time they were reported, as in Section 2.

To solve this problem, we add a mechanism that allows threads, when necessary, to report operations executed by other threads. Namely, in this case, the failing INSERT operation will first report the previous successful INSERT of T_2, and only then exit. This will ensure that the required order dependence is satisfied by the order of reports. In general, threads need to report operations of other threads if: (1) the semantics of the ADT requires that the operation of the other thread be linearized before their own operation, and (2) there is a danger that the iterator will not reflect the operation of the other thread.

3.2 Supporting Multiple Iterators

In the basic snapshot algorithm described in Section 2, only a single simultaneous scanning is allowed. To construct a useful iterator, we need to support multiple simultaneous iterators. A similar extension was also presented in [11], but our extension is more complicated because the construction in [11] does not need to even support a read, whereas we support INSERT, DELETE, and CONTAINS.

In order to support multiple iterators, we can no longer use the same memory for all the snapshots. Instead, the data structure will hold a pointer to a special object denoted the *snap-collector*. The snap-collector object holds the analogue of both arrays B and C in the single scanner snapshot, meaning it will hold the "copied" data structure, and the reports required to "fix" it. The snap-collector will also hold a Boolean equivalent to `ongoingScan`, indicating whether the iteration has already been linearized.

4   The Iterator Algorithm

The pseudo-code for the iterator is depicted in Figure 2. This algorithm applies as is to the wait-free linked-list [15], the lock-free linked-list [9], and the lock-free skiplist [10].

When a thread wishes to execute an iteration over the data structure elements, it will first obtain a snapshot of the data structure. To optimize performance, we allow several concurrent threads executing an iteration to cooperate in constructing the same snapshot. For this purpose, these threads need to communicate with each other. Other threads, which might execute other concurrent operations, also need to communicate with the iterating threads and forward to them reports regarding operations which the iterating threads might have missed. This communication will be coordinated using a snap-collector object.

The snap-collector object is thus a crucial building block of the iterator algorithm. During the presentation of the iterator algorithm, we will gradually present the interface the snap-collector should support. The implementation of the snap-collector object that supports the required interface is deferred to Section 5. All snap-collector operations are implemented in a wait-free manner so that it can work with wait-free and lock-free iterator algorithms.

To integrate an iterator, the data structure holds a pointer, denoted *PSC*, to a snap-collector object. The PSC is initialized during the initialization of the structure to point to a dummy snap-collector object. When a thread begins to take a (new) snapshot of the data structure, it allocates and initializes a new snap-collector object. Then, it attempts to change the PSC to point to this object using a compare-and-swap (CAS) operation.

4.1   The Reporting Mechanism

A thread executing INSERT, DELETE or CONTAINS operation might need to report its operation to maintain linearizability, if a snapshot is being concurrently taken. It firsts executes the operation as usual. Then it checks the snap-collector object, using the later's IsActive method, to see whether a concurrent snapshot is afoot. If so, and in case forwarding a report is needed, it will use the snap-collector Report method. The initial dummy snap-collector object should always return false when the IsActive method is invoked.

There are two types of report. An *insert-report* is used to report a node has been inserted into the data structure, and a *delete-report* used to report a removal. A report consists of a pointer to a node, and an indication which type of report it is. Using a pointer to a node, instead of a copy of it, is essential for correctness (and is also space efficient). It allows an iterating thread to tell the difference between a relevant delete-report to a node it observed, and a belated delete-report to a node with the same key which was removed long ago.

Reporting a Delete Operation. It would have been both simple and elegant to allow a thread to completely execute its operation, and only then make a report if necessary. Such is the case in all of Jayanti's snapshot algorithms presented in [11]. Unfortunately, in the case of a DELETE operation, such a complete separation between the "normal" operation and the submission of the report is impossible because of operation dependence. The following example illustrates this point.

Suppose a thread S starts taking a snapshot while a certain key x, is in the data structure. Now, another thread T_1 starts the operation DELETE(x) and a third thread T_2 concurrently starts the operation CONTAINS(x). Suppose T_1 completes the operation and removes x, but the scanner missed this development because it already traversed x, and suppose that now T_1 is stalled and does not get to reporting the deletion. Now T_2 sees that there is no x in the list, and is about to return false and complete the CONTAINS(x) operation. Note that the CONTAINS operation must linearize before it completes, whereas the snapshot has not yet linearized, so the snapshot must reflect the fact that x is not in the data structure anymore. Therefore, to make the algorithm linearizable, we must let T_2 first report the deletion of x (this is similarly to the scenario discussed in Section 3.1.). However, it cannot do so: to report that a node has been deleted, a pointer to that node is required, but such a pointer is no longer available, since x has been removed.

We solve this problem by exploiting the delete mechanism of the linked-list and skiplist (and other lock-free data structures as well). As first suggested by Harris in [9], a node is deleted in two steps. First, the node is marked. A marked node is physically in the data structure, and still enables traversing threads to use it in order to traverse the list, but it is considered *logically deleted*. Second, the node is physically removed from the list. The linearization of the DELETE operation is in the first step. We will exploit this mechanism by reporting the deletion between these two steps (lines 11-13 in Figure 2).

Any thread that is about to physically remove a marked node will first report a deletion of that node (given a snapshot is concurrently being taken). This way, the report is appropriately executed *after* the linearization of the DELETE operation. Yet, if a node is no longer physically in the list, it is guaranteed to have been reported as deleted (if necessary). Turning back to the previous scenario, if T_2 sees the marked node of x, it will be able to report it. If it doesn't, then it can safely return. The deletion of x has already been reported.

Reporting an Insert Operation. After inserting a node, the thread that inserted it will report it. To deal with operation dependence, a CONTAINS method that finds a node will report it as inserted before returning, to make sure it did not return prior to the linearization of the corresponding insertion. Furthermore, an INSERT operation that fails because there is already a node N with the same key in the list will also report the insertion of node N before returning, for similar reasons.

However, there is one additional potential problem: an unnecessary report might cause the iterator to see a node that has already been deleted. Consider the following scenario. Thread T_1 starts INSERT(3). It successfully inserts the node, but get stalled before checking whether it should report it (between lines 22 and 23). Now thread T_2 starts a DELETE(3) operation. It marks the node, checks to see whether there is an ongoing iteration, and since there isn't, continues without reporting and physically removes the node. Now thread S starts an ITERATION, announces it is scanning the structure, and starts scanning it. T_1 regains control, checks to see whether a report is necessary, and reports the insertion of the 3. The report is of course unnecessary, since the node was inserted before S started scanning the structure, but T_1 does not know that. T_2 did see in time that no report is necessary, and that is why it did not report the deletion. The trouble is that, since the deletion is not reported, reporting the insertion is not only unnecessary, but also harmful.

We solve this problem by exploiting again the fact that a node is marked prior to its deletion. An insertion will be reported in the following manner (lines 31-35).

- Read PSC, and record a private pointer to the snap-collector object, SC.
- Check whether there is an ongoing iteration, by calling SC.IsActive().
- If not, return. If there is, check whether the node you are about to report is marked.
- If it is, return without reporting. If it is not marked, then report it.

The above scheme solves the problem of harmfully reporting an insertion. If the node was unmarked after the relevant ITERATION has already started, then a later delete operation that still takes place before the linearization of the iteration will see that it must report the node as deleted. There is, however, no danger of omitting a necessary report; if a node has been deleted, there is no need to report its insertion. If the delete occurred before the linearization of the iteration, then the iteration does not include the node. If the delete occurred after the linearization of the iteration, then the insert must be present after the linearization of the iteration as well (since it had a chance to see the node is marked), and therefore it is possible to set the linearization of the insertion after the iteration as well.

4.2 Performing an Iteration

A thread that desires to perform an ITERATION first reads the PSC pointer and checks whether the previous iteration has already been linearized by calling the IsActive method (line 53). If the previous iteration has already been linearized, then it cannot use the same snapshot, and it will allocate a new snap-collector. After allocating it, it will attempt to make the global PSC pointer point to it using a CAS (line 56). Even if the CAS fails, the thread can continue by taking the new value pointed by the PSC pointer, because the linearization point of the new snap-collector is known not to have occurred before the thread started its ITERATION operation. Therefore, this CAS doesn't interfere with wait-freedom, because the thread can continue even if the CAS fails.

A snapshot of the data structure is essentially the set of nodes present in it. The iterating thread scans the data structure, and uses the snap-collector to add a pointer to each node it sees along the way (lines 62-68), as long as this node is not marked as logically deleted. The iterating thread calls the AddNode method of the snap-collector for this purpose.

When the iterating thread finishes going over all the nodes, it is time to linearize the snapshot (and iteration). It calls the Deactivate method in the snap-collector for this purpose (this is similar to setting ongoingScan to zero in Jayanti's algorithm). Afterwards, further calls to the IsActive method will return false. An INSERT, DELETE, or CONTAINS operation that will start after the deactivation will not report to this snap-collector object. If a new ITERATION starts, it is no longer able to use this snap-collector, and so it allocates a new one.

To ensure proper linearization in the presence of multiple iterating threads, some further synchronization is required between them. A subtle implied constraint is that all threads that iterate concurrently and use the same snap collector object must decide on the same snapshot view. This is needed, because the linearization point of operations that occur concurrently with the closure of the snapshot picture is determined by whether they appear in the snapshot or not. So if an operation appears in the snapshot view of one thread but not in a snapshot view of another, then the linearization argument fails.

To assure the snapshot is consistent for all threads we enforce the following. First, before a thread calls the Deactivate method, it calls the BlockFurtherNodes (line 66). The snap-collector ensures that after a call of BlockFurtherNodes returns, further invocations of AddNode cannot install a new pointer, or have any other effect. Second, before the first iterating thread starts putting together the snapshot according to the collected nodes and reports, it blocks any further reports from being added to the snap-collector. This is achieved by invoking the BlockFurtherReports method (line 69). From this point on, the snap-collector is in a read-only mode.

Next, the iterating thread assembles the snapshot from the nodes and reports stored in the snap-collector. It reads them using the `ReadPointers` and `ReadReports` methods. A node is in the snapshot iff: 1) it is among the nodes added to the snap-collector OR there is a report indicating its insertion AND 2) there is no report indicating its deletion.

Calculating the snapshot according to these rules can be done efficiently if the nodes and reports in the snap-collector are sorted first. As explained in Section 5.1, the snap-collector is optimized so that it holds the nodes sorted throughout the execution, and thus sorting them requires no additional cost. The reports, however, still need to be sorted. Finally, once the iterating thread assembled the snapshot, it can trivially perform an iteration, by simply going over the nodes present in the snapshot one after the other. Thus, the overall complexity of an ITERATION is O(#nodes + #reports*log(#reports)).

5   The Snap-Collector Object

One can think of the snap-collector object as holding a list of node pointers and a list of reports. The term *install* refers to the act of adding something to these lists. Thus, the snap-collector enables the iterating threads to install pointers, and the modifying threads to install reports. It supports concurrent operations, and it must be wait-free since it is designed as a building block for wait-free and lock-free algorithms. The semantics and interface of the snapshot object follow. To relate the new algorithm to the basic one, we also mention for each method (*in italics*), its analogue in the single scanner snapshot. *Tid* is short for Thread Identifier.

- NewSnapCollector(). *No equivalent.* Allocates a new snap-collector object.
- AddNode(Node* node, int tid). *Analogue to copying a register into array C.* Installs a pointer to the given node. May fail to install the pointer if the BlockFurtherPointers() method (see below) has previously been invoked.
- Report(Report* report, int tid). *Analogue to reporting a new value in array B.* Installs the given report. May fail to install the report if the BlockFurtherReports() method (see below) has previously been invoked.
- IsActive(). *Analogue to reading the ongoingScan binary field.* Returns true if the Deactivate() method has not yet been called, and false otherwise. (True means the iteration is still ongoing and further pointers might still be installed in the snapshot object.)
- BlockFurtherPointers(). *No analogue. Required to synchronize between multiple iterators.* After this method is completed, any further calls to AddNode will do nothing. Calls to AddNode concurrent with BlockFurtherPointers may fail or succeed arbitrarily.
- Deactivate(). *Analogue to setting ongoingScan to false.* After this method is complete, any call to IsActive returns false, whereas before this method is invoked for the first time, IsActive returns true.
- BlockFurtherReports(). *No analogue. Required to synchronize between multiple iterators.* After this method is completed, any further calls to Report will do nothing. Calls to Report concurrent with BlockFurtherReports may succeed or fail arbitrarily.

General: The data structure will hold an additional field, PSC, which is a pointer to a snap-collector object.	37. Contains(int key)
1. Initialize()	38. search for a node n with the key
2. Initialize the data structure as usual	39. if not found then return false
3. PSC = (address of) NewSnapCollector()	41. else if n is marked
4. PSC->Deactivate()	42. ReportDelete(pointer to n)
5.	43. return false
6. Delete(int key)	44. else ReportInsert(pointer to n)
7. search for a node with required key	45. return true
8. if not found	
9. return false	46. TakeSnapshot()
10. else // found a victim node with the key	47. SC = AcquireSnapCollector()
11. mark the victim node	48. CollectSnapshot(SC)
12. ReportDelete(pointer to victim)	49. ReconstructUsingReports(SC)
13. physically remove the victim node	50.
14. return true	51. AcquireSnapCollector()
15.	52. SC = (dereference) PSC
16. Insert(Node n)	53. if (SC.IsActive())
17. search for the place to insert the node n as usual, but before removing a marked node, first call ReportDelete()	54. return SC
	55. newSC = NewSnapCollector()
	56. CAS(PSC, SC, newSC)
18. If n.key is already present in the data data structure on a different node h	57. newSC = (dereference) PSC
	58. return newSC
19. ReportInsert(pointer to h)	59.
20. return false	60. CollectSnapshot(SC)
21. else	61. Node curr = head of structure
22. Insert n into the data structure	62. While (SC.IsActive())
23. ReportInsert(pointer to n)	63. if (curr is not marked)
24. return true	64. SC.AddNode(pointer to curr)
25.	65. if (curr.next is null) // curr is the last
26. ReportDelete(Node *victim)	66. SC.BlockFurtherNodes()
27. SC = (dereference) PSC	67. SC.Deactivate()
28. If (SC.IsActive())	68. curr = curr.next
29. SC.Report(victim, DELETED)	69. SC.BlockFurtherReports()
30.	70.
31. ReportInsert(Node* newNode)	71. ReconstructUsingReports(SC)
32. SC = (dereference) PSC	72. nodes = SC.ReadPointers()
33. if (SC.IsActive())	73. reports = SC.ReadReports()
34. if (newNode is not marked)	74. a node N belong to the snapshot iff:
35. Report(newNode, INSERTED)	75. ((N has a reference in nodes OR N has an INSERTED report) AND (N does not have a DELETED report)
36.	

Fig. 2. The Iterator

- ReadPointers(). *No analogue*. Returns a list of all the pointers installed in the snapshot object. Should be called only after BlockFurtherPointers is completed by some thread.
- ReadReports(). *No analogue*. Returns a list of all the reports installed in the snapshot object. Should be called only after BlockFurtherReports is called by some thread.

5.1   The Snap-Collector Implementation

The implementation of the snap-collector object is orthogonal to the iterator algorithm, but different implementations can affect its performance dramatically. This section briefly explains the particulars of the implementation used in this work.

The proposed implementation of the snap-collector object maintains a separate linked-list of reports for each thread. It also maintains a single linked-list of pointers to the nodes of the data structure, and one boolean field indicating whether it is currently active (not yet linearized).

IsActive, Deactivate.   The IsActive method is implemented simply by reading the boolean field. The Deactivate method simply writes false to this field.

AddReport.   When a thread needs to add a report using the AddReport method, it adds it to the end of its local linked-list dedicated to this thread's reports. Due to the locality of this list its implementation is fast, which is important since it is used also by threads that are not attempting to iterate over the data structure. Thus, it facilitates low overhead for threads that only update the data structure.

Although no other thread may add a report to the thread local linked- list, a report is still added via a CAS, and not a simple write. This is to allow the iterating threads to block further reports in the BlockFurtherReports method. However, when a thread adds a report, it does not need to check whether the CAS succeeded. Each thread might only fail once in adding a report for every new iteration. After failing such a CAS, it will hold that the IsActive method will already return false for this iteration and therefore the thread will not even try to add another report.

BlockFurtherReports.   This method goes over all the threads local linked-lists of reports, and attempts by a CAS to add a special dummy report at the end of each to block further addition of reports. This method should only be invoked after the execution of the Deactivate method is completed. The success of this CAS need not be checked. If the CAS succeeds, no further reports can be added to this list, because a thread will never add a report after a dummy. If the CAS fails, then either another iterating thread has added a dummy, or a report has just been added. The first case guarantees blocking further repots, but even in the latter case, no further reports can now be added to this list, because the thread that just added this report will see that the snap-collector is inactive and will not attempt to add another report.

AddNode.   The basic idea in the implementation of AddNode is to use the lock-free queue of Michael and Scott [12]. To install a pointer to a node, a thread reads the tail pointer. If the tail node is last, it attempts to add its node after the last node and then fix the tail to point to the newly added node. If the tail node is not the last node, i.e., its next field hold to a non-null node, then the thread tries by a CAS to change the tail to point to the next node (similarly to [12]), and retries adding its node again.

Clearly, this implementation is not wait-free as the thread may repeatedly fail to add its node and make progress. We therefore use a simple optimization that slightly alters the semantics of the AddNode method. To this end, we note that nodes should be added to the snapshot view in an ascending order of keys. The AddNode method will (intentionally) fail to add any node whose key is smaller than or equal to the key of the last node added to the snap-collector. When such a failure happens, AddNode returns a pointer to the data structure node that was last added to the snap-collector view of the snapshot. This way, an iterating thread that joins in after a lot of pointers have already been installed, simply jumps to the current location. This also reduces the number of pointers in the snap-collector object to reflect only the view of a single sequential traverse, avoiding unnecessary duplications. But most importantly, it allows wait-freedom.

The snap-collector object still holds a tail pointer to the queue (which might at times point to the node before last). To enqueue a pointer to a node that holds the key k, a thread reads the tail pointer. If the tail node holds a key greater than or equal to k, it doesn't add the node and simply returns the tail node. If the tail node is not the last node, i.e., its next field hold to a non-null node, then this means that there is another thread that has just inserted a new node to the snapshot view. In this case, this new node is either the same node we are trying to add or a larger one. So in this case the thread tries by a CAS to change the tail to point to the next node (similarly to [12]), and then it returns the new tail, again without adding the new node.

This optimization serves three purposes: it allows new iterating threads to jumps to the current location; It makes the AddNode method fast and wait-free; and it keeps the list of pointers to nodes sorted by their keys, which then allows a simple iteration over the keys in the snapshot.

BlockFurtherNodes. This method sets the tail pointer of the nodes list to point to a special dummy with a key set to the maximum value and the node set to null. Combined with our special implementation of AddNode, further calls to AddNode will then read the tail's special maximum value and will not be able to add additional nodes.

ReadPointers, ReadReports. These methods simply return a list with the pointers / reports stored in the snap-collector. They are normally called only after the BlockFurtherNodes, Deactivate, and BlockFurtherReports methods have all been completed, thus the lists of pointers and reports in the snap-collector are immutable at this point.

5.2   Some Simple Optimizations

The implementation used for the performance measurements also includes the following two simple optimizations.

Elimination of many of the reports. An additional binary field was added to each node, initialized to zero. When a thread successfully inserts a node, and after reporting it if necessary, this binary field is set to 1. Future INSERT operations that fail due to this node, and future CONTAINS operations that successfully find this node, first check to see if this bit is set. If so, then they know that this node has been reported, and therefore, there is no need to report the node's insertion.

If a large portion of the operations are CONTAINS operations, as is the case in typical data structure usage, this optimization avoids a significant portion of the reports. This is because in such cases most of the reports are the result of successful CONTAINS operations. However, note that this optimization is not always recommended, as it adds overhead to the INSERT operations even if ITERATION is never actually called.

Avoidance of repeated sorting. After a single thread has finished sorting the reports, it posts a pointer to a sorted list of the reports, and saves the time it would take other threads to sort them as well, if they haven't yet started to do so.

6 Performance

In this section we report the performance of the proposed iterator, integrated with the lock-free linked-list and skiplist in Java. We used the linked-list implementation as included in the book "The Art of Multiprocessor Programming" by Herlihy and Shavit [10], and added to it the iterator mechanism described in this paper. For the skiplist, we used the Java code of ConcurrentSkipListMap by Doug Lea, and added our mechanism. We also measured the performance of the CTrie, which is the only other lock-free data structure with comparable semantics that supports ITERATION. The CTrie is included in the Scala 2.10.0 distribution, and we used this implementation to measure its performance.

All the tests were run on SUN's Java SE Runtime, version 1.6.0, on a system that features 4 AMD Opteron(TM) 6272 2.1GHz processors. Each processor has 8 cores (32 cores overall), and each core runs 2 hyper-threads (i.e., 64 concurrent threads overall). The system employs a memory of 128GB and an L2 cache of 2MB per processor.

The algorithms were tested on a micro-benchmark in which one thread repeatedly executes ITERATION operations, going over the nodes one by one continually. For the other threads, 50% of the operations are CONTAINS, 25% are INSERT, and 25% are DELETE, with the number of threads varying between 1-31. In each test the keys for each operation were randomly and uniformly chosen in the ranges $[1, 32]$, $[1, 128]$, or $[1, 1024]$. In each test, all the threads were run concurrently for 2 seconds. All the tests were run in one long execution. The different data structures were run alternately: for a specific test-case parameters (i.e., the number of threads and the key range) first the linked-list was run for a 2 seconds interval, then the CTrie, and then the skiplist. After a single 2 seconds interval run of each data structure, the next test-case was run for all the three. After all the test-cases were completed once, a second iteration of the tests was initiated. The execution consisted of overall 16 such iterations; however, the first iteration was omitted from the results, and only served to allow the JVM the time to warm up. The averages of the other 15 iterations are reported in the figures.

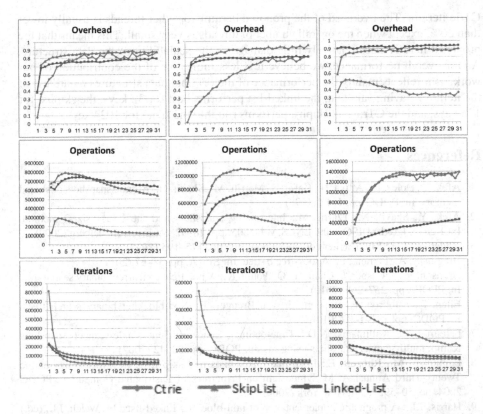

Fig. 3. Results for 32 possible keys (left) 128 possible keys (middle) 1024 possible keys (right)

For each key range, we present three different graphs. In the first graph, we measure the number of operations executed as a fraction of the number of operations executed without the additional iterating thread. For example, for a range of keys $[1, 32]$, for 16 threads, the number of operations executed while an additional thread is continually iterating the nodes is 86% of the number of operations executed by 16 threads in the skiplist data structure that *does not support iteration* at all. Thus, this graph presents the cost of adding the support for an iterator, and having a single thread continually iterate over the structure. For the CTrie, there is no available lock-free implementation that does not support iteration at all, so we simply report the number of operations as a fraction of the number of operations executed when there is no additional concurrent thread iterating over the structure. In the second graph, we report the absolute number of INSERT, DELETE, and CONTAINS operations executed in the different data structures while a single thread was iterating, and in the third graph we report the number of ITERATION operations that the single thread completed. This last measure stands for the efficiency of the iterator itself.

The results appear in Figure 3. In general, the results show that the iterator proposed in this paper has a small overhead on the other threads (which execute INSERT, DELETE and CONTAINS), and in particular, much smaller than the overhead imposed by the

CTrie iterator. The overhead of the proposed iterator for other threads is usually lower than 20%, except when the overall number of threads is very small. This means that the proposed iterator does relatively little damage to the scalability of the data structure. As for overall performance, we believe it is less indicative of the contribution of our work, as it reflects mainly the performance of the original data structures regardless of the iterator. Having said that, the linked-list performs best for 32 keys, the skiplist for 128 keys, and the CTrie and skiplist performs roughly the same for 1024 keys.

References

1. Afek, Y., Dolev, D., Attiya, H., Gafni, E., Merritt, M., Shavit, N.: Atomic snapshots of shared memory. In: PODC, pp. 1–13 (1990)
2. Afek, Y., Shavit, N., Tzafrir, M.: Interrupting snapshots and the java™ size() method. In: Keidar, I. (ed.) DISC 2009. LNCS, vol. 5805, pp. 78–92. Springer, Heidelberg (2009)
3. Anderson, J.H.: Multi-writer composite registers, pp. 175–195 (1994)
4. Braginsky, A., Petrank, E.: A lock-free b+tree. In: SPAA, pp. 58–67 (2012)
5. Bronson, N.G., Casper, J., Chafi, H., Olukotun, K.: A practical concurrent binary search tree. In: PPOPP, pp. 257–268 (2010)
6. Ellen, F., Fatourou, P., Ruppert, E., van Breugel, F.: Non-blocking binary search trees. In: PODC, pp. 131–140 (2010)
7. Fatourou, P., Kallimanis, N.D.: Time-optimal, space-efficient single-scanner snapshots & multi-scanner snapshots using cas. In: PODC, pp. 33–42 (2007)
8. Fomitchev, M., Ruppert, E.: Lock-free linked lists and skip lists. In: Proceedings of the Twenty-Third Annual ACM Symposium on Principles of Distributed Computing, PODC 2004, pp. 50–59. ACM, New York (2004)
9. Harris, T.L.: A pragmatic implementation of non-blocking linked-lists. In: Welch, J.L. (ed.) DISC 2001. LNCS, vol. 2180, pp. 300–314. Springer, Heidelberg (2001)
10. Herlihy, M., Shavit, N.: The Art of Multiprocessor Programming. Morgan Kaufmann (2008)
11. Jayanti, P.: An optimal multi-writer snapshot algorithm. In: STOC, pp. 723–732 (2005)
12. Michael, M.M., Scott, M.L.: Simple, fast, and practical non-blocking and blocking concurrent queue algorithms. In: Proc. ACM Symposium on Principles of Distributed Computing (PODC), pp. 267–275 (1996)
13. Prokopec, A., Bronson, N.G., Bagwell, P., Odersky, M.: Concurrent tries with efficient non-blocking snapshots. In: PPOPP, pp. 151–160 (2012)
14. Riany, Y., Shavit, N., Touitou, D., Touitou, D.: Towards a practical snapshot algorithm. In: ISTCS, pp. 121–129 (1995)
15. Timnat, S., Braginsky, A., Kogan, A., Petrank, E.: Wait-free linked-lists. In: PPOPP, pp. 309–310 (2012)

Practical Non-blocking Unordered Lists

Kunlong Zhang[1], Yujiao Zhao[1], Yajun Yang[1], Yujie Liu[2], and Michael Spear[2]

[1] Tianjin University
{zhangkl,zyj0131,yangyajun}@tju.edu.cn
[2] Lehigh University
{yul510,spear}@cse.lehigh.edu

Abstract. This paper introduces new lock-free and wait-free unordered linked list algorithms. The composition of these algorithms according to the fast-path-slow-path methodology, a recently devised approach to creating fast wait-free data structures, is nontrivial, suggesting limitations to the applicability of the fast-path-slow-path methodology. The list algorithms introduced in this paper are shown to scale well across a variety of benchmarks, making them suitable for use both as standalone lists, and as the foundation for wait-free stacks and non-resizable hash tables.

1 Introduction

Linked lists are fundamental data structures that are widely used both on their own and as building blocks for other data structures. While a sequential linked list is easy to implement, concurrent linked lists that achieve both strong progress guarantees and good performance are challenging to design [3,7–9,16,19,22,24]. Herlihy [10] demonstrated the existence of universal constructions for wait-free concurrent objects, yet it remains an open problem whether all such objects can be made practical: wait-free data structures implemented from universal constructions [4,6,11] tend to incur significant overhead, increased time and space complexity, and/or static bounds on the size of the data structure. Although many lock-free concurrent implementations [5,12,20,21] have been proposed for sequential data structures, practical wait-free versions are relatively rare [14,23].

We introduce the first practical implementation of an unordered linked list that supports *wait-free* insert, remove, and lookup operations. The implementation is linearizable [13] and uses only a single-word compare-and-swap (CAS) primitive. Furthermore, the implementation does not require marking the lower bits of pointers [8]. Our implementation is built from a novel lock-free unordered list algorithm, where each insert and remove operation first linearizes by appending an intermediate "request" node at the head of the list, followed by a lazy search phase that computes the return value of the operation (which depends on whether the key value is already in the set); lookup operations have no side-effects on the shared memory. The implementation achieves scalable wait-freedom by adapting a technique originally designed for wait-free queues [14], and to further improve performance, we applied a recently-devised fast-path-slow-path methodology [15] to construct adaptive variants of our algorithm.

In this paper, we introduce the first practical wait-free unordered linked list, which is immediately usable in applications as-is, and can be employed in the creation of

Y. Afek (Ed.): DISC 2013, LNCS 8205, pp. 239–253, 2013.
© Springer-Verlag Berlin Heidelberg 2013

wait-free non-resizable hash tables and stacks. [1] We discuss our experience and find-ings in applying the fast-path-slow-path methodology, identifying both strengths and limitations of the approach. In Section 2, we present background and related work. In Section 3 we present a lock-free unordered list algorithm that serves as the basis for the wait-free algorithm discussed in Section 4. We evaluate performance in Section 5. Section 6 concludes with guidelines for using the fast-path-slow-path methodology.

2   Related Work

The first lock-free list to require only atomic compare-and-swap (CAS) operations was developed by Valois [24], who employed a technique in which auxiliary nodes en-coded in-progress operations. Harris [8] implemented a lock-free ordered list by using a pointer marking technique, in which a node is logically deleted by marking the least significant bit of its next pointer; the node is then physically removed from the list in a separate phase. Michael [16] improved memory reclamation in the Harris algorithm us-ing hazard pointers [17]. Heller et al. [9] designed a lock-based linked list with wait-free lookup operations. Their wait-free technique can also be incorporated into the Harris-Michael algorithm to improve performance. Kogan and Petrank [14] proposed a wait-free queue implementation and a more efficient variant based on the fast-path-slow-path methodology [15] which composes the slower wait-free algorithm with a faster lock-free implementation [18]. Timnat et al. [23] designed a wait-free ordered linked list based on the fast-path-slow-path methodology, using the Harris-Michael algorithm as its fast path.

Subsequent efforts have contributed to our general understanding of lock-free list implementations, but have neither improved progress guarantees nor delivered supe-rior performance to that attainable by combining the Harris, Michael, and Heller tech-niques. Fomitchev and Ruppert [7] presented a lock-free list with worst-case linear amortized cost. Attiya and Hillel [1] presented a lock-free doubly-linked list that relies on a double-compare-and-swap (DCAS) operation. Sundell and Tsigas [22] presented a lock-free doubly-linked list using only CAS. Braginsky and Petrank [2] presented the first lock-free unrolled linked list.

Herlihy [10, 11] presented the first universal construction to convert sequential ob-jects to wait-free concurrent implementations. Fatourou and Kallimanis [6] provided a universal construction that can be used to implement highly efficient stacks and queues.

3   A Lock-Free Unordered List

We now present a lock-free unordered list algorithm, which serves as the basis for our wait-free implementation. The algorithm implements a set object, where the elements can be compared using an equality operator ($=$), even if they can not be totally ordered.

The list supports three operations: INSERT(k) attempts to insert value k into the set and returns true (success) if k was not present in the set, and returns false otherwise. REMOVE(k) returns true if it successfully removes value k from the set and returns false if k does not exist in the set. CONTAINS(k) indicates whether k is contained by the set.

---

[1] Presentation of these algorithms is included in a companion technical report [25].

```
datatype NODE
  key    : ℕ      // integer data field
  state  : ℕ      // INS, REM, DAT, or INV
  next   : NODE   // pointer to the successor
  prev   : NODE   // pointer to the predecessor
  tid    : ℕ      // thread id of the creater

global variables
  head   : NODE   // initially nil

 1  function INSERT(k : ℕ) : 𝔹
 2    h ← new NODE⟨k, INS, nil, nil, threadid⟩
 3    ENLIST(h)

 4    b ← HELPINSERT(h, k)
 5    if ¬CAS(&h.state, INS, (b? DAT : INV)) then
 6      HELPREMOVE(h, k)
 7      h.state ← INV
 8    return b

 9  function REMOVE(k : ℕ) : 𝔹
10    h ← new NODE⟨k, REM, nil, nil, threadid⟩
11    ENLIST(h)

12    b ← HELPREMOVE(h, k)
13    h.state ← INV
14    return b

15  function CONTAINS(k : ℕ) : 𝔹
16    curr ← head
17    while curr ≠ nil do
18      if curr.key = k then
19        s ← curr.state
20        if s ≠ INV then
21          return (s = INS) ∨ (s = DAT)

22      curr ← curr.next
23    return false

24  procedure ENLIST(h : NODE)
25    while true do
26      old ← head
27      h.next ← old
28      if CAS(&head, old, h) then
29        return
```

```
30  function HELPINSERT(h : NODE, k : ℕ) : 𝔹
31    pred ← h
32    curr ← pred.next

33    while curr ≠ nil do
34      s ← curr.state
35      if s = INV then
36        succ ← curr.next
37        pred.next ← succ
38        curr ← succ

39      else if curr.key ≠ k then
40        pred ← curr
41        curr ← curr.next

42      else if s = REM then
43        return true

44      else if (s = INS) ∨ (s = DAT) then
45        return false

46    return true

47  function HELPREMOVE(h : NODE, k : ℕ) : 𝔹
48    pred ← h
49    curr ← pred.next

50    while curr ≠ nil do
51      s ← curr.state
52      if s = INV then
53        succ ← curr.next
54        pred.next ← succ
55        curr ← succ

56      else if curr.key ≠ k then
57        pred ← curr
58        curr ← curr.next

59      else if s = REM then
60        return false

61      else if s = INS then
62        if CAS(&curr.state, INS, REM) then
63          return true

64      else if s = DAT then
65        curr.state ← INV
66        return true

67    return false
```

Fig. 1. A Lock-free Unordered List

3.1 Overview

Figure 1 presents the basic algorithm. The list is comprised of NODE objects, where each NODE stores a key value, a $next$ pointer to the successor node, and a $state$ field for coordinating concurrent operations. The $prev$ and tid fields are reserved for the wait-free algorithm (Section 4). We maintain a global pointer $head$ that points to the first element of the list. Elements are always inserted at the head position.

The key insight of the algorithm is to maintain a refinement mapping function that maps a linked list object (starting from node h) to an abstract set object AbsSet(h):

$$
\text{AbsSet}(h) \equiv \begin{cases} \emptyset & \text{if } h = \textbf{nil} \\ \text{AbsSet}(h.next) & \text{if } h.state = INV \\ \text{AbsSet}(h.next) \cup \{h.key\} & \text{if } h.state = INS \vee h.state = DAT \\ \text{AbsSet}(h.next) \setminus \{h.key\} & \text{if } h.state = REM \end{cases}
$$

To maintain this property, an INSERT or REMOVE operation first places a node with an intermediate state (*INS* or *REM*) at the head of the list. Then it searches the list for the value being inserted or removed, removing logically deleted nodes along the way. Finally, it sets the intermediate node to a final state (*DAT* or *INV*).

In more detail, an INSERT operation allocates an *INS* node (h) and links it to the head of the list by invoking ENLIST (lines 2 - 3). It then invokes HELPINSERT (line 4) to determine whether the insertion is effective, that is, to check whether the key is already present in the set. The return value of HELPINSERT dictates the return value of the INSERT operation, as well as the final state of h (line 5): if the key was absent from the set, $h.state$ is set to *DAT*, and the insertion becomes effective; otherwise, $h.state$ is set to *INV*, indicating that the insertion failed due to the key already being present in the set, and h becomes a garbage node that will be physically removed by some subsequent operation. The update of $h.state$ must use a CAS instruction (line 5), since a concurrent REMOVE that deletes the same key may attempt to change $h.state$ concurrently. If the CAS fails, it means the key was deleted concurrently and the thread will invoke HELPREMOVE (lines 6 - 7) to help the deleting thread to clean up the list.

Similarly, a REMOVE operation starts by inserting a *REM* node at the head position (lines 10 - 11). The real work of removal is delegated to the HELPREMOVE operation (line 12), which traverses the list to delete the specified key and returns a boolean value indicating whether the key was found (and deleted). Then node h is set to the *INV* state (line 13), allowing some subsequent operation to remove it from the list.

The CONTAINS operation has no side effect on shared memory (it is read-only). The operation traverses the list to find the specified key and skips any *INV* nodes (lines 18 - 20). If a non-*INV* node with the specified key is encountered, the operation returns true (found) if the node is in state *DAT* or *INS* (line 21). Otherwise, the node is in *REM* state, which represents a REMOVE operation that can be thought of as having already deleted the key from the suffix of the list, and hence, the CONTAINS operation immediately returns false.

3.2 ENLIST Operation

Both INSERT and REMOVE use the ENLIST operation to insert a node at the head position. In the lock-free algorithm, ENLIST repeatedly performs a CAS operation (line 28), attempting to change *head* to point to h, until the CAS succeeds. However, this approach fails to provide *wait-freedom*: since the CAS operation at line 28 of a specific thread may fail repeatedly, for an unbounded number of times (due to contention), the thread may starve in the ENLIST operation and make no progress. In Section 4, we introduce a wait-free ENLIST implementation, and show the algorithm can be made wait-free without any change to the other parts.

3.3 Coordination Protocol

The core protocol of coordinating concurrency is encapsulated by the HELPINSERT and HELPREMOVE operations. The two operations share a similar code structure: each takes a pointer parameter h, which points to the node inserted by the prior ENLIST operation. In both operations, the thread traverses the list starting from h, and reacts to the different types of nodes it encounters.

As a common obligation of both operations, logically deleted nodes are purged during the traversal (lines 35 - 38 and lines 52 - 55). That is, once an *INV* node is encountered (pointed to by $curr$), the node is physically removed from the list by setting the predecessor's next pointer to the successor of $curr$. Note that since new nodes cannot be added to the list at any point other than the head, the problems that plague node removal in sorted lists do not apply. In particular, it is not possible that removing one node can inadvertently lead to a new arrival disappearing from the list. While it is possible for a removed node to re-appear in the list on account of conflicting writes to the next pointer, such a node will necessarily already be marked *INV*, and thus there will be no impact on the correctness of the list.

During the traversal, the $curr$ node is skipped if $curr.key \neq h.key$ (lines 39 - 41 and 56 - 58). Otherwise, we say the $curr$ node is a "related node" with respect to the current operation. There are three possibilities if $curr$ is a related node: $curr$ is a *DAT* node, an *INS* node, or a *REM* node. In the latter two cases, the related node was created by some concurrent INSERT or REMOVE operation. We call such operations "related operations".

In HELPINSERT, if a related *REM* node is encountered, there is a concurrent REMOVE operation finalizing a removal of the same key. Hence, the HELPINSERT returns true (success) immediately (lines 42 - 43), since the concurrent REMOVE operation ensures that the key is absent in the set. Otherwise (lines 44 - 45), if the related node is an *INS* node, then the related INSERT operation inserted the same key earlier (or is determining that the key already exists in the list) and the HELPINSERT operation must return false. Finally, if the related node is a *DAT* node, HELPINSERT returns false since the key already exists in the set.

In HELPREMOVE, if a related *REM* node is found (lines 59 - 60), the operation returns false immediately since the key was already deleted by a concurrent REMOVE operation. If the related node is an *INS* node (lines 61 - 63), then the key was inserted by a concurrent INSERT operation. In this case, the thread attempts to change the node from *INS* to *REM* (line 62); a CAS instruction is needed to prevent data races on the *state* field (i.e., line 5). In the last case, the related node is a *DAT* node, meaning that the key is in the set, and the node is deleted by setting its *state* to *INV* (line 65).

3.4 Lock-Freedom

To show that the algorithm is lock-free, we show that *some* operation completes when any thread executes a bounded number of local steps. We first notice that the ENLIST operation is lock-free: a thread's CAS at line 28 may fail only due to another thread performing a CAS and completing its ENLIST operation. Since ENLIST is invoked exactly once in each INSERT and REMOVE, for n threads, at least one list operation will complete if some thread fails the CAS for n times in its ENLIST operation.

To show that every HELPINSERT and HELPREMOVE operation terminates, it is sufficient to show the list is acyclic. There are three places where the *next* pointer of a node is changed: executing line 27 cannot form a cycle, since the node h is newly allocated and is not reachable from any other node; when a thread executes line 37 or line 54, *pred* is clearly always a predecessor of *succ* in some total order R, which can be defined as the order in which nodes are inserted to the list (by the CAS at line 28).

Since the size of the list is bounded by E, the total number of completed ENLIST operations, every HELPINSERT and HELPREMOVE operation finishes in $O(E)$ steps. Note that in HELPREMOVE, a thread never executes the CAS at line 62 twice on the same node: if the CAS failed, the *curr* node is turned into a final state (*DAT* or *INV*) and will cause the loop to exit or skip the node in the next iteration. Thus, for n threads, either a thread completes its own list operation in $O(n + E)$ local steps, or some other thread completes a list operation during this period of time.

3.5 Linearizability

Due to space constraints, a complete proof of linearizability is provided in a companion technical report [25]. We define the linearization point for each operation: An INSERT(k) or REMOVE(k) operation linearizes at the successful CAS at line 28 in ENLIST. A CONTAINS(k) linearizes at line 16 if $k \notin$ AbsSet(*head*) when p executes this line. In cases where $k \in$ AbsSet(*head*) when p executes this line, the CONTAINS(k) linearizes at line 16 if the operation returns true. If the operation returns false, we show that there exists a concurrent REMOVE(k) that linearizes after p executes line 16 and before p's CONTAINS(k) returns. We let p's CONTAINS(k) linearize *immediately after* the linearization point of this REMOVE(k). Note that multiple CONTAINS(k) operations may be required to linearize after the same REMOVE(k) operation, and any two of these CONTAINS(k) operations can be ordered arbitrarily.

4 Achieving Wait-Freedom

The major challenge of the wait-free list algorithm lies in the implementation of a wait-free ENLIST operation. In this section, we present a wait-free ENLIST implementation adapted from a wait-free enqueue technique introduced by Kogan and Petrank [14]. We also introduce an adaptive wait-free algorithm which allows applications to trade off between average latency and worst-case latency of operations.

4.1 Wait-Free ENLIST Implementation

The enqueue technique introduced by Kogan and Petrank [14] provides a wait-free approach to append nodes at the tail of a list, but it is not immediately available as a solution to the ENLIST problem where nodes are appended at the head position. We employ *prev* fields to solve this problem. The additional code for implementing a wait-free ENLIST is presented in Figure 2.

```
datatype DESC
    phase    : N       // integer phase number
    pending  : B       // whether operation is pending
    node     : NODE    // pointer to the enqueueing node

global variables
    head     : NODE
    dummy    : NODE
    counter  : N
    status   : DESC[THREADS]

initially
    head ← new NODE⟨-1, REM, nil, nil, -1⟩
    dummy ← new NODE⟨-, -, -, -, -⟩
    counter ← 0
    foreach d in status do
        d ← new DESC⟨-1, false, nil⟩

68  procedure ENLIST(h : NODE)
69    phase ← F&I(&counter)
70    status[threadid] ← new DESC⟨phase, true, h⟩
71    for tid ← 0 ... (THREADS - 1) do
72        HELPENLIST(tid, phase)
73    HELPFINISH()

74  function ISPENDING(tid : N, phase : N) : B
75    d ← status[tid]
76    return d.pending ∧ (d.phase ≤ phase)
```

```
77  procedure HELPENLIST(tid : N, phase : N)
78    while ISPENDING(tid, phase) do
79        curr ← head
80        pred ← curr.prev
81        if curr = head then
82            if pred = nil then
83                if ISPENDING(tid, phase) then
84                    n ← status[tid].node
85                    if CAS(&curr.prev, nil, n) then
86                        HELPFINISH()
87                        return
88            else
89                HELPFINISH()

90  procedure HELPFINISH()
91    curr ← head
92    pred ← curr.prev
93    if (pred ≠ nil) ∧ (pred ≠ dummy) then
94        tid ← pred.tid
95        d ← status[tid]
96        if (curr = head) ∧ (pred = d.node) then
97            d' ← new DESC⟨d.phase, false, d.node⟩
98            CAS(&status[tid], d, d')
99            pred.next ← curr
100           CAS(&head, curr, pred)
101           curr.prev ← dummy
```

Fig. 2. A Wait-free ENLIST Implementation

The basic idea of the wait-free ENLIST algorithm is to let different ENLIST operations help each other to complete. The helping mechanism must ensure that every ENLIST operation reaches the response point in bounded number of steps (wait-freedom). This requires every thread to announce its intention by creating a descriptor entry in a *status* array before starting an operation. During its operation, the thread must visit each entry in the status array, helping other threads to make progress. To prevent starvation, each operation is assigned a *phase* number from a strictly increasing counter, and an operation only helps those with smaller phase numbers.

The wait-free ENLIST operation goes through six steps, as depicted in Figure 3:

(a) The thread first announces its operation by creating a descriptor entry in its slot (indexed by its thread id) in the *status* array (line 70). The descriptor contains the *phase* number of the operation, a boolean *pending* field that indicates whether the operation is incomplete, and a pointer to the enlisting node. Once the descriptor is announced, the subsequent steps can be performed by the thread itself or by some helper thread.

(b) The thread finds the node pointed to by *head*, and attempts to change its *prev* field to the enlisting node h by a CAS instruction (line 85).

(c) The thread sets the *pending* flag of the operation descriptor to false by installing a new descriptor (line 98); this prevents concurrent helpers from retrying after the node is enlisted.

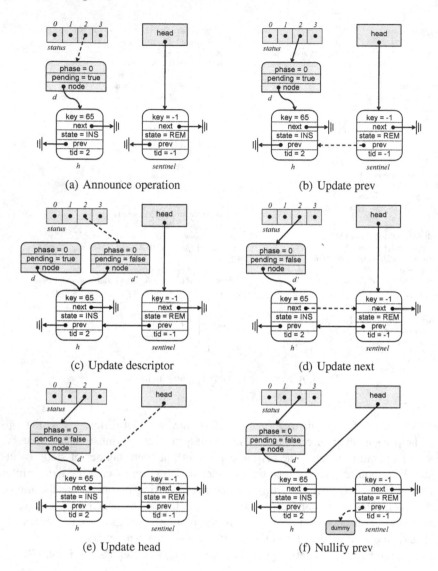

Fig. 3. Wait-free ENLIST Implementation Extended from the Kogan-Petrank Algorithm

(d) The thread sets $h.next$ to point to the original head node (line 99), which is the linearization point of the ENLIST operation. The ordering of this step is important with respect to steps (b) and (e). That is, the update of $h.next$ must be ordered after $head.prev$ is set to h, since the correct successor of h is "unknown" until then. On the other hand, $h.next$ must be updated before $head$ is changed to h, since otherwise a concurrent CONTAINS operation may start traversing from h and erroneously end by discovering $h.next$ is **nil**.

(e) The thread fixes $head$ by changing it to h using a CAS (line 100).

(f) Finally, the thread clears the *prev* field of the original head by setting it to a *dummy* state (line 101). This is necessary for allowing the garbage collector to recycle deleted nodes. Since the *prev* pointers are installed by the wait-free ENLIST implementation, and the lock-free algorithm is unaware of their existence, keeping the *prev* pointers prevents the garbage collector from reclaiming a node even if the node is considered "unreachable" by the lock-free algorithm. It is worth noting that we must invalidate the *prev* pointer by setting it to a *dummy* state instead of **nil**, since the latter would admit ABA problems for the CAS instruction (line 85). Once the *prev* field of a node is set to *dummy*, it never changes.

4.2   An Adaptive Algorithm

Although the wait-free algorithm provides an upper bound on the steps required to complete an operation in the worst case, it imposes overhead in the common cases when contention is low. We employed the "fast-path-slow-path" methodology [15] to construct an adaptive algorithm that performs competitively in the common case while retaining the wait-free guarantee.

In the adaptive algorithm, a thread starts by executing a fast path version of the ENLIST operation, and falls back to the wait-free slow path if the fast path fails too many times (bounded by constant F). To prevent a thread from repeatedly taking the fast path while another thread starves, every thread checks the global status array after completing D operations, and performs helping if necessary. As shown in [15], for n threads, the adaptive algorithm ensures that every ENLIST operation completes in $O(F + D \cdot n^2)$ local steps. The F and D parameters can be adjusted to balance between the worst-case and common-case latency of operations.

It is worth noting that the fast path ENLIST of the adaptive algorithm is *not* equivalent to the lock-free ENLIST implementation in Figure 1. Instead, the fast path algorithm resembles the wait-free protocol, but excluding the announcing and helping steps.

5   Performance Evaluation

We evaluate performance of the lock-free and wait-free list algorithms via a set of microbenchmarks. These experiments allow us to vary the ratio of INSERT, REMOVE and CONTAINS operations, the range of key values, and the initial size of the list. We compare the following list-based set algorithms:

HarrisAMR: Implementation of the Harris-Michael algorithm [16] which also incorporates the wait-free CONTAINS technique introduced in [9]. The implementation uses Java `AtomicMarkableReference` objects to atomically mark deleted nodes.

HarrisRTTI: Optimized implementation of HarrisAMR in which Java run-time type information (RTTI) is used in place of `AtomicMarkableReference`. This is the best-known lock-free list implementation.

LazyList: Lock-based optimistic list implementation proposed by Heller et al [9].

LFList: The lock-free unordered list algorithm discussed in Section 3.

	Harris	LazyList	LFList	WFList	Adaptive
INSERT Cost	1 CAS	2 CAS	2 CAS	4 CAS + 1 F&I	3 CAS
REMOVE Cost	2 CAS	2 CAS	1 CAS	3 CAS + 1 F&I	2 CAS
Traverse Distance	$\frac{1}{2}k$		$(1 - \frac{\alpha}{2})k$		

Fig. 4. Update Cost and Average Traversal Distance (in uncontended cases)

WFList: The basic wait-free unordered list algorithm discussed in Section 4.

Adaptive: The adaptive wait-free unordered list algorithm discussed in Section 4.2.

FastPath: The fast-path portion of the Adaptive algorithm from Section 4.2.

In all implementations (except "HarrisAMR"), we use Java "FieldUpdaters" to perform CAS instructions on object fields. This approach provides better performance than simply using atomic fields (i.e. `AtomicInteger` and `AtomicReference`), which require expensive heap allocation cost and extra indirection overhead.

Experiments were conducted on an HP z600 machine with 6GB RAM and a 2.66GHz Intel Xeon X5650 processor with 6 cores (12 total threads) running Linux kernel 2.6.37 and OpenJDK 1.6.0. Each data point is the median of five 5-second trials. Variance was always below 5%.

5.1 Expected Overheads

Figure 4 enumerates the expected overheads of each of the algorithms. The cost of a successful list operation is affected by the update cost and the traversal cost. We measure the cost of an update operation (INSERT or REMOVE) by the number of atomic instructions required in the uncontended case. Compared to the Harris algorithm, LFList uses an extra CAS instruction in INSERT and one less in the REMOVE operation. The WFList requires 2 more CAS instructions to provide wait-freedom, though this cost is reduced in the Adaptive algorithm by leveraging the lock-free fast path.

The traversal cost is the average number of nodes that must be accessed. Suppose the list contains k elements uniformly selected from range $[0...M)$ and let $k = \alpha M$ ($0 \leq \alpha \leq 1$). The average traversal distance for searching a random key value in an ordered list is: $D_o = \frac{1}{2}k$. In unordered lists, the average traversal distance is averaged among successful and unsuccessful search operations: $D_u = \alpha \cdot \frac{1}{2}k + (1 - \alpha)k = (1 - \frac{\alpha}{2})k$. This suggests that ordered lists have an increasing advantage over unordered lists when the set is sparse. For instance, when $\alpha = \frac{1}{2}$ (half of key space is in the set), the average traversal distance in an unordered list is 50% longer than its ordered permutation. Note too that in the ordered lists, an unsuccessful insert/remove does not perform a CAS, whereas every insert/remove in the unordered list performs a CAS.

5.2 x86 Performance

In Figures 5–7, we assess the performance of the lists for a variety of workloads. The "L" parameter indicates the percentage of operations that are lookups, with the

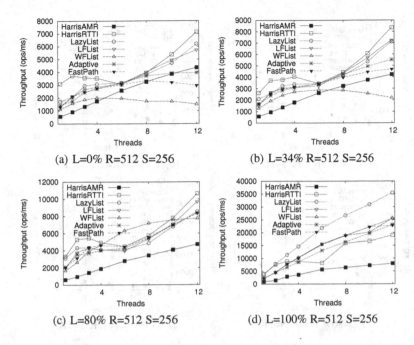

(a) L=0% R=512 S=256   (b) L=34% R=512 S=256

(c) L=80% R=512 S=256   (d) L=100% R=512 S=256

Fig. 5. Microbenchmark - Short Lists (L: Lookup Ratio, R: Key Range, S: List Size)

remainder evenly split between inserts and removals. "R" indicates the key range, and "S" indicates the average size of the list. In every case, the list is pre-populated with a random selection of S unique elements in the range [0, R). These elements are chosen at random, without replacement. Thus in the unordered lists, they will not be ordered.

The x86 processor features an aggressive pipeline, a deep cache hierarchy, and low-latency CAS operations. On this platform, the cost of write-write sharing is high, and thus both the wait-free enlistment mechanism and conflicting CAS operations on the head of the list are potential scalability bottlenecks. Nonetheless, our lock-free and wait-free algorithms scale well in all but a few cases. Indeed, the difference in performance appears to be much more a consequence of the increased traversal distance in the unordered algorithm than a consequence of increased cache misses due to frequent updates to the head of the list.

The most immediate and consistent finding is that the Harris list without RTTI optimizations has substantially higher latency and worse scalability than all other algorithms. We include this result as a reminder that concurrent data structures must be implemented using state-of-the-art techniques. Merely showing improved performance relative to the canonical Harris list presented in [12] does not give any indication of real-world performance. In particular, we caution that a direct comparison between our list and the wait-free ordered list [23] is not possible until that list is redesigned to use these modern optimizations.

We also see that long-running and read-only operations significantly reduce the cost of wait-free enlistment. When lists are small and updates are frequent, the enlistment

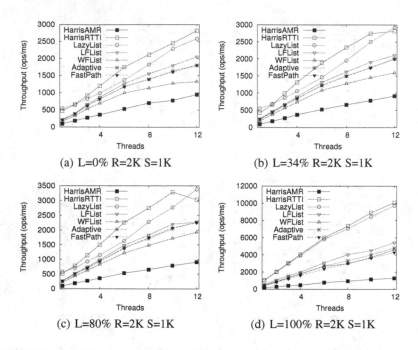

Fig. 6. Microbenchmark - Medium Lists (L: Lookup Ratio, R: Key Range, S: List Size)

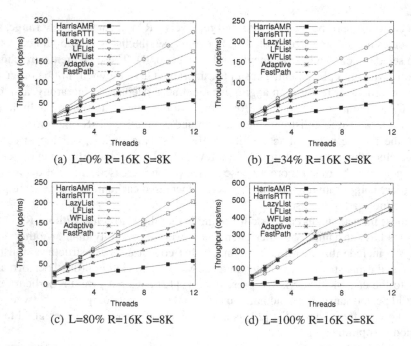

Fig. 7. Microbenchmark - Long Lists (L: Lookup Ratio, R: Key Range, S: List Size)

table and counter themselves become a bottleneck. Otherwise, the adaptive algorithm and its FastPath component are nearly identical.

The FastPath lock-free list is always a constant factor slower than the lock-free unordered list, but the Adaptive algorithm remains close to FastPath. This finding confirms Kogan and Petrank's claim [15] that the fast-path-slow-path technique can provide worst-case wait-freedom with lock-free performance. Furthermore, since the average operation in our list accesses many locations, contention on the head node of the list, while significant, does not dominate. Thus we observed that even for small thresholds, the adaptive algorithm rarely fell back to wait-free mode. However, it is important to observe that the lock-free FastPath algorithm itself is slower than our best lock-free unordered list. We shall return to this point in Section 6.

6   Discussion and Future Work

In their paper introducing the fast-path-slow-path methodology, Kogan and Petrank state that "...each operation is built from a fast path and a slow path, where the former is a version of a lock-free implementation of that operation, and the latter is a version of a wait-free implementation. Both implementations are customized to cooperate with each other [15, Sec. 3]."

Given a lock-free algorithm L, the question then is how to apply the methodology to produce a wait-free algorithm that does not sacrifice performance. We will consider L as consisting of three phases: a prefix (instructions that occur before the linearization point), a CAS operation (the linearization point), and a suffix (clean-up operations that follow the linearization point). Considering the three existing fast-path-slow-path algorithms (this work, ordered lists [23], and queues [15]), we see a pattern emerge.

First, a correct wait-free algorithm W must be constructed. This entails adding an announcement operation and operation descriptors to L. However, this step introduces the possibility of helping in the prefix, and thus makes it possible for helping operations to race (particularly if there are stores to memory that would not be shared in L). To correct these races, extra fields must be added to nodes of the data structure, stores must be upgraded to CAS instructions, and these CAS instructions must be sequenced by performing intermediate updates (via CAS) to a descriptor after each prefix step. It appears that changes to the suffix of the operation are not required, since the suffix is either clean-up operations that already support helping (e.g., the second CAS in the M&S queue [18]), or else operations that do not affect data structure invariants (e.g., the list traversal in HELPINSERT).

The second step is to perform a reduction that yields a lock-free algorithm L' that remains compatible with W. The first step of the reduction is to elide the announce operation and descriptor updates in L'. Then W must be analyzed, step-by-step, and simplified in an ad-hoc manner. In the ideal case, the result is the original lock-free algorithm L. Currently, it appears that the ideal case only occurs when the prefix is empty and the linearization point is the first CAS. Otherwise (as is the case in our list and the ordered list [23]), L' will need additional CAS instructions (relative to L) to keep its prefix compatible with the prefix of W.

Nonetheless, the ability to create low-latency wait-free data structures is valuable, particularly data structures as fundamental as linked lists. To emphasize the significance of our wait-free unordered list, note that our list can be extended to support a REMOVEHEAD operation. Such an operation would resemble our REMOVE operation, but using a wildcard as its key value, and would immediately yield a wait-free stack. In contrast to stacks, constructing wait-free resizable hash tables based on our lists will be nontrivial. One challenge is that the shared descriptor array may become a bottleneck; were it not for resizing, each bucket could have its own descriptor array. However, the unordered nature may simplify other aspects of the design, for example, easing the implementation of list merging/splitting since the resulting lists need not be sorted.

Acknowledgements. We would like to thank Tim Harris, Alex Kogan, Victor Luchangco and our anonymous reviewers for their helpful suggestions during the preparation of our final manuscript.

References

1. Attiya, H., Hillel, E.: Built-In Coloring for Highly-Concurrent Doubly-Linked Lists. In: Dolev, S. (ed.) DISC 2006. LNCS, vol. 4167, pp. 31–45. Springer, Heidelberg (2006)
2. Braginsky, A., Petrank, E.: Locality-Conscious Lock-Free Linked Lists. In: Proceedings of the 12th International Conference on Distributed Computing and Networking, Bangalore, India (January 2011)
3. Colvin, R., Groves, L., Luchangco, V., Moir, M.: Formal verification of a lazy concurrent list-based set algorithm. In: Ball, T., Jones, R.B. (eds.) CAV 2006. LNCS, vol. 4144, pp. 475–488. Springer, Heidelberg (2006)
4. Ellen, F., Fatourou, P., Kosmas, E., Milani, A., Travers, C.: Universal Constructions that Ensure Disjoint-Access Parallelism and Wait-Freedom. In: Proceedings of the 2012 ACM Symposium on Principles of Distributed Computing (July 2012)
5. Ellen, F., Fatourou, P., Ruppert, E., van Breugel, F.: Non-blocking Binary Search Trees. In: Proceedings of the 29th ACM Symposium on Principles of Distributed Computing, Zurich, Switzerland (July 2010)
6. Fatourou, P., Kallimanis, N.D.: A Highly-Efficient Wait-Free Universal Construction. In: Proceedings of the 23rd ACM Symposium on Parallelism in Algorithms and Architectures, San Jose, CA (June 2011)
7. Fomitchev, M., Ruppert, E.: Lock-Free Linked Lists and Skip Lists. In: Proceedings of the 23rd ACM Symposium on Principles of Distributed Computing, St. John's, Newfoundland, Canada (July 2004)
8. Harris, T.L.: A Pragmatic Implementation of Non-Blocking Linked Lists. In: Welch, J.L. (ed.) DISC 2001. LNCS, vol. 2180, pp. 300–314. Springer, Heidelberg (2001)
9. Heller, S., Herlihy, M.P., Luchangco, V., Moir, M., Scherer III, W.N., Shavit, N.N.: A Lazy Concurrent List-Based Set Algorithm. In: Anderson, J.H., Prencipe, G., Wattenhofer, R. (eds.) OPODIS 2005. LNCS, vol. 3974, pp. 3–16. Springer, Heidelberg (2006)
10. Herlihy, M.: Wait-Free Synchronization. ACM Transactions on Programming Languages and Systems 13(1), 124–149 (1991)
11. Herlihy, M.: A Methodology for Implementing Highly Concurrent Data Objects. ACM Transactions on Programming Languages and Systems 15(5), 745–770 (1993)
12. Herlihy, M., Shavit, N.: The Art of Multiprocessor Programming. Morgan Kaufmann (2008)
13. Herlihy, M.P., Wing, J.M.: Linearizability: A Correctness Condition for Concurrent Objects. ACM Transactions on Programming Languages and Systems 12(3), 463–492 (1990)

14. Kogan, A., Petrank, E.: Wait-Free Queues with Multiple Enqueuers and Dequeuers. In: Proceedings of the 16th ACM Symposium on Principles and Practice of Parallel Programming, San Antonio, TX (February 2011)
15. Kogan, A., Petrank, E.: A Methodology for Creating Fast Wait-Free Data Structures. In: Proceedings of the 16th ACM Symposium on Principles and Practice of Parallel Programming, New Orleans, LA (February 2012)
16. Michael, M.: High Performance Dynamic Lock-Free Hash Tables and List-Based Sets. In: Proceedings of the 14th ACM Symposium on Parallel Algorithms and Architectures, Winnipeg, Manitoba, Canada (August 2002)
17. Michael, M.: Hazard Pointers: Safe Memory Reclamation for Lock-Free Objects. IEEE Transactions on Parallel and Distributed Systems 15(6), 491–504 (2004)
18. Michael, M.M., Scott, M.L.: Simple, Fast, and Practical Non-Blocking and Blocking Concurrent Queue Algorithms. In: Proceedings of the 15th ACM Symposium on Principles of Distributed Computing (May 1996)
19. O'Hearn, P.W., Rinetzky, N., Vechev, M.T., Yahav, E., Yorsh, G.: Verifying Linearizability with Hindsight. In: Proceedings of the 29th ACM Symposium on Principles of Distributed Computing, Zurich, Switzerland (July 2010)
20. Prokopec, A., Bronson, N., Bagwell, P., Odersky, M.: Concurrent Tries with Efficient Non-Blocking Snapshots. In: Proceedings of the 17th ACM Symposium on Principles and Practice of Parallel Programming (February 2012)
21. Sundell, H., Tsigas, P.: Fast and Lock-Free Concurrent Priority Queues for Multi-Thread Systems. Journal of Parallel and Distributed Computing 65, 609–627 (2005)
22. Sundell, H., Tsigas, P.: Lock-Free Deques and Doubly Linked Lists. Journal of Parallel and Distributed Computing 68(7) (July 2008)
23. Timnat, S., Braginsky, A., Kogan, A., Petrank, E.: Wait-Free Linked-Lists. In: Baldoni, R., Flocchini, P., Binoy, R. (eds.) OPODIS 2012. LNCS, vol. 7702, pp. 330–344. Springer, Heidelberg (2012)
24. Valois, J.: Lock-free linked lists using compare-and-swap. In: Proceedings of the Fourteenth Annual ACM Symposium on Principles of Distributed Computing, Ottawa, Ontario, Canada (August 1995)
25. Zhang, K., Zhao, Y., Yang, Y., Liu, Y., Spear, M.: Practical Non-blocking Unordered Lists. Technical Report LU-CSE-13-003, Lehigh University (2013)

Atomic Snapshots in $O(\log^3 n)$ Steps Using Randomized Helping

James Aspnes[1] and Keren Censor-Hillel[2]

[1] Yale University, Department of Computer Science
aspnes@cs.yale.edu
[2] Department of Computer Science, Technion
ckeren@cs.technion.ac.il

Abstract. A randomized construction of unbounded snapshots objects from atomic registers is given. The cost of each snapshot operation is $O(\log^3 n)$ atomic register steps with high probability, where n is the number of processes, even against an adaptive adversary. This is an exponential improvement on the linear cost of the previous best known unrestricted snapshot construction [7,8] and on the linear lower bound for deterministic constructions [9], and does not require limiting the number of updates as in previous sublinear constructions [4]. One of the main ingredients in the construction is a novel *randomized helping* technique that allows out-of-date processes to obtain up-to-date information without running into covering lower bounds.

1 Introduction

An **atomic snapshot** object allows processes to obtain the entire contents of a shared array as an atomic operation. The first known wait-free implementations of snapshot from atomic registers [1,2,6] required $\Theta(n^2)$ steps to carry out a snapshot with n processes; subsequent work [7,8] reduced this cost to $O(n)$, which was shown to be optimal in the worst case for non-blocking deterministic algorithms by Jayanti *et al.* [9].

Limitations of the Jayanti *et al.* lower bound became apparent with the development of wait-free sublinear-complexity **limited-use** variants of objects to which the lower bound applied. These included deterministic implementations of **max registers** (which, when read, return the largest value written to them) and **counters** [3], and even snapshot objects [4], all with individual step complexity polylogarithmic in the number of operations applied to them.[1] These objects still have linear cost in the worst case, but the worst case is reached only after exponentially many operations.

---

[1] In the case of snapshot, this requires both registers large enough to hold a complete snapshot and the cooperation of updaters. The assumption of large registers may be avoidable for some applications of snapshot where only summary information is needed.

Y. Afek (Ed.): DISC 2013, LNCS 8205, pp. 254–268, 2013.

The dependence on the number of operations was shown to be necessary initially for max registers [3], and later for a variety of objects satisfying a perturbability condition similar to that used in the Jayanti *et al.* lower bound [5]. Curiously, for randomized implementations these lower bounds were not larger than $O(\log n)$ for any number of processes. This appeared to be a weakness of the particular proof technique used to obtain the randomized lower bounds.

We show that it is not the case that other techniques may produce larger lower bounds. Using a new randomized helping procedure along with a simple approximate max register implementation, it is possible to accelerate the max register implementation of [3] so that every operation finishes in $O(\log n)$ steps with high probability, regardless of the number of previous operations, provided the max register value does not change too quickly. Applying the same techniques to the **max array** of [4] (a pair of max registers supporting an atomic snapshot operation) yields a max array with $O(\log^2 n)$ step complexity with high probability, under the same restriction. This can be used in the snapshot implementation of [4] to obtain atomic snapshots with $O(\log^3 n)$ step complexity with high probability. Because the use of the max array within the atomic snapshot satisfies the restriction on changes in value, the complexity of the snapshot implementation holds without restrictions. The end result is a polylogarithmic snapshot implementation in which the cost of each operation does not depend on the number of operations but only on the number of processes.

1.1 Previous Constructions

Before giving more detail on our construction, we give a quick review of the previous work on which it is based. The basic building block of the bounded snapshot construction in [4] is a 2-component max array. This object supports a write operation, which specifes a value and a component, and a read operation, which returns a pair of the maximal values written to the two components in all write operation linearized before it. To directly build an unbounded snapshot object we need an unbounded version of a max register, and an unbounded version of a 2-component max array.

The max register construction of [3] is based on a tree of *switches*, which are one-bit registers that initially hold the value 0 and can only be set to 1. Each leaf represents a value for the register. A write operation sets the switches on the path toward the respective leaf, while a read operation follows the rightmost path of set switches to get the largest value written. The problem with an unbounded max register according to this construction is that the length of an operation reading the rightmost path in the infinite tree construction is unbounded. This is because this operation is searching for the first node on the rightmost path whose switch is 0, and the depth of this node depends on the values that have been written, which are now unbounded. Even worse, such an operation is not guaranteed to be wait-free, as it might not terminate if new writes keep coming in with greater values, forcing it to continue moving down the tree to the right. To handle this, the tree is backstopped with a linear snapshot object that is used for larger values in order to bound the number of steps. Formally, this means that at some threshold level, the node on the rightmost path of switches no longer points to an infinite subtree of switches but rather to a single linear-time snapshot object, and all write operations set the switch at this node after writing their value to the snapshot object, and all read operations accessing this node continue by reading the snapshot object. In total, this gives a complexity of $O(\min(\log v, n))$ steps per operation that reads or writes the value v.

The max array construction of [4] builds upon the above max register construction by combining the trees of the two components in a subtle manner. The data structure consists of a main tree, corresponding to the tree of the first component. The tree of the second component is embedded in the main tree at *every* node. That is, each switch of the main tree is associated with a separate copy of the tree of the second component. Writing to the first component is done by writing to the main tree, ignoring the copies of the second component at the switches. Writing to the second component is done by writing to the copy associated with the root of the main tree. The coordination between the pairs of values is left for the read operations. Such an operation travels the main tree in order to read the value of the first component, while dragging along the maximal value it reads for the second component along its path. It is proven in [4] that this implementation gives a linearizable 2-component max array.

1.2   Our Contributions

Our first contribution is an $O(\log n)$ construction of an unbounded max register, which overcomes the obstacle of the construction of [3] by combining a new **approximate max-register** with a novel technique of **randomized helping**. In essence, this technique allows an operation that is traveling down the tree to the right (we refer to the rightmost path of the tree as the **spine** of the tree) for too long to jump farther ahead to a point on the spine that is the correct one, that is, the first point on the spine for which the switch is unset. This is done by adopting a location in the spine used by another operation, with the challenge of making sure that this value is **fresh**—recent enough that the first operation can use it without violating linearizability. The only condition we place on the usage of the max register in order for this to work is that operations write values that are not increasing too fast. We need this condition in order to argue that once the operation found the correct node on the spine, it can safely continue to the left subtree without the worry that a new write operation is now writing a much larger value that is placed farther down the spine. While at first glance this might seem as a strong restriction, this is actually a very reasonable condition in applications that use max registers, and in particular it is satisfied by our implementation of an unbounded snapshot object.

Our second contribution is a 2-component max array that is unbounded, and whose cost per operation does not depend on the number of operations. The natural thing to try is embedding the unbounded max register construction in the 2-component max array construction of [4]. However, this does not work directly, since the main insight there is that values of the second component need to be propagated down while traveling the tree of the first component in order to guarantee that returned pairs are comparable. This cannot be done within our randomized helping technique because operations may jump down the spine without accessing each node along the way. We address this problem by restructuring the 2-component max array implementation such that operations that go right on the spine re-read the value of the second component that is located at the root. The main observation here is that a single re-reading of the root is inexpensive, and that we do not care that this information skips the nodes between the root and the target node since the second component of these nodes will never be accessed again (because their switches are either set or skipped).

Plugging these two contributions into the snapshot implementation of [4] gives an implementation of an unbounded snapshot object with an $O(\log^3 n)$ step complexity (with high probability) for updating or scanning the object.

2   Unbounded Max Registers with Bounded Increments

A **max register** [3] supports operations WriteMax(v) and ReadMax(), where WriteMax(v) writes the value v to the max register and ReadMax() returns the largest value previously written. The purpose of a max register is typically to avoid lost updates, by ensuring that old values (tagged with smaller timestamps) cannot obscure newer values, regardless of the order in which they are written. In this section, we show how to construct an unbounded max register that is linearizable in all executions and wait-free with $O(\log n)$ step complexity with high probability in executions with bounded increments.

2.1   Bounded Max Registers

We begin by reviewing the max register implementation of Aspnes et al. [3]. The idea is to implement the register as a fixed binary tree of one-bit atomic registers, referred to as **switch** bits. Initially these bits are all 0, which is interpreted as pointing to the left child of the register, while a 1 points to the right child. Each value of the max register corresponds to a leaf of the tree (which does not get a register). A ReadMax operation follows the path determined by the values of the switch bits until it reaches a leaf; the number of leaves to the left of this leaf (its **rank**) gives the return value. (See Algorithm 1.)

An unbalanced tree backed by a linear-time snapshot implementation gives a cost of $O(\min(\log v, n))$ for an operation that read or writes the value v. Aspnes et al. [3] show that $O(\min(\log v, n))$ is optimal for deterministic obstruction-free max register implementations from atomic registers. For randomized implementations, they show a weaker lower bound of $O(\log n / \log \log n)$ steps for n-bounded max registers. This lower bound is obtained as a trade-off between the complexities of ReadMax and WriteMax operations.

We will show that with randomization, the dependence on v can be eliminated. It is possible to build a snapshot object (and thus a max register), whose cost is polylogarithmic in n with high probability for all operations, regardless of the size of the values it contains.

```
1  Shared data:
2  switch: a single bit multi-writer register, initially 0
3  left: a MaxRegister_m object, where m = ⌈k/2⌉, initially 0,
4  right: a MaxRegister_{k-m} object, initially 0
5
6  procedure WriteMax(r, v)
7  │   if v < m then
8  │   │   if r.switch = 0 then
9  │   │   └   WriteMax(r.left, v)
10 │   else
11 │   │   WriteMax(r.right, v - m)
12 │   └   r.switch ← 1
13
14 procedure ReadMax(r)
15 │   if r.switch = 0 then
16 │   │   return ReadMax(r.left)
17 │   else
18 │   └   return ReadMax(r.right) + m
```

Algorithm 1. Implementation of WriteMax(r, v) and ReadMax(r) for a MaxRegister$_k$ object called r

2.2   An Unbounded Max Register Implementation

We now show how to extend the results of [3] to allow an unbounded max register that nonetheless has fixed cost per operation with high probability. The first step is to bound the cost of WriteMax operations. We will do this under the assumption of k-**bounded increments**, which we will define by the rule that each new WriteMax operation writes a value v that is at most k more than the largest input to any previously initiated WriteMax operation.[2] This assumption will be justified later by the details of our unbounded snapshot construction.

As in a standard max register, the core of our unbounded max register is a binary tree of switch bits. But now the tree is infinite, consisting of an infinite **spine** forming the rightmost path through the tree, each node of which has an m-valued max register (implemented as a balanced $⌈\log m⌉$-depth tree), where m is an integer that will be chosen later, rooted at its left child (see Figure 1). Using this tree with the original algorithm, a WriteMax(v) operation must walk all the way from the root of the tree to the corresponding leaf, which will be found in the $⌈v/m⌉$-th m-valued max register. It must then walk back up to the root, setting switch bits as needed, giving a cost of $O(v/m + \log m)$.

In our algorithm, we assume that the tree is packed in memory so that a WriteMax(v) operation can access the root of the $⌈v/m⌉$-th max register directly. Within this subtree, it executes the standard algorithm; but along the spine, it sets only as many switch bits as are needed to guarantee that all ancestors are set;

---

[2] Note that we do not require that this previous WriteMax operation finished.

this is checked by performing an embedded ReadMax operation. This optimization does not affect correctness, because setting switches that are already set farther up the spine has no effect. What it does give is an improvement to the step complexity under the assumption of k-bounded increments, since between the n processes v can have increased by at most kn above the value of the last complete WriteMax, meaning that only kn/m steps up the spine are needed.

Setting aside for the moment the cost of the ReadMax, this gives a cost for the WriteMax of $O(\log m)$ for updating the m-valued max register plus $O(kn/m)$ for updating the segment of the spine. We will later choose k and m in a way for which the above results in $O(\log n)$ steps per WriteMax operation. Note that assuming bounded increments, this procedure gives this complexity for WriteMax operations without dependence on the value being written and that this implementation is deterministic. However, the ReadMax operations still suffer from the problem mentioned earlier: they are not wait-free in the presence of concurrent WriteMax operations with increasing values. For this we add an additional mechanism of randomized helping. Algorithm 2 is a pseudo-code of our implementation, where WrapWriteMax$_i$ and WrapReadMax$_i$ are the operations for process i, which invoke WriteMax and ReadMax operations as in [3] on the m-values max registers (in which the process id does not matter).

We now provide a high-level description of the helping mechanism. Each WriteMax operation is wrapped with a WrapWriteMax$_i$ procedure, as follows. WrapWriteMax$_i$ operations by process i cycle over the PIDs, helping one process at a time. The operation then reads the *timestamp*, TS[s], associated with the current helped process, s, written to TS[s] by a WrapReadMax$_s$ operation. It then reads the value v' of the max register, and if the value v it needs to write is larger than v' it goes ahead and writes it into the max register. It then records the maximum between v and v' into a helping array, along with the timestamp it saw for s, and updates a random location in a pointer array with its pid. A WrapReadMax$_i$ operation first increments its timestamp and then takes a certain amount of steps reading the max register. If it does not finish within that number of steps, it tries to get help from a random process chosen from a random location in the pointer array. Getting help is done by checking whether the chosen helping process, j, holds the current timestamp of process i, performing the WrapReadMax$_i$ operation, and if so, taking its value from its helping array.

The idea behind the proof is that if a ReadMax operation takes too many steps trying to read the max register without finishing, it must be that there are many concurrent WriteMax operations that keep sending it down the spine. But in such a case, the WrapReadMax$_i$ operation finds a value in one of the helping arrays that it may use, in the sense that it was updated by one of these concurrent WrapWriteMax$_j$ operations – specifically, after the WrapReadMax$_i$ operation started.

Next, we proceed with the formal proof. Let *spine* be the array induced by the switch bits on the spine of the tree. Let M_i be the m-valued max register whose root is *spine*[i].

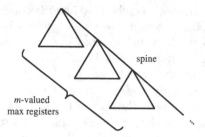

Fig. 1. An unbounded max register

```
1  Shared Data:
2  array TS[1..n] where TS[i] = timestamp for process i
3  array pointer[1..n³]; each entry is a pid
4  array help[i]; each entry consists of
5     value = integer, most recent value seen by a WrapWriteMaxᵢ operation
6     TS[j] = integer, most recent timestamp of pⱼ seen by a WrapWriteMaxᵢ
       operation
7  procedure WrapWriteMaxᵢ(v)
8  |   s ← s + 1 mod n // initialized to 0
9  |   t ← TS[s]
10 |   v′ ← WrapReadMaxᵢ()
11 |   if v > v′ then
12 |   |   WriteMax(M⌊v/m⌋, v mod m) // Write to the corresponding m-valued
       |   |   max register
13 |   |   for j = ⌊v/m⌋ to ⌊v′/m⌋ do
14 |   |   |   spine[j] ← 1
15 |   help[i].value ← max(v, v′)
16 |   help[i].TS[s] ← t
17 |   pointer[random()] ← i
18 procedure WrapReadMaxᵢ()
19 |   TS[i] ← TS[i] + 1
20 |   while true do
21 |   |   for t = 1 to c′ log m // For a constant c′, to be fixed in the step
       |   |   complexity proof do
22 |   |   |   Take a step of ReadMax()
23 |   |   if finished (initially false) then
24 |   |   |   return value
25 |   |   else
26 |   |   |   j ← pointer[random(1, ..., n³)]
27 |   |   |   if help[j].TS[i] = TS[i] then
28 |   |   |   |   return help[j].value
```

Algorithm 2. Max register with randomized helping; code for process i

We linearize a WrapWriteMax$_i$ operation writing a value v at the first time in which all the relevant switches on the path from the root to the leaf corresponding to v are set. We linearize a WrapReadMax$_i$ operation that returns in Line 24 at the time the corresponding original ReadMax is linearized. We linearize a WrapReadMax$_i$ operation that returns in Line 28 at the linearization point of the WrapReadMax$_j$ operation by p_j that is part of the WrapWriteMax$_j$ operation that wrote to help$[j].TS[i]$ the value read by WrapReadMax$_i$ in Line 27.

It is worth mentioning that, as the proof below shows, we do not need the assumption of k-bounded increments for linearizability of the construction. This assumption is used only for bounding the step complexity.

Lemma 1. *Algorithm 2 is a linearizable implementation of an unbounded max register.*

Proof. We base our proof on the correctness proof of the max register construction in [3]. We need to address two issues that differ in our implementation. First, we need to address WrapWriteMax$_i$ operations and show that the switches leading to a written value are indeed set by the time it terminates, showing that our linearization is well defined. The second issue is that we need to address WrapReadMax$_i$ operations that return in Line 28.

We use an induction on the order of linearization points to prove the correctness of the linearization. We add to the inductive claim the invariant that all switches on the path from the root to a leaf corresponding to a value v written by a WriteMax operation op are set if the path descends to their right child on the tree, by the time op finishes. This clearly holds for the base case, when no operation has yet been performed.

Assume that the linearization is correct up to some operation $t-1$ in the total order it induces. Let op be the t-th operation, and assume it is a WrapWriteMax$_i$ operation. By construction, all appropriate switches inside $M(\lfloor v/m \rfloor)$ are set in Line 12. By the induction hypothesis, all spine switches from the root down to location $\lfloor v'/m \rfloor$, where v' is the value read by op in Line 10, are set. The loop in Line 13 then shows that the invariant still holds.

Next, since correctness for WrapReadMax$_i$ operations that return in Line 24 now follows from the proof in [3], let op be a WrapReadMax$_i$ operation that returns in Line 28. Let op' be a WrapWriteMax$_j$ operation by p_j that writes to help$[j].TS[i]$ the timestamp read by op in Line 27. Let op'' be the WrapReadMax$_j$ operation performed by op' in Line 10. Since op'' is performed after op writes to $TS[i]$ and before op' writes to help$[j].TS[i]$, the linearization point of op'' is within the execution interval of op. By the correctness of the linearization points of the construction in [3], the value returned by op, which is the maximum between the value returned by op'' and the value written by op', is the largest value written by operations that are linearized before op.

Having shown that this implementation is linearizable, we turn to prove its logarithmic step complexity. Here we choose $m = 3cn^3 \log n \leq O(n^4)$ and $k = O(n^2 \log^2 n)$ for some fixed constant c that is required by the proof.

Lemma 2. *The step complexity of operations in Algorithm 2 is $O(\log n)$ with high probability, when taking $m = O(n^3 \log n)$ and assuming k-bounded increments for $k = O(n^2 \log^2 n)$.*

Proof. Let op_i be a `WrapReadMax`$_i$ operation by p_i. We say that a process p_j is **current for operation** op_i if $\mathsf{help}[j].\mathsf{TS}[i] = \mathsf{TS}[i]$, where $\mathsf{TS}[i]$ is the timestamp written by op. Every process p_j can perform at most n `WrapWriteMax`$_j$ operations before it becomes current for op_i, since j iterates over the processes to help.

By a coupon collector argument (see, e.g., [10, Chapter 2]), there is a constant c such that after $cn^3 \log (n^3)$ executions of Line 26, op_i covers all elements of the array *pointer*. Suppose that $3cn^3 \log n$ wrapped `WriteMax` operations begin after $\mathsf{TS}[i]$ is incremented. Then, at most n^2 of these operations are by processes that are not current for op_i. There can be at most n^2 different locations in the *pointer* array written by such process, plus at most $n - 1$ locations that have operations by current processes pending to write them, but still contain previous values. The rest of the $\Theta(n^3)$ locations hold values written by processes that are current for op_i. This implies that the probability of op_i choosing a random location in *pointer* that holds a value written by a process that is current for it is at least $1 - (n + n^2)/n^3 = 1 - O(1/n)$.

Assume now that op_i does not complete its `ReadMax` operation in Line 21 within $c' \log m$ steps, where the constant is such that the number of steps is enough to read a spine segment and an m-valued max register covering km values. For this to happen, op_i takes at least $O((c' - 1) \log m)$ steps down the spine (otherwise, it goes down some m-valued max register and terminates within another $O(\log m)$ steps). By the k-bounded increments assumption, there are at least m values being written for this to happen. Taking m to be $3cn^3 \log n \leq O(n^4)$ now gives that the probability of op_i choosing a random location in *pointer* written by a process current for it is at least $1 - O(1/n)$. Therefore, with high probability, op_i finishes within $O(\log m) = O(\log n)$ steps.

A `WrapWriteMax`$_i$ operation op_i takes $O(\log m + kn/m)$ steps in addition to calling `WrapReadMax`$_i$. We choose $k = O(n^2 \log^2 n)$ such that $kn/m = O(\log n)$ and therefore the number of steps required for this operation is also $O(\log n)$, completing the proof. $\square$

3   Unbounded Max Arrays with Bounded Increments

To present our unbounded 2-component max array, we first describe the implementation in [4] and then show how to overcome the obstacles that arise when embedding our unbounded max register in that construction. The [4] 2-component max array roughly works as follows. It has a main tree for the max register of the first component, where each of the switches is associated with a MaxRegister variable tail, that holds copy of the max register of the second component. A write operation to the first component simply ignores these copies, and travels up the main tree from the relevant leaf to the root, setting the required switches along the way. A write operation to the second component writes only to the tail copy associated with the root of the main tree. A read operation travels down the main tree reading the first component, while reading the tail copy of the second component at every switch and updating it if it saw a greater value earlier up the tree.

Propagating the values of the second component down the main tree is the key ingredient in guaranteeing that returned pairs are comparable. The main invariant that needs to be maintained is that a reader does not go right at a switch of the main tree returning a value for the second component that is smaller than that returned by a reader who goes left at that switch. In [4], this is guaranteed by having the reader re-read the tail copy of a switch that is set, and propagating this fresher value down to the right subtree.

However, embedding our max register in this construction does not work: in our max register implementation, a read operation does not travel all the way down from the root to the leaf, therefore it cannot drag the value of the second component with it. This causes gaps in the values of the tail copies of the second component along the tree, violating the required invariant.

To solve this, our observation is that we can re-read the tail copy of the second component associated with the root of the main tree, instead of reading the tail component of the current spine node, which may not have been updated. This guarantees that the value returned for the second component is always updated to the largest one written. Notice that we can only do this with read operations that go down the rightmost path of the main tree, that is, the spine. Otherwise, an operation that started early and goes left at some switch of the main tree might read a value for the second component that is too large: larger than the one read by a quicker operation that goes right. But the fact that we can do this only for the spine fits our goals, and our approach to handle the above issue is to re-read the tail variable at the root only when traveling the spine. At other switches the reader copies the values down the tree as in the original construction, which is unaffected by our max register implementation since gaps in switches can only occur on the spine, as a process going down some m-valued max register travels an entire path from its root to a leaf. Algorithms 3 and 4 show the pseudo-code.

Instead of repeating the linearizability proof of the 2-component max array in [4] (denoted by Alg hereafter), we reduce the algorithm in Algorithms 3 and 4 to Alg. In particular, we show that any execution of the algorithm can be translated to an execution of Alg in a way which preserves returned values, implying that the linearization of Alg also applies to the algorithm in Algorithms 3 and 4. The intuition is that whenever a `ReadMaxArray` operation goes down the spine of the main tree, just before it is about to read the copy of the second component again before going right, we imagine that a very quick `ReadMaxArray` operation in Alg starts and runs solo, going down the spine of the main tree, propagating the value of the second component that is at the copy of the second component associated with the root. If we then let the first `ReadMaxArray` operation do its read then it gets exactly the value associated with the root at that time. Hence, it cannot distinguish between these two executions, and we can take its linearization point as that of its corresponding operation in Alg. Following is the formal proof of the above argument.

```
1  Shared Data:
2  switch: a 1-bit multi-writer register, initially 0
3  left, right: two MaxArray objects with an unbounded second component, initially
   (0,0); at the spine, left has an m-bounded first component and right has an
   unbounded first component; at a MaxArray with a b-bounded first component
   for any integer b, the first component of both left and right is b/2-bounded
4  tail: an unbounded MaxRegister object, initially 0
5  array TS[1..n] where TS[i] = timestamp for process i
6  array pointer[1..n³]; each entry is a pid
7  array help[i]; each entry consists of
8     value = most recent value seen by pᵢ
9     TS[j] = most recent timestamp seen by pᵢ for pⱼ
10 procedure WriteMaxArray0(r, v)  // Write to the first component
11 │   s ← s + 1 mod n  // initialized to 0
12 │   t ← TS[s]
13 │   (v′, v″) ← ReadMaxArray(r)
14 │   if v > v′ then
15 │   │   WriteMax(M⌊v/m⌋, v mod m)
16 │   │   for j = ⌊v/m⌋ to ⌊v′/m⌋ do
17 │   │   └   spine[j] ← 1
18 │   help[i].value ← max(v, v′)
19 │   help[i].TS[s] ← t
20 └   pointer[random(1, ..., n³)] ← i
21
22 procedure WriteMaxArray1(r, v)  // Write to the second component
23 │   WrapWriteMaxᵢ(r.tail, v)
```

Algorithm 3. Writing to the 2-component max array; code for process i

Theorem 1. *The algorithm in Algorithms 3 and 4 is a linearizable implementation of a 2-component max array. It has a step complexity of $O(\log^2 n)$ per operation with high probability, when taking $m = O(n^3 \log n)$ and assuming k-bounded increments for $k = O(n^2 \log^2 n)$.*

Proof. Let α be an execution of the algorithm in Algorithms 3 and 4 with processes $\{p_0, \ldots, p_{n-1}\}$. We construct a sequence of executions $\alpha_0, \alpha_1, \ldots, \alpha'$, which ends in an execution α' of Alg, for which the return values of all operations are the same as in α.

Every execution α_j in the sequence is an execution with $n + 1$ processes, such that every process $p_i \in \{p_0, \ldots, p_{n-1}\}$ invokes the same operations as in α, and process p_n is an extra process that performs only ReadMaxArray operations. If in α the process p_i reads the copy of the second component associated with the root in Line 8, then starting from some α_j it reads the copy associated with the current switch (notice that this difference only occurs when reading locations on spine).

Even though p_i reads different locations in α and α_j, steps by p_n are used to make it obtain the same values. We define the behavior of p_n by induction. In α_0

```
1  procedure ReadMaxArrayDirect(r)
2  │   x ← WrapReadMax_i(r.tail)
3  │   if r.switch = 0 then
4  │   │   WrapWriteMax_i(r.left.tail, x)
5  │   │   return ReadMaxArrayDirect(r.left)
6  │   else
7  │   │   if on spine then
8  │   │   │   x ← WrapReadMax_i(root.tail)
9  │   │   else
10 │   │   └   x ← WrapReadMax_i(r.tail)
11 │   │   WrapWriteMax_i(r.right.tail, x)
12 │   └   return ReadMaxArrayDirect(r.right) + (m, 0)
13
14 procedure ReadMaxArray(r)
15 │   TS[i] ← TS[i] + 1
16 │   while true do
17 │   │   for t = 1 to c' log m  // For a constant c' as in Algorithm 2 do
18 │   │   └   Take a step of ReadMaxArrayDirect(r)
19 │   │   if finished then
20 │   │   │   return pair
21 │   │   else
22 │   │   │   j ← pointer[random(1, . . . , n^3)]
23 │   │   │   if help[j].TS[i] = TS[i] then
24 │   │   │   │   firstComponent ← help[j].value
25 │   │   │   │   return ReadMaxArrayDirect(spine[firstComponent/m])
26
```

Algorithm 4. Reading the 2-component max array; code for process i

the process p_n is not used, therefore it is the execution described above. Assume executions $\alpha_0, \ldots, \alpha_j$ are defined and define execution α_{j+1} as follows. Let p_i be the first process in α_j that reads root.tail in Line 8 corresponding to some location x on the spine. Denote $\alpha_j = \alpha'_j s_i \alpha''_j$ such that s_i is that step of p_i (note that we can assume an operation on a max register is an atomic operation). We define $\alpha_{j+1} = \alpha'_j \sigma s'_i \alpha''_j$, where in σ process p_n performs a read operation and s'_i is a step by p_i reading the copy of the second component associated with location x.

Our claim is that all operations return the same values in α_j and in α_{j+1}. The reason is that p_n reads the copy of the second component associated with the root of the main tree and copies it down the spine at least until location x since it starts after p_i reaches x and hence all switches toward it are set. Therefore, when p_i reads the copy in x in s'_i in α_{j+1} it gets the same value it reads from the root in s_i in α_j. Finally, for some j we reach an execution $\alpha' = \alpha_j$ of Alg, for which all returned values of processes $\{p_0, \ldots, p_{n-1}\}$ are the same as in α. This execution α' is linearizable by the proof of [4].

Because p_n performs only `ReadMaxArray` operations, removing these operations from the linearization of α' does not affect the return values of any other operations; this reduced linearization is thus a linearization of α.

4   Unbounded Snapshots

Given our unbounded 2-component max array implementation, we can now obtain an unbounded snapshot object.

We use the construction from [4], which for convenience we restate here in Algorithm 5 The shared data is:

- leaf_j, for $j \in \{0, \ldots, n-1\}$: the leaf node corresponding to process j, with fields:
  - parent: the parent of this leaf in the tree
  - view$[0, 1, \ldots]$: an infinite array, each of whose entries contains a partial snapshot, view$[0]$ contains the initial value of component j and view$[\ell]$ contains the ℓ-th value of component j
  - root: the root of the tree
- Each internal node has the fields:
  - left: the left child of the node in the tree
  - right: the right child of the node in the tree
  - view$[0, 1, \ldots]$: an infinite array, each of whose entries contains a partial snapshot, view$[0]$ contains the concatenation of leaf_j.view$[0]$ for all leaves leaf_j in the subtree rooted at this node, and view$[\ell]$ contains the concatenation of views of the leaves after ℓ updates
  - ma: an infinite MaxArray object, initially (0,0)
- The root also has the field mr: an infinite MaxRegister object, initially 0
- Each non-root internal node also has the field parent: the parent of the node in the tree

We use this algorithm with our implementations of unbounded max registers and unbounded max arrays from the previous sections. Loosely speaking, the construction is based on a balanced binary tree with n leaves, one for each process. Each intermediate node holds a 2-component max array object for its two children, that counts the number of update operations performed on each. It also stores the (unique) view corresponding to this number. A process that updates its location does so by updating the nodes from its leaf to the root, and a process scans the object by reading the view held by the root. We emphasize that correctness is always guaranteed in the above implementation, therefore the proof from [4] shows that this gives an unbounded snapshot object. It remains to show the step complexity of our construction. For this, we only need to show that the k-bounded increment assumption holds, and use the complexity analysis of the previous sections. Intuitively, this is because every MaxRegister is used only to store the number of operations observed in the subtree of processes that it represents. If the difference between two values written to a MaxRegister is more than n, then some processes completed a `WriteMax` operation between these two `WriteMax` operations, implying that the maximal difference was smaller to begin with. Formally, we prove this claim in the following lemma.

```
 1  procedure Update(s, i, v)
 2  │   count_i ← count_i + 1
 3  │   u ← leaf_i
 4  │   ptr ← count_i
 5  │   u.view[ptr] ← v
 6  │   while u ≠ root do
 7  │       if u = u.parent.left then
 8  │       └   WriteMaxArray0(u.parent.ma, ptr)
 9  │       if u = u.parent.right then
10  │       └   WriteMaxArray1(u.parent.ma, ptr)
11  │       u ← u.parent
12  │       (lptr, rptr) ← ReadMaxArray(u.ma)
13  │       lview ← u.left.view[lptr]
14  │       rview ← u.right.view[rptr]
15  │       ptr ← lptr + rptr
16  │       u.view[ptr] ← lview · rview
17  └   WriteMax(root.mr, ptr)
18  procedure Scan(s)
19  │   ptr ← ReadMax(root.mr)
20  └   return root.view[ptr]
```

Algorithm 5. Unbounded snapshot object; code for process i

Lemma 3. *In Algorithm 5, all* MaxRegister *and* MaxArray *objects are accessed according to the n-bounded increments assumption.*

Proof. A process that performs WriteMaxArray on u.ma for some node u writes the value of its ptr variable. We show that ptr holds a value which is at most the number of Update operations invoked by processes corresponding to this subtree, hence a value being written to u.ma is larger by at most n than the largest value previously written to it. The claim follows by a simple induction on the height of the node that holds the object. When accessing a leaf, ptr holds the value of $count_i$, which is the number of operations performed by process p_i. For an intermediate node u, ptr holds the sum of the values of its two children, which, by the induction hypothesis are the number of Update operations invoked by processes corresponding to these subtrees, which proves the claim. Finally, the same holds for the value of ptr when the root is accessed, implying the claim also for the MaxRegister object there.

Combining Lemma 3 with Theorem 1 gives our main theorem.

Theorem 2. *Algorithm 5 is an implementation of an unbounded snapshot object, with a step complexity of $O(\log^3 n)$ per operation with high probability.*

5   Discussion

This paper gives the first sub-linear unbounded snapshot implementation from atomic read/write registers. It is a randomized algorithm, with a step complexity of $O(\log^3 n)$ with high probability for each operation, where n is the number of processes. The main component of the construction is a new randomized implementation of an unbounded max register with a complexity of $O(\log n)$ steps per operation with high probability. The novelty of the construction is a randomized helping technique, which allows slow processes to obtain fresh information from other processes. The use of randomization avoids in most cases the linear worst-case lower bound based on covering of Jayanti *et al.* [9], because the adversary cannot predict what locations a process will read from the helper array and thus cannot guarantee to cover those locations with old values. Conversely, the lower bound shows that some use of randomization is necessary.

Acknowledgement. The authors thank the anonymous reviewers for careful comments and suggestions that helped improve the presentation of this work. The first author is supported in part by NSF grant CCF-0916389. The second author is a Shalon Fellow.

References

1. Afek, Y., Attiya, H., Dolev, D., Gafni, E., Merritt, M., Shavit, N.: Atomic snapshots of shared memory. J. ACM 40(4), 873–890 (1993)
2. Anderson, J.H.: Multi-writer composite registers. Distributed Computing 7(4), 175–195 (1994)
3. Aspnes, J., Attiya, H., Censor-Hillel, K.: Polylogarithmic concurrent data structures from monotone circuits. J. ACM 59(1), 2:1–2:24 (2012)
4. Aspnes, J., Attiya, H., Censor-Hillel, K., Ellen, F.: Faster than optimal snapshots (for a while). In: 2012 ACM Symposium on Principles of Distributed Computing, pp. 375–384 (July 2012)
5. Aspnes, J., Attiya, H., Censor-Hillel, K., Hendler, D.: Lower bounds for restricted-use objects. In: Twenty-Fourth ACM Symposium on Parallel Algorithms and Architectures, pp. 172–181 (June 2012)
6. Aspnes, J., Herlihy, M.: Wait-free data structures in the asynchronous PRAM model. In: Second Annual ACM Symposium on Parallel Algorithms and Architectures, pp. 340–349 (July 1990)
7. Attiya, H., Fouren, A.: Adaptive and efficient algorithms for lattice agreement and renaming. SIAM J. Comput. 31(2), 642–664 (2001)
8. Inoue, M., Chen, W.: Linear-time snapshot using multi-writer multi-reader registers. In: Tel, G., Vitányi, P.M.B. (eds.) WDAG 1994. LNCS, vol. 857, pp. 130–140. Springer, Heidelberg (1994)
9. Jayanti, P., Tan, K., Toueg, S.: Time and space lower bounds for nonblocking implementations. SIAM Journal on Computing 30(2), 438–456 (2000)
10. Mitzenmacher, M., Upfal, E.: Probability and Computing: Randomized Algorithms and Probabilistic Analysis. Cambridge University Press (2005)

Adaptive Register Allocation
with a Linear Number of Registers

Carole Delporte-Gallet[1], Hugues Fauconnier[1], Eli Gafni[2], and Leslie Lamport[3]

[1] U. Paris Diderot, France
[2] Computer Science Department, UCLA, USA
[3] Microsoft Research

Abstract. We give an adaptive algorithm in which processes use multi-writer multi-reader registers to acquire exclusive write access to their own single-writer, multi-reader registers. It is the first such algorithm that uses a number of registers linear in the number of participating processes. Previous adaptive algorithms require at least $\Theta(n^{3/2})$ registers.

Keywords: shared memory, read/write registers, distributed algorithms, wait-free, space complexity, renaming.

1   Introduction

One way to implement multiprocess synchronization is by providing each process with a single-writer, multi-reader atomic register (SWMR) that it can write and other processes can read. We present an adaptive algorithm to implement such a system of registers with an array of multi-writer multi-reader atomic (MWMR) registers whose length is linear in the number of participating processes. The algorithm is non-blocking unless an unbounded number of processes initiate operations.

An adaptive algorithm, also called a uniform algorithm [13], is one that does not know the number of potentially participating processes. Equivalently, it is an algorithm whose cost is a function not of the total number of processes but of the number of processes that actually participate in the algorithm. For the SWMR registers, this is the number of processes that actually perform a read or write operation. Our goal is to minimize the number of MWMR registers, and our algorithm uses a number that is linear in the number of participants. No *a priori* bound on this number is assumed.

Why do we find this algorithm interesting? There are simpler algorithms that assume stronger communication primitives—for example, test and set registers—but MWMR registers are the weakest ones for which we know that an adaptive algorithm is possible. More efficient randomized algorithms are possible, but our algorithm is always correct, not just correct with high probability. There is a trivial way to implement a collection of SWMR registers with an array C of MWMR registers. The ith process simply uses $C[i]$ as its register. Of course, this algorithm uses an unbounded number of registers. The obvious way to

Y. Afek (Ed.): DISC 2013, LNCS 8205, pp. 269–283, 2013.
© Springer-Verlag Berlin Heidelberg 2013

make the number of registers linear in the number of participating processes is by having the processes first execute an adaptive renaming algorithm [7,10] in which each participating process is assigned a unique number from 0 to M for some M that depends linearly on the number of participants. A process assigned the number j then uses $C[j]$ as its register. However, we know of few renaming algorithms that do not assume a collection of SWMR registers already allocated to processes [6,8,19]. Those algorithms are all based on the grid-network of "splitters" proposed by Anderson and Moir [19]. Of these, the more space-efficient is an improvement of Aspnes [6] that requires $\Theta(k^{3/2})$ MWMR registers for k participating processes. Even though the renaming algorithm is used only to determine the assignment of processes to elements of the array C, the values in those $\Theta(k^{3/2})$ registers must be maintained forever because additional processes may enter the system at any time. (Reclaiming the space requires knowing an *a priori* bound on the number of processes that might participate.) Thus, our algorithm is the first that implements a collection of SWMR registers with $O(k)$ MWMR registers.

Almost all previous methods for making an algorithm adaptive start by using one of several renaming algorithms [2,3,4,7,10]. It has generally been assumed that this is the only way to implement an adaptive algorithm [9]. Based on an idea in [11], our implementation avoids the use of a renaming algorithm to begin reliable communication. Instead, participating processes first announce their presence by using a non-blocking one-shot limited-snapshot algorithm that we call the GFX (Generalized Fast eXclusion) protocol, which can be viewed as generalizing [16] from 1-concurrency to k-concurrency. The snapshot is limited to having the property that two snapshots of the same size coincide. It need not ensure that snapshots of different sizes are related by containment. To perform a read or write operation to a register, a process first reads the posted snapshots to find the number n of participants that have announced their presence, and it executes an algorithm [11] that assumes at most n processes. It then reads the number of participants again, finishing the operation if that number still equals n. Otherwise, the process repeats the n-process algorithm for the new value of n. While we use this approach to implement renaming, it can be used to provide an adaptive implementation of any task.

By using our adaptive algorithm for implementing a collection of SWMR registers, we can solve any task under the assumption of finite arrival [14]. In particular, using existing algorithms, we can implement adaptive renaming with a linear range [7,10]. This in turn allows us to allocate unique registers to processes with a number of registers linear in the number of participants. With register allocation, we can implement a collection of SWMR registers with wait-free read and write operations rather than just non-blocking ones. For many tasks of high read-write complexity, doing renaming first may reduce the step complexity of an adaptive algorithm.

We ignore time complexity—the number of steps taken by the algorithm. Our algorithm is executed just once, to assign SWMR registers to processes; it adds nothing to the cost of using those registers. Since space used by an adaptive algorithm cannot be reclaimed, it is perhaps more important than time complexity. Still, optimal time complexity is an interesting problem that remains unsolved.

In the non-adaptive case, it has been shown that at least n registers are required to implement n SWMR registers [11], so the linear number of registers used by our algorithms is optimal up to a constant factor. We originally believed that adaptive algorithms required more than a linear number of registers, and we tried to derive such a lower bound on the number of registers, independent of their size. When the difficulty is caused by processes stepping on each other because of the lack of *a priori* coordination, size of the registers is not a factor. (See the lower bound for consensus [12].) We were therefore surprised to discover our algorithm.

Section 2 describes our implementation and sketches an informal proof of its correctness. (Some might call this sketch a proof.) In Section 3, the two key algorithms used in the implementation are precisely described in the PlusCal algorithm language [18]. The section also describes formal TLA$^+$ correctness proofs of the safety properties of these algorithms. The complete mechanically-checked proofs are available on the Web [15].

2 An Informal Proof of the Algorithm

A sequence of SWMR registers is easily implemented using an algorithm we call *SnapShot*. We obtain this algorithm via two intermediate algorithms: the Leaky Repository Protocol and Algorithm *GFX*. We give here informal proofs of these algorithms; formal proofs of algorithms *GFX* and *SnapShot* are described in Section 3.

2.1 Preliminaries

Our algorithms assumes a small constant number of infinite arrays of MRMW registers, indexed by natural numbers, all registers containing the same initial value that we take to be { } (the empty set). The algorithms write into only the first k elements of the arrays, where k is a linear function of the number of participating processes. Hence, they can be implemented by finite arrays, given a bound on the number of possible participants.

Since we are interested only in space complexity, for simplicity we never read a single array entry; we always atomically read the entire array, using the double scan method of [2]. To allow scanning an infinite array A, we use an auxiliary infinite array $\overline{A}$, where a process writes $A[i]$ by first writing some value other than { } into $\overline{A}[0], \ldots, \overline{A}[i]$. A scan of A can assume $A[i] = \{ \}$ for all $i \geq j$ if $\overline{A}[j] = \{ \}$.

2.2 The Leaky Repository

The Leaky Repository Protocol maintains a repository of facts using an infinite array A of MWMR registers, where the value of a register can be any finite set of facts. At any time, the contents of the repository is the set $A[0] \cup A[1] \cup \ldots$ of facts, which can be obtained by atomically reading the array A. The repository is leaky because facts stored in it may be lost. We would like a process to be able to add facts to the repository and have them remain there forever, but that is hard to do. Instead, we describe a protocol that tries to do this. It doesn't succeed, but it does provide a property that makes it a useful building block for the *GFX* and *SnapShot* algorithms.

Here is how process p tries to add a set F of facts to the repository. To try to avoid destroying previously added facts, p writes to a register only by performing a read-then-write operation that first atomically reads the entire array A and then writes the facts in F together with all the other facts it has ever read or written. To try to keep the facts in F from being overwritten by other processes, p performs such read-then-write operations to put the facts in F into multiple registers. To use as little of the array A as possible, p writes into the first n registers of A, for some n that it hopes is large enough.

Process p hopes that, if an atomic read of A shows the facts in F in each of the first n registers of A, then that ensures they will remain in the repository forever. Of course, it doesn't—the repository is leaky. Here's what can go wrong. Suppose that there are n processes other than p, each of which has performed the read of a read-then-write operation to a different one of the first n registers and is about to do the write. Process p can then perform read-then-write operations to the first n registers and read A to find that those registers all contain the facts in F. The n other processes can then perform their writes, destroying all traces of the facts in F. Before the nth process writes, the contents of the repository satisfies:

R1. It contains all the facts in F.

This property is falsified by the nth process's write. Each register i then contains a set F_i of facts written by a different process p_i. Moreover, each of those n read-then-write operations was begun before p's final read of A. Therefore, the contents of the repository at that moment satisfies the following property, where R is the read of A by p that found the facts of F in all those n registers.

R2. It contains all the facts in $F_0 \cup \ldots \cup F_{n-1}$, for sets F_i such that there are n distinct processes $p_0, \ldots, p_{n-1}$ different from p, where each p_i wrote F_i with a read-then-write operation that began before R.

We now generalize from this scenario. Note that R1 and R2 assert properties (that may be true or false) of an arbitrary read R of the repository by a process p that obtains a set F of facts. R2 asserts the existence of some sets F_i and processes p_i, not the ones from any particular scenario. Note also that if a set S of facts satisfies R1 or R2, then any superset of S also satisfies R1 or R2. We will prove the following:

Property R If a read R of A by process p finds $F \subseteq A[i]$ for $i = 0, \ldots, n-1$, then at all times after that read, the contents of the array A satisfies R1 or R2.

Property R allows R2 to be satisfied with different sets F_i and processes p_i at different times, and it allows R1 to become true again after it has become false. , If there are at most n participants when p performs R, then R2 can never be true, so the facts in F must remain in the repository forever.

Property R is true of any protocol in which a process writes to a register of A using only a read-then-write operation that first reads A and then writes all the facts it has ever read from or written to A (perhaps writing additional facts too). We say that any such algorithm obeys the Leaky Repository Protocol for repository A.

We could use the Leaky Repository Protocol in an obvious way to implement an *add F* operation that always satisfies R1 or R2 after it has completed. However, we instead implement an *add & read f* operation that adds a single fact f to the repository and returns a set F such that F is the contents of the repository when the operation completes and thereafter always satisfies R1 or R2, for some "suitable" n. What n is suitable varies with the application, and it may depends on the *add & read* operation and on F. To perform an *add & read f* operation, process p executes the Leaky Repository Protocol to keep writing f in registers. The operation completes and returns the set F of facts when a read of A finds that F is the contents of the repository and $A[0] = \cdots = A[n-1] = F$ for some suitable n.

The *add & read* operation is used by Algorithm *SnapShot* with the "suitable" value of n being the number of participants. In that case, R2 cannot be true, so the set of facts returned by the *add & read* remain in the repository forever. To determine the number of participants, *SnapShot* uses Algorithm *GFX*, which uses *add & read* operations in which the "suitable" value of n is one plus the number of facts in the repository. Property R then implies that if the facts that a process read from the repository are no longer all there, then facts added by $n + 1$ other processes are.

A process p's *add & read* operation need never complete. It can forever keep doing read-then-write operations if other processes keep performing *add & read* operations that add new facts. However, with a bounded number of participating processes and a bound on the number of registers that each operation writes, the entire collection of *add & read* operations is non-blocking—meaning that if some process is performing an *add & read* operation then some *add & read* operation will eventually complete. To prove this, we suppose that some set of processes is forever trying to perform *add & read* operations, none of which complete, and we obtain a contradiction. Since each process writes non-decreasing sets of facts and there are only a finite number of facts being added, eventually each process p forever reads only a fixed set F_p of facts and keeps writing F_p. If all the sets F_p are the same, every process will write only that set. Since there is a bound on the number of registers that an operation writes, this implies that all the operations will finish. If all the F_p are not the same, choose a minimal set F_q. Since q's operation doesn't finish, it must eventually read a set F_r different from F_q. Minimality of F_q implies that F_r contains a fact not in F_q, contradicting the assumption that q reads only facts in F_q. Hence, the algorithm is non-blocking.

We now prove Property R. We must show that R1 or R2 holds forever after the read R of p finds $F \subseteq A[i]$ for all $i < n$. Define $W(i)$ to be the set (whose elements are sets of facts) that contains every set of facts that some process is about to write into $A[i]$, having completed the read of A in a read-then-write operation. Let $W0(i)$ be the value of $W(i)$ when p performs R. We show that the following invariant is true upon completion of p's read R and is left true by every further step of the algorithm:

> For all $i < n$, the value of $A[i]$ and every element of $W(i)$ contains (as a subset) either F or an element of $W0(i)$.

The invariant is true upon completion of R because then $W0(i) = W(i)$ and $F \subseteq A[i]$ for all $i < n$. A step that writes a value from $W(i)$ into $A[i]$ obviously cannot falsify the invariant. A step that adds a value to $W(i)$ cannot falsify the invariant because the value being added to $W(i)$ contains all the facts obtained by reading the repository after read R, which includes the value of $A[i]$. This completes the proof of invariance. The invariant implies that the contents of the repository satisfies R1 or R2, since either (i) some $A[i]$ contains F, so R1 holds, or else (ii) each $A[i]$ with $i < n$ contains an element of $W0(i)$, which by definition of $W0(i)$ implies that the union of the $A[i]$ satisfies R2. This proves Property R.

2.3   Algorithm *GFX*

Algorithm *GFX* is a one-shot algorithm, meaning that it is executed at most once by any process. It solves the following weaker version of the snapshot task [2]: A process p that executes the algorithm must return a set F_p of participants such that

- $p \in F_p$ for any p.
- $|F_p| = |F_q|$ implies $F_p = F_q$ for any p and q, where $|F|$ is the cardinality of the set F.

To implement the algorithm, we use the Leaky Repository Protocol with a single infinite array $A1$, where the repository's facts are (names of) processes. A process p executes the *GFX* algorithm by executing an *add & read* p operation that completes and returns a set of facts/processes F until it reads $A1[0] = \cdots = A1[|F|] = F$. Thus, the suitable n for this *add & read* operation is $1 + |F|$, where F is the set of facts being returned.

Now suppose a process p's execution of the *GFX* algorithm completes and returns the value F. Every write by a process q writes the fact/process q. Property R therefore implies that after the read by p that completes its execution of the *GFX* algorithm, the repository $A1$ forever contains either (by R1) all the processes in F or (by R2) $|F| + 1$ distinct processes. Any execution of the *GFX* algorithm that then completes cannot return a set $G \neq F$ of facts with $|G| = |F|$. This proves that the *GFX* algorithm satisfies its required properties.

Each execution of the *GFX* algorithm is an execution of an *add & read* operation for the leaky repository that writes a number of registers at most one greater than the total number of participants. The algorithm is therefore non-blocking if there is a bounded set of participants. In a non-blocking one-shot algorithm with a finite set of participants, every execution of the algorithm by a participant completes.

2.4   Algorithm *SnapShot*

Algorithm *SnapShot* implements a non-leaky repository that provides an add-and-read operation we call *snap f* that atomically adds the single fact f and returns the new contents of the repository. More precisely, in addition to the obvious properties that *snap f* adds fact f and returns only facts that have been added, the algorithm satisfies the property that if a *snap* operation op_p by process p returns set F_p and a *snap* operation op_q by process q returns F_q, then:

- $F_p \subseteq F_q$ or $F_q \subseteq F_p$.
- If op_p finishes before op_q starts, then $F_p \subseteq F_q$.

The idea of the *SnapShot* algorithm is to use the Leaky Repository Protocol on an array $A3$, and to implement a *snap f* operation by an *add & read f* operation to the repository, where the "sufficient" number n of registers is greater than the total number of participants. Property R then implies that if the *add & read f* operation succeeds, the value returned remains forever in the repository (because R2 cannot hold).

Let's suppose that there is a *count* operation that a process p can call to learn the number of participants that can be executing a *snap* operation. To perform a *snap f* operation, a process p first executes *count* to obtain a bound n on the number of participants. It then executes the Leaky Repository Protocol to add f to the repository, writing in the first n registers of $A3$. If a read of the repository obtains a value F such that $A[0] = \cdots = A[n-1] = F$, process p executes the *count* operation again. If that execution returns the same number n of participants, then the *snap f* operation completes and returns the value F. Otherwise, the process continues the procedure, replacing n with the new value returned by *count*.

If a *snap f* operation by process p completes and returns the set F of facts, Property R holds for the final read of the repository that obtains F. Since F was in n registers and the read occurred when there were at most n participants, R2 cannot hold. Hence R1 holds forever, so F remains forever in the repository. Every *snap* operation that completes after p's *snap f* operation sees the facts in F and therefore returns a set G with $F \subseteq G$. This implies that the *SnapShot* algorithm satisfies its requirement.

We still have to implement the *count* operation. We do that by using algorithm *GFX* and a second array $A2$ of registers. When a participant p arrives, before performing any *snap* operation it (i) executes *GFX* to obtain a set S of participants, which includes itself, and (ii) writes (the processes in) S in $A2[|S| - 1]$. The correctness property of *GFX* implies that no other value can ever be written in $A2[|S| - 1]$. Since the processes written in $A2$ are all participants and every participant is written in $A2$, the set of all processes in $A2$ includes all participants that can write to $A3$. The *count* operation is then performed by reading $A2$ and counting the number of (distinct) processes read.

A *snap* operation executes a leaky repository's *add* & *read* operations that write a number of registers at most equal to the number of participating processes. Therefore, if there are a bounded number of participants, then the *SnapShot* algorithm is non-blocking.

2.5   Implementing the SWMR Registers

Using algorithm *SnapShot*, the collection of SWMR registers is implemented as follows. To write x as the ith write to its (simulated) SWMR register, a process p performs the operation *snap* $\langle p, i, x \rangle$, ignoring the value returned by the *snap* operation. To atomically read all processes' SWMR registers, a process executes a *snap* $\perp$ operation for a special fact $\perp$. (Algorithm *SnapShot* allows multiple *snap* f operations with the same fact f.) The current value of process q's register is the value x in the triple $\langle q, i, x \rangle$ with the largest value of i in the set returned by the *snap* operation. If no such triple exists, then q has not yet written to its SWMR register. It follows easily from the properties of the *SnapShot* algorithm that this implements a collection of SWMR registers with an atomic operation that reads all the registers.

3   The Formal Safety Proofs

We believe that our implementation of SWMR registers from algorithm *Snap-Shot* is obvious enough that a precise description of it and a formal proof of its correctness are not necessary. However, algorithms *GFX* and *SnapShot* are subtle. In this section, we precisely describe these algorithms in the PlusCal algorithm language [18]. PlusCal constructs whose meanings may not be obvious are briefly explained as they are introduced. A PlusCal expression can be any TLA⁺ formula [17], and a PlusCal algorithm is automatically translated to a TLA⁺ specification that defines the algorithm's formal meaning.

We have written formal, mechanically-checked TLA⁺ correctness proofs of the safety properties of the *GFX* and *SnapShot* algorithms. Those proofs are sketched here; the complete proofs are available on the Web [15]. Unlike the informal proofs of Section 2, which use behavioral reasoning, the formal proofs use purely assertional reasoning. They are therefore not a direct formalization of the informal proofs. Since we have given informal proofs of liveness and space complexity in Section 2, we discuss only safety here.

Algorithms *GFX* and *SnapShot* are written in terms of the set *Proc* of all processes that eventually participate. We assume that this set is finite (otherwise the algorithms would not be non-blocking). Processes that perform no actions are not represented in our specifications. Since processes do not use the value of *Proc*, our algorithm does not assume any *a priori* knowledge of the number of participating processes.

3.1   Algorithm *GFX*

The Specification

The specification of what algorithm *GFX* is supposed to do is given by algorithm
GFXSpec of Figure 1. The **variable** statement declares the global variable *result*

```
--algorithm GFXSpec
{ variable result = [p ∈ Proc ↦ {}]
  process(Pr ∈ Proc)
    { A: with (P ∈ {Q ∈ SUBSET Proc :
                      ∧ self ∈ Q
                      ∧ ∀p ∈ Proc \ {self} :
                            ∨ Cardinality(result[p]) ≠ Cardinality(Q)
                            ∨ Q = result[p]
                   } )
        {result[self] := P}
    }
}
```

Fig. 1. Specification of Algorithm *GFX*

and initializes it to be an array indexed by the set *Proc* of processes, with $result[p]$
initially the empty set $\{\}$ for each process p. The **process** statement declares
there to be one process for each element of *Proc*, the statement's body giving
the code for process *self*. The statement **with** $(x \in S)\{\Sigma\}$ executes Σ with an
arbitrary element of S substituted for x. The expression SUBSET *Proc* denotes
the set of all subsets of *Proc*. TLA$^+$ allows conjunctions and disjunctions to
be represented as lists of formulas bulleted with $\wedge$ or $\vee$, using indentation to
eliminate parentheses. (This notation makes large formulas easier to read.)

In PlusCal, an atomic action is the execution of code from one label to the
next, where there is an implicit label *Done* at the end. Thus, the entire body of
the process is executed as a single atomic action A (named by the label). The
with statement sets $result[self]$ to P, which is an arbitrarily chosen element Q
in the set of subsets of *Proc* such that (i) *self* is in Q and (ii) for each other
process p, either the cardinality of Q is unequal to the cardinality of $result[p]$, or
else Q equals $result[p]$. Thus, a process p that does not execute its A action has
$result[p]$ always equal to the empty set. A process p that executes its A action
terminates with $result[p]$ equal to a set of processes containing p such that for
any other process q, either $result[p]$ and $result[q]$ have different cardinalities,
or $result[p] = result[q]$. The TLA$^+$ translation of the algorithm introduces a
variable pc, where $pc[p]$ equals the label at which control is in process p, so $pc[p]$
equals either the string "A" or the string "Done".

The Algorithm

Algorithm *GFX* is described in Figure 2. The variables *known* and *notKnown*
are local to *self* (the current process) and cannot be read or written by other
processes. Variable *known* stores the set of processes known to process *self*,

--algorithm GFX
  { **variables** $A1 = [i \in Nat \mapsto \{\}]$, $result = [p \in Proc \mapsto \{\}]$;
    process $(Pr \in Proc)$
      variables $known = \{self\}$, $notKnown = \{\}$;
      { a: $known := known \cup NUnion(A1)$;
           $notKnown := \{i \in 0 \,..\, (Cardinality(known)) : known \neq A1[i]\}$;
           if $(notKnown \neq \{\})$
              { b : **with** $(i \in notKnown)$ $\{A1[i] := known\}$;
                  goto a
              }
           else $\{result[self] := known\}$;
      }
  }

Fig. 2. Algorithm *GFX*

and *unKnown* stores a set of array indices (natural numbers). In the TLA$^+$ translation, the values of these process-local variables are arrays indexed by the set *Proc*. The other new notation used in this algorithm is: *Nat* is the set of natural numbers, $i\,..\,j$ is the set of integers k with $i \le k \le j$, and the operator *NUnion* is defined (in the TLA$^+$ module containing the algorithm) by

$$NUnion(A) \triangleq \text{UNION}\{A[i] : i \in Nat\}$$

where the UNION expression is commonly written by mathematicians as $\bigcup_{i \in Nat} A[i]$. Evaluation of that expression is implemented by atomically reading the array A. Observe that although *result* is a global variable, $result[p]$ is accessed only by process p.

There are two atomic actions that a process p can execute. Action a sets $known[p]$ and $notKnown[p]$, executes the **if** test, and then either goes to label b or else executes the **else** clause, setting $result[p]$, and terminates. Action b writes to one element of $A1$ and goes to label a.

The safety property satisfied by the *GFX* algorithm is that it implements algorithm *GFXSpec* under the refinement mapping [1] that substitutes expressions of *GFX*'s variables for the variables of *GFXSpec* as follows:

  $result \leftarrow result$
  pc $\leftarrow [p \in Proc \mapsto \text{IF } pc[p] = \text{"Done" THEN "Done" ELSE "A"}]$

Implementation under this refinement mapping means that in any execution of algorithm *GFX*, the sequence of values assumed by the substituting expressions is one that algorithm *GFXSpec* allows for its variables.

This safety property is a fairly direct consequence of the invariance of the assertion *GFXCorrect* defined as follows. Let two sets of processes be *compatible* iff they are either equal or have different cardinality. We define *GFXCorrect* to assert that, for any processes p and q of *Proc*, if p and q have terminated then $result[p]$ and $result[q]$ are compatible.

To understand why *GFXCorrect* is an invariant of algorithm *GFX*, observe that process p terminates and sets $result[p]$ to $known[p]$ after using the *GFX* protocol to write $known[p]$ into registers $A1[0], \ldots, A1[Cardinality(known[p])]$. Any process q that reads $known[p]$ will set $known[q]$ to be a superset of that value, so $known[p]$ and $known[q]$ are compatible because the definition of compatibility implies that two sets are compatible if one is a superset of the other. If no process reads the value $known[p]$, then $Cardinality(known[p]) + 1$ processes must have written their $known$ values into $A1$. Since $known[r]$ contains r, for each process r, the union of all $A1[i]$ therefore has cardinality greater than that of $known[p]$, and any process q that then terminates will do so with $result[q]$ having cardinality greater than $known[p]$.

To make this reasoning completely rigorous requires an inductive invariance proof [5]. Define $PA1$ to be the set of *potential* values of the array $A1$, meaning the values that $A1$ could have after some subset of the processes at control location b execute their b action. The key part of the inductive invariant is:

$$\forall p \in Proc, P \in PA1:$$
$$\lor\ Cardinality(known[p]) < Cardinality(NUnion(P))$$
$$\lor\ known[p] \subseteq NUnion(P)$$

A machine-checked formal proof of safety is available on the Web [15].

3.2   Algorithm *SnapShot*

The Specification

The *SnapShot* algorithm maintains a set S of values that is initially empty. It provides a *snap* operation whose argument is a value v. Executing $snap(v)$ atomically adds v to S and returns the current value of S. Algorithm *SnapSpec* is specified in Figure 3. The only additional PlusCal construct it introduces is **either**, where the statement **either** Σ_1 **or** Σ_2 is executed by nondeterministically choosing either Σ_1 or Σ_2 and executing it.

```
--algorithm SnapSpec
{ variables myVals = [i ∈ Proc ↦ {}], nextout = [i ∈ Proc ↦ {}] ;
  process (Pr ∈ Proc)
    variable out = {} ;
    { A: while (TRUE)
         {    with (v ∈ Val) { myVals[self] := myVals[self] ∪ {v} } ;
           B: with (V ∈ { W ∈ SUBSET PUnion(myVals) :
                              ∧ myVals[self] ⊆ W
                              ∧ PUnion(nextout) ⊆ W })
                { nextout[self] := V } ;
           C: either out := nextout[self]
              or      goto B ;
         }
    }
}
```

Fig. 3. Algorithm *SnapSpec*, the specification of *SnapShot*

The algorithm appears in a TLA$^+$ module that declares $Proc$ as for the GFX algorithm, declares the set Val, which represents the set of all possible values that can be added to S, and defines the operator $PUnion$ by

$$PUnion(A) \;\triangleq\; \text{UNION } \{A[p] : p \in Proc\}$$

The body of the **while** loop describes the $snap(v)$ operation, where the value v is chosen by executing the **with** $(v \in Val)$ statement. The result returned by the operation is written to the process-local variable out. The set S of values maintained by the algorithm equals $PUnion(nextout)$. Thus, action A represents choosing the value v; action B represents adding v to S and reading the current value of S (into $nextout[self]$); and action C represents returning the value read.

The Algorithm

Algorithm $SnapShot$ appears in Figure 4. It uses two infinite arrays $A2$ and $A3$ of MWMR registers. The code contains no notation that hasn't appeared in previous algorithms. The single atomic action c atomically reads both $A2$ and $A3$ in evaluating $NUnion(A2)$ and $NUnion(A3)$. However, the value of $A2$ that it reads is used only in the statement that writes to $nextout$, a "history" variable that is never read. This variable is used only to reason about the algorithm. The **else** clause in which $nextout$ is set is not meant to be implemented.

A process p begins the algorithm by executing the GFX algorithm and writing the value $result[p]$ it obtains into $A2[Cardinality(result[p]) - 1]$. Since GFX ensures that two processes cannot obtain different values of $result$ having the same cardinality, a value written in any register $A2[i]$ remains there forever. Since $result[p]$ contains p and is a subset of the participating processes, this implies that $NUnion(A2)$ is a subset of the participating processes containing all processes that have finished executing the GFX algorithm.

The execution of algorithm GFX and writing into $A2$ is represented by action a of $SnapShot$. Action a consists of action A of algorithm $GFXSpec$ plus the assignment to $A2$. Having proved that GFX implements $GFXSpec$, we can represent the code of GFX by the corresponding code of $GFXSpec$. More precisely, we proved that algorithm GFX implements $GFXSpec$ under a refinement mapping in which $result$ is implemented by variable $result$ of GFX. From this, it follows that proving the correctness of algorithm $SnapShot$ proves the correctness of an algorithm in which the code from $GFXSpec$ in step a is replaced by the corresponding code of GFX.

The **while** loop at label b implements the **while** loop of $SnapSpec$. Action b, the first action of the loop, first chooses the value v for which the process is performing the $snap$ operation and adds it to $known$. It then writes $Cardinality(NUnion(A2))$, which is an upper bound on the number of processes executing the **while** loop, into $nbpart$. The loop body then executes the Leaky Repository Protocol to write $known$ into registers $A3[0], \ldots, A3[nbpart - 1]$. The properties of the protocol ensure that if the write succeeds, then the value that was written will remain forever a subset of $NUnion(A3)$ if there are still at most

```
--algorithm SnapShot
  { variables result = [p ∈ Proc ↦ {}],
              A2 = [i ∈ Nat ↦ {}],  A3 = [i ∈ Nat ↦ {}];
    process (Pr ∈ Proc)
      variables myVals = {}, known = {}, notKnown = {},
                lnbpart = 0, nbpart = 0, nextout = {}, out = {} ;
    { a: with (P ∈ {Q ∈ SUBSET Proc :
                        ∧ self ∈ Q
                        ∧ ∀p ∈ Proc \ {self} :
                            ∨ Cardinality(result[p]) ≠ Cardinality(Q)
                            ∨ Q = result[p]
                   } )
         { result[self] := P } ;
         A2[Cardinality(result[self]) − 1] := result[self] ;
      b: while ( TRUE )
         {     with (v ∈ Val) { myVals := myVals ∪ {v} } ;
               known := myVals ∪ known ;
               nbpart := Cardinality(NUnion(A2)) ;
           c: lnbpart := nbpart ;
               known := known ∪ NUnion(A3) ;
               notKnown := {i ∈ 0 .. (nbpart − 1) : known ≠ A3[i]} ;
               if (notKnown ≠ {}) { d: with (i ∈ notKnown)
                                          { A3[i] := known };
                                    goto c }
               else if (nbpart = Cardinality(NUnion(A2)))
                      { nextout := known } ;
           e: nbpart := Cardinality(NUnion(A2)) ;
               if (lnbpart = nbpart) {out := known}
               else {goto c}
         }
    }
}
```

Fig. 4. Algorithm *SnapShot*

nbpart processes executing the **while** loop. If so, the *snap* operation finishes and returns that value (by writing *out*); otherwise, the process tries again.

Observe the similarity of actions *c* and *d* of algorithm *SnapShot* and the process code (actions *a* and *b*) of algorithm *GFX*. If you understand why algorithm *GFX* is correct, you will see why algorithm *SnapShot* is. In fact, algorithm *SnapShot* is less subtle because it makes use of a possibly incorrect upper bound on the number of participants, trying again if the bound was not correct.

The safety property satisfied by algorithm *SnapShot* is that it implements *SnapSpec* under a suitable refinement mapping. However, a single process of *SnapShot* executing its *a* action can implement the simultaneous execution of action *C* by multiple processes of *SnapSpec*, each executing the action's **or** clause. To define the refinement mapping, we would have to add a special kind of auxiliary variable that adds "stuttering steps" to algorithm *SnapShot* [1].

Instead of doing that, we modify our specification to allow such simultaneous steps. The necessary specification cannot be expressed in PlusCal, but it is easily written in TLA$^+$ starting with the translation of the PlusCal algorithm in Figure 3.

The modified specification is implemented under the refinement mapping that substitutes the variables *myVals*, *nextout*, and *out* of *SnapShot* for the corresponding variables of *SnapSpec*, and that substitutes the following expression for variable *pc* of *SnapSpec*:

$$[p \in Proc \mapsto \text{CASE } pc[p] \in \{\text{``a''}, \text{``b''}\} \rightarrow \text{``A''}$$
$$\square \; pc[p] \in \{\text{``c''}, \text{``d''}\} \rightarrow \text{``B''}$$
$$\square \; pc[p] = \text{``e''} \rightarrow \text{IF } lnbpart[p] = Cardinality(NUnion(A2))$$
$$\text{THEN ``C'' ELSE ``B''} \;]$$

As usual, the proof of this implementation rests on an invariance proof. The key part of the inductive invariant is:

$$\forall p \in Proc : \forall P \in PA3 : nextout[p] \subseteq NUnion(P)$$

where *PA3* is the set of potential values of *A3*, defined the same way as the set *PA1* of potential values of *A1* for algorithm *GFX*. A rigorous proof is available on the Web [15].

4   Conclusion

We have built on earlier work of Delporte-Gallet et al. (DFGR) [11]. Unlike previous implementations of SWMR registers using arrays of MWMR registers, DFGR provided a non-blocking implementation that did not first solve the renaming problem to allocate registers to processes. However, their implementation required a known bound n on the number of participating processes. It used the Leaky Repository Protocol with n registers, so there were not enough different processes to destroy all traces of a write. To eliminate this requirement, we take full advantage of the protocol in algorithm *GFX*, which allows all traces of a write to be destroyed if each register's value is overwritten by a different process. Using algorithm *GFX*, processes can determine the current number n of participants. We then use a variant of the DFGR algorithm that assumes there are at most n participants, but that aborts and retries if n changes while performing an operation.

We have tried to make our algorithm easier to understand by breaking it into the *GFX* algorithm and the *SnapShot* algorithm that uses *GFX* as a "subroutine". The proof that the two algorithms are non-blocking is straightforward. The safety properties of both algorithms depend on their use of the Leaky Repository Protocol. Here, we have given informal correctness proofs. We have written short, completely formal PlusCal descriptions of the algorithms. Formal machine-checked proofs of their safety properties are available [15].

We have considered only complexity in the number of registers. DFGR showed that at least n registers are required to implement n SWMR registers, so the linear number of registers used by our algorithms is optimal up to a constant factor. The question of step complexity is still completely open. We conjecture that there is an adaptive snapshot algorithm with a linear number of registers with cubic step complexity.

References

1. Abadi, M., Lamport, L.: The existence of refinement mappings. Theoretical Computer Science 82(2), 253–284 (1991)
2. Afek, Y., Attiya, H., Dolev, D., Gafni, E., Merritt, M., Shavit, N.: Atomic snapshots of shared memory. Journal of the ACM 40(4), 873–890 (1993)
3. Afek, Y., Stupp, G., Touitou, D.: Long-lived adaptive collect with applications. In: FOCS, pp. 262–272. IEEE Computer Society (1999)
4. Anderson, J.H.: Multi-writer composite registers. Distributed Computing 7(4), 175–195 (1994)
5. Ashcroft, E.A.: Proving assertions about parallel programs. Journal of Computer and System Sciences 10, 110–135 (1975)
6. Aspnes, J.: Slightly smaller splitter networks. CoRR, abs/1011.3170 (2010)
7. Attiya, H., Bar-Noy, A., Dolev, D., Peleg, D., Reischuk, R.: Renaming in an asynchronous environment. Journal of the ACM 37(3), 524–548 (1990)
8. Attiya, H., Fouren, A.: Adaptive and efficient algorithms for lattice agreement and renaming. SIAM J. Comput. 31(2), 642–664 (2002)
9. Attiya, H., Welch, J.: Distributed Computing. Fundamentals, Simulations, and Advanced Topics. McGraw-Hill (1998)
10. Borowsky, E., Gafni, E.: Immediate atomic snapshots and fast renaming. In: PODC, pp. 41–51. ACM Press (1993)
11. Delporte-Gallet, C., Fauconnier, H., Gafni, E., Rajsbaum, S.: Linear Space Bootstrap Communication Schemes. In: Frey, D., Raynal, M., Sarkar, S., Shyamasundar, R.K., Sinha, P. (eds.) ICDCN 2013. LNCS, vol. 7730, pp. 363–377. Springer, Heidelberg (2013)
12. Fich, F.E., Herlihy, M., Shavit, N.: On the space complexity of randomized synchronization. Journal of the ACM 45(5), 843–862 (1998)
13. Gafni, E.: A simple algorithmic characterization of uniform solvability. In: FOCS, pp. 228–237. IEEE Computer Society (2002)
14. Gafni, E., Merritt, M., Taubenfeld, G.: The concurrency hierarchy, and algorithms for unbounded concurrency. In: PODC, pp. 161–169. ACM (2001)
15. Lamport, L.: Proofs for adaptive register allocation with a linear number of registers, http://research.microsoft.com/en-us/um/people/lamport/tla/snapshot.html
16. Lamport, L.: A fast mutual exclusion algorithm. ACM Transactions on Computer Systems 5(1), 1–11 (1987)
17. Lamport, L.: Specifying Systems, The TLA+ Language and Tools for Hardware and Software Engineers. Addison-Wesley (2002)
18. Lamport, L.: The PlusCal Algorithm Language. In: Leucker, M., Morgan, C. (eds.) ICTAC 2009. LNCS, vol. 5684, pp. 36–60. Springer, Heidelberg (2009)
19. Moir, M., Anderson, J.H.: Wait-free algorithms for fast, long-lived renaming. Sci. Comput. Program. 25(1), 1–39 (1995)

An Optimal Implementation
of Fetch-and-Increment*

Faith Ellen[1] and Philipp Woelfel[2]

[1] University of Toronto
faith@cs.toronto.edu
[2] University of Calgary
woelfel@ucalgary.ca

Abstract. We present a new wait-free implementation of a FETCH&INC object shared by n processes from read-write registers and load-linked/store-conditional (LL/SC) objects. The step complexity of each FI operation is $O(\log n)$, which is optimal. Our implementation uses $O(\max\{m,n\})$ objects, each of which stores $O(\log m)$ bits, where m is the number of FI operations that are performed. For large m, the number of objects can be reduced to $O(n^2)$. Similar implementations of other objects, such as FETCH&ADD and SWAP, are also obtained.

Our implementation uses a new object, called an AGGREGATOR. It supports an operation which, if successful, puts a value into its in-buffer that can depend on the value that is currently there, an operation that copies the value in its in-buffer to its out-buffer, provided its out-buffer is empty, and an operation that empties its out-buffer. We show how to implement an AGGREGATOR from a small constant number of LL/SC objects so that all three operations have constant step complexity.

1 Introduction

The FETCH&INC object is fundamental in distributed computing. It stores an arbitrary non-negative integer. Processes can perform one operation, FI(), that returns the value of the object and increments it. Implementing FETCH&INC is closely related to the mutual exclusion problem. Using FI(), processes can determine an order in which they enter the critical section. Conversely, a solution to mutual exclusion can be used as a lock for accessing a FETCH&INC object implemented using a shared register.

In strong renaming, processes that have names in a large universe want to acquire new distinct names from a range of minimum size, without knowing the number of processes. This is equivalent to implementing single-shot FETCH&INC, where each process is restricted to performing at most one FI().

The consensus number of FETCH&INC is two [7], so it has no deterministic, wait-free, linearizable implementation using only shared registers and counters, both of which have consensus number one. Like FETCH&INC, the counter

---

* This research was supported in part by Discovery Grants and the Canada Research Chair Program of the Natural Sciences and Engineering Research Council of Canada (NSERC), and in part by the HP Innovation Research Program.

Y. Afek (Ed.): DISC 2013, LNCS 8205, pp. 284–298, 2013.
© Springer-Verlag Berlin Heidelberg 2013

stores an arbitrary non-negative integer. However, it supports two operations: incrementing the value of the object and reading it. Allowing a process to do both in one atomic operation makes the FETCH&INC object more powerful than the counter.

A wait-free implementation of a FETCH&INC object shared by n processes can be implemented from any object with consensus number at least two [2]. However, the complexity of such implementations are less well understood. Jayanti [8] proved that the expected step complexity of any randomized wait-free linearizable implementation of an n-process, single-shot FETCH&INC object from LL/SC objects is in $\Omega(\log n)$ against the strong adaptive adversary.

Jayanti [8] also mentioned how a universal construction (for implementing any object given its sequential specifications) by Afek, Dauber, and Touitou [1] that uses only LL/SC objects could be modified to have $O(\log n)$ worst case step complexity. However, he pointed out that this modification requires atomic access to words containing $\Omega(n \log n)$ bits, making the construction impractical, even for the special case of implementing a FETCH&INC object.

Recently, Ellen, Ramachandran, and Woelfel [6] gave an implementation of a FETCH&INC object from $O(\log m)$-bit registers and LL/SC objects with $O(\log^2 n)$ worst case step complexity, where m is the number of FI() operations that are performed. Efficient randomized implementations of FETCH&INC also exist [4], but it is not known how to derandomize them.

Jayanti left open the problem of obtaining an asymptotic improvement to his lower bound when the word size of the LL/SC objects is restricted to $O(\log n)$ bits. In this paper, we show that this is impossible by presenting a wait-free, linearizable implementation of a FETCH&INC object with $O(\log n)$ worst case step complexity from $O(\log m)$-bit registers and LL/SC objects. Our implementation uses $O(\max\{n, m\})$ objects. Using a new memory reclamation scheme [3], we can reduce the number of LL/SC objects to $O(n^2)$. For a single-shot FETCH&INC object, our implementation uses $O(n)$ registers and LL/SC objects each storing $O(\log n)$ bits.

More generally, if f is an arbitrary binary associative function, we can implement a FETCH&f object that supports one operation, which, on input x, returns the value v of the object and updates its value to $f(v, x)$. For example, FETCH&ADD is a FETCH&f object, where $f(v, x) = v + x$, and SWAP is a FETCH&f object, where $f(v, x) = x$.

Our implementation of FETCH&INC is built using AGGREGATOR objects, which we define in Section 2. We also give a linearizable wait-free implementation of an AGGREGATOR object from three LL/SC objects so that each operation it supports has constant worst case step complexity. In Section 3, we describe our implementation of a FETCH&INC object using AGGREGATOR objects. The extension to FETCH&f objects is briefly described at the end of the paper.

2   The AGGREGATOR Object

An AGGREGATOR object stores data in two areas, the in-buffer and the out-buffer, and maintains a bit, $flag$. The object allows a value to be put into its in-buffer, the value in its in-buffer to be copied to its out-buffer, and the out-buffer to be emptied. The *flag* is used to indicate whether the contents of the in-buffer has been successfully copied to the out-buffer.

The in-buffer is accessed using the operation pair LLIn() and SCIn() which are similar to LL() and SC() in that an LLIn() returns the value of the in-buffer and the *flag*, and SCIn(v) stores the value v in the in-buffer and resets *flag*, provided that neither the in-buffer nor the *flag* were changed since its preceding LLIn() operation. A successful Copy() operation copies the value of the in-buffer to the out-buffer and sets the *flag*, provided that the in-buffer is non-empty, *flag* is not set, and the out-buffer is empty. Otherwise, it fails and does not change the AGGREGATOR object. The out-buffer can be read using the operation LLOut(). The operation RCOut() resets the out-buffer to empty (indicated by $\perp$), provided the out-buffer has not changed since the preceding LLOut() operation by the process that called RCOut().

The name AGGREGATOR comes from the fact that the in-buffer can be used to aggregate information. More precisely, processes can use LLIn() and SCIn() operations to read information from the in-buffer and to modify or add to the information that is already there. Since writes are conditional, they don't inadvertently destroy data that is in the in-buffer. After aggregating information in the in-buffer, processes can try to copy the data from the in-buffer to the out-buffer. They do this using the Copy() operation, which guarantees that any data in the out-buffer does not get overwritten. If successful, this operation sets the *flag* to indicate that the in-buffer has been copied. (However, the next successful SCIn() operation will reset the *flag*.) Once there is information in the out-buffer, processes can read it, process the data, store the result somewhere else (for example, in the in-buffer of a different AGGREGATOR object), and reset the out-buffer to $\perp$ using the RCOut() operation. If LLOut() and RCOut() are used properly, their semantics ensure that the data in the out-buffer has been processed by some process before the out-buffer gets reset.

2.1   Formal Specification

Formally, an AGGREGATOR object $\mathcal{O}$ with domain D stores a triple of values $(in, flag, out) \in (D \cup \{\perp\}) \times \{\text{True}, \text{False}\} \times (D \cup \{\perp\})$, where $\perp \notin D$. Initially, $in = \perp$, $flag = \text{False}$, and $out = \perp$. The objects supports five operations:

LLIn() returns the values of in and $flag$, and LLOut() returns the value of out.

SCIn(v) changes the value of in to $v \neq \perp$ and sets the value of $flag$ to False, provided no successful SCIn() or successful Copy() (on $\mathcal{O}$) by any process has been performed since the calling process last performed LLIn(). This operation can only be performed by a process if it has previously performed LLIn(), when it last did so, it received a value other than v for in, and it has not performed Copy() since its last LLIn() operation. If the value of in changes as a result of this operation, we say the operation is *successful*. If not, we say it is *unsuccessful*. In either case, SCIn() does not return anything.

RCOut() resets the value of *out* to $\perp$, provided no successful RCOut() or Copy() (on $\mathcal{O}$) by any process has been performed since the calling process last performed LLOut(). This operation can only be performed by a process if it has previously performed LLOut(), when it last did so, it received a value other than $\perp$, and it has not performed Copy() since its last LLOut() operation. If the value of *out* changes as a result of this operation, we say the operation is *successful*. If not, we say it is *unsuccessful*. In either case, RCOut() does not return anything.

Copy() sets the value of *out* to *in* and the value of *flag* to True, provided *out* $= \perp$, *in* $\neq \perp$, and *flag* $=$ False. In this case, we say the operation is *successful*. If not, we say it is *unsuccessful*. In either case, Copy() does not return anything.

Note that, if a process performs two SCIn() operations without performing LLIn() between them, the second SCIn() operation is always unsuccessful. Similarly, if a process performs two RCOut() operations without performing LLOut() between them, the second RCOut() operation is always unsuccessful.

2.2 Implementation

Our implementation of an AGGREGATOR object is presented in Figure 1. For clarity, it uses three LL/SC objects that also support an *invalidate link* operation, IL(). If a process calls LL() followed by IL() and then SC(), all on the same object, then the SC() operation will fail. Note that an IL() operation by process p only affects SC() operations of p, not those of other processes. A process can implement IL() locally using a persistent local variable for each LL/SC object it accesses to record whether it has performed IL() on the object since it last performed LL() on it.

One of the LL/SC objects, which we denote by the pair (X, F), is responsible for storing the pair $(in, flag)$ of the AGGREGATOR. Both X and F are stored in the same LL/SC object because an SCIn(v) operation may have to reset F when it writes v to X. Another LL/SC object, Y, is used to keep track of the contents of the out-buffer. The naive approach would be to implement LLIn() and SCIn() using LL()/SC() operations on (X, F) and to implement LLOut()/RCOut() using LL()/SC() operations on Y. However, the problem is the Copy() operation, which has to succeed as long as the out-buffer is empty, the in-buffer is non-empty, and the *flag* is not set. For example, to set the *flag* during a Copy() operation, a process would have to perform a successful SC() on (X, F), but this may never happen if other processes repeatedly write data into (X, F) using SCIn() operations.

Therefore, we use a third LL/SC object, B, which stores one bit that is initially False. A process that wants to perform a Copy() operation sets the bit B to True to indicate that other processes should not continue executing SC() operations on (X, F) or Y until the Copy() operation has completed. To ensure linearizability, processes instead help to finish the tasks that have to be performed during a Copy() operation. This helping mechanism is realized by a method Helper(), which processes call only when they see that $B =$ True.

Function LLIn	**Procedure** SCIn(v)

Function LLIn

1 $(x, f) := (X, F).\text{LL}()$;
2 if $B.\text{LL}()$ then Helper();
3 $(x', f') := (X, F).\text{LL}()$;
4 if $B.\text{LL}()$ then
5   Helper();
6   return (x, f);
7 return (x', f');

Procedure SCIn(v)

20 **Precondition:** $v \neq \bot$;
21 **Precondition:** *The process previously performed* LLIn()*, when it did so last the value of in was not v, and the process has not performed* Copy() *since then.*;
22 if $\neg B.\text{LL}()$ then $(X, F).\text{SC}(v, \text{False})$;
23 if $B.\text{LL}()$ then Helper();

Function LLOut

8 $y := Y.\text{LL}()$;
9 if $B.\text{LL}()$ then
10   Helper();
11   return $\bot$;
12 return y;

Procedure RCOut

24 **Precondition:** *The process previously performed* LLOut()*, when it did so last the value returned was not $\bot$, and the process has not performed* Copy() *since then.*;
25 if $\neg B.\text{LL}()$ then $Y.\text{SC}(\bot)$;
26 if $B.\text{LL}()$ then Helper();

Procedure Copy

13 $b := B.\text{LL}()$;
14 $y := Y.\text{LL}()$;
15 $(x, f) := (X, F).\text{LL}()$;
16 if $y = \bot \neq x \wedge b = f = \text{False}$ then
17     $B.\text{SC}(\text{True})$;
18 if $B.\text{LL}()$ then Helper();
19 $Y.\text{IL}()$; $(X, F).\text{IL}()$;

Procedure Helper

27 **repeat** three times
28     $y := Y.\text{LL}()$;
29     $(x, f) := (X, F).\text{LL}()$;
30     $b := B.\text{LL}()$;
31   if b then
32   if $\neg f$ then $(X, F).\text{SC}(x, \text{True})$;
33        $(x, f) := (X, F).\text{LL}()$;
34   if f then
35   if $y = \bot$ then $Y.\text{SC}(x)$;
36           $y := Y.\text{LL}()$;
37   if $y \neq \bot$ then $B.\text{SC}(\text{False})$

38 $Y.\text{IL}()$; $(X, F).\text{IL}()$;

Fig. 1. Implementation of an AGGREGATOR object

The implementation guarantees that each Helper() call finishes only after a Copy() operation completes and B is reset to False. The interval that starts when a process sets B to True and which ends when some process (not necessarily the same one) resets B to False is called a *helper interval*.

We now explain the implementation in more detail. Consider the Copy() operation. First, a process reads B, Y, and (X, F) using LL() operations (lines 13-15). If the values of X, F, and Y are such that the Copy() should succeed and $B = \text{False}$, the process tries to write True to B using an SC() operation (lines 16-17). Thus, while a helper interval is in progress, no other process writes

True to B. The Copy() operation of the process that successfully changes the value of B from False to True succeeds and will be linearized at the end of the helper interval that this process started. A Copy() operation which does not change B to True fails and can be linearized immediately after the successful Copy(), since $flag$ is then True. To ensure an unsuccessful Copy() doesn't finish too early, it calls Helper() on line 18 if it sees that B is still True. At the end of Copy(), each process needs to invalidate its links to Y and (X, F) (line 19), so that SC()s performed in its subsequent RCOut() or SCIn() operations are not linked to the LL()s it performed on Y and (X, F) during Copy().

Now consider LLOut(). First, a process uses LL() to read Y (line 8), which usually stores the contents of the out-buffer. Then it checks B to see whether a Copy() operation is in progress (line 9). If not, then the process simply returns the value it read from Y (line 12). Otherwise, it helps the ongoing Copy() operation finish by calling Helper(), and then returns $\perp$ (lines 10–11). In this case, the LLOut() is linearized immediately before this successful Copy() operation is linearized, at which point the out-buffer is empty.

Similarly, during LLIn() a process first reads (X, F) into the local variables (x, f) using LL() (line 1). Then, it checks B and calls Helper() if a Copy() operation is in progress (line 2). But now the process cannot simply return the pair (x, f). For example, suppose the process read $F = $ True and $B = $ True near the end of a helper interval. Then the LLIn() has to be linearized after the successful Copy() that is linearized at the end of this interval. At the point that it is linearized, the LLIn() must have a valid link to (X, F). However, for reasons explained later, the process invalidates the link it has to (X, F) at the end of Helper() (line 38). Therefore, the process performs another LL() operation on (X, F) (line 3). Then it checks B one more time (line 4). If B is not set, then, in line 7, the process simply returns the pair it read from its second LL() operation, which is its linearization point. If B is set, the process calls Helper() (line 5) and, in line 6, returns the pair (x, f) it received from its first LL() operation. In this case, the LLIn() can be linearized immediately following the first successful Copy() after it began. This is because at least one more Copy() operation will be linearized at or before the LLIn() completes its second call to Helper(). Hence, it is correct that the process does not have a valid link to (X, F) when it returns from LLIn().

Operations SCIn() and RCOut() are rather simple: The calling process checks whether B is set and, if not, it executes the corresponding SC() operation on (X, F) or Y, respectively. Then the process checks B one more time and calls Helper() if B is set. If the SC() operation succeeds, the SCIn() or RCOut() is successful and is linearized at the SC() operation. Otherwise, the operation fails. If its operation interval includes the end of a helper interval, the failed operation can be linearized there, immediately after a successful Copy() operation. If not, $B = $ False when the process performed the first of these LLs and the operation can be linearized at its unsuccessful SC().

The task of Helper() is to change the in-buffer, the out-buffer, and $flag$ as required by a Copy() operation. The idea is to first set F to True while $Y = \perp$

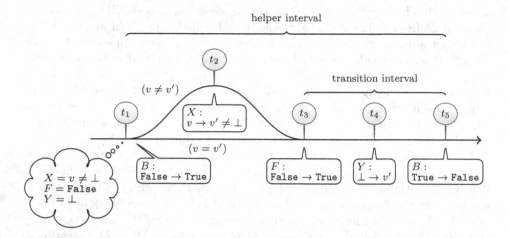

Fig. 2. Illustration of state changes during a helper interval. No changes to the shared objects occur, other than the ones depicted.

and then copy X to Y. The interval while $F = \text{True}$ and $Y = \perp$ is called a *transition interval*. This is the only interval during which the state (X, F, Y) does not correspond to a valid state of the AGGREGATOR object. Instead, for our proof of linearizability (in the full version of the paper), we consider the *interpreted state* of the object, which is $(X, \text{False}, \perp)$ during the transition interval, corresponding to the state of an AGGREGATOR object just before a successful Copy() operation.

The SC() operations required to update (X, F) and Y may fail, so a process has to repeat the sequence of steps in lines 28–37 three times. First, the process reads Y, (X, F), and B with LL() operations and then checks whether $B = \text{True}$ (lines 28–31). If $B = \text{False}$, the helper interval has already ended, and the process no longer needs to update (X, F) or Y. Now suppose $B = \text{True}$. In this case, the process first checks whether F was already True when it read it and, if not, it sets it to True using an SC() operation (line 32). Then, it reads (X, F) again using a LL() operation and verifies that F is now True (lines 33–34). If so, then, in line 35, the process tries to store the value of X it read on line 33 into Y, provided $Y = \perp$. Then, the process reads Y again and, if $Y \neq \perp$, indicating that its or some other process performed a successful SC() on Y, it tries to reset B (line 37). The proper nesting of LL and SC operations ensures that once $F = \text{True}$, X no longer changes. Moreover, Y is only changed once during a helper interval and the value to which it is changed is the value X had when F changed to True. Finally, B is only reset after all of this has happened.

Figure 2 illustrates how the values of the LL/SC objects (X, F), Y, and B may change during a helper interval. The full proof of linearizability is omitted due to space constraints and will be provided in the full version of the paper.

3   Fetch-and-Increment

There is a simple non-blocking implementation of a FETCH&INC object shared by n processes using one LL/SC object with initial value 0: Each process performs FI() by repeatedly applying LL() and then trying to increment the value of the object by applying SC(), until it is successful. Its result is the value returned by its last LL(). If each process is not allowed to perform more than one FI(), this construction gives a wait-free implementation of single-shot FETCH&INC, where FI() has worst case step complexity $\Theta(n)$.

Another approach, which we use here, is to represent a FETCH&INC object by a list of process identifiers. To perform FI(), a process appends its identifier to the end of the list and returns the number of elements in the list that precede the last occurrence of its identifier. We represent this list by an ordered in-tree, with one node per element. The list is the sequence of elements in the nodes, listed according to a preorder traversal of the in-tree. Each subtree represents a sublist beginning with the element stored at the root of the subtree. The element stored at the root of the tree is the head of the list. It is followed by the sublists represented by each child of the root, in order from oldest to youngest (i.e. left to right).

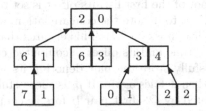

Fig. 3. An in-tree representing the list 2,6,7,6,3,0,2

Each node contains a process identifier, *id*, a pointer to its parent, *ptr*, and an integer, *offset*. The parent pointer of the root is NIL and its offset is 0. The offset of any other node is the number of elements that precede it in the list represented by the subtree rooted at its parent. The number of elements in the list preceding the element in a given node can be obtained by summing all the offsets of all the nodes on the path from the node to the root. The time to do this is proportional to the depth of its node. Therefore, we want the height of the in-tree to be small. The in-tree in Figure 3 represents the list 2,6,7,6,3,0,2. The first component of each node of the in-tree is the process identifier and the second component is the offset.

If h is a pointer to the root of an in-tree of size at least ℓ, then the pair (h, ℓ) denotes the prefix of length ℓ of the list represented by this in-tree. For example, in Figure 3, if h is a pointer to the root of the in-tree and h' is a pointer to the node with identifier 3, then $(h, 7)$ denotes the entire list, $(h, 4)$ denotes the list 2,6,7,6, and $(h', 3)$ denotes the list 3,0,2. The pair (NIL, 0) denotes an empty list. If (h_1, ℓ_1) and (h_2, ℓ_2) denote nonempty lists and the trees rooted at h_1 and h_2

have no nodes in common, they can be concatenated by atomically setting h_2's parent pointer and offset to h_1 and ℓ_1, respectively. The resulting list is denoted by the pair $(h_1, \ell_1 + \ell_2)$.

As an introduction to our wait-free implementation, we present a non-blocking implementation of FETCH&INC based on this representation. Figure 4 gives the code for process p_i. Each node of the list is stored in a pair of registers, one containing its *id* and the other containing its *ptr* and *offset*. There is also a single LL/SC object, Q, that stores a quadruple, $(h_1, \ell_1, h_2, \ell_2)$, which is initially (NIL, 0, NIL, 0). If (h_1, ℓ_1) and (h_2, ℓ_2) both denote empty lists, we say that the quadruple denotes the empty list. If exactly one of them denotes a nonempty list, we say that the quadruple denotes that list. If they both denote nonempty lists then the quadruple denotes their concatenation.

To perform FI(), a process p_i creates a node containing its identifier i, a NIL parent pointer, and offset 0 (lines 40–42). Then it tries to store the pair denoting this list into Q's second pair, provided Q's second pair denotes an empty list (line 47). If it is successful, the FI() can be linearized at this point. Next, p_i tries to concatenate the list denoted by Q's second pair to the the list denoted by its first pair. There are two cases: When Q's first pair denotes an empty list, then the two lists are simply interchanged (line 51). When both pairs in Q denote nonempty lists (and Q denotes their concatenation), the root of the second list is made a child of the root of the first list, its offset is set to be the length of the first list, Q's first pair is set to denote the concatenation, and Q's second pair is set to denote an empty list (lines 53–54). This ensures that only one element is appended to the list at a time and its offset is computed correctly.

If p_i does not successfully store the pair denoting its one node list into Q's second pair on line 47, then it tries again. If p_i is successful, its node is concatenated onto the list denoted by Q's first pair before p_i completes the rest of the iteration of the loop and p_i returns the offset stored at its node. Although many processes may try to do this concatenation, each writing to the *ptr* and *offset* fields of p_i's node on line 53, they all write the same values and, thereafter, no other values are written to p_i's node.

To obtain a wait-free implementation of FI(), the approach in [1,8] and [6] is to use a fixed, balanced binary tree T with n leaves, one per process. A process p_i that wants to perform FI() begins by putting information in the list at its leaf. Then it tries to propagate this information up the tree to the root. It tries to propagate information from a child to its parent using a constant number of steps. Specifically, a process p_i gets the new information from a vertex and its sibling after performing an LL() at their parent. Then it tries to add that information to their parent using an SC(). If the SC() is not successful because another process did a successful SC() between p_i's LL() and SC(), p_i repeats this a second time. If its second SC() is also unsuccessful, then the information it wanted to propagate is guaranteed to have been propagated to the parent by another process. To see why, suppose the first SC() by process p_i was unsuccessful because of a successful SC() by process p_j and the second SC() by process p_i was unsuccessful because of a successful SC() by process p_k. Then the LL() by

Function FI
39 $s := $ **False**
40 $h := $ new Node
41 $h.id := i$
42 $h.(ptr, offset) := (\text{NIL}, 0)$
43 **repeat**
44        $(h_1, \ell_1, h_2, \ell_2) := Q.\text{LL}()$
45   **if** $h_2 = \text{NIL}$ **then**
46   **if** $Q.\text{SC } (h_1, \ell_1, h, 1)$ is successful **then**
47                    $s := $ **True**
48              $(h_1, \ell_1, h_2, \ell_2) := Q.\text{LL}()$
49   **if** $h_2 \neq \text{NIL}$ **then**
50   **if** $h_1 = \text{NIL}$ **then**
51                    $Q.\text{SC } (h_2, \ell_2, \text{NIL}, 0)$
52   **else**
53                    $h_2.(ptr, offset) := (h_1, \ell_1)$
54                    $Q.\text{SC } (h_1, \ell_1 + \ell_2, \text{NIL}, 0)$
55 **until** $s = $ **True**
56 **return** $h.offset$

Fig. 4. A non-blocking implementation

Function FI
57 $v := T.leaf[i]$
58 $h := $ new Node
59 $h.id := i$
60 $h.(ptr, offset) := (\text{NIL}, 0)$
61 $v.\text{LLIn}()$
62 $v.\text{SCIn}(h, 1, \text{NIL}, 0, left)$
63 $v.\text{Copy}()$
64 **while** $v \neq T.root$ **do**
65        $v := v.parent$
66   **for** 5 *times* **do**
67              $\text{CopyUpInto}(v)$
68 $(h_1, \ell_1, h_2, \ell_2, c, f) := v.\text{LLIn}()$
69 **if** $h_2 \neq \text{NIL}$ **then**
70        $h_2.(ptr, offset) := (h_1, \ell_1)$
71 $result := h.offset$
72 **while** $h.ptr \neq \text{NIL}$ **do**
73        $h := h.ptr$
74        $result := result + h.offset$
75 **return** $result$

Fig. 5. A wait-free implementation

process p_k occurred after the SC() by process p_j, so process p_k gets at least all the information that was in the children immediately prior to the first of the two LL()s by process p_i.

We do something similar in our wait-free implementation. The code for process p_i is presented in Figure 5. Each vertex of T contains two pairs denoting lists. To perform FI(), a process p_i creates a node containing its identifier i, a NIL parent pointer, and offset 0 (lines 58–60) and puts a pair denoting this one element list into its leaf (lines 61–63). Then it progresses up the tree T, one vertex at a time. At each vertex v, it performs CopyUpInto(v) five times (lines 66–67). CopyUpInto(v), which is presented in Figure 6, tries to copy a pair into v from one of its children and change which child should be considered next.

When a process p_i performs CopyUpInto(v) five times, it ensures that the pair denoting the list containing its node has been moved to vertex v. Thus, when process p_i reaches the root of T, its node is in a list denoted by a pair in the root of T. If both the first pair (h_1, ℓ_1) and second pair (h_2, ℓ_2) denote non-empty lists, process p_i concatenates them (line 70). At this point, its node is in the list denoted by the first pair in the root of T. Then it computes its result by adding the offsets of all nodes on the path from its node to the root of the in-tree representing this list (lines 71–74). The FI() is linearized when its node becomes part of the in-tree representing the list at the root of T. If multiple operations are linearized at the same time, they are linearized in the same order as they appear in the list.

Procedure CopyUpInto(v)

76 Precondition: v is not a leaf
77 $(h_1, \ell_1, h_2, \ell_2, c, f) := v.\text{LLIn}()$
78 if $f = \text{True}$ then
79 $\quad$ $h_1 := \text{NIL}$
80 $\quad$ $\ell_1 := 0$
81 else if $h_2 \neq \text{NIL}$ then
82 $\quad$ if $h_1 = \text{NIL}$ then
83 $\quad\quad$ $h_1 := h_2$
84 $\quad\quad$ $\ell_1 := \ell_2$
85 $\quad$ else
86 $\quad\quad$ $h_2.(ptr, \mathit{offset}) := (h_1, \ell_1)$
87 $\quad\quad$ $\ell_1 := \ell_1 + \ell_2$

88 Let w be the child of v on side c and let $\bar{c}$ be the other side
89 $w.\text{Copy}()$
90 $wout := w.\text{LLOut}()$
91 if $wout = \bot$ then
92 $\quad$ $v.\text{SCIn}(h_1, \ell_1, h_2, \ell_2, \bar{c})$
93 else if $wout.h_1 = \text{NIL}$ then
94 $\quad$ $v.\text{SCIn}(h_1, \ell_1, wout.h_2, wout.\ell_2, \bar{c})$
95 else
96 $\quad$ $wout.h_2.(ptr, \mathit{offset}) := (wout.h_1, wout.\ell_1)$
97 $\quad$ $v.\text{SCIn}(h_1, \ell_1, wout.h_1, wout.\ell_1 + wout.\ell_2, \bar{c})$

98 $(h_1, \ell_1, h_2, \ell_2, c, f) := v.\text{LLIn}()$
99 Let w be the child of v on side $\bar{c} \neq c$
100 $wout := w.\text{LLOut}()$
101 if $wout \neq \bot$ then
102 $\quad$ $h := wout.h_1$
103 $\quad$ if $h = \text{NIL}$ then $h := wout.h_2$
104 $\quad$ if $h \in \{\text{NIL}, h_1, h_2\}$ then $w.\text{RCOut}()$

105 return

Fig. 6. A procedure used in the wait-free implementation of FI

To ensure that the same pair doesn't get copied up from a child to its parent more than once, we use an AGGREGATOR at each vertex of the tree T. The domain D of each AGGREGATOR consists of quintuples containing two pairs, (h_1, ℓ_1) and (h_2, ℓ_2), that denote lists and a bit, $c \in \{\mathit{left}, \mathit{right}\}$, that indicates which child of v should be considered next. Initially, $v.in = (\text{NIL}, 0, \text{NIL}, 0, \mathit{left})$, $v.\mathit{flag} = \text{False}$ and $v.out = \bot$ for all vertices v. Since $v.in \neq \bot$ initially, it follows from the specifications of AGGREGATOR that $v.in$ is never $\bot$. After a list has been copied from the out-buffer of a child to the in-buffer of its parent, the out-buffer of that child is reset to $\bot$, before any further lists are copied to the in-buffer of the parent. The semantics of an AGGREGATOR ensure that the out-buffer has been reset before another list can be copied into it. We maintain the following invariants for all non-leaf vertices v:

1. If w is the child of v on side $v.in.c$ and $w.out \neq \perp$, then the list denoted by $w.out$ has not been copied to $v.in$.
2. If w is the sibling of the child of v on side $v.in.c$, $w.out \neq \perp$, and $w.out$ denotes a nonempty list with head h that has been copied to $v.in$, then $h = v.in.h_1$ or $h = v.in.h_2$.

A process p_i begins $\texttt{CopyUpInto}(v)$ by performing $v.\texttt{LLIn}()$ (line 77). If $v.flag = \texttt{True}$, then $v.in$ has already been moved to the out-buffer, so $v.in$ is treated as if it denotes an empty list. Otherwise, it concatenates the lists denoted by the first and second pairs of v (lines 81–87), to make room for a list from w, the child of v on the c side. This is similar to lines 49–54 in the non-blocking implementation of $\texttt{FI}()$.

Next, process p_i considers w, the child of v from the side that was not most recently considered. First p_i tries to copy the quintuple from $w.in$ to $w.out$ (line 89). If $w.out \neq \perp$ immediately beforehand, the copy is unsuccessful. In this case, by Invariant 1, the list denoted by $w.out$ has not been copied to $v.in$. Second, p_i reads the value of w's out-buffer (line 90). If it is $\perp$, then p_i only tries to change the value of $v.in.c$ (line 92). In this case, one possibility is that, in the meantime, some other process has copied a quintuple from w to v and $w.out$ has been reset. The other possibility is that, immediately prior to the $\texttt{Copy}()$, $w.out = \perp$ and $w.flag = \texttt{True}$, which indicates that nothing has been copied into $w.in$ since the last time $w.\texttt{Copy}()$ was performed. If $wout \neq \perp$, p_i concatenates the lists denoted by the first and second pairs of w. Then it tries to atomically copy the pair denoting this list into the second pair in v and change $v.in.c$ (lines 93–97).

Finally, p_i checks whether the out-buffer of the child w that was most recently considered contains an empty list or a nonempty list that has already been copied to v (lines 100–104). If so, it tries to reset $w.out$ to $\perp$ using $\texttt{RCOut}()$ (line 104). Either the $\texttt{RCOut}()$ will be successful or some $\texttt{RCOut}()$ or $\texttt{Copy}()$ performed on w by another process was successful since p_i last performed $w.\texttt{LLOut}()$ on line 100. In either case, $w.out = \perp$ at some point after p_i last performed $w.\texttt{LLOut}()$. This ensures that the information in $w.out$ won't be copied up a second time and makes room for new information to be copied into $w.out$ by a later call to $\texttt{CopyUpInto}(v)$. It also ensures that when $v.in.c$ is next changed, Invariant 1 will be true.

After a process p_i performs $\texttt{CopyUpInto}(v)$ five times consecutively, its current node is in an up-tree that has reached node v. To see why, consider an execution and suppose that, at the point, t_0, immediately before p_i performs the first of these instances, its node is in an in-tree denoted by a pair in $w.in$, for some child w of v. Let t' be the point immediately after the next successful $v.\texttt{SCIn}()$ (on line 92, 94, or 97) by any process, and, for $j = 1, \ldots, 5$, let t_j be the point immediately after the $v.\texttt{SCIn}()$ by process p_i during the j'th of these instances. If it is unsuccessful, then there is a successful $v.\texttt{SCIn}()$ or $v.\texttt{Copy}()$ performed by some other process between t_{j-1} and t_j. Between two successful instances of $v.\texttt{Copy}()$, there must be a successful instance of $v.\texttt{SCIn}()$, to reset

$v.flag$ from True to False. Thus, there are at least two successful instances of
v.SCIn() that occur before t_5 and whose matching instances of v.LLIn() occurred after t'. Since the successful instances of v.SCIn() alternate between the
children from which they try to take a pair, at least one of them will try to copy
a pair from w. This instance will perform w.Copy() between its v.LLIn() and
its v.LLOut(), so it will move the list containing p_i's node from $w.in$ to $w.out$,
if it has not already been moved. Although more elements may be added to the
list at $w.in$ before it is moved to $w.out$, it is not deleted from $w.out$ until after
it has been copied to $v.in$.

3.1   Complexity

CopyUpInto contain no loops or recursive calls, so it has constant step complexity. In the wait-free implementation of FI(), the first while loop is performed
height(T) $\in O(\log n)$ times and the number of times the second while loop is
performed is equal to the depth of the node pointed to by h. By the following
lemma, the in-tree representing the list at the root of T has height bounded
above by height(T). Thus, every node has $O(\log n)$ depth and the worst case
step complexity of the wait-free implementation of FI() is in $O(\log n)$.

Lemma 1. *If $(v.in.h_1, v.in.\ell_1)$ denotes a nonempty list that has not been copied
to its parent, then $height(v.in.h_1) \leq height(v)$. If $(v.in.h_2, v.in.\ell_2)$ denotes a
nonempty list, then $height(v.in.h_2) \leq height(v) - 1$.*

The final in-tree, namely, the in-tree representing the list at the root of T has size
at most m, where m is the number of FI() operations that have been linearized.
A process doesn't complete an instance of FI() until the new node it created
at the beginning of the instance is part of the final in-tree. Hence, the sum of
the sizes of all other in-trees is at most n. As in the two simple, non-blocking
implementations, each *offset* field must store $\Theta(\log m)$ bits, to be large enough
to store the result of an operation. There are m nodes in the data structure,
so each *ptr* field stores $\Theta(\log m)$ bits. If $m \in n^{O(1)}$, then each node contains
$O(\log n)$ bits.

Since T contains $\Theta(n)$ vertices, the total number of objects used by our implementation is $\Theta(\max\{n, m\})$. Using a new memory reclamation scheme by
Aghazadeh, Golab, and Woelfel [3], the number of nodes in use can be bounded
by $O(n^2)$, even as m grows large. In their scheme, each process has a pool of
$2n + O(1)$ nodes from which it allocates a node for each FI() operation it performs. These are all initially in its local free list. There is a local reference counter
associated with each of its nodes (which only it can access). Each process has
two local n-element queues, RECENT$_i$ and ANNOUNCED$_i$, containing NIL
pointers and pointers to its nodes. Initially, they each contain n NIL pointers.
In addition, each process has a local modulo n counter d_i.

When a process p_i performs FI(), it allocates a node j from its free list. If it
makes node j a child of another node (excluding the root of the final in-tree), it
first stores a pointer to that node in the i'th component of an array REF$[0..n-1]$

to announce that it is being referenced by a node owned by process i. After p_i computes the result of this operation, it atomically changes $j.\textit{offset}$ to be that result and $j.\textit{ptr}$ to point directly to the root of the final in-tree. Then it removes the pointer from REF[i].

Process p_i's free list can contain every node in its pool that is not pointed to by any element of REF[$0..n-1$]. However, scanning through this entire array each time it needs to allocate a node is too expensive. Instead, process p_i spends a constant amount of time after each FI() it performs looking for nodes from its pool to add to its free list. First it dequeues a pointer from RECENT$_i$. If it is not NIL, it decrements the local counter associated with the node to which it points and, if it becomes 0, it adds the node to its free list. Then, it does the same thing to ANNOUNCED$_i$. Next, it increments the counter associated with the node it most recently allocated and enqueues a pointer to it in RECENT$_i$. If $REF[d_i]$ contains a pointer to a node from its pool, process p_i increments the counter associated with this node and enqueues a pointer to it in ANNOUNCED$_i$. Otherwise, it enqueues a NIL pointer in ANNOUNCED$_i$. Finally, it increments d_i modulo n. Essentially, process p_i amortizes the work of scanning the announcement array REF over n FI() operations.

3.2 FETCH&f

Our implementation of FI can easily be extended to compute FETCH&$f(x)$ for any binary associative function f. Such a function f can be extended to sequences $x_1, \ldots, x_k$ over its domain by defining $f(x_1) = x_1$ and $f(x_1, \ldots, x_k) = f(f(x_1, \ldots, x_{k-1}), x_k)$ for $k \geq 3$. For the empty sequence, f can be assigned a default value such as 0 or $\perp$.

The idea of this extension is to use the second component of a pair denoting a list of nodes to store f applied to the sequence of inputs to the instances represented by the nodes in the list. Likewise, the offset of any non-root node can be used to store f applied to the sequence of input arguments of all nodes that precede it in the list represented by the in-tree rooted at its parent. To concatenate two lists denoted by the pairs (h_1, ℓ_1) and (h_2, ℓ_2), it suffices to set $h_2.(\textit{ptr}, \textit{offset}) := (h_1, \ell_1)$ and the resulting list is denoted by the pair $(h_1, f(\ell_1, \ell_2))$.

4 Conclusions

In the full version of the paper, we show that our implementation of FI() can be made adaptive, with step complexity $O(\min\{k, \log n\})$, where k denotes the contention. This is optimal, even for randomized algorithms against a strong adaptive adversary [5]. It is not known whether there are faster randomized algorithms against an oblivious adversary.

Jayanti and Petrovic [9] have a wait-free implementation of M different LL/SC objects shared by n processes from $O(M+n^2)$ CAS objects and registers so that each LL and SC operation has $O(1)$ worst-case step complexity. Combined with our implementation, this gives a wait-free implementation of a FETCH&INC object with $O(\log n)$ worst-case step complexity from $O(n^2)$ CAS objects and registers, each of which stores $O(\log m)$ bits. However, a direct implementation would be nice.

References

1. Afek, Y., Dauber, D., Touitou, D.: Wait-free made fast. In: Proceedings of the 27th Annual ACM Symposium on Theory of Computing (STOC), pp. 538–547 (1995)
2. Afek, Y., Weisberger, E., Weisman, H.: A completeness theorem for a class of synchronization objects. In: Proceedings of the 12th SIGACT-SIGOPS Symposium on Principles of Distributed Computing (PODC), pp. 159–170 (1993)
3. Aghazadeh, Z., Golab, W., Woelfel, P.: Brief announcement: Resettable objects and efficient memory reclamation for concurrent algorithms. In: Proceedings of the 32nd SIGACT-SIGOPS Symposium on Principles of Distributed Computing (PODC) (2013)
4. Alistarh, D., Aspnes, J., Censor-Hillel, K., Gilbert, S., Zadimoghaddam, M.: Optimal-time adaptive strong renaming, with applications to counting. In: Proceedings of the 30th SIGACT-SIGOPS Symposium on Principles of Distributed Computing (PODC), pp. 239–248 (2011)
5. Buss, J.F., Kanellakis, P.C., Ragde, P.L., Shvartsman, A.A.: Parallel algorithms with processor failures and delays. J. Algs. 20, 45–86 (1996)
6. Ellen, F., Ramachandran, V., Woelfel, P.: Efficient fetch-and-increment. In: Aguilera, M.K. (ed.) DISC 2012. LNCS, vol. 7611, pp. 16–30. Springer, Heidelberg (2012)
7. Herlihy, M.: Wait-free synchronization. ACM Transactions on Programming Languages and Systems 13(1), 124–149 (1991)
8. Jayanti, P.: A time complexity lower bound for randomized implementations of some shared objects. In: Proceedings of the 9th SIGACT-SIGOPS Symposium on Principles of Distributed Computing (PODC), pp. 201–210 (1998)
9. Jayanti, P., Petrovic, S.: Efficiently implementing a large number of LL/SC objects. In: Anderson, J.H., Prencipe, G., Wattenhofer, R. (eds.) OPODIS 2005. LNCS, vol. 3974, pp. 17–31. Springer, Heidelberg (2006)

On Barriers and the Gap
between Active and Passive Replication

Flavio P. Junqueira[1] and Marco Serafini[2]

[1] Microsoft Research, Cambridge, UK
fpj@apache.org
[2] Yahoo! Research, Barcelona, Spain
serafini@yahoo-inc.com

Abstract. Active replication is commonly built on top of the atomic broad-cast primitive. Passive replication, which has been recently used in the popular ZooKeeper coordination system, can be naturally built on top of the primary-order atomic broadcast primitive. Passive replication differs from active replication in that it requires processes to cross a *barrier* before they become primaries and start broadcasting messages. In this paper, we propose a barrier function τ that explains and encapsulates the differences between existing primary-order atomic broadcast algorithms. We also show that implementing primary-order atomic broadcast on top of a generic consensus primitive and τ inherently results in higher time complexity than atomic broadcast, as witnessed by existing algorithms. We overcome this problem by presenting an alternative, primary-order atomic broadcast implementation that builds on top of a generic consensus primitive and uses consensus itself to form a barrier. This algorithm is modular and matches the time complexity of existing τ-based algorithms.

1 Introduction

Passive replication is a popular approach to achieve fault tolerance in practical systems [3]. Systems like ZooKeeper [8] or Megastore [1] use primary replicas to produce state updates or state mutations. Passive replication uses two types of replicas: primaries and backups. A primary replica executes client operations, without assuming that the execution is deterministic, and produces state updates. Backups apply state updates in the order generated by the primary. With active replication, by contrast, all replicas execute all client operations, assuming that the execution is deterministic. Replicas execute a sequence of consensus instances on client operations to agree on a single execution sequence using atomic broadcast (abcast). Passive replication has a few advantages such as simplifying the design of replicated systems with non-deterministic operations, *e.g.*, those depending on timeouts or interrupts.

It has been observed by Junqueira *et al.* [9] and Birman *et al.* [2] that using atomic broadcast for passive, instead of active, replication requires taking care of specific constraints. State updates must be applied in the exact sequence in which they have been generated: if a primary is in state A and executes an operation making it transition to state update B, the resulting state update δ_{AB} must be applied to state A. Applying it to a different state $C \neq A$ is not safe because it might lead to an incorrect state, which

Y. Afek (Ed.): DISC 2013, LNCS 8205, pp. 299–313, 2013.
© Springer-Verlag Berlin Heidelberg 2013

is inconsistent with the history observed by the primary and potentially the clients. Because a state update is the difference between a new state and the previous, there is a causal dependency between state updates. Unfortunately, passive replication algorithms on top of atomic broadcast (*abcast*) do not necessarily preserve this dependency: if multiple primaries are concurrently present in the system, they may generate conflicting state updates that followers end up applying in the wrong order. Primary-order atomic broadcast (*POabcast*) algorithms, like Zab [9], have additional safety properties that solve this problem. In particular, it implements a *barrier*, the *isPrimary* predicate, which must be crossed by processes that want to broadcast messages.

Interestingly, the only existing passive replication algorithm using consensus as a communication primitive, the semi-passive replication algorithm of Defago *et al.* [7], has linear time complexity in the number of concurrently submitted requests. Recent algorithms for passive replication have constant complexity but they directly implement *POabcast* without building on top of consensus [2,9].

During our work on the ZooKeeper coordination system [8] we have realized that it is still not clear how these algorithms relate, and whether this trade-off between modularity and time complexity is inherent. This paper shows that existing implementations of passive replication can be seen as instances of the same unified consensus-based *POabcast* algorithm, which is basically an atomic broadcast algorithm with a barrier predicate implemented through a *barrier function* τ we define in this work. The τ function outputs the identifier of the consensus instance a leader process must decide on before becoming a primary.

Existing algorithms constitute alternative implementations of τ; the discriminant is whether they consider the underlying consensus algorithm as a black-box whose internal state cannot be observed. Our τ-based algorithm exposes an inherent trade off. We show that if one implements τ while considering the consensus implementation as a black box, it is *necessary* to execute consensus instances sequentially, resulting in higher time complexity. This algorithm corresponds to semi-passive replication.

If the τ implementation can observe the internal state of the consensus primitive, we can avoid the impossibility and execute parallel instances. For example, Zab is similar to the instance of our unified algorithm that uses Paxos as the underlying consensus algorithm and implements the barrier by reading the internal state of the Paxos protocol. We experimentally evaluate that using parallel instances almost doubles the maximum throughput of passive replication in stable periods, even considering optimizations such as batching. Abstracting away these two alternatives and their inherent limitations regarding time complexity and modularity is one of the main observations of this paper.

Finally, we devise a τ-*free POabcast* algorithm that makes this trade off unnecessary, since it enables running parallel consensus instances using an unmodified consensus primitive as a black box. Unlike barrier-based algorithms, a process becomes a primary by proposing a special value in the next available consensus instances; this value marks the end of the sequence of accepted messages from old primaries. Table 1 compares the different PO abcast algorithms we discuss in our paper.

Table 1. Time complexity of *POabcast* algorithms presented in this paper - see Sect. 5.4 and 6 for detail. We consider the use of Paxos as the underlying consensus algorithm since it has optimal latency [12]. However, only the third solution *requires* the use of Paxos; the other algorithms can use any implementation of consensus. For the latency analysis only, we assume that message delays are equal to Δ. The *Stable periods* column reports the time, in a passive replication system, between the receipt of a client request and its delivery by a single broadcasting primary/leader (c is the number of clients). The *Leader change* column reports idle time after a new single leader is elected by Ω and before it can broadcast new messages.

	Stable periods	Leader change
Atomic broadcast [11]	2Δ	2Δ
τ-based *POabcast* (Sect. 5.1)	$2\Delta \cdot c$	4Δ
τ-based *POabcast* with white-box Paxos (Sect. 5.3)	2Δ	4Δ
τ-free *POabcast* (Sect. 6)	2Δ	4Δ

Our barrier-free algorithm shows that both active and passive replication can be implemented on top of a black-box consensus primitive with small and well understood changes and without compromising performance.

2 Related Work

Traditional work on passive replication and the primary-backup approach assumes synchronous links [3]. Group communication has been used to support primary-backup systems; it assumes a $\Diamond P$ failure detector for liveness [6]. Both atomic broadcast and *POabcast* can be implemented in a weaker system model, *i.e.*, an asynchronous system equipped with an Ω leader oracle [5]. For example, our algorithms do not need to agree on a new view every time a non-primary process crashes.

Some papers have addressed the problem of reconfiguration: dynamically changing the set of processes participating to the state machine replication group. Vertical Paxos supports reconfiguration by using an external master, which can be a replicated state machine [13]. This supports *primary-backup* systems, defined as replicated systems where write quorums consist of all processes and each single process is a read quorum. Vertical Paxos does not address the issues of passive replication and considers systems where commands, not state updates, are agreed upon by replicas. Virtually Synchronous Paxos (VS Paxos) aims at combining virtual synchrony and Paxos for reconfiguration [2]. Our work assumes a fixed set of processes and does not consider the problem of reconfiguring the set of processes participating to consensus. Shraer *et al.* have recently shown that reconfiguration can be implemented *on top* of a *POabcast* construction as the ones we present in this paper, making it an orthogonal topic [15].

While there has been a large body of work on group communication, only few algorithms implement passive replication in asynchronous systems with Ω failure detectors: semi-passive replication [7], Zab [9] and Virtually synchronous Paxos [2]. We relate these algorithms with our barrier-based algorithms in Sect. 5.5.

Pronto is an algorithm for database replication that shares several design choices with our τ-free algorithm and has the same time complexity in stable periods [14]. Both algorithms elect a primary using an unreliable failure detector and have a similar notion of epochs, which are associated to a single primary. Epoch changes are determined using an agreement protocol, and values from old epochs that are agreed upon after a new epoch has been agreed upon are ignored. Pronto, however, is an active replication protocol: all replicas execute transactions, and non-determinism is handled by agreeing on a per-transaction log of non-deterministic choices that are application specific. Our work focuses on passive replication algorithms, their difference with active replication protocols, and on the notion of barriers in their implementation.

3 System Model and Primitives

Throughout the paper, we consider an asynchronous system composed of a set $\Pi = \{p_1, \ldots, p_n\}$ of processes that can fail by crashing. They implement a passive replication algorithm, executing requests obtained by an unbounded number of client processes, which can also fail by crashing. *Correct* processes are those that never crash. Processes are equipped with an Ω failure detector oracle.

Definition 1 (Leader election oracle). *A leader election oracle Ω operating on a set of processes Π outputs the identifier of some process $p \in \Pi$. Instances of the oracle running on different processes can return different outputs. Eventually, all instances of correct processes permanently output the same correct process.*

Our algorithms build on top of (uniform) consensus, which has the following properties.

Definition 2 (Consensus). *A consensus primitive consists of two operations:* propose(v) *and* decide(v) *of a value v. It satisfies the following properties:*

Termination. *If some correct process proposes a value, every correct process eventually decides some value.*
Validity. *If a processes decides a value, this value was proposed by some process.*
Integrity. *Every correct process decides at most one value.*
Agreement. *No two processes decide differently.*

Since our algorithms use multiple instances of consensus, *propose* and *decide* have an additional parameter denoting the identifier of the consensus instance.

Primary order atomic broadcast (*POabcast*) is an intermediate abstraction used by our unified passive replication algorithm. *POabcast* provides a broadcast primitive *POabcast* and a delivery primitive *POdeliver*. *POabcast* satisfies all safety properties of atomic broadcast.

Definition 3 (Atomic broadcast). *An atomic broadcast primitive consists of two operations:* broadcast *and* deliver *of a value. It satisfies the following properties:*

Integrity. *If some process delivers v then some process has broadcast v.*
Total Order. *If some process delivers v before v' then any process that delivers v' must deliver v before v'.*

Agreement. *If some process p_i delivers v and some other process p_j delivers v', then either p_i delivers v' or p_j delivers v.*[1]

POabcast extends atomic broadcast by introducing the concept of primary and a *barrier:* the additional *isPrimary()* primitive, which *POabcast* uses to signal when a process is ready to broadcast state updates. This predicate resembles $Prmy_s$ in the specification of Budhiraja *et al.* [3]. However, as failure detectors are unreliable in our model, primary election is also unreliable: there might be multiple concurrent primaries at any given time, unlike in [3].

A *primary epoch* for a process p is a continuous period of time during which *isPrimary()* is true at p and therefore p is a *primary*. Multiple primaries can be present at any given time: the *isPrimary()* predicate is local to a single process and multiple primary epochs can overlap in time. Let P be the set of primaries such that at least one value they propose is ever delivered by some process. A *primary mapping* Λ is a function that maps each primary epoch in P to a unique *primary identifier* λ, which we also use to denote the process executing the primary role. We consider primaries as logical processes: saying that event ϵ occurs at primary λ is equivalent to saying that ϵ occurs at some process p during a primary epoch for p having primary identifier λ.

Definition 4 (Primary order atomic broadcast). *A primary order atomic broadcast primitive consists of two operations* broadcast(v) *and* deliver(v), *and of a binary* isPrimary() *predicate, which indicates whether a process is a primary and is allowed to broadcast a value. Let Λ be a primary mapping and $\prec_\Lambda$ a total order relation among primary identifiers. Primary order broadcast satisfies the Integrity, Total order, and Agreement properties of atomic broadcast; furthermore, it also satisfies the following additional properties:*

Local Primary Order. *If λ broadcasts v before v', then a process that delivers v' delivers v before v'.*

Global Primary Order. *If λ broadcasts v, λ' broadcasts v', $\lambda \prec_\Lambda \lambda'$, and some process p delivers v and v', then p delivers v before v'.*

Primary Integrity. *If λ broadcasts v, λ' broadcasts v', $\lambda \prec_\Lambda \lambda'$, and some process delivers v, then λ' delivers v before it broadcasts v'.*

These properties are partially overlapping, as we show in the full version of the paper [10]. For example, Global primary order is very useful in reasoning about the behaviour of *POabcast*, but it can be implied from the other *POabcast* properties. It is also worth noting that Local primary order is weaker than the single-sender FIFO property, since it only holds within a single primary epoch.

The above properties focus on safety. For liveness, it is sufficient to require the following:

Definition 5 (Eventual Single Primary). *There exists a correct process such that eventually it is elected primary infinitely often and all messages it broadcasts are delivered by some process.*

Definition 6 (Delivery Liveness). *If a process delivers v then eventually every correct process delivers v.*

---

[1] We modified the traditional formulation of agreement to state it as a safety property only.

```
initially
    dec ← 0;
    prop ← 0;
upon POabcast(v) ∧ isPrimary()
    prop ← max(prop + 1, dec + 1);
    propose(v, prop);
upon decide(v, dec + 1)
    dec ← dec + 1;
    POdeliver(v);
function isPrimary()
    return (dec ≥ τ) ∧ (Ω = p);
```

Algorithm 1. *POabcast* based on the barrier function and consensus - process p

4 Unified *POabcast* Algorithm Using the Barrier Function

In passive replication, a primary replica is responsible for executing client operations and for broadcasting state updates. All replicas apply the state updates they deliver to their local state. As we argued in the introduction, atomic broadcast is not sufficient to preserve a correct ordering of state updates. In the full version of this paper, we give an example of incorrect ordering with atomic broadcast and show that using *POabcast* is sufficient to guarantee correctness [10]. In addition to the *POabcast* and *POdeliver* primitives, replicas use the *isPrimary()* predicate to determine whether they should take the primary role.

We now introduce our unified τ-based *POabcast* algorithm (Algorithm 1). It uses three underlying primitives: consensus, the Ω leader oracle, and a new *barrier function* τ we will define shortly.

Like typical atomic broadcast algorithms, our *POabcast* algorithm runs a sequence of consensus instances, each associated with an instance identifier [4]. Broadcast values are proposed using increasing consensus instance identifiers, tracked using the *prop* counter. Values are decided and delivered following the consensus instance order: if the last decided instance was *dec*, only the event $decide(v, dec + 1)$ can be activated, resulting in an invocation of *POdeliver*. This abstracts the buffering of out-of-order decisions between the consensus primitive and our algorithm.

The most important difference between our algorithm and an implementation of atomic broadcast is that it imposes an additional barrier condition for broadcasting messages: it must hold *isPrimary*. In particular, it is necessary for safety that $dec \geq \tau$. The barrier function τ returns an integer and is defined as follows.

Definition 7 (Barrier function). *Let σ be an infinite execution, Λ a primary mapping in σ, $\prec_\Lambda$ a total order among the primary identifiers, and λ a primary such that at least one value it proposes is delivered in σ. A barrier function τ for λ returns:*[2]

$$\tau = \max\{i : \exists v, p, \lambda' \ s.t. \ decide_p(v, i) \in \sigma \wedge propose_{\lambda'}(v, i) \in \sigma \wedge \lambda' \prec_\Lambda \lambda\}$$

---

[2] Subscripts denote the process that executes the *propose* or *decide* steps.

An actual implementation of the τ function can only observe the finite prefix of σ preceding its invocation; however, it must make sure that its outputs are valid in any infinite extension of the current execution. If none of the values proposed by a primary during a primary epoch are ever delivered, τ can return arbitrary values.

We show in the full paper [10] that this definition of τ is sufficient to guarantee the additional properties of *POabcast* compared to atomic broadcast. In particular, it is key to guarantee that the primary integrity property is respected. Local primary order is obtained by delivering elements in the order in which they are proposed and decided.

The key to defining a barrier function is identifying a primary mapping Λ and a total order of primary identifiers $\prec_\Lambda$ that satisfy the barrier property, as we will show in the following section. There are some important observations to do here. First, we use the same primary mapping Λ and total order $\prec_\Lambda$ for the barrier function and for *POabcast*. Note also that a primary might not know its identifier λ: this is only needed for the correctness argument.

5   Implementations of the Barrier Function τ

5.1   Barriers with Black-Box Consensus

We first show how to implement τ using the consensus primitive as a black box. This solution is modular but imposes the use of sequential consensus instances: a primary is allowed to have at most one outstanding broadcast at a time. This corresponds to the semi-passive replication algorithm [7].

Let *prop* and *dec* be the variables used in Algorithm 1, and let τ_{seq} be equal to $\max(prop, dec)$. We have the following result:

Theorem 1. *The function τ_{seq} is a barrier function.*

Proof. We define Λ as follows: if a leader process p proposes a value $v_{i,p}$ for consensus instance i and $v_{i,p}$ is decided, p has primary identifier $\lambda = i$. A primary has only one identifier: after $v_{i,p}$ is broadcast, it holds $prop > dec$ and $dec < \tau_{seq}$, so *isPrimary()* stops evaluating to true at p. The order $\prec_\Lambda$ is defined by ordering primary identifiers as regular integers.

If a process p proposes a value v for instance $i = \max(prop + 1, dec + 1)$ in Algorithm 1, it observes $\tau_{seq} = \max(prop, dec) = i - 1$ when it becomes a primary. If v is decided, p has primary identifier $\lambda = i$. All primaries preceding λ in $\prec_\Lambda$ have proposed values for instances preceding i, so τ_{seq} meets the requirements of barrier functions. $\square$

5.2   Impossibility

One might wonder if this limitation of sequential instances is inherent or not. Indeed, this is the case as we show in the following.

Theorem 2. *Let Π be a set of two or more processes executing the τ-based POabcast algorithm with an underlying consensus implementation C that can only be accessed through its propose and decide calls. There is no local implementation of τ for C allowing a primary p to propose a value for instance i before p reaches a decision for instance $i - 1$.*

Proof. The proof is by contradiction: we assume that a barrier function τ_c allowing primaries to propose values for multiple concurrent consensus instances exists.

Run σ_1: The oracle Ω outputs some process p as the only leader in the system from the beginning of the run. Assume that p broadcasts two values v_1 and v_2 at the beginning of the run. For liveness of *POabcast*, p must eventually propose values for consensus instances 1 and 2. By assumption, τ_c allows p to start consensus instance 2 before a decision for instance 1 is reached. Therefore p observes $\tau_c = 0$ when it proposes v_1 and v_2. The output of τ_c must be independent from the internal events of the underlying consensus implementation C, since τ_c cannot observe them. We can therefore assume that no process receives any message before p proposes v_2.

Run σ_1': The prefix of σ_1 that finishes immediately after p proposes v_2. No process receives any message.

Run σ_2: Similar to σ_1, but the only leader is $p' \neq p$ and the proposed values are v_1' and v_2'. Process p' observes $\tau_c = 0$ when it proposes v_1' and v_2'.

Run σ_2': The prefix of σ_2 that finishes immediately after p' proposes v_2'. No process receives any message.

Run σ_3: The beginning of this run is the union of all events in the runs σ_1' and σ_2'. No process receives any message until the end of the union of σ_1' and σ_2'. The Ω oracle is allowed to elect two distinct leaders for a finite time. Process p (resp. p') cannot distinguish between run σ_1' (resp. σ_2') and the corresponding local prefix of σ_3 based on the outputs of the consensus primitive and of the leader oracle. After the events of σ_1' and σ_2' have occurred, some process decides v_1' for consensus instance 1 and v_2 for consensus instance 2.

Regardless of the definition of Λ and $\prec_\Lambda$, the output of τ_c in σ_3 is incorrect. Let p and p' have primary identifiers λ and λ' when they proposed v_2 and v_1', respectively. If $\lambda \prec_\Lambda \lambda'$, τ_c should have returned 2 instead of 0 when p' became primary. If $\lambda' \prec_\Lambda \lambda$, τ_c should have returned 1 instead of 0 when p became primary.   □

5.3 Barriers with White-Box Paxos

An alternative, corresponding to Zab [9], to avoid the aforementioned impossibility is to consider the internal states of the underlying consensus algorithm. We exemplify this approach considering the popular Paxos algorithm [11]. A detailed discussion of Paxos is out of the scope of this work and we only present a summary for completeness.

Overview of Paxos. In Paxos, each process keeps, for every consensus instance, an *accepted value*, which is the most current value it is aware of that might have been decided. A process p elected leader must first read, for each instance, the value that may have been decided upon for this instance, if any. To obtain this value, the leader selects a unique *ballot number b* and executes a *read phase* by sending a read message to all other processes. Processes that have not yet received messages from a leader with a higher ballot number b reply by sending their current accepted value for the instance. Each accepted value is sent attached to the ballot number of the previous leader that proposed that value. The other processes also promise not to accept any message from leaders with ballots lower than b. When p receives accepted values from a majority of processes, it *picks* for each instance the accepted value with the highest attached ballot. Gaps in the sequence instance with picked values are filled with empty *no op* values.

After completing the read phase, the new leader proposes the values it picked as well as its own values for the instances for which no value was decided. The leader proposes values in a *write* phase: it sends them to all processes together with the current ballot number b. Processes accept proposed values only if they have not already received messages from a leader with a ballot number $b' > b$. After they accept a proposed value, they send an acknowledgement to the leader proposing it. When a value has been written with the same ballot at a majority of processes, it is decided.

In a nutshell, the correctness argument of Paxos boils down to the following argument. If a value v has been decided, a majority of processes have accepted it with a given ballot number b; we say that the proposal $\langle v, b \rangle$ is *chosen*. If the proposal is chosen, no process in the majority will accept a value from a leader with a ballot number lower than b. At the same time, every leader with a ballot number higher than b will read the chosen proposal in the read phase, and will also propose the v.

Integrating the Barrier Function. We modify Paxos to incorporate the barrier function. If a process is not a leader, there is no reason for evaluating τ. Whenever a process is elected leader, it executes the read phase. Given a process p such that $\Omega = p$, let $read(p)$ be the maximum consensus instance for which any value is picked in the last read phase executed by p. The barrier function is implemented as follows:

$$\tau_{\text{Paxos}} = \begin{cases} \top & \text{iff } \Omega \neq p \lor p \text{ is in read phase} \\ read(p) & \text{iff } \Omega = p \land p \text{ is in write phase} \end{cases}$$

The output value $\top$ is such that $dec \geq \tau_{Paxos}$ never holds for any value of dec. This prevents leaders from becoming primaries until a correct output for τ_{Paxos} is determined.

We now show that this τ implementation is correct. The proof relies on the correctness argument of Paxos.

Theorem 3. *The function τ_{Paxos} is a barrier function.*

Proof. By the definition of τ_{Paxos}, a process becomes a primary if it is a leader and has completed the read phase. Let Λ associate a primary with the unique ballot number it uses in the Paxos read phase and let $\prec_\Lambda$ be the ballot number order.

Paxos guarantees that if any process ever decides a value v proposed by a leader with ballot number smaller than the one of λ, then v is picked by λ in the read phase [11]. This is sufficient to meet the requirements of τ.   □

5.4 Time Complexity of τ-Based *POabcast* with Different Barrier Functions

We now explain the second and third row of Table 1. Just for the analysis, we assume that there are c clients in the system, the communication delay is Δ, and Paxos is used as underlying consensus protocol since it is optimal [12].

We first consider the barrier function of Sect. 5.1. If a primary receives requests from all clients at the same time, it will broadcast and deliver the corresponding state updates sequentially. Delivering a message requires 2Δ, the latency of the write phase of Paxos. Since each message will take 2Δ time to be delivered, the last message will be delivered in $2\Delta \cdot c$ time. During leader change, Paxos takes 2Δ time to execute the read phase and 2Δ to execute the write phase if a proposal by the old primary has been chosen and potentially decided in the last consensus instance.

With the barrier function of Sect. 5.3, consensus instances are executed in parallel with a latency of 2Δ. The complexity for leader changes is the same, since the write phase is executed in parallel for all instances up to τ.

Note that the longer leader change time of *POabcast* algorithms compared to atomic broadcast (see Table 1) is due to the barrier: before it becomes a primary, a process must *decide* on all values that have been proposed by the previous primaries and potentially decided (chosen). This is equivalent to executing read and write phases that require 4Δ time. In atomic broadcast, it is sufficient that a new leader *proposes* chosen values from previous leaders.

5.5   Relationship between τ Functions and Existing *POabcast* Algorithms

The *POabcast* algorithm with the barrier function of Sect. 5.1 is similar to semi-passive replication [7] since both enforce the same constraint: primaries only keep one outstanding consensus instance at a time. The time complexity of the two protocols using Paxos as the underlying consensus protocol is the same (Table 1, second row).

If the barrier function implementation selects a specific consensus protocol and assumes that it can access its internal state, as discussed in Sect. 5.1, our barrier-based *POabcast* algorithm can broadcast state updates in the presence of multiple outstanding consensus instances. This is the same approach as Zab, and indeed there are many parallelisms with this algorithm. The time complexity in stable periods is the same (see Table 1, third row). A closer look shows that also the leader change complexity is equal, apart from specific optimizations of the Zab protocol. In Zab, the read phase of Paxos corresponds to the *discovery phase*; the CEPOCH message is used to implement leader election and to speed up the selection of a unique ballot (or epoch, in Zab terms) number that is higher than any previous epoch numbers [9]. After the read phase is completed, the leader decides on all consensus instances until the instance identifier returned by τ_{Paxos} - this is the *synchronization phase*, which corresponds to a write phase in Paxos; in our implementation, the barrier function returns and the leader waits until enough consensus instances are decided. At this point, the necessary condition $dec \geq \tau_{Paxos}$ of our generic *POabcast* construction is fulfilled, so the leader crosses the barrier, becomes a primary, and can proceed with proposing values for new instances. In Zab, this corresponds to the *broadcast phase*.

Virtually-synchronous Paxos is also a modified version of Paxos that implements *POabcast* and the τ_{Paxos} barrier function, but it has the additional property of making the set of participating processes dynamic [2]. It has the same time complexity during stable periods and leader changes as in Table 1.

6   *POabcast* Using Consensus Instead of τ for the Barrier

The previous section shows an inherent tradeoff in τ implementations between modularity, which can be achieved by using sequential consensus instances and using consensus as a black box, and performance, which can be increased by integrating the implementation of the barrier function in a specific consensus protocol. In this section, we show that this tradeoff can be avoided through the use of an alternative *POabcast* algorithm.

Algorithm. Our τ-free algorithm (see Algorithm 2) implements *POabcast*, so it is an alternative to Algorithm 1. The algorithm is built upon a leader election oracle Ω and consensus. The main difference with Algorithm 1 is that the barrier predicate *isPrimary* is implemented using consensus instead of τ: consensus instances are used to agree not only on values, but also on primary election information. Another difference is that some decided value may not be delivered. This requires the use of additional buffering, which slightly increases the complexity of the implementation.

When a process p becomes leader, it picks a unique epoch number *tent-epoch* and proposes a ⟨NEW-EPOCH, *tent-epoch*⟩ value in the smallest consensus instance *dec* where p has not yet reached a decision (lines 5-9). Like in Algorithm 1, we use multiple consensus instances. All replicas keep a decision counter *dec*, which indicates the current instance where a consensus decision is awaited, and a proposal counter *prop*, which indicates the next available instance for proposing a value. Another similarity with Algorithm 1 is that decision events are processed following the order of consensus instances, tracked using the variable *dec* (see lines 10 and 29). Out-of-order decision events are buffered, although this is omitted in the pseudocode.

Every time a NEW-EPOCH tuple is decided, the sender of the message is elected primary and its epoch *tent-epoch* is *established* (lines 10-23). When a new epoch is established, processes set their current epoch counter *epoch* to *tent-epoch*. If the process delivering the NEW-EPOCH tuple is a leader, it checks whether the epoch that has been just established is its own tentative epoch. If this is the case, the process considers itself as a primary and sets *primary* to true; else, it tries to become a primary again.

When p becomes a primary, it can start to broadcast values by proposing VAL tuples in the next consensus instances, in parallel (lines 24-28). Ensuring that followers are in a state consistent with the new primary does not require using barriers: all processes establishing *tent-epoch* in consensus instance i have decided and delivered the same sequence of values in the instances preceding i. This guarantees that the primary integrity property of *POabcast* is respected.

Processes only POdeliver VAL tuples of the last established epoch until a different epoch is established (lines 29-33, see in particular condition $epoch_m = epoch$). The algorithm establishes the following total order $\prec_\Lambda$ of primary identifiers: given two different primaries λ and λ' which picked epoch numbers e and e' respectively, we say that $\lambda \prec_\Lambda \lambda'$ if and only if a tuple ⟨NEW-EPOCH, e⟩ is decided for a consensus instance n, a tuple ⟨NEW-EPOCH, e'⟩ is decided for a consensus instance m, and $n < m$. Suppose that p is the primary λ with epoch number e_λ elected in consensus instance dec_λ. All processes set their current epoch variable e to e_λ after deciding in instance dec_λ. From consensus instance number $dec_\lambda + 1$ to the next consensus instance where a NEW-EPOCH tuple is decided, processes decide and deliver only values that are sent from λ and included in VAL tuples with $epoch_m = e_\lambda$. Replicas thus deliver messages following the order $\prec_\Lambda$ of the primaries that sent them, fulfilling the global primary order property of *POabcast*.

```
 1  initially                            24  upon POabcast( v)
 2  |  tent-epoch, dec, decseq, prop,     25  |  propose(⟨VAL, v, epoch,
    |  seqno ← 0;                              |  seqno⟩, prop);
 3  |  epoch ← ⊥;                         26  |  pa[prop] ← ⟨ v, seqno⟩;
 4  |  primary ← false;                   27  |  prop← prop+1;
 5  upon Ω changes from q ≠ p to p       28  |  seqno ← seqno+1;
 6  |  try-primary();                     29  upon decide(⟨VAL, v, epoch_m,
 7  procedure try-primary()                  seqno_m⟩, dec)
 8  |  tent-epoch ← new unique epoch      30  |  if epoch_m = epoch then
    |  number;                            31  |  |  da[seqno_m] ← v;
 9  |  propose(⟨NEW-EPOCH,                32  |  |  while da[decseq] ≠ ⊥ do
    |  tent-epoch⟩, dec);                 33  |  |  POdeliver(da[decseq]);
10  upon decide(⟨NEW-EPOCH,              34  |  |  decseq← decseq+1;
    tent-epoch_m⟩, dec)                  35  |  if primary ∧ epoch_m ≠ epoch
11  |  dec ← dec+1;                       36  |  ∧ prop ≥ dec then
12  |  epoch ← tent-epoch_m;             37  |  |  ⟨ v', seqno'⟩ ← pa[dec];
13  |  da ← empty array;                  38  |  |  pa[prop] ← pa[dec];
14  |  pa ← empty array;                  39  |  |  propose(⟨VAL, v', epoch,
15  |  decseq ← dec;                          |  |  seqno'⟩, prop);
16  |  if Ω = p then                      40  |  |  prop← prop+1;
17  |  |  if tent-epoch = tent-epoch_m   41  |  if ¬ primary ∧ Ω = p then
    |  |  then                            42  |  |  try-primary();
18  |  |  |  prop ← dec;                  43  |  dec← dec+1;
19  |  |  |  seqno ← dec;                 44  upon Ω changes from p to q ≠ p
20  |  |  |  primary ← true;              45  |  primary← false;
21  |  |  else                            46  function isPrimary()
22  |  |  |  primary ← false;             47  |  return primary;
23  |  |  |  try-primary();
```

Algorithm 2. Barrier-free *POabcast* using black-box consensus - process p

The additional complexity in handling VAL tuples is necessary to guarantee the local primary order property of *POabcast*. VAL tuples of an epoch are not necessarily decided in the same order as they are proposed. This is why primaries include a sequence number *seqno* in VAL tuples. In some consensus instance, the tuples proposed by the current primary might not be the ones decided. This can happen in the presence of concurrent primaries, since primaries send proposals for multiple overlapping consensus instances without waiting for decisions. If a primary is demoted, values from old and new primaries could be interleaved in the sequence of decided values for a finite number of instances. All processes agree on the current epoch of every instance, so they do not deliver messages from other primaries with different epoch numbers. However, it is necessary to buffer out-of-order values from the current primary to deliver them later. That is why processes store decided values from the current primary in the *da* array (line 31), and deliver them only if a continuous sequence of sequence numbers, tracked by *decseq*, can be delivered (lines 32-34).

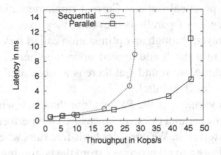

Fig. 1. Latency and throughput with micro benchmarks. Request and state update sizes were set to 1kb, which is the typical size observed in ZooKeeper. Both protocols use batching.

Primaries also need to resend VAL tuples that could not be decided in the correct order. When values are proposed, they are stored in the pa following the sequence number order; this buffer is reset to the next ongoing consensus instance every time a new primary is elected. Primaries resend VAL tuples in lines 35-40. Primaries keep a proposal instance counter $prop$, indicating the next consensus instance where values can be proposed. If an established primary has outstanding proposals for the currently decided instance dec, it holds $prop \geq dec$. In this case, if the decided VAL tuple is not one such outstanding proposal but has instead been sent by a previous primary, it holds that $epoch_m \neq epoch$. If all the previous conditions hold, the established primary must resend the value that has been skipped, $pa[dec].v'$, using the same original sequence number $pa[dec].seqno'$ in the next available consensus instance, which is $prop$.

The arrays da and pa do not need to grow indefinitely. Elements of da (resp. pa) with position smaller than $decseq$ (resp. dec) can be garbage-collected.

For liveness, a leader which is not a primary keeps trying to become a primary by sending a NEW-EPOCH tuple for every consensus instance (lines 22-23). The $primary$ variable is true if a leader is an established primary. It stops being true if the primary is not a leader any longer (lines 44-45).

Algorithm 2 correctly implements *POabcast*, as shown in our full paper [10].

Time Complexity. As before, we use Paxos for the consensus algorithm and assume a communication delay of Δ. During stable periods, the time to deliver a value is 2Δ, which is the time needed to execute a Paxos write phase. When a new leader is elected, it first executes the read phase, which takes 2Δ. Next, it executes the write phase for all instances in which values have been read but not yet decided, and for one additional instance for its NEW-EPOCH tuple. All these instances are executed in parallel, so they finish within 2Δ time. After this time, the new leader crosses the barrier, becomes a primary, and starts broadcasting new values.

7 Experimental Evaluation

Our τ-free algorithm combines modularity with constant time complexity. Since our work was motivated by our work on systems like ZooKeeper, one might wonder whether this improvement has a practical impact. Current implementations of replicated systems can reach some degree of parallelism even if they execute consensus instances sequentially. This is achieved through an optimization called *batching*: multiple clients requests are aggregated in a batch and agreed upon together using a single instance. Even in presence of batching, we found that there is a substantial advantage of running multiple consensus instances in parallel.

We implemented two variants of the Paxos algorithm, one with sequential consensus instances and one with parallel ones, and measured the performance of running our *POabcast* algorithms on top of it. We consider fault-free runs where the leader election oracle outputs the same leader to all processes from the beginning. We used three replicas and additional dedicated machines for the clients; all servers are quad-core 2.5 GHz CPU servers with 16 GB of RAM connected through a Gigabit network.

The experiments consist of micro-benchmarks where the replicated object does nothing. These benchmarks are commonly used in the evaluation of replication algorithms because they reproduce a scenario in which the replication protocol, rather than execution, is the bottleneck of the system so its performance is critical.

We used batching in all our experiments. With sequential consensus instances, we batch all requests received while a previous instance is ongoing. In the pipelined version, we start a new consensus instance when either the previous instance is completed or b requests have been batched. We found $b = 50$ to be optimal. Every measurement was repeated five times at steady state, and variances were negligible.

Figure 1 reports the performance of the two variants with a growing number of clients. Messages (requests and state updates) have size 1 kB, which is a common state update size for ZooKeeper and Zab [9].

The peak throughput with the parallel consensus instances is almost two times the one with sequential instances. The same holds with messages of size 4 kB. The difference decreases with smaller updates than the ones we observe in practical systems like ZooKeeper. In the extreme case of empty requests and state updates, the two approaches have virtually the same request latency and throughput: they both achieve a maximum throughput of more than 110 kops/sec and a minimum latency of less than 0.5 ms.

These results show that low time complexity (see Table 1) is very important for high-performance passive replication. When there is little load in the system, the difference in latency between the two variants is negligible. In fact, due to the use of batching, running parallel consensus instances is not needed. As the number of clients (c in Table 1) increases, latency grows faster in the sequential case, as predicted by our analysis. With sequential consensus instances, a larger latency also results in significantly worse throughput compared to the parallel variant due to lower network and CPU utilization.

8   Conclusions

Some popular systems such as ZooKeeper have used passive replication to mask crash faults. We extracted a unified algorithm for implementing *POabcast* using the barrier function that abstracts existing passive replication approaches. The barrier function is a simple way to understand the difference between passive and active replication, as well as the characteristics of existing *POabcast* algorithms, but it imposes a tradeoff between parallelism and modularity. We have proposed an algorithm that avoids such a limitation by not relying upon a barrier function. This algorithm is different from existing ones in its use of consensus, instead of barrier functions, for primary election.

Acknowledgement. We would like to express our gratitude to Alex Shraer and Benjamin Reed for the insightful feedback on previous versions of the paper, and to Daniel Gómez Ferro for helping out with the experiments.

References

1. Baker, J., Bond, C., Corbett, J., Furman, J.J., Khorlin, A., Larson, J., Léon, J.-M., Li, Y., Lloyd, A., Yushprakh, V.: Megastore: Providing scalable, highly available storage for interactive services. In: CIDR, vol. 11, pp. 223–234 (2011)
2. Birman, K., Malkhi, D., Van Renesse, R.: Virtually synchronous methodology for dynamic service replication. Technical Report MSR-TR-2010-151, Microsoft Research (2010)
3. Budhiraja, N., Marzullo, K., Schneider, F.B., Toueg, S.: The primary-backup approach, pp. 199–216. ACM Press/Addison-Wesley (1993)
4. Chandra, T.D., Toueg, S.: Unreliable failure detectors for reliable distributed systems. Journal of the ACM 43(2), 225–267 (1996)
5. Chandra, T.D., Hadzilacos, V., Toueg, S.: The weakest failure detector for solving consensus. Journal of the ACM 43(4), 685–722 (1996)
6. Chockler, G.V., Keidar, I., Vitenberg, R.: Group communication specifications: a comprehensive study. ACM Compututing Surveys 33(4), 427–469 (2001)
7. Défago, X., Schiper, A.: Semi-passive replication and lazy consensus. Journal of Parallel and Distributed Computing 64(12), 1380–1398 (2004)
8. Hunt, P., Konar, M., Junqueira, F.P., Reed, B.: Zookeeper: Wait-free coordination for Internet-scale systems. In: USENIX Annual Technical Conference, pp. 145–158 (2010)
9. Junqueira, F.P., Reed, B., Serafini, M.: Zab: High-performance broadcast for primary-backup systems. In: IEEE Conference on Dependable Systems and Networks, pp. 245–256 (2011)
10. Junqueira, F.P., Serafini, M.: On barriers and the gap between active and passive replication (full version). arXiv:1308.2979 [cs.DC] (2013)
11. Lamport, L.: The part-time parliament. ACM Transactions on Computing Systems (TOCS) 16(2), 133–169 (1998)
12. Lamport, L.: lower bounds for asynchronous consensus. Distributed Computing 19(2), 79–103 (2006)
13. Lamport, L., Malkhi, D., Zhou, L.: Vertical paxos and primary-backup replication. In: ACM Symposium on Principles of Distributed Computing, pp. 312–313 (2009)
14. Pedone, F., Frolund, S.: Pronto: A fast failover protocol for off-the-shelf commercial databases. In: IEEE Symposium on Reliable Distributed Systems, pp. 176–185 (2000)
15. Shraer, A., Reed, B., Malkhi, D., Junqueira, F.: Dynamic reconfiguration of primary/backup clusters. In: USENIX Annual Technical Conference, pp. 425–438 (2012)

Conflict Resolution and Membership Problem in Beeping Channels

Bojun Huang and Thomas Moscibroda

Microsoft Research Asia, Beijing, China
{bojhuang,moscitho}@microsoft.com

Abstract. Consider a group of nodes connected through multiple-access channels and the only observable feedback on the channel is a binary value: either one or more nodes have transmitted (busy), or no node has transmitted (idle). The channel model thus described is called *Beeping Model* and captures computation in hardware using a group of sequential circuit modules connected by a logic-OR gate. It has also been used to study chemical signaling mechanisms between biological cells and carrier-sensing based wireless communication.

In this paper, we study the distributed complexity of two fundamental problems in the Beeping Model. In both problems, there is a set of nodes each with a unique identifier $i \in \{1, 2, \ldots, n\}$. A subset of the nodes $A \subseteq \{1, 2, \ldots, n\}$ is called *active nodes*. In the *Membership Problem*, every node needs to find out the identifiers of all active nodes. In the *Conflict Resolution Problem*, the goal is to let every active node use the channel alone (without collision) at least once.

We derive two results that characterize the distributed complexity of these problems. First, we prove that in the Beeping Model the two above problems are equally hard. This is in stark contrast to traditional channel models with ternary feedback in which the membership problem is strictly harder than conflict resolution. The equivalence result also leads to a randomized lower bound for conflict resolution, which shows a relative powerlessness of randomization in the beeping model. Secondly, we give a new deterministic algorithm for the problems that achieves the best known parallelization among all practical algorithms.

Keywords: circuit algorithms, multiple access channel, beeping model, conflict resolution, membership detection, lower bounds.

1 Introduction

Consider a logical-OR gate in hardware circuit with n inputs $N = \{1, 2, \ldots, n\}$, in which each of the input $i \in N$ is controlled by a sequential logic module that listens to the output of the OR gate, as illustrated in Figure 1(a). Now, assume that there is a subset $A \subseteq N$ of the inputs; let us call them the *active inputs*. Only active inputs can transmit. Our goal is to determine which of the inputs are active, by repeatedly using the logical-OR gate. The problem thus described

Y. Afek (Ed.): DISC 2013, LNCS 8205, pp. 314–328, 2013.

occurs as a core component in many circuit-based algorithm implementations[1]. It is also an archetypical problem that arises in a variety of settings and systems where entities or nodes communicate using a shared communication channel, and the only observable feedback on the channel is a binary value: either "someone has transmitted" or "none has transmitted".

This channel model has been called *Beeping Model*. In this model a group of nodes communicate through beeping channels. Communication is in discrete synchronous time slots and all nodes have access to a global clock (common in hardware applications). In each time slot, a node first does some local computation, then decides to either keep sending a "beep" signal or be quiet in the rest of that time slot. At the end of the time slot, the node receives a binary *feedback* from the channel: "busy" if at least one node is beeping on the channel; and "idle" otherwise. All nodes see the same channel feedback, and the channel feedbacks in all time slots are collectively called the *channel feedback history*.

The Beeping Model has recently found a lot of attention in the distributed computing community. It is one of the fundamental models for *multiple access channels*. Such models can be distinguished by the feedback the participants (nodes) can sense from the channel. In the traditional channel model (also called the model *with Collision Detection*) [15] [9] [3] [14] [8] [16] [10] [11], nodes receive ternary feedback about the channel state: no one is sending (*idle*), exactly one node is sending (*success*), or two or more nodes are sending (*collision*). In contrast, the Beeping Model has only binary feedback: no one is sending (*idle*) or, one or more nodes are sending (*busy*). This binary model captures the computation with circuit modules connected by a logic-OR gate, and it has also been used to study chemical signaling mechanisms between biological cells [2] and carrier-sensing based wireless communication [5]; several distributed graph problems (e.g., MIS [1], coloring [5]) have been studied in this model.

Membership Problem and Conflict Resolution. In this paper, we study the distributed complexity of two fundamental problems in the Beeping Model. Let $N = \{1, 2, \ldots, n\}$. In both problems, there is a group of nodes each with a unique identifier (ID) $i \in N$. A subset of the nodes $A \subseteq N$ of size $|A| \leq k$ is called *active nodes*. Only active nodes can send out beep signals. Initially, each node knows whether itself is active, as well as its ID i, the size of the name space n, and the upper bound k. [2]

- The *Conflict Resolution Problem* (CR), also called k-*Selection Problem*, asks to coordinate the nodes' accesses to the channel such that for any $A \subseteq N$, each active node $i \in A$ obtains *exclusive access* to the channel in at least one time slot if $|A| \leq k$. A node $i \in N$ obtains exclusive access to the channel in

---

[1] Our specific motivation has been our work on building customized hardware machines to play the game of GO, one of the few classic boardgames in which computers are still unable to compete with the best human players [7].

[2] In case either i or n is unknown, we can apply standard tricks of letting node choose random IDs (when i is unknown) or exponentially estimating n based on the IDs in the system (when n is unknown). If such a k is unknown, we just iteratively run an algorithm with $k = 2^r$ in round r, until k is large enough to be an upper bound.

time slot t" if and only if i is the only node *allowed to beep* in time slot t. A time slot t is *exclusively-used* if and only if any $i \in N$ obtains exclusive access to the channel in time slot t. In the Beeping Model, the CR problem further asks every node $i \in N$ to correctly recognize all such exclusively-used time slots (since otherwise they cannot distinguish the real message from noise).

- The *Membership Problem* (MP), also called *Node Identification* or *Station Identification*, asks to learn the set A if $|A| \leq k$, i.e., to let every node $i \in N$ know the IDs of all the (at most k) active nodes.

We derive two results that characterize the distributed complexity of these problems. First, we prove that in the Beeping Model the two problems are equally hard, which is unlike in traditional access channel models in which the membership problem is strictly harder than conflict resolution. And secondly, we design a new deterministic parallel algorithm that takes significantly less time than previous solutions. We now discuss these contributions in detail.

Equivalence of MP and CR. Intuitively, one may think that the Membership Problem requires more time than Conflict Resolution for at least two reasons: First, in CR, an active node that has managed to successfully transmit can stop sending out any additional beeps; while this is not the case in MP. In other words, while the CR problem merely asks to arrange k "successful" time slots, the MP further asks to identify *who* is beeping in each successful time slot. Secondly, reducing CR to MP is trivial (by simply letting the active nodes beep successfully one-by-one in the order of their IDs), but the reversed reduction from MP to CR comes at an extra cost: A node can only transmit a single beep during one iteration of a CR protocol, which is not sufficient to transmit an entire identifier of length $O(\log n)$ bits, as required in MP.

Interestingly, the intuition that MP is strictly harder than CR is known to be true in the traditional ternary-feedback (idle, success, collision) model of access channels. Specifically, there is a known separation of the two problems for randomized algorithms. With ternary feedback, the expected running time of any Las Vegas membership algorithm is $\Omega(k \log \frac{n}{k})$ (by the entropy argument), while there are Las Vegas collision resolution algorithms with expected running time of $\leq 2.89k$ [15] [14].

In this paper, we show that the above intuition does not hold in the beeping model, i.e., that the membership problem is *not* harder than conflict resolution. This reveals two fundamental differences between the two basic models for multiple access channels: the binary Beeping Model and the ternary traditional model. (i) First, whereas MP is strictly harder than CR in the ternary model, the two problems are equally hard in the binary Beeping Model, which means the only way to achieve reliable (or collision-free) communication in the Beeping Model is to identify all the nodes competing for the channel. (ii) And secondly, we prove that there is a difference between the two models in the power of randomization for reliable communication. Specifically, Greenberg and Winograd proved in [8] a lower bound of $\Omega(k \log_k n)$ for any deterministic conflict resolution algorithm in the ternary model, which established the separation between deterministic algorithms and randomized algorithms in this problem (recall that there are $\Theta(k)$

Table 1. Known Bounds on the (Sequential) Time Complexity for CR and MP

	Ternary Feedback – $\{0, 1, 2^+\}$	Beeping Model – $\{0, 1^+\}$
Membership Problem (rand.)	$\Theta(k \log \frac{n}{k})$	$\Theta(k \log \frac{n}{k})$
Collision Resolution (rand.)	$\Theta(k)$	$\Theta(k \log \frac{n}{k})$ (*)
Membership Problem (det.)	$\Theta(k \log \frac{n}{k})$	$\Theta(k \log \frac{n}{k})$
Collision Resolution (det.)	$\Omega(k \log_k n)$, $O(k \log \frac{n}{k})$	$\Theta(k \log \frac{n}{k})$ (*)

randomized algorithms in the ternary model [15] [14]). In this paper we show that this gap disappears in the Beeping Model. We prove that in the Beeping Model any deterministic conflict resolution algorithm is also an algorithm that solves MP. This result yields the lower bound $\Omega(k \log \frac{n}{k})$ for CR with respect to both deterministic and randomized algorithms in the beeping model, which is tight since there exist deterministic algorithms that run in $O(k \log \frac{n}{k})$ time [6]. Table 1 summarizes the performance bounds in the two models. Results marked with asterisks are new. Finally, our proof techniques are nontrivial. As a by-product, we prove that in the Beeping Model, one cannot count the number of active nodes without identifying them (i.e. solving MP).

Efficient Parallel Algorithm. So far, we have assumed that there is a single channel connecting the nodes. In many applications, however, nodes can access more than one beeping channel in parallel. For example, hardware circuits are typically 32-bit or 64-bit wide (i.e., there are 32 or 64 beeping channels in parallel, see Fig. 1(a)); chemical interactions between biological cells may be activated by multiple types of proteins; and a wireless communication channel may be partitioned into multiple sub-bands (e.g., OFDM used in Wi-Fi partitions each channel into so-called *sub-carriers* that are all accessed simultaneously). In each time-slot, a node can decide to beep or not independently in *each* of the beeping channels, and listen to the feedbacks of *all* channels at the same time.

Clearly, the number of channels plays an important role in how much time is required to solve the problems. For example, with n parallel channels, both problems can be solved in $O(1)$ time with a simple round robin algorithm. However, this is unrealistic as in many applications n is the size of the name space, which may grow exponentially with the length of node identifiers (e.g., $n = 2^{64}$ for 64-bit identifiers). For this reason, we seek efficient parallel algorithms that use polylog(n) number of channels and have polylog(n) computational complexity (e.g. avoiding full scans of the whole name space). Seems the fastest such solutions in the literature is by Chou Hsiung Li [12], in which an efficient algorithm was proposed in the context of experimental variables screening. Li's algorithm turns out to be essentially a parallel algorithm which, when used in beeping model, terminates in $O(\log \frac{n}{k})$ time with $O(k)$ channels, and has computational complexity of $O(k^2 \log \frac{n}{k})$.

The second main contribution of this paper is a novel and practical *deterministic* algorithm for both CR and MP. The basic idea of the algorithm is to iteratively reduce the problem size n by renaming each node to a smaller name space in each iteration. We show that when the algorithm terminates, each

Table 2. Algorithms for CR and MP in Beeping Model with Multiple Channels

	# Time Slots	# Channels	Computation
Round-robin	$O(1)$	$O(n)$	$O(n)$
Adaptive GT [9] [3] [16] [6]	$O(k \log \frac{n}{k})$	$O(1)$	$O(k \log \frac{n}{k})$
Li's Algorithm [12]	$O(\log \frac{n}{k})$	$O(k)$	$O(k^2 \log \frac{n}{k})$
Our Algorithm (*)	$O(\log k \log \log_k n)$	$O(k \log_k n + k^2)$	$O(k^2 \log \frac{n}{k} + k^3)$

active node has an ID $i' \in \{1, \ldots, k\}$, and that each of them can locally recover the original IDs of all active nodes from the channel feedback history. The algorithm terminates in $O(\log k \log \log_k n)$ time slots in the worst case, which is *exponentially* better than Li's algorithm [12] for $k \in \text{polylog}(n)$. The algorithm uses $O(k \log_k n + k^2)$ parallel channels, and the computational complexity of the algorithm is $O(k^2 \log \frac{n}{k} + k^3)$ – both are logarithmic in n and polynomial in k. Table 2 summarizes our results relative to previous work.

In addition to its efficiency, our algorithm is also tolerant to arbitrary crash-failures in the parallel model, and always correctly returns the set of nodes that remain active when the algorithm terminates. Finally, the core component of the algorithm is a *strong renaming/coloring* process, which may be of interest in its own right. The strong renaming problem asks to assign each active node a unique ID $i' \in \{1, ..., d\}$, where d is the number of active nodes. Our algorithm, when used as a strong renaming algorithm, is *invertible* and *order-preserving* (i.e. for any two original ID's $i < j$, we have $i' < j'$).

Notations: Let $\gamma \in \{0, 1\}^*$ be a bit vector, we denote $|\gamma|$ as the length of γ, $\|\gamma\|$ as the number of bit "1" in γ, and $\gamma[i]$ for $i \in \{1, \ldots, |\gamma|\}$ as the i-th bit of γ. For a set of bit vectors $\gamma_1, \gamma_2, ..., \gamma_n$, $(\gamma_1, \cdots, \gamma_n)$ is the concatenation of these n vectors; $\gamma_i \vee \gamma_j$ is the bitwise Boolean Sum (i.e. logical-OR) of γ_i and γ_j; ϵ denotes the empty vector. For a natural number n, $[n]_q$ denotes the q-nary representation of n.

2 The Equivalence of Membership and Conflict Resolution

In this section we show the equivalence between MP and CR in the Beeping Model. The equivalence leads to a tight lower bound for both problems, and for both deterministic and randomized algorithms (Las Vegas and Monte Carlo). As discussed, both the equivalence of the problems and the relative powerlessness of randomization are in contrast to the traditional ternary channel access model. Without loss of generality, we assume the model has single channel in this section. We denote a problem instance (of any problem considered here) by a bit vector $\pi \in \{0, 1\}^n$, where $\pi[i] = 1$ means node i is active, and $\pi[i] = 0$ otherwise. For any deterministic algorithm $\mathcal{A}$, we denote by the bit vector $r_\mathcal{A}(\pi)$ the channel feedback history of algorithm $\mathcal{A}$ under problem instance π, where $r_\mathcal{A}(\pi)[t] = 1$ means the node hear a beep signal ("busy") from the channel in time-slot t.

The reduction from conflict resolution to membership is straightforward – once every node knows who is active, active nodes can send messages one by one without any conflict in k time-slots. However, an efficient reduction in the opposite way is non-trivial because through a single successful transmission a node can only convey 1 bit of information. A conflict resolution algorithm enables each node to transmit once, which seems insufficient to communicate a full $O(\log n)$-bit node ID, as required in the membership problem. We nevertheless show that the two problems are equivalent by resorting to reduce the membership problem to an intermediary problem, the *counting problem*, in which each node has to learn the exact *number of active nodes*. We prove that a conflict resolution algorithm can be used to solve the counting problem, and that–in the beeping model–every counting algorithm effectively solves the membership problem. This implies that instead of letting every active node explicitly report its $O(\log n)$-bit ID, in the beeping model we can infer every active node's ID as long as each of them can transmit *one single bit* successfully.

The following arguments are based on a general property of the beeping model, presented by Lemma 1. It asserts that, if any deterministic algorithm $\mathcal{A}$ generates the same channel feedback for two instances π and π', it must also generate exactly the same channel feedback for the instance $\pi \vee \pi'$. In other words, the equivalent class of π with respect to $r_{\mathcal{A}}(\pi)$ must be a *closure* under the logical-OR operation. The key insight behind Lemma 1 is that active nodes act according to the channel feedback history. Given the same feedback history before time-slot t, each active node in $\pi \vee \pi'$ is also either active in π or in π' (or in both), so none of them can lead to a different channel feedback at time t.

Lemma 1. *In the beeping model, for any deterministic algorithm $\mathcal{A}$, let π and π' be two instances of the problem to be solved, if $r_{\mathcal{A}}(\pi) = r_{\mathcal{A}}(\pi')$, then $r_{\mathcal{A}}(\pi) = r_{\mathcal{A}}(\pi \vee \pi')$.*

Proof. The proof is by induction. Given algorithm $\mathcal{A}$, let $\gamma_t(\pi) = < r_{\mathcal{A}}(\pi)[1], r_{\mathcal{A}}(\pi)[2], ..., r_{\mathcal{A}}(\pi)[t] >$ be the channel feedback history of $\mathcal{A}$ under π until time-slot t. So $\gamma_t(\pi)$ is a prefix of $r_{\mathcal{A}}(\pi)$ if $\mathcal{A}$ is still running in time-slot t and $\gamma_t(\pi) = r_{\mathcal{A}}(\pi)$ if $\mathcal{A}$ has terminated before time-slot t. To prove $r_{\mathcal{A}}(\pi) = r_{\mathcal{A}}(\pi \vee \pi')$, it is sufficient to prove $\gamma_t(\pi) = \gamma_t(\pi \vee \pi')$ for any $t \geq 1$.

If node i is inactive, it keeps quiet all the time; if node i is active, its decision to beep or not at time $t + 1$ fully depends on γ_t. By the indicator function $G_i(\gamma_t)$ we denote the decision of node i at time $t+1$, where $G_i(\gamma_t) = 1$ if node i chooses to beep and $G_i(\gamma_t) = 0$ if it keeps quiet. Note that G_i is determined once the deterministic algorithm $\mathcal{A}$ is given. By the definition of the Beeping Model we have

$$\gamma_{t+1}(\pi) = \Big(\gamma_t(\pi), \bigvee_i \pi[i] \cdot G_i(\gamma_t(\pi))\Big), \tag{1}$$

which also holds for π' and $\pi \vee \pi'$.

Clearly we have $\gamma_1(\pi) = \gamma_1(\pi \vee \pi') = \epsilon$, since there is no feedback history at the first time slot. By induction, suppose at time t we have $\gamma_t(\pi) = \gamma_t(\pi \vee \pi')$, we only need to prove $\gamma_{t+1}(\pi) = \gamma_{t+1}(\pi \vee \pi')$, or equivalently, by Eq.(1), to prove

$$\bigvee_i \pi[i] \cdot G_i(\gamma_t(\pi)) = \bigvee_i (\pi \vee \pi')[i] \cdot G_i(\gamma_t(\pi \vee \pi')). \tag{2}$$

Since $r_A(\pi) = r_A(\pi')$, we have $\gamma_{t+1}(\pi) = \gamma_{t+1}(\pi')$ for any $t \geq 1$, which means, again by Eq.(1),

$$\bigvee_i \pi[i] \cdot G_i(\gamma_t(\pi)) = \bigvee_i \pi'[i] \cdot G_i(\gamma_t(\pi')). \tag{3}$$

Combining Eq.(3) and the condition that $\gamma_t(\pi) = \gamma_t(\pi') = \gamma_t(\pi \vee \pi')$, we arrive at Eq. (2) after the following transformations:

$$\begin{aligned}
\bigvee_i \pi[i] \cdot G_i(\gamma_t(\pi)) &= \Big(\bigvee_i \pi[i] \cdot G_i(\gamma_t(\pi))\Big) \vee \Big(\bigvee_i \pi'[i] \cdot G_i(\gamma_t(\pi'))\Big) \\
&= \bigvee_i \Big(\pi[i] \cdot G_i(\gamma_t(\pi))\Big) \vee \Big(\pi'[i] \cdot G_i(\gamma_t(\pi'))\Big) \\
&= \bigvee_i \Big(\pi[i] \cdot G_i(\gamma_t(\pi))\Big) \vee \Big(\pi'[i] \cdot G_i(\gamma_t(\pi))\Big) \\
&= \bigvee_i (\pi[i] \vee \pi'[i]) \cdot G_i(\gamma_t(\pi)) \\
&= \bigvee_i (\pi \vee \pi')[i] \cdot G_i(\gamma_t(\pi \vee \pi')).
\end{aligned}$$

$\square$

Some problems can be defined by a function of π, denoted by $\lambda(\pi)$ here, so that the goal of the problem is to let every node learn the value of $\lambda(\pi)$. For example, $\lambda(\pi) = \pi$ for the membership problem, and $\lambda(\pi) = \|\pi\|$ for the counting problem. For any algorithm solving these kind of problems, the information available for a node to infer $\lambda(\pi)$ includes the channel feedback history $r(\pi)$ and the local initial state $\pi[i]$. Lemma 2 asserts that the inference of $\lambda(\pi)$ in any deterministic algorithm A must solely rely on analyzing the channel feedback $r_A(\pi)$, and the knowledge of $\pi[i]$ cannot be effectively utilized by any node in the inference. The proof of Lemma 2 is based on Lemma 1.

Lemma 2. *In the beeping model, for any deterministic algorithm A that lets every node learn $\lambda(\pi)$, let π and π' be two instances of the problem to be solved, if $r_A(\pi) = r_A(\pi')$, then $\lambda(\pi) = \lambda(\pi')$.*

Proof. For contradiction, suppose $\lambda(\pi) \neq \lambda(\pi \vee \pi')$ and $r_A(\pi) = r_A(\pi')$. We know $r_A(\pi) = r_A(\pi \vee \pi')$ by Lemma 1. In addition, there exists i^* for which $\pi[i^*] = (\pi \vee \pi')[i^*]$. So, all information for node i^* to distinguish the two different values of $\lambda(\pi)$ and $\lambda(\pi \vee \pi')$ is the same, which means it cannot distinguish them. Thus, the algorithm A fails to let *every* node learn $\lambda(\pi)$. This contradiction implies that any algorithm must have $\lambda(\pi) = \lambda(\pi \vee \pi')$ when $r_A(\pi) = r_A(\pi')$. In the same way we also get $\lambda(\pi') = \lambda(\pi \vee \pi')$, so $\lambda(\pi) = \lambda(\pi')$. $\square$

Lemma 2 implies that the number of different channel feedback histories generated by a deterministic algorithm computing $\lambda(\pi)$ is no less than the number of possible values of $\lambda(\pi)$. For the membership problem, there are $\sum_{i=0}^{k} \binom{n}{i}$ different values of $\lambda(\pi)$, so we have a lower bound of $\Omega(\log \binom{n}{k}) = \Omega(k \log \frac{n}{k})$ for any algorithm that correctly solves it. For the counting problem, however, two different instances may have the same number of "1" (i.e., $\lambda(\pi) = \lambda(\pi')$ for some $\pi \neq \pi'$), so one might expect an efficient algorithm that beats the lower bound of $\Omega(k \log \frac{n}{k})$ by "sharing" the same channel feedback history between different instances. Theorem 1 proves that this is impossible: In the beeping model, it is not easier to count the number of active nodes than to identify them all.

Theorem 1. *For any deterministic algorithm $\mathcal{A}$ and any problem instance π with $\|\pi\| > 1$ (i.e. $k > 1$), if $\mathcal{A}$ lets every node learn $\|\pi\|$ with channel feedback history $r_{\mathcal{A}}(\pi)$, then we can construct an algorithm $\mathcal{A}'$ that lets every node learn π with exactly the same channel feedback history $r_{\mathcal{A}}(\pi)$.*

Proof. We prove that the mapping from π to $r_{\mathcal{A}}(\pi)$ for any deterministic counting algorithm $\mathcal{A}$ must be injective, i.e., if $r_{\mathcal{A}}(\pi) = r_{\mathcal{A}}(\pi')$ then $\pi = \pi'$. Since every instance π has a different channel feedback history $r_{\mathcal{A}}(\pi)$ when $\mathcal{A}$ terminates, $\mathcal{A}'$ simply remembers the entire table of the one-to-one mapping from $r_{\mathcal{A}}(\pi)$ to π, thus solving the membership problem once $r_{\mathcal{A}}(\pi)$ is given.

The proof of injectivity is by contradiction. Since $r_{\mathcal{A}}(\pi) = r_{\mathcal{A}}(\pi')$, by Lemma 2 we have $\|\pi\| = \|\pi'\|$. Suppose $\pi \neq \pi'$, then there must be some i^* with $\pi[i^*] = 0$ and $\pi'[i^*] = 1$, so we have $\|\pi \vee \pi'\| > \|\pi\|$. On the other hand, since $r_{\mathcal{A}}(\pi) = r_{\mathcal{A}}(\pi')$, by Lemma 1 we have $r_{\mathcal{A}}(\pi \vee \pi') = r_{\mathcal{A}}(\pi)$, and then by Lemma 2 we have $\|\pi \vee \pi'\| = \|\pi\|$, a contradiction. $\qquad\square$

We remark that Theorem 1 can be naturally generalized to prove the equivalence with the membership problem for more problems defined by $\lambda(\pi)$ in the beeping model. Actually, any deterministic algorithm solving a problem defined by $\lambda(\pi)$ can be used to solve the membership problem with the same channel feedback history, as long as the function $\lambda(\cdot)$ has the property that, for any two different instances π and π', $\lambda(\pi) = \lambda(\pi \vee \pi') \Rightarrow \lambda(\pi) \neq \lambda(\pi')$.

Moreover, for problems that cannot be directly represented by a function of π, we may still prove their equivalence with MP by proving that an algorithm for this problem can solve the counting problem. This allows us to prove the main theorem of this section.

Theorem 2. *For any problem instance π with $\|\pi\| > 1$ (i.e. $k > 1$) and any positive integer T, if any deterministic algorithm $\mathcal{A}$ solves conflict resolution under π in T time slots, then we can construct an algorithm $\mathcal{A}'$ that lets every node learn π in exactly T time slots.*

Proof. The idea is to construct a counting algorithm $\tilde{\mathcal{A}}$ from the conflict resolution algorithm $\mathcal{A}$. Recall that a time slot is "exclusively-used" if only one single node is allowed to beep in that time slot. Given a deterministic conflict resolution algorithm $\mathcal{A}$, the algorithm $\tilde{\mathcal{A}}$ runs $\mathcal{A}$, and lets each active node beep in the first exclusively-used time slot it has and keep quiet since then. When $\mathcal{A}$ terminates, $\tilde{\mathcal{A}}$ lets each node count the number of beep signals in all the exclusively-used time slots, which is also the number of active nodes. So $\tilde{\mathcal{A}}$ is a valid counting algorithm (and $|r_{\tilde{\mathcal{A}}}(\pi)| = T$). By Theorem 1 we know that the information of $r_{\tilde{\mathcal{A}}}(\pi)$ is already enough to solve the membership problem. $\qquad\square$

Theorem 2 shows that MP can be reduced to CR at no additional cost in time-slots. Reversely, the reduction from CR to MP requires k additional time-slots.

Since any CR algorithm needs at least k time-slots to let every node transmit successfully once, the reduction to the MP does not change the performance bound for any deterministic CR algorithm. Thus, the two problems share the same upper and lower bounds in beeping model. As mentioned before, a simple counting argument gives the lower bound $\Omega(k \log \frac{n}{k})$ for the membership problem, which therefore also applies to conflict resolution. Furthermore, Theorem 3 shows that the same lower bound also applies to any *randomized* algorithm that solves either problem of CR and MP with constant probability.

Theorem 3. *In the Beeping Model with single channel, for any constant* $0 \leq \lambda < 1$, *every randomized algorithm requires at least* $\Omega(k \log \frac{n}{k})$ *time slots to solve Conflict Resolution or the Membership Problem with success probability* λ *under the worst-case distribution of problem instances.*

Proof. By the so-called *entropy argument*, we prove that any randomized algorithm that always correctly solves the Membership Problem when terminating (i.e. Las Vegas algorithms) has the expected run time of $\Omega(k \log \frac{n}{k})$. Specifically, due to Yao's principle, a distributed Las Vegas algorithm $\mathcal{A}$ is a stochastic distribution over a set of correct deterministic algorithms, where each deterministic algorithm $\mathcal{A}'$ in this set owns a different table $R_{\mathcal{A}'} : [n] \to \{0,1\}^*$ and simulates $\mathcal{A}$ by using the *fixed* sequence $R_{\mathcal{A}'}(i)$ to replace the random numbers used in node i. On the other hand, due to Shannon's encoding theorem, no deterministic membership algorithm can have an expected performance better than $\log_2 \binom{n}{k} = \Omega(k \log \frac{n}{k})$ under the uniform distribution over the $\binom{n}{k}$ different problem instances, thus any stochastic distribution over any subset of deterministic membership algorithms, i.e., any Las Vegas membership algorithm, must need $\Omega(k \log \frac{n}{k})$ time slots under the uniform distribution over problem instances.

Due to Theorem 2, every deterministic conflict resolution algorithm must have an average performance of $\Omega(k \log \frac{n}{k})$ (for otherwise we will find a deterministic membership algorithm beating this bound), and thus every Las Vegas conflict resolution algorithm also has a worst-case performance of $\Omega(k \log \frac{n}{k})$.

Finally, for any randomized algorithm $\mathcal{A}$ that solves either the membership problem or conflict resolution with constant success probability $0 < \lambda < 1$ in T time slots (under the worst-case distribution of problem instances), we can verify its correctness in one single time slot by letting active nodes to report whether anyone is missing, and thus can construct a Las Vegas algorithm by repeatedly running $\mathcal{A}$ until it is correct. The Las Vegas algorithm thus constructed has the expected running time of $\sum_{i=1}^{\infty} (1 - \lambda)^{i-1} \lambda \cdot i \cdot T = T/\lambda$. As proved above, any Las Vegas algorithm for either problem has expected running time of $\Omega(k \log \frac{n}{k})$ under the uniform distribution of problem instances, so $T = \Omega(k \log \frac{n}{k})$. $\square$

3   Efficient Algorithm in Beeping Model with Parallel Channels

In last section we proved a lower bound of $\Omega(k \log \frac{n}{k})$ for both MP and CR when only one single beeping channel is available. In this section we give an

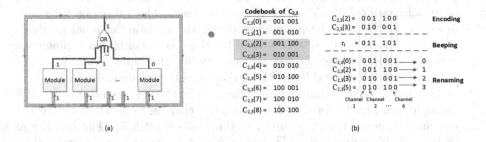

(a)   (b)

Fig. 1. (a) The hardware circuit correspondence of the Beeping Model (b) Illustration of the encoding-beeping-renaming procedure when $n_t = 9$, $d_t = 2$, $q_t = 3$. The left side is the codebook of the $(2,3)$-identity code. The right side illustrates how the encoding/beeping/renaming subroutines work in the case that nodes 2 and 3 are active.

efficient algorithm for the parallel case. We call our algorithm *the Funnel Algorithm*. The algorithm has a time complexity of $O(\log k \log \log_k n)$, yet only uses $O(\max\{k \log_k n, k^2\})$ parallel channels. As we have already shown that MP and CR are equally hard problems, we describe our algorithms in the context of the Membership Problem.

3.1 The Funnel Algorithm

The algorithm runs in a sequence of *iterations*, and the idea is to gradually reduce the problem size n by renaming the active nodes to the name space $\{0, ..., k^{d_t} - 1\}$ in iteration t. The values $d_1, d_2, ...$ decrease gradually during the iteration and the algorithm terminates when $d_t = 1$, at that time each active node has an ID $i' \in \{0, ..., k-1\}$, and then each node locally recovers the original ID's of all active nodes based on the channel feedback history. The sequence $D = \{d_1, d_2, ...\}$ is called an *iteration policy*, which has significant impact on the algorithm's performance. We now present the general iteration framework first, and then define the concrete iteration policy we use to achieve our results.

Iteration Framework. Given an iteration policy $D = \{d_1, d_2, ...\}$, in each iteration t, the algorithm works by running the following encoding-beeping-renaming procedure at each active node (see Fig. 1(b) for an illustration):

- *Encoding.* Suppose the name space is $\{0, ..., n_t - 1\}$ in iteration t. Let $q_t = \lceil n_t^{\frac{1}{d_t}} \rceil$, each node locally encodes its current ID u_t with the so-called (d_t, q_t)-*identity code*. The (d, q)-identity code encodes an integer $u \in \{0, ..., q^d - 1\}$ into a bit vector $C_{d,q}(u)$ by first transforming u into the q-nary format $[u]_q = (\mu_1, ..., \mu_d)$, then encoding each μ_j with a q-bit vector that is 1 in the μ_j'th position and "0" everywhere else. For example, $C_{2,3}(2) = C_{2,3}((0,2)) = 001\ 100$, and $C_{2,3}(3) = C_{2,3}((1,0)) = 010\ 001$. The code length of $C_{d_t, q_t}(u_t)$ is denoted by $L(n_t, d_t)$, where

$$L(n_t, d_t) = d_t \cdot q_t = d_t \lceil n_t^{1/d_t} \rceil < d_t n_t^{1/d_t} + d_t. \tag{4}$$

- *Beeping.* Each active node "beeps out" all bits of its codeword $C_{d_t, q_t}(u_t)$ in parallel, using $L(n_t, d_t)$ single-channel accesses. This takes one time slot. Since all active nodes beep simultaneously, the resulting channel feedback $r_t = (\gamma_1, ..., \gamma_{d_t})$ is the bitwise OR of all these codewords. Note that each segment γ_j in r_t is a q_t−bit vector that may have multiple "1"s in it.
- *Renaming.* Given channel feedback r_t, the "possible" codewords of any active node u_t can only be a combination of the "1"s in *different* segments of r_t. For example (see Fig. 1), for the $(2,3)$-code, the channel feedback $r_t = 011\ 101$ can only be generated by a subset of the nodes $\{0, 2, 3, 5\}$. The number of these "possible" codewords is $\prod_j \|\gamma_j\| = k^{d_t}$ in the worst case. So each active node can locally rename itself with a new unique ID $u_{t+1} \in \{0, ..., k^{d_t} - 1\}$, where u_{t+1} is the order of its original ID u_t among all the (at most k^{d_t}) possible ID's. For example, for the node with $u_t = 3$, there is two possible ID's smaller than u_t (i.e., 0 and 2), so $u_{t+1} = 2$.

Note that a node can locally recover $C_{d_t, q_t}(u_t)$ for *any* given u_{t+1} (u_{t+1} doesn't necessarily belong to the node itself) as long as d_t, q_t, and r_t are known. With $C_{d_t, q_t}(u_t)$, the node can further recover u_t locally. Therefore, when the algorithm terminates with $d_T = 1$, every node can locally recover the original identifier of each active node by sequentially recover $u_T, u_{T-1}, ...,$ down to until u_1.

Iteration Policy. Any iteration policy ending with $d_T = 1$ and having $d_{t+1} \leq d_t$ for any $t < T$ returns the correct answer to the problem. Among them, we choose the iteration policy D^* for performance consideration.

Definition 1. *Let T be the maximal integer satisfying $(1 + \frac{1}{\ln k})^T \leq \log_k n$. Define $\tilde{d}_t = (1 + \frac{1}{\ln k})^{T-t}$ for $t \geq 0$. The iteration policy $D^* = \{d_1, ..., d_T\}$, where*

$$d_t = \begin{cases} \lceil \tilde{d}_t \rceil & when\ \tilde{d}_t \geq \ln k \\ d_{t-1} - 1 & when\ \tilde{d}_t < \ln k \end{cases} . \tag{5}$$

3.2   Performance Analysis

In the Funnel Algorithm, each node makes $L(n_t, d_t)$ single-channel accesses in each iteration t, which takes one single time slot when $L(n_t, d_t)$ number of channels are available. Therefore, the algorithm's time complexity corresponds to the number of iterations, and the number of channels it requires corresponds to the maximal number of single-channel accesses in all iterations, i.e., $\max_t L(n_t, d_t)$. In the following, we first prove bounds for the time slots the Funnel Algorithm needs (Theorem 4), then characterizes its efficiency in channel usage and computational complexity (Theorem 5).

Theorem 4. *The Funnel Algorithm takes $O(\log k \log \log_k n)$ time slots to terminate in the worst case.*

Proof. Clearly the algorithm terminates in one time slo twhen $k = 1$ (i.e. at most one node is active). For $k \geq 2$, by Definition 1, the Funnel Algorithm terminates in no more than $T + \ln k + 1$ time slots in any case, and we have $((1 + \frac{1}{\ln k})^{\ln k})^{T/\ln k} \leq \log_k n$, which means

$$T \leq \ln k \cdot \ln \log_k n / \ln \left((1 + \frac{1}{\ln k})^{\ln k} \right). \tag{6}$$

Since $1.85 < (1 + \frac{1}{\ln k})^{\ln k} < e$ for $k \geq 2$, we have $T \leq 1.63 \cdot \ln k \cdot \ln \log_k n$.   □

Lemma 3. *The Funnel Algorithm makes* $O(k \log \frac{n}{k} + k^2)$ *single-channel accesses in the worst case, that is,* $\sum_{t=1}^{T} L(n_t, d_t) = O(k \log \frac{n}{k} + k^2)$.

Proof. To prove the bound on the total number of channel accesses, we show that the iterations with $\tilde{d}_t \geq \ln k$ collectively have $O(k \log \frac{n}{k})$ channel-accesses, and the remaining iterations (i.e. with $\tilde{d}_t < \ln k$) collectively have $\Theta(k^2)$ channel-accesses, thus the sum of channel accesses over all iterations is $O(k \log \frac{n}{k} + k^2)$.

When $\tilde{d}_t \geq \ln k$: Since $d_t = \lceil \tilde{d}_t \rceil$, we have $\tilde{d}_t \leq d_t \leq \tilde{d}_t + 1$ and $1 \leq \frac{\tilde{d}_t}{\ln k} \leq \frac{d_t}{\ln k}$. By Definition 1 we also have $(1 + \frac{1}{\ln k})\tilde{d}_t = \tilde{d}_{t-1}$. Combining these results together yields a chain of inequalities

$$\tilde{d}_t \leq d_t \leq (1 + \frac{1}{\ln k})\tilde{d}_t = \tilde{d}_{t-1} \leq d_{t-1} \leq (1 + \frac{2}{\ln k})\tilde{d}_t. \tag{7}$$

We know by Eq.(4) that the number of single-channel accesses made in iteration t is less than $d_t(k^{\frac{d_{t-1}}{d_t}} + 1)$. Then, by (7), we have

$$d_t(k^{\frac{d_{t-1}}{d_t}} + 1) \leq (1 + \frac{1}{\ln k})\tilde{d}_t(k^{\frac{(1+\frac{2}{\ln k})\tilde{d}_t}{d_t}} + 1) \leq (1 + \frac{1}{\ln 2})\tilde{d}_t(e^2 k + 1) \leq 2.45(e^2 k + 1)\tilde{d}_t.$$

Let t^* be the last iteration with $\tilde{d}_t \geq \ln k$. We know that the total number of single-channel accesses made from iteration 1 through iteration t^* is less than

$$\sum_{1}^{t^*} d_t(k^{\frac{d_{t-1}}{d_t}} + 1) \leq \sum_{1}^{T} d_t(k^{\frac{d_{t-1}}{d_t}} + 1) \leq \sum_{1}^{T} 2.45(e^2 k + 1)\tilde{d}_t$$

$$= 2.45(e^2 k + 1) \sum_{0}^{T-1}(1 + \frac{1}{\ln k})^t = 2.45(e^2 k + 1)\ln k((1 + \frac{1}{\ln k})^T - 1)$$

$$\leq 2.45(e^2 k + 1)\ln k(\log_k n - 1) = 2.45(e^2 k + 1)\ln \frac{n}{k} = O(k \log \frac{n}{k}).$$

When $\tilde{d}_t < \ln k$: Let t^* be the first iteration with $\tilde{d}_t < \ln k$, we have $d_{t^*} = d_{t^*-1} - 1$ and $d_{t^*-1} = \lceil \tilde{d}_{t^*-1} \rceil = \lceil \tilde{d}_{t^*}(1 + \frac{1}{\ln k}) \rceil < \lceil \ln k(1 + \frac{1}{\ln k}) \rceil$, and thus $d_{t^*} < \lceil \ln k + 1 \rceil - 1 \leq \lfloor \ln k \rfloor + 1$. Then we know that the number of single-channel accesses used in all iterations with $\tilde{d}_t < \ln k$ is

$$\sum_{\{t:\tilde{d}_t < \ln k\}} L(n_t, d_t) = \sum_{d=1}^{\lfloor \ln k \rfloor + 1} d(k^{\frac{d+1}{d}} + 1) = \sum_{d=1}^{\lfloor \ln k \rfloor} dk^{\frac{d+1}{d}} + O(k \log k) + O(\log^2 k)$$

$$= k^2 + 2k^{\frac{3}{2}} + k \sum_{d=3}^{\lfloor \ln k \rfloor} dk^{\frac{1}{d}} + O(k \log k) + O(\log^2 k)$$

Now it is sufficient to prove that $\sum_{d=3}^{\lfloor \ln k \rfloor} dk^{\frac{1}{d}} = o(k)$. By using Euler's Approximation,

$$\sum_{d=3}^{\lfloor \ln k \rfloor} dk^{\frac{1}{d}} < \int_2^{\ln k} xk^{\frac{1}{x}} dx = \frac{1}{2} xk^{\frac{1}{x}} (\ln k + x) - \frac{1}{2} (\ln k)^2 \mathrm{Ei}(\frac{\ln k}{x}) \Big|_2^{\ln k}$$

$$= \frac{1}{2} (\ln k)^2 \mathrm{Ei}(\frac{\ln k}{2}) - \sqrt{k}(\ln k + 2) + (e - \frac{\mathrm{Ei}(1)}{2})(\ln k)^2, \qquad (8)$$

where $\mathrm{Ei}(x)$ is the *Exponential Integral* function defined as $\mathrm{Ei}(x) = \int_{-\infty}^x \frac{e^t}{t} dt$, which is known to have no closed form expression. However, by noticing that $\frac{e^t}{t}$ is monotonically increasing for $t > 1$, we can derive an upper bound of $\mathrm{Ei}(x)$:

$$\mathrm{Ei}(x) = \int_{-\infty}^x \frac{e^t}{t} dt = \mathrm{Ei}(1) + \int_1^x \frac{e^t}{t} dt < \mathrm{Ei}(1) + \frac{e^x}{x}(x - 1). \qquad (9)$$

Substituting Eq.(9) back to Eq.(8), we get

$$\sum_{d=3}^{\lfloor \ln k \rfloor} dk^{\frac{1}{d}} < \frac{1}{2}(\ln k)^2 \frac{2e^{\frac{\ln k}{2}}}{\ln k}(\frac{\ln k}{2} - 1) - \sqrt{k}(\ln k + 2) + e(\ln k)^2 = \Theta\left(\sqrt{k}(\ln k)^2\right).$$

$\square$

Theorem 5. *The Funnel Algorithm uses $O(k \log_k n + k^2)$ parallel channels and has computational complexity of $O(k^2 \log \frac{n}{k} + k^3)$.*

Proof. We first prove upper bound about channel usage, i.e., $\max_{t \in [T]} L(n_t, d_t) = O(k \log_k n + k^2)$. Recall that we already proved in Lemma 3 that $\sum_t L(n_t, d_t) = \Theta(k^2)$ for the iterations with $\tilde{d}_t < \ln k$, which means $L(n_t, d_t) = O(k^2)$ for any t with $\tilde{d}_t < \ln k$. For iterations with $\tilde{d}_t \geq \ln k$, we have

$$\max_t L(n_t, d_t) \leq \max_t d_t(n_t^{\frac{1}{d_t}} + 1) = \max_t d_t(k^{\frac{d_t - 1}{d_t}} + 1) \qquad (10)$$

From Inequality (7) we know $\frac{d_t - 1}{d_t} \leq 1 + \frac{2}{\ln k}$. Substituting this to Eq. (10) yields

$$\max_t L(n_t, d_t) \leq d_t(k^{1 + \frac{2}{\ln k}} + 1) = d_t(k \cdot e^2 + 1).$$

By Definition 1 we have $d_t \leq \log_k n$ for any t, which concludes with $L(n_t, d_t) = O(k \log_k n)$ for any t with $\tilde{d}_t \geq \ln k$.

Finally, since the local computation of every subroutine (encoding/ beeping/ renaming/ decoding) in the Funnel Algorithm is linear to the code length $L(n_t, d_t)$, the computational complexity for the Funnel Algorithm to recover k identifiers is $O(k \cdot S)$, where $S = \sum_t L(n_t, d_t)$ is the total number of single-channel accesses. Then by Lemma 3, the Funnel Algorithm has computational complexity of $O(k \cdot S) = O(k^2 \log \frac{n}{k} + k^3)$.

$\square$

3.3   Crash Tolerance

In addition to its efficiency, the Funnel Algorithm is also *resilient to crash failures (fail-stops)*, in the sense that the algorithm guarantees to identify all active nodes that remain alive (not crashed) when the algorithm terminates, assuming an adversary crashes an arbitrary subset of nodes in any time slot. This is because the Funnel Algorithm maintains a candidate list until the last iteration, without making any irreversible decisions regarding the activeness of any node in the list (=no false positives). Also, the crash of an active node never leads to the removal of any other active node from the candidate list (=no false negatives).

Theorem 6. *Let $N = \{1, ..., n\}$, and let $A_t \subseteq N$ be the active set at the end of time slot t for any $t > 0$ and A_0 be the active set when the Funnel Algorithm starts. For any infinite sequence $A_0, A_1, A_2, ...$ satisfying $A_t \subseteq A_{t-1}$ for any $t > 0$, the Funnel Algorithm terminates no later than in the case of given sequence $\{A_t = A_0$ for any $t > 0\}$, and returns A_T if it terminates at time slot T.*

4   Discussion

We have proved two new results on the distributed complexity of computation in Beeping Channels. We present a new algorithm that improves upon the best-known existing solutions; and we show that two key problems in this model are equally hard. The latter result, in particular, sheds new light not only on the Beeping Model itself, but also on its relationship to the most well-studied model for medium access channels: the collision-detection model with ternary feedback. Our results prove that even for such basic problems such as conflict resolution and the membership problem, the two models behave fundamentally differently.

Moreover, there is another well-known binary-feedback model, called the *radio network model without collision detection*, where nodes are unable to distinguish collisions (the conflict state) from the random background noise (the idle state). Although also assuming binary feedbacks, the radio-network model returns whether a time slot is a success (in contrast, the beeping model returns whether a time slot is idle). Interestingly, we can also observe in the radio-network model the separation in hardness between the problems of CR and MP, as well as the separation in efficiency between deterministic and randomized CR algorithms [3] – both disappear in the beeping model.

It seems that the inability to detect successful communications (partially due to the lack of sophisticated modulation and coding schemes) has made the beeping model quite different from traditional models. As future works, it may be interesting to further investigate the relationship between these (and other) channel access models.

---

[3] In the radio-network model, there exist $O(k + \log n)$ randomized CR algorithms [13], while there is the entropy lower bound of $\Omega(k \log \frac{n}{k})$ for randomized MP algorithms and a lower bound of $\Omega(k \log \frac{n}{k})$ for deterministic CR algorithms [4].

Acknowledgements. The authors thank Dongxiao Yu and Wei Chen for the inspiring discussions about this work. We also thank all the anonymous reviewers who gave valuable comments on the previous drafts of this paper.

References

1. Afek, Y., Alon, N., Bar-Joseph, Z., Cornejo, A., Haeupler, B., Kuhn, F.: Beeping a maximal independent set. In: Peleg, D. (ed.) DISC 2011. LNCS, vol. 6950, pp. 32–50. Springer, Heidelberg (2011)
2. Afek, Y., Alon, N., Barad, O., Hornstein, E., Barkai, N., Bar-Joseph, Z.: A biological solution to a fundamental distributed computing problem. Science 331(6014), 183–185 (2011)
3. Capetanakis, J.: Tree algorithms for packet broadcast channels. IEEE Transactions on Information Theory 25(5), 505–515 (1979)
4. Clementi, A.E.F., Monti, A., Silvestri, R.: Selective families, superimposed codes, and broadcasting on unknown radio networks. In: Proceedings of the Twelfth Annual ACM-SIAM Symposium on Discrete Algorithms, SODA 2001 (2001)
5. Cornejo, A., Kuhn, F.: Deploying wireless networks with beeps. In: Lynch, N.A., Shvartsman, A.A. (eds.) DISC 2010. LNCS, vol. 6343, pp. 148–162. Springer, Heidelberg (2010)
6. Du, D., Hwang, F.: Combinatorial group testing and its applications. World Scientific (2000)
7. Gelly, S., Kocsis, L., Schoenauer, M., Sebag, M., Silver, D., Szepesvári, C., Teytaud, O.: The grand challenge of computer go: Monte carlo tree search and extensions. Commun. ACM 55(3), 106–113 (2012)
8. Greenberg, A.G., Winograd, S.: A lower bound on the time needed in the worst case to resolve conflicts deterministically in multiple access channels. J. ACM 32(3) (July 1985)
9. Hayes, J.: An adaptive technique for local distribution. IEEE Transactions on Communications 26(8), 1178–1186 (1978)
10. Komlos, J., Greenberg, A.: An asymptotically fast nonadaptive algorithm for conflict resolution in multiple-access channels. IEEE Transactions on Information Theory 31(2), 302–306 (1985)
11. Kowalski, D.R.: On selection problem in radio networks. In: Proceedings of the Twenty-Fourth Annual ACM Symposium on Principles of Distributed Computing, PODC 2005 (2005)
12. Li, C.H.: A sequential method for screening experimental variables. Journal of the American Statistical Association 57(298), 455–477 (1962)
13. Martel, C.U.: Maximum finding on a multiple access broadcast network. Information Processing Letters 52, 7–13 (1994)
14. Massey, J.L.: Collision-resolution algorithms and random-access communications. Technical Report UCLA-ENG-8016 (April 1980)
15. Tsybakov, B.S., Mikhailov, V.A.: Free synchronous packet access in a broadcast channel with feedback. Prob. Inf. Transmission 14(4) (April 1978)
16. Wolf, J.K.: Born again group testing: Multiaccess communications. IEEE Transaction on Information Theory 2 (March 1985)

Frequency Hopping
against a Powerful Adversary

Yuval Emek[1] and Roger Wattenhofer[2]

[1] ETH Zurich, Switzerland
emek@tik.ee.ethz.ch
[2] Microsoft Research, Redmond, WA and ETH Zurich, Switzerland
wattenhofer@tik.ee.ethz.ch

Abstract. Frequency hopping is a central method in wireless communication, offering improved resistance to adversarial interference and interception attempts, and easy non-coordinated control in dynamic environments. In this paper, we introduce a new model that supports a rigorous study of frequency hopping in adversarial settings. We then propose new frequency hopping protocols that allow a sender-receiver pair to essentially use the full communication capacity, despite a powerful adversary that can scan and jam a significant amount of the ongoing transmissions.

1 Introduction

The term *frequency hopping (FH)* in wireless communication refers to a century old method [31–33] of rapidly switching the carrier of a transmitted radio signal among many frequency channels. This method offers various advantages in comparison to traditional fixed frequency transmissions: it is highly resistant to narrow-band interference, it is much more difficult to intercept, and it allows for easy non-coordinated control in dynamic environments. Because of these advantages, FH is omnipresent in modern wireless communication standards such as GSM. Nevertheless, state-of-the-art FH schemes typically use "cryptographic heuristics" whose security is not mathematically established and sometimes turns out to be compromised. For example, using an off-the-shelf device that costs less than 100 EUR [27], the FH scheme that lies at the heart of Bluetooth can be breached within less than a second [17].

In this paper, we hope to bring the state of analysis of FH to the next level. In particular, we ask ourselves what kind of interference a FH protocol can withstand on an information theoretic level (without making any cryptographic assumptions). It turns out that the right tools enable us to design a FH protocol that can cope with adversarial interference, where the adversary can not only jam a constant fraction ϕ of the bandwidth, but also intercept the protocol's transmissions with a small delay. The price to pay for implementing this protocol is a constant additive overhead on the size of each transmitted message. Surprisingly, our protocol manages to utilize the bandwidth up to that ϕ fraction.

Y. Afek (Ed.): DISC 2013, LNCS 8205, pp. 329–343, 2013.
© Springer-Verlag Berlin Heidelberg 2013

1.1 Model

The Cast. Consider the setting of a uni-directional wireless communication
from Alice (the transmitter) to Bob (the receiver) in an adversarial environment.
There are n available *channels* and in each *round* $t \in \mathbb{Z}_{>0}$, Alice chooses a single
channel $a(t) \in [n]$ over which she transmits her message and Bob chooses a
single channel $b(t)$ on which he listens; $b(t) = a(t)$ is a necessary condition for
Bob to receive Alice's message in round t.

Eve (the adversary) wishes to disturb the communication from Alice to Bob.
In each round $t \in \mathbb{Z}_{>0}$, Eve chooses to *jam* a channel subset $E(t) \subset [n]$ of size
at most ϕn, $0 < \phi < 1$: if $b(t) \in E(t)$, then Bob does not receive Alice's message
even if $b(t) = a(t)$. We distinguish between two types of jamming, differing in the
exact effect that $b(t) \in E(t)$ has on Bob's input in round t: *overwriting* means
that Bob receives a message that was tailored by Eve which may be confused
with Alice's messages; *blocking* means that Bob receives *static noise* which in
particular, indicates to Bob that he did not receive Alice's message. Eve is called
an *overwriting* (respectively, *blocking*) adversary if her jamming capabilities are
suited for overwriting (resp., blocking) Alice's transmissions. For completeness
of the model, we assume that if Bob listens on a wrong channel which is not
jammed by Eve, i.e., $b(t) \notin E(t) \cup \{a(t)\}$, then he also receives static noise.
Note that Alice does not get any feedback regarding the channel on which Bob
listened or the actual message he received (if any).

In attempt to avoid Eve's channel jamming, Alice and Bob must use randomness in their channel choices.[1] This should be done in a coordinated fashion to
ensure, above everything else, that they both choose the same channel. For that
purpose, they both have access to a total of s *shared* random bits generated
(once) prior to round 1. Alice can also generate as many *private* random bits as
she needs in each round; these cannot be (directly) accessed by Bob, however,
Alice may append to each message she transmits up to k additional bits that
can be used to communicate some information regarding her (private) random
choices. In fact, since the actual content of Alice's messages is irrelevant to the
current paper, we shall subsequently consider these k bits as Alice's (whole)
message, so in what follows we assume that all messages are of size k.

The setting described so far is trivial to cope with if Eve is an *oblivious*
adversary: Alice and Bob can simply follow a random permutation of the channels (assuming that s is sufficiently large to support this random choice, i.e.,
$s = \Omega(n \log n)$). However, in our model Eve also enjoys the benefit of some
sort of *delayed adaptiveness*. It is assumed that Eve can *scan* the spectrum and
extract the channel $a(t)$ over which Alice transmitted in round t, but this information is revealed to Eve with a certain *lag* λ, that is, in round $t + \lambda$.

Notice that according to our basic model, Eve's scanning reveals the channel
$a(t)$ over which Alice transmitted in round t, but it does not reveal the content of
the transmitted message. (Although this issue is abstracted away in our model,
note that it is a valid assumption in settings with encrypted messages.) A variant

---

[1] As usual, we assume that Eve knows Alice and Bob's protocol, but not their
random bits.

of the model in which Eve's scanning reveals both the channel and the message content, referred to as *enhanced scanning*, is discussed in Sec. 4.

Grouping the Parameters. We refer to Alice and Bob's channel choosing strategy as an (n, s, k)-*FH protocol*, where n denotes the number of channels, s denotes the number of shared random bits, and k denotes the size (in bits) of the messages. Eve is referred to as a (λ, ϕ)-*adversary*, where λ denotes the delayed adaptiveness lag and ϕ denotes the fraction of channels she jams. It is important to point out that these five parameters may exhibit inter-dependencies (in particular, we shall express s and λ as functions of n), however, unless stated otherwise, they do not grow as a function of the execution length.

Round t is said to be *successful* if $b(t) = a(t) \notin E(t)$, namely, if Bob listens on the channel over which Alice transmits and this channel is not jammed by Eve. The quality of a FH protocol is measured in terms of the fraction of successful rounds captured by the probability that an arbitrary round is successful. Clearly, no FH protocol can guarantee a success probability larger than $1 - \phi$; this is demonstrated already by an (oblivious) adversary that in every round t, chooses $E(t)$ uniformly at random out of all channel subsets of size ϕn.[2] Therefore, at best, we can hope for FH protocols that guarantee success probability close to $1 - \phi$.

Resilience. Formally, an (n, s, k)-FH protocol is said to be ϵ-*resilient* to blocking/overwriting (λ, ϕ)-adversaries if round t is successful with probability at least $1 - \phi - \epsilon$ for every $t \in \mathbb{Z}_{>0}$ against any blocking/overwriting (λ, ϕ)-adversary, respectively. Note that the requirement on the success probability should hold, in particular, as t goes to infinity (fixing all other parameters). This can be thought of as requiring that the guarantees of the FH protocol hold for infinitely long executions, even though all other parameters (including the number s of shared random bits) are finite.

Motivation. The role of the shared random bits is similar to that of a *secret key* in cryptographic systems, generated and exchanged between the collaborating parties before the execution commences. Under our model, the situation is clearly hopeless without shared random bits: if $s = 0$, then Eve knows everything Bob knows already in round 1 and can easily jam the communication. On the other hand, if Alice and Bob have access to infinitely many shared random bits and in particular, can use fresh $\lceil \lg n \rceil$ shared random bits per round,[3] then they can trivially choose $a(t) = b(t) \in [n]$ uniformly at random in every round t, thus ensuring an optimal success probability of $1 - \phi$. To a large extent, the challenge in this paper is to to deal with the case of a finite, yet positive, number s of shared random bits, while trying to keep s small (as a function of n).

---

[2] By Yao's principle, the existence of an oblivious probabilistic adversary that guarantees a success probability of at most $1 - \phi$ against all FH protocols implies that for every FH protocol, there exists an oblivious deterministic adversary with the same guarantee.

[3] We use $\lg x$ to denote $\log_2 x$.

One may wonder whether the delayed adaptiveness feature of our model can be justified in practical applications. To that end, note that with dedicated hardware, Eve can scan all n channels, however, extracting the information regarding the channels over which Alice transmitted from the perceived signals is a difficult challenge, likely to incur a significant delay. Moreover, in practical FH scenarios, the spectrum is usually shared between many concurrently communicating Alice-Bob pairs (e.g., secondary users in cognitive radio networks [24]), thus adding another level of complexity to the challenge of obtaining the FH channels used by one specific pair.

1.2   Related Work

Several people are credited with inventing FH. In 1903 Nikola Tesla was granted two U.S. patents [31, 32], where in the second patent, he states: *"To overcome [several drawbacks such as electrical disturbance] and to enable a great number of transmitting and receiving stations to be operated selectively and exclusively and without any danger of the signals or messages being disturbed, intercepted, or interfered with in any way is the object of my present invention."* Jonathan Zenneck [33] claimed in his textbook on wireless telegraphy that the newly founded company Telefunken tested FH around the same time.

The first applications of FH were probably for military purposes. It is reported that the German Reichswehr used FH during World War I to prevent eavesdropping by British forces. During World War II, FH was already pretty common, e.g. in a system called SIGSALY that provided a secure communication infrastructure between Roosevelt and Churchill. Perhaps the most well known FH related martial invention was that of star actress Hedy Lamarr (Markey) and composer George Antheil for preventing the detection of radio guided torpedoes [21]. Nowadays, FH is used by essentially all military radio systems.

FH is well studied in the context of information and coding theory, e.g. [15, 22, 5]. These studies typically aim to provide algebraic hopping sequences with various properties, such as good Hamming correlation or near linear span. However, to the best of our knowledge, this body of work does not deal with adversarial interference.

In contrast, the wireless algorithms community has recently developed an increasing interest in adversarial jamming. Often, the jammer must live on a limited energy budget, which may [16] or may not [13] be known. Dolev et al. [9] studied jamming in the context of multi-channel gossip and presented tight bounds for the ϵ-gossip problem, where the adversary may jam 1 frequency per round. They also study a setting allowing the nodes to exchange authenticated messages despite a malicious adversary that can cause collisions and spoof messages [10], and present new bounds on broadcasting [11]. Another line of work focuses on the *bootstrap problem* where nodes have to find each other despite adversarial jammers [23, 8, 4]. Awerbuch et al. [3] present a MAC protocol for single-hop networks that is provably robust to an adaptive adversary that can jam (in a blocking style) a $(1 - \epsilon)$-fraction of the rounds. This work was later extended to self-stabilization [29, 30]. In [2], the adversary controls both packet injections and jamming, according to a leaky bucket process. Richa et al. [28] recently introduced a reactive jammer that can in addition learn from the protocol history. Hopping sequences with cryptographic guarantees on the resilience to adversarial jamming is studied, e.g., in [19].

Due to their asymptotic approach, theoretical works are typically deemed successful once they manage to exploit a constant fraction of the available communication capacity. In contrast, wireless protocol designers are rarely willing to sacrifice a constant fraction of the precious capacity for protocol overhead. In that regard, we would like to emphasize that our protocols use the available communication capacity up to an ϵ-fraction that can be made arbitrarily small.

1.3 Our Results

Our main technical contribution is a FH protocol that guarantees success probability near $1 - \phi$ with constant size messages, logarithmically many shared random bits, and a logarithmic lag. This protocol is suitable for any constant $0 < \phi < 1$ if Eve is a blocking adversary; and for any constant $0 < \phi < 1/16$ if Eve is an overwriting adversary.

We then turn to study the enhanced scanning variant of the model, where the content of Alice's messages is revealed to Eve together with the channel over which these messages were transmitted. In this variant we prove that resilience cannot be achieved as long as the adaptiveness lag is bounded. On the other hand, we show that if the lag *grows* logarithmically with time, then our FH protocol works even when Eve enjoys the benefit of enhanced scanning.

1.4 Techniques

Our FH protocols are inspired by pseudo-random generators à la Impagliazzo and Zuckerman [14]. The sequence of channels over which Alice transmits corresponds to a random walk on an n-vertex constant degree expander. On the one hand, this sequence seems sufficiently random to fool Eve; on the other hand, Bob only needs a constant number of bits per round in order to follow Alice's choices. Since a ϕ-fraction of Alice's messages are doomed to be lost, she encodes her transmissions using a family of error-correcting codes with suitably chosen parameters.

In contrast to the method of Impagliazzo and Zuckerman, where the subset of bad vertices is fixed, we have to deal with an adaptive adversary that dynamically changes the bad vertex subset. This issue is handled in our analysis through a careful examination of the spectral properties of the underlying expander.

2 Preliminaries

In this section, we describe the main ingredients used in the design of our FH protocols, namely, expander graphs and error-correcting codes.

Ramanujan Graphs. Consider some n-vertex d-regular connected non-bipartite graph G. Let $A \in \{0,1\}^{n \times n}$ be G's adjacency matrix and let $W = \frac{1}{d}A$ be the corresponding *walk* matrix. Since W is symmetric, it has n real eigenvalues $\omega_1 \geq \cdots \geq \omega_n$, and since G is d-regular, connected, and non-bipartite, we know that $1 = \omega_1 > \omega_2 \geq \cdots \geq \omega_n > -1$. Moreover, the all 1s vector $\mathbf{1}$ is an eigenvector of W of eigenvalue $\omega_1 = 1$, thus the stationary distribution of the random walk w is uniform in $[n]$.

Let $\omega(G) = \max_{2 \leq i \leq n}\{|\omega_i|\} = \max\{\omega_2, |\omega_n|\}$. The parameter $\omega(G)$ captures some important properties of the graph G, and in particular, the speed of convergence of a random walk to the stationary distribution. This is cast in the following lemma which is a well known fact in spectral graph theory (see, e.g., [7]).

Lemma 1. *Let w be a random walk in an n-vertex regular connected non-bipartite graph G and let $\mathbf{w}_t$ be the distribution vector of w after t steps. Then for every $i \in [n]$ and $t \in \mathbb{Z}_{>0}$, we have $\left|\mathbf{w}_t(i) - \frac{1}{n}\right| \leq \omega(G)^t$. Note that this inequality holds regardless of the initial distribution $\mathbf{w}_0$.*

The graphs in an infinite family $\mathcal{G}$ of d-regular connected non-bipartite graphs are called *expanders* if they all have a small $\omega(G)$, that is, if there exists some constant $0 < c < 1$ such that $\omega(G) \leq c$ for all graphs $G \in \mathcal{G}$. In particular, the graphs in $\mathcal{G}$ are said to be *Ramanujan graphs* (a.k.a. *Ramanujan expanders*) if they all satisfy $\omega(G) \leq 2\sqrt{d-1}/d$ [18]. The Alon-Boppana theorem (cf. [26]) essentially states that Ramanujan graphs are the best possible expanders in terms of their small $\omega(G)$.

Theorem 2 **([18, 20, 25]).** *For every prime power q and integer $n_0 > 0$, there exist an integer $n = \Theta(n_0)$ and an explicitly constructable n-vertex Ramanujan graph of degree $d = q + 1$.*

Error-Correcting Codes. An *error-correcting code* C over an alphabet Σ is an injective mapping $C : \Sigma^m \to \Sigma^n$, where m and n, $m < n$, are called the *dimension* and the *length* of the code, respectively. We refer to the $|\Sigma|^m$ strings in the image of C as *codewords*. The *minimum distance* of C is the minimum Hamming distance between any two codewords. The ratio of the minimum distance to the length, referred to as the *relative distance* δ of the code, indicates the quality of the code in terms of the number of errors that can be corrected: any number smaller than $\delta n/2$. The ratio of the dimension to the length, referred to as the *rate* $r = m/n$ of the code, indicates the quality of the code in terms of the number of different messages that can be encoded, also known as the *size* of the code: $|\Sigma|^{rn}$.

Fixing some alphabet Σ of size $|\Sigma| = q$, one typically seeks an infinite family $\mathcal{C}_q$ of codes such that both the relative distance and the rate of every code $C \in \mathcal{C}_q$ are bounded below by some constant. Our construction requires an explicit such family in which the relative distance can be made arbitrarily close to 1 by increasing q (and decreasing the rate). Such a family $\mathcal{C}_q$ is designed, e.g., in [1].

Theorem 3 ([1]). *For every real $\xi > 0$, prime power q, and sufficiently large integer n, there exist a real $0 < r = r(\xi) < 1$ and an explicitly constructable error-correcting code over $GF(q)$ of length n, rate at least r, and relative distance at least $1 - \frac{1}{q} - \xi$.*

3   Resilient FH Protocols

Our goal in this section is to establish the following theorem.

Theorem 4. *Consider some constant real $0 < \phi < 1$ (respectively, $0 < \phi < 1/16$). There exist constant integers $k = k(\phi) > 0$ and $n_0 = n_0(\phi) > 0$ such that for every real $\epsilon > 0$ and integer $n \geq n_0$, there exist an integer $\lambda = O(\log(n/\epsilon))$, an integer $s = O(\log(n/\epsilon))$, and an (n, s, k)-FH protocol with ϵ-resilience to blocking (resp., overwriting) (λ, ϕ)-adversaries.*

The basic protocol, presented in Sec. 3.1 and analyzed in Sec. 3.2, is resilient to overwriting (and hence also blocking) adversaries with $0 < \phi < 1/16$. Section 3.3 is dedicated to tuning up our protocol so that it can cope with the whole range of parameter $0 < \phi < 1$ when restricted to blocking adversaries only.

3.1   The Basic Protocol

In a preprocessing stage, Alice and Bob deterministically construct an n-vertex d-regular Ramanujan graph G as promised by Theorem 2, where $d = d(\phi)$ is a constant integer whose value will be determined later on, and identify the vertices of G with the n channels. Note that Theorem 2 does not promise that such a graph exists for every choice of n, however, by taking a graph G of size $n' > n$, and identifying each channel with either $\lfloor n'/n \rfloor$ or $\lceil n'/n \rceil$ vertices, we do not lose more than an (n/n')-term in the guaranteed success probability, and this can be made arbitrarily small. For the sake of simplicity, we shall subsequently assume that the graph G has exactly n vertices. Since the construction of G is deterministic, we are forced to assume that Eve knows G; this will not affect our analysis.

The Phases. Our protocol relies on two parameters: a constant real $\rho = \rho(\phi)$, $0 < \rho < 1$, and an integer $L = O(\log(n/\epsilon))$; the exact values of these two parameters will be determined later on. The rounds of the execution are partitioned into *phases* indexed by the non-negative integers, where phase $j \in \mathbb{Z}_{\geq 0}$ consists of the first

$$\ell(j) = L + \left\lceil 2 \log_{1/\rho}(j+1) \right\rceil$$

rounds not belonging to any phase $j' < j$. Note that this fully determines the phase to which round t belongs for every $t \in \mathbb{Z}_{>0}$.

Alice's channel choices follow a random walk w in G: The channels used in phase 0, namely, the initial vertex $a(1)$ (chosen uniformly at random) and the first $L - 1$ steps of w, are dictated by the $s = \lceil \lg n + (L - 1) \lg d \rceil = O(\log(n/\epsilon))$

shared random bits. The steps of w in phase $j + 1$, $j \in \mathbb{Z}_{\geq 0}$, are dictated by Alice's private random bits and communicated to Bob via the $\ell(j)$ messages sent in phase j. Recall that some of the messages received by Bob in phase j may be transmitted over channels jammed by Eve; to compensate for that, Alice's messages in phase j are encoded by a carefully designed error-correcting code.

Communicating w's Steps. Using the terminology of Theorem 3, we take $\xi = \xi(\phi)$ and $q = q(\phi)$ to be a constant real, $0 < \xi < 1/4$, and a constant (integer) prime power, respectively, whose exact values will be determined later on. Employing Theorem 3, let C_j be the error-correcting code over $GF(q)$ with length $\ell(j)$, relative distance $\delta \geq 1 - \frac{1}{q} - \xi$, and rate $r \geq r(\xi)$, where $0 < r(\xi) < 1$ is the real promised by the theorem.

Let μ denote the $\ell(j + 1) \leq \ell(j) + 1 \leq 2\ell(j)$ steps of the random walk w in phase $j + 1$. We set the size of Alice's messages to $k = k(\phi) = \lceil \lg q \rceil$; this allows Alice to encode μ using the error-correcting code C_j and to transmit the resulting codeword in phase j, a single letter of the alphabet $GF(q)$ in each round. For that to work, we must make sure that the size of C_j is sufficiently large to encode μ, i.e., that $q^{r\ell(j)} \geq d^{\ell(j+1)}$, which is guaranteed by requiring that the parameter $q = q(\phi)$ satisfies $q \geq d^{2/r(\xi)} \geq d^{2/r}$, and hence $q^{r\ell(j)} \geq d^{2\ell(j)} \geq d^{\ell(j+1)}$. This completes the description of our FH protocol.

3.2   Analysis of the Basic Protocol

For the sake of simplicity, we will prove that our FH protocol is $O(\epsilon)$-resilient (rather than ϵ-resilient). Our analysis relies on the fact that with probability at least $1 - O(\epsilon)$, all phases admit many successful rounds. To formally state this fact (and establish it), we first need some more definitions.

Successful Phases. We say that phase $j \in \mathbb{Z}_{\geq 0}$ is *successful* — an event denoted by A_j — if less than a $(\delta/2)$-fraction of the rounds in the phase are unsuccessful. Note that this implies that if Bob listened on the right channels, then he can successfully decode the codeword transmitted by Alice in phase j. By induction on j, we conclude that the event $A_0 \wedge \cdots \wedge A_{j-1}$ implies that $b(t) = a(t)$ for every round t in phase j. We are now ready to state the two main lemmas of our analysis.

Lemma 5. *Consider some round $t \in \mathbb{Z}_{>0}$ and let $j \in \mathbb{Z}_{\geq 0}$ be the phase to which this round belongs. Conditioned on the event $A_0 \wedge \cdots \wedge A_{j-1}$, round t is successful with probability at least $1 - \phi - \epsilon$.*

Lemma 6. *The event $A_0 \wedge \cdots \wedge A_j$ holds with probability at least $1 - O(\epsilon)$ for every $j \in \mathbb{Z}_{\geq 0}$.*

The remainder of Sec. 3.2 is dedicated to establishing Lemmas 5 and 6, but first, we should convince ourselves that the correctness of our protocol indeed follows from these two lemmas. To that end, consider some round $t \in \mathbb{Z}_{>0}$ in phase

j and let B denote the event that round t is successful. By Lemmas 5 and 6, we have

$$\mathbb{P}(B) \geq \mathbb{P}(B \mid A_0 \wedge \cdots \wedge A_{j-1}) \cdot \mathbb{P}(A_0 \wedge \cdots \wedge A_{j-1})$$
$$\geq (1 - \phi - \epsilon) \cdot (1 - O(\epsilon)) \geq 1 - \phi - O(\epsilon)$$

as required.

Our first step towards establishing Lemmas 5 and 6 is to observe that

$$\mathbb{P}(A_0 \wedge \cdots \wedge A_m) = \mathbb{P}(A_m \mid A_0 \wedge \cdots \wedge A_{m-1}) \cdot \mathbb{P}(A_0 \wedge \cdots \wedge A_{m-1})$$
$$= \mathbb{P}(A_m \mid A_0 \wedge \cdots \wedge A_{m-1}) \cdot \mathbb{P}(A_{m-1} \mid A_0 \wedge \cdots \wedge A_{m-2}) \cdots$$
$$\cdots \mathbb{P}(A_1 \mid A_0) \cdot \mathbb{P}(A_0).$$

Fixing $F_j = \mathbb{P}(\neg A_j \mid A_0 \wedge \cdots \wedge A_{j-1})$, we have

$$\mathbb{P}(A_0 \wedge \cdots \wedge A_m) = (1 - F_0) \cdots (1 - F_m) \geq 4^{-F_0} \cdots 4^{-F_m} = 4^{-\sum_{j=0}^{m} F_j},$$

where the inequality holds by ensuring that $F_j \leq 1/2$ for every $j \in \mathbb{Z}_{\geq 0}$.

Bounding $\sum F_j$. Lemma 6 will be established by showing that $\exp_4(-\sum_{j=0}^{m} F_j) \geq 1 - O(\epsilon)$, or alternatively, that $\exp_4(\sum_{j=0}^{m} F_j) \leq 1 + O(\epsilon) \iff \sum_{j=0}^{m} F_j \leq \log_4(1 + O(\epsilon))$. Since $\log_4(1 + x) > x/2$ for all $0 < x < 1$, it suffices to show that

$$\sum_{j=0}^{m} F_j \leq O(\epsilon) \tag{1}$$

Take $d = d(\phi)$ to be sufficiently large to ensure that $\frac{2}{\sqrt{d}} \leq \frac{1/4 - \sqrt{\phi}}{2}$, which is possible as ϕ is a constant strictly smaller than $1/16$. The following three *auxiliary constants* play a major role in setting the parameters introduced in Sec. 3.1:

$$\alpha = \alpha(\phi) = \frac{1/2 - 2\sqrt{\phi}}{4\sqrt{\phi} + 1}, \quad \beta = \beta(\phi) = (1 + \alpha)\left(\sqrt{\phi} + \frac{2}{\sqrt{d}}\right),$$

$$\gamma = \gamma(\phi) = \frac{1}{\log_4\left(\frac{1}{\beta}\right)}.$$

Since $\sqrt{\phi} < 1/4$, it follows that $0 < \alpha < 1/2$. Moreover, we have $0 < \beta \leq \left(1 + \frac{1/2 - 2\sqrt{\phi}}{4\sqrt{\phi} + 1}\right)\left(\sqrt{\phi} + \frac{1/4 - \sqrt{\phi}}{2}\right) = \frac{2\sqrt{\phi} + 3/2}{8} < \frac{1}{4}$, and hence $0 < \gamma < 1$.

Recall the parameters $\rho = \rho(\phi)$ and $\xi = \xi(\phi)$ introduced in Sec. 3.1 and fix

$$\rho = 2\beta^{\delta/2} \quad \text{and} \quad \xi = \frac{1 - \gamma}{4}.$$

Note that since $0 < \gamma < 1$, it follows that $0 < \xi < 1/4$ as promised. Moreover, by requiring that $q \geq \frac{4}{1-\gamma}$, we ensure that $\delta \geq 1 - \frac{1}{q} - \xi \geq \frac{1+\gamma}{2} > \gamma = \frac{1}{\log_4\left(\frac{1}{\beta}\right)}$.

This implies that $4^{1/\delta} < \frac{1}{\beta}$, hence $0 < \rho = 2\beta^{\delta/2} < 1$ as promised. Fix the integer parameter L introduced in Sec. 3.1 to be

$$L = \max\left\{\left\lceil \log_{1/\rho}\left(\frac{1}{\epsilon}\right)\right\rceil, \left\lceil \log_{\sqrt{d}/2}\left(\frac{\phi n}{\epsilon}\right)\right\rceil, \left\lceil \log_{\sqrt{d}/2}\left(\frac{n}{\alpha}\right)\right\rceil\right\},$$

which yields $L = O(\log(n/\epsilon))$ as promised.

We shall establish (1) by showing that

$$F_j \le \rho^{\ell(j)} ; \tag{2}$$

indeed, this suffices since it implies that

$$\sum_{j=0}^{m} F_j \le \sum_{j=0}^{m} \rho^{L + \lceil 2\log_{1/\rho}(j+1)\rceil} \le \rho^L \cdot \sum_{j=1}^{\infty} j^{-2} \le \epsilon \cdot O(1),$$

where the last inequality follows from the requirement that $L \ge \log_{1/\rho}\left(\frac{1}{\epsilon}\right)$.

The Adaptiveness Lag. Recalling that $L = O(\log(n/\epsilon))$, we require that the lag $\lambda = O(\log(n/\epsilon))$ satisfies $\lambda \ge L$. For the sake of the analysis, we think of Eve's scanning as the ability to know in round t, the vertices visited by w in all rounds up to $t - L$. In fact, since the random walk w is memoryless, we may think of Eve as a function that maps the current round index t and the vertex visited by w in round $t - L$ to $E(t)$.

Recall that $\omega(G) \le \frac{2\sqrt{d-1}}{d} < \frac{2}{\sqrt{d}}$. Since $L \ge \log_{\sqrt{d}/2}\left(\frac{\phi n}{\epsilon}\right)$, we can employ Lemma 1 to conclude that Eve's delayed adaptiveness does not allow her to boost the probability of hitting $a(t)$ by more than an additive term of $\frac{\epsilon}{\phi n}$ per channel, which sums up to an additive term of at most ϵ for all channels jammed by Eve, thus yielding Lemma 5. So, it remains to establish Lemma 6 which is executed by proving that (2) holds. Since $L \ge \log_{\sqrt{d}/2}\left(\frac{n}{\alpha}\right)$ as well, we can employ Lemma 1 once more to establish the following observation.

Observation 7. *Conditioned on Eve's knowledge of the vertex visited by w in round $t - L$, the probability that w visits vertex $i \in [n]$ in round t is at most $\frac{1}{n} + \frac{\alpha}{n} = \frac{1}{n}(1 + \alpha)$.*

Consider some phase $j \in \mathbb{Z}_{\ge 0}$ and let $t_1 \le \cdots \le t_\ell$ denote the indices of the $\ell = \ell(j)$ rounds in this phase. Assume that all previous phases were successful, i.e., event $A_0 \wedge \cdots \wedge A_{j-1}$ occurs, so, in particular, Bob knows the random walk w up to the end of phase j, that is, $b(t_h) = a(t_h)$ for every $h \in [\ell]$. Inequality (2) can be established by letting $\mathcal{E} = \{h \in [\ell] \mid E(t_h) \ni a(t_h)\}$ and showing that

$$\mathbb{P}\left(|\mathcal{E}| \ge \delta\ell/2\right) \le \rho^\ell \tag{3}$$

subject to the assumption that Eve knows $a(t - L)$ at round t.

Given some subset $S \subseteq [\ell]$, let $p_S = \mathbb{P}(\mathcal{E} = S)$. We can express $\mathbb{P}(|\mathcal{E}| \ge \delta\ell/2)$ as

$$\mathbb{P}\left(|\mathcal{E}| \ge \delta\ell/2\right) = \mathbb{P}\left(\bigvee_{S \subseteq [\ell], |S| \ge \delta\ell/2} \mathcal{E} = S\right) \le \sum_{S \subseteq [\ell], |S| \ge \delta\ell/2} p_S.$$

Inequality (3) can now be established by showing that

$$p_S \le \beta^{\delta\ell/2} \tag{4}$$

for every $S \subseteq [\ell]$, $|S| \ge \delta\ell/2$; indeed, (4) implies that $\mathbb{P}\left(|\mathcal{E}| \ge \delta\ell/2\right) \le 2^\ell \cdot \beta^{\delta\ell/2} = \left(2\beta^{\delta/2}\right)^\ell = \rho^\ell$ as required.

A Linear Algebraic View. Fix some subset $S \subseteq [\ell]$, $|S| \ge \delta\ell/2$. For every $h \in [\ell]$, let D_h be a diagonal $n \times n$ real matrix defined by setting

$$D_h(i,i) = \begin{cases} 1 & \text{if } h \notin S \\ 1+\alpha & \text{if } h \in S \text{ and } i \in E(t_h) \\ 0 & \text{if } h \in S \text{ and } i \notin E(t_h) \end{cases}$$

for every $i \in [n]$. In other words, D_h is the identity matrix if $h \notin S$; and a matrix having $1 + \alpha$ on the diagonal entries corresponding to $E(t_h)$ and 0 elsewhere if $h \in S$. Observe that in the latter case, multiplying a vector by D_h increases all entries corresponding to $E(t_h)$ by a factor of $1+\alpha$ and zeros out all other entries.

Lemma 8. *Denoting the uniform distribution vector on $[n]$ by $\boldsymbol{u} = \frac{1}{n}\mathbf{1}$, we have*

$$p_S \le \mathbf{1}^T D_\ell W D_{\ell-1} W \cdots D_2 W D_1 \boldsymbol{u}.$$

Proof. Let N_h denote the vertex subset $E(t_h)$ if $h \in S$; and the vertex subset $[n] - E(t_h)$ otherwise. Taking B_h to be the event that the random walk w visited (a vertex of) N_h in round t_h, we can express the event $S = \mathcal{E}$ (whose probability we would like to bound) as $B_1 \wedge \cdots \wedge B_\ell$. By Observation 7, the ith entry $D_1\boldsymbol{u}(i)$ of the vector $D_1\boldsymbol{u}$ bounds from above the probability that event B_1 occurred and w visits vertex i in round t_1, given that w is in its stationary distribution $\boldsymbol{u}$ in the beginning of the phase. Employing Observation 7 again, we notice by induction on h that

$$D_h W D_{h-1} \cdots W D_1 \boldsymbol{u}(i)$$

serves as an upper bound on the probability that event $B_1 \wedge \cdots \wedge B_h$ occurred and w visits vertex i in round t_h, given that w is in its stationary distribution $\boldsymbol{u}$ in the beginning of the phase. The assertion follows as multiplying by $\mathbf{1}^T$ simply sums up the entries.

Lemma 8 allows us to complete the proof of Lemma 6 by linear algebraic arguments; indeed, we shall establish (4) by showing that

$$\mathbf{1}^T D_\ell W D_{\ell-1} W \cdots D_2 W D_1 \boldsymbol{u} \le \beta^{\delta\ell/2}. \tag{5}$$

based solely on the definition of the matrices $D_1, \ldots, D_\ell$ and on the assumption that W is the walk matrix of a Ramanujan graph. To that end, observe that

$$\begin{aligned} \mathbf{1}^T D_\ell W D_{\ell-1} W \cdots D_2 W D_1 \boldsymbol{u} &= \mathbf{1}^T D_\ell W D_{\ell-1} W \cdots D_2 W D_1 W \boldsymbol{u} \\ &\le \|\mathbf{1}\| \cdot \|D_\ell W\| \cdots \|D_1 W\| \cdot \|\boldsymbol{u}\| \\ &= \|D_\ell W\| \cdots \|D_1 W\|, \end{aligned}$$

where $\|v\| = \sqrt{\sum_{i=1}^{n} v(i)^2}$ denotes the ℓ_2 norm of vector v, $\|M\| = \max_{v \in \mathbb{R}^n - \{0\}} \frac{\|Mv\|}{\|v\|}$ denotes the induced norm of matrix M, and the inequality follows from Cauchy-Schwarz and from some well known properties of the induced matrix norm (see, e.g., [6]).

Bounding $\|D_h W\|$. Since W is symmetric, we know that $\|W\| = \max_{i \in [n]} |\omega_i| = 1$, and since D_h is the identity matrix for every $h \notin S$, it follows that

$$\|D_\ell W\| \cdots \|D_1 W\| = \prod_{h \in S} \|D_h W\| .$$

Recalling that $|S| \geq \delta\ell/2$, inequality (5), and hence, also Lemma 6, are established due to Lemma 9, whose proof is deferred to the full version.

Lemma 9. *The walk matrix W satisfies $\|D_h W\| \leq \beta$ for every $h \in S$.*

3.3 Extending the Range of Parameter ϕ

Our goal in this section is to adapt the FH protocol presented in Sec. 3.1 and the analysis presented in Sec. 3.2 to blocking adversaries while allowing for any constant $0 < \phi < 1$. The main observation en route to this adaptation is that an error-correcting code that can recover from up to k errors, can alternatively recover from *wiping-off* up to $2k$ letters.

More formally, given some alphabet Σ and a word $u \in \Sigma^n$, let $\mathcal{B}_d(u)$ be the set of all words that can be obtained from u by replacing less than d letters with the designated letter $\flat \notin \Sigma$. In other words, $v \in \mathcal{B}_d(u) \subseteq (\Sigma \cup \{\flat\})^n$ if and only if v disagrees with u on less than d entries in which v has the designated letter $\flat$. The proof of the following observation is deferred to the full version.

Observation 10. *If C is an error-correcting code of length n and minimum distance d, then $\mathcal{B}_d(u) \cap \mathcal{B}_d(v) = \emptyset$ for every two codewords u, v of C.*

The application of Observation 10 is rather straightforward: We can use the error-correcting code C to recover from any number smaller than d of wiped-off letters. In the context of our FH protocol, Alice and Bob can recover from any number smaller than d of blocked rounds. So, except from adjusting some of the parameters, we use here the same protocol that we used against overwriting adversaries, only that this time, Bob can reconstruct the codeword that Alice transmitted in phase j as long as the fraction of unsuccessful rounds is smaller than the relative distance of the code (rather than half the relative distance).

Adjusting the Parameters. The FH protocol presented in Sec. 3.1 and analyzed in Sec. 3.2 relies on the parameters d, ρ, L, ξ, q, δ, and r, and on the three auxiliary constants α, β, and γ. We will use the primed versions d', ρ', L', ξ', q', δ', r' and α', β', γ' to describe the adaptation of this protocol to blocking adversaries. The reader is encouraged to read the remainder of this section in conjunction with Sec. 3.1 and 3.2.

Recall that in the context of overwriting adversaries, we assumed that ϕ is a constant satisfying $0 < \phi < 1/16$ and chose d and $0 < \alpha < 1/2$ so that $0 < \beta = (1 + \alpha)\left(\sqrt{\phi} + \frac{2}{\sqrt{d}}\right) < 1/4$. In the context of blocking adversaries, we assume that ϕ is a constant satisfying $0 < \phi < 1$ and choose the parameter $d' = d'(\phi)$ and the auxiliary constant $0 < \alpha' = \alpha'(\phi) < 1$ so that

$$0 < \beta' = \beta'(\phi) = (1 + \alpha')\left(\sqrt{\phi} + \frac{2}{\sqrt{d'}}\right) < 1.$$

Let $H(x) = -x \lg(x) - (1 - x) \lg(1 - x) = H(1 - x)$ be the binary entropy function defined for every $0 < x < 1$. Observe that $\lim_{x \to 1^-} 2^{H(x)} \beta'^x = \beta'$ and take $\gamma' = \gamma'(\phi)$ to be the smallest real $1/2 \le \gamma' < 1$ such that $2^{H(\gamma')} \beta'^{\gamma'} \le \frac{\beta' + 1}{2}$. Let $\xi' = \xi'(\phi) = \frac{1 - \gamma'}{2}$ and let $q' = q'(\phi)$ be the smallest prime power that satisfies

$$q' \ge \max\left\{\frac{2}{1 - \gamma'}, d'^{2/r(\xi')}\right\},$$

where $0 < r(\xi') < 1$ is the real promised by Theorem 3. The error-correcting codes C'_j over $GF(q')$ we use have rate $r' \ge r(\xi')$ and relative distance $\delta' \ge 1 - \frac{1}{q'} - \xi'$. Finally, let $\rho' = \rho'(\phi) = 2^{H(\gamma')} \beta'^{\gamma'}$ and

$$L' = \max\left\{\left\lceil \log_{1/\rho'}\left(\frac{1}{\epsilon}\right)\right\rceil, \left\lceil \log_{\sqrt{d'}/2}\left(\frac{\phi n}{\epsilon}\right)\right\rceil, \left\lceil \log_{\sqrt{d'}/2}\left(\frac{n}{\alpha'}\right)\right\rceil\right\}.$$

Modified Analysis. Using the adapted parameters, the analysis presented in Sec. 3.2 carries over quite smoothly. The one part that does require some changes is that involving inequalities (3) and (4) and the transition between them. Recalling that a phase is now considered to be successful if less than a δ'-fraction of its rounds are unsuccessful, we rewrite (3) as

$$\mathbb{P}(|\mathcal{E}| \ge \delta'\ell) \le \rho'^\ell, \tag{6}$$

(again, subject to the assumption that Eve knows $a(t - L')$ at round t). So, our goal is to prove that (6) follows from $p_S \le \beta'^{\delta'\ell}$ (the equivalent of (4)) for every $S \subseteq [\ell], |S| \ge \delta'\ell$.

As in Sec. 3.2, we express $\mathbb{P}(|\mathcal{E}| \ge \delta'\ell)$ as

$$\mathbb{P}(|\mathcal{E}| \ge \delta'\ell) = \mathbb{P}\left(\bigvee_{S \subseteq [\ell], |S| \ge \delta'\ell} \mathcal{E} = S\right) \le \sum_{S \subseteq [\ell], |S| \ge \delta'\ell} p_S,$$

only that this time, we use the fact that $\sum_{k=\lceil xn \rceil}^{n} \binom{n}{k} \le 2^{H(x) \cdot n}$ for every $n \ge 1$ and $1/2 \le x < 1$ (see, e.g., [12]) to bound the number of subsets S that should be accounted for. Specifically, we get

$$\mathbb{P}(|\mathcal{E}| \ge \delta'\ell) \le 2^{H(\delta') \cdot \ell} \beta'^{\delta'\ell} = \left(2^{H(\delta')} \beta'^{\delta'}\right)^\ell.$$

This concludes our proof as $\delta' \ge 1 - \frac{1}{q'} - \xi' \ge \gamma'$, and hence $2^{H(\delta')} \beta'^{\delta'} \le 2^{H(\gamma')} \beta'^{\gamma'} = \rho'$.

4 Enhanced Scanning

The FH protocols developed in Sec. 3 are ϵ-resilient to (blocking and overwriting) (λ, ϕ)-adversaries that have access in round $t + \lambda$ to the channel $a(t)$ over which Alice transmitted in round t, but not to the actual content $m(t)$ of Alice's message. We now turn our attention to adversaries with *enhanced scanning*, namely, both $a(t)$ and $m(t)$ are revealed to Eve in round $t + \lambda$. On the negative side, we prove that no FH protocol can be resilient to such adversaries as long as we stick to the model introduced in Sec. 1.1, requiring that the lag λ is fixed with respect to the time t. On the positive side, we show that a FH protocol with resilience to enhanced scanning adversaries does exist if the lag λ grows logarithmically with t. Due to space limitations, these proofs are deferred to the full version.

References

1. Alon, N., Bruck, J., Naor, J., Naor, M., Roth, R.M.: Construction of asymptotically good low-rate error-correcting codes through pseudo-random graphs. IEEE Transactions on Information Theory 38, 509–516 (1992)
2. Anantharamu, L., Chlebus, B.S., Kowalski, D.R., Rokicki, M.A.: Medium access control for adversarial channels with jamming. In: Kosowski, A., Yamashita, M. (eds.) SIROCCO 2011. LNCS, vol. 6796, pp. 89–100. Springer, Heidelberg (2011)
3. Awerbuch, B., Richa, A., Scheideler, C.: A Jamming-Resistant MAC Protocol for Single-Hop Wireless Networks. In: Proc. 27th Symposium on Principles of Distributed Computing, PODC (2008)
4. Azar, Y., Gurel-Gurevich, O., Lubetzky, E., Moscibroda, T.: Optimal discovery strategies in white space networks. In: Demetrescu, C., Halldórsson, M.M. (eds.) ESA 2011. LNCS, vol. 6942, pp. 713–722. Springer, Heidelberg (2011)
5. Chu, W., Colbourn, C.: Optimal frequency-hopping sequences via cyclotomy. IEEE Transactions on Information Theory 51(3), 1139–1141 (2005)
6. Demmel, J.W.: Applied numerical linear algebra. Society for Industrial and Applied Mathematics, Philadelphia (1997)
7. Diaconis, P., Stroock, D.: Geometric Bounds for Eigenvalues of Markov Chains. The Annals of Applied Probability 1(1), 36–61 (1991)
8. Dolev, S., Gilbert, S., Guerraoui, R., Kuhn, F., Newport, C.: The wireless synchronization problem. In: Proceedings of the 28th ACM Symposium on Principles of Distributed Computing, PODC, New York, NY, USA, pp. 190–199 (2009)
9. Dolev, S., Gilbert, S., Guerraoui, R., Newport, C.: Gossiping in a Multi-Channel Radio Network (An Oblivious Approach to Coping With Malicious Interference). In: Pelc, A. (ed.) DISC 2007. LNCS, vol. 4731, pp. 208–222. Springer, Heidelberg (2007)
10. Dolev, S., Gilbert, S., Guerraoui, R., Newport, C.: Secure Communication over Radio Channels. In: Proc. 27th ACM Symposium on Principles of Distributed Computing (PODC), pp. 105–114 (2008)
11. Dolev, S., Gilbert, S., Khabbazian, M., Newport, C.: Leveraging channel diversity to gain efficiency and robustness for wireless broadcast. In: Peleg, D. (ed.) DISC 2011. LNCS, vol. 6950, pp. 252–267. Springer, Heidelberg (2011)
12. Flum, J., Grohe, M.: Parameterized Complexity Theory, vol. 7. Springer (2006)

13. Gilbert, S., Guerraoui, R., Newport, C.: Of Malicious Motes and Suspicious Sensors. In: Proc. 10th Conference on Principles of Distributed Systems, OPODIS (2006)
14. Impagliazzo, R., Zuckerman, D.: How to recycle random bits. In: Proceedings of the 30th Annual Symposium on Foundations of Computer Science, Washington, DC, USA, pp. 248–253 (1989)
15. Knopp, R., Humblet, P.: On coding for block fading channels. IEEE Transactions on Information Theory 46(1), 189–205 (2000)
16. Koo, C.Y., Bhandari, V., Katz, J., Vaidya, N.H.: Reliable Broadcast in Radio Networks: the Bounded Collision Case. In: Proc. 25th ACM Symposium on Principles of Distributed Computing, PODC (2006)
17. Köppel, S.: Bluetooth jamming. Bachelor's Thesis supervised by Michael König and Roger Wattenhofer, ETH Zurich (2013)
18. Lubotzky, A., Phillips, R., Sarnak, P.: Ramanujan graphs. Combinatorica 8, 261–277 (1988)
19. Mansour, I., Chalhoub, G., Quilliot, A.: Security architecture for wireless sensor networks using frequency hopping and public key management. In: ICNSC, pp. 526–531. IEEE (2011)
20. Margulis, G.A.: Explicit group-theoretic constructions of combinatorial schemes and their applications in the construction of expanders and concentrators. Problemy Peredachi Informatsii 24(1), 51–60 (1988)
21. Markey, H.K., Antheil, G.: Secret communication system, U.S. Patent 2292387 (1942)
22. Medard, M., Gallager, R.: Bandwidth scaling for fading multipath channels. IEEE Transactions on Information Theory 48(4), 840–852 (2002)
23. Meier, D., Pignolet, Y.A., Schmid, S., Wattenhofer, R.: Speed Dating despite Jammers. In: 5th IEEE International Conference on Distributed Computing in Sensor Systems (DCOSS), Marina del Rey, California, USA (June 2009)
24. Mitola, J., Maguire, G.Q.: Cognitive radio: making software radios more personal. IEEE Personal Communications 6(4), 13–18 (1999)
25. Morgenstern, M.: Existence and Explicit Constructions of q + 1 Regular Ramanujan Graphs for Every Prime Power q. Journal of Combinatorial Theory, Series B 62(1), 44–62 (1994)
26. Nilli, A.: On the second eigenvalue of a graph. Discrete Math. 91, 207–210 (1991)
27. Project Ubertooth, http://ubertooth.sourceforge.net/
28. Richa, A., Scheideler, C., Schmid, S., Zhang, J.: Competitive and fair medium access despite reactive jamming. In: 2011 31st International Conference on Distributed Computing Systems (ICDCS), pp. 507–516 (June 2011)
29. Richa, A., Scheideler, C., Schmid, S., Zhang, J.: A jamming-resistant MAC protocol for multi-hop wireless networks. In: Lynch, N.A., Shvartsman, A.A. (eds.) DISC 2010. LNCS, vol. 6343, pp. 179–193. Springer, Heidelberg (2010)
30. Richa, A., Scheideler, C., Schmid, S., Zhang, J.: Self-stabilizing leader election for single-hop wireless networks despite jamming. In: Proceedings of the Twelfth ACM International Symposium on Mobile Ad Hoc Networking and Computing. MobiHoc, New York, NY, USA (2011)
31. Tesla, N.: Method of signaling, U.S. Patent 723188 (1903)
32. Tesla, N.: System of signaling, U.S. Patent 725605 (1903)
33. Zenneck, J.: Leitfaden der drahtlosen Telegraphie. Enke, Stuttgart, Germany (1909)

Sleeping Experts in Wireless Networks[*]

Johannes Dams[1], Martin Hoefer[2], and Thomas Kesselheim[3]

[1] Dept. of Computer Science, RWTH Aachen University, Germany
dams@cs.rwth-aachen.de
[2] Max-Planck-Institut für Informatik and Saarland University, Germany
mhoefer@mpi-inf.mpg.de
[3] Dept. of Computer Science, Cornell University, United States
kesselheim@cs.cornell.edu

Abstract. We consider capacity maximization algorithms for wireless networks with changing availabilities of spectrum. There are n sender-receiver pairs (called *links*) and k channels. We consider an iterative round-based scenario, where in each round the set of channels available to each link changes. Each link independently decides about access to one available channel in order to implement a successful transmission. Transmissions are subject to interference and noise, and we use a general approach based on affectance to define which attempts are successful. This includes recently popular interference models based on SINR.

Our main result is that efficient distributed algorithms from sleeping-expert regret learning can be used to obtain constant-factor approximations if channel availability is stochastic and independently distributed among links. In general, sublinear approximation factors cannot be obtained without the assumption of stochastic independence among links. A direct application of the no-external regret property is not sufficient to guarantee small approximation factors.

1 Introduction

One of the most important problems in the development of wireless networks is to overcome spectrum scarcity resulting from the static allocation schemes currently used by national regulators. This poses a variety of important regulatory and, in particular, algorithmic challenges. The idea is that licensed *primary users* open up their spectrum bands temporarily in local areas where it is unused. This creates spectrum opportunities for *secondary users* and results in much more efficient usage. A prominent approach that is currently discussed in industry is based on a database that records which channels are currently available for secondary usage in which areas. Primary users announce whether the channel is available to secondary users via this database organized by regulatory

---

[*] This work has been supported by DFG through Cluster of Excellence MMCI, UMIC Research Centre at RWTH Aachen University, and grant Ho 3831/3-1 and it has been supported by a fellowship within the Postdoc-Programme of the German Academic Exchange Service (DAAD).

Y. Afek (Ed.): DISC 2013, LNCS 8205, pp. 344–357, 2013.
© Springer-Verlag Berlin Heidelberg 2013

authorities. In this case, secondary users obtain information about the channels available to them querying the database and then decide independently about channel access.

In this paper, we study an underlying algorithmic problem in this scenario and analyze the performance of distributed regret-based learning algorithms. In our model, there are k channels and n secondary users represented by *links*, i.e., by sender-receiver pairs located in a metric space. We consider a round-based approach, where in each round the set of channels available to each link can change, e.g., due to changing usage of the licensed primary users. Each link gets informed about the channels available to him and then decides about making a transmission attempt on an available channel. Transmissions are subject to interference and noise, and the success of a transmission attempt depends on conflicts defined using an interference model. Instead of relying on a particular model, we use a general approach to define conflicts based on a notion of affectance. This approach encompasses a variety of graph-based interference models, like disk graphs or the protocol model, as well as more realistic models based on the signal-to-interference-plus-noise-ratio (SINR).

We consider distributed learning algorithms that are executed for each link independently. The algorithms receive as input in each round the set of available channels and, in case they decide to transmit, a binary feedback if the transmission was successful or not. In particular, they do not need to know the exact SINR or whether and which other links made a (successful) transmission attempt. The decision for transmission follows an evaluation based on a natural utility function, which rewards previous successful transmissions and punishes failed attempts. Each no-regret algorithm aims at optimizing these utilities in a unilateral fashion, and therefore this scenario also has connections to game-theory.

While each link uses a no-regret algorithm to optimize his own successful transmissions, the obvious overall goal is *capacity maximization*, i.e., to maximize the total number of successful transmissions in the system. Our main result is that if all links use algorithms that satisfy a no-regret property resulting from a sleeping expert learning model [3], the number of successful transmissions converges to a constant-factor approximation for capacity maximization. For example, the surprisingly simple protocol of [12] can be used to obtain this result with high probability after a polynomial number of rounds. The analysis is based on a novel formulation of distributed capacity maximization using linear programming duality.

All our algorithms require channel availabilities to be stochastic and independently distributed for each link. This includes as a special case also the natural deterministic variant, where each link has a subset of available channels that does not change over time. We show that independence of the availability distributions among links is necessary, because the no-regret properties do not suffice to guarantee similar bounds when distributions are correlated. In addition, we show that a direct application of no-external regret as in previous work [6] does not provide similar results.

1.1   Contribution and Related Work

Capacity maximization, i.e., the task of maximizing the number of simultaneous transmissions, has been a prominent algorithmic problem over the last decade, e.g., in graph-based interference models [7, 16, 18]. With the seminal work of Moscibroda and Wattenhofer [15] attention has shifted to more realistic settings based on signal-to-interference-plus-noise-ratio (SINR).

We consider no-regret learning algorithms to solve capacity maximization with stochastic channel availabilities. As our main result, we show in Section 3 that no-ordering-regret algorithms converge to a constant-factor approximation for capacity maximization if availabilities are drawn independently at random for each link. Our analysis is based on a conflict graph representation of the interference model and, in particular, on a notion of a C-independence. C-independence turns out to be a key parameter for the performance of no-ordering-regret algorithms in this setting. If channel availabilities are stochastically independent for each link, the Sleeping-follow-the-perturbed-leader algorithm of [12] guarantees polynomial convergence time. This also holds when for each single link the availabilities of the different channels are arbitrarily correlated.

In contrast to this result for no-ordering-regret, we observe in Section 4 that for a direct application of the simpler no-external-regret condition, the successful transmissions can on average still be a factor of $\Omega(k)$ or $\Omega(n)$ smaller than in the optimum, where k is the number of channels and n the number of links. In addition, we highlight that without independence of channel availabilities among different links, there exist examples where even the no-ordering-regret property guarantees only a $\Omega(n)$-factor, as well.

Our main result is shown using a novel technique to analyze the performance of regret learning algorithms based on linear programming. This approach extends related works on capacity maximization on a single channel with uniform powers in SINR [1, 9] and Rayleigh-fading models [5], for which no-external regret algorithms are known to converge to constant-factor approximations [2, 5, 6]. Closest to our approach is our companion paper [4], in which we introduce a general framework based on the LP technique to study no-external regret learning with adversarial jamming on a single channel. The jammer yields more restrictive feedback, as availability of the channel remains unknown. Instead, an unavailable channel yields the same feedback to the link as being unsuccessful because of interference.

In this paper, we make a first step towards capacity maximization with multiple channels. For static availability, it is easy to see that previous results on no-external regret learning in [2, 5] directly extend to multiple channels. When we consider varying availabilities, however, multiple channels represent a significant complication. For a single channel and availabilities, our LP technique can be applied using no-external regret algorithms and the more challenging jammer feedback [4]. The main idea is to repeat a chosen action sufficiently long in order to obtain a "representative" feedback. For multiple channels, a similar approach is unlikely to work as we must learn on some channels while others are unavailable. This changes the regret and feedback conditions, and the connection between regret, feedback, and optimal solution value becomes more intricate to establish. In this paper, we resort to a stronger notion of no-ordering regret and use stochastic independence assumptions among links to obtain a constant-factor approximation. Omitting the independence assumptions constitutes a major open problem. Still, our work is a strong indication that efficient capacity maximization with availabilities and multiple channels is achievable in practice.

Action availabilities are the subject of a recent line of literature in online learning [12–14]. The actions of a game (or the experts in the learning setting) are not always available, and availability is based on adversarial decisions or random coin flips. The stochastic availabilities in our setting are similarly defined, and we use no-regret learning algorithms from the sleeping-experts setting to design a protocol for capacity maximization. Designing learning algorithms for sleeping expert settings started with Blum [3] and Freund et al. [8]. For definition of regret many works in this area do not use the best single strategy in hindsight. Instead, they resort to the best ordering of actions in hindsight [12–14], where unavailable actions can be accounted for. This has led to the design of multiple no-ordering-regret learning algorithms for the sleeping-experts setting. We will use ordering regret in our analysis as well.

2 Formal Description

2.1 General Problem Statement

We assume our network to consist of a set V of n wireless links $\ell_v = (s_v, r_v)$ for $v \in V$, each consisting of a sender and a respective receiver. We denote the set of channels by K and the number of channels by k. In each step, the availability of a channel $\kappa \in K$ to a link ℓ_v is the result of a random trial. We will assume throughout that the distributions for the random availabilities are independent among the links. However, among the channels of a link the availabilities can be arbitrarily correlated in our model. We justify this assumption by giving a lower bound, where we assume channel availabilities correlated among the links, in Section 4.

In a specific time step t and a specific link ℓ_v, some subset of channels is available. For any subset of channels M we define $p_{v,M}$ to be the probability that at least one channel out of M is available to ℓ_v. Then the random variable $P_{v,M}^{(t)}$ is defined to be 1 if and only if at least one channel out of the set M is available to link ℓ_v in time slot t. Let $p_{\min} = \min\{p_{v,M} \mid v \in V, M \neq \emptyset, p_{v,M} > 0\}$ be the minimal probability of a channel to be available. We can define $p_{\min}$ such that $p_{\min} > 0$ as channels which are never available to ℓ_v can be removed from consideration because they are neither available to the optimum nor the algorithm.

In each step t, each link first gets to know the outcome of the random trial and his set of available channels. It then has to decide whether and on which channel to send. Thus, a link can either not attempt transmission or transmit on one chosen channel. Success of transmissions can be defined in various ways, e.g., using the SINR model. In fact, our proofs rely on a more general condition which is also fulfilled by other interference models, e.g., based on bounded-independence graphs like unit-disk graphs [17].

In particular, we formally rely on conflict graphs to model interference (see, e.g., [11]). A *conflict graph* is a directed graph $G = (V, E)$ consisting of the links as vertices and weights $b_v(w)$ for any edge $(v, w) \in E$. We assume the weights to be defined such that a link ℓ_w can transmit successfully if and only if $\sum_{v \in L} b_v(w) \le 1$, where L is the set of other links transmitting. We consider the conflict graph to be the same for all channels. Actually, this is only to simplify notation. It is easy to observe that our proofs also hold when the conflict graph is different in different channels. A subset of links is called *feasible* (on a channel) if all links in this set can transmit simultaneously (i.e., fullfil the condition above on that channel). The overall goal in this setting is to do *capacity maximization* in every single time step. That is to select for every time step depending on the availabilities a maximal cardinality subset of links and one available channel for those link such the sets of links are feasible on their respective channel.

We define the following notion of *C-independence* inspired by [2] as a key parameter to identify the connection between the specific interference model and the performance of our algorithm.

Definition 1 (cf. [2]). *A conflict graph is called C-independent if for any feasible set L there exists a subset $L' \subset L$ with $|L'| = \Omega(|L|)$ and $\sum_{v \in L'} b_u(v) \le C$ for all $u \in V$.*

C-independence generalizes the bounded-independence property popular in the distributed computing literature. To embed the SINR model into this framework, let us outline how we can construct such a conflict graph. Let ϕ_v be the transmission power of link ℓ_v. Success of transmissions is defined in the SINR model as follows. Each sending link w emits a signal from sender s_w. This signal is received by receiver r_v at a strength of $\frac{\phi_w}{d_{w,v}^\alpha}$, where $d_{w,v}$ is the distance from sender s_w to receiver r_v and $\alpha > 0$ the path-loss exponent. The receiver r_v can successfully decode the signal transmitted by its sender s_v, if the SINR is above a certain threshold β. Using a constant $\nu \ge 0$ to denote ambient noise, the SINR condition formally reads

$$\frac{\frac{\phi_v}{d_{v,v}^\alpha}}{\sum_{w \neq v} \frac{\phi_w}{d_{w,v}^\alpha} + \nu} \ge \beta .$$

To turn this condition into appropriate edge weights of a conflict graph, we can use the notion of *affectance* as a measure of interference. It was defined for the SINR model in [10] as follows.

Definition 2. *The affectance $a(w, v)$ of link ℓ_v caused by another link ℓ_w is*

$$a(w, v) = \min \left\{ 1, \beta \frac{\frac{\phi_w}{d_{w,v}^\alpha}}{\frac{\phi_v}{d_{v,v}^\alpha} - \beta \nu} \right\} .$$

If all links use the same uniform power for transmission, this results in C-independence with a constant C. This was proven by Ásgeirsson and Mitra [2]. Using affectance it is straightforward to construct the corresponding conflict graph by simply setting weights $b_u(v) = a(u, v)$.

For simplicity we will assume that the conflict graphs satisfy C-independence for constant C throughout the paper. Nevertheless, losing a factor of C in the approximation guarantee our main theorem on the performance of regret learning can be directly generalized to arbitrary conflict graphs.

2.2 No-Regret Learning

We apply no-regret learning algorithms to solve capacity maximization. The links independently decide in every time slot whether and on which channel to transmit using appropriate learning algorithms. Every algorithm adjusts its decisions based on the outcome of its previous decisions. To measure the quality of an outcome every link i uses an utility function $u_i(a_i, a_{-i})$ depending on action a_i chosen by player i and a_{-i}, the vector of actions of all other players. Throughout this paper we define the utility of a link i as follows. This utility function was already used for a single channel case where the channel is always available by Andrews and Dinitz [1] and later by Ásgeirsson and Mitra [2].

$$u_i(a_i, a_{-i}) = \begin{cases} 1 & \text{if } i \text{ transmits successfully,} \\ -1 & \text{if } i \text{ attempts and the transmission fails,} \\ 0 & \text{otherwise.} \end{cases}$$

This utility reflects that the best a link can achieve in one time slot is successful transmission, for which is rewarded with a utility of 1. The worst that can happen is an unsuccessful attempt, which is penalized by a utility of -1. This strikes a balance between reducing interference on other links (when not being successful) and increasing the number of transmissions (when being successful).

For our utility functions we can consider different notions of regret. The easiest notion is external regret given as follows.

Definition 3. *Let* $a^{(1)}, \ldots, a^{(T)}$ *be a sequence of action vectors. The* external regret *of this sequence for link i is defined by*

$$\max_{a_i' \in \mathcal{A}} \sum_{t=1}^{T} u_i(a_i', a_{-i}^{(t)}) - \sum_{t=1}^{T} u_i(a_i^{(t)}, a_{-i}^{(t)}),$$

where $\mathcal{A}$ denotes the set of actions.

This notion of regret can only be used if the utilities are defined also for actions that are not available in a time slot. We assume that choosing an unavailable channel is equivalent to choosing not to send at all, which is an action that we assume to be always available. This allows to directly apply no-external-regret algorithms in our scenario.

In addition, let us also consider a different notion of regret from sleeping experts learning. This notion of regret is introduced by Kanade et al. [12].

Definition 4 (Kanade et al. [12]). *Let $a^{(1)}, \ldots, a^{(T)}$ be a sequence of action vectors. The ordering regret of this sequence for link i in the sleeping experts setting is defined as*

$$\max_{\sigma \in S_{\mathcal{A}}} \mathbb{E} \left[\sum_{t=1}^{T} u_i(\sigma(\mathcal{A}^{(t)}), a_{-i}^{(t)}) \right] - \sum_{t=1}^{T} u_i(a_i^{(t)}, a_{-i}^{(t)}) \ ,$$

where the expectation is over the random availabilities. Here, $\mathcal{A}$ denotes the set of actions, $S_{\mathcal{A}}$ the set of all permutations on $\mathcal{A}$, and $\sigma(\mathcal{A}^{(t)})$ the action ordered topmost in σ of the actions available in time slot t.

In contrast to external regret, ordering regret does not measure the utility difference to the best action in hindsight but to the utility resulting from the best ordering in hindsight. The utility for an ordering is computed by assuming that in every step the topmost available action in the ordering is played. Additionally, the expectation over the availabilities is considered for comparison. Note that we do not consider the expectation in this definition to be taken over the random choices of the algorithm as, e.g., in [14]. Considering the expectation this way is possible due to the stochastic independence assumption. Thus, we can keep the choices of other players and also their availabilities fixed and just take the expectation over the availabilities of one player i.

An infinite sequence of actions or an algorithm has the *no-external regret property* if external regret grows in $o(T)$. We analogously define the *no-ordering-regret property*. Throughout this paper we will, whenever it is clear from context, use regret as a synonym for either ordering regret or external regret.

3   Convergence with No-Ordering-Regret Learning

In this section we show our main result that using no-ordering-regret algorithms the number of successful transmissions converges to a constant-factor approximation of the optimal capacity. As discussed before, the optimum is different in different time slots depending on available channels. Let us denote by $OPT_\kappa^{(t)}$ the set of links transmitting on channel κ in time slot t in the optimal solution. Thus, we compare the number of successful transmissions of the no-regret algorithms to the empirical average capacity of all optima, i.e., $\overline{|OPT|} = \frac{1}{T} \sum_t \sum_{\kappa \in K} |OPT_\kappa^{(t)}|$.

For simplicity we assume that conflict graphs are $O(1)$-independent and highlight the places at which the factor C comes into play if this assumption does not hold. Note that, in particular, conflict graphs resulting from the SINR model under uniform power yield constant C [2].

Theorem 1. *If all links use no-ordering-regret algorithms, the average number of successful transmissions becomes a constant-factor approximation for capacity maximization after a number of time steps polynomial in n and linear in k with high probability, i.e., with probability at least $1 - \frac{1}{n^c}$ for any constant c. More generally, in C-independent conflict graphs the same result holds for convergence to an $O(C)$-approximation.*

While the overall approach is in the spirit of previous work, our setting is quite different and the notion of regret also differs. Similar to [2,6], our analysis starts with the observation that a constant fraction of all transmission attempts are successful. Afterwards, we combine this with the result that the number of transmission attempts is in $\Omega\left(\overline{|OPT|}\right)$. Especially the proof of this latter statement in Lemma 2 below needs more advanced techniques. Together both statements prove our theorem.

In the remainder of this section, we denote the fraction of time slots in which link ℓ_v transmits on channel κ by $q_{v,\kappa}$. The sum over the channels is denoted by $q_v = \sum_\kappa q_{v,\kappa}$. The fraction of time slots in which link ℓ_v transmits successfully is denoted by $w_{v,\kappa}$, and the sum over channels by w_v. In the following, we will denote the fraction of all time steps in which link ℓ_v (no matter whether it attempted to transmit) would not be able to be successful on channel κ by $f_{v,\kappa}$ no matter if κ was actually available to link ℓ_v. Throughout this section, we assume that for each link the ordering regret after T time slots is at most $\varepsilon \cdot T$.

First of all, let us bound the number of successful transmissions by the number of transmission attemps.

Lemma 1 (cf. [2, 5]). *It holds* $w_v \leq q_v \leq 2 \cdot w_v + \varepsilon$ *and* $\sum_v w_v \leq \sum_v q_v \leq 2 \cdot \sum_v w_v + \varepsilon n$.

Proof. The first inequality follows by definition. For the second inequality, we use the fact that for each link v the average regret is at most ε. Therefore, not to send at all can increase the average utility per step by at most ε. Formally this means $(q_v - w_v) - w_v = q_v - 2w_v \leq \varepsilon$. Taking the sum over all v we get $\sum_v q_v - 2 \cdot \sum_v w_v \leq \varepsilon n$. This yields the claim.   □

Lemma 1 shows that the number of successful transmissions and the number of transmission attempts only differ by a constant factor. Together with the following lemma this proves Theorem 1.

Lemma 2. *Every sequence of length* $T \in \Omega\left(\frac{1}{p_{\min}}(\ln n + k)\right)$ *with ordering regret at most* $\varepsilon \cdot T < \frac{1}{4n} \cdot T$ *yields* $\sum_v q_v = \Omega\left(\overline{|OPT|}\right)$ *with high probability.*

To prove Lemma 2, we use a primal-dual approach using an appropriately defined linear program. Recall that $p_{\min} = \min\{p_{v,M} \mid v \in V, M \neq \emptyset, p_{v,M} > 0\}$ is the minimal availability probability of all the channels.

Let us start by showing in Lemma 3 that for a number of time slots $T \in \Omega\left(\frac{1}{p_{\min}}(\ln n + k)\right)$ with high probability the empirical fraction of slots $\bar{P}_{v,M}$ in which at least one channel out of M was available to link ℓ_v is close to the probability $p_{v,M}$, for every set of channels M and every link ℓ_v. Afterwards, we will use this result to draw a connection between transmission attempts, availabilities, and experienced affectances in Lemma 4 finally proving Lemma 2.

Lemma 3. *After a number of time steps* $T \in \Omega\left(\frac{1}{p_{\min}} \cdot (\ln n + k)\right)$ *it holds* $|\bar{P}_{v,M} - p_{v,M}| \leq \frac{1}{2}\bar{P}_{v,M}$ *for all sets of channels* M *and all links* ℓ_v *with high probability.*

Proof. Consider the random variable $P_{v,M}^{(t)} \in \{0,1\}$ indicating whether any channel of the set M is available for link ℓ_v in time slot t. Let $Y = \sum_t P_{v,M}^{(t)}$. Thus, we need $|\mathbb{E}(Y) - Y| < \frac{1}{2} Y$ to hold, because this directly yields $|\bar{P}_{v,M} - p_{v,M}| \leq \frac{1}{2} \bar{P}_{v,M}$ by division with T. Equivalently we need $\frac{1}{2} Y < \mathbb{E}(Y) < \frac{3}{2} Y$ to hold.

As the channel availabilities are drawn independently in every time slot, we can apply a Chernoff bound. This yields $\mathbf{Pr}\left[Y \geq (1+\delta)\mathbb{E}(Y)\right] \leq \exp\left(\frac{-\delta^2}{3}\mathbb{E}(Y)\right)$ and $\mathbf{Pr}\left[Y \leq (1-\delta)\mathbb{E}(Y)\right] \leq \exp\left(\frac{-\delta^2}{2}\mathbb{E}(Y)\right)$ for every $\delta \in [0,1]$.

Using this we get $\mathbf{Pr}\left[Y \geq 2\mathbb{E}(Y)\right] \leq \exp\left(-\frac{1}{3}\mathbb{E}(Y)\right)$ and $\mathbf{Pr}\left[Y \leq \frac{2}{3}\mathbb{E}(Y)\right] \leq \exp\left(-\frac{1}{18}\mathbb{E}(Y)\right)$. With a union bound, the probability that $|\bar{P}_{v,M} - p_{v,M}| \leq \frac{1}{2}\bar{P}_{v,M}$ does not hold for a particular set M is

$$\mathbf{Pr}\left[|\bar{P}_{v,M} - p_{v,M}| > \frac{1}{2}\bar{P}_{v,M}\right] \leq \exp\left(-\frac{p_{v,M}T}{3}\right) + \exp\left(-\frac{p_{v,M}T}{18}\right) .$$

This is at most $2 \cdot \exp\left(-\frac{1}{18}p_{v,M}T\right)$. Applying another union bound yields

$$\sum_{v \in V} \sum_{M \subseteq K} \mathbf{Pr}\left[|\bar{P}_{v,M} - p_{v,M}| > \frac{1}{2}\bar{P}_{v,M}\right] \leq 2^k n \cdot 2 \cdot \exp\left(-\frac{1}{18}p_{\min} \cdot T\right) .$$

Setting $T \geq \frac{18}{p_{\min}}\left((c+1)\ln n + (k+1) \cdot \ln 2\right)$ shows that the probability that for any arbitrary set of channels M the property $|\bar{P}_{v,M} - p_{v,M}| \leq \frac{1}{2}\bar{P}_{v,M}$ does not hold is at most n^{-c}. $\square$

Consider the set of channels with a low congestion where a link will be unsuccessful in a small fraction of time slots. For these channels we will show that the number of transmission attempts yields an upper bound on the availabilities. This fact will be used in the proof of Lemma 2.

Lemma 4. *Let M be any set of channels such that for every channel $\kappa \in M$ it holds $f_{v,\kappa} \leq \frac{1}{4}$. If regret is at most ε and $|\bar{P}_{v,M} - p_{v,M}| \leq \frac{1}{2}\bar{P}_{v,M}$, then it follows*

$$4\sum_{\kappa \in K} q_{v,\kappa} + 4\varepsilon \geq \bar{P}_{v,M} .$$

Proof. The expected utility of the best ordering in hindsight is obviously at least as high as the expected utility of the ordering in which all $\kappa \in M$ are ordered above the action 'not sending' followed by all other channels.

First, we consider just one channel. On any channel $\kappa \in M$ link ℓ_v is not successful in an $f_{v,\kappa}$-fraction of all time steps. That leaves $T \cdot (1 - f_{v,\kappa})$ time steps possibly successful each yielding a utility of $+1$ for choosing κ if it was available. Choosing κ in contrast also yields -1 as a utility in $T \cdot f_{v,\kappa}$ time steps if κ was available. Thus ordering only κ before not sending yields a total expected utility of $p_{v,\kappa}(T \cdot (1 - f_{v,\kappa}) - T \cdot f_{v,\kappa})$. We extend this argument to the set M such that it depends on $p_{v,M}$ instead of $p_{v,\kappa}$ in the following way.

For any ordering with all $\kappa \in M$ ordered above not sending (and all other channels below), we get in expectation at least the utility of the worst channel

$\kappa \in M$ if any channel of M is available. This only holds due to the independence of the availabilities between different links as we can fix the actions of other links. This way, considering the expectation over ℓ_v's own availabilities we yield at least $\min_\kappa ((1 - f_{v,\kappa}) - f_{v,\kappa})$ for time steps where any channel in M is available. For the expected utility of the best ordering in hindsight this yields

$$\max_{\sigma \in S_A} \mathbb{E}\left[\sum_{t=1}^{T} u_v(\sigma(\mathcal{A}^{(t)}), a_{-v}^{(t)})\right] \geq \min_\kappa ((1 - f_{v,\kappa}) - f_{v,\kappa}) p_{v,M} \cdot T .$$

Note that as discussed above we can only bound the expected utility by that of one channel due to the availabilities of channels between links being stochastically independent. Otherwise those could be correlated in such a way that the expected unsuccessful time steps are not at most $T \cdot \max_\kappa f_{v,\kappa} p_{v,M}$ but could be worse. This is due to correlation, for example, being able to force all interference of other links on a channel (even if it occurs in few time steps in total) occur in available time steps only.

This yields $\frac{1}{T} \max_{\sigma \in M_A} \mathbb{E}\left[\sum_{t=1}^{T} u_v(\sigma(\mathcal{A}^{(t)}), a_{-v})\right] \geq \left(\frac{3}{4} - \frac{1}{4}\right) p_{v,M} = \frac{1}{2} p_{v,M}$. Using $|\bar{P}_{v,M} - p_{v,M}| \leq \frac{1}{2}\bar{P}_{v,M}$ we can easily bound this from below by $\frac{1}{4}\bar{P}_{v,M}$. With the fact that the regret is at most ε and that the utility is at most q_v we get $\frac{1}{4}\bar{P}_{v,M} \leq q_v + \varepsilon$.   □

This connection between the availability of a set, its interference, and the actions played now allows us to prove Lemma 2.

Proof (Proof of Lemma 2). Recall the definition of C-independence. Note that the conditions given in Definition 1 can be transfered for each channel κ from the single time steps to all time steps by averaging as follows. Let $OPT_\kappa'^{(t)}$ be L' out of Definition 1 when setting $L = OPT_\kappa^{(t)}$ yielding $|OPT_\kappa'^{(t)}| \geq \Omega\left(|OPT_\kappa^{(t)}|\right)$ and $\sum_{v \in OPT_\kappa'^{(t)}} b_u(v) \leq C$ for every time step t. By averaging over all time steps this is

$$\frac{1}{T}\sum_t |OPT_\kappa'^{(t)}| \geq \Omega\left(\frac{1}{T}\sum_t |OPT_\kappa^{(t)}|\right) \quad \text{and} \quad \frac{1}{T}\sum_t \sum_{v \in OPT_\kappa'^{(t)}} b_u(v) \leq C .$$

As C-independence holds in the given network for any feasible set on each channel, it also holds in this averaged variant for the optimum on each channel.

We will prove our lemma with the following primal-dual approach. For the following primal LP we will essentially consider the optimum averaged over all time steps and utilize C-independence. The above result is this way useful to show feasibility of the primal solution.

$$\text{Max.} \sum_{v \in V} \sum_{\kappa \in K} x_{v,\kappa}$$

$$\text{s.t.} \sum_{v \in V} b_u(v) x_{v,\kappa} \leq C \quad \forall u \in V, \kappa \in \mathcal{K}$$

$$\sum_{\kappa \in M} x_{v,\kappa} \leq \bar{P}_{v,M} \; \forall v \in V, M \subseteq K$$

$$x_v \geq 0 \quad \forall v \in V$$

Observe that $x_{v,\kappa} = \frac{|\{t | v \in OPT'^{(t)}_\kappa\}|}{T}$ represents a feasible solution to this LP. The first constraint is fulfilled as C-independence is fulfilled for every single time slot. The second constraint is fulfilled due to the fact that at most one channel is used at a time. Thus, we get $\sum_{v \in V} \sum_{\kappa \in K} x_{v,k} \geq \Omega\left(\overline{|OPT|}\right)$ by the definition of C-independence for the single-slot optima.

Constructing the dual to this primal LP yields

$$\text{Min.} \sum_{v \in V} \sum_{\kappa \in K} C \cdot y_{v,k} + \sum_{v \in V} \sum_{M \subseteq K} \bar{P}_{v,M} \cdot z_{v,M}$$

$$\text{s.t.} \sum_{u \in V} b_u(v) y_{u,\kappa} + \sum_{M:\kappa \in M} z_{v,M} \geq 1 \; \forall v \in V, \kappa \in K$$

$$y_{v,\kappa}, z_{v,M} \geq 0 \; \forall v \in V, \kappa \in K, M \subseteq K$$

We construct the following dual solution that gives an upper bound to the solution of the primal LP. Let $M_v = \left\{\kappa \in K \mid f_{v,\kappa} \leq \frac{1}{4}\right\}$, where $f_{v,\kappa}$ again denotes the fraction of all time steps in which link ℓ_v would not be able to transmit successfully on channel κ. So M_v represents the set of channels with low congestion. We set $y_{v,\kappa} = 4 \cdot q_{v,\kappa}$, $z_{v,M_v} = 1$, and $z_{v,S} = 0$ for all $S \neq M_v$.

First, let us observe that this is a feasible solution and the constraints are fulfilled. Recall the definition of $f_{v,\kappa}$ being the fraction of time steps ℓ_v would have been unsuccessful on channel κ no matter whether the channel was available to ℓ_v. Thus, for any channel κ in which $f_{v,\kappa} \geq \frac{1}{4}$, it holds $\sum_{u \in V} b_u(v) q_{u,\kappa} \geq \frac{1}{4}$. So $\sum_u b_u(v) \cdot y_{u,\kappa} \geq 1$ with the chosen $y_{u,\kappa}$. For the other case with $f_{v,\kappa} < \frac{1}{4}$ we set $z_{v,M_v} = 1$ and by definition $\kappa \in M_v$. Therefore, the constraint is fulfilled.

Using Lemma 4 leads to an upper bound on the objective function of the dual LP of

$$\sum_v \left(4Cq_v + \bar{P}_{v,M_v}\right) \leq \sum_v (4Cq_v + 4q_v) + 4\varepsilon n \; .$$

Combined with the primal LP this yields $\sum_v q_v = \Omega\left(\overline{|OPT|}\right)$ for $\varepsilon < \frac{1}{4n}$. In particular, for arbitrary C-independence the last derivation obviously implies $C \cdot \sum_v q_v = \Omega\left(\overline{|OPT|}\right)$ and directly yields an approximation factor in $O(C)$. $\square$

We have seen that after a number of time slots linear in k and logarithmic in n a sequence with low regret converges to a constant-factor approximation with high probability. Additionally, this time bound depends on the minimal probability of the availabilities $p_{\min}$. It is clear that a similar parameter must occur in the convergence time as links may not learn in time slots in which they have no channel available at all.

Theorem 1 and Lemma 2 show that the no-ordering-regret property allows to converge to constant-factor approximations. The algorithms in [12] have this property, which allows to directly use them for capacity maximization in our scenario. The sleeping-follow-the-perturbed-leader algorithm of [12] yields an ordering regret of at most $\sqrt{T \log k}$ in expectation after T time slots. While this algorithm runs in the full-information model getting feedback also for actions not chosen, Kanade et al. also propose an algorithm yielding low regret roughly the size $(k \cdot T \cdot \log T)^{4/5}$ in the partial-information model, where only feedback for chosen actions is given. To reach $\varepsilon < \frac{1}{4n}$ we therefore need only an additional factor polynomial in n for the number of time slots.

4 Lower Bounds

In this section, we show that a direct application of no-external-regret algorithms does not necessarily yield a constant-factor approximation. In fact, we will give an example that shows approximation factors in $\Omega(k)$ and $\Omega(n)$. Note that these factors can already be reached by algorithms where just one channel is utilized or just one link transmits, respectively. Additionally, we show that our assumption of stochastic independence in the availabilities among links is necessary. All our lower bound constructions can trivially be embedded into 1-independent conflict graphs. Thus, they establish linear lower bounds even in cases, where no-ordering-regret obtains constant-factor approximations.

Theorem 2. *For every number of channels k there is an instance such that for a sequence yielding 0 external regret the number of successful transmissions is at least a factor of k smaller than in an optimal schedule.*

Proof. Let us assume that all n links can be successful simultaneously on every channel. This allows us to consider only a single link. We first consider a sequence of deterministic availabilities in which channel κ is available in time slots t with $(t \mod k + 1) = \kappa$. Here there is a 0-external-regret sequence in which exactly one channel is chosen. The link will transmit only in every k-th time step, choosing exactly one channel. In contrast, in the optimum the link can simply choose another channel in every single time step. This yields the factor of k.

To reproduce the same arguments with stochastic availability, we set the probabilities for each channel availability to $\frac{1}{k}$. This yields the same structure. Again, if the link chooses only a single channel for transmission, it will encounter vanishing external regret as in the long run all channels have the same availability and success. However, it will only transmit in an $\frac{1}{k}$-fraction of all time slots. In contrast, in expectation in every time slot there is at least one channel available. This implies that in the long run a factor of k. $\square$

This result also implies an $\Omega(n)$ bound by setting $k = n$. Therefore, using no-external regret in this direct way does not imply a constant-factor approximation.

Corollary 1. *For every number of links n there is a network such that for a sequence yielding 0 external regret the number of successful transmissions is at least a factor of n smaller than in an optimal schedule.*

In contrast to directly applying the no-external-regret property, one might consider using multiple such no-external-regret algorithms. It is an interesting open problem if this allows to establish similar properties as for the sleeping-follow-the-perturbed-leader algorithm leading to a constant-factor approximation.

In the previous sections, we have assumed that the channel availabilities of different links are independent. We will use a similar example as in the proof above to see that this assumption is necessary to achieve convergence to a constant-factor approximation, even for no-ordering-regret algorithms.

Theorem 3. *For every number of links n there exists a network with correlated availabilities such that for a sequence yielding 0 ordering regret the number of successful transmissions is at least a factor of n smaller than in an optimal schedule.*

Proof. Suppose there is only one channel. We construct the network as follows. No pair of links can transmit simultaneously on the channel. This can easily be achieved be placing links (almost) in the same location and constructing the interference appropriately.

The channel is either available for all n links simultaneously or for only one single link ℓ_v with $v \in \{2, \ldots, n\}$. The probability for each of these n cases is $\frac{1}{n}$.

We construct a 0-ordering-regret sequence by scheduling link ℓ_1 to send whenever the channel is available to him. All other links choose not to send at all. The dependence of the availabilities implies that the expected utility of the best response in hindsight for all links $\ell_2, \ldots, \ell_n$ becomes 0 because, in the long run, for each of these links every second available slot is occupied by ℓ_1.

In contrast, in the optimum letting every link $\ell_2, \ldots, \ell_n$ transmit when the channel is available to him alone yields a successful transmission in every time slot. This proves the theorem. □

The one-or-all structure of availabilities used in the proof of Theorem 3 can still occur with a very low probability if we do not assume correlation and instead let the channel be available to each link independently with probability $\frac{1}{n}$. In this case, however, the transmission choices in the proof of Theorem 3 do not yield 0 ordering regret.

With a slight adjustment of the one-or-all structure, it is possible to show even slightly stronger lower bounds close to $3n/2$. We proved our positive results under the assumption that availabilities of links are independent and encounter no correlation at all. In contrast, the lower bound in Theorem 3 heavily relies on correlation. It is an interesting open problem to characterize influence of correlation of availability distributions on the performance of no-regret learning algorithms (e.g., when correlation results from a locality structure of primary and secondary users).

References

1. Andrews, M., Dinitz, M.: Maximizing capacity in arbitrary wireless networks in the SINR model: Complexity and game theory. In: Proc. 28th IEEE Conf. Computer Communications (INFOCOM), pp. 1332–1340 (2009)
2. Asgeirsson, E.I., Mitra, P.: On a game theoretic approach to capacity maximization in wireless networks. In: Proc. 30th IEEE Conf. Computer Communications (INFOCOM), pp. 3029–3037 (2011)
3. Blum, A.: Empirical support for winnow and weighted-majority algorithms: Results on a calendar scheduling domain. Machine Learning 26(1), 5–23 (1997)
4. Dams, J., Hoefer, M., Kesselheim, T.: Jamming-resistant learning in wireless networks. CoRR, abs/1307.5290 (2013)
5. Dams, J., Hoefer, M., Kesselheim, T.: Scheduling in wireless networks with Rayleigh-fading interference. In: Proc. 24th Symp. Parallelism in Algorithms and Architectures (SPAA), pp. 327–335 (2012)
6. Dinitz, M.: Distributed algorithms for approximating wireless network capacity. In: Proc. 29th IEEE Conf. Computer Communications (INFOCOM), pp. 1397–1405 (2010)
7. Erlebach, T., Jansen, K., Seidel, E.: Polynomial-time approximation schemes for geometric graphs. SIAM J. Comput. 34(6), 1302–1323 (2005)
8. Freund, Y., Schapire, R., Singer, Y., Warmuth, M.: Using and combining predictors that specialize. In: Proc. 29th Symp. Theory of Computing (STOC), pp. 334–343 (1997)
9. Goussevskaia, O., Halldórsson, M., Wattenhofer, R., Welzl, E.: Capacity of arbitrary wireless networks. In: Proc. 28th IEEE Conf. Computer Communications (INFOCOM), pp. 1872–1880 (2009)
10. Halldórsson, M., Wattenhofer, R.: Wireless communication is in APX. In: Albers, S., Marchetti-Spaccamela, A., Matias, Y., Nikoletseas, S., Thomas, W. (eds.) ICALP 2009, Part I. LNCS, vol. 5555, pp. 525–536. Springer, Heidelberg (2009)
11. Hoefer, M., Kesselheim, T., Vöcking, B.: Approximation algorithms for secondary spectrum auctions. In: Proc. 23rd Symp. Parallelism in Algorithms and Architectures (SPAA), pp. 177–186 (2011)
12. Kanade, V., McMahan, B., Bryan, B.: Sleeping experts and bandits with stochastic action availability and adversarial rewards. J. Machine Learning Res. - Proc. Track 5, 272–279 (2009)
13. Kanade, V., Steinke, T.: Learning hurdles for sleeping experts. In: Proc. 3rd Symp. Innovations in Theoret. Computer Science (ITCS), pp. 11–18 (2012)
14. Kleinberg, R., Niculescu-Mizil, A., Sharma, Y.: Regret bounds for sleeping experts and bandits. Machine Learning 80(2-3), 245–272 (2010)
15. Moscibroda, T., Wattenhofer, R.: The complexity of connectivity in wireless networks. In: Proc. 25th IEEE Conf. Computer Communications (INFOCOM), pp. 1–13 (2006)
16. Nieberg, T., Hurink, J., Kern, W.: Approximation schemes for wireless networks. ACM Trans. Algorithms 4(4) (2008)
17. Schneider, J., Wattenhofer, R.: Coloring unstructured wireless multi-hop networks. In: Proc. 28th Symp. Principles of Distrib. Comput. (PODC), pp. 210–219 (2009)
18. Schneider, J., Wattenhofer, R.: An optimal maximal independent set algorithm for bounded-independence graphs. Distributed Computing 22(5-6), 349–361 (2010)

Broadcast in the Ad Hoc SINR Model

Sebastian Daum[1], Seth Gilbert[3,*], Fabian Kuhn[1], and Calvin Newport[2,**]

[1] Department of Computer Science, University of Freiburg, Germany
{sdaum,kuhn}@cs.uni-freiburg.de
[2] Department of Computer Science, Georgetown University, USA
cnewport@cs.georgetown.edu
[3] Department of Computer Science, National University of Singapore, Singapore
seth.gilbert@comp.nus.edu.sg

Abstract. An increasing amount of attention is being turned toward the study of distributed algorithms in wireless network models based on calculations of the *signal to noise and interference ratio* (SINR). In this paper we introduce the *ad hoc SINR* model, which, we argue, reduces the gap between theory results and real world deployment. We then use it to study upper and lower bounds for the canonical problem of broadcast on the graph induced by both *strong* and *weak* links. For strong connectivity broadcast, we present a new randomized algorithm that solves the problem in $O(D \log(n)\text{polylog}(R))$ rounds in networks of size n, with link graph diameter D, and a ratio between longest and shortest links bounded by R. We then show that for *back-off* style algorithms (a common type of algorithm where nodes do not explicitly coordinate with each other) and *compact* networks (a practice-motivated model variant that treats the distance from very close nodes as equivalent), there exist networks in which centralized algorithms can solve broadcast in $O(1)$ rounds, but distributed solutions require $\Omega(n)$ rounds. We then turn our attention to weak connectivity broadcast, where we show a similar $\Omega(n)$ lower bound for all types of algorithms, which we (nearly) match with a back-off style $O(n \log^2 n)$-round upper bound. Our broadcast algorithms are the first known for SINR-style models that do not assume synchronous starts, as well as the first known not to depend on power control, tunable carrier sensing, geographic information and/or exact knowledge of network parameters.

1 Introduction

In this paper, we study distributed broadcast in wireless networks. We model this setting using an *SINR-style* model; i.e., communication behavior is determined by the ratio of signal to noise and interference [6, 8–11, 15, 17, 19, 21]. While we are not the first to study broadcast in an SINR-style model (see *related work* below), we are the first to do so under a specific set of assumptions which we call the *ad hoc SINR* model. It generalizes the SINR-style models previously used to study broadcast by eliminating or reducing assumptions that might conflict with real networks, including, notably, idealized uniform signal propagation and knowledge of exact network parameters or geographic information. In this setting, we produce new efficient broadcast upper bounds as well as new lower bounds that prove key limitations. In the remainder of this section, we detail and motivate our model, then describe our results and compare them to existing work.

* Supported by the Singapore Academic Research Fund MOE2011-T2-2-042.
** Supported in part by the Ford University Research Grant program.

Y. Afek (Ed.): DISC 2013, LNCS 8205, pp. 358–372, 2013.

The Ad Hoc SINR Model. In recent years, increasing attention has been turned toward studying distributed wireless algorithms in *SINR-style* models which determine receive behavior with an *SINR formula* (see Section 2) that calculates, for a given sender/receiver pair, the ratio of signal to interference and noise at the receiver. These models differ in the assumptions they make about aspects including the definition of distance, knowledge of network parameters, and power control constraints. In this paper we study an SINR-style model with a collection of assumptions that we collectively call the *ad hoc SINR* model, previously studied (however not named yet) e.g. in [7]. Our goal with this model is to capture the key characteristic of wireless communication while avoiding assumptions that might impede the translation of theoretical results into practical algorithms. The ad hoc SINR model is formally defined in Section 2, but we begin by summarizing and motivating it below.

We start by noting that a key parameter in the SINR formula is the distance between nodes. Distance provides the independent variable in determining signal degradation between a transmitter and receiver. In the ad hoc SINR model, we do not assume that distance is necessarily determined by Euclidean geometry. We instead assume only that the distances form a metric in a "growth-bounded metric space"—describing, in some sense, an *effective distance* between nodes that captures both path loss and attenuation. Crucially, we assume this distance function is *a priori* unknown—preventing algorithms that depend on advance exact knowledge of how signals will propagate.

Another key assumption in the definition of an SINR-style model is the nodes' knowledge of network parameters. In the ad hoc SINR model, we assume nodes do not know the precise value of the parameters associated with the SINR formula (i.e., α, β, N), but instead know only reasonable upper and lower bounds for the parameters (i.e., $\frac{\alpha_{min}}{\alpha_{max}}, \frac{\beta_{min}}{\beta_{max}}, \frac{N_{min}}{N_{max}}$). This assumption is motivated by practice where ranges for these parameters are well-established, but specific values change from network to network and are non-trivial to measure.[1] We also assume that nodes only know a polynomial upper bound on the relevant deployment parameters—namely, network size and density disparity (ratio between longest and shortest links).

Finally, we assume that all nodes use the same fixed constant power. This assumption is motivated by the reality that power control varies widely from device to device, with some chipsets not allowing it all, while others use significantly different granularities. To produce algorithms that are widely deployable it is easiest to simply assume that nodes are provided some unknown uniform power.

Results. The global broadcast problem provides a *source* with a broadcast message M, which it must propagate to all reachable nodes in the network. We study this problem under the two standard definitions of *reachable* for an SINR-style setting: weak and strong. In more detail, let d_{max} be the largest possible distance such that two nodes u and v can communicate (i.e., the largest distance such that if u broadcasts alone in the entire network, v receives its message). A link between u and v is considered *weak* if their distance is no more than d_{max}, and *strong* if their distance is no more than $\frac{d_{max}}{1+\rho}$, where $\rho = O(1)$ is a constant parameter of the problem. *Weak* (resp. *strong*)

---

[1] In addition to keeping the specific values unknown, it might be interesting to allow them to vary over time in the range; e.g., an idea first proposed and investigated in [10]. The difficulty of defining such dynamic models lies in introducing the dynamic behavior without subverting tractability. This is undoubtedly an intriguing direction for future exploration.

connectivity broadcast requires the source to propagate the message to all nodes in its connected component in the graph induced by weak (resp. strong) links.

Existing work on broadcast in SINR-style models focuses on strong connectivity. With this in mind, we begin, in Section 4, with our main result: a new strong connectivity broadcast algorithm that terminates in $O(D \log n \log^{\alpha_{max}+1}(R_s))$ rounds, with probability at least $1 - 1/n^c$, for some $c \geq 1$ (w.h.p.), where D is the diameter of the strong link graph, $\alpha_{max} = \alpha + O(1)$ is an SINR model parameter, and R_s is the maximum ratio between strong link lengths. Notice, in most practical networks, R_s is polynomial in n,[2] leading to a result that is in $O(D \operatorname{polylog}(n))$. This is also, to the best of our knowledge, the first broadcast algorithm for an SINR-style model that does not assume synchronous starts. It instead requires nodes to receive the broadcast message first before transmitting—a practical and common assumption, that prevents nodes from needing advance knowledge of exactly when broadcast messages will enter the system.

We then continue with lower bounds for strong connectivity broadcast. In the graph-based models of wireless networks, the best known broadcast solutions are *back-off style* algorithms [2,4,12], in which a node's decision to broadcast depends only on the current round and the round in which it first received the broadcast message. These algorithms are appealing due to their simplicity and ease of implementation. In this paper, we prove that back-off style algorithms are inherently inefficient for solving strong connectivity broadcast. In more detail, we prove that there exist networks in which a centralized algorithm can solve broadcast in a constant number of rounds, but any back-off style algorithm requires $\Omega(n)$ rounds. This result opens a clear separation between the graph and SINR-style models with respect to this problem.

We also prove an $\Omega(n)$ bound on a *compact* version of our model that allows arbitrarily large groups of nodes to occupy the same position. We introduce this assumption to explore a reality of many real networks: when you pack devices close enough, the differences between received signal strength fall below the detection granularity of the radio hardware, which experiences the signal strength of these nearby devices as if they were all traveling the same distance. This bound emphasizes an intriguing negative reality: efficient broadcast in SINR-style models depends strongly, in some sense, on the theoretical conceit that the ratio between distances is all that matters, regardless of how small the actual magnitude of these distance values is.

We conclude by turning our attention to weak connectivity broadcast. To the best of our knowledge, we are the first to concretely consider this version of broadcast. We formalize the intuitive difficulty of this setting by proving the existence of networks where centralized algorithms can solve broadcast in $O(1)$ rounds, while any distributed algorithm requires $\Omega(n)$ rounds. We then match this bound (within $\log^2 n$ factors) by showing that the back-off style upper bound we first presented in our study of the dual graph model [13] not only solves weak connectivity broadcast in $O(n \log^2 n)$ rounds in the ad hoc SINR model, but also does so in essentially *every reasonable model* of a wireless network.

---

[2] There are theoretically possible networks, like the exponential line, in which R_s is exponential in n, but as n grows beyond a small value, those networks become impossible to realize in practice. E.g., to deploy an exponential line consisting of ~ 45 nodes, with a maximum transmission range of $100m$, the network would have to include pairs of devices separated by a distance less than the width of a single atom.

Related Work. The theoretical study of SINR-style models began by focusing on centralized algorithms meant to bound the fundamental capabilities of the setting; e.g., [6, 8,11,15,17]. More recently, attention has turned toward studying distributed algorithms, which we discuss here. In the following, n is the network size, D is the diameter of the strong link graph, and Δ is the maximum degree in the weak link graph. Randomized results are assumed to hold with high probability.

We begin by summarizing existing work on distributed strong connectivity broadcast in SINR-style models. There exist several interesting strategies for efficiently performing strong connectivity broadcast. In more detail, in the randomized setting, Scheideler et al. [19] show how to solve strong connectivity broadcast in $O(D + \log n)$ rounds, while Yu et al. [21] present a $O(D + \log^2 n)$ round solution. In the deterministic setting, Jurdzinski et al. [9] describe a $O(\Delta \operatorname{polylog}(n) + D)$ solution, which they recently improved to $O(D \log^2 n)$ (under different assumptions) [10]. However, all of these above solutions make strong assumptions on the knowledge and capability of devices, which are forbidden by the ad hoc SINR model. In particular, all four results leverage knowledge of the exact network parameters (though in [19] it is noted that estimates are likely sufficient), and assume that all nodes begin during round 1 (allowing them to build an overlay structure on which the message is then propagated). In addition, [19] makes use of tunable collision detection, [21] allows the algorithm to specify the transmission power level as a function of the network parameters, [9] adds an additional model restriction that forbids communication over weak links,[3] and [10] heavily leverages the assumption that nodes know their positions in Euclidean space and the exact network parameters, and can therefore place themselves and their neighbors in a precomputed overlay grid with nice properties.

A problem closely related to (global) broadcast is *local* broadcast, which requires a set of senders to deliver a message to all neighbors in the strong link graph. This problem is well-studied in SINR-style models and the best known results are of the form $O(\Delta \log n)$ [7, 22]. Of these results, the algorithm in [7] is the most relevant to our work as it deploys an elegant randomized strategy that can be easily adapted to the ad hoc SINR model. Using this local broadcast algorithm as a building block yields a solution for (global) broadcast that runs in $O(\Delta D \log n)$ time. In our work, we avoid dependency on the degree of the underlying link graph as we only need to propagate a single message.

In the classical graph-based wireless network model, for distributed broadcast there is a tight bound of $\Theta((D + \log n) \log (n/D))$ rounds, if nodes start asynchronously (like in this paper) [1, 2, 4, 12, 14, 18]. For the easier case where all nodes start at the same time, it is currently unknown whether or not better bounds are possible in general graphs, but in unit disk graphs a solution of the form $O(D + \log^2 n)$ is likely possible.[4]

---

[3] In slightly more detail, their model forbids v from receiving a message from u if u is too far away, even if the SINR of the transmission is above β. This restriction makes it easier to build a useful dominating set because it eliminates the chance that you are dominated by a weakly connected neighbor.

[4] The result of [16] can build a maximal independent set in the UDG graph model in $O(\log^2 n)$ rounds. Once this set is established under these constraints, an additional $O(\log^2 n)$ rounds should be enough to build a constant-degree overlay—e.g., as in [3]—on which broadcast can be solved in an additional $O(D + \log n)$ rounds.

2   Model

We study the ad hoc SINR model, which describes a network consisting of a set of nodes V deployed in a metric space and communicating via radios. We assume time is divided into synchronous rounds and in each round a node can decide to either transmit or listen. We determine the outcome of these communication decisions by the standard *SINR formula*, which dictates that $v \in V$ receives a message transmitted by $u \in V$, in a round where the nodes in $I \subseteq V \setminus \{u, v\}$ also transmit, if and only if v is listening and

$$SINR(u, v, I) = \frac{\frac{P_u}{d(u,v)^\alpha}}{N + \sum_{w \in I} \frac{P_w}{d(w,v)^\alpha}} \geq \beta,$$

where P_x is the transmission power of node x, d is the distance formula for the under-lying metric space, and $\alpha \in [\alpha_{min}, \alpha_{max}]$, $\beta \in [1, \beta_{max}]$, and $N \in [0, N_{max}]$, where α_{max}, β_{max} and N_{max} are constants.

In this paper, we assume that: (1) Algorithms are distributed. (2) All nodes use the same constant power P. (3) Nodes do not have advance knowledge of their locations, distances to other nodes, or the specific values of the network parameters α, N, and β, though they do know the range of values from which α, N, and β are chosen. In addition, nodes only know a polynomial upper bound on the standard deployment parameters: the network size ($|V| = n$) and the density (ratio of longest to short-est link distance). (4) Nodes are embedded in a general metric space with a distance function d that satisfies the following property: for every $v \in S \subseteq V$ and constant $c \geq 1$, the number of nodes in S within distance $c \cdot d_{\min}(S)$ of v is in $O(c^\delta)$, where $d_{\min}(S) := \min_{u,u' \in V}\{d(u, u')\}$ is the minimum distance between two nodes in S and $\delta < \alpha_{\min}$ is a fixed constant roughly characterizing a dimension of the metric space. Notice, for $\delta = 2$ the model strictly generalizes the Euclidean plane. We prefer this general notion of distance over standard Euclidean distance as it can capture power degradation due to both path loss *and* attenuation (a link-specific loss of power due to the materials through which the signal travels). In this paper, to achieve the strongest possible results, we prove our upper bounds with respect to this general metric, and our lower bounds with respect to the restricted (i.e., easier for algorithms) two-dimensional Euclidean instantiation.

Compact Networks. The SINR equation is undefined if it includes the distance 0. As motivated in the introduction, a natural question is to ask what happens as distances become effectively 0 (e.g., when nodes become too close for the difference in their signal strength to be detectable). To study this case, we define the *compact ad hoc SINR* model, which allows zero-distances and specifies that whenever $SINR(u, v, I)$ is therefore undefined, we determine receive behavior with the following rule: v receive u's message if and only if u is the only node in $I \cup \{u\}$ such that $d(u, v) = 0$. We formalize the impact of this assumption in our lower bound in Section 5.1.

3   Problem and Preliminaries

In this section we define the problems we study in this paper and then introduce some preliminary results that will aid our bounds in the sections that follow.

The Broadcast Problem. In the broadcast problem, a designated source must propagate a message M to every reachable node in the network. Let $r_w := \left(\frac{P}{\beta N}\right)^{1/\alpha}$ be the maximum distance at which any two nodes can communicate. Let $r_s := \frac{r_w}{1+\rho}$, for some known constant $\rho > 0$. Fix a set of nodes and a distance metric. We define $E[\ell]$, for some distance $\ell \geq 0$, to be the set of all pairs $\{u, v\} \subseteq V$ such that $d(u, v) \leq \ell$. When defining broadcast, we consider both the *weak connectivity graph* $G_w = (V, E[r_w])$ and the *strong connectivity graph* $G_s = (V, E[r_s])$. The values $R_w = \max_{\{u,v\},\{x,y\} \in E[r_w]} \left\{\frac{d(u,v)}{d(x,y)}\right\}$ and $R_s = \max_{\{u,v\},\{x,y\} \in E[r_s]} \left\{\frac{d(u,v)}{d(x,y)}\right\}$ capture the diversity of link lengths in the connectivity graphs. For most networks, you can assume this value to be polynomial in n, though there are certain malformed cases, such as an exponential line, where the value can be larger. A subset $S \subseteq V$ of the nodes is called a *maximal independent set (MIS)*, if any two nodes $u, v \in S$ are *independent*, i.e., $\{u, v\} \notin E$, and if all nodes $v \in V$ are *covered* by some node in $s \in S$, i.e., $\forall v \in V \colon \exists s \in S \colon v \in N(s)$.

In *weak connectivity broadcast* the source is required to propagate its message to all nodes in its connected component in G_w, while in *strong connectivity broadcast* the source is required only to propagate the message to all nodes in its component in G_s. In this paper, we are interested in randomized solutions to both broadcast problems. In particular, we say algorithm $\mathcal{A}$ *solves* weak or strong connectivity broadcast in a given number of rounds if it solves the problem in this time w.h.p.; i.e., with probability at least $1 - 1/n^c$, for an arbitrary constant $c > 0$.

We assume nodes remain inactive (i.e., they do not transmit) until they receive the broadcast message for the first time, at which point they become active. We say a given network is *T-broadcastable* with respect to strong or weak connectivity, if there exists a T-round schedule of transmissions that solves the relevant broadcast problem. And finally, we say a broadcast algorithm is a *back-off style* algorithm if nodes base their broadcast decisions entirely on the current round and the round in which they first received the broadcast message (which, for the source, we say is round 0).

The (x, y)-Hitting Game. Our lower bound arguments in this paper deploy the high-level strategy of proving that solving the relevant type of broadcast is at least as hard as solving an easily bounded combinatorial game we call (x, y)-*hitting*. This game is defined for two integers, $0 < x \leq y$. The game begins with an adversary choosing some arbitrary target set $T \subseteq [y]$ where $|T| = x$. The game then proceeds in rounds. In each round the player, modeled as a probabilistic automaton $\mathcal{P}$, guesses a value $w \in [y]$. If $w \in T$ the player wins. Otherwise it moves on to the next round. It is easy to see that for small x the game takes a long time to solve with reasonable probability:

Theorem 1. *Let $\mathcal{P}$ be a player that solves the (x, y)-hitting game in $f(x, y)$ rounds, in expectation. It follows that $f(x, y) = \Omega(y/x)$.*

4 Strong Connectivity Broadcast

In this section, we present STRONGCAST, an algorithm that solves strong connectivity broadcast in the ad hoc SINR model. We prove the following:

Theorem 2. *The* STRONGCAST *algorithm solves strong connectivity broadcast in the ad hoc SINR model in $O(D(\log^{\alpha_{\max}+1} R_s)(\log n))$ rounds.*

For most practical networks, R_s is polynomial in n, reducing the above result to $O(D\,\mathrm{polylog}(n))$. In some malformed networks, however, R_s can be as large as exponential in n. Because we assume the ad hoc SINR model, our algorithm leverages no advanced knowledge of the distance metric and uses only the provided constant upper bounds on α and β, and the polynomial upper bounds on n and R_s. To avoid the introduction of extra notation, we use the exact values of n and R_s in our analysis as those terms show up only within log factors in big-O notation; for simplicity of presenting the protocol, we also assume that R_s grows at least logarithmic in n.[5] To keep the analysis of the STRONGCAST algorithm concise, in the following we only present proof sketches. Full proofs for all claims of the section appear in [5].

Algorithm Overview. The STRONGCAST algorithm consists of at most D *epochs*. In each epoch, the broadcast message is propagated at least one hop further along all shortest paths from the source. In more detail, at the beginning of each epoch, we say a node is *active* with respect to that epoch if it has previously received the message and it has not yet terminated. During each epoch, the active nodes for the epoch execute a sub-protocol we call *neighborhood dissemination*. Let S be the set of active nodes for a given epoch. The goal of neighborhood dissemination is to propagate the broadcast message to every node in $N(S)$, where N is the neighbor function over the strong connectivity graph G_s. (Notice that the high-level structure of our algorithm is the same as seen in the classical results from the graph-based setting; e.g., our neighborhood dissemination sub-protocol takes the place of the *decay* sub-protocol in the canonical broadcast algorithm of Bar-Yehuda et al. [2].)

The neighborhood dissemination sub-protocol divides time into phases. As it progresses from phase to phase, the number of nodes still competing to broadcast the message decreases. The key technical difficulty is reducing contention fast enough that heavily contended neighbors of S receive the message efficiently, but not so fast that some neighbors fail to receive the message before all nearby nodes in S have terminated. We achieve this balance with a novel strategy in which nodes in S approximate a subgraph of their "reliable" neighbors, then build an MIS over this subgraph to determine who remains active and who terminates. We will prove that if a node $u \in S$ neighbors a node $v \in N(S)$, and u is covered by an MIS node (and therefore terminates), the MIS node that covered u must be sufficiently close to v to still help the message progress.

In Section 4.1 we detail a process for constructing a reliable subgraph and analyze its properties. Then, in Section 4.2 we detail the neighborhood dissemination sub-protocol (which uses the subgraph process) and analyze the properties it guarantees. We conclude, in Section 4.3, by pulling together these pieces to prove the main theorem from above.

4.1   SINR-Induced Graphs

The neighborhood dissemination sub-protocol requires active nodes to construct, in a distributed manner, a subgraph that maintains certain properties. For clarity, we describe and analyze this process here before continuing in the next section with the description of the full neighborhood dissemination sub-protocol.

---

[5] In fact, it is sufficient to assume $\log^{\alpha_{\max}} R_s = \Omega(\log^{\star} n)$.

We start by defining graphs $H_p^\mu[S]$ which are induced by a node set S, a transmission probability p and a reliability parameter $\mu \in (0, p) \cap \Omega(1)$. Given a set of nodes S, assume that each node in S independently transmits with probability p. Further, assume that there is no interference from any node outside the set S. We define $H_p^\mu[S]$ to be the undirected graph with node set S and edge set $E_p^\mu[S]$ such that for any $u, v \in S$, edge $\{u, v\}$ is in $E_p^\mu[S]$ if and only if both: (i) u receives a message from v with probability at least μ and (ii) v receives a message from u with probability at least μ.

Computing SINR-Induced Graphs. It is difficult to compute the graphs $H_p^\mu[S]$ exactly and efficiently with a distributed algorithm. However, for given S, p, and μ, there is a simple protocol to compute a good approximation $\tilde{H}_p^\mu[S]$ for $H_p^\mu[S]$ (assuming that the reception probabilities for nodes in S do not change over time). Formally, we say that an *undirected* graph $\tilde{H}_p^\mu[S]$ with node set S is an *ε-close approximation* of $H_p^\mu[S]$ if and only if:

$$E\left[H_p^\mu[S]\right] \subseteq E\left[\tilde{H}_p^\mu[S]\right] \subseteq E\left[H_p^{(1-\varepsilon)\mu}[S]\right].$$

An ε-close approximation $\tilde{H}_p^\mu[S]$ of $H_p^\mu[S]$ can be computed in time $O\left(\frac{\log n}{\varepsilon^2 \mu}\right)$ as follows. First, all nodes in S independently transmit their IDs with probability p for $T := c \frac{\log n}{\varepsilon^2 \mu}$ rounds (where the constant c is chosen to be sufficiently large). Each node u creates a list of potential neighbors containing all nodes from which u receives a message in at least $(1 - \varepsilon/2)\mu T$ of those T rounds. For a second iteration of T rounds, each node transmits its list of potential neighbors (as before, by independently transmitting with probability p). At the end, node u adds node v as a neighbor in $\tilde{H}_p^\mu[S]$ if and only if v is in u's list of potential neighbors and u receives a message from v indicating that u is in v's list of potential neighbors as well.

The following lemma results from a basic Chernoff bound, observing that: (i) if u and v are neighbors in $H_p^\mu[S]$, then u receives at least μT messages from v, in expectation, and (ii) if u and v are not neighbors in $H_p^{(1-\varepsilon)\mu}[S]$ then u receives at most $(1 - \varepsilon)\mu T$ messages from v, in expectation.

Lemma 3. *W.h.p., the SINR-Induced Graph Computation protocol runs in $O\left(\frac{\log n}{\varepsilon^2 \mu}\right)$ rounds and returns a graph $\tilde{H}_p^\mu[S]$ that is an ε-close approximation of $H_p^\mu[S]$.*

Properties of SINR-Induced Graphs. In addition to the fact that nodes in an SINR-induced graph can communicate reliably with each other, we point out two other properties. First, we remark that the maximum degree of $H_p^\mu[S]$ is bounded by $1/\mu = O(1)$, because in a single time slot, a node u can receive a message from only one other node v. consequently the second iteration requires messages of size $O\left(\frac{\log n}{\mu}\right) = O(\log n)$. Further, as shown by the next lemma, for suitable μ, the graph $H_p^\mu[S]$ contains (at least) all the edges that are very short.

Lemma 4. *$\forall p \in (0, 1/2]$, $\exists \mu \in (0, p)$ such that: Let $d_{\min} \le r_s$ be the shortest distance between any two nodes in S. Then the graph $H_p^\mu[S]$ contains all edges between pairs $u, v \in S$ for which $d(u, v) \le \min\{2d_{\min}, r_s\}$.*

Proof Sketch. We restrict our attention to the case $d_{\min} \le r_s/2$. If the minimum distance is between $r_s/2$ and r_s, the claim can be shown by a similar, simpler argument.

Consider some node $u \in S$. Due to the underlying metric space in our model, there are at most $O(k^\delta)$ nodes in S within distance $k d_{\min}$ of node u. Let v be a node at distance at most $2d_{\min}$ from u. For any constant k_0, with probability $\Omega(1)$, node v is the only node transmitting among all the nodes within distance $k_0 d_{\min}$ from node u. Further, assuming that all nodes at distance greater than $k_0 d_{\min}$ transmit, the interference $I(u)$ at u can be bounded from above by $\kappa(k_0) \cdot P / d_{\min}^\alpha$, where $\kappa(k_0) > 0$ goes to 0 polynomially with k_0. We therefore get

$$\frac{\frac{P}{d(u,v)^\alpha}}{N + \kappa(k_o)\frac{P}{d_{\min}^\alpha}} \geq \frac{\frac{P}{(2d_{\min})^\alpha}}{N + \kappa(k_0)\frac{P}{d_{\min}^\alpha}} \geq \frac{\frac{P}{r_s^\alpha}}{\frac{P}{\beta r_w^\alpha} + \kappa(k_0)\frac{2^\alpha P}{r_s^\alpha}} = \frac{\beta}{\frac{1}{(1+\rho)^\alpha} + \kappa(k_0)\beta 2^\alpha} \geq \beta.$$

The second inequality follows from $N = \frac{P}{\beta r_w^\alpha}$ and from $d_{\min} \leq r_s/2$. The last inequality holds for sufficiently large k_0. If we choose μ to be the probability that no more than one node in a ball of radius $k_0 d_{\min}$ transmits, then node v can transmit to u with probability μ.   □

In the above proof, μ depends on the unknown parameter β, so we use $\beta_{\max}$ as the base for computing μ. Note also that since $H_p^\mu[S] \subseteq \tilde{H}_p^\mu[S]$, the lemma induces the same properties on $\tilde{H}_p^\mu[S]$ with high probability.

4.2 Neighborhood Dissemination Sub-protocol

We can now describe the full operation of our neighborhood dissemination sub-protocol (depicted in Algorithm 1). We assume the sub-protocol is called by a set $S \subset V$ of nodes that have a message M that they are trying to disseminate to all nodes in $N(S)$, where N is the neighbor function over G_s. Since every node in S has already received the message M, which originated at the source node s, we can assume that all the nodes in S have been synchronized by s and therefore align their epoch boundaries and call the sub-protocol during the same round.

The protocol proceeds in phases $\phi = 1, 2, \ldots, \Phi$, with $\Phi = O(\log R_s)$. Each phase ϕ, the protocol computes a set S_ϕ, such that $S_1 = S$ and for all $\phi \geq 2$, $S_\phi \subset S_{\phi-1}$. The nodes in S_ϕ attempt to send M to nodes in $N(S)$, while the remaining "inactive" nodes remain silent. Each phase is divided into three blocks. In block 1 of phase ϕ, the nodes compute an ε-close approximation $\tilde{H}_p^\mu[S_\phi]$ of the graph $H_p^\mu[S_\phi]$ using the SINR-induced graph computation process described in Section 4.1. We choose $\mu > 0$ appropriately as described in Lemma 4, while $\varepsilon, p \in (0, 1/2)$ can be chosen freely.[6]

In block 2, nodes in S attempt to propagate the message to neighbors in $N(S)$. In more detail, during this block, each node in S_ϕ transmits M with probability p/Q for $T_{\text{phase}} = O(Q \log n)$ rounds, where $Q = \Theta(\log^{\alpha_{\max}} R_s)$ has an appropriately large hidden constant.

In block 3, the nodes in S_ϕ compute the set $S_{\phi+1}$ by finding a maximal independent set (MIS) of $\tilde{H}_p^\mu[S_\phi]$. Only the nodes in this set remain in $S_{\phi+1}$. Notice that building this MIS is straightforward. This can be accomplished by simulating the reliable message-passing model on our subgraph and then executing the $O(\log^\star n)$ MIS algorithm from [20] on this simulated network. (This algorithm requires a growth-bounded

---

[6] By Lemma 4, μ depends on p; thus p could be chosen to maximize μ.

Algorithm 1. High-level pseudo-code for one epoch of STRONGCAST

Input: $n, R_s, \alpha_{\max}, \beta_{\max}, \varepsilon, p$

Initialization: $Q = Q(p, R_s, \alpha_{\max}) = \Theta(\log^{\alpha_{\max}} R_s), \mu = \mu(p, \beta_{\max}) = \Omega(1), \Phi = O(\log R_s), S_1 = S$

    for $\phi = 1$ to Φ **do**

        Compute SINR-induced graph $\tilde{H}_p^\mu[S_\phi]$ within $O\left(\frac{\log n}{\varepsilon^2 \mu}\right)$ rounds   ▷ Block 1

        for $O(Q \log n)$ rounds **do**   ▷ Block 2

            Each round transmit M with probability $\frac{p}{Q}$

        Compute MIS $S_{\phi+1}$ on $\tilde{H}_p^\mu[S_\phi]$ within $O\left(\frac{\log n}{\varepsilon^2 \mu} \log^* n\right)$ rounds   ▷ Block 3

---

property which is, by definition, satisfied by any sub-graph of G_s.) Turning our attention to the simulation, we note that by the definition of $\tilde{H}_p^\mu[S_\phi]$, a single round of reliable communication on $\tilde{H}_p^\mu[S_\phi]$ can be easily simulated by having each node in S_ϕ transmits with probability p for $O(\log n)$ consecutive $((1 - \varepsilon)\mu$-reliable) rounds. Therefore, the MIS construction takes $O(\log n \log^* n)$ rounds.

We now turn our attention to analyzing this protocol. The most technically demanding chore we face in this analysis is proving the following: If a node $u \in S_\phi$ has an uninformed neighbor $v \in N(S)$, then either u gets the message to v in block 2, or u remains in $S_{\phi+1}$, or there is some $w \in S_{\phi+1}$ that is sufficiently close to v to take u's place in attempting to get the message to v.

Neighborhood Dissemination Analysis. In the following, we show that for appropriate parameters μ, Q, and T_{phase}, the described algorithm solves the neighborhood dissemination problem for S, w.h.p. We first analyze how the sets S_ϕ evolve. In the following, let d_ϕ be the minimum distance between any two nodes in S_ϕ.

Lemma 5. *If the constant μ is chosen to be sufficiently small, w.h.p., the minimum distance between any two nodes in S_ϕ is at least $d_\phi \geq 2^{\phi-1} \cdot d_{\min}$.*

Proof. We prove the claim by induction on ϕ. First, by the definition of $d_{\min}$, we clearly have $d_1 \geq 2^0 d_{\min} = d_{\min}$. Also, by the definition of an ε-close approximation of $H_p^\mu[S_\phi]$ and by Lemma 4, for a sufficiently small constant μ, w.h.p., $\tilde{H}_p^\mu[S_\phi]$ contains edges between all pairs of nodes $u, v \in S_\phi$ at distance $d(u, v) \leq 2d_\phi$. Because $S_{\phi+1}$ is a maximal independent set of $\tilde{H}_p^\mu[S_\phi]$, nodes in $S_{\phi+1}$ are at distance more than $2d_\phi$ and therefore using the induction hypothesis, we get $d_{\phi+1} > 2d_\phi \geq 2^\phi d_{\min}$. □

Next we consider node v that needs the message, and its closest neighbor u in S_ϕ. We show that if u and v are sufficiently close, and if the farthest neighbor of u in S_ϕ is also "sufficiently far" away, then u can successfully transmit the message to v.

Lemma 6. $\forall p \in (0, 1/2], \exists \hat{Q}, \gamma = \Theta(1)$, *such that for all $Q \geq \hat{Q}$ the following holds. Consider a round r in phase ϕ where each node in S_ϕ transmits the broadcast message M with probability p/Q. Let $v \in N(S)$ be some node that needs to receive M, and let $u \in S_\phi$ be the closest node to v in S_ϕ. Further, let d_u be the distance between u and its farthest neighbor in $\tilde{H}_p^\mu[S_\phi]$. If $d(u, v) \leq (1 + \rho/2)r_s$ and $d_u \geq \gamma Q^{-1/\alpha} \cdot d(u, v)$, node v receives M in round r with probability $1/\Theta(Q)$.*

Proof Sketch. The lemma states under what conditions in round r of block 2 in phase ϕ a node $v \in N(S) \setminus S$ can receive the message. The roadmap for this proof is to show that if u is able to communicate with probability $(1-\varepsilon)\mu$ with its farthest neighbor u' in some round r' of block 1 in phase ϕ, using the broadcast probability p, then u must also be able to reach v with probability $1/\Theta(Q)$ in round r of block 2, in which it transmits with probability p/Q. We start with some definitions and notation, and continue with a connection between the interference at u and at v. We then analyze the interference at u created in a ball of radius $2d_u$ around u, as well as the remaining interference coming from outside that ball. Finally, we transfer all the knowledge we gained for round r' to round r to conclude the proof.

For a node $w \in V$, let $I(w) = \sum_{x \in S_\phi} \frac{P}{d(x,w)^\alpha}$, i.e., the amount of interference at node w if all nodes of S_ϕ transmit. For round r', the random variable $X_x^p(w)$ denotes the actual interference at node w coming from a node $x \in S$. The total interference at node w is thus $X^p(w) := \sum_{x \in S_\phi} X_x^p(w)$. If we only want to look at the interference stemming from nodes within a subset $A \subseteq S_\phi$, we use $I_A(w)$ and $X_A^p(w)$, respectively. Further for a set $A \subseteq S_\phi$, we define $\bar{A} := S_\phi \setminus A$.

The triangle inequality implies that $d(u,w) \leq d(u,v) + d(v,w) \leq 2d(v,w)$ for any $w \in S_\phi$. By comparing $I_{S'}(u)$ and $I_{S'}(v)$ for an arbitrary set $S' \subseteq S_\phi$ we obtain the following observation:

$$I_{S'}(u) \geq 2^{-\alpha} I_{S'}(v). \tag{1}$$

Let u' be the farthest neighbor of node u in $\tilde{H}_p^\mu[S_\phi]$. Because $\tilde{H}_p^\mu[S_\phi]$ is an ε-close approximation of $H_p^\mu[S_\phi]$, we know that $\tilde{H}_p^\mu[S_\phi]$ is a subgraph of $H_p^{(1-\varepsilon)\mu}[S_\phi]$ and therefore in round r', u receives a message from u' with probability at least $(1-\varepsilon)\mu$.

Let $A \subseteq S_\phi$ be the set of nodes at distance at most $2d_u$ from u. Note that both u and u' are in A, because $d(u, u') = d_u$. In round r', if more than $2^\alpha/\beta = O(1)$ nodes $u'' \in A$ transmit, then node u cannot receive a message from u'. Since node u receives a message from u' with probability at least $(1-\varepsilon)\mu$ in round r', we can conclude that fewer than $2^\alpha/\beta$ nodes transmit with at least the same probability.

We now bound the interference from nodes outside of A. Using the fact that node u receives a message from node u' with constant probability at least $(1-\varepsilon)\mu$ allows us to upper bound $I_{\bar{A}}(u)$ and by (1) also $I_{\bar{A}}(v)$. For node u to be able to receive a message from u', two things must hold: (I) u' transmits and u listens (event $R^{u',u}$) and (II) $\frac{P}{d_u^\alpha(N + X_{\bar{A}}^p(u))} \geq \frac{P}{d_u^\alpha(N + X^p(u))} \geq \beta$. Thus we have

$$(1-\varepsilon)\mu \leq \mathbb{P}(R^{u',u}) \cdot \mathbb{P}\left(X_{\bar{A}}^p(u) \leq \frac{P}{\beta d_u^\alpha} - N\right) \leq p(1-p) \cdot \mathbb{P}\left(X_{\bar{A}}^p(u) \leq \frac{P}{\beta d_u^\alpha}\right). \tag{2}$$

Using a Chernoff result (see [5]), we can bound $X_{\bar{A}}^p(u)$ as

$$\mathbb{P}\left(X_{\bar{A}}^p(u) \leq \frac{\mathbb{E}[X_{\bar{A}}^p(u)]}{2}\right) = \mathbb{P}\left(X_{\bar{A}}^p(u) \leq \frac{pI_{\bar{A}}(u)}{2}\right) \leq e^{-\frac{p2^\alpha d_u^\alpha}{8P} \cdot I_{\bar{A}}(u)}. \tag{3}$$

Together, (2) and (3) imply that $I_{\bar{A}}(u) = O(P/d_u^\alpha)$. Hence if each node transmits with probability p/Q, by (1), with constant probability, the interference from nodes in $\bar{A}$ at v is bounded by $O(p/Q \cdot P2^\alpha/d_u^\alpha)$. Since in addition, with probability $1/\Theta(Q)$, u is the only node in A transmitting, by choosing $Q = \Omega(2^\alpha)$ sufficiently large, node v receives M with probability $1/\Theta(Q)$.

4.3   Proof Sketch of Theorem 2

Proof Sketch. First note that by construction, every phase of the neighborhood dissemination protocol has a time complexity of $O((\log^* n + Q) \log n) = O(\log^\alpha R_s \log n)$ (recall that we assumed that R_s is at least logarithmic in n). The claim of the theorem immediately follows if we show that assuming that all algorithm parameters are chosen appropriately, (I) the number of phases Φ of the neighborhood protocol is $O(\log R_s)$, and (II) the neighborhood dissemination protocol is correct, i.e., when carried out by a set S of nodes, w.h.p., each node $v \in N(S)$ receives the broadcast message M.

We prove statements (I) and (II) together. Let v be any node in $N(S)$ and let u_ϕ be the closest node to v in S_ϕ. Since $v \in N(S)$, we have $d(u_1, v) \le r_s$. Recall that in block 2 of a phase ϕ of the neighborhood dissemination protocol, S_ϕ broadcasts M with probability p/Q for sufficiently large interval of $O(Q \log n)$ rounds. Therefore, by choosing $Q = O(\log^\alpha R_s)$ sufficiently large, by Lemma 6, for all $\phi \in \{1, \ldots, \Phi\}$, either $d(u_\phi, v) \le d(u_1, v)(1 + \phi\gamma Q^{-1/\alpha}) \le (1 + \rho/2)d(u_1, v)$ or v has already received the message at the start of phase ϕ. As we also know by Lemma 5 that the minimum distance between nodes in S_ϕ grows exponentially with ϕ, it follows that for some $\phi \le \Phi$, the minimum distance between nodes in S_ϕ exceeds r_s at which point a node within distance $(1 + \rho/2)d(u_1, v) \le (1 + \rho/2)r_s$ of v trivially reaches node v. □

5   Lower Bounds for Strong Connectivity Broadcast

In this section, we present lower bounds for strong connectivity broadcast. For complete proofs we refer to [5].

5.1   Lower Bound for Compact Networks

In the compact variant of the ad hoc SINR model (defined in Section 2 and motivated in Section 1) nodes can formally occupy the same position (have mutual distance of 0), which informally captures the real world scenario where the difference in strength of signals coming from a group of nodes packed close enough together are too small to detect, making it seem as if they are all traveling the same distance. Here we prove this assumption makes efficient broadcast impossible.

Theorem 7. *Let $\mathcal{A}$ be a strong connectivity broadcast algorithm for the compact ad hoc SINR model. There exists an $O(1 + \rho)$-broadcastable network in which $\mathcal{A}$ requires $\Omega(n)$ rounds to solve broadcast.*

Proof Sketch. We reduce the $(\lceil (1+\rho) \rceil, n)$-hitting game broadcast in a specific difficult compact network. We construct a network with $k + 2 = \lceil \rho + 1 \rceil + 2$ nodes located uniformly along a line of length $r_w + \epsilon$, for some $\epsilon > 0$, and $n - (k + 2)$ additional nodes placed at one end of the line in the same position. Broadcast to the lone node at the opposite end of the line can only succeed when exactly one node in the middle of the line decides to broadcast by itself. Until that happens, interference prevents all nodes from learning anything. Hence solving broadcast requires solving the hitting game (i.e., choosing one of the k internal nodes on the line). □

5.2 Lower Bound for Back-Off Style Algorithms

In the study of broadcast in *graph-based* models, the best known algorithms are often back-off style algorithms (e.g., the canonical solution of Bar-Yehuda et. al. [2]). We prove below that such algorithms are too simple to solve strong connectivity broadcast efficiently in the SINR setting.

Theorem 8. *Let $\mathcal{A}$ be a back-off style strong connectivity broadcast algorithm for the ad hoc SINR model. There exists an $O(1 + \rho)$-broadcastable network in which $\mathcal{A}$ requires $\Omega(n)$ rounds to solve broadcast.*

Proof Sketch. The proof is similar to that of Theorem 7 where we reduce an (x, n)-hitting game to broadcast. As before, we begin with $k + 2 = \lceil 1 + \rho \rceil + 2$ nodes distributed along a vertical line of length $r_w + \epsilon$ for some $\epsilon > 0$. Since we are no longer in a compact network, we cannot place the remaining $n - k + 2$ nodes in the same position at one end of the line. Instead, we spread the remaining nodes uniformly on a horizontal line perpendicular to one end of the existing vertical line. The spacing is small enough that the nodes remain within distance r_w of every other node, except for the one lone node at the far end of the line. Since the network is no longer compact, nodes can now succeed in communicating amongst themselves before the hitting game is won. However, since the algorithm is assumed to be back-off style, this additional communication is ignored and cannot affect their behavior. As before, the nodes are reduced to guessing which k nodes among n total with the message are among those able to solve broadcast.   □

6   Weak Connectivity Broadcast

Weak connectivity broadcast is more difficult than strong connectivity broadcast because it might require messages to move across weak links (links at distance near r_w). When communicating over such a long distance, it is possible for most other nodes in the network to be *interferers*—capable of disrupting the message, but not capable of communicating with the receiver themselves—reducing possible concurrency.

In this section we formalize this intuition by proving that there is a 2-broadcastable network in which all algorithms require $\Omega(n)$ rounds to solve weak connectivity broadcast. We then turn our attention to upper bounds by reanalyzing an algorithm we originally presented in [13], in the context of the *dual graph* model, to show that it solves weak connectivity broadcast in the ad hoc SINR model in $O(n \log^2 n)$ rounds. To the best of our knowledge, this is the first known non-trivial weak connectivity broadcast algorithm for an SINR-style model (all previous broadcast algorithms make stronger assumptions on connectivity). To help underscore the surprising universality of this algorithm, we prove that not only does it solve broadcast in this time in *this* model, but that it works in this time essentially in *every standard wireless model* (a notion we formalize below).

6.1   Lower Bound

Theorem 9. *Let $\mathcal{A}$ be weak connectivity broadcast algorithm for the ad hoc SINR model. There exists a 2-broadcastable network in which $\mathcal{A}$ requires $\Omega(n)$ rounds to solve broadcast.*

Proof Sketch. We leverage the same general approach as the lower bounds in Section 5: We reduce (x, y)-hitting to the relevant broadcast problem, and then apply the bound on hitting from Theorem 1. In our reduction, we use a *rotating lollipop* network, consisting of a circle of $n - 1$ nodes with the message and a receiver at distance r_w from some unknown *bridge* node in the circle (and strictly more distant from all others). To get the message from the circle to the receiver requires that this bridge node broadcast alone. We prove that identifying this bridge node is at least as hard as solving the $(1, n - 1)$-hitting game, which we know requires $\Omega(n)$ rounds. (See [5] for a detailed proof.) □

6.2   Upper Bound

In [13], we described a simple back-off style algorithm that solves broadcast in the *dual graph* model—a variant of the classical graph-based wireless model that includes unreliable links controlled by an adversary. In this section, we show that this algorithm solves the basic definition of broadcast in $O(n \log^2 n)$ rounds in every "standard" wireless network model. The fact that it does so in the ad hoc SINR model is an immediate corollary.

First, we consider a broadcast algorithm *universal*, if it distributes the message to every node in the *isolation graph*, defined as the directed graph $G = (V, E)$, where $(u, v) \in E$ if and only if v can receive a message M if u broadcasts M alone in the network. (See [5] for a more formal definition.)

We next describe the broadcast algorithm HARMONICCAST, first presented in [13], and show that it solves broadcast in most standard wireless network models. The algorithm works as follows: Let t_v be the round in which node v first receives the broadcast message (if v is the source, $t_v = 0$). Let H be the harmonic series on n, then each round $t \in [t_v + 1, t_v + T]$, for $T = n \lceil 24 \ln n \rceil H(n)$, v broadcasts with probability:

$$p_v(t) = \frac{1}{1 + \lceil \frac{t - t_v - 1}{24 \ln n} \rceil}.$$

After these T rounds, the node can terminate. We now establish the (perhaps surprising) universality of this algorithm.

Theorem 10. *Let $\mathcal{N}$ be a wireless network. The HARMONICCAST algorithm solves broadcast in $\mathcal{N}$ in $O(n \log^2 n)$ rounds.*

The about results follows immediately from the proof in [13], which assumes pessimistically (due to the difficulties of the dual graph model) that the message only makes progress in the network when it is broadcast alone in the entire network. Since the isolation graph for a wireless network defined with respect to the SINR equation is equivalent to $G(V, E[r_w])$, an immediate corollary of the above is that HARMONICCAST algorithm solves weak connectivity broadcast in the ad hoc SINR model.

References

1. Alon, N., Bar-Noy, A., Linial, N., Peleg, D.: A Lower Bound for Radio Broadcast. Journal of Computer and System Sciences 43(2), 290–298 (1991)

2. Bar-Yehuda, R., Goldreich, O., Itai, A.: On the Time-Complexity of Broadcast in Multi-Hop Radio Networks: An Exponential Gap between Determinism and Randomization. Journal of Computer and System Sciences 45(1), 104–126 (1992)
3. Censor-Hillel, K., Gilbert, S., Kuhn, F., Lynch, N., Newport, C.: Structuring Unreliable Radio Networks. In: Proc. ACM Symp. on Principles of Distributed Computing (PODC), pp. 79–88 (2011)
4. Czumaj, A., Rytter, W.: Broadcasting algorithms in radio networks with unknown topology. Journal of Algorithms 60, 115–143 (2006)
5. Daum, S., Gilbert, S., Kuhn, F., Newport, C.: Broadcast in the Ad Hoc SINR Model. Technical Report 274, University of Freiburg, Dept. of Computer Science (2013)
6. Goussevskaia, O., Wattenhofer, R., Halldorsson, M.M., Welzl, E.: Capacity of Arbitrary Wireless Networks. In: Proc. IEEE Int. Conf. on Computer Communications (2009)
7. Halldorsson, M.M., Mitra, P.: Towards Tight Bounds for Local Broadcasting. In: Proc.Int. Workshop on the Foundations of Mobile Computing. ACM (2012)
8. Halldorsson, M.M., Mitra, P.: Wireless Connectivity and Capacity. In: Proc. ACM-SIAM Symp. on Discrete Algorithms, SODA (2012)
9. Jurdzinski, T., Kowalski, D.R.: Distributed backbone structure for algorithms in the SINR model of wireless networks. In: Aguilera, M.K. (ed.) DISC 2012. LNCS, vol. 7611, pp. 106–120. Springer, Heidelberg (2012)
10. Jurdzinski, T., Kowalski, D.R., Stachowiak, G.: Distributed deterministic broadcasting in uniform-power ad hoc wireless networks. In: Gąsieniec, L., Wolter, F. (eds.) FCT 2013. LNCS, vol. 8070, pp. 195–209. Springer, Heidelberg (2013)
11. Kesselheim, T.: A Constant-Factor Approximation for Wireless Capacity Maximization with Power Control in the SINR Model. In: Proc. ACM-SIAM Symp. on Discrete Algorithms, SODA (2011)
12. Kowalski, D.R., Pelc, A.: Broadcasting in Undirected Ad Hoc Radio Networks. Distributed Computing 18(1), 43–57 (2005)
13. Kuhn, F., Lynch, N., Newport, C., Oshman, R., Richa, A.: Broadcasting in Radio Networks with Unreliable Communication. In: Proc. ACM Symp. on Principles of Distributed Computing, PODC (2010)
14. Kushilevitz, E., Mansour, Y.: An $\Omega(D \log(N/D))$ Lower Bound for Broadcast in Radio Networks. SIAM Journal on Computing 27(3), 702–712 (1998)
15. Moscibroda, T.: The Worst-Case Capacity of Wireless Sensor Networks. In: Proc. ACM/IEEE Int. Conf. on Information Processing in Sensor Networks, IPSN (2007)
16. Moscibroda, T., Wattenhofer, R.: Maximal Independent Sets In Radio Networks. In: Proc. ACM Symp. on Principles of Distributed Computing (PODC), pp. 148–157 (2005)
17. Moscibroda, T., Wattenhofer, R.: The Complexity of Connectivity in Wireless Networks. In: Proc. IEEE Int. Conf. on Computer Communications (2006)
18. Newport, C.: Brief Announcement: A Shorter and Stronger Proof of an $\Omega(D \log(n/D))$ Lower Bound on Broadcast in Radio Networks. In: Proc. ACM Symp. on Principles of Distributed Computing, PODC (2013)
19. Scheideler, C., Richa, A., Santi, P.: An O(log n) Dominating Set Protocol for Wireless Ad-Hoc Networks under the Physical Interference Model. In: Proc. ACM Int. Symp. on Mobile Ad Hoc Networking and Computing (2008)
20. Schneider, J., Wattenhofer, R.: A Log-Star Distributed Maximal Independent Set Algorithm for Growth-Bounded Graphs. In: Proc. ACM Symp. on Principles of Distributed Computing (PODC), pp. 35–44 (2008)
21. Yu, D., Hua, Q.-S., Wang, Y., Tan, H., Lau, F.C.M.: Distributed multiple-message broadcast in wireless ad-hoc networks under the SINR model. In: Even, G., Halldórsson, M.M. (eds.) SIROCCO 2012. LNCS, vol. 7355, pp. 111–122. Springer, Heidelberg (2012)
22. Yu, D., Hua, Q.-S., Wang, Y., Lau, F.C.M.: An O(log n) Distributed Approximation Algorithm for Local Broadcasting in Unstructured Wireless Networks. In: Proc. IEEE Int. Conf. on Distributed Computing in Sensor Systems (DCOSS), pp. 132–139 (2012)

Distributed Randomized Broadcasting in Wireless Networks under the SINR Model*

Tomasz Jurdzinski[1], Dariusz R. Kowalski[2], Michal Rozanski[1],
and Grzegorz Stachowiak[1]

[1] Institute of Computer Science, University of Wrocław, Poland
[2] Department of Computer Science, University of Liverpool, United Kingdom

Abstract. In the advent of large-scale multi-hop wireless technologies, such as MANET, VANET, iThings, it is of utmost importance to devise efficient distributed protocols to maintain network architecture and provide basic communication tools. One of such fundamental communication tasks is broadcast, also known as a 1-to-all communication. We present a randomized algorithm that accomplishes broadcast in $O(D + \log(1/\delta))$ rounds with probability at least $1 - \delta$ on *any* uniform-power network of n nodes and diameter D, when each station is equipped with its coordinates and local estimate of network density. Next, we develop algorithms for the model where no estimate of local density is available, except of the value n of the size of a given network. First, we provide a simple and almost oblivious algorithm which accomplishes broadcast in $O(D \log n(\log n + \log(1/\delta)))$ rounds with probability at least $1 - \delta$. We further enhance this algorithm with more adaptive leader election routine and show that the resulting protocol achieves better time performance $O((D + \log(1/\delta)) \log n)$ with probability at least $1 - \delta$. Our algorithms are the first provably efficient and well-scalable randomized distributed solutions for the (global) broadcast task in the ad hoc setting with coordinates. This could be also contrasted with the complexity of broadcast by weak devices, for which such scalable algorithms (with respect to D and $\log n$) cannot be obtained [11].

Keywords: Ad hoc wireless networks, Signal-to-Interference-and-Noise-Ratio (SINR) model, Broadcast, Distributed algorithms.

1 Introduction

1.1 The Model

We consider the model of a wireless network consisting of n *stations*, also called *nodes*, deployed into an Euclidean plane and communicating by a wireless medium. *Euclidean metric* on the plane is denoted $\mathrm{dist}(\cdot, \cdot)$. Each station v has its *transmission power* P_v, which is a positive real number.

---

* This work was supported by the Polish National Science Centre grant DEC-2012/07/B/ST6/01534.

Y. Afek (Ed.): DISC 2013, LNCS 8205, pp. 373–387, 2013.
© Springer-Verlag Berlin Heidelberg 2013

There are three fixed model parameters: path loss $\alpha > 2$, threshold $\beta \geq 1$, ambient noise $\mathcal{N} > 0$. We also have connectivity graph parameter $\varepsilon \in (0, 1)$. The $SINR(v, u, \mathcal{T})$ ratio, for given stations u, v and a set of (transmitting) stations $\mathcal{T}$, is defined as follows:

$$SINR(v, u, \mathcal{T}) = \frac{P_v \text{dist}(v, u)^{-\alpha}}{\mathcal{N} + \sum_{w \in \mathcal{T} \setminus \{v\}} P_w \text{dist}(w, u)^{-\alpha}} \qquad (1)$$

In the *Signal-to-Interference-and-Noise-Ratio (SINR)* model a station u successfully receives a message from a station v in a round if $v \in \mathcal{T}$, $u \notin \mathcal{T}$, and

$$SINR(v, u, \mathcal{T}) \geq \beta ,$$

where $\mathcal{T}$ is the set of stations transmitting at that round.

In order to specify the details of broadcasting task and performance analysis, we first introduce the notion of transmission ranges and communication graphs.

Ranges and Uniformity. The *communication range* r_v of a station v is the radius of the ball in which a message transmitted by the station is heard, provided no other station transmits at the same time. A network is *uniform*, when transmission powers P_v and thus ranges of all stations r_v are equal, or *nonuniform* otherwise. In this paper, only uniform networks are considered and without loss of generality we assume that $r_v = r = 1$ for any v, i.e., $(P/(\mathcal{N}\beta))^{1/\alpha} = 1$, where P is the transmission power of a station.

Communication Graph and Graph Notation. The *communication graph* $G(V, E)$ of a given network consists of all network nodes and edges (v, u) such that $\text{dist}(v, u) \leq (1 - \varepsilon)r = 1 - \varepsilon$, where $0 < \varepsilon < 1$ is a fixed model parameter. The meaning of the communication graph is as follows: even though the idealistic communication range is r, it may be reached only in a very unrealistic case of single transmission in the whole network. In practice, however, many nodes located in different parts of the network often transmit simultaneously, and therefore it is reasonable to assume that we may only hope for a slightly smaller range to be achieved. The communication graph envisions the network of such "reasonable reachability". Note that the communication graph is symmetric for uniform power networks. By a *neighborhood* of a node u we mean the set of all neighbors of u in G, i.e., the set $\{w \mid (w, u) \in E(G)\}$. The *graph distance* from v to w is equal to the length of a shortest path from v to w in the communication graph, where the length of a path is equal to the number of its edges. The *eccentricity* of a node is the maximum graph distance from this node to any other node (note that the eccentricity is of order of the diameter D).

Synchronization. It is assumed that algorithms work synchronously in rounds, each station can either act as a sender or as a receiver during a round. We do not assume global clock ticking.

Carrier Sensing. We consider the model *without carrier sensing*, that is, a station u has no other feedback from the wireless channel than receiving or not receiving a message in a round t.

Knowledge of Stations. Each station has its unique ID, which is only needed for distinguishing various stations. Each station also knows its location and the number of stations in the network, n. Our algorithms also work when stations share, instead of n, an estimate $\nu \geq n$ of this value which is $O(n)$. We assume that each sender can enclose its ID and location to each transmitted message.[1]

Broadcast Problem and Complexity Parameters. In the broadcast problem, there is one distinguished node, called the *source*, which initially holds a piece of information (also called a *source message* or a *broadcast message*). The goal is to disseminate this message to all other nodes. We are interested in minimizing the *time complexity* of this task being the minimum number of rounds after which, for all communication networks defined by some set of parameters, the broadcast occurs with the probability at least $1 - \delta$ for a given $0 < \delta < 1$. This time is counted since the source is activated. For the sake of complexity formulas, we consider the following parameters: n, D and δ.

Messages and Initialization of Stations Other Than Source. We assume that a single message sent in an execution of any algorithm can carry the broadcast message and at most logarithmic, in the size of the network, number of control bits. A station other than the source starts executing the broadcast protocol after the first successful receipt of the source message; it is often called a *non-spontaneous wake-up model*. We say that a station which receives the source message for the first time is *waken up* at this moment and it is awake afterwards. Our algorithms are described from a "global" perspective, i.e., we count rounds starting from the moment when the source sends its first message. In order to synchronize stations, we assume that each message contains the number of rounds elapsed from the beginning of the execution of the algorithm.

1.2 Our Results

We present randomized distributed algorithms for broadcasting in wireless connected networks deployed in two dimensional Euclidean space under the SINR model, with uniform power assignment and any $\varepsilon \in (0, 1)$. We distinguish two settings: one with local knowledge of density, in which each station knows the upper bound on the number of other stations in its close proximity (dependent on parameter ε) and the other when no extra knowledge is assumed.

In the former model, we develop a randomized broadcasting algorithm with time complexity $O(D + \log(1/\delta))$, where D is the eccentricity of the communication graph, and δ is the maximum error probability. In the latter model, we first provide a simple and almost oblivious algorithm that accomplishes broadcast in $O(D(\log n + \log(1/\delta)) \log n)$ rounds with probability at least $1 - \delta$. Finally, we give a solution with time complexity $O((D + \log(1/\delta)) \log n)$, with probability at least $1 - \delta$, which is only slightly worse than the complexity of the algorithm relying on the density estimates. All these results hold for model parameter $\alpha > 2$ (for $\alpha = 2$ all the solutions are slower by a factor $\log n$).

Our algorithms are the first provably efficient and well-scalable randomized distributed solutions for the (global) broadcast task, which work in the model

---

[1] For the purpose of algorithms presented in this paper, it is sufficient that each station knows only some good approximation of its coordinates.

with coordinates, without spontaneous wake-up (i.e., no preprocessing is allowed) and for arbitrary value of the parameter ε defining the communication graph. This could be also contrasted with the complexity of broadcast by weak devices, for which such scalable algorithms (with respect to D and $\log n$) cannot be obtained [11]. Due to the space limit, some proofs are deferred to the full version.

1.3   Previous and Related Results

We discuss most relevant results in the SINR-based models and in the older Radio Network model.

SINR Models. One of the first communication problems studied from algorithmic point in distributed ad hoc setting under the SINR model was *local* broadcasting, in which each node has to transmit a message only to its neighbors in the corresponding communication graph. This problem was addressed in [8,10,19] for $\varepsilon > 1/2$. Randomized solutions for contention resolution [14] and packet scheduling (with power control) [13] were also obtained. Usually, the considered setting allowed power control in which, in order to avoid collisions, stations could transmit with any power smaller than the maximal one. Recently, a distributed *randomized* algorithm for multi-broadcast has been presented [18] for uniform networks. Although the problem solved in that paper is a generalization of a broadcast, the presented solution needs the power control mechanism and it is restricted to networks having the communication graph connected for $\varepsilon = \frac{2}{3}r$, where r is the largest possible range. Moreover, spontaneous wake-up of stations is necessary in their algorithm. In contrast, our solutions are efficient and scalable for *any* networks with communication graph connected for *any* value of $\varepsilon < \frac{1}{2}$.[2] Moreover, we do not use the power control mechanism. On the other hand, unlike ours, the algorithm from [18] works even if stations do not know their coordinates (or their estimates).

As shown recently [12], there exists an efficient *deterministic* broadcasting algorithm in the model considered in this paper. More precisely, it is worse than the best algorithm in this work by only a logarithmic factor. Independently, Daum et al. [4] proposed another randomized broadcasting algorithm. Their solution works for a broader family of metrics (not only the Euclidean) and does not rely on the knowledge of coordinates by stations. However, the time complexity of this solution is poly-logarithmic with respect to the ratio R between longest and shortest distance between stations, and R might be even exponential with respect to the size n of a given network.

There is a vast amount of work on centralized algorithms under the classical SINR models. The most studied problems include connectivity, capacity maximization, and link scheduling types of problems; for recent results and references we refer the reader to the survey [9].

Radio Network Model. There are several papers analyzing broadcasting in the radio model of wireless networks, under which a message is successfully heard if

---

[2] In case of $\varepsilon \in [1/2, 1)$, one could take our algorithm for $\varepsilon' = 1/3$, which guarantees at least as good asymptotic performance.

there are no other simultaneous transmissions from the *neighbors* of the receiver in the communication graph. This model does not take into account the real strength of the received signals, and also the signals from outside of some close proximity.

The problem of broadcasting is well-studied in the setting of *graph radio model*, in which stations are not necessarily deployed in a metric space. The first efficient randomized solution was developed by Bar-Yehuda et al. [1], while the close lower bound was proved in [17]. The algorithms closing the gap between the upper and the lower bound appeared in [3,16]. Since the solutions for a graph model are quite efficient, there are only few studies of the problem restricted to the geometric setting. However, solutions for some other communication problems can be significantly faster in geometric (uniform) radio networks than in general ones [7]. There is also a vast literature on deterministic algorithms for broadcasting in graph and geometric radio models, c.f., [2,15,16,5,6].

1.4   Technical Preliminaries

In this section we formulate some properties and notation that simplify the specification and analysis of algorithms.

Message Content and Global Clock. In the broadcast problem, a round counter could be easily maintained by already informed nodes by passing it along the network with the source message, thus in all algorithms we may in fact assume having a global clock. For simplicity of analysis, we also assume that every message sent during the execution of our broadcast protocols contains the broadcast message; in practice, further optimization of a message content could be done in order to reduce the total number of transmitted bits in real executions.

Successful Transmissions. We say that a station v transmits *c-successfully* in a round t if v transmits a message in round t and this message is heard by each station u in the Euclidean distance at most c from v. A station v transmits *successfully* to u in round t if v transmits a message and u receives this message in round t. We say that a station that received the broadcast message is *informed*.

Grids. Given a parameter $c > 0$, we define a partition of the 2-dimensional space into square boxes of size $c \times c$ by the grid G_c, in such a way that: all boxes are aligned with the coordinate axes, point $(0,0)$ is a grid point, each box includes its left side without the top endpoint and its bottom side without the right endpoint and does not include its right and top sides. We say that (i,j) are the coordinates of the box with its bottom left corner located at $(c \cdot i, c \cdot j)$, for $i,j \in \mathbb{Z}$. A box with coordinates $(i,j) \in \mathbb{Z}^2$ is denoted $C_c(i,j)$ or $C(i,j)$ when the side of a grid is clear from the context. In the following sections we will always refer to boxes of the grid G_γ, where γ is a parameter specific for a considered algorithm. For a station v, $box_c(v)$ (or simply $box(v)$) denotes the box of G_c containing v.

Dilution. For the tuples (i_1, i_2), (j_1, j_2) the relation $(i_1, i_2) \equiv (j_1, j_2) \mod d$ for $d \in \mathbb{N}$ denotes that $(|i_1 - i_2| \mod d) = 0$ and $(|j_1 - j_2| \mod d) = 0$. A set of stations A on the plane is *d-diluted* wrt G_c, for $d \in \mathbb{N} \setminus \{0\}$, if for any two stations $v_1, v_2 \in A$ with grid coordinates $G_c(v_1) = (i_1, j_1)$ and $G_c(v_2) = (i_2, j_2)$, respectively, the relationship $(i_1, i_2) \equiv (j_1, j_2) \mod d$ holds.

2   An Algorithm for Known Local Density

In this section we describe our broadcasting algorithm for networks of known local density, which makes use of some properties exploited e.g., in local broadcasting [8,10]. That is, every station v knows the total number of stations $\Delta = \Delta(v)$ in its box of the grid G_γ. In this section we assume $\gamma = \frac{\varepsilon}{2\sqrt{2}}$. Without loss of generality we can assume, that for some $k \in \mathbb{N}$ the equality $(2k + 1)\gamma = 2$ holds. This means that each box B from the grid G_γ lies in the center of some square 2×2 consisting of $(2k + 1)^2 = (2/\gamma)^2$ boxes of G_γ. We call this square the *superbox* $S(B)$ of B. Note that all stations in the distance at most $1 - \varepsilon/2$ from B are in $S(B)$.

Algorithm 1. RandBroadcast(Δ, d, T)   ▷ code for node v

1: the source s transmits
2: **for** *counter* $= 1, 2, 3, \ldots, T$ **do**
3:     **for** each $a, b : 0 \le a, b < d$ **do**
4:         **if** $v \in C(i, j) : (i, j) \equiv (a, b) \mod d$ **then**
5:             v transmits with probability $1/\Delta$

Analysis of Time Performance of RandBroadcast. We define *interference* at a station u with respect to the set of transmitters $\mathcal{T}$ as $\sum_{w \in \mathcal{T} \setminus \{v\}} P\mathrm{dist}(w, u)^{-\alpha}$, see Eq. (1). The boxes $C(i_1, j_1)$ and $C(i_2, j_2)$ are *connected* if there exist stations $v_1 \in C(i_1, j_1)$ and $v_2 \in C(i_2, j_2)$ such that (v_1, v_2) is an edge of the communication graph. We start with stating three general properties regarding interference in the SINR model.

Fact 1. *If the interference at the receiver is at most $\mathcal{N}\alpha x$, then it can hear the transmitter from the distance $1 - x$.*

Proof. By the Bernoulli inequality we get $(1 + x)^\alpha \ge 1 + \alpha x$. Thus

$$SINR \ge \frac{P}{(\mathcal{N} + \mathcal{N}\alpha x)(1 - x)^\alpha} \ge \frac{P}{\mathcal{N}(1 + x)^\alpha (1 - x)^\alpha}$$

$$= \frac{P}{\mathcal{N}(1 - x^2)^\alpha} \ge \frac{P}{\mathcal{N}} = \beta .$$

where the last equality follows from the assumption that the range of stations is equal to 1 which implies $\left(\frac{P}{\mathcal{N}\beta}\right)^{1/\alpha} = 1$.   □

We say that a function $d_{\alpha,Q} : \mathbb{N} \to \mathbb{N}$ is *flat* for $\alpha \geq 2$ and a (possibly empty) sequence of constant parameters Q if

$$d_{\alpha,Q}(n) = \begin{cases} O(1) & \text{for } \alpha > 2 \\ O((\log n)^{1/2}) & \text{for } \alpha = 2 \end{cases} \tag{2}$$

Let $C(a,b)$ be a box of G_γ. Assume that, in a given round of a randomized algorithm, only stations in superboxes $S(C(i,j))$ such that $(i,j) \equiv (a,b)$ mod d transmit. In each box the expected number of transmitting stations is at most 1. We denote by I_d the average maximum of the interference over superbox $S(C(a,b))$ from transmitting stations located outside $S(C(a,b))$:

$$I_d = E\left(\max_{u \in S(C(a,b))} \sum_{v \in \mathcal{T}, v \notin S(C(a,b))} P\mathrm{dist}(u,v)^{-\alpha} \right),$$

provided the algorithm uses the dilution parameter d.

Fact 2. *If in the above described process, the expected number of transmitting stations in a superbox does not exceed x instead of 1, then for any d we have the maximum expected interference in superbox $S(C(a,b))$ equal to $x \cdot I_d$.*

Let $s_\alpha(n) = \min\left\{ \frac{\ln n}{2} + \ln 2, \frac{1}{2^{\alpha-2}(\alpha-2)} \right\} + \frac{1}{2^\alpha(\alpha-1)}$ and $d_{\alpha,I,\gamma}(n) = \left\lceil \frac{1}{\gamma} \left(\frac{8Ps_\alpha(n)}{I} \right)^{1/\alpha} \right\rceil$.

Lemma 1. *For any $I > 0$ there exists a flat function d such that $I_d \leq I$. Moreover, for $I \leq \frac{8Ps_\alpha}{2^\alpha}$ we have $I_d \leq I$ when $d = d_{\alpha,I,\gamma}(n)$.*

We proceed with the analysis of algorithm RandBroadcast.

Fact 3. *Consider a round of algorithm RandBroadcast, different from the first one. The probability that in a box $(i,j) \equiv (a,b)$ exactly one station transmits is bigger than $1/e$.*

Fact 4. *Consider a round of algorithm RandBroadcast(Δ, d, T) for $d = d_{\alpha,\mathcal{N}\alpha\varepsilon/4,\gamma}$, different from the first one. The probability that exactly one station in box $C(i,j)$, where $(i,j) \equiv (a,b)$, transmits and the interference from other stations measured in all boxes connected with box $C(i,j)$ is smaller or equal to $\mathcal{N}\alpha\varepsilon/2$ is bigger than $\frac{1}{2e}$.*

Lemma 2. *Consider a Bernoulli scheme with success probability $p < 1 - \ln 2$. The probability of obtaining at most D successes in $2D/p + 2\ln(1/\delta)/p$ trials is smaller than $(D+1)\delta$.*

We say that a subset of nodes W of a graph G is an *l-net* if any other node in G is in distance at most l from the closest node in W.

Fact 5. *If G is of eccentricity D, then there exists a $(1-\varepsilon)$-net W of cardinality at most $4(D+1)^2$.*

Proof. Let $q = 1 - \varepsilon$. Ranges q of all the stations must be all inside the circle of radius $(D + 1)q$. The area of this circle is $\pi(D + 1)^2 q^2$. Let us greedily pick a maximal set of nodes such that any two nodes are in distance at least q. This set is a q-net W. Let us estimate the cardinality of W. All the circles of radius $q/2$ and center belonging to W are disjoint and have areas πq^2. They have total area at most $\pi(D + 1)^2 q^2$, so $|W| \leq 4(D + 1)^2$. $\square$

Using the above results we conclude the analysis.

Theorem 1. *Algorithm RandBroadcast(Δ, d, T) completes broadcast in any network in time $O(d^2(D + \log(1/\delta)))$ with probability $1 - \delta$, for $d = d_{\alpha, \mathcal{N}\alpha\varepsilon/4, \gamma}(n)$ and some $T = O(D + \log(1/\delta))$.*

Proof. To complete broadcasting it is enough that all the boxes containing stations of the $(1-\varepsilon)$-net W transmit the message $(1-\varepsilon/2)$-successfully at least once. This is done for box containing $v \in W$ if the message is $(1 - \varepsilon/2)$-successfully transmitted at most D times on the shortest path from the source s to v in G, and finally is successfully transmitted by the box(v). The sufficient condition for this to happen is that a chain of altogether at most $D + 1$ $(1 - \varepsilon/2)$-successful transmissions heard by all potential receivers occurs. In each round the probability of a successful transmission within this chain is bigger than $p = \frac{1}{2e}$, by Fact 4 (recall that Fact 4 uses our assumption $d = d_{\alpha, \mathcal{N}\alpha\varepsilon/4, \gamma}$).

Now we estimate the probability that algorithm RandBroadcast completes the broadcast. Let the number of trials be $T = 2D/p + 2\ln(1/\delta')/p$, for some $\delta' \in \mathbb{R}$. By Lemma 2, Fact 1 and Fact 5, the probability that box(v) transmits $(1 - \varepsilon/2)$-successfully for each $v \in W$

$$P \geq 1 - \sum_{v \in W} \Pr(\text{box}(v) \text{ doesn't transmit successfully}) \geq 1 - 4(D + 1)^3 \delta' \,.$$

This is bigger than $1 - \delta$ for our choice of T. Note also that $T = O(D + \log(1/\delta))$. Because we have a trial every d^2 rounds, we need altogether $O(d^2(D + \log(1/\delta)))$ rounds, for $d = d_{\alpha, \mathcal{N}\alpha\varepsilon/4, \gamma}$. $\square$

We would like also to point out that the knowledge of the density with respect to the grid G_γ (and not just with respect to some small neighborhood of a station) is essential for efficiency of Algorithm 1.

3   Algorithms for Unknown Local Density

In this section we describe our broadcasting algorithms for networks of unknown local density. First, we describe a simple almost oblivious algorithm, where the probability of transmitting a message by a station depends merely on the time when it receives the broadcast message for the first time, the current time slot and the fact whether it received a message from a station in its own box. Then, a more involved algorithm is presented which is slower than the (asymptotically optimal) solution for known density only by the multiplicative factor $O(\log n)$.

3.1 A Simple and Almost Oblivious Algorithm

In this section we present an almost oblivious algorithm based only on the size of a network and nodes positions up to a box in the grid G_γ, where here γ is set to $\varepsilon/(2\sqrt{2})$ and $\alpha > 2$. A computation of the algorithm is split into *phases*. A phase consists of $T \log n + R$ rounds, where T and R are some parameters which will be determined later. A station awakes when it receives a message for the first time and after that it is waiting by the end of the current phase. It becomes *active* in the following phase, when it executes Algorithm 2. However, if the station from a box B receives a message from another station in B in *any* round, it switches off and does not transmit any message in the remaining part of the algorithm. We call our algorithm Antibackoff, as each stations starts transmitting using small probabilities and then increases them gradually. This contrasts to classical backoff protocols, where stations are trying to transmit with large probabilities first and then decrease them gradually.

Algorithm 2. Antibackoff-Phase(n, T, R, d) ▷ code for node $v \in C(i, j) = B$

1: **if** at any time v receives a message from a station in B **then** switch off
2: **for** $i = 1, 2, 3, \ldots, \lceil \log n \rceil - 1$ **do**
3:     **for** $k = 1, 2, 3, \ldots, T$ **do**
4:        transmit with probability $\frac{2^i}{n}$
5: **for** $j = 1, 2, 3, \ldots, R$ **do**
6:     transmit with probability $\frac{1}{8(d+1)^2}$

We refer to iterations of the first loop in Algorithm 2 as to *stages*. The idea behind the algorithm Antibackoff is that the i-th stage deals with boxes containing around $n/2^{i-1}$ active stations by reducing the number of active stations in such boxes to no more than $n/2^i$. Thus, after the last stage, we expect that there is (exactly) one active station in each box containing an active station (at least one) at the beginning of a phase. Then, such a station is supposed to transmit $(1 - \varepsilon/2)$-successfully in the "for j" loop, thus transmitting the broadcast message *on behalf* of all stations from its box. Indeed, if a station v transmits $(1 - \varepsilon/2)$-successfully, then the message is received by all neighbors in the communication graph of all stations from the box containing v.

Now, we formulate some properties of Algorithm 2 which will conclude in Theorem 2 establishing its time complexity.

The following lemma limits the expected interference at a station caused by stations from distant boxes, provided there is an upper bound on the expected number of transmitters in the same box of G_γ. We define the max-distance between the boxes $C(i_1, i_2)$ and $C(j_1, j_2)$ as $\max\{|i_1 - j_1|, |i_2 - j_2|\}$.

Lemma 3. *Let $I_{B,k}$ be the maximal interference in a box $B = C(i, j)$ caused by boxes in max-distance at least $k+1$ from B under condition that expected number of transmitting station in every box is at most t and let $\kappa(t, x) = \lceil (8tP(\alpha - 1)/x(\alpha - 2)\gamma^\alpha)^{1/(\alpha-2)} \rceil + 1$ for $x > 0$. Then $E[I_{B,k}] \leq x$ for $k \geq \kappa(t, x)$.*

Now, we evaluate the probability that the number of active stations in each box is at most $n/2^i$ after the ith stage of a phase.

Fact 6. *The probability that at any phase, the number of active stations in any box after the i-th iteration of the first loop is at most $n/2^i$ is at least $1 - n \log n / \exp(T/2^{16c(c+1)+5})$, where $c = \kappa(2, \mathcal{N}\alpha(1 - \sqrt{2}\gamma)/2)$.*

The proof of the above fact is obtained by bounding the probability that, for a given box B, the following events appear simultaneously in a round of the ith stage:

- exactly one station from B is transmitting a message;
- no station from boxes within max-distance at most c from B is transmitting;
- maximal interference caused by stations from boxes at max-distance greater than c from B is at most $\mathcal{N}\alpha(1 - \sqrt{2}\gamma)$);

provided at least $n/2^i$ stations are active in B and at most $n/2^{i-1}$ stations are active in any other box.

While the previous fact deals with the progress in the process of eliminating stations from dense boxes, now we concentrate on the chance that a (station from a) box containing active stations transmits $(1 - \varepsilon/2)$-successfully in the "for j" loop, provided there are no boxes with more than two active stations.

Fact 7. *Consider any phase K. Assume that, after the first loop of phase K, every box has at most two active stations. Let r be the probability that, for every box B with active stations in phase K, every station connected by an edge with a station $v \in B$ in G will receive a message from some station in B. Then, r is at least $1 - n/\exp(R/64(d + 1)^2)$ with $d = \kappa(2, \mathcal{N}\alpha\varepsilon/4)$.*

By combining the above facts, we obtain a time bound of the algorithm.

Theorem 2. *Algorithm Antibackoff(n, d, T, R) completes broadcast in any n-node network in time $O(D \log n\ (\log n + \log(1/\delta)))$ with probability at least $1 - \delta$, for some $T, R \in O(\log n + \log(1/\delta))$ and $d = \kappa(2, \mathcal{N}\alpha\varepsilon/4)$.*

Proof. If events from Fact 6 and Fact 7 occur during an execution of the algorithm, then the maximal number of phases needed for the message to be heard by every station is at most D, since after the K-th phase every node within distance K from the source (in the communication graph) receives the message. Let $c = \kappa(2, \mathcal{N}\alpha(1 - \sqrt{2}\gamma)/2)$. One can easily verify that choosing $R \geq 64(d + 1)^2(\ln n + \ln(1/\delta_1))$ and $T \geq 2^{16c(c+1)+5}(\ln n + \ln(1/\delta_2))$, the probability that one of the events did not occur is smaller than $\delta_1 + \delta_2$. With $\delta_1 = \delta_2 = \delta/2$, the probability of successful transmission in time $O(D \log n(\log n + \log(1/\delta)))$ is at least $1 - \delta$. □

3.2   A Fast Algorithm with Local Leader Election

In this section we describe our broadcasting algorithm for networks of unknown local density. To construct this algorithm we consider the grid G_γ, where $\gamma =$

$\frac{\varepsilon}{6\sqrt{2}}$. For further references observe that this choice of γ satisfies the following property. Let B and $U = C(i,j)$ be boxes of G_γ and let $v \in B, u \in U$, $(u,v) \in E(G)$ for some nodes u and v. In such a case, if any node $v' \in B$ transmits $(1 - \varepsilon/2)$-successfully, then its message is received by all stations in all boxes $C(i+a, j+b)$, where $a, b \in [-2, 2]$.

We say that two boxes B and U are *adjacent* if the Euclidean distance between any two of their points is at most $1 - \varepsilon/2$. But with one exception – boxes that are very close to each other are not adjacent. More precisely the box $C(i,j)$ is not adjacent to any box $C(i+a, j+b)$, where $a, b \in [-2, 2]$. Note that if $(u,v) \in E(G)$ and $v \in B, u \in U = C(i,j)$, then any two points $x \in B$ and $y \in C(i+a, j+b), a, b \in [-2, 2]$ are in the Euclidean distance at most $1 - \varepsilon/2$; that is, B is adjacent to all boxes $C(i+a, j+b)$, unless these boxes are also very close to B. The *neighborhood* of a box B is the set of all boxes U adjacent to B. This definition guarantees that each station $v \in B$ is connected by an edge with each station $u \in U$ if U is in the neighborhood of B. However, the Euclidean distance $\mathrm{dist}(v,u)$ for such u, v is larger than the distance between v and any other station from B. This property is essential for our method of electing leaders in boxes of G_γ.

To formulate the algorithm we define an *octant* of the neighborhood of the box $B = C(i,j)$. Let us place on the plane a Cartesian coordinate system with the origin in the center of the box B. This coordinate system is naturally subdivided into four *quadrants* i.e. the plane areas bounded by two reference axes forming the $90°$ angle. The quadrant can be divided by the bisector of this angle into two *octants* corresponding to the angle of $45°$. We attribute one of the rays forming the boundaries of the octants to each octant, so that they are disjoint (and connected) as the subsets of the plane. An *octant* of the neighborhood of B is the set of all boxes U in the neighborhood of B that have centers in a given octant of the coordinate system.

Fact 8. *Each two stations in an octant of the neighborhood of a box B are in the distance at most $(1 - \varepsilon/2)$.*

Now we give an intuition how Algorithm 3 works. A station v joins the execution of the algorithm after obtaining the broadcast message (waking up); it can learn the number of executed rounds of the algorithm from the value of the clock attached to each message. The algorithm consists of T iterations of the most external loop. Each of these iterations consists of two parts. The first part is a deterministic broadcast from the leaders of the boxes to all nodes in the distance at most $1 - \varepsilon/2$ from these leaders. It is assumed that new nodes are woken up only in the very beginning and in this first part. The second part is a probabilistic algorithm attempting to elect the leaders in all the boxes in which the message was heard in the first part and which currently do not have leaders.

Now, let us fix the values of parameters for which the algorithm will by analyzed. Let $d = d_{\alpha, \mathcal{N}\alpha\varepsilon/2, \gamma}$ which assures that, in the first "**for** each a, b", loop each leader is heard in the distance $1 - \varepsilon/2$. Moreover, we take $\bar{d} = d_{\alpha, \mathcal{N}\alpha\varepsilon/28, \gamma}$. This choice guarantees that, if there are on average less than 7 transmitting stations

Algorithm 3. RandUnknownBroadcast(d, T)

1: the source s transmits and becomes the leader of its box of G_γ
2: **for** counter $\leftarrow 1, 2, \ldots, T$ **do**
3:     **for** each $a, b : 0 \le a, b < d$ **do**
4:         **if** v is the leader of $C(i, j)$ such that $(i, j) \equiv (a, b) \mod d$ **then** v transmits
5:     **for** each $a, b : 0 \le a, b < \bar{d}$ **do**
6:         **for** each octant of neighborhood of each $B = C(i, j)$ fulfilling
7:             $(i, j) \equiv (a, b) \mod \bar{d}$ **do**
8:             $u \leftarrow$ the leader of the box with lexicographically smallest
9:                 coordinates in the octant
10:            **for** each $v \in B$: conflict(v) $\leftarrow$ false
11:            **for** $k = 0, 1, 2, 3, \ldots, \log n$ **do**
12:                **if** B has no leader, u exists and not conflict(v) **then**
13:                    K1: Each vertex $v \in B$ transmits with the probability $(1/n)2^k$
14:                    K2: **if** u hears v in K1 **then**
15:                        u transmits "v" and v becomes the leader
16:                        **if** v transmitted in K1 and hears nothing in K2 **then**
17:                            conflict(v) $\leftarrow$ true
18:                    K3: nodes v transmitting in K1 and u transmit
19:                        **if** v not transmitting in K1 does not hear u **then**
20:                            conflict(v) $\leftarrow$ true

attributed to each box $C(i', j')$ in the second loop "**for** each a, b", then we have the probability at least $1/2$ that the only station transmitting for $C(i, j)$ does it $(1 - \varepsilon/2)$-successfully. We prove that, during the second part, the probability of electing a leader is bigger than some constant. This is done for each octant in the "**for** k" loop and the result is either selecting the leader of B or silencing all stations in B till the end of this loop (in order to decrease interference in other boxes). To make such an attempt some help from the leader u of a box U adjacent to B is needed. Within an octant the leaders hear each other in the first part, so they all can determine without any additional communication which of them has lexicographically smallest coordinates. Also any node in B knows whether any leader in the octant exists. Let us emphasize here that the second loop lasts $8 \cdot 3 \cdot \bar{d}^2(1 + \log n)$ rounds, since we try to elect a leader in each $B = C(i, j)$ with help of leaders from various octants of its neighborhood separately.

In the loop "**for** k" the transmission probability in K1 grows twice per iteration starting from $1/n$. In rounds K2 and K3 stations from B are "switched off" till the end of the loop "**for** k". It is done in three cases. The first case is when the external noise causes this "switching off" (v cannot hear u in K3). We show that the probability that any stations in B is switched off this way in the whole "**for** k" loop is smaller than $1/2$. In the second case the leader is chosen, because u hears some station transmitting in K1. The station u then notifies deterministically all the stations in B who the leader is. In the third case many stations of B transmit in K1 which causes "switching off" all stations in B.

We now show, that if in some step K1 at least one station of B transmits, then after K3 all stations in B are "switched off". We already considered the case when u hears some of them and the leader is elected. So now assume, that u does not hear anything in K1. Note, that in K2 all stations v transmitting in K1 get the value conflict equal true. In K3 any station v not transmitting in K1 is closer to any of the transmitting stations in B than to u (this fact follows from the properties of neighborhood). So v does not hear u and gets the value conflict equal true.

The above discussion gives the following conclusion.

Fact 9. *Let l be the first round K1 of loop "for k" in which some station from a box B transmits a message. Then in the next rounds K2 and K3 either the leader is elected or all stations $v \in B$ set conflict$(v) =$true.*

Now we formulate an analog of Fact 5 for our algorithm.

Lemma 4. *Let G be of eccentricity D. There exists a set of boxes W of the grid G_γ of cardinality at most $4(D+1)^2$ having the two following properties*

(i) if we choose one station from each box of W then these stations form a $(1 - \varepsilon/2)$-net in the set of all the stations,
(ii) for each box B of W there exists a sequence of at most $D+1$ nonempty (i.e., containing stations) boxes, starting from box(s) and ending in B, in which each two consecutive boxes are adjacent.

In what follows, we estimate what is the average maximal number of stations transmitting in the box $C(i,j)$, then we bound the probability of successful leader election in a single call of the loop "**for** k", and finally we conclude the analysis of algorithm RandUnknownBroadcast.

Fact 10. *The expected value of the maximum number of stations transmitting in the box $C(i,j)$ in round K1 during one call of the loop "for k" is at most 6.*

Fact 11. *Assume that at least one station from a box $C(i,j)$ is awaken in the first "for each (a,b)" loop. Then, the probability, that in one call of the loop "for k" the leader of the box $C(i,j)$ is elected is at least $1/18$.*

Theorem 3. *Algorithm RandUnknownBroadcast(d,T) accomplishes broadcast in $O(\bar{d}^2(D + \log(1/\delta))\log n)$ rounds, with probability $1 - \delta$, when run for $d = d_{\alpha,\mathcal{N}\alpha\varepsilon/2,\gamma}, \bar{d} = d_{\alpha,\mathcal{N}\alpha\varepsilon/28,\gamma}$ and for some $T = O(D + \log(1/\delta))$.*

Proof. Let W be a set of boxes satisfying the properties (i) and (ii) from Lemma 4. A sufficient condition for the broadcast is that each box of $B \in W$ obtains the message and broadcasts it at least once to all stations in the range $1 - \varepsilon/2$. (We say that a box *obtains* a message when at least one station in that box receives it, and a box *broadcasts* a message in a particular range r_0 when at least one of its stations transmits the message r_0-successfully.) This happens, when the message is successfully transmitted at most D times on the shortest sequence of boxes from the source to B and finally is successfully transmitted by the box B.

The sufficient condition for this is that a chain of altogether at most D successful leader elections happen. The probability of such a successful leader election is, by Fact 11, at least $p = 1/18$.

Now we estimate the probability that our algorithm completes the broadcast. Let the number of repetitions of the most external loop be $t = 2D/p + 2\ln(1/\delta')/p$, for some $\delta' \in \mathbb{R}$. By Lemma 2,

$$\Pr(\text{some } B \in W \text{ does not transmit successfully}) \leq$$

$$\leq \sum_{B \in W} \Pr(\text{box } B \text{ does not transmit successfully}) \leq 4(D+1)^2\delta' .$$

To get this probability smaller than δ we need the number of repetitions of the most external loop

$$T = \frac{2D}{p} + \frac{2\ln(1/\delta)}{p} + \frac{2\ln(4(D+1))}{p} = O(D + \log(1/\delta)) .$$

Each run of the most external loop takes $O(\bar{d}^2 \log n)$ rounds, which yields $O(\bar{d}^2(D + \log(1/\delta)) \log n)$ rounds in total. □

4   Conclusions and Future Work

In this work we showed provably well-scalable randomized distributed solutions for the broadcast problem in any wireless networks under the SINR physical model without spontaneous wake-up and without strong assumptions about the connectivity of a given network. Our algorithms rely on the knowledge of its own coordinates by each station; some results without such knowledge were obtained in [4]. We develop a new technique for fast election of local leaders in any network, which may be adopted for the purpose of other communication problems.

Our solutions could be extended to more generalized model settings. In particular, nodes do not have to know their exact coordinates, but only with some $O(\epsilon)$ accuracy. Parameters $\alpha \geq 2$ and $\beta \geq 1$ can be set up individually for every link, which would only change constants hidden in the big-Oh formulas (these constants would depend on the upper and lower bounds on the range of individual parameters α, β). The knowledge of exact number of stations n is also not necessary — an upper bound $O(n)$ is enough to obtain asymptotically the same results.

There are several interesting directions arising from or related with our work. The main one is to extend the proposed approach to other communication problems, such as multi-broadcast, gathering, group communication and routing. The second interesting direction is to study the impact of model setting, such as knowledge of coordinates (or other parameters), or the quality parameter $1 - \epsilon$ of the communication graph on the complexity of a communication task. Finally, analyzing algorithms in more advanced models, e.g., with failures, mobility, or other forms of uncertainty, is another perspective research direction.

References

1. Bar-Yehuda, R., Goldreich, O., Itai, A.: On the Time-Complexity of Broadcast in Multi-hop Radio Networks: An Exponential Gap Between Determinism and Randomization. J. Comput. Syst. Sci 45(1), 104–126 (1992)
2. Chrobak, M., Gasieniec, L., Rytter, W.: Fast broadcasting and gossiping in radio networks. J. Algorithms 43(2), 177–189 (2002)
3. Czumaj, A., Rytter, W.: Broadcasting algorithms in radio networks with unknown topology. In: FOCS, pp. 492–501 (2003)
4. Daum, S., Gilbert, S., Kuhn, F., Newport, C.: Broadcast in the ad hoc SINR model. In: Afek, Y. (ed.) DISC 2013. LNCS, vol. 8205, pp. 358–372. Springer, Heidelberg (2013)
5. Dessmark, A., Pelc, A.: Broadcasting in geometric radio networks. J. Discrete Algorithms 5(1), 187–201 (2007)
6. Emek, Y., Kantor, E., Peleg, D.: On the effect of the deployment setting on broadcasting in euclidean radio networks. In: PODC, pp. 223–232 (2008)
7. Farach-Colton, M., Fernandez Anta, A., Mosteiro, M.A.: Optimal memory-aware Sensor Network Gossiping (or how to break the Broadcast lower bound). Theor. Comput. Sci. 472, 60–80 (2013)
8. Goussevskaia, O., Moscibroda, T., Wattenhofer, R.: Local broadcasting in the physical interference model. In: Segal, M., Kesselman, A. (eds.) DIALM-POMC, pp. 35–44.ACM (2008)
9. Goussevskaia, O., Pignolet, Y.A., Wattenhofer, R.: Efficiency of wireless networks: Approximation algorithms for the physical interference model. Foundations and Trends in Networking 4(3), 313–420 (2010)
10. Halldorsson, M.M., Mitra, P.: Towards tight bounds for local broadcasting. In: FOMC 2012, p. 2 (2012)
11. Jurdzinski, T., Kowalski, D.R., Stachowiak, G.: Distributed Deterministic Broadcasting in Wireless Networks of Weak Devices. In: Fomin, F.V., Freivalds, R., Kwiatkowska, M., Peleg, D. (eds.) ICALP 2013, Part II. LNCS, vol. 7966, pp. 632–644. Springer, Heidelberg (2013)
12. Jurdzinski, T., Kowalski, D.R., Stachowiak, G.: Distributed Deterministic Broadcasting in Uniform-Power Ad Hoc Wireless Networks. In: Gąsieniec, L., Wolter, F. (eds.) FCT 2013. LNCS, vol. 8070, pp. 195–209. Springer, Heidelberg (2013)
13. Kesselheim, T.: Dynamic packet scheduling in wireless networks. In: PODC, pp. 281–290 (2012)
14. Kesselheim, T., Vöcking, B.: Distributed contention resolution in wireless networks. In: Lynch, N.A., Shvartsman, A.A. (eds.) DISC 2010. LNCS, vol. 6343, pp. 163–178. Springer, Heidelberg (2010)
15. Kowalski, D.R.: On selection problem in radio networks. In: Aguilera, M.K., Aspnes, J. (eds.) PODC, pp. 158–166. ACM (2005)
16. Kowalski, D.R., Pelc, A.: Broadcasting in undirected ad hoc radio networks. Distributed Computing 18(1), 43–57 (2005)
17. Kushilevitz, E., Mansour, Y.: An omega($d \log (n/d)$) lower bound for broadcast in radio networks. SIAM J. Comput. 27(3), 702–712 (1998)
18. Yu, D., Hua, Q.-S., Wang, Y., Tan, H., Lau, F.C.M.: Distributed multiple-message broadcast in wireless ad-hoc networks under the SINR model. In: Even, G., Halldórsson, M.M. (eds.) SIROCCO 2012. LNCS, vol. 7355, pp. 111–122. Springer, Heidelberg (2012)
19. Yu, D., Wang, Y., Hua, Q.-S., Lau, F.C.M.: Distributed local broadcasting algorithms in the physical interference model. In: DCOSS, pp. 1–8. IEEE (2011)

Asynchronous Multiparty Computation with Linear Communication Complexity[*]

Ashish Choudhury[1,**], Martin Hirt[2], and Arpita Patra[1,***]

[1] University of Bristol, UK
{ashish.choudhary,arpita.patra}@bristol.ac.uk
[2] ETH Zurich, Switzerland
hirt@inf.ethz.ch

Abstract. Secure multiparty computation (MPC) allows a set of n parties to securely compute a function of their private inputs against an adversary corrupting up to t parties. Over the previous decade, the communication complexity of *synchronous* MPC protocols could be improved to $\mathcal{O}(n)$ per multiplication, for various settings. However, designing an *asynchronous* MPC (AMPC) protocol with linear communication complexity was not achieved so far. We solve this open problem by presenting two AMPC protocols with the corruption threshold $t < n/4$. Our first protocol is *statistically* secure (i.e. involves a negligible error) in a completely asynchronous setting and improves the communication complexity of the previous best AMPC protocol in the same setting by a factor of $\Theta(n)$. Our second protocol is *perfectly* secure (i.e. error free) in a *hybrid* setting, where one round of communication is assumed to be synchronous, and improves the communication complexity of the previous best AMPC protocol in the hybrid setting by a factor of $\Theta(n^2)$.

Like other efficient MPC protocols, we employ Beaver's circuit randomization approach (Crypto '91) and prepare shared random multiplication triples. However, in contrast to previous protocols where triples are prepared by first generating two random shared values which are then multiplied distributively, in our approach each party prepares its own multiplication triples. Given enough such shared triples (potentially partially known to the adversary), we develop a method to extract shared triples unknown to the adversary, avoiding communication-intensive multiplication protocols. This leads to a framework of independent interest.

1 Introduction

Threshold unconditionally secure multiparty computation (MPC) is a powerful concept in secure distributed computing. It enables a set of n mutually distrusting parties to jointly and securely compute a publicly known function f of their private inputs over some finite field $\mathbb{F}$, even in the presence of a *computationally unbounded*

---

[*] Full version of the paper available as Cryptology ePrint Archive, Report 2012/517.
[**] This work has been supported in part by EPSRC via grant EP/I03126X.
[***] Work supported by ERC Advanced Grant ERC-2010-AdG-267188-CRIPTO.

Y. Afek (Ed.): DISC 2013, LNCS 8205, pp. 388–402, 2013.
© Springer-Verlag Berlin Heidelberg 2013

active adversary Adv, capable of corrupting any t out of the n parties. In a general MPC protocol [7,12,20,2], f is usually expressed as an arithmetic circuit (consisting of addition and multiplication gates) over $\mathbb{F}$ and then the protocol evaluates each gate in the circuit in a shared/distributed fashion. More specifically, each party secret share its private inputs among the parties using a linear secret-sharing scheme (LSS), say Shamir [21], with threshold t; informally such a scheme ensures that the shared value remains information-theoretically secure even if upto t shares are revealed. The parties then maintain the following invariant for each gate in the circuit: *given that the input values of the gate are secret-shared among the parties, the corresponding output value of the gate also remains secret-shared among the parties.* Finally the circuit output is publicly reconstructed. Intuitively, the privacy follows since each intermediate value during the circuit evaluation remains secret-shared. Due to the *linearity* of the LSS, the addition gates are evaluated *locally* by the parties. However, maintaining the above invariant for the multiplication (non-linear) gates requires the parties to interact. The focus therefore is rightfully placed on measuring the communication complexity (i.e. the total number of elements from $\mathbb{F}$ communicated) to evaluate the multiplication gates in the circuit.

In the recent past, several efficient unconditionally secure MPC protocols have been proposed [17,3,14,5,9]. The state of the art unconditionally secure MPC protocols have *linear* (i.e. $\mathcal{O}(n)$ field elements) *amortized* communication complexity per multiplication gate for both the *perfect* setting [5] as well as for the *statistical* setting [9]. The amortized communication complexity is derived under the assumption that the circuit is large enough so that the terms that are independent of the circuit size can be ignored [9]. Moreover, these protocols have the *optimal resilience* of $t < n/3$ and $t < n/2$ respectively. The significance of linear communication complexity roots from the fact that the amortized communication done by *each* party for the evaluation of a multiplication gate is *independent* of n. This makes the protocol "scalable" in the sense that the communication done by an individual party does not grow with the number of parties in the system. We note that if one is willing to reduce the resilience t from the optimal resilience by a constant fraction of t, then by using techniques like packed secret-sharing [16], one can break the $\mathcal{O}(n)$ barrier as shown in [13]. However, the resultant protocols are quiet involved. An alternate approach to break the $\mathcal{O}(n)$ barrier was presented in [15], where instead of involving all the n parties, only a designated set of $\Theta(\log n)$ parties are involved for shared evaluation of each gate. However the protocol involves a negligible error in the privacy; on contrary we are interested in protocols with no error in the privacy.

Our Motivation. The above results are obtained in the *synchronous* network setting, where the delay of every message in the network is bounded by a known constant. However, it is well-known that such networks do not appropriately model the real-life networks like the Internet. On contrary, in the asynchronous network model [6], there are no timing assumptions and the messages can be arbitrarily delayed. The protocols in the asynchronous model are much more involved due to the following phenomenon, which is impossible to avoid in a completely asynchronous setting: if a party does not receive an expected message, then it does not know whether the sender is corrupted (and did not send the message at all) or the message is just delayed in the network. Thus, at any "stage" of an asynchronous protocol, no party can afford to listen the communication from all the n parties, as the wait may turn out to be endless and so the communication from t (potentially honest) parties has to be ignored. It is well known that perfectly-secure asynchronous MPC (AMPC) is possible if and only if $t < n/4$ [6], while statistically secure AMPC is possible if and only if $t < n/3$ [8]. The best known unconditional AMPC protocol is reported in [19]. The protocol is perfectly secure with resilience $t < n/4$ and communication complexity of $\mathcal{O}(n^2)$ per multiplication gate. Designing AMPC protocols with linear communication complexity per multiplication gate is the focus of this paper.

Our Results. We present two AMPC protocols with (amortized) communication complexity of $\mathcal{O}(n)$ field elements per multiplication gate and with resilience $t < n/4$. The first protocol is statistically secure and works in a completely asynchronous setting. Though non-optimally resilient, the protocol is the first AMPC protocol with linear communication complexity per multiplication gate. Our second protocol trades the network model to gain perfect security with optimal resilience of $t < n/4$. The protocol is designed in a *hybrid* setting, that allows a single synchronous round at the beginning, followed by a fully asynchronous setting. The hybrid setting was exploited earlier in [4] to enforce "input provision", i.e. to consider the inputs of all the n parties for the computation, which is otherwise impossible in a completely asynchronous setting. The best known AMPC protocol in the hybrid setting [4] has perfect security, resilience $t < n/4$ and communication complexity of $\mathcal{O}(n^3)$ field elements per multiplication gate. Thus, our protocol significantly improves over the hybrid model protocol of [4].

2   Overview of Our Protocols

Without loss of generality, we assume $n = 4t + 1$; thus $t = \Theta(n)$. We follow the well-known "offline-online" paradigm used in most of the recent MPC protocols [3,4,14,5,9]: the offline phase produces t-sharing[1] of c_M random *multiplication triples* $\{(a^{(i)}, b^{(i)}, c^{(i)})\}_{i \in [c_M]}$ unknown to Adv, where $c^{(i)} = a^{(i)}b^{(i)}$ and c_M denotes the number of multiplication gates in the circuit. The multiplication triples are *independent* of f; so this phase can be executed well ahead of the actual circuit evaluation. Later, during the online phase the shared triples are used for the shared evaluation of the multiplication gates in the circuit, using the standard Beaver's circuit randomization technique [2] (see Sec. 4). The efficiency of the MPC protocol is thus reduced to the efficiency of generating shared random multiplication triples. Our new proposed approach for the task of generating random triples outperforms the existing ones in terms of the efficiency and simplicity.

The traditional way of generating the shared multiplication triples is the following: first the individual parties are asked to t-share random *pairs* of values

---

[1] A value v is d-shared (see Definition 1) if there exists a polynomial $p(\cdot)$ of degree at most d with $p(0) = v$ and every party holds a distinct point on $p(\cdot)$.

on which a "randomness extraction" algorithm (such as the one based on Vandermonde matrix [14]) is applied to generate t-sharing of "truly" random pairs $\{a^{(i)}, b^{(i)}\}_{i \in [c_M]}$. Then known multiplication protocols are invoked to compute t-sharing of $\{c^{(i)}\}_{i \in [c_M]}$. Instead, we find it a more natural approach to ask individual parties to "directly" share random multiplication triples and then "extract" random multiplication triples unknown to Adv from the triples shared by the individual parties. This leads to a communication efficient, simple and more natural "framework" to generate the triples, built with the following modules:

- **Multiplication Triple Sharing (Section 7.1).** The first module allows a party P_i to "verifiably" t-share $\Theta(n)$ random multiplication triples with $\mathcal{O}(n^2)$ communication complexity and thus requires $\mathcal{O}(n)$ "overhead". The verifiability ensures that the shared triples are indeed multiplication triples. If P_i is *honest*, the shared triples remain private from Adv. Such triples, shared by the individual parties are called *local* triples.
- **Multiplication Triple Extraction (Section 7.2).** The second module allows the parties to securely extract $\Theta(n)$ t-shared random multiplication triples unknown to Adv from a set of $3t+1$ local t-shared multiplication triples with $\mathcal{O}(n^2)$ communication complexity (and thus with $\mathcal{O}(n)$ "overhead"), provided that at least $2t + 1$ out of the $3t + 1$ local triples are shared by the *honest* parties (and hence are random and private). We stress that known techniques for extracting shared *random values* from a set of shared random and non-random values fail to extract shared *random multiplication triples* from a set of shared random and non-random multiplication triples.

For our first module, we present two protocols: the first one *probabilistically* verifies the correctness of the shared multiplication triples, leading to our statistical AMPC protocol. The second protocol verifies the shared multiplication triples in an *error-free* fashion in a hybrid setting, leading to our perfectly-secure hybrid AMPC protocol. For the second module, we present an *error-free* triple-extraction protocol. We do not employ (somewhat complex) techniques like *player elimination* [17,5] and *dispute control* [3,14,9] in our protocols. These techniques have been used in the most recent synchronous unconditional MPC protocols to obtain linear complexity. Briefly, these techniques suggest to carry out a computation optimistically first assuming no corruption will take place and in case corruption occurs, fault/dispute is detected and memorized so that the same fault/dispute does not cause failure in the subsequent computation. However, their applicability is yet to be known in the asynchronous setting. Central to our protocols lie the following two building blocks.

Verifiable Secret Sharing with Linear Overhead (Section 5): We propose a *robust asynchronous verifiable secret sharing* (AVSS) protocol that allows a *dealer* D to "verifiably" t-share $(t + 1) = \Theta(n)$ secret values with $\mathcal{O}(n^2)$ communication complexity (i.e. $\mathcal{O}(n)$ overhead). The protocol is obtained by modifying the perfectly-secure AVSS protocol of [19] that allows D to 2t-share a *single* value. To the best of our knowledge, we are unaware of any robust secret-sharing protocol (with $t < n/4$) having linear overhead, even in the synchronous setting.

Transforming Independent Triples to Co-related Triples with Linear Overhead (Section 6): Taking $3t + 1 = \Theta(n)$ t-shared input triples (which may not be multiplication triples), say $\{(x^{(i)}, y^{(i)}, z^{(i)})\}_{i \in [3t+1]}$, the protocol outputs $3t + 1$ t-shared triples, say $\{(\mathbf{x}^{(i)}, \mathbf{y}^{(i)}, \mathbf{z}^{(i)})\}_{i \in [3t+1]}$, lying on three polynomials of degree $3t/2$, $3t/2$ and $3t$ respectively. Namely, there exist polynomials $X(\cdot), Y(\cdot)$ and $Z(\cdot)$ of degree at most $\frac{3t}{2}, \frac{3t}{2}$ and $3t$ respectively, where $X(\alpha_i) = \mathbf{x}^{(i)}, Y(\alpha_i) = \mathbf{y}^{(i)}$ and $Z(\alpha_i) = \mathbf{z}^{(i)}$ holds for $3t + 1$ distinct α_i values. The protocol has communication complexity $\mathcal{O}(n^2)$ (i.e. $\mathcal{O}(n)$ overhead). The protocol further ensures the following one-to-one correspondence between the input and the output triples: **(1).** the ith output triple is a *multiplication triple* if and only if the ith input triple is a multiplication triple; **(2).** the ith output triple is known to Adv if and only if the ith input triple is known to Adv. The former guarantees that the relation $Z(\cdot) = X(\cdot)Y(\cdot)$ is true if and only if all the $3t + 1$ input triples are multiplication triples, while the later guarantees that if Adv knows t' input triples, then it implies $\frac{3t}{2} + 1 - t'$ "degree of freedom" in the polynomials $X(\cdot), Y(\cdot)$ and $Z(\cdot)$, provided $t' \leq \frac{3t}{2}$. The protocol is borrowed from the batch verification protocol of [9], where the goal was to *probabilistically* check whether a set of input triples are multiplication triples.

Given the above two building blocks, our first module (of the framework) is realized by asking each party P_i to invoke the AVSS protocol to generate t-sharing of $3t + 1$ random multiplication triples $\{(x^{(i)}, y^{(i)}, z^{(i)})\}_{i \in [3t+1]}$. All that is left is to verify if the shared triples are indeed multiplication triples. This is achieved by transforming the shared triples to $\{(\mathbf{x}^{(i)}, \mathbf{y}^{(i)}, \mathbf{z}^{(i)})\}_{i \in [3t+1]}$ using the triple transformation protocol and then verifying if $Z(\cdot) \stackrel{?}{=} X(\cdot)Y(\cdot)$ where $X(\cdot), Y(\cdot)$ and $Z(\cdot)$ are the underlying polynomials, associated with $\{(\mathbf{x}^{(i)}, \mathbf{y}^{(i)}, \mathbf{z}^{(i)})\}_{i \in [3t+1]}$. Two different methods are then proposed for the verification; one leads to our statistical AMPC and the other leads to our perfect AMPC in hybrid model.

The second module takes the set of $3t + 1$ *local* t-shared multiplication triples (verifiably shared by individual parties), say $\{(x^{(i)}, y^{(i)}, z^{(i)})\}_{i \in [3t+1]}$ such that at least $2t + 1$ of them are shared by the *honest* parties. Using our triple transformation protocol, shared multiplication triples $\{(\mathbf{x}^{(i)}, \mathbf{y}^{(i)}, \mathbf{z}^{(i)})\}_{i \in [3t+1]}$ are then computed. Since all the input triples are guaranteed to be multiplication triples, the relation $Z(\cdot) = X(\cdot)Y(\cdot)$ holds. Moreover, as Adv may know at most t input local triples, t output triples are leaked, leaving $\frac{t}{2}$ "degree of freedom" in the polynomials, which is used to extract $\frac{t}{2} = \Theta(n)$ random multiplication triples.

3   Model, Definitions and Notations

We assume a set $\mathcal{P} = \{P_1, \ldots, P_n\}$ of $n = 4t + 1$ parties, connected by pairwise private and authentic channels; here t is the number of parties which can be under the control of a computationally unbounded Byzantine adversary Adv. The adversary can force the corrupted parties to deviate in any arbitrary manner during the execution of a protocol. The communication channels are asynchronous allowing arbitrary, but finite delay (i.e. the messages will reach to their destination eventually). The order of the message delivery is decided by a *scheduler*; to model the worst case scenario, we assume that the scheduler is under the control of Adv. The scheduler can schedule the messages exchanged between the honest parties, without having access to the "contents" of these messages.

The function f to be computed is specified as an arithmetic circuit C over a finite field $\mathbb{F}$, where $|\mathbb{F}| > 2n$ and $\alpha_1, \ldots, \alpha_n, \beta_1, \ldots, \beta_n$ are publicly known distinct elements from $\mathbb{F}$. For our *statistical* AMPC protocol, we additionally require that $|\mathbb{F}| \geq n^2 \cdot 2^\kappa$, for a given error parameter κ, to bound the error probability by $2^{-\kappa}$. The circuit C consists of input, addition (linear), multiplication, random and output gates. We denote by c_M and c_R the number of multiplication and random gates in C respectively. Similar to [14,5], for the sake of efficiency, we evaluate $t+1$ multiplication gates at once in our AMPC protocol by applying the Beaver's method, assuming that the circuit is well-spread, with sufficiently many "independent" multiplication gates to evaluate in parallel. By $[X]$ we denote the set $\{1, \ldots, X\}$, while $[X, Y]$ with $Y \geq X$ denote the set $\{X, X+1, \ldots, Y\}$.

Definition 1 (d-sharing [3,4,14,5]). *A value $s \in \mathbb{F}$ is said to be d-shared among a set of parties $\overline{\mathcal{P}} \subseteq \mathcal{P}$ if every (honest) party $P_i \in \overline{\mathcal{P}}$ holds a share s_i of s, such that there exists a polynomial $p(\cdot)$ of degree at most d, where $p(0) = s$ and $p(\alpha_i) = s_i$ holds for every (honest) $P_i \in \overline{\mathcal{P}}$. The vector of shares corresponding to the (honest) parties in $\overline{\mathcal{P}}$ is called a d-sharing of s and denoted by $[s]_d^{\overline{\mathcal{P}}}$. A vector $S = (s^{(1)}, \ldots, s^{(\ell)})$ of ℓ values is said to be d-shared among a set of parties $\overline{\mathcal{P}}$ if each $s^{(l)} \in S$ is d-shared among the parties in $\overline{\mathcal{P}}$.*

We write $[s]_d$ (ignoring the superscript) to mean that s is d-shared among *all* the n parties. A standard property of d-sharings is its *linearity*: given sharings $[x^{(1)}]_d, \ldots, [x^{(\ell)}]_d$ and a publicly known linear function $g : \mathbb{F}^\ell \to \mathbb{F}^m$ w $g(x^{(1)}, \ldots, x^{(\ell)}) = (y^{(1)}, \ldots, y^{(m)})$, then $g([x^{(1)}]_d, \ldots, [x^{(\ell)}]_d) = ([y^{(1)}]_d, \ldots, [y^{(m)}]_d)$. By saying that the parties compute (locally) $([y^{(1)}]_d, \ldots, [y^{(m)}]_d) = g([x^{(1)}]_d, \ldots, [x^{(\ell)}]_d)$, we mean that every party P_i (locally) computes $(y_i^{(1)}, \ldots, y_i^{(m)}) = g(x_i^{(1)}, \ldots, x_i^{(\ell)})$, where $y_i^{(l)}$ and $x_i^{(l)}$ denotes the ith share of $y^{(l)}$ and $x^{(l)}$ respectively.

4   Existing Building Blocks

Private and Public Reconstruction of d-shared Values: Let $[v]_d^{\overline{\mathcal{P}}}$ be a d-sharing of v, shared through a polynomial $p(\cdot)$, where $d < |\overline{\mathcal{P}}| - 2t$. The *online error correction* (OEC) algorithm [6], based on the Reed-Solomon (RS) error-correction allows any designated party P_R to reconstruct $p(\cdot)$ and thus $v = p(0)$. We call the protocol as $\mathsf{OEC}(P_R, d, [v]_d^{\overline{\mathcal{P}}})$, which has communication complexity $\mathcal{O}(n)$. Moreover if P_R is *honest* then no additional information about v is leaked.

Let $\{[u^{(i)}]_d^{\overline{\mathcal{P}}}\}_{i \in [t+1]}$ be a set of d-shared values where $d < |\overline{\mathcal{P}}| - 2t$. The goal is to make *every* party in $\mathcal{P}$ reconstruct $\{u^{(i)}\}_{i \in [t+1]}$. This is achieved by protocol BatRecPubl with communication complexity $\mathcal{O}(n^2)$ by using the idea of "data expansion", based on RS codes, as used in [14,5].

Batch Multiplication of ℓ Pairs of t-shared Values Using Beaver's Technique: Beaver's circuit randomization method [2] is a well known method for securely computing $[x \cdot y]_t$ from $[x]_t$ and $[y]_t$, at the expense of two *public re-constructions*, using a *pre-computed* t-shared random multiplication triple (from the offline phase), say $([a]_t, [b]_t, [c]_t)$. For this, the parties first (locally) compute $[e]_t$ and $[d]_t$, where $[e]_t = [x]_t - [a]_t = [x - a]_t$ and $[d]_t = [y]_t - [b]_t = [y - b]_t$, followed by the public reconstruction of $e = (x - a)$ and $d = (y - b)$. Since the relation $xy = ((x - a) + a)((y - b) + b) = de + eb + da + c$ holds, the parties can locally compute $[xy]_t = de + e[b]_t + d[a]_t + [c]_t$, once d and e are publicly known. The above computation leaks no information about x and y if a and b are random and unknown to Adv. For the sake of efficiency, we will apply the Beaver's trick on a batch of ℓ pairs of t-shared values simultaneously, where $\ell \geq t + 1$. BatRecPubl is then used to efficiently perform the public reconstruction of the 2ℓ (e and d) values with a communication of $\mathcal{O}(\lceil \frac{2\ell}{t+1} \rceil \cdot n^2) = \mathcal{O}(n\ell)$ field elements. We call the protocol as BatchBeaver($\{([x^{(i)}]_t, [y^{(i)}]_t, [a^{(i)}]_t, [b^{(i)}]_t, [c^{(i)}]_t)\}_{i \in [\ell]}$).

Agreement on a Common Subset (ACS) and Asynchronous Broadcast: Protocol ACS [6,8] allows the (honest) parties to agree on a *common* subset Com of $(n - t)$ parties, who have correctly shared "values"; the values may be the inputs of the individual parties or a multiplication triple or a random value. The protocol has communication complexity $\mathcal{O}(\text{poly}(n))$.

Bracha's asynchronous broadcast protocol (called A-Cast) [10] allows a sender Sen $\in \mathcal{P}$ to send some message m identically to all the n parties. If Sen is *honest* then all the honest parties eventually terminate with output m. If Sen is *corrupted* and some *honest* party terminates with output m', then every other honest party eventually does the same. The protocol needs a communication of $\mathcal{O}(n^2|m|)$ for a message of size $|m|$. We say that P_i receives m from the broadcast of P_j if P_i outputs m in the instance of A-Cast where P_j is acting as Sen.

Generating a Random Value: Protocol Rand is a standard protocol to generate a uniformly random value and has communication complexity $\mathcal{O}(\text{poly}(n))$.

5 Verifiably Generating Batch of t-shared Values

We design a protocol called Sh, which allows a dealer D $\in \mathcal{P}$ to "verifiably" t-share ℓ values $\boldsymbol{S} = (s^{(1)}, \ldots, s^{(\ell)})$, where $\ell \geq t + 1$. The "verifiability" ensures that if the honest parties terminate the protocol then the output sharings are t-sharing. Moreover the shared secrets are private if D is *honest*. The protocol communicates $\mathcal{O}(n\ell)$ field elements and broadcasts $\mathcal{O}(n^2)$ field elements. We first explain the protocol assuming that $\boldsymbol{S}$ contains $t + 1$ secrets.

The starting point of Sh is the sharing protocol of the perfectly-secure AVSS scheme of [19]. The AVSS protocol of [19] enables D to $2t$-share (note the degree of sharing) a *single* secret s. The $2t$-sharing is achieved via a univariate polynomial $F(x, 0)$ of degree at most $2t$, where $F(x, y)$ is a random bi-variate polynomial of degree at most $2t$ in x and at most t in y (note the difference in degrees), such that $F(0, 0) = s$. Initially, D is asked to pick $F(x, y)$ and hand over the ith row polynomial $f_i(x)$ of degree at most $2t$ and the ith column polynomial

$g_i(y)$ of degree at most t to the party P_i, where $f_i(x) \stackrel{def}{=} F(x, \alpha_i)$ and $g_i(y) \stackrel{def}{=} F(\alpha_i, y)$. If the sharing protocol terminates, then it is ensured that there exists a bi-variate polynomial $F'(x, y)$ of degree at most $2t$ in x and at most t in y, such that every *honest* party P_j holds a column polynomial $g_j'(y)$ of degree at most t, where $g_j'(y) = F'(\alpha_j, y)$. This makes the secret $s' \stackrel{def}{=} F'(0, 0)$ to be $2t$-shared through the polynomial $f_0'(x)$ of degree at most $2t$ where $f_0'(x) \stackrel{def}{=} F'(x, 0)$ and every *honest* party P_j holds its share s_j' of the secret s', with $s_j' = f_0'(\alpha_j) = F'(\alpha_j, 0) = g_j'(0)$. For an *honest* D, $F'(x, y) = F(x, y)$ will hold and thus s will be $2t$-shared though the polynomial $f_0(x) \stackrel{def}{=} F(x, 0)$.

	$g_1(y)$	$\cdots$	$g_j(y)$	$\cdots$	$g_n(y)$		$g_{\beta_1}(y)$	$\cdots$	$g_{\beta_{t+1}}(y)$
$f_1(x)$	$F(\alpha_1, \alpha_1)$	$\cdots$	$F(\alpha_j, \alpha_1)$	$\cdots$	$F(\alpha_n, \alpha_1)$	$\Rightarrow$	$s_1^{(1)} = f_1(\beta_1)$	$\cdots$	$s_1^{(t+1)} = f_1(\beta_{t+1})$
$\cdots$									
$f_i(x)$	$F(\alpha_1, \alpha_i)$	$\cdots$	$F(\alpha_j, \alpha_i)$	$\cdots$	$F(\alpha_n, \alpha_i)$	$\Rightarrow$	$s_i^{(1)} = f_i(\beta_1)$	$\cdots$	$s_i^{(t+1)} = f_i(\beta_{t+1})$
$\cdots$									
$f_n(x)$	$F(\alpha_1, \alpha_n)$	$\cdots$	$F(\alpha_j, \alpha_n)$	$\cdots$	$F(\alpha_n, \alpha_n)$	$\Rightarrow$	$s_n^{(1)} = f_n(\beta_1)$	$\cdots$	$s_n^{(t+1)} = f_n(\beta_{t+1})$
$f_0(x)$	$s_1 = g_1(0)$	$\cdots$	$s_j = g_j(0)$	$\cdots$	$s_n = g_n(0)$		$[s^{(1)}]_t$	$\cdots$	$[s^{(t+1)}]_t$

$$[s]_{2t}, \; s = f_0(0)$$

$$s^{(1)} = g_{\beta_1}(0) \; \cdots \; s^{(t+1)} = g_{\beta_{t+1}}(0)$$

Fig. 1. Pictorial representation of the values distributed in the AVSS of [19] and protocol Sh. The polynomials $f_1(x), \ldots, f_n(x), g_1(y), \ldots, g_n(y)$ computed from the bi-variate polynomial $F(x, y)$ of degree at most $2t$ and t in x and y are distributed in both the protocols. In the AVSS protocol, s is $2t$-shared through the row polynomial $f_0(x)$ (shown in red color) of degree $2t$, while in Sh, $t + 1$ values $s^{(1)}, \ldots, s^{(t+1)}$ are t-shared through the column polynomials $g_{\beta_1}(y), \ldots, g_{\beta_{t+1}}(y)$ (shown in blue color) of degree t.

In the above sharing protocol of [19], we note that Adv's view leaves $(t+1)(2t+1) - t(2t+1) - t = (t+1)$ "degree of freedom" in $F(x, y)$ when D is *honest*. This is because Adv receives $t(2t+1) + t$ distinct points on $F(x, y)$ through the t row and column polynomials of the corrupted parties while $(t+1)(2t+1)$ distinct points are required to completely define $F(x, y)$. While [19] used the $t+1$ degree of freedom for a *single* $2t$-sharing by embedding a single secret in $F(x, y)$, we use it to create t-sharing of $t + 1$ different secrets by embedding $t + 1$ secrets in $F(x, y)$. Namely, given $t + 1$ secrets $S = (s^{(1)}, \ldots, s^{(t+1)})$, the dealer D in our protocol fixes $F(\beta_l, 0) = s^{(l)}$ for $l \in [t + 1]$, where $F(x, y)$ is otherwise a random polynomial of degree at most $2t$ in x and at most t in y. At the end, the goal is that the secret $s^{(l)}$ is t-shared among the parties through the polynomial $F(\beta_l, y)$ of degree at most t, which we denote by $g_{\beta_l}(y)$. As depicted in Fig. 1 (in blue color), an *honest* party P_i can compute its shares of the secrets in S by local computation on the polynomial $f_i(x) = F(x, \alpha_i)$. This follows from the fact that for $l \in [t + 1]$ the ith share $s_i^{(l)}$ of the secret $s^{(l)}$ satisfies $s_i^{(l)} = g_{\beta_l}(\alpha_i) = f_i(\beta_l)$.

So all that is left is to ensure that *every honest* P_i gets $f_i(x)$ in Sh protocol. For this recall that the sharing protocol of [19] ensures that every *honest* P_j holds $g'_j(y)$ such that there exists a bi-variate polynomial $F'(x,y)$ of degree at most $2t$ in x and at most t in y where $F'(\alpha_j, y) = g'_j(y)$ holds; furthermore for an honest D, $F'(x,y) = F(x,y)$ holds. Now note that $g'_j(\alpha_i)$ is the same as $f'_i(\alpha_j)$ and thus every P_j holds a point on every $f'_i(x)$. Now P_i can reconstruct $f'_i(x)$ by asking every party P_j to send its point on $f'_i(x)$ to P_i. Since $f'_i(x)$ has degree at most $2t$ and there are $4t+1$ parties, OEC enables P_i to compute $f'_i(x)$ from the received points. Finally, we note that for a *corrupted* D, $S' = (F'(\beta_1, 0), \ldots, F'(\beta_{t+1}, 0))$ will be t-shared and for an honest D, $S' = S$ will hold.

Our idea of embedding several secrets in a single *bi-variate* polynomial is different from the notion of *packed secret-sharing* [16] where k secrets are embedded in a single *univariate* polynomial of degree t and each party receives a single share (a distinct point on the polynomial). In the latter, a single share is the share for k secrets and the robust reconstruction of the secrets is possible *only if* at most $t - k + 1$ parties are corrupted. Protocol Sh, on the other hand, ensures that *each* secret in S is *independently* t-shared and thus the robust reconstruction of each secret is possible even when the adversary corrupts t parties.

Sharing More Than $t+1$ Values Together: On having ℓ secrets for $\ell > t+1$, D can divide them into groups of $t+1$ and execute an instance of Sh for each group. This will require communication of $\mathcal{O}(\lceil \frac{\ell}{(t+1)} \rceil \cdot n^2) = \mathcal{O}(n\ell)$ field elements, since $(t+1) = \Theta(n)$. The broadcast communication can be kept $\mathcal{O}(n^2)$ (*independent* of ℓ) by executing all instances of Sh (each handling $t+1$ secrets) in parallel and by asking each party to broadcast only once for all the instances, after confirming the veracity of the "pre-condition" for the broadcast for *all* the instances of Sh. The sharing protocol of the AVSS scheme of [19] describes the same idea to keep the broadcast communication independent of ℓ when D $2t$-shares ℓ secrets. In the rest of the paper, we will say that a party t-shares ℓ values, where $\ell \geq t+1$ using an instance of Sh to mean the above.

6   Transforming Independent Triples to Co-related Triples

Protocol TripTrans takes as input a set of $(3t+1)$ "independent" shared triples, say $\{([x^{(i)}]_t, [y^{(i)}]_t, [z^{(i)}]_t)\}_{i \in [3t+1]}$, and outputs a set of $(3t+1)$ "co-related" shared triples, say $\{([\mathbf{x}^{(i)}]_t, [\mathbf{y}^{(i)}]_t, [\mathbf{z}^{(i)}]_t)\}_{i \in [3t+1]}$, such that: **(a)** There exist polynomials $\mathsf{X}(\cdot), \mathsf{Y}(\cdot)$ and $\mathsf{Z}(\cdot)$ of degree at most $\frac{3t}{2}, \frac{3t}{2}$ and $3t$ respectively, such that $\mathsf{X}(\alpha_i) = \mathbf{x}^{(i)}, \mathsf{Y}(\alpha_i) = \mathbf{y}^{(i)}$ and $\mathsf{Z}(\alpha_i) = \mathbf{z}^{(i)}$ holds, for $i \in [3t+1]$. **(b)** The ith output triple $(\mathbf{x}^{(i)}, \mathbf{y}^{(i)}, \mathbf{z}^{(i)})$ is a multiplication triple if and only if the ith input triple $(x^{(i)}, y^{(i)}, z^{(i)})$ is a multiplication triple. This further implies that $\mathsf{Z}(\cdot) = \mathsf{X}(\cdot)\mathsf{Y}(\cdot)$ is true iff all the $3t+1$ input triples are multiplication triples. **(c)** If Adv knows t' input triples and if $t' \leq \frac{3t}{2}$, then Adv learns t' distinct values of $\mathsf{X}(\cdot), \mathsf{Y}(\cdot)$ and $\mathsf{Z}(\cdot)$, implying $\frac{3t}{2} + 1 - t'$ "degree of freedom" on $\mathsf{X}(\cdot), \mathsf{Y}(\cdot)$ and $\mathsf{Z}(\cdot)$. If $t' > \frac{3t}{2}$, then Adv will completely know $\mathsf{X}(\cdot), \mathsf{Y}(\cdot), \mathsf{Z}(\cdot)$.

The protocol (see Fig. 2) is inherited from the protocol for the batch verification of the multiplication triples proposed in [9]. The idea is as follows: we assume $X(\cdot)$ and $Y(\cdot)$ to be "defined" by the first and second component of the *first* $\frac{3t}{2} + 1$ input triples, compute $\frac{3t}{2}$ "new" points on the $X(\cdot)$ and $Y(\cdot)$ polynomials and compute the product of the $\frac{3t}{2}$ new points using Beaver's technique making use of the *remaining* $\frac{3t}{2}$ input triples. The $Z(\cdot)$ is then defined by the $\frac{3t}{2}$ computed products and the third component of the first $\frac{3t}{2} + 1$ input triples. In a more detail, we define the polynomial $X(\cdot)$ of degree at most $\frac{3t}{2}$ by setting $X(\alpha_i) = x^{(i)}$ for $i \in [\frac{3t}{2} + 1]$ and get $[\mathbf{x}^{(i)}]_t = [X(\alpha_i)]_t = [x^{(i)}]_t$ for $i \in [\frac{3t}{2} + 1]$. Following the same logic, we define $Y(\alpha_i) = y^{(i)}$ for $i \in [\frac{3t}{2} + 1]$ and get $[\mathbf{y}^{(i)}]_t = [Y(\alpha_i)]_t = [y^{(i)}]_t$ for $i \in [\frac{3t}{2} + 1]$. Moreover, we set $Z(\alpha_i) = z^{(i)}$ for $i \in [\frac{3t}{2} + 1]$ and get $[\mathbf{z}^{(i)}]_t = [Z(\alpha_i)]_t = [z^{(i)}]_t$ for $i \in [\frac{3t}{2} + 1]$.

Protocol TripTrans$(\{([x^{(i)}]_t, [y^{(i)}]_t, [z^{(i)}]_t)\}_{i \in [3t+1]})$

1. The parties set $[\mathbf{x}^{(i)}]_t = [x^{(i)}]_t$, $[\mathbf{y}^{(i)}]_t = [y^{(i)}]_t$ and $[\mathbf{z}^{(i)}]_t = [z^{(i)}]_t$ for $i \in [\frac{3t}{2} + 1]$.
2. Let the points $\{(\alpha_i, \mathbf{x}^{(i)})\}_{i \in [\frac{3t}{2}+1]}$ and $\{(\alpha_i, \mathbf{y}^{(i)})\}_{i \in [\frac{3t}{2}+1]}$ define the polynomial $X(\cdot)$ and $Y(\cdot)$ respectively of degree at most $\frac{3t}{2}$. The parties locally compute $[\mathbf{x}^{(i)}]_t = [X(\alpha_i)]_t$ and $[\mathbf{y}^{(i)}]_t = [Y(\alpha_i)]_t$, for each[a] $i \in [\frac{3t}{2} + 2, 3t + 1]$.
3. The parties compute $\frac{3t}{2}$ sharings $\{[\mathbf{z}^{(i)}]_t\}_{i \in [\frac{3t}{2}+2,3t+1]}$ by executing BatchBeaver$(\{([\mathbf{x}^{(i)}]_t, [\mathbf{y}^{(i)}]_t, [x^{(i)}]_t, [y^{(i)}]_t, [z^{(i)}]_t)\}_{i \in [\frac{3t}{2}+2,3t+1]})$. Let the points $\{(\alpha_i, \mathbf{z}^{(i)})\}_{i \in [3t+1]}$ define the polynomial $Z(\cdot)$ of degree at most $3t$. The parties output $\{([\mathbf{x}^{(i)}]_t, [\mathbf{y}^{(i)}]_t, [\mathbf{z}^{(i)}]_t)\}_{i \in [3t+1]}$ and terminate.

---

[a] This is a linear function.

Fig. 2. Transforming independent shared triples to co-related shared triples

Now for $i \in [\frac{3t}{2} + 2, 3t + 1]$, we compute $[\mathbf{x}^{(i)}]_t = [X(\alpha_i)]_t$ and $[\mathbf{y}^{(i)}]_t = [Y(\alpha_i)]_t$ which requires only local computation on the t-sharings $\{([\mathbf{x}^{(i)}]_t, [\mathbf{y}^{(i)}]_t)\}_{i \in [\frac{3t}{2}+1]}$. For $i \in [\frac{3t}{2} + 2, 3t + 1]$, fixing $\mathbf{z}^{(i)}$ to be the same as $z^{(i)}$ will, however, violate the requirement that $Z(\cdot) = X(\cdot)Y(\cdot)$ holds when all the input triples are multiplication triples; this is because for $i \in [\frac{3t}{2} + 2, 3t + 1]$, $\mathbf{x}^{(i)} = X(\alpha_i) \neq x^{(i)}$ and $Y(\alpha_i) = \mathbf{y}^{(i)} \neq y^{(i)}$ and thus $z^{(i)} = x^{(i)}y^{(i)} \neq \mathbf{x}^{(i)}\mathbf{y}^{(i)}$. Here we resort to the Beaver's technique to find $[\mathbf{z}^{(i)}]_t = [\mathbf{x}^{(i)}\mathbf{y}^{(i)}]_t$ from $[\mathbf{x}^{(i)}]_t$ and $[\mathbf{y}^{(i)}]_t$, using the t-shared triples $\{([x^{(i)}]_t, [y^{(i)}]_t, [z^{(i)}]_t)\}_{i \in [\frac{3t}{2}+2,3t+1]}$. We note that the triples $\{([x^{(i)}]_t, [y^{(i)}]_t, [z^{(i)}]_t)\}_{i \in [\frac{3t}{2}+2,3t+1]}$ used for the Beaver's technique are never touched before for any computation.

It is easy to see that $(\mathbf{x}^{(i)}, \mathbf{y}^{(i)}, \mathbf{z}^{(i)})$ is a multiplication triple if and only if $(x^{(i)}, y^{(i)}, z^{(i)})$ is a multiplication triple. For $i \in [\frac{3t}{2} + 1]$, this is trivially true, as for such an i, $([\mathbf{x}^{(i)}]_t, [\mathbf{y}^{(i)}]_t, [\mathbf{z}^{(i)}]_t) = ([x^{(i)}]_t, [y^{(i)}]_t, [z^{(i)}]_t)$. For $i \in [\frac{3t}{2} + 2, 3t + 1]$, it follows from the correctness of the Beaver's technique and the fact that $([x^{(i)}]_t, [y^{(i)}]_t, [z^{(i)}]_t)$ is used to compute $[\mathbf{z}^{(i)}]_t$ from $[\mathbf{x}^{(i)}]_t$ and $[\mathbf{y}^{(i)}]_t$ and so $\mathbf{z}^{(i)} = \mathbf{x}^{(i)}\mathbf{y}^{(i)}$ if and only if $z^{(i)} = x^{(i)}y^{(i)}$. For privacy, we see that if Adv knows the ith input triple then the ith output triple will be known to Adv: for $i \in [\frac{3t}{2}+1]$ the statement is trivially true, while for $i \in [\frac{3t}{2}+2, 3t+1]$, the statement follows because Adv will know the ith input triple $(x^{(i)}, y^{(i)}, z^{(i)})$, which is used to compute $[\mathbf{z}^{(i)}]_t$ from $[\mathbf{x}^{(i)}]_t$ and $[\mathbf{y}^{(i)}]_t$. Since $(\mathbf{x}^{(i)} - x^{(i)})$ and $(\mathbf{y}^{(i)} - y^{(i)})$ are disclosed during the computation of $[\mathbf{z}^{(i)}]_t$, Adv will learn $\mathbf{x}^{(i)}, \mathbf{y}^{(i)}$ and $\mathbf{z}^{(i)}$. Thus if Adv knows t' input triples where $t' \le \frac{3t}{2}$ then Adv will learn t' output triples and hence t' values of $\mathsf{X}(\cdot), \mathsf{Y}(\cdot)$ and $\mathsf{Z}(\cdot)$, leaving $\frac{3t}{2}+1-t'$ degree of freedom in these polynomials. We note that all the honest parties eventually terminate the protocol and the protocol incurs communication of $\mathcal{O}(n^2)$ elements from $\mathbb{F}$.

7   The Framework for Generating Multiplication Triples

We are now ready to present our new framework for generating t-sharing of $c_M + c_R$ random multiplication triples unknown to Adv, which requires communication of $\mathcal{O}((c_M + c_R)n)$ and broadcast of $\mathcal{O}(n^3)$ field elements. As discussed earlier, the framework consists of two modules, elaborated next.

7.1   Module I: Verifiably Sharing Multiplication Triples

A Probabilistic Solution in a Completely Asynchronous Setting: Our protocol TripleSh allows a party $\mathsf{D} \in \mathcal{P}$ to verifiably share multiplication triples with linear "overhead", where the verification resorts to a probabilistic approach. In the protocol, D is asked to t-share $3t+1$ random multiplication triples $\{(x^{(i)}, y^{(i)}, z^{(i)})\}_{i \in [3t+1]}$ using Sh. To check if the triples are multiplication triples, the shared triples are first transformed to $\{([\mathbf{x}^{(i)}]_t, [\mathbf{y}^{(i)}]_t, [\mathbf{z}^{(i)}]_t)\}_{i \in [3t+1]}$ via TripTrans and then the relation $\mathsf{Z}(\cdot) \stackrel{?}{=} \mathsf{X}(\cdot) \cdot \mathsf{Y}(\cdot)$ is verified through a public checking of $\mathsf{Z}(\alpha) \stackrel{?}{=} \mathsf{X}(\alpha) \cdot \mathsf{Y}(\alpha)$ for a random α. To ensure that no *corrupted* D can pass this test, α should be generated using Rand once D completes sharing of the triples. It follows via the property of TripTrans that if some of the input triples $\{(x^{(i)}, y^{(i)}, z^{(i)})\}_{i \in [3t+1]}$ are not multiplication triples, then $\mathsf{Z}(\alpha) \neq \mathsf{X}(\alpha) \cdot \mathsf{Y}(\alpha)$ except with probability at most $\frac{3t}{|\mathbb{F}|}$ for a random α, since $\mathsf{Z}(\alpha)$ is of degree at most $3t$. Moreover if D is honest then Adv will learn only one point on $\mathsf{X}(\cdot), \mathsf{Y}(\cdot)$ and $\mathsf{Z}(\cdot)$ (namely at α) leaving $\frac{3t}{2}$ "degree of freedom" in these polynomials. So if the verification passes, then the parties output $\frac{3t}{2}$ shared triples $\{([\mathbf{a}^{(i)}]_t, [\mathbf{b}^{(i)}]_t, [\mathbf{c}^{(i)}]_t)\}$ on the "behalf" of D, where $\mathbf{a}^{(i)} = \mathsf{X}(\beta_i), \mathbf{b}^{(i)} = \mathsf{Y}(\beta_i)$ and $\mathbf{c}^{(i)} = \mathsf{Z}(\beta_i)$ for $\frac{3t}{2}$ β_is distinct from the random α.

In TripleSh, the above idea is applied on ℓ batches of $3t+1$ t-shared triples, where $\ell \ge t+1$ and a single random α is used for all the ℓ batches. Using BatRecPubl, we then efficiently perform the public reconstruction of 3ℓ values, namely the values of the polynomials at α. The protocol thus outputs $\ell \cdot \frac{3t}{2} = \Theta(n\ell)$ shared multiplication triples, with communication complexity $\mathcal{O}(n^2\ell)$ and requires broadcast of $\mathcal{O}(n^2)$ elements from $\mathbb{F}$.

An Error-Free Solution in a Hybrid Setting: An inherent drawback of a completely asynchronous setting is that the inputs of up to t potentially honest parties may get ignored. To get rid of this, [4] introduced a "partial synchronous" or hybrid setting wherein the very *first* communication round is a synchronous round. It was shown in [4] how to enforce "input provision" from all the n parties using the synchronous round (with some additional technicalities). We further utilize the first synchronous round to present an *error-free* triple sharing protocol called HybTripleSh for t-sharing multiplication triples.

HybTripleSh follows the footstep of TripleSh, except that it verifies the relation $Z(\cdot) = X(\cdot)Y(\cdot)$ in an error-free fashion, by leaking at most t points on the polynomials to Adv. Since this leaves at least $\frac{t}{2}$ degree of freedom on each of the polynomials for an *honest* D, the parties output $\frac{t}{2}$ shared multiplication triples $\{[\mathbf{a}^{(i)}]_t, [\mathbf{b}^{(i)}]_t, [\mathbf{c}^{(i)}]_t\}_{i \in [\frac{t}{2}]}$ on the behalf of D after successful verification, where $\mathbf{a}^{(i)} = X(\beta_i), \mathbf{b}^{(i)} = Y(\beta_i)$ and $\mathbf{c}^{(i)} = Z(\beta_i)$. The idea for the error-free verification is the following: *each* party P_i is given "access" to the triple $(X(\alpha_i), Y(\alpha_i), Z(\alpha_i))$ and is given the responsibility of confirming if it is a multiplication triple. If the confirmation comes from *all* the parties, then it can be concluded that the relation $Z(\cdot) = X(\cdot)Y(\cdot)$ is true. This is because the confirmation comes from at least $(n-t) = 3t+1$ *honest* parties and the degree of the polynomials $X(\cdot), Y(\cdot)$ is at most $\frac{3t}{2}$ and the degree of $Z(\cdot)$ is at most $3t$. Moreover, at most t values on each polynomial are leaked to Adv through the t corrupted parties (for an *honest* D). Unfortunately, in a completely asynchronous setting, we cannot wait for the confirmation from all the parties in $\mathcal{P}$, as the wait may turn out to be endless[2]. The synchronous round in the hybrid setting comes to our rescue.

In the synchronous round, every party P_i is asked to "non-verifiably" t-share a dummy multiplication triple, say $(f^{(i)}, g^{(i)}, h^{(i)})$ which is used later to verify if $(X(\alpha_i), Y(\alpha_i), Z(\alpha_i))$ is a multiplication triple on behalf of P_i, although *without further participation* of P_i. By non-verifiably we mean that neither the correctness of the t-sharing nor the fact that the shared triple is a multiplication triple is guaranteed if P_i is *corrupted*. The synchronous round however ensures that a dummy triple is non-verifiably shared on the behalf of *every* party P_i. Even if a corrupted P_i does not send the shares of the dummy triples to some party by the end of the round, the receiver can take some default value to complete the sharing. By defining "good" dummy triples as the ones that are t-shared and are multiplication triples, we now show how the verification is carried out using these dummy triples. Note that the honest parties share good dummy triples.

Given a dummy triple $(f^{(i)}, g^{(i)}, h^{(i)})$, we check if $(X(\alpha_i), Y(\alpha_i), Z(\alpha_i))$ is a multiplication triple by computing the sharing of the product of $X(\alpha_i)$ and $Y(\alpha_i)$ via the Beaver's technique and using the shared dummy triple and then publicly verifying if the resultant product is the same as $Z(\alpha_i)$. The latter can be verified by checking if the difference of the product and $Z(\alpha_i)$ is 0 or not. If P_i is *honest* then the dummy triple is random and thus no information is leaked about $(X(\alpha_i), Y(\alpha_i), Z(\alpha_i))$. If the checking fails, then the sharing of

---

[2] The confirmation is needed from all the n parties as we need $3t + 1$ "true" confirmations and t corrupted parties may provide a "false" confirmation.

$(X(\alpha_i), Y(\alpha_i), Z(\alpha_i))$ are publicly reconstructed for its public verification. Note that in such a case, either P_i or D must be *corrupted* and thus the privacy of the triple is lost already. However, if $(X(\alpha_i), Y(\alpha_i), Z(\alpha_i))$ is found to be a non-multiplication triple then D is definitely corrupted in which case the protocol is halted after outputting $\frac{t}{2}$ default sharing of multiplication triples.

When the shared triple $(f^{(i)}, g^{(i)}, h^{(i)})$ is *not* a good dummy triple due to the reason that it is a non-multiplication triple (but t-shared correctly), the checking of the corresponding multiplication triple $(X(\alpha_i), Y(\alpha_i), Z(\alpha_i))$ might fail leading to its public reconstruction and verification. But in this case P_i is surely corrupted and thus losing the privacy of the triple does not matter. Furthermore, the public verification of the multiplication triple will be successful for an *honest* D, implying that an honest D can *not* be disqualified. The case when the shared triple $(f^{(i)}, g^{(i)}, h^{(i)})$ is *not* a good dummy triple due to the reason that it is not t-shared correctly is more intricate to handle. The problem could be during the reconstruction of the values that are not t-shared, while executing the Beaver's technique. We solve this problem via a "variant" of OEC that concludes the reconstructed value upon receiving shares from *any* $3t + 1$ parties without further waiting. This however, might cause different parties to reconstruct different values when the input sharing is not t-shared. So an *asynchronous Byzantine agreement* (ABA) protocol [1] is run to agree on a unique value.

Finally we note that in the protocol HybTripleSh, the above idea is actually applied on ℓ batches of $3t + 1$ t-shared triples in parallel, where $\ell \geq t + 1$. This allows the efficient public reconstruction of all the required sharings (corresponding to the ℓ batches) using BatRecPubl. The protocol thus outputs $\ell \cdot \frac{t}{2} = \Theta(n\ell)$ shared multiplication triples.

7.2   Module II: Extracting Random Multiplication Triples

Let Com $\subset \mathcal{P}$ be a publicly known set of $3t + 1$ parties, such that every party in Com has verifiably t-shared ℓ multiplication triples among the parties in $\mathcal{P}$, where the triples shared by the honest parties are random and unknown to Adv. Protocol TripExt then "extracts" $\ell \cdot \frac{t}{2} = \Theta(n\ell)$ *random* t-shared multiplication triples unknown to Adv from these $\ell \cdot (3t + 1)$ "local" t-shared multiplication triples with a communication of $\mathcal{O}(n^2\ell)$. The idea is as follows: the input triples from the parties in Com are perceived as ℓ batches of $3t + 1$ triples where the lth batch contains the lth local triple from each party in Com. Then the transformation protocol TripTrans is executed on the lth batch to obtain a new set of $3t + 1$ triples and the three associated polynomials of degree $\frac{3t}{2}$, $\frac{3t}{2}$ and $3t$, namely $X^l(\cdot), Y^l(\cdot)$ and $Z^l(\cdot)$. Since each input triple is guaranteed to be a multiplication triple, the multiplicative relation holds among the polynomials, i.e. $Z^l(\cdot) = X^l(\cdot)Y^l(\cdot)$. Since Adv gets to know at most t input triples in the lth batch, the transformation ensures that Adv gets to know at most t points on each of the three polynomials, leaving $\frac{t}{2}$ degree of freedom on each polynomial. The random output multiplication triples for the lth batch, unknown to Adv, are then extracted as $\left\{ ([X^l(\beta_i)]_t, [Y^l(\beta_i)]_t, [Z^l(\beta_i)]_t) \right\}_{i \in [\frac{t}{2}]}$.

7.3   Module I + Module II ⇒ Preprocessing (Offline) Phase

Our preprocessing phase protocol now consists of the following steps: (1) Every party in $\mathcal{P}$ acts as a dealer and t-share $\ell = \frac{2(c_M+c_R)}{t}$ random multiplication triples, either using an instance TripleSh (if it is a completely asynchronous setting) or an an instance of HybTripleSh (if it is a hybrid setting). (2) The parties then execute an instance of ACS to decide on a common set Com of $3t+1$ dealers who have correctly shared multiplication triples in their respective instances of TripleSh/HybTripleSh. (3) Finally the parties execute the triple-extraction protocol TripExt on the triples shared by the parties in Com to extract $\ell \cdot \frac{t}{2} = (c_M+c_R)$ random shared multiplication triples. Now depending upon whether we use the protocol TripleSh or HybTripleSh above, we get either a completely asynchronous preprocessing phase protocol PreProc involving an error of at most $t \cdot \frac{3t}{|\mathbb{F}|} = \frac{3t^2}{|\mathbb{F}|}$ in the output or an error-free preprocessing phase protocol HybPrePro for the hybrid setting. The output triples will be private, as the multiplication triples of the honest dealers in Com are random and private.

8   The New AMPC Protocols

Once we have a preprocessing phase protocol, the online phase protocol for the shared circuit evaluation is straight forward (as discussed in the introduction); we refer to the full version of the paper for complete details. We note that in our hybrid AMPC protocol, during the offline phase, apart from t-sharing of $(c_M + c_R)$ random multiplication triples, the parties generate t-sharing of $n \cdot (t + 1)$ *additional* multiplication triples. The additional triples are used to enforce "input provision" from *all* the n parties during the online phase by using the method of [4]; see the full version of the paper for details.

Theorem 1 (The AMPC Theorem). Let $f : \mathbb{F}^n \to \mathbb{F}$ be a function expressed as an arithmetic circuit over a finite field $\mathbb{F}$, consisting of c_M and c_R multiplication and random gates. Then for every possible Adv, there exists a statistical AMPC protocol with error probability at most $2^{-\kappa}$ to securely compute f, provided $|\mathbb{F}| \geq \max\{3t^2 \cdot 2^\kappa, 2n\}$ for a given error parameter κ. The protocol incurs communication of $\mathcal{O}((c_M+c_R)n)$ elements and broadcast of $\mathcal{O}(n^3)$ elements from $\mathbb{F}$ and requires two invocations to ACS and n invocations to Rand.

If the first communication round is synchronous, then there exists a perfect AMPC protocol to securely compute f, provided $|\mathbb{F}| \geq 2n$. In the protocol, the inputs of all (the honest) parties are considered for the computation. The protocol requires communication of $\mathcal{O}((c_M + c_R)n + n^3)$ and broadcast of $\mathcal{O}(n^3)$ elements from $\mathbb{F}$. It also requires two invocations to ACS and n^2 invocations to ABA.

References

1. Abraham, A., Dolev, D., Halpern, J.: An almost-surely terminating polynomial protocol for asynchronous Byzantine agreement with optimal resilience. In: PODC, pp. 405–414 (2008)

2. Beaver, D.: Efficient multiparty protocols using circuit randomization. In: Feigenbaum, J. (ed.) CRYPTO 1991. LNCS, vol. 576, pp. 420–432. Springer, Heidelberg (1992)
3. Beerliová-Trubíniová, Z., Hirt, M.: Efficient multi-party computation with dispute control. In: Halevi, S., Rabin, T. (eds.) TCC 2006. LNCS, vol. 3876, pp. 305–328. Springer, Heidelberg (2006)
4. Beerliová-Trubíniová, Z., Hirt, M.: Simple and efficient perfectly-secure asynchronous MPC. In: Kurosawa, K. (ed.) ASIACRYPT 2007. LNCS, vol. 4833, pp. 376–392. Springer, Heidelberg (2007)
5. Beerliová-Trubíniová, Z., Hirt, M.: Perfectly-secure MPC with linear communication complexity. In: Canetti, R. (ed.) TCC 2008. LNCS, vol. 4948, pp. 213–230. Springer, Heidelberg (2008)
6. Ben-Or, M., Canetti, R., Goldreich, O.: Asynchronous secure computation. In: STOC, pp. 52–61 (1993)
7. Ben-Or, M., Goldwasser, S., Wigderson, A.: Completeness theorems for non-cryptographic fault-tolerant distributed computation. In: STOC, pp. 1–10 (1988)
8. Ben-Or, M., Kelmer, B., Rabin, T.: Asynchronous secure computations with optimal resilience. In: PODC, pp. 183–192 (1994)
9. Ben-Sasson, E., Fehr, S., Ostrovsky, R.: Near-linear unconditionally-secure multiparty computation with a dishonest minority. In: Safavi-Naini, R., Canetti, R. (eds.) CRYPTO 2012. LNCS, vol. 7417, pp. 663–680. Springer, Heidelberg (2012)
10. Bracha, G.: An asynchronous [(n-1)/3]-resilient consensus protocol. In: PODC, pp. 154–162 (1984)
11. Canetti, R.: Studies in secure multiparty computation and applications. PhD thesis, Weizmann Institute, Israel (1995)
12. Chaum, D., Crépeau, C., Damgård, I.: Multiparty unconditionally secure protocols. In: STOC, pp. 11–19. ACM (1988)
13. Damgård, I., Ishai, Y., Krøigaard, M.: Perfectly secure multiparty computation and the computational overhead of cryptography. In: Gilbert, H. (ed.) EUROCRYPT 2010. LNCS, vol. 6110, pp. 445–465. Springer, Heidelberg (2010)
14. Damgård, I.B., Nielsen, J.B.: Scalable and unconditionally secure multiparty computation. In: Menezes, A. (ed.) CRYPTO 2007. LNCS, vol. 4622, pp. 572–590. Springer, Heidelberg (2007)
15. Dani, V., King, V., Movahedi, M., Saia, J.: Brief announcement: Breaking the $\mathcal{O}(nm)$ bit barrier, secure multiparty computation with a static adversary. In: PODC, pp. 227–228 (2012)
16. Franklin, M.K., Yung, M.: Communication complexity of secure computation (extended abstract). In: STOC, pp. 699–710 (1992)
17. Hirt, M., Maurer, U.M., Przydatek, B.: Efficient secure multi-party computation. In: Okamoto, T. (ed.) ASIACRYPT 2000. LNCS, vol. 1976, pp. 143–161. Springer, Heidelberg (2000)
18. MacWilliams, F.J., Sloane, N.J.A.: The theory of error correcting codes. North-Holland Publishing Company (1978)
19. Patra, A., Choudhury, A., Rangan, C.P.: Communication efficient perfectly secure VSS and MPC in asynchronous networks with optimal resilience. In: Bernstein, D.J., Lange, T. (eds.) AFRICACRYPT 2010. LNCS, vol. 6055, pp. 184–202. Springer, Heidelberg (2010); full version available as Cryptology ePrint Archive, Report 2010/007
20. Rabin, T., Ben-Or, M.: Verifiable secret sharing and multiparty protocols with honest majority (extended abstract). In: STOC, pp. 73–85 (1989)
21. Shamir, A.: How to share a secret. Commun. ACM 22(11), 612–613 (1979)

Secure End-to-End Communication with Optimal Throughput and Resilience against Malicious Adversary

Paul Bunn[1] and Rafail Ostrovsky[2]

[1] Google Inc., Mountain View, CA 94043, USA
paulbunn@google.com
[2] UCLA Department of Computer Science and Department of Mathematics,
Los Angeles, CA 90095, USA
rafail@cs.ucla.edu

Abstract. We demonstrate the feasibility of end-to-end communication in highly unreliable networks. Modeling a network as a graph with vertices representing nodes and edges representing the links between them, we consider two forms of unreliability: unpredictable edge-failures, and deliberate deviation from protocol specifications by corrupt and maliciously controlled nodes.

We present a routing protocol for end-to-end communication that is simultaneously resilient to both forms of unreliability. In particular, we prove that our protocol is *secure* against arbitrary actions of the corrupt nodes controlled by a polynomial-time adversary, achieves *correctness* (Receiver gets *all* of the messages from Sender, in-order and without modification), and enjoys provably optimal throughput performance, as measured using *competitive analysis*. Competitive analysis is utilized to provide protocol guarantees again malicious behavior without placing limits on the number of the corrupted nodes in the network.

Furthermore, our protocol does not incur any asymptotic memory overhead as compared to other protocols that are unable to handle malicious interference of corrupt nodes. In particular, our protocol requires $O(n^2)$ memory per processor, where n is the size of the network. This represents an $O(n^2)$ improvement over all existing protocols that have been designed for this network model.

Keywords: Network Routing, Asynchronous Protocols, Multi-Party Computation with Dishonest Majority, Fault Localization, End-to-End Communication, Competitive Analysis, Communication Complexity.

1 Introduction

With the immense range of applications and the multitude of networks encountered in practice, there has been an enormous effort to study routing in various settings. In the present paper, we investigate the feasibility of routing in a network in which neither the nodes nor the links are reliable.

Y. Afek (Ed.): DISC 2013, LNCS 8205, pp. 403–417, 2013.

We adopt the same definition of *unreliability* (with respect to both links and nodes) as [17]. Namely, for the network links, we do not assume any form of stability: the topology of the network is *dynamic* (links may spontaneously fail or come back to life at any time), transmission time across each link may vary from link to link as well as across the same link from one transmission to the next (i.e. *asynchronous* edges), and there is no guarantee enough links are available (even over time) for communication to even be possible.

Meanwhile, unreliability of network *nodes* means that they may actively and maliciously deviate from protocol specifications, attempting to disrupt communication as much as possible. In particular, a *malicious adversary* may corrupt an arbitrary subset of nodes, taking complete control over them and coordinate attacks to interfere with communication between the uncorrupt nodes.

Admittedly, few guarantees can be achieved by any protocol that is forced to operate in networks with so few assumptions. Indeed, the absence of any assumption on connectivity means that successful routing may be *impossible*, for instance if all of the links remain forever inactive. Therefore, instead of measuring the efficacy of a given protocol in terms of its absolute performance, we will employ *competitive analysis* to evaluate protocols: the throughput-performance of a given protocol with respect to the network conditions encountered will be compared to the performance of an *ideal* protocol (one that has perfect information regarding the schedule of active/inactive links and corrupt nodes, and makes perfect routing decisions based on this information).

The combination of this strong notion of unreliability together with the use of competitive analysis provides a meaningful mechanism to evaluate routing protocols in networks that demonstrate unreliability in unknown ways. For example, we are able to compare protocols that route in networks that are susceptible to all of the above forms of unreliability, but e.g. remain stable most of the time with respect to the edges (or alternatively e.g. most of the nodes remain uncorrupted). Therefore, by allowing networks to exhibit all forms of unreliability, we compromise absolute performance for robustness. That is, no protocol will route packets quickly through a network that displays all forms of unreliability, but protocols with high competitive-ratio are guaranteed to do as well as possible, regardless of the actual network conditions.

In Section 2 we provide a formal model for unreliable networks and offer definitions of *throughput* and *security* in this model. Section 3 describes a protocol that is provably *secure* and optimal with respect to throughput-efficiency (as measured via *competitive-analysis*), and requires reasonable memory of internal nodes. We emphasize that the focus of this paper is on the theoretical feasibility of routing in highly unreliable networks, and no attempt has been made to minimize constants or prototype our protocol in live experiments.

1.1   Previous Work

Development and analysis of routing protocols relies heavily on the assumptions made by the network model. In this section, we explore various combinations of assumptions that have been made in recent work, highlighting positive and negative results with respect to each network model, emphasizing clearly which assumptions are employed in each case. Since our work focuses on theoretical results, we do not discuss the vast amount of work regarding routing issues for specific network systems encountered in practice, e.g. TCP, BGP, OSPF, etc. In the presence of adversarial conditions, these protocols often try to achieve "best effort" results instead of guaranteeing eventual delivery of all messages.

The amount of research regarding network routing and analysis of routing protocols is extensive, and as such we include only a sketch of the most related work, indicating how their models differ from ours.

End-to-End Communication: While there is a multitude of problems that involve end-to-end communication (e.g. End-to-End Congestion Control, Path-Measurement, and Admission Control), we discuss here work that consider networks whose only task is to facilitate communication between the Sender and Receiver. Some of these include a line of work developing the *Slide* protocol (the starting point of our protocol): Afek and Gafni and Rosen [2], Awerbuch et al. [11], Afek et al. [1], and Kushilevitz et al. [22]. The Slide protocol (and its variants) have been studied in a variety of network settings, including multi-commodity flow (Awerbuch and Leighton [10]), networks controlled by an online bursty adversary (Aiello et al. [3]), synchronous networks that allow corruption of nodes (Amir et al. [6]). Bunn and Ostrovsky consider in [17] an identical network model to the one considered in the present paper, and prove a matching upper and lower bound on optimal throughput performance for this model. However, the mechanisms they employ to handle malicious activity is extremely expensive (in terms of memory); indeed an open problem posed in [17] was whether a protocol can achieve security against malicious nodes at no extra (asymptotic) cost with respect to memory. We answer this question affirmatively in this paper, presenting a protocol that reduces memory requirements by a factor of n^2 (from $\Theta(n^4)$ to $\Theta(n^2)$, for networks with n nodes).

Fault Detection and Localization Protocols: There have been a number of papers that explore the possibility of corrupt nodes that deliberately disobey protocol specifications in order to disrupt communication. In particular, there is a recent line of work that considers a network consisting of a *single path* from the sender to the receiver, culminating in the recent work of Barak et al. [12] (for further background on fault localization see references therein). In this model, the adversary can corrupt any node (except the sender and receiver) in an adaptive and malicious manner. Since corrupting any node on the path will sever the honest connection between sender and receiver, the goal of a protocol in this model is *not* to guarantee that all messages sent are received. Instead, the goal is to *detect* faults when they occur and to *localize* the fault to a single edge.

Goldberg et al. [20] show that a protocol's ability to detect faults relies on the assumption that One-Way Functions (OWF) exist, and Barak et al. [12] show that the (constant factor) overhead (in terms of communication cost) incurred for utilizing cryptographic tools (such as MACs or Signature Schemes) is mandatory for any fault-localization protocol. Awerbuch et al. [9] also explore routing in the

Byzantine setting, although they do not present a formal treatment of security, and [12] gives a counter-example that challenges their protocol's security.

Fault Detection and Localization protocols focus on very restrictive network models (typically synchronous networks with fixed topology and some connectivity assumptions), and throughput-performance is usually not considered when analyzing fault detection/localization protocols.

Competitive Analysis: Competitive Analysis was first introduced by Sleator and Tarjan [26] as a mechanism for measuring the *worst-case* performance of a protocol, in terms of how badly the given protocol may be out-performed by an *off-line* protocol that has access to perfect information. Recall that a given protocol has *competitive ratio* $1/\lambda$ (or is λ-*competitive*) if an ideal off-line protocol has advantage over the given protocol by at most a factor of λ.

One place competitive analysis has been used to evaluate performance is the setting of distributed algorithms in asynchronous shared memory computation, including the work of Ajtai et al. [5]. This line of work has a different flavor than the problem considered in the present paper due to the nature of the algorithm being analyzed (computation algorithm versus network routing protocol). In particular, network topology is not a consideration in this line of work (and malicious deviation of processors is not considered).

Competitive analysis is a useful tool for evaluating protocols in unreliable networks (e.g. asynchronous networks and/or networks with no connectivity guarantees), as it provides best-possible standards (since absolute performance guarantees may be impossible due to the lack of network assumptions). For a thorough description of competitive analysis, see [14].

Max-Flow and Multi-Commodity Flow: The Max-Flow and Multi-Com- modity Flow models assume synchronous networks with connectivity guarantees and incorruptible nodes (max-flow networks also typically have fixed topology and are *global-control*: routing protocols assume nodes can make decisions based on a global-view of the network; as opposed to only knowing what is happening with adjacent links/nodes). There has been a tremendous amount of work in these areas, see e.g. Leighton et al. [23] for a discussion of the two models and a list of results, as well as Awerbuch and Leighton [10] who show optimal throughput-competitive ratio for the network model in question.

Admission Control and Route Selection: There are numerous models that are concerned with questions of admission control and route selection: The Asynchronous Transfer Model (see e.g. Awerbuch et al. [8]), Queuing Theory (see e.g. Borodin and Kleinberg [15] and Andrews et al. [7]), Adversarial Queuing Theory (see e.g. Broder et al. [16] and Aiello et al. [4]). For an extensive discussion about these research areas, see [25] and references therein.

The admission control/route selection model assumes synchronous communication and incorruptible nodes and makes connectivity/liveness guarantees. Among the other options (fixed or dynamic topology, global or local control), each combination has been considered by various authors, see the above reference for further details and results within each specific model.

1.2 Our Results

We consider the feasibility of end-to-end routing in highly unreliable networks, where unreliability is encountered with respect to both the network's edges and its nodes. In particular, we consider asynchronous networks with dynamic topology and no connectivity guarantees; comprised of corruptible nodes that may deviate from protocol specifications in a deliberately malicious manner.

We present a protocol that routes effectively in this network setting, utilizing standard cryptographic tools to guarantee *correctness* with low memory burden per node. We use *competitive-analysis* to evaluate the throughput-efficiency of our protocol, and demonstrate that our protocol achieves optimal *throughput*. Our protocol therefore represents a constructive proof of the following theorem (see Section 2 for definitions of our network model and the above terms):

Theorem 1. *Assuming Public-Key Infrastructure and the existence of a group-homomorphic encryption scheme, there exists a routing protocol that achieves correctness and optimal competitive-ratio $1/n$ in a distributed asynchronous network with bounded memory $\Theta(n^2)$ and dynamic topology (and no connectivity assumptions), even if an arbitrary subset of malicious nodes deliberately disobey the protocol specifications in order to disrupt communication as much as possible.*

As mentioned in Section 1.1, our protocol solves an open problem from [17], which was to provide provable security (while maintaining optimal throughput) at **no** additional cost (in terms of processor memory) over protocols that do not provide security against corrupt nodes. Our protocol utilizes novel techniques to achieve exactly this: memory is reduced from[1] $\Theta(n^4)$ to $\Theta(n^2)$, which matches the memory requirements of a corresponding (insecure) protocol of [1]. We provide here a brief overview of the new insights that enabled us to achieve this.

We begin by describing why the $\Theta(n^4)$ bits of memory per node was required in [17] to ensure security. Consider the packet-replacement adversarial strategy, where corrupt nodes replace new packets they receive with duplicate copies of old packets that they have already transferred, thereby effectively deleting all new packets the Sender inserts. The protocol of [17] protected against this strategy by having each node maintain a signed transaction with each of its neighbors, recording the number of times *every* packet was passed between them. While this approach ensures that a node performing packet-replacement will be caught, it is extremely costly in terms of required memory: Each node has to remember, for every packet p it encountered, the number of times it sent/received p along each of its adjacent edges. For networks with n nodes, since there were $\Theta(n^3)$ relevant packets[2] and a node may have $\Theta(n)$ neighbors, the memory burden of storing this transaction information was $\Theta(n^4)$. Not only did this large memory

---

[1] These bounds ignore the cost of security parameter k and bandwidth parameter P, which are treated as constants. Including them explicitly would yield memory costs of $\Theta(kPn^4)$ for the protocol of [17] versus $\Theta(kPn^2)$ here.

[2] The n^3 appearing here is *not* a bound on the size of the input stream of packets (which can be any arbitrarily large polynomial in n); it is an upper-bound on the number of packets being stored by the internal nodes at any time.

complexity mean the protocol of [17] was unlikely to be feasibly implemented in practice, it was also the case that the cost of n^4 for storing the transaction history (for the purpose of identifying corrupt behavior) far out-weighed the per-node memory costs of the data packets being transferred (n^2), so the memory resources were being consumed by network *monitoring* as opposed to *routing*.

The present paper overcomes both of these issues, reducing the overall memory burden to $\Theta(n^2)$, as well as allocating the majority of resources to routing instead of monitoring. In order to achieve this, we had to abandon the idea of tracking each individual packet, and develop a novel technique to address packet-replacement. We began by generalizing the per-packet tracking of [17] as follows: We partition the $D = \Theta(n^3)$ packets to be sent into K sets $\{S_1, \ldots, S_K\}$ (we will optimize for the value of $K(k)$, which depends on the security-parameter k, in Section 3), and then we have nodes record transaction information with their neighbors on a per-*set* basis rather than a per-*packet* basis. Namely, nodes maintain K counters of how many packets in each set they have transferred with each neighbor, so that if a packet $p \in S$ is transferred between two nodes, the nodes increment a counter for set S. In this way, if a malicious node replaces $p \in S$ with $p' \in S'$, the per-set counters will help in detecting this if $S \neq S'$.

With this generalization, observe that as K varies in $[1, D]$, there is a trade-off in the memory burden of storing the transactions versus the probability of protecting against packet-replacement: smaller values of K result in lower per-node memory but a higher probability that a node performing packet-replacement can get away with it. The primary technical achievement of this paper was in developing a mechanism that guarantees that *any* packet-replacement strategy performed by malicious node(s) will succeed only with negligible probability, even for small values of K.

We achieve this by first using error-correction to ensure that our protocol is robust enough to handle minor amounts of packet-replacement and still transmit messages, so that in order to impede communication via the packet-replacement strategy, a large number of packets must be replaced. Next, we observe that if a malicious node replaces a packet $p \in S$ with $p' \in S'$, then if the choices of p and p' are uniformly random (among the D total packets), then the probability that $S = S'$ is roughly $1/K$. By using cryptography, we are able to obfuscate the partitioning of packets into sets in a manner that is invisible to all nodes except the Sender, and we demonstrate how this reduces *any* adversarial strategy of packet-replacement to the uniform case of replacing one packet with a randomly chosen second packet. With this reduction in hand, it becomes a straightforward probabilistic analysis for choosing an appropriate value for the parameter K so as to minimize memory burden and still guarantee (with negligible probability of error) that packet-replacement will be detected. Details of the protocol and this analysis can be found in Section 3.

2   The Model

In this section, we describe the model in which we will be analyzing routing protocols. The network is viewed as a graph G with n vertices (or *nodes*), two of which are designated as the *Sender* and *Receiver*. The Sender has a stream of messages $\{m_1, m_2, \dots\}$ it wants to transmit through the network to the Receiver.

For ease of discussion, we assume all edges in the network have a fixed bandwidth/capacity, and this quantity is the same for all edges. We emphasize that this assumption does not restrict the validity of our claims in a more general model allowing varying bandwidths, but is only made for ease of exposition. We will use the following terminology throughout this paper (see Section 3.1 for the protocol description and explanation of these terms an how they are used):

Definition 2. *Let P denote the bandwidth (e.g. in bits) of each edge. A* packet *(of size $\leq P$) will refer to any bundle of information sent across an edge. A* message *refers to one of the Sender's input m_i, and we assume without loss of generality that each message is comprised of $\Theta(kPn^3)$ bits (k is the security parameter; see below). A (message)* codeword *refers to an encoded message, which will be partitioned into* codeword parcels, *whose size is small enough such that one codeword parcel (plus some control information) fits in the bandwidth of an edge P. More generally, we will refer to the various components of a packet as* parcels. *A (message)* transmission *consists of the rounds required to send a single codeword from Sender to Receiver.*

We model *asynchronicity* via an edge-scheduling adversary $\mathcal{A}$ that controls edges as follows. A round consists of a single edge $E(u, v)$ (chosen by the adversary) being activated:

1. If $\mathcal{A}$ has at least one packet from u to be sent to v, then $\mathcal{A}$ delivers exactly one of them (of $\mathcal{A}$'s choosing) to v; same is done for one packet from v to u
2. After seeing the delivered packet, u (respectively. v) chooses the next packet to send v (respectively. u), and gives it to $\mathcal{A}$, who will store it until the next round that $E(u, v)$ is activated

If u does not have a packet it wishes to send v in Step (2), then u can choose to send nothing. Alternatively, u may send multiple packets to $\mathcal{A}$ in Step 2, but only one of these packets (of $\mathcal{A}$'s choosing) gets delivered in Step 2 of the next round $E(u, v)$ is activated. The Adversary does not send anything to v in Step (1) if it is not storing a packet from u to v during round $E(u, v)$.

Definition 3. *A packet will be said to be in an* outstanding request *if u has sent the packet to $\mathcal{A}$ as in Step (2) of some round, but that packet has not yet been delivered by $\mathcal{A}$.*

Aside from obeying the above specified rules, we place no additional restriction on the edge-scheduling adversary. In other words, it may activate whatever edges it likes (this models the fact our network makes no connectivity assumptions), wait indefinitely long between activating the same edge twice (modeling both the dynamic and asynchronous features of our network), and do anything else it likes (so long as it respects steps (1) and (2) above each time it activates an edge) in attempt to hinder the performance of a routing protocol.

In addition to the edge-scheduling adversary, our network model also allows for a polynomially bounded (in number of nodes n and a security parameter k) node-controlling adversary to corrupt the nodes of the network. The node-controlling adversary is malicious, meaning that it can take complete control over the nodes it corrupts and force them to deviate from any protocol in whatever manner it likes. We further assume that the node-controlling adversary is adaptive, which means it can corrupt nodes at any stage of the protocol, deciding which nodes to corrupt based on what it has observed thus far. We do not impose any "access-structure" limitations on the node-controlling adversary: it may corrupt any nodes it likes (although if the Sender and/or Receiver is corrupt, secure routing between them is impossible). We say a routing protocol is correct (or secure) if the messages reach the Receiver in-order and unaltered.

The separation of the two adversaries (edge-scheduling and node-controlling) into two distinct entities is solely for conceptual purposes to emphasize the nature of unreliability in the edges versus the nodes. For ease of discussion, we will often refer to a single adversary that represents the combined efforts of the edge-scheduling and node-controlling adversaries.

Finally, our network model is on-line and distributed, in that we do not assume that the nodes have access to any information (including future knowledge of the adversary's schedule of activated edges) aside from the packets they receive during a round they are a part of. Also, we insist that nodes have bounded memory[3] which is at least $\Omega(n^2)$.

Our mechanism for evaluating the throughput performance of protocols in this network model will be as follows: Let $f_{\mathcal{P}}^{\mathcal{A}} : \mathbb{N} \to \mathbb{N}$ be a function that measures, for a given protocol $\mathcal{P}$ and adversary $\mathcal{A}$, the number of messages that the Receiver has received as a function of the number of rounds that have passed. Note that in this paper, we will consider only deterministic protocols, so $f_{\mathcal{P}}^{\mathcal{A}}$ is well-defined. The function $f_{\mathcal{P}}^{\mathcal{A}}$ formalizes our notion of throughput.

We utilize competitive analysis to gauge the throughput-performance of a given protocol against all possible competing protocols:

Definition 4. *We say that a protocol $\mathcal{P}$ has competitive-ratio $1/\lambda$ (respectively is λ-competitive) if there exists a constant c and function $g(n, C)$ (where C is the memory bound per node) such that for all possible adversaries $\mathcal{A}$ and for all $\mathbf{x} \in \mathbb{N}$, the following holds for all protocols $\mathcal{P}'$:[4]*

$$f_{\mathcal{P}'}^{\mathcal{A}}(\mathbf{x}) \leq (c \cdot \lambda) \cdot f_{\mathcal{P}}^{\mathcal{A}}(\mathbf{x}) + g(n, C) \tag{1}$$

Note that while g may depend on the network size n and the bounds placed on processor memory C, both g and c are *independent* of the round $\mathbf{x}$ and the choice of adversary $\mathcal{A}$. Also, equation (1) is only required to hold for protocols $\mathcal{P}'$ that never utilize a corrupt node once it has been corrupted.

We assume a Public-Key Infrastructure (PKI) that allows digital signatures. In particular, before the protocol begins we choose a security parameter sufficiently large and run a key generation algorithm for a digital signature scheme,

---

[3] For simplicity, we assume all nodes have the same memory bound (which may be a function of the number of nodes n and security parameter k), although our argument can be readily extended to handle the more general case.

[4] λ is taken as the infimum of all values satisfying (1), and is typically a function of n.

producing $n = |G|$ (secret key, verification key) pairs (sk_u, vk_u). As output to key generation, each node $u \in G$ is given its own private signing key sk_u and signature verification keys vk_v for each $v \in G$. In particular, this allows Sender and Receiver to sign messages to each other that cannot be forged (except with negligible probability in the security parameter) by any other node in the system.

We also assume the existence of a *group-homomorphic* encryption scheme $\mathcal{E}$:

$$\mathcal{E}: \mathcal{G} \to \mathcal{H}, \quad \text{with} \quad \mathcal{E}(g_1 \circ_{\mathcal{G}} g_2) = \mathcal{E}(g_1) \circ_{\mathcal{H}} \mathcal{E}(g_2),$$

where $\mathcal{G}$ and $\mathcal{H}$ are groups[5] and $\circ_{\mathcal{G}}$ (respectively $\circ_{\mathcal{H}}$) represents the group operation on $\mathcal{G}$ (respectively $\mathcal{H}$). Note that such a scheme exists under most of the commonly used cryptographic assumptions, including *factoring* [24], *discrete log* [19], *quadratic residuosity* [21], and *subgroup decision problem* [13]. We extend our encryption scheme to $\mathbb{Z}_N^K$ in the natural way:

$$\mathcal{E}: \mathbb{Z}_N \times \cdots \times \mathbb{Z}_N \to \mathcal{H} \times \cdots \times \mathcal{H} \quad \text{via} \quad \mathcal{E}(g_1, \ldots, g_K) := (\mathcal{E}(g_1), \ldots, \mathcal{E}(g_K))$$

Finally, we assume that internal nodes have capacity $C \in \Omega(Pn^2)$ (and in particular $C \geq 24Pn^2$), and that $P = \Omega(k^2 + \log n)$.

3   Routing Protocol

We now present a routing protocol that enjoys competitive-ratio $1/n$ with respect to throughput (which is optimal, see [17]) in networks modelled as in Section 2. We give an abbreviated description of the protocol in Section 3.1, and state the lemmas leading to Theorem 1 in Section 3.2 (due to space constraints, we present only the main features of our protocol; minor optimizations, technical details, and proofs are omitted, but can be found in the extended version [18]).

3.1   Description of the Routing Protocol

The starting point of our protocol will be the Slide Protocol, introduced by Afek et at. [2], and further developed in a series of works: [11], [1], [22], [6], and [17]. The original Slide protocol assumes that nodes have buffers (viewed as stacks) able to store $C = \Theta(n^2)$ packets at any time, and simply put, it calls for a node u to send a packet to node v across an activated edge $E(u,v)$ if v is storing fewer packets in its buffer than u.

The Slide protocol is robust in its ability to handle edge-failures (modelled here via the edge-scheduling adversary). This robustness is achieved via the use of *error-correction* to account for packets that get stuck in the buffer of a node that became isolated from the rest of the network due to edge-failures. In particular, each message is expanded into a codeword, which is then partitioned

---

[5] $|\mathcal{G}|$ should be larger than the total number of codeword parcel transfers (during any transmission) between two nodes, when at least one of the nodes is *honest*. $|\mathcal{G}| \in \Omega(kn^4)$ is sufficient (see protocol description in Section 3.1).

into $D := knC/\lambda$ parcels $\{p_i\}$, where λ is the tolerable error rate and k is the security parameter. Recall from Definition 2 that without loss of generality, messages have size $O(kPn^3)$, and more precisely, messages are small enough so that a codeword parcel (plus some control information of $\Theta(k^2 + \log n)$ bits, see below) can be transmitted in a single round; i.e. $|p_i| \leq P - \Theta(k^2 + \log n)$. The Receiver can decode the codeword and obtain the original message block provided he receives $(1 - \lambda)D$ codeword parcels.

Our protocol modifies the original Slide protocol to provide security against a node-controlling adversary at no additional (asymptotic) cost: we achieve optimal throughput (competitive-ratio $1/n$), and the memory per internal node is within a factor of two of the memory requirement of the original Slide protocol. We obtain security against malicious nodes by including extra control information (described below) with each packet transfer, and by having nodes sign all communications. As mentioned in Section 1.2, our protocol closely resembles that of [17], except the nature of the control information we use to provide security does not require any extra (asymptotic) memory costs.

In the following subsections, we present our protocol by describing the control information, routing rules, and blacklist.

Control Information. There are four components of the control information; every packet has room to store exactly one parcel of each type of control information and one codeword parcel:

1. Sender/Receiver Alerts. The Sender's alert consists of up to $2n$ parcels, all time-stamped with the index of the present codeword transmission. The first of these indicates the status (S1 or F2-F4, see below) of the previous transmission; and the next n parcels give the time-stamp of the most recent (up to) n transmissions that *failed* (F2-F4). The final $n - 1$ parcels are for each of the nodes (excluding the Sender), indicating if that node is blacklisted or eliminated (see below), and if so the transmission this happened.

   The Receiver's alert consists of a single parcel indicating either that the Receiver successfully decoded the current codeword, or that it has received inconsistent potential information (see below).

2. Potential Information. One parcel per node containing that node's potential drop Φ_u (see Definition 6).

3. Status Information. For each of its neighbors v, a node will maintain up-to-date information regarding all codeword parcel transfers with that neighbor for the current codeword transmission: the net *potential drop* $\Phi_{u,v}$ and ob-*fuscated count* $\Psi_{u,v}$ (see Definitions 6 and 7 below).

4. Testimonies. At the end of a transmission T, a node will have one final (current as of the end of the transmission) status parcel $(\Phi_{u,v}, \Phi_{v,u}, \Psi_{u,v}, \Psi_{v,u})$ for each neighbor. If the node later (in a future transmission) learns that T *failed*, then these $n - 1$ status parcels become the node's testimony for transmission T. Since nodes do not participate in routing codeword parcels until the Sender has its testimony (see blacklist below), each node will only ever have at most one transmission T for which it needs to remember its own testimony; thus, at any time, there are at most $(n - 1)^2$ testimony parcels in the network.

Each of these types of control information serve a separate function. The Sender's alert parcels mark the start of a new codeword transmission, while the Receiver's alert marks the end of one (see below). Potential parcels are used to identify inconsistencies in potential differences, in which case the Receiver alerts a failed transmission (see below). Testimony parcels are ultimately used by the Sender to identify a corrupt node.

Unlike all other control information, status parcels are *not* transferred through the network (ultimately to Sender or Receiver), but rather are only kept locally and transferred between the two nodes for which the status parcel is keeping up-to-date records for the current transmission. We now formalize these concepts.

Definition 5. *The height H_u of an internal node u is the number of codeword parcels u is currently storing in its buffer (including those in outstanding requests, of which u is maintaining a copy). The Sender's height is defined to be the constant C (the capacity of an internal node's buffer); and the Receiver's height is defined to be zero.*

Definition 6. *The potential difference $\phi_{u,v}$ of two nodes u and v is the difference in their heights (always measured as a positive quantity): $\phi_{u,v} := |H_u - H_v|$. The directional potential difference $\Phi_{u,v}$ over an edge $E(u, v)$ will be the sum of the potential differences for the rounds when u transferred v a codeword parcel minus the sum of the potential differences for the rounds when v transferred u a codeword parcel:*[6]

$$\Phi_{u,v} := \sum_{u \to v} \phi_{u,v} - \sum_{v \to u} \phi_{u,v} \tag{2}$$

The potential drop over an edge $E(u, v)$ will be the absolute value of the difference of the directional potential differences across that edge: $|\Phi_{u,v} - \Phi_{v,u}|$. The potential drop at a node u will be the sum of the potential drops over all its adjacent edges:

$$\Phi_u := \sum_{v \in G} |\Phi_{u,v} - \Phi_{v,u}| \tag{3}$$

The condition that indicates inconsistency in potential difference (see Case F3 below) is if: $\sum_{u \in G} \Phi_u > kCD$.

Recall from Section 2 the existence of a homomorphic encryption scheme $\mathcal{E}$ on $\mathbb{Z}_N^K$. At the start of each codeword transmission, the Sender randomly partitions the D codeword parcels into $K := k$ sets, making a uniform random choice for each parcel. Define the distribution $\chi_T : D \to \mathbb{Z}_N^K$ (which depends on the codeword transmission T) to represent these assignments; i.e. if parcel p has been assigned to the ith set, then $\chi(p)$ is the unit vector in $\mathbb{Z}_N^K$ with a '1' in the ith coordinate. Note that only the Sender knows χ, and it will remain

---

[6] Formally, for a packet transferred during Step (1) of an edge activation, the heights used to compute the potential difference are *not* the current heights of the nodes, but rather the heights each of the nodes had the *previous* time the edge was activated. See Figure 1, in which these heights are denoted as H_v and H_{old}.

obfuscated from all internal nodes, as the only information they will ever see are the encrypted values $\mathcal{E}(\chi(p))$ (which are computed by the Sender and bundled in the same packet as the codeword parcel, so that $(p, \mathcal{E}(\chi(p)))$ will travel in the same packet as it is transferred through the network to the Receiver).

Definition 7. *The directed obfuscated count $\boldsymbol{\Psi}_{u,v}$ between two nodes is an (encrypted) K-tuple, in which the ith coordinate represents the number of codeword parcels p with $\chi(p) = i$ that have been transferred from u to v. Since p and $\mathcal{E}(\chi(p))$ are always passed together in a single packet, it can be computed by any internal node along any of its adjacent edges as:*

$$\Psi_{u,v} := \sum_{p \in \mathcal{P}_{u,v}} \mathcal{E}(\chi(p)), \tag{4}$$

where $\mathcal{P}_{u,v}$ denotes the multiset of codeword parcels transferred from u to v. The obfuscated count $\boldsymbol{\Psi}_u$ at u is:

$$\Psi_u := \sum_{p \in u} \mathcal{E}(\chi(p)), \tag{5}$$

where the sum is taken over the (current codeword) parcels p that u is storing at the end of the current transmission. Notice that the homomorphic properties of $\mathcal{E}$ allow the nodes to compute the right-hand-side of (4) and (5).

Routing Rules. Figure 1 gives a succinct description of a node's instructions for when it is part of an activated edge.

Routing Rules for node u along $E(u, v)$
\# Notation: $(H_{old}, p_{old}, \mathcal{E}(\chi(p_{old})))$ denotes prev. ht. and codeword parcel u sent v;
Input (Received via $\mathcal{A}$):
Height H_v of v, codeword parcel p and $\mathcal{E}(\chi(p))$,
  Control Information: alert parcel, status parcel, potential parcel, testimony parcel
DO:
Verify status parcel and all signatures are valid, if not, Skip to **Send Next Packet**
Store alert parcel, potential parcel, and testimony parcel
If u or v is blacklisted or eliminated, or u hasn't rec'd all parcels from Sender's alert:
  Skip to **Send Next Packet**
If u is the Sender and $H_v < C + 2n - C/2n$:
  Insert p_{old}:   Ignore p, Delete p_{old}, Update $\Phi_{u,v}$, $\Psi_{u,v}$, and Φ_u
If u is the Receiver and $H_v > C/2n - 2n$:
  Receive p: Store p, Update $\Phi_{v,u}$, $\Psi_{v,u}$, and Φ_u
If u is not Sender or Receiver and $H_{old} > H_v - 2n + C/2n$:
  Send p_{old}:   Ignore p, Delete p_{old}, Update $\Phi_{u,v}$, $\Psi_{u,v}$, and Φ_u
If u is not Sender or Receiver and $H_{old} < H_v + 2n - C/2n$:
  Receive p: Store p (and keep p_{old}), Update $\Phi_{v,u}$, $\Psi_{v,u}$, and Φ_u
Send Next Packet

Fig. 1. Succinct Description of Packet Transfer Rules of Our Protocol

Recall that Step 2 of an activated edge calls for node u to send a packet to $\mathcal{A}$ that it wishes to deliver to v next time $E(u, v)$ is activated. The rules for how u decides which data to include in the packet (see *Send Next Packet* in Figure 1):

1. Current Height H_u: See Definition 5
2. Codeword Parcel[7] $(p, \mathcal{E}(\chi(p)))$: Randomly selected among those not in outstanding request
3. Control Information: Send up to one parcel of each type of control information, selected as follows. Let $N_1, N_2, \ldots, N_n$ denote the nodes and $A = A(u, v)$ the number of times $E(u, v)$ has been activated so far. Then u includes the following parcels of control information:
   - Alert Parcel: Receiver's alert (if u has it); else next Sender alert parcel
   - Status Information: $(\Phi_{u,v}, \Phi_{v,u}, \Psi_{u,v}, \Psi_{v,u})$
   - Potential Information: Let $i \equiv A \pmod{n}$; select parcel Φ_{N_i}
   - Testimony: Let $i \equiv A \pmod{n}$; select next testimony parcel of N_i's

The Blacklist. The end of each transmission is marked by one of the following:

S1 Sender gets Receiver alert indicating successful decoding of codeword
F2 Sender gets Receiver alert indicating inconsistency in potential differences
F3 Sender inserted all (current) codeword parcels (and S1 did not occur)
F4 Sender is able to identify a corrupt node

In the case of S1, the codeword was delivered successfully, and the Sender will begin the next codeword transmission. In the case of F4, the Sender will re-start the transmission with the same codeword and indicate (in the Sender alert) that the corrupt node has been *eliminated*. All nodes are forbidden transferring codeword parcels with eliminated nodes (a node always knows the list of eliminated nodes before it has any codeword parcels to transfer; see Figure 1).

Cases F2 and F3 correspond to failed attempts to transfer the current codeword due to corrupt nodes disobeying protocol rules. When a transmission T fails as in cases F2 and F3, the nodes (excluding the Sender) that are not already on a blacklist or eliminated will be put on transmission T's blacklist; more generally, we will say a node is on the blacklist (or blacklisted) if there is some transmission T for which the node is on T's blacklist. Thus after a transmission fails as in F2 or F3, every node (except for the Sender) is either eliminated or blacklisted. As indicated in the Routing Rules of Figure 1, packets sent to/from a blacklisted node will not contain a codeword parcel (just control information). A node is removed from the blacklist either when the Sender has received its complete testimony, or when a node is eliminated (whichever happens first). In the former case, the Sender will add a new parcel to the Sender alert, simply indicating the node has been removed from the blacklist. In the latter case, the Sender will immediately end the transmission as in F4 (described above). We will say a (non-eliminated) node participated in a transmission if that node was not on the blacklist for at least one round of the transmission.

---

[7] If at any time $\Phi_u > kCD$, then u stops transferring codeword parcels (sending a special indicator $\perp$ for its height H). Since each codeword parcel transfer corresponds in an *increase* of at least $C/n - 2n = \Theta(n)$ to Φ_u, this ensures honest nodes will transfer at most $O(k^2 n^4)$ codeword parcels, and also bounds the number of distinct signatures from u per transmission by $O(k^2 n^4)$.

If a node learns that it is on the blacklist for some transmission T (note that by construction, T will necessarily be the previous transmission that the node participated in), then the node constructs its testimony for T, which is the final values of its status parcels along all its adjacent edges: $\{\Phi_{u,v}, \Phi_{v,u}, \Psi_u, \Psi_{u,v}, \Psi_{v,u}\}_{v \in G}$.

3.2   Analysis of the Routing Protocol

We state here the main lemma that leads to Theorem 1 (due to space constraints, the proof has been relegated to the extended version [18]). This lemma states that if a corrupt node causes a transmission to fail as in F3 (e.g. by employing *packet replacement*), then with overwhelming probability it can be identified due to inconsistencies in the obfuscated counts.

Lemma 8. *Suppose a transmission fails as in Case F3, and at some later point the Sender has collected all of the testimonies from all nodes participating in that transmission. The probability that the following is satisfied is negligible in k:*

$$\sum_{u \in G \setminus \{r,s\}} \Psi_{s,u} = \sum_{u \in G \setminus \{r,s\}} (\Psi_u + \Psi_{u,r}) \tag{6}$$

More precisely, (6) is satisfied with probability at most: $\frac{\sqrt{ek}}{\left(\sqrt{2\pi}\right)^{k-1}}$.

Acknowledgments. Research supported in part by NSF grants IIS-1065276; CCF-1016540; CNS-1118126; CNS-1136174; US-Israel BSF grant 2008411, OKAWA Foundation Research Award, IBM Faculty Research Award, Xerox Faculty Research Award, B. John Garrick Foundation Award, Teradata Research Award, and Lockheed-Martin Corporation Research Award. This material is also based upon work supported by the Defense Advanced Research Projects Agency through the U.S. Office of Naval Research under Contract N00014-11-1-0392. The views expressed are those of the authors and do not reflect the official policy or position of the Department of Defense or the U.S. Government.

References

1. Afek, Y., Awerbuch, B., Gafni, E., Mansour, Y., Rosen, A., Shavit, N.: Slide– The Key to Poly. End-to-End Communication. J. of Algorithms 22, 158–186 (1997)
2. Afek, Y., Gafni, E., Rosén, A.: The Slide Mechanism with Applications in Dynamic Networks. In: PODC, pp. 35–46 (1992)
3. Aiello, W., Kushilevitz, E., Ostrovsky, R., Rosén, A.: Adaptive Packet Routing For Bursty Adversarial Traffic. J. Comput. Syst. Sci. 60(3), 482–509 (2000)
4. Aiello, W., Ostrovsky, R., Kushilevitz, E., Rosén, A.: Dynamic Routing on Networks with Fixed-Size Buffers. In: SODA, pp. 771–780 (2003)
5. Ajtai, M., Aspnes, J., Dwork, C., Waarts, O.: A Theory of Competitive Analysis for Distributed Algorithms. In: FOCS, pp. 32–40 (1994)
6. Amir, Y., Bunn, P., Ostrovsky, R.: Authenticated Adversarial Routing. In: Reingold, O. (ed.) TCC 2009. LNCS, vol. 5444, pp. 163–182. Springer, Heidelberg (2009)

7. Andrews, M., Awerbuch, B., Fernández, A., Kleinberg, J., Leighton, T., Liu, Z.: Universal Stability Results for Greedy Contention-Resolution Protocols. In: FOCS, pp. 380–389 (1996)
8. Awerbuch, B., Azar, Y., Plotkin, S.: Throughput-Competitive On-Line Routing. In: FOCS, pp. 401–411 (1993)
9. Awerbuch, B., Holmer, D., Nina-Rotaru, C., Rubens, H.: An On-Demand Secure Routing Protocol Resilient to Byzantine Failures. In: Workshop on Wireless Security, pp. 21–30 (2002)
10. Awerbuch, B., Leighton, T.: Improved Approximation Algorithms for the Multi-Commodity Flow Problem and Local Competitive Routing in Dynamic Networks. In: STOC, pp. 487–496 (1994)
11. Awerbuch, B., Mansour, Y., Shavit, N.: End-to-End Communication With Polynomial Overhead. In: FOCS, pp. 358–363 (1989)
12. Barak, B., Goldberg, S., Xiao, D.: Protocols and Lower Bounds for Failure Localization in the Internet. In: Smart, N.P. (ed.) EUROCRYPT 2008. LNCS, vol. 4965, pp. 341–360. Springer, Heidelberg (2008)
13. Boneh, D., Goh, E.-J., Nissim, K.: Evaluating 2-DNF Formulas on Ciphertexts. In: Kilian, J. (ed.) TCC 2005. LNCS, vol. 3378, pp. 325–341. Springer, Heidelberg (2005)
14. Borodin, A., El-Yaniv, R.: Online Computation and Competitive Analysis. Camb. Univ. Press (1998)
15. Borodin, A., Kleinberg, J., Raghavan, P., Sudan, M., Williamson, D.: Adversarial Queuing Theory. In: STOC, pp. 376–385 (1996)
16. Broder, A., Frieze, A., Upfal, E.: A General Approach to Dynamic Packet Routing with Bounded Buffers. In: FOCS, pp. 390–399 (1996)
17. Bunn, P., Ostrovsky, R.: Asynchronous Throughput-Optimal Routing in Malicious Networks. In: Abramsky, S., Gavoille, C., Kirchner, C., Meyer auf der Heide, F., Spirakis, P.G. (eds.) ICALP 2010. LNCS, vol. 6199, pp. 236–248. Springer, Heidelberg (2010)
18. Bunn, P., Ostrovsky, R.: Secure End-to-End Communication with Optimal Throughput in Unreliable Networks. Cornell Univ. Library arXiv, Article No. 1304.2454 (2013), http://arxiv.org/abs/1304.2454
19. ElGamal, T.: A Public Key Cryptosystem and a Signature Scheme Based on Discrete Logarithms. IEEE Transactions on Info. Theory 31, 469–472 (1985)
20. Goldberg, S., Xiao, D., Tromer, E., Barak, B., Rexford, J.: Path-Quality Monitoring in the Presence of Adversaries. SIGMETRICS 36, 193–204 (2008)
21. Goldwasser, S., Micali, S.: Probabilistic encryption. J. of Computer and System Sciences 28, 270–299 (1984)
22. Kushilevitz, E., Ostrovsky, R., Rosén, A.: Log-Space Polynomial End-to-End Communication. SIAM Journal of Computing 27(6), 1531–1549 (1998)
23. Leighton, T., Makedon, F., Plotkin, S., Stein, C., Tardos, É., Tragoudas, S.: Fast Approximation Algorithms for Multicommodity Flow Problem. In: STOC (1991)
24. Okamoto, T., Uchiyama, S.: A New Public-Key Cryptosystem as Secure as Factoring. In: Nyberg, K. (ed.) EUROCRYPT 1998. LNCS, vol. 1403, pp. 308–318. Springer, Heidelberg (1998)
25. Plotkin, S.: Competitive Routing of Virtual Circuits in ATM Networks. IEEE J. on Selected Areas in Communications 13(6), 1128–1136 (1995)
26. Sleator, D., Tarjan, R.: Amortized Efficiency of List Update and Paging Rules. Commun. ACM 28(2), 202–208 (1985)

On the Communication Complexity of Distributed Name-Independent Routing Schemes*

Cyril Gavoille[1], Christian Glacet[2], Nicolas Hanusse[3], and David Ilcinkas[3]

[1] LaBRI - University of Bordeaux, Bordeaux, France
[2] LaBRI - INRIA Bordeaux Sud-Ouest, Bordeaux, France
[3] LaBRI - CNRS, Bordeaux, France
{gavoille,glacet,hanusse,ilcinkas}@labri.fr

Abstract. We present a distributed asynchronous algorithm that, for every undirected weighted n-node graph G, constructs name-independent routing tables for G. The size of each table is $\tilde{O}(\sqrt{n})$, whereas the length of any route is stretched by a factor of at most 7 w.r.t. the shortest path. At any step, the memory space of each node is $\tilde{O}(\sqrt{n})$. The algorithm terminates in time $O(D)$, where D is the hop-diameter of G. In synchronous scenarios and with uniform weights, it consumes $\tilde{O}(m\sqrt{n} + n^{3/2} \min\{D, \sqrt{n}\})$ messages, where m is the number of edges of G.

In the realistic case of sparse networks of poly-logarithmic diameter, the communication complexity of our scheme, that is $\tilde{O}(n^{3/2})$, improves by a factor of $\sqrt{n}$ the communication complexity of *any* shortest-path routing scheme on the same family of networks. This factor is provable thanks to a new lower bound of independent interest.

Keywords: distributed routing algorithm, name-independent, compact routing, bounded stretch.

1 Introduction

Message routing is a central activity in any interconnection network. Route efficiency and memory requirements are two major central parameters in the design of a routing scheme. Routing along short paths is clearly desirable, and the storage of the routing information at each node must also be limited to allow quick routing decision, fast update, and scalability. There is a trade-off between the route efficiency (measured in terms of stretch) and the memory requirements (measured by the size of the routing tables). The shorter the routes, the larger the routing tables. It is also desirable that routing schemes are universal, i.e., they apply to any topology, as the model of large dynamic networks cannot be guaranteed. An additional desirable property of a routing scheme is to use arbitrary routing addresses (say based on processor IDs or MAC addresses), and

* All the authors are supported by the ANR-project DISPLEXITY (ANR-11-BS02-014), and the European STREP7-project EULER. The first author is also member of the "Institut Universitaire de France".

thus addresses independent of the topology. Such routing schemes are called name-independent.

This paper focuses on distributed algorithms that can construct universal and name-independent routing schemes for static networks. For practical use, it is essential that such distributed algorithms be as fast as possible (typically linear in the diameter) since the objective is to quickly update routing tables after topological changes in the network. Naturally, to optimize the network troughtput, a distributed algorithm must consume as few messages as possible. We are therefore interested in time and communication complexities of distributed routing schemes. There are well-established trade-offs between the stretch and the memory for centralized routing schemes (see the related works part in Section 1.4). In this paper we show some different trade-offs between the stretch, the memory, and the communication complexity of distributed routing schemes. The fundamental question we address is to determine whether or not theoretical optimal space-stretch trade-offs can be achieved when time and communication complexities are restricted.

1.1 Terminology and Models

We consider undirected weighted graphs with positive edge-weights. The *aspect ratio* of a weighted graph G is the maximum ratio between any two edge-weights in G. A *shortest path* between u and v in G is a path of minimum cost (the weight sum of the path edges) connecting u to v in G, and this cost is the *distance* between u and v. The *hop-distance* between u and v is the minimum number of edges in a shortest path between u and v. The *hop-diameter* is the largest hop-distance in the graph.

In the case of uniform weights, the aspect ratio is 1 and the hop-diameter corresponds to the classical notion of diameter in unweighted graphs. It is well-known that the asynchronous distributed Bellman-Ford algorithm can construct a shortest-path spanning tree rooted at a node u in time $h + 1$, where h is the height of the tree and also the maximum hop-distance between u and its leaves (see [13]). This time is thus at most the hop-diameter of G plus one. The hop-diameter plays an important role, not only in the time for computing a shortest-path tree, but in the running time of all subsequent distributed subroutines using this tree (e.g. for broadcasting).

A *routing scheme* on a family of graphs is an algorithm that produces, for every graph G of the family, a routing algorithm for G. A *routing algorithm* is in charge of delivering any message from every source to every destination node in G. A *name-independent* routing algorithm must deliver messages assuming that the destination names given at the sources are the original names of the input graph.

The *stretch factor* of a routing algorithm is the maximum, over all source-destination pairs (u, v), of the ratio between the cost of the route from u to v, and the distance from u to v in G. So, shortest-path routing algorithms have stretch factor exactly one. The *round-trip stretch factor* is the maximum ratio between the total cost of the route going from u to v and back to u, and the distance from u to v plus the distance from v to u. This notion is naturally used in the context of directed graphs [23], where the distance from u to v may differ from the one from v to u. In this paper, graphs are undirected though. Note that if the round-trip stretch is bounded above by s, then the average stretch (average over all the source-destination pairs) is at most s.

The *routing tables* are the local data structures used by the routing algorithm to perform routing. The *working memory space* (a.k.a. per-node state or topological memory) is the maximum memory space a node of the graph needs when running the distributed routing scheme. If the working memory space is S, then the routing tables have size at most S as well. The challenge is to design routing schemes with working memory space that is sub-linear in n and not significantly greater than the size of the final routing tables.

We assume a reliable asynchronous network, where a message sent along an edge is received after an unpredictable but finite time. The time complexity of a distributed algorithm A is the worst-case difference of time units between the first emission of a message and the last reception of a message during any execution of A, assuming the slowest message uses one time unit to traverse an edge. The *bit-message* complexity of A is the worst-case total number of bits exchanged along the edges of the graph during any execution of A. As in the standard asynchronous model, processors have no synchronous wake-up: they can either spontaneously wake up, or be activated when receiving a message. We make no assumptions on the number of messages that can be transmitted over a link in one time unit, and so we ignore congestion problems.

As specified by the name-independent model, we do not make any assumption on the distribution of node identifiers, which are chosen by an adversary. However, using hashing technique as explained in [4,8], we will assume that node identifiers can be represented on $O(\log n)$ bits.

Each message of our distributed algorithm has a poly-logarithmic size. More precisely, messages have size at most $B = O(\log W + \min\{D, \log n\} \cdot \log n)$ bits, where W is the aspect ratio and D is the hop-diameter of the graph. We also assume that each entry of the routing tables is large enough to receive B bits. The *size* of a routing table is the number of its entries. We assume that whenever a node receives a message on some incident edge, it can determine the weight of that edge.

1.2   Our Results

We design a new distributed routing scheme and two lower bounds.

– We propose an asynchronous distributed name-independent routing scheme for weighted n-node graphs of hop-diameter D. The stretch is 7 and the round-trip stretch is 5. The time complexity is $O(D)$, with a small hidden constant (< 10). Moreover, at each time of the algorithm, the working memory space of each node is[1] $\tilde{O}(\sqrt{n})$. In particular, the routing tables have size

---

[1] The notation $\tilde{O}(f(n))$ stands for a complexity in $O(f(n) \cdot \log^{O(1)} f(n))$.

$\tilde{O}(\sqrt{n})$. In a synchronous scenario, and in the case of uniform weights, the message complexity is $\tilde{O}(m\sqrt{n} + n^{3/2}\min\{D, \sqrt{n}\})$.

- For the realistic case of weighted sparse networks of poly-logarithmic hop-diameter, the message complexity is $\tilde{O}(n^{3/2})$. A simple variant of our algorithm shows that, for this same family of networks, we can achieve stretch 5 with sub-linear routing tables and sub-quadratic message complexity. See Table 1 for a summary.

Table 1. Fast distributed name-independent routing schemes for realistic weighted graphs, i.e., with $\tilde{O}(n)$ edges and $\log^{O(1)} n$ hop-diameter. The "Memory" column stands for working memory space and routing table size. Note that lower bounds are given in bits or bit-messages.

Schemes	Stretch	Memory	#Messages	Time	Reference
Distance or Path Vector	1	$\Omega(n)$	$O(n^2)$	$O(D)$	
DISTROUTE($n^{1/2}$)	7	$\tilde{O}(n^{1/2})$	$\tilde{O}(n^{3/2})$	$O(D)$	Corollary 1
DISTROUTE'($n^{2/3}$)	5	$\tilde{O}(n^{2/3})$	$\tilde{O}(n^{5/3})$	$O(D)$	Corollary 2
Memory lower bound	$< 2k+1$	$\Omega((n\log n)^{1/k})$	any	any	[2]
#Messages lower bound	1	any	$\Omega(n^2)$	$o(n)$	Theorem 2
Time lower bound	$\leqslant n/(3D)$	any	any	$\Omega(D)$	Theorem 1

Our lower bounds show that time $\Omega(D)$ is indeed required for any constant stretch, and that shortest-path routing requires $\Omega(n^2)$ bit-message complexity even on sparse graphs of logarithmic diameter. More precisely, we prove that:

(1) Every synchronous constant-stretch name-independent distributed routing scheme requires time $\Omega(D)$ on unweighted graphs of diameter D. This bound is independent of the bit-message complexity and the routing table size of the scheme.

(2) There are unweighted n-node graphs of diameter $O(\log n)$ and with maximum degree 3 for which every synchronous distributed shortest-path routing scheme (name-independent or not) of $o(n)$ time complexity requires $\Omega(n^2)$ bit-message complexity.

For these lower bounds, we assume a synchronous scenario which also implies the results for asynchronous scenarios. We also point the fact that we do not make any restriction on the message length.

1.3   Discussion

Our first lower bound may seem trivial at first glance. It is indeed immediate to show that a time $\Omega(D)$ is required for shortest-path routing schemes. Just consider for instance a path of D nodes and a source in the middle of the path. However, this folklore lower bound is less straightforward when *arbitrary* stretched routing schemes are considered. Let us stress that, for paths, the cowpath routing algorithm [12,18] achieves stretch 9 without any routing tables!

One may also think that the second lower bound is again folklore since clearly a shortest-path routing scheme must send at least one message on each edge. Otherwise subsequent routing queries will not be able to use all the edges of the graph (and so cannot be a shortest-path routing). This gives a communication complexity of $\Omega(n^2)$ for dense graphs. However, this quadratic bound cannot be guaranteed using the same argument for sparse graphs as stated by our lower bound. An option to prove a quadratic bound for sparse graphs might be to show that $\Omega(n)$ bits of information must be transmitted along long paths in the graph, say paths of $\Omega(n)$ edges. Again, this cannot be achieved for poly-logarithmic diameter graphs. Finally, we stress that the arguments of any formal proof must take into account the time complexity of the routing scheme. This is because a 1-bit message can carry more than one bit of information. For instance a 1-bit message can be sent during odd or even clock pulse to carry more information. Senders could also decide to send 1-bit or 2-bit messages, so encoding extra information with the message length.

Our distributed routing scheme, although universal, achieves better performance when realistic networks are considered. By realistic networks we mean sparse and small-diameter graphs, typically graphs with $\tilde{O}(n)$ edges and poly-logarithmic diameter. The classical Distance Vector and Path Vector routing protocols both achieve message complexity of $\Omega(mn) = \Omega(n^2)$ for realistic networks, whereas our scheme consumes at most $\tilde{O}(n^{3/2})$ messages. This good theoretical behavior is confirmed by experiments. We have implemented our routing scheme on a fully distributed routing scheme simulator[2]. For instance, on CAIDA-2004 map[3], our scheme[4] produces an average stretch of 1.75 for 534 entry routing tables on average (maximum size is 1002), and this after exchanging a total of 55M messages (synchronous scenario). Running Distance Vector on the simulator on the same graph generates routing tables of 16K entries after exchanging 1,617M messages. Note that our scheme reduces both the number of messages and the number of entries by a factor close to 30.

Our scheme is widely inspired from the universal name-independent routing scheme [4] that achieves the smallest possible stretch for routing tables of size $\tilde{O}(\sqrt{n})$. Following the work of [4], stretch-3 can be achieved at the price of an extra communication cost factor of roughly $\sqrt{n}$ over our stretch-7 scheme. The communication complexity becomes therefore $\Omega(mn)$, which is as high as the complexity of a shortest-path routing scheme. To implement the stretch-3 scheme of [4], we need to consider the set of vicinity balls touching the vicinity ball of a given node u. Unfortunately, there are small diameter graphs where each node has $\Theta(n)$ different touching vicinity balls, which implies a total volume of $\Omega(n^2)$ routing information to manage in the graph. This translates into a $\Omega(n^2)$ communication complexity. Designing a distributed routing scheme with stretch 3 and $o(n^2)$ message complexity on small diameter graphs, if it exists, requires another approach.

---

[2] Source code available on demand.

[3] It has 16K nodes and 32K edges.

[4] More precisely, we run DISTROUTE(k) for $k = 78$, see Section 3.

To conclude the discussion, let us stress that bounding the working memory space of each node considerably reduces the set of standard tricks to decrease communication complexity. For instance, when $o(n)$ working memory space is forced, then a simple broadcast in a spanning tree may cost $O(m)$ messages instead of $O(n)$ messages (since a node cannot store all its children in the tree). More generally, the γ-synchronizer methodology [9] cannot be applied, and the use of sparse spanners (like in [14]) on which subsequent routines consume less messages is problematic.

1.4 Related Works

The theory of name-independent routing schemes has a long history, and started early with Kleinroch's work about routing in the ARPANET. The first provable trade-off between the size of the routing tables and the stretch appeared in [11]. In the line of hierarchical routing schemes initiated by Kleinroch et al. [19], the authors have proposed a name-independent routing scheme of stretch $2^k - 1$ with routing tables of size $\tilde{O}(n^{1/k})$ on average, where $k \geqslant 1$ is an integral parameter. In [8], better space-stretch trade-offs have been proposed. In particular, the size of the routing tables is bounded by $\tilde{O}(n^{2/k})$ for each node, and not only on average, and the stretch is in $O(k^2)$. However, the schemes assume polynomial aspect ratio. They achieve a stretch 3 with routing tables of size $\tilde{O}(n^{2/3})$, and a stretch 5 for routing tables of size $\tilde{O}(\sqrt{n})$. Finally, [3] proposed a scheme with linear stretch $O(k)$ for routing tables of size $\tilde{O}(n^{1/k})$, and this for arbitrary weighted graphs. According to the best current lower bounds, a linear stretch[5] $\Omega(k)$ is optimal for routing tables of size $\tilde{O}(n^{1/k})$. More precisely, [2] showed that there are weighted depth-1 trees with edge-weights in $\{1, k\}$ such that every name-independent routing scheme of stretch $< 2k + 1$ requires $\Omega((n \log n)^{1/k})$-bit routing tables. According to this lower bound, routing schemes of stretch < 5 require routing tables of $\Omega(\sqrt{n \log n})$ bits ($k = 2$), and the best possible stretch for $o(n \log n)$-bit routing tables is $\geqslant 3$ ($k = 1$). Note that these lower bounds apply to realistic graphs. A scheme with stretch-3 and $\tilde{O}(\sqrt{n})$-bit routing tables has been proposed in [4], which is therefore optimal in space and stretch.

Better stretch-space trade-offs can be achieved for more specific classes of networks. Bounded growth [6] and bounded doubling dimension [1,20] graphs, trees [21], planar and more generally minor-free unweighted graphs [5], support name-independent routing schemes of constant stretch and poly-logarithmic routing tables.

For practical usage, several distributed routing schemes have been proposed and implemented, and first of all distributed shortest-path routing schemes (stretch 1). Distance Vector and Path Vector protocols are such distributed routing schemes. Based on Bellman-Ford algorithm, they produce after a time $O(D)$ shortest-path routing tables of linear size using $O(mn)$ messages, for small aspect ratio graphs. A variant of Bellman-Ford supporting an aspect ratio $W > 1$ uses $O(mn \log(nW))$ messages while preserving the time complexity. However paths

---

[5] This holds also for the average stretch.

are no longer shortest paths and may have stretch up to 3. The message complexity of shortest-path routing has been reduced to $O(n^2 \log n)$ in [7], degrading the time complexity to $O(D \log n)$. Actually, $2n^2$ messages are enough [17], but messages can be as large as $\Omega(n \log(nW))$ bits, whereas in Bellman-Ford based routing schemes and in [7], messages have size $O(\log(nW))$ bits.

As proved by the theoretical lower bounds, shortest-path routing has to be scrapped right away if sublinear working memory space and sublinear routing tables are required. In this spirit, [11] proposed a synchronous distributed routing scheme with stretch $2 \cdot 3^k - 1$ and working memory space of $\tilde{O}(d + n^{1/k})$ for a degree-d node. For $k = 2$, the working memory space and routing tables are $\tilde{O}(d + \sqrt{n})$, and the stretch is 17. In [24], a distributed implementation of a stretch-7 routing scheme is presented. Routing tables have size $\tilde{O}(\sqrt{n})$ but the message complexity is not analytically bounded. Moreover, each entry in the tables can be as large as $\Omega(D)$, and the working memory space as large as $\Omega(d\sqrt{n})$ for a degree-d node. [25] proposed a variant of the routing scheme of [4], and show experiments on synthetic power-law graphs and real AS-graphs. For these unweighted graphs, the stretch is asymptotically 2, but it is unbounded for general graphs, even unweighted ones. Techniques using sparse spanners, like in [14,15], can achieve almost shortest paths with message complexity $\tilde{O}(mn^{\epsilon_1} + n^{2+\epsilon_2})$ where $0 < \epsilon_1, \epsilon_2 < 1$ are constants that can be arbitrarily chosen and influence the stretch of the paths. We observe that for unweighted sparse graphs of small diameter, the scheme requires at least $\Omega(n^2)$ messages and $\Omega(n)$ working memory space.

As far as we know, no distributed name-independent routing scheme is able to guarantee a bounded stretch and a sublinear working memory space.

In the next section, we present our lower bounds on the time and message complexities. In Section 3, we formally present the performance of our distributed routing scheme and give an overview of the scheme. Due to lack of space, details of the proofs and of the distributed algorithm are omitted.

2   Lower Bounds

2.1   Time Lower Bound

We give a formal proof that $\Omega(D)$ time is required for any distributed routing scheme of constant stretch (the result extends to stretch as large as n/D). Our proof is independent of the message and routing table sizes used by the distributed routing scheme. The lower bound holds for single-source routing schemes, a sub-class of routing schemes. A *single-source* routing algorithm can only deliver messages from a fixed source node of the graph. And, a routing scheme is single-source if the routing algorithms it produces are single-source.

A (d, k)-star is a rooted tree with $dk + 1$ nodes obtained by replacing each edge of a $K_{1,d}$ graph, a star of degree d, by a path of k edges. The root is the degree-d node.

Theorem 1. *Every synchronous distributed name-independent routing scheme on the family of unweighted (d,k)-stars, and running in time $t < k$, produces a route of length at least $(2d-1)(k-t)+t$ between the root and some leaf.*

In particular, every synchronous distributed single-source name-independent routing scheme on unweighted n-node graphs of diameter at most $D \in \{2,\ldots,n-1\}$, and of stretch factor at most $\frac{1}{3}n/D$, requires a time $\Omega(D)$.

Note that for $t = 0$ (no pre-processing), the problem stated by Theorem 1 is equivalent to the d-lane cow-path problem in which the distance to the destination, here k, is known at the source. Our bound gives a stretch of $2d - 1$ which is known to be optimal if the distance is known and no pre-processing is allowed (cf. [12,18]).

2.2 Communication Complexity Lower Bound

Next, we prove that the $o(n^2)$ bit-message complexity for sparse graphs, as in Corollary 1, cannot be achieved without degrading the stretch factor. Importantly, the bound holds independently of the compactness of the routing tables, and of the message length.

Theorem 2. *There are a constant $\lambda > 0$, and some unweighted n-node graphs of diameter $O(\log n)$ and maximum degree 3, for which every synchronous distributed shortest-path routing scheme (name-independent or not) of time complexity at most λn requires $\Omega(n^2)$ bit-message complexity.*

3   An Asynchronous Distributed Routing Scheme

Our distributed routing scheme, denoted by DISTROUTE(k), assumes that each node initially receives a color[6] in $\{1,\ldots,k\}$, where k is an integral parameter of our scheme. In practice, each node picks its color independently at random in $\{1,\ldots,k\}$. However our scheme is deterministic. As we will see in Theorem 3, the correctness of our scheme is independent of the node coloring, which is not the case of the routing scheme of [4].

Theorem 3. *Let G be a connected weighted n-node graph of hop-diameter D. For every k-coloring of G, DISTROUTE(k) is a deterministic asynchronous distributed routing scheme for G. It runs in time $O(D)$. The message complexity is no more than $O(n)$ times the number of messages that a single-source distributed Bellman-Ford consumes in G.*

The routing algorithm it produces has stretch 7, round-trip stretch 5, and uses headers of $O(\min\{D,\log n\} \cdot \log n) = O(\log^2 n)$ bits. Each routing decision takes constant time, and the header of each routing message, once created at the source, is modified at most once along the path to the destination.

---

[6] We do not impose that neighbors get different colors.

Our scheme directly depends on the asynchronous distributed Bellman-Ford that can generate $\Omega(2^n)$ messages in worst-case asynchronous scenarios and for graphs of large aspect ratio (see [10]). So, in some occasions, our scheme may generate an exponential number of messages. However, in a synchronous scenario and for graphs of low aspect ratio, the message complexity is polynomial. Note that it is well-known that the message complexity of the distributed Bellman-Ford algorithm is polynomial on average, and even $O(n^2\Delta^3)$ with overwhelming probability, where Δ is the maximum degree of the graph [26].

The next result (Theorem 4) specifies the size of the routing tables and the message complexity. Both complexities depend on the node coloring, the aspect ratio W of the graph, and on synchrony. The parameters involved in the analysis, namely n, m, D, W, are not known by the nodes when the distributed scheme starts. We will essentially make the two following assumptions:

Random Coloring. The node coloring is uniformly random in $\{1, \ldots, k\}$, and $k = n^\alpha$ for some constant $\alpha \in (0, 1)$. The results claimed under this stochastic hypothesis then hold in expectation or with high probability (w.h.p.)[7], where the probabilities are computed over all k-colorings of the graph.

Synchronous Scenario. The network is synchronous. In that case, the distributed Bellman-Ford algorithm uses a polynomial number of messages.

Hereafter, we define $\xi = 1 + D(1 - 1/W)$. This value appears in the message complexity of our scheme in synchronous scenarios. It corresponds to the maximum number of times a node u changes its state when computing the hop-distance to a node v. At each change, u sends a message to its neighbors. Observe that for uniform weighted graphs $\xi = 1$ as $W = 1$.

Theorem 4. *Let G be a connected weighted n-node graph of hop-diameter D, with m edges, and with aspect ratio W. Under the random coloring hypothesis, DISTROUTE(k) on G produces w.h.p. a working memory space and routing tables of size $O(k \log k + n/k)$. Furthermore if the scenario is also synchronous, the message complexity is, in expectation,*

$$O\left(\xi m \left(k \log k + \frac{n}{k}\right) + \frac{n^2}{k} \cdot \min\{D, k\}\right) .$$

So, for $k = \sqrt{n/\log n}$ the routing tables have $O(\sqrt{n \log n})$ entries, and in the case of uniform weights ($W = \xi = 1$), the message complexity in Theorem 4 even simplifies to

$$\tilde{O}(m\sqrt{n} + n^{3/2} \cdot \min\{D, \sqrt{n}\}) .$$

Another important particular corollary of our analysis is the following:

Corollary 1. *Under random coloring and synchronous hypotheses, and for weighted n-node graphs with $\tilde{O}(n)$ edges and poly-logarithmic hop-diameter, the distributed routing scheme DISTROUTE$(\sqrt{n})$ has message complexity $\tilde{O}(n^{3/2})$, produces a stretch-7 routing algorithm, and w.h.p. a working memory space and routing tables of size $\tilde{O}(\sqrt{n})$.*

---

[7] It means that it holds with probability at least $1 - 1/n^c$ for some constant $c \geqslant 1$.

A simple variant of our algorithm, denoted by DISTROUTE$'(k)$, fulfills all the statements of Theorem 3 except that it achieves stretch 5. This is done at a price of an extra communication cost of $O(n^3/k^2 \cdot \min\{D, k\})$ messages (under the hypothesis of Theorem 4). We obtain another trade-off which is:

Corollary 2. *Under random coloring and synchronous hypotheses, and for weighted n-node graphs with $\tilde{O}(n)$ edges and poly-logarithmic hop-diameter, the distributed routing scheme* DISTROUTE$'(n^{2/3})$ *has message complexity $\tilde{O}(n^{5/3})$, produces a stretch-5 routing algorithm, and w.h.p. a working memory space and routing tables of size $\tilde{O}(n^{2/3})$.*

The message complexity that can be achieved by DISTROUTE or DISTROUTE$'$ on realistic graphs without the synchronous hypothesis is significantly higher than $\Omega(n^2)$. Observe however that by a slight modification of the algorithms, namely by adding an α-synchronizer (cf. [22]), we can still guarantee a message complexity of respectively $\tilde{O}(n^{3/2})$ and $\tilde{O}(n^{5/3})$ in the asynchronous setting while keeping a time complexity of $O(D)$.

3.1   Overview of the Scheme

Consider an initial uniformly random k-coloring of the nodes of the graph, and denote by $c(u) \in \{1, \ldots, k\}$ the color selected by node u. In parallel of the coloring, nodes are split into groups of size $O(n/k)$ thanks to a fixed balanced hash function h, as in [4], mapping in constant time and w.h.p. the node identifiers to the set $\{1, \ldots, k\}$. A node of color i will be responsible of the routing information for all the nodes of hash value i. Nodes of color 1, called *landmarks*, have a special use in the scheme.

Consider an arbitrary node u. Node u stores three types of routing information. (1) The node u stores in a table B_u the information on how to route along shortest paths to its *vicinity ball*, a set containing $O(k \log k)$ nodes closest to u. More precisely, this ball contains the smallest number of nodes closest to u such that each color has been chosen by at least one node of the ball. (2) For each landmark l, the node u stores a shortest path between l and u. These pieces of information are stored in a table L_u. (3) For each node v such that $h(v) = c(u)$, the node u stores in a table C_u the closest landmark to v, namely l_v, and a shortest path from l_v to v.

All these paths stored in the second and third tables are not arbitrary but are extracted from fixed shortest-path spanning trees T_l rooted at each landmark l. Moreover, paths are stored in a compressed way into *routing labels*, using only $O(\min\{D, \log n\} \cdot \log n)$ bits, thanks to a distributed variant of the technique of [16]. Overall, the routing table of u has size $O(k \log k + n/k)$ since there are $O(n/k)$ landmarks and nodes with the same hash value.

We now describe how the actual routing from a source s to a destination t is performed using these tables. If $t \in B_s$, then the table B_s allows s to transmit the packet along a shortest path to t. Otherwise, node s forwards the packet to the closest node $u \in B_s$ such that $c(u) = h(t)$. This is done by putting u's identifier in the header of the packet. Also, note that u may be the node s itself. Once in u, the header is replaced by l_t and the compressed path from l_t to t stored in the table C_u. Now, thanks to the header and to the tables L_v of all the intermediate nodes v, the packet will follow the unique path from u to t in the shortest-path spanning tree T_{l_t} rooted in l_t (see Fig. 1).

In practice, the routing algorithm can be improved when routing on the unique path from u to t in T_{l_t}. Each intermediate node v on this path first checks whether node t_i, the i-th nearest ancestor of t on the path from l_t to t, belongs to B_v and is not an ancestor of v in T_{l_t}. In that case, v can route directly to t_i along a shortest path, producing a shortcut in the path from v to t_i in T_{l_t}. These nodes t_i are contained in the header available at v, and they are checked in the order $t_0, t_1, t_2, \ldots$ where $t_0 = t$. Actually, due to the compressed representation of the path, only $\min\{D, \log n\}$ nodes t_i are available at v.

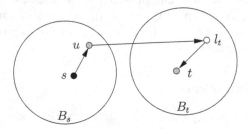

Fig. 1. Routing from s to t where $c(u) = h(t)$

The stretch analysis of the routing algorithm is as follows. If $t \in B_s$, the stretch is 1. Otherwise, assume that s and t are at distance d. Then the cost of the route $s \rightsquigarrow u$ is at most d, since $t \notin B_s$. The route $l_t \rightsquigarrow t$ is at most $2d$ since the landmark of s (that is in B_s) is at distance at most $2d$ from t, and l_t is the closest landmark to t. It follows that the cost of the route $u \rightsquigarrow l_t$ is bounded by the cost of the route $u \rightsquigarrow s \rightsquigarrow t \rightsquigarrow l_t$ which is at most $4d$. Therefore, the cost of the route $s \rightsquigarrow u \rightsquigarrow l_t \rightsquigarrow t$ is at most $d + 4d + 2d = 7d$. The round-trip stretch analysis is similar and gives an upper bound of 5.

Note that stretch 5 can be achieved if the segment of the route $u \rightsquigarrow t$ would have been done in tree T_{l_s} instead of T_{l_t}. Indeed, the route $u \rightsquigarrow t$ would not be longer that the route $u \rightsquigarrow s \rightsquigarrow l_s \rightsquigarrow s \rightsquigarrow t$ where each of the four segments is a shortest path of length at most d, yielding to a total of $5d$ from s. In other words, u could have store a better landmark tree path in C_u for v. We use this observation for the variant DISTROUTE$'(k)$ and to prove Corollary 2. Unfortunately, this consumes more messages to construct such enhanced tables C_u.

3.2   Overview of the Distributed Routing Scheme

The goal of the distributed routing scheme is to compute, for every node u, the tables B_u, L_u and C_u. The computation of the table C_u is made after every node v has computed its landmark table L_v. For that we use a weak synchronization that allows to reduce the number of messages in asynchronous environments since no unreliable information about landmark tables are sent. Thereby our algorithm can be described as two sub-algorithms that run in parallel. The first one computes B_u, and the second one computes L_u, then C_u.

The algorithm to compute vicinity balls is similar to the distributed Bellman-Ford algorithm. The main difference is that to construct B_u, the closest nodes to u start a shortest-path tree spanning u. Importantly, to save messages, tie break between candidates of the last layer for B_u is selected according to the arrival order of their discovery message received at u. This also guarantees that the monotony property of vicinity balls is respected: the next-hop w to reach any $v \in B_u$ from u verifies that $v \in B_w$. In the synchronous scenario, the construction of all vicinity balls takes $O(\xi mk \log k)$ messages.

The algorithm to construct L_u and C_u is subdivised into the following steps, each one runing in time $O(D)$.

Step 1. Each landmark l starts the construction of a shortest-path spanning tree T_l. During this process, node u stores its parents in T_l for all the landmarks, and learns the landmark of smallest identifier, the leader denoted by $l_{\min}$. In a synchronous scenario, Step 1 consumes $O(\xi mn/k)$ messages.

Step 2. After detecting termination of Step 1, the routing label of u in each tree T_l, denoted by $\ell(u, T_l)$, is computed by a process we describe in Section 3.3. After Step 2, L_u is computed, and u can determine its closest landmark denoted by l_u. The termination detection of Step 1 is done by $l_{\min}$ and takes $O(m)$ messages, and Step 2 consumes $O(mn/k)$ messages in total. Note that our bound on the working memory space prevents us from broadcasting in a tree in $O(n)$ messages, because a node cannot store all its children.

The goal of the last two steps is to construct C_u. For that, u needs to retrieve the routing label $\ell(v, T_{l_v})$ for every node v such that $h(v) = c(u)$. For that, every node v of hash value $h(v)$ sends its label to its closest node of color $h(v)$, say w. Node w is then in charge of broadcasting this message to all nodes u of color $h(v)$. It is important to note that we want a more efficient algorithm than a simple broadcast for each node, which would require $\Omega(n^2)$ messages.

Step 3. In this step, we construct an efficient broadcasting scheme composed of k *logical trees*, one for each color. We will use them in Step 4. For every color $i \in \{1, \ldots, k\}$, we build a logical tree $\mathcal{T}_i$ whose node-set is composed only of nodes of color i in G. An edge between w and w' in $\mathcal{T}_i$ represents a path from w to w' in $T_{l_{\min}}$ without any intermediate node of color i.

To construct the edge $\{w, w'\}$ in $\mathcal{T}_i$, w sends to its parent in $T_{l_{\min}}$ a message $\langle i, \ell(w, T_{l_{\min}}) \rangle$ to find a potential parent in $\mathcal{T}_i$. (There is a special treatment we do not detail whenever w has no ancestor of color i in $T_{l_{\min}}$.) Such a message is forwarded to the parent of the current node until a node w' of color i is encountered. Whenever node w' learns the existence of w, it knows how to reach w through the routing label $\ell(w, T_{l_{\min}})$. It acknowledges to w by indicating its own routing label $\ell(w', T_{l_{\min}})$.

We can prove that edges of $\mathcal{T}_i$ are composed on average of $t \leqslant 2 \min \{D, k\}$ edges of G. So, to construct $\mathcal{T}_i$ it takes $O(n_i t)$ messages, where n_i is the number of nodes of color i. For all the k logical trees, this sums to $O(\sum_i n_i t) = O(nt) = O(n \min \{D, k\})$ messages.

Step 4. Node v sends the identifier l_v and its routing label $\ell(v, T_{l_v})$ to w, its closest node of color $i = h(v)$. Node w broadcasts this label to its neighbors in $\mathcal{T}_i$. Eventually, any node u of color $i = c(u) = h(v)$ will receive all such labels to construct its table C_u. Thus v contributes to $O(\min \{D, k \log k\})$ messages for the construction of C_u, the hop-distance between v and w. Then, from w, the cost of broadcasting this label is $O(n/k \cdot t)$ messages, since there are $O(n/k)$ nodes in $\mathcal{T}_i$ connected by paths of at most t edges. Therefore, to construct all the tables C_u, and to complete Step 4, we need $O(n \cdot (\min \{D, k \log k\} + n/k \cdot t)) = O(n^2/k \cdot \min \{D, k\})$ messages since $k \leqslant n$.

The variant DISTROUTE$'(k)$ is a slight change in Step 4 only. It consists in broadcasting from v the whole collection of routing labels $\ell(v, T_l)$, for each landmarks l, instead of only $\ell(v, T_{l_v})$. These labels are already stored by v in L_v. Then node u, combining with its own routing labels in L_u can select the best landmark tree for each v. This allows u to store an enhanced table C_u producing a stretch at most 5, according to the remark in the stretch analysis of DISTROUTE(k). The counterpart of this stretch improvement is that node v sends $O(n/k)$ more messages than initially. This is $O(n^3/k^2 \cdot \min \{D, k\})$ messages in total for Step 4, the previous steps being the same.

3.3 Routing Labels

We give in this part some details about routing label computation. Let us consider a shortest-path tree T of G rooted at node r. Note that in T the path between any two nodes contains $O(D)$ edges. Every node can compute a routing label of $O(\min \{D, \log n\} \cdot \log n)$ bits such that routing can be achieved using these labels and headers of the same size. Routing decisions take a constant time. We adapt an algorithm described in [16] which allows to compute in a centralized way routing labels with similar size. However, the solution proposed in [16] would have, in a distributed setting, a time complexity of $O(n)$ due to the computation of a DFS number for every node, this DFS number is part of the routing label. Since we aim at a time complexity $O(D)$, we made some changes to the routing scheme in order to avoid this DFS construction.

In order to compute its routing label $\ell(u, T)$, every node u computes its weight (its number of descendants in T), together with its *heaviest child*. These two metrics can be computed by using a *global function* as described in [22]. Once every node has computed these metrics, node r can initiate the computation of a compact path from r to every other node. A compact path is a sequence of node identifiers in which every identifier that corresponds to an heaviest child identifier is replaced by a star $*$. This computation can be achieved by broadcasting compact paths in T from r. Once a node u has calculated its compact path, namely path$_u^*$, it can compute locally $\ell(u, T)$ with the following algorithm.

The routing label $\ell(u, T)$ is composed of (1) the cpath$_u$ which is path$_u^*$ where every star sequence is replaced by its own length; (2) and a bit-set b_u that allows to determine whether an element of cpath_u is a node identifier or a star sequence's length. An example of such a routing label is given in table 2.

Table 2. A simple example of $\ell(u, T)$ after computation, considering that u_1 heaviest child is u_2, u_2 heaviest child is u_3 and u_4 heaviest child is u_5

path in T	$u_0 = r$	u_1	u_2	u_3	u_4	$u_5 = u$
path_u^*	u_0	u_1	*	*	u_4	*
cpath_u	u_0	u_1	2		u_4	1
b_u	1	1	0		1	0

The routing algorithm at node u with destination v is performed as follows. Node u will use $\ell(u, T)$ and $\ell(v, T)$ to determine the next-hop to v. In short, using these labels, node u can determine an approximate location of v in T. To do so, u has to find the longest matching prefix of $\ell(u, T)$ and $\ell(v, T)$. This actually requires two computations: node u has to find the longest matching prefix of the two bit-sets b_u and b_v, and the longest matching prefix of cpath_u and cpath_v. Once this is done, u can determine whether v is a descendant of u or not (note that the common ancestor of u and v can be v itself). In the latter case, u routes the packet to its parent in T. Conversely, if v is a descendant, then using the first element of the bit-set b_v, node u determines whether the next-hop to v is u's heaviest child or not:

- if it is, then node u knows its heaviest child identifier and can thus route the packet to it;
- if it is not, then the next-hop is part of $\ell(v, T)$, which is contained in the header of the packet and thus, node u can route the packet.

Thus u can route to any node v in T using only $\ell(u, T)$ and $\ell(v, T)$.

References

1. Abraham, I., Gavoille, C., Goldberg, A.V., Malkhi, D.: Routing in networks with low doubling dimension. In: 26th International Conference on Distributed Computing Systems (ICDCS). IEEE Computer Society Press (July 2006)
2. Abraham, I., Gavoille, C., Malkhi, D.: On space-stretch trade-offs: Lower bounds. In: 18th Annual ACM Symposium on Parallel Algorithms and Architectures (SPAA), pp. 217–224. ACM Press (July 2006)
3. Abraham, I., Gavoille, C., Malkhi, D.: On space-stretch trade-offs: Upper bounds. In: 18th Annual ACM Symposium on Parallel Algorithms and Architectures (SPAA), pp. 207–216. ACM Press (July 2006)
4. Abraham, I., Gavoille, C., Malkhi, D., Nisan, N., Thorup, M.: Compact name-independent routing with minimum stretch. ACM Transactions on Algorithms 3, Article 37 (2008)
5. Abraham, I., Gavoille, C., Malkhi, D., Wieder, U.: Strong-diameter decompositions of minor free graphs. Theory of Computing Systems 47, 837–855 (2010)

6. Abraham, I., Malkhi, D.: Name independent routing for growth bounded networks. In: 17th Annual ACM Symposium on Parallel Algorithms and Architectures (SPAA), pp. 49–55. ACM Press (July 2005)
7. Afek, Y., Ricklin, M.: Sparser: A paradigm for running distributed algorithms. Journal of Algorithms 14, 316–328 (1993)
8. Arias, M., Cowen, L.J., Laing, K.A., Rajaraman, R., Taka, O.: Compact routing with name independence. SIAM Journal on Discrete Mathematics 20, 705–726 (2006)
9. Awerbuch, B.: Complexity of network synchronization. Journal of the ACM 32, 804–823 (1985)
10. Awerbuch, B., Bar-Noy, A., Gopal, M.: Approximate distributed Bellman-Ford algorithms. IEEE Transactions on Communications 42, 2515–2519 (1994)
11. Awerbuch, B., Bar-Noy, A., Linial, N., Peleg, D.: Improved routing strategies with succinct tables. Journal of Algorithms 11, 307–341 (1990)
12. Baeza-Yates, R.A., Culberson, J.C., Rawlins, G.J.E.: Searching in the plane. Information and Computation 106, 234–252 (1993)
13. Bertsekas, D.P., Gallager, R.G.: Data Networks, 2nd edn. Routing in Data Networks, ch. 5. Prentice Hall (1992)
14. Elkin, M.: Computing almost shortest paths. ACM Transactions on Algorithms 1, 283–323 (2005)
15. Elkin, M., Zhang, J.: Efficient algorithms for constructing $(1 + \epsilon, \beta)$-spanners in the distributed and streaming models. Distributed Computing 18, 375–385 (2006)
16. Fraigniaud, P., Gavoille, C.: Routing in trees. In: Orejas, F., Spirakis, P.G., van Leeuwen, J. (eds.) ICALP 2001. LNCS, vol. 2076, pp. 757–772. Springer, Heidelberg (2001)
17. Haldar, S.: An 'all pairs shortest paths' distributed algorithm using $2n^2$ messages. Journal of Algorithms 24, 20–36 (1997)
18. Kao, M.-Y., Reif, J.H., Tate, S.R.: Searching in an unknown environment: An optimal randomized algorithm for the cow-path problem. Information and Computation 131, 63–79 (1996)
19. Kleinrock, L., Kamoun, F.: Hierarchical routing for large networks; performance evaluation and optimization. Computer Networks 1, 155–174 (1977)
20. Konjevod, G., Richa, A.W., Xia, D.: Optimal-stretch name-independent compact routing in doubling metrics. In: 25th Annual ACM Symposium on Principles of Distributed Computing (PODC), pp. 198–207. ACM Press (July 2006)
21. Laing, K.A.: Name-independent compact routing in trees. Information Processing Letters 103, 57–60 (2007)
22. Peleg, D.: Distributed Computing: A Locality-Sensitive Approach. SIAM Monographs on Discrete Mathematics and Applications (2000)
23. Roditty, L., Thorup, M., Zwick, U.: Roundtrip spanners and roundtrip routing in directed graphs. ACM Transactions on Algorithms 3, Article 29 (2008)
24. Singla, A., Godfrey, P.B., Fall, K., Iannaccone, G., Ratnasamy, S.: Scalable routing on flat names. In: 6th International Conference on Emerging Networking EXperiments and Technologies (CoNEXT), Article No. 20. ACM Press (November 2010)
25. Tang, M., Zhang, G., Lin, T., Liu, J.: HDLBR: A name-independent compact routing scheme for power-law networks. Computer Communications 36, 351–359 (2013)
26. Tsitsiklis, J.N., Stamoulis, G.D.: On the average communication complexity of asynchronous distributed algorithms. Journal of the ACM 42, 382–400 (1995)

Convergence in (Social) Influence Networks

Silvio Frischknecht, Barbara Keller, and Roger Wattenhofer

Computer Engineering and Networks Laboratory (TIK), ETH Zürich, Switzerland
{fsilvio,barkelle,wattenhofer}@tik.ee.ethz.ch

Abstract. We study the convergence of influence networks, where each node changes its state according to the majority of its neighbors. Our main result is a new $\Omega(n^2/\log^2 n)$ bound on the convergence time in the synchronous model, solving the classic "Democrats and Republicans" problem. Furthermore, we give a bound of $\Theta(n^2)$ for the sequential model in which the sequence of steps is given by an adversary and a bound of $\Theta(n)$ for the sequential model in which the sequence of steps is given by a benevolent process.

Keywords: Social Networks, Stabilization, Democrats and Republicans, Majority Function, Equilibrium.

1 Introduction

What do social networks, belief propagation, spring embedders, cellular automata, distributed message passing algorithms, traffic networks, the brain, biological cell systems, or ant colonies have in common? They are all examples of "networks", where the entities of the network are continuously influenced by the states of their respective neighbors. All of these examples of *influence networks* (INs) are known to be difficult to analyze. Some of the applications mentioned are notorious to have long-standing open problems regarding convergence.

In this paper we deal with a generic version of such networks: The network is given by an arbitrary graph $G = (V, E)$, and all nodes of the graph switch simultaneously to the state of the majority of their respective neighbors. We are interested in the stability of such INs with a binary state. Specifically, we would like to determine whether an IN converges to a stable situation or not. We are interested in how to specify such a stable setting, and in the amount of time needed to reach such a stable situation. We study several models how the nodes take turns, synchronous, asynchronous, adversarial, benevolent.

Our main result is for synchronous INs: Each node is assigned an initial state from the set $\{R, B\}$, and in every round, all nodes switch their state to the state of the majority of their neighbors simultaneously. This specific problem is commonly referred to as "Democrats and Republicans", see e.g. Peter Winkler's CACM column [Win08]. It is well known that this problem stabilizes in a peculiar way, namely that each node eventually is in the same state every second round [GO80]. This result can be shown by using a potential bound argument, i.e., until stabilization, in each round at least one more edge becomes "more stable". This directly gives a $\mathcal{O}(n^2)$ upper bound for the

Y. Afek (Ed.): DISC 2013, LNCS 8205, pp. 433–446, 2013.

convergence time. On the other hand, using a slightly adapted linked list topology, one can see that convergence takes at least $\Omega(n)$ rounds. But what is the correct bound for this classic problem? Most people that worked on this problem seem to believe that the linear lower bound should be tight, at least asymptotically. Surprisingly, in the course of our research, we discovered that this is not true. In this paper we show that the upper bound is in fact tight up to a polylogarithmic factor. Our new lower bound is based on a novel graph family, which has interesting properties by itself. We hope that our new graph family might be instrumental to research concerning other types of INs, and may prove useful in obtaining a deeper understanding of some of the applications mentioned above.

We complement our main result with a series of smaller results. In particular, we look at asynchronous networks where nodes update their states sequentially. We show that in such a sequential setting, convergence may take $\Theta(n^2)$ time if given an adversarial sequence of steps, and $\Theta(n)$ if given a benevolent sequence of steps.

2 Related Work

Influence networks have become a central field of study in many sciences. In biology, to give three examples from different areas, [RT98] study networks in the context of brain science, [AAB$^+$11] study cellular systems and their relation to distributed algorithms, and [AG92] study networks in the context of ant colonies. In optimization theory, believe propagation [Pea82, BTZ$^+$09] has become a popular tool to analyze large systems, such as Bayesian networks and Markov random fields. Nodes are continuously being influenced by their neighbors; repeated simulation (hopefully) quickly converges to the correct solution. Belief propagation is commonly used in artificial intelligence and information theory and has demonstrated empirical success in numerous applications such as coding theory. A prominent example in this context are the algorithms that classify the importance of web pages [BP98, Kle99]. In physics and mechanical engineering, force-based mechanical systems have been studied. A typical model is a graph with springs between pairs of nodes. The entire graph is then simulated, as if it was a physical system, i.e. forces are applied to the nodes, pulling them closer together or pushing them further apart. This process is repeated iteratively until the system (hopefully) comes to a stable equilibrium, [KK89, Koh89, FR91, KW01]. Influence networks are also used in traffic simulation, where nodes (cars) change their position and speed according to their neighboring nodes [NS92]. Traffic networks often use cellular automata as a basic model. A cellular automaton [Neu66, Wol02] is a discrete model studied in many fields, such as computability, complexity, mathematics, physics, and theoretical biology. It consists of a regular grid of cells, each in one of a finite number of states, for instance 0 and 1. Each cell changes its state according to the states of its neighbors. In the popular game of life [Gar70], cells can be either dead or alive, and change their states according to the number of alive neighbors.

Our synchronous model is related to cellular automata, on a general graph; however, nodes change their opinion according to the majority of their neighbors. As majority functions play a central role in neural networks and biological applications this model was already studied during the 1980s. Goles and Olivos [GO80] have shown that a synchronous binary influence network with a generalized threshold function always leads to a fixed point or to a cycle of length 2. This means that after a certain amount of synchronous rounds, each participant has either a fixed opinion or changes its mind in every round. Poljak and Sura [PS83] extended this result to a finite number of opinions. In [GT83], Goles and Tchuente show that an iterative behavior of threshold functions always leads to a fixed point. Sauerwald and Sudholt [SS10] study the evolution of cuts in the binary influence network model. In particular, they investigate how cuts evolve if unsatisfied nodes flip sides probabilistically. To some degree, one may argue that we look at the deterministic case of that problem instead.

In sociology, understanding social influence (e.g. conformity, socialization, peer pressure, obedience, leadership, persuasion, sales, and marketing) has always been a cornerstone of research, e.g. [Kel58]. More recently, with the proliferation of online social networks such as Facebook, the area has become en vogue, e.g. [MMG+07, AG10]. Leskovec et al. [LHK10] for instance verify the balance theory of Heider [Hei46] regarding conformity of opinions; they study how positive (and negative) influence links affect the structure of the network. Closest to our paper is the research dealing with influence, for instance in the form of sales and marketing. For example, [LSK06] investigate a large person-to-person recommendation network, consisting of four million people who made sixteen million recommendations on half a million products, and then analyze cascades in this data set. Cascades can also be studied in a purely theoretical model, based on random graphs with a simple threshold model which is close to our majority function [Wat02]. Rumor spreading has also been studied algorithmically, using the random phone call model, [KSSV00, SS11, DFF11]. Using real data from various sources, [ALP12] show that networks generally have a core of influential (elite) users. In contrast to our model, nodes cannot change their state back and forth, once infected, a node will stay infected. Plenty of work was done focusing on the prediction of influential nodes. One wants to find subset of influential nodes for viral marketing, e.g. [KKT05, CYZ10]. In contrast, [KOW08] studies the case of competitors, which is closer to our model since nodes can have different opinions. However, also in [KOW08] nodes only change their opinion once. However, in all these social networks the underlying graph is fixed and the dynamics of the stabilization process takes place on the changing states of the nodes only. An interesting variant changes the state of the edges instead. A good example for this is matching. A matching is (hopefully) converging to a stable state, based on the preferences of the nodes, e.g. [GS62, KPS10, FKPS10]. Hoefer takes these edge dynamics one step further, as not only the state of the edge changes, but the edge itself [Hoe11].

3 Model Definition

An *influence network* (IN) is modeled as a graph $G = (V, E, o_0)$. The set of nodes V is connected by an arbitrary set of edges E. Each node has an initial opinion (or state) $o_0(v) \in \{R(ed), B(lue)\}$. A node only changes its opinion if a majority of its neighbors has a different opinion. One may consider several options to breaking ties, e.g., using the node's current opinion as a tie-breaker, or weighing the opinions of individual neighbors differently. As it turns out, for many natural tie-breakers, graphs can be reduced to equivalent graphs in which no tie breaker is needed. For instance, using a node's own opinion as a tie-breaker is equivalent to cloning the whole graph, and connecting each node with its clone and the neighbors of its clone.

In this paper we study both synchronous and asynchronous INs. The state of a synchronous IN evolves over a series of rounds. In each round every node changes its state to the state of the majority of its neighbors simultaneously. The opinion of a node v in round t is denoted as $o_t(v)$.

As will be explained in Section 5, the only interesting asynchronous model is the sequential model. In this model, we call the change of opinion of one node a *step*. The opinion of node v after t steps is defined as $o_t(v)$. In general, more than one node may be ready to take a step. Depending on whether we want convergence to be fast or slow, we may choose different nodes to take the next step. If we aim for fast convergence, we call this the *benevolent sequential model*. Slow conversion on the other hand we call the *adversarial sequential model*.

We say that an IN stabilizes if it reaches a state where no node will ever change its opinion again, or if each node changes its opinion in a cyclic pattern with periodicity q. In other words, a state can be stable even though some nodes still change their opinion.

Definition 1. *An IN $G = (V, E, o_0)$ is stable at time t with periodicity q, if for all vertices $v \in V : o_{t+q}(v) = o_t(v)$. A fixed state of an IN G is a stable state with periodicity 1. The* convergence time c *of an IN G is the smallest t for which G is stable.*

Note that since INs are deterministic an IN which has reached a stable state will stay stable.

In this paper we investigate the stability, the convergence time c and the periodicity q of INs in the described models. Clearly, the convergence process depends not only on the graph structure, but also on the initial opinions of the nodes. We investigated graphs and initial opinions that maximize convergence time. In the benevolent sequential in particular, we investigate graphs and sets of initial opinions leading to the worst possible convergence time, given the respectively best sequence of steps.

4 Synchronous IN

A synchronous IN may stabilize in a state where some nodes change their opinion in every round. For example, consider the graph K_2 (two nodes, connected by an edge) where the first node has opinion B and the second node has opinion R. After one round, both vertices have changed their state, which leads to a symmetric situation. This IN remains in this stable state forever with a period of length 2. As has already been shown in [GO80, Win08], a synchronous IN always reaches a stable state with a periodicity of at most 2 after $\mathcal{O}(n^2)$ rounds.

Theorem 1 ([Win08]). *A synchronous influence network reaches a stable state after at most $\mathcal{O}(n^2)$ rounds.*

Theorem 2 ([GO80]). *The periodicity of the stable state of a synchronous influence network is at most 2.*

We prove this bound to be almost tight.

Theorem 3. *There exists a family of synchronous influence networks with convergence time of $\Omega\left(\frac{n^2}{(\log\log n)^2}\right)$.*

Due to page limitations the technical proof of Theorem 3 does not fit here, but can be found in the full version of this paper. In this section, we instead present a simpler IN with convergence time $\Omega(n^{3/2})$.

The basic idea is to construct a mechanism which forces vertices on a simple path graph to change their opinion one after the other. Every time the complete path has changed, the mechanism should force the vertices of the path to change their opinions back again in the same order. To create this mechanism, we introduce an auxiliary structure called transistor, which is depicted in Figure 1.

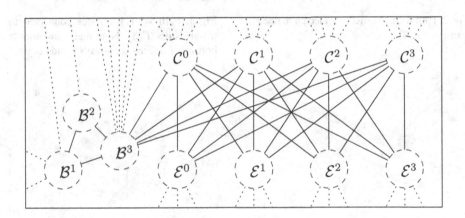

Fig. 1. A transistor $T(4)$. The dotted lines indicate how the transistor will be connected.

Definition 2. *A transistor of size k, denoted as $T(k)$, is an undirected graph consisting of three base vertices $\mathcal{B} = \{\mathcal{B}^1, \mathcal{B}^2, \mathcal{B}^3\}$, k collector vertices $\mathcal{C} = \{\mathcal{C}^i \mid 0 \leq i \leq k-1\}$ and k emitter vertices $\mathcal{E} = \{\mathcal{E}^i \mid 0 \leq i \leq k-1\}$. All edges between collector and emitter vertices, all edges between any two base vertices, and all edges between collector vertices and the third base vertex exist. Formally:*

$$T(s) = (V, E)$$
$$V = \mathcal{C} \cup \mathcal{E} \cup \mathcal{B}$$
$$E = \{\{u, v\} \mid u \in \mathcal{C}, v \in \mathcal{E}\} \cup \{\{u, \mathcal{B}^3\} \mid u \in \mathcal{C}\} \cup$$
$$\{\{u, v\} \mid u, v \in \mathcal{B}, u \neq v\}$$

All nodes in a transistor are initialized with the same opinion $X \in \{R = 1, B = -1\}$. The $3 + k + k^2$ collector edges (dotted edges pointing to the top of Figure 1, including those originating from $\mathcal{B}^1, \mathcal{B}^2$ and $\mathcal{B}^3$) are connected to vertices with the constant opinion $-X$, while up to $k^2 - k$ emitter edges (dotted edges pointing to the bottom) and the 2 base edges (dotted edges pointing to the left) may be connected to any vertex. As soon as both base edges advertise opinion $-X$, the transistor will flip to opinion $-X$ in 4 rounds regardless of what is advertised over the emitter edges, i.e., the following sets of vertices will all change their opinion to $-X$ in the given order: $\{\mathcal{B}^1\}, \{\mathcal{B}^2, \mathcal{B}^3\}, \mathcal{C}, \mathcal{E}$.

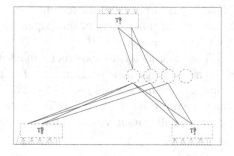

Fig. 2. Path with 4 vertices connected to one transistor $T(3)$

Fig. 3. Path with 4 vertices connected to 3 transistors $T(3)$. Note that transistors at bottom of figures are always upside down.

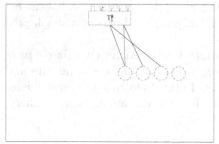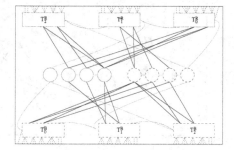

Fig. 4. Two copies of Figure 3 with inverse opinions

Fig. 5. In this graph, every time the path has run through completely the next transistor will flip, causing the path to run again

Note that $T(k)$ contains only $\mathcal{O}(k)$ many vertices, yet its emitter vertices can potentially be connected to $\Omega(k^2)$ other vertices. Given a path graph of length $\mathcal{O}(k^2)$ and a transistor $T(k)$, the emitter vertices of the transistor are connected to the path in the following way: The first vertex in the path is connected to exactly two emitter vertices, the last is connected to none and each of the remaining nodes of the path is connected to exactly one emitter vertex. Furthermore, the collector edges of transistors of opinion X are always connected to constant reservoirs of opinion $-X$. Such a reservoir can be implemented as a clique. An illustration of this graph with $k = 3$ is given in Figure 2. Without loss of generality, we set the initial state of the nodes of the path to B, and that

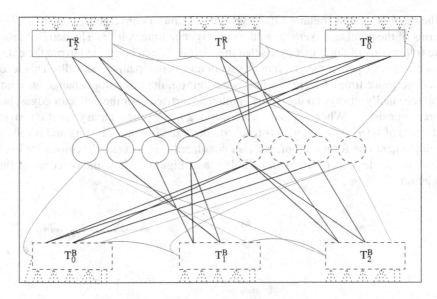

Fig. 6. Final graph in which the paths run 3 times. For an illustration with colors please refer to the electronic version of this paper.

of the transistor to R. As long as the transistor remains red, the path will turn red one vertex at a time. As soon as the transistor flips its opinion to blue (as a result of both base edges having advertised blue) the path will turn blue again, one vertex at a time. To force the path to change k times, k transistors are needed. Each of these transistors (note that we make use of red as well as blue transistors) is connected with the path in the same way as the first transistor. The resulting graph is given in Figure 3. A series of k switches of the complete path can now be provoked by switching transistors of alternating opinions in turns. For the example depicted in the Figures, the switching order of the transistors is given by their respective indices.

Now, a way is needed to flip the next transistor every time the last vertex of the path has changed its opinion. Assume the last vertex has changed to red. It is necessary to flip a red transistor to blue in order to change the path to blue; however, the path changing to red can only cause a blue transistor to turn red. To this end, the graph is extended by a copy of itself with all opinions inverted. The resulting graph is given in Figure 4. As in every round each vertex in the copy is of the opposite opinion than its original, the copy of the last vertex in the path enables us to flip a red transistor to blue as desired. The edges necessary to achieve this (highlighted in green in Figure 5) connect the end of a path to $\mathcal{B}^1$ of each transistor in the other half of the graph. To ensure that the transistors flip in the required order, additional edges (highlighted in magenta in Figure 5) are introduced, connecting an emitter node of each transistor T_i^X to the node $\mathcal{B}^1$ of transistor T_{i+1}^X.

The green edges cause an unwanted influence on the last vertex of the paths. This influence can be negated by introducing additional edges (highlighted in cyan in Figure 6). These edges connect the last vertex of each path with an emitter vertex of each transistor not yet connected to that vertex.

The resulting graph contains $\mathcal{O}(k^2)$ vertices, yet has a convergence time of $\Omega(k^3)$. In terms of the number of vertices n, the convergence time is $n^{3/2}$. The detailed proof in the full version of this paper shows that this technique can be applied to run the entire graph repeatedly, just as the graph in this section runs two paths repeatedly. This leads to a convergence time of $\Omega(n^{7/4})$. In this new graph, the transistors change back and fourth repeatedly, always taking on the opinion advertised over the collector edges, just like real transistors. When applied recursively $\log\log n$ times, an asymptotic convergence time of $\Omega(n^2/(\log\log n)^2)$ is reached. Since the full proof is long and involved, to complement our formal proof, we also simulated this recursively constructed networks for path lengths of up to 100. Table 1 and Figure 7 show the outcome of this simulation.

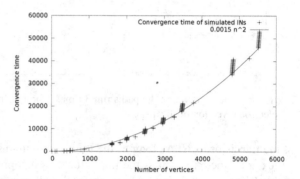

Table 1. Table summarizing the simulated results

path length	#nodes	convergence time
1	10	1
2	12	2
3	96	22
10	494	310
20	1614	3331
30	2010	5701
100	5518	45985

Fig. 7. Shows how our simulation results compare to a quadratic curve. The point clusters arise when for several consecutive path lengths no new transistor is created. Small jumps in the number of vertices indicate that a new transistor was added; big jumps indicate that a new layer of transistors was added.

5   Sequential IN

To complement our results for the synchronous model, we consider an asynchronous setting in this section. In an asynchronous setting, nodes can take steps independently of each other, i.e. subsets of nodes may reassess and change their opinion concurrently. Unfortunately, in such a setting, convergence time is not well defined. To see this, consider a star-graph where the center has a different initial opinion than the leaves. An adversary may arbitrarily often chooses the set of all nodes to reassess their opinion. After r such rounds the adversary chooses only the center node. Now this IN stabilizes, after r rounds for an arbitrary $r \to \infty$. In other words, asynchrony in its most general form is not well defined, and we restrict ourselves to sequential steps only, whereas a step is a single node changing its opinion. The sequence of steps is chosen by an adversary which tries to maximize the convergence time. Note that the convergence upper bound presented in Lemma 1 implies immediately that the IN stabilizes in a fixed state.

Lemma 1. *A sequential IN reaches a fixed state after at most $\mathcal{O}(n^2)$ steps.*

Proof. Divide the nodes into the following two sets according to their current opinion: $S_R = \{v \mid o(v) = R\}$ and $S_B : \{v \mid o(v) = B\}$. If a node changes its opinion, it has more neighbors in the opposite set than in its current set. Therefore the number of edges $X = \{\{u, v\} \mid u \in S_R, v \in S_B\}$ between nodes in set S_R and set S_B is strictly decreasing. Each change of opinion reduces the number of edges of X by at least one. Therefore the number of steps is bounded by the number of edges in X. In a graph G with n nodes $|X|$ is at most $n^2/4$, therefore at most $\mathcal{O}(n^2)$ steps can take place until the IN reaches a fixed state.   □

It is more challenging to show that this simple upper bound is tight. We show a graph and a sequence of steps in which way an adversary can provoke $\Omega(n^2)$ convergence time.

Lemma 2. *There is a family of INs with n vertices such that a fixed state is reached after $\Omega(n^2)$ steps.*

Algorithm 1. Adversarial Sequence

```
S ← ()
for i = 0 to n/3 do
    S = reverse(S);
    S ← (i, S);
    for all x ∈ S do
        take step x;
    end for
end for
```

Proof. Consider the following graph G with n nodes. The nodes are numbered from 0 to $n-1$, whereas nodes with an even id are initially assigned opinion B and nodes with an odd id are assigned opinion R. See also Figure 8. All even nodes with $id \leq n/3$ are connected to all odd nodes. All odd nodes with $id \leq n/3$ are connected to all even nodes respectively. In addition an even node with $id \leq n/3$ is connected to nodes $\{0, 2, 4, \ldots, n - 2 \cdot id - 2\}$, respectively an odd node with $id \leq n/3$ is connected to nodes $\{1, 3, 5, \ldots, n - 2 \cdot id - 3\}$. For example, node 0 is a neighbor of all nodes, whereas node 1 is neighbor of all nodes except the nodes $n - 1$ and $n - 3$. Note that each node i with $i \leq n/3$ is connected to all other nodes with $id \leq n/3$. For each node v the change potential $P(v)$ is defined as:

$$P(v) = |\{u \mid o(u) \neq o(v)\}| - |\{u \mid o(u) = o(v)\}|$$

Put differently, if the change potential of a node is larger than 0, and it is requested to reassess its opinion, it takes a step. A large change potential of a node v, means that many neighbors of v have the opposite opinion from v. If a neighbor of v with the same

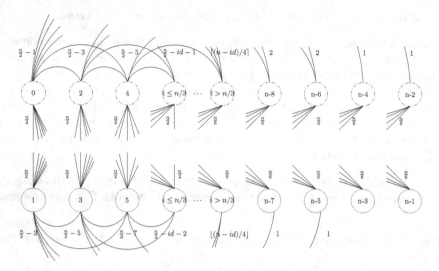

Fig. 8. In this graph an adversary can provoke $\Omega(n^2)$ changes of opinion

opinion takes a step, $v's$ change potential $P(v)$ is increased by 2. On the other hand, if a neighbor changes from the opposite opinion to the same opinion as node v, $P(v)$ is decreased by 2. If v itself changes its opinion, its change potential turns from p to $-p$. The change potential of v is basically the number of edges by which the total number of edges between set S_B and set S_R is reduced if v changes its opinion. As the total amount of steps is bounded by the number of edges between set S_B and S_R, a node v with $P(v) = p$ reduces the remaining number of possible changes by p if it takes a step. E.g. in the previously constructed graph G, the first nodes have the following change potential: $P(0) = 1, P(1) = 3, P(2) = 3, P(3) = 5$ Generally, node i has a change potential $P(i) = n/2 - (n/2 - i - 1) = i + 1$ if i is even respectively $P(i) = i + 2$ if i is odd. In order to provoke as many steps as possible, the adversary selects the nodes which have to reassess their opinion according to the following rule: He chooses the node with the smallest id for which $P(v) = 1$. Therefore each step reduces the remaining number of possible steps by 1. G is constructed in such a way, that a step from a node triggers a cascade of steps from nodes which have already changed their opinion whereas each change reduces the overall potential by 1.

The adversary chooses the nodes in phases according to algorithm 1. Phase i starts with the selection of node i followed by the selections of all nodes with $id < i$, where the adversary chooses the nodes in the reverse order than it did in round $i - 1$. Phase 0 consists of node 0 changing its opinion, in phase 1 node 1 and then node 0 make steps, and in phase 2 the nodes change in the sequence $2, 0, 1$. As a node v can only change its opinion if $P(v) > 0$, we need to show that this is the case for each node v which is selected by the adversary. It is sufficient to show that each node which is selected has a change potential of 1.

We postulate:

(i) At the beginning of phase i, it holds that: $P(i) = 1$ and $\forall v < i : o(v) = o(i)$.
(ii) Each node the adversary selects has change potential 1 and each node with $id \leq i$ is selected eventually in phase i.
(iii) At the end of phase i, all nodes with $id \leq i$ have opinion R if i is even and opinion B if i is odd.

We prove (i), (ii) and (iii) by induction. Initially, part (i) holds, as no node with $id < 0$ exists and as node 0 is connected to $n/2$ nodes with opinion R and to $n/2 - 1$ nodes with opinion B and therefore has change potential 1. In phase 0 only node 0 is selected, therefore part (ii) of holds as well. Node 0 changed its opinion and has therefore at the end of phase 0 opinion R, therefore part (iii) holds as well.

Now the induction step: To simplify the proof of part (i) of we consider odd and even phases separately. Consider an odd phase i. At the start of phase i, no node with $id \geq i$ has changed its opinion yet. Therefore node i still has its initial opinion $o(i) = R$. According to (iii), each node with $id \leq i - 1$ has at the end of phase $i - 1$ opinion $R = o(i)$. So $(i + 1)/2$ neighbors of i have compared to the initial state, changed their opinion from B to R. If a neighbor u of a node v with a different opinion than v changes it, $v's$ change potential is decreased by 2. Therefore node $i's$ initial change potential $P_{t_0}(i) = n/2 - (n/2 - i - 2) = i + 2$ is decreased by $2 \cdot (i + 1)/2 = i + 1$ and is therefore $P(i) = i + 2 - (i + 1) = 1$ at the beginning of phase i. Therefore (i) holds before an odd phase.

Now consider an even phase i. At its start, all nodes with $id \geq i$ still have their initial opinion. Therefore node i has opinion $o(i) = B$. According to (iii) each node with $id \leq i - 1$ has at the end of phase $i - 1$ opinion $B = o(i)$. As node $i's$ initial change potential was $P_{t_0}(i) = n/2 - (n/2 - i - 1) = i + 1$ and $i/2$ neighbors of i changed from opinion R to opinion B compared to the initial state, $i's$ new change potential is calculated as $P(i) = i + 1 - 2 \cdot i/2 = 1$. Therefore (i) holds before an even phase, hence (i) holds.

To prove part (ii) let v be the last node which was selected in phase $i - 1$. As v was selected, it had according to (ii) a change potential of 1. If a node changes its opinion, its change potential gets inversed. Therefore node v had at the beginning of phase i a change potential of -1. In addition, node v is by construction a neighbor of node i and has according to (i) at the start of phase i the same opinion as node i. As node i changes its opinion, node $v's$ change potential is increased by 2. Therefore $v's$ new change potential is again $-1 + 2 = 1$, when it is selected by the adversary. The same argument holds for the second last selected node u. After it was selected in phase $i - 1$ its change potential was -1. Then v has changed its opinion which led to $P(u) = -3$. As node i and node v changed their opinions in phase i, $P(u)$ was again 1. Hence if the adversary selects the nodes in the inverse sequence as in phase $i - 1$, each selected node has a change potential of 1 and is selected eventually. Therefore (ii) holds.

As node i and all nodes with $id \leq i - 1$ had at the beginning of phase i the opinion $o(i)$ according to (iii) and all nodes have changed their opinion in phase i according to (ii), all nodes with $id \leq i$ must have the opposite opinion at the end of phase i, namely R if i is even or B otherwise. Therefore (iii) holds as well.

We now have proven that in phase i, i nodes change their opinion. As the adversary starts n/3 phases, the total number of steps is $1/2 \cdot n/3 \cdot (n/3 - 1) \in \Omega(n^2)$.   □

Directly from Lemma 1 and Lemma 2, we get the following theorem.

Theorem 4. *A worst case sequential IN reaches a fixed state after $\Theta(n^2)$ steps.*

We have seen, that with an adapted graph and an adversary an IN takes up to $\Theta(n^2)$ steps until it stabilizes. But how bad can it get, if the process is benevolent instead?

Theorem 5. *An IN with a benevolent sequential process reaches a fixed state after $\Theta(n)$ steps.*

Proof. A benevolent process needs $\Omega(n)$ steps to reach a stable state. This can be seen by considering the complete graph K_n with initially $\lfloor n/2 \rfloor - 1$ red nodes and $\lceil n/2 \rceil + 1$ blue nodes. Independently of the chosen sequence this IN needs exactly $\lfloor n/2 \rfloor - 1$ steps to stabilize because the only achievable stable state is all nodes being blue. To proof that the number of steps is bounded by $\mathcal{O}(n)$ we define the following two sets: The set of all red nodes which want to change: $C_{Ri} = \{v \mid o(v) = R \wedge P(v) > 0\}$ and the set of all blue nodes which want to change: $C_B = \{v \mid o(v) = B \wedge P(v) > 0\}$. A benevolent process chooses nodes in two phases. In the first phase it chooses nodes from C_B until the set is empty. During this phase, it may happen that additional nodes join C_B (e.g. a leaf of a node $v \in C_B$, after v made a step). However, no node which left C_B will rejoin, as those nodes turned red and can not turn blue again in this phase. In the second phase, the benevolent process chooses nodes from C_R until this set is empty. The set C_B will stay empty during the second phase since nodes turning blue can only reinforce blue nodes in their opinion. Both phases take at most n steps, therefore proving our upper bound.   □

References

[AAB+11] Afek, Y., Alon, N., Barad, O., Hornstein, E., Barkai, N., Bar-Joseph, Z.: A Biological Solution to a Fundamental Distributed Computing Problem. Science, 183–185 (2011)

[AG92] Adler, F.R., Gordon, D.M.: Information Collection and Spread by Networks of Patrolling Ants. The American Naturalist, 373–400 (1992)

[AG10] Asuncion, A.U., Goodrich, M.T.: Turning Privacy Leaks into Floods: Surreptitious Discovery of Social Network Friendships and Other Sensitive Binary Attribute Vectors. In: Workshop on Privacy in the Electronic Society (WPES), pp. 21–30 (2010)

[ALP12] Avin, C., Lotker, Z., Pignolet, Y.A.: On The Elite of Social Networks. In: Personal Communication (2012)

[BP98] Brin, S., Page, L.: The Anatomy of a Large-Scale Hypertextual Web Search Engine. In: Seventh International World-Wide Web Conference, WWW (1998)

[BTZ+09] Bickson, D., Tock, Y., Zymnis, A., Boyd, S.P., Dolev, D.: Distributed Large Scale Network Utility Maximization. In: International Conference on Symposium on Information Theory, ISIT (2009)

[CYZ10] Chen, W., Yuan, Y., Zhang, L.: Scalable Influence Maximization in Social Networks under the Linear Threshold Model. In: Industrial Conference on Data Mining (ICDM), pp. 88–97 (2010)

[DFF11]   Doerr, B., Fouz, M., Friedrich, T.: Social Networks Spread Rumors in Sublogarithmic Time. In: Symposium on Theory of Computing (STOC), pp. 21–30 (2011)

[FKPS10] Floréen, P., Kaski, P., Polishchuk, V., Suomela, J.: Brief Announcement: Distributed Almost Stable Marriage. In: Principles of Distributed Computing (PODC), pp. 281–282 (2010)

[FR91]   Fruchterman, T.M.J., Reingold, E.M.: Graph Drawing by Force-Directed Placement. In: Software: Practice and Experience, pp. 1129–1164 (1991)

[Gar70]   Gardner, M.: Mathematical Games: The Fantastic Combinations of John Conway's new Solitaire Game "Life". Scientific American, 120–123 (1970)

[GO80]   Goles, E., Olivos, J.: Periodic Behaviour of Generalized Threshold Functions. Discrete Mathematics, 187–189 (1980)

[GS62]   Gale, D., Shapley, L.S.: College Admissions and the Stability of Marriage. The American Mathematical Monthly, 9–15 (1962)

[GT83]   Goles, E., Tchuente, M.: Iterative Behaviour of Generalized Majority Functions. In: Mathematical Social Sciences, pp. 197–204 (1983)

[Hei46]   Heider, F.: Attitudes and Cognitive Organization. Journal of Psychology, 107–112 (1946)

[Hoe11]   Hoefer, M.: Local Matching Dynamics in Social Networks. In: Aceto, L., Henzinger, M., Sgall, J. (eds.) ICALP 2011, Part II. LNCS, vol. 6756, pp. 113–124. Springer, Heidelberg (2011)

[Kel58]   Kelman, H.C.: Compliance, Identification, and Internalization: Three Processes of Attitude Change. Journal of Conflict Resolution, 51–60 (1958)

[KK89]   Kamada, T., Kawai, S.: An Algorithm for Drawing General Undirected Graphs. Information Processing Letters, 7–15 (1989)

[KKT05]   Kempe, D., Kleinberg, J.M., Tardos, É.: Influential Nodes in a Diffusion Model for Social Networks. In: Caires, L., Italiano, G.F., Monteiro, L., Palamidessi, C., Yung, M. (eds.) ICALP 2005. LNCS, vol. 3580, pp. 1127–1138. Springer, Heidelberg (2005)

[Kle99]   Kleinberg, J.M.: Hubs, Authorities, and Communities. ACM Computing Surveys, CSUR (1999)

[Koh89]   Kohonen, T.: Self-Organization and Associative Memory. Springer (1989)

[KOW08]   Kostka, J., Oswald, Y.A., Wattenhofer, R.: Word of mouth: Rumor dissemination in social networks. In: Shvartsman, A.A., Felber, P. (eds.) SIROCCO 2008. LNCS, vol. 5058, pp. 185–196. Springer, Heidelberg (2008)

[KPS10]   Kipnis, A., Patt-Shamir, B.: On the Complexity of Distributed Stable Matching with Small Messages. Distributed Computing, 151–161 (2010)

[KSSV00] Karp, R., Schindelhauer, C., Shenker, S., Vocking, B.: Randomized Rumor Spreading. In: Foundations of Computer Science, FOCS (2000)

[KW01]   Kaufmann, M., Wagner, D.: Drawing Graphs: methods and models. Springer (2001)

[LHK10]   Leskovec, J., Huttenlocher, D.P., Kleinberg, J.M.: Signed Networks in Social Media. In: Conference on Human Factors in Computing Systems (CHI), pp. 1361–1370 (2010)

[LSK06]   Leskovec, J., Singh, A., Kleinberg, J.M.: Patterns of Influence in a Recommendation Network. In: Ng, W.-K., Kitsuregawa, M., Li, J., Chang, K. (eds.) PAKDD 2006. LNCS (LNAI), vol. 3918, pp. 380–389. Springer, Heidelberg (2006)

[MMG+07] Mislove, A., Marcon, M., Gummadi, K.P., Druschel, P., Bhattacharjee, B.: Measurement and Analysis of Online Social Networks. In: 7th ACM SIGCOMM Conference on Internet Measurement, pp. 29–42 (2007)

[Neu66]   Von Neumann, J.: Theory of Self-Reproducing Automata. University of Illinois Press (1966)

[NS92]   Nagel, K., Schreckenberg, M.: A Cellular Automaton Model for Freeway Traffic. Journal de Physique I, 2221–2229 (1992)

[Pea82]   Pearl, J.: Reverend Bayes on Inference Engines: A Distributed Hierarchical Approach. In: Second National Conference on Artificial Intelligence (AAAI), pp. 133–136 (1982)

[PS83]   Poljak, S., Sra, M.: On Periodical Behaviour in Societies with Symmetric Influences. Combinatorica, 119–121 (1983)

[RT98]   Rolls, E.T., Treves, A.: Neural Networks and Brain Function. Oxford University Press, USA (1998)

[SS10]   Sauerwald, T., Sudholt, D.: A Self-Stabilizing Algorithm for Cut Problems in Synchronous Networks. Theoretical Computer Science, 1599–1612 (2010)

[SS11]   Sauerwald, T., Stauffer, A.: Rumor Spreading and Vertex Expansion on Regular Graphs. In: Symposium on Discrete Algorithms (SODA), pp. 462–475 (2011)

[Wat02]   Watts, D.J.: A Simple Model of Global Cascades on Random Networks. Proceedings of the National Academy of Sciences, 5766–5771 (2002)

[Win08]   Winkler, P.: Puzzled: Delightful Graph Theory. Communications of the ACM, 104 (2008)

[Wol02]   Wolfram, S.: A New Kind of Science. Wolfram Media (2002)

Trustful Population Protocols*

Olivier Bournez, Jonas Lefevre, and Mikaël Rabie

LIX, Ecole Polytechnique, 91128 Palaiseau Cedex, France
first.last-name@lix.polytechnique.fr

Abstract. Population protocols have been introduced by Angluin *et al.* as a model in which passively mobile anonymous finite-state agents stably compute a predicate of the multiset of their inputs via interactions by pairs. Stably computable predicates under this model have been characterized as exactly semi-linear predicates, that is to say exactly those definable in Presburger's arithmetic.

We consider several variants of the models. In all these variants, the agents are called *trustful*: agents with a similar opinion that meet do not change their common opinion. We provide a characterization of the computational power of the obtained models, considering both the case when agents have finitely many states, and when agents can possibly be arbitrary Turing machines. We also provide some time complexity considerations.

1 Introduction

The model of population protocol has been introduced in [5] as a model of anonymous agents, with finitely many states, that interact in pairs. One basic assumption of the model is the absence of a control over the way pairwise interactions happen: whereas the result of interactions is programmable, agents are assumed to be passively mobile.

The model has been designed in [3,5] as computing predicates: Given some input configuration, the agents have to decide whether this input satisfies the predicate. In this case the population of agents has to eventually stabilize to a configuration in which every agent is in accepting state. This must be happening with the same program for all population size.

Predicates computable by population protocols have been characterized as being precisely the semi-linear predicates; that is those predicates that are definable in first-order Presburger arithmetic [5,3].

Many works on population protocols have concentrated latter on on characterizing what predicates on the input configurations can be stably computed in different variants of the models and under various assumptions. Variants of the original model considered so far include restriction to one-way communications [3], restriction to particular interaction graphs [4], and random interactions [5]. Various kinds of fault tolerance have been considered for population

---

* Regular paper.

Y. Afek (Ed.): DISC 2013, LNCS 8205, pp. 447–461, 2013.

protocols [19], including the search for self-stabilizing solutions [7]. We refer to [8,15] for a more comprehensive survey or introduction.

As far as we know, in all already considered restrictions, agents are not restricted to be *trustful*: agents with similar opinion that meet can still change their opinion. In many contexts, and in particular in models coming from social networks [20] or natural algorithms [17], it makes sense to assume that people agreeing still agree after meeting. Notice that this is often a very basic assumption of models in all these contexts: see for example all the models in [13]. This current paper is born from an attempt to understand the impact of such a restriction on the population protocol model.

We consider in this paper several variants of population protocols where agents are *trustful*: The purpose of these restrictions is to add a notion of trust between agents: if two agents having a similar opinion meet, they do not change it. For all considered obtained variant, we provide an exact characterization of computable predicates.

More precisely, to model the notion of opinion in population protocols, we consider that the set of possible states is partitioned into finitely many subsets corresponding to the possible opinions. Once an agent has an opinion, if it meets an agent with the same opinion, then both necessarily remain with the same opinion. We distinguish *weakly* from *strongly* trustful population protocols. In the second, agents always have an opinion, and agreeing agents cannot disagree after a meeting, and cannot even change of state when they meet. In the first, agents can possibly have no-opinion before getting a opinion. We only impose that agents with an opinion keep their opinion when meeting agents with same opinion.

We characterize predicates computable by trustful population protocols in both variants. We basically prove that both variants compute exactly the same predicates that is to say boolean combination of threshold predicates with null constant.

This can also be interpreted as follows: we get first that computable predicates must be invariant by multiplication of populations: if a predicate is computed by a trustful population protocol, then its value must be the same on input E and on k times input E, where k is any integer constant. If one prefers, computable predicates are necessarily *frequency-based*, i.e. a predicate on frequencies of letters in the input. Then our results says basically that all such semi-linear predicates are indeed computable using trustful population protocols, under both variants.

We then consider the case of agents that can be non-finite state: agents can be arbitrary Turing machines. We still characterize computable predicates, as basically all frequency based computable predicates. We then go to complexity considerations, and we prove that all computable predicates can be computed using $O(n^2 \log n)$ expected interactions.

Related Work. The model of population protocols can be considered as modeling any population of indistinguishable agents interacting in pairs in a Markovian manner. This framework includes many models from nature, physics, and biology (see, e.g., [22]). Several papers have already demonstrated the benefit of using an algorithmic approach for understanding such models (see, e.g., the recent papers [10,17,18]). Conversely, models from nature, physics, and biology can be viewed as alternative paradigms of computation (see, e.g., [1,9]).

Population protocols have been introduced in [5]. In the model, interactions are not assumed to be Markovian, but a weaker (hence covering this case, if reasoning with probability one) notion of interactions is considered, based on fairness. The model was designed to decide logic predicates, and predicates computable by classical population protocols have been characterized [5,6]. Various restrictions on the initial model have been considered up to now [8,15]. As far as we know, the idea of restricting to trustful interactions has not be considered yet.

We obtain in this paper at the end that trustful interactions yield to models whose computable predicates must be frequency based. Similar results have been obtained in another model in [21]. Consequently, our paper shares many similarities with this paper. Notice that, whereas in [21] an exact characterization of the computational power of the model is still to be fully understood, we obtain here a precise characterization for trustful population protocols.

The idea of considering population protocols where agents are not finite state is not new: [14] considers for example interacting Turing machines. In particular, it is proved that if each agent is a Turing machine with a space $f(n)$ for a population of size n, then for $f = \Omega(\log n)$, the computational power of the model is exactly the class of all symmetric predicates recognizable by a nondeterministic Turing machine in space $nf(n)$. We consider here trustful versions of such protocols.

More generally, the idea that interacting agents with a similar opinion do not change their opinion is a very common assumption in all models from social networks see e.g. [13,17]. Considering that the interactions are frequency based and that the macroscopic dynamics of populations are given by laws of evolution on frequencies of agents (in possible microscopic states) in the system, it is something very natural. This is also a basic assumption in all models of nature, physics, and biology (see, e.g., [22]). That is also true for all classical models from evolutionary game theory [23]. Some connections between the dynamics of games and population protocols have been studied in [11,16].

Somehow, our paper provides a rather simple and nice explanation of the impact of assuming trustful interactions, or of why and when modeling dynamics by frequency based dynamics is natural and legitimate.

2   Models

Trustful Population Protocols are obtained as a restriction over the rules of the known model of Population Protocols.

Weakly and Strongly Trustful Population Protocols. We now introduce more formally (trustful) population protocols [3,5]: basically, a computation is always over a finite set of agents. Each agent starts with an input in Σ and has its state in Q where Σ is a finite alphabet, and Q a finite set of states. The population evolves by pairwise interactions. Each such interaction has the effect of (possibly) changing the state of the two agents according to some program, that is to say a function δ that maps couple of states (previous states of involved agents) to couple of states (next states of these agents).

A protocol computes a function (a predicate) from multisets over Σ to a finite set Y: encoding and decoding is given by two functions ι and ω. Given some input, that is to say a multiset over Σ, the initial state of the population is given by applying function $\iota : \Sigma \to Q$ element-wise. A computation can provide several outputs, each possible one being in Y. To interpret the output of an agent, it is sufficient to apply ω to its current state.

As we want to talk about trustful protocols, that is to say agents with opinions, we add to the classical model [3,5] the fact that the set of states is partitioned into a finite set of opinions.

More formally:

Definition 1 (Trustful Population Protocol). *A Trustful Population Protocol is given by 7 elements $(I, Q, \Sigma, \iota, Y, \omega, \delta)$ where:*

- *Q is a finite set of states partitioned in $|I|$ subsets: that is to say, $Q = \bigcup_{i \in I} Q_i$ with $Q_i \cap Q_j = \emptyset$ if $i \neq j$.*
- *Σ is the finite set of entry symbols.*
- *ι is a function $\Sigma \to Q$.*
- *Y is the finite set of possible outputs.*
- *ω is a function $I \to Y$.*
- *δ is a function $Q^2 \to Q^2$.*

A *Configuration* is a multiset over Q. As agents are assumed to be anonymous, a configuration can be described by only counting the number of agents in each state. In other words, a configuration can be considered as an element of $\mathbb{N}^{|Q|}$. An *input* is a multiset of Σ (i.e. an element of $\mathbb{N}^{|\Sigma|}$). The initial configuration is computed by applying ι to each agent, i.e. apply ι to the input. A *Step* is the passage between two configurations $C_1 \to C_2$, where all the agents but two do not change: we apply to the two other agents a_1 and a_2 the rule corresponding to their respective state q_1 and q_2, i.e. if $\delta(q_1, q_2) = (q'_1, q'_2)$ (also written by rule $q_1 q_2 \to q'_1 q'_2$), then in C_2 the respective states of a_1 and a_2 are q'_1 and q'_2.

Remark 1. Notice that unlike [3,5], and most following works, we do not restrict to the case where $Y = \{True, False\}$. One motivation is to be able to talk about the averaging problem: see below.

We add now two restrictions on how the interactions can happen when two agents have the same opinion to get the notion of trustful interactions. In the *strong* version, two agents do not change their state if they meet an agent with a similar opinion. The *weak* version just gives the constraint that the new states remain in the same subset of opinion and we add a subset for agents not having yet any opinion. We will prove later that these two versions compute exactly the same functions.

Definition 2 (Strongly Trustful Population Protocol). *A Strongly Trust-ful Population Protocol is such as δ does not modify two agents with the same opinion: $\forall i \in I, \forall q_1, q_2 \in Q_i, \delta(q_1, q_2) = (q_1, q_2)$.*

Definition 3 (Weakly Trustful Population Protocol). *A Weakly Trustful Population Protocol is such as δ remains stable under two agents with the same opinion, if they have one (i.e. we add a no opinion set $Q_?$, corresponding to states from which agents can change their state regardless of the state met):*

$$\forall i \in I - \{?\}, \forall q_1, q_2 \in Q_i, \delta(q_1, q_2) = (q_1', q_2') \Rightarrow q_1', q_2' \in Q_i.$$

We will use the terminology *Population Protocol* for the original model from [3,5]: that is to say, for the case when no restriction on δ is made, i.e. interactions are not restricted to be trustful.

Computing with population protocols. We now recall the notion of computation by a population protocol, and we recall known facts about the computational power of the original model.

Definition 4 (Fair Sequence of Configurations). *A Sequence of Configu-rations is a sequence $(C_i)_{i \in \mathbb{N}}$ such as for all i, $C_i \to C_{i+1}$, C_0 being an initial configuration. We say that a sequence is Fair if, for each configuration C ap-pearing infinitely often in the sequence and for each configuration C' such as $C \to C'$, C' also appears infinitely often in the sequence.*

The notion of fairness is here to avoid worst adversaries: for example, an adver-sary that would choose the same pair at each time to interact. It is also moti-vated by giving a very weak constraint that covers the case of (non-degenerated) Markovian random interactions: if pairs of agents are chosen randomly and if C appears infinitely often and $C \to C'$, then the probability for C' to appears infinitely often is 1, and hence sequence of configurations are fair almost surely.

We need to say explicitly how configurations are interpreted, in particular in our settings. This is rather natural:

Definition 5 (Interpretation of a configuration). *A configuration has an Interpretation $y \in Y$ if for every state q present in the configuration, the $i \in I$ such as $q \in Q_i$ has the property $\omega(i) = y$. If there is no $y \in Y$ such as the configuration has interpretation y, the configuration is interpreted has having no interpretation.*

Definition 6 (Function computed by a population protocol). *A popula-tion protocol Computes y on some input S, if for every fair sequence $(C_i)_{i \in \mathbb{N}}$ starting from the initial configuration corresponding to S, there exists some in-teger J such as, for all $j > J$, the configuration C_j has the interpretation y.*
A Protocol computes a function $f : \mathbb{N}^{|\Sigma|} \to Y$ if for every input $S \in \mathbb{N}^{|\Sigma|}$, the protocol computes $f(S)$ on S.

Computational power. We recall the main result from [3,5] on the computational power of population protocols: There are two ways to describe what can be computed by Population Protocols, one using Presburger's Arithmetic, and the other based on semi-linear spaces.

Definition 7 (Semi-linear set). *A* Linear *set S of* $\mathbb{N}^d$ *is a set such that one can find $k + 1$ vectors $u, v_1, \ldots, v_k \in \mathbb{N}^d$ such as $S = \{u + \sum_{i=1}^{k} a_i v_i | a_1, \ldots a_k \in \mathbb{N}\}$. A* Semi-Linear *set is a finite union of linear-sets.*

Theorem 1 ([3,5]). *Let f be a function computed by a population protocols. For every $y \in Y$, $f^{-1}(y)$, seen as a subset of $\mathbb{N}^{|\Sigma|}$, is a semi-linear sets of $\mathbb{N}^{|\Sigma|}$.*

From the equivalence between semi-linear sets and subsets definable in Presburger's Arithmetic, this can also be seen as follows:

Definition 8 (Definability in Pressburger's Arithmetic). *A subset of $\mathbb{N}^{|\Sigma|}$ is* definable in Presburger's Arithmetic *if it corresponds to a boolean combination of formulas of the form: (Here formulas are interpreted as subsets corresponding the set of elements satisfying the formula: n_i is the number of elements i in the population; the a_i, b and c's are integers. $\equiv b$ [c] denotes congruence to b modulo c.)*

$$- \sum_{s \in \Sigma} a_s n_s \geq b$$
$$- \sum_{i \in \Sigma} a_s n_s \equiv b \ [c]$$

Theorem 2 ([3,5]). *Let f be a function computed by a population protocols. For every $y \in Y$, $f^{-1}(y)$, seen as a subset of $\mathbb{N}^{|\Sigma|}$, is definable in Presburger's Arithmetic.*

3   Some Particular Trustful Protocols

We describe now two protocols that are both strongly and weakly trustful. They will be used later on in our proofs.

3.1   The Threshold Problem

Definition 9 (Threshold Problem). *The* Threshold *problem is the following problem: We have a function $g : \Sigma \to [a, b]$, an integer c, $Y = \{True, False\}$, and we want to compute the function f such as:*

$$f(input) = True \Leftrightarrow \sum_{s \in \Sigma} g(s) n_s \geq c.$$

Proposition 1. *When $c = 0$, the Threshold problem can be computed by both versions of trustful population protocols.*

Proof (Sketch). Here is the protocol:

- $Q = Q_+ \bigcup Q_-$, with $Q_+ = [a, 0[\cup \{0^-\}$ and $Q_+ = [0, b]$.
- Σ, $\iota = g$, $Y = \{True, False\}$, $\omega(+) = True$ and $\omega(-) = False$.
- δ is given by the following rules:

$$
\begin{array}{llll}
i & j \to 0 & (i+j) & \text{if } i \times j < 0 \text{ and } i+j \geq 0 \\
i & j \to 0^- & (i+j) & \text{if } i \times j < 0 \text{ and } i+j < 0 \\
0^- & i \to 0 & i & i \geq 0 \\
0 & i \to 0^- & i & i < 0
\end{array}
$$

First, it is clear that this protocol is both strongly and weakly trustful. Second, if we introduce the function $e : Q \to \mathbb{N}$ such as $e(i) = i$, $e(0^-) = 0$, we can notice that the sum of the values of e applied to the state of the agents never changes.

The proof of the correctness is perfomed by showing that: 1- In each fair sequence, there exists a time t such as, after it, either each agent keeps a positive value, either they have all a negative value (considering 0 and 0^- as both a positive and a negative integer). 2- After that point, the sequence reaches a configuration with the good interpretation which is also stable.

3.2   The Averaging Problem

Definition 10 (Averaging problem). *The* Averaging *problem is the following problem (see e.g. [21]): We have a function* $g : \Sigma \to [a, b]$, *with* $a, b \in \mathbb{N}^2$, $Y = [a, b] \bigcup_{i \in [a,b[} \{]i, i+1[\}$ *and we want to compute the function* f *such as:*

$$
f(I) = \begin{cases} s & \text{if } s \in \mathbb{N} \\ ]\lfloor s \rfloor, \lfloor s \rfloor + 1[& \text{otherwise.} \end{cases}, \quad \text{with } s = \frac{\sum\limits_{s \in \Sigma} g(s) \times n_s}{\sum\limits_{s \in \Sigma} n_s}.
$$

Proposition 2. *The Averaging problem can be computed by both versions of trustful population protocols.*

Proof (Sketch). Here is the protocol:

- $Q = \bigcup_{i \in [a,b]} \{i, i^+, i^-\}$, with $I = [a, b] \bigcup_{i \in [a,b[} \{]i, i+1[\}$ and $Q_x = \omega^{-1}(x)$.
- Σ, $\iota = g$, $Y = [a, b] \bigcup_{i \in [a,b[} \{]i, i+1[\}$, and $\omega(i^+) = \omega((i+1)^-) =]i, i+1[$, $\omega(i) = i$.
- δ is given by the following rules:

$$
\begin{array}{lll}
i* & j* \to \frac{i+j}{2} \quad \frac{i+j}{2} & \text{if } i+j \equiv 0[2] \text{ and } i \neq j \\
i & i* \to \quad i \quad i & \\
i* & j* \to k^+ \quad (k+1)^- & \text{if } i+j \equiv 1[2],\, i < j, \text{ with } k = \frac{i+j-1}{2}
\end{array}
$$

With $i* \in \{i, i^+, i^-\}$ and $j* \in \{j, j^+, j^-\}$.

First, it is clear that this protocol is both strongly and weakly trustful. Second, if we introduce the function $e : Q \to \mathbb{N}$ such as $e(i^+) = e(i^-) = e(i) = i$, we can notice that the sum of the values of e applied to the state of the agents never changes.

The proof of the correctness can be perfomed by showing that: 1- In each fair sequence, there exists a time t such as, after it, every agent keeps the same integer in its state. 2- After that point, the sequence reaches a configuration with the good interpretation which is also stable.

4   Computability

4.1   Partition of the Space

We will say that a subset X of $\mathbb{N}^{|\Sigma|}$ can be *Separated* if there exists a function $f : \mathbb{N}^{|\Sigma|} \to Y$ and $y \in Y$ such as $X = f^{-1}(y)$.

Proposition 3. *The two versions of trustful population protocols remain stable under boolean combination: if A and B are subset of $\mathbb{N}^{|\Sigma|}$ that can be separated by a trustful population protocol, then $A \cup B$ and $A \cap B$ can be separated by a trustful population protocol.*

Let $(A_j)_{j \in J}$ be a partition of $\mathbb{N}^{|\Sigma|}$ with J finite such as for each j, A_j can be separated by some trustful population protocol. There exists a trustful population protocol separating all the A_j.

Proof (Sketch). This proof is similar to the usual one for boolean combination stability. The only difference is the partition of the new Q, which remains intuitive.

We get as a consequence:

Theorem 3. *Any finite partition of $\mathbb{N}^{|\Sigma|}$ where all subset can be defined as a boolean combination of threshold with a zero constant can be separated by a Trustful Population Protocol.*

4.2   When Agents Trust on the Output

Now we consider the special case where $Y = I$ and ω is the identity function over I. Our goal is to prove that, for every $y \in Y$, $f^{-1}(y)$ is a set of elements verifying a boolean combination of inequalities of the form $\sum_{s \in \Sigma} a_i \times s_i \geq 0$ and $\sum_{s \in \Sigma} a_i \times s_i > 0$.

Theorem 4. *The partitions that can be computed by trustful population protocols when $Y = I$ is such as each partitionned set can be defined as a boolean combination of threshold problems with a nul constant (i.e. $c = 0$), where some of the inequalities can be strict.*

To prove this theorem, we will do it by double inclusion. We first need some lemmas.

Lemma 1. *Let $(A_i)_{i \in I}$ be the partition corresponding to a trustful population protocol where $Y = I$ and $\omega = Identity_I$. Each A_i satisfies the two following properties:*

- C^+*: For each $a, b \in A_i$, $a + b \in A_i$*
- C^**: For each $a \in \mathbb{N}^{|\Sigma|}$, each $\lambda \in \mathbb{N} \setminus \{0\}$(noted $\mathbb{N}^+$), $\lambda a \in A_i \Leftrightarrow a \in A_i$*

Proof. There exists a sequence that brings all agents from a into states in Q_i. Same thing happens from b. From $a + b$, we just need to use the same sequences to the two subsets, and then our configuration will be stable.

From the first point, we can deduce that $a \in A_i \Rightarrow \lambda a \in A_i$. For the converse implication, as there is a j such as $a \in A_j$, j must then be equal to i, as $\lambda a \in A_j$ and the $(A_i)_{i \in I}$ form a partition of the space.

From now on, $S \in \mathbb{N}^d$ is a semi-linear set, i.e. a union of sets of the form $\{u_i + \sum_{j \in J_i} a_j v_j | a_j \in \mathbb{N}\}$ verifying the conditions (C^+) and (C^*).

Lemma 2.

$$S = \mathbb{N}^d \cap \bigcup_{i \in I} \{(1 + a)u_i + \sum_{j \in J_i} a_j v_j | a, a_j \in \mathbb{Q}^+\}$$

Proof. Let $x \in \mathbb{N}^d \cap \bigcup_{i \in I} \{(1 + a)u_i + \sum_{j \in J_i} a_j v_j | a_j \in \mathbb{Q}^+\}$. Then there is an i_0, an a and a $a_j \in \mathbb{Q}^+$ for each $j \in J_{i_0}$ such that $x = (1 + a)u_{i_0} + \sum_{j \in J_{i_0}} a_j v_j$. For each a_j there exists p_j and q_j two non negative integers such as $a_j = \frac{p_j}{q_j}$, as a_j is in $\mathbb{Q}^+$. We get:

$$x = \left(1 + \frac{p}{q}\right) u_{i_0} + \Sigma_{j \in J_{i_0}} \frac{p_j}{q_j} v_j.$$

Let $y = (q.\Pi_{j \in J_{i_0}} q_j).x = (q.\Pi_{j \in J_{i_0}} q_j)(1 + a).u_{i_0} + \Sigma_{j \in J_{i_0}} \left(p_j.(q.\Pi_{j' \neq j} q'_j)\right) v_j$. We have:

$y - \left[(q.\Pi_{j \in J_{i_0}} q_j)(1 + a) - 1\right] .u_{i_0} = u_{i_0} + \Sigma_{j \in J_{i_0}} \left(p_j.(q.\Pi_{j' \neq j} q'_j)\right) v_j \in \{u_{i_0} + \sum_{j \in J_i} a_j v_j | a_j \in \mathbb{N}\}$.

$u_{i_0} \in S \Rightarrow \left[(q.\Pi_{j \in J_{i_0}} q_j)(1 + a) - 1\right] .u_{i_0} \in S$ (using C^*).
Hence, as y is a sum of two elements of S, by C^+, $y \in S$.
Finally, we have from C^* that $x \in S$.

The other inclusion is easy as $\mathbb{N} \subset \mathbb{Q}^+$. The conclusion follows.

For the rest of the proof, we will consider that $v_0 = u_i$ (i.e. if u_i was not in the initial set of vectors, we add it directly). From this we get that $S = \mathbb{N}^d \cap \bigcup_{i \in I} \{u_i + \sum_{j \in J_i} a_j v_j | a_j \in \mathbb{Q}^+\}$. To pursue the proof, we need a stronger version of Caratheodory's Theorem. The original version is the following:

Lemma 3 (Caratheodory's Theorem[12]). *If $x \in \mathbb{Q}^d$ is a positive linear combinations of $\{v_j\}_{j \in J_i}$ then there exists a linearly independent subset $\{v_{l_1}, \ldots, v_{l_k}\} \subset \{v_j\}_{j \in J_i}$ such that x is a positive linear combination of $v_{l_1}, \ldots v_{l_k}$.*

We need to perform our proof to be sure that the vector $v_0 = u_i$ stays after the simplification of the vectors:

Lemma 4 (Extended Caratheodory's Theorem). *If $x \in \mathbb{Q}^d$ is a positive linear combinations of $\{v_j\}_{j \in J_i}$, with $v_0 \neq 0$ and $\forall j \in J_i$ $v_j \in \mathbb{N}^d$, then there exists a linearly independent subset $\{v_{l_1}, \ldots, v_{l_k}\} \subset \{v_j\}_{j \in J_i}$ such that x is a positive linear combination of $v_0, v_{l_1}, \ldots v_{l_k}$.*

Proof. Let x be a positive of k linearly indepedent vectors $\{v_{l_1}, \ldots, v_{l_k}\}$. We have $x = \sum a_m v_{l_m}$.

We need to separate three cases here: if v_0 is already in the subset, if the new subset is still independant if we add v_0 and if v_0 can be generated by the subset:

- $v_0 = v_{l_m}$: This case is easy, as we just need to permute the numeration of the vectors.
- v_0 **is independant**: This case is also easy. Adding v_0 to the set is allowed, as the linear independance is kept.
- v_0 **is not independant**: We have $v_0 = \sum b_m v_{l_m}$. Note that the b_m are not compulsorily positives. Let M be an integer such that b_M is strictly positive and such that $\frac{a_M}{b_M}$ is minimal (for each element where $\frac{a_m}{b_m}$ has a meaning and where $b_m > 0$). M exists because if all b_m are negative or nul, v_0's coordinates would all be negative or nul. From $v_0 = \sum b_m v_{l_m}$ we get $v_M = \frac{1}{b_M} v_0 - \sum\limits_{m \neq M} \frac{b_m}{b_M} v_{l_m}$. We will now put this "value" of v_M in x:

$$x = \sum a_m v_{l_m} = \sum_{m \neq M} a_m v_{l_m} + a_M \left(\frac{1}{b_M} v_0 - \sum_{m \neq M} \frac{b_m}{b_M} v_{l_m} \right)$$
$$= \frac{a_M}{b_M} v_0 + \sum_{m \neq M} \left(a_m - a_M \frac{b_m}{b_M} v_{l_m} \right)$$

We need now to prove that all the coefficients are positive. As M is chosen such as b_M is positive, $\frac{a_M}{b_M}$ is positive. Let prove that for each $m \neq M$, $\left(a_m - a_M \frac{b_m}{b_M} v_{l_m} \right) \geq 0$.

- If $b_m \leq 0$, then $-a_M \frac{b_m}{b_M} \geq 0$, we deduce $\left(a_m - a_M \frac{b_m}{b_M} v_{l_m} \right) \geq 0$.
- If $b_m > 0$, then, as M was chosen to minimize $\frac{a_M}{b_M}$,
  $$\frac{a_m}{b_m} \geq \frac{a_M}{b_M} \Rightarrow \left(a_m - a_M \frac{b_m}{b_M} v_{l_m} \right) \geq 0.$$

This concludes the proof that v_0 can be put in the set of the linearly independant vectors. We now suppose that we always chose $v_{l_1} = v_0$.

With this lemma, we have :

$$\{ \sum_{j \in J} a_j v_j | a_j \in \mathbb{Q}^+ \} = \bigcup_{\{v_{l_1}, \ldots, v_{l_k}\} \text{ l.i.}} \{ \sum_{j \in \{l_1, \ldots, l_k\}} a'_j v_j | a'_j \in \mathbb{Q}^+ \}$$

Hence we can rewrite

$$S = \mathbb{N}^d \cap \bigcup_{i \in I | \{v_{l_1}, \ldots, v_{l_k}\} \subset J_i \text{ l.i.}} \{ u_i + \sum_{1 \leq m \leq k} a_m v_{l_m} | a_m \in \mathbb{Q}^+ \}.$$

Let consider now the set $V = \{v_{l_1}, \ldots, v_{l_k}\} \subset J_i$ of linearly independent vectors and the set $H = \{u_i + \sum_{1 \leq m \leq k} a_m v_{l_m} | a_m \in \mathbb{Q}^+\}$. We have $k \leq d$. If $k < d$, we can complete V with $k - d$ linearly independent vectors $w_{k+1}, \ldots w_d$ such that $B = V \cup \{w_{k+1}, \ldots w_d\}$ is a base of $\mathbb{Q}^d$, if $k = d$ then $B = V$.

Let swap the base to B using u_i as the new origin. Let $(x_1, \ldots, x_d)$ the coordinates of an element x in the new system. We have:

$$x \in H \Leftrightarrow \begin{cases} x_m \geq 0 \text{ if } m \leq k \\ x_m = 0 \text{ otherwise.} \end{cases}$$

We can even add the existence of vectors $y_1, \ldots, y_d$ and constants $c_1, \ldots c_d$ such as:

$$x \in H \Leftrightarrow \begin{cases} y_m.x \geq c_m \text{ if } m \leq k \\ y_m.x = c_m \text{ otherwise.} \end{cases}$$

From this we can deduce that each set $\{u_i + \sum_{1 \leq m \leq k} a_m v_{l_m} | a_m \in \mathbb{Q}^+\}$ can be caracterised as a conjunction of inequalities and equalities.

Hence we have that S can be caracterised by a disjunction (for each possible J_i) of disjunction (for each linearly independent set of vectors) of conjunctions of inequalities and equalities. We need to prove now that the right term of these formulaes is 0 (or can be replaced by 0).

First here is a last lemma that is a weaker property than C^* on our set:

Lemma 5. *If $x \in H$ then for every $\lambda \in \mathbb{N}^+$ we have $\lambda x \in H$.*

Proof. Let x be in H and $\lambda \in \mathbb{N}^+$.

We can write $x = u + \sum_{1 \leq m \leq k} x_m v_{l_m}$.

Then $\lambda x = u + (\lambda - 1)u + \sum_{1 \leq m \leq k} (\lambda x_m) v_{l_m}$.

As either u is nul, either $u = v_0 = v_{l_1}$, we can conclude that $\lambda x \in H$.

Let $y_m \cdot x = c_m$ be one of the equalities of H. As, from Lemma 5, $2x \in H$, we have $y_m \cdot 2x = c_m = 2(y_m \cdot x) = 2c_m$. We deduce from this that $c_m = 0$.

Let $y_m \cdot x \geq c_m$ be one of the inequalities verified by every element of H.

- If $c_m < 0$: Let suppose there exists an $x \in H$ such that $y_m \cdot x \in [c_m, 0[$. There exists some $\lambda \in \mathbb{N}^+$ such that $\lambda y_m \cdot x < c_m$. We deduce from it that $\lambda x \notin H$, which is a contradiction of Lemma 5 (as x is in H). We can deduce then that $y_m \cdot x \geq c_m \Leftrightarrow y_m \cdot x \geq 0$.
- If $c_m > 0$: Let suppose there exists an $x \in H$ such that $y_m \cdot x \in]0, c_m[$. There exists some $\lambda \in \mathbb{N}^+$ such that $\lambda y_m \cdot x \geq c_m$. We deduce from it that $\lambda x \in H$, which is a contradiction of Lemma 5 (as x is not in H). We can deduce then that $y_m \cdot x \geq c_m \Leftrightarrow y_m \cdot x > 0$.

From this study, we deduce the theorem :

Theorem 5. *If S is a semi-linear set verifying (C^+) and (C^*), then it can be described by a boolean combination of formulae of the form $y \cdot x \propto 0$ with $\propto \in \{\geq, >, =\}$.*

4.3   Computational Power of Trustful Population Protocols

As we know to what corresponds each $i \in I$ (in term of computability), we can now have the characterization of what can be computed by our model:

Theorem 6. *The partitions that can be computed by trustful population protocols correspond exactly to partitions where each set can be defined as a boolean combination of threshold problems with a nul constant (i.e. $c = 0$).*

Proof. We have, for $y \in Y$, $f^{-1}(y) = \bigcup_{i \in \omega^{-1}(y)} A_i$.

With the previous result, we have $a \in f^{-1}(y) \Leftrightarrow a \in \bigcup_{i \in \omega^{-1}(y)} A_i \Leftrightarrow a$ verifies the formula of an A_i. With this, $f^{-1}(y)$ is defined by the disjunction of boolean combinations of threshold problems (with a nul constant), where the inequality can be strict.

4.4   Interpretation in Terms of Frequencies

Proposition 4 (Stability under Multiplication and Division). *Both versions of trustful population protocols are stable under multiplication and division: For any function f computed by a trustful population protocol, for any input $E \in \mathbb{N}^{|\Sigma|}$, for any $k \in \mathbb{N}^+$, $f(E) = f(k \times E)$, and if every coefficient is a multiple of k, $f(E) = f(E/k)$.*

Proof. The principle of this proof is really simple: as every computation needs to have the good interpretation, we can first separate the population of $k \times E$ in k populations E. There is a sequence from E that reaches a configuration where all agents have the same interpretation. We have all of the k populations perform the same sequence. From that configuration, as every agent is in the same set Q_i for some $i \in I$, the interpretation cannot change anymore. Because of that, $f(E) = f(k \times E)$.

The case E/k is exactly the same: we use the previous result with E/k and $k \times E/k = E$.

Remark 2. With this result, there are some functions computable by population protocols that can be shown very easily not to be computable by our models:

- Is there more that two x in the input ? (it is equivalent to $n_x \geq 2$): with $E = (x, x, y, y)$, we have $f(E) = True \neq False = f(E/2)$.
- $n_x \equiv 0[2]$: With the same input E as above, $f(E) = True \neq False = f(E/2)$.

A way to interpret previous theorem, is then to observe that computable predicates are always **frequency based**: i.e. a predicate on frequencies of letters in the input.

Indeed, observe that a Threshold $\sum_{s \in \Sigma} g(s)n_s \geq c$ with $c = 0$ can always be written $\sum_{s \in \Sigma} g(s)f_s \geq 0$, where $f_s = \frac{n_s}{n}$, with $n = \sum_s n_s$. Here f_s is the frequency of agents in state s in the population.

5   Non Finitely States Agents

Now we will consider the case where the agents do not have a constant memory, and can be any arbitrary Turing machines. To understand more formally how interactions and fairness work, we consider the principles used in [14].

In this section, we show a result when agents contains $\Omega(n \log n)$ bits, where n is the number of agents in the population.

Definition 11 (Trustful Population Protocol on *Space* $f(n)$). *A Trustful Population Protocol on Space $f(n)$ is a protocol where all agents have their state in $Q = \Sigma \bigcup_{i \in I(n)} \{i\} \times \{0,1\}^{f(n)}$, where n is the number of agents in the input and $|I(n)| \leq 2^{f(n)}$; $I = \Sigma \cup \{0,1\}^{f(n)}$; $\omega = Identity_\Sigma$.*

Proposition 5. *If all agents have a space of at least $\Omega(n \log n)$, where n is the number of agents in the population, there exists a trustful population protocol that computes the exact frequency of each possible input.*

Proof (Sketch). The idea of this protocol is to run the averaging problem with different parameters at the same time. $I(n)$ will be all the possible proportions (frequencies) for populations of size smaller or equal to n (it can be represented on $\log(|\Sigma| \times n)$ bits, as it suffises to have n and $n_s \leq n$ for each s).

For each $s \in \Sigma$, each agent will run the averaging problem on $k \times n_s$ for an increasing number of k until the protocol provides an integer result. When the protocols stops on an average a_k for a given k, the population knows that the proportion n_s/n is equal to a_k/k, as $k \times n_s = a_k \times n$.

For $k = n$, we can be sure that the protocols will finish. If we separate the space in $f(n)/|\Sigma|$ bits (one portion for each $s \in \Sigma$), each portion will need $\log 1 + \log 2 + \ldots \log n \leq n \log n$ bits to compute the corresponding proportion.

We get:

Theorem 7 (Computable iff Frequency Based). *Let $F : \mathbb{N}^{|\Sigma|} \to Y$ be a function stable by multiplication computable in space $f(n)$, where $f(n) = \Omega(n \log n)$ with n corresponding to the size of the input.*

There exists a Trustful Population Protocol that computes F if all agents have $f(n)$ bits.

Proof. The agents compute the same protocol than before, but with another function ω: instead of having $\omega(n_1, \ldots, n_k) = (n_1/n, \ldots, n_k/n)$, $\omega(n_1, \ldots, n_k) = F(n_1, \ldots, n_k)$. As all the agents have enough space to compute F, they can even carry the right answer.

6   Complexity

For classic population protocols, [2] showed that computable predicates can be computed in $O(n \log^6 n)$ expected transitions if the population starts with a unique leader (and provides a protocol that seems to compute the leader election in $O(n \log n)$ expected transitions). The problem is that these protocols cannot be transposed to our model: These protocols use a probabilistic protocol which has a low probability to fail, and this failure is catched by a regular protocol computed in parallel. In our case, if the probabilistic protocol fails and give a wrong answer, as all the agents will be in the same Q_i, a regular protocol computed in parallel will not be able to correct the error.

The following can however be proved:

Proposition 6. *Any function computable by a trustful population protocol can be computed by a weakly trustful population protocol with an expected number of $O(n^2 \log n)$ interactions.*

Proof (Sketch). The idea of this protocol is to perform a leader election in parallel of the protocol. Only the leader can change the opinion of an agent when the issue is uncertain (i.e. when the agent has 0 in the memory and cannot know directly if the population has a positive or negative sum). The proof of complexity is the usual one for the classical population protocol.

Acknowledgments. We would like to thanks deeply Jérome Leroux and Jean-Philippe Méline for (sometimes indirect) help in this paper.

References

1. Adleman, L.M.: Molecular computation of solutions to combinatorial problems. Science 266(5187), 1021 (1994)
2. Angluin, D., Aspnes, J., Eisenstat, D.: Fast computation by population protocols with a leader. In: Dolev, S. (ed.) DISC 2006. LNCS, vol. 4167, pp. 61–75. Springer, Heidelberg (2006)
3. Angluin, D., Aspnes, J., Eisenstat, D., Ruppert, E.: The computational power of population protocols. Distributed Computing 20(4), 279–304 (2007)
4. Angluin, D., Aspnes, J., Chan, M., Fischer, M.J., Jiang, H., Peralta, R.: Stably computable properties of network graphs. In: Prasanna, V.K., Iyengar, S.S., Spirakis, P.G., Welsh, M. (eds.) DCOSS 2005. LNCS, vol. 3560, pp. 63–74. Springer, Heidelberg (2005)
5. Angluin, D., Aspnes, J., Diamadi, Z., Fischer, M.J., Peralta, R.: Computation in networks of passively mobile finite-state sensors. In: Twenty-Third ACM Symposium on Principles of Distributed Computing, pp. 290–299. ACM Press (July 2004)
6. Angluin, D., Aspnes, J., Eisenstat, D.: Stably computable predicates are semilinear. In: PODC 2006: Proceedings of the Twenty-fifth Annual ACM Symposium on Principles of Distributed Computing, pp. 292–299. ACM Press, New York (2006)
7. Angluin, D., Aspnes, J., Fischer, M.J., Jiang, H.: Self-stabilizing population protocols. In: Anderson, J.H., Prencipe, G., Wattenhofer, R. (eds.) OPODIS 2005. LNCS, vol. 3974, pp. 103–117. Springer, Heidelberg (2006)
8. Aspnes, J., Ruppert, E.: An introduction to population protocols. Bulletin of the EATCS 93, 106–125 (2007)
9. Berry, G.: The chemical abstract machine. Theoretical Computer Science 96(1), 217–248 (1992)

10. Blondel, V., Hendrickx, J., Olshevsky, A., Tsitsiklis, J.: Convergence in multi-agent coordination, consensus, and flocking. In: 44th IEEE Conf. on Decision and Control, pp. 2996–3000 (2005)
11. Bournez, O., Chalopin, J., Cohen, J., Koegler, X., Rabie, M.: Computing with pavlovian populations. In: Fernàndez Anta, A., Lipari, G., Roy, M. (eds.) OPODIS 2011. LNCS, vol. 7109, pp. 409–420. Springer, Heidelberg (2011)
12. Carathéodory, C., Hölder, E., Klötzler, R., Boerner, H.: Variationsrechnung und partielle Differentialgleichungen erster Ordnung. BG Teubner Leipzig, Berlin (1935)
13. Castellano, C., Fortunato, S., Loreto, V.: Statistical physics of social dynamics. Reviews of Modern Physics 81(2), 591 (2009)
14. Chatzigiannakis, I., Michail, O., Nikolaou, S., Pavlogiannis, A., Spirakis, P.G.: Passively mobile communicating machines that use restricted space. Theoretical Computer Science (2011)
15. Chatzigiannakis, I., Michail, O., Spirakis, P.G.: Algorithmic verification of population protocols. In: Dolev, S., Cobb, J., Fischer, M., Yung, M. (eds.) SSS 2010. LNCS, vol. 6366, pp. 221–235. Springer, Heidelberg (2010)
16. Chatzigiannakis, I., Spirakis, P.G.: The dynamics of probabilistic population protocols. In: Taubenfeld, G. (ed.) DISC 2008. LNCS, vol. 5218, pp. 498–499. Springer, Heidelberg (2008)
17. Chazelle, B.: Natural algorithms. In: 20th ACM-SIAM Symposium on Discrete Algorithms (SODA), pp. 422–431 (2009)
18. Cucker, F., Smale, S.: Emergent behavior in flocks. IEEE Transactions on Automatic Control 52(5), 852–862 (2007)
19. Delporte-Gallet, C., Fauconnier, H., Guerraoui, R., Ruppert, E.: When birds die: Making population protocols fault-tolerant. In: Gibbons, P.B., Abdelzaher, T., Aspnes, J., Rao, R. (eds.) DCOSS 2006. LNCS, vol. 4026, pp. 51–66. Springer, Heidelberg (2006)
20. Easley, D., Kleinberg, J.: Networks, crowds, and markets, vol. 8. Cambridge Univ. Press (2010)
21. Hendrickx, J.M., Olshevsky, A., Tsitsiklis, J.N.: Distributed anonymous discrete function computation. IEEE Transactions on Automatic Control 56(10), 2276–2289 (2011)
22. Murray, J.D.: Mathematical Biology. I: An Introduction, 3rd edn. Springer (2002)
23. Weibull, J.W.: Evolutionary Game Theory. The MIT Press (1995)

Prudent Opportunistic Cognitive Radio Access Protocols

Israel Cidon[1], Erez Kantor[2,*], and Shay Kutten[3,**]

[1] Department of Electrical Engineering, Technion, Haifa, Israel
[2] Technion & MIT
[3] Department of Industrial Engineering, Technion, Haifa, Israel
cidon@ee.technion.ac.il, erez.kantor@gmail.com, kutten@ie.technion.ac.il

Abstract. In a cognitive radio network, a Primary User (PU) may vacate a channel for intermissions of an unknown length. A substantial amount of research has been devoted to minimizing the disturbance a Secondary User (SU) may cause the PU. We take another step and optimize the throughput of an SU, even when assuming that the disturbance to the PU is indeed avoided using those other methods.

We suggest new optimization parameters the lengths of SU packets. That is, the SU fills up the intermission with consecutive packets. Each packet is associated with some fixed overhead. Hence, using a larger number of smaller packets increases the overhead ratio for each SU packet. On the other hand, it reduces the loss of throughput the SU suffers with the loss of a packet in a collision at the end of the intermission.

As opposed to previous studies, we optimize also the case where the distribution of the channel intermission is unknown. That is, we develop optimal competitive protocols. Those seek to minimize the ratio of the SU's profit compared to a hypothetical optimal algorithm that knows the intermission length in advance. We show how to compute the optimal present packets' sizes for the case that the distribution *is* known (for a *general* distribution). Finally, we show several interesting properties of the optimal solutions for several popular distributions.

1 Introduction

Cognitive Radio Networks (CRN) divide the users into Primary Users (PUs) and Secondary Users (SUs) groups. PUs are the spectrum "license holders" and have the right to use their channel at will. Various techniques have been devised to prevent SUs' transmission from disturbing the PU's transmission, e.g. by having the SU sense the channel and avoid transmission whenever the PU transmits.

---

* Supported in a part by Eshkol fellowship, the Ministry of Science and Technology, Israel and by NSF grants Nos. CCF-1217506, CCF-0939370 and CCF-AF-0937274.
** Supported in part by the Israel Science Foundation and by the Technion TASP Center.

Y. Afek (Ed.): DISC 2013, LNCS 8205, pp. 462–476, 2013.

However, collisions between the user groups not only impact the ownership rights of the PUs but also affect the performance of the SUs, reducing the effective channel usage of the SUs even during an *intermission* in the PU's transmissions. To see that, consider the extreme (rather likely) case that the PUs are allowed a much higher transmission power. Hence, an SU packet transmitted at the end of the PU intermission is likely to be lost when the packet level checksum or a CRN integrity test is conducted at the receiver. That is, even the part of the packet that was transmitted during the intermission is lost. Please observe that this SU loss may happen even if the PU's transmission is not disturbed at all (e.g. thanks to the much higher power of the PU's transmissions)!

While our work revisits one of the most basic questions in CRN, we optimize it from a different angle. To highlight that, we stress that our results are meaningful even if a negative impact on the PU is avoided (for example, avoided by using the previous methods). Our main problem is: devise optimal access algorithms that maximize the efficient usage of the channel by the SU, given the possible loss at the end of the intermission. While the above question (and our results) concentrates on the SU's throughput, our model (and some of the results) are more general than that, and can also be used to minimize the negative impact (also on the PU) caused by the collision at the end of the intermission.

Prudent Protocols. Our objective function includes a penalty for conflicts between an SU and the PUs. This penalty is traded off against a loss of SU throughput as follows. We allow an SU to break the transmission of its data to smaller packets; each packet is transmitted in a *transmission* interval that is followed by a sensing period of a *a fixed length* and (in case the intermission does not end) by the next interval. The fixed periods between the intervals are viewed as representing the fixed overhead, that may include, beside fixed length sensing, a preamble, headers, checksums, etc., associated with a packet transmission.[1]

The main optimization parameters are the lengths of the transmission intervals. Intuitively, a good sequence is not "too daring" (having too long sequences) on one hand, since we want to avoid the case that the last packet, the one that is lost, is long. On the other hand, a good sequence is not "too hesitant" (having too short messages). This is because a sequence of short packets will suffer from a relatively high overhead per packet (since the overhead per packet is fixed). Hence, we term protocols that achieve a good tradeoff-*Prudent* Optimistic protocols and the problem of finding good sequences– the problem of *Dynamic Interval Cover (DIC)*. The problem is defined formally below. We develop such protocols both for the case that the intermission length is unknown, and for the case that it is taken from a general distribution. We also highlight interesting results for several specific distributions that were not addressed before.

---

[1] We comment that in earlier work [4], the periods between the intervals were not fixed. This is because they had a different purpose– that of minimizing the probability of a collision at the end of the intermission. Recall that here, we want to emphasize the optimization that is still required for the SU's transmission, even if the collision at the end of the intermission does not harm the PU.

The Model. The issues considered in this paper are manifested even in a system with a single primary user and a single secondary user that share a single channel. Note that assuming multiple PUs would not change our results at all. (The case of multiple SUs is beyond the scope of this paper; however, we hope in a future work to fit multiple SUs into our model as follows: multiple SUs would coordinate transmissions among themselves using more traditional methods; that way, they would present the face of a single SU to the PU). The PU owns the channel and transmits over it intermittently. The SU cannot start transmitting until the PU stops. It is easy to show that optimizing for a sequence of multiple intermissions can be reduced to optimizing the SU transmission over each intermission separately. Hence, our analysis is performed per intermission.

We assume that the SU always has data. The data is divided by the SU into (variable length) packets. As opposed to some previous studies, we do not assume that the packet sizes are given ahead of time. W.L.O.G., the transmission of x bits takes x time units. When an intermission of the PU starts, the SU starts transmitting its data in packets $p_0, p_1, p_2, \ldots$ such that p_0 is transmitted using time interval ψ_0, p_1 using time interval ψ_1, etc. The sequences of time intervals $\psi_0, \psi_1, \psi_2, \ldots$ is thus, the output of the SU access control algorithms addressed in the current paper. Optimizing this sequence is the DIC problem defined below. A *prudent* protocol is an opportunistic access protocol that transmits a sequence of packets whose lengths are the result of this optimization problem.

If the PU resumes transmitting at the time that the SU is transmitting its jth packets, then the SU ceases transmission, and the jth packet is lost (an *unsuccessful transmission*). In the other case (a *successful transmission*), the SU starts and completes a packet's transmission during the intermission. The SU's benefit of such a single PU intermission is a profit for the $j-1$ successful transmissions of the first $j-1$ packets. There is also a penalty for the unsuccessful transmission of the j'th packet. Different benefits and different penalties define different profit models. In this paper, we use the following profit model.

The α-*Cost* Profit Model: Consider a constant $\alpha \geq 0$ (representing the above mentioned fixed overhead per packet). The SU's profit for a successful transmission of a single packet of time length ψ (a packet with ψ bits) is $\psi - \alpha$, i.e., the SU earns ψ and pays a fixed cost of α, for every time length $\psi > 0$. For simplicity, we ignore the cost of the last transmission. That is, for an unsuccessful transmission of a single packet, the SU earns nothing and pays nothing[2].

Definition 1. Dynamic Interval Cover (DIC) *is the optimization problem of generating a sequence of intervals according to the profit model described above.*

Our Results. A part of the novelty in this paper is the fact that we deal with case that the intermission length may be unknown at all. That is, we develop optimal $\left(1 + \frac{\sqrt{4\alpha - 3\alpha^2} + \alpha}{2(1-\alpha)}\right)$-competitive protocols (these protocols are

---

[2] Note that alternative penalty assumptions, e.g., a double loss in the case of a collision, to account also for the PU's loss, can be analyzed using this framework but are left for future research.

2.62-competitive, since $\alpha \leq 1/2$). Protocols that seek to minimize the ratio of the SU's profit compared to an optimal hypothetical algorithm that does know the intermission length in advance. We also show that the competitive ratio for the bounded intermission model is better than the one for the unbounded case, however, it is only slightly better.

For the case where the distribution of the intermission is known, we address the case of a general distribution. Previous studies assumed some specific distribution for the length of the intermission. Most assumed the exponential distribution, see e.g., [4, 10, 11]. Others [1, 5, 12], extend this assumption to distributions derived from specific Markovian system models. For a general distribution, we present (Section 3) an efficient (polynomial) algorithm to compute the optimal length of each transmission interval for the realistic case that the interval length must be discrete, and a fully polynomial-time approximation scheme (FPTAS) for computing a sequence that approximates the optimal solution.

Interestingly, one difference resulting from the general distributions we address, is that (unlike those known studies of memory-less distributions) we show that the length of the optimal intervals in a sequence is not always constant. (Our method can be used also in the case that a constant length is required.) Finally, we also found some interesting properties of an optimal solution under some popular specific distributions.

Some Related Work. A dual problem of DIC is the *buffer management* problem. In that problem, the packets arrive with different sizes. The online algorithm needs to decide which packets to drop while the size of each packet is fixed. The objective is to minimize the total value of lost packets, subject to the buffer space. Lotker and Patt-Shamir [6] studies this problem and present a 1.3-competitive algorithm.

The problem of cognitive access in a network of PUs and SUs was studied intensively. We refer to two surveys [2] and [7]. The problem of designing of sensing and transmission that maximized the throughput of the SU is studied in [4, 5, 7, 8, 10–12] under a model with collision constraints. Recall that our length optimization can be made after, and on top of, the optimizations performed by previous papers, since we optimize different parameters. Hence, a direct comparison of the the performance would not be meaningful.

Preliminaries. Consider an output $\Psi : \mathbb{N}^+ \to \mathbb{R}$ of an SU access control algorithm that defines a sequence of time intervals $\Psi = \langle \psi_0, \psi_1, \psi_2, \dots \rangle$. That is, $\psi_0 = \Psi(0), \psi_1 = \Psi(1), \psi_2 = \Psi(2), \dots$. Denote by $\Psi_{\text{INF}} = \{\Psi \in \mathbb{R}^{\mathbb{N}} \mid \Psi$ is an infinite sequence$\}$ the family of infinite sequences (of time intervals). $\Psi_{\text{FIN}} = \{\Psi \in \mathbb{R}^M \mid M \in \mathbb{N}, \Psi$ is a finite sequence$\}$ is the family of finite sequences. Denote by $\Psi_M = \{\Psi \in \Psi_{\text{FIN}} \mid |\Psi| = M\}$ (for every $M \in \mathbb{N}^+$) the family of M-*size* sequences. Let $S(\Psi, k) = \sum_{i=0}^{k} \psi_i$, and $S(\Psi) = S(\Psi, |\Psi|)$, for every $\Psi \in \Psi_{\text{FIN}}$. Let $K_{\langle \Psi, t \rangle}$ be the number of packets that SU transmitted successfully.

The profit of a sequence Ψ, with respect to an intermission of duration t, is the sum of the profits of the SU for the time intervals in the sequence Ψ:

$$\text{PFIT}_{\langle\alpha\rangle}(\Psi, t) = \sum_{i=0}^{K_{\langle\Psi,t\rangle}} (\psi_i - \alpha). \tag{1}$$

2   Unknown PU Intermission Length

We begin with a difficult case in which even the distribution of the intermission length $t' \in \mathbb{R}^+$ is unknown to the SU. As is common in analyzing competitive algorithms [3], we measure the quality of the SU protocol by comparing the profit it obtains to the profit obtained by a hypothetical optimal algorithm (the "offline" algorithm) that knows the intermission length in advance. Moreover, we make this comparison in the worst case. Informally, one may envision an "adversary" who knows in advance the sequence Ψ of transmission intervals chosen by the SU and chooses an intermission length for which the profit of the SU from Ψ is minimized relatively to the profit of the optimal offline algorithm. Formal definitions are given below, following standard notations.

It is easy to verify that if the intermission can be shorter than α, then no online protocol can achieve a positive profit. We normalize the lengths and also α such that the minimum intermission length is 1 and $0 < \alpha < 1/2$ (this implies that the first packet is of length 1 in any optimal sequence and an optimal sequence has a positive profit). Let $\Psi_\alpha = \{\Psi \in \Psi_{\text{FIN}} \cup \Psi_{\text{INF}} \mid \psi_0 = 1 \text{ and } \psi_i \geq \alpha \text{ for every } i \geq 1\}$. This family of sequences has a positive profit for any intermission time length. Moreover, it has a nonnegative profit from each interval. It is easy to make the following observation.

Observation 1. *An optimal sequence must belong to Ψ_α.*

For a sequence $\Psi \in \Psi_\alpha$ and an intermission length $t \geq 1$, the *competitive ratio* is

$$\text{C-RATIO}(\Psi, \alpha, t) = \frac{t - \alpha}{\text{PFIT}_{\langle\alpha\rangle}(\Psi, t)}. \tag{2}$$

The numerator in this ratio is the optimal (maximum) profit that could have been made by the SU had it known the intermission time length t (that is, a profit of $t - \alpha$ for the sequence $\langle t \rangle$). The denominator is the actual profit of the SU who selected sequence Ψ. The *competitive ratio* of Ψ is the maximum (over all $t \geq 1$) of the competitive ratio of Ψ with respect to t. That is,

$$\text{OPT-RATIO}(\Psi, \alpha) = \max_{t \geq 1} \text{C-RATIO}(\Psi, \alpha, t).$$

The goal of the online algorithm is to generate a sequence Ψ that minimizes the competitive ratio. We consider both infinite and finite sequence models as well as the bounded and unbounded intermission time models. Denote the optimal competitive ratio for an infinite sequence model under the unbounded intermission time model (for punishment α) by

$$\text{OPT-RATIO}(\alpha) = \min_{\Psi \in \Psi_\alpha} \text{C-RATIO}(\Psi, \alpha). \tag{3}$$

We present an optimal competitive ratio sequence and establish the following.

Theorem 1. OPT-RATIO$(\alpha) = 1 + \frac{\sqrt{4\alpha - 3\alpha^2} + \alpha}{2(1-\alpha)} \leq 2.62$.

For proving the theorem, it is convenient to define also the competitive ratio under a certain strategy of the adversary. Specifically, $f_{\langle \alpha, \Psi \rangle}(k)$ is computed as if the intermission ends just before the $(k+1)$'th interval in Ψ ends. I.e., the intermission length is $t' = \sum_{i=0}^{k+1} \psi_i - \epsilon$, where $\epsilon > 0$ is negligible. Let

$$f_{\langle \alpha, \Psi \rangle}(k) = \lim_{\epsilon \to 0^+} \text{C-RATIO}(\Psi, \alpha, S(\Psi, k+1) - \epsilon) = \frac{\sum_{i=0}^{k+1} \psi_i - \alpha}{\sum_{i=0}^{k} \psi_i - (k+1)\alpha} \quad (4)$$

$$= 1 + \frac{\psi_{k+1} + k\alpha}{\psi_0 + \ldots + \psi_k - (k+1)\alpha},$$

for every $i \in \mathbb{N}$. The usefulness of $f_{\langle \alpha, \Psi \rangle}$ becomes evident given the following.

Observation 2. *The competitive ratio of $\Psi \in \Psi_\alpha$ is*

$$\text{C-RATIO}(\alpha, \Psi) = \sup\{f_{\langle \alpha, \Psi \rangle}(k) \mid k \in \mathbb{N}\}.$$

By Eq.(3), the observation implies that the optimal competitive ratio is

$$\text{OPT-RATIO}(\alpha) = \min_{\Psi \in \Psi_\alpha} \sup\{f_{\langle \alpha, \Psi \rangle}(k) \mid k \in \mathbb{N}\}.$$

Claim 1. *There exists an optimal sequence Ψ for DIC such that $f_{\langle \alpha, \Psi \rangle}(k)$ is some constant for every $k \in \mathbb{N}$.*

Proof: Consider any optimal sequence Ψ^*. Let $\lambda = \sup\{f_{\langle \alpha, \Psi^* \rangle}(k) \mid k \in \mathbb{N}\}$ and let Ψ' be a sequence obtained from Ψ^* as follows: $\psi_0' = 1$ and $\psi_{i+1}' = (\lambda - 1)\left(\sum_{j=0}^{i} \psi_j' - (i+1)\alpha\right) - i\alpha$. By induction on i and by Eq. (4) we know that $\psi_i' \geq \psi_i$ and $f_{\langle \alpha, \Psi' \rangle}(k) = \lambda$, for every $k \in \mathbb{N}$. It remains to prove that $\Psi' \in \Psi_\alpha$, so that Observation 2 can be used. For that, we prove by induction, that $\psi_k' \geq \psi_k^*$. By Observation 1, $\psi_0' = \psi_0^* = 1$. Assume that $\psi_i^* \leq \psi_i'$, for every $i = 0, \ldots, k$. On the one hand, we have

$$\lambda \geq f_{\langle \alpha, \Psi^* \rangle}(k+1) = 1 + \frac{\psi_{k+1}^* + k\alpha}{\sum_{i=0}^{k} \psi_i^* - (k+1)\alpha} \geq 1 + \frac{\psi_{k+1}^* + k\alpha}{\sum_{i=0}^{k} \psi_i' - (k+1)\alpha},$$

where the left hand equality holds since $\sup\{f_{\langle \alpha, \Psi^* \rangle}(k) \mid k \in \mathbb{N}\} = \lambda$ and right hand inequality holds since $\sum_{i=0}^{k} \psi_i^* \leq \sum_{i=0}^{k} \psi_i'$, by the inductive assumption. On the other hand, we established above $\frac{\psi_{k+1}' + k\alpha}{\sum_{i=0}^{k} \psi_i' - (k+1)\alpha} = f_{\langle \alpha, \Psi' \rangle}(k+1) - 1 = \lambda - 1$, By the above inequality, $\lambda - 1 \geq \frac{\psi_{k+1}^* + k\alpha}{\sum_{i=0}^{k} \psi_i' - (k+1)\alpha}$. Thus, $\psi_{k+1}' \geq \psi_{k+1}^*$, as required. Since $\Psi^* \in \Psi_\alpha$, also $\Psi' \in \Psi_\alpha$. The claim follows. ∎

By Eq. (4), Claim 1 implies that, for an optimal solution Ψ,

$$\frac{\psi_k + (k-1)\alpha}{\psi_0 + \dots + \psi_{k-1} - k\alpha} = \frac{\psi_{k+1} + k\alpha}{\psi_0 + \dots + \psi_k - (k+1)\alpha},$$

hence, for every $k = 1, 2, 3, \dots$

$$\psi_{k+1} = \psi_k + \frac{(\psi_k - \alpha)(\psi_k + (k-1)\alpha)}{\psi_0 + \dots + \psi_{k-1} - k\alpha} - \alpha. \tag{5}$$

This means that for every Ψ for which $f_{\langle \alpha, \Psi \rangle}(k)$ is some constant, ψ_1 determines Ψ uniquely (since $\psi_0 = 1$). In other words, every such Ψ can be characterized as $\Psi(x) = \langle \psi_0(x), \psi_1(x), \psi_2(x), \dots \rangle$ such that $\psi_0(x) = 1$, $\psi_1(x) = x$ and $\psi_{k+1}(x) = \frac{(\psi_k(x) - \alpha)(\psi_k(x) + (k-1)\alpha)}{\psi_0(x) + \dots + \psi_{k-1}(x) - k\alpha} + \psi_k(x) - \alpha$, for every $k = 1, 2, \dots$.

The construction of $\Psi(x)$ implies that, if $\psi_i(x) \geq \alpha$ for every $i \leq k$, then

$$f_{\langle \alpha, \Psi(x) \rangle}(j) = 1 + \frac{x}{1-\alpha}, \quad \text{for every } j = 0, \dots, k. \tag{6}$$

Thus, $f_{\langle \alpha, \Psi(x) \rangle}(k)$ is smaller for smaller values of x. Unfortunately, it might be that $\Psi(x) \notin \Psi_\alpha$. By Observation 1 and by Claim 1, the optimum is,

$$\text{OPT-RATIO}(\alpha) = \min_{x \in [\alpha, \infty)} \{\text{C-RATIO}(\alpha, \Psi(x)) \mid \Psi(x) \in \Psi_\alpha\}.$$

Moreover, the fact that $f_{\langle \alpha, \Psi(x) \rangle}$ is monotonically increasing as a function of $x \in [\alpha, \infty)$, implies that, for $x^* = \min\{x \mid \Psi(x) \in \Psi_\alpha\}$,

$$\text{OPT-RATIO}(\alpha) = f_{\langle \alpha, \Psi(x^*) \rangle}(0). \tag{7}$$

We found that the optimal competitive ratio is achieved for some $x^* \in [\alpha, \infty)$, such that $\Psi(x^*) \in \Psi_\alpha$ and $x^* = \psi_1(x^*) = \psi_2(x^*) = \psi_3(x^*), \dots$. Let $x^* = \frac{\alpha + \sqrt{4\alpha - 3\alpha^2}}{2}$. We prove that $\Psi(x^*) \in \Psi_\alpha$ is optimal and $\psi_i(x^*) = x^*$, for every $i = 1, 2, \dots$. (It is easy to verify that $x^* \geq \alpha$ for every choice of $0 < \alpha < 1$.) We begin with the following claim.

Claim 2. $\psi_i(x^*) = x^*$, for every $i = 1, 2, 3, \dots$.

Proof: We prove by induction. For $i = 1$, by definition of $\Psi(x)$, it follows that $\psi_1(x^*) = x^*$, hence, the base of the induction holds. Now, assume that the claim holds for every $i \in \{1, \dots, k\}$. By Eq. (5), it suffices to prove that $\frac{(\psi_k(x^*) - \alpha)(\psi_k(x^*) + (k-1)\alpha)}{\psi_0(x^*) + \dots + \psi_{k-1}(x^*) - k\alpha} - \alpha = 0$. By assigning x^* for $\psi_i(x^*)$ (for every $i = 1, \dots, k$, using the induction hypothesis) and $\psi_0(x^*) = 1$, we get $\frac{(\psi_k(x^*) - \alpha)(\psi_k(x^*) + (k-1)\alpha)}{\psi_0(x^*) + \dots + \psi_{k-1}(x^*) - k\alpha} - \alpha = \frac{(x^* - \alpha)(x^* + (k-1)\alpha)}{1 + (k-1)x^* - k\alpha} - \alpha = \frac{(x^*)^2 + (k-2)\alpha x^* - (k-1)\alpha^2}{1 + (k-1)x^* - k\alpha} - \alpha = 0$, which implies that

$$(x^*)^2 - \alpha x^* + \alpha^2 - \alpha = 0.$$

This implies that $x^* = \frac{\alpha + \sqrt{4\alpha - 3\alpha^2}}{2}$ is the solution to the above quadratic equation under the assumption that $x^* \geq \alpha$. The claim follows.   ∎

We now show that the sequence $\Psi(x)$ is monotonically decreasing.

Claim 3. *If $\psi_i(x) \geq \alpha$ for every $i \leq k$, then $\psi_{k+1}(x) < \psi_k(x)$ for every $x \in [\alpha, x^*)$ and every $k = 1, 2, 3, \ldots$.*

(Throughout, due to lack of space, some of the proofs are deferred to the full version of this paper.)

Claim 4. $\Psi(x) \notin \Psi_\alpha$, *for every $x < x^*$.*

Proof: If $x < \alpha$, then $\psi_1(x) = x < \alpha$, and the claim holds. Consider $\alpha \leq x < x^*$, and assume by the way of contradiction that $\Psi(x) \in \Psi_\alpha$. By claim 3, it follows that $\psi_{i+1}(x) < \psi_i(x) < x$, for every $i > 1$. Hence, $\lim_{i \to \infty} \psi_i(x) = x'$, for some $x' \in [\alpha, x)$. Therefore, by Eq. (2), we get that if $x' > \alpha$, then

$$\lim_{t \to \infty} \text{C-RATIO}(\Psi(x), \alpha, t) = \lim_{t \to \infty} \frac{t - \alpha}{\text{PFIT}_{\langle \alpha \rangle}(\Psi(x), t)} = \frac{x'}{x' - \alpha},$$

but $\frac{x'}{x' - \alpha} > \frac{x^*}{x^* - \alpha} = f_{\langle \alpha, \Psi(x^*) \rangle}(0) > f_{\langle \alpha, \Psi(x) \rangle}(0)$, since $\alpha \leq x' < x^*$, (that is the competitive ratio of $\Psi(x)$ is not $f_{\langle \alpha, \Psi(x) \rangle}(0)$), which is contradiction to Observation 2. Hence $\Psi(x) \notin \Psi_\alpha$. If $x' = \alpha$, then $\lim_{t \to \infty}$ C-RATIO$(\Psi(x), \alpha, t) = \infty$, which leads to a contradiction as well. ∎

We are ready to prove that $\Psi(x^*)$ is an optimal sequence. It is easy to verify that $f_{\langle \alpha, \Psi(x^*) \rangle}(0) > f_{\langle \alpha, \Psi(x) \rangle}(0)$, for every $x > x^*$. Thus, by Observation 2, C-RATIO$(\alpha, \Psi(x)) >$ C-RATIO$(\alpha, \Psi(x^*))$, hence $\Psi(x)$ is not optimal. On the other hand, by Claim 4, $\Psi(x) \notin \Psi_\alpha$ for every $x < x^*$. Thus, by Eq. (7), we get that $\Psi(x^*)$ is an optimal sequence. Recall that C-RATIO$(\alpha, \Psi(x^*)) = 1 + \frac{x^*}{1 - \alpha} = 1 + \frac{\sqrt{4\alpha - 3\alpha^2} + \alpha}{2(1 - \alpha)}$. This yields Theorem 1.

The Bounded Intermission Time Model. Above, we have shown that for $\alpha < x < x^*$, the sequence $\Psi(x)$ is monotonically decreasing. (Actually, it can be proven that the sequence is decreasing also for $x \leq \alpha$; recall, $x^* > \alpha$). Informally, the intervals in the infinite suffix of a decreasing sequence that are "short", "pull" the competitive ratio down. Hence, intuitively, if we can stop the decrease, then we can improve the competitive ratio of a sequences $\Psi(x)$ for $\alpha < x < x^*$. In fact, the decrease of $\Psi(x)$ does stop when the intermission length is bounded. In other words, a bound on the length causes the above mentioned suffix of the sequence $\Psi(x)$ to become smaller (at least, it is finite). This allows us to choose x smaller than x^* and still not get a sequence $\Psi(x)$ with a tail of intervals that are "too small". As a result, we show that we can improve the competitive ratio to $1 + \frac{x'}{1 - \alpha}$ for the bounded intermission model by choosing a sequence $\Psi(x')$, for some $\alpha < x' < x^*$. (It should be said, though, that the value of x' is, still, close to x^*, since the sequence $\Psi(x)$ decreases very fast when x is much smaller than x^*). Still informally, the more we reduce x, the faster the intervals at the suffix of $\Psi(x)$ drop to a length that is not useful. Hence, the value of x (or "how much can x be smaller than x^*") depends on the bound we are given on the interval. This is illustrated in Figure 1.

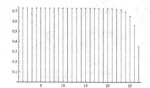
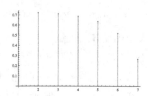

Fig. 1. In both parts of the figure, $\alpha = 0.4$. On the left, $T = 15$, and $x \approx x^* - 0.1^{10}$, a negligible improvement. On the right, $T = 5$ and $x \approx x^* - 0.1^3$, allowing a somewhat larger improvement.

Formally, the competitive ratio of Ψ with respect to time bound T is

$$\text{C-RATIO}_{\langle \alpha, T \rangle}(\Psi) = \max_{T \geq t \geq 1} \text{C-RATIO}_{\langle \alpha, T \rangle}(\Psi, t),$$

where $\text{C-RATIO}_{\langle \alpha, T \rangle}(\Psi, t) = \text{C-RATIO}(\Psi, \alpha, t)$. For a given sequence Ψ, such that $\psi_0 = 1$, and a real number x, denote by $pre_x(\Psi)$ the longest prefix of Ψ such that all intervals are of length at least x. That is, $pre_x(\Psi) = \langle \psi_0, \psi_1, ..., \psi_k \rangle$, where $\psi_i \geq x$, for every $0 \leq i \leq k$ and if the $|\Psi| > k + 1$, then $\psi_{k+1} < x$. (Note that, for $x = \alpha$, $pre_\alpha(\Psi) \in \Psi_\alpha$.)

Similarly to Observation 2, the maximum competitive ratio of $pre_\alpha(\Psi)$ is obtained even for a specific strategy of the adversary. In that strategy, the adversary chooses the intermission t to end just before the k'th interval, (for some k), or, alternatively, at $t = T$.

Observation 3. *The competitive ratio of $pre_\alpha(\Psi) \in \Psi_\alpha$ is,*
$\max \left(\text{C-RATIO}_{\langle \alpha, T \rangle}(\Psi, t = T), \max\{\lim_{\epsilon \to 0^+} \text{C-RATIO}_{\langle \alpha, T \rangle}(\Psi, \sum_{i=0}^k \psi_i - \epsilon) \mid k = 1, ..., |pre_\alpha(\Psi)| - 1\} \right)$.

Now, we prove four claims that help us find an optimal solution.

Claim 5. *Consider any $x' > x''$ and an index $i \geq 1$. Assume that $\langle \psi_0(x''), ..., \psi_{i-1}(x'') \rangle \in \Psi_\alpha$ and $\psi_i(x'') \geq 0$. Then, $\psi_j(x') > \psi_j(x'')$, for every $1 \leq j \leq i$.*

Claim 6. *There exists a sequence $x_1, x_2, x_3, ... \in \mathbb{R}$, such that*
(P1) $|pre_0(\Psi(x))| = i + 2$, for every $x \in [x_i, x_{i+1})$;
(P2) $\psi_i(x_i) = \alpha$, $\psi_{i+1}(x_i) = 0$;
(P3) $x_1 = \alpha < x_2 < x_3 < ...$, and $x_1, x_2, x_3, ... \in [\alpha, \frac{\alpha + \sqrt{4\alpha - 3\alpha^2}}{2})$; and
(P4) For every $i \leq k + 1$, $\psi_i(x)$ is continuous and strictly increasing in the range $[x_k, \frac{\alpha + \sqrt{4\alpha - 3\alpha^2}}{2}]$.

Proof: We prove properties (P2), (P3) and (P4) by induction on i. The base of the induction holds, since $\psi_1(\alpha) = \alpha$, and by Eq. (5), $\psi_2(x) = x + \frac{(x - \alpha)x)}{1 + x - \alpha} - \alpha$. thus, $\psi_2(\alpha) = 0$. Hence, properties (P2) and (P3) hold. In addition, $\psi_2(x)$ is continuous in $[\alpha, \infty]$, since $1 + x - 2\alpha > 0$, for every $x > \alpha$, and by Claim 5, $\psi_2(x)$ is strictly increasing in $[\alpha, \frac{\alpha + \sqrt{4\alpha - 3\alpha^2}}{2}]$, hence (P4) holds as well.

Assume that (P2), (P3), and (P4) holds for every $i \leq k$. For every $i = 1, ..., k$ and every $x \in [x_k, \frac{\alpha+\sqrt{4\alpha-3\alpha^2}}{2}]$, Properties (P3) and (P4) of the induction assumption imply that $\psi_i(x) \geq \psi_i(x_k) \geq \alpha$. Thus, $\sum_{i=0}^{k} \psi_i(x) - (k+1)\alpha \geq 1 - \alpha > 0$. Therefore, by Eq. (5), $\psi_{k+1}(x)$ is continuous, and by Claim 5, $\psi_{k+1}(x)$ is strictly increasing in the range $[x_k, \frac{\alpha+\sqrt{4\alpha-3\alpha^2}}{2}]$. Hence, Property (P4) holds.

In addition, by (P2) of the induction assumption, $\psi_{k+1}(x_k) = 0$, and by Claim 2, $\psi_{k+1}(\frac{\alpha+\sqrt{4\alpha-3\alpha^2}}{2}) = \frac{\alpha+\sqrt{4\alpha-3\alpha^2}}{2} > \alpha$. Hence, there exists a real number $x_{x+1} \in (x_k, \frac{\alpha+\sqrt{4\alpha-3\alpha^2}}{2})$, such that $\psi_{k+1}(x_{k+1}) = \alpha$, and by Eq. (5), $\psi_{k+2}(x_{k+1}) = 0$. Thus, (P2) and (P3) holds.

Finally, consider (P1). On one hand, by (P2), (P3) and (P4), $\psi_i(x) \geq \alpha$, for every $i = 0, 1, ..., k$, and every $x \in [x_k, \frac{\alpha+\sqrt{4\alpha-3\alpha^2}}{2}]$. On the other hand, by (P2), $\psi_{k+1}(x_k) = 0$, $\psi_{k+1}(x_{k+1}) = \alpha$; by (P3) $x_k < x_{k+1}$; and by (P4) $\psi_{k+1}(x)$ is strictly increasing in the range $[x_k, \frac{\alpha+\sqrt{4\alpha-3\alpha^2}}{2}]$. Hence, $0 < \psi_{k+1}(x) < \alpha$, which implies, together with Eq. (5), that $\psi_{k+2}(x) < 0$, for every $x \in [x_k, x_{k+1})$. ∎

Claim 7. $S(pre_0(\Psi(x)))$ *is continuous and is strictly increasing in the range* $x \in [\alpha, \frac{\alpha+\sqrt{4\alpha-3\alpha^2}}{2})$.

Proof: Let x_i be a real number such that $\psi_i(x_i) = \alpha$. (By property (P2) of Claim 6, there exists such a number.) For every $k \geq 1$, by property (P1) of Claim 6, $S(pre_0(\Psi(x))) = \sum_{i=0}^{k+1} \psi_i(x)$ in the range $[x_k, x_{k+1}]$. By property (P4) of Claim 6, $\sum_{i=0}^{k+1} \psi_i(x)$ is continuous and strictly increasing in the range $[x_k, \frac{\alpha+\sqrt{4\alpha-3\alpha^2}}{2})$. Combining this together with property (P3) of Claim 6, we get that $S(pre_0(\Psi(x)))$ is continuous and strictly increasing in the ranges $[0, x_1), [x_1, x_2), [x_2, x_3), ...$.

It remains to prove that $\lim_{\epsilon \to 0^+} S(pre_0(\Psi(x_k - \epsilon))) = S(pre_0(\Psi(x_k)))$. (This also proves that $S(pre_0(\Psi(x)))$ is strictly increasing.) We have

$$\lim_{\epsilon \to 0^+} S(pre_0(\Psi(x_k - \epsilon))) = \sum_{i=0}^{k} \psi_i(x_k - \epsilon) = \sum_{i=0}^{k+1} \psi_i(x_k) = S(pre_0(\Psi(x_k))).$$

where the second equality holds, since $\psi_{k+1}(x_k) = 0$ by property (P2) of Claim 6. The claim follows. ∎

Claim 8. *There exists an optimal sequence* Ψ *for DIC with a bound* T *on intermission time, such that* $f_{\langle \alpha, \Psi \rangle}(k)$ *is some constant for every* $k = 0, ..., |\Psi| - 2$. *(Similarly to Claim 1.)*

Proof: Consider an optimal solution Ψ^* for DIC with time bound T. Let $\lambda = \max\{f_{\langle \alpha, \Psi^* \rangle}(k) \mid k \in \{0, ..., |\Psi^*| - 1\}\}$ and let Ψ' be a sequence obtained from Ψ^* as follows: $\psi_0' = 1$ and for every $1 \leq i \leq |\Psi^*| - 2$,

$$\psi_{i+1}' = (\lambda - 1)\left(\sum_{j=0}^{i} \psi_j' - (i+1)\alpha\right) - i\alpha.$$

Note that, $|\Psi^*| = |\Psi'|$, and by induction on i and by Eq. (4) we know that $\psi_i' \geq \psi_i^*$ and $f_{\langle \alpha, \Psi' \rangle}(k) = \lambda$. Thus, $S(\Psi') \geq S(\Psi^*)$, with equality if and only if $\Psi^* = \Psi'$. If $\Psi^* = \Psi'$, then the claim follows. Assume by the way of contradiction that $\Psi^* \neq \Psi'$, thus $S(\Psi') > S(\Psi^*)$. This implies that, if $S(\Psi') \leq T$, then the profit of Ψ' is grater than the profit of Ψ^* for time T, hence C-RATIO$(\Psi', \alpha, T) \leq$ C-RATIO(Ψ^*, α, T). Otherwise, $S(\Psi') > T$, and then it follows that C-RATIO$(\Psi', \alpha, T) \leq \lambda$.

In both cases, C-RATIO$(\Psi', \alpha, T) \leq \max\{\lambda, $C-RATIO$(\Psi^*, \alpha, T)\}$. This implies that

$$\text{C-RATIO}_{\langle \alpha, T \rangle}(\Psi') \leq \max\{\lambda, \text{C-RATIO}_{\langle \alpha, T \rangle}(\Psi^*, t = T)\} = \text{C-RATIO}_{\langle \alpha, T \rangle}(\Psi^*).$$

Therefore, Ψ' is also optimal. In addition $f_{\langle \alpha, \Psi' \rangle}(k) = \lambda$, for every $0 \leq k < |\Psi'| - 1$.   ∎

Let $x_{\langle T, \alpha \rangle}$ be real such that $S(pre_0(\Psi(x_{\langle T, \alpha \rangle}))) = T$. (There exists such real, since by Claim 7 $pre_0(\Psi(x))$ is continuous, $S(pre_0(\Psi(0))) = 1$ and $\lim_{\epsilon \to 0+} S(pre_0(\Psi(\frac{\alpha + \sqrt{4\alpha - 3\alpha^2}}{2} - \epsilon))) = \infty$.)

Theorem 2. *Let $\Psi^{\langle T, \alpha \rangle} = pre_\alpha(\Psi(x_{\langle T, \alpha \rangle}))$. The sequence $\Psi^{\langle T, \alpha \rangle}$ is optimal. The competitive ratio of any access protocol using it is $1 + \frac{x_{\langle T, \alpha \rangle}}{1 - \alpha}$.*

Proof: First, we prove that

$$|\Psi^{\langle T, \alpha \rangle}| = |pre_0(\Psi(x_{\langle T, \alpha \rangle}))| - 1. \tag{8}$$

Let $last = |pre_\alpha(\Psi(x_{\langle T, \alpha \rangle}))| - 1$. By Eq. (5),

$$\text{if } \psi_i(x) \geq \alpha, \text{ then } \psi_{i+1}(x) \geq 0, \text{ and}$$
$$\text{if } \psi_i(x) \in [0, \alpha), \text{ then } \psi_{i+1}(x) < 0.$$

Hence, $\psi_{last}(x_{\langle T, \alpha \rangle}) \in [0, \alpha)$ and $\psi_{last-1}(x_{\langle T, \alpha \rangle}) \geq \alpha$, implying Eq. (8). It is easy to verify that

$$\text{C-RATIO}_T(\Psi^{\langle T, \alpha \rangle}, \alpha) = 1 + \frac{x_{\langle T, \alpha \rangle}}{1 - \alpha}. \tag{9}$$

Let Ψ^* be an optimal solution assuming the conditions of Claim 8. That is, $f_{\langle \alpha, \Psi^* \rangle}(k)$ is a constant. Let $x^* = \psi_1^*$. It follows that $\psi_i(x^*) = \psi_i^*$, for every $i = 0, 1, ..., |\Psi^*| - 1$. If $x^* > x_{\langle T, \alpha \rangle}$, then $\lim_{\epsilon \to 0+} \text{C-RATIO}_T(\Psi^*, \alpha, 1 + \psi_1^* - \epsilon) = 1 + \frac{x^*}{1-\alpha}$. This implies that, C-RATIO$_T(\Psi^*, \alpha) \geq 1 + \frac{x^*}{1-\alpha}$, and $1 + \frac{x^*}{1-\alpha} > 1 + \frac{x_{\langle T, \alpha \rangle}}{1-\alpha} = \text{C-RATIO}_T(\Psi^{\langle T, \alpha \rangle}, \alpha)$. This, is contradiction to the fact that Ψ^* is optimal. If $x^* < x_{\langle T, \alpha \rangle}$, then $S(pre_0(\Psi(x^*))) < T$ and $\Psi^* = pre_\alpha(\Psi(x^*))$. Hence, C-RATIO$_{\langle \alpha, T \rangle}(\Psi(x^*), t = T) > f_{\langle \Psi(x^*), \alpha \rangle}$ and $S(\Psi^*) < S(pre_\alpha(\Psi(x_{\langle T, \alpha \rangle})))$. Thus,

$$\text{C-RATIO}_{\langle \alpha, T \rangle}(\Psi^*, t = T) > \text{C-RATIO}_{\langle \alpha, T \rangle}(pre_\alpha(\Psi(x_{\langle T, \alpha \rangle})), t = T) = 1 + \frac{x_{\langle T, \alpha \rangle}}{1 - \alpha},$$

which is contradiction to the selection of Ψ^* as the optimal. Therefore, $x^* = x_{\langle T, \alpha \rangle}$. The theorem follows.   ∎

3   Probabilistic Intermission Length

We now turn to the case that the intermission time length is taken from a general probability distribution. To be able to deal with any probability distribution P, we assume that P is given as a black box that gets a value x and returns $P(x)$. (It is easy to generate this black box when the distribution follows some known function, e.g., poisson, uniform etc.). We present a polynomial algorithm for DIC for the discrete case, that approximates (as good as we want) the optimal solution for the continuous case. As in the previous case, it is enough to optimize the protocol for each intermission separately (because of the linearity of expectations). Hence, we concentrate on one intermission.

3.1   General Probabilistic Distribution

Consider a probability distribution $P : \mathbb{N} \to [0,1]$ that represents the intermission time length, i.e., $\Pr[\text{intermission timelength} \geq t] = P(t)$. Sometimes, we assume that a priori upper bound T is known·for the intermission time length. Denote by P_T a bounded probability distribution with bound T; That is, $P(t) = 0$, for every $t > T$.

Consider a finite sequence $\Psi = \langle \psi_1, \psi_2, ..., \psi_m \rangle \in \Psi_{\text{FIN}}$ and a probability distribution P_T. By Eq. (1), the expected profit of Ψ with respect to P_T is

$$\text{Epro}_{\langle P_T, \alpha \rangle}(\Psi) = \sum_{k=1}^{|\Psi|} (\psi_k - \alpha) \cdot P_T(\text{S}(\Psi, k)).$$

We want to compute the maximal (optimal) expected profit of a sequence with respect to P_T, denoted by- $\text{OPT}(P_T) = \max\{\text{Epro}_{\langle P_T, \alpha \rangle}(\Psi) \mid \Psi \text{ is a sequence}\}$.

Bounded Discrete Domain. First, consider the model where the intermission length is discrete, (consists of t' time slots) and is bounded from above by T. Before addressing the whole intermission, let us consider just its part that starts at $T - \ell$ (for some ℓ) and ends no later than T (note that $T - \ell$ may be empty if $t' \leq T - \ell$). Let $MAX_{\langle P_T \rangle}^{TAIL}(\ell)$ (for every $0 \leq \ell \leq T$) be the expected maximal profit that any sequence may have from this part. That is,

$$MAX_{\langle P_T \rangle}^{TAIL}(\ell) = \max_{\Psi \in \Psi_{\text{FIN}}} \{\sum_{k=1}^{|\Psi|} (\psi_k - \alpha) \cdot P_T(T - \ell + \text{S}(\Psi, k))\}.$$

In particular, $\text{OPT}(P_T) = MAX_{\langle P_T \rangle}^{TAIL}(T) = MAX_{\langle P_T \rangle}^{TAIL}(T - 0)$, The recursive presentation of $MAX_{\langle P_T \rangle}^{TAIL}$ is $MAX_{\langle P_T \rangle}^{TAIL}(0) = 0$ and $MAX_{\langle P_T \rangle}^{TAIL}(\ell) = \max_{i \in \{0,1,...,\ell-1\}} \{P_T(T-i) \cdot (\ell - i - \alpha) + MAX_{\langle P_T \rangle}^{TAIL}(i)\}$. Using dynamic programming, we can compute $MAX_{\langle P_T \rangle}^{TAIL}(T) = \text{OPT}(P_T)$ and find an optimal sequence with time complexity $O(T^2)$. Thus, finding an optimal sequence is a polynomial problem in the value of T.[3]

---

[3] It is reasonable to assume that the time length T is polynomial in the size of the input. Had we assumed that T was say, exponential in the size of the input, this would have meant an intermission whose duration is so long, that in practice, it seems as being infinity, making the whole problem mute.

Bounded Continuous Domain. Let us now consider the case where the probability distribution P_T is continuous. We present a fully polynomial-time approximation scheme (FPTAS) [9] for the case that the optimal solution provides at least some constant profit. We argue that in the other case, where the profit is of a vanishing value, a solution to the problem is useless anyhow. (Still, for completeness, we derived some result for that case: we have shown that if the profit in the optimal case is "too small", then it cannot be approximated at all.)

Consider a real number $\delta > 0$ such that $\mu \equiv T/\delta$ is an integer. Let $\Psi_\delta = \{\Psi \mid \psi_i/\delta$ is an integer, for every $i\}$. Let $MAX^{TAIL}_{\langle\delta,P_T\rangle}(\ell)$ (for every integer $0 \le \ell \le \mu$) be the expected maximum profit over sequences $\Psi \in \Psi_\delta$ from the time period $[T - \ell \cdot \delta, T]$. That is,

$$MAX^{TAIL}_{\langle\delta,P_T\rangle}(\ell) = \max_{\Psi \in \Psi_\delta} \left\{ \sum_{k=1}^{|\Psi|} (\psi_k - \alpha) \cdot P_T\left(T - \ell \cdot \delta + S(\Psi, k)\right) \right\}.$$

We show that the function $MAX^{TAIL}_{\langle\delta,P_T\rangle}$ approximates the value of $\text{OPT}(P_T)$. In particular, we show that for any optimization parameter $\epsilon > 0$, there exists a $\delta > 0$ such that $MAX^{TAIL}_{\langle\delta,P_T\rangle}(T) \ge (1 - \epsilon)\text{OPT}(P_T)$. Intuitively, we first show that a large fraction of the expected profit of an optimal sequence Ψ^* is made from intervals whose lengths are "sufficient greater" than α. (A long interval can be approximated well by dividing it into smaller intervals, whose lengths are multipliers of δ; dividing a short interval is not profitable because of α.)

Consider an optimal sequence $\Psi^* = \langle\psi^*_1, ..., \psi^*_{|\Psi^*|}\rangle$. Let $\text{PFIT}^{TAIL}_\delta(i) = \sum_{j=i}^{|\Psi^*|} [(\psi^*_j - \alpha) \cdot P_T(S(\Psi^*, j))]$ be the expected profit gained from the intervals $\psi^*_i, ..., \psi^*_{|\Psi^*|}$ under probability distribution P_T, for every $i \in \{1, ..., |\Psi^*|\}$.

Claim 9. *For any $\lambda > 0$, if $\text{PFIT}^{TAIL}_\delta(i) \ge \lambda$, then $\psi^*_i \ge \alpha + \min\{\frac{\lambda}{2T}, \lambda/2\}$.*

We are ready to show that $MAX^{TAIL}_{\langle\delta,P_T\rangle}(T)$ approximates $\text{OPT}(P_T)$. Assume *first* that we know some constant λ such that $\text{OPT}(P_T) \ge \lambda$. (We do not need to know how close is λ to $\text{OPT}(P_T) \ge \lambda$.)

Lemma 1. *Consider $0 < \lambda \le \text{OPT}(P_T)$ and an optimization parameter $\epsilon > 0$. Let $\mu_\lambda = \max\left\{\left\lceil\frac{16T^2}{\lambda\epsilon^2}\right\rceil, \left\lceil\frac{16}{\lambda\epsilon^2}\right\rceil\right\}$ and $\delta_\lambda = \min\{T/\mu_\lambda, 1/\mu_\lambda\}$. Then, $MAX^{TAIL}_{\langle\delta_\lambda,P_T\rangle}(T) \ge (1 - \epsilon) \cdot \text{OPT}(P_T)$. (For simplicity, we may omit λ from δ_λ and μ_λ.)*

Proof: Let $f_{left}(i)$ be the leftmost point s.t. (1) $f_{left}(i)/\delta$ is an integer, and (2) profit is at least, as large as the sum of all the elements $\psi^*_1, ..., \psi^*_{i-1}$. That is, $f_{left}(1) = 0$ and $f_{left}(i) = \min\{j \cdot \delta \mid j \cdot \delta \ge \sum_{j=1}^{i-1} \psi^*_j\}$. Similarly, $f_{right}(i)$ is the rightmost point such that (1) $f_{right}(i)/\delta$ is an integer, and (2) is at most, the sum of all element $\psi^*_1, ..., \psi^*_i$. It follows that $f_{right}(i) - f_{left}(i) > \psi^*_i - 2\delta$. Thus,

$$\frac{f_{right}(i) - f_{left}(i) - \alpha}{\psi^*_i - \alpha} > \frac{\psi^*_i - 2\delta - \alpha}{\psi^*_i - \alpha} = 1 - \frac{2\delta}{\psi^*_i - \alpha} .$$

Let $i^* = \max\{i \mid \text{PFIT}_\delta^{TAIL}(i) \geq \lambda\epsilon/2\}$. Combining the above inequality together with Claim 9 and the fact that $\delta \leq \min\{\frac{\lambda\epsilon^2}{16T}, \frac{\lambda\epsilon^2}{16}\}$, we get that

$$\frac{f_{right}(i) - f_{left}(i) - \alpha}{\psi_i^* - \alpha} > 1 - \max\left\{\frac{8T\delta}{\lambda\epsilon}, \frac{8\delta}{\lambda\epsilon}\right\} \geq 1 - \epsilon/2,$$

for every $i = 1, ..., i^*$. In addition, it follows that, if $i^* = |\Psi^*|$, then $\sum_{i=1}^{i^*} ((\psi_i^* - \alpha) \cdot P_T(S(\Psi^*, i))) = \text{OPT}(P_T)$. Otherwise, $\sum_{i=1}^{i^*} ((\psi_i^* - \alpha) \cdot P_T(S(\Psi^*, i))) = \text{OPT}(P_T) - \text{PFIT}_\delta^{TAIL}(i^* + 1) > \text{OPT}(P_T) - \lambda\epsilon/2$. In both cases, we get that

$$\sum_{i=1}^{i^*} ((\psi_i^* - \alpha) P_T(S(\Psi^*, i))) > \text{OPT}(P_T)(1 - \epsilon/2). \tag{10}$$

Therefore,

$$\sum_{i=1}^{i^*} (f_{right}(i) - f_{left}(i) - \alpha) \cdot P_T(S(\Psi, i)) \geq (1 - \epsilon/2) \cdot \left(\sum_{i=1}^{i^*} (\psi_i^* - \alpha) \cdot P_T(S(\Psi, i))\right)$$
$$\geq (1 - \epsilon/2) \cdot \text{OPT}(P_T)(1 - \epsilon/2)$$
$$\geq (1 - \epsilon)\text{OPT}(P_T).$$

For the first inequality see Ineq. (10); for the second one see Ineq. (10). Clearly, $MAX_{\langle\delta,P_T\rangle}^{TAIL}(T) \geq \sum_{i=1}^{i^*} [(f_{right}(i) - f_{left}(i) - \alpha) \cdot P_T(S(\Psi, i))]$. ∎

Let us compute $MAX_{\langle\delta,P_T\rangle}^{TAIL}$ (which, we have shown, approximates the optimal sequence). The recursive presentation of $MAX_{\langle\delta,P_T\rangle}^{TAIL}$ is $MAX_{\langle\delta,P_T\rangle}^{TAIL}(0) = 0$ and $MAX_{\langle\delta,P_T\rangle}^{TAIL}(\ell) = \max_{i\in\{0,1,...,\ell-1\}}\{P_T(T - i \cdot \delta) \cdot ((\ell - i)\delta - \alpha) + MAX_{\langle P_T\rangle}^{TAIL}(i)\}$. The $MAX_{\langle\delta,P_T\rangle}^{TAIL}$, as well as the sequence attaining it (observed in the lemma) can now be computed using dynamic programming. The time complexity is $O((T/\delta)^2)$ and $T/\delta = O(\frac{T^2}{\epsilon^2})$; thus, it is polynomial in $1/\epsilon$, $1/\lambda$ and T.

Now, let us get rid of the assumption that λ is known. Let $\lambda_i = 2^{-i}$. We compute $MAX_{\langle\delta_{\lambda_0},P_T\rangle}^{TAIL}$, then $MAX_{\langle\delta_{\lambda_1},P_T\rangle}^{TAIL}, ...$, as long as $MAX_{\langle\delta_{\lambda_i},P_T\rangle}^{TAIL} < \lambda_i$. When $MAX_{\langle\delta_{\lambda_k},P_T\rangle}^{TAIL} \geq \lambda_k$, the algorithm stops and returns a sequence attaining it. (Note that $MAX_{\langle\delta_{\lambda_k},P_T\rangle}^{TAIL} \geq \lambda_k$ implies that $\text{OPT}(P_T) \geq \lambda_k$.) The time complexity remains the same as $1/\lambda$ is a constant.

Theorem 3. *There exists a FPTAS for DIC for continuous distribution (for every instance of the problem for which the optimal solution obtains at least some constant positive profit).*

Theorem 4. *If there is no assumption on the minimum value of* $\text{OPT}(P_T)$, *i.e., it can be negligible, then no approximation algorithm for the DIC problem exists.*

Proof: Consider an algorithm ALG for the DIC problem. An adversary can select P_T after the execution of ALG, such that $\text{OPT}(P) > 0$ and $A(P_T) = 0$ (the expected profit of the sequence that made by ALG). Recall that algorithm

ALG must produce a sequence Ψ_{ALG} of intervals. While producing the sequence, ALG may query the distribution. Let $x_1, x_2, ..., x_z$ be sequence of queries ALG made while producing Ψ_{ALG}, and let $P_T(x_1), P_T(x_2), ..., P_T(x_z)$ be the answers. Let $X_{>\alpha} = \{x_i > \alpha \mid i = 1, ..., z\}$. In the execution of ALG the black box (representing the distribution) return 0, for every $x > \alpha$ and returns 1, for every $x \leq \alpha$. That is, if $x_i > \alpha$, then $P_T(x_i) = 0$, otherwise $P_T(x_i) = 0$, for every $i = 1, ..., z$.

At the end of the execution ALG returns a sequence $\langle \psi_1^{ALG}, ... \rangle$. It is clear that $\psi_1^{ALG} \geq \alpha$ (otherwise, it might have a negative profit). If $\psi_1^{ALG} > \alpha$, then let $x' = \min\{\psi_1^{ALG}, x_i \mid x_i \in X_{>\alpha}\}$. Chose $\epsilon = x' - \alpha$ and $P_T(x) = 1$, for every $x \leq \alpha + \epsilon/2$. Otherwise, $P_T = 0$. We get that $\text{OPT}(P_T) = \epsilon/2 > 0$ and $ALG(P_T) = 0$ as required. If $\psi_1^A = \alpha$, then chose $x' = \min\{1.5\alpha, x_i \mid x_i \in X_{>\alpha}\}$. Set $P_T = 1$, for every $x \leq x'$ and otherwise $P_T = 0$. Thus clearly, $A(P_T) \leq 0$ and $\text{OPT}(P_T) = x' - \alpha > 0$. The Theorem follows.   ∎

Finally, we describe some interesting observations on specific distributions (due to lack of space, this section is deferred to the full version).

References

1. Ahmad, S.H.A., Liu, M., Javidi, T., Zhao, Q., Krishnamachari, B.: Optimality of myopic sensing in multichannel opportunistic access. IEEE Tran. on Information Theory 55(9) (2009)
2. Akyildiz, I.F., Lee, W., Vuran, M.C., Mohanty, S.: Next generation/dynamic spectrum access/cognitive radio wireless networks: A survey. Computer Networks 50(13) (2006)
3. Borodin, A., El-Yaniv, R.: Online computation and competitive analysis. Cambridge University Press (1998)
4. Huang, S., Liu, X., Ding, Z.: Opportunistic spectrum access in cognitive radio networks. In: INFOCOM (2008)
5. Li, X., Zhao, Q., Guan, X., Tong, L.: Optimal cognitive access of markovian channels under tight collision constraints. IEEE J. on Selected Areas in Comm. 29(4) (2011)
6. Lotker, Z., Patt-Shamir, B.: Nearly optimal fifo buffer management for two packet classes. Computer Networks 42(4) (2003)
7. Zhao, Q., Sadler, B.M.: A survey of dynamic spectrum access. IEEE Signal Process. Mag. 24 (2007)
8. Urgaonkar, R., Neely, M.J.: Opportunistic scheduling with reliability guarantees in cognitive radio networks. IEEE Trans. Mob. Comput. 8(6) (2009)
9. Vazirani, V.V.: Approximation algorithms. Springer (2001)
10. Xiao, Q., Li, Y., Zhao, M., Zhou, S., Wang, J.: Opportunistic channel selection approach under collision probability constraint in cognitive radio systems. Computer Comm. 32(18) (2009)
11. Xiao, Q., Li, Y., Zhao, M., Zhou, S., Wang, J.: An optimal osa approach based on channel-usage estimate under collision probability constraint in cognitive radio systems. Annales des Télécommunications 64(7-8) (2009)
12. Zhao, Q., Tong, L., Swami, A., Chen, Y.: Decentralized cognitive mac for opportunistic spectrum access in ad hoc networks: A pomdp framework. IEEE J. on Selected Areas in Comm. (2007)

Braess's Paradox in Wireless Networks: The Danger of Improved Technology*

Michael Dinitz[1,2],*** and Merav Parter[1],**,***

[1] Department of Computer Science and Applied Mathematics,
The Weizmann Institute, Rehovot, Israel
{michael.dinitz,merav.parter}@weizmann.ac.il
[2] Department of Computer Science, Johns Hopkins University

Abstract. When comparing new wireless technologies, it is common to consider the effect that they have on the capacity of the network (defined as the maximum number of simultaneously satisfiable links). For example, it has been shown that giving receivers the ability to do interference cancellation, or allowing transmitters to use power control, never decreases the capacity and can in certain cases increase it by $\Omega(\log(\Delta \cdot P_{max}))$, where Δ is the ratio of the longest link length to the smallest transmitter-receiver distance and P_{max} is the maximum transmission power. But there is no reason to expect the optimal capacity to be realized in practice, particularly since maximizing the capacity is known to be NP-hard. In reality, we would expect links to behave as self-interested agents, and thus when introducing a new technology it makes more sense to compare the values reached at game-theoretic equilibria than the optimum values.

In this paper we initiate this line of work by comparing various notions of equilibria (particularly Nash equilibria and no-regret behavior) when using a supposedly "better" technology. We show a version of Braess's Paradox for all of them: in certain networks, upgrading technology can actually make the equilibria *worse*, despite an increase in the capacity. We construct instances where this decrease is a constant factor for power control, interference cancellation, and improvements in the SINR threshold (β), and is $\Omega(\log \Delta)$ when power control is combined with interference cancellation. However, we show that these examples are basically tight: the decrease is at most $O(1)$ for power control, interference cancellation, and improved β, and is at most $O(\log \Delta)$ when power control is combined with interference cancellation.

---

* A full version of this paper, including all proofs, can be found at http://arxiv.org/abs/1308.0173

** Recipient of the Google European Fellowship in distributed computing; research is supported in part by this Fellowship.

*** Supported in part by the Israel Science Foundation (grant 894/09), the I-CORE program of the Israel PBC and ISF (grant 4/11), the United States-Israel Binational Science Foundation (grant 2008348), the Israel Ministry of Science and Technology (infrastructures grant), and the Citi Foundation.

Y. Afek (Ed.): DISC 2013, LNCS 8205, pp. 477–491, 2013.
© Springer-Verlag Berlin Heidelberg 2013

1   Introduction

Due to the increasing use of wireless technology in communication networks, there has been a significant amount of research on methods of improving wireless performance. While there are many ways of measuring wireless performance, a good first step (which has been extensively studied) is the notion of *capacity*. Given a collection of communication links, the capacity of a network is simply the maximum number of simultaneously satisfiable links. This can obviously depend on the exact model of wireless communication that we are using, but is clearly an upper bound on the "usefulness" of the network. There has been a large amount of research on analyzing the capacity of wireless networks (see e.g. [16,15,2,20]), and it has become a standard way of measuring the quality of a network. Because of this, when introducing a new technology it is interesting to analyze its affect on the capacity. For example, we know that in certain cases giving transmitters the ability to control their transmission power can increase the capacity by $\Omega(\log \Delta)$ or $\Omega(\log P_{\max}))$ [7], where Δ is the ratio of the longest link length to the smallest transmitter-receiver distance, and can clearly never decrease the capacity.

However, while the capacity might improve, it is not nearly as clear that the *achieved* capacity will improve. After all, we do not expect our network to actually have performance that achieves the maximum possible capacity. We show that not only might these improved technologies not help, they might in fact *decrease* the achieved network capacity. Following Andrews and Dinitz [2] and Ásgeirsson and Mitra [3], we model each link as a self-interested agent and analyze various types of game-theoretic behavior (Nash equilibria and no-regret behavior in particular). We show that a version of *Braess's Paradox* [9] holds: adding new technology to the networks (such as the ability to control powers) can actually decrease the average capacity at equilibrium.

1.1   Our Results

Our main results show that in the context of wireless networks, and particularly in the context of the SINR model, there is a version of *Braess's Paradox* [9]. In his seminal paper, Braess studied congestion in road networks and showed that adding additional roads to an existing network can actually make congestion *worse*, since agents will behave selfishly and the additional options can result in worse equilibria. This is completely analogous to our setting, since in road networks adding extra roads cannot hurt the network in terms of the value of the optimum solution, but can hurt the network since the *achieved* congestion gets worse. In this work we consider the physical model (also called the SINR model), pioneered by Moscibroda and Wattenhofer [24] and described more formally in Section 2.1. Intuitively, this model works as follows: every sender chooses a transmission power (which may be pre-determined, e.g. due to hardware limitations), and the received power decreased polynomially with the distance from the sender. A transmission is successful if the received power from the sender is large enough to overcome the interference caused by other senders plus the background noise.

With our baseline being the SINR model, we then consider four ways of "improving" a network: adding power control, adding interference cancellation, adding both power control and interference cancellation, and decreasing the SINR threshold. With all of these modifications it is easy to see that the optimal capacity can only increase, but we will show that the equilibria can become worse. Thus "improving" a network might actually result in worse performance.

The game-theoretic setup that we use is based on [2] and will be formally described in Section 2.2, but we will give an overview here. We start with a game in which the players are the links, and the strategies depend slightly on the model but are essentially possible power settings at which to transmit. The utilities depend on whether or not the link was successful, and whether or not it even attempted to transmit. In a pure Nash equilibrium every player has a strategy (i.e. power setting) and has no incentive to deviate: any other strategy would result in smaller utility. In a mixed Nash equilibrium every link has a probability distribution over the strategies, and no link has any incentive to deviate from their distribution. Finally, no-regret behavior is the empirical distribution of play when all players use *no-regret* algorithms, which are a widely used and studied class of learning algorithms (see Section 2.2 for a formal definition). It is reasonably easy to see that any pure Nash is a mixed Nash, and any mixed Nash is a no-regret behavior. For all of these, the quality of the solution is the achieved capacity, i.e. the average number of successful links.

Our first result is for interference cancellation (IC), which has been widely proposed as a practical method of increasing network performance [1]. The basic idea of interference cancellation is quite simple. First, the strongest interfering signal is detected and decoded. Once decoded, this signal can then be subtracted ("canceled") from the original signal. Subsequently, the next strongest interfering signal can be detected and decoded from the now "cleaner" signal, and so on. As long as the strongest remaining signal can be decoded in the presence of the weaker signals, this process continues until we are left with the desired transmitted signal, which can now be decoded. This clearly can increase the capacity of the network, and even in the worst case cannot decrease it. And yet due to bad game-theoretic interactions it might make the achieved capacity worse:

Theorem 1. *There exists a set of links in which the best no-regret behavior under interference cancellation achieves capacity at most c times the worst no-regret behavior without interference cancellation, for some constant c < 1. However, for every set of links the worst no-regret behavior under interference cancellation achieves capacity that is at least a constant fraction of the best no-regret behavior without interference cancellation.*

Thus IC can make the achieved capacity worse, but only by a constant factor. Note that since every Nash equilibrium (mixed or pure) is also no-regret, this implies the equivalent statements for those type of equilibria as well. In this result (as in most of our examples) we only show a small network (4 links) with no background noise, but these are both only for simplicity – it is easy to incorporate constant noise, and the small network can be repeated at sufficient distance to get examples with an arbitrarily large number of links.

We next consider power control (PC), where senders can choose not just whether to transmit, but at what power to transmit. It turns out that any equilibrium without power control is also an equilibrium with power control, and thus we cannot hope to find an example where the best equilibrium with power control is worse than the worst equilibrium without power control (as we did with IC). Instead, we show that adding power control can create worse equilibria:

Theorem 2. *There exists a set of links in which there is a pure Nash equilibrium with power control of value at most c times the value of the worst no-regret behavior without power control, for some constant c < 1. However, for every set of links the worst no-regret behavior with power control has value that is at least a constant fraction of the value of the best no-regret behavior without power control.*

Note that the first part of the theorem implies that not only is there a pure Nash with low-value (with power control), there are also mixed Nash and no-regret behaviors with low value (since any pure Nash is also mixed and no-regret). Similarly, the second part of the theorem gives a bound on the gap between the worst and the best mixed Nashes, and the worst and the best pure Nashes.

Our third set of results is on the combination of power control and interference cancellation. It turns out that the combination of the two can be quite harmful. When compared to either the vanilla setting (no interference cancellation or power control) or the presence of power control without interference cancellation, the combination of IC and PC acts essentially as in Theorem 2: pure Nash equilibria are created that are worse than the previous worst no-regret behavior, but this can only be by a constant factor. On the other hand, this factor can be super-constant when compared to equilibria that only use interference cancellation. Let Δ be the ratio of the length of the longest link to the minimum distance between any sender and any receiver. [1]

Theorem 3. *There exists a set of links in which the worst pure Nash with both PC and IC (and thus the worst mixed Nash or no-regret behavior) has value at most $O(1/\log \Delta)$ times the value of the worst no-regret behavior with just IC. However, for every set of links the worst no-regret behavior with both PC and IC has value at least $\Omega(1/\log \Delta)$ times the value of the best no-regret behavior with just IC.*

This theorem means that interference cancellation "changes the game": if interference control were not an option then power control can only hurt the equilibria by a constant amount (from Theorem 2), but if we assume that interference

---

[1] Note that this definition is slightly different than the one used by [18,3,17] and is a bit more similar to the definition used by [2,12]. The interested reader can see that this is in fact the appropriate definition in the IC setting, namely, in a setting where a receiver can decode multiple (interfering) stations.

cancellation is present then adding power control can hurt us by $\Omega(\log \Delta)$. Thus when deciding whether to use both power control and interference cancellation, one must be particularly careful to analyze how they act in combination.

Finally, we consider the effect of decreasing the SINR threshold β (this value will be formally described in Section 2.1). We show that, as with IC, there are networks in which a decrease in the SINR threshold can lead to *every* equilibrium being worse than even the worst equilibrium at the higher threshold, despite the capacity increasing or staying the same:

Theorem 4. *There exists a set of links and constants $1 < \beta' < \beta$ in which the best no-regret behavior under threshold β' has value at most c times the value of the worst no-regret behavior under threshold β, for some constant $c < 1$. However, for any set of links and any $1 < \beta' < \beta$ the value of the worst no-regret behavior under β' is at least a constant fraction of the value of the best no-regret behavior under β.*

Our main network constructions illustrating Braess's paradox in the studied settings are summarized in Fig. 1.

1.2   Related Work

The capacity of *random* networks was examined in the seminal paper of Gupta and Kumar [16], who proved tight bounds in a variety of models. But only recently has there been a significant amount of work on algorithms for determining the capacity of *arbitrary* networks, particularly in the SINR model. This line of work began with Goussevskaia, Oswald, and Wattenhofer [14], who gave an $O(\log \Delta)$-approximation for the uniform power setting (i.e. the vanilla model we consider). Goussevskaia, Halldórson, Wattenhofer, and Welzl [15] then improved this to an $O(1)$-approximation (still under uniform powers), while Andrews and Dinitz [2] gave a similar $O(\log \Delta)$-approximation algorithm for the power control setting. This line of research was essentially completed by an $O(1)$-approximation for the power control setting due to Kesselheim [20].

In parallel to the work on approximation algorithms, there has been some work on using game theory (and in particular the games used in this paper) to help design distributed approximation algorithms. This was begun by Andrews and Dinitz [2], who gave an upper bound of $O(\Delta^{2\alpha})$ on the price of anarchy for the basic game defined in Section 2.2. But since computing the Nash equilibrium of a game is PPAD-complete [11], we do not expect games to necessarily converge to a Nash equilibrium in polynomial time. Thus Dinitz [12] strengthened the result by showing the same upper bound of $O(\Delta^{2\alpha})$ for no-regret behavior. This gave the first distributed algorithm with a nontrivial approximation ratio, simply by having every player use a no-regret algorithm. The analysis of the same game was then improved to $O(\log \Delta)$ by Ásgeirsson and Mitra [3].

There is very little work on interference cancellation in arbitrary networks from an algorithmic point of view, although it has been studied quite well from an information-theoretic point of view (see e.g. [13,10]). Recently Avin et al. [5] studied the topology of *SINR diagrams* under interference cancellation, which

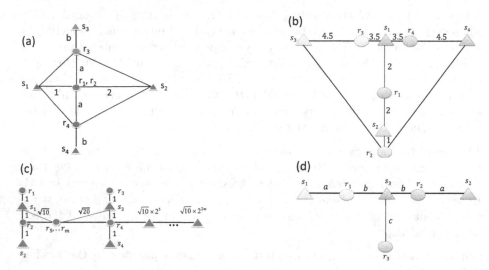

Fig. 1. Schematic illustration of the main lower bounds illustrating the Braess's paradox with (a) IC: a network in which every no-regret behavior without IC is better than any no-regret behavior solution with IC; (b) PC: a network in which there exists a pure Nash equilibrium with PC which is worse than any no-regret behavior with IC; (c) PIC: a network with a pure Nash equilibrium in the PIC setting which is $\Omega(\log \Delta)$ worse than any no-regret behavior in the IC setting but *without* power control; and (d) Decreased SINR threshold $\beta' < \beta$: a network in which every no-regret behavior with β' has a smaller value than any no-regret behavior with higher SINR threshold β. Edge weights represent distances.

are a generalization of the SINR diagrams introduced by Avin et al. [6] and further studied by Kantor et al. [19] for the SINR model without interference cancellation. These diagrams specify the reception zones of transmitters in the SINR model, which turn out to have several interesting topological and geometric properties but have not led to a better understanding of the fundamental capacity question.

2   Preliminaries

2.1   The Communication Model

We model a wireless network as a set of links $L = \{\ell_1, \ell_2, \ldots, \ell_n\}$ in the plane, where each link $\ell_v = (s_v, r_v)$ represents a communication request from a sender s_v to a receiver r_v. The n senders and receivers are given as points in the Euclidean plane. The Euclidean distance between two points p and q is denoted $d(p, q)$. The distance between sender s_i and receiver r_j is denoted by $d_{i,j}$. We adopt the physical model (sometime called the SINR model) where the received signal strength of transmitter s_i at the receiver r_j decays with the distance and it is given by $P_{i,j} = P_i/d_{i,j}^\alpha$, where $P_i \in [0, P_{\max}]$ is the transmission power of sender s_i and $\alpha > 0$ is the path-loss exponent. Receiver r_j successfully receives a message from sender s_j iff $\mathrm{SINR}_j(L) = \frac{P_{j,j}}{\sum_{\ell_i \in L} P_{i,j} + \eta} \geq \beta$, where η denotes the amount of background noise and $\beta > 1$ denotes the minimum SINR required for a message to be successfully received. The *total interference* that receiver r_j suffers from the set of links L is given by $\sum_{i \neq j} P_{i,j}$. Throughout, we assume that all distances $d_{i,j}$ are normalized so that $\min_{s_i, r_j} d_{i,j} = 1$ hence the maximal link length is Δ, i.e., $\Delta = \max_i d_{i,i}$ and any received signal strength $P_{i,j}$ is bounded by $P_{i,j} \leq P_{\max}$.

In the vanilla SINR model we require that P_i is either 0 or $P_{\max}$ for every transmitter. This is sometimes referred to as *uniform* powers. When we have power control, we allow P_i to be any integer in $[0, P_{\max}]$.

Interference cancellation allows receivers to cancel signals that they can decode. Consider link ℓ_j. If r_j can decode the signal with the largest received signal, then it can decode it and remove it. It can repeat this process until it decodes its desire message from s_j, unless at some point it gets stuck and cannot decode the strongest signal. Formally, r_j can decode s_i if $P_{i,j} / (\sum_{\ell_k : P_{k,j} < P_{i,j}} P_{k,j} + \eta) \geq \beta$ (i.e. it can decode s_i in the presence of weaker signals) and if it can decode s_k for all links ℓ_k with $P_{k,j} > P_{i,j}$. Link ℓ_j is successful if r_j can decode s_j.

The following key notion, which was introduced in [18] and extended to arbitrary powers by [21], plays an important role in our analysis. The *affectance* $a_w^P(v)$ of link ℓ_v caused by another link ℓ_w with a given power assignment vector P is defined to be $a_w^P(v) = \min\{1, c_v(\beta) P_{w,v} / P_{v,v}\}$, where $c_v(\beta) = \beta / (1 - \beta \eta d_{v,v}^\alpha / P_v)$. Informally, $a_w^P(v)$ indicates the amount of (normalized) interference that link ℓ_w causes at link ℓ_v. It is easy to verify that link ℓ_v is successful if and only if $\sum_{w \neq v} a_w^P(v) \leq 1$.

For a set of links L and a link ℓ_w, the total affectance caused by ℓ_w is $a_w^P(L) = \sum_{\ell_v \in L} a_w^P(v)$. In the same manner, the total affectance caused by L on the link ℓ_w is $a_L^P(w) = \sum_{\ell_v \in L} a_v^P(w)$. When the powers of P are the same $P_u = P_{\max}$ for every ℓ_u, (i.e. uniform powers), we may omit it and simply write $a_w(v)$, $a_w(L)$ and $a_L(w)$. We say that a set of links L is β-*feasible* if $\mathrm{SINR}_v(L) \geq \beta$ for all $\ell_v \in L$, i.e. every link achieves SINR above the threshold (and is thus successful even without interference cancellation). It is easy to verify that L is β-feasible if and only if $\sum_{\ell_w \in L} a_w^P(v) \leq 1$ for every $\ell_v \in L$.

Following [17], for the uniform power setting, we say that a link set L is *amenable* if the total affectance caused by any single link is bounded by some constant, i.e., $a_u(L) = O(1)$ for every $u \in L$. The following basic properties of amenable sets play an important role in our analysis.

Fact 5. *[3] (a) Every feasible set L with uniform powers contains a subset $L' \subseteq L$, such that L' is amenable and $|L'| \geq |L|/2$. (b) For every amenable set L' that is β-feasible with uniform powers, for every other link u, it holds that $\sum_{v \in L'} a_u(v) = O(1)$.*

2.2   Basic Game Theory

We will use a game that is essentially the same as the game of Andrews and Dinitz [2], modified only to account for the different models we consider. Each link ℓ_i is a player with $P_{\max} + 1$ possible strategies: broadcast at power 0, or at integer power $P \in \{1, \ldots, P_{\max}\}$. A link has utility 1 if it is successful, has utility -1 if it uses nonzero power but is unsuccessful, and has utility 0 if it does not transmit (i.e. chooses power 0). Note that if power control is not available, this game only has two strategies: power 0 and power $P_{\max}$. Let S denote the set of possible strategies. A *strategy profile* is a vector in S^n, where the i'th component is the strategy played by link ℓ_i. For each link ℓ_i, let $f_i : S^n \to \{-1, 0, 1\}$ be the function mapping strategy profiles to utility for link i as described. Given a strategy profile a, let a_{-i} denote the profile without the i'th component, and given some strategy $s \in S$ let $f_i(s, a_{-i})$ denote the utility of ℓ_i if it uses strategy s and all other links use their strategies from a.

A pure Nash equilibrium is a strategy profile in which no player has any incentive to deviate from their strategy. Formally, $a \in S^n$ is a pure Nash equilibrium if $f_i(a) \geq f_i(s, a_{-i})$ for all $s \in S$ and players $\ell_i \in L$. In a mixed Nash equilibrium [25], every player ℓ_i has a probability distribution π_i over S, and the requirement is that no player has any incentive to change their distribution to some π'. So $\mathbb{E}[f_i(a)] \geq \mathbb{E}[f_i(\pi', a_{-i})]$ for all $i \in \{1, \ldots, n\}$, where the expectation is over the random strategy profile a drawn from the product distribution defined by the π_i's, and π' is any distribution over S.

To define no-regret behavior, suppose that the game has been played for T rounds and let a^t be the realized strategy profile in round $t \in \{1, \ldots, T\}$. The *history* $\mathrm{H} = \{a^1, \ldots, a^T\}$ of the game is the sequence of the T strategy profiles. The *regret* $\mathcal{R}_i$ of player i in an history H is defined to be

$$\mathcal{R}_i(\mathrm{H}) = \max_{s \in S} \tfrac{1}{T} \sum_{t=1}^{T} f_i(s, a_{-i}^t) - \tfrac{1}{T} \sum_{t=1}^{T} f_i(a^t).$$

The regret of a player is intuitively the amount that it lost by not playing some fixed strategy. An algorithm used by a player is known as a *no-regret* algorithm if it guarantees that the regret of the player tends to 0 as T tends to infinity. There is a large amount of work on no-regret algorithms, and it turns out that many such algorithms exist (see e.g. [4,23]). Thus we will analyze situations where every player has regret at most ϵ, and since this tends to 0 we will be free to assume that ϵ is arbitrarily small, say at most $1/n$. Clearly playing a pure or mixed Nash is a no-regret algorithm (since the fact that no one has incentive to switch to any other strategy guarantees that each player will have regret 0 in the long run), so analyzing the worst or best history with regret at most ϵ is more general than analyzing the worst or best mixed or pure Nash. We will call a history in which all players have regret at most ϵ an ϵ-regret history. Formally an history $\mathrm{H} = \{a^1, \ldots, a^T\}$ is an ϵ-*regret* history if $\mathcal{R}_i(\mathrm{H}) \leq \epsilon$ for every player $i \in \{1, \ldots, n\}$.

A simple but important lemma introduced in [12] and used again in [3] relates the average number of *attempted* transmissions to the average number of *successful* transmissions. Fix an ϵ-regret history, let s_u be the fraction of times in which u successfully transmitted, and let p_u be the fraction of times in which u attempted to transmit. Note that the average number of successful transmissions in a time slot is exactly $\sum_u s_u$, so it is this quantity which we will typically attempt to bound. The following lemma lets us get away with bounding the number of attempts instead.

Lemma 1 ([12]). $\sum_u s_u \leq \sum_u p_u \leq 2 \sum_u s_u + \epsilon n \leq O(\sum_u s_u)$.

Notation: Let L be a fixed set of n links embedded in $\mathbb{R}^2$. Let $\mathcal{N}_{\min}(L)$ denote the minimum number of successful links (averaged over time) in any ϵ-regret history, and similarly let $\mathcal{N}_{\max}(L)$ denote the maximum number of successful links (averaged over time) in any ϵ-regret history. Define $\mathcal{N}_{\max}^{IC}(L)$, and $\mathcal{N}_{\min}^{IC}(L)$ similarly for the IC setting, $\mathcal{N}_{\max}^{PC}(L)$ and $\mathcal{N}_{\min}^{PC}(L)$ for the PC setting, and $\mathcal{N}_{\max}^{PIC}(L)$ and $\mathcal{N}_{\min}^{PIC}(L)$ for the setting with both PC and IC. Finally, let $\mathcal{N}_{\max}^{\beta}(L)$, $\mathcal{N}_{\min}^{\beta}(L)$ be for the corresponding values for the vanilla model when the SINR threshold is set to β (this is hidden in the previous models, but we pull it out in order to compare the effect of modifying β).

While we will focus on comparing the equilibria of games utilizing different wireless technologies, much of the previous work on these games instead focuses on a single game and analyzes its equilibria with respect to OPT, the maximum achievable capacity. The *price of anarchy* (PoA) is the ratio of OPT to the value of the worst mixed Nash [22], and the *price of total anarchy* (PoTA) is the ratio of OPT to the value of the worst ϵ-regret history [8]. Clearly PoA $\leq$ PoTA. While it is not our focus, we will prove some bounds on these values as corollaries of our main results.

3   Interference Cancellation

We begin by analyzing the effect on the equilibria of adding interference cancellation. We would expect that using IC would result equilibria with larger values, since the capacity of the network might go up (and can certainly not go down). We show that this is not always the case: there are sets of links for which even the *best* ϵ-regret history using IC is a constant factor worse than the *worst* ϵ-regret history without using IC.

Theorem 6. *There exists a set of links L such that $\mathcal{N}_{\max}^{IC}(L) \leq \mathcal{N}_{\min}(L)/c$ for some constant $c > 1$.*

Proof. Let L' be the four link network depicted in Figure 1(a), with $b = 3/2$ and $a = \sqrt{8.8} - b$. We will assume that the threshold β is equal to 1.1, the path-loss exponent α is equal to 2, and the background noise $\eta = 0$ (none of these are crucial, but make the analysis simpler). Let us first consider what happens without using interference cancellation. Suppose each link has at most ϵ-regret, and for link ℓ_i let p_i denote the fraction of times at which s_i attempted to transmit. It is easy to see that link 1 will always be successful, since the received signal strength at r_1 is 1 while the total interference is at most $(1/4)+2(1/8.8) = 1/\beta$. Since ℓ_1 has at most ϵ-regret, this implies that $p_1 \geq 1 - \epsilon$.

On the other hand, whenever s_1 transmits it is clear that link ℓ_2 cannot be successful, as its SINR is at most $1/4$. So if s_2 transmitted every time it would have average utility at most $-(1 - \epsilon) + \epsilon = -1 + 2\epsilon < 0$ (since $\epsilon < 1/2$), while if it never transmitted it would have average utility 0. Thus its average utility is at least $-\epsilon$. Since it can succeed only an ϵ fraction of the time (when link 1 is not transmitting), we have that $\epsilon - (p_2 - \epsilon) \geq -\epsilon$ and thus $p_2 \leq 3\epsilon$. Since the utility of s_2 is at least $-\epsilon$, it holds that the fraction of times at which both s_1 and s_2 are transmitting is at most 2ϵ.

Now consider link ℓ_3. If links ℓ_1 and ℓ_2 both transmit, then ℓ_3 will fail since the received SINR will be at most $\frac{1/b^2}{(1/(1+a^2))+(1/(4+a^2))} \approx 0.92 < 1.1$. On the other hand, as long as link ℓ_2 does not transmit then ℓ_3 will be successful, as it will have SINR at least $\frac{1/b^2}{(1/(1+a^2))+(1/(2a+b)^2)} \geq 1.2 > 1.1$. Thus by transmitting at every time step ℓ_3 would have average utility at least $(1-2\epsilon)-2\epsilon = 1-4\epsilon > 0$ (since $\epsilon < 1/4$), and thus we know that ℓ_3 gets average utility of at least $1 - 5\epsilon$, and thus successfully transmits at least $1 - 5\epsilon$ fraction of the times. ℓ_4 is the same by symmetry. Thus the total value of any history in which all links have regret at most ϵ is at least $\mathcal{N}_{\min}(L) \geq 1 - \epsilon + 2(1 - 5\epsilon) = 3 - 11\epsilon$.

Let us now analyze what happens when using interference cancellation and bound $\mathcal{N}_{\max}^{IC}(L)$. Suppose each link has at most ϵ-regret, and for link ℓ_i let q_i denote the fraction of times at which s_i attempted to transmit. As before, ℓ_1 can always successfully transmit and thus does so in at least $1 - \epsilon$ fraction of times. But now, by using interference cancellation it turns out that ℓ_2 can also always succeed. This is because r_2 can first decode the transmission from s_1 and cancel it, leaving a remaining SINR of at least $\frac{1/4}{2/(a+b)^2} = \beta$. Thus ℓ_2 will also transmit in at least $1 - \epsilon$ fraction of times and hence so far $1 - \epsilon \leq q_1, q_2 \leq 1$. Note that since $a^2 +1 < b^2$, it holds that r_3 cannot cancel s_1 or s_2 before decoding s_3 (i.e., $P_{1,3}, P_{2,3} < P_{3,3}$). Hence, cancellation is useless. But now at r_3 the strength of s_1 is $1/(1 + a^2) > 0.317$, the strength of s_2 is $1/(4 + a^2) > 0.162$, and the strength of s_3 is $1/b^2 = 4/9$. Thus r_3 cannot decode any messages when s_1, s_2, and s_3 are all transmitting since its SINR is at most $0.92 < \beta$, which implies that ℓ_3 can only succeed on at most 2ϵ fraction of times. The link ℓ_4 is the same as the link ℓ_3 by symmetry. Thus the total value of any history in which all links have an ϵ-regret is at most $\mathcal{N}_{\max}^{IC}(L) \leq 2 + 4\epsilon$. Thus $\mathcal{N}_{\min}(L)/\mathcal{N}_{\max}^{IC}(L) \geq 3/2 - o(1)$ as required.

It turns out that no-regret behavior with interference cancellation cannot be much worse than no-regret behavior without interference cancellation – as in Braess's paradox, it can only be worse by a constant factor.

Theorem 7. $\mathcal{N}_{\min}^{IC}(L) \geq \mathcal{N}_{\max}(L)/c$ *for any set of links L and some constant $c \geq 1$.*

Proof. Consider an ϵ-regret history without IC that maximizes the average number of successful links, i.e. one that achieves $\mathcal{N}_{\max}(L)$ value. Let p_i denote the fraction of times at which s_i attempted to transmit in this history, so $\sum_{i \in L} p_i = \Theta(\mathcal{N}_{\max}(L))$ by Lemma 1. Similarly, let q_i denote that fraction of times at which s_i attempted to transmit in an ϵ-regret history *with* IC that achieves value of only $\mathcal{N}_{\min}^{IC}(L)$, and so $\sum_{i \in L} q_i = \Theta(\mathcal{N}_{\min}^{IC}(L))$.

Note that since the best average number of successful connections in the non-IC case is $\mathcal{N}_{\max}(L)$, there must exist some set of connections $A \subseteq L$ such that $|A| \geq \mathcal{N}_{\max}(L)$ and A is feasible without IC. Let $B = \{i : q_i \geq 1/2\}$ and let $A' = A \setminus B$. If $|B \cap A| \geq |A|/2$ then we are done, since then

$$\mathcal{N}_{\max}(L) \leq |A| \leq 2|B| \leq 4\sum_{\ell_i \in L} q_i = 4 \cdot \mathcal{N}_{\min}^{IC}(L)$$

as required. So without loss of generality we will assume that $|B \cap A| < |A|/2$, and thus that $|A'| > |A|/2$. Note that A' is a subset of A, and so it is feasible in the non-IC setting.

Now let $\widehat{A} = \{i \in A' : \sum_{j \in A'} a_i(j) \leq 2\}$ be an amenable subset of A'. By Fact 5(a), it holds that $\widehat{A} \geq |A'|/2 \geq |A|/4$. Fact 5(b) then implies that for any link $i \in L$, its total affectance on A is small: $\sum_{j \in A} a_i(j) \leq c'$ for some constant $c' \geq 0$. Thus we have that

$$\sum_{i \in L} \sum_{j \in \widehat{A}} q_i a_i(j) \leq c' \cdot \left(\sum_{i \in L} q_i \right). \tag{1}$$

On the other hand, we know that the q_i values correspond to the worst history in which every link has regret at most ϵ (in the IC setting). Let $j \in A'$. Then $q_j < 1/2$, which means the average utility of link ℓ_j is at most $1/2$. Let y_j be the fraction of time s_j would have succeeded had it transmitted in every round. Since the average utility of the best single action is at most $1/2 + \epsilon$ it holds that $y_j - (1 - y_j) \leq 1/2 + \epsilon$ or the that $y_j \leq \frac{3}{4} + \frac{\epsilon}{2}$. In other words, in at least $1 - y_j = \frac{1}{4} - \frac{\epsilon}{2}$ fraction of the rounds the affectance of the other links on the link ℓ_j must be at least 1 (or else j could succeed in those rounds even without using IC). Thus the expected affectance (taken over a random choice of time slot) on ℓ_j is at least $\sum_{i \in L} a_i(j) q_i \geq \frac{1}{4} - \frac{\epsilon}{2}$. Summing over all $j \in \widehat{A}$, we get that

$$\sum_{j \in \widehat{A}} \sum_{i \in L} a_i(j) q_i \geq \sum_{j \in A} \frac{1-2\epsilon}{4} \geq \Omega(|\widehat{A}|). \tag{2}$$

Combining equations (1) and (2) (and switching the order of summations) implies that $|\widehat{A}| \leq O(\sum_{i \in L} q_i)$. Since $|\widehat{A}| \geq |A|/4 \geq \Omega(N_{\max}(L)) \geq \Omega(\sum_{i \in L} p_i)$, we get that $\sum_i p_i \leq O(\sum_{i \in L} q_i)$ as desired.

As a simple corollary, we will show that this lets us bound the price of total anarchy in the interference cancellation model (which, as far as we know, has not previously been bounded). Let $OPT \subseteq L$ denote some optimal solution without IC, i.e., the set of transmitters forming a maximum β-feasible set, and let $OPT^{IC} \subseteq L$ denote some optimal solution with IC. Due to lack of space, missing proofs are deferred to full version.

Corollary 1. *For every set of links L it holds that the price of total anarchy with IC is $O(\log \Delta)$, or $|OPT^{IC}|/\mathcal{N}_{\min}^{IC}(L) = O(\log \Delta)$.*

4 Power Control

In the power control setting, each transmitter s_v either broadcasts at power 0 or broadcasts at some arbitrary integral power level $P_v \in [1, P_{\max}]$. Our main claim is that Braess's paradox is once again possible: there are networks in which adding power control can create worse equilibria. For illustration of such a network, see Fig. 1(b). We first observe the following relation between no-regret solutions with or without power control.

Observation 8. *Every no-regret solution in the uniform setting, is also a no-regret solution in the PC setting.*

Hence, we cannot expect the best no-regret solution in the PC setting to be smaller than the worst no-regret solution in the uniform setting. Yet, the paradox still holds.

Theorem 9. *There exists a configuration of links L satisfying $\mathcal{N}^{PC}_{\min}(L) \leq \mathcal{N}_{\min}(L)/c$ for some constant $c > 1$.*

We now prove that (as with IC) that the paradox cannot be too bad: adding power control cannot cost us more than a constant. The proof is very similar to that of Thm. 7 up to some minor yet crucial modifications.

Theorem 10. $\mathcal{N}^{PC}_{\min}(L) \geq \mathcal{N}_{\max}(L)/c$ *for any set of links L and some constant $c \geq 1$.*

Corollary 2. *The price of total anarchy under the power control setting with maximum transmission energy $P_{\max}$ is $\Theta(\log \Delta)$.*

5 Power Control with Interference Cancellation (PIC)

In this section we consider games in the power control with IC setting where *transmitters* can adopt their transmission energy in the range of $[1, P_{\max}]$ and in addition, *receivers* can employ interference cancelation. This setting is denote as *PIC* (power control+IC). We now show that Braess's paradox can once again happen and begin by comparing the PIC setting to the setting of power control without IC and to the most basic setting of uniform powers, as illustrated in Fig. 2.

Lemma 2. *There exists a set of links L and constant $c > 1$ such that*
(a) $\mathcal{N}^{PIC}_{\min}(L) \leq \mathcal{N}^{PC}_{\min}(L)/c$.
(b) $\mathcal{N}^{PIC}_{\min}(L) \leq \mathcal{N}_{\min}(L)/c$.

Moreover, we proceed by showing that PIC can hurt the network by more than a constant when comparing PIC equilibria to IC equilibria. For an illustration of such a network, see Fig. 1(c).

Theorem 11. *There exists a set of links L and constant $c > 1$ such that the best pure Nash solution with PIC is worse by a factor of $\Omega(\log \Delta)$ than the worst no-regret solution with IC.*

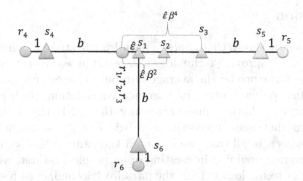

Fig. 2. Schematic illustration of a network in which playing IC with power control might generate no-regret solutions that are worse by a factor of $\Omega(1)$ than no-regret solution in a setting without interference cancellation, with or without power control.

Corollary 3. *There exists a set of links L satisfying that $\mathcal{N}_{\min}^{PIC}(L) \leq (c/\log\Delta)\cdot$ $\mathcal{N}_{\min}^{IC}(L)$.*

As in the previous sections, we show that our examples are essentially tight.

Theorem 12. *For every set of links L it holds that there exists a constant $c \geq 1$ such that*
(a) $\mathcal{N}_{\min}^{PIC}(L) \geq \mathcal{N}_{\max}(L)/c$.
(b) $\mathcal{N}_{\min}^{PIC}(L) \geq \mathcal{N}_{\max}^{PC}(L)/c$.
(c) $\mathcal{N}_{\min}^{PIC}(L) \geq \mathcal{N}_{\max}^{IC}(L)/(c\log\Delta)$.

Finally, as a direct consequences of our result, we obtain a tight bound for the price of total anarchy in the PIC setting.

Corollary 4. *For every set of links L it holds that the price of total anarchy with PIC is $\Theta(\log(\Delta \cdot P_{\max}))$.*

6   Decreasing the SINR Threshold

We begin by showing that in certain cases the ability to successfully decode a message at a lower SINR threshold results in *every* no-regret solution having lower value than *any* no-regret solution at higher β. For an illustration of such a network, see Fig. 1(d).

Theorem 13. *There exists a set of links L and constants $1 < \beta' < \beta$ such that $\mathcal{N}_{\max}^{\beta'}(L) \leq \mathcal{N}_{\min}^{\beta}(L)/c$ for some constant $c > 1$.*

We now show that the gap between the values of no-regret solution for different SINR threshold values is bounded by a constant.

Lemma 3. *For every $1 \leq \beta' \leq \beta$ and every set of links L satisfying that $P_{vv} \geq 2\beta \cdot \eta$ for every $\ell_v \in L$, it holds that $\mathcal{N}_{\min}^{\beta'}(L) \geq \mathcal{N}_{\max}^{\beta}(L)/c$ for some constant $c \geq 1$.*

7 Conclusion

In this paper we have shown that Braess's paradox can strike in wireless networks in the SINR model: improving technology can result in worse performance, where we measured performance by the average number of successful connections. We considered adding power control, interference cancellation, both power control and interference cancellation, and decreasing the SINR threshold, and in all of them showed that game-theoretic equilibria can get worse with improved technology. However, in all cases we bounded the damage that could be done.

There are several remaining interesting open problems. First, what other examples of wireless technology exhibit the paradox? Second, even just considering the technologies in this paper, it would be interesting to get a better understanding of when exactly the paradox occurs. Can we characterize the network topologies that are susceptible? Is it most topologies, or is it rare? What about random wireless networks? Finally, while our results are tight up to constants, it would be interesting to actually find tight constants so we know precisely how bad the paradox can be.

References

1. Andrews, J.G.: Interference cancellation for cellular systems: a contemporary overview. IEEE Wireless Communications 12, 19–29 (2005)
2. Andrews, M., Dinitz, M.: Maximizing capacity in arbitrary wireless networks in the SINR model: Complexity and game theory. In: Proc. 28th Conf. of IEEE Computer and Communications Societies, INFOCOM (2009)
3. Ásgeirsson, E.I., Mitra, P.: On a game theoretic approach to capacity maximization in wireless networks. In: INFOCOM (2011)
4. Auer, P., Cesa-Bianchi, N., Freund, Y., Schapire, R.E.: The nonstochastic multi-armed bandit problem. SIAM J. Comput. 32(1), 48–77 (2003)
5. Avin, C., Cohen, A., Haddad, Y., Kantor, E., Lotker, Z., Parter, M., Peleg, D.: Sinr diagram with interference cancellation. In: SODA, pp. 502–515 (2012)
6. Avin, C., Emek, Y., Kantor, E., Lotker, Z., Peleg, D., Roditty, L.: SINR diagrams: Towards algorithmically usable sinr models of wireless networks. In: Proc. 28th Symp. on Principles of Distributed Computing, PODC (2009)
7. Avin, C., Lotker, Z., Pignolet, Y.-A.: On the power of uniform power: Capacity of wireless networks with bounded resources. In: Fiat, A., Sanders, P. (eds.) ESA 2009. LNCS, vol. 5757, pp. 373–384. Springer, Heidelberg (2009)
8. Blum, A., Hajiaghayi, M., Ligett, K., Roth, A.: Regret minimization and the price of total anarchy. In: Proceedings of the 40th Annual ACM Symposium on Theory of Computing, STOC 2008, pp. 373–382. ACM, New York (2008)
9. Braess, D.: über ein paradoxon aus der verkehrsplanung. Unternehmensforschung 12(1), 258–268 (1968)
10. Costa, M.H.M., El Gamal, A.A.: The capacity region of the discrete memoryless interference channel with strong interference. IEEE Trans. Inf. Theor. 33(5), 710–711 (1987)
11. Daskalakis, C., Goldberg, P.W., Papadimitriou, C.H.: The complexity of computing a nash equilibrium. In: Proceedings of the Thirty-Eighth Annual ACM Symposium on Theory of Computing, STOC 2006, pp. 71–78. ACM, New York (2006)

12. Dinitz, M.: Distributed algorithms for approximating wireless network capacity. In: INFOCOM, pp. 1397–1405 (2010)
13. Etkin, R.H., Tse, D.N.C., Wang, H.: Gaussian interference channel capacity to within one bit. IEEE Trans. Inf. Theor. 54(12), 5534–5562 (2008)
14. Goussevskaia, O., Oswald, Y.A., Wattenhofer, R.: Complexity in geometric SINR. In: Proc. 8th ACM Int. Symp. on Mobile Ad Hoc Networking and Computing (MobiHoc), pp. 100–109 (2007)
15. Goussevskaia, O., Wattenhofer, R., Halldórsson, M.M., Welzl, E.: Capacity of arbitrary wireless networks. In: INFOCOM, pp. 1872–1880 (2009)
16. Gupta, P., Kumar, P.R.: The capacity of wireless networks. IEEE Trans. Information Theory 46(2), 388–404 (2000)
17. Halldórsson, M.M., Mitra, P.: Wireless connectivity and capacity. In: SODA, pp. 516–526 (2012)
18. Halldórsson, M.M., Wattenhofer, R.: Wireless communication is in APX. In: Albers, S., Marchetti-Spaccamela, A., Matias, Y., Nikoletseas, S., Thomas, W. (eds.) ICALP 2009, Part I. LNCS, vol. 5555, pp. 525–536. Springer, Heidelberg (2009)
19. Kantor, E., Lotker, Z., Parter, M., Peleg, D.: The topology of wireless communication. In: Proceedings of the 43rd Annual ACM Symposium on Theory of Computing, STOC 2011, pp. 383–392. ACM (2011)
20. Kesselheim, T.: A constant-factor approximation for wireless capacity maximization with power control in the sinr model. In: Proc. ACM-SIAM Symp. on Discrete Algorithms, SODA 2011 (2011)
21. Kesselheim, T., Vöcking, B.: Distributed contention resolution in wireless networks. Distributed Computing (2010)
22. Koutsoupias, E., Papadimitriou, C.: Worst-case equilibria. In: Meinel, C., Tison, S. (eds.) STACS 1999. LNCS, vol. 1563, pp. 404–413. Springer, Heidelberg (1999)
23. Littlestone, N., Warmuth, M.K.: The weighted majority algorithm. Inf. Comput. 108(2), 212–261 (1994)
24. Moscibroda, T., Wattenhofer, R.: The complexity of connectivity in wireless networks. In: Proc. 25th Conf. of IEEE Computer and Communications Societies, INFOCOM (2006)
25. Nash, J.F.: Equilibrium points in n-person games. Proceedings of the National Academy of Sciences 36(1), 48–49 (1950)

Fast Structuring of Radio Networks
Large for Multi-message Communications

Mohsen Ghaffari and Bernhard Haeupler

MIT
{ghaffari,haeupler}@mit.edu

Abstract. We introduce collision free layerings as a powerful way to structure radio networks. These layerings can replace hard-to-compute BFS-trees in many contexts while having an efficient randomized distributed construction. We demonstrate their versatility by using them to provide near optimal distributed algorithms for several multi-message communication primitives.

Designing efficient communication primitives for radio networks has a rich history that began 25 years ago when Bar-Yehuda et al. introduced fast randomized algorithms for broadcasting and for constructing BFS-trees. Their BFS-tree construction time was $O(D \log^2 n)$ rounds, where D is the network diameter and n is the number of nodes. Since then, the complexity of a broadcast has been resolved to be $T_{BC} = \Theta(D \log \frac{n}{D} + \log^2 n)$ rounds. On the other hand, BFS-trees have been used as a crucial building block for many communication primitives and their construction time remained a bottleneck for these primitives.

We introduce collision free layerings that can be used in place of BFS-trees and we give a randomized construction of these layerings that runs in nearly broadcast time, that is, w.h.p. in $T_{Lay} = O(D \log \frac{n}{D} + \log^{2+\epsilon} n)$ rounds for any constant $\epsilon > 0$. We then use these layerings to obtain: (1) A randomized algorithm for gathering k messages running w.h.p. in $O(T_{Lay} + k)$ rounds. (2) A randomized k-message broadcast algorithm running w.h.p. in $O(T_{Lay} + k \log n)$ rounds. These algorithms are optimal up to the small difference in the additive poly-logarithmic term between T_{BC} and T_{Lay}. Moreover, they imply the first optimal $O(n \log n)$ round randomized gossip algorithm.

1 Introduction

Designing efficient communication protocols for radio networks is an important and active area of research. Radio networks have two key characteristics which distinguish them from wired networks: For one, the communications in these networks have an inherent broadcast-type nature as the transmissions of one node can reach all nearby nodes. On the other hand, simultaneous transmissions interfere and this interference makes the task of designing efficient communication protocols challenging. A standard model that captures these characteristics is the *radio networks model* [4], in which the network is abstracted as a graph $G = (V, E)$ with n nodes and diameter D. Communication occurs in synchronous

Y. Afek (Ed.): DISC 2013, LNCS 8205, pp. 492–506, 2013.

rounds, where in each round, each node either listens or transmits a message with bounded size. A node receives a message if and only if it is listening and exactly one of its neighbors is transmitting. Particularly, a node with two or more transmitting neighbors cannot distinguish this collision from background noise. That is, the model assumes *no collision detection*.

Communication problems in radio networks can be divided into two groups: single-message problems like single-message broadcast, and multi-message problems such as k-message broadcast, gossiping, k-message gathering, etc. By now, randomized single-message broadcast is well-understood, and is known to have asymptotically tight time-complexity of $T_{BC} = \Theta(D \log \frac{n}{D} + \log^2 n)$ rounds [1, 7,16,17][1]. On the other hand, multi-message problems still remain challenging. The key issue is that, when aiming for a time-efficient protocol, the transmissions of different messages interfere with each other. Bar-Yehuda, Israeli and Itai [3] presented an $O(D \log^2 n)$ round construction of Breadth First Search trees and used this structure to control the effects of different messages on one another in multi-message problems. Since then, BFS trees have become a standard substrate for multi-message communication protocols (see, e.g., [5,6,9,15]). However, the best known construction for BFS trees remains $O(D \log^2 n)$ and this time-complexity has become a bottleneck for many multi-message problems.

1.1 Our Results

As the main contribution of this paper we introduce collision-free layering which are simple node numberings with certain properties (see Section 3 for definitions). Layerings are structures that can be viewed as relaxed variants of BFS trees and can replace them in many contexts while having an efficient randomized construction. We present a randomized construction of these layerings that runs in $T_{Lay} = O(D \log \frac{n}{D} + \log^{2+\epsilon} n)$ rounds for any constant $\epsilon > 0$. This round complexity is almost equal to the broadcast time, i.e., $T_{BC} = \Theta(D \log \frac{n}{D} + \log^2 n)$ rounds, and is thus near-optimal.

Using collision free layerings, and with the help of additional technical ideas, we achieve the following near-optimal randomized algorithms for the aforementioned multi-message problems:

(A) A randomized algorithm for k-message single-destination gathering that with high probability gathers k messages in $O(T_{Lay} + k)$ rounds.

(B) A randomized algorithm for k-message single-source broadcast with complexity $O(T_{Lay}+k \log n)$ rounds, w.h.p. This algorithm uses network coding.

(C) The above algorithms also lead to the first optimal randomized all-to-all broadcast (gossiping) protocol, which has round complexity $O(n \log n)$ rounds[2].

---

[1] We remark that, throughout the whole paper, when talking about randomized algorithms, we speak of the related time-bound that holds with high probability (w.h.p), where w.h.p. indicates a probability at least $1 - \frac{1}{n^\beta}$ for an arbitrary constant $\beta \geq 2$.

[2] We remark that an $O(n \log n)$ gossiping solution was attempted in [18], for the scenario of known topology, but its correctness was disproved [19].

Note that modulo the small difference between T_{Lay} and T_{BC}, the time complexity of the above algorithms are optimal, and that they are the first to achieve the optimal dependency on k and D.

1.2 Related Work

Communication over radio networks has been studied extensively since the 70's. In the following, we present a brief overview of the known results that directly relate to the setting studied in this paper. That is, randomized algorithms[3], with focus on with high probability (whp) time and under the standard and least demanding assumptions: without collision detection, unknown topology, and with messages of logarithmic size.

Single-Message Broadcast: Bar-Yehuda, Goldreich, and Itai (BGI) [2] gave a simple and efficient algorithm, called Decay, which broadcasts a single message in $O(D \log n + \log^2 n)$ rounds. Alon et al. [1] proved an $\Omega(\log^2 n)$ lower bound, which holds even for centralized algorithms and graphs with constant diameter. Kushilevitz and Mansour [17] showed an $\Omega(D \log \frac{n}{D})$ lower bound. Finally, the remaining gap was closed by the simultaneous and independent algorithms of [7] and [16], settling the time complexity of single-message broadcast to $T_{BC} = \Theta(D \log \frac{n}{D} + \log^2 n)$.

k-Message Gathering and k-Unicasts: Bar-Yehuda, Israeli and Itai (BII) [3] presented an algorithm to gather k messages in a given destination in whp time $O(k \log^2 n + D \log^2 n)$, using the key idea of routing messages along a BFS tree via Decay protocol of [2]. The bound was improved to $O(k \log n + D \log^2 n)$ [5] and then to $O(k + D \log^2 n)$ [15], using the same BFS approach but with better algorithms on top of the BFS. A deterministic $O(k \log n + n \log n)$ algorithm was presented in [6], which substitutes the BFS trees with a new concept of Breadth-Then-Depth.

k-Message Broadcast: BII [3] also used the BFS-based approach to broadcast k-message in whp time $O(k \log^2 n + D \log^2 n + \log^3 n)$. Khabbazian and Kowalski [15] improve this to $O(D \log^2 n + k \log n + \log^3 n)$ using network coding. Ghaffari et al. [12] showed a lower bound of $\Omega(k \log n)$ for this problem, even when network coding is allowed, which holds even for centralized algorithms.

Gossiping: Gasieniec [8] provides a good survey. The best known results are $O(n \log^2 n)$ algorithm of Czumaj and Rytter [7] and the $\Omega(n \log n)$ lower bound of Gasieniec and Potapov [10]. The lower bound holds for centralized algorithms and also allows for network coding. Same can be inferred from [12] as well. An $O(n \log n)$ algorithm was attempted in [18], for the scenario of known topology, but its correctness was disproved [19].

---

[3] We remark that typically the related deterministic algorithms have a different flavor and incomparable time-complexities, with $\Omega(n)$ often being a lower bound.

2   Preliminaries

2.1   The Model

We consider the standard *radio network model* [2,4]: The network is represented by a connected graph $G = (V, E)$ with $n = |V|$ nodes and diameter D. Communication takes place in synchronous rounds. In each round, each node is either listening or transmitting a packet. In each round, each listening node that has exactly one transmitting neighbor receives the packet from that neighbor. Any node that is transmitting itself or has zero or more than one transmitting neighbor does not receive anything. In the case that two or more neighbors of a listening node $v \in V$ are transmitting, we say a *collision* has happened at node v. We assume that each transmission (transmitted packet) can contain at most one message as its *payload* plus an additive $\Theta(\log n)$ bits as its *header*. Since we only focus on randomized algorithms, we can assume that nodes do not have original ids but each node picks a random id of length $4 \log n$ bits. It is easy to see that, with high probability, different nodes will have different ids.

2.2   The Problem Statements

We study the following problems:

- **k-message Single-Destination Gathering:** k messages are initially distributed arbitrarily in some nodes and the goal is to gather all these messages at a given *destination* node.

- **Single-Source k-Message Broadcast:** A single given *source* node has k messages and the goal is to deliver all messages to all nodes.

- **Gossiping:** Each node has a single message and the goal is for each node to receive all messages.

In each problem, when stating a running time for a randomized algorithm, we require that the algorithm terminates and produces the desired output within the stated time with high probability (in contrast to merely in expectation).

We make the standard assumptions that nodes do not know the topology except a constant-factor upper bound on $\log n$. From this, given the algorithms that we present, one can obtain a constant factor estimation of D and k using standard double-and-test estimation techniques without more than a constant factor loss in round-complexity. We skip these standard reductions and assume that constant-factor approximations of D and k are known to the nodes. For simplicity, we also assume that k is at most polynomial in n.

2.3   A Black-Box Tool: The CR-Braodcast Protocol

Throughout the paper, we make frequent use of the optimal broadcast protocol of Czumaj and Rytter (CR) [7]. Here, we present a brief description of this protocol. To describe this protocol, we first need to define a specific infinite sequence of positive integers BC with the following properties:

(1) Every consecutive subsequence of $\Omega(\log \frac{n}{D})$ elements in BC contains a subsequence $1, 2, \ldots, \log \frac{n}{D}$.

(2) For every integer $k \in [\log \frac{n}{D}, \log \frac{n}{D} + \log \log n]$, any consecutive subsequence of $\Omega(\log \frac{n}{D} \cdot 2^k)$ elements in BC contains an element of value k.

(3) Every consecutive subsequence of $\Omega(\log n)$ elements in BC contains a subsequence $1, 2, \ldots, \log n$.

These properties were defined in [7, Definition 7.6] under the name *D-modified strong deterministic density property*[4]. Furthermore, it can be easily verified that the following sequence, which is again taken from [7], satisfies these properties.

For any n and D, we define the sequence $BC = BC_0, BC_1, \ldots$ such that for each $j = 0, 1, \ldots$, we have:

$$BC_{3j} = \log \frac{n}{D} + k, \text{ where } k \text{ is such that } (j \mod \log n) \overset{\mod 2^{k+1}}{\equiv} 2^k$$
$$BC_{3j+1} = j \mod \log \frac{n}{D} \text{ and}$$
$$BC_{3j+2} = j \mod \log n.$$

We now present the pseudo-code of the broadcast protocol of [7], which will be used throughout the rest of the paper. This protocol has 4 key parameters: two disjoint sets A, R and two integer values δ and T. It is assumed that each node v knows the values of δ and T and it also knows whether it is in A and R, via Boolean predicates of the form $(v \in A)$ and $(v \in R)$. Each node $v \in A$ has a message μ_v (which is determined depending on the application of the protocol). The protocol starts with nodes in A where each active node $v \in A$ forwards its message. The nodes in R become active (join A) at the end of the first phase in which they receive a message, and retransmit this message in the next phases. Algorithm 1 presents the pseduo-code for algorithm CR-Broadcast(A, R, δ, T):

We will use the following lemma from [7] and [2]:

Lemma 1. *For any connected network $G = (V, E)$ with diameter D and for any node v, an execution of μ_v CR-Broadcast$(\{v\}, V \setminus \{v\}, \delta, T)$ with $T = \Theta(D(\log \frac{n}{D} + \delta) + \log^2 n)/\delta$ leads with high probability to $S_0 = V$ and $\mu_u = \mu_v$. That is, broadcasting a message from v to all nodes takes with high probability at most T rounds.*

Lemma 2. *In each execution of CR-Broadcast protocol, for any two neighboring nodes u and v, if $(u \in A) = true$ and $(v \in A) = false$ at round r, then in round $r + \Theta(\log^2 n)$, w.h.p., node v has received a message from some node.*

---

[4] We remark that the Property 3 stated here is slightly stronger than the property 3 of [7, Definition 7.6], but is satisfied by the sequence provided in [7]. This modification is necessary to achieve the $k \log n$ dependence on number of messages k in the k-message broadcast problemSection 5. Using the original definition would lead to a time bound of $\Omega(k \log n \log \frac{n}{D})$

Algorithm 1. Algorithm CR-Broadcast(A, R, δ, T) @ node v:

Syntax: each TRANSMIT or LISTEN corresponds to one communication round

1: **if** $(v \in A) = false$ **then** $\mu_v \leftarrow \emptyset$
2: **for** phase $i = 1$ to T **do**
3:    **for** $j = 1$ to δ **do**
4:       **if** $(v \in A) = true$ **then**
5:          **with probability** $2^{-BC_{i\delta+j}}$ **do**
6:             TRANSMIT $(v.id, \mu_v)$
7:          **otherwise**
8:             LISTEN
9:       **else**
10:          LISTEN
11:          **if** received a message $(u.id, \mu)$ **then** $\mu_v \leftarrow \mu$
12:       **if** $\mu \neq \emptyset$ & $(v \in R)$ **then** $(v \in A) \leftarrow true$

3   Layerings

Here, we introduce *layerings* and we provide a set of algorithms for constructing layerings with desirable properties.

3.1   Definitions

In short, layerings are particular types of numbering of nodes; they organize and locally group nodes in a way that is useful for multi-message gathering and broadcasting tasks and for parallelzing and pipelining communications. In this subsection, we present the formal definitions.

Definition 1. *(layering)* A layering ℓ of graph $G = (V, E)$ assigns to each node $u \in V$ an integer layer number $\ell(u)$ such that *(a)* there is only one node s with $\ell(s) = 0$, known as the source; and *(b)* every node u, except the source, is connected to a node v such that $\ell(v) < \ell(u)$. We define the depth of layering ℓ to be equal to $\max_{u \in V} \ell(u)$. In the distributed setting, for a layering ℓ, we require each node u to know its layer number $\ell(u)$, and also, for each node u other than the source, we require u to know (the ID of) one node v such that $\ell(v) < \ell(u)$ and u is a neighbor of v. In this case, we call v the parent of u.

Definition 2. *(C-collision-free layering)* A layering ℓ together with a C-coloring of the nodes $c : V \to \{0, \ldots, C-1\}$ is C-collision-free if for any two nodes u and v such that $\ell(u) \neq \ell(v)$ and $dist_G(u, v) \leq 2$, we have $c(u) \neq c(v)$. In the distributed setting, we require each node v to know the value of C and also its own color $c(v)$.

Definition 3. *(d-stretch layering)* A layering ℓ is d-stretch if for any two neighboring nodes u and v, we have $|\ell(u) - \ell(v)| \leq d$.

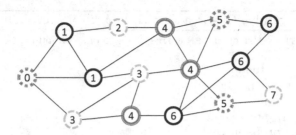

Fig. 1. A 4-collision-free layering with depth 7 and stretch 3. The number in each node indicates its layer number.

We remark that a *BFS-layering* in which each node is labeled by its distance from the source is a simple example for a layering with stretch 1 and depth D. We also remark that any d-stretch layering ℓ can also be made $(2d+1)$-collision-free by choosing $C = 2d+1$ and $c(u) = \ell(u) \mod C$. This makes BFS-layerings 3-collision free. In the next sections we show that *pseudo-BFS layerings*, that is, layerings with similar collision freeness and depth, can be constructed efficiently and can replace BFS layerings in many scenarios:

Definition 4. *(pseudo-BFS layering) A layering (and a related coloring) is a pseudo-BFS layering if it is $O(1)$-collision-free and has depth $O(D + \log n)$.*

3.2 Layering Algorithms

Here, we show that pseudo-BFS layerings can be constructed in almost broadcast time, that is, $T_{BC} = O(D \log \frac{n}{D} + \log^2 n)$ rounds. This is faster than the best known construction time of BFS layerings, which remains $O(D \log^2 n)$ rounds.

Theorem 1. *There is a distributed randomized algorithm that for any constant $\epsilon > 0$, constructs a pseudo-BFS layering w.h.p., in $O(D \log \frac{n}{D} + \log^{2+\epsilon} n)$ rounds.*

Starter: A construction with round-complexity $O(D \log \frac{n}{D} + \log^3 n)$

Theorem 2. *There is a distributed randomized algorithm that w.h.p. constructs a pseudo-BFS layering from a given source node s in $O(D \log \frac{n}{D} + \log^3 n)$ rounds.*

The high-level outline of this construction is to start with a crude basic layering obtained via a broadcast and then refining this layering to get a pseudo-BFS layering. Given the broadcast protocol presented in Section 2.3, we easily get the following basic layerings:

Lemma 3. *For any $\delta \in [\log \frac{n}{D}, \log^2 n]$ there is a layering algorithm that computes, w.h.p., an $O(D + \frac{\log^2 n}{\delta})$-depth layering with a given source s and stretch $O(\frac{\log^2 n}{\delta})$ in $O(D\delta + \log^2 n)$ rounds.*

Proof. We run the CR-Broadcast algorithm with parameter δ, $T = \Theta(D(\log \frac{n}{D} + \delta) + \log^2 n)/\delta$, $A = s$ and $R = V \backslash s$. For each non-source node v we then set $\ell(v)$ to be the smallest phase number in which v receives a message, and the parent of v to be the node w from which v receives this first message. Lemma 1 guarantees that indeed after $T\delta$ rounds all nodes are layered. The depth of the layering can furthermore not exceed the number of iterations $T = \Theta(D\delta + \log^2 n)/\delta$. The stretch part of the lemma follows from Lemma 2 which guarantees that two neighboring nodes receive their messages at most $O(\log^2 n)$ rounds and therefore at most $O(\frac{\log^2 n}{\delta})$ iterations apart.

Next we give the algorithm to refine the basic layerings of Lemma 3 to a pseudo-BFS layering. We present the algorithm but defer the correctness proof to the full version.

Lemma 4. *Given a d-stretch layering l with depth D', the Layer Refinement Algorithm (LRA) computes a 5-collision-free $O(d)$-stretch layering l' with depth $O(D')$ in $O(d \log^2 n)$ rounds.*

Layer Refinement Algorithm (LRA): Throughout the presentation of the algorithm, we refer to Figure 2 as a helper tool and also present some intuitive explanations to help the exposition.

As the first step of the algorithm, we want to divide the problem into small parts which can be solved in parallel. For this purpose, we first run the CR-broadcast protocol with parameters $T = 1$, $\delta = \Theta(\log^2 n)$, A equal to the set of nodes u such that $\lceil \frac{l(u)}{d} \rceil \equiv 1 \pmod 5$, and $R = \emptyset$. Each node $u \in A$ sets message μ_u equal to $l(u)$. In Figure 2, these nodes are indicated by the shaded areas of width d layers. Since layering l has stretch at most d, each shaded area cuts the graph into two non-adjacent sets, above and below the area (plus a third part of the shaded area itself). After these transmissions, each node v becomes a *boundary node* if during these transmissions, v was not transmitting but it received a message from a node w such that $l(w) > l(v)$. In Figure 2, the boundary nodes are indicated via red contour lines. These boundaries divide the problem of layering into strips each containing at most $5d$ layers, and such that two nodes at different strips are not neighbors. For each boundary node v, we set $l'(v) = 2d(\lceil \frac{l(v)}{d} \rceil + 1)$ and color it with color 0, i.e., $c(v) = 0$.

Next, we indicate the direction starting from the boundary which moves in the increasing direction of layer numbers l. For this, we run the CR-broadcast protocol with parameters $T = 1$, $\delta = \Theta(\log^2 n)$, A equal to the set of boundary nodes, and $R = \emptyset$, where each boundary node u sets μ_u equal to $(l(u), l'(u))$. A non-boundary node v that receives a message from a boundary node w such that $l(w) < l(v)$ is called a *start-line* node. In Figure 2, start-line nodes are indicated via green contour lines. Every such node v sets it l'-layer number to $l'(v) = l'(w) + 1$ and its color $c(v) = 1$, and records $w.id$ as the id of its parent.

Next, we assign l' layer numbers to nodes inside the strips, starting from the start-line nodes and moving upwards in (l-layer numbers) till reaching the next layer of boundary nodes. This is done for different strips in parallel, using

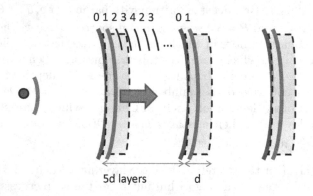

Fig. 2. Layer Refinement

the CR-Broadcast protocol with parameter $T = 5d$, $\delta = \Theta(\log^2 n)$, A equal to the set of start-line nodes and R equal to the set of nodes that are neither boundary nor start-line. As a result, in each phase of the CR-Broadcast, all non-boundary nodes that have received an l' layer number by the start of that phase try transmitting their l' layer number and their id. In every phase, a node v that does not have an l' layer number yet and receives a transmission from a node w records $w.id$ as the id of its parent and sets its l'-layer number $l'(v) = l'(w) + 1$ and $c(v) = 2 + ((c(w) + 1) \mod 3)$. In other words, the color number is incremented every time modulo 5, but skipping colors 0 and 1 (preserved respectively for boundary and start-line nodes). In Figure 2, the numbers at the top part indicate these color numbers. From Lemma 2, we get that the wave of the layering proceeds exactly one hop in each phase. Since in each phase, only nodes that do not have an l' layer get layered, the waves of layering stop when they reach boundary nodes. Finally, each boundary node v records the id of the node w from which v hears the first message as the id of its parent.

Next, we present the proof of Theorem 2 which uses the Layer Refinement Algorithm (LRA) on top of the basic layering provided by Lemma 3.

Proof (Proof of Theorem 2). If $D < n^{0.1}$, we construct a basic layering with stretch $O(\log n)$ and depth $O(D + \log n)$ in $O(D \log n + \log^2 n)$ rounds by using Lemma 3 with parameter $\delta = \Theta(\log n)$. Then, we use the LRA to get to an $O(1)$-collision-free layering with depth $O(D + \log n)$ in additional $O(\log^3 n)$ rounds (Lemma 4). The total round complexity becomes $O(D \log n + \log^3 n) = O(D \log \frac{n}{D} + \log^3 n)$.

If $D \geq n^{0.1}$, we construct a basic layering with stretch $O(\log^2 n/\delta) = O(\log^2 n)$ and depth $O(D + \log^2 n/\delta) = O(D)$ in $O(D \log \frac{n}{D} + \log^2 n)$ rounds by using Lemma 3 with parameter $\delta = \log \frac{n}{D}$. Then, we use the LRA to get to an $O(1)$-collision-free layering with depth $O(D)$, in additional $O(\log^4 n)$ rounds. The total round complexity becomes $O(D \log \frac{n}{D} + \log^2 n + \log^4 n) = O(D \log \frac{n}{D})$.

In both cases the round complexity is $O(D \log \frac{n}{D} + \log^3 n)$ and the depth is $O(D + \log n)$.

Reducing the Round Complexity to $O(D \log \frac{n}{D} + \log^{2+\epsilon} n)$: The construction time in Theorem 2 is asymptotically equal to the broadcast time T_{BC}, for all values of $D = \Omega(\log^2 n)$. Here we explain how to achieve an almost optimal round complexity for smaller D by reducing the pseudo-BFS construction time to $O(D \log \frac{n}{D} + \log^{2+\epsilon} n)$ rounds, for any constant $\epsilon > 0$.

Recursive Layering Refinement Algorithm: In the LRA algorithm, we used the CR-Broadcast protocol with parameter $\delta = O(\log^2 n)$ to refine the layering numbers inside each strip, in $O(\log^3 n)$ rounds. The key change in RLRA is that, we perform this part of refinement in a faster manner by using a recursive refinement algorithm with $O(1/\epsilon)$ recursion levels. We remark that, this speedup comes at a cost of a $2^{O(1/\epsilon)}$ factor increase in the depth and $O(1/\epsilon)$ factor increase in the round complexity, and also in using $O(1/\epsilon)$ colors (instead of just 5), for the final layering. However, since we assume ϵ to be constant, these costs do not effect our asymptotic bounds.

Let $r = \lceil 1/\epsilon \rceil$ and $\tau = \alpha \log^{\frac{1}{r}} n$ for a sufficiently large constant α. In the ith level of recursion, we get an algorithm A_i that layers a graph with depth τ^i using $2i+1$ colors, in $i \cdot \Theta(\log^{2+\frac{1}{r}})$ rounds.

For the base case of recursion, algorithm A_1 is simply using the CR-Broadcast algorithm with parameter $\delta = \Theta(\log^2 n)$, and $T = \tau$ phases. Then, we assign layer numbers $\ell_1()$ based on the phase in which each node receives its first message, and set $c(v) = \ell_1(v) \pmod 3$.

We get algorithm A_i using algorithm A_{i-1} as follows: First, use the CR-Broadcast algorithm with parameter $\delta = \Theta(\log^{2-\frac{i-1}{r}})$ and $T = \tau^i$ phases. From this broadcast, we get a layering ℓ^* that has stretch at most $d_i = \Theta(\log^{\frac{i-1}{r}} n) \le \delta^{i-1}/5$. Then, using this layering, similar to the LRA, we break the graph into $\Theta(\delta)$ strips which each contain $\Theta(\delta^{i-1})$ layers. It is easy to see that, each strip has depth at most $\Theta(\delta^{i-1})$. Next, we determine boundary and start-line nodes as in the LRA and layer and color them. In particular, we assign color $2i+1$ to the boundaries of these strips and set their layer number $\ell_i(v) = 2\delta^{i-1}(\lceil \frac{\ell^*(v)}{\delta^{i-1}} \rceil + 1)$. Moreover, we assign color $2i$ to the start-lines of these strips and layer each start-line node v with $l_i(v) = l_i(w) + 1$, where w is the first boundary node from which v receives a message. Inside each strip, which is a graph with depth δ^{i-1}, we use algorithm A_{i-1} with colors 1 to $2(i-1)+1 = 2i-1$.

Following r recursion steps, we get algorithm A_r, which layers a graph with depth $\tau^r = \Theta(\log n)$ using $2r+1 = O(r)$ colors, in $r \cdot \Theta(\log^{2+\frac{1}{r}} n) = \Theta(\log^{2+\epsilon} n)$ rounds. In the LRA, if we substitute the part that layers each strip in $\Theta(\log^3 n)$ rounds with A_r, we get the recursive layering refinement algorithm.

Proof (Proof of Theorem 1). For the case where $D \ge n^{0.1}$, we simply use the LRA algorithm and calculations are as before. For the case where $D < n^{0.1}$, the proof is similar to that of Theorem 2 with the exception of using the Recursive Layering Refinement Algorithm instead of the LRA.

4   Gathering

In this section, we present a k-message gathering algorithm with round complexity $O(T_{Lay} + k)$. This round complexity is near optimal as k-message gathering has a lower bound of $T_{BC} + k$. The additive k term in this lower bound is trivial. The T_{BC} term is also a lower bound because the lower bounds of single-message broadcast extend to single-message unicast from an adversarially chosen source to an adversarially chosen destination, and single-message uni-cast is a special case of k-message gathering where $k=1$.

Theorem 3. *There is a distributed randomized algorithm that, w.h.p., gathers k messages in a given destination node in $O(T_{Lay} + k)$ rounds.*

The result follows from using the pseudo-BFS layering from Theorem 1 with the following lemma:

Lemma 5. *Given a C-collision-free layering $\ell(.)$ with a C-coloring $c(.)$, depth D', and source node s, Algorithm 2 gathers k messages in s with high probability, in $C \cdot \Theta(D' + k + \log^2 n)$ rounds.*

The full algorithm is presented in Algorithm 2. Here, we give an intuitive explanation of our approach. The formal arguments are deferred to the proof of Lemma 5 in the full version. Consider the hypothetical scenario where simultaneous transmissions are not lost (no collision) and packet sizes are not bounded, i.e., a node can transmit arbitrary many messages in one round. Consider the simple algorithm where (1) each node u transmits exactly once and in round $D' - \ell(u)$, where it transmits all the messages that it has received by then, (2) a node v accepts a received packet only if v is the parent of the sender. It is easy to see that this is like a wave of transmissions which starts from nodes at layer D' and proceeds exactly towards source, one hop in each round. This wave sweeps the network in a decreasing order of the layer numbers and every message m gets picked up by the wave, when the wave reaches the node that holds m initially. Then, messages are carried by the wave and they all arrive at the source when the wave does, i.e., after exactly D' rounds.

Things are not as easy in radio networks due to collisions and bounded size messages; each node can only transmit one message at a time, and simultaneous transmissions destined for a common parent collide. We say that *"transmission of message m at node u failed"* if throughout the progress of a wave, message m fails to reach from node u to the parent of u because either (i) a collision happens at u's parent, or (ii) u has other messages scheduled for transmission in the same round as m. To overcome these, we use two ideas, namely C-collision-free layering $\ell()$ with coloring $c()$, and random delays. We use a C-collision-free layering by scheduling the transmissions based on colors. This takes care of the possible collisions between nodes of different layer numbers (at the cost of increasing round complexity to $C \cdot D'$).

Even with the help of a C-collision-free layering, we still need to do something for collisions between the transmission of the nodes of the same layer, and packets

---

Algorithm 2. Gathering Algorithm @ node u

Given: Layer $\ell(u)$, color $c(u)$, parent-ID $parent(u)$, a set of initial messages M
Semantics: each packet is 4-tuple in form (message, destination, wave, delay)

1: $P \leftarrow \emptyset$
2: **for** each message $m \in M$ **do**
3:       Choose delay $\delta \in_{\mathcal{U}} [8 \max\{2^{-wave}k, 4 \log n\}]$
4:       Create packet $\tau \leftarrow (m, parent(u), 0, \delta)$ and add τ to P
5: **for** $epoch = 0$ to $\Theta(D' + 16k + \log^2 n)$ **do**   ▷ Main Gathering Part
6:       **for** $cycle = 1$ to C **do**
7:             **if** $c(u) = cycle$ **then**
8:                   **if** $\exists$ exactly one $\pi \in P$ such that $epoch = D' - \ell(u) + \pi.delay$ **then**
9:                         TRANSMIT packet π
10:                        LISTEN
11:                        **if** received acknowledgment **then**
12:                              remove π from P
13:                  **else**
14:                        LISTEN
15:                        LISTEN
16:                        **for** $\pi \in P$ s.t. $epoch = D' - \ell(u) + \pi.delay$ **do**
17:                              Choose random delay $\delta' \in_{\mathcal{U}} [8 \max\{k2^{-wave-1}, 4 \log n\}]$
18:                              $MaxPreviousDelay \leftarrow \sum_{1 \leq i \leq wave} 8 \max\{k2^{-i}, 4 \log n\}$
19:                              remove π from P
20:                              $\pi' \leftarrow (\pi.m, \pi.destination, \pi.wave + 1, MaxPreviousDelay + \delta')$
21:                              add packet π' to P
22:             **else**
23:                   LISTEN
24:                   **if** received a packet σ such that $\sigma.destination = ID(u)$ **then**
25:                         add packet $\sigma' = (\sigma.m, parent(u), \sigma.wave, \sigma.delay)$ to P
26:                         TRANSMIT acknowledgment packet
27:                   **else**
28:                         LISTEN

---

scheduled for simultaneous transmission from the same node. The idea is to add a random delay to the transmission time of each message. If there are k active messages and we add a random delay chosen from $[8k]$ to each message, then for each message m, with probability at least $7/8$ no transmission of m fails, i.e., the wave delivers m to the source with probability at least $7/8$. A formal argument for this claim would be presented in the proof. With this observation, one naive idea would be to repeat the above algorithm on a C-collision-free layering $\ell()$, by having $\Theta(\log n)$ non-overlapping waves, where each time each message starts from the node that it got stuck in while being carried by the previous wave. With this, we succeed with high probability in delivering all k messages to the source and in time $C \cdot O(D' \log n + k \log n)$.

Now there are two ideas to improve upon this. First, we can *pipeline* the waves. That is, we do not need to space the waves D' rounds apart; instead

---

Algorithm 3. Network-Coded Multi-Message Broadcast @ node u

Given: Source node s with k messages

1: **if** $u = source$ **then**
2:     **for** all $i \in [k]$ **do**
3:         $v_i \leftarrow (e_i, m_i)$ ▷ $e_i \in \{0,1\}^k$ is the ith basis vector
4:         put v_i in P
5: **else**
6:     $P \leftarrow \emptyset$

7: **for** $i = 1$ to $\Theta(D' \log \frac{n}{D'} + k \log n + \log^2 n)$ **do**
8:     **for** $cycle = 1$ to C **do**
9:         **if** $cycle \equiv c(u)$ **then**
10:             **with probability** $2^{-BC_i \bmod L}$ **do**   ▷ BC is the Broadcast sequence
from Section 2.3
11:                 choose a uniformly random subset S of P
12:                 TRANSMIT $\bigoplus_{v \in S} v$
13:             **otherwise**
14:                 LISTEN
15:         **else**
16:             LISTEN
17:             **if** received a packet v **then** add v to P

18: decode $v_1, \ldots, v_k$ from $span(P)$ by Gaussian Elimination

---

the spacing should be just large enough so that two waves do not collide. For that, a spacing of $8k$ between the waves is enough. With this improvement, we go down to time complexity of $C \cdot O(D' + k \log n)$. Second, note that in each wave, each message succeeds with probability at least $7/8$. Thus, using Chernoff bound, we get that as long as the number of remaining messages is $\Omega(\log n)$, whp, in each wave, the number of remaining messages goes down by at least a $\frac{1}{2}$ factor. Hence, in those times, we can decrease the size of the interval out of which the random delays are chosen by a factor of two in each new wave. Because of this, the spacing between the waves also goes down exponentially. This second improvement, with some care for the case where number of remaining messages goes below $\Theta(\log n)$ (where we do not have the Chernoff-type high probability concentration anymore) gives time complexity of $C \cdot O(D' + k + \log^2 n)$.

5   Multi-message Broadcast, and Gossiping

In this section we show how to combine psuedo-BFS layerings, the broadcat protocol of Section 2.3, and the idea of random linear network coding to obtain a simple and optimal $O(T_{Lay} + k \log n)$ k-message broadcast algorithm. Note that the $\Omega(k \log n)$ lower bound of [12], along with the $\Omega(D \log \frac{n}{D} + \log^2 n)$ broadcast lower bound of [17] and [1], show the near optimality of this algorithm.

Theorem 4. *Given k messages at a single source, there is a randomized distributed algorithm that broadcasts these k messages to all nodes, w.h.p, in $O(T_{Lay} + k \log n)$ rounds.*

The result follows from using the pseudo-BFS layering from Theorem 1 with the following lemma:

Lemma 6. *Given a C-collision free layering ℓ with depth D' and k messages at source s, the Network-Coded Multi-Message Broadcast algorithm delivers all messages to all nodes, w.h.p., in $C \cdot O(D' \log \frac{n}{D'} + k \log n + \log^2 n)$ rounds.*

The algorithm is presented in Algorithm 3. The main ideas are as follows. To schedule which node is sending at every time, we first restrict the nodes that are sending simultaneously to have the same color. To resolve the remaining collisions, we let nodes send independently at random with probabilities chosen according to the CR-Broadcast protocol of [7] with parameter $\delta = \log \frac{n}{D'}$. Lastly, if a node is prompted to send a packet, we create this packet using the standard distributed packetized implementation of random linear network coding as described in [14]. Given such a random linear network code, decoding can simply be performed by Gaussian elimination (see [14]).

The proof uses several ideas stemming from recent advances in analyzing random linear network coding. The key part is the *projection analysis* of [14] and its modification and adaption to radio networks [13], titled *backwards projection analysis*. This allows us to reduce the multi-message problem to merely showing that, for each particular node v, one can find a path of successful transmissions from the source to v with exponentially high probability. The required tail-bound follows from a slightly modified analysis of the CR-Broadcast protocol [7]. We remark that the additive coefficient overhead in Algorithm 3, which is one-bit for each of the k messages, can be reduced to $O(\log n)$ bits using standard techniques explained in [13]. The proof of Lemma 6 appears in the appendix.

Lastly, we present our gossiping result.

Theorem 5. *There is a randomized distributed algorithm that, with high probability, performs an performs all-to-all broadcast in $O(n \log n)$ rounds.*

Proof. First, we elect a leader node in $O(n)$ rounds using the algorithm of [11]. Then, we construct a pseudo-BFS layering around this leader in time $O(n)$ using Theorem 1. We then gather the n messages in the leader node in $O(n)$ rounds using Lemma 5. Finally, we broadcast the n messages from the leader to all the other nodes in time $O(n \log n)$ using Lemma 6.

Remark: Similar to the approach of the proof of Theorem 5 one can combine the leader election algorithm of [11] with the pseudo-BFS layering, gathering, and single-source broadcast algorithms of this paper and obtain a near optimal randomized distributed algorithm for the multi-source k-message broadcast problem with round complexity $O((D \log \frac{n}{D} + \log^3 n) \cdot \min\{\log \log n, \log \frac{n}{D}\} + k \log n)$.

References

1. Alon, N., Bar-Noy, A., Linial, N., Peleg, D.: A lower bound for radio broadcast. J. of Computer and System Sc. 43(2), 290–298 (1991)
2. Bar-Yehuda, R., Goldreich, O., Itai, A.: On the time-complexity of broadcast in multi-hop radio networks: An exponential gap between determinism and randomization. J. of Computer and System Sc. 45(1), 104–126 (1992)
3. Bar-Yehuda, R., Israeli, A., Itai, A.: Multiple communication in multi-hop radio networks. SIAM Journal on Computing 22(4), 875–887 (1993)
4. Chlamtac, I., Kutten, S.: On broadcasting in radio networks: Problem analysis and protocol design. IEEE Transactions on Communications 33(12), 1240–1246 (1985)
5. Chlebus, B., Kowalski, D., Radzik, T.: Many-to-many communication in radio networks. Algorithmica 54(1), 118–139 (2009)
6. Christersson, M., Gąsieniec, L., Lingas, A.: Gossiping with bounded size messages in *adhoc* radio networks. In: Widmayer, P., Triguero, F., Morales, R., Hennessy, M., Eidenbenz, S., Conejo, R. (eds.) ICALP 2002. LNCS, vol. 2380, pp. 377–389. Springer, Heidelberg (2002)
7. Czumaj, A., Rytter, W.: Broadcasting algorithms in radio networks with unknown topology. In: Proc. IEEE Symp. on Foundations of Computer Science, pp. 492–501 (2003)
8. Gąsieniec, L.: On efficient gossiping in radio networks. In: Kutten, S., Žerovnik, J. (eds.) SIROCCO 2009. LNCS, vol. 5869, pp. 2–14. Springer, Heidelberg (2010)
9. Gasieniec, L., Peleg, D., Xin, Q.: Faster communication in known topology radio networks. In: Proc. ACM Symp. on Principles of Distributed Computing, pp. 129–137 (2005)
10. Gasieniec, L., Potapov, I.: Gossiping with unit messages in known radio networks. In: Baeza-Yates, R., Montanari, U., Santoro, N. (eds.) TCS 2002. IFIP, vol. 96, pp. 193–205. Springer, Boston (2002)
11. Ghaffari, M., Haeupler, B.: Near-optimal leader election in multi-hop radio networks. In: Proc. ACM-SIAM Symp. on Discrete Algorithms, pp. 748–766 (2013)
12. Ghaffari, M., Haeupler, B., Khabbazian, M.: A bound on the throughput of radio networks. ArXiv Preprint abs/1302.0264 (2013)
13. Ghaffari, M., Haeupler, B., Khabbazian, M.: Broadcast in radio networks with collision detection. In: Proc. ACM Symp. on Principles of Distributed Computing (2013)
14. Haeupler, B.: Analyzing network coding gossip made easy. In: Proc. ACM Symp. on Theory of Computing, pp. 293–302 (2011)
15. Khabbazian, M., Kowalski, D.: Time-efficient randomized multiple-message broadcast in radio networks. In: Proc. ACM Symp. on Principles of Distributed Computing, pp. 373–380 (2011)
16. Kowalski, D., Pelc, A.: Broadcasting in undirected ad hoc radio networks. In: Proc. ACM Symp. on Principles of Distributed Computing, pp. 73–82 (2003)
17. Kushilevitz, E., Mansour, Y.: An $\Omega(D\log(N/D))$ lower bound for broadcast in radio networks. SIAM Journal on Computing 27(3), 702–712 (1998)
18. Manne, F., Xin, Q.: Optimal gossiping with unit size messages in known topology radio networks. In: Erlebach, T. (ed.) CAAN 2006. LNCS, vol. 4235, pp. 125–134. Springer, Heidelberg (2006)
19. Xin, Q.: Personal communication (May 2012)

In-Network Analytics for Ubiquitous Sensing*

Ittay Eyal[1], Idit Keidar[2], Stacy Patterson[2], and Raphi Rom[2]

[1] Department of Computer Science, Cornell
ittay.eyal@cornell.edu
[2] Department of Electrical Engineering, Technion
{idish,stacyp, rom}@ee.technion.ac.il

Abstract. We address the problem of in-network analytics for data that is generated by sensors at the edge of the network. Specifically, we consider the problem of summarizing a continuous physical phenomenon, such as temperature or pollution, over a geographic region like a road network. Samples are collected by sensors placed alongside roads as well as in cars driving along them. We divide the region into sectors and find a summary for each sector, so that their union is a continuous function that minimizes some global error function. We designate a node (either virtual or physical) that is responsible for estimating the function in each sector. Each node computes its estimate based on the samples taken in its sector and information from adjacent nodes.

The algorithm works in networks with bounded, yet unknown, latencies. It accommodates the addition and removal of samples and the arrival and departure of nodes, and it converges to a globally optimal solution using only pairwise message exchanges between neighbors. The algorithm relies on a weakly-fair scheduler to implement these pairwise exchanges, and we present an implementation of such a scheduler. Our scheduler, which may be of independent interest, is *locally quiescent*, meaning that it only sends messages when required by the algorithm. It achieves quiescence on every link where the algorithm ceases to schedule pairwise exchanges; in particular, if the algorithm converges, it globally quiesces.

1 Introduction

As we enter the era of ubiquitous sensing, we have the opportunity to monitor the world around us with unprecedented resolution and to leverage this vast wealth of data to make our environment smarter. On-board sensors and computers in new vehicles can sense road and traffic conditions and use this information in

---

* This research was supported by the Intel Collaborative Research Institute for Computational Intelligence (ICRI-CI), the Israeli Ministry of Trade and Labor Rescue Consortium, the Sidney Goldstein Research Fund, the Israeli Science Foundation, the Arlene & Arnold Goldstein Center at the Technion Autonomous Systems Program, a Technion Fellowship, two Andrew and Erna Finci Viterbi fellowships, the Lady Davis Fellowship Trust, and the Hasso-Plattner Institute for Software Systems Engineering.

Y. Afek (Ed.): DISC 2013, LNCS 8205, pp. 507–521, 2013.
© Springer-Verlag Berlin Heidelberg 2013

route planning, smart meters enable fine-grained power usage monitoring and can assist in demand-response in the smart grid, and cheap wireless motes that measure noise, light, and air pollution can be used as input into urban planning and public health decisions.

To fully realize this vision, we must be able to process this massive amount of data and generate meaningful summaries that can be used in planning and response. The field of machine learning offers a range of tools for such data analytics, but these tools typically assume all data is present at a centralized location. As this data is generated at the edge of the network at an ever-increasing rate, transmitting the data over a long distance to a central facility is both expensive and energy consuming, especially in wireless networks [1]. Moreover, the high latency incurred by these long-distance transmissions may prove problematic to time-sensitive applications. Finally, even after collecting all data, processing it requires costly and time-consuming computation. Thus, we need distributed solutions for in-network data analytics.

A few very recent works in the field of control theory and machine learning have proposed distributed algorithms for data analytics, however, these works use a naïve model of the distributed system and thus do not offer a realistic solution for our setting. On the other hand, brute force distribution does not work. To develop realistic distributed data-analytics tools requires both an understanding of machine learning and distributed computing.

In this extended abstract, we present a distributed data analytics technique using a novel combined approach and illustrate it using a specific application of in-network analytics, motivated by our work with a major automotive corporation on *vehicular sensor networks*. The objective is to generate a compact estimate of a continuous physical phenomenon from samples measured throughout a region, for example, the road network in Western Europe. These samples are collected by vehicles driving through the region as well as by fixed infrastructure (e.g., roadside units) with compute, storage, and local communication capabilities. We leverage this fixed infrastructure as nodes in a distributed computing platform. This infrastructure may be unreliable, and so our solution must accommodate the arrival and departure of nodes. Moreover, the measured phenomenon changes over time, hence the estimate is generated from a dynamic set of samples. We detail our system model in Section 2.

From these requirements, we generate a formal problem definition for this application setting. We describe how we architect this formal problem in Section 3. Our approach is based on machine learning fundamentals, namely linear regression. Since the data is geographically distributed, care must be taken to ensure that this formalization is amenable to a distributed solution. To achieve this, we employ *selective* learning; each node learns an estimate for its local area, or *sector*, based on its samples and communication with its neighbors. (The division of the region and assignment of nodes can be done with known techniques [2,3,4,5] and is outside the scope of this paper.) We thus define an optimization problem where each node's estimate has to minimize some convex error function related to collected samples, while requiring that the union of these estimates is continuous over the entire region. The continuity requirement stems from the fact the sampled phenomenon is known to be continuous. Generating the *global* estimate is a *convex optimization problem* whose objective is to minimize the sum of the local error functions, with equality constraints that match the structure of the network. The nodes' estimates should converge to a global optimal estimate once changes cease. Note that since nodes do not know when changes stop, they must make a best effort to converge at all times. This problem structure opens the door to a solution based on *local* communication. However, it still requires multi-way coordination between all nodes sharing a sector boundary (for details see the technical report [6]). To eliminate such costly coordination, we transform the problem to its dual form to obtain a decomposable (unconstrained) problem that can be solved using only pairwise coordination between neighbors. While transforming to the dual is a common optimization technique, we have not seen it used for this purpose before.

We then present, in Section 4, a novel, distributed optimization algorithm for our formal problem based on the method of coordinate ascent. In general, coordinate ascent is not amenable to distribution, and a naïve implementation requires global synchronization and does not accommodate dynamic behavior (see related work below). In contrast, our distributed coordinate ascent algorithm deals with dynamic inputs and requires neither global information nor synchronization.

The algorithm progresses in steps, and to schedule these steps in the distributed environment we implement a *locally quiescent weakly-fair scheduler*. This scheduler executes pairwise message exchanges in a weakly-fair manner and only when they are required by the algorithm. Unlike with standard synchronizer-based approaches, if the algorithm ceases to schedule pairwise exchanges (i.e., it reaches the optimum), the scheduler achieves quiescence. This scheduler, described in Section 5, may be important in and of itself where communication is expensive and relaxed scheduling is sufficient.

We believe that our approach to distributed, in-network analytics without global communication or synchronization can prove useful in many additional settings. Section 6 concludes the paper and touches on some directions for future research. Some formal details and more elaborate examples are given in the technical report [6]. While, in the sequel, we consider estimation over a road network, our approach can also be applied to estimation over a two-dimensional region, as detailed in the technical report.

Related Work. Previous work on distributed convex optimization can be divided into two categories: averaging-based algorithms (based on the framework of [7]), and sequential algorithms. Averaging-based algorithms have been proposed for unconstrained convex optimization problems [7,8,9], and for constrained convex optimization problems where all constraints are known globally [10,11] or where constraints are purely local [11]. To satisfy the continuity constraints in our problem formulation, these algorithms would require that all nodes know the continuity constraints for the entire network, which induces a prohibitive per node storage cost and a need for global information. In sequential algorithms [12,13], there is

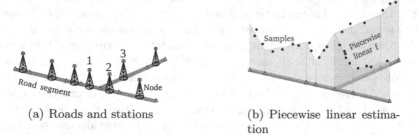

(a) Roads and stations   (b) Piecewise linear estima-
                                tion

Fig. 1. Piecewise linear estimation in a road system. We see a junction of three roads. (a) The roads are divided into sectors (e.g., 1, 2 and 3), each with its node. The sectors meet at vertices (triangles). (b) The samples are shown as dots, and a curtain above the roads shows the continuous piecewise linear estimate f.

a single copy of the optimization variables, and every node has its own objective function and constraints. Both approaches require storage for *all* variables at every node, which is infeasible for large networks of the type we consider (e.g., a road network of an entire country). Furthermore, none of these algorithms can tolerate node arrivals and departures.

In this work, we present a distributed optimization algorithm based on the method of coordinate ascent. Coordinate ascent is an iterative method where, in each step, a single variable is updated. The algorithm converges to the optimal solution only if the order in which the variables are updated obeys certain properties. A few recent works have proposed parallel implementations of coordinate descent for solving large optimization problems [14,15]. While the update operations occur in parallel, these implementations still require that updates are executed in globally specified order, thus requiring centralized coordination. They also require that the set of participating nodes does not change during the algorithm execution. In contrast, our distributed coordinate ascent algorithm requires no global information or coordination, and it operates correctly even if the set of participating nodes changes.

2   System Model

We consider a finite region, for example, a road network. Sensors collect *samples* in the region, each comprised of a geographic location and a value. There is also a computing network in the region consisting of a dynamic set of nodes. Each node may be part of a physical infrastructure, for example, a base station, or it may be a virtual node implemented by a dynamic set of mobile agents. Neighboring nodes are connected with bidirectional, reliable FIFO links.

We take a hierarchical approach and divide the region into a fixed set of non-overlapping *sectors*. In the road network, a sector is a segment of a road, and its end points are two vertices, as shown in Figure 1(a); a single vertex may be shared by several adjacent sectors. Each vertex has a unique ID. Each sector also has a unique ID, and these IDs are totally ordered. Each sector is assigned at most one node at any given time, and this node maintains a dynamic set of samples that have been taken in its sector. Each node has a unique ID and it knows the ID of the sector for which it is responsible. We assume a fail-stop model, i.e., a node that fails does not recover, and its neighbors are notified of the failure. A new node may arrive and take responsibility for the failed node's sector. When a node becomes active, its sample set is initially empty. Following its activation, a node is notified of all its neighbors, and they all receive notifications of its arrival.

Notation. We employ the following notation throughout this work:

- The set of vertices for sector i is denoted $\mathcal{V}_i$, and the set of vertices for all sectors is denoted $\mathcal{V}$.

- The dynamic set[1] of active (non-failed) nodes is denoted $\mathcal{N}$.

- The set of active nodes whose sectors share a vertex v is called the *member set* of v, denoted $\mathcal{M}(v)$. We say that nodes i and j are *neighbors* if there exists a vertex v such that both i and j are elements of $\mathcal{M}(v)$.

- Each sample is represented by a tuple (x, z) where x is the distance along the segment from the vertex with the smaller ID, and z is the value of the sample at that location.

- The set of samples at node i is denoted $\mathcal{S}_i$. The dynamic set of all samples, denoted $\mathcal{S}$, is the union of the sample sets belonging to the nodes in $\mathcal{N}$.

Stabilization. For the sake of analysis, we assume that the system eventually stabilizes.

Definition 1 (Global Stabilization Time). *The **global stabilization time** (**GST**) is the earliest time after which the following properties hold: (1) no nodes are informed of neighbor changes, (2) samples are neither added nor deleted, and (3) the message latency of all outstanding and future messages is bounded between δ and Δ. Nodes do not know when GST has been reached, nor do they know δ or Δ.*

Before GST (if it exists), there are no time bounds on message latency or on notifications of neighbor set changes or sample set changes.

3   Architecting the Problem

In this section, we develop a formal problem definition that is compatible with the system model, generates a meaningful summary of the collected samples, and is amenable to a distributed solution that scales to the size of an immense road network. Each node generates an estimate for its sector that is optimal with respect to its samples, while also ensuring that the union of these local estimates is a piecewise continuous function over the region. The global estimation problem is defined by a convex optimization problem whose objective is to minimize

---

[1] The dynamic sets $\mathcal{N}$, $\mathcal{M}(v)$, $\mathcal{S}_i$, and $\mathcal{S}$ are all functions of time. Since the time can always be deduced from the context, we omit the superscript t.

the sum of the local error functions, with equality constraints that match the structure of the network. This convex optimization problem is detailed in Section 3.1. A distributed algorithm that addresses the problem directly requires expensive coordination among all nodes that share a sector boundary (for example, at an intersection). In Section 3.2 we transform the problem to its dual form and obtain a decomposable problem that can be solved using only pairwise communication between neighbors.

3.1   Formal Problem Definition

We define the estimate for sector i to be a real-valued function f_i over the sector. The global estimate f is the union of these individual estimates. We illustrate our algorithm for the case where each f_i is a linear function defined over a single-dimensional road segment. Such a function is shown in Figure 1(b); the estimate f is drawn as a curtain above the roads. It is straightforward to extend our approach to estimation with higher order polynomials, as shown in the technical report [6].

Let u and v be the IDs of the vertices of the sector belonging to node i, with $u < v$. The function f_i is parameterized by the values at its vertices, denoted $\theta_{i,u}$ and $\theta_{i,v}$, and is given by,

$$f_i(x; \theta_{i,u}, \theta_{i,v}) \triangleq (1 - x/d_i)\,\theta_u + (x/d_i)\,\theta_v.$$

Here, d_i is the length of sector i. Define $\theta_i \triangleq [\theta_{i,u}\ \theta_{i,v}]^\mathsf{T}$, and let θ denote the vector of all $\theta_{i,u}$ variables, $i \in \mathcal{N}$, $u \in \mathcal{V}_i$. Each node must generate an optimal estimate of its sector from its samples. Specifically, each node i must determine the values θ_i that minimize a convex error function. As an example, we consider the least squares error,

$$C_i(\theta_i; \mathcal{S}_i) \triangleq \sum_{(x,z) \in \mathcal{S}_i} (f_i(x; \theta_i) - z)^2.$$

We also require that the estimates f_i are continuous at the sector boundaries. This requirement means that nodes must collaborate to perform the estimation so that they agree on the values for shared vertices.

The problem of learning the function f after GST can be formulated as a convex optimization problem with a global, separable objective function and linear constraints that capture the continuity requirements,

$$\underset{\theta}{\text{minimize}}\ \ C(\theta; \mathcal{S}) \triangleq \sum_{i \in \mathcal{N}} C_i(\theta_i; \mathcal{S}_i) \tag{1}$$

$$\text{subject to}\ \ \theta_{i,v} = \theta_{j,v},\ \ \text{for } v \in \mathcal{V},\ \ i,j \in \mathcal{M}(v), i \neq j. \tag{2}$$

The constraints (2) state that every pair of nodes in $\mathcal{M}(v)$ has the same value for vertex v, or equivalently, all nodes in $\mathcal{M}(v)$ learn the same value for vertex v. These constraints ensure that the estimate is continuous within each connected component of the network of nodes in $\mathcal{N}$.

Our goal is to design a distributed algorithm for finding the values of the parameters θ that solve the optimization problem defined above. A node i knows only its own sample set $\mathcal{S}_i$ and communicates only with its neighbors. Each node is responsible for obtaining an estimate of its sector by learning values for θ_i. After GST, these estimates must converge to a globally optimal estimate.

In the problem (1)–(2), all members of a vertex must agree on the value of θ for that vertex. An algorithm that addresses the problem directly would require that all members coordinate to maintain this constraint. In the next section, we show that by transforming to the dual, we obtain a problem formulation that only requires coordination between pairs of neighboring nodes.

3.2   Problem Decomposition

We now show how to transform the constrained convex optimization into its unconstrained dual form. We note that, typically, one transforms a problem to its dual because the dual can be solved in a more computationally efficient manner in a centralized setting. Our use of the dual is unconventional; we use the dual problem because it opens the door to a distributed solution with reduced communication costs.

Given a constrained optimization problem, the dual problem is formed by defining the Lagrangian, where the constraints are incorporated into the objective function. The Lagrangian for (1)–(2) is,

$$\mathcal{L}(\theta, \lambda; \mathcal{S}) = \sum_{i \in \mathcal{N}} C_i(\theta_i; \mathcal{S}_i) + \sum_{v \in \mathcal{V}} \sum_{i,j \in \mathcal{M}(v), i \neq j} \lambda_{i,j}^v \left(\theta_{i,v} - \theta_{j,v} \right). \tag{3}$$

Here, each equality constraint $\theta_{i,v} = \theta_{j,v}$ in (2) is assigned a Lagrange multiplier $\lambda_{i,j}^v \in \mathbb{R}$. The dual function is then defined as follows,

$$q(\lambda; \mathcal{S}) \triangleq \inf_\theta \mathcal{L}(\theta, \lambda; \mathcal{S}), \tag{4}$$

where λ denotes the vector of all Lagrange multipliers.

In our case, (4) can be decomposed as a sum over the nodes in $\mathcal{N}$. Let λ_i denote the vector of Lagrange multipliers associated with a constraint involving a component of θ_i. We can rewrite q as $q(\lambda; \mathcal{S}) = \sum_{i \in \mathcal{N}} q_i(\lambda_i; \mathcal{S}_i)$, where each function q_i is

$$q_i(\lambda_i; \mathcal{S}_i) \triangleq \inf_{\theta_i} C_i(\theta_i; \mathcal{S}_i) + \sum_{v \in \mathcal{V}_i} \left(\sum_{j \in \mathcal{M}(v), j \neq i} \text{sgn}(j - i) \lambda_{i,j}^v \right) \theta_{i,v}. \tag{5}$$

The function $\text{sgn}(j - i)$ returns 1 if $i < j$ and returns -1 otherwise. The function q_i depends only on information local to node i, specifically, $\mathcal{S}_i$ and the location of of the vertices of sector i. Therefore, given λ_i, each node i can solve for q_i independently. For the least squares error cost function, (5) is a quadratic minimization problem (over θ_i) and thus can be solved analytically. The full expression for q_i is given in the technical report [6].

The dual problem is

$$\underset{\lambda}{\text{maximize}} \quad q(\lambda; \mathcal{S}) = \sum_{i \in \mathcal{N}} q_i(\lambda_i; \mathcal{S}_i). \tag{6}$$

For a square error minimization of the form (1)–(2), strong duality holds (see [16]). Therefore, the solution to (6) gives the solution to the primal problem, $\hat{\theta} = \text{argmin}_\theta \, \mathcal{L}(\theta, \hat{\lambda}; \mathcal{S})$.

We note that each Lagrange multiplier $\lambda_{i,j}^v$ appears in both λ_i and λ_j since node i and node j share the vertex v. Therefore, the objective in (6) is not separable over the nodes in $\mathcal{N}$. While the nodes can solve (5) independently for a given vector λ_i, the dual problem contains pairwise dependences between neighbors, and so the nodes must collaborate to find the optimal $\hat{\lambda}$.

4   Distributed Algorithm

We now present our distributed algorithm for generating the optimal estimate defined in the previous section. Our algorithm is based on the coordinate ascent method for nonlinear optimization [17,18]. We briefly review this method in Section 4.1. We then describe the details of our algorithm in Section 4.2 and sketch its correctness in Section 4.3. Formal proofs are given in the technical report [6].

4.1   Preliminaries - The Method of Coordinate Ascent
Consider an unconstrained optimization problem

$$\hat{x} = \underset{x \in \mathbb{R}^m}{\text{argmax}} \quad h(x_1, x_2, \ldots, x_m).$$

The method of coordinate ascent is an iterative optimization algorithm that proceeds as follows. Let $x(k) = [x_1(k) \ \ldots \ x_m(k)]$ be the vector of the values in iteration k. The algorithm begins with an initial $x(1)$. In each step k, a coordinate i is selected, and $x_i(k)$ is updated by finding its maximum while all other values of $x(k)$ are fixed. The update step is,

$$\bar{x}_i = \underset{\xi \in \mathbb{R}}{\text{argmax}} \quad h(x_1(k), \ldots x_{i-1}(k), \xi, x_{i+1}(k), \ldots, x_m(k)) \tag{7}$$

$$x(k+1) = [x_1(k) \ \ldots \ x_{i-1}(k) \ \bar{x}_i \ x_{i+1}(k) \ \ldots \ x_m(k)]. \tag{8}$$

We note that it is possible that the execution of an update step may not result in any change to x (i.e., $x(k+1) = x(k)$) if the selected coordinate is already optimal with respect to the rest of $x(k)$.

The convergence of the above algorithm depends on the properties of h and the order in which the coordinates are evaluated: an arbitrary update order may not converge. In this paper, we consider the *essentially cyclic policy* [19], which states that there exists a constant integer $T > 0$, such that every coordinate $i \in \{1, \ldots, m\}$ is chosen at least once between the rth iteration and the $(r+T-1)^{th}$ iteration, for all r. The following theorem gives the relevant convergence result for the method of coordinate ascent with an essentially cyclic policy (see [17,19]).

Theorem 1. *Let $h(x_1, \ldots, x_m)$ be a concave function that is strictly concave in each x_i when the other variables $x_j, j \neq i$ are held constant, and let h have continuous first partial derivatives. If the coordinate update policy follows an essentially cyclic order, then the algorithm (7)–(8) converges to an optimal solution. Furthermore, if the algorithm executes a cycle of updates, where each coordinate is evaluated at least once, and no evaluation results in a change to x, then the algorithm has found an optimal solution.*

The objective in (6) is concave, has continuous first partial derivatives, and is strictly concave in each $\lambda_{i,j}^v$ when the other values of λ are fixed. So, we can solve this problem using the method of coordinate ascent. We next present a distributed algorithm, based on coordinate ascent, that solves the dual problem (6).

4.2 Distributed Optimization Algorithm

In our distributed algorithm, each node i stores its set of samples $\mathcal{S}_i$, a list of its current neighbors, and its Lagrange multipliers λ_i. Per the problem decomposition, a coordinate $\lambda_{i,j}^v$ appears in two vectors, λ_i and λ_j. Here, each $\lambda_{i,j}^v$ is a *shared variable*, and in the distributed algorithm, and nodes i and j each store a copy of $\lambda_{i,j}^v$. The goal is for nodes to converge to the optimal values for their shared variables, thus solving the dual problem (6).

To implement a distributed version of coordinate ascent for this dual problem, every pair of nodes i and j that share a coordinate $\lambda_{i,j}^v$ must collaborate to update their shared variables for $\lambda_{i,j}^v$, and the distributed algorithm must execute these pairwise updates in an order that guarantees convergence. We now show that a coordinate update can be performed with a pairwise message exchange, where each message contains two coefficients.

Distributed Coordinate Update. For an update of the shared variable $\lambda_{i,j}^v$, its new value γ depends only on the dual functions for nodes i and j,

$$\gamma = \operatorname*{argmax}_{\lambda_{i,j}^v} q(\lambda; \mathcal{S}) = \operatorname*{argmax}_{\lambda_{i,j}^v} \left(q_i(\lambda_i; \mathcal{S}_i) + q_j(\lambda_j; \mathcal{S}_j) \right).$$

The value of γ is the root of the equation

$$\frac{\partial}{\partial \lambda_{i,j}^v} (q_i + q_j) = \frac{\partial}{\partial \lambda_{i,j}^v} q_i + \frac{\partial}{\partial \lambda_{i,j}^v} q_j = 0.$$

To find this value, each node sends information about its partial derivative to the other. For the least square error cost function, this information can be encapsulated in two coefficients α_i^v and β_i^v. The values of these coefficients are given in the technical report [6]. After exchanging these coefficients, each node then independently computes $\gamma = -(\beta_i^v + \beta_j^v)/(\alpha_i^v + \alpha_j^v)$ and updates its copy of $\lambda_{i,j}^v$.

The values of the α_i^v and β_i^v are determined by the node's samples and the values of its other shared variables. These shared variables, in turn, depend on additional shared variables with other nodes. For the coordinate update step to be performed correctly, both nodes involved in the update must compute their coefficients using a consistent shared state.

Scheduler. Each node determines which coordinates should be updated by detecting which of its shared variables are not optimal with respect its current state, and it schedules pairwise exchanges on the corresponding links. Our algorithm relies on a *weakly-fair scheduler* (implemented in Section 5) as a black box to implement the pairwise message exchange on scheduled links. We give the specification for the scheduler below, followed by the details of our distributed algorithm execution.

The scheduler provides a `notify`(j) function by which a node i schedules a pairwise message exchange on a link (i, j) to update the shared variable $\lambda_{i,j}^v$. It provides functions `addNeighbor`(j) and `delNeighbor`(j) for indicating when a neighbor has been added or removed, and it provides a `getLink`() function by which a node requests a neighbor for a pairwise message exchange. The node sends messages directly to its neighbor, and the scheduler receives incoming messages. The scheduler provides the function `deliver`(j) by which a calling node delivers a message from node j. If j fails, the scheduler delivers the token FAIL.

We assume that the algorithm is notified on the addition or removal of a neighbor and invokes the appropriate function on the scheduler, `addNeighbor` or `delNeighbor`. We also assume that the algorithm executes the following infinite loop, with only non-blocking operations interleaved (as in our algorithm):

> **while** TRUE **do**
> $j \leftarrow$ scheduler.getLink()
>   send(j, msg_1)
> $msg_2 \leftarrow$ scheduler.deliver(j)

In this loop, a node requests the ID of neighbor, and it then exchanges messages with that neighbor. The scheduler must execute this message exchange atomically and provide some weak degree of "fairness" in executing scheduled exchanges. We now make these requirements precise.

We define a *step* of the distributed algorithm to be the delivery of a message at a single node. Without loss of generality, we assume that no two steps are executed concurrently. An *execution* of the distributed algorithm is a sequence of steps. We associate the invocation `scheduler.notify`(j) by a node i with the most recent step s that resulted in a message delivery at node i. In this case we say that the update of link (i, j) was scheduled in step s.

Definition 2 (Weakly-fair scheduler). *A scheduler is a* weakly-fair *scheduler if it guarantees the following for an algorithm that respects the above assumptions:*

1. *Every message is returned by* `scheduler.deliver` *at most once.*

2. *If* `scheduler.deliver`(j) *returns message m at time t then, if m is* FAIL, *j is failed at time t. If m is not* FAIL, *then m was previously sent by j.*

3. *If node i invokes* `scheduler.notify`(j), *and neither i nor j fail, then eventually i completes* `scheduler.deliver`(j) *and j completes* `scheduler.deliver`(i).

4. Let $\bar{s}$ be the last step before GST. There exists a bound B such that, if a node i invokes scheduler.notify(j) at step s, then if i does not fail, i completes scheduler.deliver(j) by step $\max(s, \bar{s}) + B$, and if j does not fail, j completes scheduler.deliver(i) by step $\max(s, \bar{s}) + B$.

Algorithm Execution. Each node is responsible for detecting when one of its shared variables is not optimal with respect to its sample set and other shared variables. A shared variable requires an update whenever a sample is added or deleted, a shared variable is added or removed, or any other shared variable is updated by pairwise exchange with another node. When one of these events occurs, the node schedules an update for that shared variable by invoking scheduler.notify.

A separate thread at each node handles the scheduled updates of shared variables, one at a time. In an infinite loop, the process requests a node ID from the scheduler by invoking scheduler.getLink, and it performs a pairwise message exchange with that node, e.g., node j. It sends its coefficients (as specified above) to j, and it delivers coefficients from j with scheduler.deliver. The node then updates its shared variable with j using the coefficients contained in the messages. If j fails before sending its coefficients, then the scheduler eventually delivers FAIL, and the node does not update the shared variable. The pseudocode for the distributed algorithm is given in the the technical report [6].

4.3   Proof Sketch of Algorithm Convergence

We now sketch the convergence proof for our distributed algorithm with a weakly-fair scheduler. The lemmas and theorem stated here are proven in the technical report [6].

We first show that, after GST, the distributed algorithm with a weakly-fair scheduler simulates the execution of the centralized coordinate ascent algorithm on the dual problem in (6). We define a mapping $\mathcal{F}$ between the state of the distributed algorithm and the state of the centralized algorithm; for a given state of the distributed algorithm at step t, $\mathcal{F}$ returns a state where the value of each coordinate $\lambda_{i,j}^v$ in λ is the value at the first node to update the shared variable for $\lambda_{i,j}^v$ in the most recent (possibly incomplete) pairwise exchange.

Lemma 1. *After GST, the algorithm simulates the centralized coordinate ascent algorithm, under the mapping $\mathcal{F}$.*

Next we show that any execution C of the centralized algorithm that is generated under the mapping $\mathcal{F}$ from an execution of the distributed algorithm is equivalent to an essentially cyclic execution of the centralized coordinate ascent algorithm. The key to this result is the observation that, at a step s in the distributed execution, if a shared variable is not scheduled for update at any node, then its value is optimal with respect to the values of the other shared variables at step s. This means that in the mapped step of centralized execution, the value of the corresponding value of $\lambda_{i,j}^v$ is also optimal with respect to the rest of λ. The weakly-fair scheduler guarantees that, after GST, all shared variables that are scheduled for update in step s of the distributed algorithm will be updated by in at most B steps after s (in both the distributed and the mapped centralized executions). Therefore, we can create an equivalent, essentially cyclic centralized execution (whose cycle length depends on B) by adding empty update steps for unscheduled shared variables. This result is formally stated in the following lemma.

Lemma 2. *Let D be an execution of the distributed algorithm starting after GST, consisting of the steps $\{d_1, d_2, d_3, \ldots\}$, and let $C \overset{\Delta}{=} \{c_1 = \mathcal{F}(d_1), c_2 = \mathcal{F}(d_2), c_3 = \mathcal{F}(d_3), \ldots\}$ be the corresponding execution of the centralized algorithm. Then, there exists an essentially cyclic centralized execution $\overline{C}$, that is equivalent to C, i.e., $\overline{C}$ contains exactly the same non-empty updates as C, and these updates are executed in the same order.*

Lemmas 1 and 2 show that the shared variables mapped under $\mathcal{F}$ converge to an optimal solution. What remains is to show that the other shared variables converge to the same solution. This result follows directly from the definition of a weakly-fair scheduler (Definition 2). We therefore conclude that the algorithm, run with a weakly-fair scheduler, solves the dual problem.

Theorem 2. *If the scheduler is weakly-fair, then, after GST, the algorithm converges to an optimal solution of the dual problem in (6).*

Since we have convergence in the dual, each node's estimate of θ_i converges to the optimal solution of the primal problem in (1)–(2). We note that, if at a time t after GST, no shared variable is scheduled for update, then every coordinate is optimal with respect to the values of the other coordinates, and thus, the algorithm has found an optimal solution.

5   Locally Quiescent Scheduler

Our algorithm, described above, requires a weakly-fair scheduler to order communication. A naturally appealing approach for such a scheduler is to use a self-stabilizing edge-coloring [20] or other synchronizer-based methods. However, this kind of approach would require the continuous exchange of messages to maintain the synchronization pulses, and these control messages would be sent regardless of whether the algorithm needed to exchange information over the links (unless some external mechanism were used to terminate the synchronizer). Furthermore, before GST, when the network is changing, the resulting schedule might lead to deadlock, which would also require an external mechanism to break.

To complement our novel optimization algorithm described above, we propose here a weakly fair scheduler implementation that we call a *locally quiescent scheduler*. This scheduler is deadlock-free, even before GST, and it only sends messages on a link if the algorithm schedules an exchange for that link. After the algorithm stops scheduling updates, no messages are sent on any link.

The scheduler assigns a master node and slave node to each link; the node with the smaller ID is the master. Note that each node may act as a slave for

---

Algorithm 1. Locally quiescent scheduler at node i.

```
1  state                                          19  function deliver(j)
2      requestQueue, initially empty              20      wait until msgBuffer(j) ≠ ⊥
3      notificationQueue, initially empty         21      msg ← msgBuffer(j)
4      msgBuffer : ℕ → msg ∪ {⊥, FAIL}            22      msgBuffer(j) ← ⊥
5      notified, initially ∅                      23      return msg

6  function notify(j)                             24  function addNeighbor_i(j)
7      if min(i, j) ∉ notified then               25      no op
8          notified ← notified ∪ {min(i, j)}
9          if i < j then                          26  function delNeighbor_i(j)
10             push(notificationQueue, j)         27      notified ← notified \ {j}
11         else                                   28      msgBuffer(j) ← FAIL
12             send(j, NOTIFY)
                                                  29  on recv_i(j, msg)
13 function getLink()                             30      msgBuffer(j) ← msg
14     while TRUE do                              31      if j < i then   (j is the master)
15         if requestQueue not empty              32          notified ← notified \ {j}
           then                (slave)            33          push(requestQueue, j)
16             return pop(requestQueue)
17         else if notificationQueue not          34  on recv_i(j, ⟨NOTIFY⟩)
           empty then                             35      push(notificationQueue, j)
18             return
               pop(notificationQueue)
```

---

some links and as a master for others. Whenever the algorithm schedules an exchange on a link, it calls the scheduler's notify function, which either places the link in the node's notificationQueue (if it is the master), or sends a NOTIFY message to the master of that link (if it is the slave). In this case, when the master receives the NOTIFY message, it places the link in its notificationQueue.

We now explain how the scheduler executes a pairwise message exchange for a scheduled link. Consider a link (i, j), where i is the master and j is the slave. When the master asks for a link with getLink, its scheduler processes the next entry in its notificationQueue and returns a neighbor j. The master proceeds by sending a message to the slave, invoking deliver(j), and blocking until the message from j is delivered. While the master is blocked, its scheduler queues incoming notifications and requests from masters on other links. When the slave receives the message from the master, its scheduler buffers the message in its msgBuffer and registers it in its requestQueue. Once getLink returns the ID of the master, the slave sends its message to the master and delivers the master's message to it. The slave's call to deliver returns instantly since the message from the master is already in its scheduler's buffer. Once the slave's message arrives, the deliver call at the master returns the message, and the pairwise exchange is complete. The scheduler is given in Algorithm 1.

The following theorem states that the scheduler is weakly-fair. The result follows from the fact that scheduled updates are handled in the order that the notifications arrive at the master and nodes only wait on their slaves. The master-slave relationship assignments follow the total order of node IDs, prohibiting a deadlock due to cycles. A formal proof is given in the technical report [6].

Theorem 3. *The locally quiescent scheduler is a weakly-fair scheduler.*

We note that our locally quiescent scheduler only sends messages on a link in response to an invocation of `notify` for that link by the algorithm. After the algorithm stops scheduling updates, no messages are sent on any link.

Observation 1. *If a link is not scheduled by the algorithm, the scheduler sends no messages on the link. Therefore, if the algorithm ceases to schedule links, the scheduler achieves quiescence.*

6 Conclusion

We have presented a distributed algorithm for estimating a continuous phenomenon over a geographic region based on samples taken by sensors inside the region. While a straightforward solution to this problem would require expensive coordination among groups of nodes, we have shown how to decompose the problem so that the algorithm requires only pairwise communication between neighbors. We have then provided a novel, distributed implementation of coordinate ascent optimization that solves this estimation problem. Our algorithm accommodates the addition and removal of samples and the arrival and departure of nodes, and it converges to a globally optimal solution without any global coordination or synchronization. The algorithm relies on a weakly-fair scheduler to implement pairwise exchanges, and we have presented an implementation of such a scheduler. Our scheduler only sends message when the algorithm indicates that there are updates to perform, and if the algorithm finds the optimal solution, the scheduler achieves quiescence.

This work demonstrates the benefits and power of distributed *selective* learning, where agents cooperate to calculate a global optimum, while each of them learns only a part of the solution. These results call for future work, studying the possibility of relaxing the communication patterns even further and extending the algorithm to other optimization problems with different objective functions and constraints, for example, estimation of non-continuous phenomena and tracking of phenomena that change over time.

Acknowledgements. The authors thank Isaac Keslassy for his good advice.

References

1. Chong, C., Kumar, S.: Sensor networks: Evolution, opportunities, and challenges. Proceedings of the IEEE 91(8), 1247–1256 (2003)
2. Gilbert, S., Lynch, N., Mitra, S., Nolte, T.: Self-stabilizing mobile robot formations with virtual nodes. In: Kulkarni, S., Schiper, A. (eds.) SSS 2008. LNCS, vol. 5340, pp. 188–202. Springer, Heidelberg (2008)

3. Dolev, S., Tzachar, N.: Empire of colonies: Self-stabilizing and self-organizing distributed algorithm. Theoretical Computer Science 410(6-7), 514–532 (2009)
4. Fernandess, Y., Malkhi, D.: K-clustering in wireless ad hoc networks. In: Proceedings of the Second ACM International Workshop on Principles of Mobile Computing, pp. 31–37. ACM (2002)
5. Lee, D.Y., Lam, S.S.: Efficient and accurate protocols for distributed Delaunay triangulation under churn. In: IEEE International Conference on Network Protocols, pp. 124–136 (2008)
6. Eyal, I., Keidar, I., Patterson, S., Rom, R.: Global estimation with local communication. Technical Report CCIT 809, EE Pub. No. 1766, Technion, Israel Institute of Technology (May 2012)
7. Tsitsiklis, J., Bertsekas, D., Athans, M.: Distributed asynchronous deterministic and stochastic gradient optimization algorithms. IEEE Transactions on Automatic Control 31(9), 803–812 (1986)
8. Nedic, A., Ozdaglar, A.: Distributed subgradient methods for multi-agent optimization. IEEE Transactions on Automatic Control 54(1), 48–61 (2009)
9. Srivastava, K., Nedic, A.: Distributed asynchronous constrained stochastic optimization. IEEE Journal of Selected Topics in Signal Processing 5(4), 772–790 (2011)
10. Ram, S., Nedic, A., Veeravalli, V.: A new class of distributed optimization algorithms: Application to regression of distributed data. Optimization Methods and Software 27(1), 71–88 (2012)
11. Nedic, A., Ozdaglar, A., Parrilo, P.: Constrained consensus and optimization in multi-agent networks. IEEE Transactions on Automatic Control 55(4), 922–938 (2010)
12. Johansson, B., Rabi, M., Johansson, M.: A randomized incremental subgradient method for distributed optimization in networked systems. SIAM Journal on Optimization 20(3), 1157–1170 (2009)
13. Ram, S., Nedic, A., Veeravalli, V.: Asynchronous gossip algorithms for stochastic optimization. In: Proceedings of the 48th IEEE Conference on Decision and Control, pp. 3581–3586 (2009)
14. Elad, M., Matalon, B., Zibulevsky, M.: Coordinate and subspace optimization methods for linear least squares with non-quadratic regularization. Applied and Computational Harmonic Analysis 23, 346–367 (2007)
15. Bradley, J.K., Kyrola, A., Bickson, D., Guestrin, C.: Parallel coordinate descent for l1-regularized loss minimization. In: Proceedings of the 28th International Conference on Machine Learning, pp. 321–328 (2011)
16. Boyd, S., Vandenberghe, L.: Convex Optimization. Cambridge University Press (2004)
17. Luenberger, D.G.: Linear and Nonlinear Programming, 2nd edn. Addison-Wesley Publishing Company, Inc. (1984)
18. Bertsekas, D.P.: Nonlinear Programming, 2nd edn. Athena Scientific (1999)
19. Tseng, P.: Convergence of a block coordinate descent method for nondifferentiable minimization. Journal of Optimization Theory and Applications 109(3), 475–494 (2001)
20. Tzeng, C., Jiang, J., Huang, S.: A self-stabilizing ($\delta+$ 4)-edge-coloring algorithm for planar graphs in anonymous uniform systems. Information Processing Letters 101(4), 168–173 (2007)

A Super-Fast Distributed Algorithm for Bipartite Metric Facility Location*

James Hegeman and Sriram V. Pemmaraju**

Department of Computer Science
The University of Iowa
Iowa City, Iowa 52242-1419, USA
{james-hegeman,sriram-pemmaraju}@uiowa.edu

Abstract. The *facility location* problem consists of a set of *facilities* $\mathcal{F}$, a set of *clients* $\mathcal{C}$, an *opening cost* f_i associated with each facility x_i, and a *connection cost* $D(x_i, y_j)$ between each facility x_i and client y_j. The goal is to find a subset of facilities to *open*, and to connect each client to an open facility, so as to minimize the total facility opening costs plus connection costs. This paper presents the first expected-sub-logarithmic-round distributed $O(1)$-approximation algorithm in the $\mathcal{CONGEST}$ model for the *metric* facility location problem on the complete bipartite network with parts $\mathcal{F}$ and $\mathcal{C}$. Our algorithm has an expected running time of $O((\log \log n)^3)$ rounds, where $n = |\mathcal{F}| + |\mathcal{C}|$. This result can be viewed as a continuation of our recent work (ICALP 2012) in which we presented the first sub-logarithmic-round distributed $O(1)$-approximation algorithm for metric facility location on a *clique* network. The bipartite setting presents several new challenges not present in the problem on a clique network. We present two new techniques to overcome these challenges.

1   Introduction

This paper continues the recently-initiated exploration [2,1,7,9,16] of the design of sub-logarithmic, or "super-fast" distributed algorithms in low-diameter, bandwidth-constrained settings. To understand the main themes of this exploration, suppose that we want to design a distributed algorithm for a problem on a low-diameter network (we have in mind a clique network or a diameter-2 network). In one sense, this is a trivial task since the entire input could be shipped off to a single node in a single round and that node can simply solve the problem locally. On the other hand, the problem could be quite challenging if we were to impose reasonable constraints on bandwidth that prevent the fast delivery of the entire input to a small number of nodes. A natural example of this phenomenon is provided by the *minimum spanning tree* (MST) problem. Consider a clique network in which each edge (u, v) has an associated weight $w(u, v)$ of which only

---

* This work is supported in part by National Science Foundation grant CCF 0915543.
** Corresponding author.

Y. Afek (Ed.): DISC 2013, LNCS 8205, pp. 522–536, 2013.

the nodes u and v are aware. The problem is for the nodes to compute an MST of the edge-weighted clique such that after the computation, each node knows all MST edges. It is important to note that the problem is defined by $\Theta(n^2)$ pieces of input and it would take $\Omega\left(\frac{n}{B}\right)$ rounds of communication for all of this information to reach a single node (where B is the number of bits that can travel across an edge in each round). Typically, $B = O(\log n)$, and this approach is clearly too slow given our goal of completing the computation in a sub-logarithmic number of rounds. Lotker et al. [9] showed that the MST problem on a clique can in fact be solved in $O(\log \log n)$ rounds in the $\mathcal{CONGEST}$ model of distributed computation, which is a synchronous, message-passing model in which each node can send a message of size $O(\log n)$ bits to each neighbor in each round. The algorithm of Lotker et al. employs a clever merging procedure that, roughly speaking, causes the sizes of the MST components to square with each iteration, leading to an $O(\log \log n)$-round computation time. The overall challenge in this area is to establish the round complexity of a variety of problems that make sense in low-diameter settings. The area is largely open with few upper bounds and no non-trivial lower bounds known. For example, it has been proved that computing an MST requires $\Omega\left((\frac{n}{\log n})^{1/4}\right)$ rounds in the $\mathcal{CONGEST}$ model for diameter-3 graphs [10], but no lower bounds are known for diameter-2 or diameter-1 (clique) networks.

The focus of this paper is the *distributed facility location* problem, which has been considered by a number of researchers [12,4,14,15,2,1] in low-diameter settings. We first describe the sequential version of the problem. The input to the facility location problem consists of a set of *facilities* $\mathcal{F} = \{x_1, x_2, \ldots, x_{n_f}\}$, a set of *clients* $\mathcal{C} = \{y_1, y_2, \ldots, y_{n_c}\}$, a (nonnegative) *opening cost* f_i associated with each facility x_i, and a (nonnegative) *connection cost* $D(x_i, y_j)$ between each facility x_i and client y_j. The goal is to find a subset $F \subseteq \mathcal{F}$ of facilities to *open* so as to minimize the total facility opening costs plus connection costs, i.e. $FacLoc(F) := \sum_{x_i \in F} f_i + \sum_{y_j \in \mathcal{C}} D(F, y_j)$, where $D(F, y_j) := \min_{x_i \in F} D(x_i, y_j)$. Facility location is an old and well-studied problem in operations research that arises in contexts such as locating hospitals in a city or locating distribution centers in a region. The *metric facility location* problem is an important special case of facility location in which the connection costs satisfy the following "triangle inequality:" for any $x_i, x_{i'} \in \mathcal{F}$ and $y_j, y_{j'} \in \mathcal{C}$, $D(x_i, y_j) + D(y_j, x_{i'}) + D(x_{i'}, y_{j'}) \geq D(x_i, y_{j'})$. The facility location problem, even in its metric version, is NP-complete and finding approximation algorithms for the problem has been a fertile area of research. There are several constant-factor approximation algorithms for metric facility location (see [8] for a recent example). This approximation factor is known to be near-optimal [5].

More recently, the facility location problem has also been used as an abstraction for the problem of locating resources in wireless networks [3,13]. Motivated by this application, several researchers have considered the facility location problem in a distributed setting. In [12,14,15], as well as in the present work, the underlying communication network is a complete bipartite graph $G = \mathcal{F} + \mathcal{C}$, with $\mathcal{F}$ and $\mathcal{C}$ forming the bipartition. At the beginning of the algorithm, each node, whether a facility or client, has knowledge of the connection costs ("distances") between itself and all nodes in the other part. In addition, the facilities know their opening costs. The problem is to design a distributed algorithm that runs on G in the $\mathcal{CONGEST}$ model and produces a subset $F \subseteq \mathcal{F}$ of facilities to *open*. To simplify exposition we assume that every cost in the problem input can be represented in $O(\log n)$ bits, thus allowing each cost to be transmitted in a single message. Each chosen facility will then open and provide services to any and all clients that wish to connect to it (each client must be served by some facility). The objective is to guarantee that $FacLoc(F) \leq \alpha \cdot OPT$, where OPT is the cost of an optimal solution to the given instance of facility location and α is a constant. We call this the BIPARTITEFACLOC problem. In this paper we present the first sub-logarithmic-round algorithm for the BIPARTITEFACLOC problem; specifically, our algorithm runs in $O((\log \log n_f)^2 \cdot \log \log \min\{n_f, n_c\})$ rounds in expectation, where $n_f = |\mathcal{F}|$ and $n_c = |\mathcal{C}|$. All previous distributed approximation algorithms for BIPARTITEFACLOC require a logarithmic number of rounds to achieve near-optimal approximation factors.

1.1   Overview of Technical Contributions

In a recent paper (ICALP 2012, [2]; full version available as [1]), we presented an expected-$O(\log \log n)$-round algorithm in the $\mathcal{CONGEST}$ model for CLIQUEFACLOC, the "clique version" of BIPARTITEFACLOC. The underlying communication network for this version of the problem is a clique with each edge (u, v) having an associated (connection) cost $c(u, v)$ of which only nodes u and v are aware (initially). Each node u also has an opening cost f_u, and may choose to open as a facility; nodes that do not open must connect to an open facility. The cost of the solution is defined as before – as the sum of the facility opening costs and the costs of established connections. Under the assumption that the connection costs form a metric, our algorithm for CLIQUEFACLOC yields an $O(1)$-approximation. We had hoped that a "super-fast" algorithm for BIPARTITEFACLOC would be obtained in a straightforward manner by extending our CLIQUEFACLOC algorithm. However, it turns out that moving from a clique communication network to a complete bipartite communication network raises several new and significant challenges related to information dissemination and a lack of adequate knowledge. Below we outline these challenges and our solutions to them.

Overview of Solution to CliqueFacLoc. To solve CLIQUEFACLOC on an edge-weighted clique G [2,1] we reduce it to the problem of computing a 2-ruling set in an appropriately-defined spanning subgraph of G. A *β-ruling set* of a graph is an independent set S such that every node in the graph is at most β hops away from some node in S; a *maximal independent set* (MIS) is simply a 1-ruling set. The spanning subgraph H on which we compute a 2-ruling set is induced by clique edges whose costs are no greater than a pre-computed quantity which depends on the two endpoints of the edge in question.

We solve the 2-ruling set problem on the spanning subgraph H via a combination of deterministic and randomized sparsification. Briefly, each node selects itself with a uniform probability p chosen such that the subgraph H' of H induced by the selected nodes has $\Theta(n)$ edges in expectation. The probability p is a function of n and the number of edges in H. We next deliver all of H' to every node. It can be shown that a graph with $O(n)$ edges can be completely delivered to every node in $O(1)$ rounds on a clique and since H' has $O(n)$ edges in expectation, the delivery of H' takes expected-$O(1)$ rounds. Once H' has been disseminated in this manner, each node uses the same (deterministic) rule to locally compute an MIS of H'. Following the computation of an MIS of H', nodes in the MIS and nodes in their 2-neighborhood are all deleted from H and H shrinks in size. Since H is now smaller, a larger probability p can be used for the next iteration. This increasing sequence of values for p results in a doubly-exponential rate of progress, which leads to an expected-$O(\log \log n)$-round algorithm for computing a 2-ruling set of H. See [1] for more details.

Challenges for BipartiteFacLoc. The same algorithmic framework can be applied to BIPARTITEFACLOC; however, challenges arise in trying to implement the ruling-set computation on a bipartite communication network. As in CLIQ-UEFACLOC [1], we define a particular graph H on the set of facilities with edges connecting pairs of facilities whose connection cost is bounded above. Note that there is no explicit notion of connection cost between facilities, but we use a natural extension of the facility-client connection costs $D(\cdot, \cdot)$ and define for each $x_i, x_j \in \mathcal{F}$, $D(x_i, x_j) := \min_{y \in C} D(x_i, y) + D(x_j, y)$. The main algorithmic step now is to compute a 2-ruling set on the graph H. However, difficulties arise because H is not a subgraph of the communication network G, as it was in the CLIQUEFACLOC setting. In fact, initially a facility x_i does not even know to which other facilities it is adjacent in H. This adjacency knowledge is collectively available only to the clients. A client y *witnesses* edge $\{x_i, x_j\}$ in H if $D(x_i, y) + D(x_j, y)$ is bounded above by a pre-computed quantity associated with the facility-pair x_i, x_j. However, (initially) an individual client y cannot certify the *non-existence* of any potential edge between two facilities in H; as, unbeknownst to y, some other client may be a witness to that edge. Furthermore, the same edge $\{x_i, x_j\}$ could have many client-witnesses. This "affirmative-only" adjacency knowledge and the duplication of this knowledge turn out to be key obstacles to overcome. For example, in this setting, it seems difficult to even figure out how many edges H has.

Thus, an example of a problem we need to solve is this: without knowing the number of edges in H, how do we correctly pick a probability p that will induce a random subgraph H' with $\Theta(n)$ edges? Duplication of knowledge of H leads to another problem as well. Suppose we did manage to pick a "correct" value of p and have induced a subgraph H' having $\Theta(n)$ edges. In the solution to CLIQUEFACLOC, we were able to deliver all of H' to a single node (in fact, to every node). In the bipartite setting, how do we deliver H' to a single node given that even though it has $O(n)$ edges, information duplication can cause the sum of the number of adjacencies witnessed by the clients to be as high as $\Omega(n^2)$?

We introduce new techniques to solve each of these problems. These techniques are sketched below.

– **Message dissemination with duplicates.** We model the problem of delivering all of H' to a single node as the following message-dissemination problem on a complete bipartite graph.

> **Message Dissemination with Duplicates (MDD).**
> Given a bipartite graph $G = \mathcal{F} + \mathcal{C}$, with $n_f := |\mathcal{F}|$ and $n_c := |\mathcal{C}|$, suppose that there are n_f messages that we wish to be known to all client nodes in $\mathcal{C}$. Initially, each client possesses some subset of the n_f messages, with each message being possessed by at least one client. Suppose, though, that no client y_j has any information about which of its messages are also held by any other client. Disseminate all n_f messages to each client in the network in expected-sub-logarithmic time.

We solve this problem by presenting an algorithm that utilizes probabilistic hashing to iteratively reduce the number of duplicate copies of each message. Note that if no message exists in duplicate, then the total number of messages held is only n_f, and each can be sent to a distinct facility which can then broadcast it to every client. The challenge, then, lies in coordinating bandwidth usage so as to avoid "bottlenecks" that could be caused by message duplication. Our algorithm for MDD runs in $O(\log \log \min\{n_f, n_c\})$ rounds in expectation.

– **Random walk over a probability space.** Given the difficulty of quickly acquiring even basic information about H (e.g., how many edges does it have?), we have no way of setting the value of p correctly. So we design an algorithm that performs a random walk over a space of $O(\log \log n_f)$ probabilities. The algorithm picks a probability p, uses this to induce a random subgraph H' of H, and attempts to disseminate H' to all clients within $O(\log \log \min\{n_f, n_c\})$ rounds. If this dissemination succeeds, p is modified in one way (increased appropriately), otherwise p is modified differently (decreased appropriately). This technique can be modeled as a random walk on a probability space consisting of $O(\log \log n_f)$ elements, where the elements are distinct values that p can take. We show that after a random walk of length at most $O(\log \log n_f)$, sufficiently many edges of H are removed, leading to $O(\log \log n_f)$ levels of progress. Thus we have a total of $O((\log \log n_f)^2)$ steps and since in each step an instance of MDD is solved for disseminating adjacencies, we obtain an expected-$O((\log \log n_f)^2 \cdot \log \log \min\{n_f, n_c\})$-round algorithm for computing a 2-ruling set of H.

To summarize, our paper makes three main technical contributions. (i) We show (in Section 2) that the framework developed in [1] to solve CLIQUEFACLOC can be used, with appropriate modifications, to solve BIPARTITEFACLOC. Via this algorithmic framework, we reduce BIPARTITEFACLOC to the problem of computing a 2-ruling set of a graph induced by facilities in a certain way. (ii) In order to compute a 2-ruling set of a graph, we need to disseminate graph adjacencies whose knowledge is distributed among the clients with possible duplication.

We model this as a message dissemination problem and show (in Section 3), using a probabilistic hashing scheme, how to efficiently solve this problem on a complete bipartite graph. (iii) Finally, we present (in Section 4) an algorithm that performs a random walk over a probability space to efficiently compute a 2-ruling set of a graph, without even basic information about the graph. This algorithm repeatedly utilizes the procedure for solving the message-dissemination problem mentioned above.

Note: This paper does not contain any proofs, due to space restrictions. All proofs appear in the archived full version of the paper [6].

2 Reduction to the Ruling Set Problem

In this section we reduce BIPARTITEFACLOC to the ruling set problem on a certain graph induced by facilities. The reduction is achieved via the distributed facility location algorithm called LOCATEFACILITIES and shown as Algorithm 1. This algorithm is complete except that it calls a subroutine, RULINGSET(H, s) (in Step 4), to compute an s-ruling set of a certain graph H induced by facilities. In this section we first describe Algorithm 1 and then present its analysis. It is easily observed that all the steps in Algorithm 1, except the one that calls RULINGSET(H, s) take a total of $O(1)$ communication rounds. Thus the running time of RULINGSET(H, s) essentially determines the running time of Algorithm 1. Furthermore, we show that if F^* is the subset of facilities opened by Algorithm 1, then $FacLoc(F^*) = O(s) \cdot OPT$. In the remaining sections of the paper we show how to implement RULINGSET$(H, 2)$ in expected $O((\log \log n_f)^2 \cdot \log \log \min\{n_f, n_c\})$ rounds. This yields an expected $O((\log \log n_f)^2 \cdot \log \log \min\{n_f, n_c\})$-round, $O(1)$-approximation algorithm for BIPARTITEFACLOC.

2.1 Algorithm

Given $\mathcal{F}$, $\mathcal{C}$, $D(\cdot, \cdot)$, and $\{f_i\}$, define the *characteristic radius* r_i of facility x_i to be the nonnegative real number satisfying $\sum_{y \in B(x_i, r_i)}(r_i - D(x_i, y)) = f_i$, where $B(x, r)$ (the *ball* of radius r) denotes the set of clients y such that $D(x, y) \leq r$. This notion of a characteristic radius was first introduced by Mettu and Plaxton [11], who use it to drive their sequential, greedy algorithm. We extend the client-facility distance function $D(\cdot, \cdot)$ to facility-facility distances; let $D : \mathcal{F} \times \mathcal{F} \to \mathbb{R}^+ \cup \{0\}$ be defined by $D(x_i, x_j) = \min_{y_k \in \mathcal{C}}\{D(x_i, y_k) + D(x_j, y_k)\}$. With these definitions in place we are ready to describe Algorithm 1. The algorithm consists of three stages, which we now describe.

Stage 1. (Steps 1-2) Each facility knows its own opening cost and the distances to all clients. So in Step 1 facility x_i computes r_i and broadcasts that value to all clients. Once this broadcast is complete, each client knows all of the r_i values. This enables every client to compute the same partition of the facilities into classes as follows (Step 2). Define the special value $r_0 := \min_{1 \leq i \leq n_f}\{r_i\}$. Define the class V_k, for $k = 0, 1, \ldots$, to be the set of facilities x_i such that

---

Algorithm 1. LOCATEFACILITIES

Input: A complete bipartite graph G with partition $(\mathcal{F},\mathcal{C})$; (bipartite) metric $D(\cdot,\cdot)$; opening costs $\{f_i\}_{i=1}^{n_f}$; a sparsity parameter $s \in \mathbb{Z}^+$

Assumption: Each facility knows its own opening cost and its distances to all clients; each client knows its distances to all facilities

Output: A subset of facilities (a *configuration*) to be declared open.

1. Each facility x_i computes and broadcasts its radius r_i to all clients; $r_0 := \min_i r_i$.
2. Each client computes a partition of the facilities into classes $\{V_k\}$ such that
   $$3^k \cdot r_0 \le r_i < 3^{k+1} \cdot r_0 \text{ for } x_i \in V_k.$$
3. For $k = 0, 1, \ldots$, define a graph H_k with vertex set V_k and edge set:
   $$\{\{x_i, x_{i'}\} \mid x_i, x_{i'} \in V_k \text{ and } D(x_i, x_{i'}) \le r_i + r_{i'}\}$$
   (Observe from the definition of facility distance that such edges may be known to as few as one client, or as many as all of them.)
4. All nodes in the network use procedure RULINGSET($\cup_k H_k$, s) to compute a 2-ruling set T of $\cup_k H_k$. T is known to every client. We use T_k to denote $T \cap V_k$.
5. Each client y_j sends an **open** message to each facility x_i, if and only if both of the following conditions hold:
   (i) x_i is a member of the set $T_k \subseteq V_k$, for some k.
   (ii) y_j is not a witness to the existence of a facility $x_{i'}$ belonging to a class $V_{k'}$, with $k' < k$, such that $D(x_i, x_{i'}) \le 2r_i$.
6. Each facility x_i opens, and broadcasts its status as such, if and only if x_i received an **open** message from every client.
7. Each client connects to the nearest open facility.

$3^k \cdot r_0 \le r_i < 3^{k+1} \cdot r_0$. Every client computes the class into which each facility in the network falls.

Stage 2. (Steps 3-4) Now that the facilities are divided into classes having comparable r_i's, and every client knows which facility is in each class, we focus our attention on class V_k. Suppose $x_i, x_{i'} \in V_k$. Then we define x_i and $x_{i'}$ to be *adjacent* in class V_k if $D(x_i, x_{i'}) \le r_i + r_{i'}$ (Step 3). These adjacencies define the graph H_k with vertex set V_k. Note that two facilities $x_i, x_{i'}$ in class V_k are adjacent if and only if there is at least one client *witness* for this adjacency. Next, the network computes an s-ruling set T of $\cup_k H_k$ with procedure RULINGSET() (Step 4). We describe a super-fast implementation of RULINGSET() in Section 4. After a ruling set T has been constructed, every client knows all the members of T. Since the H_k's are disjoint, $T_k := T \cap V_k$ is a 2-ruling set of H_k for each k.

Stage 3. (Steps 5-7) Finally, a client y_j sends an **open** message to facility x_i in class V_k if (i) $x_i \in T_k$, and (ii) there is no facility $x_{i'}$ of class $V_{k'}$ such that $D(x_i, y_j) + D(x_{i'}, y_j) \le 2r_i$, and for which $k' < k$ (Step 5). A facility opens if it receives **open** messages from all clients (Step 6). Lastly, open facilities declare themselves as such in a broadcast, and every client connects to the nearest open facility (Step 7).

2.2 Analysis

The approximation-factor analysis of Algorithm 1 is similar to the analysis of our algorithm for CLIQUEFACLOC [1]. Here we present a brief summary.

First we show a lower bound on the cost *any* solution to BIPARTITEFACLOC. For $y_j \in C$, define $\bar{r}_j$ as $\bar{r}_j = \min_{1 \leq i \leq n_f} \{r_i + D(x_i, y_j)\}$. See [1] for a motivation for this definition.

Lemma 1. $FacLoc(F) \geq (\sum_{j=1}^{n_c} \bar{r}_j)/6$ *for any subset* $F \subseteq \mathcal{F}$.

To obtain an upper bound on the cost of the solution produced by Algorithm 1 we start by "charging" the cost of a facility location solution to clients in a standard way [11]. For a client $y_j \in C$ and a facility subset F, define the *charge* of y_j with respect to F by $charge(y_j, F) = D(F, y_j) + \sum_{x_i \in F} \max\{0, r_i - D(x_i, y_j)\}$.

Simple algebraic manipulation can be used to show that for any facility subset F, $FacLoc(F)$ is equal to $\sum_{j=1}^{n_c} charge(y_j, F)$. Finally, if F^* is the subset of facilities selected by Algorithm 1, we show the following upper bounds.

Lemma 2. $D(F^*, y_j) \leq (s+1) \cdot 15 \cdot \bar{r}_j$.

Lemma 3. $\sum_{x_i \in F^*} \max\{0, r_i - D(x_i, y_j)\} \leq 3 \cdot \bar{r}_j$.

Putting the lower bound, charging scheme, and upper bound together gives $FacLoc(F^*) \leq (15s + 33) \cdot \sum_{j=1}^{n_c} \bar{r}_j \leq 6 \cdot (15s + 33) \cdot OPT$. Also, noting that all the steps in Algorithm 1, except the one that calls RULINGSET$(\cup_k H_k, s)$ take a total of $O(1)$ communication rounds, we obtain the following theorem.

Theorem 1. *Algorithm 1 (*LOCATEFACILITIES*) computes an $O(s)$-factor approximation to* BIPARTITEFACLOC *in* $O(\mathcal{T}(n, s))$ *rounds, where* $\mathcal{T}(n, s)$ *is the running time of procedure* RULINGSET(H, s), *called an n-node graph H.*

3 Dissemination on a Bipartite Network

In the previous section we reduced BIPARTITEFACLOC to the problem of computing an s-ruling set on a graph $H = \cup_k H_k$ defined on facilities. Our technique for finding an s-ruling set involves selecting a set M of facilities at random, disseminating the induced subgraph $H[M]$ to every client and then having each client locally compute an MIS of $H[M]$ (details appear in Section 4). A key subroutine needed to implement this technique is one that can disseminate $H[M]$ to every client efficiently, provided the number of edges in $H[M]$ is at most n_f. In Section 1 we abstracted this problem as the **Message Dissemination with Duplicates** (MDD) problem. In this section, we present a randomized algorithm for MDD that runs in expected $O(\log \log \min\{n_f, n_c\})$ communication rounds.

Recall that the difficulty in disseminating $H[M]$ is the fact that the adjacencies in this graph are witnessed only by clients, with each adjacency being witnessed by at least one client. However, an adjacency can be witnessed by many clients and a client is unaware of who else has knowledge of any particular edge. Thus, even if $H[M]$ has at most n_f edges, the total number of adjacency observations by the clients could be as large as n_f^2. Below we use iterative probabilistic hashing to rapidly reduce the number of "duplicate" witnesses to adjacencies in $H[M]$. Once the total number of distinct adjacency observations falls to $48n_f$, it takes only a constant number of additional communication rounds for the algorithm to finish disseminating $H[M]$. The constant "48" falls out easily from our analysis (Lemma 7, in particular) and we have made no attempt to optimize it in any way.

3.1   Algorithm

The algorithm proceeds in iterations and in each iteration a hash function is chosen at random for hashing messages held by clients onto facilities. Denote the universe of possible adjacency messages by $\mathcal{U}$. Since messages represent adjacencies among facilities, $|\mathcal{U}| = \binom{n_f}{2}$. However, it is convenient for $|\mathcal{U}|$ to be equal to n_f^2 and so we extend $\mathcal{U}$ by dummy messages so that this is the case. We now define a family $\mathcal{H}_{\mathcal{U}}$ of hash functions from $\mathcal{U}$ to $\{1, 2, \ldots, n_f\}$ and show how to pick a function from this family, uniformly at random. To define $\mathcal{H}_{\mathcal{U}}$, fix an ordering $m_1, m_2, m_3, \ldots$ of the messages of $\mathcal{U}$. Partition $\mathcal{U}$ into groups of size n_f, with messages $m_1, m_2, \ldots, m_{n_f}$ as the first group, the next n_f elements as the second group, and so on. The family $\mathcal{H}_{\mathcal{U}}$ is obtained by independently mapping each group of messages onto $(1, 2, \ldots, n_f)$ via a cyclic permutation. For each group of n_f messages in $\mathcal{U}$, there are precisely n_f such cyclic maps for it, and so a map in $\mathcal{H}_{\mathcal{U}}$ can be selected uniformly at random by having each facility choose a random integer in $\{1, 2, \ldots, n_f\}$ and broadcast this choice to all clients (in the first round of an iteration). Each client then interprets the integer received from facility x_i as the image of message $m_{(i-1) \cdot n_f + 1}$.

In round 2, each client chooses a destination facility for each adjacency message in its possession (note that no client possesses more than n_f messages), based on the hash function chosen in round 1. For a message m in the possession of client y_j, y_j computes the hash $h(m)$ and marks m for delivery to facility $x_{h(m)}$. In the event that more than one of y_j's messages are intended for the same recipient, y_j chooses one uniformly at random for *correct* delivery, and marks the other such messages as "leftovers." During the communication phase of round 2, then, client y_j delivers as many messages as possible to their correct destinations; leftover messages are delivered uniformly at random over unused communication links to other facilities.

In round 3, a facility has received a collection of up to n_c messages, some of which may be duplicates of each other. After throwing away all but one copy of any duplicates received, each facility announces to client y_1 the number of (distinct) messages it has remaining. In round 4, client y_1 has received from each facility its number of distinct messages, and computes for each an index (modulo n_c) that allows facilities to coordinate their message transfers in the next round. Client y_1 transmits the indices back to the respective facilities in round 5.

In round 6, facilities transfer their messages back across the bipartition to the clients, beginning at their determined index (received from client y_1) and working modulo n_c. This guarantees that the numbers of messages received by two clients y_j, $y_{j'}$ in this round can differ by no more than one. (Although it is possible that some of these messages will "collapse" as duplicates.) Clients now possess subsets of the original n_f messages, and the next iteration can begin.

Algorithm 2. DISSEMINATEADJACENCIES

Input: A complete bipartite graph G, with partition $(\mathcal{F}, \mathcal{C})$; an overlay network H on $\mathcal{F}$ with $|E[H]| \leq n_f$
Assumption: For each adjacency e' in H, *one or more* clients has knowledge of e'
Output: Each client should know the entire contents of $E[H]$

1. **while** *true* **do**
    Start of Iteration:
2. Each client y_j sends the number of distinct messages currently held, n_j, to facility x_1.
3. **if** $\sum_{j=1}^{n_c} n_j \leq 48 n_f$ **then**
4.   Facility x_1 broadcasts a *break* message to each client.
5.   Client y_1, upon receiving a *break* message, broadcasts a *break* message to each facility.
    end-if-then
6. Each facility x_i broadcasts an integer in $\{1, \ldots, n_f\}$ chosen uniformly at random; this collection of broadcasts determines a map $h \in \mathcal{H}_\mathcal{U}$.
7. For each adjacency message m' currently held, client y_j maps m' to $x_{h(m')}$.
8. For each $i \in \{1, \ldots, n_f\}$, if $|\{m' \text{ held by } y_j : h(m') = i\}| > 1$, client y_j chooses one message to send to x_i at random from this set and marks the others as *leftovers*.
9. Each client y_j sends the messages chosen in Lines 7-8 to their destinations; *leftover* messages are delivered to other facilities (for whom y_j has no intended message) in an arbitrary manner (such that y_j sends at most one message to each facility).
10. Each facility x_i receives a collection of at most n_c facility adjacency messages; if duplicate messages are received, x_i discards all but one of them so that the messages held by x_i are distinct.
11. Each facility x_i sends its number of distinct messages currently held, b_i, to client y_1.
12. Client y_1 responds to each facility x_i with an index $c(i) = (\sum_{k=1}^{i-1} b_k \mod n_c)$.
13. Each facility x_i distributes its current messages evenly to the clients in the set $\{y_{c(i)+1}, y_{c(i)+2}, \ldots, y_{c(i)+b_i}\}$ (where indexes are reduced modulo n_c as necessary).
14. Each client y_j receives at most n_f messages; the numbers of messages received by any two clients differ by at most one.
15. Each client discards any duplicate messages held.
    End of Iteration:
16. At this point, at most $48 n_f$ total messages remain among the n_c clients; these messages may be distributed evenly to the facilities in $O(1)$ communication rounds.
17. The n_f facilities can now broadcast the (at most) $2n_f$ messages to all clients in $O(1)$ rounds.

3.2   Analysis

Algorithm 2 is proved correct by observing that (i) the algorithm terminates only when dissemination has been completed; and (ii) for a particular message m', in any iteration, there is a nonzero probability that all clients holding a copy of m' will deliver m' correctly, after which there will never be more than one copy of m' (until all messages are broadcast to all clients at the end of the algorithm). The running time analysis of Algorithm 2 starts with two lemmas that follow from our choice of the probabilistic hash function.

Lemma 4. *Suppose that, at the beginning of an iteration, client y_j possesses a collection S_j of messages, with $|S_j| = n_j$. Let $E_{i,j}$ be the event that at least one* *message in S_j hashes to facility x_i. Then the probability of $E_{i,j}$ (conditioned on all previous iterations) is bounded below by $1 - e^{-n_j/n_f}$.*

Lemma 5. *Suppose that, at the beginning of an iteration, client y_j possesses a collection S_j of messages, with $|S_j| = n_j$. Let $M_j \subseteq S_j$ be the subset of messages that are correctly delivered by client y_j in the present iteration. Then the expected value of $|M_j|$ (conditioned on previous iterations) is bounded below by $n_j - \frac{n_j^2}{2n_f}$.*

By Lemma 5, the number of incorrectly delivered messages in S_j is bounded above (in expectation) by $\frac{n_j^2}{2n_f}$. Informally speaking, this implies that the sequence $n_f, \frac{n_f}{2}, \frac{n_f}{2^3}, \frac{n_f}{2^7}, \ldots$ bounds from above the number of incorrectly delivered messages (in expectation) in each iteration. This doubly-exponential rate of decrease in the number of undelivered messages leads to the expected-doubly-logarithmic running time of the algorithm.

We now step out of the context of a single client and consider the progress of the algorithm on the whole. Using Lemma 5, we derive the following recurrence for the expected total number of messages held by all clients at the beginning of each iteration.

Lemma 6. *Suppose that the algorithm is at the beginning of iteration I, $I \geq 2$, and let T_I be the total number of messages held by all clients (i.e. $T_I = \sum_{j=1}^{n_c} n_j(I)$, where $n_j(I)$ is the number of messages held by client y_j at the beginning of iteration I). Then the conditional expectation of T_{I+1} given T_I, $\mathbf{E}(T_{I+1} \mid T_I)$, satisfies*

$$\mathbf{E}(T_{I+1} \mid T_I) \leq \begin{cases} n_f + \frac{(T_I + n_c)^2}{2n_f \cdot n_c} & \text{if } T_I > n_c \\ n_f + \frac{T_I}{2n_f} & \text{if } T_I \leq n_c \end{cases}$$

We now define a sequence of variables t_i (via the recurrence below) that bounds from above the expected behavior of the sequence of T_I's established in the previous lemma. Let $t_1 = n_f \cdot \min\{n_f, n_c\}$, $t_i = \frac{1}{2}t_{i-1}$ for $2 \leq i \leq 5$, and for $i > 5$, define t_i by

$$t_i = \begin{cases} 2n_f + \frac{(t_{i-1} + n_c)^2}{n_f \cdot n_c} & \text{if } t_{i-1} > n_c \\ 2n_f + \frac{t_{i-1}}{n_f} & \text{if } t_{i-1} \leq n_c \end{cases}$$

The following lemma establishes that the t_i's fall rapidly.

Lemma 7. *The smallest index i for which $t_i \leq 48n_f$ is at most $\log\log \min\{n_f, n_c\} + 2$.*

Lemma 8. *For $i > 5$, if $T_I \leq t_i$, then the conditional probability (given iterations 1 through $I - 1$) of the event that $T_{I+1} \leq t_{i+1}$ is bounded below by $\frac{1}{2}$.*

Theorem 2. *Algorithm 2 solves the dissemination problem in $O(\log\log \min \{n_f, n_c\})$ rounds in expectation.*

4   Computing a 2-Ruling Set of Facilities

In this section, we show how to efficiently compute a 2-ruling set on the graph H (with vertex set $\mathcal{F}$) constructed in Algorithm 1 (LOCATEFACILITIES). Our algorithm (called FACILITY2RULINGSET and described as Algorithm 3) computes a 2-ruling set in H by performing *iterations* of a procedure that combines randomized and deterministic sparsification steps. In each iteration, each facility chooses (independently) to join the *candidate set* M with probability p. Two neighbors in H may both have chosen to join M, so M may not be independent in H. We would therefore like to select an MIS of the graph induced by M, $H[M]$. In order to do this, the algorithm attempts to communicate all known adjacencies in $H[M]$ to every client in the network, so that each client may (deterministically) compute the same MIS. The algorithm relies on Algorithm DISSEMINATEADJACENCIES (Algorithm 2) developed in Section 3 to perform this communication.

Algorithm 3. FACILITY2RULINGSET

Input: Complete bipartite graph G with partition $(\mathcal{F}, \mathcal{C})$ and H, an overlay network on $\mathcal{F}$.
Output: A 2-ruling set T of H

1. $i := 1;\ p := p_1 = \frac{1}{8 \cdot n_f^{1/2}};\ T := \emptyset$
2.   **while** $|E(H)| > 0$ **do**
     Start of Iteration:
3. $M := \emptyset$
4.   Each facility x joins M with a probability p.
5.   Run Algorithm DISSEMINATEADJACENCIES for $7 \log \log \min\{n_f, n_c\}$ iterations
        to communicate the edges in $H[M]$ to all clients in the network.
6.   **if** DISSEMINATEADJACENCIES completes in the allotted number of iterations **then**
7.   Each client computes the same MIS L on M using a deterministic algorithm.
8. $T := T \cup L$
9.   Remove $M \cup N(M)$ from H.
10. $i := i + 1;\ p := p_i = \frac{1}{8 \cdot n_f^{2^{-i}}}$
11.   **else**
12. $i := i - 1;\ p := p_i = \frac{1}{8 \cdot n_f^{2^{-i}}}$
13.   **if** $|E(H)| = 0$ **then break**;
        End of Iteration:
14. Output T.

For Algorithm DISSEMINATEADJACENCIES to terminate quickly, we require that the number of edges in $H[M]$ be $O(n_f)$. This requires the probability p to be chosen carefully as a function of n_f and the number of edges in H. Due to the lack of aggregated information, nodes of the network do not generally know the number of edges in H and thus the choice of p may be "incorrect" in certain iterations. To deal with the possibility that p may be too large (and hence $H[M]$ may have too many edges), the dissemination procedure is not allowed to run indefinitely – rather, it is cut off after $7 \log \log \min\{n_f, n_c\}$ iterations of disseminating hashing. If dissemination was successful, i.e. the subroutine completed prior to the cutoff, then each client receives complete information about the adjacencies in $H[M]$, and thus each is able to compute the same MIS in $H[M]$. Also, if dissemination was successful, then M and its neighborhood, $N(M)$, are removed from H and the next iteration is run with a larger probability p. On the other hand, if dissemination was unsuccessful, the current iteration of FACILITY2RULINGSET is terminated and the next iteration is run with a smaller probability p (to make success more likely the next time).

To analyze the progress of the algorithm, we define two notions – *states* and *levels*. For the remainder of this section, we use the term *state* (of the algorithm) to refer to the current probability value p. The probability p can take on values $\left(\frac{1}{8 \cdot n_f^{2^{-i}}}\right)$ for $i = 0, 1, \ldots, \Theta(\log \log n_f)$. We use the term *level* to refer to the progress made up until the current iteration. Specifically, the jth level L_j, for $j = 0, 1, \ldots, \Theta(\log \log n_f)$, is defined as having been reached when the number of facility adjacencies remaining in H becomes less than or equal to $l_j = 8 \cdot n_f^{1+2^{-j}}$. In addition, we define one special level L_* as the level in which no facility adjacencies remain. These values for the states and levels are chosen so that, once level L_i has been reached, one iteration run in state $i+1$ has at least a probability-$\frac{1}{2}$ chance of advancing progress to level L_{i+1}.

4.1   Analysis

It is easy to verify that the set T computed by Algorithm 3 (FACILITY2RULINGSET) is a 2-ruling set and we now turn our attention to the expected running time of this algorithm. The algorithm halts exactly when level L_* is reached (this termination condition is detected in Line 15), and so it suffices to bound the expected number of rounds necessary for progress (removal of edges from H) to reach level L_*. The following lemmas show that quick progress is made when the probability p matches the level of progress made thus far.

Lemma 9. *Suppose $|E(H)| \leq l_i$ (progress has reached level L_i) and in this situation one iteration is run in state $i+1$ (with $p = p_{i+1}$). Then in this iteration, the probability that Algorithm DISSEMINATEADJACENCIES succeeds is at least $\frac{3}{4}$.*

Lemma 10. *Suppose $|E(H)| \leq l_i$ (progress has reached level L_i). Then, after one iteration run in state $i+1$ (with $p = p_{i+1}$), the probability that level L_{i+1} will be reached (where $|E(H)| \leq l_{i+1}$) is at least $\frac{1}{2}$.*

Thus, once level L_i has been reached, we can expect that only a constant number of iterations run in state $i+1$ would be required to reach level L_{i+1}. Therefore, the question is, "How many iterations of the algorithm are required to execute state $i+1$ enough times?" To answer this question, we abstract the algorithm as a stochastic process that can be modeled as a (non-Markov) simple random walk on the integers $0, 1, 2, \ldots, \Theta(\log \log n_f)$ with the extra property that, whenever the random walk arrives at state $i+1$, a (fair) coin is flipped. We place a bound on the expected number of steps before this coin toss comes up heads.

First, consider the return time to state $i + 1$. In order to prove that the expected number of iterations (steps) necessary before either $|E(H)| \leq l_{i+1}$ or $p = p_{i+1}$ is $O(\log \log n_f)$, we consider two regimes – $p > p_{i+1}$ and $p < p_{i+1}$. When p is large (in the regime consisting of probability states intended for fewer edges than currently remain in H), it is likely that a single iteration of Algorithm 3 will generate a large number of adjacencies between candidate facilities. Thus, dissemination will likely not complete before "timing out," and it is likely that p will be decreased prior to the next iteration. Conversely, when p is small (in the regime consisting of probability states intended for more edges than currently remain in H), a single iteration of Algorithm 3 will likely generate fewer than n_f adjacencies between candidate facilities, and thus it is likely that dissemination will complete before "timing out." In this case, p will advance prior to the next iteration. This analysis is accomplished in the following lemmas and leads to the subsequent theorem.

Lemma 11. *Consider a simple random walk on the integers $[0, i]$ with transition probabilities $\{p_{j,k}\}$ satisfying $p_{j,j+1} = \frac{3}{4}$ $(j = 0, \ldots, i-1)$, $p_{j,j-1} = \frac{1}{4}$, $(j = 1, \ldots, i)$, $p_{i,i} = \frac{3}{4}$, and $p_{0,0} = \frac{1}{4}$. For such a random walk beginning at 0, the expected hitting time of i is $O(i)$.*

Lemma 12. *When $j \leq i$, the expected number of iterations required before returning to state $i + 1$ is $O(\log \log n_f)$.*

Lemma 13. *When $j > i$, the expected number of iterations required before returning to state $i + 1$ or advancing to at least level L_{i+1} is $O(\log \log n_f)$.*

Lemma 14. *Suppose that Algorithm 3 has reached level L_i, and let T_{i+1} be a random variable representing the number of iterations necessary before reaching level L_{i+1}. Then $\mathbf{E}(T_{i+1}) = O(\log \log n_f)$.*

Theorem 3. *Algorithm 3 has an expected running time of $O((\log \log n_f)^2 \cdot \log \log \min\{n_f, n_c\})$ rounds in the $\mathcal{CONGEST}$ model.*

References

1. Berns, A., Hegeman, J., Pemmaraju, S.V.: Super-fast distributed algorithms for metric facility location. CoRR (archived on August 11, 2013), http://arxiv.org/abs/1308.2473
2. Berns, A., Hegeman, J., Pemmaraju, S.V.: Super-fast distributed algorithms for metric facility location. In: Czumaj, A., Mehlhorn, K., Pitts, A., Wattenhofer, R. (eds.) ICALP 2012, Part II. LNCS, vol. 7392, pp. 428–439. Springer, Heidelberg (2012)
3. Frank, C.: Algorithms for Sensor and Ad Hoc Networks. Springer (2007)
4. Gehweiler, J., Lammersen, C., Sohler, C.: A distributed $O(1)$-approximation algorithm for the uniform facility location problem. In: Proceedings of the Eighteenth Annual ACM Symposium on Parallelism in Algorithms and Architectures, SPAA 2006, pp. 237–243. ACM Press, New York (2006)

5. Guha, S., Khuller, S.: Greedy strikes back: Improved facility location algorithms. In: Proceedings of the Ninth Annual ACM-SIAM Symposium on Discrete Algorithms, pp. 649–657. Society for Industrial and Applied Mathematics (1998)
6. Hegeman, J., Pemmaraju, S.V.: A super-fast distributed algorithm for bipartite metric facility location. CoRR (archived on August 12, 2013), http://arxiv.org/abs/1308.2694
7. Lenzen, C.: Optimal deterministic routing and sorting on the congested clique. CoRR, abs/1207.1852 (2012)
8. Li, S.: A 1.488 approximation algorithm for the uncapacitated facility location problem. In: Aceto, L., Henzinger, M., Sgall, J. (eds.) ICALP 2011, Part II. LNCS, vol. 6756, pp. 77–88. Springer, Heidelberg (2011)
9. Lotker, Z., Patt-Shamir, B., Pavlov, E., Peleg, D.: Minimum-weight spanning tree construction in O(log log n) communication rounds. SIAM J. Comput. 35(1), 120–131 (2005)
10. Lotker, Z., Patt-Shamir, B., Peleg, D.: Distributed mst for constant diameter graphs. Distributed Computing 18(6), 453–460 (2006)
11. Mettu, R.R., Plaxton, C.G.: The online median problem. SIAM J. Comput. 32(3), 816–832 (2003)
12. Moscibroda, T., Wattenhofer, R.: Facility location: distributed approximation. In: Proceedings of the Twenty-Fourth Annual ACM Symposium on Principles of Distributed Computing, pp. 108–117. ACM Press, New York (2005)
13. Pandit, S., Pemmaraju, S.V.: Finding facilities fast. Distributed Computing and Networking, 11–24 (2009)
14. Pandit, S., Pemmaraju, S.V.: Return of the primal-dual: distributed metric facility location. In: Proceedings of the 28th ACM Symposium on Principles of Distributed Computing, PODC 2009, pp. 180–189. ACM Press, New York (2009)
15. Pandit, S., Pemmaraju, S.V.: Rapid randomized pruning for fast greedy distributed algorithms. In: Proceedings of the 29th ACM SIGACT-SIGOPS Symposium on Principles of Distributed Computing, pp. 325–334. ACM (2010)
16. Patt-Shamir, B., Teplitsky, M.: The round complexity of distributed sorting: extended abstract. In: PODC, pp. 249–256. ACM Press (2011)

CONE-DHT: A Distributed Self-Stabilizing Algorithm for a Heterogeneous Storage System[*,**]

Sebastian Kniesburges, Andreas Koutsopoulos, and Christian Scheideler

Department of Computer Science, University of Paderborn, Germany
seppel@upb.de, {koutsopo,scheideler}@mail.upb.de

Abstract. We consider the problem of managing a dynamic heterogeneous storage system in a distributed way so that the amount of data assigned to a host in that system is related to its capacity. Two central problems have to be solved for this: (1) organizing the hosts in an overlay network with low degree and diameter so that one can efficiently check the correct distribution of the data and route between any two hosts, and (2) distributing the data among the hosts so that the distribution respects the capacities of the hosts and can easily be adapted as the set of hosts or their capacities change. We present distributed protocols for these problems that are self-stabilizing and that do not need any global knowledge about the system such as the number of nodes or the overall capacity of the system. Prior to this work no solution was known satisfying these properties.

1 Introduction

In this paper we consider the problem of designing distributed protocols for a dynamic heterogeneous storage system. Many solutions for distributed storage systems have already been proposed in the literature. In the peer-to-peer area, distributed hash tables (DHTs) have been the most popular choice. In a DHT, data elements are mapped to hosts with the help of a hash function, and the hosts are organized in an overlay network that is often of hypercubic nature so that messages can be quickly exchanged between any two hosts. To be able to react to dynamics in the set of hosts and their capacities, a distributed storage system should support, on top of the usual data operations, operations to join the system, to leave the system, and to change the capacity of a host in the desired way. We present self-stabilizing protocols that can handle all of these operations in an efficient way.

1.1 Heterogeneous Storage Systems

Many data management strategies have already been proposed for distributed storage systems. If all hosts have the same capacity, then a well-known approach called *consistent hashing* can be used to manage the data [6]. In consistent hashing, the data elements are hashed to points in $[0, 1)$, and the hosts are mapped to disjoint intervals in

---

[*] This work was partially supported by the German Research Foundation (DFG) within the Collaborative Research Centre "On-The-Fly Computing" (SFB 901).

[**] The full version of the paper can be found in [32].

Y. Afek (Ed.): DISC 2013, LNCS 8205, pp. 537–549, 2013.
© Springer-Verlag Berlin Heidelberg 2013

$[0, 1)$, and a host stores all data elements that are hashed to points in its interval. An alternative strategy is to hash data elements and hosts to pseudo-random bit strings and to store (indexing information about) a data element at the host with longest prefix match [31]. These strategies have been realized in various DHTs including CAN [7], Pastry [8] and Chord [9]. However, all of these approaches assume hosts of uniform capacity, despite the fact that in P2P systems the peers can be highly heterogeneous.

In a heterogeneous setting, each host (or node) u has its specific capacity $c(u)$ and the goal considered in this paper is to distribute the data among the nodes so that node u stores a fraction of $\frac{c(u)}{\sum_{\forall v} c(v)}$ of the data. The simplest solution would be to reduce the heterogeneous to the homogeneous case by splitting a host of k times the base capacity (e.g., the minimum capacity of a host) into k many virtual hosts. Such a solution is not useful in general because the number of virtual hosts would heavily depend on the capacity distribution, which can create a large management overhead at the hosts. Nevertheless, the concept of virtual hosts has been explored before (e.g., [20,19,21]). In [20] the main idea is not to place the virtual hosts belonging to a real host randomly in the identifier space but in a restricted range to achieve a low degree in the overlay network. However, they need an estimation of the network size and a classification of nodes with high, average, and low capacity. A similar approach is presented in [21]. In [18] the authors organize the nodes into clusters, where a super node (i.e., a node with large capacity) is supervising a cluster of nodes with small capacities. Giakkoupis et al. [3] present an approach which focuses on homogeneous networks but also works for heterogeneous one. However, updates can be costly.

Several solutions have been proposed in the literature that can manage heterogeneous storage systems in a centralized way, i.e. they consider data placement strategies for heterogeneous disks that are managed by a single server [22,23,27,26,24,25] or assume a central server that handles the mapping of data elements to a set of hosts [2,5,4]. The only solution proposed so far where this is not the case is the approach by Schindelhauer and Schomaker [2], which we call *cone hashing*. Their basic idea is to assign a distance function to each host that scales with the capacity of the host. A data element is then assigned to the host of minimum distance with respect to these distance functions. We will extend their construction into a self-stabilizing DHT with low degree and diameter that does not need any global information and that can handle all operations in a stable system efficiently with high probability (w.h.p.)[1].

1.2 Self-stabilization

A central aspect of our self-stabilizing DHT is a self-stabilizing overlay network that can be used to efficiently check the correct distribution of the data among the hosts and that also allows efficient routing. There is a large body of literature on how to efficiently maintain overlay networks, e.g., [28,29,8,30,7,9]. While many results are already known on how to keep an overlay network in a legal state, far less is known about self-stabilizing overlay networks. A self-stabilizing overlay network is a network that can recover its topology from an arbitrary weakly connected state. The idea of self-stabilization in distributed computing was introduced in a classical paper by E.W.

---

[1] I.e., a probability of $1 - n^{-c}$ for any constant $c > 0$.

Dijkstra in 1974 [1] in which he looked at the problem of self-stabilization in a token ring. In order to recover certain network topologies from any weakly connected state, researchers have started with simple line and ring networks (e.g. [10,16]). Over the years more and more network topologies were considered [13,12,11]. In [14] the authors present a self-stabilizing algorithm for the Chord DHT [9], which solves the uniform case, but the problem of managing heterogeneous hosts in a DHT was left open, which is addressed in this paper. To the best of our knowledge this is the first self-stabilizing approach for a distributed heterogeneous storage system.

1.3 Model

Network Model. We assume an asynchronous message passing model for the CONE-DHT which is related to the model presented in [15] by Nor et al. The overlay network consists of a static set V of n nodes or hosts. We further assume *fixed identifiers* (ids) for each node. These identifiers are *immutable* in the computation, we only allow identifiers to be compared, stored and sent. In our model the identifiers are used as addresses, such that by knowing the identifier of a node another node can send messages to this node. The identifiers form a unique order. The communication between nodes is realized by passing messages through channels. A node v can send a message to u through the channel $Ch_{v,u}$. We denote the channel Ch_u as the union of all channels $Ch_{v,u}$. We assume that the capacity of a channel is unbounded and no messages are lost. Furthermore we assume that for a transmission pair (v, u) the messages sent by v are received by u in the same order as they are sent, i.e. $Ch_{v,u}$ is a FIFO channel. Note that this does not imply any order between messages from different sending nodes. For the channel we assume *eventual delivery* meaning that if there is a state in the computation where there is a message in the channel Ch_u there also is a later state where the message is not in the channel, but was received by the process. We distinguish between the *node state*, that is given by the set of identifiers stored in the internal variables u can communicate with, and the *channel state*, that is given by all identifiers contained in messages in a channel Ch_u. We model the network by a directed graph $G = (V, E)$. The set of edges E describes the possible communication pairs. E consists of two subsets: the *explicit edges* $E_e = \{(u, v) : v$ is in u's node state$\}$ and the *implicit edges* $E_i = \{(u, v) : v$ is in u's channel state$\}$, i.e. $E = E_e \cup E_i$. Moreover we define $G_e = (V, E_e)$.

Computational Model. An action has the form $< guard > \rightarrow < command >$. *guard* is a predicate that can be true or false. *command* is a sequence of statements that may perform computations or send messages to other nodes. We introduce one special guard predicate τ called the *timer predicate*, which is periodically true and allows the nodes to perform periodical actions, i.e. τ is always true after a specific number of internal clock cycles and false all the other times. A second predicate is true if a message is received by a node. The *program state* is defined by the node states and the channel states of all nodes, i.e. the assignment of values to every variable of each node and messages to every channel. We call the combination of the node states of all nodes the *node state of the system* and the combination of the channel states of all nodes is called the *channel* *state of the system.* An action is enabled in some state if its guard is true and disabled otherwise. A *computation* is a sequence of states such that for each state s_i the next state s_{i+1} is reached by executing an enabled action in s_i. By this definition, actions can not overlap and are executed atomically giving a sequential order of the executions of actions. For the execution of actions we assume *weak fairness* meaning that if an action is enabled in all but finitely many states of the computation then this action is executed infinitely often.

We state the following requirements on our solution: *Fair load balancing*: every node with x% of the available capacity gets x% of the data. *Space efficiency*: Each node stores at most

$\mathcal{O}(|\text{data assigned to the node}| + \log n)$ information. *Routing efficiency*: There is a routing strategy that allows efficient routing in at most $\mathcal{O}(\log n)$ hops. *Low degree*: The degree of each node is limited by $\mathcal{O}(\log n)$. Furthermore we require an algorithm that builds the target network topology in a *self-stabilizing* manner, i.e., any weakly connected network $G = (V, E)$ is eventually transformed into a network so that a (specified) subset of the explicit edges forms the target network topology (*convergence*) and remains stable as long as no node joins or leaves (*closure*).

1.4 Our Contribution

We present a self-stabilizing algorithm that organizes a set of heterogeneous nodes in an overlay network such that each data element can be efficiently assigned to the node responsible for it. We use the scheme described in [2] (which gives us good load balancing) as our data management scheme and present a distributed protocol for the overlay network, which is efficient in terms of message complexity and information storage and moreover works in a self-stabilizing manner. The overlay network efficiently supports the basic operations of a heterogeneous storage system, such as the joining or leaving of a node, changing the capacity of a node, as well as searching, deleting and inserting a data element. In fact we show the following main result:

Theorem 1. *There is a self-stabilizing algorithm for maintaining a heterogeneous storage system that achieves fair load-balancing, space efficiency and routing efficiency, while each node has a degree of $\mathcal{O}(\log n)$ w.h.p. The data operations can be handled in $O(\log n)$ time in a stable system, and if a node joins or leaves a stable system or changes its capacity, it takes at most $\mathcal{O}(\log^2 n)$ structural changes, i.e., edges that are created or deleted, until the system stabilizes again.*

1.5 Structure of the Paper

The paper is structured as follows: In Section 2 we describe our target network and its properties. In Section 3 we present our self-stabilizing protocol and prove that it is correct. Finally, in Section 4 we describe the functionality of the basic network operations.

2 The *CONE*-DHT

2.1 The Original CONE-Hashing

Before we present our solution, we first give some more details on the original CONE-Hashing [2] our approach is based on. In [2] the authors present a centralized solution for a heterogeneous storage system in which the nodes are of different capacities. We denote the capacity of a node u as $c(u)$. We use a hash function $h : V \mapsto [0, 1)$ that assigns to each node a hash value. A data element of the data set D is also hashed by a hash function $g : D \mapsto [0, 1)$. W.l.o.g. we assume that all hash values and capacities are distinct. According to [2] each node has a capacity function $c(u)(g(x))$, which determines which data is assigned to the node. A node is *responsible* for those elements d with $c(u)(g(d)) = \min_{v \in V}\{c(v)(g(d))\}$, i.e. d is assigned to u. We denote by $R(u) = \{x \in [0, 1) : c(u)(x) = \min_{v \in V}\{c(v)(x)\}\}$ the *responsibility range* of u (see Figure 1 in the full version [32]). Note that $R(u)$ can consist of several intervals in $[0, 1)$. In the original paper [2], the authors considered two special cases of capacity functions, one of linear form $C_u^{lin}(x) = \frac{1}{c(u)}|x - h(u)|$ and of logarithmic form $C_u^{log}(x) = \frac{1}{c(u)}(-log(|1 - (x - h(u))|))$. For these capacity functions the following results were shown by the authors [2]:

Theorem 2. *A data element d is assigned to a node u with probability* $\frac{c(u)}{\sum_{v \in V} c(v) - c(u)}$ *for linear capacity functions $C_u^{lin}(x)$ and with probability* $\frac{c(u)}{\sum_{v \in V} c(v)}$ *for logarithmic capacity functions $C_u^{log}(x)$. Thus in expectation fair load balancing can be achieved by using a logarithmic capacity function $C_u^{log}(x)$.*

The CONE-Hashing supports the basic operations of a heterogeneous storage system, such as the joining or leaving of a node, changing the capacity of a node, as well as searching, deleting and inserting a data element.

Moreover, the authors showed that the fragmentation is relatively small for the logarithmic capacity function, with each node having in expectation a logarithmic number of intervals it is responsible for. In the case of the linear function, it can be shown that this number is only constant in expectation.

In [2] the authors further present a data structure to efficiently support the described operations in a centralized approach. For their data structure they showed that there is an algorithm that determines for a data element d the corresponding node u with $g(d) \in R(u)$ in expected time $\mathcal{O}(\log n)$. The used data structure has a size of $\mathcal{O}(n)$ and the joining, leaving and the capacity change of a node can be handled efficiently.

In the following we show that CONE-Hashing can also be realized by using a distributed data structure. Further the following challenges have to be solved. We need a suitable topology on the node set V that supports an efficient determination of the responsibility ranges $R(u)$ for each node u . The topology should also support an efficient *Search(d)* algorithm, i.e. for a *Search(d)* query inserted at an arbitrary node w, the node v with $g(d) \in R(v)$ should be found. Furthermore a *Join(v)*, *Leave(v)*, *CapacityChange(v)* operation should not lead to a high amount of data movements, (i.e. not more than the data now assigned to v or no longer assigned to v should be moved,) or a high amount of structural changes (i.e. changes in the topology built on V). All these challenges will be solved by our CONE-DHT. In the CONE-DHT, the same sets of capacity functions can be used as discussed here, and thus our system can inherit the same properties.

2.2   The *CONE*-DHT

In order to construct a heterogeneous storage network in the distributed case, we have to deal with the challenges mentioned above. For that, we introduce the *CONE*-graph, which is an overlay network that, as we show, can support efficiently a heterogeneous storage system.

The Network Layer. We define the *CONE* graph as a graph $G^{CONE} = (V, E^{CONE})$, with V being the hosts of our storage system.

For the determination of the edge set, we need following definitions, with respect to a node u:

- $succ_1^+(u) = argmin\{h(v) : h(v) > h(u) \wedge c(v) > c(u)\}$ is the next node at the right of u with larger capacity, and we call it the first larger successor of u. Building upon this, we define recursively the i-th larger successor of u as: $succ_i^+(u) = succ_1^+(succ_{i-1}^+(u)), \forall i > 1$, and the union of all larger successors as $S^+(u) = \bigcup_i succ_i^+(u)$.
- The first larger predecessor of u is defined as: $pred_1^+(u) = argmax\{h(v) : h(v) < h(u) \wedge c(v) > c(u)\}$ i.e. the next node at the left of u with larger capacity. The i-th larger predecessor of u is: $pred_i^+(u) = pred_1^+(pred_{i-1}^+(u)), \forall i > 1$, and the union of all larger predecessors as $P^+(u) = \bigcup_i pred_i^+(u)$.
- We also define the set of the smaller successors of u, $S^-(u)$, as the set of all nodes v, with $u = pred_1^+(v)$, and the set of the smaller predecessors of u, $P^-(u)$ as the set of all nodes v, such that $u = succ_1^+(v)$.

Now we can define the edge-set of a node in G^{CONE}.

Definition 1. $(u, v) \in E^{CONE}$ *iff* $v \in S^+(u) \cup P^+(u) \cup S^-(u) \cup P^-(u)$

We define also the neighborhood set of u as $N_u = S^+(u) \cup P^+(u) \cup S^-(u) \cup P^-(u)$. In other words, v maintains connections to each node u, if there does not exist another node with larger capacity than u between v and u (see Figure 2 in the full version [32]). We will prove that this graph is sufficient for maintaining a heterogeneous storage network in a self-stabilizing manner and also that in this graph the degree is bounded logarithmically w.h.p..

The Data Management Layer. We discussed above how the data is assigned to the different nodes. That is the assignment strategy we use for data in the *CONE*-network.

In order to understand how the various data operations are realized in the network, we have to describe how each node maintains the knowledge about the data it has, as well as the intervals it is responsible for. It turns out that in order for a data item to be forwarded to the correct node, which is responsible for storing it, it suffices to contact the closest node (in terms of hash value) from the left to the data item's hash value. That is because then, if the *CONE* graph has been established, this node (for example node u in Figure 1 in the full version [32]) is aware of the responsible node for this data item. We call the interval between $h(u)$ and the hash value of u's closest right node I_u. We say that u is *supervising* I_u. We show the following theorem.

Theorem 3. *In G^{CONE} a node u knows all the nodes v with $R(v) \cap I_u \neq \emptyset$.*

The proof can be found in the full version of the paper [32].

So, the nodes store their data in the following way. If a node u has a data item that falls into one of its responsible intervals, it stores in addition to this item a reference to the node v that is the closest from the left to this interval. Moreover, the subinterval u thinks it is responsible for (in which the data item falls) is also stored (as described in the next section, when the node's internal variables are presented). In case the data item is not stored at the correct node, v can resolve the conflict when contacted by u.

Now we can discuss the functionality of the data operations. A node has operations for inserting, deleting and searching a datum in the CONE-network.

Let us focus on **searching** a data item. As shown above, it suffices to search for the left closest node to the data item's hash value. We do this by using greedy routing. Greedy routing in the *CONE*-network works as follows: If a search request wants to reach some position *pos* in $[0, 1)$, and the request is currently at node u, then u forwards *search(pos)* to the node v in N_u that is closest to *pos*, until the closest node at the left of *pos* is reached. Then this node will forward the request to the responsible node.

In that way we can route to the responsible node and then get answer whether the data item is found or not, and so the searching is realized. Note that the **deletion** of a data item can be realized in the same way, only that when the item is found, it is also deleted from the responsible node. **Inserting** an item follows a similar procedure, with the difference that when the responsible node is found, the data item is stored by it.

Moreover, the network handles efficiently structural operations, such as the joining and leaving of a node in the network, or the change of the capacity of a node. Since this handling falls into the analysis of the self-stabilization algorithm, we will discuss the network operations in Section 3, where we also formally analyze the algorithm.

It turns out that a single data or network operation (i.e greedy routing) can be realized in a logarithmic number of hops in the *CONE*-network, and this happens due to the structural properties of the network, which we discuss in the next section, where we also show that the degree of the *CONE*-network is logarithmic.

2.3   Structural Properties of a Cone Network

In this section we show that the degree of a node in a stable CONE-network is bounded by $\mathcal{O}(\log n)$ w.h.p, and hence the information stored by each node (i.e the number of nodes which it maintains contact to, $|E_e(u)|$) is bounded by $\mathcal{O}(\log n + |\text{amount of data stored in a node}|)$ w.h.p..

Theorem 4. *The degree of a node in a stable CONE network is $\mathcal{O}(\log n)$ w.h.p.*

The proof can be found in the full version of the paper [32].

Additionally to the nodes in $S^+(u)$, $S^-(u)$, $P^+(u)$ and $P^-(u)$ that lead to the degree of $\mathcal{O}(\log n)$ w.h.p. a node u only stores references about the closest nodes left to the intervals it is responsible for, where it actually stores data. A node u stores at most one reference and one interval for each data item. Thus the storage only has a logarithmic overhead for the topology information and the following theorem follows immediately.

Theorem 5. *In a stable CONE network each node stores at most $\mathcal{O}(\log n + |amount\ of\ data\ stored\ in\ a\ node|)$ information w.h.p.*

Once the CONE network G^{CONE} is set up, it can be used as an heterogeneous storage system supporting inserting, deleting and searching for data. The CONE Greedy routing implies the following bound on the diameter:

Lemma 1. *CONE Greedy routing takes on a stable CONE network w.h.p. no more than a logarithmic number of steps, i.e. the diameter of a CONE network is $\mathcal{O}(\log n)$ w.h.p..*

The proof can be found in the full version of the paper [32].

3 Self-stabilization Process

3.1 Topological Self-stabilization

We now formally describe the problem of topological self-stabilization. In topological self-stabilization the goal is to state a protocol P that *solves* an overlay problem OP starting from an initial topology of the set IT. A protocol is *unconditionally* self-stabilizing if IT contains every possible state. Analogously a protocol is *conditionally* self-stabilizing if IT contains only states that fulfill some conditions. For topological self-stabilization we assume that IT contains any state as long as $G^{IT} = (V, E^{IT})$ is weakly connected, i.e. the combined knowledge of all nodes in this state covers the whole network, and there are no identifiers that don't belong to existing nodes in the network. The set of target topologies defined in OP is given by $OP = \{G_e^{OP} = (V, E_e^{OP})\}$, i.e. the goal topologies of the overlay problem are only defined on explicit edges and E_i^{OP} can be an arbitrary (even empty) set of edges. We also call the program states in OP *legal states*. We say a protocol P that solves a problem OP is topologically self-stabilizing if for P convergence and *closure* can be shown. *Convergence* means that P started with any state in IT reaches a legal state in OP. *Closure* means that P started in a legal state in OP maintains a legal state. For a protocol P we assume that there are no oracles available for the computation.

3.2 Formal Problem Definition and Notation

Now we define the problem we solve in this paper in the previously introduced notation. We provide a protocol P that solves the overlay problem *CONE* and is topologically self-stabilizing.

In order to give a formal definition of the edges in E_e, E_i we first describe which internal variables are stored in a node u, i.e. which edges are in E_e:

- $u.S^+ = \{v \in N_u : h(v) > h(u) \wedge c(v) > c(u) \wedge \forall w \in N_u : h(v) > h(w) > h(u) \implies c(v) > c(w)\}$
- $u.succ_1^+ = \text{argmin}\{h(v) : v \in u.S^+\}$: The first node to the right with a larger capacity than u
- $u.P^+ = \{v \in N_u : h(v) < h(u) \wedge c(v) > c(u) \wedge \forall w \in N_u : h(v) < h(w) < h(u) \implies c(v) > c(w)\}$
- $u.pred_1^+ = \text{argmax}\{h(v) : v \in u.P^+\}$: The first node to the left with a larger capacity than u
- $u.S^- = \{v \in N_u : h(v) > h(u) \wedge c(v) < c(u) \wedge \forall w \in N_u : h(v) > h(w) > h(u) \implies c(v) > c(w)\}$
- $u.P^- = \{v \in N_u : h(v) < h(u) \wedge c(v) < c(u) \wedge \forall w \in N_u : h(v) < h(w) < h(u) \implies c(v) > c(w)\}$
- $u.S^* = \{u.S^- \cup \{u.succ_1^+\}\}$: the set of right neighbors that u communicates with. We assume that the nodes are stored in ascending order so that $h(u.S^*[i]) < h(u.S^*[i + 1])$. If $|u.S^*| = k$, then $u.S^*, u.S^*[k] = u.succ_1^+$.
- $u.P^* = \{u.P^- \cup \{u.pred_1^+\}\}$: the set of left neighbors that u communicates with. We assume that the nodes are stored in descending order so that $h(u.P^*[i]) > h(u.P^*[i + 1])$ If $|u.P^*| = k$, then $u.P^*[k] = u.pred_1^+$.
- $u.DS$ the data set, containing all intervals $u.DS[i] = [a, b]$, for which u is responsible and stores actual data $u.DS[i].data$. Additionally for each interval a reference $u.DS[i].ref$ to the supervising node is stored

Additionally each node stores the following variables :

- τ: the timer predicate that is periodically true
- $u.I_u$: the interval between u and the successor of u. u is supervising $u.I_u$.
- m: the message in Ch_u that now received by the node.

Definition 2. *We define a valid state as an assignment of values to the internal variables of all nodes so that the definition of the variables is not violated, e.g. $u.S^+$ contains no nodes w with $h(w) < h(u)$ or $c_w < c(u)$ or $h(u) < h(v) < h(w)$ and $c(v) > c_w$ for any $v \in N_u$.*

Now we can describe the topologies in the initial states and in the legal stable state. Let $IT = \{G^{IT} = (V, E_{IT} = E_e^{IT} \cup E_i^{IT}) : G^{IT}$ is weakly connected$\}$ and let $CONE = \{G^C = (V, E^C)\}$, such that for E^C the following conditions hold: (1) $E^C = E_e - \{(u, v) : v \in u.DS\}$, (2) E^C is in a valid state and (3) $E^C = E^{CONE}$.

Note that we assume E_e to be a multiset, i.e in E^C an edge (u, v) might still exists, although $v \in u.DS$ if e.g. $v \in u.S^+$. Further note that, in case the network has stabilized to a $CONE$-network, it holds for every node that $u.S^+ = S^+(u), u.P^+ = P^+(u), u.S^- = S^-(u)$ and $u.P^- = P^-(u)$.

3.3   Algorithm

In this section we give a description of the the distributed algorithm. The algorithm is a protocol that each node executes based on its own node and channel state. The protocol contains periodic actions that are executed if the timer predicate τ is true and actions that are executed if the node receives a message m. In the periodic actions each node performs a consistency check of its internal variables, i.e. are all variables valid according to Definition 2. If some variables are invalid, the nodes causing this invalidity are delegated. By *delegation* we mean that node u delegates a node $v : h(v) > h(u)$ (resp. $h(v) < h(u)$) to the node $w' = \text{argmax}\{h(w) : w \in u.S^* \wedge h(w) < h(v)\}$ (resp. $w' = \text{argmin}\{h(w) : w \in u.P^* \wedge h(w) > h(v)\}$) by a message $m = (build - triangle, v)$ to w'. The idea behind the delegation is to forward nodes closer to their correct position, so that the sorted list (and the *CONE*-network) is formed. Furthermore in the periodic actions each node introduces itself to its successor and predecessor $u.S^*[1]$ and $u.P^*[1]$ by a message $m = (build - triangle, u)$. Also each pair of nodes in $u.P^*$ and $u.S^*$ with consecutive ids is introduced to each other. u also introduces the nodes $u.succ_1^+$ and $u.pred_1^+$ to each other by messages of type $build - triangle$. By this a *triangulation* is formed by edges $(u, u.pred_1^+), (u, u.succ_1^+), (u.succ_1^+, u.pred_1^+)$ (see Figure 2 in the full version [32]). To establish correct P^+ and S^+ lists in each node, a node u sends its $u.P^+$ (resp. $u.S^+$) list periodically to all nodes v in $u.S^-$ (resp. $u.P^-$) by a message $m = (list-update, u.S^+\cup\{u\})$ (resp. $m = (list-update, u.P^+\cup\{u\})$) to v. The last action a node periodically executes is to send a message to each reference in $u.DS$ to check whether u is responsible for the data in the corresponding interval $[a, b]$ by sending a message $m = (check - interval, [a, b], u)$.

If the message predicate is true and u receives a message m, the action u performs depends on the type of the message. If u receives a message $m = (build-triangle, v)$ u checks whether v has to be included in it's internal variables $u.P^+$, $u.S^+$, $u.P^-$ or $u.S^-$. If u doesn't store v, v is delegated. If u receives a message $m = (list - update, list)$, u checks whether the ids in $list$ have to be included in it's internal variables $u.P^+$, $u.S^+$, $u.P^-$ or $u.S^-$. If u doesn't store a node v in $list$, v is delegated. If u stores a node v in $u.S^+$ (resp. $u.P^+$) that is not in $list$, v is also delegated as it also has to be in the list of $u.pred_1^+$ (resp. $u.succ_1^+$). The remaining messages are necessary for the data management.

If u receives a message $m = (check - interval, [a, b], v)$ it checks whether v is in $u.S^+$ or $u.P^+$ or has to be included, or delegates v. Then u checks whether $[a, b]$ is in $u.I_u$ and if v is responsible for $[a, b]$. If not, u sends a message $m = (update - interval, IntervalSet)$ to v containing a set of intervals in $[a, b]$ that v is not responsible for and references of the supervising nodes. If u receives a message $m = (update-interval, IntervalSet)$ it forwards all data in intervals in $IntervalSet$ to the corresponding references by a message $m = (forward - data, data)$. If u receives such a message it checks whether the data is in its supervised interval $u.I_u$. If not u forwards the data according to a greedy routing strategy, if u supervises the data it sends a message $m = (store - data, data, u)$ to the responsible node. If u receives such a message it inserts the data, the interval and the corresponding reference in $u.DS$. Note that no identifiers are ever deleted, but always stored or delegated. This ensures the connectivity of the network.

In the full version we give the pseudocode for the protocol executed by each node.

3.4   Correctness

In this section we show the correctness of the presented algorithm. We do this by showing that by executing our algorithm any weakly connected network eventually converges to a CONE network and once a CONE network is formed it is maintained in every later state. We further show that in a CONE network the data is stored correctly.

Convergence.   To show convergence we will divide the process of convergence into several phases, such that once one phase is completed its conditions will hold in every later program state. For our analysis we additionally define $E(t)$ as the set of edges at time t. Analogous $E_e(t)$ and $E_i(t)$ are defined. We show the following theorem.

Theorem 6. *If $G = (V, E) \in IT$ at time t then eventually at a time $t' > t$ $G^{CONE} \subset G_e(t')$.*

The proof can be found in the full version of the paper. We divide the proof into 3 phases. First we show the preservation of the connectivity of the graph, then we show the convergence to the sorted list and eventually the convergence to the *CONE*-network.

Closure and Correctness of the Data Structure.   We showed that from any initial state we eventually reach a state in which the network forms a correct CONE network. We now need to show that in this state the explicit edges remain stable and also that each node stores the data it is responsible for.

Theorem 7. *If $G_e = G^{CONE}$ at time t then for $t' > t$ also $G_e = G^{CONE}$.*

Theorem 8. *If $G_e = G^{CONE}$ eventually each node stores exactly the data it is responsible for.*

These proofs can be found in the full version of the paper.

4   External Dynamics

Concerning the network operations in the network, i.e. the joining of a new node, the leaving of a node and the capacity change of a node, we show the following:

Theorem 9. *In case a node u joins a stable CONE network, or a node u leaves a stable CONE network or a node u in a stable CONE network changes its capacity, we show that in any of these three cases $\mathcal{O}(\log^2 n)$ structural changes in the explicit edge set are necessary to reach the new stable state.*

The proof can be found in the full version of the paper.

5 Conclusion and Future Work

We studied the problem of a self-stabilizing and heterogeneous overlay network and gave an algorithm of solving that problem, and by doing this we used an efficient network structure. We proved the correctness of our protocol, also concerning the functionality of the operations done in the network, data operations and node operations. This is the first attempt to present a self-stabilizing method for a heterogeneous overlay network and it works efficiently regarding the information stored in the hosts. Furthermore our solution provides a low degree, fair load balancing and polylogarithmic updates cost in case of joining or leaving nodes. In the future we will try to also examine heterogeneous networks in the two-dimensional space and consider heterogeneity in other aspects than only the capacity, e.g. bandwidth, reliability or heterogeneity of the data elements.

References

1. Dijkstra, E.W.: Self-stabilizing systems in spite of distributed control. Commun. ACM 17, 643–644 (1974)
2. Schindelhauer, C., Schomaker, G.: Weighted distributed hash tables. In: SPAA 2005, pp. 218–227 (2005)
3. Giakkoupis, G., Hadzilacos, V.: A Scheme for Load Balancing in Heterogenous Distributed Hash Tables. In: PODC 2005 (2005)
4. Brinkmann, A., Salzwedel, K., Scheideler, C.: Compact, adaptive placement schemes for non-uniform distribution requirements. In: SPAA 2002, pp. 53–62 (2002)
5. Brinkmann, A., Salzwedel, K., Scheideler, C.: Efficient, distributed data placement strategies for storage area networks. In: SPAA 2000, pp. 119–128 (2000)
6. Karger, D., Lehman, E., Leighton, T., Levine, M., Lewin, D., Panigrahy, R.: Consistent hashing and random trees: Distributed caching protocols for relieving hot spots on the World Wide Web. In: STOC 1997, pp. 654–663 (1997)
7. Ratnasamy, S., Francis, P., Handley, M., Karp, R., Shenker, S.: A scalable content-addressable network. In: SIGCOMM, pp. 161–172 (2001)
8. Rowstron, A., Druschel, P.: Pastry: Scalable, decentralized object location, and routing for large-scale peer-to-peer systems. In: Guerraoui, R. (ed.) Middleware 2001. LNCS, vol. 2218, pp. 329–350. Springer, Heidelberg (2001)
9. Stoica, I., Morris, R., Karger, D., Frans Kaashoek, M., Balakrishnan, H.: Chord: A scalable peer-to-peer lookup service for internet applications. In: SIGCOMM, pp. 149–160 (2001)
10. Cramer, C., Fuhrmann, T.: Self-stabilizing ring networks on connected graphs. In: Technical report, University of Karlsruhe (TH), Fakultaet fuer Informatik (May 2005)
11. Dolev, S., Tzachar, N.: Empire of colonies: Self-stabilizing and self-organizing distributed algorithm. Theor. Comput. Sci. 410(6-7), 514–532 (2009)
12. Jacob, R., Richa, A.W., Scheideler, C., Schmid, S., Täubig, H.: A distributed polylogarithmic time algorithm for self-stabilizing skip graphs. In: PODC 2009, pp. 131–140 (2009)
13. Jacob, R., Ritscher, S., Scheideler, C., Schmid, S.: A self-stabilizing and local delaunay graph construction. In: Dong, Y., Du, D.-Z., Ibarra, O. (eds.) ISAAC 2009. LNCS, vol. 5878, pp. 771–780. Springer, Heidelberg (2009)
14. Kniesburges, S., Koutsopoulos, A., Scheideler, C.: Re-chord: a self-stabilizing chord overlay network. In: SPAA 2011, pp. 235–244 (2011)

15. Nor, R.M., Nesterenko, M., Scheideler, C.: Corona: A stabilizing deterministic message-passing skip list. In: Défago, X., Petit, F., Villain, V. (eds.) SSS 2011. LNCS, vol. 6976, pp. 356–370. Springer, Heidelberg (2011)
16. Onus, M., Richa, A.W., Scheideler, C.: Linearization: Locally self-stabilizing sorting in graphs. In: ALENEX 2007, pp. 99–108 (2007)
17. Harvey, N.: CPSC 536N: Randomized Algorithms, Pages 5. Lecture 3. University of British Columbia (2011-2012)
18. Shena, H., Xub, C.-Z.: Hash-based proximity clustering for efficient load balancing in heterogeneous DHT networks. J. Parallel Distrib. Comput. 68, 686–702 (2008)
19. Rao, A., Lakshminarayanan, K., Surana, S., Karp, R., Stoica, I.: Load balancing in structured P2P systems. In: Kaashoek, M.F., Stoica, I. (eds.) IPTPS 2003. LNCS, vol. 2735, Springer, Heidelberg (2003)
20. Godfrey, P.B., Stoica, I.: Heterogeneity and Load Balance in Distributed Hash Tables. In: IEEE INFOCOM (2005)
21. Bienkowski, M., Brinkmann, A., Klonowski, M., Korzeniowski, M.: SkewCCC+: A heterogeneous distributed hash table. In: Lu, C., Masuzawa, T., Mosbah, M. (eds.) OPODIS 2010. LNCS, vol. 6490, pp. 219–234. Springer, Heidelberg (2010)
22. Santos, J.R., Muntz, R.: Performance Analysis of the RIO Multimedia Storage System with Heterogeneous Disk Configurations. In: ACM Multimedia Conference 1998, pp. 303–308 (1998)
23. Miranda, A., Effert, S., Kang, Y., Miller, E.L., Brinkmann, A., Cortes, T.: Reliable and randomized data distribution strategies for large scale storage systems. In: HiPC 2011, pp. 1–10 (2011)
24. Didi Yao, S.-Y., Shahabi, C., Zimmermann, R.: BroadScale: Efficient scaling of heterogeneous storage systems. Int. J. on Digital Libraries 6, 98–111 (2006)
25. Brinkmann, A., Effert, S., Meyer auf der Heide, F., Scheideler, C.: Dynamic and Redundant Data Placement. In: ICDCS 2007, p. 29 (2007)
26. Cortes, T., Labarta, J.: Taking advantage of heterogeneity in disk arrays. J. Parallel Distrib. Comput. 63, 448–464 (2003)
27. Mense, M., Scheideler, C.: SPREAD: An adaptive scheme for redundant and fair storage in dynamic heterogeneous storage systems. In: SODA 2008 (2008)
28. Awerbuch, B., Scheideler, C.: The hyperring: a low-congestion deterministic data structure for distributed environments. In: SODA 2004, pp. 318–327 (2004)
29. Bhargava, A., Kothapalli, K., Riley, C., Scheideler, C., Thober, M.: Pagoda: A dynamic overlay network for routing, data management, and multicasting. In: SPAA 2004, pp. 170–179 (2004)
30. Kuhn, F., Schmid, S., Wattenhofer, R.: A self-repairing peer-to-peer system resilient to dynamic adversarial churn. In: van Renesse, R. (ed.) IPTPS 2005. LNCS, vol. 3640, pp. 13–23. Springer, Heidelberg (2005)
31. Plaxton, C.G., Rajaraman, R., Richa, A.W.: Accessing nearby copies of replicated objects in a distributed environment. In: SPAA 1997, pp. 311–320 (1997)
32. Kniesburges, S., Koutsopoulos, A., Scheideler, C.: CONE-DHT: A distributed self-stabilizing algorithm for a heterogeneous storage system (Pre-Print) In: arXiv:1307.6747 [cs.DC] (2013)

Brief Announcements

Brief Announcement: Distributed MST
in Core-Periphery Networks

Chen Avin[1], Michael Borokhovich[1,*], Zvi Lotker[1,*], and David Peleg[2,**]

[1] Ben-Gurion University of the Negev, Beer-Sheva, Israel
{avin,borokhom,zvilo}@cse.bgu.ac.il
[2] The Weizmann Institute, Rehovot, Israel
david.peleg@weizmann.ac.il

Abstract. Motivated by the structure of social networks, this paper initiates a study of distributed algorithms in networks that exhibit a *core-periphery* structure. Such networks contain two distinct groups of nodes: a large and sparse, group identified as the *periphery*, which is loosely organized around a small, and densely connected group identified as the *core*. We identify four basic properties that are relevant to the interplay between core and periphery. For each of these properties, we propose a corresponding axiom that captures the behavior expected of a social network based on a core-periphery structure. We then address their usefulness for distributed computation, by considering a nontrivial algorithmic task of significance in both the distributed systems world and the social networks world, namely, the distributed construction of a minimum-weight spanning tree.

1. Axiomatic Approach. Most existing approaches to modeling social networks are based on creating a set of mathematical rules for gradually constructing a member of a given class of social networks (e.g., the Preferential Attachment model). A complementary approach that we promote, and adopt in this paper, is to base our characterization of social (and complex) networks in general, and their main structural components in particular, on *axiomatic* grounds, where the axioms are chosen so as to capture fundamental structural and computational properties of the modeled network.

2. Notations and Axioms. Let $G(V, E)$ denote our network, where V is the set of nodes, $|V| = n$, and E is the set of edges, $|E| = m$. We consider a synchronous model of communication with messages of bounded (logarithmic) size, such as CONGEST model ([2]). Let $N(v)$ denote the set of neighbors of node $v \in V$. For a set $S \subset V$ and a node $v \in S$, let $N_{\text{in}}(v, S) = N(v) \cap S$ denote its set of neighbors within S and denote the number of neighbors of v in the set S by $d_{\text{in}}(v, S) = |N_{\text{in}}(v, S)|$. Analogously, let $N_{\text{out}}(v, S) = N(v) \cap V \setminus S$ denote v's set of neighbors outside of S and let $d_{\text{out}}(v, S) = |N_{\text{out}}(v, S)|$. For a set $S \subset V$, let $\partial(S)$ be the *edge boundary* of S, namely the set of edges with one endpoint in S and the other outside of S and $|\partial(S)| = \sum_{v \in S} |N_{\text{out}}(v, S)|$. We define the four properties of a core-periphery network.

α-Influence. A subset of nodes S is α-Influential if $|\partial(S)| \geq \alpha \cdot m$.

* Michael Borokhovich and Zvi Lotker were supported in part by the Israel Science Foundation (grant 894/09).
** David Peleg was supported in part by the Israel Science Foundation (grant 894/09), the United States-Israel Binational Science Foundation (grant 2008348), the I-CORE program of the Israel PBC and ISF (grant 4/11), and the Citi Foundation.

Y. Afek (Ed.): DISC 2013, LNCS 8205, pp. 553–554, 2013.

β-Balanced Boundary. A subset of nodes S is said to have a β-balanced boundary *iff for every node* $v \in S$, $\frac{d_{\text{out}}(v,S)}{d_{\text{in}}(v,S)+1} = O(\beta)$.

γ-Clique Emulation. The task of clique emulation *on an n-node graph G involves delivering a distinct message* $M_{v,w}$ *from v to w for every pair of nodes* v, w *in* $V(G)$. An n-node graph G is an γ-clique-emulator *if it is possible to perform the task in γ rounds.*

δ-Convergecast. The task of $\langle S, T \rangle$-convergecast *on a graph G involves delivering* $|S|$ *distinct messages* M_v, *originated at the nodes* $v \in S$, *to some nodes in T. The sets* $S, T \subset V$ *form a* δ-convergecaster *if it is possible to perform the task in δ rounds.*

We assume our network has two disjoint sets of nodes, the *core* C ($|C| = n_c$) and the *periphery* $\mathcal{P}$ ($|\mathcal{P}| = n_p$), with $V = C \cup \mathcal{P}$, and propose the following set of *axioms*.

A1. **High Core Influence.** The core C is $\Theta(1)$-Influential.
A2. **Core Boundary.** The core C has a $\Theta(1)$-balanced boundary.
A3. **Clique emulation.** The core C is a $\Theta(1)$-clique emulator.
A4. **Periphery-Core convergecast.** $\mathcal{P}$ and C form a $\Theta(1)$-convergecaster.

Axiom A1 was first proposed in [1] in the study on the *elite* of social networks. It captures the idea that the core (or elite) has a strong influence on the network in the sense that a constant fraction of the edges in the network are "controlled" by the core. Axiom A2 talks about the boundary between the core and periphery. It states that while not all nodes in the core must have many links to the periphery, i.e., serve as *ambassadors* of the core, if a node is indeed an ambassador, then it must also have many links within the core. Axiom A3 talks about the flow of information within the core, and postulates that the core must be dense, and in a sense behave almost like a complete graph: "everyone must know everyone else". Axiom A4 also concerns the boundary between the core and periphery, but in addition it refers also to the structure of the periphery. It postulates that information can flow efficiently from the periphery to the core. The last three axioms imply a number of simple properties of the network structure that we exploit in the efficient MST algorithm ($C\mathcal{P}$-MST) proposed here.

Theorem 1. *If the core C satisfies Axioms A2, A3 and A4, then:*

1. *The size of the core satisfies* $\Omega(\sqrt{n}) \le n_c \le O(\sqrt{m})$.
2. *For every node v in the core:* $d_{\text{out}}(v, C) = O(n_c)$ *and* $d_{\text{in}}(v, C) = \Omega(n_c)$.
3. *The number of outgoing edges from the core is* $|\partial(C)| = \Theta(n_c^2)$.
4. *The number of edges within the core is* $\sum_{v \in C} d_{\text{in}}(v, C) = \Theta(n_c^2)$.

3. MST on Core-Periphery Network. We present a time-efficient randomized distributed algorithm for computing an MST on a core-periphery network. Our $C\mathcal{P}$-MST algorithm is based on Boruvka's algorithm, and runs in $O(\log n)$ phases, each consisting of several non-trivial steps that require extensive inter-node communication.

Theorem 2. *In a network that satisfies Axioms A2-A4, Algorithm $C\mathcal{P}$-MST terminates in $O(\log^2 n)$ rounds with high probability.*

References

1. Avin, C., Lotker, Z., Pignolet, Y.A., Turkel, I.: From caesar to twitter: An axiomatic approach to elites of social networks. CoRR, abs/1111.3374 (2012)
2. Peleg, D.: Distributed Computing: A Locality-Sensitive Approach. SIAM (2000)

Brief Announcement: Enhancing Permissiveness in Transactional Memory via Time-Warping

Nuno Diegues and Paolo Romano

INESC-ID Lisboa / Instituto Superior Técnico
Universidade de Lisboa, Portugal
ndiegues@gsd.inesc-id.pt, romano@inesc-id.pt

Abstract. The notion of permissiveness in Transactional Memory (TM) translates to only aborting a transaction when it cannot be accepted in any history that guarantees a target correctness criterion. Achieving permissiveness, however, comes at a non-negligible cost. This desirable property is often neglected by state of the art TMs, which, in order to maximize implementation's efficiency, resort to aborting transactions under overly conservative conditions. We identify a novel sweet spot between permissiveness and efficiency by introducing the Time-Warp Multi-version algorithm (TWM), which allows for drastically minimizing spurious aborts with respect to state of the art, highly efficient TMs, while introducing minimal bookkeeping overheads. Further, read-only transactions are abort-free, and both Virtual World Consistency and lock-freedom are ensured.

1 Overview of Time-Warping

Typical MVCC algorithms for TM allow read-only transactions to be serialized "in the past", i.e., before the commit event of any concurrent write transaction. Conversely, they serialize a write transaction T committing at time t "in the present", by: (1) attempting to order the versions produced by T after all versions created by transactions committed before time t; and (2) performing what we call a "classic validation", which ensures that the snapshot observed by T is still up-to-date considering the updates generated by all transactions that committed before t. This results in aborting any write transaction T that missed the writes of a concurrent, committed transaction T', also called an anti-dependency in the literature. We note that this approach is a conservative one, as it guarantees serializability by systematically rejecting serializable histories in which T might have actually been safely serialized before T'.

The key idea of TWM is to allow a write transaction, which missed the write committed by a concurrent transaction T', to be serialized "in the past", namely before T'. This is in contrast with the approach taken by most practical TM algorithms (designed to minimize overhead), which only allow the commit of transactions "in the present". Unlike TMs that ensure permissiveness [2], TWM tracks solely direct anti-dependencies developed by a committing transaction, hence avoiding onerous validation of the entire conflicts' graph [3]. TWM's novel validation is sufficiently lightweight to ensure efficiency, while accepting far more histories than state of the art, practical TMs.

To efficiently implement the time-warp abstraction, TWM maintains two totally ordered time lines: $\mathcal{N}$ for the natural order of commit requests and $\mathcal{TW}$ for the time-warp

Y. Afek (Ed.): DISC 2013, LNCS 8205, pp. 555–556, 2013.

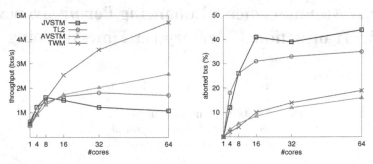

Fig. 1. Comparison of throughput (left) and aborts (right) in a skip-list

commit order that results in the version order of data. In a conflict-free execution both orders coincide. Otherwise, a transaction B is time-warped when it anti-depends on a set of concurrent transactions A. In such case, B is serialized (along $\mathcal{TW}$) before the transaction in A with the least natural commit order. Note that if B has no anti-dependencies, then the natural and time-warp commit order coincide (as B is serialized in the present). To ensure only safe executions (virtual world consistent ones), the validation scheme of TWM detects a specific pattern that we call a *triad*. A triad exists whenever there is transaction T that is both the source and target of anti-dependency edges from two concurrent transactions T' and T'' (where, possibly, $T' = T''$). We call T a *pivot*, and define the TWM validation scheme as follows: A transaction fails its validation if, by committing, it would create a triad whose *pivot* time-warp commits.

Results. We conducted an experimental study against four representative TMs. TL2 and JVSTM use the *classic validation* (the latter is also multi-version), and AVSTM is probabilistic permissive. We provide a sample of the evaluation for a contended skip-list in Fig. 1. Our overall results in typical TM benchmarks yielded an average improvement of 81% in high concurrency scenarios, with gains extending up to 8×. Further, we observed limited overheads, even in worst-case scenarios entailing no contention or patterns that cannot be optimized using TWM. More details can be found in [1].

Acknowledgements. This work was supported by national funds through Fundação para a Ciência e Tecnologia under project PEst-OE/EEI/LA0021/2013 and Cloud-TM project (co-financed by the European Commission through the contract no. 257784).

References

1. Diegues, N., Romano, P.: Enhancing Permissiveness in Transactional Memory via Time-Warping. Technical Report RT/10/2013, INESC-ID Lisboa (July 2013)
2. Guerraoui, R., Henzinger, T.A., Singh, V.: Permissiveness in Transactional Memories. In: Taubenfeld, G. (ed.) DISC 2008. LNCS, vol. 5218, pp. 305–319. Springer, Heidelberg (2008)
3. Keidar, I., Perelman, D.: On avoiding spare aborts in transactional memory. In: Proceedings of the 21st Annual Symposium on Parallelism in Algorithms and Architectures, SPAA 2009, pp. 59–68 (2009)

Brief Announcement: ParMarkSplit: A Parallel Mark-Split Garbage Collector Based on a Lock-Free Skip-List

Nhan Nguyen[1], Philippas Tsigas[1], and Håkan Sundell[2]

[1] Chalmers University of Technology, Sweden
{nhann,tsigas}@chalmers.se
[2] University of Borås, Sweden
Hakan.Sundell@hb.se

Abstract. This brief announcement provides a high level overview of a parallel mark-split garbage collector. Our parallel design introduces and makes use of an efficient concurrency control mechanism based on a lock-free skip-list design for handling the list of free memory intervals. We have implemented the parallel mark-split garbage collector in OpenJDK HotSpot as a parallel and concurrent garbage collector for the old generation. We experimentally evaluate the collector and compare it with the default concurrent mark-sweep garbage collector in OpenJDK HotSpot, using the DaCapo benchmarks.

1 Motivation

Garbage collection (GC) is an important component of many modern programming languages and runtime systems. As parallelism has become a core issue in the design and implementation of software systems, garbage collection algorithms have been parallelized and evaluated for their potential a range of scenarios. However, none of them can outperform the other in all use cases and researchers are still trying to improve different aspects of garbage collection.

Mark-split is a new GC technique introduced by Sagonas and Wilhelmsson [1] that combines advantages of mark-sweep and copying algorithms. Mark-split evolves from mark-sweep but removes the sweep phase. Instead, it creates the list of free memory while marking by using a special operation called *split*. Mark-split does not move objects, uses little extra space and has time complexity proportional to the size of the live data set. These advantages help it outperform mark-sweep in certain scenarios in sequential environment [1]. Whether it can maintain the advantages in a parallel environment remains an open question.

As mark-split repeatedly searches for and splits memory spaces, a high performance concurrent data structure to store the spaces is essential to the parallel design of mark-split. Lock-free data structures offer scalability and high throughput, guarantee progress, immune to deadlocks and livelocks. Several lock-free implementations of data structures have been introduced in the literature [2] [3], and included in Intels Threading Building Blocks Framework, the PEPPHER

Y. Afek (Ed.): DISC 2013, LNCS 8205, pp. 557–558, 2013.

framework [4], the Java concurrency package, and the Microsoft .NET Framework. Skip-list is a search data structure which provides expected logarithmic time search without the need to rebalance like balanced trees. The skip-list algorithm by Sundell and Tsigas [5] [6] is the first lock-free skip-list introduced in the literature. It is an efficient and practical lock-free implementation that is suitable for both fully concurrent (large multi-processor) systems as well as pre-emptive (multi-process) systems. We opt to extend it to store free memory spaces in our parallel mark-split.

2   Our Results

We extend the lock-free skip-list so that it is capable to handle the free memory intervals for mark-split. It is because the basic operations supported by the original lock-free skip-list, e.g *search*, *insert*, *remove*, are not strong enough to satisfy the functionality requirement of mark-split in concurrent environment. Our extension including a sophisticated concurrency control allows the skip-list to execute more complex operations such as *split* in mark-split algorithm.

Using the extended skip-list, we implement a parallel version of mark-split, namely ParMarkSplit, as a garbage collector in the OpenJDK HotSpot virtual machine. The collector performs marking and splitting in parallel to take advantage of multi-core architectures. In addition, a lazy-splitting mechanism is designed to improve the performance of the parallel mark-split.

The ParMarkSplit was evaluated and compared against a naive parallelized mark-split and the Concurrent Mark-Sweep collector bundled with the HotSpot. The former was a parallel mark-split implementation using a balanced search tree based on coarse-grained locking. The experiments were done on two contemporary multiprocessor systems, one has 12 Intel Nehalem cores with Hyper-Threading and the other has 48 AMD Bulldozer cores. A detailed version of our results will appear in a subsequent version of this brief announcement.

References

1. Sagonas, K., Wilhelmsson, J.: Mark and split. In: Proceedings of the 5th International Symposium on Memory Management, ISMM 2006, pp. 29–39. ACM (2006)
2. Herlihy, M., Shavit, N.: The Art of Multiprocessor Programming. Morgan Kaufmann (2008)
3. Cederman, D., Gidenstam, A., Ha, P., Sundell, H., Papatriantafilou, M., Tsigas, P.: Lock-free concurrent data structures. In: Pllana, S., Xhafa, F. (eds.) Programming Multi-Core and Many-Core Computing Systems, Wiley-Blackwell (2014)
4. Benkner, S., Pllana, S., Larsson Traff, J., Tsigas, P., Dolinsky, U., Augonnet, C., Bachmayer, B., Kessler, C., Moloney, D., Osipov, V.: PEPPHER: Efficient and Productive Usage of Hybrid Computing Systems. IEEE Micro (99), 1 (2011)
5. Sundell, H., Tsigas, P.: Fast and lock-free concurrent priority queues for multi-thread systems. J. Parallel Distrib. Comput. 65(5), 609–627 (2005)
6. Sundell, H., Tsigas, P.: Scalable and lock-free concurrent dictionaries. In: Proceedings of the 2004 ACM Symposium on Applied Computing, pp. 1438–1445. ACM (2004)

Brief Anouncement: The Topology of Asynchronous Byzantine Colorless Tasks

Hammurabi Mendes[1], Christine Tasson[2], and Maurice Herlihy[1]

[1] Computer Science Deptartment, Brown University – 115 Waterman Street, 02912, Providence, Rhode Island, USA
{hmendes,mph}@cs.brown.edu
[2] Université Paris Diderot, Sorbonne Paris Cité – PPS, UMR 7126, CNRS, F-75205, Paris, France
Christine.Tasson@pps.univ-paris-diderot.fr

1 Introduction

Tools adapted from combinatorial topology have been successful in characterizing task solvability in synchronous and asynchronous *crash-failure* models [2]. We extend the approach to asynchronous *Byzantine* systems: we give the first theorem with necessary and sufficient conditions to solve *arbitrary colorless tasks* in such model, capturing the relation between the total number of processes, the number of faulty processes, and the topological structure of the task's simplicial complexes.

Our focus on colorless tasks [1] encompasses well-studied problems such as consensus, k-set agreement, and approximate agreement. Informally, a colorless task is one that can be defined entirely in terms of *sets* of assigned input and output values, with no need to specify which value is assigned to which process, or how many times an assigned value appears. Therefore, the *renaming* task is *not* colorless, as each process must choose a distinct name.

Our first contribution is to **extend** the application of the topological model from [2], formerly used to characterize solvability in crash-failure systems, to colorless tasks in asynchronous Byzantine systems. Our second contribution is to give **new protocols** for k-set agreement and barycentric agreement in the Byzantine-failure model. These protocols fundament a general procedure solving arbitrary colorless tasks in Byzantine asynchronous systems, and underlie our proof of the solvability characterization in the described scenario. In other words, these protocols limn the boundary between the possible and impossible in light of asynchronous communication and Byzantine failures. Finally, our principal contribution is to give the **first theorem** with necessary and sufficient conditions to solve *arbitrary colorless tasks* in the asynchronous Byzantine model, which is described below.

2 Model

Informally, in our model for Byzantine colorless tasks, we require that outputs of non-faulty processes depend solely on inputs of non-faulty processes. So, we

Y. Afek (Ed.): DISC 2013, LNCS 8205, pp. 559–560, 2013.
© Springer-Verlag Berlin Heidelberg 2013

only care about inputs and outputs of non-Byzantine processes, and Byzantine inputs do not "influence" outputs of non-Byzantine processes.

The task itself is defined in terms of a pair of combinatorial structures called *simplicial complexes* [2]. Whether a task is solvable is equivalent to the existence of a certain structure-preserving map between the task's simplicial complexes. This equivalence captures the relation between $n + 1$, the number of processes, t, the number of failures, and the topological structure of the task's simplicial complexes.

A *colorless task* [1] is a triple $(\mathcal{I}, \mathcal{O}, \Delta)$, where $\mathcal{I}$ is the *input complex*, $\mathcal{O}$ is the *output complex*, and $\Delta : \mathcal{I} \to 2^{\mathcal{O}}$ is a carrier map. Each simplex in $\mathcal{I}$ represents possible *initial configurations*, i.e., possible sets of initial values taken by *non-faulty processes*, with possible initial configurations closed under inclusion. The output complex is analogous in regard to *final configurations*. Given an initial configuration, the carrier map Δ specifies which final configurations are legal given a particular initial configuration. For $\sigma_I \in \mathcal{I}$ and $\sigma_O \in \mathcal{O}$, a Byzantine colorless task requires $\sigma_O \in \Delta(\sigma_I)$, so the admissible non-faulty outputs depend *solely* on the starting non-faulty inputs. This condition, sometimes called *strong validity* in the literature, can be relaxed, requiring staightforward adaptations in our necessary/sufficient conditions.

Note that the *same* task definition triple $(\mathcal{I}, \mathcal{O}, \Delta)$ is used both for crash and Byzantine failure models, with the nature of the failures affecting only *protocols* (algorithms), but not *specifications* (models) – failures only alter the specification *scope*, but not its *definition*.

In our main theorem, a *non-trivial* task is one that requires communication in order to be solved. The formal definitions and details are discussed in [4].

Theorem 1 (Solvability). *A non-trivial colorless task $(\mathcal{I}, \mathcal{O}, \Delta)$ has a t-resilient protocol in the asynchronous Byzantine model if and only if*

1. *$n + 1 > t(\dim(\mathcal{I}) + 2)$ and*
2. *there is a continuous map $f : |\operatorname{skel}^t(\mathcal{I})| \to |\mathcal{O}|$ carried by Δ.*

While an analogous characterization has long been known for crash failures [2], our solvability theorem is the first such characterization for Byzantine failures. Furthermore, our theorem applies to the core/survivor-set failure model discussed in [3]. We invite the reader for the details in [4], and warmly welcome further comments and suggestions.

References

1. Borowsky, E., Gafni, E., Lynch, N., Rajsbaum, S.: The BG distributed simulation algorithm. Distributed Computing 14(3), 127–146 (2001)
2. Herlihy, M., Shavit, N.: The topological structure of asynchronous computability. J. ACM 46(6), 858–923 (1999)
3. Junqueira, F.P., Marzullo, K.: Designing Algorithms for Dependent Process Failures. Technical report (2003)
4. Mendes, H., Tasson, C., Herlihy, M.: The topology of asynchronous byzantine colorless tasks. CoRR, abs/1302.6224 (2013)

Brief Announcement:
Revisiting Dynamic Distributed Systems *

Carlos Gómez-Calzado[1], Alberto Lafuente[1], Mikel Larrea[1], and Michel Raynal[2]

[1] University of the Basque Country UPV/EHU, Spain
{carlos.gomez,alberto.lafuente,mikel.larrea}@ehu.es
[2] Institut Universitaire de France & IRISA, Université de Rennes, France
michel.raynal@irisa.fr

1 Introduction

Many of today's distributed systems are highly dynamic, and processes execute in different types of devices, some of them mobile and connected via wireless networks. As a consequence, communication can fail, messages can get lost, and the system can even partition. A number of agreement algorithms for such dynamic systems with mobile processes have been proposed. However, each proposal is based on specific system assumptions, which makes it difficult to compare them.

Clearly, system dynamicity and process mobility could be such that it prevents the success of any attempt to reach agreement due to the lack of connectivity. Hence, the system model considered should provide a sufficient degree of stability, reliability and synchrony, while embracing the many faces of dynamicity. Specifically, in this work we propose that the system alternates periods of "good" and "bad" behavior, in the line of the timed asynchronous model of Cristian and Fetzer [4]. However, while that work assumed good/bad periods for a known and non-mobile set of processes, we extend the assumption to both system dynamicity and process mobility.

We model a dynamic distributed system by means of a Time-Varying Graph [2]. We characterize a period of good behavior as a *connected interval*, in which processes are able to communicate (either directly or indirectly). Observe that during a connected interval some graph stability and communication timeliness must be satisfied. Nevertheless, we allow some link removal provided that graph connectivity is maintained, as characterized by the *Degradation Speed* metric we define in [5].

2 Categorizing Mobile Dynamic Distributed Systems

In order to characterize (mobile) dynamic distributed systems more precisely, we propose to extend the formalism of Baldoni et al. [1] by introducing an additional level, denoted by s, inspired by the good/bad period alternation of the timed asynchronous model proposed by Cristian and Fetzer [4]:

---

* Research partially supported by the Spanish Research Council, under grant TIN2010-17170, the Basque Government, under grants IT395-10 and S-PE12UN109, and the University of the Basque Country UPV/EHU, under grant UFI11/45. Also, Carlos Gómez-Calzado is recipient of a doctoral fellowship from the Basque Government.

Y. Afek (Ed.): DISC 2013, LNCS 8205, pp. 561–562, 2013.

s : the system alternates good periods, where a bound exists but it is not known a priori by processes, and bad periods, where there is no bound.

Level s combines levels n and ∞ of Baldoni et al. in good and bad periods, respectively. Moreover, other dimensions than process concurrency and network diameter characterize also mobile dynamic distributed systems, as summarized in Figure 1:

Dimension $(L: \{b,n,s,\infty\})$	Bound corresponds to...
Timeliness (T^L)	...processing and message transmission time
Process Failures $(\mathcal{P}_F^L)$	...the number of failures a process can suffer
Channel Failures $(\mathcal{C}_F^L)$	...the number of message losses on any link
Graph Partitioning $(G_\#^L)$	...the number of graphs in the system
Graph Membership (G_Π^L)	...the number of processes in any graph
Graph Diameter (G_D^L)	...the diameter of any graph
Graph Stability (G_S^L)	...the degradation speed of any graph

Fig. 1. Dimensions categorizing mobile dynamic distributed systems

As a case study of this categorization, we consider the eventual leader election problem, also known as implementing the Omega failure detector class [3]. In [5], we first adapt the definition of the Dynamic Omega class [6] to systems with process mobility. We call to the resulting new failure detector class *Mobile Dynamic Omega* (denoted by $\Delta^*\Omega$). Then, we propose a weak mobile dynamic distributed system model $\mathcal{M}^*$ where all dimensions have level s, i.e., $\mathcal{M}^* = \mathcal{M}(T^s, \mathcal{P}_F^s, \mathcal{C}_F^s, G_\#^s, G_\Pi^s, G_D^s, G_S^s)$, and a leader election algorithm implementing $\Delta^*\Omega$ in $\mathcal{M}^*$.

References

1. Baldoni, R., Bertier, M., Raynal, M., Tucci-Piergiovanni, S.: Looking for a definition of dynamic distributed systems. In: Malyshkin, V.E. (ed.) PaCT 2007. LNCS, vol. 4671, pp. 1–14. Springer, Heidelberg (2007)
2. Casteigts, A., Flocchini, P., Quattrociocchi, W., Santoro, N.: Time-varying graphs and dynamic networks. In: Frey, H., Li, X., Ruehrup, S. (eds.) ADHOC-NOW 2011. LNCS, vol. 6811, pp. 346–359. Springer, Heidelberg (2011)
3. Chandra, T.D., Hadzilacos, V., Toueg, S.: The weakest failure detector for solving consensus. Journal of the ACM 43(4), 685–722 (1996)
4. Cristian, F., Fetzer, C.: The timed asynchronous distributed system model. IEEE Transactions on Parallel and Distributed Systems 10(6), 642–657 (1999)
5. Gómez-Calzado, C., Lafuente, A., Larrea, M., Raynal, M.: Fault-Tolerant Leader Election in Mobile Dynamic Distributed Systems. Technical Report EHU-KAT-IK-07-13, University of the Basque Country UPV/EHU, http://www.sc.ehu.es/acwlaalm/
6. Larrea, M., Raynal, M., Soraluze, I., Cortiñas, R.: Specifying and implementing an eventual leader service for dynamic systems. International Journal of Web and Grid Services 8(3), 204–224 (2012)

Brief Announcement: Computing in the Presence of Concurrent Solo Executions

Sergio Rajsbaum[3], Michel Raynal[1,2], and Julien Stainer[1]

[1] Institut Universitaire de France
[2] IRISA, Campus de Beaulieu, 35042 Rennes Cedex, France
[3] Instituto de Mathematicas, UNAM, D.F. 04510, Mexico

Distributed Computability. The computability power of a distributed model depends on its communication, timing, and failure assumptions. A basic result is the impossibility to solve consensus in an asynchronous read/write or message-passing system even if only one process may crash.

The power of a model has been studied in detail with respect to *tasks*, which are the distributed equivalent of a function in sequential computing. Each process gets only one part of the input, and after communicating with the others, decides on an output value, such that collectively, the various local outputs produced by the processes respect the task specification, which is defined from the local inputs of the processes. This paper concentrates on the class of *colorless tasks*, where the specification is in terms of possible inputs and outputs, but without referring to which process gets which input or produces which output. Among the previously studied notable tasks, many are colorless, such as consensus, set agreement, approximate agreement and loop agreement, while some are not, like renaming.

Wait-Freedom and Solo Execution. This paper considers *wait-free* distributed asynchronous crash-prone computation models[1,3,6]. Wait-free has two (complementary) meanings. First, it means the model allows up to $n - 1$ processes to crash, where n is total number of processes. The term *wait-freedom* is also used to state a liveness condition, that requires every non-faulty process to progress in its computation and eventually decide (i.e., compute a result) whatever the behavior of the other processes.

In a wait-free model where processes must satisfy the wait-freedom liveness condition, a process has to make progress in its computation even in the extreme case where all other processes have crashed, or are too slow, and consequently be forced to decide without knowing their input values. Hence, for each process, there are executions where this process perceives itself as being the only process participating in the computation.

More generally, we say that a process executes *solo* if it computes its local output without knowing the input values of the other processes.

Two Extreme Wait-Free Models: Shared Memory and Message Passing. In a model where processes communicate by reading and writing to shared registers, at most one process can run solo in the same execution. This is because, while a process is running solo, its writes and reads from the shared memory, and once it finishes its computation it writes to the memory its decision. Any other process that starts running, will be able to read the history left by the solo process in the memory.

Y. Afek (Ed.): DISC 2013, LNCS 8205, pp. 563–564, 2013.

When considering message-passing communication, all processes may have to run solo concurrently in the extreme case, where messages are arbitrarily delayed, and each process perceives the other processes as having crashed. Only tasks that can be solved without communication can be computed in this model.

Investigating the Computability Power of Intermediary Models. The aim of the paper is to study the computability power of asynchronous models in which several processes may run solo in the same execution. More precisely, assuming that up to d processes may run solo, the paper addresses the following questions:

- How to define a computation model in which up to d processes may run solo? (such a model model is called d-*solo* model.)
- Which tasks can be computed in such a model?

The aim is to study these questions in a clean theoretical framework, and investigate for the first time models weaker than the basic wait-free read/write model. However, we hope that our results might be relevant to other intermediate models, such as distributed models over fixed or wireless networks, and models where processes communicate via multi-writer/multi-reader registers, when the number of registers is smaller than the number of processes. The full paper, which can be found in [5], answers all the the previous questions.

It is important to notice that our d-solo model addresses different issues than the d-concurrency model of [2], where it is shown that with d-set agreement any number of processes can emulate d state machines of which at least one remains highly available. While d-concurrency is used to reduce the concurrency degree to at most d processes that are always allowed to cooperate, d-solo allows up to d processes to run independently (i.e., without any cooperation).

References

1. Attiya, H., Welch, J.: Distributed computing: fundamentals, simulations, and advanced topics, 2nd edn. Wiley-Interscience (2004)
2. Gafni, E., Guerraoui, R.: Generalized universality. In: Katoen, J.-P., König, B. (eds.) CONCUR 2011. LNCS, vol. 6901, pp. 17–27. Springer, Heidelberg (2011)
3. Herlihy, M.P.: Wait-free synchronization. ACM Transactions on Programming Languages and Systems 13(1), 124–149 (1991)
4. Herlihy, M.P., Rajsbaum, S., Raynal, M.: Power and limits of distributed computing shared memory models. Theoretical Computer Science, 22 pages (to appear, 2013), http://dx.doi.org/10.1016/j.tcs.2013.03.002
5. Rajsbaum, S., Raynal, M., Stainer, J.: Computing in the Presence of Concurrent Solo Executions. Tech. Report 2004, 20 pages. IRISA, Université de Rennes (F) (2013)
6. Raynal, M.: Concurrent programming: algorithms, principles, and foundations, 515 pages. Springer (2013) (ISBN 978-3-642-32027-9)

Brief Announcement:
A Concurrent Lock-Free Red-Black Tree*

Aravind Natarajan and Neeraj Mittal

The University of Texas at Dallas, Richardson TX 75080, USA
{aravindn,neerajm}@utdallas.edu

We present a *lock-free* algorithm for a red-black tree that supports concurrent search and modify (insert and delete) operations, using only single-word atomic instructions. Our algorithm uses the atomic *compare-and-swap* (CAS) and *set-bit* (SB) instructions, both of which are widely supported by modern processors. To our knowledge, ours is the first lock-free red-black tree that can be directly implemented on hardware, without assuming any underlying system support such as transactional memory.

The lock-free algorithm described here builds upon our wait-free algorithm presented in [1]. As in [1], search operations traverse the tree from the root till a leaf node is reached, along a simple path referred to as the *access path*. If the key in the leaf node matches the key being searched for, the operation returns true; otherwise, it returns false. Search operations do not lock or copy any nodes.

Modify operations in our algorithm are top-down in nature, and utilize the *window* based execution idea proposed by Tsay and Li [2]. A window is a rooted sub-tree of the tree structure. The window of an operation slides down the tree as the operation progresses. For each window, the process executing the operation first makes a local copy of the nodes within it. Next, Tarjan's transformations [3] for a top-down sequential red-black tree are applied to the local copy. This may result in nodes (a) being added to or removed from the window, and/or (b) changing color. The root of a window maintains an *invariant* depending on the type of operation (insert or delete), which ensures that the transformations do not affect nodes outside the window. Finally, the original window is atomically replaced by the copy. We refer to these steps as a *window transaction*. An operation may comprise of multiple window transactions. After a window transaction succeeds, nodes in the original window are no longer reachable from the root of the tree, and are termed *passive* nodes.

Whether a node satisfies the operation invariant depends on its color, as well as that of its children or grandchildren. For an insert operation, the invariant maintained at the root of the window is that it is black and has a black child. The invariant maintained by the root of a delete window is that either it is red, or has a red child, or red grandchild. We refer to this *path* of nodes, that begins at the root of the window and ends at its child, or grandchild as the *invariant-path*.

Modify operations are based on our observation that *all* window transactions are *self-contained*. The invariant maintained by the window root ensures that applying Tarjan's transformations to the window never leaves the tree out of

---

* This work was supported in part by the NSF Grant CNS-1115733.

Y. Afek (Ed.): DISC 2013, LNCS 8205, pp. 565–566, 2013.
© Springer-Verlag Berlin Heidelberg 2013

balance. In other words, the tree is *always* a valid red-black tree. Therefore, instead of always starting at the root of the tree as in [1], the transformations can be applied starting at any internal node on the access path that satisfies the operation invariant. In our algorithm, modify operations exploit this observation and start from the *deepest* such node. We refer to this node as the *injection point*, and it is determined by traversing the tree along the access path, while checking if the invariant holds at each node. The operation starts at the root of the tree only if no such internal node is found. However, our experiments indicate that in most cases the injection point is close to the leaf, resulting in (a) lesser contention, and (b) fewer window transactions being executed by a modify operation. Consequently, modify operations are, on average, 15 times faster than those in [1].

However, a process cannot directly start executing window transactions from the injection point, once it has been determined, because the tree is modified concurrently by other operations that may: (a) cause the injection point to become passive, or (b) violate the operation invariant at the injection point by changing the color of nodes. Therefore, before a modify operation can start executing its window transaction, the entire invariant-path must be *locked* on its behalf. Failure to do so causes the operation to restart. Note that the term 'lock' is used loosely here. Whenever a node is *locked* by an operation, enough information is left behind that any process blocked by that operation can *help* move it out of the way. Helping involves locking the invariant-path as well as the execution of a window transaction. After helping, a process returns to its own operation.

To summarize, the execution of a modify operation in our algorithm can be partitioned into four phases: (i) *seek*, (ii) *validation*, (iii) *injection*, and (iv) *execution*. In the seek phase, the tree is simply traversed along the access path to determine the injection point and invariant-path. The validation phase consists of examining the nodes on the invariant-path, determined in the seek phase. If a node is locked by another operation, it is helped to ensure lock-freedom, following which the seek phase is restarted. If all nodes are free, then the process moves to the injection phase, where the invariant-path is locked on behalf of the operation. Locks are obtained in a top-down manner, and failure to acquire a lock causes the operation to restart after relinquishing all obtained locks. Finally, after the invariant-path has been locked, the process moves to the execution phase where it executes its window transaction(s), as described earlier.

References

1. Natarajan, A., Savoie, L., Mittal, N.: Brief Announcement: Concurrent Wait-Free Red-Black Trees. In: Aguilera, M.K. (ed.) DISC 2012. LNCS, vol. 7611, pp. 421–422. Springer, Heidelberg (2012)
2. Tsay, J.J., Li, H.C.: Lock-Free Concurrent Tree Structures for Multiprocessor Systems. In: Proceedings of the International Conference on Parallel and Distributed Systems (ICPADS), pp. 544–549 (December 1994)
3. Tarjan, R.E.: Efficient Top-Down Updating of Red-Black Trees. Technical Report TR-006-85, Department of Computer Science, Princeton University (1985)

Brief Announcement:
A General Technique for Non-blocking Trees

Trevor Brown[1], Faith Ellen[1], and Eric Ruppert[2]

[1] University of Toronto, Canada
[2] York University, Canada

We introduce a template that can be used to implement a large class of non-blocking tree data structures efficiently. Using this template is significantly easier than designing the implementation from scratch. The template also drastically simplifies correctness proofs. Thus, the template allows us to obtain provably correct, non-blocking implementations of more complicated tree data structures than those that were previously possible. For example, we use the template to obtain the first non-blocking balanced binary search tree (BST) using fine-grained synchronization.

Software transactional memory (STM) makes it easy to turn sequential implementations into concurrent ones, but non-blocking implementations of STM are currently inefficient. Tsay and Li [6] gave a general approach for implementing wait-free trees using LL and SC primitives. However, their technique severely limits concurrency, since it requires every process accessing the tree (even for read-only operations) to copy an entire path of the tree starting from the root. For library implementations of data structures, and applications where performance is critical, it is worthwhile to expend effort to get more efficient implementations than those that can be obtained using these techniques.

The Tree Update Template. We can implement any down-tree, which is a directed acyclic graph with indegree one. Each update operation on the data-structure replaces a contiguous part of the tree with a new tree of nodes (which can point to nodes that were previously children of the replaced nodes). As with all techniques for concurrent implementations, our method is more efficient if the operations are smaller. For instance, an insertion into a (leaf-oriented) chromatic tree is performed by one update operation to replace a leaf by a new internal node and two new leaves, followed by a sequence of rotations, each of which is an update operation. If an operation has to access several nodes, implementing it in a non-blocking way requires synchronization among processes. Our template takes care of all process coordination, so provably correct implementations can be obtained fairly mechanically.

The template uses the recently introduced LLX and SCX primitives [2], which are extended versions of LL and SC that can be efficiently implemented from CAS. At a high level, an update operation built using the template consists of a sequence of LLXs on a small set V of nodes, the creation of a (typically small) tree of new, replacement nodes, and an SCX, which atomically swings a pointer to do the replacement, only if no node in V has changed since the aforementioned LLX on it. If the SCX successfully swings the pointer, it also prevents any removed nodes from undergoing any further changes.

Y. Afek (Ed.): DISC 2013, LNCS 8205, pp. 567–568, 2013.

The operations of a data structure built using the template are automatically linearizable. Moreover, simply reading an individual field of a node always returns the result of the most recently linearized operation that modified the field. Some queries can be performed efficiently using only reads. For example, in a BST where the keys of nodes are immutable, a search can follow the appropriate path by simply reading keys and child pointers, and the value in the node reached. Such a search is linearizable even if concurrent update operations occur along the path. The implementation of LLX/SCX also provides an easy way to take a snapshot of a set of nodes. This facilitates the implementation of more complex queries, such as successor or range queries. The template allows some update operations to fail, but guarantees that update operations will continue to succeed as long as they continue to be performed. Moreover, if all update operations in progress apply to disjoint parts of the tree, they will not prevent one another from succeeding.

Implementing Non-blocking Balanced BSTs. Chromatic trees [4] are a relaxation of red-black trees which decouple rebalancing operations from operations that perform the inserts and deletes. Rebalancing operations can be performed in any order, and can be postponed and interleaved freely with operations that perform the inserts and deletes. Amortized O(1) rebalancing operations per insert or delete are sufficient to rebalance the tree into a red-black tree. Using the template, we implemented a non-blocking chromatic tree. The height of a tree containing n keys is $O(\log n + c)$, where c is point contention. Our implementation is easily described in 10 pages, and rigorously proved in five pages. In contrast, a non-blocking implementation of a B+tree (a considerably simpler sequential data structure) is described in 30 pages and proved correct in 33 pages [1].

We are presently working on relaxed versions of (a, b)-trees and AVL trees. Performance experiments (available in the full paper, at http://www.cs.utoronto.ca/~tabrown) indicate that our Java implementations rival, and often significantly outperform, highly tuned industrial-strength data structures [3,5].

References

1. Braginsky, A., Petrank, E.: A lock-free B+tree. In: Proc. 24th ACM Symposium on Parallelism in Algorithms and Architectures, pp. 58–67 (2012)
2. Brown, T., Ellen, F., Ruppert, E.: Pragmatic primitives for non-blocking data structures. In: Proc. 32nd ACM Symp. on Principles of Distr. Comput. (2013)
3. Lea, D.: Java's java.util.concurrent.ConcurrentSkipListMap
4. Nurmi, O., Soisalon-Soininen, E.: Chromatic binary search trees: A structure for concurrent rebalancing. Acta Informatica 33(6), 547–557 (1996)
5. Spiegel, M., Reynolds Jr., P.F.: Lock-free multiway search trees. In: Proc. 39th International Conference on Parallel Processing, pp. 604–613 (2010)
6. Tsay, J.-J., Li, H.-C.: Lock-free concurrent tree structures for multiprocessor systems. In: Proc. Int. Conf. on Parallel and Distributed Sys., pp. 544–549 (1994)

Brief Announcement: Communication-Efficient Byzantine Consensus without a Common Clock

Danny Dolev[1] and Christoph Lenzen[2]

[1] Hebrew University of Jerusalem, 91904 Jerusalem, Israel
[2] Massachusetts Institute of Technology, MA 02139 Cambridge, USA

Abstract. Many consensus protocols assume a synchronous system in which all processes start executing the protocol at once and in the same round. However, such a common start requires to establish consensus among the correct processes in the first place, making this assumption questionable in many circumstances. In this work, we show that it is possible to consistently initiate consensus instances without a common round counter. Every correct node can initiate consistent consensus instances, without interfering with other nodes' instances. Furthermore, by bounding the frequency at which nodes may initiate instances, Byzantine faulty nodes can be prevented from initiating too many instances.

Keywords: communication complexity, simulation framework.

Consensus is a fundamental fault-tolerance primitive in distributed systems, which has been introduced several decades ago [3]. Both in asynchronous and synchronous models, it is a very common assumption that all nodes start to execute the algorithm at a given point in time.[1]

We provide a self-stabilizing solution to this problem. In this brief announcement, we assume a synchronous model and a deterministic binary consensus algorithm. Furthermore, output 0 is supposed to mean "take no action", bearing no effect on the system; it can thus be used as a save fallback value. All of these restrictions are dropped in the full paper [2]. Moreover, our results can be used to derive new algorithms for Byzantine-tolerant self-stabilizing pulse synchronization (cf. [1]). This is subject to future publication.

Problem Statement. We assume that executions proceed in rounds, where in each round, each node may perform local computations and send a message to each other node, where all messages sent by correct nodes are received before the end of the round. Up to $f < n/3$ faulty nodes are controlled by an adversary that can disobey the algorithm in any fashion. In the following we assume that a consensus protocol $\mathcal{P}$ is given. The goal of the *initiation problem* is to enable correct nodes to initiate independent executions of $\mathcal{P}$. More precisely:

---

[1] If in an asynchronous setting nodes unconditionally wake up and join an instance upon receiving the "first" message, this essentially means to *always* run *any* possible instance, concurrently, resulting in unbounded message complexity in case of Byzantine faults.

Y. Afek (Ed.): DISC 2013, LNCS 8205, pp. 569–570, 2013.

1. Each instance carries a label $(r, v) \in \mathbb{N} \times V$, where r is a round and v a node. We say that the corresponding instance is *initialized* by node v in round r (note that the nodes do not know r).
2. For each instance, each correct node decides whether it *participates* in the instance at the beginning of round $r + 2$.
3. We assume that for each instance (r, v), each participating node $w \in V$ can compute some input $i_w(r, v) \in \{0, 1\}$.
4. If correct node w participates in instance (r, v), it terminates this instance at the latest in round $r + R + 4$ and outputs some value $o_w(r, v) \in \{0, 1\}$.
5. If correct nodes w, w' participate in instance (r, v), then $o_w(r, v) = o_{w'}(r, v)$.
6. If all correct nodes participate in an instance with input b, all output b.
7. If $o_w(r, v) \neq 0$ for some correct node participating in instance (r, v), then all correct nodes participate in this instance (and output $o_w(r, v)$).
8. If a correct node v initializes instance (r, v), all correct nodes w participate in this instance with input $i_w(r + 2, w)$.

Compared to "classical" consensus, property 4 corresponds to *termination*, property 5 to *agreement*, and property 6 to *validity*. Note that validity is replaced by a safety property in case not all correct nodes participate: property 7 states that non-zero output is feasible only if no correct node is left out. Finally, property 8 makes sure that all nodes participate in case a non-faulty node initializes an instance, therefore ensuring validity for such instances.

Theorem 1. *Given a synchronous, deterministic R-round consensus protocol resilient to f faults, we can construct an algorithm solving the initiation problem that self-stabilizes within $R + 4$ rounds.*

Communication Complexity. In case of crash faults, our solution is efficient in the sense that for each initiated instance, there is an overhead of 4 rounds and 4 broadcasts per node. However, Byzantine faults may result in each faulty node initiating an instance every round, even if correct nodes are known to do so very infrequently.

If we decide that correct nodes may initialize an instance at most once within T rounds, we can force faulty nodes to do so as well. The modified algorithm can be implemented such that it self-stabilizes in $\min\{T, R + 4\}$ rounds. Note that the choice of $T = R$ is particularly attractive, enabling nodes to initiate and complete an instance within $2R + 4$ rounds, yet ensuring that never more than one instance per node causes communication.

References

1. Dolev, D., Hoch, E.N.: Byzantine Self-Stabilizing Pulse in a Bounded-Delay Model. In: Masuzawa, T., Tixeuil, S. (eds.) SSS 2007. LNCS, vol. 4838, pp. 234–252. Springer, Heidelberg (2007)
2. Dolev, D., Lenzen, C.: Communication-Efficient Byzantine Consensus Without a Common Clock. Computing Research Repository abs/1307.7976 (2013)
3. Pease, M., Shostak, R., Lamport, L.: Reaching Agreement in the Presence of Faults. Journal of the ACM 27, 228–234 (1980)

Brief Announcement: Consistency and Complexity Tradeoffs for Highly-Available Multi-cloud Store

Gregory Chockler[1], Dan Dobre[2], and Alexander Shraer[3]

[1] Royal Holloway, University of London
Gregory.Chockler@rhul.ac.uk
[2] NEC Labs Europe, Heidelberg, Germany
dan.dobre@neclab.eu
[3] Google, Inc.
shralex@google.com

1 Introduction

Cloud storage services are becoming increasingly popular due to their flexible deployment, convenient pay-per-use model, and little (if any) administrative overhead. Today, they are being offered by a growing number of Internet companies, such as Amazon, Google, Microsoft as well as numerous smaller providers, such as Rackspace, Nirvanix and many others. Although cloud storage providers make tremendous investments into ensuring reliability and security of the service they offer, most of them have suffered from well-publicized outages where the integrity and/or availability of data have been compromised for prolonged periods of time. In addition, even in the absence of outages, the customers can still lose access to their data due to connectivity problems, or unexpected alterations in the service contract (*data lock-in*).

To address these concerns, *multi-cloud* storage systems whereupon data is replicated across multiple cloud storage services have become a hot topic in the systems community. Despite the significant progress in building practical multi-cloud storage systems [1], as of today, little is known about their fundamental capabilities and limitations. The primary challenge lies in the variety of the storage interfaces and consistency semantics offered by different cloud providers to their external users. For example, whereas Amazon S3 supports a simple read/write interface, other storage services expose a selection of more advanced transactional primitives, such as conditional writes.

In this paper, we outline the results of our recent study [2] that explored the space and time complexity of building reliable multi-cloud storage services.

2 Overview of the Results

Space Bound for Multi-Writer Register Emulations. Our first result establishes a lower bound on the space overhead associated with reliably storing a *single* data item, such as a single key/value pair in a key-value store, supporting basic *put* and *get* operations. For this lower bound we assume underlying storage services exposing put, get, and list primitives (such as those supported by Amazon S3), which we model as multi-writer/multi-reader (MWMR) *atomic snapshot* objects. We formalize this setting using the fault-prone shared memory model [4], and prove the following [2]:

Theorem 1. *Let A be a t-tolerant emulation of a wait-free k-writer/1-reader safe register, supporting a set of values V, $|V| > k$, out of a set of $n > t$ wait-free atomic MWMR snapshot objects which can store vectors of length $m > 0$. Then, $k \leq \lfloor (nm - t - 1)/t \rfloor$.*

Y. Afek (Ed.): DISC 2013, LNCS 8205, pp. 571–572, 2013.

Our proof constructs a failure and contention-free run α in which all k writers take turns writing into the emulated register each leaving t low-level writes "hanging" on t distinct snapshot objects. We then show that α cannot be extended with another write W as the hung writes may terminate at any time, and in particular, after W returns, erasing all traces of W. Thus, the emulation space overhead is not adaptive to contention. Our result explains the space overheads incurred by recently published practical implementations of reliable multi-cloud stores (e.g., [1]). Their worst-case space complexity is proportional to the total number of writers, which matches our lower bound.

Space-Efficient Emulations Using Conditional Writes. We next turn to emulating reliable registers over storage services supporting transactional update primitives. First, it is well known that a constant number of *read-modify-write* (RMW) objects is indeed sufficient to reliably emulate multi-writer atomic register [5]. However, the RMW objects employed by the existing implementations are too specialized to be exposed by the commodity cloud storage interfaces. Instead, the cloud storage providers typically expose *general purpose* read-modify-write primitives which are variants of *conditional writes*, and therefore, essentially equivalent to *compare-and-swap (CAS)*. In [2], we show that there exist reliable *constant* space implementations of *(i)* multi-writer atomic register, which requires the underlying clouds to only support a *single CAS* object per stored value, is *adaptive to point contention*, and tolerates a minority of cloud failures and *(ii)* Ranked Register [3] using a single fault-prone *CAS* object. A collection of such Ranked Registers can be used to construct a reliable Ranked Register, from which agreement is built [3]. Our construction thus can be leveraged to implement multi-cloud state machine replication capable of supporting infinitely many clients with constant space.

Our work opens several avenues for future research. For example, the step complexity of our atomic register implementation is adaptive to point contention. Is this optimal? Interestingly, if this question can be answered in the affirmative, this would imply that there is a time complexity separation between *CAS* and generic read-modify-write primitive, which have been previously thought to be equivalent (e.g., in terms of their power to implement consensus).Furthermore, our space bound in [2] does not rule out constant space algorithms in which all writers are correct. Since the writer reliability can be enforced in many practical settings, it will be interesting to see whether a constant memory algorithm can be constructed under the assumption of reliable writers, or the space bound can be further strengthened to also apply in this case.

References

1. Basescu, C., Cachin, C., Eyal, I., Haas, R., Sorniotti, A., Vukolic, M., Zachevsky, I.: Robust Data Sharing with Key-Value Stores. In: DSN, pp. 1–12 (2012)
2. Chockler, G., Dobre, D., Shraer, A.: Consistency and Complexity Tradeoffs for Highly-Available Multi-Cloud Store (2013),
   http://people.csail.mit.edu/grishac/mcstore.pdf?
3. Chockler, G., Malkhi, D.: Active Disk Paxos with infinitely many processes. Distrib. Comput. 18(1), 73–84 (2005)
4. Jayanti, P., et al.: Fault-tolerant wait-free shared objects. Journal of the ACM 45(3) (1998)
5. Gilbert, S., et al.: Rambo: a robust, reconfigurable atomic memory service for dynamic networks. Distrib. Comput. 23(4), 225–272 (2010)

Brief Announcement:
BFT Storage with $2t + 1$ Data Replicas

Christian Cachin[1], Dan Dobre[2], and Marko Vukolić[3]

[1] IBM Research - Zurich, Switzerland
cca@zurich.ibm.com
[2] NEC Labs Europe, Heidelberg, Germany
dan.dobre@neclab.eu
[3] EURECOM, Sophia Antipolis, France
marko.vukolic@eurecom.fr

Byzantine Fault Tolerant (BFT) protocols are notoriously costly to deploy. This cost stems from the fact that, in many applications, tolerating Byzantine faults requires more resources than tolerating less severe faults, such as crashes. For example, in the asynchronous communication model, BFT read/write storage [2] protocols are shown to require at least $3t + 1$ replicas in different storage servers so that t Byzantine server faults can be tolerated [5]. This is to be contrasted with the requirement for $2t + 1$ replicas in the asynchronous crash model for protocols used in production cloud-storage systems. This resource gap is one of the main concerns for practical adoption of BFT systems.

In this paper we briefly state the results of our recent study [1] in which we show that perhaps surprisingly, this gap may in fact be significantly smaller. Namely, in [1] we show a fundamental separation of data from metadata for BFT storage which we use to design *MDStore*, a novel protocol that reduces the number of *data replicas* to as few as $2t + 1$, maintaining $3t_M + 1$ *metadata replicas* at (possibly) different servers. Here, t and t_M are thresholds on the number of Byzantine data and metadata replicas, respectively. To achieve lower replication cost, *MDStore* does not sacrifice other functionalities. Namely, *MDStore* implements multi-writer multi-reader (MWMR) wait-free atomic [2] storage that tolerates any number of Byzantine readers and crash-faulty writers. *MDStore* is the first asynchronous BFT storage protocol that does not assume any trusted components to reduce its resource cost. Moreover, being a fully asynchronous read/write storage protocol, *MDStore* is fundamentally different from the existing consensus and state-machine replication protocols that employ similar separation of control and data planes [6], which are subject to the FLP impossibility result and require partial synchrony.

The key technique that allows *MDStore* to achieve lower replication cost, is separation of data from metadata, where metadata holds: (i) a hash of a value, (ii) a timestamp, and (iii) pointers to data replicas that store a value. *MDStore* has modular architecture: a client reads and writes metadata through an abstraction of a *metadata service*: an array of single-writer multi-reader (SWMR) safe wait-free storage objects [2] and a novel MWMR atomic wait-free storage object variant, we call *timestamped storage*. This object is very similar to classical atomic storage, except that it exposes a timestamp of stored values to clients

Y. Afek (Ed.): DISC 2013, LNCS 8205, pp. 573–574, 2013.
© Springer-Verlag Berlin Heidelberg 2013

as well. In an array of safe storage objects, indexed by timestamps, *MDStore* stores hashes of data values, whereas in atomic timestamped storage, *MDStore* stores pointers to $t+1$ (out of $2t+1$) data replicas storing the most recent value. On the other hand, data replicas simply store timestamp/value pairs. Finally, we show in [1] that the *MDStore* metadata service can be implemented from asynchronous BFT SWMR safe (e.g., [3]) and SWMR atomic (e.g., [4]) storage protocols using $3t+1$ replicas for tolerating t faults; in the context of *MDStore*, these replicas are exactly the $3t_M + 1$ *metadata replicas*.

We further prove in [1] that at least $2t+1$ data replicas are necessary for implementations that leverage a metadata service, even if data replicas can fail only by crashing. This shows not only that *MDStore* is optimally resilient, but also that it incurs no additional data replication cost compared to crash-tolerant storage. Our $2t+1$ lower bound has a very broad scope: it applies to any obstruction-free single-writer single-reader safe storage [2]. Moreover, for the purpose of the lower bound, we define in [1] a metadata service very loosely as a fault-free oracle, that can implement arbitrary functionality with a single limitation: roughly speaking, metadata service can not be used for storing and/or forwarding data. We believe that this definition of a metadata service is of an independent interest.

Finally, we show in [1] that separating data from metadata for reducing the cost of BFT storage is not possible without limiting the power of the Byzantine adversary. Namely, for an unrestricted, unbounded Byzantine adversary, our lower bound on the number of data replicas extends to $3t+1$, despite the metadata service oracle. However, this $3t+1$ lower bound does not apply to a practically relevant, bounded adversary that cannot subvert the collision-resistance property of cryptographic hash functions. Intuitively, this explains why our *MDStore* protocol stores value hashes in its metadata service.

Our work opens multiple avenues for future work. We show in [1] that with the design that separates data and metadata, the cost of BFT storage, traditionally a major impediment to its practical deployment, is on par with that of crash tolerant storage. For BFT storage this is a paradigm shift since it requires rethinking all the aspects of BFT storage including complexity, erasure coding techniques and practical implications, all of which have been extensively studied in the traditional "unified" model of data and metadata.

References

1. Cachin, C., Dobre, D., Vukolic, M.: BFT Storage with 2t+1 Data Replicas. CoRR, abs/1305.4868 (2013)
2. Lamport, L.: On Interprocess Communication. Distr. Comp. 1(2), 77–101 (1986)
3. Malkhi, D., Reiter, M.K.: Byzantine Quorum Systems. Distr. Comp. 11(4), 203–213 (1998)
4. Malkhi, D., Reiter, M.K.: Secure and scalable replication in Phalanx. In: Proc. SRDS, pp. 51–58 (1998)
5. Martin, J.-P., Alvisi, L., Dahlin, M.: Minimal Byzantine Storage. In: Malkhi, D. (ed.) DISC 2002. LNCS, vol. 2508, pp. 311–325. Springer, Heidelberg (2002)
6. Yin, J., Martin, J.-P., Venkataramani, A., Alvisi, L., Dahlin, M.: Separating agreement from execution for Byzantine fault tolerant services. In: Proc. SOSP, pp. 253–267 (2003)

Brief Announcement: Private Channel Models in Multi-party Communication Complexity*

Faith Ellen, Rotem Oshman, Toniann Pitassi, and Vinod Vaikuntanathan

University of Toronto

Introduction. Communication complexity lower bounds have found many applications in distributed computing. For the most part, these applications have involved lower bounds on *two-player* communication complexity. However, there are limits to the usefulness of two-player lower bounds: reductions from the two-player model cannot prove certain results (see, e.g., [4]). Multi-player communication complexity has been studied extensively, but the models most commonly studied are not suitable for modeling distributed computation, because the inputs are not private (e.g., the number-on-forehead model) or players communicate by *shared blackboard*. Recently, though, some lower bounds have been obtained on multi-player communication complexity for several different models with private channels and inputs [2, 5–7].

One hurdle in reasoning about private-channel models is that there is no *shared transcript* that all players observe, which makes them tricky to define. In this paper, we give formal definitions for private-channel models used in [2, 5–7], taking into account such factors as the network topology (e.g., the message passing model vs. the coordinator model) and timing (synchrony vs. asynchrony). Our first main contribution is to prove that these models are all equivalent up to polylogarithmic factors, thus simplifying the diverse landscape of private-channel models. Our second is the development of a randomized protocol, based on a simulation of the AKS sorting network [1], that can exactly compute the t-th frequency moment of n-bit inputs using $O(tk \operatorname{polylog}(n, k))$ bits and $O(\operatorname{polylog}(n, k))$ rounds, with high probability.

Models. All our models have k players, each with private randomness and n bits of input. We consider both synchronous models, in which computation proceeds in rounds, and asynchronous models, in which the order of events is controlled by a scheduler. In all cases, we are interested in the total number of bits sent by all participants. We consider the following variants.

SYNC-MP [3]. In each round, each player sends a (possibly different) message of any length (including 0) directly to each of the other players. All messages are delivered simultaneously, and then the next round begins.

SYNC-COORD. There is a *coordinator* in addition to the k players. In each round, each player sends a message of any length to the coordinator and the coordinator sends a (possibly different) message of any length to each player. The players cannot communicate directly with each other.

* This research was partially supported by NSERC Discovery Grants, a donation from Sun Microsystems, DARPA Grant FA8750-11-2-0225, a Connaught New Researcher Award, and an Alfred P. Sloan Fellowship.

Y. Afek (Ed.): DISC 2013, LNCS 8205, pp. 575–576, 2013.

ASYNC-MP. There is a communication channel from every player to every other player, which we model as a queue. Initially, each player selects a (possibly empty) subset of the other players and sends/enqueues a (possibly different) non-empty message to each. Then, at each step, the scheduler, which is adversarial, selects a non-empty channel, dequeues a message, and and delivers it to its recipient. The recipient may then send a (possibly different) non-empty message to any number of the other players.

ASYNC-COORD. In addition to the k players, there is a *coordinator*, which also acts as the scheduler. At each step, the coordinator sends a non-empty message to one player of its choice, which must respond with a non-empty message.

The Simulations. The SYNC-MP and ASYNC-MP models can trivially simulate the SYNC-COORD and ASYNC-COORD models, respectively, with no overhead. In the other direction, the models can easily simulate each other with a factor of $O(\log k)$ more bits and we show that no better simulations exist. Synchronous models are at least as powerful as the corresponding asynchronous models, but they seem more powerful because players can convey information by *not* sending any bits in a given round. Nevertheless, we show that with a multiplicative overhead logarithmic in the number of rounds, T, the number of players, and $1/B$, where B is the communication complexity, the ASYNC-COORD model can simulate the SYNC-COORD model. We also show that communication by *push*, where players send each other messages, is roughly equivalent to communication by *pull*, where, instead, players select a subset of players from which they wish to receive information.

$$\text{ASYNC-MP} \underset{\text{no overhead}}{\overset{O(\log k)}{\rightleftarrows}} \text{ASYNC-COORD} \underset{O(\log(\frac{Tk}{B}))}{\overset{\text{no overhead}}{\rightleftarrows}} \text{SYNC-COORD} \underset{O(\log k)}{\overset{\text{no overhead}}{\rightleftarrows}} \text{SYNC-MP}$$

References

1. Ajtai, M., Komlós, J., Szemerédi, E.: Sorting in c log n parallel sets. Combinatorica 3(1), 1–19 (1983)
2. Braverman, M., Ellen, F., Oshman, R., Pitassi, T., Vaikuntanathan, V.: Tight bounds for set disjointness in the message passing model. In: FOCS 2013 (2013)
3. Cover, T.M., Thomas, J.A.: Elements of information theory. Wiley (2006)
4. Kuhn, F., Oshman, R.: The complexity of data aggregation in directed networks. In: Peleg, D. (ed.) DISC 2011. LNCS, vol. 6950, pp. 416–431. Springer, Heidelberg (2011)
5. Phillips, J.M., Verbin, E., Zhang, Q.: Lower bounds for number-in-hand multiparty communication complexity, made easy. In: SODA 2012, pp. 486–501 (2012)
6. Woodruff, D.P., Zhang, Q.: Tight bounds for distributed functional monitoring. In: STOC 2012, pp. 941–960 (2012)
7. Woodruff, D.P., Zhang, Q.: Distributed computation does not help. CoRR, abs/1304.4636 (2013)

Brief Announcement: Certified Impossibility Results for Byzantine-Tolerant Mobile Robots*

Cédric Auger, Zohir Bouzid[4], Pierre Courtieu[2],
Sébastien Tixeuil[4,5], and Xavier Urbain[1,3]

[1] École Nat. Sup. d'Informatique pour l'Industrie et l'Entreprise (ENSIIE), Évry, F-91025
[2] CÉDRIC – Conservatoire national des arts et métiers, Paris, F-75141
[3] LRI, CNRS UMR 8623, Université Paris-Sud, Orsay, F-91405
[4] UPMC Sorbonne Universités
[5] Institut Universitaire de France

Negative results such as impossibility results are fundamental in Distributed Computing to establish what can and cannot be computed in a given setting, or permitting to assess optimality results through lower bounds for given problems. Two notorious examples are the impossibility of reaching consensus in an asynchronous setting when a single process may fail by stopping unexpectedly [5], and the impossibility of reliably exchanging information when more than one third of the processes can exhibit arbitrary behaviour [8]. As noted by Lamport, Shostak and Pease [7], correctly proving results in the context of Byzantine (*a.k.a.* arbitrary behaviour capable) processes is a major challenge, as they knew *of no area in computer science or mathematics in which informal reasoning is more likely to lead to errors than in the study of this type of algorithm.*

An attractive way to assess the validity of distributed algorithm is to use *tool assisted* verification. Networks of static and/or mobile sensors (that is, robots) [6] received increasing attention in the past few years from the Distributed Computing community. Preliminary attempts for automatically proving impossibility results in robot networks properties are due to Devismes *et al.* [4] and to Bonnet *et al.* [2]. The first paper uses the LUSTRE formalism and model-checking to search exhaustively all possible 3-robots protocols that explore every node of a 3×3 grid (and conclude that no such algorithm exists). The second paper uses an ad hoc tool to generate all possible unambiguous protocols of k robots operating in an n-sized ring (k and n are given as parameters) and check exhaustively the properties of the generated protocols (and in the paper conclude that no protocol of 5 robots on a 10 sized ring can explore all nodes infinitely often with every robot). Those two proposals exhibit shortcomings we wish to address: *(i)* they are limited to a so called *discrete space*, where the robots may only occupy a *finite* number of positions, *(ii)* they are restricted to a particular setting (*e.g.* 3 robots on a 3×3 grid), and *(iii)* they do not integrate the possibility of misbehaving robots (*e.g.* robots crashing or exhibiting arbitrary and potentially malicious behaviour).

Our Contribution. We developed a general framework relying on the COQ proof assistant to prove possibility and impossibility results about mobile robotic networks. Proof assistants are environments in which a user can express programs, state theorems and develop interactively proofs that will be mechanically checked (that is

---

* This work was supported in part by the Digiteo Île-de-France project PACTOLE 2009-38HD.

Y. Afek (Ed.): DISC 2013, LNCS 8205, pp. 577–578, 2013.
© Springer-Verlag Berlin Heidelberg 2013

machine-checked). The key property of our approach is that its underlying calculus is of higher order: instead of providing the code of the distributed protocols executed by the robots, we may quantify universally on those programs/algorithms, or just characterize them with an abstract property. This genericity makes this approach complementary to the use of model-checking methods for verifying distributed algorithms [4,2] that are highly automatic, but address mainly particular instances of algorithms. In particular, quantifying over algorithms allows us to express in a natural way *impossibility results*.

We illustrate how our framework allows for such certification by providing COQ proofs of two earlier impossibility and lower bound theorems by Bouzid *et al.* [3], guaranteeing soundness of the first one, and of the SSYNC fair version of the second one. More precisely, in the context of oblivious robots that are endowed with strong global multiplicity detection and whose movements are constrained along a rational line, and assuming that the demon (that is, the way robots are scheduled for execution) is fair, the convergence problem cannot be solved if respectively at least one half and at least one third of robots are Byzantine. To our knowledge, these are the first certified (in the sense of formally proved) impossibility results for robot networks. The interestingly short size of the COQ proofs we obtained using our framework not only makes it easily human-readable, but also very encouraging for future applications and extensions of our framework.

Resources. A research report [1] describing our approach (LRI 1560) as well as the actual development for COQ 8.4pl3 are both available from the project's webpage: http://pactole.lri.fr

References

1. Auger, C., Bouzid, Z., Courtieu, P., Tixeuil, S., Urbain, X.: Certified impossibility results for byzantine-tolerant mobile robots. CoRR, abs/1306.4242 (2013)
2. Bonnet, F., Défago, X., Petit, F., Potop-Butucaru, M.G., Tixeuil, S.: *Brief Announcement:* Discovering and Assessing Fine-Grained Metrics in Robot Networks Protocols. In: Richa, A.W., Scheideler, C. (eds.) SSS 2012. LNCS, vol. 7596, pp. 282–284. Springer, Heidelberg (2012)
3. Bouzid, Z., Potop-Butucaru, M.G., Tixeuil, S.: Optimal Byzantine-Resilient Convergence in Uni-Dimensional Robot Networks. Theoretical Computer Science 411(34-36), 3154–3168 (2010)
4. Devismes, S., Lamani, A., Petit, F., Raymond, P., Tixeuil, S.: Optimal Grid Exploration by Asynchronous Oblivious Robots. In: Richa, A.W., Scheideler, C. (eds.) SSS 2012. LNCS, vol. 7596, pp. 64–76. Springer, Heidelberg (2012)
5. Fischer, M.J., Lynch, N.A., Paterson, M.: Impossibility of Distributed Consensus with One Faulty Process. J. ACM 32(2), 374–382 (1985)
6. Flocchini, P., Prencipe, G., Santoro, N.: Distributed Computing by Oblivious Mobile Robots. Synthesis Lectures on Distributed Computing Theory. Morgan & Claypool Publishers (2012)
7. Lamport, L., Shostak, R., Pease, M.: The Byzantine Generals Problem. ACM Transactions on Programming Languages and Systems 4(3), 382–401 (1982)
8. Pease, M.C., Shostak, R.E., Lamport, L.: Reaching Agreement in the Presence of Faults. J. ACM 27(2), 228–234 (1980)

Brief Announcement: Distributed Compressed Sensing for Sensor Networks

Stacy Patterson, Yonina C. Eldar, and Idit Keidar

Department of Electrical Engineering, Technion, Haifa, Israel
{stacyp,yonina,idish}@ee.technion.ac.il

Distributed Compressed Sensing. Compressed sensing is a new and popular signal processing technique for efficient signal acquisition, or sampling, and reconstruction from these samples [3]. The signal is an N-vector, with N typically very large, and it is assumed that the signal has a sparse representation in some basis with only $K \ll N$ non-zero components. The signal is simultaneously sampled and compressed into measurements, each of which is a linear combination of the components of the signal. For a general (non-sparse) signal, N measurements are needed to reconstruct the signal. The power of compressed sensing lies in the fact that, if the measurements are taken appropriately, it is possible to reconstruct the signal exactly from only $O(K \log N)$ measurements and to do so in an efficient manner.

One application setting that is beginning to receive attention from the compressed sensing community is estimation and monitoring in sensor networks. Recent works have shown that compressed sensing is applicable to a variety of sensor networks problems, including urban environment monitoring [5] and traffic speed estimation [8]. In these works, sensors distributed throughout a region take measurements of the signal. The measurements are then collected at a fusion center where signal recovery is performed using a centralized algorithm.

While the vast majority of recovery algorithms for compressed sensing consider a centralized setting, a centralized approach is not always feasible, especially in sensor networks where no powerful computing center is available and where bandwidth is limited. Since the measurements are already distributed throughout a network, it is desirable to perform the reconstruction within the network itself. This problem of in-network sparse signal recovery from distributed measurements is known as *distributed compressed sensing*. Here, each node has a set of measurements, known only to it. Nodes must recover the signal from their collective measurements using only communication between neighbors.

Distributed Iterative Hard Thresholding. We propose an approach for distributed compressed sensing in sensor networks that outperforms previously proposed solutions in both message and time complexity [7]. To develop our algorithm, we first looked inside the "black boxes" of the centralized recovery algorithms to identify a good candidate for distribution. We selected a greedy algorithm called *Iterative Hard Thresholding* (IHT) [2] as the basis for our distributed solution, which we call Distributed IHT (D-IHT).

We show how to decompose IHT into iterations that consist of a simple *local computation* at each node to compute an intermediate vector, followed by a *global*

Y. Afek (Ed.): DISC 2013, LNCS 8205, pp. 579–580, 2013.
© Springer-Verlag Berlin Heidelberg 2013

computation over the intermediate vectors at all nodes Each global computation requires finding the components of the sum of these intermediate vectors that have the K largest magnitudes. This global computation is nearly identical to the distributed top-K problem [4], and so we leverage a solution to this problem to perform this global computation with minimized communication cost.

By decomposing IHT in this manner, D-IHT simulates centralized IHT exactly. Furthermore, each local computation consists of a few matrix-vector multiplications, and thus the computational cost is low. This is in contrast with competing works which all solve the problem using distributed convex optimization (e.g., [1,6]). These algorithms do not optimize for metrics that are important in a distributed setting, most notably, bandwidth consumption. In addition, they introduce computational complexity on top of their centralized counterparts, as they have each node solve an optimization problem in each iteration, and moreover require more iterations than D-IHT to converge.

Results and Conclusion. We compared the performance of D-IHT with the best-known convex optimization-based distributed compressed sensing algorithm on several problems in various network topologies. For every recovery problem and every topology, D-IHT required far fewer total messages (between one and three orders of magnitude) to achieve the same recovery accuracy. D-IHT also required less total time to perform the recovery, between one and two orders of magnitude fewer time steps [7].

We are currently working to extend D-IHT to time-varying network topologies. We also plan to explore applications of distributed compressed sensing in the Smart Grid.

References

1. Bazerque, J.A., Giannakis, G.B.: Distributed spectrum sensing for cognitive radio networks by exploiting sparsity. IEEE Transactions on Signal Processing 58(3), 1847–1862 (2010)
2. Blumensath, T., Davies, M.E.: Iterative hard thresholding for compressed sensing. Applied and Computational Harmonic Analysis 27(3), 265–274 (2009)
3. Eldar, Y.C., Kutyniok, G.: Compressed Sensing: Theory and Applications. Cambridge University Press (2012)
4. Fagin, R., Lotem, A., Naor, M.: Optimal aggregation algorithms for middleware. Journal of Computer and System Sciences 66(4), 614–656 (2003)
5. Li, Z., Zhu, Y., Zhu, H., Li, M.: Compressive sensing approach to urban traffic sensing. In: 31st International Conference on Distributed Computing Systems, pp. 889–898 (2011)
6. Mota, J., Xavier, J., Aguiar, P., Püschel, M.: Distributed basis pursuit. IEEE Transactions on Signal Processing 60(4), 1942–1956 (2012)
7. Patterson, S., Eldar, Y.C., Keidar, I.: Distributed sparse signal recovery in sensor networks. In: IEEE International Conference on Acoustics, Speech, and Signal Processing (2013)
8. Yu, X., Zhao, H., Zhang, L., Wu, S., Krishnamachari, B., Li, V.O.K.: Cooperative sensing and compression in vehicular sensor networks for urban monitoring. In: IEEE International Conference on Communications, pp. 1–5 (2010)

Brief Announcement: Towards Distributed and Reliable Software Defined Networking*

Marco Canini[1], Petr Kuznetsov[2], Dan Levin[1], and Stefan Schmid[1]

[1] TU Berlin / T-Labs
[2] Télécom ParisTech

Software-defined networking (SDN) is a novel paradigm that out-sources the control of packet-forwarding switches to a set of software controllers. The most fundamental task of these controllers is the correct implementation of the *network policy*, *i.e.*, the intended network behavior. In essence, such a policy specifies the rules by which packets must be forwarded across the network. This paper initiates the study of the SDN control plane as a distributed system.

We consider a *distributed* SDN control plane which accepts *policy updates* (*e.g.*, routing or access control changes) issued *concurrently* by different controllers and whose goal is to *consistently* compose these updates. One of our contributions is precisely the notion of consistency of concurrent policy composition. We introduce a formal model for SDN under fault-prone concurrent control. In particular, we seek to ensure *per-packet consistency* [3]. Informally, this property ensures that every packet is processed at every switch it encounters in the data plane according to just one and same policy, which is the composition of policy updates installed by the time when the packet entered the network.

We present the abstraction of *Consistent Policy Composition (CPC)* which offers a *transactional* interface. A policy-update request returns *commit* if the update is successfully integrated in the current network policy or *abort* if the update cannot be installed. Our correctness property informally requires that the abstraction, regardless of the actual interleaving of concurrent policy updates and data packets' arrivals, *appears* sequential to every data packet, as though all the committed requests (and possibly a subset of incomplete ones) are applied atomically and no data packet is in flight while an update is being installed.

We show that it is generally impossible to implement the CPC abstraction in the presence of a single controller's crash failure. The requirement of per-packet consistency allows us to introduce an interesting variant of the bivalency argument [2], where the valency of an algorithm's execution accounts for all possible *paths* a packet may take in all extensions of the execution. Since typically the controllers do not have influence on the network traffic workload, our impossibility proof is able to exploit the intertwined combination of two kinds of concurrency: overlapping policy updates arbitrarily interleaving with traffic.

Accordingly, we investigate stronger model abstractions which enable fault-tolerant CPC implementations. We find that a slightly more powerful SDN switch interface supporting an atomic read-modify-write allows for a *wait-free* CPC solution, and we investigate the tag complexity of such a solution.

---

* A full version of this paper can be found at [1].

Y. Afek (Ed.): DISC 2013, LNCS 8205, pp. 581–582, 2013.
© Springer-Verlag Berlin Heidelberg 2013

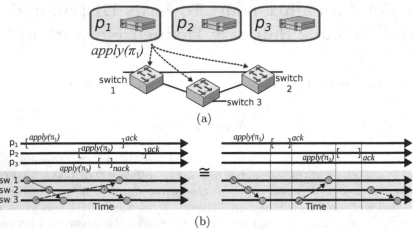

Fig. 1. Example of a policy composition: (a) 3-process control plane and 3-switch data plane, (b) a concurrent history H and its sequential equivalent H_S.

Policy Composition in SDN: Example. Consider a network consisting of three switches sw1, sw2 and sw3 (Figure 1(a)), and controlled by p_1, p_2, and p_3. The controllers' function is to try to install policy-update requests on the switches. An example of a concurrent history H is presented in Figure 1(b). The three controllers try to concurrently install three different policies π_1, π_2, and π_3. Imagine that π_1 and π_2 are applied to disjoint fractions of traffic (*e.g.*, π_1 affects only http traffic and π_2 only ssh traffic) and, thus, can be installed independently of each other. In contrast, let us assume that π_3 is conflicting with both π_1 and π_2 (*e.g.*, it applies to traffic from address 1.2.3.4). In this history, π_1 and π_2 are committed (returned *ack*), while π_3 is aborted (returned *nack*).

While the concurrent policy-update requests are processed, three packets are injected to the network (at switches sw1, sw2, and sw3) leaving three *traces* depicted with dotted and dashed arrows. Each trace is in fact the sequence of ports which the packet goes through while it traverses the network. For example, in one of the traces (depicted with the dotted arrow), a packet arrives at sw1, then it is forwarded to sw2, and then to sw1. Next to H we present its "sequential equivalent" H_S. The traffic on the data plane is processed *as though* the application of policy updates is *atomic* and packets cross the network *instantaneously*.

The full paper [1] presents a formal specification of concurrent policy composition and explores its implementation costs. We believe that this work opens a new and exciting problem area with a number of unexplored concurrency issues.

References

1. Canini, M., Kuznetsov, P., Levin, D., Schmid, S.: The case for reliable software transactional networking. Technical report, arXiv TR 1305.7429 (2013)
2. Fischer, M.J., Lynch, N.A., Paterson, M.S.: Impossibility of distributed consensus with one faulty process. J. ACM 32(2), 374–382 (1985)
3. Reitblatt, M., Foster, N., Rexford, J., Schlesinger, C., Walker, D.: Abstractions for network update. In: SIGCOMM (2012)

Brief Announcement:
Dynamic Forwarding Table Aggregation without Update Churn: The Case of Dependent Prefixes*

Marcin Bienkowski[1], Nadi Sarrar[2], Stefan Schmid[2], and Steve Uhlig[3]

[1] Institute of Computer Science, University of Wrocław, Poland
[2] Telekom Innovation Laboratories & TU Berlin, Germany
[3] School of EE and CS, Queen Mary University, United Kingdom

Abstract. This paper considers the problem of a route or SDN controller which manages a FIB table. The controller wants to aggregate the FIB entries as much as possible while minimizing the interactions with the FIB. We present a $O(w)$-competitive online algorithm for the aggregation of FIB tables in presence of routing updates, where w is the maximum length of an IP address. Our result is asymptotically optimal within a natural class of algorithms.

Introduction and Model. This paper studies a new online problem arising in the context of forwarding table aggregation in a router or *Software Defined Network (SDN)* switch. The *Forwarding Information Base (FIB)* contains the rules used by the router to decide, for each packet, to which port it should be forwarded; a rule is simply an (IP prefix, port) pair. We will identify ports with colors.

More specifically, any packet has a destination (IP) address which is a binary string of length w (e.g., $w = 32$ for IPv4 and $w = 128$ for IPv6). For any packet processed by the router, a decision is made on the basis of its destination IP address x using the *longest prefix match* policy: among the FIB rules $\{(p_i, c_i)\}_i$, the router chooses the longest p_i being a prefix of x, and forwards the packet to the port of color c_i. Unlike [1], we allow *dependent* prefixes, i.e., the address ranges described by prefixes stored in the FIB may be contained in each other.

In order to save memory, we let the online algorithm aggregate this table, i.e., replace the current set of rules by an *equivalent* but smaller set. In addition to reducing the number of FIB rules, an online algorithm should minimize the number of rule updates. Precisely speaking, the router consists of two parts: the *controller* (e.g., implemented on the route processor) and the *(compressed) FIB* (stored in a fast and expensive memory). The controller keeps a copy of the *uncompressed FIB (U-FIB)* and receives dynamic routing updates to this structure (that may change the color of an existing prefix). Right after such an update occurs, the controller must ensure that the U-FIB and the FIB are equivalent. To this end, the controller can insert, delete or update individual rules in the FIB, cf Fig. 1a.

---

* A full version of this paper can be found at [2].

Y. Afek (Ed.): DISC 2013, LNCS 8205, pp. 583–584, 2013.

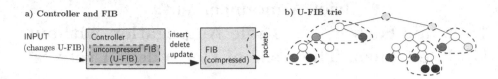

Fig. 1. *On the left:* Controller and FIB; the controller updates the rules in the FIB. This paper focuses on online algorithms for the controller. *On the right:* Example U-FIB trie. Stick boundaries are marked with dashed lines.

For presentation purposes, we represent both U-FIB and FIB as colored binary tries. These tries may contain blank nodes that do not correspond to existing rules.

Costs. We associate a fixed cost α with a change of a single rule in FIB. This paper focuses on the minimization of the sum of the total update cost and the total memory cost, where the latter is defined as the size of the FIB integrated over time.

Our Result. We present the online algorithm HiMs (HIDE INVISIBLE AND MERGE SIBLING). HiMs is based on the concept of *sticks*: roughly speaking, a stick is a maximal part of the U-FIB trie that — if cut out of the trie — will constitute a trie of its own, with all leaves colored and all internal nodes blank. An example is given in Fig. 1b.

HiMs employs two time-delayed optimization rules: (1) If there are two siblings in a stick that are of the same color for time α, then they are removed and a rule corresponding to their parent is inserted. (2) If all colored nodes of a stick are of the same color and of the same color as their least colored ancestor in the trie (again for time α), then all these stick rules become removed from the trie. These optimizations are rolled back only when necessary to assure that the forwarding behavior of FIB is the same as that of U-FIB. A precise definition of the algorithm and its analysis are given in [2].

Theorem 1. HiMs *is $O(w)$-competitive. This is optimal in the class of all algorithms (even offline ones) that do not create dependent prefixes within a single stick. Furthermore,* HiMs *can be implemented using a data structure, whose amortized complexity for a single operation is at most $O(w)$ times the number of updates* OPT *performs in its FIB.*

References

1. Bienkowski, M., Schmid, S.: Competitive FIB aggregation for independent prefixes: Online ski rental on the trie. In: Proc. of the 20th Colloquium on Structural Information and Communication Complexity, SIROCCO (to appear, 2013)
2. Sarrar, N., Bienkowski, M., Schmid, S., Uhlig, S., Wuttke, R.: Exploiting Locality of Churn for FIB Aggregation. In TR 2012/12, TU Berlin (2012)

Author Index